THE ULTIMATE SOUTHERN AFRICAN GARDENING BOOK

KRISTO PIENAAR
Introduces

THE ULTIMATE SOUTHERN AFRICAN GARDENING BOOK

SOUTHERN
BOOK PUBLISHERS

Chief consultant	KRISTO PIENAAR
Consultants	STIRLING MACOBOY
	ROGER MANN
	IAN PERCY
	TONY RODD

Writers

Text

Your Garden	Roger Mann
Annuals & Perennials	Dalys Newman
	Robin Simon
Shrubs	Peter Lavelle
Trees	Henry Barrkman
Bulbs, Corms & Tubers	Julie Silk
Lawns, Ground Covers & Ornamental Grasses	Robin Simon
Vegetables & Herbs	Gina Schien (vegetables)
	Denise Greig (herbs)
Fruit Trees, Nut Trees & Other Fruits	Gina Schien
Indoor Plants	Marnie Roper
Cacti & Succulents	Henry Barrkman
Orchids	Roger Mann
Ferns, Palms & Cycads	Gina Schien
Climbers & Creepers	Denise Greig
Chapter Introductions	Roger Mann
	Judy Moore

Field Trips

Andy Clements (*Dochu La*); Tony Curry (*Tengchong*); **John Forlonge** (*Magallanes Region*); **Maurie Kellett** (*Fortin de las Flores*); John Manning (*Darling and Malmesbury*); Kristo Pienaar (*Cape Floral Kingdom*); **Graeme Platt** (*Coromandel Peninsula*); **Julie Silk** (*Blue Mountains, Mount Kinabalu, Norfolk Island*); **Paul Sterry** (*Grindelwald, Lundy*); **Angus Stewart** (*Guadalupe Mountains National Park, Anza-Borrego Desert State Park*).

Publisher	Gordon Cheers
Managing editor	Margaret Olds
Senior editor	Marie-Louise Taylor
Copy editors	Deb Brown
	Susan Page
	Stephanie Campion
	Kate Etherington
	Margaret McAllister
	Marnie Roper
	Dawn Cockle
	Lisa Foulis
	Heather Jackson
	James Young
Art director	Stan Lamond
Designers	Joy Eckermann
	Linda Christie
Maps	Stan Lamond

Published in South Africa by
Southern Book Publishers
PO Box 3103, Halfway House, 1685, RSA

First published 1994

ISBN 1–86812–550–5.

Typesetting: Jan Greenville, Leonie Draper

Production: Marc Nolan

Film separation: Pica Colour Separation Overseas Pte Ltd

Printed by: Tien Wah Press (Pte) Ltd
977 Bukit-Timah Road, Singapore 2158

Page 1: *Kniphofia praecox,* the red-hot poker. (Kristo Pienaar)
Page 2: *Protea cynaroides,* the king protea. (Joy Harland)
Page 5: The romance and beauty of old roses. (Gil Hanly)
Pages 8–9: A lush, cool-climate garden. (Gil Hanly)

Contents

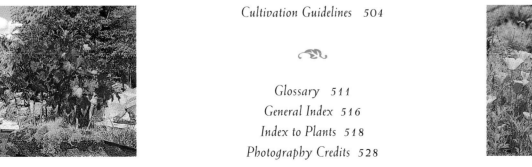

CHAPTER 1

Your Garden

*Everything You Need to Know to Plan,
Develop and Maintain Your Garden*

*W*e walk in a world of our own
creation; and the pleasures of
the gardens we create are many and
lasting. True, the flower fades, the
perfect tomato is brought to the
table and is no more: but tomorrow
there will be new flowers, other
fruit; still the sunshine will sparkle
on the lawn; the newly dug earth
gives its sweet smell, rich with
promise; and as the years and
seasons pass, the garden matures in
beauty. In our hectic and alienated
times, what price an activity that
brings us back in touch with the
slow rhythms of nature?

But first we must begin to create
our garden. A beautiful garden
grows out of the interaction between
the site, the climate, the soil, and
the needs and desires of its owner;
and there are as many ways to
bring these together as there are
gardeners. There is no 'right' way to
make a garden—there is only the
one that works best for you.

PLANNING THE GARDEN

Design for living

Most of us make our garden on the land
about our house, and it augments the
house's living space. Thinking about
how you (and your family) want to live
in your garden is as good a starting
point for planning as any. Do you need
a place to wash the car, to entertain
friends at a braai, for children to play;
to hang out the washing, hide the
dustbin, make a compost heap; to
sunbathe, to sit in the cool of a summer
evening with a cold drink? Would you
like a swimming pool, a spa, a place to
grow vegetables and fruit? To grow
flowers for cutting? Do you need a
shed, or can tools, the lawn-mower,
portable garden furniture and what
have you be kept in the garage? How
important is privacy to you?

Think, if you like, in terms of 'garden
rooms', remembering, however, that
'rooms' in a garden need not have the
clearly defined functions that those in a
house normally do. A sunny lawn can
serve just as well for the children to
throw a ball as it can for adults to

sunbathe; and if you have a party,
guests can wander out on to it and sit
on the grass. On the other hand, the
feet of chairs and tables tend to sink
into grass if it is soggy from rain, and
you may find yourself wishing for a
paved area—a stoep, patio, call it what
you will. Paving can get uncomfortably
hot in summer, so this suggests the
patio should be shaded: but you will
probably want the winter sun, so you
start thinking in terms of deciduous
trees or of vines on pergolas. The patio
probably should link up in some easy
way with the living rooms, and in turn
open out onto the lawn; perhaps it is
the spot to display some extra-choice
flowers or a piece of sculpture … or
should the flowers or the sculpture go
at the other side of the lawn to draw
people out to admire them? Before you
know it, a design for a garden room is
taking shape …

Plan for the climate

When gardeners think of climate, it is
usually in terms of how it affects the
choice of plants, but it influences the
basic layout of a garden also. Braais and

Vine-covered arbours, favourite sitting places since the days of the Romans, are still an effective way to link house with garden.

swimming pools flourish where summers are sunny and pleasant; in a hot climate shade is a necessity; in any climate you will almost certainly face winds, hot or cold, that you want to break.

If you can arrange a balance of sun and shade, you have the option of sitting in either, and you gain a greater choice of plants you can grow. But shade doesn't stay in one place—the sun moves around all the time. It moves daily from east to west of course; but it also shifts with the seasons, being higher in the sky in summer than in winter. So the pool of shade cast by a tree, for instance, is larger in winter than in summer—and a corner behind the shed may get sun in summer but not in winter.

It is a general rule that (in the southern hemisphere) the north side of the house is the sunny one, and the south is in the shade of the house itself. Most of us like the morning sun, but on a hot summer day the last thing we want is the hot afternoon sun streaming in the windows. If you can arrange trees on your western side to shade the house on summer afternoons, it will make life more comfortable. The north side can do with summer shade too, but here you will probably welcome the winter sun. Deciduous trees, which drop their leaves as the summer cools into autumn and clothe themselves again in spring, will fill the bill here, and so might grapes or wisteria trained on pergolas. Beneath them is the ideal place for a terrace for sitting out and entertaining: but what if your living rooms face some other aspect? It doesn't really matter. An easy link with the living rooms is more important. (You don't really want to be taking guests out through the bedrooms or laundry, do you?)

East is marginally better than west or south; most people entertain in the evenings and in summer a west aspect will still be hot. But it doesn't really matter; arrange suitable shade and you can make yourself comfortable on most aspects. (My own two patios face east and west, which gives me one for the morning and one for the afternoon.) The south side of the house can be tricky. For most of the year it is in shade, but in midsummer the sun will have moved around enough to reach it. A south side patio should also have deciduous shade.

When you are planning for sun and shade, think of your comfort inside the

A spot for outdoor living amidst lush greenery, the brightly painted walls adding colour.

house as well as in the garden. Curtains or no, once the sun has got in through a window, its heat is in too, and it is very difficult to evict; shading the outside of the glass is the only way to keep it out. Architects employ a variety of devices—cornices, eaves, verandahs —to achieve this. Gardeners use plants: trees, shrubs, climbers which can be allowed to climb the walls and hang trails of greenery over the windows (few sights are more romantic) or trained over pergolas to form green roofs. Plants give cooler shade than structures do, by virtue of their constant transpiration of water which makes them natural air-conditioners.

Climbers can provide much-needed shade.

Climbers soften the front of this colonial home.

An inviting white summer house stands out against varied greens.

A modern interpretation of formal style.

Wind

Say 'windbreak' and most people immediately think of the rows of Lombardy poplars or *Pinus radiata* that march across the fields in the country. If you have a country garden you'll probably be thinking of belts of large trees. In the suburbs there is unlikely to be room for them, and so you'll be thinking of shrubs, small trees, and maybe fences and trellises. Nonetheless, you will want to screen the garden from the cold winds in winter and the hot ones of summer. Not only for your own comfort, but because wind dries out the garden as effectively as it does the washing on the line. Trees and shrubs

are more effective than structures for the purpose. If the wind hits a wall it just rebounds and comes down with renewed force, but foliage filters the wind and gives you shelter for a distance downwind about eight times the height of the planting. In a hot climate, you can use greenery as an air-conditioner simply by turning a sprinkler on it, converting a hot dry breeze into a gentle cool one.

Not all wind is undesirable. In most areas there are evening summer breezes that you won't want to block, and you'll be thinking of less dense plantings on that aspect. It isn't possible to give rules for all this, as wind patterns vary so much from place to place. On the east coast, the hot summer winds come from the west; in Durban or East London they blow from the north. Everywhere, it is the local geography that determines the prevailing winds. A strong wind off the sea is a major factor in garden-making, but gardens by the sea are a special case and we will look at them later.

It can be a problem when the prevailing wind (or the hot summer sun) comes from the same direction as a wonderful view. Perhaps the best way to deal with it is to use fairly open-growing trees which will break the wind or sun a bit but not block the view too much, or to group the plants

so that they frame segments of the view, the way a photographer arranges interesting things in the foreground of a picture. If the problem is essentially a summer one, you might use deciduous trees, which will at least give you back the view in winter. However you deal with the problem, the answer will inevitably be a compromise between view and shelter—but in gardening, as in life, compromises can often have the happiest results.

Privacy

How much privacy you need in the garden is a matter of temperament; some people like more seclusion than others. A new garden is apt to be dominated by fences and the neighbours' houses, but before you rush to surround yourself with dense growth like Sleeping Beauty in the fairy tale, take a careful look. Ignore the fence for a moment—you can mask it with creepers and shrubs—and concentrate on the neighbours' houses. If you arrange some trees or tall shrubs to mask these from your view, leaving the skyline open elsewhere, will that be sufficient?

It can be difficult to visualize how this is going to look; try taking some photographs and sketching some foliage on them to get an idea how much cover you'll need. (This can be a good way of visualizing any changes you propose to the garden—and before-and-after pictures of the garden are well worth taking.)

Front gardens

Almost always, the house is set on the land so that you have front and back gardens. As it is usually more private, the back garden is frequently where most people enjoy their family activities. It is very difficult to contrive privacy in a front garden. The front garden is still basically a threshold to your property, a link between the street and the front door. It may be possible to screen a section to make a front patio, but there is still the need to have access to the house, and that really can't be forbidden to the person who comes to read the meters, let alone your invited guests. You do need to have a clear path from the entrance to the front door, and to ensure it is well lit at night.

The front garden is the scene of the visitor's first and last impressions. Also

Detail counts: here, the fence and gate match the period colour scheme of the house, and the gareden.

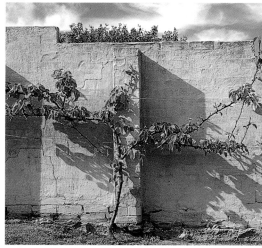

A cherry tree trained espalier to soften a wall.

One fine jacaranda lifts a row of terraces.

it is neighbourly to have a garden that looks pleasing from the street and you will want to show off the architecture of the house to advantage. If you are a keen gardener, you may seize the opportunity to show off your skills. But on the other hand you may not want to spend a high proportion of your gardening time on an area you don't use much yourself and you may opt for a low maintenance design. It's up to you, but a word to the wise: in these days of high crime, it isn't a good idea to shroud the front of your house too much in greenery or with high fences. Burglars appreciate privacy too!

Inner-city gardens

The return to the inner city is no longer a new phenomenon. These days if you look out over the old inner suburbs, you see trees and greenery where once there was an unbroken landscape of iron roofs and telephone poles. People are discovering that they can make delightful gardens in back yards which were simply spaces for outhouses, washing lines and coal heaps when the houses were originally built in the days of Queen Victoria and King Edward VII.

In some ways, a city garden is the ideal for busy people—there simply isn't room to overindulge in gardening! But a confined space does call for some

editing of the wish list—you just can't include all the activities or all the plants you might want. The answer is to develop the garden as a living room; think of it as a courtyard and pave most of it—a garden that is all patio, in fact (and it is interesting to recall that the Spanish word 'patio' originally meant a paved courtyard garden just like this).

The walls and fences can be clad with climbing plants or with shrubs trained espalier. If space allows, you might be able to contrive a pocket-handkerchief-sized lawn; but city conditions are against it. Surrounding buildings often block the sun, and few lawn grasses like shade. Chances are you'll wear the grass out underfoot anyway; and you'll need to consider where you are going to store the lawn mower.

The big problem is quite likely to be privacy. The dominant feature of your view is likely to be the neighbours' walls and windows. Sure, they will be as much concerned about you as you might be about them: but it is still desirable to screen them. Pergolas might do it; trees are effective too, though they will probably eventually confine your choice of plants to shade lovers. Also you need to choose carefully to be sure that the trees don't have structure-damaging roots. One splendid tree spreading its leafy (and why not flow-

ery?) canopy over the whole garden can set the style far more effectively than several smaller ones.

Side gardens

If the areas beside the house are large enough to use as living spaces, you can usually extend a screen (built or planted) from the facade of the house to the side fence and thus incorporate the area into the back garden. Depending on aspect, this can be a nice place for a secluded patio, for the vegetable garden or for the compost heap; and trees planted there can be useful in framing the house. Often, however, it is simply a narrow strip, just wide enough to separate the house from the neighbours. Here there is little to do but treat it as a passageway, putting down a path and training plants on the fence and the house. Make the plants interesting enough to be worth visiting. Watering a long narrow area can be difficult and tedious. Even if you elect to use hand-held hoses and movable sprinklers elsewhere in the garden, consider an in-ground system here.

Country gardens

A garden in the country gives you more scope than one in the suburbs; you don't have to worry about being over-looked by neighbours, and you can develop just as much ground as you please. Sweeping driveways, vistas through trees and across whole fields of flowers to the countryside beyond are all possible; but beware lest ambition outrun resources. If you are dependent on water from dams or rainwater tanks, the sweeping lawns can all too easily go brown and the flowers wilt in a dry summer. There is a tradition in England of country gardens divided by hedges into distinct flower-filled rooms; many people feel that this doesn't suit our sparser, more open landscape and wider horizons. They suggest a freer style, open to the surrounding country, is more appropriate.

You will almost certainly need to plant windbreak trees if they don't exist already; hot winds will dry the garden faster than you can keep the water up to it. In many dry areas of the country, lawns are something of a luxury and people save their bath water to water them—they make such a pleasant relief to the eye from the glare of summer dryness and dust. You could try laying the area in gravel, which needs no water; but shade it, or the glare and reflected heat will be ferocious. And be very conscious of the danger of bushfires. The idea of having the country sweep right up to the windows in the manner of the great country estates of Britain or the eastern United States of America is of limited relevance in South Africa, where the bush is usually inflammable. It is important to provide yourself with as much water as possible in event of the worst, and maintain your firebreaks!

In a large garden, a variety of places to sit—and a whole succession of different pictures.

Making a plan

The easiest way of developing a layout for the garden is to make a plan on paper. An empty yard is apt to look larger than it is, and a plan can tell you whether you can in fact fit in all the things you want to accommodate. Start by making a plan showing the land as it exists. It doesn't have to be a work of art, but it is desirable that it be fairly accurately to scale, and that it shows the features that might influence your design. These include the boundaries and fences; any pavings, paths, drive-ways, immovable rocks and trees that might already be there; and, of course, the house itself, with its external doors and windows.

Don't forget to note desirable views that you will want to frame, undesirable ones that should be screened; the location of such nuisances as overhead wires or underground sewers and telephone lines; and the direction of north, which tells you where the sun comes from. You may have builder's plans for the house that show many of these things; your local council may still have them; or you may need to spend a few hours with a long tape measure and paper to create the plan for yourself.

A formal vista like this needs a focal point—here, the comfortable white-painted seat.

Then you can start to arrange your garden rooms—the patio near the living room, the vegetable patch in that sunny place near the kitchen door, the swimming pool, the path to the front door. Get them in the right places first, and then the decisions about what shapes they are to take, where the trees and shrubs are to go to frame them (and block out the view of that nosy neighbour), whether to give them floors of paving or grass, and what sort of plants to have, can follow.

Plan generously, allowing yourself room to move. If you make a lawn or terrace for sitting out, 3 sq m is about as small as you can get away with; paths less than about 1.5 m wide are too narrow for two people to stroll along; a row of shrubs tall enough to give privacy will grow at least 2 m wide.

Remember that a plan is flat, and most blocks of land are, at most, flattish. It is a rare garden that will not have some changes of level to negotiate, even if only the provision of a couple of steps leading up into the house. Welcome them, and make them features in your design. People have been known to contrive level changes just for the sake of the interest they add!

Two hints on plan making: Don't make your plans too big in scale or you'll spend an inordinate amount of time drawing on unmanageably large sheets of paper. A scale of 1:100 (used on most builders' drawings) is quite large enough. Do your basic 'as is' plan on good stout paper (graph paper makes setting out easier), and develop your ideas on tracing paper laid over it—it saves redrawing the house and fences all the time.

CHOOSING A STYLE

Don't worry that this care over the plan and layout will lead to a stereotyped garden. You can develop your ideas in any style you like, and clothe them with your favourites among the plants that your soil and climate allow. You might opt for a rigidly formal, symmetrical design, like the old gardens of Italy and France, making much use of clipped hedges and statuary, with flowers used only as accents at key points: or you might go to the opposite extreme, and make flowers the theme, disposing them with total informality in drifts and masses, maybe in English-style borders. If you concentrate on 'old-fashioned'

Brick steps, simply designed but generously proportioned.

The formal garden at its most magnificent; the Chateau de Villandry in France.

The green on the painted shutters and door is echoed in the colours of the plants.

flowers, blending them (perhaps) with scented herbs and maybe the more decorative vegetables and fruit trees, you have a cottage garden. (Picket fences and arches covered with climbing roses are very much a part of the cottage style.) Taking your cue from the presence of a tree or several, you might decide on a woodland theme, treating your living spaces as woodland glades. Here you have several possibilities—you might use mostly deciduous trees with such plants as camellias, azaleas or bluebells beneath; or you might prefer to use indigenous trees and shrubs to re-create a patch of bush or forest; or you might go tropical with palm trees and exotic foliage.

The different styles of gardening are more about the kinds of plants you choose and how you display them than about how you cultivate them. But, in deciding which you would like, do be realistic about the time you will be prepared to devote to your garden. If sports or family activities already take most of your leisure hours, will you be able to cope with extensive plantings of flowers or vegetables? Might you not be wiser to develop a love for easy-care trees and ground covers?

REMODELLING

What if you are remodelling an existing garden? The procedure is in fact the same as if you were planning a new one on a clean slate; start with considering how the existing garden fits your lifestyle. What changes would help it fit better? To some extent, the style will be already set, though garden styles aren't rigid categories. Your predecessors may, for instance, have been indigenous plant buffs while you long for a cottage garden—who says you can't keep the best of the indigenous trees and shrubs and blend them with your cottage flowers?

It is always wise to proceed slowly when you take over an established garden; live with it for at least a year before deciding on major changes. Mature trees and shrubs are assets that take time to replace, and you should give them time to reveal their beauties, especially if they are species you aren't familiar with. Who knows what hidden treasures may appear and flower with the change of season; that sunny place behind the shed (why didn't they put the vegetable garden there?) may turn out to be in heavy shade all winter …

Engaging a professional

Designing a garden can be one of life's most rewarding challenges, but there is no shame in deciding that you need some assistance. A professional has done it all before, many times, and will be placing the benefit of that experience at your disposal. He (or she) will be doing for a living what you do for a hobby, so don't begrudge him his fee—chances are, he will save you that much money and more. Anyone with a truck and a shovel can set himself up as a landscaper, so you need to be careful in your search; but there are trained professionals around. There are landscape architects, many of whom specialize in big projects like airports or parks, though equally many are only too delighted to take on the more intimate challenge of domestic gardens; many of the bigger nurseries and landscape contractors offer a design service, sometimes as a part of a design-and-build package, sometimes not; and there are smaller, independent designers also. Feel free to shop around, asking to see some of that firm's work to see whether you like their style, talking to previous clients if you wish; and don't be shy about discussing money. Be clear about your wishes and tastes, and your budget—mental telepathy isn't part of a designer's skills.

BUILDING THE GARDEN

Having made your plans for the garden, you can elect to have your designs carried out professionally. Financial institutions are far more willing to finance landscaping than they used to be. Or you can save money—and gain a great deal of personal satisfaction—by doing some or all the work yourself. This will mean that you will have to make a considerable input in time and energy, so it will save much frustration and back-tracking if you develop a game plan for doing the work in stages, perhaps over two or three years.

If you are impatient, remember that staging the work allows you time to ponder and to add the touches that lift a garden out of the ordinary. These can be difficult to anticipate on paper. They might be unusual and effective combinations of plants, pieces of furniture or sculpture, cleverly arranged lighting, even something as simple as laying a paving pattern in one way and not another—the sorts of inspirations that strike only while you are getting your hands dirty.

If you are starting from scratch, the best plan is the one that most landscape contractors follow. First, do any major reshaping of the ground which will need heavy equipment, build any retaining walls needed to hold the reshaped earth in place, and lay any soil drains needed. (All this is disruptive, messy work if you do it later.) Then you might lay your basic pavings: the driveway comes first or you will be getting the car bogged on the way to the garage. (Chances are, the builder will have installed a basic, concrete drive as part of the house package.) If you can afford to lay paths and terraces at this stage, do it, but if not, you'll need to at least provide some cover for the bare ground; this needn't be the final lawn; there is sense in growing a cover crop of clover to improve the soil—and this won't cause heartache if it gets dug up or torn around later.

Then, as early as possible, you should plant your most important trees: the earlier you get them in, the earlier you'll be enjoying their shade. This might be enough for your energy and

budget in the first year. If the garden looks a bit unfinished, fill in with inexpensive, fast return annuals to give you something to look at.

If you haven't laid your pavings already, they should be the big project for the second year, with the final grading and installation of the lawn to follow. However if your budget calls for it, you can sow the lawn now, leaving the future terraces simply in gravel or grass. Structures like pergolas might also form part of this second stage.

Stage three involves the more detailed planting of things such as shrubberies and ground covers. Stage four is the fine-tuning, the trying out of new plants, the adjusting of colour schemes, and so on. This can go on for as long as the garden is yours.

This sort of plan, whether carried out over two years, three or more, works for most people and situations, but don't treat it as obligatory. Use it as a basis for tailoring a strategy that will suit you.

Garden construction

The actual construction of fences, walls, pergolas and their like is a matter both of taste and flair in design, and of handyperson skill. While much garden construction is well within the scope of the amateur carpenter, if you're at all doubtful about your skills, it is better to call in a professional. Nothing looks worse than clumsy workmanship—and surprisingly often, you don't save all that much money; not when you factor in the cost of your own time and of hiring the equipment which the professional builder already owns. But don't let this put you off. Doing your own building can be fun, and if your work isn't as finely finished as it might be, you can always call on foliage to camouflage this.

Fences and walls

Fences are worth spending time on, as they can set the tone and feeling of the garden. You need them for privacy and to keep out intruders, but you want them to work for your design, not against you.

Most builders and developers provide a basic fence with the house. Usually, this is tallest around the back garden, though surprisingly often it is only about 1.5 m high, tall enough to keep the children and the dog from straying but not really tall enough for

A beautifully detailed trellis fence.

privacy, for which it really ought to be 2 m or a shade taller.

The material used will vary from one part of the country to the other, but brick, wire or concrete slabs are quite usual. Though in theory the maintenance of boundary fences is the joint responsibility of the two adjoining property owners, in practice if you want to heighten the fence, or replace it with a more decorative material, it is likely you'll be bearing the cost yourself. Don't despair; a coat of paint (choose the sort of olive drab, khaki, dark brown or grey the army uses for camouflage rather than green which stands out in the landscape instead of receding) or the application of a timber trellis can work wonders in dressing up the fence; or you can attach a wire-mesh trellis and cover the lot with creepers. Alternatively, call on foliage to provide some screening—2 m or taller shrubs or small trees will do the trick. They needn't be evergreen; many deciduous shrubs are sufficiently thick in growth to provide screening.

It might not be wise to build a high, opaque front wall. They aren't called the

Adding a panel of trellis at the top of the paling fence has gained greater privacy without making the whole thing too dominating.

burglar's friends for nothing. Here, the fence is part of the foreground to the house, and its style will depend very much on that of the house itself. Timber pickets, plain or fancy, suit colonial style cottages, whether colonial in date or not; cast-iron pickets are the standard accompaniment to a Victorian house; and modern houses can be flattered by brick walls and stone as well as timber. The choice is limited only by your imagination.

Also, any type of fence can be decorated with flowering climbers and creepers. Be careful, though, with thorny plants like roses and bougainvilleas: if they injure a passer-by, you will be liable.

Fences are usually thought of as fairly light constructions; when they are made of masonry (brick or stone) or precast concrete they are walls. Walls can look mighty handsome, but cost usually limits their use. There is no reason why you shouldn't put windows or gates in them to allow access or to frame a view. Unless you really are skilled at building, leave masonry and its heavy foundations to the professional.

Gates go with fences, and they offer nearly as infinite a range of options. The only rule is that the gate should not look stronger than the fence it interrupts.

While we usually think first of boundary fences, don't forget that fences and walls can be used within the garden too, to set off and enclose your garden rooms. Here, where security is not the issue, they can be open, light and decorative in construction, but not flimsy. You don't want them blowing down in the first storm.

Retaining walls and steps

Retaining walls are heavy engineering rather than art, and you shouldn't attempt to design or build one more than about a metre high without the assistance of a professional. Lower walls are safer, provided you adhere to two rules.

First, the wall should be battered, that is leant back into the earth that it supports. The pressure of the earth is constantly trying to push the wall over, and once a vertical wall starts leaning outwards, it not only looks unstable, it is unstable.

Second, water builds up behind the wall and, unless you give it somewhere to go, its pressure will endanger the

Spaced laths, painted white.

A cream picket fence hung with bougainvillea.

stability of the wall. You can lead it away by a drain behind the foot of the wall, or provide holes so that it can flow out through the wall face; either is effective.

With these two rules in mind, you can make your wall from a variety of materials—brick, stone, concrete blocks, treated pine logs. All can look effective, and all can be clothed with plants to soften their appearance. Often, there is no need to make the wall in one lift; you can make it as a series of steps, with plants growing at each level—a terraced bank if you like. If you have the room to simply make a bank at a slope of 1:1 (no steeper), you can dispense with the wall altogether, using a dense ground cover to hold the bank against erosion. There will be run-off at the foot of any bank so it is important to ensure that there is some way of carrying the water away—either a drain or a slope.

Whether you have retaining walls or banks, changes of level call for steps to get from one level to the other. They can be focal points in the garden design, but need to be designed with care, because they should not only be attractive to look at, they *must* be safe and comfortable to use. If you are going to use them at night, ensure they are well lit; but it is even more important that they should fit the feet of those who walk up and down them. The rule to ensure good, comfortable steps is that twice the height of the step (the riser) plus its length (the tread), in centimetres, equals 66. The maximum height for a garden step is 16 cm, but the ideal proportion is a riser of 12 cm with a tread of 42 cm. It is important to try to have an uneven number of steps, and to keep all in the same flight the same dimensions; if you must change the proportions to accommodate a changing slope, separate the two lots with a landing.

The width of steps is a matter of proportion, though it is an accepted rule that the fewer you have, the wider they should be. The steps must not be slippery when wet; usually you can make them in any material which is suitable for paving. If they are wide enough, you could make the risers in brick or timber and the treads in grass—but that will involve you in some rather careful trimming. Whatever you make them of, ensure they are firm; a wobbly step is as dangerous as a slippery one.

Paths and paving

A path needn't be made of paving (in situations like a formal rose or vegetable garden you may well want to make your paths of grass) but they usually are, so we can consider them as narrow strips of paving, to be made of the same sorts of materials as you might use for a more extensive terrace or patio.

The choice of paving materials is enormous, but they can be broken down into two main categories: those you lay as a continuous sheet and those

you assemble from small blocks.

The continuous sheet pavings start with gravel, the oldest of all, and the cheapest. It has the disadvantages of being uncomfortable to bare feet, tending to track into the house and onto the lawn, and on any but the very slightest of slopes it washes away. But it does look soft and natural and flatters any plants associated with it. (It can look very attractive to plant a few plants in the gravel itself, to look as though they have escaped the adjacent planting beds, but don't overdo it.) If you have a

A rockery looks best planted so lavishly that the rocks are almost hidden.

A long flight of steps needs to be well lit for night-time safety and well upholstered with plants.

choice, a fine, well-rounded river gravel is the best. Initially it should be laid to give you a layer about 8 cm deep. Lay the gravel on a weed-free, well-rolled bed of soil. Keep some Roundup handy to zap the occasional weed that tries to grow in it. It will bed down into the soil over time, so you'll need to top it up occasionally. To look its best it should be raked smooth every so often. Japanese gardens often feature a very fine white gravel which is raked daily into patterns. Nothing looks so authentic in a Japanese style garden—but unless you are a Zen monk you may find the constant raking a bore.

Wood chips and tanbark are softer equivalents of gravel and can look very pleasing in an informal woodland style garden—but are they pavings or mulches?

Then there is bitumen or asphalt, a functional pavement, and, alas, looking it—it is very hard to make it look like anything except a car park. Bitumen needs professional laying, so it isn't really cheap. Few gardeners would want to use it.

Last of the continual sheet paving is concrete. Plain grey concrete is a bore. You can colour it, but it is a bit like a bore at a party who hopes that a martini or two is going to make him witty. The only really attractive surface is 'exposed aggregate', achieved by using a good quality gravel and gently hosing off the surface excess before the concrete is quite set. This is a skilled job. If you would like to try it, you should practise behind the shed before tackling the patio where your visitors will see it. You can buy the sand, cement and gravel and mix the concrete yourself, but these days most gardens are within reach of a ready-mix place that will supply small orders. They will make a better, stronger mix than you can. Have everything in readiness before the truck arrives. This involves levelling your bed and placing the timber formwork that will hold the concrete in place while it sets. You can't cast concrete paving in wide, seamless sheets—it will crack even if it is reinforced. Divide it with expansion joints every couple of metres. These can be the formwork, left in place; and you can have great fun arranging patterns. If this all sounds

like a stretching of handyman skills to the limit, you hear correctly; if you are planning a cast concrete patio or driveway, you'll be thinking of calling in an expert to lay it for you.

Concrete can be coloured to look like brick, but why not lay the paving in brick anyway? The real thing always looks better. Brick is probably the most popular of the pavings you can assemble yourself. And brick is just the thing for the do-it-yourselfer; it's easy to lay, and you can do just as much at a time as you have the time and energy for. The easiest way to lay it is on a carefully levelled bed of sand 10 cm deep. The sand should be held in place with the same sort of timbers you use for concrete formwork. Start at one end, and tap your bricks into place with a mallet, and when you are finished, spread more sand over the top and sweep and water it in to fill the joints. There are many patterns in which you can lay the bricks, but the easiest, and in many ways the most attractive, is basket weave. Stretcher bond, the kind you use in walls, is dependent on high accuracy, both in the making of the bricks and in

A simple gravel pathway, edged with an equally simple planting in white, yellow and blue.

the laying if the lines of the pattern aren't to go crooked. The same is true of 'herringbone', which gives the strongest pavement, a factor that might be important if you are planning a brick driveway. The South African climate isn't so severe that frost damage to paving bricks is a problem, but you should tell your supplier that you are going to use the bricks for paving, to ensure you do get good, well-burnt ones. The actual colour is a matter of taste, and it will soften with weathering and dirt. One that matches or is a darker tone than the brick walls of the house is always a good choice.

Concrete blocks ('cobblestones') are an artificial brick and are laid in the same way, though their proportions are such that the variety of possible patterns is less. They come in a range of colours, and which to choose is a matter of personal taste. They all fade a bit with age and sunlight, and that is usually an improvement.

You can also buy precast concrete slabs, usually about 6 cm thick, in a variety of sizes and proportions. They are cast in steel moulds. Plain-surfaced slabs can be so smooth they get slippery when wet; try laying them upside down (the bottom is rougher) or pay the extra for an exposed aggregate finish. They look very well laid a couple of centimetres apart, with grass growing in between. A sand bed is best, and two pairs of hands will make the laying of the heavy slabs a lot easier.

Stone is the choicest of paving materials, but it isn't cheap. The type available will depend on what your local quarry can supply, and you can either set big, squared slabs with wide grassed joints the way you lay concrete slabs or butt them closer and point up the joints in cement. Or you can lay slasto, which calls for much care in arranging the irregular pieces of stone to fit the space. Some trimming is usually called for. A sand bed will normally suffice, but you might prefer the added strength of an 8 cm concrete base.

Slate, whose grey surface can be very sympathetic to plants, must be laid on concrete as it is very brittle. The same is true of marble—but if you can afford marble, the expense of having a marble mason lay it for you won't be a problem! Be careful of stone and brick in shaded places, as they can develop a surface growth of algae in wet weather. This is not only dirty looking and

Low plantings on either side of this mellow brick path enhance the feeling of space.

A long flight of steps, but of such an easy grade that they aren't tiring. The material is bluestone.

Swimming pools need both a sunny, paved 'beach' for sunbathing and a shaded place out of the sun—here provided by the trellised pavilion.

unsightly, but it makes the paving as slippery as glass. If it starts to develop, you should wash the paving down with either swimming pool chlorine or diluted bleach, sweeping it on with a stiff broom to remove as much of the algae as possible. A pale blue solution of copper sulphate is even better, but neither treatment is permanent—in wet weather cleaning the pavement can be a regular chore. Concrete isn't so troubled by the problem.

Finally, no pavement except gravel should be perfectly level or there will be puddles everywhere when it rains. There should always be a fall, not less than about 1:200 (1:150 is better) to carry the water away—to a lawn, to planting beds, anywhere but towards the house.

Swimming pools

Building a swimming pool is not a do-it-yourself project, and the local swimming pool company (choose carefully; the trade is notorious for attracting cowboys) is the best source of advice on styles and whether you should go for the traditional chlorinated fresh-water pool or a salt-water pool, fibreglass or concrete. Let us here only note a couple of factors that might affect the garden.

Plan for the pool from the very beginning, even if it is a to-be-done-later project. Unless you have a vast acreage where you can tuck it away, it will be the dominant feature of the garden. It should look as though it belongs, and not be an afterthought. It's difficult to make a pool look natural, and a simple shape is almost always the best. Try to arrange the pool itself to be in the sun, but some shade nearby will be a pleasure to retreat to. You don't want plants overhanging the water and dropping leaves into the pool. Allow room for the pool builder to get in later with his equipment—don't plan some feature like a patio or a major planting that will obstruct him or the price will sky-rocket. Many local authorities these days require swimming pools to be securely fenced. So make sure you plan for enclosure. Finally, make sure that the surrounding pavements drain *away* from the pool, or every time it rains it will be flooded with dirty water and your filter system will be forced to work overtime.

Getting the soil in shape

If the builder has just left you with a brand new house, the first thing to do is to get rid of the inevitable heaps of rubbish. Call in a rubbish removal contractor, or yell at the builder to come and clean up after himself. You will, hopefully, have remembered to put it in his contract to remove the topsoil from the areas he is building over so that you can spread it on the garden-to-be. But before you can spread topsoil, you need to do some thorough cultivating. His trucks and heavy equipment will have been driving everywhere, and they will have compacted the soil. Digging with a spade is hard work, though good exercise for the young and fit. You may prefer to hire a rotary hoe, complete with operator, for a day. This is the time to do the shaping of the ground, so that your lawns won't be full of bumps and hollows. Then you can spread your reserved topsoil. If you are in the position of having to buy in soil, buy the best 'garden' grade. Imported soil is often dug deep from beds near rivers and is lacking in humus. 'Garden' grade should have some (usually composted sawdust) added.

This is part of the joy of a brand new house, and buyers of old houses are spared it. But it is still worth checking your soil and cultivating if need be. Before you plant is the best time to improve soil in old garden beds, and the best way to do that is to dig by hand, to a spade's depth—as far, that is, as the blade of the spade will go. Turn the soil over and incorporate as much organic matter—manure, compost and the like—as you can lay your hands on. Leave it to settle a few days, and you're ready to plant. (More about soil and how to improve it in the section 'Looking after the garden'.)

Installing the lawn

Most of us think of installing a lawn as part of the construction of the garden—after all, you need to have something to keep the dust down. You can do it at any time of year, but remember that grass takes longer to establish in winter, and at the height of summer you will be driving yourself crazy keeping the new lawn watered. Spring and autumn are the best times, with a preference for spring if you have the choice.

The bed for a lawn should be prepared as scrupulously as you would for any other plants, by cultivating and enriching the soil as much as you can; but you also need to ensure that it is properly even in grade, with no bumps and hollows. Dragging a long straight piece of timber over it helps, and for the final grading you need a fine-tined rake. Pick up any stones lying on the surface and get rid of them—you don't want the mower to find them later. Then, you water. Not only will this help show up any spots that still need levelling, it will encourage the weeds to germinate. When they have come up and are looking dreadful, zap them with Roundup. Yes, we know: this takes a month or so, and you are impatient to be getting on with the lawn; but starting clean will be a great help in keeping

things that way in the years to come.

With the weeds gone, it is time to think about grass. Different parts of the country have their own favourites, and this is one area where you should be guided by local custom. The only thought we offer is that you should go for the finest grass mixture available, even if it is more expensive and slower to establish than cheaper, fast-growing blends designed for parks and playgrounds. Think of all the time you'll save by having to mow less frequently.

The cheapest way to establish the lawn is by sowing seed. Follow the directions on the packet as to quantity, and then divide your seed supply in two. You can hire a gadget like a carpet-sweeper that dribbles the seed out evenly, or you can broadcast by hand. Either way, you do it twice, first going up and down and then from side to side—you get a more even coverage that way. Follow up with a light raking which will cover the seed, and instruct the cat to chase the birds away from it. Water with the finest spray the hose will give, and keep the bed evenly moist until the grass is well up. Normally germination takes about ten days, but you need to keep watering (twice a day if needed in hot weather) until it is about 5 cm high, when you can taper off. About then, you can give the grass

its first mowing to encourage it to branch low, but set the mower blades as high as they will go. By the second or third mowing you should be down to your regular watering schedule of no more than once a week.

Turf is easier and faster—'instant lawn'—but very much more expensive, and you are likely to have a more limited selection of grasses than you would find on the seed shelf. Still, if you are laying only a fairly small lawn, or don't have the time to devote to nursing seedling grass, it will be worthwhile. The bed needs to be prepared as before, but laying the turf is easy. You just unroll it and put it on the ground face up like so much carpet, trimming it around the edges with scissors. Stand back and admire while you can, for the next job is to spread fine topsoil over it until the green almost disappears. Water it in and most of the green will return, and keep it all well watered at least until the grass is due for its first mowing.

For economy, you can cut each turf into plugs about 3 cm square, which you then plant out like seedlings about 10 cm apart, watering them in and keeping an eye out for weeds that might grow in while the grass is growing together. Or you could pull the turf apart into runners, which you sprinkle

A lawn always looks best uncluttered; here, the promontory of bright flowers sets off the perfect sward.

all over the bed and then rake over to cover with soil. You have to work fast though, for the runners dry out quickly, and you'll have to water nearly as assiduously as you water seed.

Remember, turf doesn't keep. If you are planning to lay it on Saturday or Sunday, order delivery for Thursday at the earliest.

PLANT SELECTION

Choosing plants for the design

Half the art of successful planting design is learning to see plants as a whole. Don't just focus on the flowers, however gorgeous. Does the plant have attractive foliage, and what is more, is it attractive for a long time, even all year? If it isn't, is its moment of glory sufficient to keep you looking fondly at it during its off-days? Does it have an attractive habit, graceful and open, or neat, rounded and compact, boldly upright, cascading or whatever: or is it just a scruffy support for the flowers? What sort of texture does it suggest to the eye: fine, medium, coarse or bold, matt or glossy? Does it offer features other than flowers or fancy leaves— interesting bark or fruit perhaps, or fragrance? Is it easy to grow in your soil and climate, or will it be an unhappy invalid, needing constant attention? And, if your temperament suggests, does it carry pleasant associations, childhood memories perhaps? There are some plants that will seem to have that indefinable quality of distinction, that makes you say, 'Yes, I want to grow you!' and those are the ones you should choose to plant.

The other half is learning to think of plants in terms of the role you want them to play in your garden design. This is particularly useful if you don't know everything there is to know about plants—and there are so many in the world that none of us can have even a nodding acquaintance with them all. It's much easier to talk to someone from a nursery or search through an illustrated book like this one if you have already focused your desires by thinking in terms of, say, a deciduous shrub, about 3 m tall, with yellow flowers, or an evergreen, cascading ground cover to trail over the retaining wall, than if you just ask 'What would look pretty?'

The art of all art is simplicity. Don't think you will be bored by having

In a sloping garden, steps and paths of neatly tailored concrete pavers are softened by lavish plantings.

Proteas make spectacular cut flowers.

Kniphofia praecox, *ideal for waterside clumps.*

several plants of the one kind; it is much easier to arrange just a few species effectively than to try to weave an intricate tapestry with just one plant each of many.

A word of warning. The commonest mistake in planting is to crowd your plants. Sure, the baby plants look so lonely; but space them in accordance with their spread when they grow up or you'll end up with a tangle. Where we have given the width of a plant take note; where it isn't given, assume that it will spread to a width about two-thirds to three-quarters of its height, unless it is noted as 'spreading' or 'upright', in which case you can assume a greater or lesser figure.

Indigenous or exotic?

Gardeners have always used their indigenous plants. The cypresses, umbrella pines and box of the great formal Italian gardens are all indigenous to Italy and the camellias and chrysanthemums of Japanese gardens are indigenous to Japan, though after centuries of cultivation they can scarcely be described as wildflowers. So the idea that South African gardens should contain South African plants and that their presence will help to create a distinctive South African style of gardening, in harmony with the South African landscape as the gardens of Italy and Japan are with theirs, is not radical.

On the other hand, gardeners have always taken delight in importing choice plants from foreign lands—there are carvings on ancient Egyptian and Assyrian temples praising the rulers who had the benevolence to introduce trees and flowers that had never grown in those countries before. So whether you belong to the 'indigenous only' school, prefer the beautiful garden plants of other countries, or prefer to blend the two, you will have plenty of tradition behind you.

It is true that indigenous plants can create a feeling that the garden belongs to this land which is hard to achieve with exotics (using the term in the strict scientific sense of 'coming from a foreign place or environment'). However this is a big country with many diverse climates and ecosystems. Can you really call a tree from the Mariepskop rainforests 'indigenous' in Cape Town or Bloemfontein; or pretend that a Namaqualand wildflower is anything other than foreign to the very different soils and climates of the east coast? True, it is South African, and thus pleasing to the patriotic breast in a way that a plant from, say, California won't be; but it isn't indigenous in the sense that a *local* wildflower is.

Local plants do have the practical advantage that they are born to your own environment, and the chances are that they will flourish with little attention. And wherever you might live there will be indigenous plants of great beauty to choose from: trees, shrubs or flowers, and even grasses—many of our favourite grasses originated here.

Most gardeners ignore the debate and grow what they like, no matter where it comes from, mixing indigenous and exotic plants as their fancy suggests. And why not?

Trees

Trees are the most important plants in any garden—they grow bigger, and live longer than any others, and they are the main creators of the form and structure of your garden. More than any other plants, they are the ones that enhance not only your garden but the entire street. They can provide, according to the type and how you place them, shade, shelter or privacy. Some give flowers in their season, and there is no better way of having the sensation of swimming in flowers than from a flowering tree. However flowers are not

Big trees can lend dignity to a house the way no combination of smaller plants can; provided there is room.

the prime consideration: elegant habit, attractive foliage and suitability for the position and use are more important.

Think of deciduous trees for summer shade and winter sun; of evergreens for screening and backdrops. Think too of trees that branch high enough to walk under, so that you can look up and see the sun shining through the branches as well as those that sweep the ground to be looked at from the outside as it were. Don't forget to think of the mature height and spread of your chosen tree, and how quickly it will reach full size. Scale is important: will it be too big for the garden, or just right? If you garden on a grand scale, you can think of forest giants; in small gardens, small trees are more appropriate.

Shrubs

Shrubs are the workhorses of the garden, filling in the structure at and below eye level. They can act as screens

for privacy, soften the lines of the house, or be given starring roles by virtue of their flowers, fruit or handsome foliage. They provide detailed interest for less expense and work than any other plant. But don't forget to allow them room to do their job; most shrubs will grow nearly as tall as they are wide, and it would be a pity if you have to be constantly trimming to get past them.

Try to value shrubs as much for their habit and foliage as for their flowers. It can be very telling to set some small, rounded shrubs in front of a tall, arching one; to set dense foliage against shrubs which feature an open tracery of branches; to contrast an upright grower against one of spreading, prostrate habit.

And don't forget those shrubs which can be clipped to form hedges, or which lend themselves to training flat against a wall, in the fashion known as espalier. These can create a note of

Whether low or tall, hedges introduce long horizontal lines to a garden and call for trees to balance them.

Seaside daisies set off the intricate patterns of tiled pavings. A mix of flowers would look restless here.

formality as nothing else can, and there are times when that is just what is needed.

Ground covers

Low plants that carpet the ground with foliage, suppressing weeds, ground covers will grow in the dense shade beneath low branching trees and shrubs where few other plants will grow. They are often modest in foliage and flower,

and their great asset is the unity and simplicity they can bring to a garden. Always planted in masses of a single species (you can make patterns of several types, but you'll always be fighting to keep them apart), they tie together collections of disparate plants that rise above them. If you have a fine tree or group of trees, their beauty will be enhanced by allowing them to rise unencumbered by a clutter of fancy plants at their feet. Simple panels of

ground cover can relieve the arid appearance of large areas of paving.

Climbing plants

Do you have an unsightly fence or shed that you wish would vanish from your sight? Climbing plants to the rescue. Do you want to soften the lines of the house and make it blend with the garden? Try decorating the walls with a climber. Do you want shade in a hurry, and can't wait for a tree to grow? Build a pergola and grow a creeper over it. In two or three years you will have the shade, while a shade tree is still a sapling.

You can train some climbing plants to grow flat on the ground as ground covers—ivy is the classic example—or place them at the top of retaining walls to cascade down in a foam of greenery and flowers. Or, if you have a worthy but dull tree, try climbing some flowery climber into it to wreathe it in colour. Just beware that it doesn't grow so heavy that it brings the tree down on top of you. English gardeners are fond of training climbers over dead trees, but this isn't a wise idea here, where we have white ants. Should they get into the dead tree, the whole thing could come crashing down without warning.

Annuals and perennials

They don't have permanent woody stems, but annuals and perennials bear some of the brightest and most beautiful of all flowers, and no flower lover would be without them. The distinction according to the botanist is that annuals don't live to see their first birthday, ensuring their future by setting abundant seed; perennials live and flower for years. But matters in the garden are not as clear cut as that. There are many subtropical plants, perennial in frost-free climates but always grown as annuals where winter cold cripples them—petunias, gazanias, scarlet salvias and the busy lizzie (*Impatiens wallerana*) for instance. Conversely, other perennials need winter cold and rarely flourish beyond their first summer in mild climates. A notable example is the delphinium; long-lived in Britain where it is one of the glories of the classic perennial border, but best discarded after flowering in all but the coolest parts of South Africa. The Iceland poppy is another; and then there are such plants as gaillardias, carnations and rudbeckias, which come in both truly annual and perennial versions. So we have decided to list all our annual and perennial flowers together. And there is no reason other than horticultural convention why you shouldn't mix and match them in your plantings also.

Some gardeners are prejudiced against annuals, which only live for a few months and thus put their owners to the bother of replacing them when they die. But if annuals' lives are short, they are filled with gaiety; some of the world's best loved flowers are annuals—sweet peas, petunias, poppies, larkspurs, everlasting daisies. Annual flowers are generous with their blooms, and they are a great boon to the owner of a new garden. They grow quickly and give you something to admire while your slower growing, permanent plants are developing. In an established garden, they provide continuity of flower while perennials and shrubs are coming into bloom and passing out

again, and you can use them to draw attention to focal points in your design. Cluster them at the front door, around the patio, on either side of steps; they don't call for a permanent commitment, and you can change your colour schemes from year to year, even season to season. If you love novelty and variety, they are for you. Just don't make the mistake of building the garden around them—you do need those permanent plantings!

With the current fashion for cottage gardens, perennials are enjoying a great revival. No wonder, for they are the flowers of Grandma's garden, and if you have childhood memories of beautiful flowers there, chances are that many of them were perennials. Coming up unfailingly year after year, they can be displayed in borders in the English manner, or you can just tuck a few here and there among and in front of shrubs, or beside a path: or blend them with annuals and shrubs for a kaleidoscope

of colour. Many have handsome foliage too, and some are providers of the boldest, most architectural foliage the garden contains. Use these in the way you use pictures and accessories and ornaments in a room; they draw the eye and provide the finishing themes. Their ease of propagation allows you to expand your holdings year by year; and many a lifelong friendship has begun with the gift of a piece of some choice perennial flower.

Bulbs

If you want to initiate a friend into the joys of gardening, you could do worse than give him (or her) a packet of bulbs. If nature ever developed a foolproof way of packaging a plant it is this; just plant, add water, and before too long there will be flowers. We always associate bulbs with spring and with cool climates, but there are summer flowering bulbs and bulbs for

The unmatched brilliance of summer flowers—here zinnias, begonias and roses—calls for a simple green backdrop such as the leafy wisteria in this garden.

Formal bedding needs to be on the grand scale of this bed of tulips and white daisies to look really stunning, and is most successful in public spaces.

Daffodils can brighten a winter garden.

warm climates too. They all share a perfection of form and colour which is their own—but most only give a few flowers per plant each year. So plant them as generously as your purse will allow, in clumps, in bold masses under trees, in containers, in with other flowers. The English love great drifts of bulbs growing as though they were wildflowers in long grass, and it is an idea that works very well in cooler climates. Warm-climate grasses tend to grow so quickly as spring warms up that the bulbs get either smothered or mown prematurely. You can 'naturalize' bulbs in ground cover plantings too. They will look very nearly as good.

Vegetables and herbs

Time was, when it wasn't quite nice to admit you had a vegetable patch. The master and mistress of the house may have taken the keenest interest in the vegetable garden, but no visitor ever saw the vegetables growing. *They* only saw them after they had been harvested and the cook had had her way with them.

Nowadays, many of us take great pride in our vegetables, and for many people they are the most important part of the garden. If that includes you, why not display them with pride? Not in the front garden, perhaps (we don't want to place temptation in the way of light-fingered passers-by) but in a choice position in the back garden, where they get the sun they need and where you don't have to make a safari out to the back of the shed to admire their progress. Lay the plot out with care, casting an eye over the proportions of your beds and laying attractive paths between them (grass, brick and gravel all have their admirers) and giving them a flattering backdrop of shrubs or fruit trees, not just a bare fence or a shed.

The problem is that a vegetable bed is never full. Just as the plants are beginning to develop sufficient growth to be worth looking at, the cook descends on them, and great gaps appear in your plantings. What to do? You could edge the beds with low-growing flowers (and why not include some annuals among the cabbages, to provide cut flowers for the house?) but it is even nicer to edge the bed with herbs. Most herbs are fairly low-growing, and their scent is a pleasure as you plant and weed. Their varied greens and textures offer much scope for developing garden pictures. Think, for instance, of the grey-green of sage in front of the darker, matt green of cabbages or the brighter colour of lettuces …

There is an old tradition of growing herbs in small formal gardens by themselves, and a small herb patch can be a pleasant accompaniment to a patio, but you needn't isolate them. Plant them as edgings to flowers, or set them among the blooms in a cottage garden mix. Their soft textures and varied greens will help stop a riot of colours turning violent with clashes—and again, their fragrance is definitely to be sniffed at.

Don't forget, too, that fruit trees (unless they are pruned into grotesqueness) are as beautiful to the eye as any other trees. Let them take places of honour in your garden design.

Water gardens and water plants

In our dry climate, water in the garden adds a special dimension of pleasure. It needn't take the form of the elaborate fountains that Italian and Islamic gardens specialize in; just a simple pond reflecting the sky and cradling a water lily or two can bring great joy too.

In designing a garden pond, the important thing to remember is that it is the water that is the purpose of the exercise. It is so easy to get excited by water lilies, lotuses, Japanese irises and all the other water garden plants that the water vanishes in the greenery and you might as well have planted a regular flower bed. As a general rule, whether your pond be informal and naturalistic or frankly formal and artificial (and this is a matter of which will best suit the style of your garden as a whole), the water plants should cover no more than a third of the surface.

A second rule is to make your pond a good deal bigger than you first thought of it as being. The pond itself is just a hole in the ground with a waterproof liner. You can buy ready-made fibreglass pool liners, though they tend to be sized for portability and to end up looking like puddles. The choice for liners is really between concrete and plastic sheeting. Both have their devotees. Plastic is certainly easier and

Herbs lend themselves wonderfully to formal treatment as in this traditionally styled herb garden.

Tropical waterlilies. A pond yielding flowers such as these is a garden in itself.

cheaper, though you must hold down its edges and conceal them with rocks or a strip of paving. If you choose blue plastic the pool will always look unnatural. Simply lay plastic over a sand base, taking great care that there is no unevenness or any sharp objects that will tear it. A layer of pebbles over the bottom will mask it from sight. Pebbles will help the appearance of a concrete pool too.

The plants need rich soil to grow in, and this is usually provided by planting in containers, wooden boxes being

traditional. (You can't use plastic pots, which tend to float; it is a bit disconcerting to see a water iris topple over in full growth because its roots are trying to rise to the surface.) Give the plants rich soil, and, at the point where the pond can overflow when it rains, plant some of the many desirable perennials that love wet feet. If the water garden bug really bites, you could make it the theme for the entire garden, taking your cue from some of the old gardens of China and Japan, where the 'lake' occupies most of the garden and the

Even in the tiniest of ponds, you need to allow sufficient clear water to catch the light.

A butterfly on a scarlet canna.

viewers stroll around it. If you fancy artificial waterfalls and rock work, go ahead. But first, spend a day or two in the bush, looking at natural streams and waterholes to see how nature arranges rocks, water and plants. You'll learn more from her than from a torrent of words; but don't come back with the car loaded up with rocks. Those rocks are part of the ecology of the bush, and are home to many wild creatures. It is scandalous to dispossess them.

Don't forget when you plant the pond to include as well as the water lilies some floating and submerged plants to provide oxygen to the water. These are essential if you aren't to have the pond all choked up with algae, and they are needed for the fish. Of course, you will have fish to keep the pond from becoming infested with mosquitoes. Goldfish in their various forms and varieties are the easiest to keep as well as the most decorative. Buy them from a good aquarium supplier, and, as

soon as you introduce any new fish to your pond, treat it against fish diseases with methylene green. The people who raise fish take every care, but it is better to be overcautious. The aquarium shop will advise you about all these things.

Birds and butterflies

While there are some forms of wildlife that you won't want to encourage in the garden—poisonous snakes, black, and brown button spiders, and the assorted bugs that will try to eat your plants— you will want to encourage birds and butterflies. This is easy to do.

Most of the birds we want to see are indigenous, and the recipe for encouraging them to visit the garden and hopefully take up residence is simple. First, you put a bell (or preferably two) on the cat. It's surprising how cats can learn to silence one bell when the urge to go hunting seizes them. Then, you plant as wide a variety of indigenous

plants as you can accommodate. Grevilleas, banksias and their relatives, and tecomarias and aloes are much loved by honey-eating birds, and so are such plants as New Zealand flax. Seed-eaters will go for their fruits, and for those of such things as eucalypts and tea-trees; but they will eat the berries of cotoneasters and their like too. Insect-eaters will come too, for the indigenous plants and trees provide their food without asking. Regular spraying not only cleans out the insects, it can poison the birds too. If you don't spray, the birds may well act as pest-control agents for you.

Don't forget that many indigenous birds nest in hollow trees and branches, and you should think twice about removing these unless they are really unsafe.

We always think of providing food for adult butterflies. Any flat-faced summer flowers will attract them, not just the buddleias that are so much frequented by them they are called the butterfly bush. (The New South Wales Christmas bush is another great butterfly plant.) But don't forget that they start out life as caterpillars, and if you want butterflies in the garden there has to be a source of caterpillar food somewhere nearby. Most of the preferred caterpillar plants are weeds, and a lazy gardener will often be rewarded with more butterflies than an industrious, conscientious one. It's not fair, is it?

A pleasing arrangement of colour is a personal thing; some may not have placed the yellow tulips in this display.

Colour

It is fashionable for gardening books to give learned dissertations on the 'rules' of arranging colour schemes, so that you are burdened with terms like 'analogous harmonies', 'complementary contrasts' and 'colour wheels'; and to give lists of colours that do and don't, in the opinion of the writer, go together. This book won't do any such thing, because the careful colour schemes which might be appropriate in arranging wall-paper and furnishing fabrics fail to take into account that colour in the garden (by which most people mean the colours of flowers) are displayed and arranged against a background of green. The green of foliage comes in infinite variety, from the brilliant green of grass to the dark, almost black-green of some tropical plants to yellow-greens, olive greens, grey-greens, and the steely tones that gardeners are pleased to describe as 'blue', as in the blue spruce and some eucalypts. All these greens are constantly changing with the time of year and time of day.

In any case, pleasing arrangement of colour is such a personal thing; some people adore bright pink flowers, others don't; some find bright yellow shrill, others think it cheerful and sunny.

Fragrance

It used to be common to make scented gardens for the delectation of blind people, but the fashion has lapsed, fortunately, for most blind people found such gardens patronizing. They like to smell the flowers in the same sort of gardens that everyone else does. Indeed, scent on the air is one of the great delights of gardening.

The problem with writing about scent is that you can't describe it in any meaningful way except by comparison—and most flowers smell more like themselves than anything else. Nor can you photograph it.

Francis Bacon suggested that scented flowers should be planted along paths where you can sniff them as you pass

A quiet scheme in greys and pale colours.

by, and that still holds good. But he also reminded us that there are many plants whose fragrance is in the leaves, not to be released unless they are brushed against or crushed, and that these should be planted right at the edge of paths, 'where you may enjoy them as you walk and tread'.

In this book, we have noted when a plant is fragrant. In choosing plants for the delight they offer to the eye, don't forget the nose. Develop the habit of sniffing every new plant you meet, and plant your favourites in your garden with a lavish hand.

Climate

We have discussed the influence of climate on the design of the garden, but mainly from the point of view of your, the garden user's, comfort. But your climate also determines, more than anything else, the selection of plants you can grow. The earth has many types of climate, from tropical to arctic, and nature has evolved plants to grow in all of them. Take those plants from the wild and bring them into a garden, and they will be happiest and easiest to grow where the climate matches that of their homeland. If it is markedly different, the plant will either not grow at all or it will lose its character. And it is not only the familiar phenomenon of a tropical plant freezing to death when struck by frost; the reverse is true too. Cold-climate plants need their winters to flourish. For example, we always say that cherries need a cold climate to grow, but this is not strictly true. There was, some years ago, a cherry tree in the Botanic Gardens in Singapore. It grew, but it never flowered or even lost its leaves; in the tropical climate it had become over time a non-flowering evergreen.

Nevertheless, it is frost that provides the sharpest division. Though it is true that plants that can stand frost vary in the amount they can survive, plants from warm climates with no frosts have never evolved defensive mechanisms to allow themselves to cope with being frozen. Take them to a frosty climate, and they die from having their cell walls ruptured by the freezing and expansion of their sap. In the USA, 'hardiness zones' have been worked out for the entire country, based on the minimum temperatures expected and how long they occur. American gardeners have developed the habit of saying that a

plant is hardy to zone 7 (or 3 or whatever) or 'suitable for zones 5 to 9'. They are not of great relevance to South Africa, most of which has relatively mild climates (certainly by the standards of the continental USA), and the problem is just as likely to be trying to grow some cool-climate plant in a climate too warm for it as the reverse and the limiting factors are likely to be drought and heat. We have simply noted minimum winter temperatures in our Cultivation Guidelines at the back of this book.

So for this book, in the plant entries we have described the growing conditions each plant requires, and any particular characteristics, such as whether it is hardy or frost-tender. And we have also noted if a plant is drought-tolerant, remembering that summer humidity is important here, not just rainfall.

Buying plants

These days, gardening is big business. Every suburb, even inner-city ones, has its garden centre; florists do a flourishing trade in pot plants; even supermarkets sell plants. It has never been easier to buy what you need to furnish the garden. If you can't find just what you are looking for, you can often find it advertised in the gardening press by one of the many mail-order nurseries.

Supermarkets and chain stores tend to buy nationally from one or more of the big wholesale growers. The fact they are selling a particular plant doesn't guarantee its suitability for your climate—you need to use your own knowledge. Also, conditions in an artificially lit, air-conditioned store aren't always ideal for plants (except indoor plants, usually a good buy). It is good fortune to find a salesperson who knows anything about them. Try to buy as soon as possible after the plants arrive. Walk by any that look as though they are suffering stress. Bulbs and perennials in picture packets can often be a good buy here, but check them carefully—sometimes stock gets left on the shelves long after the planting season has finished and the poor things are dead.

At garden centres and nurseries, you can expect the staff to be able to give good advice about the plants they sell. Often they will also have encyclopedic knowledge of what does well in their area, knowledge that can save you making costly mistakes. You should still

look carefully at the quality and condition of the plants. Are they healthy, vigorous-looking and free from disease. Not potbound from hanging around too long (telltale signs are a plant that's just too big for the pot, with roots poking out of the drainage holes or at the surface), or obviously having suffered drought at some stage? Naturally, there won't be weeds in the pots. Be prepared to pay a fair price; bargains are often plants left over from last season, offered cheap to get rid of them. They may grow well, or they may not; why spend money to take the risk?

Bare-rooted stock, like roses, fruit trees and perennials in season, should be plump and healthy, with plenty of roots. Reject any that look shrivelled and dried out, or which seem to be trying to grow prematurely. Bulbs should be firm; if you find any that feel squashy or mildewed, examine the others even more carefully. But a good nursery knows that it trades on its reputation for quality …

The same is true of the mail-order houses. Here you can't examine before you buy, but you should take a critical look at the plants the minute they arrive. Notify the nursery at once if they arrive in less than perfect condition. (A nursery that regularly supplies inferior stock won't stay in business for long.) Don't forget, however, that the nursery may be a very long way from you, and it is up to you to be sure that your chosen plants will grow in your area. The mail-order nurseries are often the best places to find rare, choice plants your local nursery may not even have heard of. When you find yourself reading their catalogues with the same eagerness as movie fans do the latest gossip about the stars, you know that gardening has you hooked.

LOOKING AFTER THE GARDEN

Preparing and cultivating the soil

Just what sort of soil you have doesn't influence the basic planning of the garden much as there are trees, ground covers and grasses suitable for just about any soil. But it does matter when it comes to choosing your plants, and then when you look after them. Geologists have developed many different

A display of annuals like these pansies and double daisies takes a lot from the soil, which you have to put back if you want to repeat it season after season.

classifications for soils, but the gardener needn't learn them. Garden soils are classed as light (or sandy), medium (or loam) and heavy (or clay), the terms referring to how easy they are to dig. (Sand is in fact weightier than clay.) Then, we want to know how deep our topsoil is before we strike the less-fertile subsoil or even rock; how well-drained it is; whether it be acid or alkaline; and, finally, how fertile it is.

Let us look at each in turn. To find out whether you have sand, loam or clay is easy. Make a ball of just-moist soil in your hand. Does it feel gritty and crumble as soon as you open your hand? Sand. Does it feel gritty, but holds its shape, more or less? Sandy loam. Does it feel just slightly sticky and holds its shape but crumbles if you poke it? Medium loam—and go and open a bottle of champagne, because this is the sort of soil that gardeners' dreams are made of. Does it feel greasy, holds its shape, and polishes if you rub

it with your fingers? Clay loam, heavy to work but not to worry; it will grow most things. Can you not only polish it, but mould it into delicate shapes like modelling clay? Clay. Be prepared for hard work, but don't despair—clay soils are usually fertile. Away from the beach, pure sand is rare, and so is pure clay; most soils will fall in the range from sandy to heavy loam.

Strictly speaking, you should measure the average size of the rock particles that make up your soil to arrive at a more scientific classification. But these are measurements you can't make outside a laboratory, and for practical purposes the ball in the hand will tell you what you need to know.

Below the topsoil, you'll find the subsoil, which is usually, but not always, of the same type, but distinguished from it by a different colour, due to its lesser humus content. It is normally more tightly packed than the topsoil, so that plant roots don't pen-

etrate it as easily. As it contains less humus, it is less fertile. You don't usually want to dig it up and mix it with the more fertile topsoil, but if a little of that happens, no great worry. Below the topsoil and subsoil you will eventually come across rock. Sometimes this is quite close to the surface, sometimes many metres down; but as long as you have about 30–50 cm of topsoil before striking it (or a solid subsoil) you have sufficient depth to grow almost anything.

It is the subsoil that normally determines how well drained your soil is. This is perhaps the most important thing to know about your soil. While plant roots need water, they also need air; if the spaces between the soil particles remain clogged with water for too long, they suffocate. Test your drainage by digging a hole about 40 cm deep, which is as deep as most of us can take a spade without strain, and fill it with water. Come back in 24 hours, and if it is quite empty, you have no worries about drainage. If there is still a puddle in the bottom, you will have to do something to improve it, unless you are content to specialize in wet ground plants. There are a lot of these; but, alas, many choice trees and shrubs, lawn grass, and most vegetables aren't included on the list.

There are two ways to improve drainage. If your garden design suits, you can make raised beds. These can be an advantage if you don't like bending. Hold the soil with a wall (brick, heavy timber or whatever) and you can sit down rather than crouch to garden. Or you can lay agricultural drain pipes, leading the excess water to a sump or to a convenient ditch or stream. Thanks to the introduction of flexible plastic pipes, this isn't the difficult job it used to be, but it's still heavy work to dig a network of trenches to lay the pipes in. The usual arrangement is to lay branch lines across the slope, feeding to a main which should direct the water away from the house.

Happily, poor drainage is rare in suburban gardens—wet ground is not prime land for building development. Generally, the sandier the soil, the better drained it will be—sometimes too well, so that you barely seem to have finished watering before you have to start again—and sloping sites are usually well drained too. Poorly drained soils are often clays.

Then there is the matter of acidity and alkalinity to consider. This is a great business for show-off gardeners who like to be 'scientific' and say things like 'Oh, my soil is ideal—slightly acid; pH 6.8, you know.' The pH scale measures acidity and alkalinity, with 1 representing a strong acid, strong enough to eat the end off your spade, 14 an alkali just as strong. The mid-point, 7, is completely neutral, like pure water, and each step is ten times as large as the next; thus a soil of pH 5 is ten times as acid as one of pH 6. Most soils fall within the range of 5.6 to approximately 8.6. The significance is that the higher the pH, the more lime there is in the soil.

Some plants, like rhododendrons, azaleas, camellias and blueberries, dislike the stuff and prefer their soil acid (i.e., with pH less than 7); others, notably bearded irises, the cabbage tribe, and some of the choicer Namaqualand wildflowers, are lime-lovers and like a soil with a pH of about 8. If your soil is too acid for these, it is simply a matter of adding a little lime; if it is too alkaline (limy) for the acid-lovers, you are in trouble, as it isn't easy to acidify a soil. (Adding sulphur is the standard way, but worms and most soil-living micro-organisms dislike it; you can grow the acid-lovers in containers of special soil.) So the ideal is to have the soil neutral or slightly acid. (In our plant descriptions, we draw your attention to any special likes or dislikes in soil that a plant may have.)

You can buy soil-testing kits that will tell you just what the pH of your soil is, or you can send a sample away to your state department of agriculture who will test it for you. Easier, perhaps, is checking out what sort of plants are growing in the neighbourhood. If you see many camellias and azaleas flourishing, you can assume your soil to be acid; if they are looking miserable, with odd russet and yellowish tints to their foliage, you can bet it is alkaline. Hydrangeas are even better indicators: in acid soils their flowers are blue, in alkaline ones pink. As a *very* general rule, the sandstone or shale-derived soils along the humid east coast tend to be acid: those in dry areas inland, or where the parent rocks are limestones, alkaline.

Finally, there is the big question: is the soil fertile? To an extent, this depends on its type. Sandy soils tend to be 'hungry', because the large spaces between their particles don't hold the water and the plant nutrients that it contains. Clay soils, with their smaller pores, hold the water and nutrients more readily and are often more fertile. Loam is the perfect balance. But fertility depends even more on the amount of humus the soil contains. This sub-stance, the end-product of the rotting of the remains of plants and animals—organic matter for short—gives fertile

The arum lily (Zantedeschia aethiopica), an obliging plant that actually loves wet, poorly drained soil.

Raised beds are a classic way to overcome less than perfect drainage—but they also are a great showcase for flowers.

soil its instantly recognizable dark colour. It provides the nourishment for all the microscopic life (bacteria, fungi, algae, tiny insects) which hold and release nutrients to the plants we grow. It also improves the soil texture, simultaneously aiding its water-holding capacity and its drainage. So if you want to improve your soil and maintain its fertility, the recipe is simple: add as much organic matter in the form of compost, old manure, and what have you, as often as you can. (Yes, we know it might be possible to overdo it; but where is the lucky gardener who has that much compost available?)

It used to be said that soil wasn't properly prepared for planting unless it had been dug to two spades' depth by a laborious process called 'double digging'. These days we are content to dig it over to as deep as the spade will go, breaking up the clods, softening and opening up the structure and just folding in (as a cook would put it) our compost. After the bed is planted, it is impossible to dig that deep without disturbing the roots of our plants, so we cultivate more shallowly, just sufficient to break up the crust that tends to develop on the surface with the pres-

sure of rain and watering. And if we put a protective blanket of mulch on the surface, we don't have to do that very often.

Don't fret about the type of soil you have. Sure, a slightly acid, crumbly medium loam is the ideal, but few desirable plants insist on it. Attend, if needed, to the drainage; and then, with regular cultivation, and keeping up the humus supply, and any soil will become more fertile as the years go by.

Fertilizing

To listen to some of the advertising fertilizer manufacturers have put out since factory-made fertilizers were invented about a hundred and fifty years ago, plants are made up entirely of the things they market. Not so; most of a plant's substance is made up of hydrogen, carbon and oxygen—elements that don't appear on the analyses given on fertilizer packages. The plant extracts these from air and water by the wonderful process known as photosynthesis. As a by-product, green plants release oxygen into the air, thus making life possible for animals, including ourselves. Both the oxygen

and hydrogen are derived from water. That's why plants grow ahead so strongly after a drought breaks; a plant deprived of water isn't just thirsty, it's starving too.

But living things are more complex than that, and there are many other elements that a plant needs to live. These it gets from the soil, absorbing them in very dilute solutions through its roots. Chief among these are nitrogen, phosphorus, potassium and calcium. Others, like magnesium, manganese, boron, iron, copper and what have you, are only wanted in tiny amounts and so are called trace elements.

Calcium is pretty abundant in most soils, and it is only if we want to grow lime-loving plants in acid soils that we need to add it in the form of lime. Lime (calcium oxide) comes in various forms. There is quicklime, the pure oxide; slaked lime is prepared by putting quicklime in water. Both of these will burn the skin off your hand if you are silly enough to touch them. Leave them to builders for their mortar mixes. If you want to apply lime use it in the form of pulverized limestone (calcium carbonate). Better yet, use dolomite, which contains magnesium as well. Not that magnesium (a vital component of the green pigment chlorophyll which makes photosynthesis work) is usually in short supply, but it won't hurt to top it up. The other three elements, nitrogen, phosphorus and potassium, are used up by plants. In nature most of these elements are eventually returned to the soil when plants die and decay. But in the garden there is always some waste—we harvest our vegetables and eat them, flowers are cut and taken into the house, prunings burnt or carted away. A prudent gardener establishes a recycling depot, otherwise known as the compost heap.

Nitrogen forms most of the air, but in that form it is no use to plants. They need to absorb it in combination with oxygen (as nitrates) or with hydrogen (as ammonia). These come into the soil by several routes: they are formed by lightning in thunderstorms; they are released by the decay of once-living organisms; and they can be formed ('fixed') out of atmospheric nitrogen by certain bacteria that live in nodules on the roots of legumes, plants of the pea family. Nitrogen is a vital part of proteins, without which life can't exist.

It is essential to plants if they are to grow and make abundant foliage. This is why high-nitrogen fertilizers are prescribed for lawns and for leafy crops like lettuces and cabbages. Sulphate of ammonia is the standard source of nitrogen in artificial fertilizers; blood and bone (which is mostly protein) is the richest organic source. Compost and manure contain nitrogen too, in varying amounts depending on their origin, how old they are, and so on.

Phosphorus and potassium are needed for almost all life processes, but they play especially important roles in flowering and fruiting, and in the creation of woody tissue. Consequently, plants that we grow for their flowers, or which we want to make firm branches (trees and shrubs) need them in abundance. A fertilizer designed for them will be proportionately higher in these two elements than in nitrogen, too much of which can promote luxuriant leaves and few flowers. Nitrogen deficiency shows up in stunted growth and pale, wan-looking leaves, which usually drop prematurely.

Phosphorus doesn't occur pure in the soil, but in various salts. Most of

these are very insoluble, and it is something of a mystery how plants actually get hold of them. It is thought that the soil micro-organisms are involved—and as these need humus to thrive, this is another reason for the compost heap. Soluble or not, phosphorus eventually leaches from the soil. Many South African soils, especially along the coast, are apt to be short on this element. This is why our farmers have been so lavish in their use of superphosphate, the standard phosphorus-containing fertilizer. They have, however, sometimes overdone it; and the consequence has been phosphate pollution of rivers and streams. The main organic sources of phosphorus are bone meal and blood and bone. Phosphorus deficiency manifests itself in stunted growth, with leaves showing odd russet tones.

Potassium salts are highly soluble, and the element washes from the soil very easily. Fortunately, micro-organisms can fix it; but if you let a potassium-containing fertilizer get wet, you'll have lost much of its nourishment. Various potassium salts are used in the making of fertilizers; the main

Here a raised bed takes the place of a front fence. Scarlet cannas bring bright colour, contrasted with the soft blue of trailing Convolvulus sabatius.

homemade source is wood ash (not coal ash!), which should always be kept under cover if it isn't going to be spread on the garden as soon as the fire has died. Seaweed is very rich in potash and kelp solutions are available at nurseries and garden centres. Potassium deficiency shows first in yellowing of the tips and edges of older leaves, which eventually die.

These are the big three. An artificial fertilizer containing all of them can be described on the label as 'complete'. The amount the fertilizer contains is usually given as a percentage by weight, and you will see such indications as N:P:K 2:3:2 or N:P:K 3:2:1 on the bag. (K stands for potassium which was originally known to eighteenth-century chemists as kalium.) Most companies make a range of blends for different purposes. Thus a nitrogen-high blend like 3:2:1 might be recommended for lawns, the lower-nitrogen 3:1:5 for shrubs or roses. Whether it is economical to have different bags for different plants is up to you to decide; many people find it easier to just buy a standard, evenly balanced mix, say 2:3:2, and use it for everything except indigenous plants. While you're at it, you might as well look for one that contains trace elements too.

The various trace elements each have their own functions, and each deficiency has its own symptoms (like the mottled yellow pallor of young leaves caused by iron deficiency or the between-the-veins yellowing of older leaves associated with lack of manganese). So if you suspect a trace element deficiency—and they aren't common, these elements being needed only in tiny amounts—it is better to give the plants a complete trace element mix or a general fertilizer containing them. Treat just the one you suspect and the chances are you will overdo it and throw the soil out of balance, leading to a deficiency of something else: and your last state will be worse than the first.

ORGANIC OR ARTIFICIAL?

So we are going to fertilize our soil. The question is whether to do it with organic materials (the various forms of manure, compost, blood and bone) or with factory-made artificial fertilizers. In the short term, it makes little difference to the plants, which can only take in their nourishment in the form of solutions of chemical salts, and don't discriminate as to how they got there. In

Spring bulbs are ideal for the busy gardener; dormant in summer, they need no water when it is scarcest.

the long term it matters very much indeed, because if the soil is to *remain* fertile, it must have its humus content continually replenished so that the soil micro-organisms continue to flourish. So the thinking gardener always prefers organic fertilizers. Never mind that their N:P:K ratios are much lower than those of the artificials. They are feeding all the life of your soil; the plants you planted are only a part of this. Take an analogy, but don't stretch it too far—vitamin pills are richer in vitamins than food, but would you try to live on a diet of pills? You can give your plants a quick boost with artificial fertilizers occasionally, but make their main diet organic. The analogy holds good in terms of quantity too—artificial fertilizers must always be used with a sparing hand or you will overdose. It's really better to halve the manufacturer's recommended dose and apply it in two lots a fortnight or so apart. Don't increase the dose—a little may be good but more won't be better! Never apply artificial fertilizer to dry ground, and water heavily as soon as you have spread it. Otherwise you risk burning roots and stems it comes in contact with.

MANURE

There's a story told of Mrs Harry Truman, in the audience while her husband the American president was lecturing a group of farmers on the virtues and uses of manure. A prim friend leant over and whispered to her, 'Can't you get him to say something politer than "manure"?', to which Mrs Truman replied, 'Honey, if you only knew how hard it was to get him to say "manure"!'

Even now, primness becomes us; let us simply note that manure is the *rotted* dung of animals. Until it has been rotted (mellowed if you like), it is far too sharp and strong to put on the garden. It will burn any plant it touches, and the neighbours will turn up their noses as they go by. If you do acquire it fresh, put it in a heap in an out of the way place, or spread it on top of the compost heap, and leave it to settle for six weeks or so, throwing an old tarpaulin or a piece of plastic sheet over it to keep rain from washing out the soluble nitrogen and discourage flies. When it stops smelling like … when it starts to smell less offensive, it is ready to use.

Dig it into the beds you are preparing to plant, or spread it as a mulch. Or make liquid manure out of it; simply put some in a hessian bag and steep it in a dustbin full of water like a tea bag. When the water is the colour of tea, it will be as rich in nitrogen as any artificial fertilizer. You can pour it around plants that need a quick boost, and throw the bag and its contents on the compost heap. Artificial fertilizers designed to be mixed up in water are available to give much the same effect without making you hold your nose. They are usually applied diluted enough to be absorbed by the leaves as well as the roots, and shouldn't burn. Even so, the makers usually suggest you pour them on in the cool of the evening. They can be applied with a hose-end sprayer or with a watering can.

Manure varies in richness and 'heat' according to the animal it comes from. Pig manure, not often seen for hygienic reasons, is the 'coldest', poultry manure the 'hottest'. Horse and cow manure fall somewhere in between. If in doubt, heap it up and wait; well-rotted manure is almost always safe to use. Exception: human manure. Only use it if you have a compost toilet that works properly; there is too great a risk of horrible diseases like cholera and dysentery otherwise. The Chinese have used 'night soil' for centuries, and fertile stuff it is, but they always compost it first—and even so the history of China is studded with epidemics. Treated sewage sludge is indeed safe to use on paddocks and fields, but that has been prepared under skilled attention.

How much manure? Old garden books that assumed you had a horse or two give recipes that boggle the mind, calling for layers of manure 15 or 20 cm deep to be spread over beds and dug in, and this often twice a year. Nobody can

afford to buy the stuff in such quantities these days, but take the point: you can feel free to be as lavish as you can afford.

Dehydrated, pelleted, fairly odor-free poultry manure is a recent development. It's great stuff, but concentrated, and it needs to be applied nearly as carefully as an artificial fertilizer. Follow the suggestions on the bag, and store it in a dry place—if it gets wet in the bag it will putrefy.

Blood and bone is a by-product of the meat industry, and is the strongest organic source of nitrogen, with some potassium and phosphorus. It should be used as sparingly as an artificial fertilizer, just colouring the ground with the powder (think of a cook sprinkling icing sugar on a cake) and watering it in thoroughly. Keep the dog off for a few days, or the smell will have him digging like crazy. Bone meal is the same stuff, without the blood. It is slow acting and the best purchasable organic source of phosphorus, the best being wood ash. (Wood in this case includes paper.)

Compost

No garden should be without its compost heap. Compost is the most readily available source of organic matter, and it is free but for the labour in making it. That isn't all that great either; you can simply gather together all the fallen leaves, grass clippings, cabbage stalks and other once-living debris of the garden, throw them on a heap in an out-of-the-way corner, and come back a little while later to find compost. That may be several months or even a year, but sooner or later you'll find, under a skin of leaves and twigs that haven't completely rotted, a pile of the black, moist crumbly stuff that works such magic on any soil.

Compost freaks will throw up their hands in horror. 'Compost making is a scientific process!' they'll say. 'A heap like that takes too long to rot, half the nitrogen will have evaporated as ammonia, and the compost won't be as rich as manure, as it would have been had it been made properly.' True; but compost isn't all that rich in N:P:K— that is not the point. It is mainly intended to keep the soil supplied with humus, its direct value as fertilizer being only secondary. Let us, however, look at the standard recipe for compost making, with the understanding that apart from piling up the heap just about all the manipulations directed are optional.

First, you gather together roughly a cubic metre of compostable stuff. This can be almost anything of organic origin, though the bulk will be plant matter. (Don't put meat in the heap or you'll attract blowflies and rude remarks from the neighbours.) Ideally, you want a mix of coarse and fine material, so that the heap will neither be too open to rot properly nor so well-packed that air can't get into it. Coarse stuff includes cabbage and tomato stalks from the vegetable garden, straw, weeds complete with roots and a bit of dirt, twiggy prunings (no thorns, please) and the like; fine includes lawn clippings, shredded paper, small fallen leaves and their like. Cooked vegetables are apt to go soggy and putrefy, and left-overs from the salad bowl are dubious—the oil tends to set like lacquer and preserve the vegetables. Perfectionists will keep the coarse and fine stuff separate, so that they can put them on in layers, like a layer cake.

You need to keep the heap compact. The best way to do this is to put it in a compost bin. Better yet, have two, side by side. Bins can be made of wood,

A small compost heap held with bricks.

A plastic compost bin.

The traditional, triple compost heap.

bricks, or chicken wire stretched between four stakes, as you please and as your handyperson skills allow. (Several commercial types of composting bins are available.) No need for a concrete floor; sitting the bin on the ground allows worms to enter the heap and assist with the rotting.

Into the bin, you throw about 20 cm of stuff, and on that you sprinkle a nitrogen-rich chemical activator, to encourage the bacteria and fungi that will do the rotting to begin their work. Fairly fresh animal manure (horse, pig, cow or chicken) incorporated with every cubic metre of vegetable waste will ensure a compost which will be richer in plant nutrients and much more alive with beneficial soil bacteria.

Keep piling, in layers of stuff and starter, and when the bin is full, water it. Then you should cover it with a tarpaulin to keep the rain off; you don't want it all to get too wet or it may putrefy and smell of rotten eggs and worse. (If it does, it's a sign of it being too compact and too wet. Take the tarpaulin off, and stab the heap several times with a sharp stake to let some air in. That is really the only thing that can go radically wrong.)

Almost at once, there will be frantic activity from the bacteria and friends, the heap will start to get very hot in the middle, and there will be a smell of ammonia. No doubt this represents nitrogen being lost, but most of it will stay in the heap. Don't get obsessive … When the ammonia smell passes off (in a couple of weeks to a month) the heap is ready to be turned inside out, so that the bits on the outside get the benefit of the heat and activity of the middle. This is what the second bin is for—simply pitchfork everything into it, and the compost should be well turned. (Then you can start on making a new heap in the first bin.) Once again, the smell of ammonia; but this time when it fades there is no need to turn. That would disturb the worms, which will now come in and polish the compost. When most of them leave, it is ready to be shovelled out onto the garden. It will be black, crumbly and sweet-smelling, and free from weeds and diseases, which will have been killed by the heat of fermentation.

Even so, it isn't wise to count on this last quality—diseased material and such horrors as small tubers of yellow nut grass are better burnt to make ash. They should not be added to compost heaps.

While bark chips are a favourite mulch, they rot very slowly and don't add much to the soil.

The compost will keep for a while, but don't just sit and gloat over how gorgeous it is. Compost is not an end in itself; it is meant to be put on the garden to improve the soil. The lazy gardener can make compost without even going to the trouble to make a heap. Just spread your compostable material straight on your beds as mulch, sprinkle it with a bit of blood and bone to ensure it doesn't take nitrogen from the soil as it starts to rot, and let it rot down in place. This has the fancy name of 'sheet composting'. There are neater mulches, more suitable for putting in the front garden where the neighbours might see them, but it's fine for the vegetable garden.

Shredders, alias chippers, are useful gadgets—they chop up prunings and other garden waste into small pieces. This allows you to compost bigger, woodier stuff than otherwise, and the neat same-sized pieces are great for sheet composting. The mulch looks so much better than when it is thrown on as it came. Like dishwashers a few years ago, they are moving up from being just gadgets to don't-know-what-I-did-without-it status. Most of us will only need a smallish, electric model.

Mulching

Mulches have become so much a part of gardening that it is hard to realize our parents found them a novelty. Basically, a mulch is a blanket you lay across the surface of bare soil to protect it against the crusting effect of rain and watering, to conserve moisture by blocking its evaporation from the surface, and to smother weed seedlings, and it can be of any of a wide variety of materials.

Cut-rate landscapers are fond of black plastic, which certainly holds moisture in and stops weeds; but it also blocks moisture getting in, and eventually suffocates the soil. It is a fine way to kill off weeds without digging or using weedkillers, but don't leave it on for more than six months or so. It is usually hidden beneath a layer of pebbles, which would make an effective mulch by themselves. Gravel, scoria or crushed rock or brick would serve too. These conserve a surprising amount of moisture, and by reflecting heat they keep the soil cool. But they are apt to be glary, and they look artificial except in a desert-style landscape.

Rocks don't add any fertility to the soil; organic mulches eventually rot down and add humus. There is an enormous variety you can use: grass clippings (don't pile these on more than a centimetre thick at a time, or they will ferment, get hot, and clog into a thatch that suffocates the soil), fallen leaves, pine needles; compost, well-rotted manure; shredded prunings; straw; bark chips; shredded bark; old mushroom compost (careful, it tends to make the soil alkaline) and others which you'll find at the garden centre, the precise selection varying from place to place. Sawdust is common, but it takes a lot of nitrogen to start it rotting, and it is best heaped up with a bit of compost starter and left for a few months.

Which of these you choose depends on which is easy and cheap to get, and how you like the look of it. Some, like straw or bark chips, can look a bit raw when they are new, but will presently weather into inconspicuousness. Just be wary of nitrogen starvation unless, like compost, the rotting process has already taken place. Sprinkle some blood and bone over the mulch when you lay it.

How thick to apply mulch depends on how much you can afford, but the ideal with most materials is to have the mulch 3–4 cm thick, thinning it out a bit immediately around the stems of the plants. Less isn't so effective at smothering the weed seeds. Notice weed *seeds*; if weeds are already established, they will *benefit* from the mulch. Remove them first, and water the soil. Never, never, mulch dry soil—there has to be water to conserve! And a dry mulch will rob moisture from the soil beneath; water it after you spread it. That's it; but don't forget that the rotting eventually attenuates the mulch. You'll need to top it up from time to time, though there's no need to use the same material as before.

You can, as our grandparents used to do, hoe the soil after every rain to create a dust mulch. The hoeing encourages the top centimetre or two to dry out, and the dust acts as a mulch, stopping further evaporation. It does work, but it's scarcely labour saving, and the dust blows about in the wind.

Planting

The actual planting of a plant only takes a few minutes, but how you do it is as important as anything else you ever do to it. Plant with care, and you get it off to a good start; do it carelessly and badly and you can cripple it for life. Don't be alarmed; the rules only number four.

Rule 1. Never put a ten rand plant in a one rand hole. If you haven't been able to dig the whole bed, dig as much as you can. Make your hole generously wider than the plant's roots, so that it has plenty of nice, soft soil to spread its roots into. People often dig a small hole in the middle of a lawn, pop a tree into it, and then wonder why it doesn't

Planting seedlings into well-prepared soil.

grow. They should have made a bed at least a metre wide, preferably wider, and planted the tree in that. Plenty of time to let the grass grow up to the trunk when the tree has had a chance to become established.

Rule 2. Disturb the roots as little as possible. If the plant is growing in a container, it has to be removed, and there is a right and wrong way to do it. The wrong way is to grab the poor thing by the stalks and tug. You'll get it out of the pot all right, but like as not you'll leave half the roots behind. The right way is to tip the pot upside down, holding the plant in the fingers of one hand, and give the rim a sharp tap to release the pot from the root ball. It can then just be lifted off. If the pot is too big to do this, lie it on its side and tap; the plant should slide out sideways. Advanced trees and shrubs are often grown in large plastic bags. These are best cut away with scissors, and then you can lift the plant (cradling the roots, not grabbing the stem and expecting it to take the weight of the soil) off the bottom.

If the plant is at all potbound and the roots are showing signs of going around in circles, gently release them and tease them out, or they will continue to circle forever and not break out into the surrounding ground. (Eucalypts are very prone to this.) This might sound like breaking the rule, but not so if you do it gently and quickly, so that the

Well-spaced plantings of ageratums.

roots don't get a chance to dry out. (If you're nervous about this, simply cut the circling roots by slashing the root ball in two or three places with a sharp knife; new, outward-going roots will grow where you cut.)

Seedlings growing in trays are tipped out the same way as other plants are removed from pots.

Growing bags are on the way to superseding the technique of growing trees in the field and then lifting them and bundling up their root balls in hessian and string, but if you do acquire a 'balled and burlapped' tree, they are easy to handle. Simply carry them by the root ball and undo the string when the tree is safely in its hole. Leave the hessian in place; it will soon rot and the roots will grow through its remains.

Fruit trees and roses are often sold bare-root, that is, without soil. These need care to ensure they don't dry out. Plan on planting them as soon as you get them home. Once they are unwrapped, keep them in a bucket of water. If need be, disentangle the roots, and trim any broken ones with sharp secateurs. (Planting is simple enough: make your hole, spread the roots out over a small mound in the bottom, fill up the hole with crumbly soil and water heavily to settle the soil around the roots.)

Drying out is the worst disturbance you can inflict on any roots—once you

Nemesias, ideal for spring bedding.

Cinerarias, almost always sown in punnets (the seed is very small) and then planted out.

have plants out of their containers, don't dawdle.

Rule 3. Set the plant at the same depth as it was originally. This is simple enough with container grown plants, and balled-and-burlapped and bare-rooted trees usually show a mark on the stem where the soil was in the nursery. Add or take soil to adjust the hole's depth. With most plants, a whisker or two too deep or shallow won't matter, but do try not to set the roots too deep or there is a real danger of smothering them.

Grafted plants are normally set with the graft union just at soil level, though there are two major exceptions, citrus and lilac. Citrus are prone to collar rot, which is almost certain to occur if the graft is buried. Lilac, on the other hand, must have the graft set well below the surface. This is because it is normally grafted on the closely related privet, which is really too vigorous for it. Burying the graft enables the lilac to make its own roots and eventually smother the privet, which otherwise would push the lilac off after a few years.

Annuals can go in a shade deeper than they were in the tray, and most perennials are set with 5–8 cm of soil above the crown. Bulbs, as a general rule, are set so they have as much soil over their noses as they are tall, though most won't mind if they are a bit shallower or deeper. Many have the

remarkable ability to pull themselves down to where they feel comfortable.

Rule 4. Water the plant in well. First of course you need to fill the hole in around the roots with well-crumbled soil, and many people like to enrich this with a bit of compost to help the plant make the transition from the enriched soil of its container to the garden soil. Time was when people told you to trample it well to stick it to the roots, but that is no longer the fashion. Just water in well with the hose or water poured from a bucket, and that will settle the soil well enough. Some people like to water with a plant hormone to encourage new roots; others think it makes no difference. Naturally, you'll water and mulch the new plant for as long as it needs it.

A few don'ts. Don't plant any plant while it is making active growth if you can avoid it. Even minimal disturbance to the roots will affect their ability to support the activity above, though if the choice is between planting and any risk of the plant drying out in its pot, plant. Don't plant out of the correct season for the plant unless you really have to, but especially not when the weather is hot and dry. *Warm* weather planting from containers is fine, and most plants will establish quicker than they would in winter; but you do need to take extra care—its new home is probably less sheltered than the nursery was. Give it some shade for a few days (a newspaper

teepee is just the thing for seedlings, a few leafy twigs or some shade cloth for a shrub) and water regularly at least until autumn.

Watering and conserving water

It may seem superfluous to suggest that watering is a skill; after all, any child can turn on a tap and wave a hose around. Yet it is a skill. The water we put on our gardens accounts for a surprisingly high percentage of our total water usage, and an alarming percentage of that water is, in fact, wasted.

The golden rule is to water only when the plants actually need it and then to water thoroughly, so that the water actually penetrates to where the roots are. Frequent light sprinklings only encourage roots to stay near the surface, where they suffer as soon as the soil dries out again; deep watering sends them deep where the soil dries out more slowly.

It isn't possible to give rules like 'water twice a week for twenty minutes'. It depends on the weather and even more on your soil. Sandy soils absorb moisture more quickly than clay soils do, but they don't absorb so much, so excess runs away more easily and what has been held is used up the faster. Clay soils are the opposite; they only absorb water slowly (especially when they are quite dry) but they hold onto it for longer. Watering heavy soils takes patience—you can't apply the water as fast as you can on sand. Loam, as in so much else, is the best balance, absorbing the water fairly quickly and holding onto it well. On any soil, you shouldn't apply water faster than the soil can absorb it—if the water is running away it is being wasted.

Similarly, you shouldn't waste water by evaporation. This will happen if you water in the heat of the day, especially if a dry wind is blowing, and the loss will be worse if you deliver the water in a fine spray. Much of it will evaporate even before it hits the ground! Early morning or evening, when the air is cooler and stiller, is better; better yet is the middle of the night, when the air is coolest and water pressure highest.

Not that anyone would want to leave a plant that is actually wilting till the evening—water at once! Plants send signals that they are suffering water stress long before they actually wilt, and the observant gardener learns to recognize them and act promptly. Leaves and flowers go, not exactly limp, but unhappy-looking and lustreless; grass retains your footprints instead of springing back; in many plants the stems and leaves lose the appearance of firm plumpness they have when they are well-filled with water. Some plants react faster than others, and you may want to plant such things as hydrangeas or acanthus as an early warning system. When they start to droop, it is a signal to get out the hose.

In drought prone areas (and that includes most of the country!), it is wise to make the backbone of your plantings species that will survive and flourish with little assistance beyond the local rainfall. It is frustrating not to be able to give lists of these, but so much depends on your climate. For instance: in Durban, with its fairly reliable summer rainfall and high humidity, one can regard camellias as reasonably drought-hardy; inland, where summer drought is the rule and summer humidity is low, they are no such thing—to survive, let alone give their full beauty, they must be watered regularly in summer.

The best way to find out what plants are drought-hardy in your area is to make a tour of the neighbourhood next time a summer drought strikes, and note the plants that are obviously bearing up without assistance. There will be plenty, and they should form the basis of your planting designs, with the more tender plants concentrated at key positions where they will give the best value for water.

WATERING SYSTEMS

Watering by hand can be a relaxing way to spend time in the evening, but to do it thoroughly takes more time than you would think. It can save time and water to install a fixed sprinkler system. Thanks to modern developments in plastics these are not the luxury they used to be. Almost every big hardware store these days can give you a choice of do-it-yourself systems, and if you want something more sophisticated there are plenty of more complex ones which need professional design and installation. These can be of mind-boggling complexity, with sprinklers that pop up out of the ground, electronic gadgets that sense when the soil is dry, and timers that can be set to turn the system on late at night when conditions are optimum and the chances of giving a visitor a surprise shower are least.

Somewhere along the range is one that will suit your needs and pocket. Designs and gadgetry are always changing and you should take the advice of the people who market the systems or an independent irrigation consultant. Let us only note here that in most gardens do-it-yourself systems can be perfectly adequate, and that the 'trickle' systems are the most economical of water, though the most fiddly to install (you need far more tricklers than you do sprinklers) and to maintain, the tiny pipes clogging up easily and the absence of water only being noticed when a choice plant dies. If you install any watering system, do give it a test run every few weeks to ensure all is working properly, and install an in-line filter unless you can swear on the Bible to the purity of your water supply. And do arrange your system so you aren't watering pavings and driveways. They don't need it, you know!

Often thirsty and prone to wilt if the soil gets a bit dry, hydrangeas tell you the garden needs watering.

Night time is a good time to water—and it makes a great picture.

You may prefer the old-fashioned but still effective method of sprinklers on the ends of hoses. Shifting these about is troublesome, and it is best to have several strategically placed taps rather than just one. That way you can run two or three sprinklers simultaneously. Short hoses last longer and are less fuss to handle than long ones too. Place a timer on each tap. They are quite cheap, and save the annoyance of finding that you have left the sprinkler on all night.

Three final thoughts on saving water. Mulching protects the soil from drying out; a single dripping tap or leaking pipe wastes thousands of litres a year; and the single most important thing you can do to save water is to keep your garden weeded. One of the things that allows a plant to become a weed is super-efficiency at taking water from

the soil. Why allow plants you don't even want to rob water from the garden?

Looking after a lawn

Ask anyone who announces a dislike of gardening what they dislike about it, and chances are 'mowing the lawn' will be high on the list. This is understandable; it is a chore with little creativity about it. Yet it is the most important part of managing a lawn. Leave the grass unmown, and eventually it becomes a meadow—the grass gets long, and the weeds come in. How often and how short to mow depends on the type of grass and also, to an extent, on the season. Fine grasses like Florida and Kentucky blue can take closer cropping than the coarser types like buffalo or

kikuyu, and in a dry summer it is wise to leave the grass a little longer than usual.

As with any plant, cutting back the foliage takes strength from it, and when it is growing slowly you shouldn't weaken it too much. As a general rule, the fine grasses can be cropped to 2 cm or a shade more, the coarser ones to 3 cm. Don't make the mistake of cutting as short as the mower will go in the hope of mowing less often. This only weakens the grass and allows weeds to get in; and then you'll be mowing more often, as the weeds grow taller and faster than the grass and look dreadful.

The actual layout of the lawn can make mowing easier or more difficult. Don't clutter it with flower beds and specimen trees any more than you really have to; and avoid sharp corners and

Dragging a long hose like this around the garden is a bore. It would be better to have several taps, so that you could have two or three shorter hoses.

wriggly curves, which make it difficult to get the mower right to the edge without much backing off and returning. Ideally, no corner should be sharper than a right angle, no curve smaller than you can easily sweep the mower round. If you fancy grass paths, in the vegetable garden or in a formal rose garden for instance, don't make them narrower than the mower! It is easy to make them exactly the same width, and that way you only have to push the machine down them once: but in practice that requires such careful handling that you might as well have them wider and make two passes. The same applies to the space between two trees, should you plant a grove on the lawn. Here don't forget to allow for the eventual thickening of the trunks. A gentle slope is easy enough to mow, but anything steeper than about 1 in 4 is both uncomfortable and dangerous. Consider planting banks with no-mow ground covers rather than grass.

THE LAWNMOWER

The mower itself is probably the most expensive item of gardening equipment you'll buy, so choose with care and look after it. There is nothing that gives the perfect velvet sward better than the old-fashioned hand-mower with its cylinder

of blades kept razor sharp; but it needs cleaning and oiling after every use, the blades are fiddly to sharpen, and it takes energy to push it. Most of us aren't such perfectionists (or can think of more enjoyable ways to get our exercise) and will opt for a power-driven mower. Petrol or electric is up to you. Electric mowers are quieter and save the bother of storing fuel and they aren't as useful for a big or rugged lawn as the commoner petrol-driven type. These come in either reel-cut or rotary models, the reel-cut being essentially a mechanized hand-mower. The rotary is easier to maintain, and better at tackling thick or wet grass; but it doesn't give the striped effect that is so admired in English gardens. For that you must have a cylinder. Most people aren't that fussy, and opt for a rotary, with a grass catcher to save raking up. (Leaving the clippings on the lawn, to filter down between the grass blades and rot, is a better idea in theory than in practice. In reality they don't rot properly, and the grass shoots get choked with 'thatch', which has to be removed with a special rake—leaving the lawn looking like a child's attempts to cut his own hair.)

Whichever mower you buy, look after it as the manufacturer directs, and develop an obsession with safety in its

use. Make sure the blades of rotaries are screwed on properly lest they fly off and amputate your foot; remove sticks, stones, children and toys from the lawn before you start; don't go away and leave the mower running, even for a minute; wear solid, protective shoes; and never, never, put your hand down near the business end while the machine is running.

EDGES

Trimming edges is as time consuming a job as mowing. There is no real substitute for the old-fashioned edging shears for this, though the mechanical edgers that operate with a flailing nylon line are adequate for the non-perfectionist. You can save a lot of work if you make your edges such that you can ride the mower over them. If you don't like the effect of brick, timber or concrete edging strips, at least keep the edges of your beds level with the grass and avoid the gutter so admired by municipal gardeners. And don't edge your plantings with fragile things like lobelias or wax begonias that can't take the odd bump from the mower wheels! Beware the junction of ground cover and grass. They will tend to invade each other and have you down on your hands and knees separating them. You can just mow over the edge, but it will get messy-looking. If you can't make a mowing strip without introducing an unwanted element of formality, use ground covers or massed shrubs tall enough to have an overhang under which the mower can be tucked and which will hide the planting/grass interface.

KEEPING WEEDS OUT

The second arduous job is weeding. It sounds like 'I told you so', but most sessions of hands-and-knees labour on the lawn could have been avoided, simply by starting with clean soil and keeping the grass growing strongly enough so that weeds don't get a chance to get in. (Yes, we know it will then need mowing!) If you do need to weed, it is often easier to cut the weeds out with a heavy kitchen knife than to use a trowel or hand fork. Just make sure you get all the root. Or you can try painting the weed with a small brush dipped in Roundup, relying on the vigour of your grass to cover the bare patch. (If you are unfortunate enough to inherit a lawn that is more than 35 per cent weeds, you might be better off ploughing the whole thing under and starting again.)

How to encourage the grass to grow strongly enough to be weed repellent? First, you need to water it: and here, more than ever, the golden rule of watering—infrequently but heavily—applies. A few minutes' sprinkling will revive the grass and have it looking fresh after a hot day, but grass roots are lazy, and this will only encourage them to stay close to the surface where they will suffer as soon as the surface soil dries out.

Thorough watering, sufficient to wet the soil down deep, and only repeating it when the surface soil has really dried, will force the roots deeper and you'll have a much more vigorous, drought-resistant lawn. Water properly and you shouldn't have to water more than once a week, even at the height of summer.

Fertilizing is easy. Choose a good brand of lawn fertilizer, and apply it according to the manufacturer's directions. Better yet, halve the quantity, and put it on in two lots a fortnight apart. Spring and autumn are the best times; and don't forget to water the fertilizer in thoroughly and at once, or you'll burn the grass. Organic fertilizers like manure and compost aren't really much use on the lawn—too bulky—but you might try blood and bone. Old-time

One of the greatest joys of Camellia japonica *is that it needs so little pruning!*

gardeners used to set much store by an annual top-dressing with sandy soil, but this is more a ritual than any real benefit; fertilizer is better unless you want to even out any hollows.

Lawn pests are basically two. Various grubs live under the soil, eat the roots and leave dead, brown patches. You can usually dig them up and leave them for the birds, or simply water the scene of their activities with a strong insecticide. (See the section on caterpillars later in this chapter.) Dollar spot is a fungus that attacks the grass and is worst in wet weather. It tends to leave lawn both dead and mildewed-looking; water with a fungicide. If dead patches are more than 30 cm wide, it's desirable to sow some fresh grass on them; if less, the lawn will usually grow over them, but watch for weeds trying to get in first!

Constant traffic can compact the soil so that it sets like cement and water and air can't get in to the roots. The grass, no matter what you do, just doesn't grow vigorously. The solution is to hire an aeriator, a kind of spiked roller, roll it over the lawn a couple of times to break the crust, and resolve not to park the car on the grass in future. The problem is worst on heavy soils, where it is a good idea to aerate every spring.

Pruning

It may seem paradoxical, but the reason we cut bits of plants is to encourage growth. Yet that is the purpose of pruning. Bear it in mind, asking yourself, 'If I cut here, what sort of growth will come?', and you should be able to prune just about any tree or shrub with confidence.

Indiscriminately 'cutting back' isn't pruning; it's butchery, and the usual result is a misshapen, unhappy plant. Still, some gardeners love cutting back, and can never see a shrub or tree flourishing without saying, 'That is getting beyond itself. It needs cutting back!' There is no need to become one of their company.

The golden rule is always to prune to a place where growth will come. Most trees and shrubs grow by first extending their branches, and then making side shoots from growth buds in the axils (the 'armpits') of the leaves. To encourage these buds (the lateral buds) to grow, you shorten the branch, cutting to just above a leaf; to encourage the main branch (or the trunk of a young tree) to grow taller, you shorten any side shoots to divert the plant's energy into the end shoot, the terminal bud. And if you want to remove the branch altogether, you cut it right back to a junction with another, diverting the energy to that branch. However you cut, don't leave stubs. If you are cutting to above a leaf, cut just above it; if back to another branch, cut close. Stubs and stumps won't grow, they'll only rot, and the rot may spread into the living wood. Cut at the right place, and the wound will heal over.

That's really all there is to it—to encourage side shoots, shorten leading shoots; to encourage leading shoots, shorten side shoots. The art is in deciding which to do. Many shrubs, though not all, bear most of their flowers and fruit on side shoots, and shortening the leaders encourages not only a bushier plant, it leads to more flowers. On the other hand, you might want to encourage the leading shoots, as when you are trying to get a young tree to grow tall in a hurry. Then you would shorten the side branches.

When do you remove a branch altogether? It might be dead, when it is no use to the plant; it might be senile, and the plant is already replacing it with strong new growth, as when you remove a branch of a mock-orange, say, or a rambling rose that has already flowered; it might be weak and feeble, its energy better diverted to other branches; it might be spoiling the desired shape of the plant, when you might want to shorten it simply for symmetry; or it might be crowding out other, better placed or stronger branches.

This last is the key to pruning trees. Usually, trees can grow perfectly well without pruning, though the prudent gardener removes dead branches before they fall on someone; but often a tree is a bit too big or too densely shady for its position. All too often, it gets cut back (lopped) to make it smaller. This is usually a disaster. Lopping may indeed make the tree smaller, but at the cost of ruining its shape; and the poor thing usually responds by making great bunches of new shoots, so that it is shadier than before. Controlled, regular lopping, called pollarding, certainly has its place in European city streets, where a lollipop-shaped tree can look appropriate: in a garden, you are almost always better to thin out the crown of the tree, removing superfluous branches to let in the light.

With shrubs, thinning is often the wisest course also, as it reveals the lines of the branches and allows the light into the plant to encourage strong new growth; but every species is different, and you need to study how the plant grows. If, like a mock-orange, a hydrangea, a poinsettia, a raspberry or a rose, it grows by renewing itself, annually making new shoots to take the place of those that have spent their energy in flowers, then the basic job is thinning out the old wood to make way for the

new, and these are the plants that call for the most attention from the pruning shears. (You can usually recognize them by their thicketing, multi-stemmed habit, with unbranched young stems and twiggy older ones.) If it grows more like a miniature tree, as camellias, bottlebrushes, hibiscus or crepe myrtles do, then it will need less pruning; usually the judicious removal of weak or overcrowded branches is all that is needed.

Nature doesn't prune, and you shouldn't get the idea that it is something that you must do every year or your plants will languish. Even roses, normally pruned each winter, can be let go for a while, and you only have to see a neglected rosebush covered with roses in some old garden to wonder whether we don't prune too much. When a description says 'prune in winter', take it as meaning that is the time to prune if you think the plant will benefit from it. Many trees and shrubs can flourish without ever feeling the secateurs or the saw.

Fruit trees are a special case. Here the aim is to keep the tree small enough to make spraying and harvesting of the fruit easy, as well as to encourage the plant to put its energy into maximum numbers of fruit. You can leave fruit trees unpruned (this is the rule with citrus, avocados, and most subtropical fruit) if you don't mind getting out the ladder to tend them. They can look very romantic growing naturally.

The next question is when to prune. First, never prune anything during the period when it is actively growing and the sap is running; you risk having it bleed to death. There are a few exceptions; you can pinch back the tips of such things as lavender, rosemary and the bushier local plants to encourage the growth to be bushy, and you can pinch the long shoots of wisteria to keep the plant from getting out of bounds; but if you find yourself cutting into strong wood at this time, you will regret it.

The golden rule here is that unless you are hoping for fruit or berries to follow, prune after flowering and before growth begins. This means that spring bloomers, almost all of which bloom on the growth they made last year, are pruned in late spring or summer; they include such things as forsythia, weigelas, flowering peaches and their ilk, and wild roses. Prune them in winter, and you are cutting away the

wood that will shortly be flowering. (You can do your pruning while the plants are in bloom, taking the cut off branches inside for flower arrangements.) Summer bloomers usually flower on growth made in spring, and in their case 'after flowering' means in winter.

Unless you expect spring flowers from them, most trees can be thinned in winter; but the after-flowering rule applies here also, so you can do the job in late summer or early autumn after growth has slowed down. This can be the better time if the aim is to let in sunshine; you can see the effect more easily if you prune a deciduous tree with the leaves on.

The next rule is to use the right tools; you'll do far more harm by tearing your plant about with the wrong tool than from ignorance. If the branch is too big for secateurs, you will need long-handled loppers or a pruning saw—if you find yourself wishing for a chain-saw, call in a professional. Tree surgery is dangerous work, and chainsaws lethal in the hands of the inexperienced. What price falling out of a tree and breaking a leg or worse? And keep your tools *sharp* so they cut cleanly. Ragged cuts heal poorly and infections can get in. If you aren't used to using a whetstone, send your tools to be sharpened professionally.

Propagating

It has never been so easy to buy plants, but there is still satisfaction to be had in propagating your own—it's cheaper too. The basic way is from seed, the way most plants propagate themselves in the wild. Almost any garden plant can be grown from seed (unless hybridity or doubling, which transforms the reproductive organs into petals, has made it sterile), and seed-grown plants have the advantage that they start out life healthy—very few plant diseases are transmitted through the seed. But gardeners can be an impatient lot, and don't always want to wait for seedlings to take their time about flowering, as most trees shrubs and perennials do. Also, many highly bred plants don't 'come true' from seed. These we propagate by division, from cuttings, or by layering or grafting, according to the type of plant. Collectively, these are known as 'vegetative' means of propagation, and they give you new plants exactly the same as their parents. A group of plants propagated vegetatively from a single original is called a 'clone'. The named varieties of roses or fruit trees are examples.

GROWING SEEDS

Plants differ in the ease with which they can be raised from seed, but basically it isn't difficult. The first thing to note is that your seeds must be fresh. If you have bought them, they should be fine if sown by the 'sow by' date, provided you haven't broken the seal on the packet. Don't try to save unsown seeds for next year; the germination rate falls off markedly. (Saving some for a second sowing in a few weeks, as one does with many vegetables, is fine.) If you save your own seeds from the garden, make sure they are quite dry before you store them, a sealed container in the vegetable drawer of the fridge being the best place. Sow at the right time of year, which will be given on the seed packet or can be looked up in books like this one.

Whether you sow your seeds in a nursery bed or in pots, the soil should be fine and crumbly. A bed can be improved by the addition of some sand or vermiculite. For sowing in pots you can buy special seed-raising composts. Naturally, you'll make sure there are no weeds or weed seeds to confuse matters. Water your seed bed well to encourage weeds to germinate and zap them with Roundup, then wait a few days before sowing. The basic rule is to sow seeds so that they are covered by their own thickness of soil, and this is easiest if you make furrows to sow them in. A pointed stick will do the job nicely. Very fine seeds need only a light dusting of soil to cover them, and it can be easier to distribute them along the furrow if you bulk them up with some dry sand. Large seeds like nasturtiums or pumpkins can be placed individually. Such plants are often sown where they are to spend their lives, in the regular garden beds, as are many vegetables. Smooth the soil over, pat it down very gently, and water with the finest spray your hose or watering can deliver. Until the seeds have germinated, you need to keep them constantly, evenly moist, which will mean daily attention in warm weather.

How long the seedlings will take to come up depends on the species. Most annuals, including vegetables, appear in ten days or so, but perennials and shrubs can take much longer, some

Impatiens are easy to propagate—just pick a few stems and stand them in a glass of water to root.

preferring to be sown in autumn and given a spell of cold before germinating in spring. Be patient!

If germination is as good as it should be, the baby seedlings will be crowded. As soon as they are big enough to handle, prick them off into another container or another bed until they are big enough to transplant to their final homes. If they are already in their permanent bed, thin them out, leaving only the strongest at the required spacing.

The biggest problem with young seedlings is damping off, a fungus that rots them. Poor drainage in the seedling bed encourages it, and so does too close an atmosphere which you might get if you are sowing in a greenhouse or have enclosed the pots in plastic bags to keep them from drying out. Take the precaution of watering with a dilute fungicide as soon as you see signs of germination.

DIVISION

Division is the easiest method of vegetative propagation. At the appropriate planting time, you dig up a clump of perennials or bulbs, and shake the excess soil off its roots. The clump may simply fall into pieces, but often you'll have to pull it apart or cut it apart with a sharp knife or secateurs. The result is several new plants, which you can plant in their new homes immediately. Don't try to make the divisions any smaller than what comes easily, and give

preference to the strong new sections from the outside of the clump.

CUTTINGS

Cuttings are the standard means of propagating most shrubby plants. All they are is a piece of stem about 15–20 cm long, detached from the plant and put in soil in the expectation that it will make roots. Not all shrubs will strike from cuttings—eucalypts are impossible and rhododendrons and lilac recalcitrant—but most are easy enough. Cuttings are classed as follows: softwood or tip cuttings, taken from the ends of actively growing shoots in spring or summer (fuchsias, impatiens, lavender); semi-mature or half-ripe cuttings, taken after growth is complete but before it is quite ripe, usually about the middle of summer (for example, camellias); and hardwood cuttings, taken in autumn or winter from wood which has fully matured and might even be dormant. Roses are the classic example of these.

All cuttings are prepared in much the same way. Take the piece of stem you want, allowing about 4 to 6 joints where the leaves arise, and trim the bottom end of the stem just below a leaf, using a razor sharp knife or blade so as not to bruise it. Cut off any leaves that will be buried, and trim the remainder in half to stop moisture loss. Then you simply insert your cutting in a very sandy soil, either in a pot or a suitably sheltered bed, and keep it moist. Softwood and semi-mature cuttings are best given some protection from dry air, the standard way being to enclose pot and all in a clear plastic bag. Nurseries now use misting systems that keep the air of a greenhouse as humid as a Turkish bath, and these have allowed many plants to be propagated from cuttings that were regarded as too difficult before.

Dipping the end of the cutting in rooting hormone does help the 'take', but make sure the stuff is fresh. It loses potency quickly and has a short shelf life.

The speed with which roots will form varies greatly. Be patient; as long as your cutting hasn't withered it will be trying to root. After a fortnight or so, you can tip the cuttings out of a pot to check on progress provided you don't disturb them. When you see roots growing, the plants can be potted on or transplanted, treating them as gently as seedlings.

LAYERING

Layering is used for shrubs that don't root easily from cuttings, but it is useful also for any shrub when you only want a couple of new plants. It's simple to do; you bend a branch down to the ground and bury a section, holding it firmly in place with a short stake. Roots will form—eventually—where the stem was buried. Then the new plant can be severed from its parent and transplanted. Some shrubs like rhododendrons will take their time about it. You can nick the stem where you want the roots, but take care not to cut right through. A wipe with rooting hormone won't go astray.

Many sprawling or creeping plants—raspberries, rambling roses, hypericum, ivy ground covers—will layer themselves naturally, and they are the easiest of all plants to propagate. Rummage around the base of an old plant, and chances are you will find new ones waiting for you.

AIR-LAYERING

The only problem with layering is that you have to be able to bend the stem down to the ground. If this isn't possible, you can try air-layering, sometimes called by its old French name of *marcottage*. This always looks like magic, but isn't difficult. Spring or early summer is usually the best time. Select a suitable branch, and trim off any leaves, then cut it part-way through, being careful not to cut it off. If you are worried about it breaking, brace it with a stick for reinforcement. Then pack around the cut with wet sphagnum moss, and wrap that in a sheet of plastic, tying it on firmly. You'll need to check that the moss doesn't dry out; when it is evidently full of roots, you can detach the new plant, unwrap, and plant it in a pot.

GRAFTING

Grafting is one of the high points of the gardener's art, and also one of the most ancient. It has many different techniques, but they all involve the uniting of a piece of stem from one plant to the roots of another. It seems a lot of fiddling; why not just take a cutting? The answer is that by selection of the plant that provides the roots (the understock), you can influence the growth of the plant grafted on it (the scion). Thus you might want to give a cultivated plant the strength of wild roots, which is why roses are almost always grafted despite many of them doing quite well from cuttings. Conversely, you might want to reduce the vigour of the scion. This is the often the case with fruit trees. A cutting-grown apple tree, for instance, will normally grow unmanageably tall: but graft it onto a less vigorous, 'dwarfing' stock, and you produce a smaller (and often more fruitful) tree. But the two plants keep their genetic identity—graft a white grape onto a red one, and you'll get white grapes, not pink ones.

Grafting needs to be done at the optimum time, when the stock is growing strongly and the sap will run straight up into the scion and keep it alive while the tissues are growing together. To make the union requires exquisite care in matching the cambium layers, the band of green tissue just beneath the bark where the sap runs and cells are dividing. Fail in this, and the graft won't take. This is delicate surgery, calling for sharp knives and a steady hand.

Budding, the method used for roses and fruit trees, is the simplest form of grafting, and the one you should start with before graduating to cleft grafting and the more exotic types like veneer and approach grafting.

MERICLONAL PROPAGATION

There is yet another method of vegetative propagation which we should note, though you probably won't be able to use it yourself. This is mericlonal propagation, which involves cutting out, under a microscope, the very tip of a growing shoot—just the few cells that are actively dividing—and placing them on a sterile growing medium. The tip gives rise to a mass of undifferentiated cells called callus, which can be cut into pieces that then are placed in a different growing medium to grow into plants. The method has had huge success in

Ivy cuttings will often root in water, but ground-cover plantings usually layer themselves.

making such formerly intractable plants as kangaroo paws readily available, and has allowed outstanding orchids to be propagated in quantity much more quickly and cheaply than before. It can also be used to create virus-free clones of old cultivars whose vigour has declined through infection. We will be hearing a lot more of mericlonally propagated plants in the future.

Controlling pests and diseases

Nothing is more off-putting than a long list of the bugs, grubs and fungi that are just lying in wait to attack your plants and destroy your garden in the twinkling of an eye—unless it be an equally long list of the dangerous chemicals that you have to douse them with. Some of these kill one bug, some another. Identification of the precise nature of the trouble is evidently crucial; you wouldn't want to mistake a greenfly for a blackfly, or brown rot for black rot.

Happily, things aren't nearly as bad as that. For one thing, many pests are specific in the plants they attack, and unless you grow these you'll never see them. Then, most plants do have a certain amount of resistance—it's rare for major harm to be done before you can notice and take action. The multifarious pests and diseases really only fall under a few headings; and once you have decided what group the problem falls into, deciding the appropriate remedy is usually easy.

SNAILS AND SLUGS

Perhaps the most bothersome of all pests are in a group of their own: snails and slugs. They eat leaves, any sort of leaves that are soft enough, with a particular fondness for newly planted seedlings. They'll climb into plants to get their dinner, and have no compunction about eating flowers. If you can catch them, you can simply squash them; but that calls for constant vigilance. Night-time and wet weather (the times when most of us prefer to stay indoors) are the best times to go snail hunting. The standard way to control slugs and snails is to scatter anti-snail pellets, which you can buy in many suburban supermarkets as well as at garden centres. Some people worry about them, as there is a risk of poisoning a bird that eats a dying snail. You can protect delicate plants by surrounding them with a circle of ash or poultry grit, across which the snails can't

Snails.

A 'snail trap'.

Slugs.

Lily borers.

Cabbage butterfly caterpillars love nasturtiums.

slither; or you can use salt for the purpose if you don't mind its disastrous effects on the soil. Also time-honoured is setting saucers or small dishes up to their rims in the soil, and filling them with beer, which snails adore. They drown in it, making a revolting mess …

CATERPILLARS

Perhaps the next tribe of pests is the caterpillars, the juvenile stage of moths and butterflies. No one would like to be without butterflies in the garden, but happily the most desirable and decorative butterflies rarely come in such numbers that their caterpillars do much damage. It is usually the ones which are least attractive as adults that cause the most trouble as juveniles. A nasty caterpillar is the lily borer which attacks members of the Amaryllis family. Also troublesome are the caterpillars of the cabbage moth (diamond-back moth) which chew up the leaves of not only cabbages but their kith (broccoli,

cauliflowers, Brussels sprouts and the various Chinese cabbages) and kin (wall flowers, stocks, honesty) and other plants as well. They are especially fond of nasturtiums. Then there are the processional caterpillars, hairy brutes that march single file along the twigs of trees and shrubs; American bollworms, the tiny pests that curl up in the young leaves of roses and other plants and eat the developing growth; the tomato caterpillar or corn earworm, which eats the young fruit of tomatoes and the developing ears of corn; the loopers, which walk by doubling themselves up as they eat just about anything green; and finally the cutworms and white grubs that live below the soil and eat roots. These curl up if you dig them up and expose them to the air, a defence that might protect them against birds, but leaves them defenceless against the gardener who promptly squashes them.

Squashing them if you can catch the beasts—fortunately very few caterpillars

The caterpillar of the painted apple moth.

Tomato caterpillars.

A cut worm.

Codling moth damage.

Borer damage.

Sawdust evidence of borers.

Borers in an angophora branch.

move quickly—is the easiest way of dealing with caterpillars if there aren't many. Two words of caution: if you see a shoot rolled up by a bollworm, squash the shoot before you open it up, or the caterpillar will escape; and don't touch any processional caterpillars, which defend themselves either by sticking itchy hairs into your fingers or squirting vile juices at you. Processional caterpillars are best sprayed. You will want to spray any kind of caterpillar if they invade in greater numbers than can be controlled by squashing. The standard anti-caterpillar spray is carbaryl, which is certainly effective but poisonous both to people and birds that might eat a dying caterpillar. Also use Dipterex and Dursban for loopers, Garden Ripcord for American boll-worm, and Bexadust for white grub.

Borers, which burrow into the stems of trees, are caterpillars too. Their activities are revealed by masses of stuck-together sawdust around the entries to their tunnels, and if you see this take action at once, as a severe borer attack can kill a tree. The stand-ard treatment is to poke a wire down the tunnel in the hope of impaling the caterpillar; if you can't reach it, squirt some kerosene or methylated spirits into the hole. (It is very hard to get any sort of spray into the holes.) Borers are particularly fond of wattles and of some conifers. There are types that molest cherry, fig and pear trees too.

Borers usually have trouble invading a vigorous and otherwise healthy tree, and borer attack is often a sign that the tree is unhappy. Water and fertilizer are called for. If the tree under attack is a wattle, don't forget that wattles are short-lived, and when borers start to wreak havoc on an old tree it is a sign that you should think about removing it and planting a new one.

Another caterpillar that gets inside the plant is that of the codling moth, a major pest of apples, pears and quinces. The moth lays its eggs on the develop-ing fruit, which by the time it ripens is ruined by being full of little grubs. When the caterpillars are fully grown, they leave the fruit to pupate in crevices in the bark and in litter at the base of the tree. The first step in controlling them is to clean off loose bark and rubbish from the base of the trees. If you like, you can tie a collar of sacking around the trunk, where the pupas will make themselves at home; you can then

burn sacking, pupas and all, before they turn into moths. But if the moth is bothersome in your area, you will have to spray with carbaryl or Garden Ripcord every two or three weeks from the time the flower petals fall until the fruit is approaching ripeness.

SUCKING INSECTS

Caterpillars and their ilk are chewing insects, which need to be poisoned directly—you have to get the poison onto them, which means thorough spraying. The big tribe of sap-sucking

A stinkbug.

Red spider mite damage.

Mealy bug.

A yellow-black fruit beetle.

Aphids on a rose bush.

White wax scale.

Red scale on a lemon.

insects includes beetles, aphis (also known as greenfly), mealy bugs and scale insects. They don't do the immediately obvious damage that caterpillars do, but they can severely stunt the growth of a plant. Just as importantly, they can spread virus diseases. The suckers can be controlled by most insecticides, but their control has been made much simpler by the development of systemic insecticides, the most important of which is dimethoate (Aphicide). These are absorbed by the plant and render its sap poisonous to the pests. (To people too, so you need to be very careful about using these on plants which you plan to eat. The poison dissipates after a while, and you should be scrupulous about observing the 'withholding period' noted on the label.) The great advantage of systemic insecticides is that not only do they not get washed off by rain, they protect parts of the plants which the spray didn't reach. They are most effective against the sap-sucking tribe; the chewers have to do a fair amount of damage before they take in enough poison to affect them, and there is no substitute for dousing them with insecticide. Effective biodegradable insecticides, such as Eco Trounce and Biokill are highly recommended.

BEETLES
Beetles aren't usually a great nuisance, with one exception—the yellow-black fruit beetle. These beetles attack all kinds of fruit, garden flowers and especially roses. The adult is a large (20–30 mm) brightly coloured beetle with a conspicuous black and yellow pattern. *Pachnoda sinuata* is the species. They attack ripe or ripening fruit, eating large chunks out of these. They are also fond of many flowers and are a really troublesome pest during summer. Removing them by hand and dropping them in water with a little paraffin, is a very effective method of control. You could also spray them with Folithion. Specially made beetle traps are also available.

Fruit beetles breed in compost heaps. It is very easy to remove their larvae (big white grubs) from the heaps and kill them.

Other beetles like stinkbugs or twig wilters, leaf beetles, chafer beetles and CMR beetles are fairly common in many South African gardens. Spray with Folithion.

SCALE INSECTS
The grand exception to all this is the scale insects, sap-suckers which live sedentary lives, secreting a carapace of wax to protect themselves. This it does very effectively, and they don't seem to pick up systemic insecticides much. The most familiar are the white wax scale and red scale which affect citrus and many other shrubs, and the white scale of roses. The gardener's strategy here is to wreck the carapace, destroying the tiny breathing tubes the insect

builds into it, so that the insect suffocates in its own wax, and this is done by spraying with white oil, which dissolves the wax. This is tricky stuff to use, as it can burn the foliage in summer heat—check whether you are about to use 'summer' or 'winter' oil. If the plant or the infestation is small, you can avoid using white oil by brushing methylated spirits onto the scales. An old toothbrush is ideal, and if it scrubs the insects off, so much the better—they can't crawl back on.

EELWORMS
Nematodes or eelworms are microscopic worm-like creatures that live in the soil and attack the roots or bulbs of a range of plants. The destruction of the roots causes the plant to wilt and often die, and they cause bulbs to rot. They are especially fond of tomato roots and daffodil bulbs, but they are not very common. Fortunately, as they are very difficult to eradicate. The soil can be

fumigated to kill them, but this calls for professional help; the chemicals are too dangerous for you and me. African and French marigolds secrete substances into the soil that drive the nematodes away, which is why they are often planted with tomatoes. Daffodil bulbs can be treated in hot water. But if you are unfortunate enough to suffer eelworms, crop rotation is the only real defence.

BACTERIA

The bacterial diseases are the rarest, which is just as well as they are difficult to treat. The most common bacterial diseases are those that cause cankers and galls on the stems and sometimes the leaves of stone fruit, tomatoes and oleanders. Here you can do little except remove and burn the affected parts in the hope of destroying all the bacteria, a course of action to follow too if you get bacterial leaf spots on ivy or geraniums. Gladiolus bulbs are sometimes affected by bacterial scab, which manifests itself in black, rooted areas. If this happens, burn any affected bulbs, and don't replant any new ones in the same place.

FUNGI

The fungi are the main diseases. There are many of them and they tend to be specific in their choice of plants to attack. They fall into two categories: those that spread through the soil and those that attack the leaves, flowers or stems. Let us look at the latter first, as they are the most common.

The fungi that attack leaves, flowers and stems fall into two categories: those that stay mostly on the surface and those that burrow into the plant to do their damage from within.

The surface-living types like the assorted mildews, moulds and rusts, are simple enough to deal with. Spray at the first signs of infection, using the fungicide currently fashionable for the particular fungus, and keep spraying at weekly or ten-day intervals until the problem clears up. The important thing is to get in as early as possible and spray thoroughly, making sure that all the leaf surfaces, including the undersides, are coated with the spray. Fungicides are mostly based on copper, the old standby being copper oxychloride, though this is pretty potent stuff and can damage soft foliage. Many old-time gardeners swear by Bordeaux mixture, originally developed in the nineteenth century to protect the French vineyards against mildew; it incorporates both copper and sulphur, another traditional fungus killer, but it needs to be applied in large quantities and is anything but biodegradable. More recent fungicides are less damaging to the environment and need less chemical to do their job, which is of course a good thing. They aren't all copper based, some incor-

porating manganese (Dithane M45). Don't worry over much about what goes into a fungicide—read the label and it will tell you which fungus it is designed to kill.

The systemic fungicides, which work in much the same way as systemic insecticides, are no longer new, and they have proved the best defence against the fungi that get into the plant tissues the way black spot of roses and some vegetable rots do. They are effective against the surface dwellers also. Like systemic insecticides, they don't have to be applied quite so meticulously. Fungi mutate and develop resistance to chemicals even faster than insects do, so any list of remedies for specific fungi becomes outdated surprisingly quickly. The best way to deal with any disease (or insect) is to take the advice of the people at your local nursery, showing them a sample of the problem if you are uncertain about it, and then read the directions on the packet with care.

Soil-borne fungi, like soil-dwelling insects, are a headache to deal with. Drenching the soil with fungicide is not very effective and can wreak havoc on the humus-producing micro-organisms. The most feared is root rot, *Phytophthora cinnamomi*, alias cinnamon fungus, the cause of die-back of members of the protea family and Australian tea bushes. This can kill and cripple the roots of a

Mildew on a grape leaf.

Sooty mould.

Hollyhock rust.

very wide range of trees and shrubs. By the time you see the plant suddenly wilting, it is too late to save it. The fungus flourishes best in damp ground, and the best preventive and remedy is to improve drainage, or to plant plants that like wet feet, which are often resistant to the fungus, and to be obsessive about not transferring infected soil to other parts of the garden. Club root affects the cabbage tribe and their relatives. Sufficient to note that it cripples the plants and crop rotation is your best defence.

VIRUSES

It is a general rule that viruses are untreatable. The only thing to do is to destroy the infected plant before the virus gets a chance to spread, which it can do by the activities of aphids and by careless gardeners exchanging plant fluids by way of unclean secateurs. But don't act in haste. Some viruses, such as rose wilt and the viruses that affect lilies and tomatoes, are indeed fatal and to be viewed with fear and loathing; others are more-or-less harmless. But they do generally reduce the vigour of an infected plant. Where you are offered the choice of certified virus-free stock of *anything*, pay the extra money for it. Some viruses are indeed viewed as desirable: many variegated-leaved plants get that way through virus infection, as do some striped and blotched camellias; and the classic desirable virus is the one that 'breaks' the colour of tulip blossoms into stripes. (In seventeenth century Holland, these 'broken' flowers were much prized, and were so expensive that speculators started trading in tulip bulb futures, to the enrichment of some and the ruin of many. Eventually the government had to step in to stop the 'tulipomania'.)

Happily, few virus diseases are transmitted through the seed, and you can often save your stock of a plant dying of a virus by saving some seeds and growing them.

SAFETY FIRST

It is easy to speak glibly as we have been doing about spraying, but all these chemicals are poisonous and you need to handle them with care. Don't even try to spray if there is a breeze blowing, or you'll get spray everywhere you don't want it, including on yourself. Wear protective clothing. Long trousers, long sleeves, gloves and a bandanna—Western bad-guy fashion over your

Black spot on a rose leaf.

mouth and nose to guard against breathing in the spray—are the minimum. When you have finished spraying, wash both your clothes and yourself. This even applies if you are using the relatively non-toxic insecticides like pyrethrum or its derivatives. And take great care when mixing different chemicals as they may not be compatible. At best they may not work; at worst the mixture may be poisonous to plants. If you want to mix, say, an insecticide and a fungicide, check the labels on the packets. If that doesn't give you clear answers, phone the manufacturers or the local office of the Department of Agriculture and ask their advice.

Naturally, keep all garden chemicals securely stored out of the reach of children and pets. There is no need to arm yourself with a whole arsenal of spray guns. For small jobs you can often buy the sprays ready mixed in aerosol cans; medium-sized jobs can be adequately dealt with by a pump-up pressure gun which holds a litre or so of spray. For big tasks like a whole bed of roses or a fruit tree, there is nothing easier than one of the gadgets that attaches to the end of the hose. These are apt to only give a coarse spray, but that probably won't bother you much. It is important to wash your equipment thoroughly with warm water and detergent when you have finished spraying; and if you are in the habit of spraying weedkiller, keep a separate

Mosaic virus on an apple tree.

gun, prominently marked, for this purpose.

Don't forget that there are many, many beautiful plants that are not bothered by pests and diseases. Concentrate on these, and you won't have to be alarmed by what you have just been reading.

Weeds

Console yourself. *Every* year is a dreadful one for weeds. If your soil won't support a decent crop of weeds, it won't grow anything else.

Weeding is still everyone's least favourite gardening chore, and it is one that you can't really design away. No matter what you do, weeds *will* appear, to rob your desired plants of light, nourishment and water.

What is a weed? There is an old saying that it is simply a plant in the wrong place. The classic example is couch, one of the most desirable of lawn grasses but apt to provoke the gardener to unprintable language should it escape from the lawn into nearby flower beds. Another definition is that it is a plant which a local government authority has declared to be a weed and which you are, therefore, obliged to remove from your land should it appear. One such is yellow sorrel, admittedly a pest in South Africa, but considered a desirable ground cover in California! Not all such 'declared weeds' meet the usual gardener's definition of an uninvited, unlovely plant that would take over the garden (and the bush!) if you let it. Your local council should be able to give you a list of the declared weeds for your area, and the fines, if any, for harboring them.

While the invention of the non-persistent herbicides like Roundup, that do not poison the soil, has given the gardener the upper hand in the battle against weeds, the victory still goes to the swift. Pull weeds out as soon as they come up and they won't get a chance to go to seed. Eventually, the reservoir of weed seeds in your soil will diminish and the standing army will go away. Seeds will still blow in from next door or down the road, but you will be ahead. Just remember that most weed plants have long-lived seeds and there is truth in the old adage, 'One year's seeding, seven years weeding.' You can either pull by grasping the weed at its base, or dig it out with a trowel—just

make sure you get the whole plant.

Mulching, provided the stuff you do it with isn't full of weed seeds, gives you an advantage in the war, as mulches smother most weed seeds and prevent them germinating. If any do come up, the soft texture of the mulch makes it easier to pull them out.

Weeds can be annuals, perennials, or even shrubs or trees. The annuals are perhaps the easiest to deal with. Pull them up before they go to seed and put them on the compost heap. Then you can mulch to smother the germination of any seeds that might still be lurking. (Don't leave any weed just lying there; they have an alarming ability to re-root themselves.) Paradoxically, the shrubs and trees like sesbania, Port Jackson and rooikrans are nearly as simple, as they grow slowly in their youth. All you have to do is make sure you get all the roots when you pull them up. (This does get harder as they get bigger!) The

most difficult are the perennial weeds that proliferate from underground runners or bulbs—horrors like oxalis, onion weed, and worst of all, nut grass, *Cyperus rotundus.* With these, you must, must get every last root, tuber or bulb or there will shortly be an even bigger crowd of baby weeds there. You can't get rid of them by mulching; they just come up and grow all the stronger.

Dealing with these is when Roundup really comes into its own. Spray it on, and it should kill the whole plant. But watch you don't overspray and kill plants you want. In close country, you might want to paint the weed with a small paint brush. This is worth doing in lawns too; if you are careful you won't kill so much grass that it can't grow quickly over the bare spot where the weed was growing. There are selective weedkillers that will kill broad-leafed weeds and not the grass.

Weedkillers, like all garden chemi-

Rooikrans (Acacia cyclops).

Creeping oxalis (Oxalis corniculata).

Buffalo killed by herbicides.

Onion weed (Nothoscordum inodorum).

Couch escaping from the lawn.

The edible dandelion (Taraxacum officinale).

cals, are poisonous. Take the greatest care in using them. Don't breathe the fumes; don't get them on your skin; wash up thoroughly after using them; and don't store them where they might fall into the hands of children.

One last thought on weeds: before you pull out a tiny seedling, do make sure it *is* a weed. Sometimes garden plants seed themselves, and you might be pulling out something choice by mistake. Give the suspect a chance to identify itself first; if it turns out to be a weed after all, no harm will be done unless you have waited so long that it has started to go to seed.

ORGANIC GARDENING

With the growing awareness of the importance of conserving the environment, organic gardening has become fashionable. We may not, as individuals at least, be able to do much about saving the Amazon rainforests, but we can do something about the patch of land we have in our own stewardship, keeping it healthy and free from poisons, in harmony with nature.

After such a lofty beginning, it can be a disappointment to find that organic gardening has no hidden secrets. It is easier to define organic gardening in terms of what it is not. Basically, it is gardening without the (often dubious) benefits of modern chemicals. Organic gardeners don't use weedkillers; they pull weeds out by hand. They don't spray bugs and fungi with chemicals, or at least not with the newer ones developed by the petrochemical industry. They prefer to squash caterpillars or, when spraying can't be avoided, to use old-fashioned chemicals like Bordeaux mixture or home-made sprays like garlic water. (Infuse a few garlic cloves in 2 cupfuls or so of boiling water, as though you were making tea; when it reeks of garlic, it is ready to use. Tobacco water is made the same way, using the highest-tar cigarettes you can buy.) They don't use chemical fertilizers, relying on compost and on manure.

In many ways, this is just a return to the ways of our forebears before the rise of modern technology, and so organic gardening has attracted its share of people who look at the past through rose-tinted glasses. For some, old-fashioned ways are, simply because they *are* old-fashioned, the best ways. They tend to forget that two hundred years ago most gardens were in the veld, and that manure was more readily available than it is now. These days, it is an expensive commodity bought in plastic bags; then, it was available for the sweeping from the farmyard and the stables.

The basic philosophy of organic gardening—returning what we can to

Wandering jew (Tradescantia albiflora).

The prickly bindii.

Yellow clover (Trifolium dubium).

Paspalum (P. dilatatum).

The unpleasant, asthma-causing sticky weed or pellitory (Pellitoria judaica).

the soil and avoiding chemicals that might damage the environment—is simply common sense. A fertile soil is one which contains a flourishing population of micro-organisms, and they cannot long endure without the constant replenishment of humus that comes from compost or manure. Chemical fertilizers don't help them, and, what is more, fertilizers do leach from the soil to pollute waterways and other soils. Sprays, no matter how non-toxic their manufacturers hope them to be, should always be regarded as poisonous and dangerous to the environment until proved otherwise. It was only thirty-five years ago, after all, that parathion, an insecticide now banned as too dangerous to use, was considered 'safe as rainwater'.

Any gardeners who really cares about their soil and garden will make compost; will give preference to organic fertilizers like manure and blood and bone rather than chemicals like super-phosphate and sulphate of ammonia; and will use chemical sprays only when absolutely necessary, after less drastic

controls of pests and diseases have failed. Most gardeners garden like this. The days when people used to spray their gardens from fence to fence every season just in case there might be a bug lurking somewhere are long over.

Whether the result of strict organic gardening practices is indeed more flavourful, more nutritious vegetables and healthier, prettier flowers is hard to say. Some scientific research suggests no, that the nourishment contained in an orange is the same whether it was 'organically' or 'chemically' grown. But it will be as free as it might be of chemical residues: and the soil that grew it will, or should, be still healthy and fertile—and that is certainly worth aspiring to.

COMPANION PLANTING

The idea that some plants exert a beneficial effect on others growing nearby and others inhibit their growth is an ancient one that is enjoying

renewed popularity. Many of the companion plantings suggested even now tend to be among the vegetables and herbs that interested the old herbalists and alchemists. There is indeed scientific evidence that there is some basis for the belief. It is known, for example, that African and French marigolds secrete substances from their roots that drive away eelworms (nematodes) the minute soil-living creatures that eat plant roots. Planted among tomatoes, which are notoriously prone to nematode attack, the marigolds offer some protection. Some of the widely accepted companionships follow.

HAPPY

Roses and garlic (the garlic protects the roses from aphids, and it is claimed, intensifies the roses' perfume)

Beans and mealies (train the beans up the cornstalks, and remember to water and fertilize for both); beans also grow well with potatoes

Tomatoes and marigolds; tomatoes like onions and garlic also

Potatoes and cabbages; and maybe

The most widely accepted marriage of companion plants—French marigolds protecting tomatoes against soil-dwelling nematodes (eelworms).

Nasturtiums are said to enhance the growth of most vegetables. Here they are with broccoli.

the other members of the cabbage tribe also

Nasturtiums and most vegetables

UNHAPPY

Walnuts and most other plants (fallen walnut leaves are said to poison the soil and prevent other plants growing beneath the trees)

Sunflowers and almost everything else

Cabbages and beans

Peas and onions

Some people suggest that irises and roses get on famously together. They certainly look good together. And what about the scent of *Nicotiana* which is disliked by many insects— it should have a place in the garden. Parsley is

another plant disliked by snails and rose beetles.

LOW-MAINTENANCE GARDENING

Non-gardeners are apt to wish for no-maintenance gardening. 'I want a beautiful garden that never needs any work!' is one of the cries most familiar to a professional garden designer's ears. Gardeners know better; gardening, even the boring bits like weeding, is one of the happiest of hobbies. Even so, there are times when we would prefer to be doing something else with our spare time; just as houses should be labour-

saving, so gardens should be too.

There are two ways to achieve the low-maintenance garden.

The celebrated English garden designer Russel Page used to say 'trees, grass and water'. That sums up one approach, that of concentrating on plants that need little attention to grow well and look handsome. (Grass might seem an odd inclusion; but unless you are a perfect-lawn freak, it isn't really all that demanding to maintain, not compared with beds of annuals or vegetables, anyway.) The best trees fit the bill nicely, but there are many shrubs, and indeed ground-cover plants too, that need little care other than admiration.

You need to take your climate and soil into account here. Any plant that needs extra watering, sheltering from the cold, or spraying because it is growing in conditions that aren't exactly right for it can't be called 'low maintenance', however it might behave in other climates and gardens. Neither is one which needs constant pruning, dividing, or dead-heading to look presentable.

This may sound awfully boring, but in fact there is a good range of beautiful, easy-care plants: and if limiting your choice leads to simplicity of design, so much the better. There is no need to be purist and banish your own favourite flowers—just don't go overboard on them, and place them at key points where they give maximum effect for the work you put into them. Search among the flowers, and you'll find many that need only once- or twice-a-year attention, among them the evergreen day-lilies, the shrub roses, the daffodils that come up, flower, and then obligingly disappear beneath ground covers or mulches. Remember though, that if a plant doesn't appeal to you, you will resent *any* care it asks for …

Indigenous plants are often touted as easy-care, as they were bred by nature to our soils and climates. Moreover, few have been subjected to the ministrations of the plant breeder which can so often lead to bigger flowers or fruit at the expense of health and vigour. True, but only up to a point. Many of the most desirable indigenous (by this we mean South African) plants are easy-care but short-lived, and after 10 or 15 years lazy gardeners may find themselves facing the major job of replanting much of the garden.

The other approach is to be meticu-

These brick pavers are set slightly below the level of the grass, so the mower can just ride onto it and trim the edges automatically.

A raised stone edge like this keeps the lawn out of the flower bed.

lous in your layout, so that the chores of gardening are zed. Thus you would arrange to surround a messy tree like a eucalypt (gums always seem to be dropping something!) with a ground cover planting into which its fallen leaves, twigs and so on will vanish to make a mulch, rather than a paving or lawn where they would have to be swept up. Lawns can be given mowing strips of brick or concrete to eliminate the chore of trimming the edges, and to keep the grass from invading nearby plantings. Paving should be set so that it meets the lawn at the same level, instead of a few centimetres higher, for the same purpose. Pavings and ground covers could take the place of some areas of grass; neat, dense shrubs that of clipped hedges.

The prudent gardener combines both approaches, and remembers that no garden can truthfully be called 'low maintenance' until it is well established. Baby trees and shrubs will need water-

Where potted plants are being massed like these regal pelargoniums, unattractive plastic pots will be largely hidden by foliage.

ing, fertilizing, protecting from such nasties as snails and caterpillars, and maybe pruning; ground covers won't be weedproof until they have grown to make a solid mat of foliage, and newly planted grass needs pampering. Any garden, low maintenance or not, needs some attention from time to time—wouldn't it be boring if it didn't?

GARDENING IN CONTAINERS

At first thought, growing plants in containers seems a perverse thing to do. Why imprison a plant in a pot where it is utterly dependent on you to water and fertilize it, and where it will need more care than it would if it were growing in the ground? There are many reasons.

First, you can give a potted plant individual care, with a soil mix de-signed to suit it, watering or not just as it needs it, and a position in sun or shade as it needs. Some plants with specialized needs such as epiphytic orchids and some cacti are usually grown as pot plants for this reason. Baby plants, whether grown from seeds or cuttings, are usually brought on in pots while they are too delicate to take their chances in the competition of the open garden. They will suffer less shock when they are transplanted than they would if they were lifted from the open ground; and most modern nurseries grow most of their plants in pots for this very reason. You and I can buy them, take them home and plant them at almost any time with reasonable certainty of success.

Then, you might want to grow your plant on a paved terrace, on a verandah, even on a balcony or roof. Here, pots can make the difference between having plants or not having them. Or you might be renting your house on a short lease, and want to be able to take your plants with you when you go—plant them in the ground and you are making a present of them to your landlord.

Put a plant in a handsome container, and you give it importance. It's a bit like setting a statue on a plinth or a picture in a frame. And you might want to use a potted plant or a group of them to create a focal point—next to the front door, at the head of a set of steps, around a swimming pool for instance. You might then want to take advantage of container plants' portability to arrange a changing display, retiring one plant as its flowers fade and bringing in another that is just coming into bloom. This way you can have interest all year.

Just about any plant can be grown in a pot, at least for the time being. Full-sized trees can be grown in containers, and many a city tree is growing in a huge planter box while cars park in a basement beneath its roots; but few gardeners will want to deal with something so cumbersome. A half-barrel is about as big as most of us can cope with—and even that will need two people to shift it—but it is quite big enough to grow a shrub. Bearing in mind that a container plant like this will draw the eye, choose one that looks good for as much of the year as possible. Think of long-flowering, handsome evergreens like oleanders, hibiscus, camellias, azaleas, allamandas, even citrus. There are also many others just as suitable.

Smaller pots offer their own possibilities. Annuals, spring bulbs (which often flower a week or two earlier in the warmth of a pot than they do in the open ground), those frustrating autumn bulbs like nerines and blood lilies that won't bloom without summer drought (shift them out of the rain when they die down); ferns; even vegetables and

climbing plants. (Try training a moonflower or a pink mandevilla up a tripod of tall stakes to make a column of bloom—an eye-catcher indeed.)

A cluster of small or medium-sized pots has more impact than just one, and you can mix and match your plants just as the mood takes you—one of the joys of container gardening.

Window boxes are a European idea we don't see as much in South Africa as we should. They dress up the front of a plain house like nothing else can, and to an ornate one they add an extra touch of gaiety. Pelargoniums and petunias are the traditional plants for them, but you can plant any sort of low or trailing things you fancy. Ferns and fuchsias would be nice in a shaded spot; and what about some herbs conveniently outside the kitchen window? The important things are to

make the box itself generous in size—20 cm is not too wide or deep—and to fix it securely in place.

The containers themselves offer great choice. Plastic pots have been much improved in recent years, and there are more to choose from than just the old black ones, useful as they are as temporary homes for plants that are going to be planted out. The material doesn't age well, however, and though its lightness is usually an asset, it won't be if you are planning a tall plant which might get blown over in a high wind.

Terracotta is the material with several thousand years' tradition behind it, and even in the plainest models its warm colour is flattering to almost any plant displayed in it. It has an advantage over plastic in that it is porous; it is harder to overwater a plant in terracotta. Salts from fertilizer tend to make a white

A complete garden growing in containers on a balcony. The pink and white flowers are petunias, which take very happily to container life.

This handsome glazed Chinese pot holds a complete spring garden of primulas, violas and lobelias (which haven't started to flower yet).

bloom on the surface, which isn't pretty. It does wash off easily, but also it can be minimized by painting the inside of the pot with olive oil before you plant—a trick practised by the ancient Romans. As long as you don't have an accident, terracotta will last for hundreds of years, mellowing in beauty all the time.

Glazed earthenware and porcelain pots have been fashionable for years. The best come from Italy (very expensive) and the Orient (rather cheaper), though there are potters making attractive ones here. They offer good accommodation for plants, with three caveats: they are sometimes rather fragile; the fancier ones are apt to distract from the plants they are supposed to be showing off; and some of the large Chinese ones have no drainage holes. That's because they aren't flower pots at all, but goldfish bowls. You can drill holes in them, but it's a risky

Bring potted spring bulbs out to show them off, then retire them after they have finished flowering.

Nothing dresses up a facade the way window boxes do, and the simplest plantings are always the most effective, like the impatiens and lobelias here.

A collection of different terracotta pots, given unity by a common theme of grey foliage—catnip (Nepeta), lamb's ears (Stachys) and sun roses (Helianthemum).

Some of the variety of sizes and shapes available in terracotta. The bright flowers in the centre are Colchicum autumnale.

business. Better to make mini-water gardens in them.

Wood is traditional for containers too, whether in the form of cut-down barrels (harder to come by than they used to be) or in more elaborate designs like the *caisses de versailles* originally designed for the gardens of Louis XIV. It has the great ability to keep the roots of any plant growing in it cool, no matter how hot the summer. Choose wooden containers as much for their durability as their looks. Teak and oak are the timbers of choice; treated pine is a reasonably economical alternative. All will last longer if they are oiled or painted. Wood is the material of choice for window boxes.

Reinforced concrete is the material of the most daring modern architecture, but did you know it was first developed to make flower pots? That was back around 1800, and concrete pots have been with us ever since. Their walls have to be thick, so there is no point in

trying to make them small; most concrete pots are tub-sized and heavy. The weight is a disadvantage; few concrete tubs are truly portable. So is the ease with which the material can take moulded decoration, usually with unhappy results. The most attractive concrete pots are simple in design, and these days are often coloured and finished to resemble stone. You can paint them, though moisture from inside usually flakes the paint off in a couple of years and they then look tatty. Asbestos pots are the most commonly available plant containers.

Splendidly carved urns and vases of stone and marble are sometimes available, though they are fabulously expensive. Should you be fortunate enough to have one, you have a work of art which could be the focal point of the entire garden.

Whatever the material, make sure your container has adequate drainage holes; nothing will kill your plants

faster than wet feet. For the same reason, it isn't wise to stand an outdoor pot in a saucer, which will stay full in wet weather. Only do this for real water lovers such as arum lilies, willows or Louisiana irises. Over the holes it is customary to place a few pieces of broken pot to keep the soil from washing out. (Unless you are in the habit of breaking pots, these crocks are hard to come by; also use pieces of broken brick and try pieces of brass or aluminium fly wire, which will also keep out worms, which rapidly wear out their welcome in the confines of a pot.) Cover the pieces of broken pot with a layer of gravel for drainage; and then add your potting soil and plant. When planting, make sure there are a couple of centimetres between the finished level of the soil and the rim for water.

A good time-honoured potting mix, suitable for most plants, can be made from equal parts of good garden soil,

A container need not sit in splendid isolation. This decorative urn filled with pansies adds a graceful note to a bed of flowers in fetching blue and yellow tones.

sharp sand, and peat moss or the coarser stuff from the compost heap, with a handful of complete fertilizer added to each barrowful. Unless you are planning on a lot of pot plants, you'll probably find it easier to buy one of the ready-made potting mixes which every garden centre carries these days. Premium grade is worth the extra money, and you can buy special mixes for acid-loving plants like azaleas. Recently, water-retaining granules which you add to the potting mix have become available. They aren't all that cheap, but they do reduce the need for frequent watering a little. A point to watch: always use fresh potting mix; it can be tempting to re-use soil that has held annuals or bulbs, but this is not wise. It will have lost structure and nutrients and the new plants will suffer accordingly.

Planting is just the same as when planting in the open ground—follow the four rules. Make sure your plant is accurately centred in the container, or it will annoy you every time you look at it. Looking after container plants is simple. Water them when they need it (in summer this can mean every day) and fertilize them regularly, as the constant watering leaches nutrients from the soil rather quickly. In this situation slow-release fertilizers are well worth their high cost.

Annuals are simply discarded at the end of their season, but other plants will eventually need repotting when they exhaust their soil. If they can go into a larger container, fine; if not, you may have to prune the roots. This is easy—simply tip the plant out of its container, shave a centimetre or so off the sides of the root ball with a sharp knife, and replant.

Right: A garden seat is the perfect place to sit and enjoy the fruits of your labour.

CHAPTER 2

Annuals &
Perennials

*A*nnuals and perennials, the mainstay of a garden, can provide year-round colour and interest. Horticulturally, annuals are those plants which complete their life cycle, from seed to seed, in a season, while perennials generally live for three years or more.

Within the vast group of perennials are evergreens, such as the hardy agapanthus and iris, which are ideally suited to temperate climates, and the herbaceous types, such as asters and gentians, which are able to cope with severe winters as they die back at the end of the summer and form new shoots after a dormant period.

Traditionally these plants were used for massed displays called carpet bedding, where plants were selected to form disciplined colour displays. Today this type of formal, high maintenance display is usually restricted to very large private gardens or parks for special events, while the keen gardener experi-

ments with plants to provide varied and interesting combinations.

Annuals are ideally suited to this experimentation as they are not permanent. One summer the garden could be a subtle combination of creams and soft blues of the newer viola hybrids, another season a completely different effect could be achieved by using bright blue salvias and bold yellow marigolds in the same position. In this way the novice gardener can decide which colour combination is the most pleasing and go on to repeat these colours in the permanent planting of a garden.

Planting Combinations

By combining perennials with annuals in a more informal manner the garden loses that 'all or nothing' effect which is so evident when a bed of annuals has 'finished' and is again planted out with tiny seedlings. By placing clumps of perennials besides drifts of annuals the eye is drawn from one accent to another, say from a group of low-growing

annuals in front to the taller perennial flower spikes behind. Annuals are marvellous for providing a festive welcome to an entrance or a splash of colour to a shrub border when the garden is to be used for a special event. For a continuous effect, group them with perennials, staggering the flowering times of the plants so that when a small pocket of annuals is nearly past its prime a perennial just behind is about to strut its stuff. This complementary display can take a few seasons to achieve as many perennials need two years to bloom, but don't give up as experimenting in this way is one of the most rewarding aspects of gardening.

Apart from colour combinations within a garden, try to tie in the house colour to that of a garden display so they complement one another—a red or red-orange toned house looks good surrounded by bright oranges/yellow/rusty reds and creams while a white or muted pastel painted house blends well with soft blue, mauve, pink and white flowers plus masses of silver foliage.

Chrysanthemums can provide a spectacular display of colour.

Just as important as linking the house to the garden, is the overall siting of the garden beds. Most annuals demand full sun to flower well so be sure to choose an aspect where the plants will receive as much light, particularly morning sun, as possible. Give them generously wide beds ensuring the colourful display will not be overwhelmed by shrub foliage or robbed of nutrients by the roots of nearby permanent plants.

Instant Colour Effects

One of the most welcome developments in recent years is the increase in the number of annuals and perennials available in 'instant colour' pots. Once red geraniums were the only available way to provide a splash of colour in early spring, now, right through the seasons a pot or tray of mature, flowering annuals can be purchased to add instant colour to a garden dead spot or patio. And don't overlook hanging baskets filled with annuals to highlight a garden colour scheme. If potting up seedlings to make your own instant colour, take care to choose plants that fall gracefully over the edge of the basket. Both upright and sprawling types can produce a very decorative display in large pots or tubs.

As discussed earlier, annuals, by their very nature, aim to set as many seeds as possible within a very short life span. Gardeners can extend the flowering period by cutting the blooms for indoor use or nipping off faded flowers before they set seed and so decide it's all over for another year. Remember, if you follow this procedure it is good practice to provide regular nourishment to the plants in the form of a quick-acting fertilizer designed to promote flowers, rather than foliage growth.

Soil Preparation and Planting

To ensure good strong growth and maximize flowering, prepare your garden beds soundly. If the area to be planted has not been dug over before, it is a good idea to double dig. This means that the topsoil, say a fork's depth, is weeded and put aside and the soil under this layer is dug over to the depth of a fork. Humus, such as well-rotted manure, or compost can be added to this layer to help break up heavy clay

With their large spikes of showy, pea flowers, Lupinus *species will enhance any garden.*

particles or to add moisture retentive qualities to sandy soils. This double digging is particularly beneficial to perennials which can be left in the same position for some years. Replace the top layer of soil and prepare this surface in accordance with your planting needs. If planting perennials, a dressing of well-rotted manure or compost or a complete fertilizer can be added while roughly digging the soil over, whereas if hardy annual seeds are to be sown directly into the soil in temperate areas this top layer needs to be well dug over to remove any clods, then raked evenly to ensure a smooth, even surface.

In many areas the local climate determines when and if seeds can be planted directly into the ground. A much greater success rate is ensured, should there be a possibility of a late frost, if seeds are sown in a greenhouse or on a warm, weather-proof veranda or

similar sheltered spot. This guarantees that the seedlings are ready to be transplanted as soon as weather permits.

Whereas annuals are grown from seed each season, perennials have various ways of being propagated. Most can be grown from seed, however this usually takes longer for blooms to form. If established crowns or rhizomes are divided, new plants, true to form, are generally established more quickly and often produce flowers the following season.

For gardeners in all climatic zones annuals provide welcome displays of colour, especially in the early spring, while perennials put on a colour parade once a year, often as a bonus to distinctive foliage. What's more, perennials pay handsome dividends, providing the gardener with a source of plant material with which to experiment with design and colour combinations each season.

Achillea filipendulina 'Gold Plate'

Achillea millefolium

Acanthus spinosus

Aconitum napellus

Abelmoschus moschatus 'Mischief'

Acanthus mollis

ABELMOSCHUS
moschatus 'Mischief'

MALLOW

This bushy, fast-growing annual grows to 50 cm (about 20 in) high with a spread of 30 cm (about 12 in). It has narrow green leaves, sometimes tinged with pink, and bears red and white flowers over a prolonged period in summer and autumn/fall. The flowers show affinity to the hibiscus and, when crushed, both flowers and foliage have a musty smell. It grows well as a pot plant and is also ideal for naturalizing in a wild garden or odd corner. The plant is half-hardy, doing best in sun and a good, well-drained soil. Propagate from seed in spring. Rust disease can be a problem; spray with fungicide.

ACANTHUS

BEAR'S BREECHES, OYSTER PLANT

These ancient Mediterranean perennials are grown mainly for their handsome leaves and curious spikes of flowers. They make spectacular feature plants and are useful for covering steep banks. They are fully hardy, doing best in sun but tolerating semi-shade. They need a rich, well-drained soil and are best suited to temperate gardens. Flowers appear in early summer, after which the plant dies back. Remove spent flowers, stems and dead leaves and propagate by division in autumn/fall or from seed sown in spring. Watch for snails and other insect pests and water well except when dormant. They have deep roots and are therefore difficult to eradicate if incorrectly planted. This genus has been immortalized by the Greeks, who used the motif to decorate the capitals of their Corinthian columns.

A. mollis

This strong, upright-growing, semi-evergreen has large, deeply serrated and veined, bright green leaves. It produces 1 m (about 3 ft) tall, densely clustered spikes of funnel-shaped, light rosy purple flowers in summer. It grows to 1.2 m (about 3½ ft) high with a 45 cm (about 18 in) spread. It likes partial shade.

A. spinosus

This species has very large, deeply divided, arching dark green leaves with spiny points. In summer it bears bold spikes of white flowers tinted with purple. It grows to 1.2 m (about 3½ ft) high with a spread of 60 cm (about 24 in).

ACHILLEA

YARROW, MILFOIL

There are about 200 species of *Achillea*, most native to Europe, Asia and North America. Foliage is fern-like, and masses of large, flat heads of tiny daisy flowers are borne in summer in shades of white, yellow, pink and red. They are hardy perennials, easily grown and tolerant of poor soils, but doing best in sunny, well-drained sites in temperate climates. They multiply rapidly and are easily propagated by division in late winter or from softwood cuttings in early summer. Flowering stems may be cut when spent or left to die down naturally in winter, when the clumps should be pruned to stimulate strong spring growth. Fertilize in spring. Achilleas are suitable for massed border planting and rockeries, and flowerheads can be dried—retaining their colour—for winter decoration. This genus is named after Achilles, who in Greek mythology used the plant to heal wounds. On St John's Eve, the Irish traditionally hang yarrow in the house to ward off evil.

A. filipendulina 'Gold Plate'

A strong-growing, erect cultivar reaching 1.2 m (about 3½ ft) or more with a spread of 60 cm (about 24 in). It has aromatic, bright green foliage, and in summer bears flat, rounded heads of golden-yellow flowers, 10–15 cm (about 4–6 in) wide. It is a valuable border plant.

A. millefolium

A shrubby plant growing to 60 cm (about 24 in) tall with feathery, dark green foliage and crimson flowers in summer. Cultivars include 'Cerise Queen', cherry red with pale centres, and the pink 'Rosea'. This species may become invasive in some areas and needs controlling.

ACONITUM
napellus

HELMET FLOWER, FRIAR'S-CAP

Native to Asia, Europe and America, this autumn/fall-flowering perennial is good for cooler climates. Plant in bold groups or allow to naturalize in woodland conditions. It has tall slender spires of helmet-shaped violet-blue flowers (some forms have pink or white flowers) and deeply divided mid-green leaves. It grows to 1.5 m (about 4½ ft) in height with a spread of 30 cm (about 12 in). It will do best in a moderately rich well-drained soil, in sun or partial shade, and must not be allowed to dry out during the growing season. Plants are easily increased by root division in winter, but once established they are best left undisturbed for several years. Transplant when dormant in winter. *A. napellus* is fully hardy. The poison aconite is extracted from the roots of this plant.

ACORUS
calamus
SWEET FLAG

This grass-like plant is a marginal water plant, needing a depth of up to 25 cm (about 10 in) of water. It is a semi-evergreen perennial with aromatic tangerine-scented leathery sword-like leaves. *Acorus* grows to 75 cm (about 30 in) high with a spread of 60 cm (about 24 in). It is fully hardy and grows best in full sun in an open position. Propagation is by division of the rhizomes in winter or early spring. Plants should be divided every three or four years. Cut away dead foliage in autumn/fall. The leaves of the cultivar *A. calamus* 'Variegatus' have cream variegation and take on a rosy tinge in spring.

ACTINOTUS
helianthi
FLANNEL FLOWER

Native to Australia, this short-lived perennial grows from 30 cm to 1 m (about 1–3 ft) high with a spread of 60 cm (about 24 in). It has divided grey-green foliage. Furry erect stems appear in spring and summer, topped by star-like flowerheads which consist of a cluster of pink-stamened, greenish florets surrounded by flannel-textured dull white bracts with greyish green tips. Flannel flowers prefer a well-drained soil in full sun and grow well in arid, sandy situations. It is frost-hardy. Propagate from seed or stem cuttings in spring or summer. It is a popular perennial for native gardens.

ADONIS
aestivalis

This fully hardy herbaceous perennial has ranunculus-like red blooms in early spring, and feathery mid-green foliage. It grows in clumps with a height and spread of 25–30 cm (about 10–12 in). Best results are obtained when planted in a moist, fairly light soil that contains a considerable amount of composted material, peat or leafmould. It flowers in sun or light shade but wilts badly in extreme heat. Fertilize and water regularly and propagate from seed

Aethionema 'Warley Rose'

Agapanthus 'Blue Baby'

in late summer or by division after flowering.

AETHIONEMA
'Warley Rose'

A member of the Brassicaceae (which includes cress) family, and native to the Mediterranean area, this low evergreen short-lived sub-shrub is grown for its profusion of small bright rose-pink flowers in spring and summer. Foliage is handsome, with narrow, elongated bluish green leaves. It is a compact 15 cm (about 6 in) high and wide, making it an ideal plant to grow between paving stones or in a rock garden. It is fully hardy, and enjoys well-drained coarse-textured soil and full sun. Trim lightly after flowering and propagate by softwood cuttings in spring or by seed in autumn/fall. It will self-seed readily.

AGAPANTHUS
AFRICAN LILY, AGAPANTHUS

Native to southern Africa, these strong-growing perennials are

Actinotus helianthi

popular for their fine foliage and showy flowers produced in abundance over summer. They have dark green, glossy, gracefully arching strap-shaped leaves. Flowers are blue or white, in many flowered umbels, borne on a long erect stem, often 1 m (about 3 ft) or more tall. Agapanthus are ideal for background plants or for edging along a wall, fence or driveway. Cut flowers are useful for bold arrangements in large containers and the plants also make excellent tub and container specimens. The genus is extremely tough, thriving in conditions of neglect, on hillsides and near the coast. The plants enjoy full sun but will tolerate some shade, and will grow in any soil as long as it is well watered. They naturalize readily, soon forming large clumps. Propagate by division in late winter, or from seed in

spring or autumn/fall. Remove spent flower stems and dead leaves at the end of winter. Frost-hardy to half-hardy.

A. 'Blue Baby'

Growing 45–60 cm (about 18–24 in) high with a spread of 30 cm (about 12 in), this frost-hardy cultivar bears light blue flowers on rather open heads in summer.

A. praecox subsp. orientalis

A half-hardy species, this is probably the best known agapanthus. It has large dense umbels of rich blue flowers carried on strong stems over broad dark green leaves in late summer. It grows to 1 m (about 3 ft) high and 60 cm (about 24 in) wide, and is an ideal pot plant species. Prefers full sun and moist soil.

Acorus calamus

Adonis aestivalis

Agapanthus praecox subsp. *orientalis*

Alcea rosea

Agrostemma githago

Alchemilla mollis

Ajuga reptans

Alpinia purpurata

Ageratum houstonianum

AGERATUM
houstonianum

FLOSS FLOWER

Native to tropical Mexico, this member of the Asteraceae family (which also contains daisies) is a popular and easily grown annual with dull hairy heart-shaped leaves and showy blue, lavender, mauve-pink or white fluffy flowerheads. It should flower throughout summer and into autumn/fall if the ground is kept moist and dead flowerheads are removed regularly. The tall cultivars form clumps of 30 cm (about 12 in) high and wide and are useful for bedding and cut flowers. The dwarf varieties form clumps of 15 cm (about 6 in) high and wide and are excellent for edging and containers. Any well-drained soil is suitable, preferably compost-enriched. They are half-hardy and prefer a sunny position with protection from cold wind. Keep moist, especially during spring and summer. Young plants benefit from tip pruning and spent flowers should be removed. Propagate from seed sown in spring.

AGROSTEMMA
githago

CORN COCKLE

This fast-growing showy annual reaches a height of 1 m (about 3 ft), with a spread of 30 cm (about 12 in), making it ideal for planting at the back of an annual border. It has a slender, many branched, willowy habit with lance-shaped leaves. Open, trumpet-shaped pink flowers, 8 cm (about 3 in) in diameter, appear throughout summer. It is fully hardy, growing best in full sun in a well-drained soil. Propagate from seed sown in early spring or autumn/fall. Young plants should be thinned to about 25 cm (10 in) spacing and may need light staking if growing in exposed areas. The tiny, round, dark brown seeds are poisonous.

AJUGA
reptans

CARPET BUGLEWEED, BLUE BUGLE

This excellent perennial ground cover forms a showy carpet in sun or part shade. Bright blue flower spikes appear in early spring above the metallic green crinkled leaves. There are various cultivars with different coloured leaves: 'Burgundy Lace' has cream and maroon variegated leaves; 'Atropurpurea', dark purplish bronze; 'Multicolor', white and pink and purple; 'Variegata', light green and creamy white; and 'Jungle Beauty', dark green with a tinge of purple. They grow 10–30 cm high (about 4–12 in) and spread rapidly from runners. Fully hardy, they grow in most conditions but prefer shade and cool moist soil. Those with variegated foliage do better in sun. Propagate by division in spring. Remove spent flowerheads and watch for fungus disease. *Ajuga* has been widely used as a healing agent for wounds.

ALCEA
rosea

syn. *Althaea rosea*

HOLLYHOCK

A native of the eastern Mediterranean and central Asia, this stately biennial was one of the first flowers to be cultivated in the southern hemisphere. They are popular for their tall spikes of flowers which can reach 2 m (about 6 ft). Flowers appear in summer and early autumn/fall, and come in a range of colours including pink, cream and yellow. Foliage is roundish and rough and the plant spreads to about 60 cm (about 24 in). They are fully hardy but need shelter from wind, benefiting from staking in exposed positions. They prefer sun, a rich, heavy well-drained soil and frequent watering in dry weather. Propagate from seed in late

summer or spring. Rust disease can be a problem; spray with fungicide.

ALCHEMILLA
mollis

LADY'S MANTLE

This old-fashioned, low-growing perennial is ideal for ground cover, the front of borders or for rock gardens. It is clump-forming, growing to a height and spread of 40 cm (about 16 in). It has decorative, wavy-edged leaves which hold dew or raindrops to give a sparkling effect. In summer, it bears masses of small sprays of greenish yellow flowers, similar to *Gypsophila*. They are fully hardy, preferring partial shade, moist, well-drained soil and a humid atmosphere. Propagate from seed or by division in spring or autumn/fall, and cut back to 3 cm (about 1½ in) when they finish flowering.

ALPINIA

ORNAMENTAL GINGER

A genus named in honour of the sixteenth-century Italian botanist Prospero Alpino, it is grown for its very showy flowers. Gingers are not easy to grow successfully in pots and will only flower in a warm, moist position. They prefer a mild to subtropical climate, although all but *A. purpurata* will grow in a mild temperate climate. They need full sun to part-shade. Frost-tender, they will not survive below 16–18°C (about 61–64°F). Propagate by division of rhizomes in spring or early summer. Although edible, it is not the ginger used commercially. The flowers are used in the Pacific islands to make garlands.

A. purpurata

RED GINGER

From Polynesia, the showy spikes of fairly inconspicuous, small white flowers in scarlet bracts, bloom throughout the year and bring a vivid splash of colour to the garden. The glossy leaves are narrow and lance-shaped. New plantlets sprout among the flower bracts and take root when the dying flower stems fall to the ground under the weight of the growing plantlets.

A. zerumbet
syn. A. speciosa, A. nutens
SHELL GINGER, SHELL FLOWER

A tall plant, originally from China, in summer it bears racemes of waxy, ivory or white flowers with yellow lips and pink or red throats. It can grow to 3 m (about 9 ft) and needs partial shade, good soil and plenty of water to flower well.

ALSTROEMERIA
PERUVIAN LILY

Native to South America, these tuberous plants are among the finest of all perennials for cutting, but they do drop petals. Flowers are showy and multi-coloured, resembling miniature trumpet lilies held on thin wiry stems. They flower profusely from spring to summer. About 50 species exist, all growing well in sun or light shade in a well-enriched, well-drained acid soil. They soon form large clumps, bearing dozens of heads of flowers. Propagate from seed or by division in early spring. They are frost-hardy, but in cold winters protect the dormant tubers by covering with loose peat or dry bracken. Best left undisturbed when established, but one-year-old seedlings transplant well. Alstroemerias do well naturalized under trees or on sloping banks.

A. aurea
syn. A. aurantiaca

This is the most common and easily grown species, with heads of orange flowers, tipped with green and streaked with maroon. Leaves are twisted, narrow and lance-shaped. Several cultivars exist; 'Majestic' and 'Bronze Beauty' both have deep orange or bronzy orange flowers. They reach a height of 1 m (about 3 ft) with a spread of 60 cm–1 m (about 2–3 ft).

A., Ligtu hybrids

Leaves are narrow and twisted and flowers are widely flared in shades of pink, salmon, yellow or orange, sometimes streaked and spotted with other colours. They grow 60–80 cm tall (about 24–32 in) with a spread of 60 cm–1 m (about 2–3 ft).

AMARANTHUS

These bright showy annuals, native to the tropics, are grown for their brilliant foliage, curious flowers and adaptability to hot, dry conditions. They are popular bedding plants, with large and attractively coloured leaves and minute flowers borne in drooping tassel-like spikes. A sunny, dry position with protection from strong winds is essential, and they enjoy a fertile, well-drained soil, mulched during hot weather. Half-hardy. Prune when young to

Alpinia zerumbet

Alstroemeria, Ligtu hybrid

Alstroemeria aurea

Amaranthus tricolor 'Joseph's Coat'

Amaranthus caudatus

Anagallis linifolia

thicken growth and propagate from seed sown in spring. Prepare soil for planting with plenty of manure, and water seedlings regularly. Protect from snails when young and watch for caterpillars and aphids.

A. caudatus
LOVE-LIES-BLEEDING, TASSEL FLOWER

This tall species, growing to 1.2 m (about 3½ ft) high and 50 cm (about 20 in) wide, has oval, pale green leaves and dark red flowers in long, drooping cords, their ends often touching the ground. Flowers appear in summer through to autumn/fall. In many old gardens this plant was used to give height in the centre of circular beds.

A. tricolor 'Joseph's Coat'

A bushy annual, growing to 1 m (about 3 ft) and 50 cm (about 20 in) wide. This plant is grown for its brilliant bronze, gold, orange and red variegated 20 cm (8 in) long leaves which retain their colouring into the late autumn/fall. Tiny red flowers appear in summer.

ANAGALLIS
linifolia
PIMPERNEL

This charming little plant is grown for its brilliant blue flowers of 1 cm (about ½ in) in diameter. They are excellent small rockery plants or can be used for edging large containers. They flower during summer and are low-growing, rarely exceeding 5 cm (about 2 in) in height, with a spread of 15 cm (about 6 in) or more. This species requires a sunny, well-drained spot in fertile, moist soil. They benefit from some shade in hot areas. Propagate from seed or by division in spring. Fully hardy.

ANAPHALIS
margaritacea
syn. A. yedoensis
PEARL EVERLASTING

Native to the northern hemisphere this perennial member of the Asteraceae family (which includes daisies) is valued for its papery, small white flowers which can be dried for

Anaphalis margaritacea

indoor decoration. It has lance-shaped, silvery grey leaves and the flowers are borne on erect stems in late summer. Bushy in habit, it grows to 60–75 cm (about 24–30 in) high and 60 cm (about 24 in) wide. Easily grown, it prefers a sunny situation (but will grow in semi-shade) and well-drained chalky soil. Do not allow to dry out. They are fully hardy. Propagate from seed in autumn/fall or by division in winter or spring. Prune back hard in winter.

Antirrhinum majus

Anchusa capensis 'Blue Angel'

Anchusa azurea

Anthemis tinctoria

ANCHUSA

SUMMER FORGET-ME-NOT, ALKANET

Natives of Europe, north and south Africa and western Asia, this genus consists of about 50 species of annuals, biennials and perennials. They are larger than the forget-me-not (*Myosotis*) and have clearer, true blue flowers that do not fade easily. All species are suitable for herbaceous borders and are easily grown in beds and containers. Fully to frost-hardy, they grow best in a sunny position in deep, rich, well-drained

soil. In very hot areas planting in semi-shade helps maintain the flower colour. Feed sparingly and water generously. The taller species benefit from staking and the plants require plenty of room as they make large root systems. Cut flower stalks back after blooming to promote new growth. Propagate perennials by division in winter, annuals and biennials from seed in autumn/fall or spring. Transplant perennials when dormant in winter. These plants are popular with bees.

A. azurea
syn. A. italica

This fully hardy perennial grows to 1–1.2 m (about 3–3½ ft) high and 60 cm (about 24 in) wide. It has coarse, hairy leaves and an erect habit with tiers of brilliant blue flowers borne in spring to summer. Cultivars include the rich blue 'Morning Glory', light blue 'Opal' and deep blue 'Loddon Royalist'.

A. capensis 'Blue Angel'

A bushy biennial, grown as an annual, this *Anchusa* reaches a height

Anigozanthos 'Bush Gems'

Anigozanthos manglesii

and spread of 20 cm (about 8 in). A native of southern Africa, it forms a compact pyramid of shallow, bowl-shaped sky-blue flowers in early summer. Frost-hardy. 'Blue Bird' is a taller—50 cm (about 20 in)—but equally striking cultivar.

ANIGOZANTHOS

KANGAROO PAW

Native to south-western Australia, these perennials are noted for their unique paw-shaped, bird-attracting flowers. A low-growing tufted plant, it reaches a height of 1.2 m (about 3½ ft) and spread of 30–60 cm (about 12–24 in). Flowers come in many colours including green, gold, deep red and orange-red, and bicolours including green and red, orange and burgundy, and yellow and lime. They prefer warm, very well-drained sandy or gravelly soil and a hot, sunny, open position. Water well during dry seasons. Half-hardy, they will tolerate some frost and do well in coastal regions. Propagate by division in spring or from fresh seed. Plants are often affected by ink disease, a fungus disease which blackens the foliage.

A. 'Bush Gems'

This plant grows to 70 cm (about 28 in) tall and 30–60 cm (about 12–24 in) wide. It comes in a variety of hybrid colours, ranging from yellow, gold and green through to orange, red and burgundy.

A. manglesii
RED-AND-GREEN KANGAROO PAW

This regal plant has blue-green, strap-like leaves. Green flowers with

a red base and stem appear mainly in spring. It grows to 1 m (about 3 ft) in height and has a spread of 45 cm (about 18 in).

ANTHEMIS
tinctoria

GOLDEN MARGUERITE, YELLOW CHAMOMILE

A fully hardy easily grown perennial that is covered in late spring and summer with a dazzling display of daisy-like yellow flowers above fern-like, crinkled green leaves. The foliage of *Anthemis*, very aromatic when crushed, is used to make chamomile tea. They prefer sun and will thrive even in poor sandy or clay soils as long as they are well-drained. Strong growers, they form clumps 1 m (about 3 ft) high and wide and need cutting back and breaking up into smaller clumps each season. Propagate by division in spring, or basal cuttings in spring or late summer. Prolong flowering by cutting back the spent stems.

ANTIRRHINUM
majus

SNAPDRAGON

Native to the Mediterranean region, this perennial is valued for its showy flowers that are borne over a long period from spring to autumn/fall. There are many cultivars (usually grown as annuals), ranging from tall—75 cm (about 30 in); to medium—50 cm (about 20 in); to dwarf—25 cm (about 10 in). They have a spread of 30–50 cm (about 12–20 in). Erect plants, they form dense bushes of many upright stems carrying spikes of frilly, two-lipped, sometimes double, flowers, in a range of colours including orange, yellow, red, purple, pink and white. They prefer a fertile, well-drained soil in full sun with some protection from wind. Plants should be dead-headed to prolong flowering and early buds can be pinched out to increase branching. Half-hardy. Propagate from seed in spring or early autumn/fall. Rust disease can be a problem.

AQUILEGIA

COLUMBINE

These graceful, clump-forming perennials, native to Europe, North America, Asia and the Orient, are grown for their interesting form and varied colour range. They are also useful cut flowers, and the dwarf and alpine species make good rock garden plants. Foliage is fern-like and the flowers are mainly bell-shaped and spurred. Fully to frost-hardy, they flower during early summer and prefer a well-drained light soil, enriched with animal manure. Plant in an open, sunny site, protected from strong winds and with some shade in hot areas. They look their best in bold clumps with a foreground planting of other annuals. Keep moist and give plenty of liquid Fertilizer during growth. In cold climates columbines are perennial and need to be cut to the ground in late winter, but growing them as annuals usually gives best results. Propagate from seed in autumn/fall and spring. The plants are short-lived, but self-seed readily. The species name, 'columbine', comes from the Latin for dove, as the flowers were thought to resemble a cluster of doves.

A. caerulea
BLUE COLUMBINE

This alpine species is a short-lived, upright perennial growing to 45 cm (about 18 in) in height with a spread of 15 cm (about 6 in). Big, powdery blue or white nodding flowers on branching stems appear in spring and early summer. It sometimes produces a few blooms in autumn/fall. It is fully hardy, and does best in rich soil. *A. alpina* is similar but has short spurs and usually all blue flowers.

A., McKana hybrids

A clump-forming, leafy perennial growing to 75 cm (about 30 in) tall with a spread of 30 cm (about 12 in). This strain includes an extensive range of pastel shades and bicolours. Flowers are large and noted for their delicate long spurs behind the petals. Fully hardy, they flower in spring or early summer.

A. vulgaris
GRANNY'S BONNETS

This is the true columbine, one of the parents of the modern hybrids. It is a variable species, growing to 1 m (about 3 ft) high with a spread of 50 cm (about 20 in). It bears funnel-shaped, short spurred flowers in colours of pink, crimson, white and purple, on long stems from the centre of a loose rosette of grey-green foliage that resembles maidenhair fern. Fully hardy, it flowers from spring to early summer.

ARABIS
caucasica 'Plena'
syn. A. albida

This fully hardy, evergreen perennial is suitable for ground cover in the rock garden, crevices in walls or bedding. It is sometimes used to overplant spring flowering bulbs. Easily grown, it forms dense clusters of thick foliage, up to 15 cm (about 6 in) high with a spread of 45 cm (about 18 in). It has loose, mid-green leaf rosettes and white, fragrant, double flowers appear in early to late spring. It requires a light, well-drained soil, rich in organic matter. Plant in full sun (semi-shade in

warmer climates) and cut back hard after flowering. Propagate from softwood cuttings in summer, or from seed or by division in autumn/fall.

ARCTOTIS
× hybrida
AFRICAN DAISY, AURORA DAISY

Native to southern Africa, these colourful, profusely blooming flowers are excellent for ground cover or mass planting on sloping sites. They are compact perennials, often grown as annuals, and reach a height of 50 cm (about 20 in) or more, and spread of 40 cm (about 16 in). Daisy-like 8 cm (about 3 in) flowers in shades of pink, white, yellow, red and orange, all with contrasting black and gold centres, are produced abundantly from winter until late summer. The blooms close in dull weather and in late afternoon. Leaves are chrysanthemum-like. These plants require full sun, regular watering, and a well-drained light soil with well-rotted compost and sharp sand added. Frost-tender. Propagate from seed in spring or autumn/fall, or from year-round stem cuttings.

ARGEMONE
mexicana
PRICKLY POPPY

This half-hardy perennial has prickly, white-marked greyish green leaves, and fragrant, yellow or white poppy-like flowers. The flowers are 8 cm (about 3 in) wide and appear in summer. It has a spreading habit, growing to 60 cm (about 24 in) high and 30 cm (about 12 in) wide. They grow best in full sun and very well-drained soil. Remove spent flowers to prolong flowering and propagate from seed in early summer. Transplant in autumn/fall. This species self-seeds readily and tends to become invasive. Native to North America, the genus is named from the Greek *argema*, a cataract, as the local Indians believed the plants had medicinal properties that would cure cataracts.

ARGYRANTHEMUM
frutescens
syn. Chrysanthemum frutescens
MARGUERITE, PARIS DAISY

Native to the Canary Islands, this bushy evergreen perennial is available in many colours. They bear many daisy-like flowerheads, both single and double, in spring and summer. Most grow to a height and spread of 1 m (about 3 ft). A. *frutescens* is half-hardy. Pinch out growing tips regularly to maintain shape, and cut back severely in summer.

Aquilegia, McKana hybrid

Aquilegia caerulea

Aquilegia vulgaris

Argemone mexicana (white form)

Arabis caucasica 'Plena'

Arctotis × *hybrida*

Argyranthemum frutescens

Armeria maritima

ARMERIA
maritima
SEA PINK, THRIFT

One of the best of the old cottage garden plants, thrift was in cultivation as early as 1578. It is a tufted evergreen perennial with a mound-like mass of narrow, dark green leaves, and dense flowerheads of small white to pink flowers. Flowers are produced in a flush in early spring and continue to bloom for most of the year. The plant grows to 10 cm (about 4 in) high and spreads to 20 cm (about 8 in), making it good for edging. Sandy soil and good drainage are essential and they thrive in hot, dry, sunny situations, particularly near the coast. The species is native to the mountains and rocky coasts of the Mediterranean and Asia Minor and resents wet conditions or heavy soils. Fully hardy. Propagate from seed in autumn/fall, or semi-ripe cuttings in summer.

Asclepias physocarpa

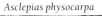

Artemisia arborescens

ARTEMISIA
WORMWOOD

This is a large genus of plants and herbs, mostly native to arid regions in the northern hemisphere. Grown for their decorative silvery foliage that is often aromatic and sometimes repellent to insects. They have insignificant flowers but are an attractive addition to a flower border where their feathery foliage provides interest throughout the year. There are both shrubby and herbaceous, evergreen and deciduous species. Mostly fully to half-hardy, they prefer an open, sunny situation with light, well-drained soil. Prune back lightly in spring to stimulate growth. Propagate from softwood or semi-ripe cuttings in summer or by division in spring. Transplant during winter.

A. arborescens

Evergreen perennial with silvery white foliage, reaching a height of 1.2 m (about 3½ ft) and spread of 75 cm (about 30 in). Small bright yellow flowers are borne in summer and early autumn/fall. Half-hardy. Trim well in spring. This is a good plant for the back of a border.

A. lactiflora
WHITE MUGWORT

A tall-growing, attractive Chinese species which grows like a Michaelmas daisy with many-branched heads of tiny milky white flowers blooming in summer. Foliage is fern-like and aromatic. This is a useful plant to contrast with stronger colours in a garden. Needs staking. It grows 1.2–1.5 m tall (about 3½ to 4½ ft) with a spread of 50 cm (about 20 in). Fully hardy.

A. stelleriana

Excellent planted in light sandy soils, this evergreen perennial has serrated, white-haired silver leaves, and slender sprays of small yellow flowers are borne in summer. It has a rounded habit and grows 30–60 cm (about 12–24 in) high and spreads up to 1 m (about 3 ft). Fully hardy.

ARUNCUS
dioicus
syn. *A. sylvester*, *Spiraea aruncus*
GOAT'S BEARD

A graceful woodland perennial useful for shady spots and moist situations. The clump-forming plants produce a mass of rich green, fern-like foliage and arching plumes of tiny silky white flowers in summer. Grows to a height of 2 m (about 6 ft) and spread of 1.2 m (about 3½ ft). It is a good specimen for planting beside a pool or creek. Fully hardy, the plant naturalizes readily and thrives in any well-drained moist soil, in full light or partial shade. Propagate from seed in spring or by division in spring or autumn/fall. Cut flowering stems back hard in autumn/fall.

ASCLEPIAS
physocarpa
SWAN PLANT

Native to southern Africa, this evergreen sub-shrub is best suited to warm climate gardens. Where frosts are severe it should be treated as an annual. From late spring it bears small white flowers. These are not very showy but the bladder-like, swan-shaped, seed pods that follow are interesting novelties which appeal to children. The narrow lanceolate leaves are light to mid-green and about 10 cm (about 4 in) long. Frost-tender, it prefers a sunny situation and a well-drained soil. Drought tolerant once established. Frequently planted as a food source for monarch butterflies (*Danaus plexippus*), which can totally defoliate the plant: this is one of the few occasions where the gardener is unlikely to object. Propagate from seed or tip cuttings.

ASTELIA

Native to the South Pacific, this genus contains 25 species of thicket-forming perennial shrubs and herbs admired for their leaves. The plants develop basal rosettes of slender, shiny, evergreen leaves with prominent midribs and downy reverses. The insignificant flowers are produced in branched terminal clusters and are followed by round fruit. They require a rich, moisture-retentive soil. In spring, propagate by division. The genus name comes from the Greek *a*, without, and *steele*, a pillar, referring to the epiphytic nature of the plants.

A. chathamica 'Silver Spear'

This is the most striking of the 13 New Zealand species of this Pacific genus of flax-like, strap-leaved, clump-forming evergreen perennials.

Artemisia lactiflora

Aruncus dioicus

Artemisia stelleriana

Its bright, almost metallic, silver leaves are unique. It forms a dense foliage clump 1.5 m (about 4½ ft) in height with a spread of up to 2 m (about 6 ft). Tiny flowers are followed by bright orange berries on some plants. Only female plants bear fruit but, as 'Silver Spear' comes in both fruiting and non-fruiting forms, it is most likely that several different plants are cultivated under this name. Best in full sun and moist well-drained soil. Propagate by division in late winter to early spring.

A. nervosa
KAKAHA

Spreading out to 1.5 m (about 4½ ft) and reaching up to 60 cm (about 25 in) high, this vigorous New Zealand species is valued for its pendent, lanceolate, frosted grey leaves. In summer, starry light brown fragrant flowers form in clusters on the ends of long slender stems. These are followed by small green fruit, which turn orange-red when ripe.

ASTER
MICHAELMAS OR EASTER DAISY, ASTER

Native to the northern hemisphere, this large genus of perennials and deciduous or evergreen sub-shrubs contains over 250 species. Easily grown, they vary in height from miniatures suitable for rock gardens to 2 m (about 6 ft) tall giants suitable for the back of a herbaceous border. Leaves are sometimes dark coloured, sometimes hairy. Showy, daisy-like flowerheads are usually produced in late summer or

autumn/fall, in a wide range of colours, including blue, violet, purple, pink, red or white, all with a central disc of yellow or black. Grow in sun or partial shade in hot areas in a well-drained soil, preferably enriched with leafmould. Keep moist at all times and feed complete plant food in spring and summer. Shelter from strong winds and stake the taller species. Cut the long stems down to ground level and tidy the clumps when flowers have faded. Propagate by division in spring or late autumn/fall, or from softwood cuttings in spring. Replace plants about every three years; the most vigorous types are best lifted annually, and two or three strong side shoots planted again.

A. alpinus

A clump-forming plant, growing 15 cm (about 6 in) high and spreading to 45 cm (about 18 in). Large violet-blue daisies with yellow centres appear from late spring until early summer and the foliage is dark green. This species is from the higher mountains of Europe and is popular as a rock garden plant. Fully hardy, it prefers full sun and is easily grown in any but very light soil.

A. frikartii 'Mönch'

A bushy free-branching plant, producing large, single soft lavender-blue daisy-like flowers with yellowish centres over a long period from mid-summer until late autumn/fall. Grows to a height of 75 cm (about 30 in) and spread of 45 cm (about 18 in). Fully hardy. One of the best asters for garden display and picking.

A. novae-angliae 'Barr's Pink'

An erect plant growing to 1 m (about 3 ft) tall, this cultivar produces bright rose pink flowers from late summer until autumn/fall. Fully hardy and mildew resistant. May need staking.

A. novae-angliae 'Harrington's Pink'

The best-known of the *A. novae-angliae* cultivars, this cultivar produces lovely salmon-pink flowers with yellow centres in autumn/fall. Fully hardy, it grows to 1.2 m (about 3½ ft) tall, so it may need staking. It is well-branched and very showy when in bloom.

A. novi-belgii 'Mulberry'
NEW YORK ASTER

An upright plant bearing large, daisy-like semi-double, rich mulberry-red flowers with yellow centres in autumn/fall. Leaves are small, lance-shaped and dark green. Grows to 75 cm (about 30 in) tall with a spread of 45 cm (about 18 in). Fully hardy. Watch for mildew.

ASTILBE
GOAT'S BEARD

Native to the Orient, these easily grown fully hardy perennials are ideal used as a trouble-free ground cover in damp spots. They grow best on the edge of ponds and in damp hollows, but are also suitable for borders and rock gardens. Foliage is attractive and fern-like, and in young plants often a coppery red. Flowers appear in summer, in tall, fluffy plume-like

Astelia nervosa

Astelia chathamica 'Silver Spear'

panicles, in white, cream, many shades of pink, red and purple. Plant in rich, deep soil with plenty of water, in partial shade and do not allow to dry out. Propagate by division of established clumps from late winter to spring, or from seed or division in autumn/fall. Yearly winter top-dressing or rich compost maintains vigor. Cut down to ground level in late autumn/fall and lift and divide every three years. Astilbes make good cut flowers.

Aster frikartii 'Mönch'

Aster alpinus

Aster novi-belgii 'Mulberry'

Aster novae-angliae 'Barr's Pink'

Aster novae-angliae 'Harrington's Pink'

Astilbe chinensis 'Pumila'

Astilbe 'Fanal'

Aubrieta deltoidea

Aurinia saxatilis

Begonia semperflorens

Begonia metallica

Begonia 'Orange Rubra'

A. 'Fanal'

A leafy, clump-forming plant growing to 1 m (about 3 ft) high and wide. Spring-flowering, it bears feathery spikes of small, star-shaped, scarlet long-lasting flowers. It has broad leaves with oval, toothed leaflets.

A. chinensis 'Pumila'

An attractive clump-forming plant with toothed, hairy, dark green leaves and dense, fluffy spikes of small, star-shaped mauve-red flowers. It grows to a height of 30 cm (about 12 in) and spreads quickly. Ideal for moist, shady borders or rock gardens. Will benefit from extra Fertilizer during the summer flowering period.

AUBRIETA
deltoidea
ROCK CRESS

This miniature trailing perennial is an ideal plant for rock gardens, sunny dry banks, chinks in stone paving and walls or for border edges. It is a compact plant with greenish grey leaves and masses of starry flowers in mauve-pinks, mauve-blues and violets. It flowers for a long period in spring, often repeat flowering in autumn/fall. It forms a dense mat to 5 cm (about 2 in) high with a spread of 20 cm (about 8 in), and spills prettily over the edges of beds or containers. Fully hardy, it thrives in sun and any well-drained soil. Propagate from semi-ripe cuttings in late summer or autumn/fall or from seed sown in spring. Cut back hard after flowering. Aubrieta was named for an eighteenth-century French botanical artist.

AURINIA
saxatilis
syn. Alyssum saxatile
YELLOW ALYSSUM

Native to south-eastern Europe, this perennial blooms in early spring. It forms a neat mound of greyish green leaf rosettes and has showy flower sprays in shades of vivid yellow and gold that last for months. It is a woody rooted evergreen plant growing to 25 cm (about 10 in) high with a spread of 30 cm (about 12 in). Fully hardy, it needs sun and a moderately fertile, coarse, gritty, well-drained soil. It is highly regarded as a rock garden or wall plant and makes a good companion plant to tulips. Propagate from seed in autumn/fall or softwood or greenwood cuttings in early summer. Self-seeds readily. Cut back immediately after flowering.

BEGONIA
BEGONIA

This large genus of perennial plants are grown for their colourful flowers and ornamental foliage. Most of the 1000-odd species can be grown outdoors only in areas with temperate to subtropical climates. Tuberous rooted or fibrous, they range in habit from dwarf to tall and scandent, some are hardy and others very sensitive to frost. All require a light, rich well-drained soil that is slightly acidic. They need shelter from wind and strong sunlight. There are various groups of begonias, each with different cultivation requirements.

Semperflorens group
BEDDING BEGONIA, WAX BEGONIA

Bushy, evergreen perennials, cultivars within this group are often grown as bedding annuals. They are also useful for bordering, especially in shaded gardens. Freely branching plants, with soft succulent stems, they have rounded glossy green, bronze or variegated 5 cm (about 2 in) long leaves. Flowers are showy, single or double in colours of bright rose-pink, light pink, white or red. They grow best in partial sun or shade and a well-drained soil. Propagate in spring from seed or stem cuttings and pinch out growing tips to encourage bushy growth. Frost-tender, these begonias can be dug up and potted for indoor winter use in frosty areas.

B. semperflorens

Evergreen, with glossy rounded dark green leaves, this begonia flowers all year round, but mainly in summer, and is widely used as a bedding plant. Slow-growing, it reaches a height of 30 cm (about 12 in) and spread of 25 cm (about 10 in). Small waxy single pink flowers, sometimes with a white centre, are borne on the leaf axils. Prefers semi-shade. Hybrids are available in white, pink and red.

B. metallica
METAL-LEAF BEGONIA

A tall-growing, shrub-like begonia from Mexico with bronze-green leaves often splashed with white. The leaves are borne from white-haired stems and are covered with fine silver hairs, red beneath. In summer to autumn/fall pink flowers with red bristles appear.

B. 'Orange Rubra'

This cane-stemmed begonia can reach 60 cm (about 24 in). It has large, oval, light green leaves, sometimes with white spots that disappear with age. Clusters of orange flowers are produced throughout the year.

B. scharffii
syn. B. haageana

A shrub-like begonia that grows up to 1.2 m (about 3½ ft) tall with hair-covered stems and leaves. The large, oval, soft olive-green leaves

Begonia scharffii

Bergenia cordifolia

Bellis perennis

Browallia americana

Brachycome iberidifolia

Blandfordia grandiflora

have tapered tips and reddish green on the underside. The flowers are pinkish white with small pink-red hairs like a beard, and are produced throughout the year.

BELLIS
perennis

DOUBLE DAISY, ENGLISH DAISY

A slow-growing, fully hardy perennial with fully double flowerheads of red, crimson, pink or white, all with a gold centre. It grows to a height and spread of 15–20 cm (about 6–8 in) and makes an ideal front border, edging or rockery plant. It flowers in spring and both large flowered and miniature flowered cultivars are available. Grows in sun or semi-shade and prefers well-drained, rich moist soil. Plants will die out if allowed to become dry in the autumn/fall. Watch for rust disease. Propagate by division after flowering or from seed in summer, and remove spent flowerheads regularly to prolong flowering. The golden centre of the daisy gave the flower its name 'Deus eye', or the eye of god.

BERGENIA
cordifolia

HEARTLEAF, SAXIFRAGA

Native to Siberia, this tough perennial has large, roundish, crinkle-edged, heart-shaped leaves and produces racemes of rosy red flowers on 30–40 cm (about 12–16 in) stems in spring. It is long-flowering and useful for cutting. Cultivars include 'Red' with deep carmine flowers and 'Purpurea', magenta pink. It grows to a height of 45 cm

(about 18 in) and spread of 60 cm (about 24 in). Fully hardy, it makes an excellent border plant or trouble-free ground cover among deciduous trees and shrubs. Thrives in sun or shade and requires a fairly good soil with plenty of humus. Propagate by division from autumn/fall through to spring, after flowering. Water well in hot weather and remove spent flowerheads to prolong flowering.

BLANDFORDIA
grandiflora
syn. *B. flammea*

CHRISTMAS BELLS

Native to Australia, this colourful perennial is grown for its showy, hanging bell-like flowers which vary from deep red with yellow tips to pure yellow. Flowers appear in summer on slim stems up to 50 cm (about 20 in) tall, rising out of clumps of grassy leaves that spread to 30 cm (about 12 in). Frost-hardy, it requires warm, moist, climatic conditions with well-drained acid soil in full sun or partial shade. Keep consistently moist. Grows naturally in peaty bogs in partial shade. Plants seed freely and are easy to raise, usually blooming the second season after sowing. Transplant during winter and early spring.

BRACHYCOME

Native to Australia, these low-growing annuals and evergreen perennials are suitable for use as ground cover. They are mound-forming plants with finely divided, soft, fern-like foliage and bear hundreds

of daisy-like flowers in many shades of blue, mauve, pink and white, centred in black and gold. They are showy border or bedding plants, the smaller species being excellent for rock gardens. Frost-hardy to half-hardy, they require a sunny situation, sandy loam or well-drained garden soil. A sheltered position is preferable, with plenty of root protection. Do not overwater as they prefer dry conditions. Pinch out early shoots to encourage branching and propagate from ripe seed or by divisions or stem cuttings in spring or autumn/fall. The Swan River daisy (*B. iberidifolia*) grows to a height and spread of 50 cm (about 20 in). It is fairly fast growing with lacy green foliage. Small, fragrant daisy-like flowers of blue, pink, mauve, purple or white appear in summer and early autumn/fall.

BROWALLIA
americana
syn. *B. elata*

This moderately fast-growing perennial, related to the petunia, is usually grown as an annual. A bushy plant, it grows to a height of 60 cm (about 24 in) and spread of 15 cm (about 6 in). Makes a good pot or basket plant as well as growing well outdoors. In summer and early autumn/fall it bears clusters of showy semi-star shaped 4 cm (about 2 in) wide flowers in a rare shade of intense blue. It has oval, mid-green leaves. It can withstand temperatures down to 4°C (40°F), and grows best in partial shade in a rich soil with good drainage. Do not allow to completely dry out. Propagate from

seed in spring, or in late summer for winter flowers. Pinch out young growing tips to encourage bushiness. The cultivar 'Vanja' has deep blue flowers with white eyes; 'White Bells' has ice white flowers.

Callistephus chinensis

Calceolaria integrifolia

Calocephalus brownii

Calceolaria herbeohybrida

Calendula officinalis

CALCEOLARIA

LADIES' PURSE, SLIPPER FLOWER

Mostly native to Central and South America, these charming annuals, biennials, evergreen perennials, subshrubs and scandent climbers make spectacular pot plants and garden plants, and are valued for their ability to flower profusely in partial shade. Flowers are pouch-like, usually yellow, sometimes red and heavily spotted on the lower lip. They are fully hardy to frost-tender. Most prefer sun, but several species will flower well in a shady cool site in moist, well-drained soil, with added compost and sharp sand. Propagate from seed in autumn/fall or softwood cuttings in summer or late spring. Provide shelter from heavy winds as the flowerheads are easily damaged. Needs to be pruned back to half height each winter.

C. herbeohybrida

A compact bushy annual popular for spring display indoors. There are many named varieties, growing to a height of 20–40 cm (about 8–16 in) and spread of 15–25 cm (about 6–10 in). Flowers during spring and summer, bearing heads of red and yellow pouched flowers about 4 cm (2 in) wide. Leaves are oval and slightly hairy. Half-hardy.

C. integrifolia

An evergreen, sub-shrubby perennial, growing to 1.2 m (about 3½ ft) high with a spread of 60 cm (about 24 in). It has soft green, heavily wrinkled, clammy leaves, rust-coloured beneath, and in summer bears crowded clusters of wide, brilliant yellow to red-brown flow-

ers. Half-hardy. It is sometimes grown as an annual and during very cold winters may die down to near ground level. Prefers crowded conditions, an acid soil and only occasional watering.

CALENDULA
officinalis

POT MARIGOLD

This is a popular winter and spring flowering annual that remains in bloom for a long time. There are tall and dwarf forms, both bushy, the tall growing to a height and spread of 60 cm (about 24 in) and the dwarf to 30 cm (about 12 in). These fast-growing plants are among the easiest of all annuals to grow, and are useful for filling gaps in the winter and spring garden. They also provide good cut flowers for the cooler months. All forms have lance-shaped, strongly scented pale-green leaves and daisy-like single or double flowerheads. Tall cultivars include 'Geisha Girl' with double orange flowers; 'Pacific Beauty', pastel-shaded double flowers; 'Princess', crested orange, gold or yellow flowers; and the Touch of Red Series, double flowers in tones of deep orange-red. Dwarf cultivars include the Fiesta Series, double flowers in colours ranging from cream to orange; and 'Honey Babe', apricot, yellow and orange flowers. All cultivars are fully hardy and will thrive in almost any well-drained soil in a sunny situation. Propagate from seed sown in spring or autumn/fall. They also self-seed readily. Remove spent flowerheads to encourage prolonged flowering. Watch for mildew, snails and slugs.

CALLISTEPHUS
chinensis

CHINA ASTER

An erect, bushy annual that is reputedly difficult to grow. This species needs sun, protection from wind and extremes of heat and a light sandy, fertile, well-drained soil with added lime. Water plants well and mulch in hot weather to keep the root system cool. It is a fairly fast-growing plant. There are various cultivars available, ranging from tall, up to 60 cm (about 24 in) with a spread of 45 cm (about 18 in) to very dwarf, up to 20 cm (about 8 in) with a spread of 30 cm (about 12 in). Leaves are oval, toothed and mid-green and the plants flower in summer and early autumn/fall in a wide range of colours including white, blue, pink and red. *C. chinensis* is half-hardy. Stake tall cultivars and remove spent flowers regularly. Propagate from seed in

mid-spring and watch for virus disease, aphids, foot rot and root rot.

CALOCEPHALUS
brownii

CUSHION BUSH

This dwarf, evergreen, spreading low shrub is native to Australia. It has a rounded habit, growing to 1 m (about 3 ft) high and wide, and makes a silvery mound with its intricate velvety grey branches and tiny scale-like leaves. It flowers in summer with pale cream rounded knobs that appear silver when in bud. Useful as an accent plant, a striking ground cover or a dwarf hedge. Frost-hardy, it prefers a sunny situation and well-drained soil. Propagate from semi-ripe cuttings or seed in late summer. Trim after flowering, pinch tips of young plants to promote bushy growth and watch for botrytis in damp conditions.

Caltha palustris

Campanula isophylla

Campanula portenschlagiana

Campanula persicifolia 'Alba'

CALTHA
palustris
KINGCUP, MARSH MARIGOLD

Native to the temperate and cold regions of the northern hemisphere, this hardy marginal water plant is grown for its attractive flowers. It is a deciduous or semi-evergreen perennial, with glistening, buttercup-like golden yellow flowers borne in spring, and dark green, rounded leaves. Grows to a height and spread of 30 cm (about 12 in). Fully hardy, it is suitable for the margins of streams or ponds or in any damp spots. Prefers an open, sunny position and wet soil. Propagate by division in early spring, or from seed or by division in autumn/fall. Watch for rust which should be treated with a fungicide.

CAMPANULA
BELLFLOWER

Native to the temperate parts of the northern hemisphere, this large genus includes about 250 species of annuals, biennials and perennials. They are among the most showy of plants and are useful specimens for rockeries, borders, wild gardens and hanging baskets. Many of the species are classed as rock and alpine plants. Leaves vary in shape and size, sometimes appearing on upright stems and sometimes only as a cluster at the base. Flowers are mostly bell-shaped and blue, with some whites. All do best in a moderately enriched, moist, well-drained soil. They grow in sun or shade, but flower colour remains brightest in shady situations. Protect from drying winds and stake the taller varieties, which make good cut flowers. Remove spent flower stems. Feed regularly, particularly during the growing season. Propagate from seed or by division in spring or autumn/fall, or by softwood or basal cuttings in spring or summer. They are fully to half-hardy. Transplant during winter. Watch for slugs.

C. isophylla
ITALIAN BELLFLOWER

A dwarf, evergreen trailing perennial, growing to 10 cm (4 in) high with a spread of 30 cm (12 in). Native to

Campanula poscharskyana

the mountain slopes of northern Italy, it has star-shaped blue or white flowers in summer. Leaves are small and heart-shaped. 'Alba' has white flowers. Half-hardy. This is an ideal hanging basket specimen.

C. lactiflora

A strong growing perennial reaching a height of 1.2 m (about 3½ ft) and a spread of 60 cm (about 24 in). In summer, it produces immense pyramidal spikes containing large, nodding, bell-shaped lilac blue, occasionally pink or white, flowers. Leaves are narrowly oval. If cut back straight after flowering they may bloom again in late autumn/fall. Fully hardy, these plants can be naturalized among light grass and will thrive in either sun or semi-shade.

C. medium
CANTERBURY BELL

A biennial species, this is a slow-growing, erect clump-forming plant. It produces spires of bell-shaped single or double, white, pink or blue flowers, towering 1 m (3 ft) over a rosette of lance-shaped fresh green leaves that spreads to 30 cm (about 12 in). Dwarf cultivars grow to 60 cm (about 24 in). Flowers in spring and early summer. Grow as border plants in semi-shade. The name is derived from the harness bells worn by medieval pilgrims' horses as they journeyed to Canterbury Cathedral in England.

C. persicifolia

Perhaps the best known *Campanula* with nodding, bell-shaped blue or white flowers borne above narrow,

Campanula lactiflora

lance-shaped bright green leaves in summer. *C. p.* 'Alba' has white flowers. Pinch individual spent flowers off upright stems as soon as they fade. Fully hardy, it is a spreading, rosette forming perennial reaching a height of 1 m (about 3 ft) and spread of 30 cm (about 12 in).

C. portenschlagiana

Native to the mountains of southern Europe, this is a low-growing evergreen plant, well suited to rock gardens. Grows to a height of 15 cm (about 6 in) with an indefinite spread. It has dense, small, ivy-shaped leaves, and a profusion of open, bell-shaped, violet flowers are borne in late spring and early summer. Plant in cool, part-shaded positions with good drainage. Fully hardy.

C. poscharskyana

A rampant, low-growing, spreading perennial with sprays of bell-shaped mauve-blue flowers from late spring onwards. It mounds up from 10 to 15 cm (about 4–6 in) with an indefinite spread and is fully hardy. Ideal for use as a ground cover, on walls, banks and in the front of mixed borders. Partial shade will prolong flowering.

Campanula medium

Catharanthus roseus

Canna × generalis

Celmisia semicordata

Carthamus tinctorius

Celosia cristata

Celmisia asteliifolia

CANNA
× generalis

Native to tropical America and Asia, these robust, showy perennials grow from rhizomes and are valued for their striking flowers and foliage. Ideally suited to summer bedding displays and containers, they grow from 1.5–2 m (about 4½–6 ft) tall and spread to 60 cm (about 24 in). The sturdy stems have bold, lance-shaped, green or bronze leaves and the summer flowers are red, pink, orange or yellow. Frost-tender, they require a sunny position and moist soil with plenty of well-decayed animal manure. Water well during summer to prolong flowering. Propagate in spring by division. In cold areas protect roots with mulch.

CARTHAMUS
tinctorius
SAFFLOWER

A fast-growing annual, this thistle is valued for its yellowy orange flowers in summer and for the oil contained in its seeds. It grows to a height of 1 m (about 3 ft) and spreads to 50 cm (about 20 in). Its leaves are spiny and oblong, half gripping the stems. Safflower is frost-hardy and grows best in full sun and a fertile, well-drained soil. Propagate from seed in spring.

CATHARANTHUS
roseus
syn. *Vinca rosea*
MADAGASCAR PERIWINKLE

A native of Africa, this small relative of the frangipani is an evergreen spreading shrub, valued for its rose-pink to white, phlox-like flowers, which bloom from spring through to autumn/fall—and into winter as well in warmer areas. Grows to 60 cm (about 24 in) in height and spread. Frost-tender, it requires full light and a well-drained, compost-enriched soil. It will tolerate considerable heat. Older plants may become untidy and require pruning to promote a bushy habit. A useful summer bedding plant in cool climates, it is often grown annually from seed in spring, or greenwood or semi-ripe cuttings in summer.

CELMISIA
SNOW DAISY, MOUNTAIN DAISY

These attractive, evergreen daisies have tufted silvery grey leaves and a profuse display of yellow centred white flowers. In most species the stalks and undersides of the leaves are covered with a thick silvery fur. Fully hardy, they demand full sun to partial shade and moist, well-drained sandy, acid soil. This genus, which is primarily native to New Zealand and south-eastern Australia, includes many spectacular species but they are difficult to cultivate outside their natural range. Most are true alpine plants that resent lowland conditions, but a few will grow successfully in rockeries, peat beds or scree gardens in colder areas. Propagate from seed in autumn/fall or by division in late spring.

C. asteliifolia
syn. *C. longifolia*

This plant forms a clump of strappy, silvery grey leaves and flowers heavily in early summer. The flower stems are 30 cm (about 12 in) in height and the clump spreads to 60 cm (about 24 in) in diameter. It is one of the easier species to cultivate but needs ample summer moisture.

C. semicordata
syn. *C. coriacea*

This is the largest species and generally regarded as the easiest to cultivate. The flower stems are 40 cm (about 14 in) in height and the clumps may reach 1.5 m (about 4½ ft) in diameter with individual leaves up to 40 cm (about 18 in) long. It is more heat and drought tolerant than most species but does best with ample summer moisture.

CELOSIA
cristata
COCKSCOMB

Native to tropical Asia, this fairly fast-growing perennial is cultivated as an annual for summer bedding displays. Erect and bushy, it reaches 30–60 cm (about 12–24 in) high with a 30 cm (about 12 in) spread. Leaves are mid-green; rippled coral-shaped flowerheads appear in summer. Flowers are usually vivid red or yellow, though other colours are available. They are long lasting and make excellent cut flowers. Half-hardy they require a rich, well-drained soil and constant moisture. Grows best in a sunny position and does well in hot summers. Propagate from seed in spring.

CENTAUREA
KNAPWEED

Mostly native to Europe, Asia and Africa, this large genus of annuals and perennials are grown for their graceful flowerheads which have thistle-like centres surrounded by finely rayed petals in shades of bright red, deep purple, blue and golden yellow. Some species are inclined to sprawl and need trimming back. All are suitable for cutting. Fully hardy, they need sun and well-drained soil. They are particularly useful in dryish conditions on chalky soil. Propagate by division or seed in autumn/fall, late winter or spring.

Transplant during winter or spring. Centaureas have been grown since ancient times and were once used as a love divination.

C. cyanus
CORNFLOWER

One of the best known annuals, this fast-growing upright plant reaches a height of 1 m (about 3 ft) with a spread of 30 cm (12 in). It is a hardy species with lance-shaped grey-green leaves and a spring or early summer display of double daisy-like flowerheads in shades of pale and deep pink, cerise, crimson, white, purple and blue. Tall and dwarf cultivars are available. Best displayed in large clumps and will flower for months if deadheads are removed regularly. Once known as bluebottle, the wild form was used to make ink.

C. dealbata

A very leafy plant with light greyish green, deeply cut foliage. Lilac-purple to lilac-pink flowerheads appear in a mass from late spring onwards. An erect perennial, it grows to 1 m (about 3 ft) high with a spread of 60 cm (about 24 in). The cultivar 'Steenbergii' has larger, deep pink flowers.

C. moschata
SWEET SULTAN

A sweet-scented cottage garden plant introduced to cultivation over 350 years ago, this is a fast-growing, upright annual with lance-shaped, greyish green leaves. Large, delicate, fluffy flowers to 8 cm (about 3 in) across are produced in a wide range of colours in summer and early autumn/fall. Grows to 50 cm (about 20 in) high and spreads to 20 cm (about 8 in). An open position with protection from hot afternoon sun is best.

CENTRANTHUS
ruber
RED VALERIAN, KISS-ME-QUICK

Native to Europe, this perennial is often seen as a naturalized plant on dry banks and is ideal for dry rock gardens. It is grown for its dense clusters of small, star-shaped, deep reddish pink flowers that are borne

for a long period from late spring to autumn/fall. The cultivar 'Albus' has white flowers. Forms loose clumps of fleshy leaves and grows to a height of 60 cm to 1 m (about 2–3 ft) and spread of 50–60 cm (about 20–24 in). One of the easiest plants to grow, it requires sun and good drainage and will tolerate exposed positions and poor, alkaline soil. It is fully hardy. Propagate from seed in autumn/fall or spring; it self-seeds readily and may naturalize.

CERASTIUM
tomentosum
SNOW-IN-SUMMER

A vigorous, fast-growing ground cover, this perennial is ideal for a well-drained hot dry bank or rockery. It has tiny, silvery grey leaves, and masses of star-shaped white flowers are borne in late spring and summer. It is particularly attractive when used as an underplanting against darker backgrounds. The foliage is dense and an effective weed-suppressant. It grows to 8 cm (about 3 in) high and spreads indefinitely, and is fully hardy. Water regularly but allow to dry out between soakings. Fertilize in early spring and propagate by division in spring. After flowering, remove spent flowers by clipping the top of the plant with shears.

CERATOSTIGMA
plumbaginoides
CHINESE PLUMBAGO, PERENNIAL LEADWORT

Native to western China, this bushy perennial grows to 45 cm (about 18 in) high with a spread of 20 cm

(about 8 in). Valued for its tough constitution and attractive foliage and flowers, it has oval, mid-green leaves that turn a rich orange and red in autumn/fall. Flowers are plumbago-like, with small clusters of single cornflower blue blooms appearing on reddish, branched stems in late summer and autumn/fall. Fully hardy, it requires an open sunny position, preferably sheltered from salty winds, and a well-drained light soil. Keep moist. Cut back severely in early winter to stimulate strong spring growth. Propagate by division in spring. It is useful to grow in front of a border or as a ground cover.

CHEIRANTHUS
WALLFLOWER

These perennial flowering plants are well-known as winter and spring bedding subjects and have been part of the cottage garden for centuries. Some species are suitable for rock gardens. Short-lived species are best grown as biennials. The older types

are sweetly scented while the newer cultivars have no fragrance but bloom well in the winter months. Fully to half-hardy, they do best in fertile soil in an open sunny position. Propagate from seed in spring or greenwood or softwood cuttings in summer. Cut plants back occasionally so only a few leaves remain on each stem.

Centaurea cyanus

Ceratostigma plumbaginoides

Centaurea moschata

Centaurea dealbata

Cerastium tomentosum

Centranthus ruber

Cheiranthus cheiri

Cheiranthus mutabilis

C. cheiri
ENGLISH WALLFLOWER

A bushy perennial grown as an annual or biennial. Cultivars vary in height from tall, up to 60 cm (about 24 in) with a spread of 40 cm (about 16 in), to dwarf, with a height and spread of 20 cm (about 8 in). Fragrant 4-petalled flowers appear in spring in colours ranging from pastels to deep browns, bronze, orange, bright yellow, dark red and scarlet. All have lance-shaped leaves. Fully hardy and self-seeding. They must not be allowed to dry out in summer and should be cut back after blooming and again in autumn/fall. They grow best in cooler areas.

C. mutabilis
WINTER WALLFLOWER

This quaint perennial sub-shrub flowers for much of the year and gives colour and fragrance to the winter garden. Fully hardy, it flowers best in sheltered sunny spots. Colours range from yellow to mauve and purple. There is a form with variegated leaves.

CHELIDONIUM
majus 'Flore Pleno'

A quick-growing perennial that forms a good ground cover. It is an upright plant about 60 cm (24 in) high and spreading to 30 cm (12 in).

Chelidonium majus 'Flore Pleno'

Clarkia amoena

Chrysanthemum carinatum

In late spring and early summer, a profusion of small, cup-shaped, double yellow flowers appear on branching sprays from a basal rosette of bright green, deeply lobed foliage. The plant self-seeds readily and can become invasive. Fully hardy, it grows in sun or shade and does well in all except very wet soils. Propagate by seed or division in autumn/fall and cut back after flowering to keep under control.

CHRYSANTHEMUM
CHRYSANTHEMUM

Native to temperate zones, this large genus is valued for its ease of culture, rapid growth and showy flowers. It includes annuals, perennials and sub-shrubs, most of which are evergreen. All have daisy-like flowers, each flowerhead in fact made up of a large number of individual florets. Colour range includes yellow, orange, brown, white, pink, red and purple. Leaves are usually deeply cut or divided, often feathery, and oval to lance-shaped. Stems are upright and often

woody. Fully to half-hardy, chrysanthemums grow best in an open, sunny site in a rich, friable, well-drained soil. Feed and water regularly. Stake tall plants with canes and pinch out growing tips of young plants to encourage lateral branching. Suckers should not be allowed to develop until the plants have flowered. Propagate annuals by seed sown in spring; perennials by dividing basal growth or by striking cuttings taken from plant material that is in active growth in spring; and sub-shrubs by softwood cuttings in spring or hardwood cuttings in winter. The genus *Chrysanthemum* is currently undergoing revision. Some species have been re-classified and will be found in this chapter under their new names. Diseases include chrysanthemum rust, white rust (difficult to control—the plant should be destroyed), powdery mildew, petal blight, and botrytis. Insect pests can also be a problem.

C. carinatum
syn. *C. tricolor*
PAINTED DAISY

This spectacular annual species is from Morocco and grows to 60 cm (about 24 in), spreading to 30 cm (about 12 in) with banded, multi-coloured flowers in spring and early summer. Hardy to half-hardy. 'Monarch Court Jesters' comes in red with yellow centres or white with red centres, and the Tricolor Series has many colour combinations. Excellent as bedding plants and cut flowers.

C. frutescens see
Argyranthemum frutescens

C. maximum see
Leucocanthemum maximum

C. morifolium see
Dendranthema grandiflora

CLARKIA
amoena
syn. *C. elegans*
FAREWELL-TO-SPRING

A free-flowering, hardy annual, this American native is fast-growing to a height of 60 cm (about 24 in) and spread of 30 cm (about 12 in). It has lance-shaped, mid-green leaves, thin upright stems, and in summer bears spikes of open, cup-like single or double flowers, in shades of pink. They make excellent cut flowers but remove leaves before putting them in water as they have an offensive smell. The plants require a sunny situation and a well-drained sandy soil that has low fertility; they do not flower well in rich soil. Allow to dry out between watering. Propagate by seed sown in autumn/fall or in spring in cool areas. Watch for botrytis. *Clarkiae* are named after Captain William Clark, a Rocky Mountains explorer.

CLEOME
hassleriana
syn. *C. spinosa*
SPIDER FLOWER

Mainly native to tropical America, this fast-growing, bushy annual is valued for its unusual spidery flowers. An erect plant, it grows to 1.2 m (about 3½ ft) tall with a spread of 45 cm (about 18 in). It has hairy spiny stems and large, palmate leaves topped in summer with heads of airy, pink or white flowers with long protruding stamens. Flowers will last until winter. A good background bedding plant and useful in new gardens for their rapid growth. Half-hardy, they require sun and fertile, well-drained soil. Shelter from strong winds and water regularly. Taller growth can be encouraged by removing side branches and dead flowers should be removed. Propagate by seed in spring or early summer. Watch for aphids.

CLIANTHUS
formosus
syn. *C. dampieri*
STURT'S DESERT PEA

Native to the dry outback of Australia, this slow-growing, trailing annual can be cultivated in warm climates in well-drained sandy or gritty loam in full sun. In cooler areas it should be grown under glass. It does not do well in humid or coastal climates. It has unusually large and showy, brilliant red, black blotched spring flowers and small grey, pea-like leaves. It grows to a height of 12 cm (about 5 in) and spread of 1 m (about 3 ft), and is frost-tender. Propagate by seed in spring or by stem cuttings in late summer. Prune out growing tips in spring to increase bushiness, and cut out dead wood.

COBAEA
scandens
CUP-AND-SAUCER VINE

Native to Mexico and tropical Central America, this vigorous quick-growing perennial vine has dense foliage and abundant bell-shaped flowers that open yellow-green and turn from mauve to a translucent purple with age. There is an all-green version, usually sold as 'white'. Flowers throughout the year in mild climates and makes an attractive screen on a netting fence or trellis. It is a woody stemmed tendril climber growing to a height of 4–5 m (about 12–15 ft). Frost-tender, it is best grown as an annual in colder climates. It requires full sun, protection from cold winds and a rich, well-drained soil, kept moist. Propagate by seed in spring. Needs constant control in a confined space.

COLEUS

Native to Indonesia and tropical North Africa, these annuals, perennials and evergreen sub-shrubs are grown for their brightly coloured and variegated foliage. In milder climates, they are popular pot plants and useful for bedding in sheltered places. *Coleus* grow best in bright, indirect light or partial shade and rich, well-drained or moist soil in a sheltered position. Feed and water liberally during the growing season to encourage strong leafy growth. In winter the soil should be kept almost dry. Potted plants develop brightest colours when pot bound. Pinch out young shoots to promote bushy growth. Frost-tender. Propagate from seed sown under glass in late winter or spring, or from softwood cuttings in spring or summer.

C. blumei

Native to Java, this bushy, fast-growing perennial is grown as an annual in more temperate climates. Leaves are a bright mixture of pink, green, red or yellow and are a pointed oval shape with serrated edges. It grows to 50 cm (about 20 in) high with a spread of 30 cm (about 12 in), and prefers partial shade. Remove flower spikes.

C. thyrsoideus

Fast-growing, bushy perennial, also grown as an annual. This is a larger species, growing to 1 m (about 3 ft) high with a spread of 60 cm (about 24 in). Leaves are oval, mid-green with serrated edges and panicles of tubular bright blue flowers are borne in winter.

CONVOLVULUS

This is a large genus of dwarf, bushy and climbing perennials, annuals, evergreen shrubs and sub-shrubs from warm to temperate climates. Some species are now naturalized and strongly invasive; others, of only moderate vigour, are useful for spilling over walls, for rock gardens, hanging baskets and as a ground cover. They are fully hardy to frost-tender, flowering most prolifically in a sunny situation in poor to fertile well-drained soil. Little pruning is needed. Dead-head plants to prolong flowering. Propagate from seed sown in mid-spring, or from softwood cuttings in late spring and summer for perennials and sub-shrubs.

C. cneorum
SILVERBUSH

A dense, shrubby, evergreen, growing to 60 cm (about 24 in) or more, with narrow, silky, silvery green leaves and large white flowers, sometimes tinged with pink or cream, with yellow centres. Flowers from mid-spring to late summer. It is a useful plant for hot dry places and average soil, and is frost-hardy. It flowers best if lightly trimmed back every year.

Convovulus cneorum

Coleus blumei

Cleome hassleriana

Cobaea scandens 'White' form

Coleus thyrsoideus

Clianthus formosus

Coreopsis verticillata

Convolvulus sabatius

Convolvulus tricolor

Coreopsis tinctoria

Corydalis cashmeriana

Coreopsis maritima

Cosmos atrosanguineus

C. sabatius
syn. *C. mauritanicus*
MOROCCAN GLORY VINE, BINDWEED

A trailing perennial with profuse, open, trumpet-shaped mauve-blue flowers from spring to autumn/fall. Slender stems and small, oval leaves. An excellent specimen for draping over walls and hanging baskets, it grows to a height of 15–20 cm (about 6–8 in) and spread of 30 cm (about 12 in). Half-hardy.

C. tricolor
syn. *C. minor*

An interesting bedding annual with profuse trumpet-shaped blue or white flowers with banded yellow and white throats. Leaves are lance-shaped and mid-green. Grows to a height of 20–30 cm (about 8–12 in) and spread of 20 cm (about 8 in). Fully hardy, it blooms continuously through the warm weather.

COREOPSIS

This genus of easily grown annuals and perennials is valued for its daisy-like flowers in shades of gold or yellow, some bicolours. They are mainly summer-flowering and fully to frost-hardy. The perennials make excellent herbaceous border plants, looking striking with shasta daisies and blue delphiniums. They prefer full sun and a fertile well-drained soil but also grow well in coastal regions and on poor, stony soil. Propagate perennials by division of old clumps in winter or spring, or by spring cuttings. The annuals also prefer full sun and a fertile, well-drained soil; they will not tolerate a heavy clay soil. Taller varieties may need staking. Propagate annuals from seed in spring or autumn/fall, and dead-head regularly.

C. maritima
syn. *Leptosyne maritima*
WINTER MARGUERITE

A bushy annual with fern-like leaves that grows to 75 cm (about 30 in) high with a spread of 50 cm (about 20 in). It is long-flowering, bearing 10 cm (about 4 in) wide, daisy-like yellow flowers in late winter and spring. Frost-hardy and fast-growing.

C. tinctoria
TICKSEED

A fast-growing showy annual that produces clusters of bright yellow daisy-like flowerheads with red centres throughout summer and autumn/fall. Grows to a height of 60–90 cm (about 24–36 in) and spread of 20 cm (about 8 in). Fully hardy. Provide support with branched twigs or fine bamboo stakes. Makes good cut flowers.

C. verticillata

A strong, tall perennial, growing to 75 cm (about 30 in) with a spread of 60 cm (about 24 in). Produces abundant, large, daisy-like rich yellow flowers on elegant stems and is useful for cutting. Flowers from late spring until winter and does best in light, poorish soil. Leaves are bright green, divided and lance-shaped. It is fully hardy.

CORYDALIS
cashmeriana

Native to the northern hemisphere and South Africa, this delicate peren-nial is a relative of the poppy. It is an excellent rock garden plant, also growing well in wall crevices. Summer-flowering, it produces dense spikes of brilliant blue flowers. It is tuft-forming and fibrous rooted, growing to a height of 10–25 cm (about 4–10 in) with a spread of 8–10 cm (about 3–4 in). It is fully hardy and prefers a cool, partially shaded rich, damp soil that is also well-drained. Propagate by division when dormant or by seed in autumn/fall. The plant dies down in winter. The botanical name means crested lark.

COSMOS
MEXICAN ASTER

Native to Mexico and Central America, this small genus of annu-als and perennials has been grown in gardens for over a century. Some annual species are particularly tall, ideal for the back of borders and excellent for late summer and autumn/fall cutting. They require a sunny situation with protection from strong winds and will grow in any well-drained soil as long as it is not over-rich. Mulch with compost or animal manure and water well in hot, dry weather. Fully to half-hardy. Propagate annuals by seed in spring and autumn/fall, half-hardy species by basal cuttings in spring. Remove dead-heads regularly, and in humid weather watch for insect pests and moulds.

C. atrosanguineus
BLACK COSMOS, CHOCOLATE COSMOS

A clump-forming perennial grow-ing to 60 cm (about 24 in) in height and spread, black cosmos has very dark, blackish red flowers that have a chocolate scent, which is most noticeable on warm days. It flowers from late spring to autumn/fall. The pinnate foliage is broad compared to that of the annuals. Partially evergreen but it may die back com-pletely in cold areas. Near hardy but demands excellent winter drainage or the rootstock may rot.

C. bipinnatus

An upright, bushy annual, growing to nearly 2 m (about 6 ft) in height with a spread of 50 cm (about 20 in). Though too tall for bedding, it is a fine border plant with large rose-pink, white or maroon flowerheads held against delicate feathery foliage. Half-hardy, it flowers in late summer and autumn/fall. In South Africa, it is often seen growing in grasslands along roads on the Transvaal Highveld in autumn/fall.

C. sulphureus

This annual has coarser foliage and blooms in many shades of yellow and orange in summer and early autumn/fall. Half-hardy, it is moderately fast-growing, reaching a height of 60 cm (about 24 in) and spread of 50 cm (about 20 in).

CRAMBE
maritima
SEA KALE

This robust, small perennial forms a mound of wide silvery green leaves and carries branching sprays of tiny white flowers in summer. Fully hardy, sea kale prefers an open sunny position, but will tolerate light shade, and a well-drained, neutral to alkaline soil. It grows to a height and spread of 60 cm (about 24 in). The leaf shoots are edible. Propagate from seed in spring or autumn/fall or by division in early spring. *C. cordifolia* is very similar.

CREPIS
incana
HAWKWEED

This dandelion-like, rosette-forming perennial is a good subject for a

sunny rock garden or border and looks pretty in cracks and crevices. It grows to a height of 20 cm (about 8 in) and spread of 10 cm. Summer-flowering, with ragged, pink to orange flowerheads on stiff stems. Leaves are oblong, greyish green and hairy. Fully hardy, it is easily grown in either sun or shade and prefers a well-drained soil. Propagate by root cuttings in late winter. Self-seeds readily.

CYPERUS
papyrus
PAPER REED, PAPYRUS

This large perennial evergreen sedge has an indefinite spread and grows 3–5 m (about 9–15 ft) tall. Its sturdy leafless stems carry enormous umbels of spikelets in summer. Prefers a sunny situation in wet soil and can be grown in water. It is half-hardy.

DAHLIA
DAHLIA

This genus of bushy, tuberous perennials, native to Mexico, is named after the Swedish botanist, Andreas Dahl, a pupil of Linnaeus. Grown as bedding plants, they are valued for the wide range of colours, colour combinations, sizes and shapes of their flowers, which are excellent as cut flowers. Named varieties come and go with amazing speed, and every country has a different selection. So we have simply given representative examples of each type. Dwarf forms are also suitable for containers. Half-hardy and fast-growing, they have a

long flowering period from late spring to late autumn/fall. They grow best in a warm sunny position, preferably sheltered from strong winds, and in well-fertilized, well-drained soil. They must be fed monthly and watered well when in flower. Old and faded blooms should be removed to help prolong the flowering season. Flower size can be increased by disbudding—pinch out the two buds that grow with the centre bud on each stem and cut off the immediate laterals and all superfluous shoots. In very hot weather they benefit from a mulch of straw around the stems. All dahlias except for the dwarf forms will require staking. In areas prone to frost, the tubers should be lifted in late autumn/fall after foliage has died down, stored covered with

straw, and replanted when all frost danger has passed. In frost-free areas they can be treated as normal herbaceous perennials and left in the ground. Propagate dwarf forms from seed; others in spring from seed, basal shoot cuttings or by division of tubers. Watch for virus infection, thrips, earwigs, aphids and red spider mite.

Cactus dahlias

Derived from crosses between *D. variabilis* and *D. juarezii* from northern Mexico, this most popular type is distinguished by the long, recurved ray florets which give the flower a graceful outline. The varieties are classed as miniature, medium and giant, the size range being about the same as the decoratives. All are tall and need staking.

Cactus dahlia

Cosmos bipinnatus

Crambe maritima

Crepis incana

Cosmos sulphureus

Cyperus papyrus

A Field Trip to Lundy

Viewed from the mainland on a clear day, the windswept island of Lundy looms out of the sea haze, providing a tantalizing and imposing view of its fortress-like profile. A safe haven for pirates and marauders in centuries past, Lundy is now a sanctuary for wildlife, both land-based and marine. It has been owned by the National Trust for the past 25 years. As a measure of its importance, the surrounding waters were recently declared Britain's first Marine Nature Reserve.

Lundy lies 17 km (about 11 miles) off the coast of Devon in south-western England. Boat trips there operate regularly from the small, north Devon port of Bideford. After an invariably choppy sea-crossing lasting a couple of hours, the towering cliffs of Lundy are a welcome sight. After stepping ashore, regain your land legs and climb the steep slopes to admire stunning coastal scenery of granite headlands and cliffs stretching into the distance. The island comprises a flattish plateau, which in places rises almost 120 m (about 400 ft) from the sea, some cliffs being almost sheer. The eastern side is relatively sheltered from prevailing westerly winds while the western side is often battered by the full force of Atlantic gales. If your visit coincides with the peak flowering period, many of the views are framed by a foreground carpet of purple foxgloves (*Digitalis purpurea*).

Lundy's flowers are fascinating and varied. In May and June, thrift, or sea pink (*Armeria maritima*), and sea campion

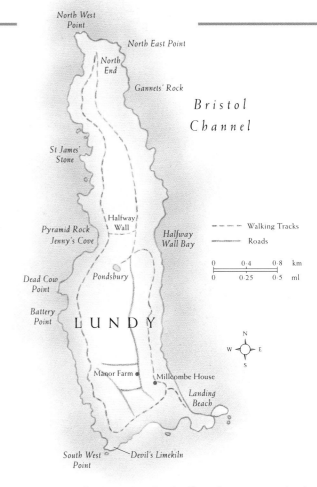

Foxgloves grow profusely on the islands off south-western England.

(*Silene vulgaris* subsp. *maritima*) provide a floral display on the western side, while short-cropped turf on the top of the island harbours Britain's best population of the intriguingly named dwarf adder's tongue-fern (*Ophioglossum azoricum*). There is even an endemic plant here—the Lundy cabbage (*Coincya wrightii*), which is found nowhere else in the world. The impact of these is diminished, however, by the abundant spikes of purple foxgloves that thrive in the eastern and southern parts of the island.

Although the foxglove is sometimes perennial, especially in ornamental settings, it is mostly considered a biennial in the wild. In the first year it produces rosettes of broad, oval to lanceolate leaves up to 30 cm (about 12 in) long with a distinctly hairy upper surface. In the second year a tall flowering spike is produced, which is usually branched and stands up to 2 m (about 6 ft) in height. Flowers appear on the spike over a period of a few weeks between May and August, opening from the bottom of the spike upwards as the spike itself lengthens. The individual flowers, lasting approximately one to two weeks, are tubular with an elongated, bell-shaped appearance. In the wild they are usually deep pink or purple, although white flower spikes are occasionally seen. In cultivation, the paler varieties tend to be more popular. The inner surface of the flower is usually spotted and hairy; this latter assists bees to pollinate the flowers.

Foxgloves are common along the north Devon coast and grow wild in a wide range of habitats. They do, however, prefer comparatively well-drained, neutral to acid soil. Typical sites would include sunny woodland glades, forest clearings, hillsides with broken or rocky soils and coastal cliffs; they will grow quite happily on recently disturbed ground. On Lundy they thrive on slopes which, although covered with bracken (*Pteridium aquilinum*), are almost completely lacking in tree cover. Growing in these conditions, the plant has to be tolerant of salt-spray and constant, sometimes violent, wind.

Rainfall in the west of Britain is comparatively high—1000–1200 mm (about 40–50 in) per year is not unusual—so the plant will need regular watering in a garden setting; however it will not tolerate becoming waterlogged. Foxgloves will also grow both in the open and in a sheltered position although they will not survive for long where the shade is too dense. Since it occurs from sea-level to moderate elevations inland, the foxglove is clearly tolerant of climatic variation.

If you want to see foxgloves at their best on Lundy, visit in mid-June. One of their most attractive settings is among the quarries and spoil workings halfway along the eastern side. Here you can see signs of where blocks of granite were hewn from the cliffs, although much of the evidence is now masked by plant growth, including introduced clumps of rhododendrons. For an alternative view, make your way to the top of the island where you may see small numbers of the rare Soay sheep and Lundy ponies (a breed exclusive to the island). A track runs north–south down the island's spine.

Whether you visit Lundy to see garden plants such as the foxglove growing in their native setting, or simply to experience the rugged splendour of the untamed coastal scenery, you will find it a captivating island, one which few visitors can bear to see only once.

Digitalis purpurea

Digitalis

Digitalis, the foxglove genus, consists of around 18 species of biennials and perennials and a few soft-wooded shrubs. Geographically they are centred on the Mediterranean (including North Africa), the majority growing wild in Britain and Europe. Apart from *D. purpurea*, several other *Digitalis* species are sometimes grown for ornament.

Despite being poisonous, the foxglove is one of Britain's most striking and distinctive plants, both in overall size and flower structure. The medicinal properties of *D. purpurea* are important—the leaves are a source of the drug digitalin, which is used to control and alleviate the symptoms of heart disease.

Foxgloves are represented in gardens chiefly by the ornamental strains of *D. purpurea*, for example, the well-known 'Excelsior' strain. The garden forms are more robust than the wild *D. purpurea* plants, and the flowers are packed more closely on the stem. Breeders have aimed for larger, more widely flared and richly spotted flowers displaying a more varied mix of colours. Garden foxgloves are also remarkably adaptable, thriving almost anywhere in temperate zones and in any normal, well-drained garden soil.

Digitalis is just one of almost 250 genera of the worldwide Scrophulariaceae family. Snapdragons (*Antirrhinum* spp.), a genus of annuals popular among gardeners, also belong to this family.

Digitalis purpurea

Collarette dahlias

These old-fashioned dahlias have single flowers which have a ruffle of short petals surrounding the disk like a lace collar. Usually they are in a contrasting colour from the main ray petals. Both tall, 2 m (about 6 ft), and dwarf, 35 cm (about 12 in), forms are available.

Decorative dahlias

Growing to about 2 m (about 6 ft), these have informal, fully double flowers with broad ray petals. They come in giant, medium and miniature varieties, the miniatures having flowers about 10 cm (about 4 in) across and the giants 35 cm (about 15 in) or more. All need staking.

Dwarf or bedding dahlias

Often grown as annuals, dwarf dahlias grow 35–40 cm (about 16 in) tall and do not need staking. The flowers are about 10 cm (about 4 in) across and either semi-double or fully double, like small editions of the tall decoratives. They are much

used for bedding and may be grown from seed sown in spring or by division of the tubers.

Pompon dahlias

These are tall growing—2 m (about 6 ft)—but bear small flowers, 4–5 cm (about 2 in) across. They are usually fully double, so much so that the flowers open into perfect spheres. They are very useful for cutting, to contrast with the larger types. Show dahlias, not often seen now, are similar in form but three times the size.

Waterlily or Nymphaea dahlias

These have fully double flowers with broad ray petals, smaller and more formal than the decoratives; most varieties are about 12–15 cm (about 5–6 in) wide. They grow 1.5–2 m (about 4½–6 ft) tall and need staking.

DELPHINIUM

This is a large genus of annuals and herbaceous perennials, most native to the northern hemisphere. The splendid mainly blue, pink, purple or

white spikes of cup-shaped, spurred flowers are useful for massed displays or for cutting. They range from tall spikes up to 2 m (about 6 ft) to dwarfs suitable for bedding. Best suited to cooler climate gardens, they can be grown as annuals in warmer climates. Grow in a sunny position, preferably sheltered from wind—the taller cultivars will need to be staked. A well-drained, moist, slightly alkaline, rich loam is ideal. Fully to half-hardy, they will not tolerate drought conditions. Feed with a complete fertilizer, water well, and provide a surface mulch of compost during the growing season. Remove flower spikes after they fade to encourage a second flush in late summer, and remove stems at the end of the flowering period. Spray with fungicide for mildew and black spot, and protect from slugs and snails. The name delphinium derives from the Greek *delphin*, for the dolphins the buds were thought to resemble.

D. belladonna

Fully hardy perennials with an upright branching form and 2 cm (about 1 in) wide, flowers in shades of blue or white. The single, sometimes semi-double, flowers which appear in summer on 30 cm (about 12 in) long spikes, are useful for cutting. It grows to a height of 1–1.5 m (about 3–4½ ft) and spread of 60 cm (about 24 in). Propagate by division or basal cuttings in spring.

D. elatum hybrids

These fully hardy, erect perennials flower in a range of colours from white to purple, usually with con-

trasting eyes. They grow to 1.5–2.2 m (about 4½–6½ ft) high with a spread of 75 cm–1 m (about 2½–3 ft). Tall, tapering spikes of evenly spaced semi-double flowers appear from summer through to autumn/fall. Cultivars include: 'Blue Bird', medium blue flowers with a white eye; 'Galahad', pure white; 'King Arthur', royal-purple with a white eye; 'Summer Skies', light blue with a white eye; 'Black Knight', violet-blue with a black eye; and 'Astolat', blush pink to rose. Propagate *D. elatum* hybrids by cuttings only; selections by seed in spring or autumn/fall.

D. grandiflorum
syn. *D. chinense*
BUTTERFLY DELPHINIUM

Perennial in its native Asian home, this plant is best treated as an annual in mild winter climates. It grows to a height of 45 cm (about 18 in) and spread of 30 cm (12 in). It has bright blue flowers and is useful as a bedding plant as it flowers over a long period during the summer months. Remove spent flowerheads regularly. 'Azure Fairy' is a pale blue form; 'Blue Butterfly', deep blue. Fully hardy.

DENDRANTHEMA
grandiflora
syn. *Chrysanthemum morifolium*
FLORIST'S CHRYSANTHEMUM

Hybrids of this perennial species make up the vast majority of cultivated chrysanthemums, and include a variety of flower forms, sizes and growth habits. Most

Waterlily or Nymphaea dahlia

Decorative dahlia

Dwarf or bedding dahlias

Pompon dahlia

Delphinium belladonna

Collarette dahlia

Delphinium elatum hybrid

flower in mid- or late autumn/fall, but flowering is often artificially delayed to fit in with exhibition seasons. The best cultivars for garden display and cut flowers are the intermediate decorative (e.g. 'Pink Poolys'), reflexed decorative (e.g. 'Amethyst'), anemone-centred (e.g. 'Powder Puff'), single (e.g. 'Kathleen Olsen'), pompon (e.g. 'Ping Pong'), spider (e.g. 'Nightingale') and charm (e.g. 'Ringdove'). Potted chrysanthemums can be planted out after the flowers have faded. *Dendranthema grandiflora* is the national flower of Japan.

DIANELLA
tasmanica
FLAX LILY

Native to Australia and New Zealand, this upright perennial is fibrous-rooted, spreading from underground rhizomes and sending up evergreen, strap-like leaves. Nodding, star-shaped, bright blue or purple-blue flowers are borne in branching sprays in spring and early summer, followed by shining deep blue berries. The plants grow from 50 cm to 1.2 m (about 20 in– 4¹/₂ ft) in height with a spread of 50 cm (about 20 in), and are frost-hardy. They make interesting accent plants in sun or partial shade and require a well-drained, neutral to acid soil. Propagate by division, rooted offsets, or seed in spring and autumn/fall. It is invasive, but useful for naturalizing. Named after Diana, the ancient Roman goddess of hunting.

DIANTHUS
PINK

A very large genus including the carnation, maiden pink, cottage pink, sweet William, Chinese or Indian pink and many other cultivated annuals, biennials and evergreen perennials. Most species are popular as massed border plants and for cutting. Perennial species include some small-flowered plants, excellent for rock gardens and chinks in stone walls and between paving stones. The taller perpetual and spray carnations are generally grown in glasshouses. Fully to halfhardy, *Dianthus* likes a sunny position, preferably protected from strong wind, and well-drained, slightly alkaline, soil. Regular watering and twice-monthly feeding produces good flowers. The taller varieties will require staking. Prune stems back after flowering to encourage new growth. Propagate perennials by layering or cuttings in summer; annuals and biennials by seed in autumn/ fall or early spring. Watch for aphids, thrips and caterpillars. Also susceptible to rust and virus infections. The name dianthus means heavenly flower.

Dianthus caryophyllus cultivars

D. × allwoodii
PERPETUAL FLOWERING PINK

Densely leafed, tuft-forming perennials of hybrid origin, with greygreen foliage and an abundance of erect flowering stems each carrying four to six fragrant, single to fully double flowers in shades of white, pink or crimson, often with dark centres and with plain or fringed petals. Flowers over a long season from late spring until early autumn/ fall. Grows 30–50 cm (about 12–20 in) high with a spread of 20–25 cm (about 8–10 in). Frost-hardy.

D. barbatus
SWEET WILLIAM

A short-lived perennial, usually treated as a biennial, it self-sows readily and is useful for bedding and cut flowers. It is slow growing, to a height of 50 cm (about 20 in) and spread of 15 cm (about 6 in). In late spring and early summer, it bears many small, fragrant flowers, in bright reds, pinks and bicolors, on a flat-topped crown. It has bright green, grassy leaves. Frost-hardy. The dwarf cultivars, to about 10 cm (about 4 in), are usually treated as annuals.

D. caryophyllus cultivars
CARNATION

Fairly fast-growing evergreen perennials of short duration, carnations have a tufted erect habit with lanceshaped grey-green leaves and showy, perfumed, semi-double or double flowers. The range of colours includes pink, yellow, white and red. Striped flowers are called fancies; those edged in a contrasting colour,

Dendranthema grandiflora

Dianthus × allwoodii

Delphinium grandiflorum

Dianthus barbatus

Dianella tasmanica

picotees. The numerous cultivars are classified under 3 groups.

Annual or marguerite carnations

Evergreen perennials, usually grown as annuals. The 6 cm (about 2¹/₂ in) wide flowers appear in sprays in spring to autumn/fall. They grow to 75 cm (about 30 in) high with a spread of 20 cm (about 8 in). Frosthardy. 'Enfants de Nice' has fancy or picotee flowers; 'Chabaud', fringed, solid coloured flowers.

Border carnations

Bushy evergreen perennials, growing to a height of 80 cm (about 32 in) and spread of 30 cm (about 12 in). Frost-hardy, they are best suited to cooler climates. Flowers are smooth-edged or fringed, 8 cm (about 3 in) wide, and come in many colours. Spring or early summer flowering. Most varieties of border carnations carry a decided clove perfume.

Perpetual-flowering carnations

Evergreen perennials growing to 1 m (about 3 ft) high or more with a spread of 30 cm (about 12 in). They have a straggly habit and may need staking. Fully double flowers, usually fringed, are produced throughout the year. Half-hardy. Cultivars include: 'William Sim', bright red; 'Exquisite', deep pink; 'Arthur Sim', white with red markings; 'Harvest Moon', pale yellow; 'Calypso', pale pink; 'Mini Star', apricot. Disbud large-flowered varieties to give one flower per stem. Spray types produce about five flowers per stem and do not need disbudding.

D. chinensis

INDIAN PINK

This popular annual has a short, tufted growth habit, and grey-green lance-shaped leaves. In late spring and summer it bears masses of tubular, single or double, sweetly scented flowers in shades of pink, red, lavender and white. Slow growing to a height and spread of 15–30 cm (about 6–12 in), and fully hardy.

D. deltoides

MAIDEN PINK

Ideal for a rock garden or ground cover, this dwarf, mat-forming evergreen perennial is easily grown from seed or cuttings. It has tiny, lance-shaped leaves and bears small, single, fringed flowers in pink, cerise or white, mostly with a red eye, in spring and early summer. Grows to 15 cm (about 6 in) high with a spread of 30 cm (about 12 in), and is fully hardy. Cut back after flowering.

D. plumarius

GARDEN OR COTTAGE PINK

A loosely tufted, evergreen perennial growing 30–50 cm (about 12–20 in) in height with a spread of 25 cm (about 10 in). There are many named cultivars, bearing sprays of single or fully double sweetly scented flowers in red, pinks, purple-reds, mauves and whites. Many have fringed petals and a contrasting eye. Late spring flowering and frost-hardy. Useful at the front of the border or in rockeries.

DIASCIA
barberae

This low growing, rather fragile perennial, native to South Africa, is a useful addition to rock gardens and borders. It has small heart-shaped, pale green leaves, and bears clusters of twin-spurred, salmon pink flowers in spring through to early autumn/fall. Grows to a height of 15–20 cm (about 6–8 in) with a spread of 20 cm (about 8 in). They

do best in rich, well-drained soil, in a sunny position in temperate climates and in partial shade in hotter areas. Fertilize lightly and water regularly when flowers are forming. Pinch out growing tips to increase bushiness and cut back old stems after flowering has finished. Propagate from seed in autumn/fall, softwood cuttings in late spring or from semi-ripe cuttings in summer.

DICENTRA

Herbaceous perennials native to the colder regions of northern Asia and North America, they are grown for their attractive sprays of pendent, heart-shaped pink, red or white flowers, which are carried on arching stems above lacy grey-green leaves. They flower from spring through summer. They grow to a height of from 8 cm (about 3 in) to 5 m (about 15 ft) and have a spread of up to 60 cm (about 24 in). Plant in a rich, well-drained soil of coarse texture with a liberal dressing of organic matter. Propagate by late winter divi-

sions, from spring basal cuttings or seed in autumn/fall.

D. formosa

WESTERN BLEEDING HEART

This spreading plant grows to 45 cm (about 18 in) high and has a spread of 30 cm (about 12 in). Dainty pink and red flowers appear throughout spring and summer. *D. f.* 'Alba' is a white-flowered form.

D. spectabilis

BLEEDING HEART

This species is a popular garden perennial. It grows to a height and spread of 60 cm (about 24 in). Pink and white flowers appear in late spring and summer.

DICHORISANDRA
thyrsiflora

BLUE GINGER, BRAZILIAN GINGER

An evergreen perennial with glossy, dark leaves which grow on their stems in spirals. Tall spikes of deep purple-blue flowers are produced

Dichorisandra thyrsiflora

Dicentra formosa 'Alba'

Dianthus chinensis

Dicentra spectabilis

Dianthus plumarius

Diascia barberae

Dianthus deltoides

in summer and autumn/fall. Grows well in a temperate or subtropical area in the shade, such as beneath trees. Needs well-drained soil with acid peat and leaf mould. This plant will not tolerate frost and needs a minimum temperature of 15–20°C (about 59–68°F). Requires adequate moisture at all times and high humidity in summer. Propagate by division in early spring or from stem cuttings taken during summer.

DICTAMNUS
albus
BURNING BUSH

Native to southern Europe and Asia, this long-lived, herbaceous perennial is grown for its early summer spikes of fragrant star-shaped white flowers with long stamens. Flowers are good for cutting. It has an upright habit, growing to 1 m (about 3 ft) tall with a spread of 60 cm (about 24 in) with lemon-scented, glossy, leathery, light green leaves. Fully hardy, it requires full sun, fertile well-drained soil and regular water. It is a slow-growing plant, taking 3 or 4 years to reach flowering size. Propagate from seed sown in late summer. Resents being disturbed once established. The whole plant gives off an inflammable oil which may ignite if a flame is held near it.

DIERAMA
pulcherrimum
LADY'S WAND, WANDFLOWER, ANGEL'S FISHING ROD

South African members of the same family (Iridaceae) as the Iris, these upright, summer-flowering corms have evergreen, strap-like foliage and arching stems which bear long, swinging tassels of tubular or bell-shaped deep pink flowers. The effect is particularly enchanting in a breeze or reflected in a pool. Grows to a height of 1.5 m (about 4½ ft) and spread of 30 cm (about 12 in). Requires sun and deep, rich, moist well-drained soil—water well in summer when in growth. Frost-hardy, it dies down partially in winter. Propagate by division of corms in spring or from seed in spring and autumn/fall. They resent disturbance and may be left in the ground for years.

DIETES

Native to southern Africa, these ever-green, rhizomatous perennials are grown for their attractive iris-shaped flowers. The flowers usually last only for a day but new buds open over a long period in spring and early summer. They have strong, sword-like leaves which form large and attractive clumps. All species will thrive in semi-shade or sun, and in humus-

rich, well-drained soil that does not dry out too quickly. Do not remove flower stems as they continue to flower for several years. Half-hardy, they are tough enough to use as low hedges and, once established, self-seed readily. Propagate from seed in spring or autumn/fall or by division in spring.

D. grandiflora
WILD IRIS

Wild Iris grows to a height and spread of 1 m (about 3 ft) and bears 10 cm (about 4 in) wide, white, iris-like flowers marked with mauve and orange-yellow. Its blooms last several days in summer.

D. iridioides
syn. D. vegeta

A smaller version of D. grandiflora, it has branching wiry stems carrying 6–8 cm (about 2½–3 in) wide, iris-like flowers, white with central yellow marks. Grows to a height of 60 cm (about 24 in) and spread of 30–60 cm (about 12–24 in), forming dense clumps. Its native habitat is in semi-shade under tall open trees.

DIGITALIS
FOXGLOVE

Natives of Europe, northern Africa and western Asia, these biennials and perennials, some of which are evergreen, are grown for the strong accent value of their tall flower spikes in the summer border. They are very effective planted in groups in a shrub border under taller trees to provide shade and wind protection. They come in many colours including magenta, purple, white, cream, yellow, pink and lavender. Fully to frost-hardy, they grow in most conditions, doing best in cool, humid climates in semi-shade and moist, well-drained soil. Cut flowering stems down to the ground after the spring flowering to encourage development of secondary spikes. Propagate from seed in autumn/fall; they self-seed readily. The medicinal properties of digitalis have been known since ancient times, and these plants are still used in the treatment of heart ailments today.

D. × mertonensis

Clump-forming, this perennial grows to 60 cm (about 24 in) in height with a spread of 30 cm (about 12 in). Summer-flowering, it bears spikes of tubular, cherry rose to salmon rose flowers over a rosette of soft, hairy, oval leaves. Divide after flowering. Fully hardy.

D. purpurea

The common foxglove, this short-lived perennial is grown as a biennial.

Digitalis purpurea

Dietes iridioides

Dietes grandiflora

Digitalis × mertonensis

Dictamnus albus

Dierama pulcherrimum

It is ideal for providing a backdrop in a border or for naturalizing in open woodlands because of its upright habit, reaching a height of 1–1.5 m (about 3–4½ ft) and spread of 60 cm (about 24 in). Tall spikes of tubular flowers in shades of purple, white, pink, rosy magenta and pale yellow appear between late spring and early autumn/fall, above a rosette of rough, oval, deep green leaves. D. purpurea is fully hardy. All parts of the plant, especially the leaves, are poisonous.

Dorotheanthus bellidiformis

Dimorphotheca sinuata

DIMORPHOTHECA

AFRICAN DAISY, CAPE MARIGOLD

Indigenous to South Africa, these
annuals, perennials and evergreen
sub-shrubs are valued for their glossy
daisy-like flowers which appear over a
long season from early spring. They
are useful for rock gardens, dry banks
and the front row of borders—particularly as temporary fillers. They
require an open sunny situation and a
fertile, well-drained soil. Ideal for
beach gardens. They are not good as
cut flowers as they close on cloudy
days and remain closed indoors.
Light pruning after flowering helps
extend the life of the plants. Dead-
head to prolong flowering. Propagate
annuals from seed sown in spring and
perennials from semi-ripe cuttings in
summer. Watch for botrytis.

D. pluvialis

RAIN DAISY

This annual is an excellent bedding
plant producing small flowerheads,
snowy white above, purple beneath, with brownish purple centres.
It is low growing, reaching 20–30 cm

Dodecatheon meadia

(about 8–12 in) high with a spread
of 15 cm (about 6 in) and half-
hardy.

D. sinuata

syn. D. aurantiaca, D. calendulacea

This expansive annual species
grows up to 30 cm (about 12 in).
Its roughly serrated spoon-shaped
leaves grow to 8 cm (about 3 in)
long. Daisy-like flowers with yellow
centres and orange outer petals
which occasionally have yellow
bases, appear from the beginning of
spring until autumn/fall.

DIPLARRHENA

moraea

This iris-like perennial features
elegant clusters of white flowers with
yellow and purple centres, borne on
wiry stems. Flowers are short-lived
but appear in quick succession during spring and early summer. It has
fans of strong, long, green strap-
shaped leaves. Clump forming, it
quickly grows to a height of 50 cm
(about 20 in) and spread of 25 cm
(about 10 in). Frost-hardy, it requires

Dimorphotheca pluvialis

a sunny position and well-drained,
moist soil. Propagate by division in
spring or autumn/fall, or by seed in
spring.

DODECATHEON

meadia

SHOOTING STAR

This perennial, a member of the
Primulaceae family (which includes
the primrose) and native to North
America, is good for hillside and
mountain gardens, and is a beautiful poolside or bog plant. In spring
it bears distinctive, nodding,
cyclamen-pink flowers with reflexed
petals and extended stamens. It has
primula-like, clumped rosettes of pale
green leaves, and ranges in height
from 15 to 50 cm (about 6–20 in)
with a spread of 50 cm (about 20 in).
Best grown in semi-shade in a moist,
well-drained acid soil. Fully hardy.
Propagate from seed in autumn/fall or
by division in winter. Dormant after
flowering and difficult to transplant as
it resents disturbance. The plant's
common name derives from the fact
that, once fertilized, the flowers turn
skywards.

DOROTHEANTHUS

bellidiformis

ICE PLANT, LIVINGSTONE DAISY,
BOKBAAI VYGIE

Native to South Africa, this small
succulent annual is ideal for massed
summer display in rockeries,
banks, beds and planter boxes,

Diplarrhena moraea

Duchesnea indica

particularly if sown thickly so the
plants can intermingle. It has daisy-
like flowerheads in dazzling shades of
yellow, white, red or pink. Grows to a
height of 15 cm (about 6 in) and
spread of 30 cm (about 12 in). Plant
in an open sunny position—the
flowers close in dull weather or if
grown in shade. Grows well in poor
but well-drained soil, and because
of its salt-resistance is good for seaside gardens. Do not overwater.
Half-hardy. Propagate from seed in
autumn/fall. Dead-head regularly
and watch for slugs and snails.

DORYANTHES

excelsa

GYMEA LILY, SPEAR LILY, GIANT LILY

A bold plant from Queensland and
New South Wales in Australia. It
has stiff rosettes of 10–15 cm
(about 4–6 in) wide, lance-shaped,
light green leaves which at maturity
can reach 1–2 m (about 3–6 ft) long.
Globular heads of long-lasting, bright
red flowers are borne on 5 m (about
15 ft) stems in summer. These eye-
catching flowers drip with nectar. A
half-hardy perennial preferring light,
well-drained but moist soil in full sun
or semi-shade. Propagate from seed
in spring or suckers after flowering.

DUCHESNEA

indica

syn. Fragaria indica

A semi-evergreen trailing perennial
that spreads rapidly by runners and is

Doryanthes excelsa

Echium wildpretti

Echinacea purpurea

Echinops ritro

Epilobium nummularifolium

Epimedium alpinum

Echium vulgare [dwarf]

useful for ground cover, bed edging, hanging baskets and pots. It has dark green leaves and bright, 2.5 cm (about 1 in) wide, yellow flowers from spring to early summer. Ornamental, strawberry-like small red fruits appear in late summer. Grows to a height of 10 cm (about 4 in) with an indefinite spread. Fully hardy, it is best grown in sun or semi-shade in well-drained, rich, cultivated soil. Propagate by division in spring, from seed in autumn/fall, or by rooting plantlets formed at the ends of runners in summer.

ECHINACEA
purpurea
syn. *Rudbeckia purpurea*
PURPLE CONEFLOWER

Native to North America, this showy summer-flowering perennial has large daisy-like, rosy purple flowers with high, orange-brown central cones. The 10 cm (about 4 in) wide flowers, borne singly on strong stems, are useful for cutting. Leaves are lance-shaped and dark green. Of upright habit, it grows to 1.2 m (about 4 ft) and spreads 50 cm (about 20 in). Fully hardy, it prefers a sunny situation and a rich, moist but well-drained soil. Regular dead-heading prolongs flowering, and in cold climates the entire plant can be cut back in autumn/fall. Propagate by division or root cuttings from winter to early spring.

ECHINOPS
ritro
GLOBE THISTLE

This perennial of a genus native to northern Africa, Europe and western

Asia, from Spain to India, is a useful plant for the herbaceous border, and its globe-like spiky flowers can be cut and dried for winter decoration. It has large, deeply cut, prickly leaves, downy beneath, with silvery white stems and round, thistle-like, purplish blue heads of flowers in summer. Of an upright habit, it grows to 1.2 m (about 4 ft) in height with a spread of 75 cm (about 30 in). Fully hardy, it requires full sun and a well-drained soil, and is generally drought resistant. Propagate from seed in spring, by root cuttings or division in autumn/fall, or by division in late winter. Transplant during the winter or early spring months.

ECHIUM

Indigenous to the Mediterranean, Canary Islands and Madeira, this genus of annuals and evergreen shrubs, perennials and biennials is grown for their spectacular tall spires and bright blue or pink flowers in late spring and summer. Fully hardy to frost-tender, they require a dry climate, full sun or semi-shade, and a well-drained soil of light to medium quality. They grow unwieldly in soil that is too rich or damp. Coastal planting is ideal. Propagate from seed or cuttings in spring or summer. In mild climates they self-sow readily.

E. vulgare [dwarf]

This biennial has an erect, bushy habit. In its dwarf form it grows to a height of 30 cm (about 12 in) and a spread of 20 cm (about 8 in). It has lance-shaped, dark green leaves, and white, blue, pink or purple tubular flowers. Fully hardy, it is fast growing and may become invasive.

E. wildpretti
syn. *E. bourgaeanum*

A striking biennial from the Canary Islands, this evergreen plant makes a lovely rosette of narrow, silvery leaves and, in its second season, bears a single, bold spike of small, funnel-shaped, rich coral flowers. Frost-hardy, it needs perfect drainage and dies after fruiting. It has an erect habit, growing to a height of 2.5 m (about 7½ ft) or more with a spread of 60 cm (about 24 in).

EPILOBIUM
nummularifolium
WILLOW HERB

This alpine perennial is grown for its attractive foliage and white flowers, and is a useful plant for rock gardens. Leaves are tiny, shining and coppery coloured and the minute flowers are borne on 5 cm (about 2 in) stems in spring and summer. Of a creeping, mat-forming habit, it grows 2–3 cm (about 1–1½ in) high with a spread

of 1 m (about 3 ft) or more. Quick-growing and frost-hardy, it prefers a position in partial shade and a moist but well-drained lime-free soil. Propagate from seed in spring or autumn/fall.

EPIMEDIUM
alpinum

An evergreen, low-growing perennial, this plant makes a good ground cover under azaleas and rhododendrons. The finely toothed, glossy leaves are bronze-red when young, turning to mid-green with age. In spring it bears racemes of pendent yellow and crimson flowers. Grows to a height of 25 cm (about 10 in) and spread of 30 cm (about 12 in). Fully hardy, this plant prefers cooler climates, partial shade and rich, moist, well-drained soil. Remove old or damaged leaves in spring just before new growth appears. It is easily divided and increased from the many-crowned clumps in spring or autumn/fall.

Erigeron glaucus

Erigeron 'Charity'

Erinus alpinus

Eryngium giganteum

Erigeron karvinskianus

Eremurus, Shelford hybrids

Eryngium agavifolium

EREMURUS,
Shelford hybrids
FOXTAIL LILY

This group of perennials is grown for its lofty spikes of close-packed flowers, magnificent for floral displays. They produce rosettes of strap-like leaves and in mid-summer each crown yields spikes of bloom with strong stems and hundreds of shallow cup-shaped flowers in a wide range of colours including white, pink, salmon, yellow, apricot and coppery tones. Grows to 1.5 m (about 4¹/₂ ft) in height with a spread of 60 cm (about 24 in). Frost-hardy, they prefer a sunny, warm position, protection from heavy winds, and well-drained soil. May require staking. Protect roots with a layer of mulch in cold winters. Propagate from seed in autumn/fall or by division in late winter and early spring. Transplant when dormant.

ERIGERON
FLEABANE

This is a large genus of annuals, biennials and perennials, some evergreen, that are predominantly native to North America. They have mainly erect stems, capped by masses of pink, white or blue, daisy-like flowers that are striking in the front row of a mixed herbaceous border or rock garden. They flower between late spring and mid-summer. Fully to frost-hardy, they prefer a sunny position, sheltered from strong winds, and moderately fertile, well-drained soil. Do not allow to dry out during the growing season. Propagate by division of an established clump in spring or autumn/fall and remove spent stems after flowering. Can become invasive. Erigeron became popular garden plants for their supposed ability to repel fleas.

E. 'Charity'

A perennial with a profusion of pale pink flowers with yellowy green centres borne over a long period in summer. Clump-forming, it grows to a height and spread of 60 cm (about 24 in) and it may require support.

E. glaucus
ALPINE FLEABANE

A perennial bearing lilac-pink flowers in summer. Clump-forming, it grows to 25 cm (about 10 in) in height with a spread of 20 cm (about 8 in). Leaves are long and hairy. Fully hardy.

E. karvinskianus
syn. E. mucronatus

This frost-hardy, spreading perennial is useful as an informal ground cover and in mild climates will bloom profusely throughout the year. The small 2 cm (about 1 in) wide, daisy-like flowers open white, fading to pink and wine-red. Grows 10–15 cm (about 4–6 in) in height with an indefinite spread. It has lax stems and narrow, lance-shaped, hairy leaves. Cut back hard from time to time. Native to Mexico. This plant is becoming a noxious weed in New Zealand.

ERINUS
alpinus

This small semi-evergreen perennial is native to the European alps and ideal for planting in wall crevices and rock gardens. It forms rosettes of soft, medium green leaves, and bears a profusion of starry, rosy purple or white flowers in late spring and summer. Grows 5–8 cm (about 2–3 in) in height and spread. It is short-lived but self-seeds freely. Fully hardy, E. alpinus grows well in either full sun or partial shade and requires a well-drained soil. Propagate from seed in autumn/fall.

ERYNGIUM
SEA HOLLY

Native to South America and Europe, these biennials and perennials are members of the same family as the carrot (Apiaceae), and are grown for their interesting foliage and spiny-collared blooms that usually have a bluish metallic sheen. They flower over a long period in summer and may be cut and dried for winter decoration. Fully to half-hardy, they require a sunny situation, good drainage and a sandy soil. Plants tend to collapse in wet, heavy ground during winter. Propagate species from fresh seed; selected forms by root cuttings in winter or by division in spring. Transplant when dormant in winter. The spiny appearance of the strongly coloured thistle-like bracts that surround the central flower give rise to the common name 'holly'.

E. agavifolium

A tall, clump-forming perennial with narrow, spiny, rich green leaves and greenish white thistle heads borne on branched stems in summer. It grows to a height of 1.5 m (about 4¹/₂ ft) with a spread of 60 cm (about 24 in). It is evergreen and half-hardy.

E. giganteum

This short-lived perennial dies after its late-summer flowering but is free-seeding. It is clump-forming, growing to a height of 1–1.2 m (about 3–3¹/₂ ft) and spread of 75 cm (about 30 in). Foliage is heart-shaped and mid-green, and it bears large, rounded blue or pale green thistle heads, surrounded by spiny, silvery bracts. It is fully hardy.

E. × oliverianum

This fully hardy upright perennial grows to a height of 60 cm–1 m (about 2–3 ft) and spread of 45–60 cm (about 18–24 in). In late summer it bears large, rounded, lavender blue thistle heads. Leaves are jagged, mid-green and heart-shaped.

ERYSIMUM
hieraciifolium
syn. *Cheiranthus* × *allionii*
SIBERIAN WALLFLOWER

Found in all parts of the northern hemisphere, this bushy evergreen perennial is suitable for rock gardens, banks and borders. It is short-lived and should be grown as a biennial. It has toothed, mid-green leaves and bears bright yellow or orange flowers in spring, putting on a dazzling display for a long period. Slow-growing, it reaches a height and spread of 30 cm (about 12 in). It is fully hardy, preferring light, well-drained fertile soil and a sunny position. Propagate in summer by cuttings, which root very easily, or from seed in spring—it self-seeds freely. Cultivars include 'Orange Bedder' which has scented, brilliant orange flowers.

ESCHSCHOLZIA
californica
CALIFORNIAN POPPY

This, the official floral emblem of California, is one of the brightest garden annuals, suitable for rock gardens, the front of borders, and gaps in paving. The cup-shaped flowers open out from grey-green feathery foliage into vivid shades of orange, bronze, yellow, cream, scarlet, mauve and rose. They flower from summer through to autumn/fall but close in dull weather so should be planted in a sunny situation. Of a slender, erect habit, they grow to 30 cm (about 12 in) high with a spread of 15 cm (about 6 in). Fully hardy, they grow well in poor, very well-drained soil and should be dead-headed regularly to prolong flowering. Propagate from seed sown in spring. They do not transplant easily so sow where the plants are to remain. Watch for snails.

EUPHORBIA
MILKWEED, SPURGE

This large and varied genus of shrubs, succulents, perennials and annuals have in common a milky sap which may irritate the skin and can be poisonous. The spectacular flowerheads consist of a series of highly coloured cup-shaped bracts or modified leaves. There are many succulent species which are suitable for pot plants and for sandy or desert gardens. Fully hardy to frost-

tender, they require either sun or partial shade and a moist but well-drained soil. Plants are increased from young basal cuttings in spring, division in early spring or early autumn/fall. They may also self-seed if conditions at flowering time are suitable.

E. amygdaloides subsp. robbiae
WOOD SPURGE

This perennial forms rosettes of dark green leaves and in spring is covered with yellowish green flowerheads. Very useful as a ground cover in shade and beneath shrubs. It is evergreen, with a spreading habit, and grows to 50–60 cm (about 20–24 in) in height with a spread of 60 cm (about 24 in). Fully hardy, it does well in poor, dry, well-drained soil and semi-shade.

E. griffithii 'Fireglow'

A bushy, summer-flowering perennial that produces soft, green-veined, dense red young spring growths and branches topped with heads of copper-red bracts. Grows to 1 m (about 3 ft) in height with a spread of 50 cm (about 20 in). This cultivar is fully hardy and prefers full sun and a well-drained soil.

E. marginata
SNOW-ON-THE-MOUNTAIN, GHOSTWEED

Native to central areas of North America, this bushy annual makes an excellent foil for brighter flowers. It has pointed oval, bright green leaves, sharply margined with white, and broad petal-like white bracts surrounding small flowers in

Euphorbia marginata

Eryngium × oliverianum

summer. Fairly fast-growing to 60 cm (about 24 in) tall with a 30 cm (about 12 in) spread. Half-hardy, it will endure colder conditions.

EUSTOMA
grandiflorum
syn. *Lisianthus russellianus*
PRAIRIE GENTIAN

Native to America's mid-west, right down to Texas and New Mexico, this annual is grown for its flowers which are excellent for cutting, lasting up to 3 weeks in water. They are also useful as container plants. It has lance-shaped deep green leaves and 5 cm (about 2 in) wide, flared tulip-like flowers in colours of rich purple, pink, blue or white. Flowers appear in spring and again in autumn/fall. Of an upright habit, the plant is slow growing to a height of 60 cm (about 24 in) and spread of 30 cm (about 12 in). It is frost-tender, requiring a sunny situation and well-drained soil. In frost-free areas propagate from seed sown in early autumn/fall.

Euphorbia griffithii 'Fireglow'

Erysimum hieraciifolium

Euphorbia amygdaloides subsp. *robbiae*

Eschscholzia californica

Eustoma grandiflorum

EXACUM
affine
PERSIAN VIOLET

Native to the Yemeni island of Socotra, this showy miniature is useful both as an indoor pot plant and as a plant for outdoor sun or semi-shaded positions. It has shining, oval dark leaves and bears a profusion of tiny, fragrant, 5-petalled, saucer-shaped purple flowers with yellow stamens throughout summer. A biennial usually treated as an annual, it has a bushy habit and grows to a height and spread of 20–30 cm (about 8–12 in). It is frost-tender and enjoys rich, moist but well-drained soil. Indoors, they like diffused sun and a night temperature not below 15°C (60°F). Propagate from seed sown in early spring or late summer.

FELICIA

Native to South Africa, these annuals and evergreen sub-shrubs include some of the finest species of blue daisy flowers. They are particularly useful as container plants as they are seldom without blooms. They are fully hardy to frost-tender and require full sun and a dryish, well-drained gravelly soil enriched with organic matter; they will not tolerate wet conditions. Flowers are produced throughout spring and summer, and dead-heading can prolong the season. Prune straggly shoots regularly. Propagate by cuttings taken in autumn/fall and spring or from seed in spring.

F. amelloides
BLUE MARGUERITE

A bushy, evergreen shrub with roundish, bright green leaves and sky-blue flowerheads with bright yellow centres borne on long stalks. It has a spreading habit, growing to 60 cm (about 24 in) in height and width. Half-hardy, it is fast growing in temperate climates and useful for small formal hedges, rock gardens, path edgings, indoor pot plants or as a seaside plant. The flowers cut well for posies. Prune hard as soon as it becomes straggly to encourage new growth.

F. bergeriana
KINGFISHER DAISY

This mat-forming annual bears a mass of bright cobalt-blue daisy flowers with yellow centres, above hairy, lance-shaped grey-green leaves. The flowers only open in sunshine so plant in a sunny situation. It can be used for bedding or edging, window boxes or balcony containers. It is fast growing to a height and spread of 15 cm (about 6 in), and fully hardy.

FILIPENDULA
vulgaris
syn. *F. hexapetala*
DROPWORT

This fully hardy herbaceous perennial is grown for its attractive, deeply cut, fern-like foliage, and showy, crowded heads of tiny white flowers; some garden varieties are pink. Flowers are long-lasting and the foliage remains lovely long after flowering. These plants do well at the back of larger perennial borders, as long as the soil remains moist, and in waterside positions. Upright in habit, it grows to a height of 1 m (about 3 ft) and spread of 45 cm (about 18 in) and has fleshy, swollen roots. Fully hardy, this species will tolerate fairly dry conditions but prefers a moist soil in full sun or in semi-shade. Propagate by division in winter or from seed in spring and autumn/fall, and cut back when dormant in colder areas. Watch for powdery mildew.

GAILLARDIA
BLANKET FLOWER, INDIAN BLANKET

These annuals and perennials from the central and western United States have vividly coloured, daisy-like flowers. Some varieties make good cut flowers. The perennials are often short-lived and are better grown as biennials in cooler climates. They are easy to grow, requiring sun and any ordinary well-drained garden soil. Suits coastal areas. Fully to frost-hardy. Propagate from spring cuttings taken before the plants have bloomed or from seed in autumn/fall or spring.

G. aristata

A showy perennial with large, single, daisy-like cheerful orange flowers with red centres, and aromatic, divided leaves. Flowers are borne freely from early summer until early winter, and their bright colours enhance the shades of autumn/fall leaves. Grows to a height of 60 cm (about 24 in) with a spread of 50 cm (about 20 in) and may require staking. It is fully hardy but may be short-lived in damp conditions.

G. pulchella

An annual or short-lived perennial, this upright species has hairy, lance-shaped, grey-green leaves and ball-like flowers. Garden forms are usually double with many tubular flowers, creating a pompon effect. It is summer-flowering and comes in shades of crimson, red or pink, and yellow. Useful for creating bright patches in the border. Fast-growing to a height of 30–50 cm (about 12–20 in) and spread of 30 cm (about 12 in) and fully hardy.

Exacum affine

Felicia bergeriana

Gaillardia aristata

Gaillardia pulchella

Felicia amelloides

Filipendula vulgaris

GALEGA
officinalis
GOAT'S RUE

Indigenous to the goat country of
southern Europe and Asia Minor,
this fully hardy perennial has spikes
of small, pea-like mauve, pink or
white flowers over a long period in
summer. These are followed by
erect, long, narrow pods. It has an
upright habit with erect stems and
divided, lance-shaped, bright green
leaves. Grows to a height of 1.5 m
(about 4¹/₂ ft) and spread of 1 m
(about 3 ft) and requires staking.
Thrives in an open, sunny situation
in any deep, well-drained soil.
Propagate by division in winter or
from seed in autumn/fall and cut
faded flower stems to the ground.

Galega officinalis

GALEOBDOLON
argentatum
syn. *Lamiastrum galeobdolon*
'Variegatum', *Lamium galeobdolon*
'Variegatum'

This semi-evergreen carpeting perennial is much favoured as ground
cover in shaded places, particularly
under deciduous trees. It spreads fast
from runners, producing long trailing
stems of oval, coarsely-toothed, sil-
ver-marked mid-green leaves. It is
inclined to be rampant but can be
easily controlled. In summer it bears
racemes of tubular, two-lipped,
golden-yellow flowers. It grows to 30
cm (about 12 in) high with an indefinite spread. Fully hardy, it will grow
in sun or shade and any well-drained
soil. Propagate by division of rooted
runners in winter and cut back after
flowering.

GAURA
lindheimeri

Native to North America, this
bushy, long-flowering perennial is
useful for backgrounds and mixed
flower borders. It has loosely
branched stems covered with tiny
hairs, and from spring to autumn/
fall produces beautiful, pink-suf-
fused, small white flowers which
give a misty pink effect. Leaves are
lance-shaped and mid-green.
Grows to 1.2 m (nearly 4 ft) in height
with a spread of 1 m (about 3 ft), and
is fully hardy. It is easily grown, thriving in hot dry climates and preferring
full sun and a light sandy, well-
drained soil. Propagate from seed in
spring or autumn/fall or from cuttings
in summer.

GAZANIA

These low-growing perennials,
some grown as annuals, are valued
for their ease of culture and large,
brightly coloured flowers. Most modern variants are hybrids from a
number of South African species.

Galeobdolon argentatum

They are useful for bedding, rock
gardens, pots and tubs, and for binding soil on sloping land. Leaves are
either entire or deeply lobed, long
and narrow, and dark green on top,
silver-grey and woolly beneath. The
large daisy flowers are in a range of
colours from cream to yellow, gold,
pink, red, buff, brown and intermediate shades, usually marked with
bands or spots of contrasting colour
at the base of the petals. They open
in full sun and glow with a metallic
sheen. Flowering is over a long period
from early spring until summer. Grow
in full sun in sandy, fairly dry, soil.
Give an annual mulch of compost
and water during dry periods. They
are half-hardy and salt resistant so are
useful in coastal areas. Propagate by
division or from cuttings in autumn/
fall, or from seed in late winter to
early spring. Remove spent flowers
and dead leaves, and tidy up at the
end of the growing season.

G. 'Daybreak'

This carpeting perennial grows to a
height and spread of 20 cm (about 8
in). In cooler districts it is better
grown as an annual. Produces large,
orange, yellow, pink and bronze
daisy-like flowers. Unlike most
Gazania, flowers of this species remain open even in cloudy weather.

G. krebsiana

Originating in South Africa, this
stemless perennial has slender
lance-shaped leaves with a smooth
upper surface and a white downy
underside. Flowers are yellow to
orange-red with a contrasting darker
colour around their centres. Plant in
light, well-drained soil in full sun.

Gazania, Sunshine hybrids

G., Sunshine hybrids

Another carpeting perennial that is
better grown as an annual in cooler
climates. Grows to a height and
spread of 20 cm (about 8 in). There
is a large range of colours, many of
them with dark centres. The hybrids are often not quite as hardy as
the older species.

GENTIANA
GENTIAN

Natives of alpine meadows
throughout the world, these fully
hardy annuals, biennials and perennials, some of which are evergreen, are
valued for their brilliant blue flowers.
They are useful plants for rock gardens, peat beds and sloping hillside
gardens, doing best in cooler regions.
They prefer a well-drained, acid,
peaty-sandy soil with some humus.
Some species grow naturally on

Gaura lindheimeri

limestone soils. Plant in either sun
or semi-shade. Propagate by division in spring or from seed in au-
tumn/fall. Divide autumn/
fall-flowering species every 3 years
in early spring, planting out in fresh
soil. They are named after Gentius,
an Illyrian king who discovered the
medicinal value of their bitter roots.

Gazania 'Daybreak'

Gazania krebsiana

G. acaulis
syn. G. excisa, G. kochiana
STEMLESS GENTIAN

An evergreen, clump-forming perennial suitable for edgings or rockeries. In spring, and sometimes autumn/fall, it forms a striking carpet of trumpet-shaped, vivid blue flowers with green-spotted throats. Its foliage is compact, with tufted clumps of glossy green, narrow leaves. Grows to 2 cm (about 1 in) in height with a spread of 5–8 cm (about 2–3 in). Needs a deep root run and benefits from a light application of lime.

G. lutea
GREAT YELLOW GENTIAN

This perennial produces tubular yellow flowers in summer. Erect and unbranched, it grows to 1–2 m (about 3–6 ft) high and spreads to 60 cm (about 24 in). Its oval leaves grow to 30 cm (about 12 in) in length. This species is the main commercial source of gentian root which is used medicinally and as a flavouring in vermouth.

G. sino-ornata

An evergreen perennial, flowering in autumn/fall, bearing trumpet-shaped, deep blue flowers that are paler at the base and banded purplish blue. It is an easily grown species of prostrate, spreading habit, reaching a height of 5 cm (about 2 in) and spread of 30 cm (about 12 in). Prefers a moist, acid soil.

GERANIUM
CRANESBILL, GERANIUM

There are over 400 species of perennial geraniums, some of which are evergreen, found all over the world in cool, temperate and alpine regions. Grown for their attractive flowers, they are useful for rock gardens, informal ground covers and plants for the front of the border. They make small, showy clumps with pink to blue or purple flowers about 3 cm (1½ in) across. All flower in spring to summer. Fully to half-hardy, most species prefer a sunny situation and damp, well-drained soil. Propagate from semi-ripe cuttings in summer; seed in spring or by division in autumn/fall. Tidy up regularly to encourage bushy growth. Transplant during winter.

G. incanum

This half-hardy South African evergreen perennial grows up to 40 cm (about 16 in) in height and broadly spreads up to 1 m (about 3 ft). Its greyish green leaves are heavily lobed and have a spicy aroma. This frost-hardy plant produces cup-shaped individual blooms, usually crimson in colour with deeper coloured veins.

G. 'Johnson's Blue'

Fully hardy, this rhizomatous perennial has cup-shaped lavender-blue flowers throughout summer. Leaves are deeply divided. It has a spreading habit, growing to a height of 30 cm (about 12 in) and spread of 60 cm (about 24 in). Propagate by division or cuttings only.

G. sanguineum
BLOODY CRANESBILL

A fully hardy perennial useful as ground cover. It bears cup-shaped, bright purple-crimson, notched-petalled flowers throughout spring and summer. A much-branched species, it has deeply divided, dark green leaves. Grows to 25 cm (about 10 in) in height with a spread of 30 cm (about 12 in) or more and has a hummock-forming, spreading habit. A pretty pink version called 'Lancastriense' is also available.

GERBERA
jamesonii
BARBERTON DAISY

Native to the Transvaal in South Africa, but much developed and improved in Holland, this is one of the most decorative of all daisies and is an excellent cut flower. It has orange-red or flame-scarlet flowerheads up to 10 cm (about 4 in) wide, borne singly on long stems in spring and summer from basal rosettes of large, jagged leaves. An evergreen perennial of upright habit, it grows to 60 cm (about 24 in) in height with a spread of 45 cm (about 18 in). Half-hardy, it requires an open, sunny position and a light, fibrous soil with free drainage. Keep somewhat dry during autumn/fall and winter. Fertilize monthly in spring and summer to produce large blooms. Propagate from cuttings of side shoots in summer, from seed in autumn/fall or early spring, or by division from late winter to early spring. Watch for white rust, root rot and wire worms.

GEUM

These evergreen and herbaceous perennials are valued for their long flowering period from late spring until early autumn/fall. Flowering can be prolonged by regular dead-heading, and in frost-free areas they will flower almost continuously all year. They form basal rosettes of hairy, lobed leaves and bear masses of red, orange and yellow, single or double flowers with prominent yellow sta-

Geranium sanguineum

Geranium 'Johnson's Blue'

Gentiana acaulis

Gentiana sino-ornata

Geranium incanum

Gentiana lutea

Gerbera jamesonii

mens. Good plants for mixed herbaceous borders and rock gardens, but require a lot of room to produce a good display. Fully hardy, they prefer a sunny, open position and moist, well-drained soil. Propagate by division or from seed in autumn/fall. Easily transplanted from divisions of older plants during winter or seedlings planted out in spring or autumn/fall.

G. × borisii

A clump-forming perennial with a constant succession of single, bright orange flowers borne on slender, branching stems above irregularly lobed leaves. Low-growing, it reaches a height and spread of 30 cm (about 12 in). A good rock garden plant.

G. 'Mrs Bradshaw'

A taller cultivar with rounded, double, orange-scarlet flowers borne in small sprays. Grows to a height of 60 cm (about 24 in) and spread of 45 cm (about 18 in) and is good for mixed herbaceous borders. Water well during hot weather.

GILIA
capitata
QUEEN ANNE'S THIMBLES

Native to the western mountains of the Americas, this erect, branching annual has mid-green, fern-like leaves and tiny, soft lavender-blue flowers that appear in a pincushion-like mass in summer and early autumn/fall. It is a good cut flower and useful border plant. It grows to a height of 50 cm (about 20 in) and spread of 20 cm (about 8 in). Fully hardy, it prefers a cool climate and requires full sun and a fertile, well-drained soil. Water lightly and regularly. The intensity of flower colour can vary with soil type and situation. Propagate from seed sown outdoors in spring, or under glass in autumn/fall.

GLECHOMA
hederacea
GROUND IVY, RUNAWAY ROBIN

A European native, this evergreen perennial makes a good carpeting ground cover but is very invasive and should be kept away from heavily planted beds. Useful as a container and hanging basket plant. It has heart-shaped leaves and bears small clusters of insignificant mauve-blue trumpet flowers in summer. A pretty variegated cultivar has white marbling on the leaves. It grows to a height of 15 cm (about 6 in) and spreads rapidly. Fully hardy, it can be grown in either sun or shade in a moist, well-drained soil. Propagate by division in spring or autumn/fall, or by softwood cuttings in spring.

Geum × borisii

Gomphrena globosa

Glechoma hederacea

GLOBULARIA
cordifolia
GLOBE DAISY

An evergreen dwarf shrub found in Europe and the Mediterranean, this plant is ideal for sunny rockeries in cool temperate climates. It has creeping woody stems with unusual, tiny, spoon-shaped leaves, and produces solitary stemless round heads of fluffy mauve stamens from late spring until early summer. It forms a dome-shaped hummock, growing to a height of 2–5 cm (about 1–2 in) and gradually spreading to 20 cm (about 8 in). Fully hardy, it requires full sun and well-drained neutral to alkaline soil. Water sparingly. Propagate by division or from seed in autumn/fall, or softwood cuttings in summer.

GOMPHRENA
globosa
GLOBE AMARANTH, BACHELOR'S BUTTONS

This bushy bedding annual from South-East Asia is valued for its papery, pompon-like flowers which

Geum 'Mrs Bradshaw'

Globularia cordifolia

are attractive dried for winter decoration. Cut flowering stems just before blooms are fully open and hang upside down in a cool, well-ventilated place until dry. The plant has oval hairy leaves and produces clover-like flowerheads in shades of pink, purple, yellow, orange or white in summer and early autumn/fall. Of an upright habit, it reaches a height of 30 cm (about 12 in) and spread of 20 cm (about 8 in) and is moderately fast growing. Half-hardy, it prefers a sunny situation and light, well-drained soil. Propagate from seed in spring when danger of frost is passed. The plants benefit from mulching in hot weather.

GYPSOPHILA
BABY'S BREATH

Native to Europe, Asia and North Africa, these annuals and perennials, some of which are semi-evergreen, are grown for their masses of small, dainty, white or pink flowers which make an excellent foil for bolder flowers. They are also a valuable cut

Gilia capitata

flower for use with other flowers or foliage. Plant in full sun with shelter from strong winds. Fully hardy, they will tolerate most soils but do best in deep, well-drained soil that contains some organic matter in the form of compost or peat. They will grow well on limestone soils. Cut back after flowering to encourage a second flush of flowers. Propagate from cuttings of small lateral shoots in summer or from seed in spring or autumn/fall. Transplant when dormant during winter.

Helianthemum nummularium

Gypsophila elegans

Hedychium gardnerianum

Hedychium coronarium

Helenium 'Moerheim Beauty'

G. elegans

Of dainty, erect habit, this bushy annual grows to a height of 60 cm (about 24 in) and spread of 30 cm (about 12 in). It makes delicate, pretty clumps in the garden and bears masses of tiny purplish white flowers in branching heads from summer to early autumn/fall. Leaves are lance-shaped and greyish green.

G. paniculata 'Bristol Fairy'

A short-lived perennial, mostly used as an annual. It has small, dark green leaves and bears sprays of tiny, white, double flowers in spring. An excellent garden plant, it should be resown every 3 weeks for continuous warm weather bloom. Grows 60–75 cm (about 24–30 in) in height with a spread of 1 m (about 3 ft).

HEDYCHIUM
GINGER LILY

Natives of South-East Asia, these semi-tropical perennials with fleshy rhizomes and sweetly scented flowers are ideal for sheltered borders. The large deep-green, paddle-shaped leaves are attractive in summer and die down in winter in cold areas. The showy flowers are short lived but borne profusely. In some species the flowers are followed by capsules with red or orange seeds. Grow in full sun or partial shade and rich, moist soil with a little sand for drainage. Water well in summer. Propagate by division of rhizomes from late winter to spring. Cut down to ground level as soon as flowers have finished and keep barely moist over winter. Ginger lilies are frost-hardy to frost-tender.

H. coronarium
WHITE GINGER LILY

A satiny white-flowered, sweet-scented species that in summer bears dense spikes of butterfly-like flowers with pastel yellow blotches. Leaves are lance-shaped with downy undersides. It has an up-right habit and grows to 1.5 m (about 4½ ft) in height with a spread of up to 1 m (about 3 ft). Frost-tender.

H. gardnerianum
KAHILI GINGER

The best-known and easiest grown species, this plant produces spikes of short-lived, fragrant scarlet and yellow blossoms in late summer and early autumn/fall. Its leaves are greyish green and lance-shaped. It grows to 1.5 m (about 4½ ft) in height with a spread of 75 cm (about 30 in). Frost-tender. This plant is becoming a noxious weed in northern New Zealand.

HELENIUM
'Moerheim Beauty'
SNEEZEWEED

This upright perennial, native to North America, is grown for its sprays of daisy-like, rich orange-red flowers with prominent, chocolate-brown central discs. Flowers are borne in summer and early autumn/fall above dark green foliage. Easily grown, they give a vivid splash of colour to borders and are useful as cut flowers. They are slow growing to a height of 1 m (about 3 ft) and spread of 60 cm (about 24 in). Fully hardy, they enjoy hot summers and

Gypsophila paniculata 'Bristol Fairy'

are best grown in full sun with shelter from strong wind, otherwise staking may be necessary. A rich, moist, well-drained soil is ideal. Dead-head regularly to prolong the flowering period, and propagate by division of old clumps in winter or from seed in spring or autumn/fall.

HELIANTHEMUM
nummularium
SUN ROSE, ROCK ROSE

Native mostly to the Mediterranean countries and North America, these evergreen, sun-loving sub-shrubby perennials are grown in rock gardens or as a ground cover for their brightly coloured flowers and neat, prostrate habit. The double cultivars retain their flowers until the evening, but the petals of the singles drop off in the afternoon. They have attractive foliage, varying from deep to greyish green and in spring are smothered with flowers in shades of red, pink, orange and yellow. They should be lightly cut back as soon as flowers fade to encourage a second flush of bloom in autumn/fall. Fully hardy,

they enjoy a warm sunny position in a freely drained, coarse soil; add a little peat or compost during dry periods. They do not do well in strongly acid soils. Good for cold winter areas and temperate climates. Propagate by semi-ripe cuttings in late summer and autumn/fall.

HELIANTHUS
SUNFLOWER

Native to the Americas, these tall, showy-flowered annuals and perennials are grown for their large daisy-like, golden-yellow blooms, which are on prolonged display from summer to autumn/fall. The plants have coarsely hairy, sticky-feeling leaves, and tall, rough stems which bear mostly yellow flowers with brown or yellow discs. They are effective planted against a dark green background. Fully hardy, they prefer full sun and protection from wind, otherwise staking will be necessary to support the tall stems. Soil should be well-drained. Fertilize in spring to promote large blooms and water deeply in dry conditions. They may become invasive and should be cut down to the base when they finish flowering. Propagate from seed or by division in autumn/fall or early spring. Watch for snails. These flowers were once worshipped by the Incas as living images of their Sun God.

H. annuus

An upright annual, fast growing to a height of 3 m (about 9 ft) or more. Large daisy-like, 30 cm (about 12 in) wide, yellow flowerheads with brown centres are borne in summer. They are coarse, leggy plants with heavily veined, mid-green leaves. The seeds produce a vegetable oil that has economic uses and are also used to feed parrots and poultry.

H. salicifolius

An upright perennial that is valuable for background planting. It grows to 2.2 m (about 6½ ft) in height and bears brilliant yellow, 7.5 cm (about 3 in) wide, single daisy-like flowers on branching stems in late summer or autumn/fall. The rich, dark green shining leaves are willow-like. They look good planted with late-flowering blue asters or salvias.

HELICHRYSUM

EVERLASTING, STRAWFLOWER, PAPER DAISY, IMMORTELLE

This large genus of mainly annuals and short-lived perennials are notable for their papery, daisy flowers, commonly called everlastings. The most spectacular species occur in Australia. They are fully hardy to frost-tender and require a warm, sunny situation and a moderately fertile sandy or gravelly soil with free drainage. The plant adapts to most soils except heavy clay. Water regularly and shelter from strong winds. To use as dried decoration, cut flowers when just open, tie in bundles loosely wrapped in a paper sheath and hang upside-down in a well-ventilated place. Propagate perennials by division, seed or suckers in spring and annuals from seed in spring.

H. bracteatum
STRAWFLOWER, EVERLASTING DAISY

Native to Australia, this annual or short-lived perennial has an upright, branching habit and grows to a height and spread of 75 cm (about 30 in). It has tough, hollow stems, rough narrow leaves and from summer to early autumn/fall bears clusters of daisy-like blooms. Flowers are multi-coloured and have a crackly, papery finish. Half-hardy. 'Dargan Hill Monarch' is the name of the golden-flowered cultivar commonly grown which often lives for two or three years, while the many-coloured garden hybrids raised in Europe (red, pink, white, yellow) are definitely annuals.

H. hookeri

An evergreen shrub with a compact habit, growing to 1 m (about 3 ft) in height with a spread of 60 cm (about 24 in). Clusters of white flowers with greenish yellow bracts are borne in summer. Leaves are tiny and dark green. This species is frost-hardy.

HELICONIA

Beautiful, exotic plants from South America, they have large leaves and spikes of colourful bracts enclosing relatively insignificant flowers. Grow only in a warm, tropical garden with a winter minimum of 18°C (about 64°F). Plant in a humus-rich, well-drained soil in filtered sun and summer humidity. Water well during growing season. To encourage new growth remove all dead leaves and flowers. Propagate by division of rootstock in spring, ensuring there are two shoots on each division.

H. humilis
LOBSTER CLAW

The large, paddle-shaped, green leaves surround a flower stem of pointed, scarlet bracts tipped with green and inconspicuous white flowers. They are popular for flower arrangements.

H. psittacorum
PARROT'S FLOWER

A smaller species good for mass planting, H. psittacorum has long-stalked, lance-like, rich green leaves. Narrow, glossy, orange-red bracts surrounding orange flowers with green tips, are produced in summer.

HELIOPSIS
'Light of Loddon'

Native to North America, this fully hardy, herbaceous perennial puts on a bright display in the summer border. It has rough, hairy leaves and strong stems which carry neatly shaped, bright yellow, double flowers in late summer. The flowers are dahlia-like and are good cut flowers, particularly in large arrangements. The plant grows to a height of 1.2 m (about 3½ ft) and spread of 60 cm (about 24 in). Fully hardy, it requires sun and a moist but well-drained soil. Dead-head regularly to prolong the flower display and cut back to ground level after flowering finishes. Propagate from seed or by division in spring or autumn/fall.

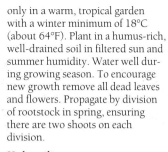
Helianthus salicifolius

Heliconia humilis

Heliconia psittacorum

Helichrysum hookeri

Helichrysum bracteatum

Helianthus annuus

Heliopsis 'Light of Loddon'

Helipterum anthemoides

HELIPTERUM
anthemoides
PAPER DAISY

This perennial, particularly in its forms 'Paper Baby' and 'Paper Cascade', is very popular for rockeries, hanging baskets and dried arrangements. It has thin, wiry stems with small, greyish green leaves. The papery, daisy-like, 2.5 cm (about 1 in) wide flowers are carried throughout the year in most areas. It has a mounding habit and grows to 20 cm (about 8 in) in height with a spread of 30 cm (about 12 in). Near-hardy, it grows best in sun and poor, very well-drained soil. The species may be propagated from seed but the selected forms are propagated from cuttings taken in spring. Dead-head regularly to stimulate flower display and cut back occasionally to maintain dense growth.

HELLEBORUS
LENTEN ROSE

Native to southern Europe and western Asia, these perennials, some of which are evergreen, are useful winter and spring-flowering plants for cooler climates. They bear beautiful, open, cup-shaped flowers in shades of green and purple and are effective planted in drifts or massed in the shade of deciduous trees. Fully to half-hardy, they grow best in semi-shade and a moisture-retentive, well-drained soil that is heavily enriched with organic matter. Never let the plants dry out in summer. Cut off old leaves of deciduous species in early spring just as buds start to appear. A top-dressing of compost

or manure after flowering is beneficial. Propagate from seed or by division in autumn/fall or early spring, and watch for aphids. The plants have poisonous properties.

H. lividus subsp. corsicus
CORSICAN HELLEBORE

This is one of the earliest flowering *Helleborus*, with blooms appearing in late winter and early spring. It is a robust evergreen which produces large clusters of cup-shaped, nodding, 5 cm (about 2 in) wide, green flowers on an upright spike above divided, spiny, dark green foliage. It has a clump-forming habit, growing to a height of 60 cm (about 24 in) and spread of 45 cm (about 18 in). Frost-hardy, the flowers are long-lasting when cut.

H. orientalis

The most easily grown of the genus, this species is evergreen and clump-forming, growing to a height and spread of 45 cm (about 18 in). The large nodding flowers come in a great variety of colours from white, green, pink and rose to purple, sometimes with dark spots. Fully hardy, it flowers in winter or early spring. The dense foliage fades and can be trimmed back before flowering. Good cut flowers.

HEMEROCALLIS
DAYLILY

Native to Europe, eastern Asia and the Orient, these perennials, some of which are semi-evergreen or evergreen, are grown for their showy, often fragrant flowers, which come in a vibrant range of

Hemerocallis fulva

Helleborus lividus subsp. *corsicus*

colours. Individual blooms last only for a day, but they are borne in great numbers on strong stems above tall, grassy foliage and continue flowering from early summer to autumn/fall. Grow in the herbaceous border, among shrubs, or naturalize in grassy woodland areas. Position carefully when planting as the flowers turn their heads towards the sun and the equator. Fully hardy, they prefer sun but will grow well and give brighter colours in part shade. Plant in a reasonably good soil that does not dry out. Propagate by division in autumn/fall or spring and divide clumps every 3 or 4 years. Cultivars raised from seed do not come true to type. Watch for slugs and snails in early spring. Plants may also suffer from aphid or spider mite attack. The botanical name derives from the Greek and means beautiful for a day.

H. fulva

Clump-forming, growing to a height of 1 m (about 3 ft) and spread of 75 cm (about 30 in). It bears rich orange-red, trumpet-shaped, 7.5–12.5 cm (about 3–5 in) wide, flowers from mid to late summer. This plant has been in cultivation for centuries. 'Kwanso Flore Plena' is double-flowered.

H., hybrids

In the last 50 years, plant breeders in the USA, and lately Australia and the UK, have developed a huge range of daylilies. These bloom in late spring and intermittently until autumn/fall, and have flowers 8–15 cm (about 3–6 in) wide on plants ranging in height from 50 cm to 1 m (about 20–36 in) or more. Col-

Hemerocallis hybrid

Helleborus orientalis

Hesperis matronalis

ours vary from cream to brilliant yellow, pale pink to red; many have contrasting shades in the throat. Evergreen types are best suited to mild climates; deciduous to cool areas. Catalogues carry an ever-changing selection.

HESPERIS
matronalis
SWEET ROCKET

This perennial, found mainly in the northern hemisphere, is grown for its flowers which become very fragrant on humid evenings. It has smooth, narrowly oval leaves and branching flowerheads with white to lilac flowers borne in summer. Upright in habit, it grows to 75 cm (about 30 in) in height with a spread of 60 cm (about 24 in). Fully hardy, it prefers a sunny situation and will tolerate poor soil as long as it is well-drained and is not allowed to completely dry out. Plants have a tendency to become woody and are best renewed every few years. Propagate by division or from seed in spring or autumn/fall.

HETEROCENTRON

elegans
syn. *Schizocentron elegans*
SPANISH SHAWL

Native to Central America, this prostrate, evergreen perennial is a well-known ground cover, and is seen at its best when cascading over a bank or wall. It is also suitable for hanging baskets and rock gardens. Foliage is dense, trailing and mid-green, and masses of bright carmine-purple flowers cover the plant in summer. Grows to a height of 5 cm (about 2 in) with an indefinite spread. Frost-tender, it prefers filtered sun or partial shade. A sheltered humid position is best. Soil should be rich and well-drained but kept moist in dry periods. Propagate from softwood cuttings in late winter or early spring.

HEUCHERA
ALUM ROOT, CORAL BELLS

These evergreen perennials, indigenous to North America, are useful cultivated as ground cover or as rock garden or edging plants. They form neat clumps of scalloped leaves, often tinted bronze or purple, from which arise very slender stems bearing masses of dainty, nodding white, crimson or pink bell flowers over a long flowering season. Fully to frost-hardy, they grow well in either full sun or semi-shade, and like a well-drained, coarse, moisture-retentive soil. Propagate species from seed in autumn/fall or by division in spring or autumn/fall; cultivars by division in autumn/fall

or early spring. Remove spent flower stems and divide established clumps every 3 or 4 years.

H. 'Palace Purple'

This species is grown for its striking, purple, heart-shaped foliage and sprays of small white flowers in summer. It is clump forming, growing to a height and spread of 50 cm (about 20 in). The leaves last well for indoor decoration. Fully hardy.

H. sanguinea
CORAL BELLS

This is the most important species, with sprays of scarlet or coral-red flowers over round dark leaves. British and American gardeners have developed strains with a wider colour range—from pale pink to deep red—and slightly larger flowers. Bressingham hybrids are typical.

HIBISCUS
moscheutos
MALLOW ROSE

Native to North America, this herbaceous perennial grows to a height of 2 m (about 6 ft) and spread of 1–1.5 m (about 3–3½ ft). Single, hollyhock-like flowers, 10–20 cm (4–8 in) wide, are carried on robust, unbranched stems in late summer and autumn/fall. Colours vary from white to pink, some with deeper throat markings. Leaves are large, toothed, and softly hairy beneath. Suitable for the back of the herbaceous border and should be protected from strong winds. Frost-hardy, this hibiscus requires full sun and a well-drained, moder-

ately rich soil. Remove spent canes in winter after the wood has died back to ground level. Transplant when dormant during winter. Fertilize in spring to encourage growth and water well during the flowering season. Prune to maintain shape and extend flowering. Propagate from seed or cuttings. Watch for root and collar rot, and for attacks by aphids, the hibiscus beetle, white fly and caterpillars.

HOSTA
PLANTAIN LILY

Natives of Japan and China, these easily grown, fully hardy perennials are valued for their decorative foliage. They all produce wide, handsome leaves, some being marbled or marked with white, others a bluish green. All-yellow foliage is also available. They do well in large pots or planters, are excellent for ground cover, and add an exotic touch planted on the margins of lily ponds or in bog gardens. Tall stems of nodding white, pink or mauve bell flowers appear in warmer weather. Both leaves and flowers are popular for floral arrangements. They prefer shade, and rich, moist, neutral, well-drained soil. Feed regularly during the growing season. Propagate by division in early spring, and guard against snails and slugs.

H. fortunei

This group of clump-forming hybrid perennials has oval to heart-shaped leaves in different colours. 'Aurea Marginata' has mid-green leaves with creamy yellow edges and

tolerates full sun; 'Marginata Alba' has sage green leaves with white margins, grey beneath, good for waterside planting; 'Albopicta', pale green with a creamy yellow centre. All bear racemes of trumpet-shaped violet flowers in summer. They grow to a height of 75 cm–1 m (about 2½–3 ft).

H. lancifolia

A clump-forming plant growing to 50 cm (about 20 in) with a spread of 75 cm (about 30 in). It has narrow, lance-shaped, glossy, mid-green leaves and is one of the smaller leaved species. Racemes of trumpet-shaped pale lilac flowers are borne in late summer and early autumn/fall.

H. sieboldiana

A robust, clump-forming plant growing to a height of 1 m (about 3 ft) and spread of 1.5 m (about 4½ ft). It has large, puckered, heart-shaped bluish grey leaves and bears racemes of trumpet-shaped white flowers in early summer. There are many beautiful variegated cultivars.

Hosta fortunei

Hosta sieboldiana

Heuchera 'Palace Purple'

Heuchera sanguinea

Heterocentron elegans

Hosta lancifolia

Hibiscus moscheutos

Iberis sempervirens

Hypericum calycinum

Iberis umbellata

Hypericum cerastoides

Hunnemannia fumariifolia

Iberis amara

Houttuynia cordata 'Chamaeleon'

HOUTTUYNIA
cordata 'Chamaeleon'
syn. *H.c.* 'Variegata', 'Court Jester', 'Harlequin'

A native of the Himalayas, Indonesia and Japan, this water-loving deciduous perennial makes a good ground cover but may become invasive. It is a vigorous plant, growing to 10 cm (about 4 in) in height with an indefinite spread. It grows from underground runners which send up bright red branched stems bearing aromatic leathery, heart-shaped leaves splashed with yellow and red. Small sprays of white flowers are borne in summer. Fully hardy, it prefers a damp, semi-shaded position and will grow in shallow water at the edge of streams and ponds. Propagate from runners in spring.

HUNNEMANNIA
fumariifolia
MEXICAN TULIP POPPY

One of the best yellow-flowered perennials, this relative of the Californian poppy is usually grown as an annual. It has an upright habit and is fast growing to a height of 60 cm (about 24 in) and spread of 20 cm (about 8 in). It has decorative, oblong, divided, bluish green leaves and bears rich, glowing yellow, single or semi-double, 8 cm (about 3 in) wide, tulip-shaped flowers in summer and early autumn/fall. Half-hardy, it prefers a warm, sunny position and slightly alkaline, well-drained soil. Dead-head plants regularly to prolong flowering and provide support in exposed areas. Water liberally during hot weather. Propagate from seed in spring—the plants do not transplant well so seed should be sown where the plants are to remain.

HYPERICUM

This large genus of perennials and deciduous, semi-evergreen or evergreen sub-shrubs and shrubs are grown for their bright yellow flowers with prominent showy stamens. In a mild temperate climate they provide year-round colour. There are prostrate species excellent for rock gardens and large flowered species striking in garden displays. Larger species need semi-shade and a fertile, not too dry, soil; the smaller types prefer full sun and well-drained soil. Most are frost resistant. Propagate perennials by seed or division in spring or autumn/fall, and sub-shrubs and shrubs by softwood cuttings in summer. Leaves are occasionally attacked by rust and should be sprayed with a fungicide if this occurs. Most species benefit from winter mulching.

H. calycinum
AARON'S BEARD, ROSE OF SHARON

An evergreen or semi-evergreen dwarf shrub with dark green foliage that grows to a height of about 30 cm (about 12 in) with an indefinite spread. It is a good ground cover and bears large yellow flowers, up to 10 cm (about 4 in) wide, from midsummer to mid-autumn/fall. It is frost-hardy, grows in sun or shade, and is ideal for massed planting.

H. cerastoides

A deciduous sub-shrub with dense, oval, grey-green leaves, and terminal clusters of bright yellow, cup-shaped flowers in late spring and early summer. It has an upright, slightly spreading habit and grows to 30 cm (about 12 in) tall with a 50 cm (about 20 in) spread. Fully hardy, it is useful in rock gardens.

IBERIS
CANDYTUFT

These annuals and perennials are mainly from southern Europe, western Asia and the Mediterranean area. They are highly regarded as decorative plants and are excellent for rock gardens, bedding and bordering. Showy flowers are borne in either flattish heads in colours of white, red and purple, or in erect racemes of pure white flowers. They are widely used in floral arrangements. Fully to half-hardy, they require a warm, sunny position and a well-drained, light soil, preferably with added lime or dolomite. Water regularly. Propagate from seed in autumn/fall—they may self-sow but are unlikely to become invasive—or semi-ripe cuttings in summer.

I. amara
CANDYTUFT, HYACINTH-FLOWERED CANDYTUFT

Native to the United Kingdom and Europe, this fast-growing, fully hardy, annual has lance-shaped, mid-green leaves and produces showy, flattish heads of numerous, fragrant, small pure white flowers in early spring and summer. Of an erect, bushy habit, it reaches a height of 30 cm (about 12 in) and spread of 15 cm (about 6 in). Various strains are available. The Hyacinth-flowered Series has flowers in a variety of colours.

I. sempervirens

A low, spreading, evergreen perennial, this species is ideal for rock gardens. It has narrow, dark green leaves and dense, rounded heads of white flowers in spring. It is fully hardy, and grows to a height of 15–30 cm (about 6–12 in) and spread of 50–60 cm (about 20–24 in). The cultivar 'Snowflake' is most attractive. Lightly trim after flowering.

I. umbellata
GLOBE CANDYTUFT

Native to the Mediterranean region, this upright annual has lance-shaped, mid-green leaves and flattish heads of mauve, lilac, pink, purple, carmine or white flowers in late spring and summer. Of a bushy habit, it grows to a height of 15–30 cm (about 6–12 in) and spread of 20 cm (about 8 in). It is fully hardy. A useful cut flower.

IMPATIENS

This large genus of succulent annuals and mainly evergreen perennials are from the subtropics and tropics of Asia and Africa. They are useful for colourful summer bedding displays and for indoor and patio plants. Flowers come in an ever-increasing range of colours. Many hybrid strains are perennial in mild climates but in colder climates are usually grown as annuals. Frost-tender, they will grow in sun or semi-shade, many species doing well under over-hanging trees. They prefer a moist but freely drained soil, and need protection from strong winds. Tip prune the fast-growing shoots to encourage shrubby growth and more abundant flowers. Propagate from seed or stem cuttings in spring or summer. Their botanic name refers to the impatience with which they grow and multiply.

I. balsamina
GARDEN BALSAM

An erect, bushy annual with lance-shaped bright green leaves and small, camellia-like single or double spurred flowers produced in abundance throughout summer and early autumn/fall. Colour range includes blood-red, purple-red, pink, yellow and white, some spotted. It is fairly fast-growing to a height of 30–50 cm (about 12–20 in) and spread of 18–25 cm (about 7½–10 in). It is half-hardy and good for bedding displays in sunny situations.

I., New Guinea hybrids
BUSY LIZZIE

A group of fast-growing perennials that are also grown as annuals in cool climates. The result of extensive hybridizing from a New Guinean species, they are frost-tender and grow to a height and spread of 30–50 cm (about 12–20 in). Leaves are oval, pointed and bronze-green, or they may be variegated with cream, white or yellow. Flowers are flat, spurred, pink, orange, red or cerise, sometimes with white markings. 'Cheers' has coral flowers; 'New Guinea F1 Tango', deep orange; and 'Red Magic', scarlet. They do well in brightly lit positions indoors.

I. sodenii
syn. I. oliveri

This vigorous and profusely flowering, softwooded perennial has whorls of 4 to 10 waxy, oval, pale green leaves with toothed margins. Many white or pale lilac single flowers appear in autumn/fall to winter.

I. wallerana
syn. I. sultanii
BUSY LIZZIE

Native to tropical East Africa, this succulent, evergreen perennial is grown as an annual in cool climates. It has soft, fleshy stems with reddish stripes, oval, fresh green leaves and flattish spurred flowers ranging through crimson, ruby red, pink,

Impatiens balsamina

Incarvillea delavayi

Impatiens sodenii

Impatiens wallerana

Inula oculis-christi

orange, lavender and white, some variegated. There are many cultivars. Half-hardy, fast-growing and bushy to a height and spread of 30–35 cm (about 12–14 in). Flowers from late spring to late autumn/fall. A popular indoor plant and useful for bedding in partial shade. Water well.

INCARVILLEA
delavayi
PRIDE OF CHINA

This fleshy-rooted, clump-forming perennial is useful for rock gardens and borders. It has handsome, fern-like foliage and erect stems bearing 7.5 cm (about 3 in) long, trumpet-shaped, rosy purple flowers in summer. Best suited to cool, temperate climates, the plants grow to a height of 60 cm (about 24 in) and spread of 30 cm (about 12 in), but die down early in autumn/fall. Fully hardy, but should be protected with a compost mulch during cold winters. Grow in a sunny situation in rich, well-drained soil. Propagate from seed or by division of old clumps in spring or autumn/fall.

INULA
oculis-christi
EYE OF CHRIST

This showy, daisy-like perennial has lance-shaped, hairy, mid-green leaves, 8.5 cm (about 3 in) wide, yellow flowerheads, and blooms freely in summer. It is a spreading, fleshy-rooted plant growing to 45 cm (about 18 in) in height with a spread of a little more than that. Fully hardy, it requires a sunny position and fertile, moisture-retentive soil. Propagate from seed or by division of old plants in spring or autumn/fall. The genus is native to Asia, Africa and Europe and has been in cultivation since ancient times.

IRIS
IRIS

This genus of more than 200 species, almost all of which are worth cultivating, is native to the temperate regions of the northern hemisphere. The majority are clump-forming, rhizomatous perennials, although a significant number grow from bulbs (these can be found in

that chapter). The rhizomotous irises are divided into four groups: the bearded irises, sometimes called 'flag irises' and distinguished by the tuft of hairs (the 'beard') on the three lower petals; the beardless irises, which have none; the crested or Evansia irises, which have a raised crest in lieu of a beard and are mostly rather tender in cold climates; and the very rare and beautiful Oncocyclus irises, allied to the bearded types. These last are native to the eastern Mediterranean and need cold winters and hot, dry summers to flourish; the pale grey *I. susiana* is the most likely to be seen in specialist catalogues. All the rhizomatous irises have sword-shaped leaves, sometimes evergreen. As a rule they are cold hardy and prefer sun: some of the beardless types like very moist soil. All are easily grown and are propagated by division in late summer after flowering. There are many hybrids in all divisions, and the selection is constantly being updated. The varieties illustrated are simply indicative of the range available.

A Field Trip to the Guadalupe Mountains National Park

The prairie country of the USA is home to a host of wild-flowers, a number of which have found their way into gardens all over the world. Although the prairies are large, relatively flat expanses of many different grasses, extensive stands of one or a few wildflower species can sometimes occur, creating a wildflower lover's delight.

Driving along any of the major highways in Texas from March through to May, particularly following a season of good rainfall, you are likely to be greeted with a kaleidoscope of wildflowers.

Although the prairie country consists mainly of vast flat regions, you are always close to mountains, and the adventurous wildflower lover can move between different elevations to extend the viewing range, as the delayed spring of higher altitudes causes the lowland species to flower later.

One of the most distinctive of these prairie wildflowers is the daisy, Indian blanket (*Gaillardia pulchella*), with its bright, almost gaudy, colour scheme. Native to a wide area of the southern and central USA—from Arizona to Texas, north to Colorado and Nebraska and south into Mexico—it is found

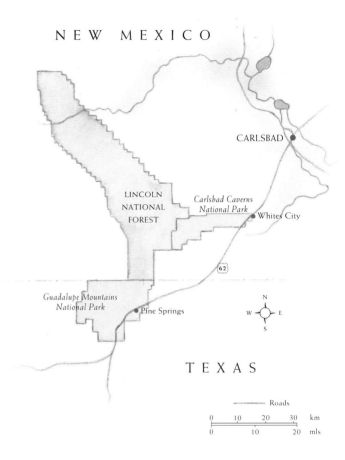

A huge drift of Indian blanket creates a colourful expanse.

mainly on the sandy prairies and in the desert regions. Its scientific name, *Gaillardia pulchella*, which incorporates the name of Gailard de Charentoneau, a French patron of botany, and the Latin word for 'pretty', hardly conveys the vividness of its floral display. Its common name, Indian blanket, more appropriately describes its habit, after a good rainfall season, of spreading over wide areas of the prairie in a series of flamboyant patterns.

One of the best places to view *G. pulchella* is in the Guadalupe Mountains National Park, on the border between New Mexico and Texas. Travelling east from El Paso, take Route 62 for approximately 160 km (about 100 miles) until you reach the town of Pine Springs, just inside the park. From here, drive in a north-easterly direction, skirting the southern side of the park through the foothills of the Guadalupe Mountains and up to the border with New Mexico, which forms the park's northern boundary. Among these foothills, you will see that the Indian blanket is well-adapted to colonizing roadside verges, making it easy to find. At first you will see the odd flash of colour on a roadside bank and then, if you are lucky, a large expanse of pure Indian blanket will appear over a meadow or a disturbed area of soil. It is worth stopping at these spots to explore the subtle variations in size and colour of each population. These areas usually run into larger expanses of wildflowers further from the roadside—walking through these is a memorable experience.

The prairies often produce spectacular fields of wildflower mixtures and you may find the adaptable *G. pulchella* near other equally appealing flowers, such as the delicate white Queen Anne's lace (*Daucus carota*) and the strikingly blue Texas bluebonnet (*Lupinus texensis*).

The Indian blanket can grow on high plains to 1000 m (about 3300 ft) above sea level, where there are dramatic fluctuations between day and night temperatures, and is adaptable enough to grow in conditions ranging from desert to humid coastal areas. Being a prairie species, the Indian blanket needs full sun and room to spread. It is best suited to porous, well-drained soils which mimic those found in its natural habitat.

A fascinating aspect of the Indian blanket is the natural variation it shows when it is grown from seed. A wonderful range of colours is obtained with interesting zigzag patterns on the florets. It is frequently grown as an annual, and seed should be sown in autumn/fall. Alternatively, it can be easily propagated from soft-tip cuttings which, if renewed every six months or so, can produce flowers all year round. The Indian blanket itself can form a sprawling specimen up to 80 cm (about 32 in) if not kept in check by tip pruning. The flowers are, of course, its most outstanding feature, the individual heads being 4–6 cm (about 1.5–2.5 in) wide, with bristly scales found among the florets. The leaves are a pleasing greygreen, approximately 7 cm (about 3 in) in length, often with toothed margins.

The Indian blanket is a star attraction of the prairie wildflower country. Whether you wish to appreciate its ephemeral charm in the wild or cultivate it in your own garden, *G. pulchella* will always reward the you with both its adaptability and inspirational colouring.

Gaillardia pulchella

Gaillardia

Gaillardia is a genus of about 28 species of annuals and perennials in the daisy (Asteraceae) family, within which it falls into the sunflower tribe (Heliantheae). *Gaillardia* is centred in the USA and Mexico, with three of its species also being found in South America. Only two species are generally known in gardens, the yellow-flowered perennial *G. aristata* and the bicoloured annual Indian blanket, *G. pulchella*. Both have been selected over a hundred years for their size and for the colouring of the flowers. A range of hybrids has arisen between them, the earliest of which were believed to have appeared spontaneously. The results of deliberate breeding for new strains are known collectively as *G. × grandiflora*.

The most distinctive feature of *Gaillardia* is the circle of 'petals' (the ray-florets), which are wedge-shaped and toothed at the apex. These contrast in colour with the prominent dark centre of the flowerhead. Cultivated gaillardias are among the hardiest of garden flowers, tolerating extreme heat as well as cold and dryness, strong winds and poor soils.

Daisies form one of the largest flowering plant families with some 25 000 species in 1100 genera, including *Coreopsis*, *Cosmos*, *Rudbeckia* and *Echinacea*.

Gaillardia pulchella

Iris Pacific Coast hybrids

Iris Louisiana hybrid

Iris pallida 'Variegata'

Iris japonica

Iris ochroleuca

Iris ensata

Iris bearded hybrid

I. bearded hybrids

Often classed under *I. germanica*, which is only one of their ancestral species, the bearded irises are among the most beautiful and widely grown of late-spring flowers. Their sword-shaped, greyish foliage is handsome in its own right and the flower stems bear several flowers. They are available in an enormous range of colours—everything but true red—with many varieties featuring blended colours, contrasting 'standards' and falls, or a broad band of colour around basically white flowers (this pattern is called 'plicata'). They are divided into three groups: the dwarfs which grow to 15–20 cm (about 6–8 in) tall and flower earlier than the others; the intermediates which are usually about 1.5 m (about 4å ft) tall and flower a fortnight or so later; and the tall bearded irises, last to bloom and growing 1 m (about 3 ft) tall or slightly higher. These are the most popular, and new introductions are available every year from breeders in the United States, the United Kingdom, and Australia and New Zealand. Some of the newer varieties, described as 'remontant', flower a second time in late summer or autumn, though rather erratically. All prefer a temperate climate, sun, and milky alkaline, well-drained soil, and flower most freely where they are not over-watered in summer.

I. ensata
syn. *I. kaempferi*
JAPANESE IRIS, HIGO IRIS

Native to Japan and cultivated there for centuries, the beardless *I. ensata* grows to a height of 1 m (about 3 ft) and bears purple flowers with yellow blotches in late spring. The many named garden varieties bear huge flowers, sometimes as much as 25 cm (about 10 in) wide, in shades of white, lavender, blue and purple, often blending two shades. The foliage dies down for the winter. The plants prefer rich, acid soil and plenty of moisture, even growing happily in shallow water, provided they are not submerged in winter. The similar but slightly smaller flowered *I. laevigata* can grow in water all year. Both feature in Japanese paintings.

I. japonica
syn. *I. fimbriata*
CRESTED IRIS

This 50 cm (about 20 in) tall species from Japan is the best known of the crested species. It forms large clumps of almost evergreen, mid-green leaves and bears sprays of many 7 cm (about 2½ in) wide, exquisitely ruffled, pale blue or white flowers in late winter and spring. It likes acid soil and a lightly shaded spot, and prefers a more or less frost-free climate. There is a variety with white-striped leaves, although this is rather shy flowering.

I. Louisiana hybrids

Mainly derived from *I. louisiana* and its allied species from the United States, these beardless irises are evergreen and bear flat, often ruffled flowers. In late spring several flowers appear together on stems which are usually a little over 1 m (about 3 ft). They come in a very wide range of colours—white, cream, yellow, blue, mauve, magenta and purple. They prefer sun and very moist soil and will grow permanently in shallow water at the edge of a pond. The flowers are excellent for cutting.

I. ochroleuca
SWAMP IRIS

This 1.2 m (about 3½ ft) tall, almost evergreen beardless iris from western Asia has mid-green leaves and produces white and yellow flowers in early summer. There is an all yellow variety called *monnieri*. Although they will grow in damp ground, they are perfectly happy in any rich, well-watered garden soil and sun.

I. Pacific Coast hybrids

These almost evergreen, beardless irises are mainly derived from *I. innominata, I. douglasiana* and other species native to the west coast of the United States. In late spring they bear 8 cm (about 3 in) wide flowers, usually beautifully marked and veined in a wide range of colours—cream, yellow, blue, mauve and bronze. They prefer acid soil and sun or light shade, and have the reputation of being difficult to transplant. Once a clump is established, leave it undisturbed. Water freely while the plants are growing, less generously in winter. Foliage is narrow and dark green.

I. pallida 'Variegata'

This splendid bearded iris from the Middle East features handsome leaves which are striped in grey-green and cream. Its pale blue, lightly scented flowers are borne on 1.2 m (about 3½ ft) high stems in late spring. Cultivation is the same as for the bearded irises.

I. pseudacorus

WATER FLAG

A beardless iris from Europe, the water flag has handsome, mid-green leaves and profuse bright yellow flowers in late spring. There is also a form with variegated leaves. Both prefer to grow in shallow water and rich soil, and are delightful, easily grown plants for a garden pond.

I. spuria hybrids

While *I. spuria, I. sibirica* and their allied species, mainly from eastern Europe and western Asia, are beautiful plants in their own right, they have been much hybridized. The more common hybrids bear many flowers on 1.2 m (about 3½ ft) high stems in early summer. The colours are mainly in the white to blue range. All prefer sun, rich soil, and lavish watering while they are growing and flowering.

I. unguicularis

syn. I. stylosa

WINTER IRIS, ALGERIAN IRIS

This evergreen, beardless species from north Africa is valued for its habit of bearing its scented flowers from autumn to spring. Whenever the weather is mild they are lovely for cutting and will last 3 or 4 days if cut in bud. The typical form is pale blue but there are also white and darker blue varieties available. Although frost-hardy, all flower best in a warm, sunny position where they don't get too much summer sun, and in slightly alkaline soil. The flowers on their 20 cm (about 8 in) stems will be more conspicuous if the luxuriant foliage is cut back in late autumn. They are much loved by snails and precautions must be taken.

KAEMPFERIA

rotunda

ORIENTAL CROCUS

This member of the ginger family belongs to a large genus native to tropical Africa and tropical Asia. A delightful cluster of stemless flowers appears before the patterned foliage. The delicate purple and white flow-

ers are scented. The rhizomes should be planted in a rich, moist soil in partial shade; they need a lot of water through summer, but like to dry out when dormant. The plant is very sensitive to frost, so grow in a greenhouse in cool areas. It does best in subtropical conditions. Propagate by division in spring. The roots of some species of *Kaempferia* are used as spices and the Swazis have used the rhizomes as a treatment for malaria.

KNIPHOFIA

RED-HOT POKER, TORCH LILY, TRITOMA

Native to southern Africa, these stately perennials, some of which are evergreen, can be relied upon to make a brilliant display in the garden for a long time. They are upright, tufted plants with long, grass-like foliage and tall bare stems carrying showy, brightly coloured, tubular flowers in dense racemes. Fully to half-hardy, they require an open position in full sun and a well-drained soil with plenty of water in summer. They tolerate wind well and are often seen growing close to the coast. From spring on, fertilize monthly to increase size and quality of blooms. Remove dead flower stems and leaves in late autumn/fall. They are excellent cut flowers, looking very good when combined with agapanthus. Propagate species from seed or by division in spring; cultivars by division in spring. Attractive to bellbirds, tuis and other nectar-feeding birds.

K. ensifolia

WINTER POKER

This frost-hardy evergreen perennial forms a dense clump, growing to 1.5 m (about 4å ft) in height with a spread of 60 cm (about 24 in). It has slender, sword-shaped, mid-green leaves and bears torches of prolific, lemon-yellow flowers in late autumn/fall and winter.

K. 'Maid of Orleans'

This summer-flowering cultivar has dense racemes of yellow buds that open into creamy white flowers. It is frost-hardy and grows to a height of

Iris pseudacorus

Kaempferia rotunda

1.3 m (about 4 ft). Basal, strap-shaped leaves spread to 45 cm (about 18 in).

K. praecox

RED-HOT POKER

This South African perennial is the most common species in the wild and reaches up to 1.5 m (about 4½ ft) tall when in bloom. It has distinctive slender leaves up to 60 cm (about 25 in) long, heavily keeled and serrated. Vivid red or yellow flowers appear in early summer. It is able to survive long dry periods and enjoys full sun.

K. uvaria

A tall perennial with large, strap-shaped, strongly channelled leaves and dense racemes of tubular scarlet flowers that become orange-yellow with age. Flowers in late summer and autumn/fall and grows to a height of 1.2 m (about 3½ ft) with a spread of 50 cm (about 20 in). It is fully hardy.

Iris spuria hybrid

Kniphofia uvaria

Kniphofia ensifolia

Kniphofia praecox

Iris unguicularis

Kniphofia 'Maid of Orleans'

Lavatera trimestris

Lamium maculatum

Lathyrus odoratus

Leucocanthemum maximum

Leonotis leonurus

Kochia scoparia f. trychophylla

KOCHIA
scoparia f. trychophylla
SUMMER CYPRESS, BURNING BUSH

This very bushy annual, native to southern Europe, is grown for its narrow, lance-shaped, 5–8 cm (about 2–3 in) long, soft, light green leaves that turn a brilliant reddish brown in autumn/fall. The flowers are dull and inconspicuous. It is useful for bedding and for pot plants. Moderately fast-growing, it reaches a height of 90 cm (about 36 in) and spread of 60 cm (about 24 in). It is half-hardy and prefers an open, sun-exposed position, warm and sheltered from harsh winds—provide support in very windy areas. Soil should be moderately fertile and well-drained. Tip-prune young plants to encourage denser growth. Propagate from seed in spring.

LAMIUM
maculatum
DEAD NETTLE

A semi-evergreen perennial, native to Europe and the Middle East, where they are often treated as weeds, this plant is a popular flowering ground cover. It has mauve-tinged, deeply toothed leaves with central silvery stripes and carries clusters of pinkish flowers in spring and summer. Mat-forming, it grows to a height of 25 cm (about 10 in) with a spread of 1 m (about 3 ft). It can be invasive. Fully hardy, the plants prefer full or partial shade and a moist, well-drained soil. Propagate by division of the root mass in autumn/fall or early spring. There are several cultivars.

LATHYRUS
odoratus
SWEET PEA

Native to Italy but much 'improved' by gardeners, this vigorous, climbing annual is grown for its abundant and sweetly scented flowers. Flowers 5 cm (about 2 in) wide and in colours of white, cream, pink, blue, mauve, lavender, maroon and scarlet bloom, several to the stem, from late winter to early summer. It is an excellent cut flower. The plant has oval, mid-green leaves with compound tendrils and grows to 2 m (about 6 ft) in height. There are dwarf non-climbing cultivars available, suitable for bedding. Fully hardy, the climbers will need a good support such as wire netting or lattice, and are ideal for covering sunny walls or fences. They should be grown in full sun and a deep, well-fertilized soil with plenty of lime. Water regularly. Propagate in autumn/fall from seed, which should be soaked for an hour or two before planting.

LAVATERA
trimestris
ANNUAL MALLOW

This shrubby annual, native to the Mediterranean, is grown mainly for its silken, trumpet-shaped, brilliant white or pink flowers that closely resemble a hibiscus. Flowers are 8 cm (about 3 in) wide and appear from summer to early autumn/fall. They are short-lived but are borne in profusion, benefiting from regular dead-heading. Leaves are oval, lobed and mid-green. It has an erect, branching habit and is moderately fast-growing to a height of 60 cm (about 24 in) and spread of 50 cm (about 20 in). Fully hardy, mallows are best in temperate climates and require a sunny position and well-drained soil. Propagate from seed in spring or early autumn/fall. L. trimestris 'Silver Cup' has lovely dark pink flowers.

LEONOTIS
leonurus
LION'S EAR, WILD DAGGA

Native to Africa, this semi-evergreen shrubby perennial is popular in all temperate climates. A striking plant, growing to 2 m (about 6 ft), it bears tall stems with whorls of tawny orange, furry, tubular flowers in late summer and autumn/fall. Leaves are lance-shaped and aromatic. It requires a sunny position and rich well-drained soil. Do not over water. These plants are fairly drought resistant and do well in coastal situations. They are half-hardy, and if damaged by frost will usually come into new growth in spring. Propagate from seed in spring or greenwood cuttings in early summer, and cut back to 15 cm (about 6 in) above ground level in early spring. There is a white variety.

LEUCOCANTHEMUM
maximum
syn. *Chrysanthemum maximum*
SHASTA DAISY

This robust perennial grows to a height and spread of 1 m (about 3 ft). It has large, daisy-like white flowerheads with golden centres. The flowers are carried high over the dark, shiny, toothed leaves in summer. Cultivars are always white but there are many single and double flowers, some with fringed petals. Divide and replant every 2 years.

LIATRIS
spicata
syn. *L. callilepis*
GAY FEATHER, BLAZING STAR

This low-growing perennial from the USA is a desirable cut flower and a good butterfly and bee-attracting plant. The flowers are lilac-purple and are produced in crowded, fluffy spikes—like a feather duster—in late summer. They open from the top downwards, the opposite of most flowering spikes. The species has thickened, corm-like rootstocks and basal tufts of grassy, mid-green foliage. Clump-forming, it grows to a height of 60 cm (about 24 in) with a spread of 30 cm (about 12 in). The plants require a sunny situation and well-drained light soil of reasonable quality. They are fully hardy but do not like high humidity. Propagate by division in early spring or from seed in spring or autumn/fall. Transplant when dormant during winter.

LIBERTIA
grandiflora
NEW ZEALAND IRIS

An easily grown, rhizomatous perennial, native to New Zealand and valued for its foliage, decorative seed pods and flowers. It has grass-like, brown-tipped, dark green leaves. In early summer it produces tall, wiry, lightly branched flower stems with dainty white flowers, followed in autumn/fall by golden brown seed capsules. Loosely clump-forming, it grows to a height of 75 cm (about 30 in) and spread of 60 cm (about 24 in). Frost-hardy, it requires a sheltered, sunny or partially shaded position and well-drained, peaty soil with plenty of moisture in spring and summer. Propagate by division in spring or from seed in spring or autumn/fall. They naturalize freely.

LIGULARIA

Originally from the temperate regions of Europe and Asia, these perennials produce large, daisy-like flowers in summer. Some species grow up to 2.5 m (about 7½ ft) and 1 m (about 3 ft) wide. Fully hardy to half-hardy, they prefer a moist, well-drained soil and will grow in either sun or semi-shade. Propagate by division in spring or from seed in spring or autumn/fall. Prone to attack by slugs and snails.

L. dentata 'Desdemona'
syn. *Senecio clivorum* **'Desdemona'**

A compact perennial, grown for its striking foliage and showy heads of daisy flowers. It has kidney-shaped, long-stalked, leathery, brownish green leaves and bears clusters of large, 7.5 cm (about 3 in) wide, orange-yellow flowerheads on long branching stems in summer. Clump-forming, it grows to a height of 1.2 m (about 4 ft) and spread of 60 cm (about 24 in). Fully hardy, this species will grow happily at the edge of ponds.

L. tussilaginea 'Aureomaculata'
LEOPARD PLANT

This herbaceous perennial is grown for its foliage and flowers. It has variegated gold and white leaves with clusters of daisy-like flowers arising from branched stems in late summer. This species grows to a height and spread of 60 cm (about 24 in). A frost-tolerant plant ideal for a damp, shady area although it will also grow in the sun. Plant in damp fertile soil. Cut stems down to the base in autumn/fall.

LIMONIUM
STATICE, SEA LAVENDER

These sub-shrubs and perennials, sometimes grown as annuals, are popular for their papery, many coloured flowers, which can be cut and dried for decoration. Flowers should be cut just as they open and hung upside down to dry in a cool, airy place. They are good mixed border plants and are easily grown in full sun and well-drained, sandy soil. Their tolerance to seaspray and low rainfall make them a good choice for seaside and low maintenance holiday house gardens. Plants will benefit from light fertilizing in spring while flowerheads are developing. Propagate by division in spring, from seed in early spring or autumn/fall, or from root cuttings in late winter. Transplant during winter or early spring.

L. latifolium

A fully hardy, tall-stemmed perennial bearing clusters of lavender-blue or bluish white flowers for a long period over summer. Clump-forming, it grows to a height of 30 cm (about 12 in) and spread of 45 cm (about 18 in), with large leaves. The dried flower stems have a delicate, misty appearance.

L. sinuatum

This statice is a bushy, upright perennial, almost always grown as an annual. It produces dense rosettes of oblong, deeply-waved, dark green leaves and bears masses of tiny blue, pink or white papery flowers on winged stems. Flowers in summer and early autumn/fall. It is fairly slow-growing to a height of 50 cm (about 20 in) and spread of 30 cm (about 12 in).

Liatris spicata

Libertia grandiflora

Limonium latifolium

Limonium sinuatum

Ligularia dentata 'Desdemona'

Ligularia tussilaginea 'Aureomaculata'

LINARIA

maroccana 'Fairy Bouquet'

TOADFLAX

Native to Morocco, this fast-growing, bushy annual is a useful bedding plant, giving a long and colourful display of flowers in spring. It bears sprays of small, snapdragon-like flowers in colours of gold, pink, mauve, apricot, cream, purple and yellow. It has lance-shaped, pale green leaves, and grows to a height of 10–15 cm (about 4–6 in) and spread of 10 cm (about 4 in). Fully hardy, it prefers sun or light shade and a well-drained, neutral soil. Water well in early stages of growth. Propagate from seed in spring or autumn/fall. It self-seeds freely. Cut back hard after the first flush to encourage plants to flower again.

LINDHEIMERA

texana

STAR DAISY

This fully hardy annual is grown for its dainty daisy-like, yellow flowers, borne in late summer and early autumn/fall. It is moderately fast-growing with hairy stems and oval, serrated, hairy fresh-green leaves. Of an erect, branching habit, it grows from 30–60 cm (about 12–24 in) in height with a spread of 30 cm (about 12 in). Plant in a sunny situation in fertile, well-drained soil, and propagate from seed in early spring.

LINUM

FLAX

These annuals, biennials, perennials, sub-shrubs and shrubs, some of which are evergreen, are distributed widely in temperate regions. They are grown for their profusely blooming flowers. The plants are useful in a rock garden or border. They are fully to half-hardy; some species need shelter in cool climates. Grow in a sunny spot in humus-rich, well-drained, peaty soil. Prune the perennial species back hard after flowering. Propagate the annuals, biennials and perennials from seed in autumn/fall and perennials by divi-sion in spring or autumn/fall. Most self-sow readily. Transplant from late autumn/fall until early spring.

L. grandiflorum 'Rubrum'

SCARLET FLAX

Native to Algeria, this annual has small, rounded, flattish, deep red flowers and lance-shaped, grey-green leaves. Flowers best in cool summers. The flowering period is short but can be extended by sowing seed at monthly intervals. It has a slim, erect habit and is fairly fast-growing to a height of 50 cm (about 20 in) and spread of 15 cm (about 6 in). It is fully hardy.

L. perenne

syn. *L. sibiricum*

A vigorous, upright perennial, forming a shapely bushy plant 30 cm (about 12 in) high with a spread of 15 cm (about 6 in). It has slender stems with grass-like leaves and clusters of open, funnel-shaped light blue flowers are borne throughout summer. A pure white cultivar, 'Alba', is also available. It is fully hardy.

LIRIOPE

spicata

MONDO GRASS

This clumping, rhizomatous evergreen perennial—one of 5 species of a genus native to Vietnam, Japan and China—is a useful ground cover and edging plant. It has grass-like, shining, dark green leaves (*L. s.* 'Variegata' has variegated leaves), and bears erect spikes of rounded, bell-shaped, pale lavender flowers in late summer. Grows to a height of 25 cm (about 10 in) with a spread nearly double that. Fully hardy, it will grow in sun but prefers shade and well-drained, moderately fertile soil. Foliage should be cut back hard in late winter when it becomes ragged. Propagate by division in early spring or from seed in autumn/fall.

LOBELIA

This large genus of annuals and perennials is widely distributed in temperate regions, particularly America and Africa. Growth habits vary from low bedding plants to tall herbaceous perennials. They are all grown for their ornamental flowers and neat foliage and make excellent edging, flower box, hanging basket and rock garden specimens. Some are suitable in wild gardens or by the waterside. They are best grown in a well-drained, moist, light loam enriched with animal manure or compost. Most grow in sun or semi-shade but resent wet conditions in winter. Prune after the first flush of flowers to encourage repeat flowering, and fertilize weekly with a liquid manure during the season. Fully hardy to frost-tender. Propagate annuals from seed in spring, perennial species from seed or by division in spring or autumn/fall and perennial cultivars by division only. Transplant from late autumn/fall until early spring.

L. cardinalis

CARDINAL FLOWER

A clump-forming perennial, useful for growing in wet places and beside streams and ponds. From late summer to mid-autumn/fall it produces spikes of brilliant scarlet-red

Linum perenne

Linaria maroccana 'Fairy Bouquet'

Lindheimera texana

Lobelia cardinalis

Liriope spicata 'Variegata'

Linum grandiflorum 'Rubrum'

Lobelia erinus 'Cambridge Blue'

flowers on branching stems above green or deep bronzy purple foliage. Grows to a height of 1 m (about 3 ft) and spread of 30 cm (about 12 in). It requires moist soil and semi-shade and is half-hardy. 'Queen Victoria' is a well-known cultivar.

L. erinus 'Cambridge Blue'
EDGING LOBELIA

This slow-growing compact annual is native to South Africa. It has a tufted, sometimes semi-trailing, habit with dense oval to lance-shaped leaves. It bears small, 2-lipped blue flowers continuously through spring, summer and early autumn/fall. Grows to a height of 10–20 cm (about 4–8 in) and spread of 10–15 cm (about 4–6 in), and is half-hardy. Water sparingly and feed regularly. Excellent for edging, rockeries, pots and hanging baskets.

L. 'Vedrariensis'

A clump-forming perennial that is an excellent border plant, growing to a height of 1 m (about 3 ft) and spread of 30 cm (about 12 in). It produces racemes of 2-lipped violet-blue flowers in late summer. Leaves are dark green and lance-shaped. Frost-hardy, it prefers full sun, but should not be allowed to get too dry.

LOBULARIA
maritima
syn. *Alyssum maritimum*
SWEET ALYSSUM, SWEET ALICE

Native to southern Europe and western Asia, this fast-growing, spreading annual is a widely popular edging, rock garden or window box plant. It produces masses of tiny, honey-scented, 4-petalled white flowers over a long season from spring to early autumn/fall. Lilac, pink and violet shades are also available. It has a low, rounded compact habit with lance-shaped greyish green leaves and grows to a height of 8–15 cm (about 3–6 in), and a spread of 20–30 cm (about 8–12 in). Fully hardy, it grows best in a dryish position in full sun and likes a fertile, well-drained soil. Good for coastal and beach situations. Shear back after flowering to encourage continuous flowering. Propagate from seed in spring.

Lobularia maritima

LOTUS
berthelotii
CORAL GEM

Native to the Cape Verde and Canary Islands, this semi-evergreen, trailing perennial is suitable for hanging baskets, ground cover or spilling over rockeries, banks or the tops of walls. It has hairy, silvery branches of fine needle leaves and clusters of pea-like scarlet flowers cover the plant in spring and early summer. Grows to 30 cm (about 12 in) tall with an indefinite spread. It requires a fairly sunny situation and well-drained coarse soil, preferably with a little added peat or other organic matter. Frost-tender, it suits warm coastal gardens. Tip-prune young shoots to encourage dense foliage. Propagate from cuttings taken in summer or from seed in spring or autumn/fall.

LUNARIA
annua
syn. *L. biennis*
HONESTY

A fast-growing biennial, native to southern Europe and the Mediterranean coast, this plant is grown for its attractive flowers and curious fruits. It has pointed oval, serrated, bright green leaves, and bears heads of scented, four-petalled rosy magenta, white or violet-purple flowers in spring and early summer. These are followed by circular seed pods with a silvery, translucent membrane, which are used in dried floral arrangements. Erect in habit, it grows to a height of 75 cm (about 30 in) and spread of 30 cm (about 12 in). Fully hardy, it will grow in either

Lobelia 'Vedrariensis'

sun or shade, but prefers partial shade and a moderately fertile, well-drained soil. Propagate from seed in spring or autumn/fall. This plant self-sows readily in most climates.

LUPINUS
LUPIN

A large genus of annuals and perennials mainly native to North America and southern Europe, grown for their ease of culture, rapid growth and large spikes of showy pea flowers in a range of colours including blue, purple, pink, white, yellow, orange and red. They are useful grouped with bearded irises in bedding schemes and are good naturalized. Grow in cool climates in an open, sunny position and a well-drained alkaline soil. They enjoy high humidity and should be mulched in dry areas. Spent flowers should be cut away to prolong plant life and to prevent self-seeding. Fully to frost-hardy. Propagate species from seed in autumn/fall and selected forms from cuttings in early spring. Watch for

Lotus berthelotii

Lupinus hartwegii

Lunaria annua

slugs and snails. The foliage adds nitrogen to the soil when dug in.

L. hartwegii
HAIRY-FOLIAGED LUPIN

Native to Mexico, this annual has compact, erect growth to 70 cm (about 28 in) high with a spread of 40 cm (about 16 in). It has hairy, palmate, dark green leaves, and slender spikes of pea flowers in shades of blue, white or pink are borne abundantly in late winter, spring and early summer. Fast-growing.

L., Russell hybrids

This fine strain of strong-growing perennial lupins bear long spikes of large brilliant, strongly coloured flowers (in shades of cream, pink, orange, blue or violet), some of which are bicoloured, in late spring and summer. They produce a magnificent clump of handsome, deeply divided, mid-green leaves, growing to a height of 90 cm (about 3 ft) with a spread of half that. There are also dwarf strains, such as the 60 cm (24 in) high 'Lulu'. Cut back flowering stems to ground level in late autumn/fall and divide and replant clumps between autumn/fall and early spring every two or three years.

L. texensis
TEXAS BLUE BONNET

A fast-growing, bushy annual reaching a height of 30 cm (about 12 in) and spread of 20 cm (about 8 in), this species has bright green palmate leaves and bears dark blue and white flowers in late spring. Easily grown, it thrives in poor soils, and is quick to flower from seed. This is the state flower of Texas.

LYCHNIS

Native to the temperate regions of the northern hemisphere, these annuals, biennials and perennials are grown for their attractive summer flowers, borne in cymes in white through to reds and magenta. They are fully hardy, and easily grown in cool, elevated places, preferably on sunny sites with an easterly or southerly slope to minimize soil temperatures. They grow in any well-drained soil and an annual feeding in late winter to early spring is beneficial. Remove spent stems after flowering and dead-head frequently to prolong the flowering period. Propagate by division or from seed in autumn/fall or early spring. They self-seed readily. These plants have been cultivated for many centuries.

L. coronaria
ROSE CAMPION

A clump-forming perennial, sometimes grown as a biennial, this plant grows to a height of 60 cm (about 24 in) and a spread of 45 cm (about 18 in). It forms a dense clump of silvery, white, woolly leaves, and branched grey stems carry bright scarlet flowers throughout summer. Fully hardy, it thrives in most areas and self-sows readily. 'Alba' is a white-flowered cultivar. In ancient times the flowers were used for garlands and crowns.

L. × haagena
MALTESE CROSS

A short-lived, clump-forming perennial, growing to a height of 45 cm (about 18 in) with a spread of 30 cm (about 12 in). In summer it bears clusters of large, 5-petalled white, salmon, flame and scarlet flowers. Foliage is mid-green. It is weak-growing and should be regularly propagated from seed.

LYSICHITON
camtschatcensis
SKUNK CABBAGE

Native to Siberia and northern Japan, this deciduous perennial is a marsh plant, useful for planting in damp, boggy soils and on pond edges. It has handsome, arum-like, pure white spathes surrounding spikes of small insignificant flowers. These are borne in spring and are followed by tufts of bold, bright green foliage, arising from a creeping rhizome. Grows to a height of 75 cm (about 30 in) and spread of 60 cm (about 24 in). Fully hardy, it prefers full sun but will tolerate semi-shade. They require a cold and frosty winter climate and are happy growing in both running and still water. Propagate from seed in late summer.

LYSIMACHIA
punctata
GARDEN LOOSESTRIFE, GOLDEN LOOSESTRIFE

A clump-forming perennial seen at its best planted in bold drifts or groups. It has mid-green leaves and lightly branched stems that in summer carry a great massed display of brilliant yellow, starry flowers, produced in whorls near the top of the stem. They are suitable for bedding, rock gardens or beside pools and streams. It grows erect to a height and spread of around 70 cm (around 28 in). Fully hardy, it prefers a sunny situation and moist but well-drained soil. Propagate by division in autumn/fall, winter or early spring, or from seed in autumn/fall. Its common name is derived from 'louse-strife', as the plant was grown to repel lice.

MACLEAYA
cordata
syn. *Bocconia cordata*
PLUME POPPY

Native to China and Japan, this tall perennial grows to 1.5 m (nearly 5 ft) or more. It belongs to the Papaveraceae family, which includes poppies. It has large, rounded, deeply veined, heart-shaped grey-green leaves, and bears large, feathery, terminal flower spikes of cream tinted with pink in summer. An evergreen, it is one of the most attractive foliage plants available for the herbaceous border. Fully hardy, it requires

Lysichiton camtschatcensis

Lychnis coronaria

Lychnis × haagena

Lysimachia punctata

Lupinus, Russell hybrids

Lupinus texensis

Macleaya cordata

Matthiola incana

a sunny, sheltered situation and well-drained soil, and prefers a cool climate. Water well during the growing season and mulch during winter. It exudes a yellow sap when cut. Propagate by division in early spring or from root cuttings in winter. It spreads from underground stems and may become invasive.

MALCOLMIA
maritima

VIRGINIA STOCK, VIRGINIAN STOCK

An attractive little annual from the Mediterranean, this plant is valued for its ability to flower quickly from seed as soon as 4 to 6 weeks after seed is sown. It is very useful for edging, for paths, crevices and window boxes, and for growing over spring-flowering bulbs. It has oval, grey-green leaves, and bears 2 cm (1 in) wide, fragrant flowers in shades of pink, red, mauve and white from spring to autumn/fall. It has an erect habit and is fast-growing to a height of 20 cm (about 8 in) and spread of 5–8 cm (about 2–3 in). Fully hardy, it requires sun and fertile, well-drained soil. Propagate from seed sown at frequent intervals from spring to early autumn/fall for a long flowering season. Self-seeds readily.

MALVA
moschata

MUSK MALLOW

Useful for naturalizing in a wild garden or odd corner, this fully hardy perennial has narrow, lobed, divided

leaves with a sticky, hairy texture, which emit a musky, cheesy odour when crushed. A native of Europe, it bears profuse spikes of saucer-shaped pink flowers in summer. 'Alba', the white cultivar, is also very popular. It has a bushy, branching habit and can grow to a height of 1 m (about 3 ft). It requires a sunny situation and will thrive in a wide range of soil and climatic conditions. Propagate from seed in autumn/fall and cut plants back after first flowers have faded. Watch for rust disease.

MATTHIOLA

STOCK

This genus of annuals, biennials and perennials is native to the Mediterranean region. They are grown for their soft grey-green foliage and densely clustered, highly scented flowers in shades of white, lilac and purple, deep reds and pinks, and yellow. They are fragrant

Malva moschata

and long-lasting as cut flowers. Grow in a sheltered position in sun or semi-shade, and in a fertile, well-drained new soil that has been freshly turned with manure and lime. Tall and dwarf, single and double varieties have been developed. Tall cultivars may need support. Over fertilizing will encourage leaf growth at the expense of the flowers. Fully hardy to frost-tender. Sow seed of annuals in late summer to early autumn/fall; perennials under glass in spring. Watch for botrytis, downy mildew, club root, aphids and flea beetle.

M. incana
STOCK

This upright biennial or short-lived perennial from southern Europe is best grown as an annual. It has a bushy habit and grows up to 60 cm (about 24 in) in height with a spread of 30 cm (about 12 in). These stocks are fully hardy with lance-shaped, grey-green leaves, and fragrant, 7–15 cm (about 3–6 in) long spikes of mauve flowers borne in spring. There are many varieties and strains available, the best selected for a high percentage of double flowers.

M. 'Mammoth Column'
syn. M. 'Giant Column'

This is a cultivar from *M. incana* which grows taller, reaching 75 cm (about 30 in) in height. Each plant produces a single, 30–40 cm (about 12–16 in) tall spike of scented flowers in spring, in mixed or separate colours. When the main spike is finished, cutting the plant back will promote more flowers.

MAZUS
radicans

This prostrate carpet-forming New Zealand perennial has a strong stem and stout upright branches. The limbs are covered with egg-shaped to linear foliage which often has a downy reverse. In summer, bluish purple to pink or white 5-lobed cylindrical flowers with a yellow centre appear. These are followed by egg-shaped seed pods containing many seeds. Plant in medium soil allowing full sun. Propagate from seed or by division at the beginning of spring.

Malcolmia maritima

Mazus radicans

Matthiola 'Mammoth Column'

MECONOPSIS
betonicifolia

BLUE POPPY, TIBETAN POPPY

Native to the Himalayas, this clump-forming perennial bears pure, sky-blue, saucer-shaped, 5–8 cm (about 2–3 in) wide, satiny flowers with yellow stamens in late spring and early summer. Oblong, hairy, mid-green leaves are produced in basal rosettes. Grows to a height of 1 m (about 3 ft) and spread of 45 cm (about 18 in). A fully hardy woodland species, it must be grown in a sheltered position in humus-rich, moist, neutral to acid soil and in a cool climate. Plants do not bloom in the first season, die down completely over winter, and produce fine flowerheads the next spring. Propagate from seed in late summer.

MERTENSIA
virginica

VIRGINIA BLUEBELL

Native to the cooler parts of North America, this perennial is one of the loveliest of all blue spring flowers. It has smooth, oblong, soft blue-green foliage, and bears clusters of rich blue, tubular 2.5 cm (about 1 in) long flowers, 20 or more on each stem. It is effective planted with daffodils and polyanthus and is seen at its best naturalized in woodlands or alongside streams. Fully hardy, it grows to a height and spread of around 45 cm (about 18 in). Plant in shade and a deep, well-drained soil. Propagate by division in spring or from seed or by division in autumn/fall. Watch for slugs. *V. ciliata* is very similar.

Meconopsis betonicifolia

MIMOSA
pudica

HUMBLE PLANT, SENSITIVE PLANT, TOUCH-ME-NOT

Native to Brazil, this short-lived evergreen sub-shrub is usually treated as an annual. It is grown for its curiosity value—the fern-like leaves close up and droop when touched, usually re-opening within minutes. It has prickly stems and small, fluffy, ball-shaped pink flowers in summer. Grows to a height and spread of around 1 m (about 3 ft). Frost-tender, it is best grown in partial shade in fertile, well-drained soil. Can be grown indoors as a pot plant. Keep plants well-ventilated and moist and feed with liquid fertilizer. Avoid over watering. Propagate from seed in spring or semi-ripe cuttings in summer. In some areas this plant is becoming a noxious weed.

MIMULUS

These annuals and perennials are characterized by tubular flowers with flared mouths, often curiously spotted and mottled, which have been likened to grinning monkey faces. The flowers come in a large range of colours including brown, orange, yellow, red and crimson. Mainly native to the cool Pacific coastal areas of Chile and the USA, most species are suited to bog gardens or other moist situations, although some are excellent rock garden plants. The bright flowers are particularly effective in containers and in groups at the edge of flower beds. Grow in full sun or partial shade in a wet or moist soil. Propagate perennials by division in spring and annuals from seed in autumn/fall or early spring.

M. luteus

YELLOW MUSK

A spreading perennial often grown as an annual, this plant bears a profusion of snapdragon-like yellow flowers above mid-green foliage throughout summer. It grows to a height and spread of 30 cm (about 12 in). It is frost-hardy, and needs partial shade and a moist soil.

M. moschatus

MONKEY MUSK

A small, creeping, water-loving perennial growing to a height and spread of 15–30 cm (about 6–12 in). It bears snapdragon-like, pale yellow flowers, lightly dotted with brown, in summer to autumn/fall. It is fully hardy. This plant was once grown for its musk scent but, mysteriously, it has been odourless for many years.

MINA
lobata

syn. *Ipomoea versicolor, Quamoclit lobata*

Native to Mexico and Central America, this vigorous, short-lived twining climber is a perennial usually grown as an annual. It is deciduous or semi-evergreen with three-lobed bright green leaves, and bears racemes of small, tubular, dark red flowers fading to orange then creamy yellow. Flowers appear from late summer until late autumn/fall. The plant climbs to a height of 5 m (about 15 ft) and quickly provides a dense leafy cover over a suitable supporting structure. Half-hardy, it requires a warm, sun-exposed position and a rich well-drained soil that does not dry out. In cold climates the plant rarely survives the winter and should be replaced by fresh sowings in spring.

MIRABILIS
jalapa

MARVEL OF PERU, FOUR-O'CLOCK-FLOWER

This bushy tuberous perennial is grown for its fragrant, trumpet-shaped, crimson, pink, white or yellow flowers that open in late afternoon and remain open all night, closing again at dawn. Good as pot plants, bedding plants or as a dwarf hedge. They are native to tropical America, summer-flowering, and grow to around 1 m (about 3 ft) high with a spread of 60–75 cm (about 24–30 in). They require a sheltered position in full sun with a fertile well-drained soil. In frosty areas tubers are best lifted and stored like dahlias over winter; in mild climates

Mimulus luteus

Mimosa pudica

Mertensia virginica

Mina lobata

Mimulus moschatus

they can be left undisturbed and gradually make large clumps. Propagate from seed or by division of tubers in early spring.

MOLUCCELLA
laevis
BELLS OF IRELAND, SHELL FLOWER

This summer-flowering annual, native to Syria, is grown for its spikes, surrounded by shell-like, apple green calyces which are very popular for fresh or dried floral work; the tiny white flowers are insignificant. Rounded leaves are pale green and nettle-like. The plant is fairly fast growing to a height of 60 cm (about 24 in) and spread of 30 cm (about 12 in), and has an erect, branching habit. Half-hardy, it grows best in a sunny, open position and a rich very well-drained soil. Propagate by sowing seed directly into its flowering position in early spring. Water moderately and feed monthly with a balanced fertilizer.

MYOSOTIDIUM
hortensia
CHATHAM ISLAND FORGET-ME-NOT

Native to the Chatham Islands off the coast of New Zealand, this evergreen, clump-forming perennial is the giant of the forget-me-not family, growing to a height and spread of around 60 cm (about 24 in). It has a basal mound of large, glossy, rich-green, pleated leaves, and in spring and summer bears large clusters of bright blue flowers, slightly paler on the edges, on tall flower stems. Half-hardy, it requires semi-shade and a humus-rich moist soil. It can withstand salt winds and benefits from a mulch. Propagate by division in spring or from seed in summer or autumn/fall. Once growing well, they should not be disturbed and will naturalize freely.

MYOSOTIS
FORGET-ME-NOT

This genus of annuals and perennials includes 34 New Zealand natives among its 50 or so species, but those most commonly cultivated come from the temperate regions of Europe, Asia and the Americas. They are grown for their dainty blue (sometimes pink or white) flowers that complement plants of stronger colour in the spring garden. Most species are useful in rock gardens, border displays or as ground cover under trees and shrubs.Fully hardy, they prefer either a semi-shaded woodland setting or a sunny spot with the protection of other larger plants. Soil should be fertile and well-drained. They are rarely affected by pests or diseases and respond well to feeding in the pre-flowering period. Discard plants

after flowering. Propagate from seed in autumn/fall. Once established they self-seed freely. Myosotis is derived from the Greek for 'mouse ear', referring to the pointed leaves. The flowers have long been associated with love and remembrance.

M. alpestris
ALPINE FORGET-ME-NOT

This fully hardy, short-lived perennial (usually grown as an annual or biennial) forms clumps to a height and spread of 10–15 cm (about 4–6 in). In late spring and early summer, it bears clusters of dainty, bright blue, pink or white flowers with creamy yellow eyes. Plant in gritty soil in semi-shade.

M. 'Blue Ball'

This fully hardy, slow-growing perennial is usually grown as an annual. It has a bushy, compact habit, growing to a height of 20 cm (about 8 in) with a spread of 15 cm (about 6 in), and bears tiny, deep blue flowers in spring and early summer. It is good for edging.

M. colensoi
NZ FORGET-ME-NOT

The best known New Zealand forget-me-not, it adapts well to garden conditions, unlike most of the other species. It has rounded, slightly hairy, greyish green to silver leaves and small white flowers in late spring and summer. It forms a dense clump 5 cm (about 2 in) tall with a 30 cm (about 12 in) spread. Grow in sun or partial shade and moist well-drained soil. Suits rockeries or alpine pans. Propagate from seed in autumn/fall, by division in early spring or from rooted offsets.

M. scorpioides
syn. M. palustris
WATER FORGET-ME-NOT

A deciduous to semi-evergreen perennial, ideally grown as a marginal water plant for muddy situations or in very shallow water. It grows to a height and spread of 30 cm (about 12 in). It bears small blue flowers, with a yellow, pink or white eye, throughout summer. It is fully hardy.

Myosotis alpestris

Myosotis scorpioides

Mirabilis jalapa

Moluccella laevis

Myosotis colensoi

Myosotidium hortensia

Myosotis 'Blue Ball'

Nepeta × faassenii

Nemophila insignis

Nertera granadensis

Neomarica caerulea

NELUMBO
nucifera
SACRED LOTUS

A deciduous, perennial, marginal water plant, this is the giant of the Nymphaeaceae (water lily) family, growing 1–1.4 m (about 3–4½ ft) above the water surface and spreading to 1.2 m (about 3½ ft). Large fragrant, pink or white 25 cm (about 10 in) wide flowers are borne above large, shield-shaped, pale green leaves. It is a subtropical species and requires an open, sunny position and 60 cm (about 24 in) depth of water. Flowers develop into unusual seed pods, resembling salt-shakers. Remove faded foliage and divide overgrown plants in spring. Propagate from seed in spring. This vigorous plant grows well in large ponds. Buddha is often depicted in the centre of a lotus.

NEMESIA
strumosa

Indigenous to southern Africa, this colourful, fast-growing annual is a popular bedding plant. They are also useful for planting between summer-flowering bulbs, in rock gardens and window boxes. They are bushy plants with lance-shaped, pale green and prominently toothed leaves, growing to a height of 20–30 cm (about 8–12 in) and spread of 25 cm (about 10 in). Large, trumpet-shaped flowers in colours of yellow, white, red or orange are borne in spring on short terminal racemes. The plants prefer a well-dug, moderately fertile, mildly acid or neutral, well-drained soil, and a wind-sheltered, sunny position.

Nemesia strumosa

They cannot tolerate very hot, humid climates. Prune spent flowers to prolong flowering and pinch out growing shoots of young plants to encourage a bushy habit. Propagate from seed in early autumn/fall. The most cultivated of its genus, *N. strumosa* has spawned a range of hybrids and cultivars of varying heights and colours. 'Blue Gem' is a compact annual, fast-growing up to 20 cm (about 8 in). It bears trumpet-shaped, small, clear blue flowers that are a good foil for stronger coloured spring plants.

NEMOPHILA
insignis
syn. *N. menziesii*
BABY BLUE-EYES

A charming little Californian wildflower, this fast-growing, spreading annual is a useful ground cover under shrubs such as roses, in rock gardens and edges, and is particularly effective overplanted in a bed with spring bulbs. It bears small, bowl-shaped, sapphire-blue flowers with a well-defined concentric ring of white in the centre. It has dainty, serrated mid-green foliage, and grows to a height of 20 cm (about 8 in) and spread of 15 cm (about 6 in). It is best planted in a cool, partly shaded site in fertile, well-drained soil that does not dry out in summer. These plants dislike heat and transplanting. Propagate from seed sown outdoors in early autumn/fall. Watch for aphids.

NEOMARICA
caerulea
WALKING IRIS

Native to Brazil, this iris-like, rhizomatous, evergreen perennial yields an amazing number of flowers, but is essentially a garden plant as they are not suitable for cutting. It has tall, straight, sword-like leaves in basal fans, and produces a succession of triangular sky-blue flowers with white, yellow and brown central marks. Flowers are short-lived but are borne over a long period in summer. The plant grows to a height of 1 m (about 3 ft) and spread of 1–1.5 m (about 3–4½ ft),

Nelumbo nucifera

and is frost-tender. Plant in a fertile, moist, humus-rich soil in a partially shaded position. Water well in summer and ensure the soil does not dry out in winter. Propagate from seed in spring or by division in spring or summer. Transplant from late autumn/fall until early spring.

NEPETA
× faassenii
CATMINT

A bushy, clump-forming perennial, useful for separating strong colours in the shrub or flower border, and very effective when used with stone, either in walls, paving or rock gardens, or as an edging plant. It forms spreading mounds of greyish green leaves that are aromatic when crushed, and the numerous flower stems carry hundreds of small, pale violet-blue flowers throughout summer. Grows to a height and spread of 45 cm (about 18 in). Fully hardy, it prefers cool conditions and a sunny situation but will grow in semi-shade. Any moderately fertile, well-drained soil will suit. Cut back old growth to within 15 cm (about 6 in) of soil level in winter when the plants become untidy. Propagate by division in early spring or from softwood cuttings in spring and summer.

NERTERA
granadensis
syn. *N. depressa*
BEAD PLANT

A carpeting perennial, grown for the mass of spherical, orange or red, bead-like berries it bears in autumn/fall. It has a prostrate habit, growing to 1 cm (about ½ in) in height with a spread of 10 cm (about 4 in) and forming compact cushions of tiny bright green leaves with extremely small, greenish white flowers in early summer. Half-hardy, it thrives in a cool, sheltered, semi-shaded site in gritty, moist but well-drained sandy soil. Water well in summer but keep dryish in winter. It is an excellent alpine house plant. Propagate by division or from seed or tip cuttings in spring. There is a variety with purple-tinged foliage.

NICOLAIA
elatior
syn. *Phaeomeria magnifica*
TORCH GINGER

A magnificent plant from Indonesia for the subtropical garden only. Sixty centimetre (about 24 in) long, oblong leaves are borne on 6 m (about 18 ft) bamboo-like leaf stalks. In spring a cluster of small, gold-rimmed, scarlet flowers are embedded in a waxy, pyramid-like cone of pink-edged, bright red bracts, sometimes opening to 25 cm (about 10 in) across. The flowers are borne on a 1.5 m (about 4 ¹/₂ ft) leafless stem that comes straight out of the ground. Grow in moist, humus-rich soil in full sun or part-shade with a minimum temperature of 18°C (about 64°F). Water well during growth and less when dormant. Propagate by division—they can be invasive so lift and divide as they outgrow an area.

NICOTIANA
FLOWERING TOBACCO

These annuals and perennials, some of which are grown as annuals, are mainly of South American origin and are an ornamental species of tobacco. The older species are grown for the fragrance of their warm-weather flowers which usually open at night; the newer strains have flowers that remain open all day but have limited perfume. They are half-hardy to frost-tender, requiring full sun or light shade and a fertile, moist, but well-drained soil. Propagate from seed in early spring. The flowers are good for cutting, although the plants are sticky to handle. Watch for snails and caterpillars.

Nigella damascena

N. alata
syn. N. affinis

A short-lived perennial, often grown as an annual, this half-hardy plant bears clusters of attractive, tubular flowers in white, red or various shades of pink. The flowers open towards evening and fill the garden with scent on warm, still nights. Rosette-forming, it has oval, mid-green leaves and grows to a height of 1 m (about 3 ft) with a spread of 30 cm (about 12 in). It flowers through summer and early autumn/fall.

N. × sanderae

A half-hardy, slow-growing bushy annual, reaching to a height of 40 cm (about 16 in) and spread of half that. In summer and early autumn/fall it bears long, trumpet-shaped flowers in shades of white, pink, red, cerise, bright crimson and purple. Flowers stay open during the day and are fragrant in the evening.

NIEREMBERGIA
hippomanica var. *violacea*
'Purple Robe'
syn. N. caerulea

Native to Argentina, this small, bushy perennial, best grown as an annual, is ideal for edgings and massed beddings, rock gardens and window boxes. In summer and early autumn/fall it bears a profusion of cup-shaped, open, dark bluish purple flowers with yellow throats. It has much-branched, thin, stiffly erect stems and narrow, lance-shaped, deep-green, slightly hairy leaves. Moderately fast-growing to a height

Nicolaia elatior

and spread of 15–20 cm (about 6–8 in). Half-hardy, it prefers a moist but well-drained soil and a sunny situation. Cut well back after flowering. It increases readily by underground runners and may become invasive. Propagate by division in spring, from semi-ripe cuttings in summer or seed in autumn/fall. Fresh stock should be raised every two or three years.

NIGELLA
damascena
LOVE-IN-A-MIST, DEVIL-IN-A-BUSH

A fully hardy annual, grown for its attractive flowers, native to the Mediterranean and western Asia. It has spurred, many-petalled blue or white flowers in spring and early summer, almost hidden in the bright green, feathery foliage followed by rounded green seed pods that mature to brown. Both flowers and seed pods are good for floral decoration. Upright and fast-growing, it reaches 60 cm (about 24 in) high with a spread of 20 cm (about 8 in). Plant in a sunny situation in a fertile, well-drained soil; fertilize monthly and water regularly. The plants have a short blooming season and can be dead-headed to prolong flowering; successive sowings can also be made. Propagate from seed in autumn/fall. It self-sows readily.

NYMPHAEA
WATER LILY

This genus of deciduous and evergreen, perennial aquatic plants with fleshy roots is named for the Greek

goddess Nymphe. They are grown for their floating leaves and attractive brigh flowers that come in shades of white and cream, brilliant yellows and oranges, pinks and deep reds, blues and purple. There are hardy and tropical varieties. Hardy water lilies grow in all climates and flower freely throughout summer, both flowers and foliage floating on the water surface. Faded foliage should be removed. Divide the tuber-like rhizomes and replant in spring or summer every three or four years. Tropical water lilies are all frost-tender, requiring a very warm, sunny situation. They flower from mid-summer into autumn/fall, and have large, scented flowers held above the water surface. In cooler areas, the tubers should be lifted and stored in moist sand over the winter. All species need still water and annual fertilizing as they are gross feeders. Propagate from seed or by separating plantlets in spring or early autumn/fall. Watch for insects, particularly aphids; goldfish in the pool will eat most pests.

Nicotiana alata

Nicotiana × sanderae

Nierembergia hippomanica var. *violacea* 'Purple Robe'

N. *alba*

A deciduous, hardy species with floating dark green leaves and cup-shaped, semi-double, fragrant 10 cm (about 4 in) wide, white flowers with golden centres. Spreads to 3 m (about 9 ft).

N. 'Aurora'

A smaller hardy cultivar, also deciduous, with floating olive green leaves blotched with purple. Semi-double flowers are star-shaped, 5 cm (about 2 in) wide and turn from cream to yellow, to orange, to blood-red. Spreads to 75 cm (about 30 in).

N. 'Blue Beauty'

A deciduous or evergreen tropical water lily with large, brown-speckled, dark green leaves with purplish undersides. Flowers are rounded, fragrant, semi-double, 30 cm (about 12 in) across, deep purple-blue with yellow centres. Spreads to 2.5 m (about 7½ ft).

N. *nouchali* var. *caerulea*
syn. *Nymphaea caerulea*
BLUE LOTUS

Native to tropical Africa, this species has long, rounded complete leaves over 30 cm (12 in) wide. The leaves have a green surface with purple edges and markings beneath. After the first year, lightly fragrant, pale blue, lilac or pink flowers bloom in spring. This species is easily grown in a tub and is suitable for the greenhouse.

Nymphaea nouchali var. *caerulea*

OENOTHERA
EVENING PRIMROSE

Native to North America but widespread elsewhere, this genus of annuals, biennials and perennials is grown for the masses of short-lived flowers borne during summer. Most species are pollinated by night-flying insects and only release their lovely fragrance at night. Some members of the genus do not even open their petals during the day. They are fully to frost-hardy and grow best in a well-drained sandy soil in an open sunny situation. They will tolerate dry conditions. Propagate from seed or by division in spring or autumn/fall, or from softwood cuttings in late spring. Evening primrose oil has great health benefits. The oil is extracted from the plant's tiny seeds which contain essential fatty acids.

O. *biennis*

A showy plant, this upright biennial has large, scented, yellow flowers that grow in long sprays and open in the evening. Foliage is light green. It is frost-hardy and fast-growing to a height of 1.5 m (nearly 5 ft) and spread of 60 cm (about 24 in).

O. *missouriensis*

A spreading perennial that forms mats of dark green leaves and has short-stemmed, bell-shaped, 10 cm (about 4 in) wide, canary yellow flowers, sometimes spotted red. Flowers open at sundown and are borne over a long period throughout spring and summer. It is fully

hardy and grows to a height of 10 cm (about 4 in) and spread of 40 cm (about 16 in) or more.

O. *speciosa*
WHITE EVENING PRIMROSE

A short-lived rhizomatous perennial bearing spikes of fragrant, saucer-shaped, pink-tinted white flowers in profusion. Fresh flowerheads open daily throughout the summer. The small leaves often turn red in hot or cold weather. Clump-forming, it grows to 45 cm (about 18 in) in height with a spread of 30 cm (about 12 in) or more, and is frost-hardy.

OSTEOSPERMUM

This genus of annuals and evergreen, semi-woody perennials is mostly indigenous to South Africa. The tough plants are useful for rock gardens, dry embankments, or the front rows of shrub borders, particularly as temporary filler plants. They produce large daisy-like flowers in the white and violet, purple, blue range, and flower for many weeks in winter and spring. They

prefer a warm, temperate climate and require moderately fertile, well-drained soil. An open, sun-exposed position is essential. Light pruning after flowering helps maintain shape and extend the plant's life span. Propagate from cuttings of non-flowering shoots or from seed in summer.

O. *ecklonis*
SAILOR BOY DAISY, FREEWAY DAISY

An evergreen with either upright or straggling habit, this half-hardy perennial grows to a height and spread of

Oenothera speciosa

Nymphaea alba

Nymphaea 'Aurora'

Nymphaea 'Blue Beauty'

Oenothera biennis

Osteospermum ecklonis

Oenothera missouriensis

45 cm (about 18 in). It has lance-shaped, mid-green leaves and bears 7.5 cm (about 3 in) wide daisies, glistening white with deep reddish violet centres, and streaked with bluish mauve underneath the petals. Flowers from early summer to autumn/fall.

O. jucundum
syn. *O. barberae, Dimorphotheca barberae*

TRAILING MAUVE DAISY, PINK VELD DAISY, FREEWAY DAISY

This frost-hardy, evergreen perennial grows to a height and spread of 45 cm (about 18 in). It is clump-forming with mid- to dark green, lance-shaped to rectangular leaves, and produces abundant purplish pink daisies with darker central discs throughout autumn/fall and early summer. The flowers close on cloudy days. 'Whirligig' has pink or white flowers and curled petals.

OURISIA
macrophylla

Native to New Zealand, this perennial has a carpet-forming habit. It reaches up to 10 cm (about 4 in) high and 15 cm (about 6 in) wide. The light green, downy foliage is egg-shaped to elliptical and develops on long, purple-tinted stalks. In late spring to early summer an abundance of small white blossoms appear. It requires total shade and fertile, damp soil. It is reluctant to grow in dry climates, preferring moist peat beds or shady walls. Propagate from seed or by division in spring.

OXYPETALUM
caeruleum
syn. *Tweedia caerulea*

Pale blue starry flowers, ageing to purple, are borne in summer and early autumn/fall on this herbaceous twining climber. They are followed by 15 cm (about 6 in) long, boat-shaped, green seed pods. The flowers are suitable for picking but the cut stems must be burnt to seal the sticky white sap. The plant has heart-shaped grey-green leaves covered with a hairy down, and grows to a height of 1 m (about

3 ft). Frost-tender, it requires a sunny situation and rich, well-drained soil. It should be grown as an annual in cooler climates. Propagate from seed in spring and pinch out tips of buds to encourage a branching habit. This species, from Uruguay and Brazil, is the only member of its genus to be cultivated widely. It belongs to the Asclepiadaceae family, which is the favoured source of food for the monarch caterpillar.

PACHYSANDRA
terminalis

This creeping perennial, a native of Japan, has leathery, ovate leaves with saw-tooth tips, clustered at the ends of short stems. Tiny white flowers, sometimes pink or purple-tinted, appear in terminal clusters in early summer. This frost-resistant evergreen makes good ground cover and likes moist, well-drained soil in a shady site. It grows to a height of 10 cm (about 4 in) with a spread of 20 cm (about 8 in). Propagate by division in early spring.

PAEONIA
PEONY

Some species of these deciduous shrubs and perennials display showy seed pods in addition to the lobed foliage and full round flowerheads for which this genus is renowned. Many species are from western China and the Himalayas; some from Siberia and Mongolia. Others are of European origin, including *P. officinalis* which, although poisonous, has been used as a remedy for everything from gout, cramps and asthma to bladder and kidney problems, as well as serving as a diuretic, sedative and antispasmodic. Sow seed in autumn/fall or propagate by division in autumn/fall or early spring. Germination from seed can take as long as three years. Use root cuttings from tuberous species in winter. To start the deciduous tree peonies, use grafts in winter or semi-ripe cuttings late in summer. Soil should be moist and fertilized, although too much animal manure or

poorly drained soil may bring on botrytis.

P. 'Bowl of Beauty'

Big flowers appear on this perennial between late spring and mid-summer. A dense cluster of slender, creamy-white petaloids nest in the

centre of broad, pink outer petals. The plant grows to a height and spread of 1 m (about 3 ft). This frost resistant perennial enjoys semi-shade. The variety is typical of the Chinese peonies, derived mainly from *P. lactiflora* which comes in a huge range of colours and forms.

Osteospermum jucundum

Oxypetalum caeruleum

Paeonia 'Bowl of Beauty'

Pachysandra terminalis

Ourisia macrophylla

A Field Trip to Grindelwald

Visit the picture-postcard town of Grindelwald between December and March and you will find thousands of brightly clad skiers trudging through the slush and ice. Return again in July and Grindelwald will have undergone a transformation, with colourful windowboxes full of geraniums adorning attractive alpine houses.

The town nestles in the mountains of the Bernese Oberland, sitting against the backdrop of the Swiss Alps. These mountains, with their wooded lower slopes, alpine meadows and snow-capped peaks, include among their number the towering Eiger.

Although Grindelwald at times suffers from an inundation of visitors, it does have two important advantages for the plant enthusiasts who visit. Firstly, it is surrounded by some superb alpine meadows and pastures which are incredibly rich in colourful species; secondly, the same chairlifts that

The great yellow gentian, with a spectacular mountain backdrop.

transport hopeful skiers to the *piste* during the winter months operate throughout the year and can save hours of foot-slogging toil. Within a few short minutes, you can be free of the hustle and bustle of urban Grindelwald below and admire the clear views and brilliant flowers which in summer include one of the Alps' most spectacular species, the great yellow gentian (*Gentiana lutea*).

The Grindelwald chairlift has intermediate stations before you reach the highest point. One of the best ways to explore the region, assuming you are sufficiently fit and energetic, is to walk down the slopes from one of these stop-off points. The network of paths and tracks are signposted and route maps are available.

The highest ski-station is well above the tree-line and in the highest zone of vegetation before areas of permanent snow are reached. A succession of flowers appears from May onwards, as the snows retreat, and these include the spring gentian (*G. verna*) and the trumpet gentian (*G. acaulis*). One of the region's most enchanting plants also occurs here, the aptly named alpine snowbell (*Soldanella alpina*), and it is one which usually cannot wait for the snow to melt. Nodding flower-spikes of these fringed flowers often force their way through the snow itself.

After you descend a hundred metres or so (a few hundred feet) you come to some truly vivid alpine meadows. Throughout the summer months these flower-rich pastures are home to small herds of cattle, noisily identified by their jangling cow-bells. Everywhere you look there are such plants as alpine pasque-flower (*Pulsatilla alpina*), alpine bartsia (*Bartsia alpina*) and alpine butterwort (*Pinguicula alpina*), as well as numerous cranesbills, bedstraws, cinquefoils and orchids. It is in this region, on slopes and banks, that you are most likely to come across some brightly coloured stands of great yellow gentian.

Further down the mountainside, towards Grindelwald, the meadows become increasingly lush and full of grasses and rich flowers such as red campion (*Silene dioica*) and dandelion (*Taraxacum officinale*).

Here and there, as you are descending the slopes above Grindelwald, you walk through stands of native conifer forest. These are mainly comprised of white fir (*Abies alba*)—in winter their sagging, snow-laden branches make a delightful spectacle. On the forest floor colourful plants such as the yellow wood violet (*Viola lutea*) and the twinflower (*Linnaea borealis*) are there to be seen. If you look carefully you may find the diminutive and easily overlooked lesser twayblade orchid (*Listera cordata*).

Gentiana lutea is among the most striking and distinctive of all these plants, and its appearance is enhanced by the invariably stunning settings in which it grows.

The species produces a robust basal rosette, each leaf of which is broadly lanceolate or ovate in outline and pointed at the tip. The leaves are bluish green in colour with strongly marked veins, and can be up to 30 cm (about 12 in) long. From June until August, stout and upright flower-bearing spikes appear, rising from the basal rosette. These reach a height of up to 2 m (about 6 ft) or more and are hollow and unbranched. Whorls of large, bright yellow flowers are arranged up the stem with pairs of clasping leaves below. These are similar in appearance to the basal leaves but smaller in size. The individual flower corollas are coloured deep yellow, or occasionally reddish, and are about 2 cm (about 1 in) long; they have five to nine lobes which spread out in star-shaped fashion.

Great yellow gentian is a hardy, long-lasting perennial, like all the species that grow in the Alps and central European mountains, Here the combination of a short growing season and a prolonged winter has favoured the adaptation of very hardy plants indeed. The first heavy snows in the Alps can come as early as October, although the lower slopes are not usually covered until Christmas. Sub-zero temperatures and a blanket of snow are then the norm until April, when the thaw begins.

Great yellow gentian can be found in many of the mountainous areas of Europe, but while some of these may rival the Bernese Oberland for scenic splendour, few can match it for the ease with which you can reach the plant's natural habitat. Whether you visit Grindelwald or one of the many other alpine resorts, you will surely have a botanical field trip to remember and cherish.

Gentiana

Gentians are members of the genus *Gentiana* and its more recent sister-genera *Gentianella* and *Gentianopsis*. The group consists of around 400 species of mostly perennial herbs found in most parts of the world, although in the tropics only in higher mountain regions. The areas richest in gentian species are the mountains of western China and the neighbouring Himalayas. The Alps of Europe boast equally attractive species, including *G. lutea* which is widespread throughout the upland and mountain regions of central Europe. The roots of *G. lutea* are important in herbal medicine and its infusions and brews serve as useful tonics; a potent liqueur is also distilled from the fermented root.

Intense deep blues and sky blues are the flower colours most commonly associated with gentians, but whites and creams are also frequent, and *G. lutea* has a brilliant yellow flower.

The family Gentianaceae contains about 80 genera, including woody shrubs, annuals and perennials. Others that may be familiar to gardeners include the prairie gentian (*Eustoma*), popular as a cut flower, and the Persian violet (*Exacum*), which is grown as an indoor plant.

Gentiana lutea

Gentiana lutea

P. mlokosewitschii

From late spring to mid-summer, this European perennial bears big, open, pale to bright yellow flowers atop soft green leaves with hairy undersides that are sometimes tinged purple at the edges. Grows to a height and spread of 75 cm (about 30 in). The species enjoys semi-shade and is resistant to frosts.

P. officinalis

A tuberous species, this perennial reaches 60 cm (about 24 in) in height and spread, bearing single, purple or red, rose-like flowers in spring through mid-summer. Frost-hardy, it is a native of Europe and likes good soil and ample water. Of similar size, the hybrid 'Rubra Plena' bears flowers that are fulsome clusters of many small, mid-magenta petals. A more compact hybrid, 'China Rose', bears darker green foliage and flowers with yellow-orange anthers.

PAPAVER

POPPY

With their characteristic cupped petals, and nodding buds turning skywards upon opening, poppies are popular bedding flowers. They are fully hardy and prefer little or no shade and moist, well-drained soil. Sow seed in spring or autumn/fall; many species self-seed readily.

P. alpinum

This alpine poppy is a miniature Iceland poppy. A short-living perennial, this tuft-forming semi-evergreen grows 20 cm (about 8 in) high with a spread of half that, and has fine, greyish leaves. It bears white or yellow flowers through summer. Use on banks or in rock gardens.

P. nudicaule

ICELAND POPPY

This tuft-forming perennial is in fact almost always grown as an annual. It bears large scented flowers, coloured white, yellow, orange and pink and with a crinkled texture, in winter and spring. The plant has pale green leaves, long hairy stems, and grows to a height of 30–60 cm (about 12–24 in) with a 10 cm (about 4 in) spread. Give this native of North America and Asia Minor full sun. Sow in late summer to early autumn. The species is good for rock gardens and cutting.

P. orientale

ORIENTAL POPPY

This frost-hardy perennial bears spectacular single or double flowers in early summer. Originally from Asia, varieties offering different colours abound, but a common feature is the dark basal blotch on each petal. Foliage of hairy, lance-like, bluish green leaves can become straggly. The plant will grow to a height and spread of 45 cm (about 18 in) and may need support.

P. rhoeas

CORN POPPY, FIELD POPPY

The cupped flowers on this fast-growing annual from Asia Minor are small, delicate, scarlet and single, although cultivated varieties (Shirley poppies) offer hues including reds, pinks, whites and bicolours. Double-flowered strains are also available. It will grow 60 cm (about 24 in) high with a 30 cm (about 12 in) spread. Flowering time is early summer, and the leaves are light green and lobed. Give them all full sun.

P. somniferum

OPIUM POPPY

The green leaves on this fast-growing annual have a greyish cast, are lobed and elliptical with serrated edges. It blooms in summer, displaying big flowers in white, pink, red or purple, usually as doubles. The fully hardy species from the Middle East likes sun. Opium poppies are cultivated for the milky sap extracted from their seed capsules, source of the narcotic drug opium and its derivatives. Garden varieties are not very potent, but homemade opium is still illegal, and nervous nursery owners can be reluctant to stock the opium poppy.

PARADISEA

liliastrum

ST BRUNO'S LILY, ST BERNARD'S LILY

Racemes of scented, white, funnel-shaped flowers bloom on long, thin stems in early summer on this perennial from Italy. The leaves have a greyish cast and are strap-like, ar-

Paeonia mlokosewitschii

Papaver somniferum

Paeonia officinalis

Papaver orientale

Papaver rhoeas

Papaver nudicaule

Papaver alpinum

Paradisea liliastrum

Parochetus communis

Pelargonium cucullatum

Pelargonium × domesticum

ranged in a basal rosette. The roots are fleshy clusters. Fully hardy, plant where it is sunny but cool, or in semi-shade. Its soil must drain well but retain moisture. Propagate by division or from seed in spring or autumn/fall, although with division you might miss one season of flowering.

PAROCHETUS
communis
SHAMROCK PEA

It is the flowers that are pea-like on this evergreen, ground-hugging, wide-spreading perennial. The flowers are bright blue and bloom for most of the year. The leaves resemble clover. An alpine house environment best suits this half-hardy species, although in moderate climates it is a successful ground cover. Plant it in partial shade in moist, coarse soil. Use rooted runners to propagate by division at any time of year. Don't be alarmed if it vanishes without apparent cause; marginal bits will live from which you can make divisions to re-establish it.

PATERSONIA
glabrata
AUSTRALIAN IRIS, SNAKE FLOWER

Violet 3-lobed flowers appear on this upright perennial in spring and summer. Its leaves are strap-like and clump-forming. Plant this frost-hardy species in well-drained soil in full sun. Sow seed in autumn/fall, and once planted, don't disturb it. It will grow to 30 cm (about 12 in) or more with a similar spread. This is a native of the eastern states of Australia.

Patersonia glabrata

PELARGONIUM
GERANIUM

These frost-tender perennials are often grown as annuals for summer bedding in colder climates. In warmer climates with long hours of daylight, they flower almost all the time, although they do not do well in extreme heat and humidity. Plant in pots or beds. The site should be sunny with light, well-drained, neutral soil. If in pots, fertilize regularly and cull dead-heads. Avoid over watering. Use softwood cuttings for propagation in spring through autumn/fall. The species in this genus are mainly from South Africa. Including hybrids and culti-vated varieties, the genus is divided into three large groups: zonal, ivy-leaved and regal or show geraniums.

P. crispum
LEMON GERANIUM, FINGER-BOWL GERANIUM

The lemon-scented leaves on this upright plant are small and lobed with crinkled margins. Pink flowers up to 25 mm (about 1 in) across often have darker markings. Grows

to 1 m (about 3 ft) with a 30–50 cm (about 12–20 in) spread. *P. c.* 'Variegatum' has variegated leaves.

P. cucullatum

This South African upright perennial grows to 2 m (about 6 ft) high. It has readily branching downy stems cov-ered with broad, light green foliage. The erect leaves are funnel-shaped and have wavy edges. In spring to summer, lustrous reddish purple flowers with deeper coloured veins appear. The flowers are up to 5 cm (about 2 in) in diameter.

P. × domesticum
REGAL GERANIUM, REGAL PELARGONIUM, MARTHA WASHINGTON GERANIUM

Often just called 'pelargonium', the regal types are shrubby perennials with stiff, pleated leaves and clusters of large flowers, wide open and often blotched or parti-coloured. They flower in late spring and come in shades from white through pink to red and purple. They are much grown as pot plants, and are tender—in cool areas a greenhouse is needed. Cut back hard after blooming to keep the bushes compact.

Pelargonium × zonale

Peltiphyllum peltatum

Pelargonium rodneyanum

Pelargonium peltatum

Pelargonium 'Orange Ricard'

Pelargonium × fragrans

Pelargonium echinatum

Pelargonium tomentosum

P. echinatum

SWEETHEART GERANIUM, CACTUS GERANIUM

The leaves drop off this upright ivy-leaved geranium at the end of the growing season, exposing fleshy, prickly looking branches. The toothed leaves are hairy, white and composed of 3 to 5 lobes. White, pink, mauve or purple flowers bloom in late winter. Their upper petals often carry a red blotch in a heart shape. Reaching 50 cm (about 20 in) in height, this species spreads to 30 cm (about 12 in). Water it less for three months after the leaves yellow.

P. × fragrans

APPLE GERANIUM

A strong spicy smell comes off the small, roughly heart-shaped, lobed, grey-green leaves of this very bushy, many branched geranium, which reaches a height and spread of 30 cm (about 12 in). The flowers it bears are small and white, sometimes with red veins in the upper petals.

P. 'Orange Ricard'

Masses of large, semi-double coral flowers bloom on this variegated-leaved zonal geranium. It grows vigorously to 60 cm (about 24 in), spreading over half that.

P. peltatum

IVY-LEAVED GERANIUM, HANGING GERANIUM

Originating in South Africa, this species has narrow trailing or climbing stems up to 1 m (about 3 ft) long. Its bright green leaves have five sharp lobes and are up to 7 cm (about 3 in) across. The foliage is similar in appearance to ivy. Flowers can range from purplish red-pink to white and appear in spring and summer.

P. rodneyanum

STORK'S BILL

Well suited to rock gardens, this ground-hugging, herbaceous species has a thick tap root. Its small mid-green leaves, which form a basal rosette, are lobed ellipses. It bears clusters of magenta flowers in spring. An Australian evergreen, it grows 30 cm (about 12 in) in spread and height. It is resistant to both frost and drought.

P. tomentosum

PEPPERMINT GERANIUM

A strong refreshing smell of peppermint comes from the large-lobed, heart-shaped, greyish green velvety leaves on this sprawling geranium. It produces insignificant, purple-veined white flowers in clusters. Give it at least partial shade. The species climbs to 60 cm (about 24 in), spreads widely or hangs. Limit its spread by pinching out the growing tips. Older plants present poorly and are better replaced.

P. × zonale

ZONAL GERANIUM

These popular hybrids of several South African species are bushy aromatic perennials, with round leaves, often marked with a darker zone, and clusters of bright flowers all year in frost-free climates. Elsewhere, they are grown as summer annuals, propagated from either seed or cuttings. Flowers can be single or double, in red, purple, pink or white, and there are several cultivars with variegated leaves.

PELTIPHYLLUM
peltatum

UMBRELLA PLANT

A good plant for around ponds, this perennial, indigenous to North America, has lobed, peltate leaves (hence the species name, meaning shield-shaped) that grow up to 60 cm (about 24 in) across. In spring it bears pale pink flowers, some forming into panicles, on hairy stems. Foliage growth follows flowering. It grows 1.2 m (about 4 ft) in height and half that in spread. Plant this fully hardy species in moist soil in a sunny or shaded location. Propagate by division in spring. In full growth it is not easily contained.

PENSTEMON

This large genus includes shrubs, sub-shrubs, annuals and perennials, all of which do best in fertile, well-drained soil and full sun. Most of the species are native to North America, but hybrids are grown worldwide for their showy flower spikes in blues, reds, white and bicolours. Tall varieties suit sheltered borders; dwarf strains are bright in bedding schemes. Cut plants back hard after flowering. Propagate from seed in spring or autumn/fall, by division in spring, or from cuttings of non-flowering shoots in late summer (the only method for cultivars). The genus comprises mainly evergreens and semi-evergreens.

P. barbatus
syn. Chelone barbata
CORAL PENSTEMON, BEARD-LIP PENSTEMON

The scarlet flowers on this frost-hardy perennial are tubular with 2 lips. They bloom on racemes from the middle of summer to early in autumn/fall above narrow, lance-shaped, green leaves. The plant grows to 1 m (about 3 ft) high, with a spread of 30 cm (about 12 in). Plant this semi-evergreen in well-drained soil in a sunny location.

P. × gloxinioides
BEARD TONGUE

These hybrids between P. hartwegii and P. cobaea are the most widely grown penstemons in gardens. They include the two-toned, strong-growing 'Huntington Pink'; the tall, dark 'Midnight' and not-so-tall but also dark 'Prairie Dusk'; and one that flowers profusely called 'Apple Blossom'. All grow about 80 cm (about 32 in) tall and are fine plants for the middle of a border.

P. heterophyllus 'True Blue'
VIOLET PENSTEMON

A good addition to rock gardens, this frost-hardy semi-evergreen shrub reaches 25 cm (about 10 in) in height and somewhat more in spread. In late spring through early summer, blue tube-shaped flowers bloom from short side shoots. Its lanceolate leaves are pale green. Used for ground cover, this North American native has been dubbed 'Blue Bedder' in some regions.

PETUNIA
PETUNIA

'Petun' means 'tobacco' in a South American Indian dialect; and petunias are indeed relatives of the tobaccos (Nicotiana), their leaves having a similar narcotic effect on humans, and both genuses belonging to the same family as potatoes (Solanaceae). Always grown as annuals, these perennials like well-drained, fertile soil and a sunny location. They thrive where summers are hot, but need shelter from the wind. Available are hues of white, purple, red, blue, pink and a mix. Fairly fast-growing, the branching plant has dark green elliptical leaves. Flowers of some of the larger grandiflora hybrids are damaged by rain but others, mainly the multiflora hybrids, are more resistant. Sow seed early in spring. Pinching back hard encourages branching. Give fertilizer every month only until the onset of hot weather. Cucumber mosaic and tomato spotted wilt can attack these species, which need regular dead-heading. Petunias are some of the most popular flowers in the world, finding widespread use as bedding plants and in window boxes, hanging baskets and planters.

P. 'Bonanza'

A multiflora type, this has frilly double flowers in trumpet shapes which display in a multitude of colours.

P. 'Cascade'

A wide range of colours is available from this grandiflora series. The plants bear their flowers singly and have trailing stems, most suitable for hanging baskets.

P. 'Giants of California'

Although not a profuse bloomer, this petunia produces fine individual blossoms. The ruffled flowers are large, coloured white, pink and mauve.

Petunia 'Bonanza'

Penstemon barbatus

Petunia 'Giants of California'

Petunia 'Cascade'

Penstemon × gloxinioides

Penstemon heterophyllus 'True Blue'

PHACELIA
campanularia
CALIFORNIA BLUEBELL

True to its common name, the flowers on this fast-growing annual are blue and shaped like bells. Appearing in spring and early summer, the flowers are small, only 2.5 cm (about 1 in) across. The bushy, branching plant is delightful in a rock garden or border; it grows about 20 cm (about 8 in) high, with a 15 cm (about 6 in) spread. Its leaves are dark green and serrated. Plant in well-drained, fertile soil and full sun, to approximate the conditions of its native home, California's Mojave Desert. Propagate from seed in spring or early autumn/fall.

PHLOX

These evergreen and semi-evergreen annuals and perennials, mostly native to North America, are grown for their profuse, fragrant flowers. The name phlox means 'flame', an appropriate epithet for these brightly coloured, showy flowers, popular in bedding and border displays. Grow in fertile soil that drains well but remains moist. Choose a sunny or partially shaded location.

P. drummondii
ANNUAL PHLOX

This annual grows fairly rapidly to a bushy 40 cm (about 16 in) height, half that in spread. The species has a number of cultivars, including some dwarf strains which grow to 10 cm (about 4 in). *P. drummondii* bears closely clustered, small flattish flowers with 5 petals in summer and autumn/fall, in reds, pinks, purples and creams, and has lanceolate light green leaves. It is resistant to frosts but not to droughts. Sow seed in spring.

P. paniculata
SUMMER PHLOX, PERENNIAL

This tall perennial can grow to more than 1 m (about 3 ft), although height varies a little among the many named varieties. In summer it bears long-lasting, terminal flowerheads comprising many small, 5-lobed flowers. Colours range through violet, red, salmon and white according to variety. Eelworm is this species' enemy. Watch out also for spider-mites and mildew. Propagate from root cuttings in winter or by division early in spring. Give it mulch in winter. It is fully hardy.

P. subulata
MOSS PHLOX, CREEPING PHLOX

The flowers that bloom through spring in terminal masses on this prostrate alpine perennial are mauve, pink, white and shaped like stars, the petals being notched and open. The fully hardy, evergreen species is suited to growing in rock gardens where it will get sun. Its fine-leaved foliage will grow carpet-like to 10 cm (about 4 in) high with a spread twice that. Start in spring or summer using cuttings from non-flowering shoots. Trim back after flowering.

PHORMIUM
NEW ZEALAND FLAX

Grown for the dramatic effect of their stiff, vertical leaves, these large, clumping plants are extremely hardy in most conditions. In summer they produce panicles of flowers which are attractive to nectar-feeding birds. *P. tenax* grows to 2 m (about 6 ft) tall, while *P. colensoi* about half that height. They make splendid container plants as well as useful garden plants in almost any climate as they are fairly frost-hardy. They respond well to generous watering and permanently moist conditions. Propagate from seed or by division in spring. The plants produce a fibre which has been used commercially but which is now largely confined to traditional Maori crafts.

P. 'Dawn'

The stiff, sword-shaped dark green leaves of this cultivar have red, bronze, salmon-pink and yellow vertical stripes. In summer, panicles of tubular, dull red flowers are produced on short green stems. Grows well by the sea.

P. tenax 'Bronze Baby'

Wide, fibrous, strap-like, copper-toned leaves with sharply pointed ends grow to about 1 m (about 3 ft) long. Panicles of tubular, bronze-red flowers grow on a strong stem from the base of the clump in summer. Grows well by the sea.

P. tenax 'Purpureum'

The stiff, pointed, strap-like leaves of this cultivar are plum-purple to dark copper, and grow to 2.5 m (about 7½ ft) long. Panicles of reddish flowers on purplish blue stems appear in summer.

Phlox subulata

Phlox paniculata

Phormium 'Dawn'

Phlox drummondii

Phormium tenax 'Bronze Baby'

Phormium tenax 'Purpureum'

Phacelia campanularia

Polemonium caeruleum

Polygonatum x *hybridum*

Polygonum affine

Plectranthus parviflorus

PHYSOSTEGIA
virginiana
OBEDIENT PLANT, GALLIPOLI HEATH

If you move a flower on this herbaceous perennial, it will not spring back into position but will obediently stay put, thanks to a stalk with a hinge-like structure. The showy flowers, which bloom in erect terminal spikes late in summer, are tubular, have 2 lips and are available in pale pink, magenta ('Vivid') or white. The leaves are lance-shaped and serrated. Plant this fully hardy species in sun in fertile soil that drains well but remains moist. Propagate by division in spring. This native of North America will grow to 1 m (about 3 ft) and make a striking display planted in clumps in a mixed border.

PLATYCODON
grandiflorus
BALLOON FLOWER, CHINESE BELL FLOWER

This perennial originates from Japan and China. In summer, balloon-like buds open out into 5-petalled flowers like bells, coloured blue, purple, pink or white. The serrated elliptical leaves with a silvery blue cast form in a neat clump up to 60 cm (about 24 in) high and half that in spread. Plant the fully hardy species in full sun in well-drained sandy soil. Use rooted basal cuttings of non-flowering shoots to propagate in summer, sow seed in spring or autumn/fall, or divide clumps in spring.

Physostegia virginiana

PLECTRANTHUS
parviflorus
COCKSPUR

The large, scented leaves on this evergreen perennial have a texture like felt. With age, their grey colour becomes silver. The stems are woody and robust. Growing to a height of 40 cm (about 16 in) and a spread of 1 m (about 3 ft), this native of Australia bears loose heads of flowers, ranging from pale blue to purple, in spring to summer. Frost-tender, the plant does not do well below 10°C (about 50°F). Plant it in semi-shade or full light and keep moist. Trim tips to keep it neat in the growing season. Use stem cuttings or division to propagate in spring or summer.

POLEMONIUM
caeruleum
JACOB'S LADDER

Yellowy orange stamens provide a colourful contrast against the blue of this perennial's bell-shaped flowers when they open in summer. The flowers cluster among lance-shaped leaves arranged in many pairs like the rungs of a ladder, hence its common name. The plant grows in a clump to a height and spread of up to 60 cm (about 24 in) or more. The stem is hollow and upstanding. Grow this species in well-drained soil in sun or semi-shade. Propagate by division in early spring, from seed or by division in autumn/fall. A native of temperate Europe, it suits cooler climates.

POLYGONATUM
x hybridum
syn. *P. multiflorum*
SOLOMON'S SEAL

The elegant Solomon's seal is native to temperate areas of the northern hemisphere. A hardy plant, it does best in cool to cold areas where it will produce tubular, bell-shaped flowers in spring. A drooping stem grows to about 90 cm (about 36 in). White, green-tipped flowers hang down from the stem at the leaf axils. The broadly oval leaves rise off the stem like sets of wings. Rhizomes should be planted in autumn/fall to winter in a moist, shady spot in well-drained soil. The rhizomes can be divided in winter. It is difficult to grow from seed.

Platycodon grandiflorus

POLYGONUM
affine
KNOTWEED

The green of this evergreen perennial's small, shiny, lance-like leaves becomes bronze in winter. It spreads 30 cm (about 12 in) or more, forming a mat to about the same height. The flowers it bears in dense spikes in late summer and autumn/fall are small, red and funnel-shaped. Sunny or shady locations are fine for this fully hardy plant, but not damp conditions, so plant in soil that drains well, and a dry position in a bank or rock garden. Sow seed or propagate by division in spring or autumn/fall. The genus name means 'many knees', referring to the plant's swollen nodes.

Pontederia cordata

Portulaca grandiflora

Potentilla nepalensis

Pratia pedunculata

Pratia angulata

Potentilla 'Monsieur Rouillard'

PONTEDERIA
cordata
PICKEREL RUSH, PICKEREL WEED

This fully hardy marginal water plant from North America grows to 75 cm (about 30 in) with a 45 cm (about 18 in) spread. Its tapered, heart-shaped leaves are dark green and shiny. Blooming in summer, the deciduous perennial produces intense blue flowers in dense, terminal spikes. Plant it in full sun in up to 25 cm (about 10 in) of water. Cull flowers as they fade. Sow seed or propagate by division in spring.

PORTULACA
grandiflora
MOSS ROSE, SUN PLANT

This annual, native to South America, grows slowly, attaining a height of up to 20 cm (about 8 in) and a spread of 15 cm (about 6 in). Its small, lance-shaped, fleshy leaves are bright green and its branching stems are prostrate. Its large open flowers, which may be single or double, bloom in red, pink, yellow or white, in summer through early autumn/fall. Plant this half-hardy plant as ground cover or in a rockery or border, in well-drained soil in a sunny location. The flowers close in dull conditions and overnight. Sow seed in spring. Watch out for aphids.

POTENTILLA
CINQUEFOIL

The flowers of this large genus of deciduous shrubs and perennials are small and rounded, growing in clusters. Although the species all thrive in full sun in temperate climates, cultivars producing pink, red and orange blooms will be better coloured if protected from very strong sun. Plant all in well-drained, enriched soil. The species are indigenous to the northern hemisphere, from temperate to arctic regions. Perennials are generally frost-hardy and propagated by division in spring or from seed or by division in autumn/fall. Some species are used medicinally for such ailments as diarrhoea, cramps, mouth sores, enteritis, fever and jaundice. The root bark of one species is said to stop nose-bleeds, and even internal bleeding.

P. 'Monsieur Rouillard'

The flowers borne on this cultivar through summer are saucer-shaped and double, in deep red hues. Its dark green leaves resemble those of a strawberry plant. This perennial matures into a clump 45 cm (about 18 in) wide and high.

P. nepalensis

A profusion of flowers in shades of pink or apricot with cherry-red centres appears on the slim branching stems of this Himalayan perennial throughout summer. With bright green, strawberry-like leaves, this frost-hardy species reaches a height of 30 cm (about 12 in) or more and twice that in breadth. Plant it in well-drained soil.

PRATIA

This genus includes 20 species of predominantly carpet-forming perennials native to New Zealand, Australia, Africa and South America. The species have multiple branching stems and little lobed leaves. A profusion of starry flowers is followed by globular berries. These plants range from frost- to semi-hardy and generally enjoy damp but porous soil, total sun or partial shade and protection from the elements. Water liberally during the growth period and sparingly in winter. Some species are susceptible to slugs if over moist. They make excellent rockery specimens, but they have a tendency to overrun the garden. Propagate by division or from seed in autumn/fall.

P. angulata

This frost-hardy New Zealand creeper has wide, rounded, deep green leaves with roughly serrated edges. In spring white starry flowers with purple veins appear in the leaf axils, followed in autumn/fall by globular, reddish purple fruits. This species will tolerate full sun and enjoys damp soil.

P. pedunculata

A creeping perennial with small leaves, this species is good for ground cover as it is low-growing and spreads widely into a carpet, taking root at its nodes. A native of the coast and tablelands of eastern Australia, it blooms profusely in spring and early summer. Its 5-petalled flowers are star-shaped and usually mid-blue or paler to the point of white, although sometimes of a more purple hue. It also bears small berries. The species prefers moist soil in a sunny position, with partial shade from hot noonday sun. It is frost-resistant. Propagate from seed or by division in autumn/fall.

PRIMULA
PRIMULA, PRIMROSE

Fragrant, colourful flowers on stems above a rosette of basal leaves is characteristic of this genus, mostly from the temperate regions of the northern hemisphere. The flowers can be flat, trumpet-shaped or bell-shaped. Primulas like fertile, well-drained soil, partial shade and ample water. Propagate from seed in spring, early summer or autumn/fall, or by division or from root cuttings. Remove dead-heads and old foliage after blooming. There is a primula for virtually every position and purpose. Primula groups include: Candelabra, Polyanthus and Auricula. A floury substance called 'farina'—the term for the flour ground from cereal grains—covers the leaves, stems and sepals of some primulas.

P. denticulata
DRUMSTICK PRIMULA, DRUMSTICK PRIMROSE

The name of this frost-hardy Himalayan perennial refers to the toothed profile of the leaves, which are mid-green and broadly lanceolate. A neat and vigorous grower, it reaches a height and spread of 30 cm (about 12 in). It blooms in early to mid-spring, when open flowers of pink, purple or lilac, with yellow centres, crowd in rounded terminal clusters atop thick hairy stems.

P. florindae
HIMALAYAN PRIMROSE

Growing 60 cm–1 m (about 2–3 ft) high, this fully hardy perennial blooms in spring. The flowers—up to 60 of them to an umbel—are bright yellow and hang like little bells against a backdrop of broad, mid-green leaves with serrated edges.

P. japonica
JAPANESE PRIMROSE

Forming a clump up to 60 cm (about 24 in) high and 50 cm (about 20 in) across, this fully hardy native of Japan blooms from thick stems in spring to early summer. Its shiny flowers are pink or deep red, although the cultivar 'Postford White' offers a white, flattish round flower. This perennial has elliptical, serrated, pale green leaves.

P. malacoides
FAIRY PRIMROSE

Small, open flowers bloom in spiral masses on this frost-tender perennial, sometimes grown as an annual. It is a native of China. The single or double flowers range in colour from white to pink to magenta. Its oval-shaped, light green leaves have a hairy texture, as does its erect stem. The species reaches a height and spread of 30 cm (about 12 in) or more.

Primula vulgaris

Primula florindae

P. obconica
POISON PRIMROSE

Dense flower clusters grow in an umbellate arrangement on hairy, erect stems on this perennial. A native of China, it grows to 30 cm (about 12 in) high and as much or more in spread. Flowering time is winter through spring. The yellow-eyed, flattish flowers, 2.5 cm (about 1 in) across, range in colour from white through pink to purple. The light green leaves are elliptical, serrated and form a basal rosette. This is popular as a container plant.

P. × polyantha
POLYANTHUS

This fully hardy perennial, sometimes grown as an annual, reaches 30 cm (about 12 in) in spread and height. Large, flat, scented flowers in every colour but green bloom on dense umbels in winter through spring. Polyanthus are cultivars derived from *P. vulgaris* crossed with the cowslip (*P. veris*) and have been grown since the seventeenth century.

Primula malacoides

P. viallii

This 60 cm (about 24 in) tall perennial species from Yunnan Province in China is remarkable for carrying its purple flowers in short spikes, quite unlike any other primula. The buds are paler than the open flowers, giving the inflorescence a two-tone effect. Foliage is lush and bright green. A cool, moist climate is needed.

P. vulgaris
ENGLISH PRIMROSE, COMMON PRIMROSE

This is one of the most familiar wildflowers in Europe and it likes its cultivated conditions to mirror its cool woodland native environment. It is low-growing to around 30 cm (about 6 in), usually frost-resistant, and produces a carpet of bright flowers in spring. The flattish flowers are pale yellow with dark eyes (but the garden forms come in every colour), and bloom singly on hairy stems above rosettes of crinkled, lance-shaped, serrated leaves. Both leaves and flowers are edible.

Primula obconica

Primula denticulata

Primula viallii

Primula japonica

Primula × polyantha

PRUNELLA
grandiflora
LARGE SELF-HEAL

Purple, 2-lipped flowers grow in erect spikes above leafy stubs in spring and summer on this hardy, semi-evergreen perennial. A native of Europe, it is good for ground cover or rock gardens, having a spread and height of 50 cm (about 20 in). Plant in moist, well-drained soil in a sunny location. Propagate by division in spring. Trim out old flower stems before they seed. The species is a member of the Lamiaceae family (as is mint), of a genus that includes woundwort, and is said to be beneficial for wounds, throat irritations, thrush, diarrhoea, fits, convulsions, worms and stomatitis.

PTILOTUS
exaltatus
MULLA MULLA, TALL PUSSY-TAILS

This drought-resistant perennial, native to the arid inland of Australia, bears lilac-grey to dark pink flowers in feathery, cylindrical clusters on strong upstanding stems above lance-shaped, grey-green leaves. Flowering occurs in spring, possibly winter through summer. It grows 60 cm–1 m (about 2–3 ft) tall with a 60 cm (about 24 in) spread. The species needs well-drained, composted soil in an open, sunny location. Propagate from cuttings in spring or seed at any time of the year.

PULMONARIA
angustifolia
BLUE COWSLIP

Dark blue flowers, sometimes tinged pink, bloom through spring on this frost-resistant European perennial. The flowerheads have a 5-lobed tubular shape and are held above basal rosettes of mid-green foliage. The plant grows to a height and spread of 25–30 cm (about 10–12 in). Plant in moist, well-drained soil in shade. Propagate by division in spring or autumn/fall. It is a relative of lungwort, used by ancient herbalists to treat wounds, diarrhoea, haemorrhoids and respiratory ailments; its effectiveness for the last condition having been inferred from its lung-shaped leaves.

PULSATILLA
vulgaris
syn. *Anemone pulmonaria*
PASQUE FLOWER

Nodding, six-petalled flowers bloom in spring on this fully hardy perennial from Europe. The yellow centres of the flowers are a stark colour contrast to the petals, which can range through white, pink and red to purple. The finely divided leaves are pale green. Reaching 25 cm (about 10 in) in height and spread, the species is good in a sunny rock garden, in well-drained soil rich in humus. Avoid disturbing the roots. Sow seed when fresh or propagate using root cuttings in winter.

RAMONDA
myconi
syn. *R. pyrenaica*
BALKAN PRIMROSE, PYRENEAN PRIMROSE, ROSETTE MULLEIN

From branched, reddish brown stems this perennial produces flattish flowers—5-petalled and resembling African violets—in hues of white, pink, blue, lavender or purple, with yellow, pointed anthers. The flowers bloom late in spring and early in summer. Reaching a height and spread of 8–10 cm (about 3–4 in), this fully hardy evergreen, from the mountains of southern Europe, bears rosettes of rounded leaves that are wrinkled and hairy (more so on the undersides), with wavy and toothed edges. Grow in a rock garden or shallow pot. Add fragments of limestone to a potting mix of sand, loam and leafmould. Keep moist and shade from full sun.

RANUNCULUS
BUTTERCUP

This is a genus of some 250 species, mostly annuals and perennials, grown for their colourful flowers. The name derives from the Latin for 'frog' as some of the genus are aquatic plants, although these are not widely cultivated. Most species are tuberous and thrive in cool moist conditions, in sunny or shady locations. They are fully to half-hardy. Sow seed when fresh or propagate by division in spring or autumn/fall. The genus includes two species of buttercups that are popular folk cures for arthritis, sciatica, rheumatism and skin conditions including the removal of warts.

R. aconitifolius
FAIR MAIDS OF FRANCE

Cultivated to produce pure white, single or double flowers, this perennial flowers in terminal clusters on robust branched stems from spring to summer. Its dark green leaves have 3 or 5 lobes with saw-edges. The plant grows to 60 cm (about 24 in) high over a slightly lesser spread. The species is native to southern and central Europe.

R. gramineus

With bluish green leaves like grass, this perennial has a compact spread

Pulsatilla vulgaris

Ramonda myconi

Ranunculus gramineus

Prunella grandiflora

Pulmonaria angustifolia

Ranunculus aconitifolius

Ptilotus exaltatus

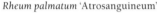

Rheum palmatum 'Atrosanguineum'

Ranunculus lyallii

Rhodochiton atrosanguineum

Reinwardtia indica

Raoulia australis

and grows 50 cm (about 20 in) tall. It blooms in late spring and early summer producing yellow, cupped flowers. Plant it in rich soil.

R. lyallii
MT COOK LILY, MOUNTAIN LILY

Native to the high altitude regions of the South Island of New Zealand, this erect thicket-forming perennial grows to 1 m (about 3 ft) tall. Its broad woody foliage can be up to 7 cm (about 3 in) wide and is a lustrous deep green. Attractive glossy, white, cup-shaped flowers appear in branched clusters on tall stems in summer. This fully hardy species will not bloom in arid conditions and rarely produces seeds in cultivation. It requires the cold conditions of high altitude, plentiful water and porous fertile soil.

RAOULIA
australis

GOLDEN SCABWEED

Suitable for rock gardens, this native of New Zealand lays down a solid carpet of silvery leaves 1 cm (about ½ in) deep over a spread of 25 cm (about 10 in). In summer it produces miniscule flowerheads of fluffy yellow blooms. Plant this perennial in moist, well-drained, acidic soil that has been well composted. Give it an open, sunny location. Sow seed when fresh or propagate by division in spring.

REINWARDTIA
indica

syn. *R. trigyna, Linum trigynum*
YELLOW FLAX

This winter-flowering native of the mountains of northern India is an evergreen shrub bearing sprays of golden flowers with overlapping petals forming a wide-flaring funnel. Its leaves are 7.5 cm (about 3 in) long, bright green ovals. Plant in semi-shade or full sun, in fertile, well-drained soil. Watch for two-spotted mite. Water well when growing, easing off when dormant. Prune tips to encourage branching in young plants. Prune severely after flowering. Propagate from soft tip cuttings late in spring.

RESEDA
odorata

MIGNONETTE, LITTLE DARLING

A moderately fast-growing annual, renowned for the strong fragrance of its flowers. The conical heads of small greenish flowers with dark orange stamens are otherwise unspectacular. Flowering is in summer through early autumn/fall. Remove dead-heads to prolong flowering. Plant it in well-drained, fertile soil in sun or partial shade. Sow seed in spring or autumn/fall. It will grow to 60 cm (about 24 in) high and about half that in spread.

RHEUM
palmatum 'Atrosanguineum'

A cousin of the rhubarb we eat, this fully hardy perennial bears panicles of small, bright red flowers that open early in summer. It has deep green leaves with decoratively cut edges, and reaches up to 1 m (about 3 ft) in height and 60 cm (about 24 in)

in spread. Grow in deep, rich soil that drains well but retains moisture. Give it a sunny or partially shaded location. Propagate from seed or by division in spring or autumn/fall. *R. palmatum* itself has white flowers.

RHODOCHITON
atrosanguineum

syn. *R. volubile*
PURPLE BELLS

A native of Mexico, this evergreen leaf-stalk climber is mostly grown as an annual. The flowers it bears in late spring through late autumn/fall comprise a long, finger-like, dark purple corolla protruding from a bell-shaped calyx in a redder hue of purple. Its leaves are ovate to heart-shaped with sparsely spiky edges. The plant is good for ground cover or for planting on trellises or fences, where it will grow to 3 m (about 9 ft). It thrives in sun and well-drained soil. Propagate from seed early in spring.

Reseda odorata

Roscoea cauteloides

Rudbeckia fulgida 'Goldsturm'

Rudbeckia hirta

Romneya coulteri

Rodgersia podophylla

Ricinus communis

RICINUS
communis
CASTOR OIL PLANT

The purgative of universal renown comes from the seeds of this species, native to Australia. The evergreen shrub, which is alone in its genus, is mostly grown as an annual. Rounded, prickly seed pods appear following the summer display of woolly clusters of red and greenish flowers. The plant's leaves are large, glossy and divided deeply into elliptical lobes. It grows rapidly, reaching 2 m (about 6 ft) in height and spread. This drought- and frost-resistant species takes to most soils and likes a sunny, open location. Propagate by sowing seed. Some warn that the whole plant (but especially the seeds) contains an irritant that can poison the blood.

RODGERSIA
podophylla

Suited to pond surrounds, this rhizomatous perennial has unusual leaves comprising 5 to 9 large leaflets,

with a touch of copper to their green colour. Multi-branched panicles of star-shaped flowers bloom in mid-summer in a froth of cream. Plant in moist soil and protect from strong wind. Tolerates full shade, but is better in partial shade. Propagate by division in early spring or from seed in autumn/fall. This frost-hardy species grows to a height of 1–1.2 m (3–4 ft) and a spread of 75 cm (about 30 in).

ROMNEYA
coulteri
CALIFORNIA TREE POPPY, MATILIJA POPPY

This summer-flowering, shrubby Californian perennial produces large sweetly scented, poppy-like flowers with white colour highlighted by the gold of fluffy stamens. The silvery green leaves are deeply divided, their edges sparsely fringed with hairs. Sensitive to disturbance but a vigorous grower once established, this fully hardy species forms a bush up to 2.4 m (about 8 ft) high, with a spread of 1 m (about 3 ft). Grow it in well-drained soil in full

sun. In colder climates, protect the roots. Sow seed in early spring.

ROSCOEA
cauteloides

Bearing a yellow flower similar to an orchid in summer, this frost-hardy tuberous perennial grows to 25 cm (about 10 in) with a 15 cm (about 6 in) spread. Glossy leaves are lance-shaped, erect and wrap into a hollow stem-like structure at their base. Grow this species in cool soil that is rich in humus. Keep the soil moist in summer. Choose a sunny or semi-shaded location. When it dies back, top-dress with mature compost or leafmould. Propagate by division in spring or from seed in winter or autumn/fall.

RUDBECKIA
CONEFLOWER

These North American annuals, biennials and perennials are popular for their bright, daisy-like flowers with a prominent dark-coloured central cone (hence their common

name). Plants range from 60 cm–2 m (about 2–6 ft) tall, depending on species, and spread up to 1 m (about 3 ft) wide. The summer and autumn/fall blooms provide good cut flowers. Grow in moist soil in a sunny position. Start from cuttings in spring. Propagate from seed or by division in spring or autumn/fall.

R. fulgida 'Goldsturm'

This upstanding perennial bears flowerheads like daisies, yellow with central black cones. Growing 60 cm (about 24 in) high with a spread of 30 cm (about 12 in) or more, the plant has narrow lanceolate green leaves. Both sunny and shaded locations are suitable. It is very fashionable for massed plantings in meadow-style gardens.

R. hirta

The flowerheads on this branching annual are big, daisy-like and bright yellow, with central cones of green or purple. Its leaves are mid-green and lance shaped. It reaches 30 cm–1 m (about 1–3 ft) tall, with a spread of 30 cm (about 12 in).

Salvia elegans

Rudbeckia laciniata 'Golden Glow'

Salvia azurea

Salvia uliginosa

Salvia splendens

R. laciniata 'Golden Glow'

The double, daisy-like flowerheads on this upstanding perennial are yellow with green centres. Each of its leaves comprises small lanceolate leaflets in mid-green. It grows to over 2 m (about 6 ft).

SALPIGLOSSIS
sinuata
PAINTED TONGUE

Offering a variety of flower colours including red, orange, yellow, blue and purple, this species from Chile blooms in summer and early autumn/fall. The 5 cm (about 2 in) wide, heavily veined flowers are like small flaring trumpets. The lanceolate leaves are light green. A fast grower, this branching annual reaches a height of 40–50 cm (about 16–20 in) and a spread of at least 40 cm (about 16 in). It is both frost- and drought-tender. Grow it in well-drained, rich soil in a sunny location, supporting its stems. Watch out for aphids. Propagate from seed early in either spring or autumn/fall.

SALVIA
BLUE SAGE

This large and widely distributed genus of annual and perennial herbs and shrubs includes species whose leaves are used as edible herbs as well as for a host of folk remedies. The genus is named from the Latin *salveo*, to save or heal. The leaves of most species are aromatic, and many produce decorative garden displays with spikes of small thimble-shaped flowers with two lips. Establish these species in fertile well-drained soil in a sunny location. Propagate annuals from seed and perennials by division in spring or from softwood cuttings in spring and summer.

S. azurea
BLUE SAGE

Dense spikes of white or deep blue flowers bloom in terminal spikes in summer and autumn/fall on this perennial. The narrow green leaves have a grey cast. This native of North America grows to 2 m (about 6 ft). It is drought-tender but resistant to frost.

S. elegans
syn. *S. rutilans*
PINEAPPLE-SCENTED SAGE

A smell of pineapples comes from this perennial's oval leaves, which are toothed and hairy. Growing to a height and spread of 1 m (about 3 ft), the half-hardy species blooms in summer and autumn/fall, producing scarlet flowers in spiral clusters.

S. farinacea 'Blue Bedder'
MEALY-CUP SAGE

This species is grown as an annual in regions that have cold winters and sometimes also in warmer climates. Growing to 45 cm (about 18 in), the perennial bears its violet-blue flowers in slender racemes on whitish stems. This cultivar was developed in North America.

S. nemorosa
syn. *S. virgata* var. *nemorosa*

Many slender, erect spikes of pinkish purple flowers bloom in summer on branching racemes on this perennial. Growing 1 m (about 3 ft)

Salvia farinacea 'Blue Bedder'

Salvia nemorosa

high, with a 45 cm (about 18 in) spread, this fully hardy species has rough leaves of narrow elliptical shape.

S. splendens
SCARLET SAGE

This native of Brazil, which is grown as an annual, produces dense terminal spikes of scarlet flowers in summer through early autumn/fall. The leaves are toothed ellipses. It grows to 30 cm (about 12 in) with a similar spread. In hotter climates, give it a little shade. This species is half-hardy.

S. uliginosa

Long racemes of blue flowers appear on this branching species in summer and autumn/fall, amid serrated, elliptical to lance-shaped leaves. Growing to 2 m (about 6 ft) with a spread of 45 cm (about 18 in), it has slender, curving stems. Its soil should be moist. This species originates in South America.

Salpiglossis sinuata

SANVITALIA
procumbens
CREEPING ZINNIA

A native of Central America, this summer-flowering, fully hardy annual produces masses of bright yellow flowerheads like 2.5 cm (about 1 in) daisies with black centres. It is a prostrate species with mid-green, ovate leaves, growing to 15 cm (about 6 in) high and spreading easily twice that. Grow it as ground cover or in a hanging basket, in fertile well-drained soil in a sunny position. Sow seed in situ in spring or early autumn/fall.

SAPONARIA
ocymoides
SOAPWORT

Ideal for banks, rock gardens or trailing over walls, this tough alpine perennial, a native of Europe, forms a thick carpet from which profuse terminal clusters of small, flattish flowers, coloured pink to deep red, bloom in late spring and early summer. Grow this fully hardy species in sun in sandy, well-drained soil. Propagate from softwood cuttings in early summer or seed in spring or autumn/fall. The common and generic names refer to the juice of the plant's crushed leaves which, lathered in water, can be used as a soap substitute.

SARRACENIA
flava
YELLOW PITCHER PLANT

This insectivorous plant, native to North America, has cylindrical, yellowish green pitchers (modified leaves) marked in red and with a hooded top. The pitchers secrete nectar which, together with the bright colours of the plant, attract insects which become trapped and are absorbed into the plant. Strongly scented, yellow or greenish yellow flowers are borne on long stems in late spring to summer. During the growth period it requires wet conditions, and in winter, when dormant, cool moist conditions are preferred. Grow in full sun or part-shade. Frost-tender, it requires a minimum temperature of 5°C (about 40°F).

SAXIFRAGA

Both the foliage and blooms on these perennials are equally appealing. The genus comprises some 370 species of evergreens and semi-evergreens. Their natural territory includes temperate, alpine and subarctic regions but many garden hybrids have been cultivated, and they serve well in rock gardens, in edges and as ground cover. The flowers are mostly white, sometimes spotted with pink, but other colours are also available. Use rooted offsets for propagation in winter or seed in autumn/fall. The genus name combines two Latin terms, 'rock' or 'stone' and 'to break', suggestive of either the hardiness of their rooting system or their reputed medicinal effect on bladder stones.

S. caespitosa
MOSSY SAXIFRAGE

This frost-hardy perennial grows low over a spread of 15 cm (about 6 in). White flecks adorn its small leaves, which cluster into leafy masses. Flowers with open, flared back petals, in white or, more commonly, a shade of pink, bloom in early spring. Grow it in moist soil in a sunny, open position.

S. paniculata
syn. S. aizoon
LIVELONG SAXIFRAGE

This summer-flowering evergreen perennial from central Europe bears terminal clusters of 5-petalled white flowers, often with spots of reddish purple on erect stalks. Other colours include pale pinks and yellows. The bluish green leaves, which are stiff and strap-like with saw edges, form a rosette below the flower stems. The species grows to a height and spread of 20–25 cm (about 8–10 in).

S. stolonifera
syn. S. sarmentosa
MOTHER OF THOUSANDS

Geranium-like leaves are a feature of this perennial, which is a native of eastern Asia. The rounded glossy leaves are olive green with silver veins, purplish pink on the under-

Saponaria ocymoides

Sarracenia flava

Saxifraga caespitosa

Sanvitalia procumbens

Saxifraga paniculata

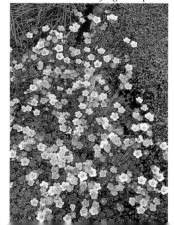

Scaevola aemula

Scabiosa atropurpurea

Schizanthus pinnatus

Scaevola 'Mauve Clusters'

Saxifraga stolonifera

sides. In spring through early summer, oddly petalled white flowers are borne in delicate panicles on thin, erect stalks. One petal on the tiny flowers seems to outgrow its 4 companion petals. This frost-tender species makes a good ground cover or container plant. It grows to a height of 15–20 cm (about 6–8 in) and spreads 30 cm (about 12 in) by runners.

SCABIOSA

SCABIONS

This genus of annuals and perennials, found widely in temperate climates, produces tall-stemmed, honey-scented flowers ideal for cutting. Blooms of multiple flowerets with protruding filaments, giving a pincushion-like effect, are a feature. Flower colours range from pinkish white to deep purple. Most species will thrive in full sun in well-drained, alkaline soil. Propagate annuals from seed in spring; perennials from cuttings in summer, seed in autumn/fall, or by division in early spring.

S. atropurpurea

This bushy annual produces flowers from summer through to early autumn/fall, provided blooms are cut or dead-headed. The dome-shaped flowerheads are some 5 cm (about 2 in) wide and fragrant, mainly crimson but also in white,

pink, purple and blue. Sizes vary from 50 cm (about 20 in) for dwarf forms, up to 1 m (about 3 ft) high for taller plants. This fully hardy species has lobed, lance-like foliage.

S. caucasica

PINCUSHION FLOWER

Flat, many petalled flowerheads in pink, red, purple or blue hues, with pincushion-like centres, often in a contrasting colour, make these summer-flowering annuals popular for borders and cut flowers. A busy plant with lobed mid-green leaves, it reaches a height and spread of 50–60 cm (about 20–24 in). The native species is from the Caucasus, and there are many fully hardy cultivars.

SCAEVOLA

FAN FLOWER

The distinctive flowers of this genus of about a hundred evergreen perennials and small shrubs found in tropical and subtropical regions, particularly of Australia and the islands of the Pacific, all have 5 petals shaped like fans. They come in many colours, from white to mauves and blue. The plants are excellent as ground cover or in rockeries or hanging baskets. They like sun or partial shade and well-drained soil. Propagate from cuttings in spring and summer.

S. aemula

FAIRY FAN FLOWER

The thick, coarsely toothed, dark green leaves on this perennial herb grow along spreading stems to form ground-hugging cover not more than 50 cm (about 20 in) high. Its spread is typically 1 m (about 3 ft). Spikes of large mauve-blue flowers with yellow throats bloom in spring and summer. This species, native to the sandy coastal regions of Australia, resists drought, frost and salt spray.

S. 'Mauve Clusters'

This spreading perennial flowers profusely in spring and summer. The small flowers present as mauve masses against a backdrop of bright green leaves. Growing very close to the ground, the frost-hardy cultivar spreads as much as 2 m (about 6 ft).

SCHIZANTHUS

pinnatus

syn. S. wisetonensis
BUTTERFLY FLOWER, POOR MAN'S ORCHID

These attractive plants, native to Chile, are grown for their exotic blooms and pale green, fern-like foliage. The orchid-like flowers come in a range of colours from white, pinks and mauves to scarlet and purple, all with speckled yellow throats. They need fertile well-drained soil, partial shade, and protection against both frost and heat. They

Scabiosa caucasica

grow into a bush up to 1 m (about 3 ft) high, with a 30 cm (about 12 in) spread, although there are more compact cultivars. They are usually grown in containers or greenhouses for winter and spring flowers, but make fine spring- and summer-flowering bedding plants in mild climates. Propagate from seed in late summer and autumn/fall. Encourage young plants into bushy growth by nipping off growing tips. A light feeding of bone meal encourages flowering. Watch for aphids.

A Field Trip to Dochu La

The flight to Bhutan from the cities of Calcutta and Delhi passes over a region of stark contrast. As your light aircraft crosses the flat expanse of the Bangladesh plains, which can be either dry and dusty or completely flooded, you will see far to the north the snow-covered peaks of the world's tallest mountains, hanging suspended above an ever-present haze. As your descent begins, you pass closely over a myriad of ridges and slopes still completely clothed in pristine forest. Soon you slip into the Paro valley and land at the airstrip which services Bhutan's capital, Thimphu, which has a population of 20 000. Walk down the steps and treat yourself to the rarified Himalayan air, with spectacular scenery whichever way you look.

This was certainly not the way that plant collectors in the nineteenth and early twentieth century arrived in the kingdom, but Bhutan's diversity of plant species was a big enough incentive for them to endure the hardship of a long overland journey through India to reach these botanical crown jewels. Many of our most attractive garden plants originated in the

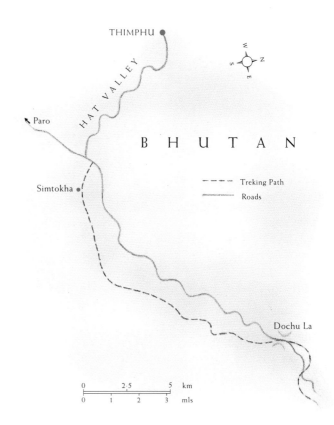

forests of Bhutan, ranging from large-flowering *Magnolia* and *Rhododendron* species, shrubby *Pieris* and *Daphne* species, to *Impatiens* and *Primula*. Nowhere else in the world can you see as many species from the *Primula* genus. The best time to see *Primula denticulata* in Bhutan is April. Spring weather is often clear and cold at night but pleasantly warm during the day.

Bhutan is a small Bhuddist country to the east of the famous Indian districts of Darjeeling and Sikkim, with Tibet to the north. The interior is protected physically by ranges of forested hills and a scarcity of roads, while its culture is maintained intact by a monarchist government committed to conservation of the environment. Fortunately for both the visitor and the Bhutanese, its policy of sustainable tourism, designed to protect the country's fragile natural and cultural riches, allows only limited access.

Thimphu, the base for your field trip, lies 30 km (about 19 miles) to the east of the airstrip. The road from here climbs east out of the Thimphu valley and, after about 20–25 km (about 12–15 miles), reaches a pass called the Dochu La. Most visitors travel to the pass by taxi, coach or jeep, the hardy returning part of the way on foot. A trekking path winds downhill for about 15 km (about 9 miles), passing through open forest with clearings. The walk back to the road junction at Simtokha takes about four hours.

The view from Dochu La at 2800 m (about 9100 ft) allows a glimpse of distant snowy peaks, but the forests in the foreground are even more spectacular. The birches, oaks and firs always make an impressive combination, but in spring the gaze is really drawn to the multiple splashes of bright colour. These include the intense red of the tree rhododendron (*Rhododendron arboreum*), the stark and beautiful candles of the

A carpet of drumstick primulas at Dochu La.

Campbell magnolia (*Magnolia campbellii*) on branches otherwise bare of leaves; and the bright pink *Rhododendron kisangi*, this last species only recognized as a separate species in the 1980s and named after the queen of Bhutan.

In clearings on the ground and along the sides of the path, the round pink heads of the drumstick primula or primrose (*Primula denticulata*) can be seen. Common throughout the mid-altitudinal range and the most easily seen member of its genus in the Himalayas, *P. denticulata* is particularly impressive, with tall, flowering stalks and large, round umbels of flowers—a growth form which gives the plant its colloquial name. The leaves form a compact rosette. At flowering time they are a fresh, pale green, often closely packed in the rosette and tending to curl downwards along the edges. After flowering the leaves become much larger, up to 30 cm (about 12 in) long. The flowers are usually pink or purple, the intensity of colour varying considerably, although occasionally they can be white. Around Dochu La, drumstick primulas are mainly tall with purplish pink flowers. In other areas, where Bhutan's wild deer and yak or domestic flocks of sheep have been grazing, the stem may be very short and the flowers appear to sit down on the leaves.

In this area the drumstick primula can be found in shrubberies and on open slopes, but not in the shade of the forest interior. Like other primulas it grows close to water, often along the damp edges of paths. In the 1930s, the plant collector, Frank Kingdon Ward, said during one of his Himalayan expeditions: 'Primulas have a strong social sense. They hate to be alone. On the other hand they loathe all but their own kind. Each primula species stands up for its own rights, but once security is attained, then it is primulas against the world; at least the alpine world.'

The drumstick primula's natural range covers a wide diversity of habitat and climate. The species can withstand heavy frosts and in its highest Himalayan locations, up to 4500 m (about 14 750 ft), it will often spend some months under snow. In summer, its presence in open, rather than shaded, situations shows its ability to withstand long days of intense sunshine and heat.

In the Dochu La pass groups of tall pink drumstick primulas compete for your attention with the wildlife. Parties of small, brightly coloured birds move through the trees and understorey of bamboo and daphne—warbler-sized babblers and flycatchers, and the iridescent red and green sunbirds which perch among the rhododendrons to sip nectar. Overhead the occasional mountain hawk-eagle soars, and yellow-billed magpies flap across to their fir tree perches. It may be possible to glimpse muntjac deer or yellow-throated marten; these forests also hold small numbers of the elusive lesser, or red, panda.

Yet despite these distractions, a swathe of *P. denticulata* is spectacular enough to halt your progress. In this area particularly, the species grow in large concentrations, making the area flush with pink, with the whole scene framed by tall Himalayan firs and a glorious blue sky. It is a scene not easily forgotten, a reminder of the magnetic attraction which originally drew explorers to these mountains—and to their botanical treasures—a hundred years ago.

Primula denticulata

Primula

Primulas, or primroses, are botanically members of the genus *Primula*, which consists of as many as 500 species. They are concentrated in temperate Asia, more particularly in China and the Himalayas; smaller numbers of species occur in other areas of the world. *Primula denticulata* occurs right throughout the Himalayas, from Afghanistan to south-eastern Tibet and to Burma in the east. Its seed only reached England in the mid-nineteenth century. Some of the most popular English wildflowers are *Primula* species, namely the primrose, cowslip and oxlip (*P. vulgaris*, *P. veris* and *P. elatior* respectively).

Hardly any other genus offers such a treasury of perennials to the cool-climate gardener. With spikes of flowers in almost every colour known in nature and often with two or more colour zones in a flower, they attract the attention of enthusiasts and collectors. Their scale is generally small though there are a few that send up spikes 1 m (about 3 ft) in height. In warmer temperate climates a few species succeed, for instance fairy primula (*P. malacoides*), which is usually treated as an annual, poison primula (*P. obconica*) and the more brilliantly coloured polyanthuses, (*P. × polyantha*), which are treated as spring annuals in warmer areas.

The Primulaceae family contains 20 or so genera, most of them confined to the northern hemisphere. Another well-known genus (*Cyclamen*) contains the tuberous cyclamens.

Primula denticulata

Sempervivum arachnoideum

Sedum spurium

Sempervivum tectorum

Schizostylis coccinea 'Grandiflora'

Sedum rosea

SCHIZOSTYLIS

coccinea 'Grandiflora'

KAFFIR LILY, RIVER LILY

Spikes of cupped, gladiolus-like flowers provide bright splashes of crimson against long grassy foliage on this rhizomatous perennial, which blooms in autumn/fall. A South African native, it grows to a height of 40 cm (about 16 in) or more and a spread of about half that. Like most of its genus, it is a good source of cut flowers. Grow this frost-hardy species in moist, fertile soil. Give it some shade only where exposed to hot weather. Water amply during summer. Propagate by division every three years in spring. There are white and pink cultivars, the best known being the pale pink 'Mrs Hegarty'.

SEDUM

STONECROP

There are about 600 species and eight groups in this genus, comprising annuals, biennials, perennials, shrubs and sub-shrubs, mostly

Sedum spectabile

succulents. They serve well along borders and in rock gardens. Common features are the small overlapping leaf and cyme-type flowering. Their natural territory is wide: from the Far East and Europe to tropical mountain regions. Any soil is suitable, but they need sun. Propagate perennials from seed in spring or autumn/fall, or by division or from softwood cuttings in spring through mid-summer. Propagate annuals and biennials from seed sown under glass in early spring or outdoors in mid-spring.

S. rosea
syn. *Rhodiola rosea*
ROSEROOT

The tightly massed heads of pink buds produced by this perennial in late spring or early summer open to small star-shaped flowers, in pale purple, green or yellow. The saw-edged, elliptical leaves are fleshy. This fully hardy species grows into a clump 30 cm (about 12 in) in height and spread. The name comes from the scent of the fleshy roots, used in making perfume.

S. spectabile
SHOWY SEDUM

Spoon-shaped, fleshy, grey-green leaves grow in clusters on the branching erect stems of this perennial. Butterflies flock to the flattish heads of little pink star-like flowers which bloom late in summer. This Asian native grows to a height and spread of 45 cm (about 18 in). It is drought- and frost-resistant.

S. spurium

This summer-flowering, semi-evergreen perennial bears small blooms in big, rounded flower-heads; colours range from white to purple. Hairy stems carrying saw-edged elliptical leaves spread widely into a carpet 10 cm (about 4 in) deep, suitable for covering banks and slopes. It is frost-hardy.

SEMPERVIVUM

HOUSELEEK

These fully hardy, evergreen perennials with distinctive small rosettes of fleshy, elliptical or strap-shaped

leaves spread into a dense carpet, making good cover for walls, banks and rock gardens. Found in Europe, northern Africa and western Asia, their star-shaped flowers comprise 8 to 16 petals. Gravelly soil and sun are preferred. Flowering does not begin for several years. Propagate in summer from offsets left after the rosettes die following flowering.

S. arachnoideum
COBWEB HOUSELEEK

The web of white hairs covering the green, triangular-leaved rosettes of this species undoubtedly inspired its name. This evergreen produces pink to crimson flowers in loose terminal clusters through summer. A native of the European Alps, it grows to a height of 30 cm (about 12 in) and about half that in spread.

S. tectorum
COMMON HOUSELEEK, ROOF HOUSELEEK, HENS AND CHICKENS

The rosettes of this species are reddish tipped, sometimes red throughout. The flowers are a purple to rosy red and appear in one-sided terminal clusters on 30 cm (about 12 in) high stems in summer. The plant has a spread of about 20 cm (about 8 in) and a height of 10–15 cm (about 4–6 in). Applying bruised leaves to the skin has a cooling effect and is said to relieve burns, insect bites, skin problems and fever. The juice is used by some on warts and freckles. Shingles, haemorrhoids, and worms are also said to benefit from houseleek. In the Middle Ages, the plant was grown on house roofs to ward off evil spirits and lightning.

SENECIO
elegans
WILD CINERARIA

This semi-hardy, hairy annual is native to South Africa and has an erect habit, growing to 60 cm (about 24 in) tall. Its branching stems are covered with variable dark green leaves that range from entire to pinnate, up to 8 cm (about 3 in) long. In spring to summer, daisy-like purplish pink flowers appear in dome-shaped terminal clusters.

SIDALCEA
'Rose Queen'

The flower spikes borne in summer by this fully hardy perennial resemble hollyhocks. The large, cupped flowers are pink. The divided leaves form a basal clump with a spread of 60 cm (about 24 in). Overall height of this species is 1.2 m (about 4 ft) and tall plants may need staking. Establish in well-drained soil in sun. Propagate from seed or by division in spring or by division in autumn/fall.

SILENE
CAMPION, CATCHFLY

These annuals and perennials feature 5-petalled summer flowers, baggy calyces and a multitude of small, elliptical, often-silky leaves. Some of the species do well potted; others make good ground cover, with numerous stems forming a mound. Widely distributed throughout temperate and cold climates of the northern hemisphere, these fully to half-hardy evergreens like fertile, well-drained soil and full or partial sun. To propagate, use seed in spring or early autumn/fall or softwood cuttings in spring.

S. coeli-rosa
syn. *Agrostemma coeli-rosa, Lychnis coeli-rosa, Viscaria elegans*

This upstanding annual bears pinkish purple flowers with white centres in summer. Its green leaves have a greyish cast. It grows rapidly to 50 cm (about 20 in), with a spread of 15 cm (about 6 in).

S. vulgaris subsp. maritima
DOUBLE SEA CAMPION

This deep-rooted perennial bears a multitude of white flowers like pompons on branched stems in spring or summer. Its calyces are greenish and balloon-like; its lanceolate leaves have a greyish cast. Reaching about 20 cm (about 8 in) in height and spread, it can be grown on top of walls, in beds or containers. Cut the stems occasionally to bring on new growth. The species grows wild on cliffs along the European seaboard.

SISYRINCHIUM

These natives of South and North America can self-destruct in seasons of prolific blooming. This is because the flower stem kills off the leaf stem from which it sprouted. The genus includes fully to half-hardy species of annuals and perennials. Establish them in moist soil that drains well. Although tolerant of semi-shade, they prefer sun. They readily self-seed, or can be propagated by division in late summer. It is easy to mistake the narrow leaves of the seedlings for grass.

Silene coeli-rosa

S. graminoides
syn. *S. angustifolium, S. bermudiana*
BLUE-EYED GRASS

This semi-evergreen perennial blooms in spring, producing terminal clusters of small pale to dark purple flowers like irises, with yellow throats; some yellow with darker veins. The stalks are flattened and winged. The plant grows to 60 cm (about 24 in).

S. striatum
SATIN FLOWER

Long, narrow and sword-shaped, the leaves on this frost-resistant, semi-evergreen perennial are grey-green. In summer it bears slender spikes of little cream flowers, striped purple. The species, which originates in Chile, grows 45–60 cm (about 18–24 in) high, with a 30 cm (about 12 in) spread. There is also an attractive variegated form.

Sidalcea 'Rose Queen'

Silene vulgaris subsp. *maritima*

Sisyrinchium graminoides

Sisyrinchium striatum

Senecio elegans

Solidago 'Golden Wings'

Soleirolia soleirolii

Solidago virgaurea subsp. *minuta*

SMILACINA
racemosa
FALSE SPIKENARD, FALSE SOLOMON'S SEAL

Red fleshy fruits appear on this perennial after it blooms in spring through mid-summer, producing lemon-scented white flowers in feathery sprays above fresh green, elliptical leaves. Growing to 90 cm (about 36 in) high and a spread of about half that, this fully hardy plant likes semi-shade and moist soil of acidic pH. It is a native of North America.

SOLANUM
pseudocapsicum
JERUSALEM CHERRY, WINTER CHERRY, CHRIST-MAS CHERRY

The small scarlet berries that appear on this species after flowering are poisonous to eat but in some northern hemisphere countries are used as Christmas decorations. The starry white flowers, precursors to the berries, bloom in summer. A native of the Mediterranean, this frost-tender evergreen grows sedately into a bushy, velvety leaved shrub about 1.2 m (about 4 ft) high and wide. It is perhaps best grown as an annual, even in wild areas, in which case it should grow to 65 cm (about 26 in) tall. Several varieties with differently coloured fruit are available. The species is related to the potato, eggplant and tomato, as well as some less edible plants. The genus name refers to the narcotic qualities of some species.

SOLEIROLIA
soleirolii
syn. *Helxine soleirolii*
BABY'S TEARS, MIND-YOUR-OWN-BUSINESS, PEACE-IN-THE-HOME

Indigenous to the Mediterranean, this creeping herbaceous perennial has small, round, bright green leaves and tiny white flowers, which occur singly in the leaf axils. Grow in moist soil and semi-shade. And will survive frost even if its leaves are killed. It spreads widely and can be invasive unless contained; hanging baskets are ideal.

SOLIDAGO
GOLDENROD

Hay fever sufferers have had cause to dread the plants in this genus, although breeders have tried to reduce their pollen output. These rhizomatous perennials are mostly natives of eastern North America and, left unchecked, become invasive and weedy. The more compact garden cultivars have good foliage. Taller species produce graceful spikes in autumn/fall. These fully hardy plants grow well in sun or shade, in any well-drained soil. Most species self-seed or can be propagated by division of the clumps in spring or autumn/fall.

S. 'Golden Wings'

This perennial grows to 1.5 m (about 5 ft) high with a spread of 1 m (about 3 ft). It has downy, lance-shaped leaves with serrated margins, and produces small bright yellow flowers in feathery panicles early in autumn/fall.

S. virgaurea subsp. *minuta*

The miniature of a species found naturally in Europe, northern Africa and Asia, this goldenrod is 10 cm (about 4 in) in height and spread, a tenth the size of the species. Its alternate green leaves are small and lance-shaped. In autumn/fall, it bears neat terminal panicles of small, yellow flowerheads. Give it moist soil and shade.

x SOLIDASTER
luteus
syn. x *S. hybridus*, *Aster luteus*
YELLOW ASTER

When the daisy-like flowers first open at their mid-summer blooming, their disk and rays are gold, although the rays quickly fade to creamy yellow. The flowers cluster in flattish heads, 10 cm (about 4 in) across, on downy stems branched near the top. Leaves are mid-green. Grows to 60 cm (about 24 in) high and spreads somewhat more than that. This fully hardy species likes well-drained soil and full sun.

Smilacina racemosa

Solanum pseudocapsicum

x Solidaster luteus

STACHYS
byzantina
syn. S. lanata, S. olympica
LAMB'S EARS, LAMB'S TONGUE

The leaves give this perennial its common name: tongue-shaped, they are thick and whitish. Unfortunately their woolly surface turns mushy if rained on heavily. Frost also does damage. Nonetheless it makes a good ground cover or border plant, growing 30–50 cm (about 12–20 in) high, with a 60 cm (about 24 in) spread. Mauve-pink flowers appear in summer; nip the buds at the onset of blooming to make the foliage lusher. Establish in well-drained soil in full sun.

STOKESIA
laevis
STOKES' ASTER

This fully hardy perennial from the south-east of North America has evergreen rosettes, its narrow leaves green, basal and divided. The summer-flowering, blue-mauve or white blooms have a shaggy appearance, reminiscent of cornflowers. They last well as cut flowers. The plants grow to a height and spread of about 40 cm (about 16 in). Establish in well-drained soil in full sun. Water regularly in summer. Propagate from seed or root cuttings.

STRELITZIA

These feature plants are grown for their architectural foliage and spectacular flowers which resemble exotic birds. Natives of South Africa, they are cultivated in frost-free areas worldwide. In mild climates, blooms appear in winter and in the spring in cooler areas. They prefer nutrient-rich, well-drained soil in a slightly shaded area and are frost-tender to a minimum 5–10°C (about 40–50°F). They benefit from abundant watering and feeding. Propagate in spring by offsets or division, although rhizomes are large and difficult to divide. Named after George III of England's wife whose family name was Mecklenberg-Strelitz.

S. nicolai

This tree-sized plant has huge banana-like leaves which grow to at least 2 m (about 6 ft) or more on stems up to 5 m (about 15 ft) long. The outer flower segments are white and the inner flowers pale blue and enclosed in boat-shaped, brownish red or dark purple bracts.

S. reginae
BIRD OF PARADISE, CRANE FLOWER

The leathery, bluish green, banana-like leaves can be 75 cm (about 30 in) long, growing on stiff, erect stems. The striking flowers look like crested birds' heads. Carried on long stems, just above the foliage, the bright orange and purple-blue flowers are in boat-shaped, red-edged bracts.

SWAINSONA
galegifolia
DARLING PEA

In Australia—where this poisonous evergreen perennial grows naturally throughout the states of New South Wales and Queensland—the Aborigines are said to make a poultice from its crushed leaves to relieve swelling and bruising. Each of its light to dark green leaves comprises a dozen or so narrow elliptical leaflets. The pea-shaped flowers bloom in spring and summer in dense terminal heads. They can be pink, purple, carmine-red or white and perhaps also red or blue. Establish in well-drained, humus-rich soil in a sunny, open location. Water freely, easing off outside the growth season. Cull the old flowered shoots late in winter. To propagate, use scarified seed in spring or semi-ripe cuttings in summer.

TAGETES
MARIGOLD

These annuals are used in beds or for edges. Plant seed in spring. To prolong flowering, cull the deadheads. Watch out for attack by botrytis and slugs.

T. erecta
AFRICAN MARIGOLD, AZTEC MARIGOLD

A strong aroma comes from the glossy dark green leaves of this bushy annual from Mexico. The leaves' margins are deeply incised. The stems are upstanding and branching. It grows to about 50 cm (about 20 in) in height and spread. Orange or yellow daisy-like flowers bloom in summer and autumn/fall. The flowers can be as large as 10 cm (about 4 in) across. The species resists frost and drought. It suits most soils and likes a sunny, open location. Propagate from seed.

Tagetes erecta

Stokesia laevis

Strelitzia reginae

Swainsona galegifolia

Stachys byzantina

Strelitzia nicolai

T. patula
FRENCH MARIGOLD

The double flowerheads produced in summer and early autumn/fall by this bushy annual resemble carnations. They bloom in reds, yellows and oranges. The leaves are deep green and aromatic. This fast-grower reaches 30 cm (about 12 in) in height and spread. Like *T. erecta*, it is a native of Mexico. This marigold was introduced to European gardens via the south of France—hence its common name.

TANACETUM

Immortality came to Ganymede as a result of drinking tansy, a species of this genus that even in recent times has been used (despite being potentially quite poisonous even when applied externally) for promoting menstruation and treating hysteria, skin conditions, sprains, bruises and rheumatism. Confined mainly to the northern hemisphere, the species of this genus are today appreciated more for their daisy-like flowers. They are relatives of the chrysanthemum. The foliage of many of the perennials carry a strong fragrance. Grow them in sun in well-drained, dryish soil. Propagate by division in spring.

T. coccineum 'Brenda'
syn. *Pyrethrum* 'Brenda', *C. coccineum*
PYRETHRUM

The leaves are feathery and scented on this perennial. Its single flowerheads are magenta, appearing from late spring to early summer. The species grows 60 cm (about 24 in) high with a spread of 45 cm (about 18 in) or more.

T. ptarmicifolium

This is a bushy perennial spreading from a woody tap root. Its silvery lanceolate leaves are strongly divided. A frost-hardy species, with a maximum height and spread of 40 cm (about 15 in), it is good for the rock garden. In summer it bears white flowerheads in terminal clusters. They are very useful in floral arrangements.

TELEKIA
speciosa
syn. *Buphthalmum spesiosum*

Not highly recommended for the garden, this coarse, invasive perennial might nonetheless find a place around pools. The shape of the leaves varies from the base, where they are shaped like hearts, to the stems, where they are elliptical. Its scented flowers, which bloom in summer, are like gold daisies. The species grows 1.2–1.5 m (about 3½–4½ ft) tall with a spread of up to 1.2 m (about 3½ ft).

THALIA
dealbata
WATER CANNA

This aquatic perennial from the south-east of North America tolerates cool water, although it is frost-tender. Growing to 2 m (about 6 ft) in height and 60 cm (about 24 in) or more in spread, it carries blue-green leaves that are broadly elliptical to lanceolate with long stalks and a mealy whitish coating. Its stems are erect and unbranching. Its summer blooms are followed by decorative seed heads. The flowers, which occur in tall spikes, are violet and waxy, their six petals forming a tube. Establish the species in loamy soil in sun.

THALICTRUM
MEADOW RUE

A genus known for its fluffy, showy flowers, these perennials overall have a delicate presentation. The branches of their slender upstanding stems often intertwine. The leaves are finely divided and columbine-like. Blooming in summer and spring, the flowers have four or five sepals and conspicuous stamen tufts. They serve well in borders, particularly as contrast to perennials with bolder blooms and foliage, and in the margins of bush gardens. Propagate from seed when fresh or by division in spring. The genus has its roots in Europe, northern Africa, northern Asia, Himalaya and Tibet.

T. aquilegiifolium
GREATER MEADOW RUE

This spring-flowering perennial bears lilac or greenish white flowers in fluffy clusters on strong stems. Each grey-green leaf comprises three or seven small, elliptical, saw-edged leaflets composed into a feather-like arrangement, something like maidenhair fern. Growing 1 m (about 3 ft) high, the species has a spread of 45 cm (about 18 in). It is resistant to frost. Establish it in rich, damp soil in a protected location with partial shade. Sow seed in spring.

T. delavayi
syn. *T. dipterocarpum* of gardens
LAVENDER SHOWER

Rather than fluffy heads, this species bears a multitude of nodding, lilac flowers in loose panicles, their yellow stamens prominent. Flowering time is from the middle to the end of summer. The finely divided leaves give the mid-green foliage a dainty appearance. Reaching 1.2 m (about 3½ ft) high, this species has a spread of 60 cm (about 24 in).

Thalictrum aquilegiifolium

Thalia dealbata

Tanacetum coccineum 'Brenda'

Tanacetum ptarmicifolium

Tagetes patula

Telekia speciosa

Thalictrum delavayi

THUNBERGIA
alata
BLACK-EYED SUSAN

A black 'pupil' at the centre of each flat, golden-orange flower gives this annual from southern and eastern Africa its common name. Flowering occurs from early summer to early autumn/fall. A twisting climber, the plant grows fairly rapidly up to 3 m (about 9 ft). Its leaves are heart- or pear-shaped, with sparsely toothed edges. It prefers well-drained soil and a sunny, protected location. It is both frost and drought tender. Use cuttings or seed for propagation.

TIARELLA
cordifolia
FOAMFLOWER, COOLWORT

This vigorous spreading evergreen, a North American native, blooms profusely in early to late spring, producing terminal spikes of tiny, pink-tinged, white flowers with 5 petals. Its leaves are mostly pale green, lobed and toothed, with dark red marbling and spots, although the basal leaves take on an orange-red hue. Its height and spread when in flower are 30 cm (about 12 in) or more. Establish in moist well-composted soil in semi-shade. Propagate from seed or by division.

TITHONIA
rotundifolia 'Torch'
MEXICAN SUNFLOWER

Flowerheads resembling bright orange or red daisies up to 8 cm (about 3 in) across appear on this slow-growing annual in summer and early autumn/fall. Growing to 90 cm (about 36 in) high with a spread of 30 cm (about 12 in), this half-hardy species carries rounded lobate leaves. Establish it in well-drained soil in full sun. Propagate by seed sown under glass in late winter or early spring.

TORENIA
fournieri
WISHBONE FLOWER

This branching annual from tropical Asia has light to dark green, ovate or elliptical leaves with toothed edges. Its flowers, borne in summer and early autumn/fall, are pansy-like and deep purplish-blue, turning abruptly paler nearer the centre, and with a touch of yellow. Frost-tender, it grows fairly rapidly to a height of 30 cm (about 12 in) and a spread of 20 cm (about 8 in). Establish in rich, moist soil that drains well, in partial shade. Propagate from seed. Red, pink and white varieties are available.

TRADESCANTIA
virginiana
COMMON SPIDERWORT

A native of eastern North America, this perennial has dull green, strap-like leaves that grow up to 40 cm (about 18 in) long. It has an erect stem with spreading branches, and reaches a height of 45–60 cm (about 18–24 in) with a spread of 60 cm (about 24 in) or more. It bears small, 5 cm (about 2 in) wide, deep blue flowers with three petals in late spring to autumn/fall. This frost-resistant species is the foundation of many cultivars. Give it a protected location, in moist to dry soil, and fertilize. Propagate by division.

TRILLIUM
grandiflorum
WAKE ROBIN

The wild wake robin, a native of North America, has 3-petalled white flowers which fade to pale pink in spring, above deep green leaves. It is a perennial for a shaded spot in a cool climate where it will be long lived and easy to grow. The double-flowered form is beautiful but very rare and expensive. There are several other species, all with 3-petalled red or pink flowers.

TROLLIUS
europaeus
GLOBE FLOWER

The stem on this perennial from northern and central Europe is smooth, hollow and upstanding, branching at the apex. Its spring flowers are yellow and terminal, its 5 to 15 petal-like sepals forming a rounded shape 5 cm (about 2 in) across. Forming each mid-green leaf are 3 to 5 lobes arranged palmately, each lobe incised deeply. This frost-resistant species grows to a height of 60 cm (about 24 in) with a 45 cm (about 18 in) spread. Establish it in moist rich soil, in a protected location with some shade. Propagate from seed in spring or autumn/fall, by division in spring or autumn/fall.

Thunbergia alata

Tradescantia virginiana

Torenia fournieri

Tithonia rotundifolia

Tiarella cordifolia

Trillium grandiflorum

Trollius europaeus

Tropaeolum majus 'Alaska'

Veratrum nigrum

Ursinia anthemoides

Tropaeolum peregrinum

x *Venidio-arctotis cultivars*

Ursinia calenduliflora

TROPAEOLUM

NASTURTIUM

Bright flowers are the attraction of this genus of annuals, perennials and twining climbers, whose natural territory extends from Chile to Mexico. Frost-hardy to frost-tender, most species prefer moist, well-drained soil and a sunny or semi-shaded location. Propagate from seed, basal stem cuttings or tubers in spring. Watch out for aphids and the caterpillars of the cabbage moth.

T. majus

GARDEN NASTURTIUM, INDIAN CRESS

The stem is trailing and climbing on this fast-growing, bushy annual. Its leaves are rounded and variegated with radial veins. It blooms in summer and autumn/fall, its 5-petalled flowers spurred, open and trumpet-shaped, in many shades of red or yellow. It grows to a spread of 30 cm (about 12 in) and a height up to twice that. Avoid fertilizing this plant, which is resistant to frost but not to drought, and let it have sun. The spicy-flavoured leaves and flowers of this species are used to add taste to salads. There are several varieties with single or double flowers and compact or trailing habit. 'Alaska' has single flowers and prettily variegated leaves.

T. peregrinum
syn. T. canariense
CANARY CREEPER

This frost-tender South American annual vine climbs to over 2 m (about 6 ft). Its grey-green leaves have 5 broad lobes and radial veins. In summer to early winter, it bears small, trumpet-shaped yellow flowers; the upper pair of its 5 petals are bigger and fringed.

URSINIA

Native to South Africa and Ethiopia, this genus contains up to 40 species of annual and perennial herbs and shrubs. The plants have pinnate fern-like foliage. Open terminal clusters of yellow, white, orange or occasionally red flowers have purple or yellow centres. The blooms are followed by tubular or club-shaped seed pods. The species range from frost-hardy to frost-tender and require full light and porous soil. Propagate from cuttings or seed in spring. This genus is prone to aphids.

U. anthemoides
STAR OF THE VELD

This bushy annual, with its pale green feathery foliage, blooms in summer and early autumn/fall. Its flowerheads are like yellow daisies with dark centres. Growing 30 cm (about 12 in) high, with a 20 cm (about 8 in) spread, this frost-tender species likes sun and well-drained soil. Use seed or greenwood cuttings for spring propagation.

U. calenduliflora

This South African annual has pinnate foliage made up of narrow to rounded leaflets. Its flowers are yellow and are frequently marked with bronze around the base.

x VENIDIO-ARCTOTIS CULTIVARS

MONARCH OF THE VELD

In summer, these branching perennials bear large flowers like daisies in numerous hues. Most commonly grown as annuals, the plants carry lobate green leaves that have a greyish cast on the upper side and are almost white beneath. They grow sedately to a height and spread of 50 cm (about 20 in). Only half-hardy, they are from a hybrid genus that enjoys well-drained, fertile soil and sun. The plants are best propagated in late summer using semi-ripe cuttings. In frosty climates they are grown as annuals.

VERATRUM

nigrum

BLACK FALSE HELLEBORE

This species is a rare perennial from southern Europe and Asia. It carries long, nar-row, terminal spikes of small, purplish brown flowers with six petals that bloom from late summer. The big, pleated, elliptical leaves are arranged spirally into a sheath around the stout, erect stems. This fully hardy species grows to a height of 2 m (about 6 ft) and a spread of about half that. Establish it in moist rich soil, in a protected location in sun or semi-shade. Propagate *V. nigrum* in early spring from seed or by division. *V. album*, with cream flowers, and *V. viride*, with pale green flowers, are very similar to this species. Protect all from snails. All species are poisonous.

VERBASCUM

MULLEIN

Large, often complex, basal rosettes develop on these evergreens from Europe and the more temperate zones of Asia. Including both very large and some very coarse species, the genus offers much variety in the foliage, with leaves ranging from glossy to velvety. Summer flowering is mainly in the form of tall narrow spikes. There are frost-resistant through to fully hardy species. Establish all species in well-drained soil, and an open, sunny location though they do tolerate shade. Propagate from seed in spring or late summer or root cuttings in winter. Some species self-seed readily.

V. nigrum

BLACK MULLEIN, HAG TAPER

Long spikes of yellow flowers with almost black centres appear on this native of Morocco in summer through autumn/fall. The species' mid-green leaves taper to a point and carry a dense layer of hairs. This semi-evergreen, which is fully hardy, grows to a height and spread of around 1 m (about 3 ft). Most well-drained soils are suitable. Give it an open sunny location. Black mullein is used as a herbal remedy for colic, coughs and spitting blood. Applied externally, it is said to relieve haemorrhoids. Witches of the Middle Ages were thought to use the plant in their love potions and brews, hence the name 'hag taper'.

V. olympican

Not a long-lasting species, this semi-evergreen perennial grows sedately up to 1.5 m (about 4½ ft) with a spread of 60 cm (about 24 in). Its stems and leaves are hairy. The rosette-forming leaves are large, elliptical and silver-grey and spikes of 5-lobed yellow flowers appear in summer.

VERBENA

VERBENA

Because of a susceptibility to mildew, these biennials and perennials are considered best grown as annuals. Originating in Europe, they are characterized by small, dark, irregularly shaped and toothed leaves. They bloom in summer and autumn/fall. Half-hardy, they do best where winters are not severe. Establish in medium, well-drained soil, in sun or at most semi-shade. To propagate, use seed in autumn/fall or spring, stem cuttings in summer or autumn/fall, or division in late winter. You can also propagate in spring by division of young shoots. An agreeably spicy aroma is associated with most verbenas.

V. × hybrida

This trailing perennial bears slightly hairy leaves. It blooms in summer to autumn/fall, its fragrant flowers appearing in dense clusters 2 cm (about 1 in) across, many showing off white centres among the hues of red, mauve, violet, white and pink. Use this species in summer beds and containers. Avoid being heavy handed with fertilizers or the plants will yield more leaves than flowers.

V. laciniata

A prolific bloomer, this perennial grows only 30–50 cm (about 12–20 in) tall but spreads widely. It bears finely divided, grey-green leaves and heads of blue, magenta or violet flowers. Trim this half-hardy species back after flowering. Avoid mildew by not over-watering.

VERONICA

SPEEDWELL

These perennials are widespread through temperate regions. Although their flowers are usually blue, they encompass a wide variety of foliage and of size, with a height range from 30 cm (about 12 in) to over 1.2 m (about 4 ft). Some are evergreens, some semi-evergreens. Hardiness ranges from frost-resistant to fully hardy. Establish them in well-drained, fertilized soil in sun. To propagate, use seed in autumn/fall or spring, division in early spring or autumn/

fall, or either softwood or semi-ripe cuttings in summer.

V. prostrata

This perennial from the alpine regions of Australia and New Zealand has woody, branching stems and variable foliage, although all tooth-edged. The flowers are small and blue, with widely flared petals, occurring in upright spikes in spring and early summer. This species spreads widely into a mat of indefinite coverage, its height only 30 cm (about 12 in).

Veronica prostrata

Verbena laciniata

Verbena × hybrida

Verbascum nigrum

Verbascum olympican

Viola reichenbachiana

Veronica spicata

Viola hederacea

Vinca minor

Viola odorata

Vinca major

V. spicata

DIGGER'S SPEEDWELL

A European species, this fully hardy perennial reaches a height of 60 cm (about 24 in) and a spread of up to 1 m (about 3 ft). Its stems are erect, hairy and branching. Spikes of small star-shaped blue flowers bloom in summer. The leaves of this species are mid-green, linear to lanceolate in shape.

VINCA

PERIWINKLE

Shiny green leaves are common on these vining perennials and sub-shrubs from Russia and Europe. The flowers are widely flared with five lobes. Hardiness ranges from frost- and drought-resistant to fully hardy. Any soil is good provided it is not too dry. If you want ground cover, provide these evergreens with shade to semi-shade. If you want flowers, let them have more sun. Propagate by division in autumn/fall through spring, or from semi-ripe cuttings in summer.

V. major

GREATER PERIWINKLE

The leaves have a dark green gloss and are heart-shaped to pointed ovate on this tenacious evergreen vine from the Mediterranean. Widely spreading, with an erect woody stem, the species climbs as high as 3 m (about 9 ft). Brilliant blue flowers, 5 cm (about 2 in) across, are borne in late spring through early autumn/fall. It is drought-resistant and frost-resistant, and can also be aggressive and invasive.

V. minor

LESSER PERIWINKLE

The slender woody stems on this European evergreen creeper will cover ground over a distance of 3 m (about 9 ft) to lay down a mat of glossy, dark green leaves of pointed elliptical shape. The small flowers it produces in mid-spring through early summer are bluish lilac, purple or white. This species, like V. major, is often aggressive and invasive.

VIOLA

VIOLET, PANSY

Although the sweet violet (V. odorata) gives one of the best loved of flower perfumes, many of the other species are less fragrant. Their leaves can be solitary or in clumps, lightly to heavily textured, kidney to heart-shaped. Their hardiness ranges from half- to fully hardy. The annuals are suited to summer bedding, although big beds of them are needed if you want sufficient yield to pick. The perennials and sub-shrubs are good in beds and rock gardens. Some species have runners and are invasive. Most species do best in lean or fertile soil that drains well and retains moisture, with some preferring an acidic pH. Grow them in sun or shade. All bloom in spring.

V. hederacea

syn. V. reniformis, Erpetion reniforme

AUSTRALIAN NATIVE VIOLET

The tiny 5-petalled, scentless flowers that bloom on short stems on this creeping perennial from the south-east of Australia are lilac or white and solitary. They appear in spring, summer and autumn/fall. The plant's stems are prostrate, suckering and mat forming, spreading widely but reaching only 5 cm (about 2 in) in height. Its leaves are rounded and kidney-shaped, deep green and with irregular edges. Partially shade this frost-resistant but drought-tender species. Propagate V. hederacea by division in spring or autumn/fall.

V. odorata

VIOLET, SWEET VIOLET

A sweet perfume wafts from the flowers on this spreading, rhizomatous perennial from Europe, which grows 7 cm (3 in) high over 15 cm (about 6 in) or more in spread. Its dark green leaves are a pointy kidney shape with shallow toothed edges. Spurred, flat-faced flowers in violet, white or rose, bloom from late winter through early spring. Boasting many cultivars, this fully hardy species readily self-seeds and can be propagated by division in autumn/fall. The plants like well-composted, moist soil and a protected location in semi-shade.

V. reichenbachiana

WOOD VIOLET

This perennial bears small, flattish, pink, mauve or pale blue flowers in spring and summer. Its kidney-shaped leaves are green. Although an invasive species—spreading widely, growing to only 5 cm (about 2 in)—it can serve over a bank or in natural settings. Propagate from rooted runners in autumn/fall.

Wachendorfia thyrsiflora

Viola × wittrockiana

V. *septemtrionalis*

CONFEDERATE VIOLET

This spring-flowering perennial is native to North America and bears large flowers with a spur, in hues usually of bluish purple but sometimes white. Its hairy, green leaves are pointed and oval to heart-shaped and have toothed edges. The plant has creeping and suckering stems and grows 15–20 cm (about 6–8 in) in height and spread. Its preference is for well-composted, moist soil and a protected location in semi-shade. Propagate the fully hardy species from seed or by division.

V. *tricolor*

HEARTSEASE, WILD PANSY, JOHNNY JUMP UP, LOVE-IN-IDLENESS, PINK OF MY JOHN

Originating in the United Kingdom, this perennial or annual produces neat flowers with appealing faces from spring to autumn/fall, displaying shades of yellow, blue, violet and white. It has soft, angular, branching stems, and lobed ovate to lanceolate leaves, and grows to a height and spread of 5–15 cm (about 2–6 in). Frost-resistant, it prefers a sunny, open location, and readily self-seeds.

V. × *wittrockiana*

PANSY, VIOLA

This group of predominantly bushy perennials are almost always grown as biennials or annuals. Offering flowers of a great many hues, the species bloom in late winter through spring and possibly into summer in cooler climates. The flowers grow up to 10 cm (about 4 in) across and have 5 petals in a somewhat flat-faced array. Its mid-green leaves are elliptical, sometimes with toothed margins. Sedate growers, these plants reach about 20 cm (about 8 in) in spread and height. Propagate from softwood cuttings in spring. The usual distinction is that pansies have black blotches, violas none, but there are now intermediate types with pale-coloured markings.

WACHENDORFIA
thyrsiflora
RED ROOT

This attractive plant from South Africa grows to 1 m (about 3 ft). It has bright yellow flowers borne in a cluster along the flower stem in spring and early summer. The lance-shaped leaves are pleated. Grow in the shade in moist soil, ensuring the roots are kept damp while flowering. It is half-hardy and may need to be potted in very cold winters, but it will not flower in a pot. Propagate by division in spring. The corms have a red sap which was sometimes used as a dye in Africa, hence the common name.

WAHLENBERGIA
gloriosa
ROYAL BLUEBELL, AUSTRALIAN BLUEBELL

The name derives from the royal blue flowers, like 3 cm (about 1½ in) wide bells, that adorn this species in summer. The flowers, the largest of any of the several species of Wahlenbergias, have 5 petals and bloom profusely at the end of slender, sprawling stems. Its leaves are dark green, 2.5 cm (about 1 in) long and ovate with wavy edges. A native of the alpine regions of the Australian states of New South Wales and Victoria, this frost-hardy perennial grows to a spread of up to 20 cm (about 8 in) and a height of half that, and prefers cooler climates. Establish it in light to medium moist soil that drains well, in an open location in sun or semi-shade. Propagate from seed.

Viola septemtrionalis

Wahlenbergia gloriosa

Viola tricolor

XANTHORRHOEA
australis
GRASS TREE, BLACKBOY

Australia's ancient grass tree is a remarkable, long-lived plant but one seldom seen outside its native habitat. A dense tuft of narrow, arching, grassy leaves 1 m (about 3 ft) long, sprout from a trunk made up of a mass of old leaf bases held together by resin. It takes 30 years or more for the leaf tuft to rise above the trunk. Spears of small white or cream flowers, smelling of honey, appear after 10 to 15 years, but then erratically; often it will bloom after a bushfire. This frost-hardy plant likes well-drained soil and full sun. Plant while young, or propagate from seed in spring and autumn/fall. The resin from the trunk was used for making varnish.

XERANTHEMUM
annum
IMMORTELLE

A good source of dried flowers, this annual blooms in summer, produc-ing heads of purple daisy-like flow-ers; whites, pinks and mauves and doubles are also available. The leaves are silvery and lanceolate on this fully hardy species, which grows 60 cm (about 24 in) high with a 50 cm (about 20 in) spread. Grow in well-drained soil and full sun.

YUCCA
YUCCA

Huge clumps—in some species reaching to 13 m (about 40 ft)—are formed by the spear-like leaves of these evergreen plants from North and Central America. Yuccas carry showy clusters of flowers, mostly white, at the end of stalks which can measure 3 m (about 9 ft) or more. They need well-drained soil and full sun. If you grow them in containers, do not over water and ease off even more outside the growth season. Propagate from seed, root cuttings or by division in spring. Although not all are desert species, the yuccas are drought resistant. They are also resistant to frost.

Yucca filamentosa

Y. filamentosa
ADAM'S NEEDLE

Like 1 m (about 3 ft) long green spears, the leaves on this evergreen plant form a basal rosette. The leaves are edged with white threads. The flowers that bloom in terminal spikes from the middle to the end of summer are white and bell-shaped. This species is native to south-eastern North America and grows to 2 m (about 6 ft) high with a 1.5 m (about 5 ft) spread. It is fully hardy.

Y. gloriosa
SPANISH DAGGER, MOUND LILY

The stout erect stem on this ever-green plant has a tufted crown of stiff, spear-like leaves, which start out with a greyish cast but, as they mature, turn a deeper green. The white bell-shaped flowers appear in very long terminal spikes in summer through autumn/fall. This native of eastern North America reaches a height and spread of 1 m (about 3 ft).

ZANTEDESCHIA
ARUM LILY, CALLA LILY, PIG LILY

These tuberous perennials, indig-enous to South Africa, are charac-terized by the classic lily shape comprising an enfolding spathe like a funnel with a central finger-like spadix. The leaves are glossy green and arrow shaped. Mostly ever-greens in warm climates, this genus includes frost-tender to frost-resistant species, most being drought-tender. Establish in well-drained soil. Some prefer full sun, others partial shade. Propagate using offsets in winter.

Z. aethiopica
WHITE ARUM LILY, LILY OF THE NILE

The large flowers that appear on this species in spring are white, the spadix yellow. Although normally deciduous, the perennial can stay evergreen if given enough moisture. You can grow it around pools in water 15–30 cm (about 6–12 in) deep. Growing 60 cm–1 m (about 2–3 ft) high with a 30–50 cm (about 12–20 in) spread, the plant produces many large broad leaves.

Z., NZ Mixed hybrids

These are hybrids from *Z. rehmannii* and *Z. elliottiana* and offer a range of colours from red, pink and bronze to orange. Some have spotted leaves. Although there are miniatures, most reach 60 cm (about 24 in) or more, with a spread of 20 cm (about 8 in). They are not as easy to grow as their parents, needing warmth and very rich soil.

Z. rehmannii
PINK ARUM LILY, PINK CALLA

The spathe on this summer-flower-ing species is rosy purple with paler

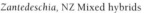
Xeranthemum annum

Zantedeschia, NZ Mixed hybrids

Xanthorrhoea australis

Yucca gloriosa

Zantedeschia aethiopica

Zinnia angustifolia

margins, enclosing a yellow spadix. Its arrow-shaped leaves are glossy green, basal, semi-erect and about a handspan long. It grows 40 cm (about 16 in) high with a spread of 30 cm (about 12 in). The species is half-hardy, and likes well-composted soil, a protected location and partial shade.

ZAUSCHNERIA
californica
CALIFORNIAN FUCHSIA

The common name refers both to the species' Californian origin and to its flowers that are indeed like fuchsias. These are bright red, appearing in terminal spikes on erect slender stems in late summer and early autumn/fall. The evergreen shrub has lance-like, 2 cm (about 1 in) long leaves, and grows to a height and spread of 50 cm (about 20 in). Give it light, well-drained soil and a sunny, open location. This species is not resistant to frost or drought.

ZINGIBER
zerumbet
WILD GINGER

A clump-forming ginger plant from India and Malaysia with very narrow, 30 cm (about 12 in) long leaves. On separate, tall stems, are overlapping cones of green bracts that age to red, surrounding white and gold flowers. Used to hot equatorial areas, it is frost-tender to a minimum 18°C (about 64°F) and needs a humid atmosphere in part-shade with plenty of water during growth period. Plant in moist, hu-

mus-rich soil. Propagate by division of rhizomes in spring. The rhizomes, unlike the edible ginger of *Zingiber officinale*, are bitter to eat, but can be used in potpourri.

ZINNIA
ZINNIA

The flowerheads on these half-hardy annuals are like dahlias. Establish them in fertile soil that drains well in a sunny position. They need frequent dead-heading. Sow seed under glass early in spring. Found through Mexico, Central and South America, this genus is an excellent source of cut flowers. Propagate by seed under glass in early spring.

Z. angustifolia
syn. Z. linearis
LITTLE STAR

This native of Central America grows hairy green leaves of elliptical shape. Its abundant flowers are orange-yellow. The plant is trailing in habit, with matt green leaves. A fast-growing annual, it reaches a height of 40 cm (about 16 in) and a spread of 30 cm (about 12 in). There is a very pretty white form.

Z. elegans
YOUTH-AND-OLD-AGE

This sturdy annual from Mexico is the best known of the zinnias. The flowerheads are purple, and bloom in summer to autumn/fall. It grows fairly rapidly to 60–75 cm (about 24–30 in), with a smaller spread. Its deep green leaves are linear to lanceolate. Hybrids offer hues of white,

Zinnia elegans

red, pink, yellow, violet, orange or crimson in flowers up to 12 cm (about 5 in) across. Grow in rich, loamy soil in an open, sunny location.

Z. haageana 'Old Mexico'
syn. Z. mexicana

The 6–8 cm (about 2½–3 in) wide single or double flowers on this annual are yellow and bronze. It flowers in summer and early autumn/fall. A fast-grower, this Mexican species reaches 60 cm (about 24 in) high, with a 20 cm (about 8 in) spread, its stem erect and branching. It is drought-resistant and frost-tender. 'Persian Carpet' is another well-known strain, with a few more petals.

Zauschneria californica

Zinnia haageana 'Old Mexico'

Zingiber zerumbet

Zantedeschia rehmannii

CHAPTER 3

Shrubs

*N*o garden is complete without the cohesive atmosphere that shrubs supply. With their multi-stemmed growth they fill in the garden picture between the lower growing annuals and perennials and the taller growing background trees. They unite the house and garden, make wonderful barriers for both sight and sound and can be grouped with one another to form eye-catching displays of colour almost all year round.

Shrubs are generally classified as deciduous or evergreen, although in more temperate areas some fall between these two groups and are termed partly or semi-deciduous.

Evergreen shrubs provide the permanent structure of a garden so necessary in the overall landscape design, especially in winter when the deciduous types are dormant. In this regard they make excellent backgrounds for deciduous plants. Also, consider the advantage of permanent plant foliage against a plain house or fence wall or where a division of garden space is needed.

Deciduous shrubs can provide the contrast elements of garden design. Their ever-changing attributes give continued interest. In winter their bare branches can look magnificent against green backgrounds or a winter skyline, then plants such as the bright yellow forsythias and the flowering quinces in the pink shades tell us the cold is almost over. We can look forward to an unsurpassed parade of colour through spring provided by a myriad of well-loved and proven shrubs. As summer progresses the shrub garden can form a dense, cool background highlighted by spectacular show stoppers like the tibouchinas, crepe myrtles and oleanders.

Keep this continuous colour show in mind when designing and choosing the plants for the shrub garden as it is possible to have a plant in bloom almost year-round.

Colour through Foliage

Colour is not the sole domain of flowers in the shrub garden. There are many plants clothed with a fantastic display of coloured leaves. Many of these make striking accents in an otherwise green shrubbery, indeed in tropical and humid subtropical areas plants such as acalyphas and crotons take the place of flowering plants and replace those that are traditionally used to provide autumn colour in colder areas.

Shrubs with silver or grey foliage can be used to create wonderful landscapes and are often combined with white flowering plants to great effect. Also there are the variegated forms, some of which need to be planted where they are sheltered from drying winds and hot afternoon sun otherwise they tend to burn. On the other hand, gold-leafed plants and those with gold markings need to be planted in full sun to retain their colour. The shade loving variegated forms of *Aucuba japonica* are the exceptions to this rule.

Roses are perhaps the best loved of all flowers.

Remember also to include in your list of essential shrubs those plants with berries which highlight the foliage and make marvellous displays indoors. Holly is one cold country favourite. Then, in warmer climates, the pigeon berry (*Durante repens*) with its display of bright yellow berries can be a real eye-catcher as can the showy ardisias with their long-lasting red or white berries providing added interest to a deeply shaded area.

Scented Shrubs

Plants not only give visual pleasure; a fragrant shrub can provide a subtle sense of joy as its scented foliage, if brushed against, or its flowers release their distinctive perfume. Daphne, boronias, lavenders, rosemary, gardenias and the lilacs are all beautifully scented and well worth including on your shopping list. They are examples of the many plants which can be placed near an outdoor living area where their perfume can be appreciated as you sit at leisure. Others, such as the night scented *Cestrum nocturnum*, some may find overpowering on a summer's evening and are best positioned where you pass by, such as beside a front gate or entrance path.

Accent Points

The dramatic statements that an accent plant can provide are sometimes overlooked. These shrubs, used sparingly, act as a focal point, drawing the eye through the landscape to another section of the garden.

They are choice plants, chosen for a particular growth pattern such as a weeping standard or for their arresting shapes like those of the *Acer palmatum* cultivars. Though usually more expensive, if well positioned they give a garden that individual look.

Soil

Most shrubs will tolerate a wide range of soil types, as long as it is well drained and reasonably fertile, however there are a number of garden favourites which need to have an acidic soil. Soil is measured on a pH scale ranging from very acid (1) to very alkaline (14) and although soil solutions don't reach these extremes a plant is considered to be acid loving if it enjoys a pH level in the low 6 range. Three that immediately

Most of the over 30 000 varieties of camellias are decended from Camellia japonica.

come to mind are camellias, azaleas and rhododendrons but there are other shrubs which will thrive in similar conditions and help to give variety to a shrub border. Other shrubs to interplant with them include the heaths and ericas, magnolias, the American laurel (*Kalmia*) and the various species of *Pieris*. These plants thrive in soils that have had loads of compost, peat moss and organic mulches added to them.

Planting

A shrub border is best planned wide enough to accommodate at least two shrubs in depth, with the taller, easy care evergreens at the back and the plants which require more attention, in the form of pruning, or which are to be grown for cutting, planted towards the front. Often there is room to interplant these with ground-hugging shrubs to act as a mulch keeping both weeding and watering requirements to a minimum. And it makes sound gardening sense to plant out a complete bed at the one time—not only do some plants resent being disturbed, but the ability for shrubs to establish a good root system within a well-established border is very limited.

Prepare a garden bed a few weeks prior to planting, digging it over well and adding well-rotted compost or other decayed organic matter. This humus helps to break up heavy soils making it more porous and so more

easily drained and provides light, sandy type soils with moisture-retentive materials.

Pruning

Pruning is often unnecessary for shrubs, but some do require annual attention to ensure continued high quality blooms. These shrubs can be divided into two categories—those that produce flowers on new or the current season's wood and those that form the flower buds in the previous season. Flowers that appear on last season's canes include forsythia, weigela and kerria. These and similar shrubs do best if the flowering canes are cut well back once the flowers are finished to enable the developing new shoots ample room to develop.

When shrubs produce flowers on the current season's growth, the flowers usually appear towards the end of summer on spring growth. These are best pruned in late winter, or in colder areas once all possibility of frost is over. Shaping is the main requirement here, taking thin or dead wood back to the main trunk and shortening vigorous shoots. Plants in this category include the late summer flowering shrubs such as tibouchina, fuchsias and abutilon as well as hibiscus and luculia. Bearing this in mind, it is possible to choose plants for a garden shrubbery that require very little attention and still be assured of a colourful display that is as easy care as a garden can possibly be.

Abelia × grandiflora

Abelia schumannii

Abutilon × hybridum

Abuliton megapotamicum 'Variegatum'

Acacia acinacea

ABELIA

Native to Japan, the Himalayas and India, these dense, low-branching evergreens are widely grown in temperate climates the world over. They flower in summer, bearing fragrant, pink or white flowers and a sprinkling of deep red bracts. They prefer sun or part-shade and do best when well watered. They flourish in all but the coldest regions, where they may survive in deciduous form. If conditions are very cold, abelias prefer the shelter of a wall or bushes. Plant out in early spring or autumn/fall. Dead-wood should be removed in late spring and older branches pruned after flowering. Trim lightly all over during winter. The fine growth that follows trimming makes it an excellent choice for a pleasantly decorative hedge. Propagate from cuttings in summer.

A. × grandiflora

This, the best known of the group, is a hybrid of a number of Chinese species. It has oval, glossy, bronze-green foliage, and fragrant, pink-tinged, white flowers which appear from mid-summer to mid-autumn/fall. When there is new foliage, or when the flowers have fallen, leaving behind red bracts, the entire bush takes on a reddish tone. It grows to a height and spread of 2–3 m (about 6–9 ft).

A. schumannii
SCHUMANN'S ABELIA

Also from China, Schumann's abelia has larger flowers which are a deeper mauve-pink than *A. grandiflora*. Its yellow-blotched, pink-and-white, bell-shaped flowers appear from mid-summer and last until mid-autumn/fall. Its dense habit makes it a suitable choice for a hedge. It grows to a height and spread of 1.5 m (about 4½ ft).

ABUTILON
CHINESE LANTERN, FLOWERING MAPLE

Grown for the beauty of their variegated, maple-like leaves as much as for their delightful, colourful, lantern-shaped flowers, these leggy evergreen or semi-evergreen shrubs are grown in glasshouses in cold conditions or in the open when warmer. They prefer full sun or part-shade and a rich, moist, fertile and well-drained soil. Improve the flower yield by regular pinching back to ensure branching and hence budding. If necessary, tie to a support if lax. Raised from seed sown at any time, *Abutilon* will germinate within 3 weeks or less and should flower within 12 months. The varieties named here however will come true only from cuttings (take these from firm, new tips later in the season and struck with heat in a sand/peat mixture). Often raised as indoor plants, they bloom best when rootbound. Popular with flea beetles and aphids.

A. × hybridum
FLOWERING MAPLE

These open, soft-wooded shrubs have green, heart-shaped leaves with a furry texture. They bear bell-shaped flowers, in shades of white, cream, pink, yellow, orange and red (often veined in contrasting tone), from spring to autumn/fall. In the growing season, young plants may need tip pruning to promote bushy growth. Mature specimens should have the previous season's stems cut back hard annually in early spring. It grows to a height and spread of 2 m (about 6 ft). Propagate from softwood or semi-ripe cuttings from summer to winter. Slightly tender, they are best grown as conservatory plants in cold climates.

A. megapotamicum 'Variegatum'
BIG RIVER ABUTILON, TRAILING ABUTILON

One of the hardiest of the genus, this sprawling evergreen is a native of Brazil. It has long, slender branches and pendant, bell-shaped, yellow and red flowers appearing in spring to autumn/fall. They appear among oval, lightly serrated leaves variegated with yellow blotches. Normally it is trained against a wall, but it may be used as a dense ground cover. Prefers sun, well-drained soil and is half-hardy. It grows to a height and spread of 3 m (about 9 ft).

ACACIA
MIMOSA, WATTLE, MYALL, ACACIA

One thousand species of evergreen, semi-evergreen and deciduous trees and shrubs, found in Africa, North America and most predominantly Australia. They grow fast and are usually short-lived. The flowering season is variable and brief, with a spectacular explosion of fragrant yellow that blows away to leave dry pea pods. The flowers are actually a mass of stamens and produce pollen in abundance—birds and bees love them. Instead of leaves, many species have phyllodes—flattened leaf-like stalks—that serve the same function. The fruits are round or extended pods containing seeds that are exceptionally resilient—they may survive for up to 30 years. Light watering in dry seasons and light pruning after flowering will prolong life. They require well-drained soil and full sun to thrive. Propagate from seed or cuttings. Borer, leaf miner, acacia scale and galls can be a problem.

A. acinacea
GOLD DUST WATTLE

This is an evergreen, many branched shrub with slender leaves, 1.3 cm (about ½ in) long. It flowers in late winter to late spring, either singly or in clusters. It grows to a height and spread of 2 m (about 6 ft). *A. acinacea* likes an open, sunny, well-drained position. It is half-hardy, tolerates periods of dryness well and prefers a light to medium soil. The obliquely oblong, bright green phyllodes grow to about 1.5 cm (about ½ in) long.

A. boormannii
syn. *A. hunteriana*
SNOWY RIVER WATTLE

This small, rounded, evergreen tree or shrub grows to a height and spread of 3–4 m (about 9–12 ft), producing bright yellow balls of flowers in spring. *A. boormannii* tolerates the cold well. It produces narrow, dark green phyllodes and is best propagated from the suckers that appear around the main trunk.

A. cardiophylla
WYALONG WATTLE

Fern-like leaves, each composed of tiny, heart-shaped leaflets in 12 to 18 pairs, give this plant its name (*cardiophylla*: with heart-shaped leaves). Its arching branches are smooth, grey and slightly ribbed. Small, bright yellow flowers appear in mid-winter. Fast-growing, adaptable and very frost-hardy, it grows to a height of 3–4 m (about 9–12 ft) with a spread of 2 m (about 6 ft).

A. floribunda
WHITE SALLOW WATTLE

This evergreen, bushy shrub or small tree flowers in late winter, producing pale yellow balls in abundant spikes. Its phyllodes are thin, smooth and green. It is half-hardy and grows to a height of 3–8 m (about 6–24 ft) and a spread of 3 m (about 9 ft).

A. howittii
STICKY WATTLE

This is a dense evergreen shrub or tree with weeping branches. It flowers in winter, producing pale yellow balls on short stalks. Half-hardy, it grows to a height of 4–7 m (about 12–21 ft) and a spread of 3 m (about 9 ft).

A. pravissima
OVENS WATTLE, ALPINE WATTLE

This arching evergreen shrub is half-hardy and grows to a height and spread of 6 m (about 18 ft). Its phyllodes are triangular, spine-tipped and dull green. Small heads of bright yellow flowers appear in late winter or early spring.

ACER
MAPLE

Maples have been grown in cool climates all over the world for centuries, but when we think of *Acer*, we think of Japan, where its cultivation reached the level of an art form. Maples are grown for the delicate beauty of their foliage, although they do have small red flowers on drooping stems, which are followed by two-winged fruits and seeds which can glide for miles. They prefer cool, moist conditions and fertile, well-drained soil. They do best when protected from full sun,

Acacia howittii

otherwise the leaves will burn. They colour beautifully in the autumn—particularly if the soil is neutral or slightly acid. Mainly deciduous, they are propagated by seed as soon as ripe, or in autumn/fall (cultivars by grafting). Avoid pruning where possible, apart from removing dead branches.

A. palmatum 'Dissectum Atropurpureum'
JAPANESE MAPLE, CUT LEAF MAPLE

This cultivar of the deciduous Japanese mountain maple has normally reddish purple leaves, which turn brilliant red in autumn/fall. The flowers are small, also reddish to purple, and appear in spring. The plant grows sideways rather than vertical, to a maximum spread of about 6 m (about 18 ft). It can only be propagated by grafting and is a slow grower—hence it is often expensive to buy. It prefers sunlight, moist soil, and is fully hardy. Protect from the sun to prevent leaf burn.

A. palmatum 'Dissectum Viridis'

The green cut-leaf maple resembles the purple, but it is slightly more able to stand the sun.

ACOKANTHERA
oblongifolia
syn. *A. spectabilis*
AFRICAN WINTERSWEET, BUSHMAN'S POISON

A native of south-east South Africa, this dense, spreading, evergreen shrub has large, oval, leathery, bronze-green leaves, which become purple in winter. In spring to summer it produces pleasant, sweet-smelling white flowers. Plum-sized fruits follow. It likes plenty of sunlight and well-drained soil, and tolerates frosts poorly. This plant grows to a height and spread of 3 m (about 9 ft). Avoid the sap at all costs—the Kalahari Bushmen traditionally used it as a poison to coat the tips of their arrows. Propagate from seed, cuttings or graft.

Acacia boormannii

Acokanthera oblongifolia

Acacia pravissima

Acer p. 'Dissectum Viridis'

Acer p. 'Dissectum Atropurpureum'

Acacia floribunda

Acacia cardiophylla

AGAPETES
serpens
syn. *Pentapterygium serpens*
FLAME HEATH

This arching climber, the most widely known of the genus, is native to the Himalayas. It is a squat, semi-epiphytic shrub, sending out slender, arching branches from a tuberous rootstock. The evergreen leaves are red-tinted on the upper side only. Bright red tubular flowers, hanging in loose pairs, appear in spring and summer. It grows to a height and spread of just under 2 m (about 6 ft). *A. serpens* prefers a well-drained, humus-rich soil (neutral to acid), and full light or part-shade. Potted specimens should be watered freely when in growth. Propagate in spring from seed, or in late summer from semi-ripe cuttings.

ALLAMANDA
neriifolia
BUSH ALLAMANDA

This exotic upright evergreen shrub is native to South America. Prized for its delightful, golden yellow, trumpet-shaped flowers, streaked with orange, it does tend to sprawl untidily. In fact it can be trained as a climber. It grows to a height and spread of 2 m (about 6 ft) and has lance-shaped, glossy, green leaves and large, shiny pods. Frost-tender, it prefers partial shade. Light watering is adequate in colder weather but during the summer months, it requires heavier watering, alternated with liquid manure. The stems will need to be tied to sup-

ports. Improve the shape by pruning heavily in spring. This is also the best time to propagate from tip cuttings. The two-spotted mite is an occasional pest.

ALYOGYNE
huegelii
syn. *Hibiscus huegelii*
LILAC HIBISCUS

A native of Western Australia, this dense, semi-deciduous desert shrub blooms in late spring and summer, bearing lilac, hibiscus-like flowers. Formerly a member of the hibiscus genus, it has now been reclassified. The leaves are lobed and slightly hairy with irregularly serrated margins. It prefers full sun, and well-drained soil. Avoid watering—normal seasonal rainfall is adequate. It grows to a height and spread of 1.5 m (about 4½ ft). Prune frequently for compact growth. Propagate from semi-hardwood cuttings in summer.

ANDROMEDA
polifolia
BOG ROSEMARY

A native of sub-arctic areas, this dainty, spreading evergreen will only grow in cool climates or mountain conditions. It has glossy, mid-green leaves and produces pitcher-shaped clusters of pink flowers in spring and early summer. It prefers full sun or partial shade and a moist, humus-rich, acid soil—it thrives naturally in peat bogs. Fully hardy, it grows to a height and spread of 60 cm (about 24 in). Propagate from seed or by

division of root runners. *Andromeda* are named after the Greek mythological figure who survived an attack by a sea monster—an apt choice given that all the other former members of the genus have been reclassified—only *A. polifolia* survives.

ARDISIA
crispa
syn. *A. crenata, A. crenulata*
CORALBERRY, SPICEBERRY

Native to the area stretching from the East Indies to Japan and Korea, this evergreen upright shrub with its slender trunk may be found in subtropical climates worldwide. It grows to a height and spread of 1 m (about 3 ft) and is a frequent feature of Japanese gardens, where its whirled arrangement of berries are used to delightful effect. Fragrant, star-shaped, white or pink flowers appear in early summer, followed by berries, which may survive a year or more. Frost-tender, it does best in partial shade and a humus-rich, well-drained soil. Sow seed in spring or plant cuttings in summer.

Allamanda neriifolia

Ardisia crispa

Andromeda polifolia

Agapetes serpens

Alyogyne huegelii

AUCUBA
japonica
JAPANESE LAUREL, GOLD-DUST TREE, SPOTTED LAUREL

Thriving in shade, while producing colourful fruits under a dense cover, this cool-climate mountain native of Japan grows in all but the most barren of soils. A bushy evergreen, it has stout, green shoots and glossy, dark green, oval leaves, heavily splashed with gold. Small, purple, star-shaped flowers appear in mid-spring. Red, egg-shaped berries follow, but only if at least one male plant is grown to every two females (the females are the ones that bear fruit). Cut old shoots back in spring to restrict growth. Hardy to frost-hardy, it grows to just under 3 m (about 9 ft) in height and spread. Propagate from semi-hardwood autumn/fall cuttings.

AZARA
microphylla

This elegant, evergreen native of Chile has deep green, oval leaves and in spring bears vanilla-scented, yellow flowers with masses of stamens. It grows to a height and spread of 5 m (about 15 ft), thriving in sun or shade. It requires fertile, well-drained soil. Frost- to half-hardy, it suits a mild, temperate garden. Propagate from semi-ripe cuttings in summer.

BACKHOUSIA
citriodora
LEMON-SCENTED MYRTLE

This dense, evergreen shrub, native to Australia, is popular world-wide, especially in southern Africa, southern USA and southern Europe. In its natural state in rainforests it grows to heights of up to 20 m (about 65 ft). Under cultivation it grows to 3–10 m (about 9 to 30 ft). It is grown for its lance-shaped, pale to dark green leaves, which give off a delightful lemon fragrance when crushed. In summer, small white flowers cover the shrub. It prefers full sun and moist soil and dislikes coastal conditions. Raise from half-ripe cuttings taken in spring.

BAECKEA
virgata

This dainty, woody, evergreen, native to Western Australia, is prized for its elegant profusion of white, tea-tree-like flowers, which appear in summer. It bears thin leaves up to 1.5 cm (about ½ in) long and prefers well-drained, moist soil and full sun or semi-shade conditions. It grows to a height of 4 m (about 12 ft) with a spread to 3 m (about 9 ft). Propagate either from young cuttings or ripe seeds, if they can be caught before dispersal.

Banksia integrifolia

Backhousia citriodora

Aucuba japonica

Baeckea virgata

Azara microphylla

Banksia coccinea

BANKSIA
BANKSIA, BUSH HONEYSUCKLE

Named after the botanist, Sir Joseph Banks, who discovered this resilient evergreen in 1770, banksias are found all over Australia, particularly in the south-western regions. Foliage and habit vary, but all species are characterized by colourful flowerheads, odd, woody follicle fruits, and adaptation to harsh conditions. The slender, tubular flowers arranged in neat, parallel rows along a spike usually appear in spring. All species prefer well-drained and sandy soil (free of nitrates and phosphates). They do best in full sun or part-shade conditions. The plants are frost-hardy to frost-tender. Containerized plants need moderate watering during growth periods, but little water at other times. Propagate from seed in early spring or autumn/fall. Take care not to allow pot seedlings to become potbound prior to planting. Banksias are closely related to the *Protea* genus, found around the Cape of Good Hope, and scientists cite this as evidence that the con-

Banksia ericifolia

tinents were once joined as part of the supercontinent 'Gondwanaland'.

B. coccinea
SCARLET BANKSIA

Scarlet banksia, from Western Australia, is one of the showiest species. It has short, wide, erect brushes, and broad, serrated foliage; the leaves are dark green and grey-green beneath. It grows to a height and spread of 3 m (about 9 ft).

B. ericifolia
HEATH BANKSIA

This wiry, freely branching shrub has fine, dark, glossy foliage and an upright, copper to orange, bottlebrush spike about 10–25 cm (about 4–10 in) long. It flowers in autumn/fall to winter. It is found freely in coastal, sandstone ridges, but adapts to inland conditions. It grows to about 4 m (about 12 ft) in height and spread.

B. integrifolia
COAST BANKSIA

This gnarled, evergreen has a lime-yellow flower spike up to15 cm (about 6 in) long. The leaves are grey-green above; white below. It grows 15 m (about 50 ft) tall with a 7 m (about 21 ft) spread.

Berberis thunbergii

Bauera ruboides

Berberis darwinii

Beaufortia sparsa

Begonia fuchsioides

Bauhinia galpinii

good light and moist but well-drained soil. Best propagated from soft tip cuttings or seed if available.

BERBERIS
BARBERRY

Species from this genus of evergreen, semi-evergreen and deciduous shrubs from Europe, Asia and the Americas are among the most popular for cool climate gardens. The leaves are shiny and saw-toothed, and the flowers, which resemble very small daffodils, are a delight, especially when offset against the red or purple foliage, which may change colour in late summer or autumn/fall. They prefer sun or part-shade, any but waterlogged soil, and are fully to frost-hardy. Smaller species are excellent in rockeries, while taller species make good, dense hedges. Propagate from seed in autumn/fall.

B. darwinii
DARWIN BARBERRY

This is a native of Chile and Argentina. It grows to a height and spread of 3 m (about 9 ft), producing an abundance of orange to yellow flowers among dark green leaves from mid- to late spring. Then blue-coloured berries appear in turn. It is fully hardy. Water heavily only in dry seasons. Prune lightly to shape after flowering if desired, but be prepared to lose some berries. Propagate from semi-ripe cuttings in summer.

B. thunbergii

This is a deciduous species from Japan. Its pale to mid-green, oval leaves turn brilliant, orange-red in autumn/fall. Small, red-tinged, pale yellow flowers erupt in mid-spring. Bright red, egg-shaped fruits follow. It is fully hardy and grows to 1.5 m (about 4½ ft) and 3 m (about 9 ft) wide. The dwarf cultivar 'Red Pygmy', with purple tinted leaves, is very popular. It grows to about 80 cm (about 32 in) tall and wide.

BORONIA
BORONIA

Native to Australia, boronias are found in lightly covered, sandy bushland, and are admired for their sweet smelling flowers. These evergreens do best in very well-drained soil with an acid pH balance (moistened peatmoss may be added to retain moisture). They prefer shady conditions and are half-hardy to frost-hardy. The genus is related to two other fragrants—*Citrus* and *Murraya*. Light pruning after flowering improves the look, and can prolong the life of short-lived species. Water potted plants lightly, less when not in full growth. Seed germination is unpredictable, so propagate from small, firm-tipped cuttings struck in coarse sand.

BAUERA
ruboides
DOG ROSE, RIVER ROSE

Native to Australia, this spreading evergreen is normally found in the sandy, peaty soil of mountain stream banks along the eastern seaboard (including Tasmania). It thrives when cultivated in a shady spot, such as among garden stonework or on the shaded side of rockeries. A well-drained, slightly acid soil suits it best. Each of its leaves have three slender, oval-shaped glossy leaflets, and in early spring or summer it bears dainty, bowl-shaped, pink or white flowers hanging from slender stems. It grows to 1 m (about 3 ft) in height and spread. Propagate from soft tip cuttings in a peat/sand mixture.

BAUHINIA
galpinii
NASTURTIUM BAUHINIA, PRIDE OF DE KAAP, PRIDE OF THE CAPE

The most spectacular shrub in the genus *Bauhinia*, this low-spreading

bush (occasionally a climber) is native to Africa. It has 2-lobed leaves and sweet smelling, bright red flowers—borne in small racemes—which appear in late summer and autumn/fall. It prefers light, fertile, well-drained soil and full sun and dislikes cold or salty wind. It grows to a height of 3 m (about 9 ft) with a spread to 2 m (about 6 ft). Prune after flowering and propagate from seed in spring.

BEAUFORTIA
sparsa
SWAMP BOTTLEBRUSH

This heath-like, evergreen shrub from Western Australia has small, oval leaves and produces delightful, bright, vermilion-to-orange, bottlebrush-like flowers in summer and autumn/fall. *B. sparsa* prefers full sun, well-drained, fertile soil and tolerates drought conditions well. Potted specimens should be watered moderately. Propagate from stem tip cuttings in summer, or from seed or suckers in spring. It grows to a height and spread of 1.5 m (about 4½ ft). The genus is named after Mary, Duchess of Beaufort, a patron of botanical pursuits in England in the early nineteenth century.

BEGONIA
fuchsioides

This evergreen, multi-stemmed begonia has dark green, oval, serrated leaves. Small, single, bright red or pink flowers are borne in spring and autumn/fall. It grows to 1 m (about 3 ft) tall with a 30 cm (about 12 in) spread. It prefers

B. heterophylla
KALGAN BORONIA

This frost-hardy species has finely divided, bright green leaves. In spring it bears fragrant, bell-shaped flowers in bright magenta-pink. It grows to a height of 1.5 m (about 4½ ft) and spread of 1 m (about 3 ft).

B. ledifolia
SYDNEY BORONIA

This rounded evergreen shrub grows to a height and spread of 1 m (about 3 ft) and bears starry, pink flowers, mid-winter to early spring. The flowers are fragrant, but not so the trifoliate leaves, which emit an unpleasant odour when crushed.

B. mollis

This species bears pink, star-shaped flowers in spring. Hairy, bronze-green leaves are divided into 3–5 leaflets. It grows to 2 m (about 6 ft) high with a 1 m (about 3 ft) spread.

Boronia mollis

B. serrulata
AUSTRALIAN OR NATIVE ROSE

This upright, evergreen shrub has small, bright green, fragrant, serrated leaves which turn a distinctive bronze in the winter months. Clusters of fragrant, pink, cup-shaped flowers appear in spring. Prefers well-drained soil and tolerates full shade. It is frost-hardy and grows to 1 m (about 3 ft) with a 70 cm (about 2 ft) spread.

BOUVARDIA

These evergreens come from Mexico and Central America and are grown for the spectacular beauty of their flowers, though they also have a reputation for fragrance (largely undeserved). Bouvardias are untidy and require pruning after flowering to maintain shape—cut back stems half- to three-quarters. Frost-tender, they prefer full light and fertile, well-drained soil. Water heavily in summer and add diluted liquid fertilizer when the shrub is flowering. Propagate in spring from softwood cuttings or root cuttings. Whitefly and mealy bug may present problems.

B. hybrids

There are a number of hybrid bouvardias available, mainly derived from *B. longiflora*. They are spreading shrubs to about 1 m (about 3 ft) tall, with clusters of flowers in shades from white to bright red; some, such as the pink 'President Garfield', have double flowers. They make excellent, long blooming pot plants, and used to be very popular conservatory plants. Scent is apt to be lacking.

B. longiflora
syn. *B.* 'Humboldtii'

This thin-stemmed, spreading evergreen is the only *Bouvardia* that is truly fragrant. It bears exquisite, white flowers, each with four tubular-shaped petals, in terminal clusters during autumn/fall and winter. It has small lance-shaped leaves and grows to a height and spread of 1 m (about 3 ft) or more. Cold resistant only to 13–15°C (55–59°F) when flowering—7°C (44°F) at other times.

Bouvardia longiflora

Boronia serrulata

Bouvardia hybrids

Boronia heterophylla

Boronia ledifolia

Brugmansia sanguinea

Brunfelsia pauciflora

Brachyglottis monroi

Brachyglottis greyi

Brugmansia suaveolens

Buddleia davidii

BRACHYGLOTTIS

RANGIORA

These evergreen shrubs and trees, native to the North Island of New Zealand, are grown for their handsome foliage and attractive appearance. The terminal panicles of tiny, greenish flowers borne in spring are insignificant. Hardiness varies considerably among the species. They do best in a damp, compost-rich soil, in full light or partial shade. Potted specimens should be watered freely in summer. Prune regularly and pinch back occasionally to maintain habit. Propagate from semi-ripe cuttings in summer.

B. greyi
syn. *Senecio greyi*

This many-branched evergreen belongs to the same family (Asteraceae) as daisies—though its petite, bright yellow, daisy-like flowers that appear in summer and autumn/fall are less interesting than its hair-covered, leathery, green-grey leaves. Half- to fully hardy, it prefers full sun or part-shade and well-drained soil. Plants in a pot should be watered freely in summer, otherwise moderately. It grows to a height and spread of 1 m (about 3 ft). Propagate from cuttings in late summer.

B. monroi
syn. *Senecio monroi*

A neat, compact shrub, *B. monroi* bears terminal racemes of bright yellow flowers in summer. Half-hardy, it grows to a height and spread of 60–90 cm (about 24–36 in). The olive- to brownish green leaves have crinkled margins.

BRUGMANSIA

ANGEL'S TRUMPET

These exotic-looking but robust, evergreen or semi-evergreen shrubs are native to the Andes mountains. Hardiness varies considerably among the species. They prefer full sun or half-shade and fertile, well-drained soil. Propagate from seed in spring, or greenwood or semi-ripe cuttings in summer. Keep moist during the growing season. Prune in early spring to maintain shape. Specimens in containers should be watered freely. Whitefly and red soldier mite may present problems. Be prepared for disoriented, 'high' snails—the sap contains a narcotic. *B. stramonium* (Jimson weed) is an annual and a fairly common weed, with white flowers and prickly seed capsules. It is dangerously hallucinogenic and poisonous.

B. sanguinea
syn. *Datura sanguinea*

This species grows cream and scarlet, trumpet-shaped flowers up to 20 cm (about 8 in) long, each with a spathe-like calyx, in summer to autumn/fall. *B. sanguinea* has oval leaves and is frost-tender. It grows to a height and spread of 4 m (about 12 ft).

B. suaveolens
syn. *Datura suaveolens*

This round-headed tree or shrub produces thin, oval leaves to 30 cm (about 12 ft) long, and funnel-shaped, double, white flowers which appear in autumn/fall and winter. Green, egg-shaped berries follow. Half-hardy, it grows to a height and spread of 2–4 m (about 6–12 ft).

BRUNFELSIA
pauciflora

BRAZIL RAINTREE, YESTERDAY-TODAY-AND-TOMORROW

This stunning, rounded, evergreen shrub from South America is widely enjoyed for the varying displays of fragrant blue flowers on the one plant. In spring, this tropical beauty produces rich, purple flowers, which gradually fade to pale blue and then to white. The shrub has lance-shaped, glossy, leathery leaves, and prefers full sun to part-shade and fertile, humus-rich, well-drained soil. It is frost-tender. Water plants in containers only moderately. It grows to 60 cm (about 2 ft) in height and spread. Propagate from summer cuttings. Mealy bug and whitefly may present problems.

BUDDLEIA

BUTTERFLY BUSH

The spicy, fragrant blooms of *Buddleia* attract butterflies from far and wide—hence the common name. Found in Asia, Africa and the Americas, there is little variation in the foliage between species—all have pointed, crepe-textured, large leaves, but the bloom varies—the tubular florets may be arranged in whorls, globes, single spikes or branched racemes. Most do best in fertile, well-drained soil, and are fully hardy to frost-tender. Propagate these arching deciduous shrubs and trees from semi-ripe cuttings in summer.

B. davidii
syn. *B. variabilis*
BUTTERFLY BUSH, SUMMER LILAC

This deciduous or semi-evergreen, arching shrub is the most widely known. It has dark-green, long, lance-shaped leaves with white-felted undersides. Small, honey-scented, purple, lilac or white flowers appear in long panicles in summer to autumn/fall. A fully hardy species from China, it grows to a height of 5 m (about 15 ft) and spread of 3 m (about 9 ft).

B. globosa

This deciduous or semi-evergreen species from South America grows to a height and spread of 4 m (about 12 ft) and is valued for its fragrant, bright orange flowers in ball-like heads which appear in spring and summer. Its leaves are long, dark green and wrinkled. It likes full sun, good drainage and is frost-hardy.

B. salviifolia

This dense, vigorous, semi-evergreen native of southern Africa bears terminal clusters of delightful, sweet-smelling, lilac flowers. It has finely serrated 12 cm (about 5 in) long grey-green leaves. Propagate from hardwood cuttings in autumn/fall. Susceptible to frosts, it grows to a height and spread of about 2 m (about 6 ft).

BURCHELLIA
bubalina
SOUTH AFRICAN POMEGRANATE

The only species in its genus, this small shrub originates in South Africa and is valued for its leaves and summer flowers. It grows 2–3 m (about 6–9 ft) high and has shiny, rounded, deep green leaves. In late spring to summer, dark orange-red, cylindrical flowers appear at the branch tips in dense terminal clusters containing up to 10 blooms. This frost-tender shrub enjoys full shade in extremely hot areas, but generally needs good light with partial shade. Prune as soon as flowering finishes. Propagate from semi-ripe cuttings in summer.

BURSARIA
spinosa
PRICKLY BOX

Australian sheep farmers hate this spiny, evergreen bush—they claim it is forever snagging the wool of passing sheep. However, the fragrance and charm of the tiny white flowers make it popular in Australian gardens and also in the USA, particularly California. In summer the flowers are massed in panicles towards the ends of the branches, after which attractive, brown fruits appear. These contrast nicely with the small, shiny leaves, making the plant an attractive choice for flower arrangements. It is also excellent for hedging, though it is of course thorny. It prefers full sun and well-drained soil. Resistant to frost, it grows to a height of 10 m (about 30 ft) and a spread of 6 m (about 18 ft). Propagate from seed or semi-ripe cuttings.

BUXUS
BOX

These densely foliaged evergreen shrubs are native to Mediterranean Europe, Japan and Central America. The flowers are insignificant but the foliage is ideal for hedging, edging and topiary; the plants have been used in this way for centuries. They thrive in sun or semi-shade and any soil that is not waterlogged. They are best set out (use semi-ripe cuttings) in early spring or late summer, watered regularly and, as they grow (which is very slowly), pinched to shape. Trim and shear regularly as separate plants grow together. Promote new growth by cutting back stems to 30 cm (about 12 in) or less in late spring.

B. microphylla var. japonica
syn. B. japonica

This evergreen, bushy variety bears a rounded mass of small, oblong, glossy, dark green leaves. It is resistant to frost, requires full sun and will tolerate moist soil. It grows to a height and spread of 2.5 m (about 7 ft). Perfect for hedging and screening.

B. sempervirens

This is almost identical to *B. microphylla* but grows to twice the height. However, the form most often seen, 'Suffruticosa', grows to only about 80 cm (about 32 in) and is the type used to make clipped edgings in formal Italian or French style gardens.

CAESALPINIA

These deciduous shrubs, trees and climbers are valued in warm climates worldwide for their brilliant flowers. Found in tropical and subtropical areas, they do best in soil that retains moisture, and prefer full sun and plenty of water. Named after a sixteenth-century Italian botanist, *Caesalpinia* are half-hardy to frost-tender. Propagate from seed in autumn/fall or spring, or from softwood cuttings in summer.

C. gilliesii
DWARF POINCIANA

C. gilliesii is sometimes incorrectly called 'Bird of paradise'—this name really belongs to *Strelizia reginae*. This rather prickly deciduous shrub or small tree is grown for the short racemes of bird-like, yellow flowers with long, red stamens that appear in summer. It has finely-divided, dark green leaves. In cooler areas it may be seen as a wall shrub. It prefers full sun, a well-drained soil and is half-hardy. It grows to a height of 4 m (about 12 ft) and a spread of 6 m (about 18 ft). Propagate from seed in autumn/fall.

Buxus microphylla var. *japonica*

Burchellia bubalina

Buxus sempervirens (variegated)

Bursaria spinosa

Caesalpinia gilliesii

Buddleia salviifolia

Buddleia globosa

C. pulcherrima
syn. *Poinciana pulcherrima*
BARBADOS PRIDE

This is the most common species of *Caesalpinia*. An erect or spreading, prickly, evergreen shrub, it has fern-like leaves and in summer bears racemes of orange-red to yellow, cup-shaped flowers for most of the year. It prefers full sun and well-drained soil. It grows to a height and spread of 3 m (about 9 ft) and tolerates the cold poorly—minimum 5°C (about 40°F). Propagate from seed in autumn/fall.

CALLIANDRA
tweedii
RED POWDER PUFF

Native to Central and South America and related to the *Acacia*, this evergreen shrub grows to a height and spread of 3 m (about 9 ft). In late autumn/fall to spring it bears striking flower heads made up of many red-stamened florets—like all species in the genus, *Calliandra*, it has no petals. Each of its leaves have 16 to 24 oval leaflets. This pictur-

esque plant prefers full sun and well-drained soil, and tolerates the cold poorly—it will not survive in temperatures below 7°C (about 44°F). The Greek genus name reflects its characteristics (*kallos*: beauty and *andros*: stamens). Propagate from seed in spring or by semi-ripe cuttings in autumn/fall.

CALLICARPA
BEAUTY BERRY

The attraction of these upright, deciduous shrubs lies in the luxurious bunches of glossy, purplish, lilac berries they bear in summer. The pale green, crepe-textured leaves (often bronze-tipped when young) and tiny, lilac flowers in spring are of little interest. Ungainly plants, they should be pruned in winter. Use the fruiting stems for indoor decoration. They grow best in fertile, well-drained soil and prefer full sun or semi-shade conditions. They grow to a height and spread of 2 m (about 6 ft) and are fully frost-hardy. Propagate from softwood cuttings in summer. There are several species, all very much

Callicarpa bodinieri

Callistemon citrinus

alike. *C. bodinieri* is usually thought to be the best.

CALLISTEMON
BOTTLEBRUSH

Native to Australia, these woody and sometimes papery-trunked evergreen shrubs are popular in Ireland, the USA, Mediterranean countries, Hong Kong and South Africa and wherever frost is not severe. Often weeping in habit, they are grown for their magnificent flowers, which closely resemble a bottle brush. From the tips of the flower spikes, new leaves grow, leaving long-lasting, woody, seed capsules behind. A favourite with birds, *Callistemon* prefer full sun and a moist soil—many species will tolerate soggy, almost boggy, conditions. Propagate from semi-ripe cuttings in summer. Tent caterpillar may present a problem about this time.

C. citrinus
LEMON BOTTLEBRUSH

The forms of this species all thrive and flower profusely in dry or damp

Callistemon viminalis 'Hannah Ray'

Callistemon viminalis

Calliandra tweedii

Caesalpinia pulcherrima

conditions. Many cultivars exist, including 'Anzac', which bears white bottlebrush-like flowers with yellow tips, and grows to 1 m (about 3 ft); 'Burgundy', with masses of burgundy bottlebrush flowers in summer, growing to 2.5 m (about 7½ ft); 'Mauve Mist', with delightful, mauve-pink flowers in spring and growing to 2 m (about 6 ft); and 'Splendens' with spikes of bright red flowers.

C. 'Harkness'
syn. *C.* 'Gawler Hybrid'

This rounded, weeping, evergreen shrub (or small tree) grows to a height of 5 m (about 15 ft). It bears large 25 cm (about 10 in) bright red flowers in early summer and autumn/fall. It has narrow, pointed, light green leaves and does best in full sun with well-drained soil. It is half-hardy and has a spread of 4 m (about 12 ft).

C. viminalis
WEEPING BOTTLEBRUSH

This graceful weeping evergreen shrub or small tree flowers mostly in spring, producing clusters of bright red flowers. It grows up to 5 m (about 15 ft) in height and spread, producing long, narrow, oblong leaves. Half-hardy, it tolerates most soil conditions.

C. viminalis 'Hannah Ray'

An evergreen, weeping shrub, grown for its beautiful, soft, grey-green foliage and scarlet flowers. It grows to a height and width of 3 m (about 9 ft) and has lance-shaped, light green leaves. The attractive, bright red to scarlet flowers grow up to 10 cm (about 4 in) long and appear in early summer and autumn/fall. It prefers full sun, well-drained soil and is half-hardy.

CALLUNA
vulgaris
SCOTTISH HEATHER, LING

A familiar sight as natural cover on moors and heaths in northern Europe, this bushy evergreen is a native of Europe and Asia Minor. A densely spreading bush, its small leaves are arranged in pairs. It has spikes of

Callistemon 'Harkness'

Camellia chrysantha

Calluna vulgaris 'Multicolor'

Camellia japonica (wild form)

Camellia japonica 'Elegans'

Camellia japonica 'Desire'

Camellia j. 'Aldolphe Audusson'

bell- to urn-shaped, single or double flowers, usually pink, mauve or white, which appear from mid-summer to late autumn/fall. The shrub does well in rockeries and where mulched with pebbles. Salt, wind and drought resistant, it makes good ground cover, preferring a gritty, well-drained, acid soil with regular water. Grows to a height of 60 cm (about 2 ft) and a width of 50 cm (about 20 in). Propagate from autumn/fall cuttings. Several cultivars with coloured leaves, e.g. 'Multicolor', are available.

CAMELLIA

CAMELLIA

Though associated with Japanese culture, the majority of this genus of evergreen, woody shrubs and trees are actually from mainland China and the Indo-Chinese peninsula. They are found in mountainous, subtropical areas, growing in partial shade. In Japan these lush plants are grown in part for the oil content of their seed capsules, but elsewhere most camellias are cultivated for their luxurious flowers and shiny foliage. Over 30 000 varieties now exist, most of which are descendants from *C. japonica*. They prefer semi-shade in the open and a well-drained, neutral to acid soil. During frost or snow periods, move in containers to the shelter of evergreen trees. White or pink varieties need to be screened from direct sun or their flowers will discolour. Propagate from cuttings in late summer or mid-winter, or graft in spring or winter. To trim the shape,

prune camellias during or immediately after flowering. *C. sinensis*, is not grown for flowers, but for its leaves, which are used to make tea. Legend has it that enterprising British East India agents attempted to export some specimens out of China, after tea had become fashionable in Europe in the mid-seventeenth century. However, Chinese officials substituted *C. japonica* instead—a beautiful plant, but quite useless for tea making. The popularity of *C. japonica* as a flowering plant took off soon after.

C. chrysantha

YELLOW CAMELLIA

A newcomer to the genus, this fast-growing, evergreen shrub comes from southern China. It grows to a height of 6 m (about 18 ft) and a spread of 3 m (about 9 ft). It does best in warm conditions, producing up to five crops of new, purple-red foliage per year. The leaves are large, oval and leathery. Delightful, small, single, cup-shaped, yellow flowers appear in spring.

C. granthamiana

This half-hardy, evergreen shrub from Hong Kong flowers in late autumn/fall. The flowers are single, up to 15 cm (about 6 in), white, and saucer-shaped, with a row of a maximum 8 petals surrounding a central boss of yellow stamens. The leaves are glossy, deep green and crinkly.

C. japonica

Native to Japan, Korea and eastern China, this evergreen shrub contains much variation in habit, foliage, floral form and colour. The

Camellia granthamiana

flowers may be single to very double, in shades from white to red. It flowers in winter in temperate conditions and in spring in very cold areas. It grows to 7 m (about 21 ft), with a similar spread. Prefers a cool soil, adequate moisture and a protected environment. Shade from the burning afternoon sun. Watering is essential in dry areas, or the buds will fail to open.

C. japonica 'Adolphe Audusson'

This well-established cultivar has better resistance to cold than other varieties. It grows large, saucer-shaped, dark red flowers, sometimes with white markings, and prominent yellow stamens. They are semi-double with 2 or more rows of

9–21 petals. The leaves are dark green and broadly lance-shaped.

C. japonica 'Elegans'

Beautiful, large, rose-pink flowers are what make this cultivar so highly prized. Often the flower has white, variegated petaloids in its centre. The petaloids are intermingled with a mass of stamens. The flower has surrounding rows of flat petals—the 'anemone' configuration. The leaves are dark green and broadly lance-shaped.

C. japonica 'Desire'

This fairly new camellia is greatly admired for its perfect formal double shape and delicate pink and white colouring. It blooms early.

Camellia sasanqua

Camellia sasanqua 'Yuletide'

Camellia japonica 'Lady Vansittart'

Camellia reticulata 'Captain Rawes'

Camellia japonica 'Kingyo-Tsubaki'

Camellia sasanqua 'Hiryu'

Camellia japonica 'Yamato Nishiki'

Camellia lutchuensis

C. japonica 'Kingyo-Tsubaki'

Sometimes called the 'Fishtail' or 'Mermaid' camellia, because of its distinctive lobed leaves, this ancient Japanese cultivar bears abundant single flowers in an attractive shade of bright pink from early in the season. It has a rather weeping habit.

C. japonica 'Lady Vansittart'

Medium-sized, saucer-shaped, 'semi-double', white flowers, flushed rose-pink, appear in winter to early spring. This upright shrub has unusual, holly-like, twisted, mid-green foliage.

C. japonica 'Yamato Nishiki'
syn. *C. japonica* 'Brocade of Old Japan'

The large, single flowers of this spreading shrub are streaked in pink and red. The centre features a flare of gold-tipped stamens. The plant's leaves are small and lance-shaped.

C. lutchuensis

This recently introduced species from China is a little tender but well worth growing for the long display of dainty, white flowers with only 3 petals but the strongest, sweetest perfume of any camellia. The plant is fairly fast growing, upright when young and spreading at maturity.

C. reticulata

A favourite among enthusiasts, with its upright habit and handsome, serrated foliage. Found naturally in the forests of southern China, it grows slowly, up to a height of 10 m (about 30 ft). The species bears large, saucer-shaped, single, rose-pink and red flowers in spring; the cultivars have large (20 cm—about 8 in—or more) double flowers in shades of pink or red. 'Captain Rawes', the oldest, has been joined by many in recent years. The leaves are large, oval and leathery. Less cold-hardy than *C. japonica*, it is a taller, more open grower.

C. sasanqua

This upright native of southern Japan is another lovely evergreen and it is the most sun-tolerant of all camellias. It is a fast-growing, slender and dense species, which produces an explosion of fragrant, single, white (occasionally red or pink) flowers in autumn/fall. These flowers usually shatter within a day or so of opening. The leaves are lance-shaped, glossy and bright green. *C. sasanqua* will thrive in a sunny spot.

C. sasanqua 'Hiryu'

Suitable for hedges, this popular cultivar bears double, pink flowers.

C. sasanqua 'Yuletide'

Suitable for formal or container planting, it bears a profusion of deep red flowers throughout the winter months.

C. sinensis
TEA

A variable shrub/tree, cultivated in warm, temperate parts of eastern and southern Asia, its processed young leaves are used to make tea. Some varieties are also used as ornamental hedge plants. The flowers are small, scented and white.

C. × williamsii

This is a hybrid group between *C. japonica* and *C. saluensis,* including numerous popular and attractive cultivars. Most popular of these are 'Donation', 'E. G. Waterhouse', 'Elsie Jury' and 'J. C. Williams', but there are many others, almost all in shades of pink.

C. × williamsii 'Donation'

This spectacular cultivar makes both an excellent tub specimen and garden plant. It is quite prolific; a compact upright shrub, it bears large, semi-double, orchid-pink flowers in the winter months.

Carissa macrocarpa

Cantua buxifolia

Camellia × williamsii 'Donation'

Camellia × williamsii

Camellia sinensis

CANTUA
buxifolia
MAGIC FLOWER, FLOWER-OF-THE-INCAS

This beautiful native of the Andes mountains develops a leggy habit with slender, weeping branches. It grows to a height and spread of 4 m (about 9 ft). An evergreen, soft-stemmed, bushy shrub, it becomes bowed down by the sheer weight of its bright red or purplish, trumpet flowers in mid- to late spring. Preferring full sun and well-drained soil, it is drought resistant and half-hardy, showing a considerable resistance to cold, especially in a sheltered position. The shrub requires support for best display. Light-tipped pruning after flowering helps keep its shape. Propagate from semi-ripe cuttings in summer.

CARISSA
macrocarpa
NATAL PLUM, AMATUNGULU

Native to South Africa, this fast-growing, dense, thorny hedge plant grows to a height of 3 m (about 9 ft) and a spread of 2 m (about 6 ft). The leaves are leathery and glossy and in spring large, white, frangi-pani-like flowers appear followed by fruit, which is rich in vitamin C. Half-hardy, it needs a well-composted soil, partial shade and regular watering. Propagate from seed.

CARMICHAELIA
odorata
SCENTED BROOM

Native to New Zealand, this leafless, broom-like, many-branched shrub bears clusters of fragrant, pea-like, purple-veined flowers from spring to summer, followed by small, ovoid pods. Instead of leaves, it bears flattened, green shoots. This shrub does best in a well-drained humus-rich soil in semi-shade. Deadwood should be cut out in spring. Frost-hardy, it grows to a height and spread of just under 2 m (about 6 ft). Propagate from seed in spring or cuttings in summer. The genus, *Carmichaelia* is named after Captain Dugan Carmichael, a Scottish army officer who collected botanical specimens in the early nineteenth century in India, South Africa and Mauritius—but curiously never in New Zealand.

Carmichaelia odorata

CARPENTARIA
californica

Like many other Californian natives, this sturdy, evergreen shrub is drought resistant, but dislikes the air pollution in city gardens. Half-hardy, it thrives in full sun and likes a rich, damp, well-drained soil. It has glossy, long, narrow, dark green leaves and fragrant, yellow-centred, white flowers which appear in summer. Withhold water in winter to prolong life, and prune regularly after flowering to prevent scragginess. Grows to a height of 3 m (about 9 ft). Propagate from seed in autumn/fall or from cuttings in summer.

CARYOPTERIS
× clandonensis

This deciduous, bushy, sub-shrub is prized for its masses of delicate, purple-blue flowers from late summer to autumn/fall. The leaves are irregularly serrated, oval, and grey-green. Frost-hardy, preferring full sun and light, well-drained soil, it grows to a height and spread of 1 m (about 3 ft). Propagate by greenwood or semi-ripe cuttings in summer or by seed in autumn/fall.

CASSIA
artemisioides

SILVER CASSIA, FEATHERY CASSIA, DESERT CASSIA

Native to Australia, this wiry, upright to spreading evergreen is a dry climate, frost-tender shrub. It is a member of the same family (Leguminosae) as peas and beans, it bears spikes of delightful, buttercup-like, yellow flowers from winter to early summer. Each leaf has 6 to 14 silver-grey leaflets covered in a fine down. It prefers an open, sunny position, and fertile, well-drained soil, although it will tolerate wetter conditions if the water is allowed to drain freely. It grows to a height and spread of 1–2 m (about 3–6 ft). Cut back hard in spring and propagate from semi-hardwood cuttings, or from seed in spring.

CEANOTHUS

CALIFORNIA LILAC

Originating in Mexico and the western states of the USA, this genus of over 50 species of evergreen or deciduous shrubs prefers cooler areas. *Ceanothus* species thrive in many parts of England, Europe and the cooler southern states of Australia. Despite the name, members of this genus are not lilacs. They bloom in much greater varieties of shades of blue, violet, mauve, pink and purple than true lilacs. They are grown for their small but densely-clustered flowers, which develop in showy terminals or panicles. The evergreen species are the more popular. Half-hardy, all species do best in a sheltered spot in an open sunny position, preferring a light, gravelly, well-drained soil. To prune, cut deadwood from evergreens in spring, and trim side shoots after flowering. Propagate from seed in spring or from leafy, semi-hardwood cuttings taken in summer.

C. 'Gloire de Versailles'

This sturdy, vigourous, deciduous shrub has mid-green leaves that are broad and oval. It does best in full sun and well-drained soil. It is fully hardy and, in mid-summer to early autumn/fall, bears racemes of pale blue flowers. Grows to a height and spread of 1.5 m (about 4½ ft).

C. impressus

This evergreen, bushy shrub does best in full sun and well-drained soil. Frost-hardy, it bears deep blue flowers which appear in clusters from mid-spring to early summer. The leaves are small, dark green, and crinkled. It grows to 1.5 m (about 4½ ft) with a spread of 3 m (9 ft).

CERATOPETALUM
gummiferum

NEW SOUTH WALES CHRISTMAS BUSH

Native to New South Wales, Australia, this erect, evergreen shrub grows to a maximum height of 5 m (about 15 ft) with a spread of 3 m

Cassia artemisioides

Ceanothus 'Gloire de Versailles'

Ceanothus impressus

Carpentaria californica

Caryopteris × clandonensis

Chamaelaucium uncinatum

Cestrum 'Newellii'

Chaenomeles speciosa

Cestrum aurantiacum

Cestrum nocturnum

(about 9 ft). Half-hardy, it likes a sunny position and well-drained soil. Water in spring and summer and fertilize in spring to increase the flower crop. The flowers are tiny and white and appear in spring, to be followed by rich, pink or red calyces in summer. The leaves are divided into three symmetrical, saw-tooth leaflets. Prune after flowering to encourage bushiness. Collect seed in summer to propagate.

CESTRUM

JESSAMINE

While some enjoy the scent from some species of this genus of deciduous/evergreen shrubs and semi-scrambling climbers, others find it overpowering and unpleasant. All agree that the showy flowers are a delight. These shrubs like a sunny position and fertile, well-drained soil. Generally not frost-hardy, they like plenty of water and regular fertilizer during the warmer months. Plants in containers should be freely watered during active growth, less at other times. Cut out the older canes every year. Propagate from soft-tip cuttings in the summer.

C. aurantiacum

Mostly evergreen, this semi-scrambling shrub is deciduous in colder climates. Frost-tender, it grows to a height and spread of 2 m (about 6 ft), though it stays a rounded shrub if cut back. In summer, tubular, bright orange flowers appear in large trusses, followed by white berries. The leaves are oval and bright green. Prune annually—and

remove dead stems by cutting to the base after flowering.

C. 'Newellii'

This arching, evergreen cultivar grows to a height and spread of 3 m (about 9 ft). It has large, green, broadly lance-shaped leaves and bears clusters of crimson flowers in late spring and summer; followed by berries in a matching shade of crimson.

C. nocturnum

NIGHT-SCENTED JESSAMINE

This spreading, evergreen tropical and subtropical shrub with dark green leaves comes originally from the West Indies. In summer, it bears clusters of greenish white to cream flowers, which give off intense fragrance, especially after dark. It prefers full sun and a well-drained soil. It grows to a height of 3 m (about 9 ft) and a spread of 2 m (about 6 ft).

CHAENOMELES

speciosa

FLOWERING QUINCE, JAPONICA

This dense, thorny, many-branched shrub from China is grown not so much for its fruit as for its flowers. The spherical, greenish fruits make excellent jelly. They follow the winter–spring bloom of attractive, clustered, red, white, pink or orange flowers. In colder climates C. speciosa is popular with flower arrangers because, when indoors, its bare but budded stems will open when placed in water. The plant prefers sun and well-drained soil and is fully hardy. After flowering,

cut back side shoots on wall-trained shrubs to two or three buds and shorten shoots growing away from the wall during the growing season. Take leafy, semi-hardwood cuttings in summer or autumn/fall, the latter also being the best time to plant seed. Fireblight and chlorosis may present problems. The shrub grows to 3 m (about 9 ft) with a spread of 5 m (about 15 ft).

CHAMAELAUCIUM

uncinatum

GERALDTON WAXFLOWER

Native to Western Australia, this dainty, attractive, evergreen, wiry-

Ceratopetalum gummiferum

stemmed shrub has a reputation for being difficult to grow—quite undeservedly, however, as it will do well in the right conditions. The plants need a slightly alkaline, gravelly, well-drained soil, and full sun. In late winter and spring it bears masses of waxy flowers, ranging in colour from pink to deep rose-purple. Each of the needle-like leaves has a tiny tip. C. uncinatum is half-hardy and grows to a height of 2 m (9 ft) and a spread of 3 m (6 ft). Propagate from seed in spring or semi-ripe cuttings in summer. The plant is half-hardy, but much grown in greenhouses in Europe for the cut flower trade.

Clerodendrum thomsoniae

Chorizema cordatum

Cistus ladanifer

Cistus salviifolius

Choisya ternata

Cistus 'Brilliancy'

Chimonanthus praecox

CHIMONANTHUS

praecox

WINTERSWEET

This twiggy, deciduous shrub, native to China and Japan, is grown for the rich, fragrant scent of its dainty, brown and pale yellow flowers with purple centres. These appear on the bare wood of the branches during milder periods in mid-winter. It has rough, glossy, oval, dark green leaves. It needs constant moisture to thrive, preferring full sun and a fertile, well-drained soil. Prune lightly to shape. Propagate from seed in late spring and early summer, and by layering in autumn/fall. It grows to 3 m (about 9 ft) in height and spread.

CHOISYA

ternata

MEXICAN ORANGE BLOSSOM

Originally from Mexico, this drought-resistant, moderately frost-hardy plant prefers a sunny but sheltered position and a fertile, well-drained soil. It grows to a height and spread of 2 m (about 6 ft). Fragrant, white flowers, similar to orange blossom, appear in spring. The bright green, glossy leaves are also scented. Propagate from semi-ripe cuttings in summer.

CHORIZEMA

cordatum

HEART-LEAFED FLAME PEA

This gaudy, popular native of Western Australia bears sprays of yellow or orange-red pea-like flowers in spring. A thin-branched, scrambling shrub, it has heart-shaped, light green leaves. It does best in a sandy loam and likes to be watered regularly. Without pruning, it turns into a climbing plant, so prune annually to keep it a tidy shape. Otherwise, grow in hanging baskets, or tie climbers to supports. If potted, water moderately in full growth, less so at other times. It prefers shady conditions and grows to a height of 1 m (about 3 ft), with a spread of 1.5 m (about 4½ ft). Propagate from seed in spring or semi-ripe cuttings in summer. Frost-free climates are preferred.

CISTUS

ROCK ROSE

This genus of spreading evergreens is famous for its drought resistance and ability to thrive in poor or sandy conditions, such as exposed banks or seaside cliffs. Equally, it does badly in moist, humid conditions. Native to the shores of the Mediterranean, Cistus species produce delightful, freely borne but short-lived flowers; these only last a day, but are quickly replaced. However in cold areas they need shelter and are frost-hardy. They do not transplant easily. Regular pinching back will maintain shape—cut out deadwood in spring, but do not prune hard. Propagate by seed in autumn/fall or by softwood or greenwood cuttings in summer (cultivars and hybrids by cuttings in summer only), and grow the young plants on in pots.

C. 'Brilliancy'

This straggling cultivar grows to 1.5 m (about 4½ ft) tall with a 1 m (about 3 ft) spread. In summer it bears pretty, little, rose-pink flowers with crimson blotches near the central stamens, set off by elliptic, grey-green leaves with downy undersides. Fully-hardy, it likes full sun and well-drained sandy soil.

C. ladanifer

LADANUM BUSH

This open, upright evergreen bears striking, large, white flowers in summer, bearing triangular, red markings at the base of each petal. The narrow leaves are dark green and sticky. Frost-hardy, it likes full sun and well-drained soil. It grows to a height and spread of 1 m (about 3 ft). The leaves are the source of the fragrant, medicinal resin ladanum; not to be confused with laudanum, a form of opium.

C. salviifolius

This is a bushy, dense, evergreen bearing white flowers in late spring and early summer. Slightly smaller than C. ladanifer, its flowers have yellow blotches at the centre. It also prefers the same conditions.

CLERODENDRUM

These picturesque flowering evergreen or deciduous shrubs are found mostly in Africa, South-East Asia and Australia. They vary tremendously in habit, from upright tree to climbing varieties. Thriving in humus-rich, well-drained soil, they all do best in full sun, with partial shade in summer. Water all year round, especially in summer. Stems will require support. Crowded growth should be thinned out in spring. Propagate from semi-hardwood cuttings in autumn/fall. Whitefly, mealy bug and red spider mite may present problems.

C. thomsoniae

BLEEDING HEART

This woody-stemmed, climbing shrub from western tropical Africa bears clusters of crimson flowers with white, bell-shaped calyces in summer. Leaves are a deep green oval shape. It reaches 3 m (about 9 ft) tall and prefers partial shade and well-drained soil. It requires temperatures above 16°C (about 61°F).

C. trichotomum

This deciduous, upright, tree-like shrub grows to a height and spread of 3 m (about 9 ft). From late summer to mid-autumn/fall it bears clusters of fragrant, tubular white flowers with red calyces. These are followed by blue berries.

C. ugandense
BLUE BUTTERFLY BUSH

This is an open, evergreen shrub, grown for its delicate flowers in two shades of blue with long, arching stamens. It grows to a height of 3 m (about 9 ft) and spread of 2 m (about 6 ft). It has serrated, oval leaves and does best in partial shade and well-drained soil. Does badly below 5°C (about 40°F). Prune after flowering to keep it compact.

CLETHRA
alnifolia
SWEET PEPPER-BUSH

This bushy, deciduous, rounded shrub, native to eastern North America, has oval, serrated leaves and bears a profusion of dainty, spicily fragrant, bell-shaped flowers in summer to autumn/fall. It prefers a well-drained, moist, peaty, acid soil in semi-shade conditions and year-round watering. Prune back after bloom by removing the oldest canes. Grows to a height and spread of 3 m (about 9 ft). Propagate from spring seed, soft-tip cuttings, or best of all, from the suckers it produces.

CLIANTHUS
puniceus
KAKA BEAK, PARROT'S BILL

Known to have been cultivated by the Maori before European settlement, this weeping evergreen is a native of New Zealand. *C. puniceus* is grown for the drooping clusters of red, claw-like flowers it bears in spring and early summer, and for its green, fern-like foliage. It is best grown outdoors in a sunny area, with well-drained, sandy, alkaline soil. It is half-hardy to hardy. In cooler areas it should be under glass. Feed with animal manure and water regularly. It has a rambling, spreading habit, so prune after flowering to maintain shape. Snails can be a problem. It grows to a height and spread of 4 m (about 12 ft). Propagate from summer cuttings or from scarified seed. In Europe it is often grafted onto *Colutea arborescens*.

COLEONEMA
pulchrum
DIOSMA, BREATH OF HEAVEN

This spreading shrub is a native of South Africa. While not a member of the same family as heath, they do have heath-like foliage and are com-

monly planted along banks or alongside lawns. They can also be trained as a low hedge. The soft, bright green leaves give off a sweet-scented fragrance when crushed. Terminal clusters of pink flowers appear from late winter to spring. The shrub does best in a well-drained, neutral to acid soil and needs a sunny to half-shaded spot. Water potted specimens moderately during the growing season, less so at other times. Winter moisture stimulates flowering. Clip after blooming to maintain shape. Grows to a little over 1 m (about 3 ft) in height and spread. Propagate from soft tip cuttings in summer.

COPROSMA
MIRROR PLANT, TAUPATA, LOOKING-GLASS PLANT

These lush, spreading, evergreen shrubs are native to New Zealand. They require both male and female plants to produce flowers and fruits, so unless planted in groups, are generally grown for their foliage. All species grow well in warm, humid conditions, in a well-drained soil that is not over-rich. They are salt resistant and do well in a seaside environment. Hardiness varies considerably, some species requiring a minimum temperature of 5°C (about 40°F). Water all plants heavily in summer and moderately at other times. A regular, light pruning helps maintain shape. Propagate from seed in spring or from semi-ripe cuttings in late summer.

C. × kirkii

The foliage of this smaller-leafed hybrid varies; most frequently narrow, oblong, glossy, bright green leaves are set opposite or in clusters. A variety with leaves variegated in grey-green is also available. Squat and densely branched, the half-hardy shrub is useful as a dense ground cover, and for erosion control, especially on coastal sites. Grows to 40 cm (about 16 in) high with a 1–2 m (about 3–6 ft) spread.

C. repens
syn. *C. baueri*
TAUPATA

This evergreen shrub, which at first has a spreading habit and then later becomes erect, grows to a height and spread of 2 m (about 6 ft). It has bright, shiny, oval leaves, often with variegations. The insignificant flowers that appear in late spring are followed (on female plants only) by orange-red, egg-shaped berries from late summer to autumn/fall. It is tolerant to all kinds of soil conditions, including sandy soil. Withstanding salt winds as well as it does, it is no surprise that it flourishes in coastal areas. Prune back to prevent dense growth.

Clianthus puniceus

Clerodendrum ugandense

Coleonema pulchrum

Clethra alnifolia

Coprosma × kirkii

Clerodendrum trichotomum

Coprosma repens

A Field Trip to the Magallanes Region

The story is told that, in the closing years of the eighteenth century, James Lee, a famous English nurseryman, was showing a client around his establishment in Hammersmith. The visitor remarked that he had seen a plant, far more beautiful than anything in Mr Lee's collection, growing in a humble house in Wapping. Lee found the house and a magnificent species of *Fuchsia*. After much negotiation he obtained the plant for the princely sum of six guineas.

The plant was *Fuchsia magellanica* and it has been one of the most important parents of our modern *Fuchsia* hybrids, thanks to its early introduction, its reputation for hardiness, the range of its different forms and colour variants and, of course, its own delicate beauty.

About 95 per cent of the naturally occurring fuchsia species are native to Central and South America, mainly in the moist, cool forests of the Andes. Two of these, including *F. magellanica*, are native to Chile and that country's most southern city, Punta Arenas, is the base for our field trip.

Torres del Paine National Park, in the Magallanes region.

As you move south of the capital, Santiago, the climate changes progressively from dry, almost Mediterranean, to a zone of heavy rainfall around Los Lagos (the Lake Region). The rainfall becomes even heavier, the further south you go, to the point where some of the western Patagonian islands receive an astonishing 4000 mm (about 158 in) annually. *F. magellanica* occurs throughout this region and down to the southern part of the continent.

Punta Arenas, with a population of 90000, is the capital of the Magallanes region of Chile, and the most southern city of this size in the world. It is a cold and windy place even in the warmer months from October through to March. Despite the cold, it is a good idea to time your visit for early autumn/fall, when the southern, or Antarctic, beech trees (*Nothofagus* species) are turning to red and gold. This also coincides with the later part of the flowering period for *F. magellanica*. As you travel toward the south of the Brunswick Peninsula, you will see many southern beeches covering the hillsides, some of them growing sideways due to the prevailing winds. The area around the Strait of Magellan has not changed greatly since its discovery by Ferdinand Magellan in 1520. Tierra del Fuego (Land of Fire) is but a line on the eastern horizon and looking south, you will see masses of snow-capped mountains above a green plain.

At various spots along the road south you are likely to find a delightful yellow violet (*Viola magellanica*), the occasional Chilean fire tree (*Embothrium coccineum*), which is a relative of grevillea and waratah and has similar red spider flowers, and a primitive flowering, glossy-leaved shrub or small tree, *Drimys winteri*.

Approximately 100 km (about 62 miles) south of Punta Arenas, in the area around Fuerte Bulnes, you will find mixed beech forests of evergreen *Nothofagus betuloides* and some

The flowers of Fuchsia magellanica *contrast well with its foliage.*

Fuchsia magellanica

deciduous *Nothofagus antarctica* and *N. pumilio*. As you glance around, you are likely to see numerous *Fuchsia magellanica* plants covered in edible black berries about 1.5 cm (about ½ in) wide. They are quite common in this open woodland, enjoying the dappled light under the beech trees, where they grow into flaky-barked shrubs 2 m (about 6 ft) high and wide. The leaves are 3–4 cm (about 1½–2 in) long, sitting in an unusual pattern on their stems—mostly in opposite pairs, but also in threes and sometimes fours. The sepals are a striking crimson and the petals themselves are a pinkish purple and form a long tube. Flowers of many unrelated plants in this part of the world are reddish and tube-like, to attract the various species of tiny hummingbird.

Other plants to be seen in this woodland include various *Acaena* species which you are likely to collect in your socks, for this ground cover member of the rose family has burrs for fruit. Some barberry shrubs (*Berberis ilicifolius*) with spiny stems and prickly leaves, are found here, as are more Chilean fire trees. Many flowering stalks of the orchid genus *Chloraea* emerge from the grazing grass that covers most of the areas between the trees.

There are patches of boggy ground where you can find a yellow-flowered *Ranunculus* (buttercup) species, and a little herb with red spikes of fruit, *Gunnera magellanica*. The tree-tops are home to an interesting group of shrubby parasites (*Missodendron* species) that only occur on the southern beech trees of Chile. Some look like old man's beard lichen; others resemble button mushrooms; and others are reminiscent of the unrelated European mistletoe. *F. magellanica* grows in parts of the forests that are well drained, though fairly moist. The soil here is a loamy type with a rich, organic top layer.

Although *F. magellanica* is fairly common throughout the southern region of Chile, nothing can compare with seeing it in the wild and majestic area of the Strait of Magellan—an area steeped in history, extreme in location, and the place where the plant was first recorded and collected over 200 years ago. Not a field trip for the faint-hearted, but one that will impress you with the splendour of the setting.

Fuchsia

The genus *Fuchsia* comprises around 100 species, from the north to the southern tip of South America centred on the Andean mountain chain. Some species are found in eastern South America and there are five species in the Pacific, one in Tahiti and four in New Zealand. *F. excorticata*, from New Zealand, forms a tree to 12 m (about 40 ft) tall with a trunk to 60 cm (about 2 ft) in diameter! Variable in flower shape and colour, *F. magellanica* is possibly the most cold-hardy species and was introduced to the British Isles as early as 1788, and has since become naturalized in some milder, wetter areas.

Fuchsias are known to most gardeners through numerous named hybrids, grown as indoor plants in cold climates or as outdoor shrubs in milder climates, where they are also popular in tubs and hanging baskets. These hybrids derive from South American species such as *Fuchsia magellanica* and *F. coccinea*, with some genes from *F. fulgens* and *F. arborescens*, both from Mexico.

Fuchsia belongs to Onagraceae, the evening primrose family, which has 21 genera worldwide, with about 640 species.

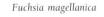

Fuchsia magellanica

Cornus nuttalli

Coronilla glauca

Corokia cotoneaster

Corokia x virgata

Cornus alba

Cordyline banksii

CORDYLINE
banksii

Native to New Zealand, this evergreen reaches a height and spread of 1.5–3 m (about 4–9 ft). In late spring and summer it bears panicles of delightfully fragrant, white flowers, set among long, drooping, dark green leaves. It does best in medium, well-drained soil in a protected, shaded position. Water potted plants moderately during active growth, less at other times. Propagate from stem cuttings in summer, or from seed in spring.

CORNUS
DOGWOOD, REDTWIG, BUNCHBERRY, CORNEL, CLUSTERBERRY

Brilliant winter bark followed by a beautiful spring bloom, and then by autumn/fall foliage and fruit bloom make this genus of twiggy, deciduous shrubs a gardener's delight. Native to the cooler regions of the USA and Asia, they are a favourite for the cold to cool-temperate climates. The main attraction is the bracts

which surround the clusters of small flowers. These later turn into fruit, giving rise to the names 'clusterberry' and 'bunchberry'. The various species all do best in sun or semi-shade and need a fertile, well-drained soil. They are fully to half-hardy. Cut back stems to almost ground level annually. Propagate from seed or rooted layers struck in a humid, sand-peat mixture.

C. alba
RED-BARKED DOGWOOD

This deciduous, upright then spreading shrub from northern Europe and Asia has shoots that turn an attractive, deep red in winter before the appearance of the foliage. The normally dark green, oval leaves turn red-orange in autumn/fall. Star-shaped, creamy white flowers appear in late spring and early summer and are followed by round white berries, which are often blue-tinted. Propagate from softwood cuttings in summer or hardwood cuttings in autumn/fall and winter. Grows to a height and spread of 3 m (about 9 ft) and is

fully hardy. Varieties with variegated leaves or yellow stems are available.

C. nuttalli
MOUNTAIN DOGWOOD, PACIFIC DOGWOOD

This spectacular, conical deciduous tree grows to a maximum height and spread of 5 m (about 12 ft). Its tiny, white flowers, surrounded by bracts, appear in spring followed by red to orange berries. The oval, green leaves turn red and gold in autumn/fall. *C. nuttali* is fully hardy.

COROKIA

These evergreen shrubs are suitable for mild coastal areas where they have a good tolerance to wind and salt. They require full sun and a fertile, well-drained soil. Propagate from softwood cuttings in summer.

C. cotoneaster
WIRE NETTING BUSH

This sparse and hardy, evergreen bush is a native of New Zealand. Difficult to control, it grows zigzag

fashion in all directions. It has small, round, dark green leaves and fragrant, yellow flowers that appear in spring and summer. *C. cotoneaster* is frost- to half-hardy, but in very cold areas it will need some protection from the wind. It grows to a height and spread of 3 m (about 9 ft). Shear regularly after flowering to promote dense growth.

C. x virgata

This evergreen shrub, native to New Zealand, bears pretty yellow, star-shaped flowers in spring followed by bright orange, egg-shaped berries. The glossy green leaves have a downy undersurface. Frost-hardy, it adapts to most soils and conditions, but does best in full sun and a fertile, well-drained soil. It grows to a height and spread of 3 m (about 9 ft). Cultivars include: 'Red Wonder', with bright red berries, 'Yellow Wonder', with golden fruits, and 'Bronze Lady', so-called for its leaf colour in maturity.

CORONILLA
glauca
CROWN VETCH

This dense shrub is a native of the Mediterranean region. If grown in a sunny spot in a well-drained soil, it will thrive and bear yellow, fragrant, pea-like flowers from mid-spring to early summer. The leaves are a pleasant, blue-grey colour, each with 5 or 7 leaflets. Frost-hardy, it grows to a height and spread a little over 1.5 m (about 4^1/2 ft). Use seed, summer cuttings, layers or divisions to propagate this delightful and rewarding, evergreen shrub.

CORREA

AUSTRALIAN FUCHSIA

The dense, evergreen Australian natives in this genus range from ground covers to 1.5 m (about 4 1/2 ft) tall shrubs. They bloom in late winter if conditions are right. Their long, bell-shaped flowers are rich in honey. They prefer a semi-shaded spot, and a fertile, moist but well-drained soil. More mature plants will tolerate a drier soil. When planting out, a slightly alka-line soil is recommended. Water potted specimens moderately when in flower, less at other times. Prune to keep them well-shaped and com-pact. Although tender to frost, they are easy to grow. Propagate from seed in spring or semi-ripe cuttings in summer. *Correa* is named for the eighteenth-century Portuguese botanist, Jose Correa de Serra.

C. alba

WHITE CORREA

This is a low, compact, rounded shrub with rounded, downy leaves 4 cm (about 1 1/2 in) long. White (sometimes pink), bell-shaped flow-ers, opening to star-shaped blooms, appear in winter. It grows to a height of 1.5 m (about 4 1/2 ft) and a spread of 1 m (about 3 ft). As it tolerates salt spray, it does well in coastal gardens, and makes an ex-cellent sand binder.

C. 'Dusky bells'

This spreading, dense, evergreen shrub takes its name from the de-lightful dusky pink, bell-shaped flowers that appear from autumn/fall to spring. It grows to 60 cm high (about 2 ft) with a spread of 1 m (about 3 ft) and does best in shady conditions. It has bright green, oval leaves.

C. reflexa

This dense, evergreen shrub grows to 1 m (about 3 ft) high, with a spread of 2 m (about 6 ft). Its pale green or pink, green tipped, bell-shaped flowers appear from autumn/fall to spring.

CORYLOPSIS

spicata

WINTER HAZEL

Native to Japan, this deciduous many-stemmed, shrub is popular in Britain, Australia and New Zealand. It grows slowly to a height of 2 m (about 6 ft) and a spread of 3 m (about 9 ft). The leaves of this spreading shrub are dull, bristle-toothed and pale green. In late win-ter, small, fragrant, lemon-green, bell-shaped flowers appear in drooping racemes. It prefers a neu-tral to mildly acid soil rich in leafmould, and semi-shady condi-tions. Propagate from softwood

cuttings in summer or from seed in autumn/fall. Purple-leaved clones are available.

CORYNABUTILON

vitifolium

syn. Abutilon vitifolium

BLUE ABUTILON

This tall, open, evergreen shrub, native to Chile, is prized for the masses of delicate, purplish blue flowers that bloom in spring. The oval, serrated leaves resemble maple foliage. One of only three species in the genus, the shrub is closely re-lated to *Abutilon* and some botanists prefer to include it in that genus. *C. vitifolium* does best in full sun or partial shade with fertile, well-drained soil. Tip prune new growth to encourage bushiness. Water well during growth, less at other times. Tie wayward-growing species to a support if necessary. The shrub grows to a height of 4 m (about 12 ft) with a spread of 3 m (about 9 ft). Propagate from semi-hardwood cuttings in summer.

COTINUS

coggygria

syn. Rhus cotinus

VENETIAN SUMACH, SMOKE TREE, WIG TREE

This tall-growing, deciduous shrub, found in southern Europe and in Asia, is grown chiefly for its splen-did autumn/fall colour and unusual flowers. Its rounded leaves, nor-mally oval and light green, turn a glorious yellow-red in autumn/fall, more so in colder areas. Its fruits are unimpressive, as are its flow-ers—masses of tiny flower stalks forming pale grey clusters from late summer. The tiny stems left after the flowers fall give the appearance of puffs of smoke—hence the name. Smoke tree does best in fertile soil that is not too rich. It needs full sun or semi-shade and is fully hardy. It grows to a height and spread of 5 m (about 15 ft). Prune back to growth buds by two thirds in winter. Propa-gate from greenwood or softwood cuttings in summer, or from seed in autumn/fall. There are purple-leaved forms available, however they aren't so bright in full colour.

Correa alba

Correa 'Dusky bells'

Corylopsis spicata

Corynabutilon vitifolium

Correa reflexa

Cotinus coggygria

Cuphea ignea

Crotolaria agatiflora

Crinodendron hookerianum

Crotolaria capensis

Cotoneaster horizontalis

Cotoneaster dammeri

Cotoneaster salicifolius

COTONEASTER
COTONEASTER, ROCKSPRAY

This genus of mostly evergreen bushes comes from Europe, North Africa and northern Asia. They are from the same family (Rosaceae) as the quince; the Greek *kotoneon* and *aster* together mean 'like a quince', and the genus name is pronounced 'kotonee-aster', not 'cotton-easter'. Cotoneasters are perhaps the most popular of berry-bearing shrubs anywhere—having the added attraction of tolerating almost any kind of soil condition (except waterlogged soil). They do thrive a little better, however, when the soil is dry and alkaline. They are also very drought resistant, and are fully frost-hardy. They are eminently suitable for use as an arching, specimen shrub, but may be used for hedging, or for ground cover. Evergreen species do well in either sun or semi-shade, but deciduous varieties and cultivars prefer full sun. Propagate from cuttings in summer or seed in autumn/fall.

C. dammeri

This trailing, evergreen shrub grows to a height of 30 cm (12 in) with a spread of 1 m (about 3 ft). In summer it bears striking, white flowers with purple anthers, followed in autumn/fall by red fruits. Frost-hardy, it is vulnerable at times to fireblight. The leaves are glossy, dark green and oval.

C. horizontalis
WALL SPRAY

This low-growing, deciduous bush from China has horizontal, herringbone branches which spread along the ground—hence the name. As the

plant matures, these branches grow in height. From late spring to early summer, it bears attractive pinkish white flowers, which are followed by bright red berries. The glossy, green leaves tend to redden in late autumn/fall. *C. horizontalis* is sturdy and makes an excellent addition to a rock garden. Fully hardy, it grows to a height of 50 cm (about 20 in) and a spread of 1.5 m (about 4½ ft).

C. salicifolius
WILLOW-LEAVED COTONEASTER

The long, slender, arching branches of this vigourous evergreen, also from China, make it a graceful addition to any garden. The small, white flowers borne in winter are not much to speak about, but the clusters of bright red berries appearing in autumn/fall are a delight. The leaves are narrow, lance-shaped and dark green, with distinct veins. Fully hardy, it grows to a height and spread of 5 m (about 15 ft).

CRINODENDRON
hookerianum
syn. *Tricuspidaria lanceolata*
LANTERN TREE

This stiff-branched, evergreen native of Chile generally grows as a bush with a rounded top. In spring, red, lantern-like flowers appear, hanging from the leaf axils. Its leaves are coarse-toothed and leathery. It prefers moist, well-drained, slightly acid soil and partial shade. Frost-hardy, it grows to a height and spread of 3 m (about 9 ft). Propagate from softwood cuttings in summer or seed in autumn/fall.

CROTOLARIA

These evergreen shrubs, annuals and perennials are popular because of their flowers. They are frost-tender to frost-hardy. Plants in containers should be freely watered when in full growth, but only moderately at other times. To keep the plant shape compact and attractive, cut back old stems after flowering.

C. agatiflora
CANARY-BIRD BUSH

This open, evergreen shrub is grown for its elegant, large, green-yellow, pea-shaped flowers that erupt in autumn/fall. It has light green leaves. Frost-hardy to frost-tender, it prefers a well-drained soil and full light. It grows to a height of 2 m (about 6 ft) and a spread of 1.5 m (about 4½ ft). Propagate from seed in spring or semi-ripe cuttings in summer.

C. capensis

Native to South Africa and Mozambique, this upright, branching, evergreen shrub bears deep yellow,

reddish tinged, pea-shaped flowers in autumn/fall, set amid pale green leaves. It prefers a light to medium soil, in an open, sunny position. Prune regularly after flowering to promote further bloom. Frost-tender, it grows to a height and spread of 2 m (about 6 ft). Propagate from scarified seed.

CUPHEA
ignea
syn. *C. platycentra*
CIGAR FLOWER, PUA KIKA

The most common of the cupheas, this native of Central America is popular in temperate to subtropical areas. A petite sub-shrub with bright green leaves, it can grow untidily however, so remove flowered shoots after bloom to maintain a compact habit. Tubular orange-red flowers appear in autumn/fall, each with a white ring at the mouth. *C. ignea* prefers fertile, well-drained soil and full sun conditions. Water freely in full growth, not too much at other times. Half-hardy to frost-tender, it does poorly in cold conditions—it will die back to the ground in frost—but when conditions are suitable, it will grow to a height and spread of 75 cm (about 30 in).

CYTISUS
BROOM, ATLAS BROOM

Among the brightest and gaudiest of the Fabaceae family, this genus of flowering, arching deciduous or evergreen shrubs is native to the Mediterranean area and the islands of the Atlantic. The abundant, pea-like flowers range in colour from shades of pink, red, cream and pure yellow to tan. They prefer full sun and well-drained soil that is not too rich. They do not transplant well, so set in the final position early on. Brooms are ideal at the back of mixed borders or as rock plants. The species are best propagated from semi-ripe cuttings in summer or from seed in autumn/fall.

C. × praecox
WARMINSTER BROOM

This semi-weeping, deciduous shrub bears pale yellow, pea-like flowers in spring. These have a characteristically acrid smell. The tiny, silky leaves are grey-green. Fully hardy, *C.* × *praecox* prefers sunny conditions and a well-drained soil. It grows to a height and spread of 1.5 m (about 4½ ft).

C. scoparius
SCOTCH BROOM

This deciduous, arching shrub is a native of Europe. A profusion of yellow flowers appear in spring and early summer. It is fully frost-hardy and prefers a well-drained soil and full sun. *C. scoparius* grows to a height and spread of 1.5 m (about 4½ ft). In New Zealand it has become a weed. 'Burkwoodii' is a garnet red cultivar.

DABOECIA
cantabrica
IRISH HEATH

This straggling, evergreen shrub, a native of Ireland, grows to a height and spread of 50 cm (about 20 in). It prefers a peaty, well-drained but moist, slightly acid soil. A slow-growing bush, it flowers throughout the year except in winter, bearing pinkish purple, urn-shaped flowers. The leaves are oval to lance-shaped, dark green above, silver-grey below. It prefers full sun in cooler areas and semi-shade elsewhere. Named after Ireland's St Dabeoc, *D. cantabrica* is frost-hardy—though the top may be damaged by cold winds and frost. Prune to produce fresh growth from the base. It makes a perfect choice for lining sandstone paths or in rockeries. Propagate from semi-hardwood cuttings kept under glass.

DAHLIA
excelsa
TREE DAHLIA

This woody, tuberous, bushy perennial is grown for its magnificent, autumn/fall bloom of single, large, pink, slender flowers with yellow centres, that grow to 10 cm (about 4 in) across. They are eminently suitable for cutting. *D. excelsa* has thick, bamboo-like stems and grows to a height of 4–5 m (about 12–15 ft). Half-hardy, it needs well-drained soil and a sunny position. Propagate in spring from seeds, basal shoot cuttings or by division of tubers. Cut the plants back hard in autumn/fall. *D. imperialis* is almost exactly the same except its flowers are white.

DAIS
cotinifolia
POMPON BUSH

Native to Africa, this handsome, neat shrub or small tree, with reddish bark and blue-green leaves, requires full sun or semi-shade to thrive. South African varieties are evergreen but in California and Australia it tends to be deciduous. In late spring it bears fragrant, tubular-shaped flowers in clusters. Its leaves are small and oval-shaped. Frost-tender, it only tolerates temperatures above 5°C (about 40°F). It prefers a well-drained, slightly acid soil. Plants in containers should be freely watered in full growth, but less so at other times. Propagate from seed in spring or semi-ripe cuttings in summer.

DAMPIERA
diversifolia

In spring and summer, this low-spreading, evergreen perennial bears beautiful, fragrant, deep blue flowers. It has narrow, crowded, mid-green leaves. A good ground cover plant, it is also suitable for rockeries. Hardy to about minus 5°C (about 23°F), provided it is kept reasonably dry, it prefers full sun and a well-drained soil. It grows to a height of 5 cm (about 2 in) with a spread of up to 1.5 m (about 4½ ft). Propagate from cuttings.

Daboecia cantabrica

Dahlia excelsa

Cytisus scoparius 'Burkwoodii'

Dampiera diversifolia

Dais cotinifolia

Cytisus × *praecox*

DAPHNE

DAPHNE, SPURGE LAUREL

Found everywhere except the tropics, these evergreen, semi-evergreen or deciduous shrubs are grown for their delightfully fragrant, tubular flowers that appear in winter and spring. They thrive in semi-shady conditions and prefer a slightly acid, fertile, peaty soil that is well-drained but not too dry. Water lightly and use a small amount of complete fertilizer after flowering. Excessive watering will cause collar rot. Transplanting is not recommended, so choose the site carefully. It is best to grow daphnes in a raised spot, with the root junction above soil level. Between summer waterings allow the soil to dry out. The genus is named after the nymph in Greek mythology, who, rather than face the unwanted affections of the pursuing sun god Apollo, turned into a flowering shrub.

Daphne odora

D. × burkwoodii

BURKWOOD'S DAPHNE

The dense clusters of fragrant, white and pink flowers of this upright, semi-evergreen shrub appear in late spring, and sometimes for a second time in autumn/fall. Its leaves are pale to mid-green and lance-shaped. Fully hardy, it prefers a sunny spot with well-drained soil. It grows to a height and spread of 1.5 m (about 4½ ft).

D. odora

syn. *D. indica*

The most popular of the genus, this moderately frost-hardy, evergreen, bushy shrub from China grows to a height and spread of 1.5 m (about 4½ ft). It bears fragrant, white to purplish pink flowers from mid-winter to early spring and has glossy, dark green, oval leaves. As a cut flower, it lasts well indoors. The form with yellow-margined leaves is said to be more tolerant of cold.

DESFONTAINEA

spinosa

PERUVIAN HOLLY

This compact, evergreen native of the Andes Mountains superficially resembles a holly with its spiny, glossy, dark green leaves—hence the name. But the delightful, showy, orange-scarlet tubular flowers appearing in mid-summer put paid to the illusion. Frost- to half-hardy, *D. spinosa* prefers moist, peaty, preferably acid soil. In dry conditions it needs some shade and in cold areas does better in shelter. Even in these optimal conditions it grows slowly, to a height and spread of 1.5 m (about 4½ ft). Propagate from semi-ripe cuttings in summer.

DEUTZIA

WEDDING BELLS, BRIDAL WREATH

These deciduous, arching bushes appear fairly nondescript until late spring or early summer, when a profusion of flowers appears—white, pink or bicoloured depending on the species. Related to *Philadelphus*, which it resembles, the genus *Deutzia* is a native of China, Japan and the Himalayas. The shrubs prefer fertile, moist but well-drained soil and do best in full sun, although they require semi-shade in warmer areas. Give fertilizer in early spring to encourage a full flower yield. Prune heavily to encourage bloom—remove about half the old wood. Propagate from softwood cuttings in summer.

D. × rosea

This compact, bushy, arching shrub produces massed clusters of beautiful, bell-shaped, pale pink flowers in spring and early summer. Its leaves are dark green, oval and deciduous and it grows to a height and spread of 75 cm (about 2½ ft). *D. × rosea* is fully hardy, and prefers a moist soil and partial shade.

D. scabra

This upright, deciduous shrub bears dense clusters of pink-tinged white blooms in spring. Its leaves are dark green and oval and it grows to a height of 3 m (about 9 ft) with a spread of 1.5 m (about 4½ ft). Fully hardy, it prefers a moist soil and partial shade.

DILLWYNIA

retorta

PARROT-PEA

This heath-like shrub, native to eastern Australia, is grown for its delightful clusters of yellow, red-centred flowers, which bloom in spring. Its stiff, narrow, leaves are twisted. It grows in most soils, as long as they are well drained and mulched all year round. Half-hardy,

Dillwynia retorta

Deutzia × rosea

Desfontainea spinosa

Daphne × burkwoodii

Deutzia scabra

it prefers dappled shade—the flowers are brightest when the shrub is grown under the shade of larger trees. It grows to a height and spread of 1.5 m (about 4½ ft). Propagate from scarified seed—soak for at least 24 hours—or semi-ripe tip cuttings in autumn/fall. It is suitable for containers but is prone to the root disease, phytophthora.

DIPELTA
floribunda

This tall, stiff, open shrub is grown for its spring appearance of fragrant, pale pink flowers, with throats flushed in yellow, and for its pale brown, peeling bark. The green, pointed leaves are deciduous. A native of China, it is not often found in Western gardens. Fully hardy, it thrives in sun or semi-shade and requires fertile, well-drained soil to do really well. A member of the same family (Caprifoliaceae) as honeysuckle, it grows to a height and spread of 4 m (about 12 ft). Prune old shoots after flowering and propagate from softwood cuttings in summer.

DODONAEA
viscosa
STICKY HOP-BUSH

This dense, fast-growing, short-lived bush is grown for the showy clusters of green fruits in summer, that follow its insignificant bloom. The sticky, glossy, pale green leaves are deciduous. Native to Australia and New Zealand, it succeeds almost anywhere outside the tropics. D. viscosa grows to a height of 3 m (about 9 ft) or more and a spread of 1.5 m (about 4½ ft), with reddish brown, peeling bark and thick branches. It prefers a well-drained soil, and sun or partial shade. To keep its shape, cut back in summer after flowering. Water specimens in containers frequently when in full growth, less at other times. Propagate from seed in spring or semi-ripe cuttings in summer; it will strike in any location.

DOMBEYA
burgessiae

This evergreen native of eastern Africa bears delightful, fragrant, pinkish white, hydrangea-like flowers, among rounded, downy leaves, in autumn/fall to winter. It needs a fertile, well-drained soil and full light or partial shade. Potted plants should be well-watered during active growth. Prune after flowering. Frost-tender, it grows to a height and spread of just over 2 m (about 6 ft). Propagate from semi-hardwood cuttings in spring. Red spider mite and whitefly may cause problems.

DREJERELLA
guttata
syn. *Beloperone guttata, Justicia brandegeana*
SHRIMP PLANT

The salmon to rose-pink, or pale yellow bracts surrounding the white flowers of this attractive, evergreen shrub, resemble a shrimp—hence its name. Native to tropical Mexico, it grows best in fertile, well-drained soil, and colours best under partial shade. It flowers mainly in summer. It can survive temperatures as low as minus 4°C (about 25°F) by behaving like a perennial when the tops are frozen back. A weak, sprawling plant, it needs regular pruning to maintain its shape and encourage new, flowering wood. Water potted plants freely when in full growth, less at other times. It grows to a height of 1 m (about 3 ft) and a spread of 60 cm (about 2 ft). Propagate from tip or semi-hardwood cuttings.

DRYANDRA

Native to Western Australia, these bushy shrubs are grown for the small, yellow or orange flowers in rounded domes, that grow in late winter to spring. Their elongated, saw-toothed leaves are evergreen. They prefer full light or partial shade, and do best in a well-drained, light, sandy soil without a large amount of nitrates or phosphates. They can withstand about minus 3°C (about 27°F). They grow to a height and spread of 2 m (about 6 ft). Water moderately. Propagate from seed in spring, and remember that these shrubs are susceptible to root rot. There are several species.

DURANTA
repens
syn. *D. plumieri*
GOLDEN DEWDROP, PIGEONBERRY, BRAZILIAN SKYFLOWER

Found naturally in the area stretching from Florida, USA, to Brazil, this handsome, weeping shrub makes an ideal windbreak or hedge in warmer climates. It bears delightful but tiny, violet-blue flowers in summer, which are followed by a shower of yellow berries. (These are poisonous, so keep children away.) The dark green, oval leaves are deciduous. Frost-tender, *D. repens* grows quickly to a height of 3 m (about 9 ft) with a spread of 2 m (about 6 ft). It does best in a well-drained soil and in full light or partial shade. Prune for shape (the plants can be clipped as a hedge) and water potted plants when growing. Propagate from seed in spring or semi-ripe cuttings in summer. Whitefly can cause problems.

Drejerella guttata

Dryandra nobilis

Dipelta floribunda

Duranta repens

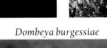

Dombeya burgessiae

Dodonaea viscosa

Elaeagnus pungens

Enkianthus campanulatus

Edgeworthia papyrifera

Elaeagnus pungens 'Maculata'

Epacris impressa

Eremophila glabra

EDGEWORTHIA

papyrifera
syn. *E. chrysantha*
PAPERBUSH, YELLOW DAPHNE

This open, rounded shrub is native to eastern Asia. Once used in Japan for paper-making, it has tough, fibrous branches, so flexible they can be knotted without breaking. In late winter and early spring, it bears sweet-smelling heads of rounded, tubular, yellow flowers. The oval, dark green leaves are deciduous. It is frost-hardy, except for the flowerheads. It likes moist, well-drained, leafy soil and full sun or partial shade. The position should be chosen carefully as it does not transplant well. It grows to a height and spread of 1.5 m (about 4¹/₂ ft). Propagate from semi-ripe cuttings in summer or seed in autumn/fall.

ELAEAGNUS

WILD OLIVE, OLEASTER, SILVERBERRY

These dense, spreading, mainly evergreen shrubs are favourites for hedging and as a backdrop. Found

all over the northern hemisphere, they grow well in poor soil and are frost-hardy. Deciduous species prefer full sun; evergreens thrive in sun or partial shade. Hedges are best trimmed in late summer. Propagate from seed in autumn/fall or semi-ripe cuttings in summer.

E. pungens
syn. *E. japonica*

This is the most common of the genus. A frost-hardy, evergreen bush with long, prickly, horizontal branches, it is excellent for hedges, growing to a height of 3 m (about 9 ft) and a spread of 5 m (about 15 ft). In autumn/fall it bears fragrant, tiny, bell-shaped, cream flowers. The glossy, oval leaves—dark green above, silvery with brown spots beneath—are deciduous.

E. pungens 'Maculata'

This bushy, slightly thorny shrub grows to a height and spread of 4 m (about 12 ft). Its glossy, dark green leaves, which feature a large, central, yellow patch, are evergreen. Mid- to late autumn/fall sees the

appearance of sweet-smelling, bowl-shaped, creamy white flowers. Half-hardy, it likes a well-drained soil and full sun.

ENKIANTHUS

campanulatus
CHINESE BELLFLOWER

Related to azaleas and heaths, these cool-climate, tree-like shrubs are originally from China and Japan where the flowers are gathered in large numbers to celebrate New Year. In spring the open, spreading habit is gaily adorned with small, bell-shaped, red-veined, creamy flowers. The shrub is deciduous; tufts of dull green leaves turn bright red in autumn/fall. Fully to frost-hardy, *E. campanulatus* does well in sun or partial shade in a moist, acid, peaty soil. Like all the species of *Enkianthus*, it does not tolerate air pollution well and does best in a country garden. Propagate from semi-ripe cuttings in summer or seeds in autumn/fall.

EPACRIS

impressa
VICTORIAN HEATH

This erect, leafless, evergreen, heath-like shrub is perfect for rock gardens as it likes fast drainage, preferring a sandy soil with full sun or partial shade. Native to south-eastern Australia and Tasmania, *E. impressa* bears pendent, tubular, white, pink or red flowers in late autumn/fall to spring. Evergreen, with short, red-tipped leaves, it grows to a height and spread of 1 m (about 3 ft). It does well in pots,

provided it is pruned back in spring after flowering, and the soil is sandy. Use liquid manure rather than chemical fertilizer. Propagate from young cuttings dipped in rooting hormone, keeping them constantly moist. It is also easily grown from seed (when this is commercially available).

EREMOPHILA

EMU-BUSH, POVERTY BUSH

Native to the outback areas of Australia, this genus is appropriately named 'lovers of lonely places'. Evergreen, bun-shaped shrubs, they do best in a sunny, open position and require well-drained, slightly alkaline soil. Frost-hardy, they dislike moist conditions and will thrive when conditions are very dry—they can go for years without water. Throughout most of the year they bear tubular flowers of varying colour. Propagate from semi-ripe tip cuttings in autumn/fall. Grow on for at least a year before planting out.

E. glabra
EMU-BUSH

This tenacious shrub bears red, yellow or green flowers mostly during spring. Frost-hardy, it grows to a height of 1.5 m (about 4¹/₂ ft) and a spread of 1–3 m (about 3–9 ft). Its lance-shaped, silvery grey leaves are evergreen. It thrives in arid conditions.

E. maculata
SPOTTED EMU-BUSH

From winter to spring, this rounded shrub produces tubular, yellow, pink, white or red flowers.

Erica carnea

Erica bauera

Erica cinerea

Erica grandiflora var. *grandiflora*

Eremophila maculata

Evergreen, with oval or linear, grey-green leaves with spotted throats, it grows to a height and spread of 2 m (about 6 ft). Half-hardy, it prefers dry, sunny conditions.

ERICA

HEATH, HEATHER

This genus of evergreen shrubs is native to southern Africa, parts of northern Africa and much of western Europe. Related to azaleas and rhododendrons, it boasts some of the most popular flowering plants, partly because of the long flowering season. They are very particular, however, requiring an acid soil that is porous and left constantly moist with unpolluted rainwater—any hint of lime in the soil and they will do badly. Avoid animal manure. They bear tubular, waxy flowers of varying lengths, and small linear leaves grouped around a stem. Propagate from seed—kept moist and sheltered—or from tip cuttings taken in autumn/fall or early winter. *E. arborea* from eastern Europe, rarely grown in gardens, supplies the 'briar' (bruyère) from which tobacco pipes are made.

E. bauera

BRIDAL HEATH

Native to South Africa, this upright, branching, evergreen shrub bears clusters of tubular, white or pink flowers for most of the year, set among tiny, narrow, grey-green leaves. Half-hardy, it grows to a height and spread of 1 m (about 3 ft).

E. carnea

syn. E. herbacea

This evergreen, spreading shrub makes good ground cover. From early winter to late spring, it bears bell-shaped to tubular flowers in shades of red and pink (sometimes white). Its mid- to dark green leaves are arranged in whorls. It will withstand some lime in the soil and shady conditions. Grows to a height of 30 cm (about 12 in) and spread of 50 cm (about 20 in) or more.

Erica cerinthoides

E. cerinthoides

This upright, fire-resistant evergreen is a native of South Africa. It bears terminal clusters of scarlet, bell-shaped flowers in winter and spring and has narrow, hairy leaves. Half-hardy, it grows to a height and spread of 1 m (about 3 ft).

E. cinerea

BELL HEATHER

From early summer through to early autumn/fall, this compact native of Europe bears bell-shaped flowers in shades of pink, white and dark red. It has mid- to deep green, needle-like, evergreen leaves. It does best in a dry, warm position with an acid soil. Numerous attractive cultivars bear blooms of varying hue.

E. grandiflora var. grandiflora

ORANGE HEATH

This sturdy, upright shrub grows to 1.5 m (about 4½ ft) high. Masses of orange, slightly curved, tubular flowers, up to 3 cm (about 1½ in) long, are borne in mid-summer. The leaves are stiff and needle-like. Plant in well-drained, acidic soil in full sun and water well during dry periods.

Erica speciosa

Erica regia

Erica mediterranea

E. mediterranea

As the name suggests, this attractive species is native to Mediterranean countries. An upright evergreen, it grows to 2.5 m (about 7 ft) high with a spread up to 2 m (about 6 ft). In winter and early spring it bears pinkish mauve, bell-shaped flowers. The mid-green leaves are shaped like a needle. Frost may damage the top of the plant, but it will recover from the base; generally it is frost-hardy. Many attractive, fragrant cultivars exist; most not more than 80 cm (about 32 in) in height or width.

E. regia
ROYAL HEATH

This upright evergreen grows to 2 m (about 6 ft) tall with a 1 m (about 3 ft) spread. In spring, it bears profuse clusters of beautiful, bell-shaped, sticky, crimson flowers set amid small, deep green, cylindrical leaves. Half-hardy, it is native to South Africa.

E. speciosa

This colourful shrub grows to a height and spread of 1 m (about 3 ft). In summer it bears red, tubular flowers with green tips. The narrow, grooved leaves are evergreen.

ERIOSTEMON
WAXFLOWER, AUSTRALIAN DAPHNE

These rounded evergreens native to Australia grow naturally as understory shrubs in forests. In cultivation they make excellent dappled shrub borders. Species prefer a neutral to acid, well-drained soil and do best in semi-shaded conditions, but will tolerate full sun. Bearing a strong resemblance to *Citrus*, to whom they are related, they bear star-shaped flowers and are frost-hardy. The foliage is often aromatic and fragrant. After flowering, prune back to the mounded foliage. Propagate from scarified seed or semi-ripe tip cuttings in autumn/fall. Scale insects may pose a problem. They are a little tender and best in a greenhouse in frosty climates.

E. australasius
syn. *E. lanceolatus*
PINK WAXFLOWER

This upright, evergreen shrub, native to New South Wales and Queensland, Australia, grows to a height of 2 m (about 6 ft) with a spread of 1 m (about 3 ft). In spring, pink flowers appear along its stems. It bears grey-green leaves.

E. myoporoides
AUSTRALIAN DAPHNE, LONG-LEAF WAXFLOWER, FAIRY WAXFLOWER

This variably shaped, evergreen, woody shrub is the most popular of the genus. In spring, pink buds open to waxy, white, star-shaped flowers. Its dark green, oval leaves are fragrant. Half-hardy, it prefers partial shade and well-drained soil. It grows to a height and spread of 2 m (about 6 ft).

ERYTHRINA
humeana

This sturdy, erect shrub, native to South Africa, bears terminal sprays of pea-shaped, scarlet flowers, set among trifoliate leaves set on prickly petioles. Knobbly pods containing hard seeds follow the bloom. It prefers an open, sunny position, in a well-drained, moist soil. Frost-hardy, it grows well in exposed, coastal areas. Potted specimens should be watered frequently in the summer months, less at other times. Propagate from semi-ripe cuttings in summer, or from seed in spring. Watch for spider mite.

Eriostemon australasius

Eriostemon myoporoides

Erythrina humeana

ESCALLONIA
'Apple Blossom'

Wind-resistant and ideal for hedging in coastal gardens, this attractive, bushy, dense evergreen bears apple-blossom pink flowers in early to mid-summer. It has dark green, glossy leaves. Half-hardy, and preferring well-drained soil and full sun, it grows to a height and spread of 2 m (about 6 ft). After flowering, trim the hedges and wall-trained plants. Propagate from softwood cuttings in summer.

EUCALYPTUS
EUCALYPTUS, FLOWERING GUM

The open, sprawling, evergreen trees and shrubs of this large genus are all native to Australia. Mostly trees, a few species are shrubby. They all do best in a sandy, slightly acidic, very well-drained soil—preferably over clay. Fully hardy to frost-tender, they require full sun to do well. Eucalyptus do not like root disturbance, so plant the smallest specimen available. Potted plants should be watered moderately, less so in winter. Planted specimens need extra water in dry spells. Cut growth back hard in spring to retain attractive, young growth. Propagate from seed in spring or autumn/fall.

E. forrestiana
FUCHSIA GUM

This large shrub or bushy small tree from Western Australia usually grows to about 3–4 m (about 9–12 ft) in height and spread. It has erect branches, olive green leaves and reddish twigs. In summer it bears pendant flowers with prominent red calyces and yellow stamens, which mature to bell-shaped woody fruit. Half-hardy, it needs protection from frost when young. One of the most widely grown of the shrubby eucalypts, it will tolerate severe pruning after flowering if it needs to be kept bushy.

E. macrocarpa
MOTTLECAH, ROSE OF THE WEST

This slow-growing species is native to Western Australia. From winter to summer, red flowers with yellow-tipped stamens appear, followed by conical capsules. Frost-hardy, it prefers full sun and well-drained soil. It grows to 5 m (about 15 ft) tall with a 2 m (about 6 ft) spread.

E. rhodantha
ROSE OF THE WEST

This shrubby eucalypt from Western Australia shares its common name with *E. macrocarpa* and resembles it in its grey leaves and rather straggling habit. It is a little taller and bushier, with smaller but equally lovely flowers in shades of deep pink. It has the reputation of being easier to grow, and is much admired in California. Prune fairly hard after flowering to keep the shrub compact.

EUONYMUS
SPINDLE BUSH

These evergreen or deciduous shrubs, with the occasional tree and climber are prized for their foliage, their odd, spindle-shaped seed pods, and the breathtaking autumn/fall colour of deciduous species. Found world-wide, the deciduous shrubs are grown in cool, temperate climates, while the evergreens are more suited to warmer conditions. Fully to frost-hardy, all need sun or semi-shade and well-drained soil. Propagate from semi-ripe cuttings in summer or seed in autumn/fall.

E. alatus
JAPANESE SPINDLE TREE

This slow-growing deciduous shrub from China and Japan is grown mainly for its splendid autumn/fall colour and display of purple fruits with scarlet seeds. It is of stiff and open habit to about 2.5 m (about 7$\frac{1}{2}$ ft) high and 2 m (about 6 ft) wide, with pointed, oval leaves which turn brilliant crimson in autumn/fall. The stems have corky wings and the tiny greenish spring flowers are insignificant. It is fully hardy.

E. europaeus
SPINDLE TREE

A 2–3 m (about 6–9 ft) tall deciduous shrub from Europe, the spindle tree takes its name from the use of its hard, perfectly straight branches in weaving in the days before the mechanical loom. Fully hardy, it is grown in gardens for its lavish display of fruits, whose carmine red calyces split to reveal orange seeds. The tiny greenish spring flowers are insignificant and although the slender pointed leaves colour in autumn/fall, they are of less account than the fruit. 'Red Cascade' is an especially fine cultivar.

Euonymus alatus

Eucalyptus forrestiana

Escallonia 'Apple Blossom'

Eucalyptus rhodantha

Euonymus europaeus

Eucalyptus macrocarpa

Euphorbia pulcherrima

Eupatorium megalophyllum

Euonymus j. 'Aureomarginatus'

Euonymus fortunei

Euphorbia milii

Euphorbia fulgens

E. fortunei
EMERALD AND GOLD

This open shrub is grown as a ground cover or shrub to about 1 m (about 3 ft) tall. As a ground cover it has an indefinite spread. From early to mid-summer it bears greenish white flowers. An evergreen, it has dark green and gold leaves.

E. japonicus 'Aureomarginatus'

This dense, upright evergreen grows to a height of 2–4 m (about 6–12 ft). It has oval, yellow-margined leaves and small, star-shaped, green flowers in summer. Frost-hardy, it makes a suitable choice for a hedge. The plain green variety is freer (on female plants) with its pretty coral pink berries.

EUPATORIUM
megalophyllum
MIST FLOWER

This erect shrub is a native of southern Mexico. In spring, it bears striking clusters of lilac flowers. The large, dark green leaves of this

evergreen shrub are veined and have pale undersides. It will not survive even the mildest of frosts. It requires full sun or partial shade and does best in a moist but well-drained soil. It seeds profusely—to prevent it taking over, prune lightly after flowering or in spring. Tip back new shoots in summer to maintain shape. Potted plants should be watered freely in full growth, less so at other times. It grows to a height of 1.5 m (about 4½ ft) and a spread of 2 m (about 6 ft). Propagate from slim, semi-hardened cuttings with short internodes. Two-spotted mite and whitefly may cause problems.

EUPHORBIA
MILKWEED, SPURGE

This genus contains over 1000 widely varying species of shrubs, perennials and succulents. Each species bears a spectacular show of coloured bracts rather than true flowers, and the milk sap is always poisonous. The shrubs do well in sun or partial shade and in moist but well-

drained soil. Propagate from seed in autumn/fall or spring, from basal cuttings in spring or summer, or by division in early spring or early autumn/fall.

E. fulgens
SCARLET PLUME

This evergreen, arching shrub grows to a height of 1.5 m (about 4½ ft) and a spread of 60 cm (about 24 in). In winter to spring, its long branches bear sprays of flowers, each cluster surrounded by red bracts. It has mid- to deep green, oval to lance-shaped leaves. It tolerates frost poorly and is suited to warmer areas only. Propagate from hardwood cuttings in summer.

E. milii
syn. *E. splendens*
CROWN OF THORNS

This slow-growing, ferociously thorny, semi-succulent shrub is a native of Madagascar. Deciduous in cooler areas, it is drought resistant and grows to a height of 1 m (about 3 ft) and a spread of 75 cm (about 2½ ft). It is excellent in rock gar-

dens or in cavities and is often used as a low hedge in coastal areas. Throughout the year and especially in spring, it bears tiny, yellowish flowers, enveloped by bright red bracts, whether there are pale green leaves on the branches or not. It does not tolerate frost well—hardy only down to 5–7°C (about 40–44°F). It prefers a sunny spot and well-drained soil.

E. pulcherrima
POINSETTIA, CHRISTMAS PLANT

The hollow-stemmed poinsettia is the showiest and most popular of the genus. A native of Mexico, it does best in well-drained soil, and plenty of water. From late autumn/fall to spring, small, greenish-red flowers appear, surrounded by bright-red, pink or white bracts. The oval, green leaves may be evergreen or deciduous. It is not at all frost-hardy—even a light frost will kill it. Prune poinsettias back hard to encourage shoot growth. Grow them in pots for pleasant, indoor, winter decoration, although the colour will not be as good as when grown out-

Fatsia japonica

doors in subtropical or tropical climates where it will grow 4 m (about 12 ft) tall and wide.

EURYOPS
pectinatus
BRIGHTEYES, RESIN BUSH

A native of South Africa, this shrubby evergreen grows well in most temperate conditions. Excellent for rock gardens and borders, it likes sun, partial shade in hot conditions, and a moist, well-drained, gravelly soil. From winter to spring it bears delightful, bright yellow, daisy-like flowers. It has a spreading habit, with grey-green leaves. Water in the hot months and prune after blooming to maintain the shape. It dislikes root disturbance so avoid transplanting. Half-hardy, it grows to a height of 1 m (about 3 ft) with a spread of 75 cm (about 2½ ft). Propagate from softwood cuttings in summer.

EXOCHORDA
racemosa
PEARL BUSH

This deciduous, arching shrub, native to China, is grown for the delightful, upright clusters of white flowers it bears in late spring. These appear from bare wood and the buds resemble a string of pearls—hence the name. *E. racemosa* has oblong, deep blue-green leaves and grows to a height and spread of 4 m (about 12 ft). Plant the shrub in loamy but well-drained, acid soil in a sunny position. If the soil is limy, chlorosis may present a problem. Thin out old shoots after flowering—this will improve the bloom. Fully hardy, it needs regular watering. Propagate from softwood cuttings in summer or seed in autumn/fall.

× FATSHEDERA
lizei
TREE IVY

This bi-generic hybrid (a botanical rarity) is the offspring of *Fatsia japonica* 'Moseri' and *Hedera helix* 'Hibernica' (Irish ivy). Popular as a house plant, it is also used extensively as ground cover; otherwise it may be trained against a wall or pillar. It prefers partial shade, and does best in moist but well-drained, fertile soil. Frost-hardy, it reaches 2 m (about 6 ft) tall with a spread of 3 m (about 9 ft). Small, white flowers appear in autumn/fall. It bears glossy, deep green leaves; on × *F. lizei* 'Variegata' the leaves have a narrow creamy white edge. Pinch back to keep from falling over, or support it with canes. Propagate in summer from semi-ripe cuttings.

FATSIA
japonica
syn. *Aralia japonica, A. sieboldii*
JAPANESE ARALIA

Japanese aralia is one of the world's most loved house plants. It may also be cultivated as a spreading bush, or trained into a single-stemmed tree. It bears splendid, large, rounded, deeply lobed, glossy, dark green leaves under almost any conditions. There is also a variegated form. Dense clusters of insignificant, tiny, white flowers appear in autumn/fall, followed by small, black berries. It does best in sunny or shaded areas and prefers a well-drained, fertile soil. Frost-hardy, it prefers shelter from cold winds. Cut back hard if it gets too leggy. Propagate by semi-ripe cuttings in summer or from seed in autumn/fall or spring.

FORSYTHIA
GOLDEN BELLS

Profuse blooms of yellow flowers are the principal attraction of this genus of deciduous shrubs. Vase-shaped and deciduous, they are easy to grow in rich, well-drained soil. They prefer regions where winter is frosty—they are frost-hardy to minus 25°C (about minus 13°F). Propagate by division or from semi-hardwood cuttings taken in summer. The genus was named in the eighteenth century in honour of William Forsyth, gardener to King George III of England.

F. × intermedia

This compact, deciduous, arching or spreading shrub bears yellow flowers in spring. Its leaves are dark green and lance-shaped. It grows to a height of 3 m (about 9 ft) with a spread of 2 m (about 6 ft).

Exochorda racemosa

Euryops pectinatus

Forsythia × intermedia

× *Fatshedera lizei*

F. × *intermedia* 'Beatrix Farrand'

This bushy, arching, deciduous shrub bears masses of yellow flowers about 6 cm (about 2½ in) across in spring. Mid-green, oval, serrated leaves soon follow. Fully hardy, it does best in full light and in a well-drained soil. It grows to a height and spread of 2 m (about 6 ft). The flower clusters are most dense on the previous year's growth, which is encouraged by pruning after flowering.

Fremontodendron californicum

FOTHERGILLA
major

MOUNTAIN WITCHHAZEL

This spreading, cool-climate shrub is native to the USA, where it thrives in remote, mountain areas. This, the best known of only 4 species in the genus, grows to a height of 2 m (about 6 ft) and a spread of 1.5 m (about 4½ ft). Fragrant, snowy white, puffball flowers appear in spring, and again in autumn/fall. The dark-green leaves, slightly blue beneath, turn yellow in autumn/fall. Fully frost-hardy, this species does best in a moist, peaty, acid soil and prefers partial shade. Propagate from softwood cuttings in summer.

FRANCOA
appendiculata

BRIDAL WREATH

From summer to early autumn/fall, this evergreen perennial bears racemes of delightful pale pink flowers on graceful erect stems. It bears

Forsythia × i. 'Beatrix Farrand'

crinkled, hairy, oval, dark green leaves. Frost-hardy, *F. appendiculata* will thrive best in full sun or partial shade. Plant in fertile, well-drained soil. It grows to a height of 60 cm (about 2 ft) with a spread of 45 cm (about 1½ ft). Propagate from seed or by division in spring .

FREMONTODENDRON
californicum

FLANNEL BUSH

This sun-loving, evergreen or semi-evergreen shrub is prized for its bright yellow flowers that bloom from spring to mid-autumn/fall. Its lobed, dark green leaves are white-felted underneath. A native of California, it thrives in arid, even desert conditions, with full sun, and a well-drained, sandy soil. Frost-hardy, it grows to a height of 6 m (about 18 ft) with a spread of 4 m (about 12 ft). It is advisable to wear gloves when handling the plant as it is covered in hairs which can cause allergic reactions. It does not transplant very well, so choose the final location carefully. Propagate from seed or softwood cuttings in summer or from seed in autumn/fall or spring.

FUCHSIA

FUCHSIA, LADIES' EARDROPS

Native to the rainforests of South America, these exotic evergreen and semi-evergreen shrubs and trees are grown for the splendid, pendulous, tubular flowers born from early summer to late autumn/fall. These hang from axils, most heavily at the

ends of arching branches. Each flower consists of four reflexed sepals and four or more petals, often in a contrasting colour. Fuchsias prefer a partially shaded, sheltered position and will thrive in almost any soil, as long as it contains plenty of organic matter. They require plenty of water (sometimes twice a day in summer)—but avoid watering in full sun. Prune back drastically to prevent the plant from becoming too woody, and to maintain shape. They are frost-hardy to frost-tender. Propagate from softwood cuttings in any season. Red spider mite may cause problems, also guard against leaf-eating caterpillars or looper.

F. 'Gartenmeister Bonstedt'

This lax shrub produces large, tubular, orange to brick-red flowers—abundantly, if conditions are mild with plenty of sun. It is quite useful as a garden hedge. Plant at intervals of 75 cm (about 2½ ft), or as a pot or garden shrub. The leaves of this cultivar are a dark, bronzed red.

F. *magellanica* var. *gracilis*

This upright, frost-hardy evergreen bears small, red, tubular flowers, with purple petals and red sepals. Black fruits follow.

F. *magellanica* var. *gracilis* 'Alba'

If growth continues unchecked, this cultivar can grow to a considerable size. Prune it back to maintain its shape. This shrub bears attractive, pale pink flowers.

Fuchsia 'Gartenmeister Bonstedt'

Fothergilla major

Francoa appendiculata

Fuchsia magellanica var. *gracilis* 'Alba'

Gamolepis chrysanthemoides

Fuchsia magellanica unnamed cultivar

Fuchsia procumbens

Fuchsia magellanica var. *gracilis*

F. magellanica cultivars

F. magellanica has given rise to a large number of cultivars, very popular as pot plants and (in mild winter areas) as garden shrubs for a shaded spot. They can have single or double flowers, in shades of white, pink, red, mauve or purple, often with the petals and sepals in contrasting colours. They range in height from less than 1 m (about 3 ft) to almost 1.5 m (about 4½ ft). They are evergreen and will thrive best in fertile, well-drained soil. Prune in late winter for bushiness and propagate from softwood cuttings.

F. procumbens

TRAILING FUCHSIA

Native to New Zealand, this prostrate, evergreen shrub grows to a height of 10 cm (about 4 in) with an indefinite spread. It bears erect, orange-tipped, purple and green flowers among small, heart-shaped leaves, followed by large, red berries. Half-hardy, it is excellent as a ground cover, or in rock gardens and hanging baskets.

GAMOLEPIS
chrysanthemoides

PARIS DAISY

Admired for its ability to flower continuously throughout the year, this rounded shrub bears delightful yellow, daisy-like flowers, carried on single stems. Its glossy, green, irregularly serrated leaves are evergreen. Half-hardy, it prefers full sun and does best in moist but well-drained, loamy soil. Prune regularly to maintain shape and water all year round. Remove wilted flowers to promote continuous blooming. It self-seeds profusely; otherwise propagate from cuttings. It grows to a height of 1.5 m (about 4½ ft) and a spread of 1 m (about 3 ft).

GARDENIA

GARDENIA, CAPE JASMINE

Gardenias provide some of the most attractive, fragrant blooms to be found in warm climate gardens world-wide. Unfortunately they are mostly frost-tender, and will not do well at temperatures below 5°C (about 40°F): in Europe and most of the USA they need greenhouse culture. They do best in full sun to partial shade, and like a rich, peaty, well-drained, neutral to acid soil. Shorten strong shoots after blooming to maintain a good shape. Water potted plants generously in full growth, less so at other times. Some pests can pose problems—notably mealybug and whitefly. Propagate from semi-ripe cuttings in summer, or greenwood cuttings in spring.

Garrya elliptica

Gardenia thunbergia

Gardenia augusta 'Radicans'

G. augusta 'Florida'

This cultivar grows slowly up to a height and spread of 1.5 m (about 4¹/₂ ft). From summer to winter it bears fragrant, double, white flowers. It is an evergreen, with glossy, oval, dark green leaves.

G. augusta 'Radicans'

DWARF GARDENIA

This cultivar, native to China, is low-growing, with a height to 50 cm (about 20 in) and spread to 2 m (about 6 ft).

G. thunbergia

TREE GARDENIA

An exceptionally beautiful and desirable shrub, this tree gardenia grows to a height and spread of 2 m (about 6 ft) or more. It does best in temperate to warm conditions. In autumn/fall, it bears fragrant, large, white, terminal flowers, set among glossy, deep green leaves.

GARRYA
elliptica

SILK TASSEL BUSH

This extraordinary, bushy, dense shrub is cultivated almost exclusively for its curtain of grey-green catkins, which grow up to 20 cm (about 8 in) in length—shorter on female plants which, however, bear decorative bluish berries. These appear from mid-winter to early spring, and may be damaged by frosts. Native to the west coast of the USA, G. elliptica may grow to a height of 5 m (about 15 ft) with a spread of 3 m (about 9 ft). Frost-hardy, it prefers full sun

Gardenia augusta 'Florida'

Gaultheria rupestris

or part-shade and well-drained soil to thrive, doing particularly well on the coast or inland. It has leaves that are dark green and leathery. Propagate from semi-hardwood cuttings taken in summer.

GAULTHERIA
rupestris

A native of New Zealand, this erect, branching, evergreen shrub bears clusters of tubular white flowers set amid oblong, leathery leaves. Succulent berries follow the bloom. It prefers a well-drained, mildly acid soil, with a year-round mulch of leaf litter, in a protected, partially shaded position. Frost-hardy, it grows to a height and spread of 2 m (about 6 ft). Propagate from seeds or cuttings.

GENISTA

DYER'S GREENWEED, BROOM

In ancient times, members of this genus of deciduous shrubs and trees were grown to make dyes. Nowadays, they are grown solely for the fragrance and beauty of their blooms. Native to the Mediterranean areas of North Africa, southern Europe and Asia Minor, they make good seaside shrubs. They do well in hot, sunny conditions but are quite hardy nonetheless, and will survive a prolonged freeze. Grow in a not-too-rich, well-drained soil. They will not do well if transplanted. Prune tips to encourage a bushy look. Propagate in spring from sown seed (soak for 24 hours first) or from semi-hardwood cuttings in summer.

G. aetnensis

MOUNT ETNA BROOM, SICILIAN BROOM

This rounded, somewhat weeping shrub/tree is native to Sicily and North Africa. Frost-hardy, it prefers full sun and a moist soil. Growing to 10 m (about 30 ft) in height and spread, it is almost leafless, but in summer bears an explosion of small, golden yellow flowers.

G. monosperma

This deciduous, broadly bushy shrub is native to Spain and North

Genista aetnensis

Grevillea banksii

Goodenia ovata

Genista monosperma

Grevillea 'Boongala Spinebill'

Gordonia axillaris

Genista tinctoria

Grevillea biternata

Africa. Spectacular in spring when in full bloom, it bears fragrant, white, pea-shaped flowers on long, arching branches. It grows to a height and spread of 3 m (about 9 ft). Propagate from semi-hardwood cuttings in autumn/fall.

G. tinctoria
DYER'S GREENWEED

Fully hardy, this squat, deciduous, spreading shrub grows to a height of 75 cm (about 2½ ft) and a spread of 1 m (about 3 ft). In summer, golden-yellow, pea-like flowers appear, set among thin, dark green leaves. It does best in full sun with a well-drained soil.

GOODENIA
ovata

This compact, low-growing, evergreen shrub grows to a height of 30 cm (about 1 ft) and a spread of 1 m (about 3 ft). In spring and summer it bears clusters of fan-shaped, bright yellow flowers. The oval leaves are bright green. It makes good ground cover—a useful plant for a shaded rock garden or slope. Prune when young to keep it from becoming straggly. It prefers full sun or semi-shade, and a mildly acid, well-drained soil. Propagate from tip cuttings in autumn/fall.

GORDONIA
axillaris

CRÊPE CAMELLIA

This handsome, glossy-leaved plant may reach tree-size after many years—up to 9 m (about 30 ft)—in mild climates. Normally, however, it is seen as a shrub, growing to 2–3 m (about 6–9 ft). A native of China, Taiwan and Vietnam, it bears cream-white, saucer-shaped flowers with a mass of yellow stamens in autumn/fall to spring. Although evergreen, sometimes a few of its leathery, lance-shaped leaves turn rich scarlet or gold at the same time. Half-hardy, it prefers a sunny spot, with a well-drained, acid soil. Potted plants should be watered moderately, less so in winter. Propagate from late summer cuttings.

GREVILLEA

GREVILLEA, SPIDER FLOWER

The most popular and decorative of native Australian shrubs and trees, this genus numbers some 250 species, and again as many cultivars. Extremely variable in habit, foliage and flowers, most grevilleas are found in the south-western part of Western Australia. There are also a few species native to Malaysia. Well sought after as garden plants, many are adaptable and easy to grow with a long flowering period. Popular with honey-seeking birds, they will grow in most soils, but do best in one that is well-drained, slightly dry, gravelly and neutral to acid. Most are only moderately frost-hardy to minus 5°C (about 23°F). They appreciate the occasional addition of a light fertilizer, but avoid using phosphorus. Flowers are borne on heads, sometimes globular, sometimes elongated and one-sided, like a toothbrush. The fruits that follow are leathery capsules that split to release one or, more commonly, two seeds. Propagate from seed in spring or from firm tip cuttings taken in late summer. They can also be grafted. Strong roots develop early and it is important not to disturb these when potting on. Grevilleas are generally pest free, but scale insects and leaf spot may pose a problem.

G. banksii

This adaptable, quick-growing species from Queensland, Australia, is a favourite among gardeners, but it does tend to become straggly, so judicious pruning is recommended. It bears abundant, upright, terminal clusters of red flowers in spring and summer. The slender leaflets have a silky down beneath. Frost-tender, it grows to a height of 3 m (about 9 ft) and a spread of 2 m (about 6 ft). Easily grown from seed, it is suitable for hedges in streets, parks and gardens or as a specimen, and is a good shrub for coastal areas. *G. banksii* is named after the botanist, Sir Joseph Banks.

G. biternata

This rapidly growing, evergreen native of Western Australia is ideal for ground cover. It grows from 50 cm to 1 m (about 20 in to 3 ft) with a spread of 2 m (about 6 ft). In winter and spring it bears fragrant, white flowers in dense, fluffy masses. The leaves are divided into needle-like segments and are yellow-green. *G. biternata* is hardy, tolerating a certain degree of frost.

G. 'Boongala Spinebill'

This attractive cultivar bears long, dense heads of deep red flowers for most of the year. A spreading, frost-hardy, evergreen shrub, it has serrated, green leaves and grows to a height of 2 m (about 6 ft) and spread of 4 m (about 12 ft).

A Field Trip to the Cape Floral Kingdom

The southern tip of the African continent encompasses the 'Cape Floral Kingdom', the name botanists have given to the southern Cape Province and its extraordinarily rich flora. This is a diverse region—the coastal plains are largely sand and limestone and further inland, the undulating landscape is formed from shales and clays. The Cape Fold Mountains dominate the skyline to the north-east of Cape Town and Table Mountain. They are composed of steeply tilted acid sandstones, which yield a shallow soil that is deficient in the nutrients required for plant growth and hence of no value for agriculture or even the grazing of livestock. On their slopes though, and in many areas of similar soil in the southern Cape, there has developed the famous 'Fynbos' vegetation—a low scrub of extraordinary botanical diversity.

Of the world's great floral kingdoms, the Cape Floral Kingdom occupies the smallest area, but for its size it has a higher concentration of plant species (about 8500) than anywhere else on earth.

A feature of the Fynbos vegetation is the concentration of genera and species of the Proteaceae family. Richest in species are the *Protea*, *Leucadendron* and *Leucospermum* genera. In spring you can travel to any one of the mountainous areas within 250 km (about 160 miles) of Cape Town and find yourself in a world of flowers.

Low-growing vegetation on the South West Cape Mountains slopes.

Of the many species of *Protea*, one of the best known and most widely distributed in Cape Province is the wagon tree (*Protea nitida*), a shrub or smallish tree of varying size and shape. It is typically small and bushy, appearing a distinct greyish white from a distance, usually 5 m (about 15 ft) high with a trunk up to 50 cm (about 18 in) in diameter. The crown of foliage is rounded and irregular. The flowerheads (inflorescences), normally creamy white, may be present all year round but their bloom peaks between May and August. They are typical protea blooms, with globes up to 16 cm (about 6½ in) wide when open.

In early colonial days in South Africa, the attractive, reddish coloured wood of the wagon tree was used for furniture, wagon building and wagon brake blocks, hence the common name. The bark was also used for tanning, while the mature leaves produced a tolerably good black writing ink extracted with a solution of iron salt.

A field trip to view the wagon tree can be made at any time, as the species flowers all year round. However the best time to visit the Cape Floral Kingdom is in spring to early summer (September to December), because there is a great profusion of other flowers to be seen at this time. Head out from Cape Town along the N1 national road towards the Transvaal. Approximately 30 km (about 18 miles) north-east of Cape Town is the town of Paarl, in the heart of one of the richest and longest-settled agricultural areas in South Africa. You will pass orchards and vineyards, for this is also the centre of the country's wine production.

From here there are two possible routes. If you proceed on the old N1 over the Du Toitskloof Pass, within 5 or 10 minutes you will be in the typically rugged sandstone mountains of the Cape. As you go up the pass you will have your first glimpse of the Fynbos flora and see *Protea nitida* almost on the shoulders of the road. There are many places to stop and stroll around, but the best is yet to come.

The wagon tree, with other Fynbos plants.

Protea nitida

As you continue over the pass and go slowly down the other side, you will find the sunny eastern slopes on your right are covered in groups and single specimens of both the wagon tree and another *Protea* species, the sugarbush (*P. repens*). The early Dutch settlers extracted a syrup from the nectar-rich flowers of this plant, and at times it was their only source of sugar.

The alternative route is via the R303 district road after Paarl, crossing the Berg River. This will take you to the historic town of Franschhoek (where French Huguenots settled at the end of the seventeenth century). From here continue on up the Franschhoek Pass where you will find a floral profusion equal to that of the Du Toitskloof Pass. Apart from proteas and other Proteaceae, the Fynbos on these mountain slopes contains many species of *Erica* (the heath genus), most of which have colourful flowers. This is an amazingly diverse genus with almost 600 species in the southern Cape Province alone. Although *Erica* is also well known in Europe and the Mediterranean, that far larger region has fewer than one-twentieth the number of species. Other colourful wildflowers in the Fynbos include some lovely members of the daisy family, and spring-flowering bulbs such as watsonias, to name but a few.

From Franschhoek it is some 50 km (about 30 miles) back to Cape Town. After your field trip, it is worthwhile visiting Kirstenbosch National Botanic Garden, famous as much for its magnificent setting on the slope of Table Mountain as for its collections of South African native plants. Stroll to the magnificent Castle Rock and then walk through the Protea Garden. Here you will again find yourself in native Fynbos vegetation, rich in a number of beautiful species, including *Protea nitida* of course. Another attraction of this wonderful garden is the view, with the Cape Peninsula laid out below and, more distantly, the mountains behind Paarl and Stellenbosch where you have already been.

Protea

When the eminent Swedish botanist Linnaeus was systematically renaming all known plant and animal species in the mid-eighteenth century, he was so impressed by the range of form in one genus of African shrubs that he named it *Protea* after the Greek god Proteus, who had the ability to change at will into any of a myriad of forms.

Protea later lent its name to a major plant family, the Proteaceae, which includes many genera and species in Australia as well as in Africa, with smaller numbers in South America, New Caledonia, New Guinea and Indonesia. It is one of the most clear-cut examples of a plant group that originated in the super-continent Gondwana, predating its break-up into the present southern hemisphere land masses.

The astoundingly beautiful, symmetrical and long-lasting flowerheads of many Proteaceae have contributed to their popularity as cut flowers, to the extent that they are now a major item of international trade. Foremost are species of *Protea* itself, grown in Australia, New Zealand, California and Israel as well as in their native South Africa. The more striking species of Proteaceae are all adapted to highly nutrient-deficient soils and their cultivation requirements are frequently specialized. Most are only suited to milder temperate areas.

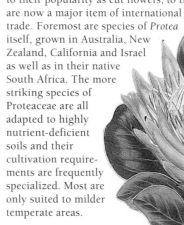

Protea cynaroides

Grevillea 'Honey Gem'

G. 'Honey Gem'

This dense, evergreen shrub grows to a maximum height of 4 m (about 12 ft) and a spread of 2 m (about 6 ft). It bears large, orange flowers for most of the year. Frost-tender, it has finely divided, dark green leaves with a silvery underside.

G. juniperina
syn.   G. trinervis

Attractive and useful in a wide range of situations, this arching shrub is native to New South Wales, Australia. It has both an upright and a prostrate form. The densely textured, upright form has arching limbs and a formal habit, growing to a height and spread of 2 m (about 6 ft). The prostrate form has long, willowy branches, broader, shorter leaves, and grows to 50 cm (about 20 in) tall with a 2 m (about 6 ft) spread. Both forms bear clusters of handsome, red flowers in winter to early summer. It has sharp, needle-like leaves. Very hardy, it is both drought and frost resistant. It is the parent of many hybrids with flowers of many other colours.

G. lavandulacea

One of the most variable of the genus, this bushy, compact shrub bears small, crowded, abundant clusters of crimson to pink (sometimes white) flowers over the entire bush for most of the year. The leaves are short and broad, silvery grey, usually covered in hairs but sometimes smooth. Hardy, frost and drought resistant, it grows to a height of 1 m (about 3 ft) or less with a spread of 2 m (about 6 ft). It is suitable for hedges in parks and gardens.

G. 'Misty Pink'

This spectacular shrub is half-hardy and grows to a height and spread of 2–3 m (about 6–9 ft). A spectacular shrub, it blooms throughout the year, bearing pink, cylindrical flowers. It has silvery, grey-green, fern-like, divided flowers.

G. 'Poorinda Royal Mantle'

This prostrate, evergreen shrub grows rapidly, to a height of 10–15 cm (about 4–6 in) with a spread of 5 m (about 15 ft) or more. Throughout the year, but especially in spring and summer, it bears red, tooth-brush-like flowers. Frost-hardy, it has dull green leaves which are sometimes lobed. It is often grafted on G. robusta to form weeping standards.

G. 'Robyn Gordon'

A popular and attractive hybrid (from G. banksii and G. bipinnatifida), this sprawling, evergreen shrub bears large, rich red, drooping flower-heads all year round. It has dark green, fern-like leaves with silky undersides. Moderately frost-hardy,

Grevillea juniperina (prostrate form, hybrid)

Grevillea 'Misty Pink'

Grevillea lavandulacea

Grevillea glabrata

Grevillea 'Poorinda Royal Mantle'

G. glabrata

This fast-growing, spreading evergreen can be trimmed to a compact, small shrub. It has attractive, lobed, prickly, grey-green leaves. Most of the year it bears small, dainty white flowers. It likes an open situation with well-drained, light to medium soil and propagates readily from cuttings—make sure these are well-rooted before potting on. Very easy, fairly frost and drought resistant, it grows to a height of 3 m (about 9 ft) and a spread of 4 m (about 12 ft).

Greyia sutherlandii

Griselinia littoralis

Grevillea 'Robyn Gordon'

it is vulnerable to leaf spot in damp conditions. Prune to encourage dense growth. It grows to a height of 1 m (about 3 ft) and a spread of up to 2 m (about 6 ft).

GREWIA
occidentalis
LAVENDER STAR, CROSSBERRY

Native to Africa, this fast-growing evergreen is widely grown in the southern USA. In summer it bears pink and mauve, star-shaped flowers. It is frost- to half-hardy and likes moist but well-mulched, well-drained soil. Grows to a height and spread of 3 m (about 9 ft). Pruning will maintain a compact habit. Propagate from seed or cuttings.

GREYIA
sutherlandii
SOUTH AFRICAN BOTTLEBRUSH, NATAL BOTTLEBRUSH, BEACONWOOD

Native to South Africa, this dome-shaped ornamental shrub grows to 3 m (about 9 ft) or more in height and spread. Clusters of woody, roughly saw-toothed leaves develop at the branch tips. These look similar to the mulberry leaf and turn red in autumn. In spring, vivid pinkish red, bottlebrush-like flowers appears as does new foliage. This half-hardy species requires full sun and porous soil. A dry spell after flowering will encourage next season's flowering. Prune flower stems after blooming. Propagate from seed or half-ripe cuttings in summer.

GRISELINIA
littoralis

Native to New Zealand, this fast-growing tree or shrub is a popular seaside plant in Ireland and in New England and California in the USA. It is grown for its shining, oval, apple-green leathery leaves. It bears insignificant tiny, yellow-green flowers in spring. Small, black berries follow the bloom. *G. littoralis* is resistant to wind and salt, making it a perfect choice for a hedge or windbreak in coastal areas. Drought resistant, it likes fertile, well-drained soil and full sun or partial shade. It is frost- to half-hardy and grows to a height and spread of 6–12 m (about 16–36 ft). Propagate from semi-ripe cuttings in summer or seed in spring and autumn/fall.

HAKEA
PINCUSHION TREE, NEEDLE BUSH

Members of this variable genus of shrubs and small trees are native to Australia but are now popular in Mediterranean areas, southern California and New Zealand. Strongly fragrant, they do best in dry, gravelly, well-drained soil that is slightly acid. The leaves vary; they are mostly hard and needle like. The flowers resemble those of grevilleas—instead of petals they have stamens sitting in cups of joined sepals. These are usually small and grow in pairs, often clustered into a long head. Frost-hardy to frost-tender, these plants like plenty of sun. Potted specimens should be watered moderately in full growth, less so at other times. Propagate from seed (pre-treated by nicking or immersion in near-boiling water) in

autumn/fall or semi-ripe cuttings in summer. Collar rot is occasionally a problem.

H. laurina
PINCUSHION PLANT

A loose, gangly plant with weeping branches, this tall, smooth-barked shrub is extremely popular. In winter to spring it bears delightfully fragrant, crimson or cherry flowers, with protruding, white styles, that resemble pins in a pincushion. The leaves are broad, stalked, and grey-green, with prominent veins. Half-hardy, it grows to a height of 3–6 m (about 9–18 ft) with a spread of 3 m (about 9 ft).

Grewia occidentalis

Hakea laurina

Hebe × franciscana 'Blue Gem'

Hebe hulkeana

Hakea sericea

Hakea saligna

Halimium lasianthum

H. saligna
syn. *H. salicifolia*
WILLOW-LEAFED HAKEA

This elegant, compact, fast-growing, bushy tree bears tiny, cream flowers that cluster along its branches in spring and autumn/fall. Small, woody fruits follow. It has pointed, pale green leaves which are bronze-red when young. Frost and drought resistant, it prefers full sun and well-drained soil. It grows to a height of 5 m (about 15 ft) and a spread of 3 m (about 9 ft).

H. sericea

This evergreen, rounded shrub grows to a height of 3–5 m (about 9–15 ft) and a spread of 2–3 m (about 6–12 ft). It bears clusters of small, fragrant, tubular white or palest pink flowers in autumn/fall and winter. Its needle-like leaflets are very sharply pointed and the plant makes a good burglar-resistant hedge. *H. sericea* is moderately hardy.

HALIMIUM
lasianthum
syn. *H. formosum*
SUNROSE

This stunning, low-spreading evergreen is a native of Spain and Portugal. It has grey-green foliage and in spring and summer bears open, golden flowers, each petal marked with a central, red blotch. Although frost-hardy, it needs shelter in colder areas. Water sparingly, except in drought conditions, ensuring it has a well-drained soil and full sun. Related to *Cistus*, it is admirably suited for coastal gardens. It grows to a height of 75 cm (about 30 in) and a spread of 1.5 m (about 4½ ft). Propagate from semi-ripe cuttings in summer.

HEBE
VERONICA, SHRUB SPEEDWELL

Most of these evergreen shrubs are native to New Zealand but some species are to be found naturally in Chile and New Guinea. They are all grown for the luxurious, dense spikes of tiny, 4-petalled, purple, white or cerise flowers. Resistance to salt and sea winds make them eminently suited to coastal areas. They are good as dense hedges or thick ground covers. Half-hardy to about minus 5°C (about 23°F), they require well-drained soil and full sun or semi-shade. Cut back in spring to shape and tidy, or to restrict growth. Propagate from semi-ripe cuttings in summer. There are a great many cultivated species and hybrids.

H. × andersonii

This is a bushy, half-hardy, evergreen shrub that grows to a height and spread of 2 m (about 6 ft). It bears dense spikes of small, lilac flowers in summer. The leaves are dark green. A form with cream-variegated leaves is available.

H. × franciscana 'Blue Gem'

From summer to early winter, this spreading evergreen bears dense spikes of small, violet-blue flowers and has oblong, densely arranged, mid-green leaves. Frost-hardy, it grows to a height of 60 cm (about 24 in) with a spread of 1 m (about 3 ft).

H. hulkeana

This upright, open, evergreen shrub bears masses of small, pale lilac flowers in spring and early summer. Its attractive, oval, serrated, glossy, dark green leaves have red margins. It grows to a height and spread of 1 m (about 3 ft).

Hebe × andersonii

H. speciosa

This desirable species boasts deep green foliage and purple brushes of flowers that appear in terminal clusters in summer and winter to spring. Half-hardy, it grows to a height of 1.5 m (about 4½ ft) with a spread of 1 m (about 3 ft). Numerous, brightly coloured cultivars exist, with flowers ranging from purple and deep red to pale lilac, pink and white.

HELICHRYSUM
selago

Native to the mountain regions of New Zealand, this erect evergreen shrub grows up to 45 cm (about 18 in). It has a conifer-like appearance; its rigid stems are covered with dense, triangular scale-like foliage. Terminal clusters of downy cream flowers sporadically appear at the tips of the branchlets.

HELIOTROPIUM
arborescens
syn. H. peruvianum
CHERRY PIE, HELIOTROPE

This attractive shrub is much-prized for the clusters of fragrant, purple to lavender flowers it bears from late spring to autumn/fall. A native of South America, it grows fast 75 cm (about 30 in) tall and 1 m (about 3 ft) wide. It is a branching, evergreen species with dark green, wrinkled leaves. Tender to frost, it needs rich, fertile, well-drained soil and full sun. In very dry areas, it is best raised in a semi-shady position and the soil kept moist. Potted specimens should be regularly watered in full growth, but moderately at other times. Cut back to half in early spring to promote a bushy look. Propagate from seed in spring or semi-ripe cuttings in early autumn/fall. The name comes from the unusual way the flowerheads turn towards the sun.

HIBISCUS
ROSE OF CHINA, ROSE MALLOW, ROSE OF SHARON, SHRUB ALTHEA

These beautifully exotic, flowering, evergreen or deciduous shrubs, perennials and annuals hail from all continents, but particularly the countries around the Indian ocean—eastern Africa, Madagascar and Malaysia—as well as the Pacific Islands, Australia and China. Popular in warm to tropical gardens, they bear large, showy flowers, many of which last as little as one day—longer in colder conditions. The flowering season is long, however, lasting from late spring into autumn/fall, and the range of colours is impressive. They thrive in full sun, in a well-drained, rich, slightly acid, sandy soil. Water regularly and fertilize during flower-

ing. Trim after flowering to maintain shape. Propagate from cuttings taken in spring and summer. Potential pests include aphids, caterpillars, whitefly, tip borer and the hibiscus beetle. The genus is the floral emblem of Hawaii, where some of the most stunning hybrids are grown, and several beautiful species grow wild.

H. mutabilis
CONFEDERATE ROSE, COTTON ROSE

This delightful native of China grows to a height and spread of 6 m (about 24 ft). Frost-hardy, it bears large, hairy, heart-shaped leaves, with single, white flowers that fade to deep rose-pink. These appear in autumn/fall. Prune regularly in winter to maintain shape.

H. rosa-sinensis
ROSE OF CHINA, SHOEFLOWER

Native to China, this tall shrub bears coral-red flowers virtually all year in a frost-free climate. The wild form is less often seen in gardens than the numerous dazzling cultivars, many bred in Hawaii, which come in single or double and every colour but blue. Plants range in height and spread from 1–3 m (about 3–9 ft) and have evergreen, glossy leaves. They prefer full sun in tropical or subtropical climates where they are as important in gardens as roses are in temperate climates. In cold climates they can be grown in tubs in a greenhouse or as indoor plants. Water freely in summer, prune in spring after cold weather is over, and propagate from cuttings in summer. The name 'shoeflower' comes from the West Indian custom of polishing shoes with a hibiscus flower.

H. rosa-sinensis 'Apple Blossom'

This cultivar bears large, single, pale pink flowers. It grows vigorously to 4 m (about 12 ft) or more.

H. rosa-sinensis 'Cooperi'

Ideal for potting and excellent as an indoor decoration, this shrub bears small, light, open, scarlet flowers. It grows to a height of 1.5–3 m (about 4½–12 ft) and has variegated white, cream and pink foliage.

Hebe speciosa

Hibiscus rosa-sinensis

Hibiscus rosa-sinensis 'Cooperi'

Helichrysum selago

Hibiscus r.-s. 'Apple Blossom'

Heliotropium arborescens

Hibiscus mutabilis

Hydrangea macrophylla

Hydrangea aspera var. *aspera*

Hovea lanceolata

H. rosa-sinensis 'Madonna'

A Hawaiian cultivar, growing to about 2 m (about 6 ft) with large single flowers, cream with cerise-red throats.

H. rosa-sinensis 'Sabrina'

This cultivar bears fully double, bright cerise-red flowers and grows about 2 m (about 6 ft) tall.

H. syriacus

ALTHEA, ROSE OF SHARON

This colourful, upright, deciduous shrub is the hardiest of the genus. It flowers freely in summer in varying shades of white, pink, soft red, mauve and violet-blue. The single, semi-double and double flowers are bell-shaped. It has small, glabrous leaves and grows to 4 m (about 12 ft) tall with a spread of 1–2 m (about 3–6 ft). Prune hard in winter to keep it healthy.

H. syriacus 'Ardens'

This popular hibiscus bears large, mauve flowers with crimson centres. An upright shrub, it grows to a height of 3 m (about 9 ft).

H. syriacus 'Blue Bird'

This shrub bears single, violet-blue flowers with red centres. It grows to a height of 2 m (about 6 ft).

HOVEA
lanceolata

PURPLE PEA-BUSH

This lovely bush, covered in purple, pea-like flowers in spring, prefers full or semi-shade—the cover of taller shrubs and trees is ideal. It does best in a fertile, well-mulched

H. rosa-sinensis 'Madonna'

soil with good drainage. After flowering, prune lightly. Half-hardy, it grows to 2 m (about 6 ft) tall and 1 m (about 3 ft) wide. Propagate from scarified seed.

HYDRANGEA

HYDRANGEA

These lush, popular, deciduous and evergreen shrubs are native to China, Japan and North America and they grow profusely in the summer months. They need constant watering, as they transpire heavily from the stems and large, saw-toothed leaves. The sun damages their foliage, so always position them in the shade, or in full sun only in areas that are frequently cloudy. They are fully to frost-hardy. Hydrangeas are grown for the striking and attractive, domed fertile flowers which appear mid-summer. Each head consists of small flowers surrounded by larger petal-like sepals. Prune immediately after flowering—this encourages strong, vigorous growth for the following season. Propagate from softwood cuttings in summer.

Hibiscus syriacus 'Blue Bird'

H. aspera var. aspera
syn. *H. villosa*
STAR HYDRANGEA

This delicate beauty, native to eastern Asia, bears broad heads of blue or purple flowers in the centre of the shrub, and larger, white flowers towards the periphery. A deciduous upright shrub, it grows to a height and spread of 3 m (about 9 ft) and is fully hardy.

H. macrophylla

HORTENSIA

This deciduous, bushy shrub from Japan flowers in mid- to late summer, the colour depending on the pH of the soil. In soils with a pH of up to about 5.5, blue or purple flowers bloom; above this level they are pink. White flowers are unaffected by soil pH. There are two types—hortensias, with dense, domed heads; and lacecaps, with flat, open heads. Trim winter-damaged growth back to new growth and in summer, remove spent flowers. It is frost-hardy, has oval, serrated, green leaves and grows to a height and spread of 2 m (about 6 ft).

Hibiscus syriacus 'Ardens'

Hibiscus syriacus

Hibiscus rosa-sinensis 'Sabrina'

Hydrangea macrophylla 'Blue Wave'

Hypericum patulum

Hydrangea paniculata 'Grandiflora'

Hydrangea quercifolia

Hypoestes aristata

Hypericum 'Rowallane'

Hymenolepsis parviflora

H. macrophylla 'Blue Wave'

This deciduous, bushy shrub with flat heads of blue to pink flowers appearing in summer, has oval, green, serrated leaves and grows to a height and spread of 1.5 m (about 4¹/₂ ft). It is the best known Lacecap type.

H. paniculata 'Grandiflora'
PEEGEE HYDRANGEA

This deciduous, open, upright shrub bears large, conical, terminal panicles of white bloom. Greenish to begin with, they gradually turn to pink as summer progresses. To obtain larger panicles, prune back hard in spring. Fully hardy, it grows to a height and spread of 3 m (about 9 ft).

H. quercifolia
OAK-LEAFED HYDRANGEA

The dark green foliage of this deciduous, bushy shrub turns red and purple in autumn/fall. It bears creamy white flowerheads from mid-summer to mid-autumn/fall. Frost-hardy, it grows to a height and spread of 2 m (about 6 ft).

HYMENOLEPSIS
parviflora
syn. *Athanasia parviflora*
COULTER BUSH

This spreading, slightly woody shrub comes from the south-western Cape of South Africa. It grows to 1.5 m (about 4¹/₂ ft) high and bears small, golden-yellow flowers on large, flattened heads in early summer. The leaves are needle-like and 'branched'. Plant in rich, well-drained soil in full sun. Prune regu-

larly to remove old stems and maintain shape.

HYPERICUM
ST JOHN'S WORT, GOLDFLOWER, AARON'S BEARD, ROSE OF SHARON

These showy perennials, annuals and shrubs are easy to grow in mild, temperate climates worldwide. Larger species require sun or semi-shade, and fertile soil that is slightly moist. Smaller species do better in full sun and well-drained soil and make excellent rock plants. They are fully to half-hardy. Prune annually to prevent legginess and to maintain shape. Prune seed-pods to maintain vigour. Propagate small species from 5 cm (about 2 in) cuttings taken in late spring; for larger shrubs, from 12 cm (about 5 in) cuttings of non-flowering shoots in summer.

H. patulum

This evergreen, upright shrub bears large, golden yellow, erect flowers from mid-summer to mid-autumn/fall. It has dark green, oval leaves

and grows to a height and spread of 1 m (about 3 ft). *H. patulum* is frost-hardy. 'Hidcote', raised in the famous English garden of that name, is the best known cultivar.

H. 'Rowallane'

In mid-summer to mid- or late autumn/fall, this attractive, arching shrub bears delightful, bowl-shaped, yellow flowers, set among green, oval leaves. Frost-hardy, it grows to a height and spread of 1.5 m (about 4¹/₂ ft).

HYPOESTES
aristata

This bushy shrub is native to South Africa, and grows to a height of 1 m (about 3 ft) with a spread of 60 cm (about 24 in). In late winter, it bears terminal spikes of attractive, small, tubular, pink to purple flowers, set among mid-green, oval leaves. It prefers full sun and a moist, well-drained soil. Prune as required, and water frequently in the summer months. Propagate from stem cuttings in spring or summer.

IBOZA

riparia
syn. *Moschosma riparia*
NUTMEG BUSH, PLUME BUSH

This aromatic, bushy, deciduous shrub is a native of South Africa. Both the serrated, grey-green leaves and the clusters of tiny, mauve flowers that appear in winter are fragrant, smelling more like a spicy mint than nutmeg. It does best in a rich, well-drained, sandy, neutral to acid soil in full sun. Frost-tender, *I. riparia* is well suited to humid summer climates. Prune hard to maintain shape—after blooming, remove three-quarters of the previous season's growth. It grows to a height of 2 m (about 6 ft) with a spread of 1.5 m (about 4½ ft). Propagate from cuttings in spring.

ILEX

HOLLY

These popular and well-known evergreen shrubs are grown for their green, spiny leaves and the red, yellow or black berries borne in summer, autumn/fall or winter by female plants. Male and female plants must be grown together to obtain the berries. The shrubs bear clusters of small, white or greenish blossoms, but these are not of much significance. They need a moist, well-drained soil with plenty of leaf mulch and prefer sun or partial shade. Half-hardy, they do best when pruned hard in late spring and do not transplant successfully. Propagate from semi-hardwood cuttings in early autumn/fall. Watch for holly leaf miner and holly aphid. Holly was invested with mystical properties by Europeans during the Middle Ages as it defied the winter, retaining both leaves and berries.

I. aquifolium
ENGLISH HOLLY, COMMON HOLLY

The bright red, winter berries and glossy, spiny, dark green leaves of this European species make popular traditional Christmas ornaments, at least in the northern hemisphere. Growing to a height of 4 m (about 12 ft), this frost-hardy evergreen shrub prefers shaded conditions and a well-drained soil.

I. cornuta
CHINESE HOLLY

This dense, rounded species from China is self-fertile and frost-hardy. Better suited than other species to mild-winter areas, it grows to a height of 4 m (about 12 ft) with a spread of 5 m (about 15 ft). The leaves are rectangular with a spine at each corner, and bright red berries appear in summer. This too is excellent as a Christmas holly.

I. 'Golden King'

This magnificent female tree or shrub is excellent, both as a specimen plant or as a hedge. Its principal attraction is the deep green, shiny leaves, with yellow borders that turn white as they get older. It tends to bear fruit poorly. Frost-hardy, it grows to a height of 6 m (about 18 ft) with a spread of 5 m (about 15 ft). Pollinate with the male cultivar 'Silver Queen'.

INDIGOFERA

FALSE INDIGO, SUMMER WISTERIA

These soft, fast-growing, evergreen or deciduous shrubs and perennials are found world-wide in warmer climates. They are grown for their delicate, pea-like flowers and light green, divided leaves. All species need full sun and fertile, well-drained soil. They are fully to frost-hardy; frosts in colder areas will cut them to the ground, but they will grow back well enough in spring. Drought resistant, they are handy plants for dry gardens where the soil is poor. Prune to shape from an early age and propagate from softwood cuttings in summer, or seed in autumn/fall.

I. australis
AUSTRALIAN INDIGO

This elegant, smooth, spreading shrub is grown as a specimen plant in parks and gardens. It bears small, mauve-pink flowers in long heads in winter to summer, followed by brown pods. It has blue-grey leaves divided into leaflets. Frost-hardy, it prefers full sun and a well-drained soil. It grows to a height and spread of 2 m (about 6 ft).

I. decora
syn. *I. incarnata*

This delightful shrub, a native of China and Japan, bears racemes of pink and white, pea-shaped flowers in summer. It has glossy, dark green leaves with oval leaflets. Frost-hardy, it grows to a height of 60 cm (about 24 in) and a spread of 1 m (about 3 ft).

Ilex 'Golden King'

Ilex cornuta

Indigofera australis

Ilex aquifolium

Indigofera decora

Iboza riparia

Juniperus sabina

Jasminum nudiflorum

Jasminum mesnyi

Juniperus conferta

Itea ilicifolia

ISOPOGON
anemonifolius
DRUMSTICKS

Native to eastern Australia, this species of bushy, evergreen plants is grown also in California and the countries bordering the Mediterranean. It bears prominent, cone-shaped, yellow flowerheads in spring, followed by cones. These and the stiff, needle-like foliage make it popular in flower arrangements. Frost- to half-hardy, it does best in plenty of sunlight in a well-drained soil. Water generously in dry periods. Propagate from well-ripened seed sown in winter (germination is slow), or by cuttings in late summer and autumn/fall. It grows to a height and spread of 2 m (about 6 ft).

ITEA
ilicifolia
SWEETSPIRE

This handsome, bushy, evergreen shrub, native to western China, has leaves resembling those of holly, only narrower. It bears long racemes of small, greenish or cream flowers in late summer to early autumn/fall. It does best in moist, deep, rich soil, preferring partial shade. Hardy to minus 15°C (about 5°F), it grows to a height and spread of 3 m (about 6 ft). Propagate from softwood cuttings in summer.

JASMINUM
JASMINE, JESSAMINE, PIKAKE

These deciduous, semi-evergreen or evergreen shrubs, and woody-stemmed, twining or scrambling climbers, are native to Asia, Europe and Africa. Grown for their yellow, white or pink, star-shaped flowers, they are fully hardy to frost-tender. Water regularly and prune occasionally to maintain their habit. The shrubs can easily be trained as climbers if their heads are not cut back. Propagate from ripe wood cuttings in summer, by layers, or from seed.

J. mesnyi
syn. *J. primulinum*
PRIMROSE JASMINE, YELLOW JASMINE

Native to China, this evergreen, rambling shrub bears large, semi-double, golden blooms on arching canes, in late winter and spring. Its dark green leaves are made up of 3 leaflets. Half-hardy, it does well in all but the hottest climates, and prefers full sun and a well-drained soil. *J. mesnyi* grows to a height and spread of 3 m (about 9 ft).

J. nudiflorum
WINTER JASMINE

This is a rambling, deciduous, arching shrub from China. It is best suited to a cool or cold climate, where it will happily bear masses of bright yellow flowers on slender, leafless, green shoots in winter and early spring. Fully hardy, it prefers a well-drained soil and full sun. It grows to about 1.5–2 m (about 4¹/₂–6 ft) tall. Propagate from semi-hardwood cuttings in spring.

JUNIPERUS
JUNIPER

These evergreen, dwarf conifers make excellent garden plants. They

Isopogon anemonifolius

provide year round interest and need little attention. Plant in rock gardens to provide scale, or to act as a foil for other plants. They do well in all but the coldest conditions, requiring full sun and a dry, sandy soil. All species and cultivars are best propagated from tip cuttings, as they root easily. Some cultivars can be propagated by grafting. Aphids are sometimes a problem.

J. conferta
SHORE JUNIPER

This shrubby, prostrate, dwarf conifer does quite well in a salty, coastal environment. It has dense, glossy, aromatic, needle-like, soft green leaves on spreading branches. Fully hardy, it grows to a height of up to 15 cm (about 6 in) and a spread of up to 2 m (about 6 ft), and makes an excellent ground cover.

J. sabina
SAVIN JUNIPER

The dark green leaves of this vigorously spreading, shrubby bush, a native to the Caucasus in Europe, give off an unpleasant odour when bruised or crushed. It has flaking, red-brown bark. Fully hardy, it can grow to 4 m (about 12 ft) but dwarf forms, about 1 m (about 3 ft) tall, are more often seen in gardens.

Justicia carnea

Kolkwitzia amabilis

Juniperus sabina 'Tamariscifolia'

Kerria japonica

Kunzea baxteri

J. sabina 'Tamariscifolia'

This bushy conifer grows to a height of 1 m (about 3 ft) with a spread of 2 m (about 6 ft). Its bright green or blue-green, needle-like leaves are arranged in tiers.

JUSTICIA
carnea
syn. *Jacobinia carnea*, *J. pohliana*
BRAZILIAN PLUME FLOWER

This strikingly handsome, ever-green shrub bears spikes of white, pink or rose-purple flowers in summer to autumn/fall. It has pointed, veined, deep green leaves. In colder climates, it needs to be grown under glass, as it is a frost-tender, tropical or subtropical plant. It does best in fertile, well-drained soil, and requires full light and partial shade. Water potted specimens freely in full growth, less so at other times. Prune back hard in early spring—this will encourage branching and prevent growth from becoming too tall and straggly. *J. carnea* grows to a height of 1.5 m (about 4½ ft) with a spread of 75 cm (about 30 in).

Kalmia latifolia

Propagate in spring or early summer by softwood or greenwood cuttings. Caterpillars and snails can be a problem.

KALMIA
latifolia
MOUNTAIN LAUREL

The charm and fragrance of this American native make it a favourite among shrub enthusiasts. It has dark, glossy, laurel-like leaves and bears small, purple-rose to rose-red flowers in late spring and early summer. *K. latifolia* grows to a height of 3 m (about 9 ft) and a spread of 3.5 m (about 10½ ft). Fully hardy, it thrives in a moist, peaty, acid soil and prefers sun or semi-shade. Propagate by layering in summer, otherwise (with more difficulty) from softwood cuttings in summer, or seed in autumn/fall.

KERRIA
japonica
JAPANESE ROSE, GLOBE FLOWER, BACHELOR'S BUTTONS

The golden blossom of this species, the only one in its genus, will light up a garden corner in spring. The flowers, which appear at the end of lateral shoots on arching branches, also make delightful cut flowers. The leaves are double-toothed and bright green. Fully hardy, it likes partial shade and a well-drained soil. Prune back heavily to promote full growth and, every now and then, give it a heavy watering. It grows to a height of 2 m (about 6 ft) and a spread of 3 m (about 9 ft). Grow from cutting layers in summer, or by division in autumn/fall.

KOLKWITZIA
amabilis
BEAUTY BUSH

The only species in its genus, this attractive plant is native to China. Its deciduous, arching branches bear delightful, bell-shaped, pink flowers with yellow throats, from late winter to early spring. It has peeling bark and dark green, oval leaves. *K. amabilis* likes a well-drained soil, rich in leafmould, and prefers full sun. Fully hardy, it grows to a height and spread of 3 m (about 9 ft). After flowering, prune old, weak or damaged shoots. Propagate from softwood cuttings in summer.

KUNZEA
baxteri
TICK BUSH

This rounded, wiry-stemmed ever-green from Australia is popular for the fluffy, bottlebrush-like, long-stamened, red flowers it bears in spring. The leaves are tiny and heath-like. Frost-tender, *K. baxteri* prefers well-drained, sandy, neutral to acid soil and does best in full light. Potted specimens should be watered moderately when in full growth, less at other times. It grows to a height and spread of 3 m (about 9 ft). Propagate from tip cuttings in summer.

Lavandula dentata

LAGERSTROEMIA
indica
CRÊPE MYRTLE, PRIDE OF INDIA

This deciduous, vase-shaped bush
bursts into bloom in spring, bearing
luxuriant trusses of pink, white or
purple petals. Its small, oval, short-
stalked leaves are deciduous and
colour prettily in autumn/fall. Half-
hardy, it prefers a fertile, well-
drained soil and full light. Cut back
the previous season's stems to maintain a bushy habit or allow the plant
to grow unpruned into a small tree.
Water potted plants freely in full
growth, less at other times. It grows
to 6 m (about 18 ft) tall with a 5 m
(about 15 ft) spread. Propagate from
hardwood cuttings in winter, semi-
ripe cuttings in summer, or seed in
spring.

LAMBERTIA
formosa
MOUNTAIN DEVIL

Native to New South Wales, Australia, this dainty and charming evergreen is best known for the seed
capsules, which resemble a devil's
face with horns (hence the common
name). The clusters of tubular, red
flowers, moderately enclosed in
bracts, bloom continuously
throughout most of the year. *L.
formosa* is hardy and prefers a sunny
position with well-drained soil. Tip
prune regularly to maintain the
shape. It grows to a height and
spread of 1.5 m (about 4½ ft).
Propagate from seed or from semi-
hardwood cuttings taken in
autumn/fall.

LANTANA
montevidensis
syn. *L. sellowiana*

The dainty, arched stems of this
trailing or mat-forming, evergreen
shrub make a wonderful ground
cover or small hedge. Throughout
the year, but particularly in summer, it bears heads of magenta or
white posy-like flowers, each with a
yellow eye. It grows to a height of
30 cm (about 12 in) and a spread of
1.5 m (about 4½ ft). Native to the
Americas, it does best in fertile,
well-drained soil and a sunny posi-

Lavandula angustifolia

tion. When in full growth, potted
specimens should be well watered,
but this is not important at other
times. To keep the habit bushy, tip
prune occasionally. Propagate from
semi-ripe cuttings in summer, or
seed in spring. Whitefly and red
spider mite may present problems.
L. camara 'Chelsea Gem' and a few
other species are considered noxious weeds in some countries.

LAVANDULA
LAVENDER

These fragrant, flower-bearing plants
come from southern Europe. Cultivated commercially for the perfume
industry, they are also grown for their
evergreen foliage and attractive
bloom. They prefer full sun and
fertile, well-drained soil, that is not
too rich in nitrates and phosphates.
Fully to half-hardy, lavender tend
not to bloom profusely in warm
conditions. Excellent as hedges,
they need a light trimming in spring
to keep the habit neat. Propagate in
summer from semi-ripe cuttings.

L. angustifolia
syn. *L. officinalis, L. spica*
ENGLISH LAVENDER

This dense, bushy, evergreen shrub
is native to the Mediterranean
countries of southern Europe. It is
grown mainly for the long-stemmed
heads of mauve, scented flowers
that appear from spring to autumn/
fall—these are easily dried for lavender sachets, pot pourri and the
like. It bears small, furry, grey leaves
that turn green as the plant ages.
Fully hardy and makes an excellent
hedge; trim it in spring to maintain
the shape. It grows to a height of
1.5 m (about 4½ ft) and a spread of
1 m (about 3 ft). The flowers of *L.
angustifolia* and *L. stoechas* are used
in the distillation of oil of lavender.

L. dentata
FRENCH LAVENDER

The dense spikes of tubular,
mauve-blue flowers of this bushy,
evergreen shrub appear in autumn/
fall to late spring. Its aromatic leaves
are serrated, fern-like and grey-

Lantana montevidensis

Lagerstroemia indica

Lavandula stoechas

Lambertia formosa

green. Frost-hardy, it grows to a
height and spread of 1 m (about
3 ft). *L. dentata* is drought resistant
and adaptable to most soils.

L. stoechas
SPANISH LAVENDER, BUSH LAVENDER

This evergreen, dense, bushy shrub
is frost-hardy and grows to a height
and spread of 60 cm (about 24 in). In
late spring and summer, it bears
terminal spikes of fragrant, deep
purple flowers. The leaves are aromatic and silver-grey.

Leptospermum laevigatum

Leucadendron salignum

Leptospermum petersonii

flowers. There are many other cultivars of this native of Australia and New Zealand, many bred in the USA. They have white, red or pink flowers.

LEUCADENDRON

SILVER TREE

This genus, native to South Africa, is grown principally for its foliage, as the bloom is insignificant. The stiff, upward-pointing leaves may be silky or smooth and, as well as green, may be coloured gold, pink or silver. The male and female flowers are borne on separate plants—the female flowers are woody cones, the male flowers a mass of stamens. Colourful bracts (modified leaves) surround both male and female plants for several months of the year. Species do best in full light and well-drained, sandy, peaty soil—preferably without too much phosphate or nitrogen. Potted specimens should be well watered during periods of growth, less at other times. Propagate from seed in spring.

L. 'Safari Sunset'

This erect, evergreen shrub grows fast, to a height and spread of 1.5 m (about 4½ ft). In winter to spring, the large, deep red bracts that surround the insignificant flowers, turn gold-yellow as the plant matures. Its leaves are oblong, deep green, and flushed a dark wine colour. Half-hardy, it prefers a slightly acid, well-drained soil.

L. salignum

A native of South Africa, this evergreen shrub with branching stems bears small, yellow to red flowers, surrounded by colourful bracts, in autumn/fall and winter. It has silvery, lance-shaped leaves (the outer foliage may turn yellow in spring). Frost-hardy, *L. salignum* may grow to a height of 1.5 m (about 4½ ft) with a spread of 1 m (about 3 ft).

LEUCOSPERMUM

PINCUSHION, SPELDEKUSSING, FLAMESPIKE

Native to South Africa, these spreading evergreen bushes have been raised successfully in warm, open temperate areas worldwide,

Lechenaultia biloba

Leucadendron 'Safari Sunset'

Leptospermum s. 'Red Damask'

LECHENAULTIA

biloba

BLUE LECHENAULTIA, FLOOR OF THE SKY

Native to Western Australia, this evergreen, erect or straggling sub-shrub has soft, light green leaves and bears striking, open flowers in varying shades of blue. It thrives in a protected, sunny position and needs a sandy, well-drained soil, preferably with few phosphates or nitrates. Cut back over-long stems after blooming. Potted specimens should be moderately watered during growth, less at other times. *L. biloba* grows to a height and spread of 60 cm (about 24 in). Propagate from tip cuttings taken at any time of the year, or from seed in spring. It is not an easy plant to grow, and short lived at the best of times.

LEPTOSPERMUM

TEA-TREE, MOONAH

Ideal for the informal landscape garden, this genus of evergreen trees and shrubs is native to Tasmania and south-eastern Australia, as well as

New Zealand. Well suited to cooler conditions, they have found their way into the gardens and parks of Europe and America, where many hybrids and cultivars have been developed. Profuse, small flowers—white, pink or red—appear in spring. Drought, wind and even salt resistant, they do well in coastal areas if not too exposed, and prefer a fertile, well-drained soil and full sun. Propagate from semi-ripe cuttings in summer. History has it that Captain James Cook prepared a brew from a New Zealand species for his crew as a remedy for scurvy—hence the common name, 'tea-tree'.

L. laevigatum

COASTAL TEA-TREE

Native to the eastern states of Australia, this tall, bushy shrub or tree bears attractive, small, white flowers in spring and early summer. The evergreen leaves are small, oval and leathery. Frost-hardy and preferring a moist soil, it grows to a height of 5 m (about 15 ft) and a spread of just under 3 m (about 9 ft). It is an ex-

cellent plant for the seaside, but not in South Africa where it has become a much-hated weed.

L. petersonii

syn. *L. citratum*

LEMON-SCENTED TEA-TREE

This evergreen shrub or small tree, a native of the eastern states of Australia, bears delightful, white flowers in spring and early summer. The narrow, lance-shaped leaves turn from red to green as the plant matures, giving off a characteristic lemon scent when bruised or crushed. It prefers light to medium, well-drained soil and does best in an open, sunny position. Drought resistant but frost-tender, *L. petersonii* grows to a height of 4 m (about 12 ft) and a spread of 2 m (6 ft).

L. scoparium 'Red Damask'

MANUKA

This upright, evergreen shrub grows to a height and spread of just under 3 m (about 9 ft). Frost-hardy, it has purple-tinged, dark green leaves and in spring and summer, bears sprays of double, dark red including western USA and Australia. Grown for both flowers and foliage, they prefer a Mediterranean-type climate and a sandy, well-drained soil with few nitrates or phosphates. A sunny, protected position suits them best. Potted plants should be watered moderately during growth, less at other times. Propagate in spring from seed.

L. cordifolium
syn. L. nutans
SPELDEKUSSING, PINCUSHION BUSH

This well-branched evergreen shrub, a native to south-west South Africa, is grown for the delightful profuse bloom of pinkish orange, pincushion-like flowers it bears. These are long lasting when cut and much sought after by florists; they are cultivated extensively in Hawaii as well as in South Africa and Australia. Its leaves are green and lanceolate. It grows to a height of 1–2 m (about 3–6 ft) with a spread of a little over 1 m (about 3 ft).

L. reflexum
ROCKET PINCUSHION

This is an evergreen erect species that grows to a height of 3 m (about 9 ft) with a spread of 2 m (about 6 ft). It bears terminal, salmon-red, yellow-tipped, spiky flowers in spring to summer, amid small, grey-green leaves.

L. tottum
FIREWHEEL PINCUSHION BUSH

This upright, branching evergreen shrub is native to South Africa. From mid-spring to late summer, it bears terminal, dome-shaped, scarlet and yellow, spiky flowers, among thick, narrow leaves. It grows to a height and spread of 1 m (about 3 ft).

LIGUSTRUM
PRIVET

These deciduous, semi-evergreen and evergreen shrubs enjoy a mixed popularity. They can be difficult to remove once established, and they spread rapidly—birds eat the berries and then excrete the seeds. Some species, however, are popular as hedge shrubs. Leaf size varies among the species, but they all have small, creamy white flowers in dense clusters with a strong odour. Fully to frost-hardy, they do best in sun or semi-shade—variegated forms require a fully sunny position. Cut back in mid-spring to restrict growth. Propagate from semi-ripe cuttings in summer.

L. ovalifolium 'Aureum'
GOLDEN PRIVET

This upright, dense shrub, native to Japan, grows to a height of 4 m (about 12 ft) with a spread of 3 m

Leucospermum cordifolium

Ligustrum sinense

(about 9 ft). In mid-summer it bears dense panicles of small, tubular, white flowers which give off a sickly odour. These are followed in turn by spherical, black fruits. The glossy, oval, green leaves have yellow borders. L. ovalifolium 'Aureum' is fully hardy. Prune out any green shoots as soon as they appear or they will take over the shrub.

L. sinense
CHINESE PRIVET

This semi-evergreen or deciduous, bushy shrub bears fragrant, tubular, white flowers in mid-summer, set among pale green, oval leaves. Small, black-purple berries follow. Fully hardy, L. sinense grows to a height of 4 m (about 12 ft) with a spread of 3 m (about 9 ft).

LONICERA
HONEYSUCKLE, WOODBINE

These woody-stemmed, twining climbers are grown for the delightful, scented flowers and the foliage

Lonicera fragrantissima

that suit them admirably as a cover for sheds and pergolas. Found worldwide in warm and temperate climates, they do best in a fertile, well-drained or moist soil in sun or semi-shade. Prune to remove dead growth or to restrict their often rampant spread—position the shrub where there is plenty of room. Mostly deciduous, the shrubby species of *Lonicera* should be propagated from cuttings taken in late summer. Aphids may pose a problem.

L. fragrantissima
WINTERSWEET

This bushy, spreading shrub, the most fragrant of the species, is native to China. It grows to a height of 2 m (about 6 ft) and a spread of 4 m (about 12 ft). Fully hardy, it bears paired, creamy, tubular, sweetly fragrant flowers in winter and early spring. Its leaves are oval, heart-shaped and green, and appear shortly after the flowers. Prune after flowering to control size and the plant's tendency to straggle.

Leucospermum tottum

Lonicera nitida

Leucospermum reflexum

Ligustrum ovalifolium 'Aureum'

L. nitida

This bushy, dense, evergreen shrub makes an excellent hedging specimen. Growing to a height of 2 m (about 6 ft) and a spread of 3 m (about 9 ft), it bears insignificant, cream flowers, in pairs, in late spring. These are followed in turn by small, rounded purple berries. Moderately frost-hardy, it has glossy, green, small, oval leaves. It can be clipped as a formal hedge.

Magnolia quinquepeta

Luculia gratissima

Mackaya bella

Macropiper excelsum

Loropetalum chinense

LOPHOMYRTUS
bullata

An evergreen, upright shrub, this native of New Zealand bears open, white flowers with prominent stamens, in late spring and early summer. These are followed by black berries. Frost resistant but drought-tender, it prefers a rich, moist, well-drained soil, preferably in a protected, shaded position. Its purple, rounded leaves turn a reddish brown as the plant matures. To restrict growth, tip prune in spring. Propagate from semi-ripe cuttings in late summer.

LOROPETALUM
chinense
FRINGE FLOWER

Native to China, this well-branched, rounded, evergreen shrub is prized for the attractive, creamy white flowers it bears in clusters all along the branches during winter and spring. The 5 cm (about 2 in) oval leaves are light green. Half-hardy, it needs full light or semi-shade, and does best in a well-drained soil that is neutral to acid. Potted specimens should be watered freely in full growth, but only moderately at other times. Little pruning is required, except to remove twiggy growth. The shrub grows to a height and spread of 1.5 m (about 4½ ft), although it can grow larger if very happy. Propagate from semi-ripe cuttings in late summer or by layering in spring.

LUCULIA
gratissima

Native to the Himalayas, this bushy evergreen shrub grows to a height and spread of 1–2 m (about 3–6 ft) and is grown mainly for the attractive, terminal clusters of pink, phlox-like, fragrant flowers that bloom in winter. The soft, green leaves, oval to oblong, are downy on their undersides. Drought- and frost-tender, it prefers a fertile, well-drained soil in full light or partial shade. Potted specimens should be watered generously during growth, less so at other times. Cut back heavily after bloom and tip prune new growth to shape. Propagate from semi-ripe cuttings in summer or from seed in spring. There is also a very handsome white-flowered species, L. grandifolia. It has the reputation of being slightly less tender.

MACKAYA
bella
ASYSTASIA, FOREST BELL BUSH

This evergreen, erect (when young) and then spreading shrub is a native of South Africa. It is prized for the clusters of delightful, bell-shaped, pale lilac flowers with purple veins that appear from spring to autumn/fall. It has pointed, oval, glossy leaves and prefers full light or partial shade—the hotter the conditions, the more shade it requires to maintain the colour of its bloom. M. bella prefers a fertile, leafy, well-drained soil and will benefit from pruning in winter. Potted specimens should be watered generously in growth, less so at other times. Frost-tender, it grows to a height and spread of 1.5 m (about 4½ ft). Propagate from semi-ripe cuttings in summer or from greenwood cuttings in spring.

MACROPIPER
excelsum
KAWA KAWA, PEPPER TREE

This evergreen shrub or small tree, a native of New Zealand, bears tiny yellow flowers followed by small, round, orange fruits clustered on spikes, set among dark green, heart-shaped, aromatic leaves. It does best in a well-drained, well-composted soil in an open sunny position. Though half-hardy, young plants should be protected from frost. Prune to maintain habit and feed potted plants regularly. It grows to a height of 6 m (about 18 ft) with a spread of 2 m (about 6 ft). Propagate from seed sown under glass, or from semi-hardwood cuttings in autumn/fall.

MAGNOLIA

These evergreen, semi-evergreen and deciduous shrubs and trees hail from China. Grown for the pleasing, often sweet-scented, waxy, tulip-shaped flowers, they thrive in a fertile, well-drained soil. If the soil is sandy, add manure and leafmould before planting. Magnolias need shelter from strong winds, and prefer full-light to shady conditions. Little pruning is required, as they continue to flower on the same wood for several years. The very old branches with woody spurs may be removed to encourage new growth. Propagate from semi-ripe cuttings in summer or from seed in autumn/fall. Alternatively, graft in winter.

M. quinquepeta
syn. M. liliiflora

This deciduous, bushy species is native to China. From mid-spring to mid-summer, it bears handsome, purple, tulip-like flowers set among dark green, oval leaves. Fully hardy, it grows to a height of 4 m (about 12 ft) and a spread of 5 m (about 15 ft).

M. stellata
STAR MAGNOLIA

This dense, slow-growing, deciduous shrub is a native of Japan. Prized for the delightful, white, star-like

Melaleuca armillaris

flowers it bears in late winter and early spring, it is fully hardy and grows to a height and spread of 3 m (about 9 ft). It has narrow, pale green, elongated, oval leaves.

MAHONIA

OREGON GRAPE, HOLLY GRAPE, MOUNTAIN GRAPE

Useful as hedges or windbreaks, these evergreen shrubs are also grown for their dense panicles of open, yellow flowers. These are followed by blue-black fruits that make excellent jam. Low-growing species are also useful for ground cover. Plant in fertile soil that is well-drained but not too dry. In cold conditions, they require full sun; in warmer climates, partial shade will see them thrive. Propagate from seed in autumn/fall or from semi-ripe cuttings in summer.

M. aquifolium

OREGON GRAPE

This evergreen, open shrub, native to North America, grows to 1 m (about 3 ft) tall with a 1.5 m (about 4½ ft) spread. In early spring, it bears attractive, yellow flowers, followed by blue-black, globular berries. Its leaves are divided into bright green leaflets and turn bronze in winter. It is fully hardy.

M. lomariifolia

MOUNTAIN GRAPE

This evergreen, moderately frost-hardy, very upright shrub, is native to Yunnan Province, China. It grows to a height of 3 m (about 9 ft) with a spread of 2 m (about 6 ft), bearing bright yellow spikes in terminal clusters in late autumn/fall to winter. These are arranged like the spokes of an inverted umbrella and are set among narrow, holly-like, spiny leaflets. Black berries appear after the bloom.

MALVAVISCUS

arboreus

TURK'S CAP, SLEEPY MALLOW

This evergreen, rounded shrub, a native of Mexico, is grown for the rich, red, hibiscus-like flowers it bears in summer, and for its bright green, soft-haired leaves. It prefers a well-

Magnolia stellata

Mahonia lomariifolia

drained but moist soil, and thrives in full sun or partial shade. Cut flower stems back hard in winter to maintain the shape. Potted specimens should be well watered in the growing season, but only moderately at other times. Frost-tender, *M. arboreus* grows to a height and spread of 3 m (about 9 ft).

MELALEUCA

HONEYMYRTLE, PAPERBARK

As well as being grown for their showy blossom, the magnificent shrubs of this genus (which also includes trees) are also useful for hedging and screening. They do best in a light, well-drained soil that is relatively free of nitrogen, but they will tolerate a wide range of soil conditions, even waterlogged soil. They do well in coastal areas and will assume interesting shapes. Many species have a fragrant, honey scent that will attract birds. Potted specimens should be watered moderately, less so in colder temperatures. Pruning into a hedge shape will encourage growth. Propagate

Mahonia aquifolium

Melaleuca fulgens

from seed sown in spring, or from semi-hardwood cuttings from summer to mid-winter.

M. armillaris

BRACELET HONEY MYRTLE

This evergreen, rounded shrub or tree grows to a height of 3–6 m (about 9–18 ft) with a spread of 1–3 m (about 3–9 ft). It bears delightful, showy clusters of creamy, bottlebrush-like flowers in summer—each consisting of a brush of white stamens, set among needle-like, deep green leaves. A native of

Malvaviscus arboreus

New South Wales and Tasmania, Australia, it is frost-tender.

M. fulgens

SCARLET HONEY MYRTLE, FIERY BOTTLEBRUSH

This erect, open, evergreen shrub comes from Western Australia. Half-hardy, it grows to a height and spread of 1.5 m (about 4½ ft) and in spring, bears lateral spikes of deep red-pink flowers with gold tips. These are followed by small, woody capsules. The leaves are lance-shaped, concave and grey-green.

M. hypericifolia

This evergreen, rounded shrub, native to New South Wales and Queensland, Australia, grows to a height and spread of 3 m (about 9 ft). In summer, it bears large, orange-red flowers in dense, bottlebrush spikes. These appear among lanceolate, mid- to pale green leaves that turn bronze-tipped in winter. The fruits are small, woody capsules. *M. hypericifolia* is half-hardy. If the

Michelia figo

Melastoma affine

Melaleuca hypericifolia

shrub is pruned back hard in spring, it will produce long stems of foliage for flower arrangements.

M. incana

This pendulous, evergreen shrub is grown for its narrow, grey-green leaves and spring appearance of dainty, creamy-yellow, bottlebrush flowers. Half-hardy, it grows to a height of 3 m (about 9 ft) with a spread of 2 m (about 6 ft). *M. incana* is native to New South Wales, Australia.

M. nesophylla

WESTERN TEA MYRTLE

This evergreen, bushy shrub is native to Western Australia and in summer, bears flowers that are brushes of mauve, gold-tipped stamens, fading to white to give the plant a multi-coloured effect. Its leaves are oval, broad, smooth and grey-green. Frost-hardy, it grows to a height of 3 m (about 9 ft) with a spread of 2 m (about 6 ft).

Melaleuca nesophylla

MELASTOMA
affine
syn. M. denticulatum, M. polyanthum
NATIVE LASIANDRA, PINK LASIANDRA

This tropical, bushy shrub from India and Australia grows to 2–3 m (about 6–9 ft) tall. The ovate, rough-textured leaves are bright green with 3–5 prominent veins. Large pinkish purple, mauve or, more rarely, white flowers up to 7 cm (about 3 in) wide, are borne on terminal clusters. The flowers are short-lived but bloom most of the year, peaking in summer, followed by purple berries which can be eaten. This plant will grow in a wide range of soils but likes well-drained soil in full light or part-shade. Can be kept in a pot and needs abundant water during growth and moderate amounts at other times. Propagate from fresh seed or cuttings which strike readily in spring or summer. It may be attacked by red spider mite or whitefly. In some countries it has run wild and in Hawaii is considered a pest.

MELIANTHUS
major
HONEY FLOWER, TOUCH-ME-NOT

This sprawling, evergreen bush is a native of South Africa. Growing to a height and spread of 2–3 m (about 6–9 ft), it is prized for the luxuriant foliage and brownish-red, tubular flowers on terminal spikes that appear in spring and summer. The leaves have oval, blue-grey, serrated leaflets. Half-hardy, it does best in fertile, well-drained soil and will

Melaleuca incana

Melianthus major

thrive in a sunny position. It can be pruned hard in early spring to keep it compact, although it will then flower less freely. Propagate from seed in spring or from greenwood cuttings in summer. The leaves have a strong, unpleasant smell when bruised, hence the common name 'touch-me-not'.

MICHELIA
figo
PORT WINE MAGNOLIA, BANANA SHRUB

Native to western China, this evergreen shrub bears small, strongly scented, wine-coloured flowers, set among glossy, oval leaves. The flowers smell strongly of bananas. It does best in a well-drained, humus rich, neutral to acid soil. Half-hardy but drought-tender, *M. figo* does best in a protected spot in full light or partial shade. Pruning is not really necessary. Keep potted specimens well watered when in growth. The shrub grows to a height and spread of 3 m (about 9 ft). Propagate from semi-hardwood cuttings taken in summer or autumn/fall.

MIMETES
cucullatus
ROOISTOMPIE

This handsome, evergreen shrub from the south-western and southern Cape area of South Africa, reaches 1.5 m (about 4½ ft) high. Striking inflorescences in bright red and yellow and white are produced from mid-winter to early summer. Plant in marshy, slightly acidic soil in full sun.

Mimetes cucullatus

Myoporum parvifolium

MIMULUS
aurantiacus
syn. *M. glutinosus, Diplacus glutinosus*
MONKEY MUSK

This evergreen shrub, native to North America, is grown for the beautiful crimson or yellow-orange, tubular flowers that appear in spring and summer, offset by narrow, glossy, lance-shaped leaves with margins that roll slightly inwards. Half-hardy, it prefers full sun to partial shade and a moist, even wet, soil (though it will adapt to most soil conditions). It grows to a height and spread of 1 m (about 3 ft). Propagate from seed in autumn/fall. Prune in early spring to keep it compact.

MURRAYA
paniculata
syn. *M. exotica*
ORANGE JESSAMINE

This rounded, evergreen shrub is native to Malaysia. It is grown for the delightful clusters of fragrant, white flowers that show throughout the year, offset by rich green leaves. Red berries ripen in autumn/fall. *M. paniculata* prefers a fertile, moist, well-drained soil, in a protected sunny position. Frost-tender, it will not survive below freezing. It grows to a height of 3 m (about 9 ft) with a spread of 2 m (about 6 ft).

MUSSAENDA
BUDDHA'S LAMP, FLAGBUSH, ASHANTI BLOOD, PAPER-CHASE TREE

These evergreen shrubs and scrambling climbers are prized more for the colour of their over-sized white or yellow sepals than for the insignificant flowers. Frost-tender, they do better in warmer climates, especially in a fertile, well-drained soil in full light. Water frequently in full growth, less so at other times, pruning heavily after bloom to produce more flowers. Propagate from soft-tip cuttings in spring, or from semi-ripe cuttings in summer.

M. erythrophylla

A native of the Congo (Zaire) area in Africa, this sprawling, vigorous, evergreen shrub is grown for the de-

Mussaenda erythrophylla

lightful, yellow flowers with red tubes, yellow petal lobes, and a single red bract, that appear during summer to autumn/fall. It has large, bright-green, rounded, oval leaves. Rich, moist soil, and a protected, shaded position suits best. Frost-tender, it grows to 2–6 m (about 6–18 ft) tall. There are many cultivars, with multiple bracts in white, pink or red.

M. frondosa
DHOBI TREE

Native to India, this evergreen shrub grows to a height and spread of 2 m (about 6 ft). In summer, it bears clusters of orange-yellow, tubular flowers inside large, white bracts, set among pale green, oval leaves; berries follow the bloom. The stem is erect and branching with a shrubby crown. *M. frondosa* is frost-tender, but both species are very popular shrubs.

MYOPORUM
parvifolium
CREEPING BOOBIALLA

This evergreen, spreading to prostrate shrub is native to southern and western Australia. Half-hardy, it grows to a height of 15 cm (about 6 in) and spread of 80 cm (about 32 in). Grow in an open, sunny position in a light to heavy, well-drained soil. Clusters of white, tubular flowers appear in summer, followed by purple, globular berries. The semi-succulent leaves are narrow, blunt and thick. Water potted plants moderately. Propagate from seed in spring, or semi-ripe cuttings in late summer.

Mimulus aurantiacus

Murraya paniculata

Myrtus communis

MYRTUS
MYRTLE

Popular for hedges and screens, most species of the evergreen genus, *Myrtus*, also make elegantly handsome, potted plants. All bear long-stamened flowers with a pleasant fragrance, followed by handsome, edible berries. The leaves give off a strong scent when crushed. Myrtles do best in full sun and fertile, well-drained soil. Trim back in spring to restrict growth. Drought resistant and half-hardy, they will survive

Mussaenda frondosa

down to minus 8°C (about 18°F). Propagate from semi-ripe cuttings in late summer.

M. communis
COMMON MYRTLE, GREEK MYRTLE

From early summer, this bushy, evergreen shrub bears dainty, fragrant, white flowers, set among glossy, dark green leaves. The flowers are followed by purple-black berries. Frost-hardy, *M. communis* grows to a height and spread of 3 m (about 9 ft). Propagate from seed.

A Field Trip to Mount Kinabalu

Mount Kinabalu in Sabah, on the island of Borneo, is a plant hunter's paradise. It is a bridge for the flora and fauna of both northern and southern hemispheres, and thousands of plant enthusiasts have made the pilgrimage to climb Mount Kinabalu, 'the botanist's Mecca'. It is also one of the places where the vireya rhododendrons can be seen. Many of these are epiphytic, and have unusual sunset colouring.

The journey from the closest town, Kota Kinabalu, takes about a day and you will then need to allow two days on the mountain, staying overnight in accommodation near the summit. You need to book an authorized guide at Kinabalu National Park Headquarters. Take warm clothing because, although this is the tropics, the upper parts of the mountain can be cold.

The journey to park headquarters will take you through typical lowland rainforest. The trees here are enormous, creating a heavy canopy that allows little or no sunlight through to the forest floor.

Park headquarters, where you start your climb, is at an altitude of 1500 m (about 5000 ft). Here in the lower montane zone, the trees, mainly oaks, are smaller than in the lowland rainforest. Lush ferns grow everywhere. The common tree fern (*Cyathea contaminans*) thrives, its graceful fronds reaching up to 4 m (about 12 ft) in length. Look up into the trees and you will see bird's nest ferns perched on forks in the branches, from which tangles of vines hang. Orchids also abound in this rich environment. The crimson and white nun's orchid (*Phaius tankervillae*) and the delicate white and gold angel orchid (*Coelogyne venusta*) are common.

After about two hours you will reach the Kamborangoh Shelter, situated at an altitude of 2286 m (about 7500 ft); then take the by-pass trail from here to Carsons Camp. The trees in this upper montane zone are smaller, up to 6 m

(about 18 ft). There are more orchids here, but it is the rhododendrons which will take your breath away. The magnificent *Rhododendron lowii* is everywhere, the shrubs almost obscured by masses of bright yellow flowers. The leaves are thick and long and the waxy, funnel-shaped flowers are 8 cm (about 3 in) wide. The flowers are usually yellow but sometimes pinkish yellow in colour. Along the track are located other *Rhododendron* species. *R. brookeanum* has smaller leaves and flowers, which are yellowish pink to red with white centres and often lemon-scented. You may see it growing as an epiphyte. *R. rugosum* and *R. fallacinum* have pink to apricot flowers. *R. stenophyllum* has orange to red, bell-shaped flowers and needle-like foliage. The carnivorous pitcher plant (*Nepenthes tentaculata*) also grows here.

Rhododendron ericoides

Rhododendron crassifolium

Rhododendron lowii

The summit of Mount Kinabalu, seen from park headquarters.

Mount Kinabalu is home to many rhododendrons, some of which are only found here. They are amazingly vigorous and luxuriant; if you take a moment to really study your surroundings you will see why. The soil is light but rich and covered in leaves. The rainfall and humidity are high and the rhododendrons are lightly shaded from the strong sun.

Mount Kinabalu is also rich in animal and birdlife, including the leopard, mongoose and Malay bear, but unfortunately these are unlikely to be seen as most keep well away from the tracks. Orang-utans are occasionally spotted near the trails and you may see small monkeys swinging in the trees.

Continuing on past Carsons Camp, at an altitude of 2713 m (about 8900 ft), the vegetation on either side of the track is thick with bamboo and more rhododendrons. At times the whole path will be clouded with mist and you will notice the temperature getting cooler.

After about two hours you reach Paka Cave, at an altitude of 3200 m (about 10 500 ft). This 'cave', not much more than the underside of a rock, is where Sir Hugh Low and Spencer St John, two of the region's earliest explorers, sheltered for several icy nights. The trees here include twisted, gnarled forms of the manuka or tea tree (*Leptospermum*). You may see green mountain blackeyes and the brown mountain bush warbler. You will also see the endemic *Rhododendron ericoides*, an unusual species with needle-like leaves and scarlet, 1 cm (about ½ in) long flowers.

As you climb higher the soil virtually disappears and the vegetation becomes sparse against the granite background. Very few plants can survive the fierce winds, strong sun and abundant rain. Some that do survive have adapted to the extreme conditions by assuming a bonsai-like form. Another unusual rhododendron grows at this altitude—*R. buxifolium*, which has leathery leaves and scarlet flowers.

Soon you reach the huts where you will spend the night. The best time to climb the rest of the way to the summit is at dawn; by late morning Lows Peak will be enveloped in mist. The last short leg of your climb is devoid of any vegetation but the stark granite landscape has a beauty all its own.

Rhododendron

In 1848 the renowned botanist Professor Lindley wrote: 'When Mr Hugh Low returned from his visit to Borneo, he was so obliging as to place in my hands some drawings and dried specimens of certain species of Rhododendron which occur in that island *growing upon trees*. They are found to be distinct from all previously known … '

Low's collections from Borneo contained some of the first botanical specimens of what we now call the vireya, or Malesian, rhododendrons, technically members of *Rhododendron* sect. *Vireya*. This group has around 280 recognized species (out of a total of around 800 for the genus *Rhododendron* as a whole), mostly confined to the region between mainland Asia and Australia. By far the largest number, over 150, occur on the island of New Guinea; Borneo has 34, Sumatra has 26, the Philippines has 24, and there are 15 on the Malay Peninsula. Australia has a single native species, *R. lochiae*.

Many vireyas grow as epiphytes on trees, while others grow on cliffs or rocky mountain summits, on raw clay landslips, or in high mountain bogs at altitudes of up to about 4500 m (about 14 760 ft). Both leaves and flowers range in size from tiny to very large, while flower colours tend towards yellows, oranges and scarlets, although whites and pinks are also frequent.

In the last 30 to 40 years many of the New Guinea species have been brought into cultivation and hybridized, and are popular in mild humid areas.

Rhododendron brookeanum

Nandina domestica 'Nana'

Nerium oleander 'Album'

Nerium o. 'Splendens Variegatum'

Nerium oleander

Myrtus ugni

Nerium oleander 'Punctatum'

Nandina domestica

M. ugni
CHILEAN GUAVA

This handsome, upright, densely branched, shrub is native to Chile. In spring, it bears cup-shaped, pink flowers, set among glossy deep, green, thick, small, round leaves. Edible dark red fruits follow the bloom. Half-hardy, it grows to a height of 1.5 m (about 4½ ft) with a spread of 1 m (about 3 ft).

NANDINA
SACRED BAMBOO, HEAVENLY BAMBOO

Not a true bamboo, the stems of these evergreen and semi-evergreen shrubs from China and Japan will grow to a height of nearly 3 m (about 9 ft) but with a spread of only about 1 m (about 3 ft). This makes the genus popular with landscape gardeners, who also grow the species for the handsome, reddish foliage which appears in autumn/fall and winter. Small, yellow-centred, white flowers appear in summer and autumn/fall, followed by glossy, red fruits. Frost-hardy,

they prefer a sheltered, sunny position, and fertile, well-drained, but not too dry soil. In spring, prune untidy, aging stems to the base, particularly on old plants. Propagate from semi-ripe cuttings or seed in summer.

N. domestica
SACRED BAMBOO, HEAVENLY BAMBOO

This upright evergreen shrub is a native of Japan and China. In summer, it bears small, white, upright, star-shaped flowers in sprays; these are followed (on female plants) by red berries. It has narrow, lance-shaped, sheathing leaves that turn purplish-red in winter. Frost-hardy, it prefers a moist soil and sunny position. *N. domestica* grows to a height and spread of just under 2 m (about 6 ft).

N. domestica 'Nana'

This dwarf shrub is particularly popular, probably because it colours so strongly in winter. An evergreen or semi-evergreen, it grows to a height of 30–60 cm (about 12–24 in) with a spread of 4 m (about

12 ft). Frost-hardy, it rarely flowers. Given sufficient direct sun, its bright green leaves will turn scarlet in autumn/fall to winter. *N. domestica* 'Nana' is eminently suitable for a mixed border or rockery.

NERIUM
OLEANDER, ROSE-BAY, ROSE LAUREL

These evergreen shrubs are grown for their delightful flowers, which bloom in a variety of colours—pink, white, red and cream. They have dark, glossy spear-shaped leaves. Although they do best in full sun and a well-drained soil, they do extremely well in a variety of conditions—dry, semi-arid; salty coastal areas; and in soil with poor drainage—and flourish from tropical to warm-temperate climates. Ideally the shrub should be pruned to promote branching, and when potted, should be watered regularly when in full growth. Propagate from semi-ripe cuttings in summer, or from seed in spring. The plant is poisonous, but so bitter even goats will not eat it.

N. oleander

This evergreen, upright, bushy shrub grows rapidly to a height of 2–4 m (about 6–12 ft) with a spread of 3 m (about 9 ft). Native to the Mediterranean, it bears open, white or pink flowers from spring to autumn/fall in terminal sprays set among narrow, long, dark green leaves. *N. oleander* is half-hardy.

N. oleander 'Album'

This cultivar bears single, white flowers with a cream centre.

N. oleander 'Punctatum'
syn. N.o. 'Monsieur Belaguier'

This upright, evergreen shrub bears clusters of delightful, pale pink, single flowers from spring through to autumn/fall. It has deep-green, leathery leaves. Frost-tender, it grows to a height and spread of 3 m (about 9 ft).

N. oleander 'Splendens Variegatum'

This evergreen cultivar bears deep pink, double flowers from spring to autumn/fall. It has leathery, dark green leaves with yellow margins. The plain-leaved version is splendid, also bearing flowers in great profusion.

NOTOSPARTIUM
carmichaeliae
PINK BROOM, NEW ZEALAND PINK BROOM

This deciduous arching shrub is grown for the dainty, lilac, pea-shaped flowers that appear in loose terminal heads, in summer. A native of New Zealand, it bears tiny, brown leaves only when young. Moderately frost-hardy, it grows best in a sheltered, sunny position in well-drained soil. More mature plants may require staking. *N. carmichaeliae* grows to a height of 2–3 m (about 6–9 ft) and a spread of 1.5 m (about 4½ ft). Propagate from seed in autumn/fall or from semi-ripe cuttings in summer.

OCHNA
serrulata
BIRD'S EYE BUSH, SMALL-LEAVED PLANE, MICKEY MOUSE PLANT

This evergreen shrub is native to Guinea, in western Africa. It is grown for the terminal clusters of attractive, yellow flowers set among oval, glossy, serrated leaves, and for the black, glossy berries set in red calyces that follow the bloom. It prefers full light in an open, sunny position, and a light, sandy, well-drained soil. Water potted plants moderately in full growth. If necessary, prune shrubs in spring. Frost-tender, it grows to a height and spread of just under 2 m (about 6 ft). Propagate

from semi-ripe cuttings in summer, seed in spring. It self-sows readily and can become a pest.

OLEARIA
DAISY BUSH

These dense, evergreen shrubs are native to Australia and New Zealand, and are grown for their foliage and delicate, pale, daisy flowers. They do well in seaside gardens, providing good, wind-resistant shelter. They do best in full sun and moist, well-drained soil. Prune annually and dead-head regularly to prevent them becoming woody and straggly. Propagate from semi-ripe cuttings in summer.

O. arborescens

In summer, this many-branched, spreading tree-like shrub bears oval, daisy-like flowers in panicles at the ends of the branches. It has oval, serrated leaves. Half-hardy, it likes a moist soil and full sun. It grows to 5 m (about 15 ft) tall and 3 m (about 9 ft) wide.

Notospartium carmichaeliae

Olearia arborescens

Ochna serrulata

O. macrodonta
LARGE-TOOTHED TREE ASTER

Native to New Zealand, this shrub is popular in the USA and UK. It grows 3–6 m (about 9–18 ft) tall and in summer bears many small, white, daisy-like flowers in terminal clusters. The ovate to oblong leaves, white felted below, have coarse toothed margins.

O. phlogopappa
DUSKY DAISYBUSH

This erect, evergreen shrub, native to New South Wales, Tasmania and Victoria, Australia, is grown for the white, pink or mauve, daisy-like flowers it bears from mid-spring to early summer. The grey-green leaves are oblong and serrated. Frost-hardy, it grows to a height and spread of 2 m (about 6 ft).

O. traversii
SILVER AKE AKE

An erect evergreen with pale fur-rowed bark, this frost-hardy shrub

Olearia traversii

grows to a height of 6 m (about 18 ft) with a spread of 3 m (about 9 ft). *O. traversii* bears small, white, daisy-like flowers in summer. The leaves are leathery and oblong.

OSMANTHUS
FRAGRANT OLIVE, KWAI FA

The slow-growing, evergreen shrubs or small trees in this genus are grown for their fragrance produced from small, almost invisible, flowers. The scent resembles that of jasmine and gardenias and lasts from autumn/fall through to spring. Frost-hardy to half-hardy, they prefer fertile, well-drained soil and tolerate either sun or shade. Cut back after flowering to restrict growth, and propagate from semi-ripe cuttings in summer. The flowers of *Osmanthus* species are traditionally used by the Chinese to scent and sweeten their tea. Hybrids between *Osmanthus* and the closely related *Phillyrea* are called *Osmarea*: they look just like *Osmanthus* and are grown in the same way.

Olearia macrodonta

Olearia phlogopappa

Paeonia suffruticosa

Paeonia lutea

Osmanthus fragrans

Parahebe lyalli

Parahebe cataractae

Pachystegia insignis

Osmanthus h. 'Variegatus'

O. fragrans
SWEET OSMANTHUS

This erect, branching, evergreen shrub is native to the Himalayas, India and Japan. It grows to a height of 5 m (about 15 ft) with a spread of 3 m (about 9 ft). Sprays of small, white, very fragrant flowers appear in spring and again in autumn/fall. O. fragrans has glossy, broad, green leaves and is half-hardy.

O. heterophyllus 'Variegatus'
syn. O. illicifolius variegatus

Native to China, this erect, branching, evergreen shrub or tree bears small, white, delightfully fragrant flowers in the leaf axils, in autumn/fall. It has holly-like leaves; there is a form with yellow-bordered foliage. Frost-hardy, it grows to a height of 6 m (about 18 ft) with a spread of 3 m (about 9 ft).

PACHYSTEGIA
insignis

This low-growing, spreading, evergreen shrub, native to New Zealand, is grown for its white, daisy-like flowers with yellow centres borne in winter. It has leathery, dark green, shiny leaves and likes a well-drained soil in a protected, sunny position; it will tolerate partial shade. Frost-hardy, it grows to 1 m (about 3 ft) tall with a 2 m (about 6 ft) spread. Propagate from seed or cuttings.

PAEONIA
PEONY

Native to Tibet, western China and Bhutan, peonies do best in colder temperatures. The shrubs of the genus (which also includes perennials) are called 'tree peonies'. These are woody and deciduous, bearing brightly coloured flowers that range from white to darkest red, to purple, orange and yellow. They do best in a cool, lightly shaded spot, especially in mild-winter climates—it is best to plant them in the shade of other shrubs, otherwise the sun will damage the blooms. However, where they are able to become properly dormant in winter, they are better with half-day sun. Peonies

like a moist, well-drained soil, rich with humus and preferably with some lime. Propagate from hardwood cuttings in autumn/fall or by grafting in winter. Protect young plants from frost and watch out for botrytis, especially in soggy soil. Difficult to propagate, plants are expensive and grafting is the usual method.

P. lutea

A deciduous, upright shrub, native to China, P. lutea bears single, yellow flowers in late spring to early summer. Its dark green leaves have sawtoothed edges. Frost-hardy, it grows to a height and spread of 2 m (about 6 ft).

P. suffruticosa
MOUTAN, TREE PEONY

This deciduous, upright shrub, a native of China, grows to a height and spread of 1–2 m (about 3–6 ft). In spring it bears single or double, cup-shaped, huge, red, pink, white or yellow flowers (depending on variety: there are many) set among large, compound, mid-green leaves. It is frost-hardy.

PARAHEBE
VERONICA

Found mainly in New Zealand, these dense, shrubby evergreens have a prostrate, decumbent habit, making them excellent for border edgings or for rock gardens. Frost-hardy, they prefer full sun, and a well-drained, peaty, sandy soil. Propagate from semi-ripe cuttings in early summer.

P. cataractae

Perhaps the most decorative of the genus, this species has at first a rapid spreading habit and then grows upwards. In spring, it bears racemes of small, white, funnel-shaped flowers tinged with purple, among oval, serrated leaves. Frost-hardy, it grows to a height and spread of 30 cm (about 12 in).

P. lyalli

This semi-evergreen, frost-hardy, prostrate shrub, a native of New Zealand, grows to a height of 15 cm (about 6 in) with a spread of up to 25 cm (about 10 in). In early summer, it bears terminal spikes of small, white or pink flowers, set among oval, serrated, leathery green leaves.

P. perfoliata
syn. Veronica perfoliata
DIGGER SPEEDWELL

A native of New South Wales and Victoria, Australia, this evergreen shrub is grown for the beautiful, deep blue flowers it bears in spring, set among broad, sessile, leathery, silver-grey leaves. Frost-hardy, it does best in a well-drained, peaty, sandy soil, in a sunny or partially shaded position. Well suited as a rockery plant or for border edging, *P. perfolia* grows to a height and spread of 60 cm (about 2 ft). Propagate from semi-ripe cuttings in early summer.

PENTAS
lanceolata
syn. *P. carnea*
EGYPTIAN STAR, STAR CLUSTER

Native to the tropics of Africa and the Arabian peninsula, this erect, straggling shrub grows to a height of 60 cm (about 24 in) and a spread of 1 m (about 3 ft). It is grown for the spring/summer appearance of clusters of tubular, red, pink, lilac or white flowers, set among bright green, hairy leaves. Frost-tender, it does best in fertile, well-drained, sandy soil—ideally, rich with leafmould—and an open, sunny position. Pinch back regularly to maintain a compact habit and to encourage bloom. Dead-head regularly and trim slightly in early spring. Water generously when in full growth. Propagate from seed in spring or from softwood cuttings in summer. Whitefly may cause problems.

PERNETTYA
mucronata
PRICKLY HEATH

Native to the southern tip of South America, this evergreen shrub bears white, urn-shaped, heath-like flowers in late spring and early summer, set among small, pointed, heath-like leaves. Small, bright berries of variable colour appear in autumn/fall and winter. It does best in a well-drained acid soil and prefers sun or semi-shade. Densely branched when young, it gets leggy when more mature and will require cutting back hard. It grows to a height and spread of 1 m (about 3 ft). Propagate by division or from seed in summer or spring, or from softwood cuttings in summer to be sure of the berry colour.

PERSOONIA
pinifolia
PINE-LEAVED GEEBUNG

This erect, evergreen shrub is a native of New South Wales and Queensland, Australia. It grows to a height of 4 m (about 12 ft) with a spread of 3 m (about 9 ft), and is grown for the terminal spikes of yellow flowers it bears in summer, and for the green, edible, grape-like berries that follow in autumn/fall. Other attractions are its pine-like, needled leaves, and red bark. It prefers a well-drained, light to medium soil in a sunny spot and is moderately frost-hardy. *P. pinifolia* is notoriously difficult to propagate—sowing seed is probably the best

way. Soak the seeds overnight for twenty-four hours before sowing.

PHILADELPHUS
MOCK ORANGE, SYRINGA

These suckering, deciduous shrubs come from Europe, Asia and the Americas and are among the most popular of flower-bearing shrubs because of their delightful orange-blossom fragrance. Very versatile plants, they are ideal for pathways, in open borders or as wall shrubs. Hardiness varies considerably among the species. They need sun and a fertile, well-drained soil. Thin out after bloom, and propagate from softwood cuttings in summer. Keep warm and moist until the roots establish themselves. Aphids may be a problem. Syringa is the old Roman name, now used by botanists as the genus name for the lilac.

P. coronarius
MOCK ORANGE

This species is a native of Europe and South-East Asia. Fully hardy, it grows to a height and spread of 3 m (about 9 ft). It bears terminal clusters of fragrant, creamy white flowers in spring, and oval leaves that have hairy veins on the undersurface.

P. 'Lemoinei'

From early mid-summer, this slightly arching, upright, deciduous shrub bears small, very fragrant, white flowers, set among oval to lance-shaped leaves. Fully hardy, it grows to a height and spread of 1.5 m (about 4½ ft).

Pentas lanceolata

Pernettya mucronata

Philadelphus coronarius

Philadelphus 'Lemoinei'

Parahebe perfoliata

Persoonia pinifolia

P. mexicanus
MEXICAN MOCK ORANGE, EVERGREEN MOCK ORANGE

Native to Mexico, this evergreen shrub bears single, cream, very fragrant flowers, set among oval green leaves. Moderately frost-tender, it grows to a height of 3 m (about 9 ft) and a spread of 2 m (about 6 ft). It prefers a partially shaded, protected position.

P. 'Virginal'

Fully hardy, this vigorous, upright shrub grows to a height and spread of a little under 3 m (about 9 ft). From late spring to early summer, it bears large, fragrant, semi-double flowers set among dark green, oval leaves.

PHILESIA
magellanica

This erect evergreen from Chile is grown for the delightful, pink, trumpet-shaped flowers it bears from mid-summer to late autumn/fall. It has dark green, narrow, ob-

long-shaped flowers with bluish white undersides. It grows to a height of 1 m (about 3 ft) with a spread of 2 m (about 6 ft). It prefers a moist, humus-rich, acid soil and does best in semi-shade. Give it a dressing of leafmould every year. Propagate from semi-ripe cuttings in summer.

PHLOMIS
fruticosa
JERUSALEM SAGE

This evergreen shrub, a native of southern Europe, is grown for the strikingly beautiful, yellow flowers it bears in whorls, from early to mid-summer, among oval, wrinkled, woolly green leaves. Frost-hardy, it does best in full sun and a well-drained soil. Drought, frost and salt resistant, it tolerates coastal areas quite well and grows to a height and spread of about 75 cm (about 30 in). Prune back to about half in autumn/fall to keep its habit neat. Propagate from seed in spring or from cuttings in summer.

Phlomis fruticosa

Philadelphus 'Virginal'

Photinia glabra

PHOTINIA
CHINESE OR JAPANESE HAWTHORN

Grown mostly for their shiny foliage, species of this genus of semi-deciduous shrubs and trees make excellent hedges. They bear insignificant, white, acrid-smelling flowers in spring followed by blue-black berries The young foliage is brilliantly coloured, maturing to rich green. Fully hardy, photinias do best in a fertile, well-drained soil and require sun or semi-shade. Prune regularly to keep their habit dense and to promote new growth. Propagate by layering, or by grafting onto hawthorn stock.

P. glabra
PHOTINIA HEDGE

A native of eastern Asia, this species grows to a height of 3 m (about 9 ft) and a spread of 2 m (about 6 ft). As its name suggests, it makes an excellent hedging shrub. The tiny white flowers appear in flat terminal clusters in late spring, followed by blue-black berries. The leaves are

Philadelphus mexicanus

Photinia serrulata

elliptical to oblong and glossy green. *P. glabra* is frost-hardy. Selected cultivars are grown for their brilliant red young leaves and make excellent hedges; clipping usually brings on several flushes of young growth.

P. serrulata

This species, native to China, has glossy, oval, serrated, dark green leaves. In spring, it bears small, white flowers and these are followed in turn by red berries. Fully hardy, it grows to a height of up to 6 m (about 18 ft) with a spread of 4 m (about 12 ft).

PHYGELIUS
CAPE FUCHSIA

Related to *Penstemon* and *Antirrhinum* (snapdragon) rather than *Fuchsia*, these erect, evergreen undershrubs—perennials in some winter conditions—are native to the Cape of Good Hope, South Africa. They are grown for the handsome, red flowers they bear in summer, set among dark green, oval leaves. They do best in sun or semi-shade and like a fertile, well-drained soil that is not too dry. Excellent in a rock garden, they grow to a height of 1 m (about 3 ft) and a spread of 50 cm (about 20 in). Propagate from softwood cuttings in summer. *P. capensis* and *P. aequalis*, both red, are the best known species; there are several hybrids available with flowers in red, yellow or orange.

PIERIS
ANDROMEDA, PEARL FLOWER, LILY-OF-THE-VALLEY BUSH

These fairly dense, bushy, evergreen shrubs, native to the colder regions of North America and Asia, are related to the *Azalea* and are grown for their small, urn-shaped flowers. Slow growing, they do best in a mildly acid soil that is well-drained and rich with leafmould. They prefer a sheltered spot in shade or semi-shade and are fully to frost-hardy, although young plants may be killed by frost in spring. They also like a humid atmosphere—this maintains the colour and freshness

Phygelius aequalis

of the foliage. Dead-head after flowering as this improves the growth. Propagate from semi-ripe or soft tip cuttings in early summer.

P. forrestii
RED LEAF PEARL FLOWER

This bushy, dense, evergreen species is a native of China. In spring it bears terminal sprays of white flowers, set among small oval leaves that are bronze when young and turn dark green when older. Frost-hardy, it grows to a height and spread of 2 m (about 6 ft).

P. japonica
JAPANESE PEARL FLOWER

This rounded, bushy, dense, evergreen shrub is a native of Japan. In spring it bears dense sprays of pendent, white flowers that resemble lily-of-the-valley. Though flower buds develop in autumn/fall, they do not open until spring. When young, the small, glossy leaves are oval, turning bronze as the plant matures. Fully hardy, *P. japonica* grows to a height and spread of 2 m (about 6 ft). There are selected cultivars with even more brilliant young foliage.

PIMELEA
prostrata

This low-spreading shrub, native to New Zealand, has small, leathery leaves and profuse white to pink, fragrant flowers appearing in terminal clusters. Frost-hardy, it prefers a light, porous soil with plenty of leafmould, and dappled sunlight. Propagate from semi-hardwood cuttings in late summer.

PINUS
mugo
DWARF PINE, MOUNTAIN PINE, SWISS MOUNTAIN PINE

This shrubby, spreading conifer is native to the Pyrenees in Europe. It bears purple, scaly, 5 cm (about 2 in) long cones that ripen over two years. Its leaves are long, dark green needles, arranged in clusters of two or three. It prefers a well-drained, light to medium, acid soil and an open, sunny position. Evergreen and frost-hardy, it grows to a height of 5 m (about 15 ft) with a spread of 3 m (about 9 ft).

PISONIA
brunoniana
syn. P. umbellifera, Heimerliodendron brunonianum
BIRDLIME TREE, BIRD CATCHER TREE

Native to New South Wales and Queensland, Australia, this erect, branching evergreen shrub grows to a height of 5 m (about 15 ft) with a spread of 3 m (about 9 ft). It has

Pimelea prostrata

large, elliptical, glossy green leaves and bears very sticky, purplish fruit all year round. The flowers are insignificant. Tolerant to most soil conditions, it does best in a humus-rich, well-drained soil in full light or partial shade. Potted plants should be well-watered when in full growth. Prune as necessary to maintain shape. Propagate from semi-ripe cuttings in summer or seed in spring.

PITTOSPORUM
MOCKORANGE, PITTOSPORUM

These handsome, evergreen, fragrant shrubs and trees are found in China, Japan, Africa, New Zealand,

Pieris japonica

Australia and the Pacific. Grown for their fragrance and ornamental foliage, they like a leaf-rich, well-drained soil and regular moisture. They are frost-hardy to frost-tender and generally do best in mild climates. Some species prefer sun, others sun or partial shade. Propagate from seed in autumn/fall or spring, or from semi-ripe cuttings in summer. There are a great many cultivated species and hybrids.

P. eugenioides 'Variegatum'

This engaging cultivar bears grey-green leaves with white borders. It is a dense shrub of pyramidal habit, growing to about 4 m (about 12 ft), and makes an excellent hedge.

Pinus mugo

Pisonia brunoniana

Pittosporum eugenioides 'Variegatum'

Pieris forrestii

Plumbago auriculata

Polygala myrtifolia 'Grandiflora'

Pittosporum tenuifolium

Podalyria calyptrata

Polygala virgata

P. tenuifolium

KOHUHU

This evergreen tree grows to a height of 10 m (about 30 ft) with a spread of 6 m (about 18 ft). A native of New Zealand, it bears glossy, oval, mid-green leaves with undulating margins, and bears dark purple, honey-scented flowers in spring. It is half-hardy. There are several cultivars, with variegated or purple-toned leaves, much sought after by flower arrangers.

PLUMBAGO
auriculata
syn. P. capensis
CAPE LEADWORT

This evergreen, lax-growing shrub, originally from South Africa, bears pale blue or white flowers in terminal clusters from spring to autumn/fall. Half-hardy, it has oblong, pale green leaves. Fast growing, it likes a fertile, well-drained soil and full light or semi-shade. It is quite suitable as an informal hedge or to disguise fences and walls, as it

climbs to a height of 5 m (about 15 ft). Water regularly in full growth, less so at other times. Whitefly may pose problems. Propagate from semi-ripe cuttings in summer. *P. auriculata* 'Alba' is a white cultivar. *P. capensis* is said to have been used by the ancient Romans as a cure for lead poisoning.

PODALYRIA
calyptrata
SWEET PEA BUSH

This rounded, fragrant, evergreen shrub, native to South Africa, is prized for the delightful, pinkish mauve, pea flowers it bears in spring, set among greyish oval leaves. Half-hardy, it is very useful in exposed positions, tolerating full light or semi-shade. It requires a fertile, well-drained soil and should be watered regularly in full growth, less at other times. *P. calyptrata* grows to a height and spread of 2 m (about 6 ft). Prune after flowering if necessary. It is best propagated from scarified seed in spring or semi-ripe cuttings in summer.

POLYGALA
MILKWORT, LANGELIER, BLUECAPS, SEPTEMBERBOSSIE

These evergreen shrubs are native to South Africa. Well branched above, somewhat leggy below, they are ideal as temporary filler behind slow-growing plants or as a background. They are grown mainly for their pea-like flowers. Fully hardy to frost-tender, plant in full light or partial shade, in moist, well-drained soil. Water potted plants well during full growth, less at other times. Cut lanky stems back hard in late winter. Propagate from semi-ripe cuttings in late summer, or seed in spring.

P. chamaebuxus
BASTARD BOX

This evergreen shrub, a native of alpine Europe, grows to a height of 20 cm (about 8 in) with a spread of 40 cm (about 16 in). Racemes of small, pea-like, yellow and white flowers appear in spring and early summer. It has tiny, oval, dark green leaves and is fully hardy.

P. myrtifolia 'Grandiflora'

From late winter to summer, this erect, evergreen shrub bears luxuriant, purple, pea-like flowers in clusters at the ends of shoots. It has small, greyish green leaves and is moderately frost-hardy.

P. virgata

This upright evergreen bears clusters of handsome, pale mauve-pink flowers in spring to summer. It has cane-like stems and narrow leaves. Frost-tender, it grows to a height of 2 m (about 6 ft) with a spread of 1.5 m (about 4½ ft).

POMADERRIS

Native to Australia and New Zealand, this genus of evergreen shrubs and small trees contains about 40 species. Some are widely grown as ornamentals. They do best in moist, well-drained, sandy or gravelly soil. Frost-hardy but drought-tender, they prefer a sunny position with protection from winds. Tip prune to maintain shape. Propagate from seed or tip cuttings in autumn/fall.

P. apetala
NEW ZEALAND HAZEL, TAINUI

This erect, evergreen shrub is grown mainly for its foliage—large, wrinkled, prominently veined leaves. Less significant are the long clusters of green flowers it bears in spring. It grows to a height of 5 m (about 15 ft) with a spread of 2 m (about 6 ft).

P. kumeraho
GOLDEN TAINUI

This erect, branching, evergreen shrub is native to New Zealand. In spring, it bears terminal rounded clusters of golden yellow flowers. The rich green, oval leaves are deeply veined on the upper surface. It grows to a height and spread of 3–4 m (about 9–12 ft).

POTENTILLA
fruticosa 'Tangerine'

The yellow flowers of this dense, deciduous shrub carry a hint of reddish orange. The flowers appear from early summer to autumn/fall amid flat, mid-green leaves comprising 5 or 7 narrow elliptical leaflets arranged palmately. Sow seed in autumn/fall or propagate using greenwood or softwood cuttings in summer. The arching shrub reaches 60 cm (about 24 in) in height with a spread of 1.5 m (about 4½ ft).

PROSTANTHERA
rotundifola
MINT-BUSH

This 3 m (about 9 ft) tall, evergreen shrub is grown for the delightful clusters of mauve or violet flowers it bears in spring. It has small, fragrant, deep green leaves. Native to the southern and south-eastern states of Australia, it needs a fertile, well-drained soil and full light or partial shade to thrive. Potted plants should be watered well, less so when not in full growth. Prune after flowering. Propagate from semi-ripe cuttings in late summer, or from seed in spring.

PROTEA
PROTEA, SUGAR BUSH, HONEY FLOWER

The beauty of the gigantic blooms of these evergreen shrubs make them a popular choice for a sunny spot in a garden with the right soil conditions—sandy, well-drained, low on phosphates and nitrates, and preferably acid (though some species tolerate an alkaline soil). Native to South Africa, the genus has relatives in South America, New Zealand and Australia. Often difficult to grow, all species need protection in the winter for a year or two after planting. Potted specimens in full growth should be watered now and then. Keep well ventilated if under glass. They last well after fading and after cutting—hence their popularity in arrangements. Proteas are half-hardy. Propagate from cuttings taken in summer (seed germination is erratic). The genus is named after the mythical Greek god, Proteus, who could change into any shape he desired. The flowers are widely grown in Hawaii for the flower shops of the USA.

P. compacta
RIVER PROTEA

This half-hardy, erect, branching evergreen grows to a height of up to 3 m (about 9 ft) with a spread of 2 m (about 6 ft). Rose-pink, silver fringed flowers appear in winter to mid-spring. It has light green, oval, heart-shaped leaves.

P. cynaroides
KING PROTEA

This species bears large, open flowerheads with pink, petal-like bracts, in winter, spring or summer. The leathery leaves are round and dark green. A lovely shrub, it is half-hardy and grows to a height and spread of 1.5 m (about 4½ ft). Like all proteas, the size of the shrub bears little relationship to that of the flowers—the flowerheads grow to 30 cm (about 12 in) wide. It is the floral emblem of South Africa.

Potentilla fruticosa 'Tangerine'

Prostanthera rotundifola

Pomaderris apetala

Pomaderris kumeraho

Protea cynaroides

Protea compacta

Protea grandiceps

Protea scolymocephala

Protea repens 'Guerna'

Protea 'Pink Ice'

P. grandiceps
PEACH PROTEA

This slow-growing, erect, branching, evergreen shrub, bears striking, peach-pink flowers with hairy fringes in winter and spring. The greyish leaves have red margins. Frost-hardy, it grows up to 2 m (about 6 ft) high, with a spread of 1.5 m (about 4¹/₂ ft).

P. neriifolia
OLEANDER-LEAVED PROTEA, BLACK PROTEA

The flowerheads of this species are fragrant, silvery pink, black-tipped and grow to 10 cm (about 4 in). These appear from autumn/fall to early spring. *P. neriifolia* has narrow, oblong, oleander-like leaves. It grows to a height and spread of 3 m (about 9 ft).

P. 'Pink Ice'

This evergreen shrub is a hybrid of *P. susannae* and *P. neriifolia*. Its shiny, pink flowers, appearing in autumn/fall and winter, resemble those of *P. neriifolia*, minus the soft,

black hairs on the bracts. Half-hardy, it grows to a height of 3 m (about 9 ft) and a spread of 2 m (about 6 ft).

P. repens 'Guerna'
SUGAR BUSH

Widely distributed in South Africa, *P. repens* is the easiest of all the proteas to grow. It reaches to 3 m (about 9 ft) high and 2 m (about 6 ft) wide. Colours vary from creamy white to dark pink and red. Nectar from the flowers is used to make syrup. 'Guerna', one of the first cultivars, bears large, upright, deep red flowers in summer.

P. scolymocephala

This erect, branching, evergreen shrub is grown for the spring growth of handsome green, cone-like, solitary flowers it bears that are ideal for indoor arrangements. Small, green, slightly hairy leaves are massed along the stems. Half-hardy, it grows to just over 1 m (about 3 ft) high, with a spread of 1.5 m (about 4¹/₂ ft).

Prunus glandulosa 'Rosea Plena'

Protea neriifolia

PRUNUS

BUSH CHERRY, CHOKEBERRY

Best known as a genus of popular, fruiting trees, *Prunus* also contains some delightful ornamental plants, mostly from North America. Grown for the autumn/fall colour of their foliage, as well as their fruits and flowers, they seem to tolerate any soil that is not excessively wet. Superficially they resemble the rose, but as would be expected in a genus with over a hundred species and cultivars, there is widespread variation. All their leaves are oval to oblong. Deciduous species prefer full sun, while the evergreens do best in sun or shade. The evergreens should be propagated from semi-ripe cuttings in summer or autumn/fall, the deciduous species from seed in autumn/fall or hardwood cuttings in winter.

P. glandulosa 'Rosea Plena'
BUSH CHERRY

In late spring, this dainty, suckering, deciduous shrub bears handsome, rose-pink flowers, set among green, oval leaves. It grows to a height and spread of 1–1.5 m (about 3–4¹/₂ ft). After flowering, prune young shoots close to the old wood.

P. laurocerasus
CHERRY LAUREL

A dense, bushy shrub that eventually becomes spreading and open, this species bears racemes of small, white flowers in mid- to late spring. These are set among glossy, dark green, oblong to oval leaves. After the bloom, grape-like clusters of glossy, black, cherry-like fruits make their

Pyracantha angustifolia

Pseudowintera colorata

appearance. Frost-hardy, *P. laurocerasus* grows to a height of 6 m (about 18 ft) with a spread of 10 m (about 30 ft). Both the cherry laurel and the Portugal laurel respond very well to clipping and make splendid hedges.

PSEUDOPANAX
syn. *Neopanax, Nothopanax*

Native to China, Chile, New Caledonia, Tasmania (Australia) and New Zealand, these evergreen shrubs and trees are grown for their unusual foliage and fruits—the flowers are insignificant. They prefer well-drained, moisture-retentive, humus-rich soil in a sheltered, sunny or partially shaded position. Perfect for growing in large pots, they also make excellent landscape plants. Propagate from seed in autumn/fall or spring, or from semi-ripe cuttings in summer.

P. lessonii
HOUPARA

This erect, branching New Zealand native has thick, leathery, bronze-coloured leaves and insignificant flowers. Frost-tender, it grows to a height of 3–6 m (about 9–18 ft) with a spread of 2–5 m (about 6–15 ft). Young specimens thrive in a cool greenhouse or indoors.

P. lessonii hybrids

These have oval, serrated, green leaves; some have yellow markings and veins.

PSEUDOWINTERA
colorata
syn. *Drimys colorata*
ALPINE PEPPER TREE, HOROPITO

A spreading, bushy, evergreen shrub, native to New Zealand, this shrub grows to a height of 1–2 m (about 3–6 ft) with a spread of 1.5 m (about 4¹/₂ ft). The aromatic green leaves, with scarlet markings and a silvery underside, are its main attraction—these turn purple in the winter months. The greenish, spring and summer bloom is insignificant. It prefers a light to medium, moist, humus-rich, well-drained soil in full light or partial shade. Potted plants should be watered frequently in

Pultenaea pedunculata

summer. Prune to maintain the shape. Propagate from seed in spring or autumn/fall, or from semi-ripe cuttings in summer.

PULTENAEA
pedunculata
BACON AND EGGS

This low-growing, trailing, evergreen shrub is native to the south-eastern states of Australia. In spring and summer, it bears a profusion of delightful, orange-yellow, pea-like flowers, set amid rigid, green, heath-like leaves. A rich, well-drained soil suits it best. Drought, frost and salt resistant, it is suitable for ground cover cultivation in coastal areas. It grows to a height of 30 cm (about 12 in) with a spread of 1.5 m (about 4¹/₂ ft). Propagate from scarified seed.

PUNICA
granatum var. nana
DWARF POMEGRANATE

This deciduous, rounded shrub grows slowly to a height and spread of 30–90 cm (about 12–36 in). Native to Asia, it bears red, funnel-shaped flowers in summer, set among light green, oblong leaves. Small, orange-red fruit follow the bloom—these fruits are edible only in warm climates. Frost- to half-hardy, it does best in a sunny, sheltered position and likes a coarse, gravelly, well-drained soil. Water well in dry conditions. Prune lightly at the end of each winter to maintain its compact habit. Propagate from semi-ripe cuttings in summer, or from seed in spring.

Punica granatum var. nana

Prunus laurocerasus

PYRACANTHA
FIRETHORN

Though these arching, evergreen shrubs bear delightful profusions of tiny, white flowers in spring, they are mostly grown for the impressive display of berries that follows in autumn/fall. These tend to colour better in cooler conditions. Dense and spiny, they do well as hedges, espaliers and ground covers. If grown against a wall, cut back long shoots after flowering. Grow in fertile soil in a sheltered, sunny position. Propagate from semi-ripe cuttings in summer. Scab and fireblight may cause problems.

P. angustifolia
FIRETHORN

This dense shrub, native to western China, grows to a height and spread of 3 m (about 9 ft). In early summer, it bears small, white, open flowers set among dark green, oblong leaves followed by orange berries. It is frost-hardy.

Pseudopanax lessonii

Pseudopanax lessonii hybrid

Rhamnus alaternus

Raphiolepis × delacourii

P. crenulata
syn. *Crataegus crenulata*
NEPAL FIRETHORN

This sturdy, erect, half-hardy shrub grows rapidly to a height and spread of 3–4 m (about 9–12 ft). Native to Nepal and China, *P. crenulata* bears numerous white, open flowers in early summer which are followed in turn by a profusion of small, dark-red berries. The glossy leaves are narrow and blunt.

RAPHIOLEPIS
INDIAN HAWTHORN, YEDDO HAWTHORN

These dense, evergreen shrubs, grown for their fragrant bloom and foliage, are native to subtropical South-East Asia. Frost- to half-hardy, they like plenty of sun but, in hot climates, prefer semi-shade. They do best in a well-drained, sandy soil and in a sheltered position, ideally against a wall. They bear panicles of five petalled flowers, followed by berries, among alternate, leathery, dark green, oblong leaves. Coastal areas suit them best but, in colder areas, they need to be grown under glass. Propagate from seed or cuttings in summer.

R. × delacourii

A rounded, evergreen shrub that grows to a height and spread of 2 m (about 6 ft), *R. × delacourii* is grown for the rose-pink flowers it bears in early summer, and the blue-black berries that follow in winter. Its oval, leathery leaves are toothed at the ends. *R. × delacourii* is a hybrid between *R. indica* and *R. umbellata*.

R. indica
INDIAN HAWTHORN

This bushy, evergreen shrub is native to the southern China. In spring or early summer it bears clusters of fragrant, star-shaped, white flowers, set among serrated, oblong leaves. Fully hardy, it grows to a height and spread of just under 1 m (about 3 ft).

RHABDOTHAMNUS
solandri
TAUREPO, NEW ZEALAND GLOXINIA, WAIUATUA

This slender, many-branched evergreen shrub has small, rough, hairy leaves with coarsely serrated margins. It bears orange-red flowers with purple-marked throats, which bloom throughout the year in favoured positions. It does best in a moist, rich, well-drained soil, in a protected, shady position. Prune back frequently to promote bushiness. Half-hardy, it grows to a height and spread of 2 m (about 6 ft). Propagate from seed or hardwood cuttings.

RHAMNUS
alaternus
BUCKTHORN

This erect, branching, evergreen shrub, native to southern Europe, grows to a height of 6 m (about 18 ft) with a spread of 3 m (about 9 ft). It bears tiny, greenish flowers in axillary racemes, which are followed by black, rounded, pea-sized fruits. The leaves are dark green and oval with saw-toothed margins. *R. alarternus* likes a protected, shady position and a light to medium, well-drained soil. Drought, frost and salt resistant, it is popular as a screening plant and makes an excellent clipped hedge in European coastal gardens. A variety with variegated leaves is popular. Propagate from semi-ripe cuttings in summer. This shrub is becoming a noxious weed in some countries.

RHODODENDRON
RHODODENDRON, AZALEA

The rhododendrons are an enormous genus of some 600 species (almost all garden-worthy) and countless cultivars, native mainly to the temperate regions of Europe, North America and Asia, although with important representatives in the highlands of tropical South-East Asia and one species (*R. lochae*) in Australia. They are admired for their handsome leaves and showy, bell or funnel-shaped flowers. The flowers are borne at the ends of the previous year's shoots, often in clusters, mainly in spring although both winter and summer flowers are fairly common. Just about all of them share an intense dislike of lime, but where soils suit they are among the most desirable of all flowering shrubs. As a general rule, they like a shaded to semi-shaded position with a cool root run and acid, perfectly drained soil with abundant humus; none can be called drought resistant. No regular pruning is required, although they can be cut back quite severely in early spring if needed. Propagation is by layering, from cuttings, or by grafting, most species being fairly slow to strike. Their usually shapely habit and compact root systems make them first rate subjects for container growing, and they are among the easiest of all shrubs to transplant, even when mature. Red spider, lace bug, thrips, caterpillars and leaf miners can be troublesome, usually in dry conditions.

The genus is divided into some forty 'series', but horticulturally there are three most important divisions. First, there are the azaleas, formerly given a genus of their own (the distinguishing mark being that azaleas usually have 5 stamens, the rest of the genus 10 or more); then the subtropical species and their

Pyracantha crenulata

Rhabdothamnus solandri

Raphiolepis indica

Rhododendron × *gandavense*

Rhododendron 'White Gumpo'

Rhododendron luteum hybrid

hybrids, mostly of the series Vireya and usually called vireya rhododendrons or simply vireyas; and the rhododendrons proper, which are very variable in habit, from dwarfs growing 25 cm (about 10 in) high or less to small trees, and, generally, preferring a cooler climate than the other two groups do. We shall deal with each in turn, illustrating merely a representative or two of each of the main types.

AZALEAS

These divide naturally into two groups, the deciduous azaleas and the evergreen kinds. The deciduous azaleas bear their flowers either on bare branches before their leaves or with the young foliage; they are available in just about every colour but blue, the yellow-to-flame range being the most distinctive and popular. The flowers are usually followed by brilliant autumn/fall foliage. Fully hardy, they are happiest in cool to cold climates. The evergreen azaleas are on the whole less cold hardy, and several of them are distinctly tender. They are of great importance in warm-temperate climates and as flowering pot plants.

R. × gandavense
GHENT AZALEAS

The Latin title is traditional, but effectively these are simply mollis-type azaleas with double flowers.

R. gumpo azaleas

These are a small group of cultivars from Japan, a trifle more hardy than the Indicas. They are prostrate shrubs about 50 cm (about 20 in)

Rhododendron simsii 'Eureka'

tall (less with pruning) but spreading about 1.5 m (about 4½ ft) wide. They are suitable for ground cover in mild-winter climates, and have 8 cm (about 3 in) flowers in shades from white to red. They are late bloomers and their flowers may be damaged by the sun.

R. indica azaleas

Derived mainly from the southern Chinese *R. simsii*, and half-hardy at best, these are the most important rhododendrons in warm-temperate climates. They make rounded shrubs from 1–3 m (about 3–9 ft) tall, according to variety, with slightly hairy, dull green leaves. There are very many named varieties. Some flower throughout winter, but most are spring blooming. Bloom is most profuse in the white to red and purple range, the flowers usually being about 8 cm (about 3 in) wide. Single-flowered cultivars tend to be bigger growers than the doubles which are, under the name 'Belgian indicas', much cultivated under glass in Europe as Christmas-flowering pot plants.

Rhododendron kurume azalea

R. kurume azaleas

Mainly derived from the Japanese *R. obtusum*, these are the most frost-hardy of the evergreen azaleas. They grow to about 2 m (about 6 ft) high and wide, but are very slow and usually seen smaller than that. Foliage is dark green and oval, and the densely bushy plants are so smothered in bloom in their spring season that the leaves are quite obscured. The individual flowers are small, about 3 cm (about 1½ in) across, single or double, and come in every shade from white through pink to red and purple. They take their name from the province of

Japan where the leading varieties originated. In Japan, they are often sheared into formal shapes, although at the cost of some bloom.

R. luteum hybrids
MOLLIS AZALEAS

These are the best known of the deciduous azaleas, bearing wide open flowers in shades from white, cream, yellow, pale to deep pink and orange to red in early spring. They grow mostly 2–3 m (about 6–9 ft) high and wide, with mid-green leaves that turn brilliant shades in autumn/fall. There are many named varieties; some are sweetly scented.

VIREYAS (Malesian rhododendrons)

Native as they mostly are to such inaccessible places as the highlands of Indonesia, Borneo and New Guinea, the vireyas are still fairly new in cultivation, and there is still much work to be done in sorting out which of the species are going to prove easy to cultivate and popular. They are, however, among the most exciting new developments in gardening, at least in warm-temperate and subtropical climates—in areas with more than the mildest of frosts they need greenhouse cultivation—and hybrids are already being raised. Evergreen, they are mostly shrubs about 1–1.5 m (about 3–4½ ft) tall, with dark green, leathery, often glossy leaves, which are apt to be tinted russet when young. They flower in spring, although many continue intermittently throughout the summer into the autumn/fall. Flower size and shape varies, from 2–8 cm (about 1–3 in), from funnels to wide open bells, and some are sweetly scented. Colours range from white to orange, taking in sunset shades of gold coral and salmon pink on the way. The usual conditions of cultivation suit them.

R. jasminiflorum
VIREYA RHODODENDRON

This small, evergreen rhododendron bears fragrant, white flowers any time of the year among mid-green, oval leaves. It grows to a height and spread of 50 cm (about 20 in).

R. javanicum
VIREYA RHODODENDRON

Growing to a height and spread of 1 m (about 3 ft), this rhododendron bears red to orange flowers with purple stamens in autumn/fall. It has oval, lightly-veined green leaves.

R. lochae
AUSTRALIAN RHODODENDRON

Notable as the only species from Australia, this is a fairly typical vireya, growing about 1.5 m (about 4½ ft) tall in gardens, although capable of much more. It has glossy dark leaves and bears 3 cm (about 1½ in) wide, bell-shaped red flowers in late spring. It is rather tender.

RHODODENDRONS

Apart from the deciduous azaleas, all the rhododendrons are evergreen and, typically, bear their flowers in large domed clusters. They are a very varied lot, and we give simply a few typical species to illustrate the range.

R. arboreum

Native to the Himalayas, this species grows to a 10 m (about 30 ft) tall tree in the wild, although in cultivation it is usually only about half that. It has long, dull green leaves, often with silvery tinted undersides, and bears big clusters of red to pink flowers in spring. It is frost-hardy and one of the chief parents of the popular Hardy hybrids.

R. augustinii

Native to central China, this fully hardy, bushy species can grow to about 3 m (about 9 ft) high and wide, although it is usually rather less in gardens. It has small leaves, giving the bush an appearance like an evergreen azalea. The wide open flowers, borne in small clusters, vary in colour from blue to violet; in the best forms they are the purest blue seen in the genus. *R. augustinii* has been the parent of several choice blue-flowered hybrids.

R. auriculatum

Another native of western China, this bushy, wide-branching shrub bears fragrant, white or pink, funnel-shaped flowers in summer. Its leaves are large, oblong and hairy. Fully hardy, it grows to a height of 6 m (about 18 ft) with a spread of 4 m (about 12 ft). It is notable for its very late season of flowering.

R. 'Chrysomanicum'

This shrubby, bud-tender specimen bears delightful, primrose-yellow flowers in spring and has hairy, green leaves. Unlike most species of

Rhododendron jasminiflorum

Rhododendron lochae

Rhododendron auriculatum

Rhododendron arboreum

Rhododendron javanicum

Rhododendron 'Chrysomanicum'

Rhododendron augustinii

Rhododendron, it does well in full sun and in warmer areas. Frost-hardy, it grows to a height and spread of just over 1 m (about 3 ft).

R. ciliicalyx

This spreading shrub grows to a height and spread of 2 m (about 6 ft). It has shiny, dark green leaves. Its fragrant white or white-tinged rose flowers bloom in spring. *R. ciliicalyx* tolerates minus 8°C (about 18°F) or lower and grows at altitudes of up to 3000 m (about 9600 ft) in the southern China–Burma–Himalaya region.

R. 'Fragrantissimum'

In the summer months this rhododendron bears trusses of fragrant, white flowers, tinted with pink. It makes an excellent plant for house decoration in a large tub, trained around a framework of bamboo. It can be susceptible to frosts; however, in a greenhouse it will give very little trouble and flower freely.

R. Hardy hybrids

The most widely grown of the rhododendrons, the Hardy hybrids are mostly large, domed shrubs 3 m (about 9 ft) or more tall, with large, dull green leaves. They flower spectacularly in spring, bearing many almost spherical clusters of wide open flowers in shades of white, pink, red or purple; very rarely cream or yellow. There are very many named cultivars, varying a little in hardiness, from frost-hardy to fully hardy. The usual conditions of cultivation apply.

R. maccabeanum

This magnificent species is typical of a group from the Himalayas which are noted for their extremely large and handsome leaves. It is an evergreen shrub or tall tree to about 10 m (about 30 ft) tall, with large leathery leaves, deeply corrugated above, woolly white beneath, and clusters of yellow flowers in spring. It is frost-hardy, but appreciates a sheltered position.

R. ponticum

Native to Spain, this is an evergreen shrub that grows to a height of 4 m (about 12 ft) and spread of 2 m (about 6 ft). It bears delightful, loose clusters of expanding, tubular, rose-pink flowers among green, oblong to lanceolate leaves. This species is one of the best rhododendrons for mild-winter climates, and it is much used as an understock on which to graft choicer species and hybrids.

R. trichostomum
syn. R. sphacranthum

One of the most desirable of dwarf rhododendrons, of which there are many, this evergreen species from western China makes a compact shrub, growing sometimes to 1.2 m (about 3½ ft) in height, but usually a bit less, spreading about 80 cm (about 32 in) wide. This species bears small leaves and white or rose pink flowers in clusters in late spring. Several varieties of wild origin are grown; they vary from half-hardy to frost-hardy. Give it sunshine in cool areas, shade elsewhere.

R. yakushimanum

This upright, dense, native of Japan bears rounded, terminal clusters of expanding, tubular flowers in late spring. It has deep green, wrinkled leaves. *R. yakushimanum* grows to a height of 1 m (about 3 ft) with a spread of 2 m (about 6 ft). It has been the parent of many hybrids, which retain its shapely, compact growth, as well as its beautiful flowers. It is perhaps the most desirable of the rhododendrons for small gardens in temperate to cool climates.

Rhododendron Hardy hybrid

Rhododendron 'Fragrantissimum'

Rhododendron ciliicalyx

Rhododendron trichostomum

Rhododendron maccabeanum

Rhododendron yakushimanum

Rhododendron ponticum

A Field Trip to the Blue Mountains

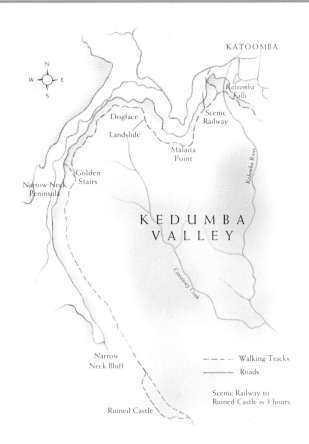

About a two-hour drive west of Sydney, Australia, takes you to the Blue Mountains, an area encompassing one of the country's most important national parks, and a haven for a variety of native plants, birds and animals. The Blue Mountains is also home to one of the largest populations of the waratah (*Telopea speciosissima*), a strikingly distinctive native shrub and the floral emblem of the state of New South Wales.

The waratah blooms from October to December (spring to early summer in Australia). This is a good time to explore the Blue Mountains as it can be quite cold in winter, sometimes down to –4°C (about 24°F), and the whole area is often covered in an eerie, dense mist. In summer the average maximum temperature is a mild 23°C (about 73°F). Even when travelling in the middle of summer you should be prepared for a sudden change in the weather—a glorious warm day can suddenly turn quite cold.

A dry winter and spring can turn the whole of the Blue Mountains into a giant tinderbox and bushfires have ravaged the area many times. The waratah is a highly fire-adapted species, sprouting rapidly from a large woody underground stem (lignotuber) which withstands the fiercest bushfires and produces new growths within a month or two. Due to the fires, most wild plants are multi-stemmed with about 1–5 flowerheads per stem.

The best way to see the waratah is to start by taking the Scenic Railway at Katoomba. The railway runs the length of

The Three Sisters —a famous landmark of the Blue Mountains.

an almost sheer cliff face to the valley below and is so steep it is more like an amusement park ride than a train trip. It once served a coal mine and you will pass by openings to old mines and the remains of a horse-drawn tramway. A walking track at the bottom of the railway leads to a rock formation known as the Ruined Castle. The round trip on this walk will take you about 6 hours.

The first part of the walk is through tall open forest which contains the white-trunked Blue Mountains ash (*Eucalyptus oreades*) and the smooth-barked apple gum (*Angophora costata*), easily recognized by its twisted, bumpy trunk. The Australian bush is quite different from the forests and woodlands of Europe and America. The abundant eucalyptus trees give an overall impression of grey rather than the green of a European forest. The trees of the open forest are taller and the soil there is deeper than on the exposed ridgetops and the extra moisture due to runoff causes many of the trees to be covered in moss.

Soon you will find yourself in a rich, cool rainforest. The lush green vegetation includes the lilly pilly (*Acmena smithii*), which bears pinkish berries in winter. These berries were once part of the local Aborigines' diet. Other plants you will see include the strap water fern (*Blechnum patersonii*) and rough tree fern (*Cyathea australis*) and rainforest trees such as the yellow sassafrass (*Doryphora sassafras*), which has fragrantly scented leaves, and the magnificent coachwood (*Ceratopetalum apetalum*). In this area and also in the open forest you may also be lucky enough to see a lyrebird preening its magnificent plumage. The lyrebird has a fanned tail of feathers which opens in similar fashion to that of a peacock. It is also a wonderful mimic.

The New South Wales waratah—a colourful note in bushland.

Telopea speciosissima

After the rainforest you climb a steep track leading to a ridge and the Ruined Castle. The trees here are smaller than those of the open forest and the vegetation more sparse. Walk a little further on and you will come upon the singularly striking red flowers of the waratah, which grows in profusion on the ridgetops and hillsides beneath the shelter of eucalypts such as red bloodwood (*Eucalyptus gummifera*). The soil is very sandy and covered in leaves and twigs. The understorey here contains a number of attractive shrubs including the old man banksia (*Banksia serrata*), which has leathery leaves and creamy yellow bottlebrush-like flowers. Like the waratah, it also blooms in spring and summer.

Undoubtedly, the most distinctive plant in the area is the waratah. Both its common and botanical names mean 'to be seen from afar'. In 1793, Sir James Smith, President of the Royal Society, wrote in his book *A Specimen of the Botany of New Holland* (Australia): 'The most magnificent plant which the prolific soil of New Holland affords is, by common consent both of Europeans and Natives, the Waratah'. It grows to about 3 m (about 9½ ft) with foliage of leathery, coarsely serrated leaves. The large heads of closely packed flowers, encircled by bright red bracts and carried on strong stems, are an adaptation to bird pollination. Large nectar-feeding birds such as the wattle-bird and noisy miner are frequent visitors, their colour vision enabling them to spot the flowerheads from a long way off.

Other birds commonly seen here are grey currawongs, striking crimson rosellas and white-eared honeyeaters. Bold currawongs come quite close, particularly if you have some food to share. The area is also home to the ring-tailed possum and another 'bat-like' possum, the sugar glider. You may also glimpse shy wallabies.

Before you start your return journey, take time to climb to the top of the Ruined Castle and enjoy the panoramic views. The plants and wildlife alone would make this walk worthwhile but the magnificent scenery makes it unforgettable.

Telopea

The waratahs belong to a remarkable group of trees and shrubs found on both sides of the South Pacific Ocean—the Proteaceae (see A Field Trip to the Cape Floral Kingdom, page 193), a family significant for its strong evolutionary association with Gondwana.

The true waratah genus (*Telopea*) consists of four or five species (an isolated population in north-eastern New South Wales may be a distinct species). *T. speciosissima* is confined to a small area on the central coast of New South Wales and inland for less than 100 km (about 62 miles). The Braidwood waratah (*T. mongaensis*) is also found in New South Wales. It has bright red, loosely packed flowerheads. The Gippsland waratah (*T. oreades*) can be found in the damp ranges of south-eastern New South Wales and eastern Victoria. It has small heads of crimson flowers. The Tasmanian waratah (*T. truncata*) is similar to the Gippsland waratah but has more conspicuous flowers. The latter has proved hardy under sheltered conditions in the British Isles.

Waratahs are grown for cut flowers in South Africa, Israel and California as well as in their native south-eastern Australia.

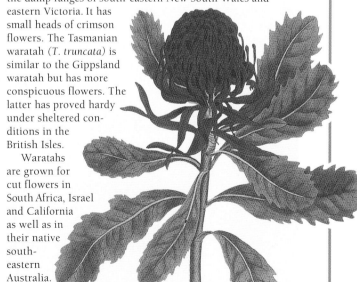

Telopea speciosissima

Rosa foetida bicolor

Ribes sanguineum

Rondeletia amoena

RIBES
sanguineum
FLOWERING CURRANT

This deciduous shrub is native to the west coast of the USA. Growing to a height and spread of about 2 m (about 6 ft), it bears handsome sprays of spicily fragrant, dainty, rose-pink flowers in spring, followed in turn by blue-black berries. The dark green, toothed leaves are also aromatic. Fully to frost-hardy, *R. sanguineum* needs full sun and fertile, well-drained soil to thrive. Straggly plants should be pruned hard in winter or early spring. Propagate from hardwood cuttings taken in autumn/fall. There are several cultivars, differing in their precise shade of pink.

RONDELETIA
amoena
RONDELETIA, YELLOW-THROATED RONDELETIA

This erect, branching, evergreen shrub is native to Central America. Growing to a height and spread of 2 m (about 6 ft), it is grown for the

Rosa glauca

dense, rounded clusters of pink, tubular, scented flowers it bears in spring. It has dark green, oval leaves. Half-hardy, it does best in a fertile, well-drained soil in full light or partial shade. Keep potted specimens well watered in full growth. Prune back annually in early spring, taking flowered shoots back to within a few nodes of the previous year's growth. Propagate from seed in spring or semi-ripe cuttings in summer.

ROSA
ROSA

The rose is perhaps the best loved of all flowers, and it is prosaic to describe the genus as one of late spring or summer flowering deciduous shrubs, with prickly branches, pinnate leaves and terminal inflorescences; the flowers being (in wild roses) almost always 5 petalled, usually pale pink or white, sometimes red, purple or yellow; often, although by no means always, fragrant; and followed by red or orange fruits called 'hips'. Such a description does not account for the charm of the flowers, which has led gardeners to develop many thousands of hybrids and garden cultivars, often flowering intermittently from late spring or early summer until the autumn/fall. Most have many more petals than 5, which are arranged in a variety of flower forms, and in a much wider variety of colours: every shade of red and pink, white, yellow, orange, mauve, purple, coral; everything that is but true blue; many cultivars feature blends and variegations of two or more colours. Scent is variable, some cultivars offering intense fragrance, others virtually none. The plants range from only a few centimetres (about an inch) tall to giant, long limbed plants which are always treated in gardens as climbing plants and so are included in this book in the chapter on climbers. Names come and go from the catalogues with alarming speed: and we shall here simply list the most important classes accepted by the World Federation of Rose Societies, illustrating a typical variety or two of each, and departing from strict alphabetical order to place them

roughly in their historical sequence. Some of the Chinese species and their hybrids are half-hardy, but most roses are fully hardy. They all prefer sun and rich, well-drained soil. Pruning consists of removing weak or elderly branches and shortening the rest, and is carried out either immediately after bloom (for spring-only types) or in winter (for 'repeat-flowering' types). Aphids, caterpillars, scale insects, mildew, black spot, rust, and various virus diseases may prove bothersome, and it is important to seek the guidance of an experienced grower as to which varieties are most resistant in one's local conditions. Roses are normally propagated by budding in summer, although many of the strongest varieties grow readily from cuttings taken in late summer or autumn/fall.

WILD ROSES

There are between one and two hundred species of *Rosa*, distributed very widely throughout the northern hemisphere. All tend to be variable and to interbreed freely, hence the uncertainty in the number. They are mostly arching shrubs, some climbers, and probably about half are garden-worthy. We describe only a few, to give an idea of the range.

R. foetida
AUSTRIAN OR PERSIAN BRIAR

This deciduous, rather rangy 1.5 m (about 4½ ft) tall shrub from Iran is of great historical importance as the chief ancestor of the modern yellow garden roses. It comes in two forms: *R. f. lutea*, the Austrian Yellow, with brilliant deep yellow flowers about 8 cm (about 3 in) across; and *R. f. bicolor*, the Austrian Copper, identical except for its brilliant orange-red petals with yellow reverses. Both flower in late spring and have a strong, sharp scent which many dislike—hence the name *foetida* meaning 'smelly'. The name Austrian briar comes from the rose having been introduced in northern Europe from Austria in the sixteenth century. There is a double yellow version known as 'Persian Yellow', introduced from Iran in 1837. All forms are frost-hardy but rather susceptible to black spot.

R. glauca
syn. R. rubrifolia

This 2–3 m (about 6–9 ft) tall, arching shrub from central Europe is grown mainly for its decorative grey foliage. It is plum-tinted when young and when the plant is grown in full sun; it is much sought after by flower arrangers. The small pink, late spring flowers are rather fleeting and of less account, but the red-brown hips are generously borne and decorative. Fully hardy, most forms are thornless or mostly so.

Rosa moyesii

Rosa pimpinellifolia

Rosa rugosa

Rosa gallica 'Cardinal Richelieu'

Rosa virginiana

R. moyesii

This tall, deciduous shrub from China is grown both for the deep red colour of its spring flowers and the spectacular display of large, bottle-shaped scarlet hips in autumn/fall. It is a gawky grower to about 3 m (about 9 ft), and several more compact selected forms have been introduced, the best known of which is the 2 m (about 6 ft) tall and wide 'Geranium'. All are fully hardy.

R. pimpinellifolia
syn. R. spinossissima
BURNET ROSE

Native to northern Europe, including the British Isles, this densely thicketing, fully hardy shrub grows to about 1 m (about 3 ft) high. It has many straight prickles and fern-like leaves (their resemblance to salad burnet gives rise to both its common and scientific names). The fragrant, 5 cm (about 2 in) wide flowers are borne in spring and are very variable in colour, from white through pale yellow, and pale pink to purple. Black hips follow in autumn/fall, when the leaves assume muted tints. Double-flowered varieties have been cultivated since the eighteenth century, and in re-

cent years the species has been used in the breeding of extremely frost-resistant garden roses.

R. rugosa
JAPANESE ROSE, RAMANAS ROSE

This 1.5–2 m (about 4 1/2–6 ft) tall, densely thicketing (and very thorny) rose from Japan, Korea and northern China is one of the very best of all flowering shrubs. It is fully hardy, densely furnished with bright green, quilted (rugose) leaves and bearing flowers from spring to autumn/fall. These are about 10 cm (about 4 in) across in the best forms, and may be white, pink or violet. They are scented of cloves, and followed by 2 cm (about 1 in) globular hips. The foliage colours clear yellow in autumn/fall. In the wild it grows within sight of the sea, and is invaluable for seaside gardens and sandy soil. It is perhaps the best of all roses for hedging. There are a number of garden varieties with single and double flowers. The species has entered into the breeding lines of modern shrub roses and climbers, giving them great resistance to disease and cold.

R. virginiana

This 1.5 m (about 4 1/2 ft) tall, clump-forming, late spring bloom-

ing shrub from eastern North America is one of the most desirable of Wild roses. The leaves are glossy and dark green. The bright pink or white flowers, 8 cm (about 3 in) across, are borne in small clusters. The leaves colour brilliantly in autumn/fall, and there is usually a lavish display of orange-red hips. It is fully hardy.

OLD GARDEN ROSES

These are the groups which were developed before the rather arbitrary date 1867, when 'La France', first of the hybrid Teas (large-flowered bush roses) was introduced. They fall into two main groups: the old European roses, mainly derived from the Mediterranean species R. gallica and spring or early summer flowering only, and including the Gallicas, Albas, Damasks, Centifolias and Moss roses; and those which were bred from crosses of these with repeat-flowering roses

from China, bred there from R. chinensis. These include the China roses, the Teas, Bourbons, Portlands, and Hybrid Perpetuals as well as the Noisettes, most of which are climbers.

R. gallica and varieties
GALLICA ROSES

Derived directly from R. gallica, these varieties are mainly upright bushes, growing to about 1.2 m (about 3 1/2 ft) high and a bit less wide, with small prickled, rough-textured leaves and flowers in shades of pink, crimson and purple, often striped or blended. The flowers are usually about 8 cm (about 3 in) wide, carried erect, and mainly very fragrant. The double varieties open flat and often 'quartered', a style of flower common in all the European old roses. Fully hardy, they are early summer flowering only. Mildew may be a problem.

Damask roses
syn. *R. damascena*

These are thought to have originated as hybrids between *R. gallica* and the otherwise insignificant *R. phoenecia*. They are rather lax growing shrubs from 1.2–2 m (about 3¹/₂–6 ft) in height, with matt-textured light green leaves and flowers in shades of pink or white. Most are very fragrant. The majority flower in summer only, although there is a small group called Autumn Damasks which repeat sparingly in autumn/fall. All are fully hardy.

Alba roses

These derive from *R. alba*, not a true species but thought to be of hybrid origin. They are strong, prickly bushes, usually about 2 m (about 6 ft) tall and wide, with grey-green leaves and flowers in refined shades of white or pink, almost always very fragrant. Fully hardy, they need only very light pruning.

Centifolia or Provence roses
syn. *R. centifolia*, *R. provincialis*, cabbage roses

These are of garden origin, and make floppy bushes, usually from 1.5–2 m (about 4¹/₂–6 ft) tall, with coarsely toothed leaves, many sharp prickles, and nodding, very double flowers in white or pink; a few show deeper tones. The term cabbage roses comes from the globular flower shape. Fully hardy, they are intensely fragrant. They benefit from discreet staking to control their lax habit.

Moss roses
syn. *R. centifolia muscosa*

These arose mainly as sports of Centifolia varieties, although some are forms of the Damask roses. They resemble their parents except for the strongly developed, resinous glands on the sepals, which resemble fragrant moss. They are available in shades of white through crimson, and a few are sparingly repeat flowering.

They were great favourites in Victorian times. Most are fully hardy.

R. chinensis and varieties
CHINA ROSES

Introduced from China at the end of the eighteenth century, the Chinas are mainly compact shrubs, from 50 cm–1.2 m (about 20 in–3¹/₂ ft) tall, with distinctively pointed leaves. They flower very continuously from spring to autumn/fall; many will flower all year in frost-free climates. The flowers are usually about 5 cm (about 2 in) wide and carried in clusters. They come in shades of true red or pink, and the flowers become deeper in colour as they age; most are only mildly fragrant. Half to frost hardy, they are pruned in winter.

Tea roses
syn. *R. odorata*

The Teas, so called because of a fancied resemblance between their

scent and that of freshly prepared tea leaves, are thought to have been derived in China from crosses between *R. chinensis* and the climbing rose *R. gigantea*. They are mainly bushes growing to about 1.5 m (about 4¹/₂ ft) high and wide (taller in mild climates) although some are climbers. Leaves are smooth and often glossy. Flowers are large, to 12 cm (about 5 in), usually carried singly on rather weak flower stalks, and borne almost all year in mild climates; from late spring to autumn/fall elsewhere. They are of elegant form, and mainly in delicate shades of pink, white, apricot or yellow. Few are more than half-hardy. Prized by Victorian gardeners, they are outstanding in sub-tropical climates.

Bourbon roses

Derived originally from crosses between China roses and Damasks, these are mainly fully hardy, arch-

Rosa 'Crested Moss' (Moss)

Rosa 'Celeste' (Alba)

Rosa damascena 'Kazanlik'

Rosa 'Coupe d'Hébé' (Bourbon)

Rosa 'Monsieur Tillier' (Tea)

Rosa chinensis

Rosa centifolia 'Bullata'

ing shrubs about 1.5 m (about 4½ ft) tall; a few are best treated as climbers. Flowers are mainly double, opening cupped or flat, and very fragrant. They are available in shades from white to red and purple. Most varieties are repeat flowering, although some are not very generous about it. Foliage is smooth, and the stems only lightly armed with prickles.

Portland roses

Derived from crosses between the gallica types and China roses, the portlands are mostly erect shrubs about 1.2 m (about 3½ ft) tall, with luxuriant, smooth leaves and 10–12 cm (about 4–5 in) wide flowers, usually fully double and quartered, in shades of white, pink, red or purple. Fully hardy, they are repeat blooming, although the amount of autumn/ fall bloom depends on how generously the bushes are fertilized and watered.

Hybrid Perpetual roses

These are derived from crosses of all the old types, and were the leading garden roses from about 1840 until World War I; few of the many thousands of varieties then raised are available now. They are mostly tall shrubs, to 2 m (about 6 ft), with long lax branches which may be bent over horizontally and tied down to short stakes to create a great mass of summer flowers. Whether there will be a comparable autumn/fall show depends on the variety; many are distinctly stingy unless very generously manured, and the term 'perpetual' is nurseryman's salesmanship. The flowers range from white through pink to crimson and purple, and most varieties are very large in flower—to 15 cm (about 6 in) or slightly more—and fragrant.

MODERN GARDEN ROSES

These include the types developed since the 1870s, and represent the bulk of roses grown today. They are classed as Bush roses (either large or cluster flowered) which make compact, upright bushes about 1 m (about 3 ft) tall (although often rather more in mild climates) and flower from late spring to autumn/ fall; Shrub roses, which are taller, less upright growers, mostly repeat-flowering; Miniatures, which are repeat-flowering bushes growing only about 30 cm (about 12 in) tall or less, with leaves and flowers reduced in proportion; and Climbers, which may or may not be repeat flowering.

Large-flowered bush roses
syn. Hybrid Tea roses

Derived originally from crosses between Hybrid Perpetuals and Tea roses, but also incorporating the blood of R. foetida and one or two

other species, these are perhaps the most important of all classes of roses. They are mainly upright bushes, displaying large, 12–18 cm (about 5–7½ in), flowers singly on strong stems from late spring or early summer to autumn/fall, and are pre-eminent for cutting. Growth varies from 1 m (about 3 ft) to twice that, depending on climate and conditions. Most are fully hardy, although some winter protection will still be needed in extreme winter climates such as those of the mid-western USA. The range of colours is enormous; just about everything but blue and bright green is available. Fragrance is variable, some varieties being very richly scented, others almost scentless. So is vigour and resistance to disease, and local knowledge should be sought in selecting varieties.

Polyantha roses

Mainly of historical importance now, these dwarf bushes grow to about 35 cm (about 14 in) tall. They bear small, scentless flowers in large clusters from late spring to autumn/ fall. They are available in shades from white through pink and salmon to red. Mildew may be a problem. The only variety to have retained general favour is the lovely pale pink 'Cécile Brünner'.

Cluster-flowered bush roses
syn. Floribunda roses, Hybrid Polyantha roses

Originated in the 1920s from crosses between large-flowered bush roses and polyanthas, the cluster roses rival the large-flowered roses in popularity, and interbreeding between the two has led to the division becoming rather indistinct; they can be mingled freely in beds if one so chooses. The cluster types are generally a little shorter in growth, and bear smaller blooms in clusters of 5 to 20 or so from early summer to autumn/fall. The individual flowers range from 6–10 cm (about 2½– 4 in), and can be single to fully double, informally shaped or in the high-centred form traditional for the large-flowered roses. Most are excellent for cutting. They are available in the full range of colours, but strong fragrance is exceptional. The best varieties are strongly disease resistant and fully hardy.

Patio roses
syn. Dwarf Floribunda roses

These are not a recognised class, but are becoming very popular. They are short-growing, cluster-flowered bush roses, usually about 50 cm (about 20 in) tall, but otherwise resemble the taller-flowered varieties. They are useful for the front of a mixed rose bed, for small spaces, or for growing in pots, but their stems are rarely long enough for cutting.

Rosa 'Peace' (Large-flowered)

Rosa 'Iceberg' (Cluster-flowered)

Rosa 'Jaques Cartier' (Portland)

Rosa 'Général Jacqueminot' (Hybrid Perpetual)

Rosa 'Cécile Brünner' (Polyantha)

Rosa 'Marlena' (Patio)

Rosa 'Flower Carpet' (Ground cover)

Rothmannia globosa

Rosa 'Rise 'n Shine' (Miniature)

Russelia juncea

Ruscus aculeatus

Miniature roses
syn. Fairy roses, *R. chinensis minima*

Derived originally from exceptionally dwarf China roses crossed with bush roses, the Miniatures are scaled down bush roses, usually growing to about 35 cm (about 14 in) with flowers about 3 cm (about 1½ in) wide. The bushes are smaller if propagated from cuttings, although budded plants, which tend to grow larger, to about 50 cm (about 20 in). Bushes grown from cuttings are excellent for growing in containers and rockeries; the larger, budded plants are useful for giving touches of low, bright colour in the garden. All the usual bush rose colours are available, but few varieties have much in the way of scent. They are usually very free and continuous in bloom, and delightful for small flower arrangements. Most are fully hardy.

Modern shrub roses

These are something of a mixed bag, with several sub-groups, but most are too tall and robust for growing in beds in the usual way;

they are placed in the garden as other deciduous flowering shrubs are, and can be used to great effect in mixed borders. Among the recognised groups are the Hybrid Musks, large, arching bushes with sprays of very fragrant flowers resembling cluster-flowered roses; 'landscape roses', a fairly new group, mostly resembling the cluster roses in habit but claimed by their originators to be exceptionally easy to grow and needing no pruning; 'English roses', raised by the English grower David Austin who has sought to unite the grace and full petalled, scented flowers of the old European roses with the repeat flowering habit and brighter colours of the bush roses.

Ground cover roses

These are a very recent development, and are best thought of as prostrate or trailing shrub roses, which can be used as ground cover, although very few (as yet) are really sufficiently dense or evergreen enough to smother weeds. They have flowers resembling the smaller and more informal cluster roses. They

are fully hardy, and most varieties are repeat flowering. Few have much fragrance.

ROTHMANNIA
globosa
TREE GARDENIA, BELL GARDENIA

This erect and branching evergreen shrub is native to South Africa. In spring, it bears a profusion of creamy white, bell-shaped, scented flowers, followed by brown seed pods, among the dark green foliage. *R. globosa* does best in full light or partial shade and in a humus-rich, well-drained, neutral to acid soil. Water regularly and feed with an acid-based fertilizer and manure. Potted specimens should be watered well in full growth. Half-hardy, it grows to a height and spread of 5 m (about 15 ft). Propagate from semi-ripe cuttings in summer, or from seed in spring.

RUSCUS
aculeatus
BUTCHER'S BROOM, BOX HOLLY

A rough, erect, branching, evergreen shrub, *R. aculeatus* is native to northern Africa. In spring it bears tiny, star-shaped, green flowers, followed by bright red berries. The 'leaves' are actually extensions of the stem,

ending in spines and the flowers and fruit are borne in the centre, apparently on the leaves. Useful for dry, shady sites, it does well in sun or shade, and prefers a heavy, moist, alkaline soil. Fully hardy, it grows to a height of 75 cm (about 2½ ft) and a spread of 1 m (about 3 ft). Propagate by division in spring but remember that male plants will not bear fruit. Butcher's broom is so called because in days gone by, butchers used the brush of the spiky stems to brush down their chopping blocks.

RUSSELIA
juncea
syn. *R. equisetiformis*
CORAL PLANT

This erect, slender shrub is a native of Mexico. It is grown for the clusters of handsome, red, tubular flowers it bears all year round, set among tiny, green leaves. *R. juncea* does best in a light, humus-rich, well-drained soil and prefers a sunny spot. Fast-growing, it is well suited to spilling over a wall, or as a seaside specimen. It is frost-tender, and grows to a height and spread of just under 1 m (about 3 ft). Propagate from stem cuttings or by division in spring.

Rosa 'Buff Beauty' (Modern shrub)

SALVIA
africana-lutea

This bushy, evergreen shrub bears bi-labiate brown flowers, fading to red then brown. The foliage is soft, light-grey and aromatic. It does best in a sunny position with a well-drained, fertile soil. Propagate from softwood cuttings in spring and summer.

SAMBUCUS
nigra 'Aurea'

This bushy, deciduous shrub is grown for the creamy white, star-shaped, fragrant flowers it bears in early summer, followed by round, black berries. The yellow leaves are each composed of five yellow leaflets. It prefers a rich, well-drained soil and plenty of sun. Fully hardy, it grows to a height and spread of 6 m (about 18 ft). Propagate from suckers or from cuttings taken in late autumn/fall. Remove old flowerheads before they set seed.

SANTOLINA
chamaecyparissus
COTTON LAVENDER, LAVENDER COTTON

This low-spreading, deciduous shrub, native to mild, coastal areas of the Mediterranean, grows to a height and spread of 1 m (about 3 ft). It bears bright yellow, rounded flowerheads on long stalks in summer, set among oblong, greyish green leaves. Cotton lavender does best in a sunny spot in soil that is well drained but not too rich. Water from time to time and dead-head continually. Straggly old plants should be pruned to a neat rounded habit in early spring. Hardy, it grows to a height of 75 cm (about 30 in) with a spread of 1 m (about 3 ft). Propagate from semi-ripe cuttings in summer.

SENECIO
petasitis
VELVET GROUNDSEL

This erect, branching, evergreen shrub bears large, terminal panicles of sparsely petalled small, yellow flowers in mid-winter. The foliage is handsome and lobed. It prefers full sun in a protected position and a rich, moist, well-drained soil. It makes an excellent coastal garden shrub. Prune annually to keep its habit compact. Frost-tender, it grows to a height and spread of 1.5 m (about 4½ ft). Propagate from semi-ripe cuttings in summer.

SENNA
corymbosa
syn. *Cassia corymbosa*
AUTUMN CASSIA

This fast-growing shrub has light green foliage and large, dense clusters of bright yellow flowers that cover the shrub in autumn/fall. It grows to a height of 2.5 m (about 7½ ft) with a spread of 2 m (about 6 ft). Plant in ordinary garden soil in a sunny position. Propagate from cuttings.

SERRURIA
florida
BLUSHING BRIDE

This short-lived native of South Africa's Cape Mountains grows to a height and spread of 1.5 m (about 4½ ft). An erect, branching, evergreen shrub, it bears white silvery-centred flowers tinged with pink. The greyish green leaves are divided into soft, needle-like segments. It does best in an open, sunny position in a light, sandy, slightly acid, well-drained soil. Prune the plant from an early age to keep it compact and replace the plant every three years. Propagate from seed—germination will occur within a few weeks and the plant will flower the following year.

SESBANIA
grandiflora
SCARLET WISTERIA TREE, VEGETABLE HUMMING-BIRD

This evergreen grows fast to 5–8 m (15–24½ ft) tall and 4 m (about 12 ft) wide. In summer it bears large, red-pink, pea-like flowers amid green, fern-like leaves. Grow in moist, well-drained soil in a sunny spot. Prune after blooming. Propagate from seed or half-ripe cuttings in late autumn/fall.

Senna corymbosa

Sambucus nigra 'Aurea'

Salvia africana-lutea

Senecio petasitis

Santolina chamaecyparissus

Sesbania grandiflora

Serruria florida

SKIMMIA
japonica

This dense, round, evergreen shrub, native to the cooler parts of Asia, is resistant to air pollution, and so is a good choice for town gardens and parks. In early spring it bears clusters of tiny, white flowers. If male and female plants have been grown together, bright red berries will follow in summer and last well into autumn/fall. The leaves are aromatic, mid- to dark green and glossy. *S. japonica* prefers a well-drained, acid soil and shade or semi-shade—poor soil or too much sun will cause chlorosis. Fully hardy, it grows to a height and spread of 1.5 m (about 4½ ft). Propagate from cuttings in summer.

SOPHORA
prostrata

This native of New Zealand is much prized for the clusters of pea-shaped, pale yellow flowers that appear in summer amid small, oval leaflets. Frost-hardy, it prefers a rich, moist, well-drained soil, in a sunny position, and grows to a maximum height and spread of 2 m (about 6 ft). Propagate by scarified seed under glass in autumn/fall.

SPARMANNIA
africana
AFRICAN HEMP

This erect, spreading, evergreen shrub or small tree, native to southern Africa, bears clusters of delightful, white flowers all year round, amid large, heart-shaped, light green leaves. It is available in both single- and double-flowered types. It does best in fertile, well-drained soil. Water freely when in full growth, less so at other times. Prune hard every few years to control size. *S. africana* is frost-tender and it grows to a height and spread of just over 3 m (about 9 ft). Propagate from cuttings in spring. The genus is named after Dr Andes Sparmann, a Swedish naturalist aboard Captain Cook's historic second voyage.

SPARTIUM
junceum
SPANISH BROOM

This sparse, twiggy, almost leafless, deciduous shrub is native to southern Europe. In spring it bears long, showy spikes of bright yellow, pea-shaped flowers. The leaves are very small and sparse. *S. junceum* does best in a sunny spot in soil that is well-drained but not too rich. It is very suitable for a ground cover or as a hedge, especially in seaside areas. Prune in early spring to maintain a compact habit. Frost-hardy, it grows to a height and spread of 3 m (about 9 ft). Propagate from seed in autumn/fall. Plants are not very long lived, but are a good choice where a fast-growing plant is needed to fill in while slower growers are maturing.

SPIRAEA
SPIREA, MAYBUSH, GARLAND FLOWER, BRIDAL WREATH

Native to the northern hemisphere, these thick, often arching, deciduous or semi-evergreen shrubs are grown for their beautiful springtime bloom of pink, white or crimson flowers. Fully hardy, they do best in a fertile, moist, well-drained soil in full sun. A layering of manure in autumn/fall and early spring will help bring out the best quality bloom. Cut back spent heads to the old wood. Propagate from softwood cuttings in summer.

S. 'Anthony Waterer'

This fully hardy, upright, deciduous shrub bears crimson-pink flowers from late spring to early summer. It grows to a height and spread of 1 m (about 3 ft). The red foliage turns green as the shrub ages.

S. cantoniensis

This deciduous shrub, with arching, slender stems, is native to China and Japan. It grows to a height and spread of 2 m (about 6 ft) and is prized for its showy clusters of white flowers that appear in spring. These are set among narrow, diamond-shaped leaves with saw-toothed margins.

Spiraea cantoniensis

Sophora prostrata

Sparmannia africana (double)

Spiraea 'Anthony Waterer'

Spartium junceum

Skimmia japonica

Staphylea colchica

Sutherlandia frutescens

Streptosolen jamesonii

Spiraea vanhouttei

Spiraea thunbergii

S. thunbergii

Another native of Japan and China, *S. thunbergii* is a dense, deciduous shrub that bears clusters of single, white flowers in early spring. The leaves are narrow and long and turn orange in autumn/fall. It grows to a height and spread of 1 m (about 3 ft).

S. vanhouttei
BRIDAL WREATH

This compact, deciduous shrub bears dense clusters of white flowers amid dark green, diamond-shaped leaves in spring. It grows to a height of 3 m (about 9 ft) with a spread of 2 m (about 6 ft).

STAPHYLEA
colchica
BLADDER NUT

This deciduous, upright shrub is native to the Caucasus in Europe. From spring to early summer it bears delicate, erect, daffodil-like, trumpet-shaped flowers, set among serrated, trifoliate leaves. Pale green inflated pods follow the bloom. *S. colchica* does best in a moist, leaf-rich soil, and in a shaded spot in hotter areas. Fully hardy, it grows to a height and spread of 3 m (about 9 ft). Propagate from cuttings in summer or seed in autumn/fall.

STREPTOSOLEN
jamesonii
FIREBUSH, ORANGE BROWALLIA, MARMALADE BUSH

This rather lax, branching evergreen, a native of Colombia, bears terminal clusters of orange, phlox-like flowers in spring; a yellow variety is also available. It has narrow, oval leaves. Full sun suits it best and it will thrive in a well-drained, humus-rich soil. Water well in full growth, less at other times. Tip prune regularly when young to help develop its shape. *S. jamesonii* is ideal as a shrub border plant. Cut back flowered shoots after the bloom. Frost-tender, it grows to a height and spread of 2 m (about 6 ft). Propagate from softwood or semi-ripe cuttings in summer.

SUTHERLANDIA
frutescens
DUCK PLANT, CANCER BUSH

Originating in South Africa, this erect semi-evergreen shrub is extremely attractive but short lived. With an expansive habit and reaching up to 1.5 m (about 4½ ft) when potted, it is valued for its foliage, flowers and fruit. The vivid green, pinnate leaves are composed of up to 21 lance-shaped downy leaflets. In late spring, pendent deep red-orange flowers appear along slender stems, followed by inflated seed pods. Locate in full sun in fertile, well-drained soil. Prune dead stems back to ground level in winter. Propagate from seed or root cuttings in spring. It is prone to two-spotted mite.

SYMPHORICARPOS
SNOWBERRY, WAXBERRY

These showy, cold-climate shrubs are grown for the clusters of long-lasting, pink-tinted or puffy white berries that follow their spring bloom of small, bell-shaped flowers. Native to the colder areas of China and North America, their arching habit bends almost double under the weight of flowers and fruit. They are fully hardy and prefer filtered sun and a rich, acid soil. Propagate from softwood cuttings in summer or by division in autumn/fall.

S. orbiculatus
CORAL BERRY, INDIAN CURRANT

Native to North America, this erect, slender, deciduous shrub bears white or pink flowers in late summer, set among dark green, oval leaves that turn bronze in autumn/fall. A variegated form is also available. Round, purple-red berries follow the bloom. It grows to a height and spread of 1–1.5 m (about 3–4½ ft).

Syringa 'Maréchal Foch'

Syringa × *persica*

Syringa 'Souvenir de Louis Spaëth'

Tamarix gallica

Symphoricarpos rivularis

S. rivularis
syn. *S. albus* var. *rivularis*

This deciduous, thicketing shrub bears pink or white flowers in summer, appearing among dark green, rounded leaves. Large, white fruits follow. It grows to a height and spread of 1.5 m (about 4½ ft). There is a form with variegated leaves.

SYRINGA
LILAC

These vigorous, open, deciduous bushes, native to Europe and northeastern Asia, are much loved. They are grown for the delightful fragrance of their flowers, which form in dense panicles in any shade of red, pink, white, mauve, purple, or even yellow, most being cultivars of the Turkish *S. vulgaris*. The leaves are oval and medium sized. Lilacs are fully hardy, and require cold, dormant winter conditions to bloom the following spring. They do best in a deep, fertile, well-drained, preferably alkaline soil, in full sun.

Prune after flowering to maintain the shape. Dead-head for the first few years. Propagate by grafting or from softwood cuttings in summer. Grafted plants should be set with the graft union well below the soil surface.

S. 'Maréchal Foch'

This deciduous, bushy, upright shrub grows to a height and spread of 3 m (about 9 ft) and bears large panicles of fragrant, crimson-pink flowers in spring, among heart-shaped, mid-green leaves.

S. × persica
PERSIAN LILAC

Native to Afghanistan, *S. × persica* is a deciduous, bushy, compact shrub. In spring it bears profuse sprays of small, delightfully fragrant flowers set amid narrow, pointed, dark green leaves. It grows to a height and spread of just under 2 m (about 6 ft). It will grow in warmer winter climates than most lilacs.

S. 'Souvenir de Louis Spaëth'

In late spring, this lilac shrub bears long, thin panicles of sweet-smelling, deep purple-red flowers set among dark green, heart-shaped leaves. It grows to a height and spread of 5 m (about 15 ft).

TAMARIX
TAMARISK

The deciduous shrubs and small trees of this genus, native to the deserts and salty areas of Europe, Africa and Asia, are grown for their impressive foliage and the panicles of small flowers they bear. Being wind and salt resistant, these shrubs do particularly well in exposed, coastal positions, and make excellent hedges. They do best in a fertile, well-drained soil in a sunny position. All are frost-hardy. Early spring-flowering species should be pruned back to about half, once the flowerheads are spent, while late spring- and summer-flowering species are best pruned in winter. Propagate from semi-hardwood cuttings in late summer or from hardwood cuttings in late autumn/fall.

T. gallica
FRENCH TAMARISK

Native to the Canary Islands and Sicily, this deciduous, irregularly branched, upright shrub grows to a height of 4 m (about 12 ft) with a spread of 6 m (about 18 ft). In spring and summer, it bears terminal racemes of pink, star-shaped flowers set amid tiny, blue-grey leaves. *T. gallica* is frost-hardy.

T. parviflora

This graceful, arching, deciduous shrub grows to a height and spread of 4 m (about 12 ft). Native to Mediterranean Europe, it bears terminal racemes of inconspicuous, pink flowers, set amid tiny, blue-green, sessile leaves. *T. parviflora* is frost-hardy.

TECOMA
stans
syn. *Bignonia stans, Stenolobium stans*
YELLOW ELDER, YELLOW BELLS

Native to Central America, this erect, branching, evergreen shrub grows to a height of 5 m (about 15 ft) with a spread of 3 m (about 9 ft). It bears gorgeous, golden yellow, tubular flowers right through the warmer months, set among fern-like leaves with narrow leaflets. Half-hardy, it thrives in a rich, moist, well-drained soil and does best in a protected, sunny position. Potted plants require an occasional watering when in full growth. Prune *T. stans* annually after blooming to maintain its habit. Propagate from soft-tip or semi-hardwood cuttings in summer.

TECOMARIA
capensis
syn. *Tecoma capensis*
FIRE FLOWER, CAPE HONEYSUCKLE

This evergreen, shrubby climber can be grown either as a shrub or climber. It bears tubular, fiery orange-red flowers in spring to summer, set among saw-toothed, dark green leaflets. Resistant to drought and salt, it does well in coastal areas, growing to a height and spread of 2–3 m (about 6–9 ft). *T. capensis* is half-hardy. It does best in fertile, well-drained soil and likes an open, sunny position. It will climb if not pruned hard annually. Crowded stems should be thinned out in spring. Propagate from semi-ripe cuttings in summer or from seed in spring. Yellow, dark red and pink forms are available.

TELOPEA
WARATAH

This is a genus of Australian bushy, tree-like shrubs, grown for their striking flowerheads. These consist of multiple, curved florets, surrounded by common bracts. Waratahs can be difficult to grow, and only really do well in a damp, sandy, neutral to acid loam, covered in leafy mulch. Half-hardy, they do best in dappled shade, though they will tolerate full sun. Potted specimens should be watered well in full growth, not so much at other times. Prune regularly to keep them compact. Propagate by layering in winter or from seed in spring. In its natural state in the Australian bush, its bright spring flowers can be easily spotted from a distance, hence the Aboriginal name of 'Waratah', meaning 'seen from afar';

the botanical name has the same significance.

T. 'Shady Lady'

This evergreen shrub grows fast to a height and spread of 3 m (about 9 ft). In spring, it bears red flowerheads up to 15 cm (about 6 in) across at the ends of the branches. These are set amid dark green, leathery, oval leaves.

T. speciosissima
NEW SOUTH WALES WARATAH

This upright, bushy, evergreen shrub bears red, globular heads 15 cm (about 6 in) across, surrounded by bright red bracts in spring and early summer. It has leathery, wedge- to oblong-shaped leaves with saw-toothed margins. It grows to a height and spread of just under 3 m (about 9 ft). *T. speciosissima* is native to and the floral emblem of the state of New South Wales, Australia. Recently, white and pink-flowered cultivars have become available.

TETRAPANAX
papyriferus
syn. *Fatsia papyrifera*
RICE PAPER PLANT

This upright, evergreen, branching shrub is grown mainly for its large, felted, deeply lobed leaves, but the creamy white flowers it bears in late summer and autumn/fall, and the small black berries that follow, are added attractions. *T. papyriferus* is the only species in the genus. It prefers a humus-rich, moist but well-drained soil and does well in either full sun or partial shade. It tolerates salt-laden winds and so is excellent for coastal gardens. Too large for pots, it is suitable for courtyards. Half-hardy, it grows to a height of 4 m (about 12 ft) with a spread of 5 m (about 15 ft). Propagate from suckers or seed in early spring, and prune as and when needed to control the plant's size.

Tetrapanax papyriferus

Tecomaria capensis

Telopea 'Shady Lady'

Telopea speciosissima

Tamarix parviflora

Tecoma stans

Thevetia peruviana

Tetratheca ciliata

Teucrium fruticans

Thuja occidentalis 'Rheingold'

Thomasia macrocarpa

Thryptomene saxicola

TETRATHECA
ciliata
PINK EYE, PINK BELLS

A compact, evergreen shrub, *T. ciliata* is native to the southern and south-eastern states of Australia. In winter and spring it bears delightful, four-petalled, pinkish purple flowers with black centres, amid small, rounded leaves arranged in whorls of three. It prefers a light, well-drained, acid soil in a shady, protected position. Add a leaf-mould or growing carpet mulch for best results. Half-hardy, it grows to a height and spread of 1 m (about 3 ft). Propagate from cuttings in late summer or autumn/fall, or from seed in spring.

TEUCRIUM
fruticans
BUSH GERMANDER

Native to southern Europe, this upright evergreen grows to a height and spread of around 1.5 m (about 4¹/₂ ft). It is mostly enjoyed for the attractive, blue, tubular, double-

lipped flowers it bears in spring, set among aromatic, oval, slivery grey leaves. Half- to frost-hardy, it needs a well-drained soil and full sun. Trim old flowerheads to promote new growth. *T. fruticans* makes a good, low, neat hedge, and does well in seaside gardens. Propagate from softwood or semi-ripe cuttings in summer.

THEVETIA
peruviana
syn. *T. neriifolia*
YELLOW OLEANDER

Native to tropical America, this upright, spreading evergreen bears fragrant, yellow, petunia-like flowers from winter to summer, set among spidery, short-stemmed, lance-shaped leaves. Frost-tender, it does best in well-watered, well-drained, sandy soil, in full sun. Potted plants should be watered moderately in full growth, less at other times. Tip young stems in winter to promote branching. Propagate from semi-ripe cuttings in summer, or from seed in spring. *T.*

peruviana is sometimes called the 'be-still bush' because of the distinctive movement of its leaves in a breeze. The plant is intensely poisonous and should not be planted where it might pose a danger to children.

THOMASIA
PAPER FLOWER

These upright, rounding, evergreen natives of southern and south-eastern Australia are grown for their summer bloom of pinkish purple, bell-shaped flowers. Their leaves are broadly oblong and greyish green. They do best in a well-drained soil in full sun, except in very hot areas, where partial shade is best. A high tolerance to salt makes them popular in seaside gardens. There are several species, all very alike: *T. macrocarpa* and *T. petalocalyx* are typical. Maintain their shape by pruning lightly after flowering. Frost-hardy, they grow to a height of 80 cm (about 32 in) and a spread of 1 m (about 3 ft). Propagate from cuttings in autumn/fall or from scarified seed.

THRYPTOMENE
saxicola
syn. *T.* 'Paynei'
ROCK THRYPTOMENE

This dense, rounded, evergreen shrub comes from the state of Western Australia. In winter and spring it bears masses of tiny, white flowers tipped with pink. Its small, oval leaves are aromatic when crushed. *T. saxicola* prefers a well-drained, slightly acid soil in full sun to partial shade. Tip prune all over after flowering to maintain its shape. Give it a regular, light watering. Half-hardy (except when young), it grows to a height of 1 m (about 3 ft) and spread of 1.5 m (about 4¹/₂ ft). Propagate from semi-hardwood cuttings in the warmer months.

THUJA
occidentalis 'Rheingold'
AMERICAN ARBOR-VITAE, NORTHERN WHITE CEDAR

This attractive little conifer grows slowly to a height of 1–2 m (about 3–6 ft) and a spread of 1.5–3 m (about 4¹/₂–9 ft). It is grown for its rounded habit and its yellow, summer foliage that turns bronze in winter. Fully hardy, it tolerates most types of soil but prefers a shady position. Prune to shape or to restrict size. Propagate from hardwood cuttings taken from a young plant and strike in humid conditions, between late autumn/fall and late winter.

TIBOUCHINA
urvilleana
syn. *T. semidecandra*
GLORY BUSH, LASIANDRA

This upright, branching native of South America is grown for the delightful clusters of purple flowers it bears from summer to early winter, set among prominently veined, hairy, oval leaves. It needs a rich, well-drained, acid soil and full sun. In very hot areas it will do reasonably well in dappled shade. To promote bushiness, pinch out growing tips regularly. Keep the soil moist during spring and summer. Frost-tender, *T. urvilleana* grows to a height of 3 m (about 9 ft) with a spread of 2 m (about 6 ft). Propagate from greenwood or semi-ripe cuttings in late spring or summer. There are several cultivars available, with flowers in varying shades of purple or strong pink.

VERTICORDIA
plumosa
FEATHER FLOWER

This small, open shrub is grown for the delightful, pink show of flowers it bears in spring. These appear singly or in spikes towards the ends of its branches amid narrow, grey-green leaves. Native to the state of Western Australia, *V. plumosa* does best in a protected, partly shaded position in a light to medium, well-drained soil. Half-hardy, it grows to a height and spread of just under 1 m (about 3 ft). Propagate from semi-ripe tip cuttings. The genus name is taken from the Latin root, *Verticordia*: to turn a heart, and indeed the feather flower has earned its rightful place in the cut-flower industry.

VIBURNUM
SNOWBALL TREE, CRANBERRY BUSH, GUELDER ROSE, LAURUSTINUS

These deciduous or evergreen shrubs and trees are grown for their fragrant flowers, fruits and beautiful autumn/fall foliage. Fully to frost-hardy, the hundred-odd species and many more varieties grow best in sun or semi-shade in a rich, moist, well-drained soil. Remove spent flowerheads regularly and prune annually to maintain shape. Propagate from cuttings in summer or from seed in autumn/fall. Mildew and spider mite may cause problems.

V. × burkwoodii
BURKWOOD VIBURNUM

This bushy, open, semi-evergreen shrub bears wide, globular clusters of scented flowers that open pink, but fade to white. Its oval, dark green leaves turn red in autumn/fall. Fully hardy, it grows to a height and spread of 2.5 m (about 7 ft).

V. carlesii
KOREAN VIBURNUM

This upright, deciduous shrub grows to a height and spread of just over 1 m (about 3 ft). In spring, it bears fragrant, snow-white and pink flowers, followed by round, black berries. Its dull green, woolly, oval leaves turn red in autumn/fall.

V. farreri
syn. *V. fragrans*

A deciduous shrub from western China, bearing the name of the great plant explorer who discovered it. It is a 3 m (about 9 ft) tall deciduous, frost-hardy shrub whose leaves turn red in the autumn/fall. Its main feature is the fragrance of its clustered pale pink flowers which are reliably borne all through the winter.

Viburnum × burkwoodii

Viburnum farreri

Viburnum carlesii

Verticordia plumosa

Tibouchina urvilleana

Viburnum tinus

Viminaria juncea

Viburnum plicatum 'Mariesii'

Vitex agnus-castus

V. opulus 'Sterile'
syn. V. o. 'Roseum'
GUELDER ROSE

This vigorous, bushy, deciduous
shrub, native to Europe, Asia and
northern Africa, grows to a height
and spread of 4 m (about 12 ft). In
spring and early summer, it bears
flattened heads of flowers that are
green at first and later turn white.
The oval, green leaves turn red in
autumn/fall. The wild form has lacy
flowerheads followed by berries.

V. plicatum 'Mariesii'

In late spring and early summer,
this bushy, deciduous shrub bears
large, rounded heads of flowers
with white bracts. The dark green
leaves turn red in autumn/fall. Fully
hardy, it grows to a height of 3 m
(about 9 ft) and a spread of 4 m
(about 12 ft).

V. tinus
LAURUSTINUS

This bushy, evergreen shrub bears
clusters of honeysuckle-fragrant,
pinkish white flowers in winter, set
amid oval, dark green, glossy leaves.
Frost-hardy, it grows to a height
and spread of 3 m (about 9 ft).
Recommended as a hedge plant,
although not for enclosed courtyards where the smell of the fallen
leaves can be offensive.

VIMINARIA
juncea
syn. V. denudata
GOLDEN SPRAY, AUSTRALIAN BLOOM

This evergreen shrub is an Australian native. It grows to a height of 5
m (about 15 ft) with a spread of 2 m
(about 6 ft). It bears many yellow,
pea-shaped flowers in long sprays
in summer. The small, trifoliate
leaves are very sparse. It prefers a
light to medium, well-drained soil
with plenty of water and full sun,
but will also tolerate shady conditions. Propagate from scarified seed.

VITEX
agnus-castus
CHASTE TREE

Native to Europe and Asia, *V. agnus-
castus* grows to a height and spread of
2–3 m (about 6–9 ft). This open,
deciduous, spreading shrub bears
dense, upright clusters of small, dark
blue or white flowers in late summer. The grey-green, compound
leaves are aromatic. It is frost- to
half-hardy and prefers full sun and
well-drained soil. It is best propagated from semi-ripe cuttings in
summer or from seed in spring.

WEIGELA
FAIRY TRUMPETS, WEIGELA

These deciduous, fountain-shaped
shrubs bear brilliant, though short-
lived, masses of pink, white or red
trumpet flowers in the warmer
months. However, their leaves fall
early in autumn/fall without
colouring, leaving the branches
bare for most of the winter. They
do best in a sunny position in a
rich, well-drained soil. Water them
well during the growing season and
prune out older branches after flowering. Propagate from softwood
cuttings in summer.

Viburnum opulus 'Sterile'

W. florida

A native of China and Korea, this deciduous, arching shrub bears delightful, deep rose-pink, trumpet-shaped flowers in late spring and early summer. The leaves are serrated, mid-green, small and oval. Fully hardy, it grows to a height and spread of 2.5 m (about 7 ft).

W. florida 'Eva Ratke'

This cultivar bears crimson flowers from purplish red buds from late spring to early summer. Fully hardy, it grows 1.5 m (about 4½ ft) tall and wide with a dense, erect habit.

W. florida 'Variegata'

In late spring and early summer, this cultivar bears an abundance of funnel-shaped, pink flowers, set among green leaves with creamy white margins.

WESTRINGIA

COAST ROSEMARY

These evergreen Australian shrubs are grown for their flowers and overall appearance. While they do grow fast—an advantage for those who wish to quickly establish a garden—they are short lived. Moderately frost-hardy, they do best in a sunny position in a fertile, well-drained soil. Potted plants are best watered regularly during full growth, less at other times. Propagate from seed in spring or from semi-ripe cuttings in late summer.

W. fruticosa
syn. W. rosmariniformis
MORNING LIGHT, COAST ROSEMARY

This rounded, compact, evergreen shrub grows to a height and spread of 1.5 m (about 4½ ft). Native to New South Wales and Queensland, Australia, it is grown for the delicate, white to pale mauve flowers it bears in spring, set among light, greyish green, broad leaves arranged in whorls of four.

W. grandifolia
COAST ROSEMARY

This, the showiest species of the genus, bears large white or mauve flowers in spring (though it may flower at any time). An evergreen shrub, it bears thin, lance-shaped leaves, close together in whorls of three. It grows to a rounded, compact habit with a height and spread of 1.5 m (about 4½ ft).

WIGANDIA

These striking, evergreen shrubs from Central to South America have huge, oval to heart-shaped, scalloped, deep green leaves with white, stinging hairs beneath. The leaves are 45 cm (about 18 in) long and the bushes grow to a height of 3 m (about 9 ft) but can be pruned. Violet-blue flowers appear in large, terminal, one-sided sprays from spring to autumn/fall. W. caracasana from Venezuela is the best known of the half-a-dozen species. Plant in moist but well-drained soil in full light. Frost-tender, they prefer temperatures above 7°C (about 44°F). They can be grown in pots and need abundant water during the growth period, and moderate amounts at other times. Propagate from seed or softwood cuttings in spring. Sometimes whitefly is a problem.

Weigela florida

Westringia fruticosa

Weigela florida 'Eva Ratke'

Westringia grandifolia

Wigandia caracasana

Weigela florida 'Variegata'

CHAPTER 4

Trees

*T*he backbone of a garden, trees are fundamental to the landscape. Whatever their size, these plants form the basis of the type of garden being aimed for, be it a lush rainforest atmosphere, a cold country woodland or a single specimen highlight for a small courtyard.

A tree is a plant, either broad leafed or coniferous, with a single, woody stem reaching to a height of at least 4 m (about 12 ft) when mature. Palms and tree ferns, although they do not have the same type of woody stem, are generally included for horticultural purposes because their growth habit and landscape uses are similar to that of trees.

Trees can form windbreaks in larger gardens, are invaluable as noise inhibitors, provide privacy from overlooking houses or unit buildings and soften the skyline in the urban environment.

They are growing structures in gardens, chosen for a particular purpose, though many will provide bonus points to add to their initial attractiveness as they mature. Trees planted to provide shade may well provide a horizontal branch to support a swing, or branches to form a climbing frame for adventurous children. Birds will soon inhabit suitable trees for nesting or food gathering among blossom and fruits while keeping a sharp eye on the insect population in the garden below.

Choosing the Right Tree

Never buy a tree on impulse. It is a permanent part of the garden structure, after all trees can take around 20 years to arrive at any semblance of maturity, so it is necessary to get the selection right first time. Take time before you go to the nursery, read as much as you can about a tree's growing habits such as its estimated mature height and spread, as well as its seasonal displays. What at first appears to be a bewildering choice will soon be whittled down to a couple of possible contenders for a particular spot in the garden.

Climate and soil requirements also need to be considered. It is preferable to grow a tree climatically suited to your area. If you're new to a neighbourhood, walk through the parks and look over garden fences to see which trees are growing well.

Evergreen or Deciduous?

Trees are most often sought after for their shade value. Consider then the choice of evergreen or deciduous. Perhaps an evergreen is what's needed in a screening situation or in the tropics where year-round sun protection over a patio is needed. A deciduous tree will provide summer shade and winter sun. There is an ever changing display each season, ranging from the fine tracery of bare branches in winter to soft green new spring growth, a welcoming dense cover in summer then a wonderful autumn/fall display, often with flowers and colourful fruit as well.

The colourful contribution trees make to the landscape often comes because of their foliage colour. Consider the soft blue-grey foliage of some of the conifers and eucalypt species or *Pyrus salicifolia* which meld so well with the

Shape and height are two important considerations when selecting trees.

white and pastel blues and pinks favoured by cottage gardeners. Then there's the variegated foliaged trees which provide a welcome accent in an otherwise green landscape, but it's the intensity of yellow/orange/red tones that really capture a gardener's heart.

Cold country gardeners have any number of trees in all sizes and shapes from which to make a rich display of colour before winter sets in. Temperate gardeners are not so fortunate. However, beautiful displays can be assured with *Nyssa sylvatica*, *Ginkgo biloba* or in larger gardens the majestic *Liquidambar styraciflua*.

Getting the Proportions Right

For the home gardener, perhaps the most important consideration in choosing a particular tree is its mature height and spread. Proportion is the catchword here for both aesthetic and practical reasons. A large, dense tree planted too close to a house may shade it too well, making rooms very dark and cutting off any perspective view through the windows. It may also rob the surrounding garden of light and root room. In such a situation it may be better to choose a smaller, more openly branched tree which both frames the view and allows ample light into a room, for example *Cassia fistula*, *Betula pendula*, *Pistacia chinensis* or *Zelkova serrata*.

Planting

It takes a few years for a tree to become self-sufficient even though it may be quite large when planted out. New roots need time to establish to forage for nutrients and to anchor the plant. Consequently, all trees, but in particular those planted as specimen trees, need to be given great care in their early years. Before planting, check the tree will not be hindered above by overhead wires or that underground pipes will not be invaded by vigorous root systems.

Good drainage is essential as few plants will thrive with wet feet. Wide planting holes, ample surrounding soil cultivation and even raising the bed are some ways of overcoming a drainage problem, but if the soil is very heavy, the addition of gypsum or coarse sand may be required as well. As soil in the container and the surrounding garden soil are often quite different in texture, it's important to combine these two to allow new roots to venture easily into

Deciduous trees provide a delightful display of autumn/fall colour.

their new surrounding. Do this by digging a shallow (just a little deeper than the container) yet wide hole, at least twice the diameter of the root ball, and fill the base with a friable mixture composed of about half the existing soil and a rich humus mix. Carefully remove the plant from the container, taking special care not to damage the main trunk, and place the root ball in position, together with up to three stakes. At this point check that the roots are not tangled or wound round in circles. If they are they need to be gently teased out and straightened, otherwise they will continue in this circular fashion eventually causing the plant to wither. Continue to fill the hole with the soil mix firming it in and around the trunk by hand, but ensuring that the tree is planted only as deep as it was in the container. Once it is firmly in position water well to get rid of any remaining air pockets. The remaining soil mix can be used to form a raised circle around the plant. Then, to conserve moisture, a layer of organic mulch can be added. This mulch, weeds and low-growing ground covers should be kept well away from the trunk to discourage collar or other root rot fungus.

If planting in a lawn, cut away a circle of turf at least 1 m (about 3 ft) in diameter to ensure the tender roots of the newly planted tree will not have to compete with those of voracious lawn grasses. Keep the surface of this area well mulched to retain as much moisture as possible and to deter weeds competing for the available nutrients.

Trees need to be staked to ensure the leader, main trunk, is not damaged while still young and tender. Place the stakes in position at the time of planting, then attach the plant to these with tree ties or a length of old rag tied in a figure of eight to ensure the trunk remains steady when buffeted by strong winds. Don't use wire as it can cut into the trunk.

Deciduous trees are usually planted in the dormant state; evergreens, in temperate areas, are best planted out in autumn/fall while the soil is still warm. In colder areas, evergreens with new, tender growth will avoid frost damage if planted out in late spring.

Pruning

Trees rarely need pruning in maturity except after storm damage or for the removal of diseased branches, however young trees often benefit from being given a helping hand to balance their shape or to develop a higher branching system where they overhang a path. If noticed early enough unwanted new shoots can be rubbed off very easily by hand, a technique which doesn't leave unsightly scars on the often beautiful trunks of these majestic garden plants.

Acacia pycnantha

Abies procera 'Glauca'

Acacia dealbata

Acacia melanoxylon

Abies cephalonica

ABIES

SILVER FIR, BALSAM

These 40 diverse species of conical conifers are cold-climate ever-greens. Prized for their aromatic wood and sap, their usefulness to the timber and pharmaceutical industries has threatened many species with extinction. Their name comes from the Latin *abeo*, 'I rise': some attain majestic heights of 100 m (about 320 ft), growing 1 m (about 3 ft) a year. In autumn/fall the spiral branches show seed-bearing cones, not pendent but growing upright, which distin-guishes *Abies* from similar conifers like the spruces. The soft, spindle-shaped leaves are flat and round-edged, often bearing two parallel silver lines on the underside. Most species are too large for the average garden, being better suited to a country property. Fully hardy, they prefer moist soil, partial shade and a cool climate. Prune in late winter to encourage shape and limit size; propagate from seeds from ripened cones. The classic European Christ-mas tree belongs to this genus.

A. cephalonica

GRECIAN FIR

This upright conifer grows to 30 m (about 95 ft) high, and has a conical crown. Its cylindrical cones are 10–15 cm (about 4–6 in) long and brown when mature. The glossy, dark green leaves have white-green undersides.

A. procera 'Glauca'

The attractive blue foliage and smooth, silvery bark identify this

Acacia baileyana

upright conifer. It grows to 30 m (about 95 ft) high. Its cylindrical cones are 15–20 cm (about 6–8 in) long and purplish brown. The leaves are glaucous. If the tree dries out cracks will appear in the wood and bark.

ACACIA

WATTLE, ACACIA

This extremely diverse genus con-tains over 1000 short-lived ever-green, semi-evergreen and deciduous species, mostly native to Australia and Africa. Growing 5–20 m (about 15–65 ft) high, they are valued for their beautiful dense golden blossoms and rapid growth. Most species have flat, spindle-shaped stalks (phyllodes) instead of conventional leaves. A few develop pinnate, fern-like fronds or compound leaves. The fruit is a long, legume-like pod. Heat-treated seeds may be used for propagation, mim-icking the way seeds are released in bushfires. Untreated seeds have been known to last 50 years. Re-nowned for their ability to survive drought, acacias grow best in warm

climates with well-drained soil and full sun; few can be described as more than half-hardy. To extend their life, completely lop dead branches and prune soon after flow-ering ends. Watch for borers, leaf miner and acacia scale. White Aus-tralian settlers used acacias to build wattle-and-daub huts; hence the common name.

A. baileyana

COOTAMUNDRA WATTLE

Native to Australia, this elegant, half-hardy evergreen grows to 6 m (about 18 ft). In late winter to early spring, soft golden blossoms appear on drooping branches. The foliage is silver-blue pinnate leaves, rather than phyllodes, 5 cm (about 2 in) long. Ugly circular swellings may appear on the limbs as a result of gall wasp; remove and burn af-fected limbs.

A. dealbata

SILVER WATTLE, MIMOSA

This frost-hardy evergreen pro-duces beautiful lemon-coloured flower clusters. It is popular in

Acacia pendula

Europe and the USA, where it is known as mimosa. While it may grow to 30 m (about 95 ft), the average height is 12 m (about 37 ft). Silver-blue compound leaves, 13 cm (about 5 in) long, contrast with the soft pink seed pods, which are 5–10 cm (about 2–4 in) long.

A. melanoxylon

BLACKWOOD

This Australian native evergreen is quite different from other acacias as it requires good rainfall and outlives most other species. Interestingly, it develops both pale green compound leaves and crescent-shaped phyllodes, 7–14 cm (about 3–5½ in) long and almost 2 cm (about 1 in) wide. Blackwood thrives in damp gullies rather than dry inland areas. It is prone to attack by grey mistletoe, which should be removed immediately. Blackwood is a very fine cabinet timber.

A. pendula

WEEPING MYALL

Growing to a height of 6–10 m (about 18–30 ft), this frost-hardy Australian native can survive in harsh climates with low rainfall. Arching limbs almost touch the ground and bear light yellow blos-soms in spring. The phyllodes are a light silvery green, 5–8 cm (about 2–3 in) long.

A. pycnantha

GOLDEN WATTLE

Originating in south-eastern Aus-tralia, this stocky, half-hardy ever-green reaches 4–8 m (about 12–24 ft). Perfumed flower clusters appear on drooping branches in late winter to early spring. This rich golden blossom is set against pale green, slightly curved phyllodes, 6–20 cm (about 2½–8 in) long and 1–5 cm (about ½–2 in) wide. Flat, scythe-shaped pods, 5–13 cm (about 2–5 in) long, contain 10–12 seeds. The species thrives in sandy soil and is useful for sand binding. Watch for borers. This wattle is Australia's floral emblem.

ACER

MAPLE

Originating in the cool-temperate zones of the northern hemisphere, these deciduous trees and shrubs are prized for their decorative bark and magnificent foliage. Species vary considerably in shape and size: some grow to 40 m (about 130 ft) in cool mountain regions; others in coastal zones reach 3–5 m (about 9–15 ft). Hand-shaped leaves with sharply pointed fingers colour dramatically in autumn/fall. Some species produce little flowers followed by 2-winged fruit, or keys, that 'fly' long distances on the wind. Maples prefer cool or temperate climates with rich, well-drained soil and will not flourish in dry heat or tropical conditions. Provide full sun or partial shade; shelter from the wind to avoid leaf burn. A neutral to acid soil encourages optimum leaf colours. Prune and graft cultivars in late winter. Propagate from seed in autumn/fall; budding in summer. *Acer*, meaning 'sharp', has been used since the days of the Romans; the name is thought to derive from the use of the wood for spears.

A. negundo 'Aureo-variegatum'

BOX ELDER, GHOST TREE

This attractive, fast-growing cultivar reaches 5–6 m (about 15–18 ft). Small yellow-green flowers appear in bunches on slender stalks in early spring. Distinctive compound leaves, 3 to 5 oval-shaped leaflets edged with yellowish gold, give the tree a remarkable appearance; it does not change colour in autumn/fall. The species itself has plain green leaves and is fast growing to 15 m (about 50 ft). It comes from North America.

A. palmatum

JAPANESE MAPLE

There are many cultivars of this popular species, both trees and shrubs, and all have striking foliage. A deciduous, shapely tree with a bushy head, it grows 3–5 m (about 9–15 ft) in mild-winter areas and can reach 15 m (about 50 ft) in cool-temperate zones. The 5-pointed leaves are deeply recessed. They turn from mid-green to bronze in spring and reddish orange in autumn/fall. Avoid pruning and provide protection from the wind.

A. platanoides 'Crimson King'

NORWAY MAPLE

Native to Europe, this grand tree grows to 15–18 m (about 50–60 ft). Immature leaves turn blood red in autumn/fall, while the mature leaf changes from bright green to yellow or orange. Deeply recessed, with few lobes, the leaves are 15 cm (about 6 in) long and 20 cm (about 8 in) wide. Small yellow flowers with red edges appear in clusters in mid-spring.

AESCULUS

x carnea

syn. A. rubicunda

RED HORSE-CHESTNUT, BUCKEYE

This deciduous hybrid between the Indian and European horse-chestnuts is valued for its beautiful foliage and well-rounded shape. It grows slowly to 10–20 m (about 30–65 ft) and is fully hardy. The dark green, divided leaves are prone to leaf spot when immature. Large, upright clusters of rich pink blossoms appear in late spring to early summer, followed by the fruit. This species prefers a cold winter to cool-temperate climate. Suitable for parks or large gardens, it needs a rich, moist, well-drained soil and full sun or partial shade. Leaves burn easily. Propagate from seed in autumn/fall; by grafting in late winter. Pruning is generally unnecessary but the tree may be lopped in winter. The white species *A. hippocastanum* is a splendid tree, larger than the red.

AGATHIS

KAURI, TENNIS BALL TREE

These tall, erect, evergreen conifers, native to the South Pacific, are slow growing and average between 40 and 60 m (about 130–190 ft) in height. Unlike most conifers, the waxy, simple leaves are deep green and slightly curved. The large cones are also unusual, resembling small pineapples or tennis balls and developing at the union of the branch and branchlet. The trees prefer warm temperatures and full sun, and will grow in most soils. Prune to encourage shape or limit size and propagate from seed. Highly valued for their timber, which is relatively straight and free of knots, the trees are a copious source of copal resin which is used in varnish.

A. australis

KAURI PINE, KAURI

Reaching heights up to 35 m (about 110 ft), this grand, long-living New Zealand evergreen has a slender, conical shape, developing a spreading level crown in maturity. Its narrow elliptical foliage is mid-green turning to coppery brown in colder weather. Inconspicuous male and female flowers develop separately on the same tree, and are followed in autumn/fall by globular, egg-shaped cones. This half-hardy species prefers moderate temperatures, damp soil and full sun. Prune regularly and propagate from cold-treated seed. This tree is highly valued worldwide as a source of Kauri gum, copal lacquer and timber.

A. robusta

QUEENSLAND KAURI, TENNIS-BALL TREE

This tall tree is a native of the Pacific region and highly valued for its knot-free timber. A frost-hardy evergreen, the species slowly reaches a lofty height of 18–30 m (about 60–95 ft). Its deep green, waxy leaves are 5–10 cm (about 2–4 in) long and ovular. Globe-shaped cones, 7–12 cm (about 3–5 in) long, grow at the union of the branches and resemble tennis balls—hence the nickname. The species also yields a gummy resin, copal, which is used to manufacture varnish. The tree prefers warm-temperate to tropical regions. Propagate from seed.

Acer palmatum

Acer platanoides 'Crimson King'

Agathis australis

Agathis robusta

Aesculus x carnea

Acer negundo 'Aureo-variegatum'

Albizia lophantha

Agonis flexuosa

Alberta magna

AGONIS
WILLOW MYRTLE

Native to Western Australia, these evergreen shrubs and trees have impressive foliage and flowers. They grow to a height of 5–15 m (about 15–50 ft) and flower in spring and summer. They are half-hardy to frost-tender, suiting cool or warm-temperate areas, and prefer full sun and well-drained soil. They are able to survive without water for long periods and are an excellent substitute for deciduous willows. Propagate from seed in spring or cuttings in summer.

A. flexuosa
WILLOW MYRTLE, PEPPERMINT TREE

Growing to a variable height of 2–15 m (about 6–50 ft), this species has rough, dark grey bark and pendulous branches and foliage. Its shiny green, narrow, lanceolate leaves are 4–15 cm (about 2–6 in) long. Tiny white, tube-shaped flowers with 4 to 5 petals blossom in late spring and summer. Fibrous, globular fruit ripen from green to red and carry small black seeds from which the plant self-propagates. The species prefers sandy, well-drained soils and tolerates dry conditions once established. It is a little frost-tender. The crushed leaves give out a peppermint smell, which explains the common name.

A. juniperina

Reaching a height of 6–12 m (about 18–37 ft), this half-hardy tree is more slender and upright than others of its genus. The rich green narrow leaves on whitish stalks are rather prickly. The small white flowers blossom in mid-winter rather than spring.

AILANTHUS
glandulosa
syn. A. altissima
TREE OF HEAVEN

Native to China, this broad, deciduous shade tree reaches 6–18 m (about 18–60 ft). It is valued for its attractive, unusual foliage: deep green, fern-like leaves, 60 cm (about 24 in) long, with 15–30 oval leaflets. Inconspicuous groups of tiny green flowers, with an unfortunate odour, bloom in mid-summer, followed by reddish orange, winged seed pods. Able to withstand the worst city smog, this fully hardy tree graces many world capitals. It does best in subtropical areas but will survive in most climates, preferring full sun or partial shade and deep, rich soil. Prune severely in spring to create a shrub. Propagate from seed in autumn/fall, and suckers or root cuttings from the female tree in winter. Because of its tendency to sucker, it is classified as a noxious weed in Victoria, Australia.

ALBERTA
magna

This small, slow-growing, evergreen tree from South Africa reaches a height of 4 m (about 12 ft). It is grown for its shiny, oval-oblong, dark green leaves that look like laurel leaves, and the erect clusters of tubular, orange-red flowers from late autumn/fall to spring, followed by scarlet calyces in summer. It prefers a moist, well-drained soil in a warm, temperate coastal climate in full sun or semi-shade. Protect against cold and salty winds and give plenty of water in summer. Frost-tender, it does best above 10°C (about 50°F). Propagate from seed in autumn/fall or separate root cuttings or suckers for true-to-type plants.

ALBIZIA
SILK TREE

This genus comprises over 100 species of deciduous trees and shrubs native to the tropical and subtropical areas of Asia, Africa and Australia, with one species in Mexico. They are distinguished from their close relatives in the *Acacia* genus by their stamens, which are knitted together. Trees vary in height, 6–25 m (18–75 ft), and are noted for their very unusual foliage: opposing pairs of bipinnate leaves form along a central stalk and fold up at night. Clusters of small flowers, spiky or downy, form large, globular crowns similar to bottlebrushes. Plants refuse to bloom in pots but are still worthwhile for their foliage. They prefer full sun with protection from the wind. Plant in a light, compost-enriched soil and propagate from seed in late autumn/fall to early spring. The genus was named after an Italian naturalist, F. degli Albizi, who first cultivated *A. julibrissin* in 1759.

A. julibrissin
PINK SILK TREE

Found in the area between Iran and Japan, this is a squat tree with a broad crown. Reaching a height of 10 m (about 30 ft), it has large, pale to mid-green pinnates. An abundance of translucent pink, downy blossom appears in late spring to early summer. The species is hardy to minus 12°C (10°F), and is valuable as the only fern-leaved tree for cool-temperate climates.

A. lophantha
CAPE LEEUWIN WATTLE, TREE-IN-A-HURRY

This 6 m (about 18 ft) evergreen tree from Western Australia is valued for its rapid growth—it can grow 3 m (about 9 ft) in its first year. The leaves are doubly pinnate, the summer flowers greenish. Frost-tender, it is rather short lived and best used for immediate effect while slower trees are growing.

Ailanthus glandulosa

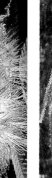

Albizia julibrissin

Agonis juniperina

ALECTRYON
excelsa
syn. *A. excelsus*
TITOKI

Native to New Zealand, this thickly foliaged, spreading evergreen grows 6–10 m (about 18–30 ft) tall. Its squat trunk is covered with distinctive, dark brown-black bark and the branches are reddish brown and downy. The foliage is asymetrically bipinnate and grows up to 40 cm (about 16 in) long. Tiny red or cream-coloured blossoms develop in multi-branched clusters, followed by brown seed pods. The fruit splits open to reveal a deep red interior and glossy black seed. Plant in light, sandy soil with full sun or partial shade and water regularly. Propagate from seed in autumn/fall. The hardwood timber is used to make carpentry tools and furniture.

ALNUS
ALDER

These birch relatives are slender, upright trees, deciduous and fully hardy. Reaching heights of 25–30 m (about 80–95 ft), they have attractive, slightly arching branches. Highly valued for their ability to survive in extremely wet locations due to their strong root system, they are often found by rivers, in moist gullies or swamps. Small, conical male flowers and pendulous, spiky female flowers appear in spring. The leaves are long stemmed and shiny. The genus will survive in a range of climates, from cool to warm-temperate to subtropical. Propagate from seed in autumn/fall, bud cultivars in late spring and hardwood cuttings in early winter. The timber is extremely water-resistant; once prized by shipbuilders, it was also used for the wooden piles that have supported the city of Venice for hundreds of years.

A. glutinosa
COMMON ALDER

This conical deciduous tree grows rapidly to 10–18 m (about 30–60 ft). Hanging yellow catkins (male) and tiny upright ones (female) are borne in early spring, followed in mid-spring by shiny, heart-shaped leaves with slim stalks. The species bears round, fruit like tiny pine cones in autumn/fall. It grows best by the water.

A. jorullensis
MEXICAN ALDER, EVERGREEN ALDER, TOORAK GUM

Native to Mexico and Central America, this fast-growing erect evergreen reaches 12–15 m (about 24–50 ft). Its drooping branches are light grey and papery. The deep green, lanceolate leaves are heavily veined and saw-toothed. Small, stretched seed pods appear in late spring and mature in summer. Conical fruit ripens in autumn/fall. It is half-hardy.

ANGOPHORA
costata
SMOOTH-BARKED APPLE, RUSTY GUM, SYDNEY RED GUM

This tall, elegant tree originates in the sandstone areas of Australia's east coast. It grows up to 30 m (about 95 ft), has a sturdy, trunk and an irregular open crown of many twisting branches. Uneven annual peeling reveals fresh pink bark, often stained red from the tree's sap; it then turns grey. The 7–16 cm (about 3–6½ in) red and green leaves are lance-shaped and pendulous. Immature foliage is bright pink or red turning to green, with a prominent yellow central rib. In spring and summer the tree produces tiny cream flowers with multiple stamens and five lobes. The woody, seed-bearing fruit is greyish brown and flat-topped, like a gumnut. A warm-temperate climate with full sun or partial shade is ideal for this half-hardy tree. Propagate from seed in winter.

ARALIA
elata
ANGELICA TREE

This deciduous South-East Asian native is valued for its abundant foliage and flowers. A small tree or tall shrub, it varies in height from 3 to 10 m (about 9–30 ft). Its enormous, shiny, deep green leaves, 1 m (about 3 ft) long and 60 cm (about 25 in) wide, divide twice into serrated leaflets. The spiny leaf stalks, covered in fine hair, turn red in autumn/fall. Small white or pink flowers cluster together forming large globe-shaped heads in late summer to early autumn/fall. The species has a tendency to sucker, sending out stocky, sharp thorny shoots, and in smaller gardens is best grown in pots. Frost-hardy, it requires full sun or partial shade and protection from the wind. Plant in a rich, well-drained soil. Propagate from seed in autumn/fall; sucker and root cutting in winter.

ARAUCARIA

The 18 conifers in this genus are native to the South Pacific region, where coniferous species rarely originate. These upright, slender trees grow 30–50 m (about 95–160 ft) tall and make popular indoor plants when immature. Stiff outstretched branches, which are shed periodically, radiate out from the trunk. Adaptable to all but cold climates, Araucarias will grow in poor soil and like full sun. Water only when the root surface appears dry. Propagate from seed in spring.

Alectryon excelsa

Alnus jorullensis

Angophora costata

Alnus glutinosa

Aralia elata

Araucaria bidwillii

Arbutus unedo

Araucaria heterophylla

Arbutus menziesii

Banksia serrata

Athrotaxis selaginoides

A. bidwillii
BUNYA BUNYA PINE

Native to the south-eastern rainforests of Queensland, Australia, this slow-growing species is valued for its shapely appearance and timber. Its upright scaly trunk supports drooping branches which umbrella out at the apex. The stiff, shiny green leaves that whorl around the ends of the radial branches are lance-shaped and stalkless. Scaly cylinders of yellowish green male flowers appear in spring; followed on the same tree in summer by oval, scaly green female flowers. Heavy upright cones, 30 cm (about 12 in) long and 20 cm (about 8 in) wide, appear at the top of the tree every two years. These scaly, pineapple-like fruit ripen from green to brown. Each scale contains an edible red seed, a traditional Aboriginal delicacy. The tree flourishes in coastal districts and reasonably moist inland areas, growing best in fertile volcanic soil.

A. heterophylla
NORFOLK ISLAND PINE, STAR PINE

Native to Norfolk Island and north-eastern Australia, this attractive species rapidly reaches 18–30 m (about 60–95 ft) on average; some grow as high as 60 m (about 190 ft). The whorled, slightly upright branches are spaced widely apart in tiers, giving the tree a triangular appearance. Bold green, scale-like, triangular leaves overlap to form cylindrical branchlets up to 30 cm (12 in) long. The species does best in well-watered sandy soil; a waxy layer on its foliage protects it from salt air. It can also be successfully grown in a pot, with occasional time in the greenhouse. Excellent sand-binders, these trees were once widely planted on Australian coasts; air pollution has taken its sad toll.

ARBUTUS

This genus contains some 20 species of frost-hardy, evergreen trees and shrubs. Valued for their attractive, egg-shaped leaves and decorative bark, they are native to an area reaching from California to the Mediterranean. Bell-shaped flower clusters bloom in spring, followed in summer by orange-red spherical fruit, 1 cm (about ½ in) in diameter, which may take up to a year to mature. Arbutus do well in both cool and warm-temperate climates. They are attractive planted in tubs, where root constriction causes earlier blooming and fruiting. Plant in a well-drained, slightly acid soil; protect from sea breezes and full sun. Propagate from seed in spring, cuttings in summer and layering in autumn/fall or spring. Arbutus is Latin for 'strawberry', but the raw fruit is tasteless. It is used to make wine and jam in Italy and Spain.

A. menziesii
MADRONE

This native of North America, Canada and Mexico is valued for its timber. Moderately fast growing, it reaches 10–15 m (about 30–50 ft) on average but may grow to 30 m (about 95 ft), making it the tallest of its genus. The knotted branches are reddish, the smooth bark a lighter red that peels away in large sheets. Smooth-edged leaves are deep-green on top and blue-grey underneath. White flowers form in triangular clusters, followed by orange or red fruit.

A. unedo
IRISH STRAWBERRY TREE, CANE APPLE

A native of Ireland and southern Europe, this small tree grows up to 8 m (about 24 ft). It is valued for its attractive foliage and its bark, used for tanning. Pink or white flowers form in clusters of 30 to 50 in autumn/fall and early winter. A species with a shrubby habit, it is suitable for hedges and backdrops.

ATHROTAXIS
selaginoides
KING WILLIAM PINE, KING BILLY PINE

Originating in the mountains of Tasmania, Australia, this evergreen conifer is frost-hardy. It grows slowly to 40 m (about 130 ft) and has tiny dark green leaves, narrow and sharply pointed. This tree only starts producing an abundance of branches and branchlets halfway up its straight trunk, which made it attractive to early boatbuilders. The reddish brown bark matures to grey and is scored with long vertical grooves. Unimpressive globe-shaped cones, containing 6 rectangular winged seeds, appear in spring and take up to a year to ripen. The tree prefers a moist, cool-temperate climate and rich, well-drained soil. Plant in full sun or partial shade.

BANKSIA
serrata
SAW BANKSIA, RED HONEYSUCKLE, OLD MAN

An evergreen Australian native, this tall shrub or medium tree grows to 3–10 m (about 9–30 ft). Its sturdy, twisted trunk is often grooved, the bark a dark grey. The gnarled branches are thinly covered with dark green, rectangular or lanceolate serrated leaves. The silvery grey flowers produce prominent whorled stigma stems, similar to bottlebrushes, and are 7–10 cm (about 3–4 in) long. Seed-bearing grey tubular cones, 13–15 cm (about 5–6 in) long, appear in summer. These contain black winged seeds, which are released during bushfires. This salt-resistant coastal species will grow in temperate or warmer climates and prefers light sandy soil with full or partial shade. It is half-hardy. Banksias are named after renowned English botanist Sir Joseph Banks.

BAUHINIA
ORCHID TREE

Native to the warm-temperate and tropical zones of Asia, Africa, America and Australia, this predominantly deciduous genus contains over 300 species. The rotund trees grow 7–12 m (about 21–37 ft) tall. Their much-valued flowers are large and unusually twin-lobed, resembling the pea's, and come in a variety of colours. Trees should be well watered during spring, when the flowers are in bloom. Frost-tender, they should be grown in full sun, protected from cold winds and sea breezes. Propagate from seed or cuttings in spring. Bauhinias are named after the brothers Jean and Gaspard Bauhin, sixteenth-century Swiss botanists.

B. variegata
MOUNTAIN EBONY

This slender, elegant species, originating in India and China, quickly reaches heights up to 7 m (about 21 ft). The most popular of its genus, it has magnificent, perfumed flowers: rose-pink, they have five overlaid petals, the fifth splashed with pink or purple. This species has a tendency to shrub and requires regular pruning. Indians consider the flower buds a delicacy. The variety 'Blakeana' has deeper pink flowers and bears no seeds.

B. variegata 'Candida'
syn. B. variegata 'Alba'
WHITE MOUNTAIN EBONY

This cultivar has large white or lemon-green flowers up to 10 cm (about 4 in) in diameter. They bloom in early spring and are most impressive after a cool winter, when leaves are prematurely shed.

BEAUCARNEA
recurvata
syn. Nolina recurvata, N. tuberculata
PONY-TAIL PALM, ELEPHANT'S FOOT

A slow-growing tree from southern USA and Mexico, it is not in fact a palm, but is related to yuccas, adapting to the arid tropics in a similar manner. The swollen base stores water in times of drought, and tapers to a smooth, palm-like trunk with 2 m (about 6 ft) long, thin, recurving leaves sprouting from the top. It is sparsely branched and makes an attractive plant for a dry spot. It will only grow outdoors in mild to warm climates and in well-drained, fertile soil, preferring full sun and a minimum temperature of 7°C (about 44°F). Water well when growing, but sparingly at other times. Potted specimens need full light and moderate water; allow to dry out between waterings. Propagate from seed or suckers in spring, or stem-tip cuttings in summer.

BETULA
BIRCH

This genus contains over 35 species, native to the northern hemi-sphere. Tall and elegant, these fully hardy deciduous trees are valued for their slender, weeping branches and shimmering foliage. Growing to 18–30 m (about 60–95 ft), they have broad serrated leaves that turn gold in autumn/fall. Pendent fruit contains winged seeds. Brightly coloured grey, red-brown, white or yellowish black bark is shed in long strips. Birches will grow in any well-drained soil, provided they receive plentiful water and full sun. Pruning is unnecessary. Propagate from seed, by grafting in late winter or from softwood cuttings in early summer. Once used to make school canes and domestic brooms, birch timber is highly prized by Scandinavia's furniture industry. North American Indians traditionally used the leathery, waterproof bark to make canoes.

B. pendula
SILVER BIRCH, EUROPEAN BIRCH, WHITE BIRCH

This popular ornamental garden tree is native to Europe and Asia. It is widely conical and rapidly grows up to 20 m (about 65 ft). The species has silvery white bark turning to black, and thinly stalked, diamond-shaped leaves 2–7 cm (about 1–3 in) long. Seed-bearing cones, lemon-green and 2 cm (about 1 in) long, appear in spring. If kept moist, the tree will survive in most climates other than the tropics and sub-tropics. It is, however, happiest in cold climates.

B. pendula 'Dalecarlica'
syn. B. pendula 'Laciniata'
CUT-LEAF BIRCH, SWEDISH BIRCH

A slim and attractive tree, this cultivar reaches a height of some 10 m (about 30 ft). It has distinctive white bark and its branches are gently arching. The leaves are deeply cut with saw-toothed margins.

BOLUSANTHUS
speciosus
SOUTH AFRICAN WISTERIA, WILD WISTERIA, TREE WISTERIA, RHODESIAN WISTERIA

This deciduous South African native is the only species in its genus. It is valued for its slender appearance and wisteria-like blooms. Averaging 6 m (about 18 ft) tall, this tree has slightly arching branches covered with uneven fern-like foliage. The immature frosted green leaflets become lustrous in maturity. In spring, beautiful bluish purple, pea-type flowers appear, followed by legume-type seed pods. This frost-tender species will thrive best in full sun and rich porous soil. Give it plenty of water. But once it is established it will survive long dry spells. Propagate from heat-treated seed in summer.

Bauhinia variegata

Bauhinia variegata 'Candida'

Betula pendula 'Dalecarlica'

Betula pendula

Bolusanthus speciosus

Beaucarnea recurvata

BRACHYCHITON

This genus consists of 12 half-hardy deciduous or evergreen trees native to the warm-temperate and tropical zones of Australia and New Guinea. They are extremely variable, growing to 9 m (about 27 ft) in dry inland areas and up to 30 m (about 95 ft) on the coast. Their sturdy trunks are covered with grey or brown bark, often swollen from moisture retention in dry conditions. The foliage is tough and changeable. Attractive, bell-shaped flowers bloom erratically in spring and summer after the leaves have been shed. Leathery brown pods, shaped like boats, split along a side seam to release their seeds. These trees prefer full sun or partial shade and rich, well-drained acid soil. They are prone to leaf tier insects. Propagate from seed or cuttings; prune if necessary. The timber is used for fencing and farmhouse roofs.

Callicoma serratifolia

Brachychiton populneus

Butea monosperma

B. acerifolius

FLAME TREE, ILLAWARRA FLAME TREE, FLAME BOTTLE TREE

One of Australia's most attractive trees, this deciduous species is prized for its brilliant red flowers. It grows slowly to 6–40 m (about 18–130 ft), with smooth grey or brown furrowed bark. The leaves, up to 30 cm (about 12 in) long, have 3 to 7 lobes and resemble the maple's. Bright green on top, lighter underneath, foliage is shed when the tree flowers. This is when the tree earns its name, seemingly aflame with magnificent clusters of scarlet flowers, 3 cm (about 1½ in) long. Water regularly when in bloom. It is rather frost-tender.

B. populneus

syn. *Sterculia diversifolia*
KURRAJONG

This cone-shaped, deciduous shade tree reaches 20 m (about 65 ft). Its

Calocedrus decurrens

Brachychiton acerifolius

grey-brown bark is orange-chocolate coloured underneath. The foliage is remarkably diverse: ovate, heart- shaped and poplar-like leaves, 5–10 cm (about 2–4 in) long, may all grow on the same specimen. Bell-shaped flowers are cream tinged with green, spotted inside with red, purple or yellow. The spring to summer flowers are followed by clusters of brown, woody follicles. The leathery pods contain irritating hairs and red seeds. The species will survive in all soil types provided there is sufficient warmth. Leaves and flowers are used to feed stock.

BUTEA

monosperma

syn. *B. frondosa*
FLAME OF THE FOREST, PALAS

This magnificent deciduous tree is valued for its flowers, foliage and sap, which is used to make astringents. A native of Bangladesh, Burma and East India, it slowly grows up to 10 m (about 30 ft). The leaves, 20 cm (about 8 in) long, are composed of three leaflets, greyish blue on the surface and silvery underneath. Big clusters of orange-red flowers, similar to the pea's, precede the foliage in spring. The grey seed pods are legume-shaped and covered in down. This species prefers a damp, warm location but also tolerates saline conditions. Frost-tender, it does best in tropical climates. Pruning is not required. This species is named after the eighteenth-century Earl of Bute. There is a yellow-flowered variety.

CALLICOMA

serratifolia

BLACK WATTLE, BUTTERWOOD

This frost-hardy Australian native evergreen is the only species in its genus. It grows up to 18 m (about 60 ft) with slim, arching branches and a dense crown. Branchlets, flower stems and leaf undersides are downy. Shiny green, serrated foliage is either wide and lanceolate or oval and narrow, with a prominent midrib. Creamy yellow blossoms cluster in thick puffballs, similar to the wattle's, in spring and early summer. This tree prefers damp, rich soils and requires plentiful water in summer. Shelter from cold winds and sea breezes. Prune when immature to encourage shape; propagate from seed in autumn/fall. Like the acacia, this tree was used by early white Australians for their wattle-and-daub constructions.

CALOCEDRUS

decurrens

syn. *Libocedrus decurrens*
INCENSE CEDAR

Valued for its shapely, conical habit and attractive foliage, this species is frost-hardy and grows slowly to 12–22 m (about 38–70 ft). Shiny, dark bluish green leaves adhere to the branches in flat clusters. The tubular cones grow in three splayed segments. This tree likes partial shade and well-drained soil of indifferent quality. It does well in the heat of summer and makes an ideal windbreak. If immature plants are liberally watered they will become drought-resistant in maturity. Propagate from seed.

CALODENDRUM

capense

CAPE CHESTNUT

This warm climate evergreen is native to South Africa. Decorative and dome-shaped, it grows to 8–15 m (about 24–50 ft). Its shiny oval leaves, 10–15 cm (about 4–6 in) long, are similar to those of the lemon tree. They are marked with dots, only discernible when held to the light. Clusters of light pink to pale

Calodendrum capense

lavender flowers appear in spring and early summer. Half-hardy, this tree prefers warm climates but not dry exposed areas and requires regular watering. Plant in rich, well-drained soil and full sun. This species will stand pruning if necessary to keep its shape. Propagate from seed in spring or, more effectively, from semi-ripe cuttings in summer.

CASSIA
CASSIA

This genus contains over 500 diverse species of evergreen, deciduous and perennial plants, ranging from fully hardy to frost-tender. Varying from 9 to 15 m (about 27–50 ft) tall, they are among the most popular and beautiful of flowering trees and shrubs. Their fern-like foliage has a variable number of alternating leaflets. Their predominantly yellow, dish-shaped flowers, some scented, bloom at different times of the year, appearing in some species in long, drooping sprigs; in others, at the end of stiff stems. All produce long, legume-like seed pods, up to 60 cm (about 24 in) long. Cassias readily cross-fertilize, producing a vast array of hybrids. They require sunny, spacious locations and like fertile, well-drained soil. Water these plants liberally when in flower and only occasionally in winter. While all species tolerate radical pruning, they are best left to grow freely. Propagate from seed in spring, and from cuttings in late summer. Cassias are used for tanning as well as in the pharmaceutical industry.

C. fistula
INDIAN LABURNUM, GOLDEN SHOWER

This attractive, tropical native of India and Sri Lanka grows rapidly up to 10 m (about 30 ft). It has pinnate leaves, 20 cm (about 8 in) long, which are composed of 4 to 18 oval leaflets. Light to vivid yellow flower clusters form in thick, drooping racemes. The seed pods are dark brown and 60 cm (about 24 in) long and give cassia pulp which is used for medicinal purposes. This frost-tender species requires full sun.

C. javanica
JAVA SHOWER, APPLE BLOSSOM CASSIA, APPLE BLOSSOM SENNA

Native to Java and Malaysia, this evergreen has either a spreading or columnar shape, depending on the climate, and grows up to 10 m (about 30 ft). Feathery, greenish grey foliage is made up of 12–24 oval-shaped leaflets, 5 cm (about 2 in) long. Pale pink flowers, becoming more vivid with age, appear in large thick sprigs during spring and summer. Black seed pods,

30–60 cm (about 12–24 in) long, form on the long arching branches. This frost-tender species will not survive in temperatures under 10°C (about 50°F).

C. multijuga
GOLDEN SHOWER

This half-hardy evergreen originates in Brazil and Guyana and grows rapidly to 7 m (about 21 ft). It is either round-crowned or tall and narrow, with pendent branches. Its fern-like leaves are made up of 36–80 rectangular leaflets, 2 cm (about 1 in) long. Attractive orange-yellow blooms form in dense clusters during spring and summer. The flat seed pods are 15 cm (about 6 in) long.

CASTANOSPERMUM
australe
BLACK BEAN, MORETON BAY CHESTNUT

This Australian species, the only one in its genus, is valued for its timber and shade. A slow grower, it reaches 9–18 m (about 27–60 ft) and develops a broad, open crown. Shiny, dark green compound leaves of 5 to 7 leaflets are 30–45 cm (about 12–18 in) long. Orange-red or occasionally yellow, the pea-type flowers bloom in spring and summer, at which time the tree should be liberally watered. Long, tubular seed pods containing big poisonous 'chestnuts', 5 cm (about 2 in) across, appear in autumn/fall. This frost-tender tree prefers warm locations. Plant in an open sunny location in well-drained soil. Propagate from seed or ripe cuttings. The attractive timber is used to make furniture.

CASUARINA
IRONWOOD, SHEOKE

Originating in Australia and the South Pacific, these 30 species of evergreen trees and shrubs are valued for their shade and extremely tough timber. Conical, with a domed crown, they grow up to 12 m (about 37 ft). Fine, spindly branchlets develop in whorls at the extremities of the rough arching branches, giving the trees a mysterious appearance. The needles are surrounded by a variable number of tiny leaf scales, depending on the species. Small red flowers grow among the twigs, appearing in late spring. These trees adapt to a wide range of conditions, from poor arid soil to swampy saltwater marshes. They are excellent sand-binders but are prone to suckering, which prevents other plants growing nearby. Propagate from seed in spring. The timber has been used for traditional Aboriginal hunting weapons as well as tool handles.

C. cunninghamiana
RIVER SHE-OAK, FIRE OAK, BEEFWOOD

Reaching heights of up to 30 m (about 90 ft), this Australian native is the tallest of its genus. It has drooping, dark green branchlets with pendent, needle-like leaves, and globular cones, 1 cm (about 1/2 in) in diameter. Flowers are reddish brown. It is frost-hardy, but only just. This species is particularly useful in preventing soil erosion along rivers and creeks.

Cassia fistula

Casuarina cunninghamiana

Castanospermum australe

Cassia multijuga

Cassia javanica

Catalpa bignonioides

Casuarina glauca

Cedrus deodara

Cedrela sinensis

Cedrus atlantica

Cephalotaxus harringtonia

C. glauca

SWAMP SHE-OAK

This triangular or conical Australian native grows 15–20 m (about 50–65 ft) tall. It has greenish blue branches and tough, deep grey bark with long vertical grooves. The small, greyish brown cones are 1 cm (about ½ in) long and tubular. This valuable timber tree, like others of its genus, has a strong tendency to sucker.

CATALPA
bignonioides

INDIAN BEAN TREE, CIGAR TREE

Native to North America, this deciduous tree is valued for its large foliage and flowers. It grows up to 15 m (about 50 ft), spreading broadly in later life. Pale green or yellow, heart-shaped leaves are 18–25 cm (about 7½–10 in) long, grouped in threes. Bell-shaped and perfumed, the flowers are white, pink or lemon, variegated with purple and yellow. They appear in summer in thick upright clusters, 18–30 cm (about 7½–12 in) tall,

later replaced by drooping tubular seed pods. This tree likes full sun, shelter from the wind and rich, well-drained soil. It is best grown alone. Propagate from seed in autumn/fall, cultivars by budding and cuttings in summer.

CEDRELA
sinensis
syn. *Toona sinensis*

CHINESE CEDAR, CHINESE TOON

This deciduous native of China is not a cedar, although in the timber trade its red timber is called cedar. Reaching heights of up to 12 m (about 38 ft), it is valued for its large foliage: beautiful pink, fern-like leaves, later changing to green, appear in early spring and grow 30–60 cm (about 12–24 in) long. Perfumed white flowers appear in drooping clusters in spring. This species likes full sun and rich, well-drained soil. Prune in winter to encourage shape. Propagate from seed in autumn/fall, cuttings in winter. In some areas locals eat the onion-scented young leaves.

CEDRUS

CEDAR

This genus of conifers contains four species of tall, conical trees greatly valued for their timber. Native from Africa to India, some species grow up to 45 m (about 145 ft) tall. The spiralled foliage is grey-green and needle-shaped. They have woody, egg-shaped cones which bear seed scales. These fully hardy trees prefer cool temperatures, full sun and rich, well-drained soil. Too large for the average garden, they are better suited to country properties. Propagate from seed; some cultivars by grafting. Cedars have an ancient lineage; their timber was used for Solomon's temple and it was greatly valued by the Greeks and Romans.

C. atlantica

MT ATLAS CEDAR, ATLANTIC CEDAR

Originating in North Africa, this fast-growing species reaches heights of up to 40 m (about 130 ft). The pale green or blue-grey, spindly foliage is distinctively short at 2 cm (about 1 in). Erect, light green to purple flowers bloom in summer. The brown male and pale green female cones take 2 years to mature. While young, this tree may be grown in a tub.

C. deodara

DEODAR, INDIAN CEDAR

The largest of its genus, this magnificent Himalayan native reaches a towering 45 m (about 145 ft). Tiered branches droop slightly at the extremities where the silvery grey leaves develop. Male and female flowers grow on separate trees

and the 5–10 cm (about 2–4 in) cones have flat tops. This species will grow in various climates, from arid inland to cooler mountain areas. Height is determined by soil quality and the amount of water the tree receives. Suitable for pots, it may be replanted when up to 2 m (about 6 ft) tall. In Britain, this species is slightly tender.

CEPHALOTAXUS
harringtonia

JAPANESE PLUM YEW

Originating in South-East Asia, this bushy, decorative conifer grows to 5 m (about 15 ft). Its slightly flattened needles are deep green on top, grey below. This upright foliage grows in whorls around the branch shoots. Male and female flowers bloom on separate trees in spring. These are followed in summer and autumn/fall by plum-sized, edible green fruit. Though the species is quite hardy, it cannot survive in climates too cold or hot. Plant in good, slightly acid, well-drained soil with protection from the midday sun. Propagate from seed.

CERCIS

REDBUD, JUDAS TREE

This genus consists of 7 small, ornamental trees and shrubs, native to North America, southern Europe and Asia. They are grown for their beautiful, pea-like flowers. Deciduous species reach 12 m (about 37 ft) with fine multiple branches. It is straight out of these limbs that the pink, white or purple, stalkless flowers appear at the end of winter.

Cercis siliquastrum

Numerous flat seed pods, 10 cm (about 4 in) long, follow the blooms and endure until the following winter. These trees prefer rich porous soils and full sun. They do not like being moved, so transplant when young. Propagate from seed in autumn/fall and bud cultivars in summer. According to legend, Judas Iscariot hanged himself from the bough of one of these trees after betraying Christ.

C. canadensis

RED BUD

Native to the USA, this erect tree or shrub grows up to 13 m (about 40 ft) tall and has heart-shaped leaves. The young, reddish purple flower buds turn light pink when open, 1 cm (about ½ in) in diameter less attractive than those of *C. siliquastrum*. Seed pods are brown and 9 cm (about 3½ in) long.

C. siliquastrum

JUDAS TREE, LOVE TREE

This small, bushy tree develops a rounded crown and is fully hardy. It originates in southern Europe and Asia Minor and grows up to 13 m (about 40 ft). An abundance of bright pinkish purple or white flowers, 2 cm (about 1 in) across, blossom in spring before the leaves appear. These are heart-shaped and 7–10 cm (about 3–4 in) long. Propagate from seed.

CHAMAECYPARIS

FALSE CYPRESS

Native to the USA and eastern Asia, the 8 conifers comprising this genus

Cinnamomum camphora

Chorisia speciosa

Chionanthus virginicus

are extremely variable in colour and custom. They may be shrubby and small, or erect and tall, up to 30 m (about 95 ft). Their small leaves vary considerably in colour, from green to greyish blue. Branches may be stiff or arching, tiered or constant. All species are easily propagated, withstand transplanting and do not require pruning—hence their popularity as possibly the most commonly cultivated genus of evergreens. They prefer cool-temperate conditions and full sun. Propagate from seed; cultivars by cuttings. Once classified as true cypresses, they were placed in their own genus early this century.

C. lawsoniana

LAWSON CYPRESS, PORT ORFORD CEDAR

This native of the USA is prized for its quality timber and impressive appearance. It has a triangular shape, later becoming open-crowned and columnar, and is variable in height, up to 30 m (about 95 ft). Tiny, deep green scales cover the slender, slightly arching

Cercis canadensis

Chamaecyparis pisifera

branches, giving the tree a felty appearance. Narrow rectangular cones of both genders appear on the same tree. The species thrives best in cool conditions and rich, damp soil. There are many garden varieties with narrower habit, or silvery or golden foliage.

C. pisifera

SAWARA CYPRESS

This fully hardy species is shaped like a pyramid. It grows to a height of 30 m (about 95 ft) and has stiff branches and reddish brown bark with raised vertical lines. The deep green leaf scales have white margins. This species bears rectangular, yellowy brown cones.

CHIONANTHUS

virginicus

FRINGE TREE, OLD MAN'S BEARD

Native to North America, this fully hardy deciduous species slowly grows to 3–10 m (about 9–30 ft) tall, as a slender small tree or large shrub. It has an open crown and is valued for its attractive flowers. The flowers are dainty and white, and appear in late spring in drooping terminal clusters, 20 cm (about 8 in) long—hence the name 'old man's beard'. The large, shiny, dark green leaves are rectangular and turn gold in autumn/fall. This species prefers cool temperatures and moist soil with full sun.

CHORISIA

speciosa

FLOSS SILK TREE, BRAZILIAN KAPOK TREE

This tree is native to the subtropical zones of Brazil and Argentina. An

Chamaecyparis lawsoniana

erect species with a lofty crown, it grows to 15 m (about 50 ft). Its tapering trunk is covered with vicious spikes and its branches are long and uplifted. Compound leaves are shaped like hands, made up of saw-toothed leaflets 12 cm (about 5 in) long. Resembling the hibiscus, the variegated flowers have 5 petals and range in colour from light pink to purple with white or yellow throats, marked with red or brown. The species needs full sun, a warm climate and well-drained soil. Water liberally when in flower, in autumn/fall. Propagate from seed in spring.

CINNAMOMUM

camphora

CAMPHOR LAUREL, CAMPHOR TREE

Originating in China, Japan and Taiwan, this evergreen is highly valued for its oil and scented timber and foliage. It grows quickly to 35 m (about 110 ft), with a rounded crown and tough grey bark. Immature foliage is rust-coloured with a greyish blue underside and matures to a shiny green. The oval-shaped leaves are 12 cm (about 5 in) long, tapering to a point. These leaves release a camphor fragrance when crushed. Inconspicuous flowers appear in spring, followed by black berries. This tree requires plentiful water and full sun or partial shade and a warm to hot climate to thrive. Pruning is tolerated. Propagate from cuttings in summer, seeds in autumn/fall. Fragrant carved chests are made with the wood, which has the ability to protect their contents from moths.

Cladrastis lutea

Cornus capitata

Clusia rosea

CITHAREXYLUM
FIDDLEWOOD

Native to South America and the Caribbean, this genus of evergreen and half-evergreen decorative timber trees grow up to 15 m (about 50 ft). They have an attractive compact appearance and a dense crown. Plant in fertile crumbly soil with good drainage. In summer, water plentifully and prune tips to encourage good shape. Propagate from ripe seed or half-ripe cuttings in spring. The timber is used in cabinet-making. The genus name was derived from the Greek *kithara*, a lyre, and *xylon*, wood, as the timber was used to make lyres in ancient times.

C. quadrangulare
JAMAICAN FIDDLEWOOD

Valued for its impressive autumn/fall foliage, this Jamaican native evergreen grows to 6–12 m (about 18–37 ft) tall. Its rectangular to elliptical leaves have distinctive elongated tips and are neither serrated nor veined. They turn a golden, reddish brown in autumn/fall and endure through winter. When young, this tree requires shelter from frost. Propagate from hardwood cuttings at the end of winter.

C. spinosum
syn. C. subserratum

Valued for its foliage, this semi-evergreen is native to the West Indies. Growing quickly to 10–15 m (about 30–50 ft), it is conical or shrubby with a broad, open crown. The vivid green, oval leaves are heavily serrated and turn a beautiful rusty bronze in winter. Tiny white flowers grow in slender erect sprays from mid-summer to winter, followed by small pendent seed pods. The species is only just frost-hardy and requires liberal water when in flower. Plant in fertile, crumbly soil with full sun. Prune tips in early summer to encourage shape. Propagate from seed or cuttings in spring.

CLADRASTIS
lutea
YELLOW WOOD

Native to east Asia and the USA, this fully hardy deciduous species has very fragrant flowers and thick foliage. It grows to 11 m (about 34 ft) or more, with a broad, dome-shaped crown. The attractive compound leaves have 7 to 9 deep-green, ovate leaflets and are 10 cm (about 4 in) long. Foliage turns from deep green to vivid yellow in autumn/fall. Magnificent white flower clusters follow, although not every year. This species takes 10 years to flower. It likes cool weather and will grow in adequate soil provided there is good drainage. Propagate from seed in autumn/fall. The common name

comes from the bright yellow colour of its freshly cut timber, which is used to make dye.

CLUSIA
rosea
COPEY, AUTOGRAPH TREE

This shrubby tree is slow-growing to 16 m (about 50 ft). The lustrous, deep green leaves are oval, and in summer it bears 5 cm (about 2 in) cup-shaped, pink flowers, followed by globe-shaped, greenish fruit with a sticky resin. Grow in well-drained soil in semi-shade with a minimum temperature of 2–5°C (about 35–40°F). If in a pot, water moderately, less during colder weather. Propagate by layering in spring or from semi-ripe cuttings in summer.

CORDYLINE
australis
NEW ZEALAND CABBAGE TREE, GIANT DRACENA, GRASS PALM, SAGO PALM, PALM LILY

A palm-like tree from New Zealand, it is extremely hardy, although slow-growing. The tall central stem has a rosette of slender, strap-like leaves growing to 1 m (about 3 ft) in length. From late spring to summer, large sprays of tiny, scented, white flowers appear. This tree grows well in almost all conditions but prefers fertile, well-drained but moist soil and full sun to part-shade. It makes an excellent potted plant that needs moderate watering with less in winter. Propagate from seed or suckers in spring or stem cuttings in summer. Among its many common names, it was called 'cabbage tree' because early settlers used the young, tender leaves instead of cabbage.

CORNUS
DOGWOOD

These 100 species of deciduous and evergreen shrubs and trees originate in Asia and the USA. A broad-crowned group, between 6 and 18 m (about 18–60 ft) tall, they are valued for their leaves, flowers and vivid stems. Small green blossoms appear in spring surrounded by a rosette of bracts. The blooms develop into clusters of vivid red, white or pink berries that last until autumn/fall. Cornus like cold temperatures, full sun or partial shade. Soil should be rich, porous, and acid or alkali depending upon the species. Prune plants back to soil level in spring.

C. capitata
syn. Dendrobenthamia fragifera
HIMALAYAN STRAWBERRY, BENTHAM'S CORNEL

This Himalayan evergreen or semi-evergreen has wide, spreading branches and grows up to 13 m

Cordyline australis

Citharexylum spinosum

Citharexylum quadrangulare

(about 40 ft) high and wide. Pendent, greenish grey leaves are 7–10 cm (about 3–4 in) long. The bracts are creamy yellow, 6–8 cm (about 2½–3 in) wide. The plump, dark pink fruit resembles strawberries. This tree does best in cool coastal climates and acid soil.

C. florida
DOGWOOD

Originating in the USA, this slim or shrubby deciduous species slowly reaches 6–18 m (about 18–60 ft). It is valued for its abundant pink or white spring flowers and deep green, egg-shaped, large veined leaves, 7–10 cm (about 3–4 in) long, that turn vivid, reddish purple in autumn/fall. It requires deep, rich, acid soil.

CORYLUS
avellana 'Contorta'
CURLY HAZEL, CRAZY HAZEL

This strange-looking deciduous bush or small tree is native to the USA and Asia. It grows to 6 m (about 18 ft), a dense mass of contorted stalks and shoots with wide serrated leaves. Sleek, greenish yellow catkins, 5 cm (about 2 in) long, appear on its bare limbs in winter. The tree also produces edible brown nuts. Fully hardy, it requires full sun or partial shade and deep, rich, well-drained soil. Propagate from cuttings in autumn/fall or by grafting in summer. The foliage is prone to mildew and the nuts susceptible to insects.

CORYNOCARPUS
laevigata
syn. *C. laevigatus*
KARAKA

This New Zealand evergreen has a dense, rounded crown and grows 6–12 m (about 18–37 ft) in height. The complete rectangular leaves are lustrous, deep green or streaky and up to 20 cm (about 8 in) long. Clusters of small, creamy green flowers are followed in autumn/fall or winter by yellowy orange, egg-shaped fruit which contain an extremely poisonous seed. This semi-hardy species prefers damp,

moderate climates and full sun or partial shade with well-drained soil. Water regularly while in flower and propagate in summer from seed or half-ripe cuttings.

CRATAEGUS
HAWTHORN, THORN

This large, diverse genus of ornamental deciduous trees and shrubs originates in Europe, Asia Minor and Africa. Members of the Roseaceae family, they have beautiful rose flowers and cruel thorns. Height varies between 5 and 14 m (about 15–45 ft). The spiky branches, usually spreading, develop finely serrated rose-type leaves, divided into lobes. Fragrant double or single flowers bloom in spring, often white but also in shades of pink, followed by long-lasting ornamental fruit, white, pink, orange, yellow or bright red and of varying size. Species enjoy a cool climate, though some are frost-tender. They will survive in most soils provided they are not too damp. Propagate from seed in autumn/fall; cultivars by budding in late summer. The genus name from the Greek *kratos*, 'strength', refers to their durable wood.

C. laevigata 'Paul's Scarlet'
syn. *C. oxyacantha*
DOUBLE-RED HAWTHORN

This decorative, deciduous tree reaches 8 m (about 24 ft). It is much admired for its flowers, ornamental fruit and dense foliage. Egg-shaped leaves with deeply cut lobes are 5 cm (about 2 in) long on spiky, broadly spreading branches. Strongly scented, double red or deep pink flowers bloom in late spring to early summer. Red fruit endures through autumn/fall. This frost-hardy tree prefers a cool climate, full sun and well-drained soil. Propagate by budding in late summer. Susceptible to fireblight.

C. phaenopyrum
syn. *C. cordata*
WASHINGTON THORN

This small, attractive species has a round shape and grows up to 10 m (about 30 ft). Its shiny deep green

foliage is heart-shaped and deeply lobed. Clusters of white flowers appear in summer, followed by shiny orange-red spherical fruit. This species is fully hardy and suitable for most gardens in cool climates.

C. pubescens
syn. *C. mexicana, C. stipulacea*
MEXICAN HAWTHORN

This frost-hardy semi-evergreen quickly reaches 6–10 m (about 18–30 ft) and has a dense crown with serrated foliage, 8 cm (about 3 in) long. The tree bears clusters of single flowers 2 cm (about 1 in) across. The leaves turn orange-red in autumn/fall; edible, golden yellow or red fruit follow.

Cornus florida

CRYPTOMERIA
japonica 'Elegans'
BRONZE JAPANESE CEDAR

This erect triangular Asian conifer up to 5–12 m (about 15–37 ft) is highly valued for its fascinating needle-like foliage that develops in soft feathery whorls and drapes to the ground. Leaves turn from deep green in summer to rich golden rust in autumn/fall. It prefers cool conditions but will survive in the heat with regular watering. Plant in cool, damp soil and shelter from cold winds; it will withstand transplanting up to a reasonable size. Propagate from cuttings. The wood is rather weak and it is rare for a mature tree not to lean.

Crataegus pubescens

Crataegus laevigata 'Paul's Scarlet'

Corylus avellana 'Contorta'

Cryptomeria japonica 'Elegans'

Corynocarpus laevigata

Crataegus phaenopyrum

CUPRESSUS
CYPRESS

Native to Europe, Asia, the USA and Central America, this diverse genus of evergreen coniferous trees and shrubs may be tall and slender or open and squat, ranging from 1 to 45 m (about 3–145 ft) high. They make symmetrical shade trees or hedges. Golden green or bluish grey needle-like foliage changes to tiny leaf scales in maturity. Their globose, scale-covered cones may hang on the branches for years. They prefer cool to warm-temperate regions, can survive in arid, sandy soil and are ideal for coastal locations where they can enjoy full sun. Prune frequently to promote fresh growth. Mature plants will not survive transplanting. Propagate from cuttings in winter or cold-treated seed from the end of autumn/fall to late winter. The trees are susceptible to leafroller caterpillars, beetles, weevils and canker. Cypresses are traditionally associated with death and mourning.

Dais cotinifolia

Cussonia spicata

C. macrocarpa
MONTEREY CYPRESS

This stately tree from California is noted for its handsome habit, conical when young and developing picturesque, spreading branches with maturity. The wild form has dark green needles, but several 'golden' leaved cultivars are popular. It is not a tree for bitterly cold climates, although it is frost-hardy. It is very resistant to salt winds and much used as a shelter tree; and, as it takes clipping very well, for tall hedges. Propagate from cuttings or seed. It is prone to cypress canker.

C. sempervirens 'Swane's Golden'
SWANE'S GOLDEN PENCIL PINE

This classic pencil-slim conifer is an Australian cultivar. Fully frost-hardy, it grows 6–27 m (about 18–85 ft), with the largest cones in the genus. With its stately appearance, this tree is ideal in large landscaped gardens or paired in tubs at entrances. Its spreading root system makes it unsuitable for smaller

Cupressus torulosa

gardens. Take cuttings from good stock; avoid overfertilizing. The plain green species is one of the finest of upright trees, an unforgettable feature of Italian gardens.

C. torulosa
HIMALAYAN CYPRESS, BHUTAN CYPRESS

This Himalayan native has an erect triangular shape, broadening in maturity, and grows 10–20 m (about 30–65 ft) tall. Thick, bluish green foliage gives it a soft appearance. Its globose cones ripen from purple to reddish brown. This conifer prefers warm conditions and does not need pruning. It will survive for many years in a tub and makes an excellent hedge tree.

CUSSONIA
spicata
SPIKED CABBAGE TREE, LITTLE CABBAGE TREE

This fascinating South African evergreen has a thick rounded crown and an upright smooth trunk. It grows to 6 m (about 18 ft) and produces extremely large, serrated compound leaves to 25 cm (about 10 in) long on dense stalks. Inconspicuous yellow flowers appear above the canopy in spring to summer. It will grow in any reasonable, well-drained soil and requires full light and liberal water while in bloom. It is frost-tender.

DAIS
cotinifolia
SOUTH AFRICAN DAPHNE, POMPON BUSH

This small deciduous tree originates in South Africa. Growing to 4–5 m

Davidia involucrata

Cupressus macrocarpa

(about 12–15 ft) tall, it has a rounded dome and multiple branches. Its greenish blue leaves grow to 8 cm (about 3 in) long and are egg-shaped. At the end of spring, convex terminal clusters of fragrant, pinkish purple, starry flowers bloom and endure after withering. This half-hardy species enjoys full sun or partial shade and porous soil. Water liberally while flowering. Propagate from seed in spring and half-ripe cuttings in summer. The stringy bark is used to make twine.

DAVIDIA
involucrata
DOVE TREE, HANDKERCHIEF TREE

This native to China, the only species of its genus, is valued for its unusual white bracts. Growing to 6–12 m (about 18–37 ft), this deciduous ornamental develops a rounded appearance. Its broad, egg-shaped leaves, up to 15 cm (about 6 in) long, are succeeded in late spring by small, deep-set, brownish red flowers. Two white bracts (commonly mistaken for petals) of unequal lengths surround the flower. The longer leaf resembles a bird or handkerchief; hence the common names. Purplish green, pear-shaped seed pods follow, each encasing a single nut. Plant in full sun or partial shade in rich, porous soil and protect the bracts from harsh winds. It is frost-hardy. Propagate (with some difficulty) from cuttings or seed in spring. The genus is named after Pére David, the French missionary who discovered it.

Cupressus s. 'Swane's Golden'

DELONIX
regia
FLAMBOYANT TREE, POINCIANA,
ROYAL POINCIANA

This tropical native of Madagascar, it is claimed, produces the most spectacular flowers of all. While it only grows up to 10 m (about 30 ft), it is often three times as broad and quickly develops a buttressed trunk and thick crown. Its extremely long, bipinnate foliage is composed of 40 light green 'feathers' with numerous leaflets. These are replaced by flaming red blooms, 10 cm (about 4 in) across, one petal variegated with white. This species will not blossom in temperatures below 10°C (about 50°F) and needs rich, well-drained loamy soil with plenty of moisture. Prune when immature to prevent the development of multiple trunks. Propagate from seed in summer and autumn/fall.

DIOSPYROS
kaki
KAKI, CHINESE PERSIMMON, DATE PLUM,
KEY FIG

Valued for its fruit, timber and stunning autumn/fall foliage, this graceful, slow-growing deciduous tree is native to China and Japan. It may reach 13 m (about 40 ft) but is more usually 6 m (about 18 ft) tall. In autumn/fall the egg-shaped leaves turn the most striking colours: scarlet, yellow, orange and purple. Insignificant, yellowish white female flowers develop into delicious, golden red fruit, or persimmons. Up to 7 cm (about 3 in) in diameter, these are the size and shape of a tomato. This tree enjoys warm summers, rich, fertile soil and frequent watering. It is best propagated by grafting, though seed may be used. A relative of the ebony, its precious timber is used to make oriental cabinets and golf 'woods'.

DOMBEYA
tiliacea
syn. *D. natalensis*
NATAL CHERRY, WILD PEAR,
CAPE WEDDING FLOWER

This evergreen is native to Africa and certain islands in the Indian Ocean. It has slim, multiple trunks and branches and grows quickly to 8 m (about 24 ft). Its bark is brownish black and the heart-shaped leaves erratically serrated. In late autumn/fall to early winter, white, fragrant flowers appear in clusters at the end of long stalks. This species prefers warm, sunny or partially shaded locations and will not survive below 5°C (about 40°F). It is susceptible to white fly and red spider mite. Water generously while flowering and prune afterwards. Propagate from seed and cuttings. The genus was named after Jacob

Delonix regia

Dombey, an eighteenth-century botanist.

ELAEOCARPUS
reticulatus
syn. *E. cyaneus*
BLUEBERRY ASH, BLUE OLIVEBERRY

This Australian evergreen is valued for its foliage, flowers and fruit. A tall shrub or small tree, it reaches 10 m (about 30 ft), with an erect trunk and spreading crown. The shiny, lanceolate foliage is sharply lobed and finely veined. In spring and summer, clusters of pink or white frilly-edged flowers appear on fine stalks. Bright blue berries follow, globe-shaped and 1 cm (about ½ in) in diameter. This frost-tender tree tolerates a minimum temperature of 5°C (about 40°F). The species requires a damp, shady location and plentiful water while in flower. Prune back summer growth at the start of winter to control its size. Propagate from seed in spring, or from cuttings in summer.

EMBOTHRIUM
coccineum
CHILEAN FIREBUSH

Native to Chile and Argentina, this evergreen or semi-evergreen small tree or spreading bush varies in height between 3 and 10 m (about 9–30 ft) and has shiny, dark green, lance-shaped leaves. These are woody and narrow, growing up to 10 cm (about 4 in) long. Terminal clusters of scarlet, tubular flowers bloom in an impressive display from late spring to early summer. The plant will produce flowers from an early age, provided it is well watered. A cool-temperate species, it enjoys a damp, cool location with acid soil and good drainage. Propagate from suckers in spring or seed in autumn/fall.

ENTELEA
arborescens
WHAU

This small evergreen tree or shrub is native to New Zealand and grows to 3–6 m (about 9–18 ft) in height. It is the only species in its genus, and is grown for its attractive foli-

Embothrium coccineum

Diospyros kaki

Entelea arborescens

Elaeocarpus reticulatus

age, fruits and flowers. It has a stocky, upright trunk and green, slightly serrated foliage with prominent veins, similar to the mulberry. Pendent clusters of dainty, white flowers with orange stamen appear in late spring. These are followed, in mid-summer, by thorny, light green seed pods. This frost-tender species prefers temperate coastal areas, semi shade and damp soil. Water frequently while in flower and propagate from seed or cuttings in summer. The timber is valued for its lighter-than-cork weightlessness.

Dombeya tiliacea

A Field Trip to Norfolk Island

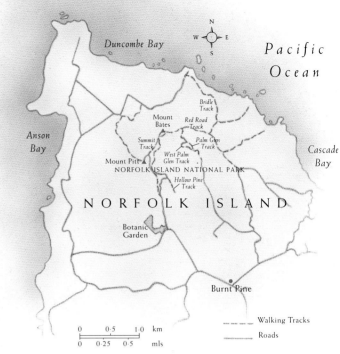

The stately splendour of Norfolk Island pines (*Araucaria heterophylla*) can't be fully appreciated until you see them growing in their own home—Norfolk Island.

Norfolk Island is a tiny island in the Pacific Ocean, about 1700 km (about 1050 miles) north-east of Sydney, Australia. You can fly to Norfolk Island from Sydney or from Auckland, New Zealand. As your aircraft approaches the island, you can see the steep basalt cliffs and gently rolling hills, and catch your first glimpse of its most dominant feature—great stands of Norfolk Island pines. They can be seen both in the open and in the densely wooded areas where they can be seen towering over the canopy.

Norfolk Island has a pleasant, mild, subtropical climate with an average yearly rainfall of 1326 mm (about 52 in). The best time to visit is in summer, when the mean temperature is 25°C (about 77°F); in winter it is about 18°C (about 65°F).

The best place to see the island's most interesting and beautiful flora is Norfolk Island National Park. There are up to 170 native plant species, about 40 of which are found only on Norfolk Island. It is a good idea to visit the Botanic Garden on Mission Road before you explore the National Park. Here you can familiarize yourself with some of the flora so you can more easily identify it when you are in the park. The National Park contains some 8 km (about 5 miles) of walking tracks. A good place to start exploring these is from the summit of Mount Pitt, the highest point of the island. You can walk or drive to this area from Burnt Pine.

As you wind your way up the mountain the towering pines and palms create a canopy that, in places, obscures the sky. The rich soil here is home to many fern species, including the smooth tree fern (*Cyathea brownii*), which is considered to be the world's tallest. The view from the summit is magnificent; you can see the whole of Norfolk Island and neighbouring Nepean and Phillip Islands, and all around an endless expanse of sea.

From Mount Pitt take the Summit Track to Mount Bates, winding your way through some thick forest. The trees here include the Norfolk Island hibiscus, also known as the white oak (*Lagunaria patersonii*), which produces splendid pink flowers in spring (September to November). The pepper tree (*Macropiper excelsum*), too, is fairly abundant. This shrub grows up to 3 m (about 9 ft), producing yellow flower spikes followed by spikes of yellow to orange fruit which was used in preserves by the early settlers.

Follow the Red Road Track from Mount Bates through more hardwood forest and large stands of Norfolk Island pines and you may see the epiphytic orchid *Taeniophyllum muellerii*, commonly known as the minute orchid, growing on the trunks and branches. On the forest floor is *Oplismenus*, a creeping native grass which has tiny reddish flowers.

Looking south from Anson Bay, Norfolk Island.

Lichen covers the limbs of some pines in the island's north-east.

Araucaria heterophylla

The Palm Glen Track leads you through one of the island's most attractive areas where you will see great stands of the Norfolk Island palm (*Rhopalostylis baueri*), a magnificent tree reaching heights of 10 m (about 30 ft). The West Palm Glen Track leads through more stands of palms and a lush tree fern forest. Here you will see the smooth tree fern again, also the smaller rough tree fern (*Cyathea australis*) and the rare king fern (*Marattia salicina*).

Wildlife in the area includes the scarlet robin, a delightful but endangered endemic bird which is black with a bright red breast. The Norfolk Island morepork (a small owl) makes its nest in a hollow of the Norfolk Island pine, as do many of the island's native birds. Another threatened species, the Norfolk Island green parrot, an attractive bird with jewel green plumage, makes its home among the branches. The white tern, a sea bird and the island's emblem, also nests here.

After you have walked back to Mount Pitt—the round trip is 4 km (about 2½ miles)—take the track to Hollow Pine. Here stands a magnificent Norfolk Island pine which is hollow at the base. An escaped convict is said to have lived for seven years in a similar pine before he was finally captured.

The area surrounding Hollow Pine is rich in native flora. Many parts of the island have been affected by the encroachment of weeds but here volunteers have assisted in the battle against unwanted introduced species.

Before European settlement, the island was almost covered in rainforest. When Captain Cook first landed, the Norfolk Island pines came right down to the water's edge. Clearing of the land started within days of settlement in 1788, and now less than 1 per cent remains as it was when Cook saw it. Planting of the pines is now being done on a large scale. These may take up to 80 years or more to reach their full height of up to 70 m (about 220 ft), but eventually the island may once again be almost covered by these magnificent trees.

As the Pitcairners of Norfolk Island say: 'If we do not live to see them grow, our children will.'

Araucaria

The unique conifer genus *Araucaria* consists of 19 species, distributed in a remarkable geographical pattern. On one side of the Pacific Ocean there are two species in eastern Australia, one of which occurs in New Guinea which also has an endemic species; Norfolk Island has just one species but nearby New Caledonia has 13 species. Across the Pacific in South America there are just two species, the spectacular 'monkey puzzle' in Chile and southern Argentina, and the Parana pine in south-central Brazil. This sort of distribution suggests the genus originated and diversified before Gondwana, the southern supercontinent, began splitting apart over 100 million years ago.

The araucarias make beautiful ornamental trees where space is sufficient and the climate is suitable. The most cold-hardy is the Chilean monkey puzzle (*Araucaria araucana*), which actually requires cool climates such as that of southern England. The next most hardy is the Australian bunya pine (*A. bidwillii*). Some of the species, such as the Norfolk Island pine and the New Caledonian pine (*A. columnaris*), are noted for their tolerance of salt-laden winds.

Araucaria heterophylla

Eucalyptus citriodora

ERYTHRINA

CORAL TREE

These deciduous and semi-ever-green trees and shrubs originate in the tropical and warm-temperate areas of Africa, Asia, Central America, the Caribbean and Hawaii. They are usually grown in these areas as ornamentals. They vary in height between 9 and 18 m (about 27–60 ft) and usually have twisted, thorny trunks. Broad, heart-shaped leaves appear on light, weak branches, prone to falling. Tubular flowers bloom in a mass of scarlet, crimson or orange at various times of year; some species in mid-winter, their flowers in striking contrast to denuded limbs. Coral trees will survive in diverse conditions pro-vided temperatures remain above 5°C (about 40°F). Many species prefer exposed coastal locations. Provide rich, porous soil and water sparingly, especially if growing in pots. Propagate from seed in spring, cuttings in summer. Prone to attack by red spider mite.

E. caffra
syn. *E. constantiana, E. insignis*
SOUTH AFRICAN CORAL TREE

This semi-evergreen African native with its spreading crown grows quickly to 12–18 m (about 37–60 ft). The compound foliage, 17 cm (about 7 in) wide, comprises three sharp oval leaflets. Orange-red flow-ers appear in late spring to early sum-mer, followed by leathery legumes containing scarlet seeds. This half-hardy species prefers cold conditions. It is the floral emblem of the city of Los Angeles.

E. crista-galli
COCKSCOMB CORAL TREE, CRYBABY TREE

Originating in Brazil, this decidu-ous species rapidly reaches 4–10 m (about 12–30 ft) and spreads broadly. Its prickly, 3-leafed foliage develops at the end of thorny stems. Rich crimson flowers bloom in loose terminal clusters from sum-mer to autumn/fall. The woody seed pods are 38 cm (about 15 in) long. This species requires full sun and moist soil. Prune in winter; an attrac-tive gnarled trunk will develop with-out pruning but then the crown will be full of dead branches. *E. crista-galli* can survive the occasional frost.

E. lysistemon

This semi-deciduous South African native grows up to 10 m (about 30 ft) tall. Terminal clusters of cylin-drical red flowers often bloom from the tips of the branchlets prior to the new season's foliage.

EUCALYPTUS

GUM TREE, EUCALYPT

This diverse genus of mainly Aus-tralian natives contains over 600 species of evergreen trees and shrubs, prized for their beauty, shade, oils, hardwood and honey. Foliage varies from linear to heart-shaped; young and adult leaves differ markedly, making identification difficult. All species have distinctively lidded flower buds with densely packed stamens, blooming in spring or summer in shades of white, red or yellow. Trees vary from frost-hardy to frost-tender and differ greatly in size, shape and habitat: some low, multi-trunked species are excellent sand-binders, able to survive for a year without rain in the arid inland; other gnarled, salt-resistant species thrive in swamps; others still, straight and tall, prefer cool moun-tain areas. Plant eucalypts in isola-tion with full sun in rich, well-drained soil; trees do not transplant well. Prune in spring and early winter. Propagate from seed in autumn/fall and late winter. Eucalypts were first brought to Europe by Captain Cook's Austral-ian expedition.

E. citriodora
LEMON-SCENTED GUM

This species grows 10–20 m (about 30–65 ft) and is valued for its slen-der beauty and lemon-scented leaves. The attractive trunk is cov-ered with smooth, pinkish grey bark that peels in patches. The deep green foliage is rough and downy when young, becoming lanceolate and smooth when mature. Flowers bloom in thick terminal clusters, 2 cm (about 1 in) across. It is half-hardy; shelter young trees from frost.

E. ficifolia
SCARLET FLOWERING GUM,
RED FLOWERING GUM

Regarded as the most beautiful of all the flowering eucalypts, this species bears enormous terminal clusters of scarlet to orange flowers in late spring to summer. It grows up to 10 m (about 30 ft) with rough bark and a spreading crown of lance-shaped foliage. The pitcher-shaped nuts contain brown winged seeds. This tree does best in a coastal location with full sun, well-drained soil and only very little frost. Seeds from cultivars will pro-duce a variety of colours. It is closely related to *E. calophylla*.

E. globulus
syn. *E. globulus* subsp. *globulus*
TASMANIAN BLUE GUM, BLUE GUM,
SOUTHERN BLUE GUM

Perhaps the most beautiful of all eucalypts, this column-shaped spe-cies is the floral emblem of its native Tasmania in Australia. A fast grower, it may exceed 70 m (about 220 ft). The thick, contorted trunk sheds its smooth, blue bark. The young leaf is silvery blue and circu-lar, maturing to a deep green sickle shape, up to 45 cm (about 18 in) long and fragrant. Single cream blossoms develop along slender stalks in spring and summer. This fully hardy, drought-resistant spe-cies occurs naturally in coastal ar-eas. It prefers a mostly frost-free climate. Probably the most fre-quently planted gum outside Aus-tralia, this species is used for paper pulp, building timber and eucalyp-tus oil.

Eucalyptus globulus

Erythrina lysistemon

Erythrina crista-galli

Erythrina caffra

Eucalyptus ficifolia

E. haemastoma
SCRIBBLY GUM

This species has multiple trunks, their white bark distinctively marked by insect larvae. It grows to 15 m (about 50 ft) with an uneven crown of thick, sickle-shaped leaves 15 cm (about 6 in) long and bears white flowers in terminal clusters year-round, and hemispherical nuts. It survives temperatures down to 5°C (about 40°F). Plant in full sun in rich, well-drained soil.

E. leucoxylon
WHITEWOOD, WHITE IRON BARK, RED-FLOWERED YELLOW GUM

With smooth, bluish white bark marked with yellow patches, this erect evergreen reaches 5–10 m (about 15–30 ft). Its rounded crown is covered with greyish green, lanceolate leaves of varying widths. White or pink flowers (according to variety) appear in long-stemmed triple clusters during winter and spring. The seed pods are 2 cm (about 1 in) long with pointed ends. This moderately frost-hardy species prefers a cool climate and rich, well-drained soil. First described by Von Müeller in 1855, leucoxylon means 'white wood'.

E. mannifera subsp. maculosa
RED-SPOTTED GUM

Erect, with an open, spreading crown, this frost-hardy evergreen grows quickly to 10–15 m (about 30–50 ft). Its powdery white bark is pinkish red when new. The blue-green, lanceolate foliage is 8–15 cm (about 3–6 in) long. Creamy white flowers appear in terminal clusters of 3 to 7 blossoms, in late spring and summer; in winter in some climates.

E. saligna
SYDNEY BLUE GUM

This magnificent evergreen grows to over 35 m (about 110 ft) and has ornamental, smooth, bluish white bark. Its wide lanceolate leaves are deep green in maturity and prominently veined. Dense white blossoms appear in summer and autumn/fall, attracting an abundance of bees. This half-hardy tree prefers temperatures above 5°C (about 40°F). Plant in deep, fertile soil. The species is grown for timber and honey.

E. torquata
CORAL GUM, COOLGARDIE GUM

A fast grower reaching only 6–12 m (about 18–37 ft), this small triangular tree is highly valued for its ornamental buds and flowers. It has a thick round crown and pendent branchlets. The mature, bluish green leaves are lance-shaped and 4–12 cm (about 2–5 in) long. Reddish pink buds appear after only 2 years, opening into red, pink or white flowers in spring and summer—sometimes enduring through winter. The small nuts are jug-shaped. Half-hardy (though it may be frost-tender when young), it is able to withstand drought.

FAGUS
BEECH

Native to Europe and North America, this small, cool-climate genus includes some of the world's most popular deciduous trees. They are valued for their autumn/fall foliage and their timber, used to make furniture. Reaching up to 30 m (about 95 ft), they are well rounded with dense crowns. Foliage varies in shape, size and colour, ranging from yellow to purple. Inconspicuous flowers bloom in late spring, followed in late autumn/fall by the pyramid-shaped nuts in their prickly, oval seed pods. Although edible, beechnuts are not particularly tasty and are usually used as stock fodder. The purple-leaved trees like full sun; the yellow-leaved prefer partial shade. All species enjoy well-drained, limed soil.

F. sylvatica
EUROPEAN BEECH

Triangular in shape with a broad spreading crown and drooping branches, this fast grower reaches up to 40 m (about 130 ft). Young foliage is oval, downy and light green, maturing to deep, glossy green. Leaves turn a vivid golden orange in autumn/fall. It prefers cold climates and partial shade, and will do best in well-drained alkaline soils. Prune in summer, and propagate from seed in autumn/fall, budding in late summer.

F. sylvatica f. purpurea
COPPER BEECH, PURPLE BEECH

This form has purple-green leaves that turn copper in autumn/fall. It requires full sun. True colour can be achieved from seed. In Germany it is considered unlucky to plant a copper beech near the house—the tree is thought to attract lightning. It stands clipping and can be used for tall hedges.

Eucalyptus saligna

Fagus sylvatica f. purpurea

Fagus sylvatica

Eucalyptus haemastoma

Eucalyptus leucoxylon

Eucalyptus torquata

Eucalyptus mannifera subsp. maculosa

FICUS

This large and extremely diverse genus consists of about 600 evergreen or deciduous tropical trees, shrubs and root climbers. These trees are grown for their foliage or for shade; some species are also grown for their fruit. The spring or summer flowers are insignificant. They prefer a fertile, well-drained soil, and sun or partial shade. They range from fully hardy to frost-tender. Propagate from seed in spring, or from cuttings or by layering in summer. Watch out for red spider mite.

F. rubiginosa
PORT JACKSON FIG, RUSTY-LEAFED FIG

This large evergreen, native to Australia, grows to 20–30 m (about 65–95 ft) high, its crown spreading almost as wide. The main trunk is buttressed; pendent branches drop aerial roots that become auxiliary trunks. The foliage is shiny deep green on top, downy and rust coloured underneath. Inconspicuous

Fuchsia excorticata

flowers form in flapped tubes in spring and summer, followed by pairs of globular, yellow fruit, covered with bumps. This salt-resistant species will not survive below 10°C (about 50°F). It is too large for the average garden.

F. sur
BROOM CLUSTER FIG, CAPE FIG

This semi-deciduous to evergreen tree reaches a height of 20 m (about 65 ft). It is an attractive wide-crowned shade tree with 10 cm (4 in) long leaves that are reddish brown when young. Large edible, orange to red fruit is borne in branched clusters. The fruit can be used to make jams and jellies. It prefers a warm climate and deep soil; water regularly. *F. sur* should be planted well away from buildings and drain pipes.

FIRMIANA
simplex
syn. *F. platanifolia, Sterculia platanifolia*
CHINESE PARASOL TREE, PHOENIX TREE

This sturdy tree, originating in Japan and China, grows up to 15 m (about 50 ft). Valued for its shade, it has large leaves with 3 to 5 lobes. Yellowy green flowers appear in spring, clustered along the tree's thin stems. The papery fruit has 5 bracts and the seeds develops on its exterior. Only just frost-hardy, this tree prefers a warm-temperate climate, with full sun. It likes damp well-drained soil. Prune if it be-

comes necessary; propagate from mature seed in spring.

FRAXINUS
ASH

Native to the northern hemisphere, this well-known genus contains about 60 deciduous timber trees and shrubs. They are extremely variable in size, ranging from 15 to 50 m (about 50 to 160 ft). Dense flower clusters which are insignificant in most species appear in early spring, followed by distinctive feathery foliage up to 30 cm (about 12 in) long, divided into 3 to 13 leaflets. Decorative drooping clusters of small, winged seeds develop from the flowers. These fully hardy trees will endure a broad range of temperatures provided that they are planted in deep, fertile soil with sufficient moisture and full sun. Propagate from heat-treated seed in autumn/fall, or by budding in summer.

F. ornus
MANNA ASH, FLOWERING ASH

Originating in southern Europe and Asia Minor, this spreading tree quickly grows up to 20 m (about 65 ft) with a rounded crown. The compound foliage comprises 5 to 9 leaflets, which turn from deep green to reddish purple in autumn/fall. Fragrant white flowers appear in abundance in early spring, during which time a sweet substance called manna is exuded from fissures in the bark.

F. oxycarpa 'Raywood'
CLARET ASH

This robust and fast-growing tree, a cultivar of Australian origin, is valued for its autumn/fall leaves and attractive shape. The tree grows to 10–15 m (about 30–50 ft), developing a stocky trunk and rounded crown. The deeply lobed foliage is made up of 7 to 9 narrow leaflets which turn from shiny deep green to a claret red in autumn/fall. This frost-hardy tree will withstand hot conditions if regularly watered.

FUCHSIA
excorticata
TREE FUCHSIA

Originating in New Zealand, this attractive evergreen is valued for its flowers and extended blooming period. Reaching up to 10 m (about 30 ft) tall, it has scaly bark and papery, rounded, mid-green leaves up to 10 cm (about 4 in) in length. Individual, elongated, green and purple flowers appear from early summer until the end of autumn/fall. The flowers have 4 petals and a glossy appearance. This tree prefers moderate temperatures and a damp, humid atmosphere. Plant in rich, peaty soil, particularly if planted in a tub, with semi-shade and shelter from stiff breezes. Propagate from soft cuttings at any time of the year. Prune severely in early spring if affected by the cold, otherwise prune annually to encourage regular form and promote fresh growth.

Ficus rubiginosa

Firmiana simplex

Fraxinus ornus

Fraxinus oxycarpa 'Raywood'

Ficus sur

GEIJERA
parviflora
WILGA

This evergreen, native to Australia and New Caledonia, is valued for its attractive shape and aromatic hardwood. Small and slender, with pendent branches and a spreading crown, it quickly reaches 3–10 m (about 9–30 ft). Its thick, lanceolate, grey-green leaves are up to 15 cm (about 6 in) long. Open clusters of creamy white flowers cover the tree in spring. Glossy black seeds follow. Prune the tree infrequently to encourage compact form. It should be propagated from seed in autumn/fall. This citrus relative enjoys full sun and grows well in dry areas, where it may be used for stock fodder in droughts. It is only just frost-hardy. The genus was named after seventeenth-century botanist J. D. Geijer.

GINKGO
biloba
MAIDENHAIR TREE

The sole member of its genus, this important deciduous conifer has been found in fossils that are over 200 million years old. Native apparently to Europe, Asia, Australia and America, it is thought to be extinct now in the wild. Fortunately, it is widely cultivated. This hardy tree, valued for its rich autumn/fall foliage and timber, grows up to 40 m (about 130 ft). Its triangular crown broadens out in maturity. The arching branches develop bright green, fan-shaped leaves, similar to the maidenhair fern but much larger, which turn deep golden yellow in autumn/fall. Little yellow flowers sprinkle the mature trees in spring, followed by orange-yellow fruits about the size of a small plum. The female tree is not popular among some gardeners as the fallen seeds have an unpleasant odour. This enduring tree survives both arid and wet climates and withstands urban pollution. The tree needs deep fertile soil and it should be propagated from seed or graft. Ginkgos are widely cultivated in China, where their edible seeds are considered a delicacy. These trees were introduced to the West in the eighteenth century.

GLEDITSIA
triacanthos 'Sunburst'
HONEY LOCUST

This deciduous North American species grows up to 15 m (about 50 ft) and develops a broad crown. It is valued for its attractive fern-like foliage, composed of up to 32 leaflets. The immature foliage is golden yellow, turning to deep green in

Grevillea robusta

summer and reverting to golden yellow in autumn/fall. Insignificant, pea-like flowers appear in green, downy clusters. These are followed by large, shiny, red-ochre seed pods, slightly curved and up to 45 cm (about 18 in) long. The pods are filled with sweet pulp, explaining the common name. This drought-resistant tree is fully hardy, though saplings may be affected by frost. Plant in rich, well-drained soil in full sun. Propagate by budding at the end of summer. The species itself is viciously thorny, and thornless cultivars like 'Sunburst' are much preferred in gardens. There are several others available also.

GREVILLEA
robusta
SILKY OAK, SILK OAK

Native to Australia, this cone-shaped evergreen tree is the tallest of its large genus. It quickly reaches 15–45 m (about 50–145 ft). It is admired for its attractive flowers, foliage and timber. The pointed, bipinnately lobed leaves are dark green on the top and silvery beneath. In late spring to early summer the tree is ablaze with brilliant orange, comb-like flowers which are followed by winged seeds. The tree likes full sun or partial shade and can be propagated readily from seed. Young specimens are used as indoor plants in Europe. Half-hardy, it is difficult to establish in dry conditions. The genus was named after botanist Charles Greville, a contemporary of the famous botanist Sir Joseph Banks.

Geijera parviflora

Harpephyllum caffrum

Ginkgo biloba

Gleditsia triacanthos 'Sunburst'

HARPEPHYLLUM
caffrum
KAFFIR PLUM, DATE

This South African evergreen grows moderately fast to 10 m (about 30 ft) with a thick, domed crown. The pretty foliage, which matures from red to shiny deep green, consists of pinnate leaves with angled, lanceolate leaflets 7 cm (about 3 in) long. Inconspicuous green-white blossoms appear in branched clusters (male and female flowers are borne on separate trees), followed by

bunches of lush, edible fruit hanging from the ends of the branches. These turn from green to red to deep purple and, though acidic when eaten raw, they are excellent in jellies and jams. This frost-tender species requires a warm climate (it does best in subtropical climates) to thrive. Plant it in full sun and deep, crumbly soil. Shelter this tree from salt winds and water frequently. Propagate from seed or cuttings. This tree's dense foliage prevents anything growing beneath it or nearby.

Hoheria populnea

HOHERIA
populnea
LACEBARK, HOUHERE

Native to New Zealand, this slender, fast-growing evergreen reaches 8–15 m (about 24–50 ft) and is one of only two in its genus. The tree is valued for its decorative flowers, foliage and bark, which is papery, pale brown and white, shedding in patches. Its glossy, deep green leaves are elliptical and deeply lobed. Thick white clusters of lightly scented, star-shaped flowers appear in late summer to early autumn/fall. This half-hardy species will survive in cool and warm conditions. Plant in rich, porous soil with full sun or partial shade and water regularly. Propagate from cuttings in summer, seed in autumn/fall.

HYMENOSPORUM
flavum
SWEETSHADE, AUSTRALIAN FRANGIPANI, WING-SEED TREE

The only species of its genus, this Australian native is valued for its attractive flowers. Up to 17 m (about 56 ft) tall, it has an erect columnar shape, spreading to triangular in maturity. The elliptical foliage is glossy deep green on sparse limbs with irregular downturned branches. Splendid long flowers, cream variegated with red and green, develop in clusters in spring. These fragrant tubular blooms mature to rich orange-yellow and are followed by flat seed pods filled with numerous seeds. This half-hardy evergreen prefers a warm climate with full sun and fertile, well-drained, acidic soil. Propagate from seed in autumn/fall, cuttings in late summer.

JACARANDA
mimosifolia
syn. J. ovalifolia
JACARANDA

Native to the high plains of Brazil, this fast grower is valued for its beautiful flowers, foliage and timber. It develops a broad, rounded crown and grows up to 17 m (about 56 ft). Vivid green, fern-like foliage is bipinnate, with 12 or more leaflets. Depending on climate, the leaves may be shed in winter or early spring before the flowers appear. These are very attractive, mauve-blue terminal clusters of tubular blossoms. Flat, leathery seed pods follow. This half-hardy species prefers dry and temperate climates. Protect the immature tree from frosts. Plant in rich, porous soil with full sun and do not over water; prune potted specimens in late winter. Propagate from seed in spring.

JUGLANS
nigra
BLACK WALNUT, CALIFORNIA WALNUT

This species from North America and is valued for its foliage, timber and edible nuts. It grows to some 30 m (about 95 ft) with an open crown and shiny, red-tinted foliage. Large, shiny foliage comprises 15 to 25 leaflets some 15 cm (about 6 in) long. These are followed by greenish yellow male catkins, inconspicuous female flowers and, finally, edible nuts. This tree is fully hardy but saplings require shelter from frosts. Plant in deep, rich, porous soil with full sun. Propagate from seed in autumn/fall. In Latin, *Juglans* means 'Jupiter's acorn', so highly did the Romans value the fruit of the European walnut, *J. regia*, which is included in this book under fruit trees.

JUNIPERUS
JUNIPER

This northern hemisphere genus contains over 50 species of slow-growing conifers of extremely diverse colour and habit, ranging in height from 9 to 25 m (about 27 to 80 ft). Adult foliage comprises short, scale-like leaves. Species are fully hardy and drought-resistant, able to survive extremes in temperature. Unusually for conifers, they prefer alkaline soil. They also prefer full sun and dry, sandy soil. Trees should be pruned regularly: as with most conifers, new growth will not sprout from brown wood. Propagate from seed or cuttings, or by grafting. Watch for aphids and leafrollers. The blue, berry-like fruit is used to flavour gin.

J. communis
COMMON JUNIPER

This shrub or tree reaches a height of 3 to 12 m (about 9 to 37 ft) and is slim or cone-shaped. It has brownish red bark and fragrant, yellowish green, needle-like foliage borne in groups of three. The globular fruit are blue-black, turning bluish green before finally maturing to black. These fruit are used for flavouring in cooking. This frost-hardy species prefers cool to cold climates.

J. virginiana
PENCIL CEDAR, EASTERN RED CEDAR

Originating in North America, this conifer is valued for its shade and timber. Triangular at first, the tree spreads in maturity and grows to 33 m (about 105 ft). The grey, needle-like foliage is prickly when young. Blue-black cones bear three seeds. The timber is used to make pencils (explaining the common name, 'Pencil cedar') and cigar boxes.

Jacaranda mimosifolia

Juniperus virginiana

Juniperus communis

Hymenosporum flavum

Juglans nigra

Koelreuteria paniculata

Lagarostrobus franklinii

Knightia excelsa

Kigelia africana

KIGELIA
africana
syn. *K. pinnata*
SAUSAGE TREE

This single-species African genus is grown for its flowers, foliage and bizarre long-stemmed fruit. A small, upright, compact tree, it quickly reaches up to 10 m (about 30 ft). The broad, shady crown has feather-like foliage, composed of 7 to 11 leaflets. Deep red, bell-shaped blossoms develop in drooping clusters from autumn/fall until spring. These open at night and smell unpleasant. They are followed by inedible, sausage-like pods which last almost the entire year. Leathery and brown, they hang from stems over 1 m (about 3 ft) long—possibly the longest stemmed fruit in the world. This tropical tree prefers temperatures above 16°C (about 60°F) and a humid climate, rich, well-drained soil, and a sunny position. Propagate from seed in autumn/fall.

KNIGHTIA
excelsa
REWAREWA, MAORI HONEYSUCKLE

This evergreen New Zealand native reaches up to 20 m (about 65 ft). Slim and columnar, it has rigid upstretched branches covered with deep green, heavily serrated leaves. This woody, lanceolate foliage grows 10–15 cm (about 4–6 in) long. Dark red, silky flowers bloom in thick, long-stemmed clusters from mid-summer to early spring. Leathery brown seed pods follow, dividing into two segments when mature. This half-hardy, cool-temper-

ate tree prefers temperatures above 5°C (about 40°F). Plant in well-drained soil with full sun or semi-shade. Propagate from seed in spring. An excellent timber tree, this species is able to withstand fires.

KOELREUTERIA
paniculata
CHINA TREE, GOLDEN-RAIN TREE, VARNISH TREE, PRIDE OF INDIA

This deciduous Asian native has a broad convex crown and grows quickly to 10–15 m (about 30–50 ft) tall. Its feathery bipinnate foliage grows up to 45 cm (about 18 in) long and turns from green to deep golden yellow in autumn/fall, particularly in cooler climates. Large decorative clusters of golden yellow flowers develop in summer, followed by pinkish brown seed pods, swollen with black seeds. This frost-hardy species survives arid inland conditions and enjoys full sun and strong alkaline soil. Propagate from seed in spring; root cuttings in winter. The flowers are used in Chinese medicine.

LABURNUM
x *watereri* 'Vossii'
VOSS'S LABURNUM, HYBRID LABURNUM, GOLDEN CHAIN TREE

Native to Europe and parts of Asia Minor, this deciduous hybrid is valued for its beautiful golden chains of flowers. Elegant and erect, it grows 3–10 m (about 9–30 ft). The compound foliage has 3 oval leaflets, shiny dark green on top, soft and downy underneath. Pendent, pea-like flowers develop in golden clusters on long stems in late

Lagunaria patersonii

spring. A few legume-like pods follow, some containing the highly poisonous seeds. This tree likes cold, damp locations with full sun and will tolerate most soil types, but it will not survive in hot climates or waterlogged soil. Propagate by budding in summer. Do not plant where animals graze, as all parts of this species are toxic.

LAGAROSTROBUS
franklinii
syn. *Dacrydium franklinii*
HUON PINE

Native to Tasmania, Australia, this magnificent timber tree lives for hundreds of years in cool-temperate forests. A very slow-growing conifer with a conical shape, it reaches up to 30 m (about 95 ft). The slim, pendent, grey branches and branchlets are covered in small, densely packed, scale-like leaves. This tree likes cold, damp climates and does very well in tubs. It requires deep, rich soil with plenty of water and good drainage. Prune regularly and propagate from seed or cuttings. The pale timber is prized by woodworkers. Unfortunately many of

Laburnum x *watereri* 'Vossii'

Tasmania's majestic specimens have been felled and it will be a long time before they are replaced. It is rare in cultivation, but well worth growing.

LAGUNARIA
patersonii
NORFOLK ISLAND HIBISCUS, WHITEWOOD, PYRAMID TREE

Native to Australia's Lord Howe Island and Norfolk Island, this attractive evergreen is the only species of its genus. Growing to 15 m (about 50 ft), it is valued for its attractive, regular triangular shape and for its timber and flowers. Its leathery, elliptical leaves are grey with a whitish underside. Hibiscus-like, 3 cm (about 1½ in) wide pink flowers appear in summer followed by inedible large fruit. These contain fine prickles, extremely irritating if touched. This half-hardy tree prefers warm climates but is unable to survive drought. It is salt-resistant, and enjoys coastal locations with sandy soil. It propagates simply from seed and tolerates pruning. The genus was named after sixteenth-century botanist Andres Laguna.

Liquidambar formosana

Maclura pomifera

Larix decidua

Liriodendron tulipifera

Lophostemon confertus

Liquidambar styraciflua

LARIX
decidua
EUROPEAN LARCH

Native to northern Europe, this enduring deciduous conifer has an attractive symmetrical conical shape, opening out in later years. It reaches an enormous height, 60 m (about 190 ft), and develops tiered, drooping branches. These are covered in pale green needle-like foliage in spring, turning to golden brown in autumn/fall. Little upright cones with round scales appear in winter, when all the limbs are bare. This cold-climate tree requires good rainfall, well-drained soil and full sun. It is prized by shipbuilders for its lofty, regular trunks and is also a valuable source of turpentine.

LIQUIDAMBAR
SWEET GUM

This deciduous genus contains three species, one each from Asia, Asia Minor and North to Central America. All are valued for their splendid autumn/fall foliage, which greatly varies in colour. Conical in shape, the trees grow to varying heights, from 8 to 38 m (about 24 to 122 ft). The leaves are palmate, resembling the maple, with 5 to 7 deeply cut, serrated lobes. Frost-hardy when fully grown, these trees can survive extremes in temperature. They prefer a warm moist location but are not salt-resistant. Nothing will grow near them as they are voracious feeders, sucking what goodness there is from the soil. Plant in rich, deep, porous earth with full sun or partial shade. Propagate from seed in autumn/fall; bud in spring. The timber is used to make furniture.

L. formosana
FORMOSA SWEET GUM, CHINESE LIQUIDAMBAR

This tough, fast-growing native of Taiwan and China has a spreading pyramidal shape and reaches some 38 m (about 122 ft). The leaves have 3 lobes and are hairy underneath. They turn from purple in spring to deep green in summer, before changing to brilliant orange-red and purple in autumn/fall. Male and female flowers bloom separately on the same tree, followed by prickly globes of pendent fruit. This valuable timber tree is also used in the manufacture of perfumes.

L. styraciflua
SWEET GUM, RED GUM, BILSTED

This deciduous native of North and Central America has an erect conical shape that may spread in maturity. It grows quickly: up to 38 m (about 122 ft), depending on conditions. The lustrous foliage, with 5 or 7 lobes, is 10–15 cm (about 4–6 in) wide. Young leaves are pale green, maturing to deep green and turning vivid red-purple and orange-yellow in autumn/fall. The branches develop corky shoots in winter. This frost-hardy tree survives hot weather with regular watering. Select seedling trees in autumn/fall as colour is very variable.

LIRIODENDRON
tulipifera
TULIP TREE, TULIP POPLAR, YELLOW POPLAR

This deciduous North American native is valued for its flowers and rich yellow autumn/fall foliage. The tree quickly attains heights of 15–30 m (about 50–95 ft), in a symmetrical pyramid; branches often do not start until halfway up. Distinctive, 4-lobed leaves have blunted middle teeth, giving the foliage a squarish appearance. In spring the tree bears green, scented flowers shaped like tulips, with orange bands encircling the stamens. These are followed by conical seed heads containing winged seeds. This fully hardy species prefers cool climates and enjoys full sun and neutral to acid soil. It may be transplanted up to a good size and is propagated from seed in autumn/fall, budding in summer. The timber, although not very durable, is much used in the USA.

LOPHOSTEMON
confertus
syn. *Tristania conferta*
BRUSH BOX, BRISBANE BOX

This evergreen Australian species is a fast grower, reaching 45 m (about 145 ft) in its rainforest habitat, but only 15–30 m (about 50–95 ft) in the average garden. The brown bark is shed in strips. It has a domed crown and deep green foliage, lanceolate and woody. Little cream flowers with dense, prominent stamens bloom in spring. It is classed as half-hardy but will survive in a broad range of climates. Plant in rich, well-drained soil with full sun; prune saplings in winter to encourage shape. Propagate from seed in spring, cuttings in summer. There is a handsome cultivar with variegated leaves.

MACLURA
pomifera
OSAGE ORANGE, BOWWOOD

Originating in North America, this single-species genus is valued for its deciduous foliage, interesting fruit and yellow timber. It grows quickly to 20 m (about 65 ft) with an open, uneven crown and arching branches. Elliptical, deep green leaves turn yellow in autumn/fall. Small clusters of yellow-green flowers appear in summer followed by large, inedible, aggregate fruits. These spherical leathery pods will only develop if both male and female trees are present. The adult tree is frost-hardy, while the immature specimen is frost-tender. Suitable for hedges, the species requires full sun and hot summer temperatures to survive cold winters. Propagate from seed in autumn/fall, cuttings in summer and root cuttings in late winter. The timber was once used to make bows.

MAGNOLIA
MAGNOLIA

This genus comprises two groups: deciduous species, native to the

Magnolia × soulangiana

Malus floribunda

Himalayan region of China, and evergreens, native to Central America and southern USA. All are valued for their beautiful large flowers. The trees grow 12–25 m (about 37–80 ft), with spreading crowns. Their elliptical leaves are lustrous green on top, pitted with brown underneath. The perfumed flowers with silky petals and densely packed stamen bloom on deciduous trees in spring, sometimes before the foliage; on the evergreens, in summer. Seed-bearing cones follow. Trees prefer full sun or partial shade and rich, well-drained soil (slightly acid for deciduous species). If using poorer soil, fertilize first with manure. Transplant with care: the roots are extremely fragile. Propagate from cuttings in summer, seed in autumn/fall; graft cultivars in winter. The genus was named after eighteenth-century botanist Pierre Magnol.

M. campbellii

PINK TULIP TREE, CHINESE TULIP TREE

This deciduous Chinese native has an erect appearance when immature, broadening out later. It grows quickly to 6–15 m (about 18–50 ft) tall. Scattered branches bear pointed, elliptical leaves up to 30 cm (about 12 in) long, powdery underneath. This species takes 15–20 years to flower. The big, scented blooms, light pink inside and darker pink outside, appear from the end of winter to mid-spring. The tree prefers a cool-temperate climate and open space.

M. grandiflora

BULL BAY, SOUTHERN MAGNOLIA, LAUREL MAGNOLIA

This evergreen species from southern USA varies broadly in size and habit: 6–20 m (about 18–95 ft) high, it may be compact and rounded or spreading and conical. It has thick, woody foliage of shiny mid- to deep green leaves, downy brown underneath. Cup-shaped white blooms with a strong citrus scent appear from mid-summer to early autumn/fall, followed by red-brown cones. This moderately frost-hardy species prefers warm climates and moist soil.

Magnolia heptapeta

M. heptapeta
syn. M. denudata, M. conspicua
YULAN, LILY TREE

Native to China, this deciduous spreading tree or tall shrub grows up to 12 m (about 37 ft). It has dark bark and egg-shaped leaves with a hairy underside. Naked branches bear scented, snow-white, tulip-like flowers in early spring. These are followed by rectangular cones containing orange seeds. This frost-hardy species prefers temperate climates.

M. × soulangiana

SAUCER MAGNOLIA, SOULANGE-BODIN'S MAGNOLIA

This deciduous tree develops slowly, reaching 3–8 m (about 9–24 ft), frequently growing multiple trunks and a rounded crown. Tulip-like blooms precede the foliage in early spring, even on young plants. The flower's interior varies from snow white to light pink; the exterior is a deeper pink. The egg-shaped foliage is up to 15 cm (about 6 in) long. This species prefers a warm climate and requires shelter from hot winds. There are several cultivars, blooms ranging in colour from pure-white to deep red. This hybrid was bred in Paris in 1820 by Étienne Soulange-Bodin, from M. heptapeta and M. liliflora.

MALUS

CRAB-APPLE, APPLE

Native to the northern hemisphere, this diverse genus contains 25 deciduous shrubs and trees, valued for their flowers, foliage and fruit. They

Magnolia campbellii

Malus 'Gorgeous'

grow 9–12 m (about 27–37 ft) tall with spreading, round crowns. Foliage ranges from bronze, hairy and wide-lobed to deep green, linear and neat, while the spring blossom varies in colour from deep purple to pure white. The acidic fruit also varies widely, from edible kinds that can be eaten cooked, to purely ornamental crab-apples. Fully hardy, the trees like full sun and cold weather and tolerate any soil that is not too wet. Prune in winter to encourage symmetry; propagate by budding in summer or grafting in winter. Watch for aphids and fireblight.

M. 'Aldenhamensis'

PURPLE CRAB

This small, fully hardy English cultivar grows only 4 m (about 12 ft) tall and is valued for its beautiful autumn/fall foliage. The little leaves have shallow-lobed margins and are purplish red when immature. An abundance of claret-coloured blossoms appear in spring, followed by very attractive purplish red crab-apples in autumn/fall.

Malus 'Aldenhamensis'

Magnolia grandiflora

M. floribunda

JAPANESE FLOWERING CRAB-APPLE, SHOWY CRAB-APPLE

This expansive, thick-crowned tree grows to 10 m (about 30 ft). Its early spring buds are crimson red, blooming into light pink blossoms. The variable foliage is egg-shaped to rectangular, some types with heavily saw-toothed edges and 3 to 5 lobes. Small, reddish yellow, scented crab-apples appear in autumn/fall. The oldest of the decorative crab-apples, this tree is thought to originate in Japan, and is the parent of many hybrids.

M. 'Gorgeous'

Bred in New Zealand, this cultivar is valued for its decorative fruit, which is also used to make jellies and preserves. A small tree of only 2–4 m (about 6–12 ft), it has elliptical green leaves 12 cm (about 5 in) long. Pink buds appear in spring, opening into snow white blossoms. Between autumn/fall and winter the branches become laden with an abundance of little crab-apples which mature from green-red to deep red.

Metrosideros excelsa

Michelia doltsopa

Malus ioensis 'Plena'

Melia azedarach

Melaleuca quinquenervia

Maytenus boaria

M. ioensis 'Plena'

BECHTEL'S CRAB, PRAIRIE CRAB, WILD CRAB

This North American tree grows slowly up to 6 m (about 18 ft) with an expansive habit. Its branches bear foliage which has an extremely downy underside and turns from vivid green to bright yellow in autumn/fall. Large, semi-double and lightly scented, the light pink flowers bloom in open clusters towards the end of spring. They are sometimes followed by inconspicuous green-yellow fruit.

MAYTENUS
boaria

MAYTEN

Originating in Chile, this small, handsome evergreen grows 6–8 m (about 18–24 ft) tall. Lustrous deep green foliage growing on slender stalks is lance-shaped and slightly lobed. Inconspicuous starry flowers bloom in late spring. Perfect for small gardens, this frost-hardy tree prefers cool climates, although saplings need protection from winter winds. Plant in full sun or partial shade. Propagate from cuttings in summer, suckers in autumn/fall and spring. Mayten is inclined to be invasive in some countries, such as New Zealand.

MELALEUCA
quinquenervia

BROAD-LEAF PAPERBARK, PUNK TREE

Native to Australia, New Caledonia and New Guinea, this vigorous evergreen reaches 10–15 m (about 30–50 ft). It is valued for its attractive orange-brown bark: papery and thin, it sheds in patches, contrasting pleasingly with the large lustrous green leaves. Little spiky flowers, resembling bottlebrushes, bloom in pink or cream clusters almost year-round, but especially in spring and autumn/fall. Although this species is frost-tender it is salt-resistant and able to survive in saturated soil. Plant in full sun and propagate from seed in spring, cuttings in summer. A medicinal oil is made from the leaves. It is a dreadful pest in the Florida Everglades.

MELIA
azedarach

PERSIAN LILAC, BEAD TREE, CHINABERRY, WHITE CEDAR

This expansive Asian native, growing 6–12 m (about 18–37 ft) tall, is valued for its foliage, flowers, fruit and timber. Deep green, bipinnate leaves have numerous leaflets. Scented, star-shaped flowers bloom in spring in bluish purple clusters, resembling lilacs. The green fruit matures to yellow-orange in autumn/fall. This frost-hardy species flourishes in warm coastal areas, tolerates arid conditions and

may be planted in any reasonable soil if given full sun. Propagate from seed in autumn/fall. Check for white cedar moth caterpillars in late summer to autumn/fall. The fine timber of this tree is used to make furniture and its fruit, although poisonous to both animals and humans, is used to make medicines. The species does occur in northern Australia, although most Australian plantings are of Iranian origin. It has become invasive in some countries, such as South Africa.

METROSIDEROS
excelsa

NEW ZEALAND CHRISTMAS TREE, POHUTUKAWA, RATA

This hardy New Zealand evergreen grows to 6–15 m (about 18–50 ft). Slow growing and compact when immature, it becomes fast growing and spreading in adult life, occasionally dropping aerial roots. The elliptical leaves are a lustrous deep green with a white downy underside. In early summer the attractive flowers appear, with erect whorls of dense, wiry, deep red stamens. This species will not survive freezing, but will grow in full sun or partial shade. It makes an excellent hedge or windbreak. Prune the young tree's lower branches to encourage a dense crown. Propagate from seed in spring, cuttings in summer. In its native country this tree flowers around Christmas time, explaining its common name.

MICHELIA
doltsopa

WONG-LAN, EVERGREEN MAGNOLIA

Originating in Tibet and West China, this triangular evergreen grows rapidly up to 15 m (about 50 ft). The attractive oval leaves are deep green, lighter underneath, and up to 15 cm (about 6 in) long. In late winter to early spring white to yellowish flowers appear in the leaf axils. Resembling the magnolia (to which Michelia is related), they have 12 petals and a strong, cloying perfume. This species is half-hardy but prefers warm climates. Plant in fertile well-drained soil with full sun or partial shade. Propagate from seed in autumn/fall or spring, cuttings in summer. The genus was named after a seventeenth-century botanist, Pietro Micheli.

MILLETTIA
grandis
syn. M. caffra

IRONWOOD TREE, TREE WISTERIA, UMZIMBEET

This evergreen member of the Leguminoseae (pea) family is native to South Africa. Fast growing, it reaches up to 9 m (about 27 ft) with a stout trunk and an expansive,

Nothofagus obliqua

Nyssa sylvatica

convex crown. The downy foliage is made up of 11 to 15 slender, feathery leaflets which mature from grey to a glossy deep green. Erect, purple and white flowers appear in branched racemes in late spring to early summer, followed by brown seed pods. This species prefers a tropical climate and will not survive below 5°C (about 40°F). Plant in rich, well-drained soil with full sun. Water regularly; prune to encourage shape. Propagate from heat-treated seed in spring. The timber is used in carpentry.

NAGEIA
falcata
syn. *Podocarpus falcatus*
OUTENIQUA YELLOW-WOOD

This grand conifer grows erect up to 50 m (about 160 ft) in the wilds of its native South Africa, but usually 15–30 m (about 50–95 ft) in cultivation. It has peeling bark and shiny, slender, dark green foliage, 2–5 cm (about 1–2 in) long. Its large, greenish blue seed pods are globe-shaped and hang from a short, thick stem (*Podocarpus* means 'footed stalk'). A frost-hardy species, it prefers a mild climate. It may be grown in most soils and requires full sun. Prune to shape and propagate from seed.

NOTHOFAGUS
SOUTHERN BEECH

Native to the southern hemisphere, this diverse genus has over 25 deciduous and evergreen species, including some extremely valuable timber trees. Dome-shaped, they range from short and shrubby to tall and columnar, reaching up to 70 m

Millettia grandis

(about 220 ft). The leaves, resembling those of their close relative the northern beech, are egg-shaped to rectangular with heavily lobed edges and are downy when young. Insignificant flowers develop in late spring, followed by seed pods containing 3 triangular beechnuts. These fully to frost-hardy trees grow in cold temperate to subtropical climates. They like full sun or partial shade and deep, rich, neutral to acid soil that is moist but porous. Protect from strong winds; propagate from seed in autumn/fall.

N. fusca
NEW ZEALAND RED BEECH

This very attractive, erect evergreen is valued for its decorative leaves and timber. It has a dome-shaped crown and averages 6–12 m (about 18–37 ft) in height when cultivated and up to 35 m (about 110 ft) in the wild. The egg-shaped foliage is roughly serrated and up to 4 cm (about 2 in) long, the immature leaves turning reddish bronze in cooler weather. Small, green flowers are followed by seed cups (involucres), each containing 3 angular seeds. This frost-hardy species prefers moderate temperatures and requires full sun or partial shade. It likes a rich, damp soil with good drainage but has an aversion to alkaline soil. Propagate from seed in autumn/fall.

N. moorei
ANTARCTIC BEECH, AUSTRALIAN BEECH

This erect Australian evergreen has a broad crown, thick foliage and brown, peeling bark. Quick growing, it reaches 18–22 m (about

Nothofagus solandri

60–70 ft). The sharp elliptical foliage matures from lustrous golden red to dark green. Seed pods and green-white flowers are inconspicuous. It prefers a mild climate and is not very drought resistant.

N. obliqua
ROBLE TREE, CHILEAN BEECH

This graceful, deciduous Chilean native grows fast to 20 m (about 65 ft). It has a wide, spreading crown, pendent branches and serrated leaves that turn from deep green to orange-red in autumn/fall. Fully hardy, it requires full sun and well-drained soil. It is much used for its timber in England.

N. solandri
BLACK BEECH

This rapidly growing species is native to New Zealand and is valued for its appearance and timber. Up to 25 m (about 80 ft) tall, it has an erect habit with a rounded crown. The rectangular to oval leaves have slightly furled margins.

Nageia falcata

Nothofagus fusca

Nothofagus moorei

Green individual blooms are followed by typical fruit.

NYSSA
sylvatica
SOUR GUM, PEPPERIDGE, BLACK GUM, TUPELO

Native to North America and Asia, this striking deciduous species is valued for its autumn/fall foliage, its timber and honey. Its shape is a wide-based pyramid, from 15 to 35 m (about 50 to 110 ft) high. Large shiny leaves are almost diamond shaped and deep green, turning vivid red and yellow in autumn/fall; although away from its native home the colours are not always reliable, in some years it just turns yellow. Little clusters of flowers, while inconspicuous, contribute to some of the finest honey in the world. This species likes very warm, humid conditions and relishes waterlogged, slightly acid soil. Plant in full sun or partial shade and avoid transplanting. Propagate from seed in autumn/fall, cuttings in summer.

Peltophorum africanum

Phellodendron
amurense   Parrotia persica

PARKINSONIA
aculeata
JERUSALEM THORN, MEXICAN PALO VERDE

Native to tropical America, this small, spreading, tree has a dome-shaped crown and averages 4 m (about 12 ft) tall and 5 m (about 15 ft) wide. Its distinctive, long bipinnate leaves have prominent midribs that produce bright green, oval leaflets. In spring, pendent clusters of scented, yellow flowers with 5 petals appear, followed by slender seed pods. This frost-tender species prefers a tropical or subtropical climate, rich porous soil and total sun. Pruning is not recommended. Propagate from seed in spring.

PARROTIA
persica
PERSIAN WITCH-HAZEL, PARROTIA, IRONWOOD

Originating in Iran, this compact deciduous species is valued for its decorative autumn/fall foliage. It grows fast, reaching some 10 m (about 30 ft), and often has pendent limbs. Upright spirals of wiry crimson stamens appear on leafless branches in early spring, followed by glossy, egg-shaped foliage. The leaves have undulating margins and turn vivid red, yellow and orange in autumn/fall. The tree is fully hardy, though frosts may damage buds, and prefers a cool climate. Plant in a protected location in deep, rich soil: it withstands lime but shows the best leaf colours in a neutral to acid soil. Propagate from seed in autumn/fall, cuttings in summer. The genus was

named after famous botanist F. W. Parrot.

PAULOWNIA

This deciduous Chinese genus is valued for its beautiful flowers and large foliage. Pyramidal in shape, the trees reach up to 12 m (about 37 ft). The cordate foliage is 30 cm (about 12 in) long and almost as wide. The elegant flowers, similar to foxgloves, develop in dense clusters along an erect common stem, preceding the foliage. These trees like cold climates, some species withstanding extremely cold temperatures, although severe frosts may damage buds and saplings. Plant in rich, porous soil and full sun. Prune severely in spring to encourage large leaves. Propagate from seed in autumn/fall and spring; cuttings in winter.

P. fortunei
FOXGLOVE TREE, FORTUNE'S PAULOWNIA

This small tree grows 7–10 m (about 21–30 ft), with a conical shape that may spread in maturity. Its elliptical leaves are covered underneath in a thick down. Trumpet-like flowers have purple exteriors, their throats a deep purple variegated with white.

P. tomentosa
syn. P. imperialis
ROYAL PAULOWNIA, EMPRESS TREE, PRINCESS TREE, KURRI

Valued for its shade and flowers, this frost-hardy, salt-resistant species quickly reaches 6–15 m (about 18–50 ft). The foliage consists of

Parkinsonia aculeata

Paulownia tomentosa

Paulownia fortunei

paired green leaves, sometimes divided into 3 lobes. Upright, conical blooms are lilac and strongly scented. The tree can be cut almost to the ground annually to develop branches about 3 m (about 9 ft) tall with huge leaves. The timber is used in Asian countries to make furniture.

PELTOPHORUM

Native to all the tropics, this genus contains 15 evergreen or deciduous species valued for their broad shady crowns, flowers and decorative fruit. The trees may grow up to 30 m (about 95 ft) in height. The compound leaves are fern-like. Golden yellow, scented flowers appear in terminal bunches in summer. Frost-tender, the trees prefer temperatures above 8°C (about 46°F) and grow well in subtropical to tropical climates. Locate in a sheltered, semi-shady position with sandy, porous soil. Pruning is not required; propagate from seed or cuttings in summer.

P. africanum

Native to the tropics and subtropics of Africa, this semi-deciduous species reaches 13 m (about 40 ft) in height. In summer, light yellow flowers are borne in terminal clusters.

P. pterocarpum
syn. P. inerme, P. ferrugineum
YELLOW POINCIANA, YELLOW FLAME TREE, RUSTY-SHIELD BEARER

Native to South-East Asia, this deciduous tropical species grows 4–18 m (about 12–60 ft) tall, its thick crown opening out in later years. Much cultivated in tropical countries, it has feathery leaves up to 30 cm (about 12 in) long, a lustrous deep green. In summer vivid reddish brown buds appear, developing into terminal clusters of attractive, wrinkled flowers, bright yellow shaded with red. These are followed by an abundance of rich red, flattened pods that endure until the next flowering. This species is frost-tender, not surviving below 8°C (about 46°F). Plant in a sheltered, partially shady location in light sandy soil. Propagate from seed and cuttings in summer.

PHELLODENDRON
amurense
AMUR CORK TREE

This deciduous Asian native grows to 12 m (about 37 ft), spreading widely. Its shiny dark green foliage has a spicy aroma and turns yellow in autumn/fall. Small green flowers appear, male and female on separate trees, followed by small black, spherical fruit. This cool-climate tree is fully hardy (though young shoots may be affected by frost) but

Pinus patula

Picea pungens 'Koster'

Pinus canariensis

enjoys warm summers. Plant in full sun and rich, porous soil. Propagate from cuttings in summer, seed in autumn/fall and root cuttings in late winter. Rather than referring to the production of cork, the common name describes the older tree's corky bark.

PICEA
pungens 'Koster'
KOSTER BLUE, COLORADO SPRUCE

This North American evergreen tree's glaucous foliage makes it one of the most attractive of all conifers. The leaves are rigid and thorny, maturing from silvery deep blue to green. Spiralled branches support tubular, scaled cones, 10 cm (about 4 in) long. This frost-hardy species likes cooler climates, well-drained soil and full sun. Prune regularly as fresh growth will not bud from deadwood. These trees dislike being moved, so transplant them young. Prone to aphids and mites. Although cutting-grown plants and bluish seedlings are available, a well-grafted plant is preferable. This is one of many cultivars of *P. pungens*; others include 'Aurea', which has golden leaves and 'Caerulea', which has bluish white leaves.

PINUS
PINE

This northern hemisphere genus comprises 80 variable evergreen conifers, between 6 and 60 m (about 18–190 ft) high. Many species are conical when immature, their crowns expanding in later life. The leaves, cylindrical needles up to

45 cm (about 18 in) long, are erect when young and develop in clustered whorls of 2, 3 or 5. Upright yellow-red male catkins and female flowers appear on the same tree. The latter develop into scaled seed-bearing cones, borne singly or in bunches depending upon type. Preferred habitats range from cold high altitudes to subtropical coasts, some fully hardy species growing in difficult positions such as wind-swept cliffs. All enjoy full sun. Prune young trees' candle-like young shoots if necessary to control shape; propagate from seed or by grafting. Prone to leafroller caterpillars. Pines are grown for their softwood, oil and resin.

P. canariensis
CANARY ISLANDS PINE

This elegant tree, native to the Canary Islands, is valued for its bark, shade and pyramidal appearance. It grows quickly to 15–24 m (about 50–77 ft) and has tan-coloured bark with black grooves. Arching branchlets are covered with long, narrow needles that mature from bluish green to a pale green. The woody cones are brown, up to 25 cm (about 10 in) long. This frost-hardy species prefers damp soil.

P. densiflora
JAPANESE RED PINE

This Japanese species grows quickly, averaging 15–25 m (about 50–80 ft), with a level crown. It has a contorted trunk and limbs, and shiny green foliage. Its yellow-purple cones are 5 cm (about 2 in) in diameter. Fully hardy, it prefers moderate climates.

Peltophorum pterocarpum

P. patula
MEXICAN YELLOW PINE, WEEPING PINE, SPREADING-LEAF PINE

This elegant Mexican native has a broad pyramid shape, sometimes with pendent branches. Valued for its timber and shade, it grows rapidly to 15–20 m (about 50–65 ft) tall. Its foliage consists of lustrous, yellowish green needles hanging in whorled clusters of three. The fruit develops in spiralled clusters of 2 to 5 egg-shaped cones. This fully hardy, temperate species requires damp soil and full sun.

P. pinea
STONE PINE, ITALIAN STONE PINE

This attractive species grows 10–18 m (about 30–60 ft) tall and is native to southern Europe and Asia Minor. Its distinctive convex crown spreads from a short, stout trunk. The paired rigid needles are deep green; blue-green when immature. The large, globular cones mature to lustrous brown and produce edible nut-like seeds. This frost-hardy tree suits coastal locations.

Pinus pinea

Pinus densiflora

Pistacia chinensis

Pittosporum undulatum

Pinus radiata

Platanus orientalis

Pittosporum rhombifolium

Platanus × acerifolia

P. radiata
syn. *P. insignis*
MONTEREY PINE, RADIATA PINE

The fastest growing pine, this species is commonly grown for its timber as well as its shelter and shade. It grows 25 m (about 80 ft) or more, its conical shape maturing into a broad, flat crown. Silky green needles, grouped in threes, grow up to 15 cm (about 6 in) long. Its long-lasting fruit is yellow and irregularly egg-shaped. This frost-hardy species is easy to grow, given full sun and sufficient water.

PISTACIA
chinensis
CHINESE PISTACHIO

This deciduous species, prized for its autumn/fall foliage, is native to Asia. A fast grower, it averages 5–12 m (about 15–37 ft), sometimes reaching 25 m (about 80 ft). Low and spreading or erect and dome-shaped, it has narrow, fern-like leaves comprising 10 or more green leaflets. These turn vivid hues of red, yellow and purple in autumn/fall. Tiny red flowers are followed by red spherical seed pods that ripen to blue. This half-hardy tree prefers moderate climates. It will flourish in most soil types, given full sun, and withstands pruning. Propagate from seed in autumn/fall and winter, cuttings in summer. The European species, *P. vera*, bears the famous pistachio nut.

PITTOSPORUM
VICTORIAN BOX, MOCK ORANGE

This genus contains about 100 evergreen trees and shrubs which are valued for their scented blooms and decorative leaves. They have a triangular appearance and a domed crown, growing 6–12 m (about 18–37 ft) tall. Flowers have a strong citrus scent and the attractive seed pods contain their seeds in a sticky resin. All species prefer moderate to tropical climates. Some like dryish, well-drained soil; others prefer damp locations. They are simple to propagate, from seed in autumn/fall and spring; mature cuttings in summer; and several species from semi-ripe cuttings in summer. *Pittosporum*, Latin for 'pitch seed', alludes to the resinous fruit.

P. rhombifolium
QUEENSLAND PITTOSPORUM,
BRISBANE LAUREL

This handsome Australian native grows moderately fast to 4–9 m (about 12–27 ft) high and about 2 m (about 6 ft) wide. Its dense foliage is diamond-shaped, with roughly serrated edges, and vivid green. Thick terminal clusters of scented white flowers bloom abundantly in spring, followed by a great display of little orange berries containing black seeds. This half-hardy species survives in temperatures down to freezing point, and prefers partial shade and damp soil.

P. undulatum
SWEET PITTOSPORUM, AUSTRALIAN DAPHNE

This popular Australian native reaches 6–12 m (about 18–37 ft) tall, with a wide domed shape. The dense green leaves are lance-shaped with scalloped edges. Clusters of creamy white, bell-shaped flowers bloom profusely in spring, followed by decorative yellow-brown fruit. Half-hardy, it prefers moderate to warm climates. Watch for white scale and sooty mould.

PLATANUS
PLANE TREE, SYCAMORE

This diverse deciduous genus of wide-crowned species reaches up to 45 m (about 145 ft). The scaly yellow, brown and white trunks are often buttressed or multiple, the lower branches are arching and gnarled. The wide, maple-like foliage consists of 5 lobes and ranges from light green to dark green. Insignificant flowers are followed in autumn/fall by hanging bunches of large, spherical fruit. Trees vary from fully hardy to frost-hardy, growing in climates from cold to warm-temperate. All like full sun. Some species prefer rich, well-drained soil; others like arid conditions. Propagate from cuttings, or from seed in autumn/fall.

P. × acerifolia
syn. *P. × hybrida, P. × hispanica*
LONDON PLANE

This popular hybrid, from Asia's *P. orientalis* and North America's *P. occidentalis*, is robust and fast growing, reaching up to 25 m (about 80 ft) with a wide, spreading crown. Shiny, pale green leaves with 3 to 5 lobes are 25 cm (about 10 in) wide. Little red flowers appear in pendent clusters, followed by paired spherical fruit. This tree is able to withstand extremes in temperature and substantial pollution. It is a common sight in England, flanking suburban avenues.

P. orientalis
CHINAR, ORIENTAL PLANE

Native to an area stretching from southern Europe to India, this tree is valued for its hardiness, shade and beauty. It grows fast, to 25 m (about 80 ft) or more. Smooth, lustrous light green leaves with 5 to 7 deeply cut teeth are up to 20 cm (about 8 in) wide. Green pendent flower clusters are followed by uneven seed pods hanging in clusters of 2 to 6. The species has a strong tendency to sucker and requires frequent pruning.

PLUMERIA

FRANGIPANI, TEMPLE TREE

Originating in Central America and the Caribbean, this evergreen or deciduous genus contains 5 species and numerous varieties, all valued for their fragrant blooms. The stocky trees grow 6–9 m (about 18–27 ft) tall with open crowns of plump, woody limbs. The waxy flowers are usually white. All species prefer warm climates and are frost-tender, not surviving below 5°C (about 40°F). In colder climates, grow them in the greenhouse or against a west-facing wall. Plant in rich well-drained soil with full sun and shelter from winds. Propagate from cuttings, or from seed (colour may vary). The frangipani symbolizes eternity for Buddhists, because cut branchlets continue to flower.

P. obtusa

SINGAPORE PLUMERIA, WHITE FRANGIPANI

Native to the Bahamas, this tropical species grows slowly to 8 m (about 24 ft) with a dome-shaped crown and expansive limbs. Deep green leaves are broad ovals, tapering to a point. Glossy snow-white blooms with orange-yellow middles appear in late summer to early autumn/fall. Usually evergreen, this species will shed its leaves in arid conditions.

P. rubra var. acutifolia
syn. P. acuminata, P. acutifolia
WEST INDIAN JASMINE, TEMPLE TREE, FRANGIPANI

This shrubby variety, native to Central America's warm-temperate and tropical zones, grows 4–9 m (about 12–27 ft) tall. Its glossy white, scented flowers have 5 petals with yellow middles. Deep green, leathery leaves are pointed ovals with prominent ribs. This frost-tender species will not survive below 5°C (about 40°F); but it is grown, in numerous cultivars with flowers ranging from white and yellow to pink and red, throughout the tropics.

PODOCARPUS

FERN PINE, YELLOW-WOOD

This diverse ornamental genus of evergreen conifers for cool to warm-temperate climates is native to Australia, New Zealand, South America and South Africa. Species vary from low and spreading to slender and erect, from 15 to 50 m (about 50 to 160 ft) tall. The dense foliage consists of very narrow leaves, long or short according to species. Vivid spherical fruit, more like berries than cones, are borne individually on short stems (*Podocarpus* means 'footed stalk'). These trees like warm conditions, full sun or partial shade and grow in most soil types. Propagate from seed or cuttings.

P. henkelii

Native to South Africa, this species has arching branches with pendent, frequently curved leaves up to 17 cm (about 7 in) in length. Its smooth green fruit is globular.

P. totara

TOTARA, MAHOGANY PINE

This New Zealand conifer, valued for its timber, gradually reaches up to 30 m (about 95 ft) and has a thick, wide convex crown. Its little pointed leaves are deep green-brown, narrow and rigid. Small red cones like berries are 1 cm (about ¹/₂ in) in diameter. This tree is frost-hardy, preferring cool climates, and withstands severe lopping. *P. t.* 'Aureus' is much admired for its brilliantly coloured leaves.

POPULUS

POPLAR, ASPEN, COTTON

These deciduous trees, native to the northern hemisphere and related to the willows, are valued for their rapid growth, autumn/fall foliage and aromatic yellow softwood. Reaching 27–55 m (about 86–175 ft), they are either conical or columnar. Brightly coloured catkins appear in the leaf axils in late winter to early spring; leaves turn vivid yellow in autumn/fall. These fully hardy trees like warm weather but will not survive in arid conditions. Plant in rich, moisture-retentive soil with full sun. Propagate from cuttings in summer or by grafting. With a strong tendency to sucker, it is unsuitable for small gardens, and is prone to canker and fungi. Cultivated for over 2000 years, it lined Roman roads, and was called *arbor populi*, the tree of the people.

P. alba

SILVER POPLAR, WHITE POPLAR, SILVER-LEAF POPLAR, ABELE

This central European species grows extremely quickly to 15–25 m (about 50–80 ft), with a very attractive conical shape and silky grey bark. The egg-shaped leaves have 3 to 5 deeply cut lobes with wavy edges. Deep green on top, frosty white and downy underneath, they turn a beautiful golden yellow in autumn/fall. This tree prefers alkaline soil and suckers very strongly.

P. deltoides

COTTONWOOD, NECKLACE POPLAR

This temperate species from the USA grows rapidly to 15–30 m (about 50–95 ft). Lofty with an expansive crown, it is valued for its timber and appearance. The cordate leaves are glossy green, lighter beneath and 18 cm (about 7¹/₂ in) long. Pendent yellow and red catkins appear in spring.

Podocarpus henkelii

Plumeria obtusa

Plumeria rubra var. *acutifolia*

Populus deltoides

Podocarpus totara 'Aureus'

Populus alba

A Field Trip to the Coromandel Peninsula

New Zealand's pohutukawa (*Metrosideros excelsa*) has the ability to grow where no other tree can—along the coastal cliffs of the hills, bays and beaches of northern New Zealand. The spreading roots of this tree allow it to grow on rock faces and other precipitous sites, totally out of the reach of any competition. To the people of northern New Zealand, a beach without a pohutukawa is considered no beach at all—such is the character that these trees add to the coastal landscape.

The pohutukawa's Latin name is *Metrosideros excelsa*—'ironwood of excellence'—a reference to the density of the pohutukawa's hard, reddish brown wood. Also known as the New Zealand Christmas tree, the pohutukawa flowers from December to early January, at the height of the summer holiday season. The display of crimson-red flowers brightens the headlands, cliffs and bays with splashes of colour that are visible for many miles. The summer climate here is mild and pleasant, rarely getting too hot or too cold—about 25°C (about 77°F) during the day. This, with bright sunshine, provides perfect conditions both for trees and holiday makers.

Across the wide Hauraki Gulf, 40 km (about 25 miles) east of Auckland, lies the Coromandel Peninsula, home to some of the greatest pohutukawa groves. Short heavy downpours

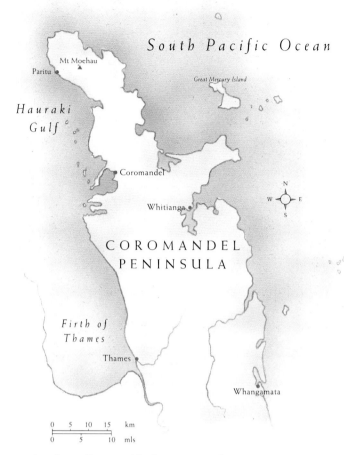

Pohutukawa flowers add colour to coastal areas in summertime.

of rain occur regularly throughout the year, creating lush growth and almost perfect conditions for these trees. From time to time harsh storms lash the coast with salt-laden air. Winds buffet the trees, crashing the odd tree on its side, where generally they regrow with a new crop of branches.

The old miners' road between Thames and Coromandel twists and bends along the coast at the foot of the steep hills and cliffs, only a few metres above the high-tide mark. It runs around many rocky bays with oyster-encrusted rocks and 400- to 800-year old shady pohutukawas at every point.

Once you reach Coromandel—a distance of 54 km (about 34 miles) from Thames—continue up the coast to the base of Mount Moehau. Here, and right along the coastal cliffs and bays, are some of the largest pohutukawas to be found anywhere. At times they grow into huge spreading trees with great branches that bend and twist to the ground, where they re-root, encouraging even more growth. In many places the road passes under their spreading branches.

Near the base of Mount Moehau is the small hamlet of Paritu which, together with Fantail Bay just to the north, is one of the best places to view the pohutukawa. Standing slightly out to sea on the granite quarry wharves at Paritu, you can look back at the stony beaches and rocky bays, along which the pohutukawas go right down to the water's edge. Granite rocks covered in lichen add to the beauty of the coastline. At Christmas, you will see bright red carpets on the ground under the trees, where the stamens have fallen.

The crimson flowers drip with nectar, attracting songbirds such as the tui and bellbird. The introduced starlings also enjoy the nectar; the pollen from the flowers often turns their chests yellow, creating great confusion as to their identity. The road continues on until you reach Fantail Bay, where you look out to sea through the pohutukawas' contorted trunks. Fantails flit and dart about, in and under the canopy, eating insects attracted to the rich nectar in the flowers. Bees swarm to the trees, creating a persistent buzzing sound.

Other animals, plants and insects find a haven in these trees. Epiphytes festoon old pohutukawas, with great clumps of *Collospermum hastatum,* a lily-like plant, growing in the crown along the branches. *Pyrrosia serpens,* a climbing fern, scrambles up the trunks. After dark, Australian brush-tailed possums come out to devour the fresh pohutukawa shoots, killing many trees in the process. Wetas—large tree-climbing insects of the cricket family—also come out at night to eat the leaves, making loud scraping noises.

If you leave the coast road and travel inland, you will see a cousin of the pohutukawa, the northern rata (*Metrosideros robusta*). This is a tree of the inland forests, often germinating as an epiphyte high on the crown of old trees. Where the pohutukawa and rata meet—most often in the steep, hilly country of Coromandel Peninsula—hybrids are produced, sharing characteristics of both trees.

To the Maori people, the pohutukawa has been esteemed from time immemorial. At Cape Reinga, the furthest promontory of land at the northern tip of New Zealand, lies the most sacred pohutukawa tree of all. According to the Maori legend it is from this point that the souls of the dead depart from this world into the life hereafter.

Metrosideros excelsa

Metrosideros

The genus *Metrosideros* consists of 20 or more species of trees and shrubs, some creeping over rocks or up trees with clinging roots. About half the species are found only in New Zealand while most of the others occur on other Pacific Islands, as far east as Hawaii. Few apart from the pohutukawa have become widely cultivated.

The beautiful pohutukawa is generally called the 'New Zealand Christmas tree' in other countries, even in the northern hemisphere where it flowers from about May to July. It is only suited to milder temperate climates.

Although the twisted, contorted shape of the stout trunk and branches is too irregular to be of any great commercial value, the pohutukawa is most highly prized for seashore planting. In South Africa, Australia and California it has been found to be one of the most resistant of all small trees to continued exposure to salt spray. Popular for beachfront parks and esplanades, it will grow at reasonable speed into a low tree with a dense, rounded canopy, even in quite poor soils such as dune sands, as long as the ground is not prone to waterlogging.

Metrosideros excelsa

Many new varieties are being produced; these have been selected for their growth and vigour. However, planted trees seldom rival those on the New Zealand seashores in the abundance of flowers and richness of colour.

P. nigra 'Italica'
syn. P. pyramidalis
LOMBARDY POPLAR

This slender, stately cultivar, said to have been developed by the ancient Romans, grows extremely quickly up to 30 m (about 95 ft). Its rhomboid-oblong leaves mature from reddish brown to lustrous green before turning deep golden in autumn/fall. Red catkins appear on male trees in spring. Fully hardy, it requires deep, damp soil, full sun and an open location.

P. tremuloides
ASPEN, QUAKING

A 20 m (about 65 ft) fast growing deciduous tree from North America, grown for its graceful habit and the way the dark green leaves flutter in the slightest breeze. They turn brilliant gold in autumn/fall. Fully hardy, it likes sun and moist soil.

Prunus × amygdalo-persica

Prunus mume

PRUNUS
CHERRY, PEACH, PLUM

This large genus contains over 200 evergreen or deciduous shrubs and trees and thousands of cultivars. They are grown either for their fruit or for their ornamental foliage, flowers and bark. Reaching 5–6 m (about 15–18 ft), their shape is inversely conical. Members of the Rosaceae family, they bear sweetly scented single or double rose-like flowers with 5 petals ranging from white to scarlet. All species are fully hardy and thrive in most well-drained soils. The evergreens like partial shade; prune in spring and propagate from cuttings in summer and autumn/fall. Deciduous types (useful for hedges) prefer full sun; prune after flowering and propagate from seed in autumn/fall or cuttings in winter. Bud or graft cultivars in spring and autumn/fall.

Prunus × blireiana

P. × amygdalo-persica
syn. P. 'Pollardii'
POLLARD ALMOND

This very attractive, squat deciduous hybrid is valued for its flowers. It reaches up to 6 m (about 18 ft) and has deep green lanceolate leaves with finely serrated margins. Broad, deep pink flowers with protruding purplish red stamens appear on leafless branches at the end of winter; inedible green almonds follow. This hybrid withstands arid conditions. Prune while in bloom and guard against peach curly-leaf fungus.

P. × blireiana
DOUBLE-ROSE, CHERRY-PLUM

This popular deciduous hybrid grows up to 4 m (about 12 ft). It has a squat appearance with slender arching branches and red-purple elliptical leaves that change to golden brown in autumn/fall. Its red-pink, semi-double flowers, blooming in early spring, are fragrant and very attractive.

P. campanulata
TAIWAN CHERRY, BELL-FLOWERED CHERRY

This deciduous Taiwanese species grows up to 8 m (about 24 ft) high and wide. In late winter it bears pendent clusters of dark red, bell-shaped flowers (*campanulata* means 'bell-shaped'). These are followed by deep green leaves, sharply elliptical with heavily serrated margins, and little spherical red seed pods. This moderately frost-hardy tree prefers cooler weather, but is the best cherry for mild-winter areas.

Prunus cerasifera 'Nigra'

P. cerasifera 'Nigra'
PURPLE-LEAF PLUM

This little Asian cultivar is admired for its impressive foliage and flowers. It has an attractive dome shape, reaching 5–10 m (about 15–30 ft) tall. Its leaves, a vibrant deep purple, stay bright until they fall. In early spring an abundance of pretty pink or white flowers bloom, one to each slender stem. These are followed by the cherry-plum fruit, which is edible when cooked. This tree tolerates arid conditions.

P. mume
UME, JAPANESE APRICOT

This small deciduous tree from China, Korea and Japan grows to about 6 m (about 18 ft). It bears abundant flowers in late winter or early spring before the leaves appear. The species is white or pink, but double-flowered cultivars in white or light or deep pink are popular. This is the 'plum blossom' which is such a favourite subject with Chinese and Japanese painters because it flowers while snow is still on the ground. It is fast growing, and trees rapidly assume quaintly gnarled trunks and branches. Frost-hardy, it prefers cool-temperate climates.

P. serrulata
JAPANESE FLOWERING CHERRY

Originating in east Asia, this deciduous species is the parent of many cultivars. It grows quickly, up to 20 m (about 65 ft), with a convex shape and spreading habit. Its scaly bark is a glossy reddish brown. The slightly lobed foliage, slender and

Populus tremuloides

Populus nigra 'Italica'

egg-shaped, turns from deep green to yellow in autumn/fall. Long-stemmed terminal clusters of white unscented flowers appear in spring, followed by little spherical fruit; but the garden varieties rarely fruit. Flowers of garden varieties range from white to bright pink. It prefers cooler climates.

P. serrulata 'Amanogawa'

This erect deciduous flowering cherry grows up to 10 m (about 30 ft) high and 4 m (about 12 ft) wide. Its deep green, sharply ellipti-cal leaves turn reddish orange in autumn/fall. Light pink, semi-dou-ble perfumed flowers appear at the end of spring.

P. serrulata 'Mount Fuji'
**syn. P. serrulata 'Kojima',
P. s. 'Shirotae'**

Reaching up to 7 m (about 21 ft) high and wide, this small spreading cultivar has a broad crown and slightly arching branches. Green, lacy edged leaves appear in early spring and turn orange-red in autumn/fall. Large, scented white flowers, single or semi-double, appear in mid-spring.

P. subhirtella 'Pendula'
HIGAN CHERRY, ROSEBUD CHERRY

This deciduous spreading tree has a wide crown and arching branches. It grows 6–12 m (about 18–37 ft) tall and develops sharply elliptical, ser-rated deep green leaves which turn yellow in autumn/fall. Light pink flowers, predominantly single with 5 petals, appear from winter to early spring before the foliage. These are followed by little spherical brown-red fruit. This cultivar prefers cooler climates. The cultivar 'Autumnalis' is more reliably winter flowering.

P. × yedoensis
YOSHINO CHERRY

This Japanese hybrid is an elegant, fully hardy deciduous tree. It grows up to 8 m (about 24 ft) tall and spreads up to 10 m (about 30 ft) wide, with a convex crown and pendent limbs. White or light pink flowers with an almond fragrance open in early spring, preceding the

deep green foliage. This tree prefers a cooler climate with full sun and well-drained soil. It is much planted in Washington DC.

PSEUDOPANAX
arboreus
**syn. Neopanax arboreus,
Nothopanax arboreus**
FIVE FINGERS

This New Zealand evergreen tree or shrub grows up to 6 m (about 18 ft). It has a domed crown and stubby limbs. Large, lustrous deep green compound leaves comprise 5 to 7 serrated leaflets, each 15–20 cm (about 6–8 in) long. Small incon-spicuous green flowers with a honey fragrance appear in summer. These are followed by bunches of purple-black, spherical fruit. This species prefers cool climates down to –5°C (about 23°F). Plant in full sun or partial shade in deep, rich, well-drained soil. It is ideal for landscaped gardens or as a tub specimen. Propagate from cuttings in summer, or seed in autumn/fall and spring.

PSEUDOTSUGA
menziesii
syn. P. douglasii, P. taxifolia
DOUGLAS FIR

This majestic species, one of North America's most impressive conifers, grows 20–70 m (about 65–220 ft) in an attractive pyramid shape. Its deeply grooved, grey-brown bark is set off by the bluish green foliage,

which comprises needles 3 cm (about 1½ in) long, arranged in whorls. Immature leaves turn claret red in winter. The woody brown cones hang down and are 7–10 cm (about 3–4 in) long. This fully hardy tree prefers cold climates, though it will survive in warm weather. It grows quickly in fertile soil. Plant in open spaces in full sun or partial shade; propagate from cold-treated seed. The Douglas fir is America's original Christmas tree. Its valuable timber is known as Oregon pine.

Prunus serrulata 'Mount Fuji'

Prunus × yedoensis

Pseudopanax arboreus

Prunus serrulata

Prunus subhirtella 'Pendula'

Prunus campanulata

Prunus serrulata 'Amanogawa'

Pseudotsuga menziesii

Pterocarya fraxinifolia

Pyrus calleryana

Pyrus ussuriensis

Pyrus salicifolia 'Pendula'

PTEROCARYA
fraxinifolia
CAUCASIAN WINGNUT

This rapidly developing deciduous tree, native to the Caucasus and Iran, is a relative of the walnut. It grows up to 35 m (about 110 ft) with a spreading convex crown. Its fern-like, compound foliage consists of up to 20 lance-shaped leaflets. Pendent yellowish green chains of attractive male and female catkins appear in summer. These are followed by drooping clusters of green, winged nuts with red markings. This species prefers warm climates and waterside locations. Prune suckers frequently and propagate from cuttings or suckers in summer; seed in autumn/fall.

PYRUS

PEAR

This genus contains small, deciduous species native to Europe, Asia and Africa. They are valued for their foliage, flowers and edible fruit. Species grow slowly to 18–25 m (about 60–80 ft) and have wide, convex crowns. Foliage is diverse, from ovate and hairy to linear and smooth. White flowers are followed by plump fruit in various shades of brown, yellow and green. Species range from fully hardy to half-hardy and enjoy well-drained soil with full sun. Propagate from seed in autumn/fall; bud cultivars in summer, graft in winter.

P. calleryana
CHINESE PEAR, BRADFORD PEAR

This fully hardy Asian native grows up to 15 m (about 50 ft). It has shiny elliptical leaves that turn from deep green to red in autumn/fall. An abundance of white blossoms appear in mid- to late spring, followed by little brown fruit. A number of selected cultivars are available.

P. salicifolia 'Pendula'
SILVER PEAR, WEEPING SILVER PEAR, WILLOW-LEAF PEAR

Native to south-eastern Europe and the Caucasus, this fully hardy tree grows to 10 m (about 30 ft), with a

Quercus lusitanica

domed shape and gracefully arching branches. The tasselled lanceolate foliage, similar to the willow's but silver-grey, emerges soon after the flower buds. Flat-topped clusters of small white flowers appear in abundance in spring, followed by small, yellowish brown fruit. It is frost-hardy but prefers a cool climate.

P. ussuriensis
MANCHURIAN PEAR

Originating in Asia, this frost-hardy deciduous species has a triangular crown and spreading habit. It grows 15–20 m (about 50–65 ft) tall and has rigid lower limbs. The circular leaves are 5–10 cm (about 2–4 in) across and shiny green, turning to vivid red, orange and yellow in autumn/fall. The tree is powdered with small white blossoms in spring and later bears little yellowish brown fruit. Fully hardy, it is the most reliable species for autumn/fall colour in mild climates.

QUERCUS

OAK

This extremely diverse genus contains some 450 species of evergreen trees and shrubs, mostly native to the northern hemisphere. Ranging from small and shrubby to very tall and erect, they grow slowly up to 30 m (about 95 ft). Foliage varies from wide, multi-lobed and leathery to lustrous, thin and papery. All species bear acorns inside woody pods, which also differ from species to species: slender and sharp or stubby and flat; sleek-shelled or downy and rough. All species prefer cooler weather and deep, damp, well-drained soil. Some like alkaline soils and full sun; others prefer semi-shade. Propagate from seed in autumn/fall—also a time to guard against oak-leaf miner. The heavily grained timber, moisture- and salt-resistant, was prized by boatbuilders and carpenters.

Q. lusitanica
syn. *Q. faginea*
PORTUGAL OAK

This deciduous, frost-hardy, southern European species grows 10–18 m (about 30–60 ft). The small changeable leaves are serrated and have a grey downy underside. The acorns are long and skinny.

Q. palustris
PIN OAK, SPANISH OAK

Originating in North America, this expansive deciduous species is valued for its timber, shade and autumn/fall foliage. A fast grower, it averages 10–24 m (about 30–77 ft) in cultivation, and up to 40 m (about 130 ft) in the wild. Slim, arching branchlets bear glossy green foliage in spring. These heavily serrated oval leaves turn scarlet then glossy brown in autumn/fall and once dead endure until the following spring. Small, slim, globe-shaped acorns are half covered by their cup. This tree's dense root system means transplanting is quite easy, as long as plenty of earth is taken.

Q. robur
ENGLISH OAK, COMMON OAK

This fully hardy species, native to Africa, Asia and Europe, is valued for its timber. It grows quickly, ranging widely in height between 10 and 35 m (about 30 and 110 ft), with an expansive crown and large, heavy branches. The leaves, inverted ovals with 6 to 12 serrations and 2 small auxiliary wing teeth, turn from deep green to golden brown in autumn/fall. Egg-shaped acorns are one-third covered by their cup and develop in small bunches on slender stems.

Q. suber
CORK OAK

Valued for its dense soft bark, used to make cork, this moderately frost-hardy evergreen has a broad, spreading crown up to 15 m (about 50 ft) high. The glossy deep green leaves are egg-shaped and serrated with a fleecy underside. Single oval acorns are half covered by their cup.

Q. virginiana
syn. Q. virens
LIVE OAK, SOUTHERN LIVE OAK

Native to Mexico and the southern USA, this moderately frost-hardy evergreen grows rapidly up to 20 m (about 65 ft), its crown level. Rigid, spreading branches bear deep green leaves with a fleecy white underside. These are predominantly oval with erratically serrated margins. Elliptical acorns are a quarter covered by their cup.

RAUVOLFIA
caffra
QUININE TREE

This fast-growing, medium-sized, deciduous to evergreen tree has a bare trunk and glossy, dark green, lanceolate leaves in whorls of five.

Rauvolfia caffra

Its wide, round crown, and branches with slightly drooping foliage, make it an ideal specimen tree on a large lawn. Plant in rich soil and keep well watered.

RHUS
SUMACH, TOXICODENDRON

This genus contains over 150 species of small deciduous trees, shrubs and climbers, valued for their vibrant autumn/fall foliage. They grow 6–9 m (about 18–27 ft) with wide, spreading crowns. The foliage consists of paired leaflets along a main branchlet. These vary from feathery fronds with serrated margins to plain, slender ovals. Small flowers bloom in thick terminal clusters, followed by pendent bunches of fruit on the female tree only. Species are fully to frost-hardy and require full sun, porous soil and protection from winds. Propagate from seed in autumn/fall, cuttings in summer or root cuttings in winter. *Toxicodendron* means 'poison tree'—avoid contact with

Quercus suber

Quercus robur

bare skin as they contain a toxic resin.

R. pendulina
syn. R. viminalis
WHITE KAREE

Native to South Africa, this deciduous, frost-hardy tree grows to a height of 8–12 m (about 24–37 ft) and a spread of 7 m (about 21 ft). The foliage is pale green, lance-shaped and trifoliate, the branches having a weeping habit. Tiny whitish green flowerets appear in terminal panicles from spring to summer. Excellent as a street tree, shade cover or windbreak, it requires full sun, well-drained soil and frequent watering. Propagate from seed or cuttings.

R. succedanea
syn. Toxicodendron succedaneum
WAX TREE

Originating in Japan and China, this popular species for moderate climates grows up to 9 m (about 27 ft). It has an open spreading crown, scattered limbs and fern-like

foliage comprising up to 14 silky leaflets. Immature foliage has a purple tint, turning shiny deep green before finishing with a splendid autumn/fall display of deep red, yellow and purple. Yellow-green flowers appear in thick terminal clusters from the leaf axils, followed by big drooping bunches of spherical fruit that ripen to brown. These are a source of wax; hence the common name. This tree is banned in some Australian states as so many people are allergic to it.

Rhus pendulina

Quercus palustris

Rhus succedanea

Quercus virginiana

Rhus typhina 'Laciniata'

Rothmannia capensis

Robinia pseudoacacia

Robinia pseudoacacia 'Frisia'

Salix alba

Salix babylonica

R. typhina 'Laciniata'
syn. R. typhina 'Dissecta'
STAG'S HORN SUMACH, VELVET SUMACH

This North American species has an expansive crown and grows quickly to 3–6 m (about 9–18 ft). Its compound pinnate foliage has up to 30 light green, tasselled leaflets which turn beautiful shades of red and orange in autumn/fall. Dense clusters of little green-white flowers appear in summer, followed by red seed pods in pendent woolly bunches. This species prefers temperate climates and has a strong tendency to sucker. The leaves are a source of tannin.

ROBINIA
BLACK LOCUST

This deciduous genus contains 20 species of trees and shrubs, native to North America but now common worldwide. They grow up to 25 m (about 80 ft) with a rounded shape and spreading habit. The scented flowers and fruit are typical of the Leguminoseae family, the peas resembling those of the locust tree (hence the common name). The species will survive in a broad range of temperatures and soils but dislikes saturated soil. Plant in full sun and protect the fragile limbs from strong winds. Propagate from seed and suckers in autumn/fall, cultivars by grafting. The genus was named after seventeenth-century herbalist Jean Robin, who first cultivated it.

R. pseudoacacia
BLACK LOCUST, FALSE ACACIA

This erect hardwood timber tree grows 10–15 m (about 30–50 ft) and has a tough grooved trunk and thorny branches. Its fern-like leaves, composed of up to 23 elliptical leaflets, turn yellow in autumn/fall. Pendent clusters of scented, wisteria-like flowers appear in spring, followed by sleek seed pods that endure until the following spring. This species has a strong suckering habit; avoid planting near pathways.

R. pseudoacacia 'Frisia'

This expansive deciduous cultivar is thornless and grows up to 15 m (about 50 ft) high and 10 m (about 30 ft) wide. Its feather-like foliage has rounded leaflets and changes from gold in spring to yellowish orange in autumn/fall. Plant this fully hardy tree in well-drained soil with full sun.

ROTHMANNIA
capensis
WILD GARDENIA, COMMON ROTHMANNIA

This small tree, native to South Africa, is related to *Gardenia*. It can reach a height of 5 m (about 15 ft) and spread of 3 m (about 9 ft) and has glossy green leaves. It is valued for its bell-shaped, scented flowers, in cream to yellow with reddish-brown throat markings, up to 4 cm (about 2 in) long. These are followed by round fruits, 60–70 mm (about 2½ in) in diameter. Half-hardy, it will develop fairly quickly in rich, well-drained, neutral to acid soil, and full sun or partial shade. Frost-tender, it is suited to tropical and subtropical areas. Propagate from seed in spring or semi-ripe cuttings in summer.

SALIX
WILLOW, OSIER

Originating in the northern hemisphere, these 250 deciduous species of trees and shrubs grow to 10–25 m (about 30–80 ft) with convex crowns, rough, twisted trunks and weeping branches. Excellent shade trees, their narrow, tassel-like foliage often drapes along the ground. Pendent male and female catkins usually develop on different trees and may be slender and soft or thick and leathery. Trees vary from fully to frost-hardy and love waterside locations, where eroded banks benefit from their strong suckering habit. They will grow in all except arid soils and require full sun, or partial shade in hot regions. Prune every two years; propagate from cuttings in summer and winter. Watch for caterpillars, gall mites, aphids and canker. The high quality timber has been used in the manufacture of cricket bats, whips and baskets.

S. alba
WHITE WILLOW

This fast-growing though rather short-lived deciduous tree from Europe reaches to about 10 m (about 30 ft) tall, but it is often pollarded to gain long, flexible shoots for basket making. The leaves are lance-shaped and turn yellow rather fitfully in autumn/fall. This is a popular tree for wet ground, holding riverbanks and the like, but its roots are greedy so it is not very popular as a garden tree. Cricket bats are made from the wood of *S. a. caerulea*. Both are fully hardy.

S. babylonica
WEEPING WILLOW, NAPOLEON'S WILLOW

This very attractive, popular tree is native to China and grows up to 15 m (about 50 ft). It has a broad dome and erect branches that support distinctively arching branchlets. The light green lanceolate leaves, brushing the ground, are slender and thinly lobed. This temperate species will grow in most conditions if planted by waterways. The name comes from the unlikely story that these were the trees growing in Babylon under which the Hebrews sat and wept.

Salix matsudana 'Tortuosa'

Salix 'Chrysocoma'

Sassafras albidum

Schinus terebinthifolia

Schinus ariera

S. caprea

PUSSY WILLOW, GOAT WILLOW,
GREAT WILLOW

Native to Asia, this dense shrub or tree grows 3–10 m (about 9–30 ft) tall. The rounded deep green leaves are 5–10 cm (about 2–4 in) long with a fleecy grey underside. Decorative grey male catkins with yellow stamens appear in spring before the foliage. This species grows well in brackish marshlands but its very strong suckering habit can cause problems in the garden.

S. 'Chrysocoma'
syn. S. alba 'Tristis'
GOLDEN WEEPING WILLOW

This French cultivar, a hybrid between S. alba and S. babylonica, grows rapidly up to 18 m (about 60 ft) with a spread of some 20 m (about 65 ft). Its pendent limbs produce long, thin, arching yellow branchlets that droop to the ground. Lance-shaped, yellow-green leaves turn golden yellow in autumn/fall. Both male and female flowers develop on the same tree. This fully hardy tree requires full sun and moist soil to thrive.

S. matsudana 'Tortuosa'
CORKSCREW WILLOW,
DRAGON CLAW WILLOW

This popular northern Asian tree resembles S. babylonica, but is smaller growing to only 15 m (about 50 ft). Its branchlets and shiny green leaves are tortuous and twisted (as the cultivar name implies). Catkins appear at the same time as the lanceolate, serrated foliage. This fully hardy tree prefers damp soil and full sun.

SAPIUM
sebiferum
CHINESE TALLOW TREE, WAX TREE

This variable deciduous tree, native to China and Japan, grows 6–13 m (about 18–40 ft) tall. Its thick crown is composed of pointed leaves, oval to diamond, which turn a beautiful lustrous crimson or orange-red in autumn/fall. Slender yellow catkins are followed by white, waxy fruit, their 3 seeds held together with wax. This warm-temperate tree will not survive below 5°C (about 40°F); the foliage is at its most vivid in hotter areas. Plant this species in rich, porous soil in a position with full sun. Prune if necessary and propagate from seed in spring, semi-ripe cuttings in summer. Wax from the fruit of S. sebiferum is used to make soap and candles.

SASSAFRAS
albidum
SASSAFRAS

This erect, deciduous North American native reaches up to 20 m (about 65 ft), widening to 12 m (about 37 ft) in maturity. The foliage, either egg-shaped or with 3 deep lobes, turns from lustrous deep green to striking red and yellow in autumn/fall. Inconspicuous yellow-green flowers bloom in spring, followed by blue fruit. This fully hardy species likes full sun or partial shade and rich, porous, slightly acid soil. Propagate from seed or suckers in autumn/fall, or from root cuttings in winter. Sassafras oil is extracted from the bark and roots of these trees.

Sapium sebiferum

SCHINUS

This genus consists of about 28 species of evergreen trees and shrubs, usually grown for their foliage and as shade trees. Half-hardy, they prefer a sunny position with some protection from winds. Plant in moist, well-drained, well-composted soil. Propagate from semi-ripe cuttings in summer or seed in spring.

S. ariera
syn. S. molle
PERUVIAN PEPPER TREE, PEPPER TREE,
PEPPERCORN TREE, MOLLE, PIRUL, MASTIC

Native to South America, this handsome evergreen grows quickly to 15 m (about 50 ft) with a broad rounded crown and elegant arching branches. Pendulous, pinnate foliage is a dark glossy green, comprising up to 40 slender lance-shaped leaflets. Little yellow flowers appear in branched racemes from late winter to summer, followed by drooping 'necklaces' of small, shiny, reddish pink berries; these are edible and can be used as a spice. This species endures extreme drought but is only half-hardy. The Incas planted this tree to shade their royal roads.

Salix caprea

S. terebinthifolia
BRAZILIAN PEPPER TREE

This stout, evergreen bushy small tree is native to tropical America and is mostly grown for its foliage. It has oval, mid- to deep green leaflets, 3 to 13 on each leaf, and bears panicles of insignificant greenish flowers. Dense clusters of round, orange berries follow the bloom, but only if male and female plants have been grown together. This species grows to a height of 8–15 m (about 24–50 ft) with a spread of 5 m (about 15 ft).

Sophora microphylla

Sequoiadendron giganteum

Sophora japonica

Sciadopitys verticillata

Sequoia sempervirens

Sophora tetraptera

Schotia brachypetela

SCHOTIA
brachypetela
WEEPING BOER-BEAN, TREE FUCHSIA

Originating in subtropical South Africa, this erect or compact semi-evergreen grows 6–12 m (about 18–37 ft) tall. It has fern-like foliage, which in colder climates is shed before the tree blossoms in spring. The shiny, deep crimson flowers have prominent stamens and develop in thick clusters. They produce an abundance of nectar irresistible to parrots (hence 'parrot tree'). This half-hardy tree is best suited to hot climates and, with regular watering, will grow in most soils. Prune saplings to encourage an erect shape. Propagate from heat-treated seed; move small plants with caution.

SCIADOPITYS
verticillata
JAPANESE UMBRELLA PINE, UMBRELLA PINE, PARASOL PINE

Native to Japan, this fully hardy evergreen conifer is valued for its perfect pyramid shape and unusual foliage. It grows very slowly up to 12 m (about 37 ft) in cultivation, and up to 40 m (about 130 ft) in the wild. Its horizontal open spirals of dark green needles look like the ribs of an umbrella. Ovate woody cones with numerous wide, curved scales mature for two years before dispersing their seeds. This tree prefers cold mountain locations with damp, acid soil and will not tolerate lime or urban smog. Plant in a protected site in full (but not hot) sun and water liberally. It will benefit from yearly mulching with its composted leaves. Propagate from seed and transplant when young. The genus name comes from two Greek words: *skias*, 'shade', and *pitys*, 'fir tree'.

SEQUOIA
sempervirens
CALIFORNIAN REDWOOD, SEQUOIA

This tough evergreen conifer, native to the western USA, is prized for its timber. It averages 30 m (about 95 ft); much taller in the wild. It is either pyramidal or columnar in shape, with rigid branches. Whorled foliage comprises 2 rows of small, light green needles which are narrow and slightly flattened, with 2 frosty bands underneath. Male and female flowers appear on the same tree followed by rectangular to obovate green cones, ripening to deep brown. This tree will survive in a wide range of climates; extremely cold weather may affect the foliage but not the plant itself. Suckers should be pruned immediately and general pruning is tolerated. Redwoods are extremely long living, with some specimens estimated to

be about 3500 years old. The genus boasts the world's tallest tree, at about 110 m (362 ft).

SEQUOIADENDRON
giganteum
syn. Sequoia gigantea, Wellingtonia gigantea
BIG TREE, MAMMOTH TREE, WELLINGTONIA

This long-living evergreen conifer, native to America's Sierra Nevada, has an attractive triangular shape and the broadest trunk of all known species. This vigorous tree averages 20–50 m (about 65–160 ft) tall and, like its redwood relative, grows taller in the wild. Its bluish green needles mature to brown and drape along the ground during the first 50 years of life, after which it develops no new lower branches. Cylindrical cones endure for 20 years—not very long, given that one specimen has been recorded as 3000 years old. These trees like cool climates, full sun and damp soil. Propagate from seed.

SOPHORA

This diverse genus belongs to the Leguminoseae (pea) family and contains semi-evergreen and deciduous species native to Chile, Hawaii, Japan, Korea, New Zealand and North America. These ornamental trees and shrubs are valued for their shape, leaves and flowers. They vary in height, 5–25 m (about 15–80 ft), and have thick fern-like foliage with differing numbers of oval leaflets. The pea-like flowers hang in thick terminal clusters during summer, generally in shades of white and yellow. Species vary from

fully to frost-hardy and prefer moderate temperatures. Plant in rich porous soil with full sun. Pruning is tolerated. Propagate deciduous species from seed or cuttings in autumn/fall; semi-evergreens from softwood cuttings in summer.

S. japonica
PAGODA TREE, SCHOLAR TREE

Native to Japan, China and Korea, this deciduous species grows 6–15 m (about 18–50 ft) high and wide. Its round crown is composed of deep green foliage with up to 16 oval leaflets. Older trees bear big, open clusters of little yellowish white pea-like flowers in late summer, followed by green elliptical seed pods. This fully hardy species enjoys hot summers.

S. microphylla
WEEPING KOWHAI

Originating in New Zealand, this short, spreading evergreen grows to 3–5 m (about 9–15 ft) in height, developing stiff branches with arching branchlets. These are covered with glossy, feather-like leaves, composed of up to 40 leaflets with downy undersides. In spring, pea-like, light yellow flowers appear along pendent stems. This species is frost-hardy but best grown beside a west-facing wall. Plant in rich soil with good drainage.

S. tetraptera
NORTH ISLAND KOWHAI

This semi-evergreen New Zealand species varies between 5 and 10 m (about 15 and 30 ft), a compact shrub or broad triangular tree. It has slender, deep green foliage with up to 40 leaflets. Golden blooms with lacy margins appear in spring, followed by winged seed pods. It is moderately frost-hardy. *S. tetraptera* is the national flower of New Zealand.

SORBUS

This genus, a member of the Rosaceae family, has deciduous and semi-evergreen species native to Europe, North America and north Asia. Shrubs or trees, growing 9–27 m (about 27–86 ft), are valued for their foliage, timber and edible fruit. Leaves vary from pinnate green to plain deep purplish red, the deciduous species displaying intense autumn/fall colours. Little white 5-petalled flowers appear in spring, followed in summer by enduring pendent bunches of berries. These cool-climate trees range from frost-hardy to frost-tender, preferring full sun or partial shade and rich, moisture-retentive soil. Propagate by grafting in winter, from buds and cuttings in summer or seed in autumn/fall. Susceptible to fireblight. Some species' edible fruit is used to make cider.

S. aria
WHITEBEAM

This European deciduous tree grows quickly up to 15 m (about 50 ft) and spreads to 10 m (about 30 ft). The single, oval, saw-toothed leaves are frosty grey when immature, maturing to deep green with downy white undersides. Sprays of spring blossoms give way to oval fruit, dark red with brown markings.

Sorbus aria

S. aucuparia
ROWAN, MOUNTAIN ASH, QUICKBEAM

Originating in Europe and Asia, this erect broad-crowned tree grows 6–12 m (about 18–37 ft) tall and is valued for its edible fruit, flowers and foliage. These green pinnate leaves comprise up to 15 leaflets and change to yellowish red in autumn/fall. Big dense sprays of white spring blossom are followed by a profusion of elliptical orange-red summer berries, turning golden yellow in autumn/fall. The fruit is used to make Rowan jelly. This deciduous species is suited to most climates and should not be replanted until of considerable size. The cultivar *S.* 'Beissneri' has attractive greenish gold foliage.

S. hupehensis
CHINESE ROWAN

This small elegant Chinese species reaches up to 12 m (about 37 ft) and is broadly expansive. The bluish green deciduous foliage, with up to 17 slightly serrated leaflets, turns reddish orange in autumn/fall. Open sprays of spring blossom are replaced by big clusters of egg-shaped white fruit, pink in winter.

SPATHODEA
campanulata
AFRICAN TULIP TREE, BATON DU SORCIER, GABON TULIP TREE, FOUNTAIN TREE

This handsome flowering evergreen, native to West Africa, grows to 17 m (about 56 ft) with an upright, spreading habit. The pinnate foliage comprises 10 to 20 dark green, lanceolate leaflets up to 14 cm (about 5½ in) long. Vivid green, downy spring buds unfurl to reveal stunning, long-lasting flowers: tulip-like and orange to deep red, their lacy edges tinged yellow inside. An all-yellow form is also grown. This frost-tender tree prefers warm coastal weather but will not tolerate stiff sea breezes. Plant in rich, damp sandy soil with full sun. Propagate from semi-ripe cuttings in summer, seed in spring. *Baton du sorcier* is French for 'magician's wand'; the tree is used in African tribal medicine.

STENOCARPUS
sinuatus
WHEEL OF FIRE, FIREWHEEL TREE

This slender erect Australian evergreen is valued for its unusual flowers, which it may take 10 years to produce. Height averages 15 m (about 50 ft); taller in warm climates. The dark shiny leaves have very wavy edges. Vivid red flowers with upright yellow stamens appear on long stems in summer, often springing directly from the trunk or limbs, and last until autumn/fall. These wheel-like blooms, up to 10 cm (about 4 in) across, increase in abundance in warmer conditions. Plant in well-drained rich soil with full sun, water liberally when in flower and shelter the immature tree from frosts; it is only half-hardy. Pruning is usually unnecessary. Propagate from semi-ripe cuttings in summer, seed in spring.

Spathodea campanulata

Sorbus aucuparia

Stenocarpus sinuatus

Sorbus hupehensis

STUARTIA
pseudocamellia
syn. *Stewartia pseudocamellia*
JAPANESE STEWARTIA

This deciduous Japanese native is valued for its foliage, flowers and decorative scaly bark. Compact or expansive, it reaches 6–12 m (about 18–37 ft) and has elliptical irregularly lobed leaves that turn attractive shades of yellow, red and purple in autumn/fall. Large, snow white,

Taxus baccata

Syzygium paniculatum

Taxodium distichum

camellia-like flowers with dense yellow stamens appear in summer, followed by downy seed pods. This fully hardy tree prefers moderate temperatures and rich acidic soil. Provide partial shade and protect from stiff winds. Propagate from seed in autumn/fall, cuttings in summer.

SYZYGIUM
LILLY PILLY, ROSE APPLE

Native to Africa, Australia and Asia, this large genus contains over 400 species of small evergreen shrubs and trees, valued for their foliage and flowers. Reaching up to 12 m (about 37 ft), they have lustrous green foliage, particularly vivid when immature. They bloom sparsely, their flowers composed of constellations of usually creamy white stamens. These are typically followed by bright pink, edible fruit. Plant in rich, damp but porous soil with full sun. Allow to grow freely, but prune if required. They are frost-tender. Propagate from semi-ripe cuttings.

Syzygium luehmannii

in summer, seed in spring. Leaf undersides are susceptible to scale insects; treat with white oil.

S. luehmannii
syn. *Eugenia luehmannii*
WATER MYRTLE, SMALL-LEAFED LILLY PILLY, CHERRY ALDER

This Australian native grows quickly, reaching 6–24 m (about 24–77 ft). Erect or spreading in habit, it is valued for its foliage and fruit. The lance-shaped leaves mature from coppery pink to deep green. White flowers bloom in late spring and early summer, followed by rose-coloured berries. This tree enjoys warm, humid locations and benefits from regular pruning; it can be used for hedging.

S. paniculatum
syn. *S. australe, Eugenia australis, E. myrtifolia*
BRUSH CHERRY, SCRUB CHERRY, CREEK LILLY PILLY

This Australian native, suitable for hedges, quickly reaches 6–18 m (about 18–60 ft) with an erect or spreading habit. Arching branches are thickly covered with shiny lance-shaped leaves, golden yellow-green when immature. The creamy white flowers are followed by deep crimson, egg-shaped fruit, scented and acidic. It will not survive below 5°C (about 40°F). The fruit is used to make jellies and conserves.

TAIWANIA
cryptomerioides
FORMOSA REDWOOD

This fully hardy evergreen conifer, native to Taiwan, grows up to 50 m

Stuartia pseudocamellia

Taiwania cryptomerioides

(about 160 ft). Its arching branches with upstretched tips do not usually start until halfway up the trunk. These are covered with narrow, greyish green, slightly curved or straight leaves, which become scales in later life. The seed-bearing cones are tubular and woody. Fresh growth will not shoot from old wood, so prune regularly. Propagate from cold-treated seed in winter, or cuttings at the end of autumn/fall and winter.

TAMARIX
aphylla
syn. *T. articulata*
ATHEL TREE, EVERGREEN TAMARISK

This short, tough evergreen originates in Africa and Asia. It reaches 6–10 m (about 18–30 ft) with an upright, slender habit and is an excellent hedge tree. Thin, greyish green leaves form in whorls around its branchlets. Racemes of pinkish white flowers bloom profusely during summer and autumn/fall. This frost-hardy species prefers warm regions but is extremely resilient, surviving stiff sea breezes and arid sandy soil. For optimum growth, plant in full sun and rich, porous soil; with insufficient drainage it is prone to borer. Propagate from hardwood cuttings in winter; semi-ripe cuttings in late spring.

TAXODIUM
distichum
SWAMP CYPRESS, BALD CYPRESS

Originating in the southern USA, this deciduous conifer quickly reaches up to 50 m (about 160 ft), erect to broadly triangular with a level crown. Soft green spirals of slender leaves and shorter ovate scales appear on the same tree and turn coppery brown in autumn/fall. Purplish brown female cones develop individually, the smaller male cones in bunches. 'Cypress humps'—protruding, cone-shaped mounds that help the tree breathe—often radiate from the roots and are 30 cm (about 12 in) tall. This fully hardy species loves water and does best in saturated soil with full sun. Propagate from seed and cuttings, and prune young trees to encourage symmetry. The valuable timber resists moisture and termites.

TAXUS
baccata
YEW

This long-living evergreen conifer originates in Europe, Africa and Asia. It grows slowly to some 25 m (about 80 ft) and almost double that in the wild, its irregular conical shape becoming level-crowned in maturity. Its slender needles are deep green with a greenish yellow underside and develop in typical

Tamarix aphylla

Thujopsis dolabrata

Thuja plicata, young tree

Thuja occidentalis

Tilia 'Petiolaris'

Tilia x *europaea*

whorls. Small pollen-rich bunches of male flowers and green globular female flowers develop on separate trees. Unusually, this conifer has no cones; the female flower develops instead into an individual seed partly enclosed in a fleshy red case. This frost-hardy tree likes full sun and tolerates pruning; it is greatly favoured for hedging and topiary. It propagates simply from seed and cuttings in spring and is prone to scale insects. The timber was once used to make longbows. The Irish yew is a narrowly upright cultivar of Irish origin. Both it and the regular type prefer moist climates.

THUJA

ARBORVITAE

This small genus comprises 5 species of evergreen conifers, native to North America or Asia. They grow up to 70 m (about 220 ft), gradually developing a pyramid shape. They have heavily grooved trunks and flat compound foliage. Woody green seed-bearing cones of varying size mature to brown before releasing their seeds. Trees tolerate pruning and will grow in most soils but prefer moderate climates and full sun. Propagate from seed or simply from cuttings. Several of the species are among the world's most valuable softwood timber trees, used extensively to build houses.

T. occidentalis

AMERICAN ARBORVITAE, WHITE CEDAR, TREE OF LIFE

This fully hardy North American native reaches up to 15 m (about 50 ft), its triangular shape becoming columnar in later life. Its bark is orange-brown and its aromatic foliage develops in flat V-shaped sprays of deep yellow-green scales with blue-green undersides. This moderate-climate species is valued for its white softwood and general appearance.

T. plicata

WESTERN RED CEDAR, GIANT ARBORVITAE, WESTERN ARBORVITAE

Native to an area spreading from California to Alaska, USA, this species grows quickly to 15–30 m (about 50–95 ft), and up to 70 m (about 220 ft) in the wild. Triangular to columnar, it has brownish red, scaly bark and upstretched limbs. Sprays of shiny green scales, backed with silver, hang from their extremities. Its extremely small, erect cones bloom like flowers to disperse their seeds. It is frost-hardy. Its softwood timber is among the most sought-after in the world.

THUJOPSIS
dolabrata

HIBA, MOCK THUJA

This handsome Japanese evergreen grows slowly to 6–14 m (about 18–45 ft). Pyramidal or low and spreading, this conifer is valued for its thick foliage: large, flat fans of shiny needles, dark green with frosted white undersides. Its little rounded cones are bluish grey and covered with dense woody scales. This frost-hardy tree prefers cool climates and damp soil. Prune to encourage shape or restrict size. Propagate from cuttings or cold-treated seed.

TILIA

LIME, LINDEN

This genus is made up of over 25 deciduous species native to Asia, Europe and North America. These elegant trees grow fast to 50 m (about 160 ft). They are generally upright with extremely wide, buttressed trunks and noticeable suckers. Their heart-shaped foliage has slightly saw-toothed, furled edges and frosted downy undersides. Five-petalled yellowish green tulip-like flowers appear in long racemes in spring to summer. The flowers are highly scented and they prove irresistible and sometimes deadly to bees. These fully hardy trees prefer cool weather and rich, porous soil. However, they will grow in most soil types, given regular water and full sun or partial shade. Propagate from seed in autumn/fall; some species and cultivars are propagated by grafting and layering in late summer. The versatile timber—a pale honey colour— is used for wood-carvings, musical instruments, clogs and blinds.

T. x europaea

COMMON LINDEN, COMMON LIME

Native to Europe, this quick-growing tree reaches 18–35 m (about 60–110 ft), erect at first and spreading in old age. The slightly serrated, cordate leaves are deep green on top, light green and smooth underneath. Terminal clusters of scented yellow-white flowers appear in late spring to early summer, followed by little spherical ribbed seed pods. The flowers can be dried and used to make linden tea.

T. 'Petiolaris'

WEEPING SILVER LINDEN, PENDENT SILVER LIME, WEEPING LIME

This weeping tree, native to southern Europe and west Asia, reaches between 18 and 25 m (about 60 and 80 ft) high. It has a triangular shape which expands in old age. The pointed, cordate leaves are 5–10 cm (about 2–4 in) long, deep green on top and silver-felted underneath. Creamy yellow flowers bloom in terminal clusters, followed by bumpy, nut-like seed pods.

Tipuana tipu

Ulmus parvifolia

Toronia toru

Trichilia emetica

Ulmus procera

Tsuga canadensis

TIPUANA
tipu
syn. *T. speciosa*
PRIDE OF BOLIVIA, TIPU TREE, ROSEWOOD

Native to subtropical and tropical South America, this predominantly evergreen genus is valued for its shade, flowers and timber. The tree quickly grows to 12–20 m (about 37–65 ft) and has a spreading habit. The dense crown is covered with attractive, feather-like foliage, composed of up to 25 rounded leaflets. In spring an abundance of pea-like, yellowish orange blooms appear on short slender stalks. These are followed in summer by leathery brown fruit up to 6 cm (about 2½ in) in diameter. Plant in full sun with rich well-drained soil. This tree is frost-tender and prefers a tropical or sub-tropical climate; it refuses to bloom in a tub. Prune immature plants in winter and propagate from seed in spring. The timber is marketed as Brazilian rosewood.

TORONIA
toru
syn. *Persoonia toru*

This New Zealand native is the only member of its genus. It grows to a height of 10 m (about 33 ft) or more. It has narrow, leathery, deep green leaves in autumn/fall. Clusters of brown felted buds opening to starry cream flowers are borne in late winter to early spring. The flowers are small but massed and have a strong honey fragrance. A member of the *Protea* family (Proteaceae), it prefers well-drained soil and full sun to partial shade. May be lightly pruned to shape if necessary. Hardy to a minimum temperature of minus 8°C (about 18°F).

TRICHILIA
emetica

This native of South Africa and tropical USA, is up to 10 m (about 30 ft) high. It has glossy, dark green foliage of 7 to 11 woody, rectangular–elliptical leaves up to 15 cm (about 6 in) long and arranged alternately. Terminal clusters of 5-lobed flowers are followed by woody pods, the seeds of which are used in the production of oil.

TRISTANIOPSIS
laurina
syn. *Tristania laurina*
WATER GUM, KANOOKA

From the east coast of Australia, this small erect evergreen grows 5–15 m (about 15–50 ft) and has sleek light brown bark. Its thick rounded crown bears lance-shaped foliage up to 10 cm (about 4 in) long. Leaves are shiny deep green with a pale green verso and may turn red in cooler climates. During summer, terminal clusters of little vivid yellow flowers develop in the leaf axils. Half-hardy, it prefers full shade and damp, rich, well-drained soil. Prune when required and propagate from seed. Suitable for small gardens and hedges, the flowers make for fine honey.

TSUGA
canadensis
CANADIAN HEMLOCK, EASTERN HEMLOCK

This elegant evergreen conifer is native to North America and Asia. It is very changeable in colour and shape, but generally grows from 15 to 25 m (about 50 to 80 ft), often developing multiple upstretched trunks. The bark is dark and heavily grooved and the foliage is deep green, comprising two ranks of flat narrow leaves. These are lightly serrated and often twist to reveal silvery white stripes underneath. Pale brown, egg-shaped cones contain little winged seeds from which the tree is propagated. It is fully hardy. The 'hemlock' in the common name apparently derives from its leaves' resemblance to those of the poisonous plant.

ULMUS
ELM

This genus contains over 15 fully hardy species of deciduous trees and shrubs native to Asia, Europe and North America. The majestic, round-crowned trees have attained heights up to 50 m (about 160 ft). The elliptical foliage varies: from slender, deep green and shiny to broad, mid-green and roughly textured; heavily or finely serrated; with or without prominent parallel ribs. Inconspicuous flowers with reddish stalks but no petals appear in early spring. Thick clusters of greenish white pods, containing single winged seeds, develop at the ends of branches in summer. Plant these moderate-climate trees in rich, well-drained soil with full sun. Propagate from seed or cuttings or by grafting the numerous suckers. The timber is used to make rustic furniture. Many of England's finest specimens were wiped out by the deadly fungus, Dutch elm disease.

U. parvifolia
CHINESE ELM

Native to China, Japan, Korea and Taiwan, this species grows fast to 10–15 m (about 30–50 ft). Its trunk and pendent branches are covered with decorative grey bark variegated with white and yellow-brown. Small, glossy, egg-shaped leaves are slightly serrated and atypically endure well into winter (in warmer climates, until the following spring). This frost-hardy species tolerates most climates but prefers warm weather. Propagate from seed or root cuttings in autumn/fall.

U. procera
ENGLISH ELM

This upright European species reaches up to 35 m (about 110 ft) high and spreads up to 15 m (about 50 ft) wide with a thick, rounded crown. It has dark, furrowed bark and wide, elliptical foliage. Seed pods, each containing one sterile seed, appear before the serrated leaves. These are deep green, textured above and felty beneath, turning yellow in autumn/fall. This fully hardy tree prefers moderate temperatures and is propagated from cuttings in summer or suckers in autumn/fall. With a very strong tendency to sucker, it is not recommended for small gardens.

U. procera 'Louis Van Houtte'
syn. *U. procera* 'Van Houttei'

This small elm has a thick rounded dome and grows up to 12 m (about 37 ft). Its vivid, light yellow foliage is lightly serrated and turns golden yellow-green in summer. This fully hardy tree requires full sun, well-drained soil and shelter from summer winds. Propagate by grafting on to non-suckering stock.

UMBELLULARIA
californica

CALIFORNIA BAY, CALIFORNIA LAUREL, OREGON MYRTLE, PEPPERWOOD

This single-species North American genus is a valuable shade tree that reaches up to 25 m (about 80 ft). Changeable in habit, it varies from compact and dome-shaped in open coastal areas to large, broadly spreading and multi-trunked in damp forests. Its glossy, bright green leaves are lanceolate and aromatic when crushed. Little clusters of insignificant yellow blossoms are followed by small, inedible purple fruit. This frost-hardy species prefers cool climates and moist, shady locations. However, it is able to survive in full sun and even extended periods of drought, once fully established. The spicy leaves of *U. californica* are similar to bay leaves, but stronger, and may be substituted for them in cooking.

VIRGILIA
oroboides

syn. *V. capensis*
CAPE VIRGILIA, KEURBOOM

This small South African evergreen grows 3–10 m (about 9–30 ft) with a shrubby or triangular shape and a spreading habit. It is valued for its beautiful flowers and extremely quick growth—up to 2 m (about 6 ft) a year. The feathery leaves comprise slender, dark green leaflets with a frosty white, felted underside. Pale bluish pink clusters of dainty, pea-like flowers appear in late spring, lasting until late autumn/fall with regular watering. This tree requires full sun, light porous soil and shelter from strong winds; otherwise staking may be necessary. It is frost-tender. Propagate from heat-treated seed in spring. Although it only lives 10 years, its rapid growth makes this tree invaluable for new gardens. The genus was named after the Roman poet Virgil.

VITEX
lucens

PURIRI

Reaching up to 18 m (about 60 ft) in height, this attractive New Zealand evergreen develops a broad convex crown and fern-like foliage composed of up to 5 dark green leaflets. From late winter to mid-spring, racemes of red, tulip-like flowers appear in profusion. This frost-hardy species prefers full sun and porous soil. Propagate from seed in autumn/fall and spring, or semi-ripe cuttings in summer.

WEINMANNIA
racemosa

KAMAHI

This New Zealand evergreen grows to 12–18 m (about 37–60 ft) in height and is valued for its flowers and shape, and its shade cover. The glossy, elm-like but symmetrical foliage is cordate with a sharp point and slightly serrated edges. During spring and summer, little white or pink, bottle brush type flowers appear. These develop in 10 cm (about 4 in) long, dense, terminal whorls around a slender stem and are followed by red fruit. This half-hardy species prefers cool climates and semi-shade or total sun. It is best grown in slightly acid, peaty soil with adequate drainage, and needs regular water while in bloom; it will withstand pruning. Propagate from semi-ripe cuttings in summer, or seed in spring.

ZELKOVA
serrata

JAPANESE ELM

Native to Japan, this expansive deciduous tree rapidly reaches 12–18 m (about 37–60 ft). Erect, with sculpted limbs, it is valued for its shade and timber. The slender cordate foliage, similar to its relative the elm's, is fine-pointed and lightly serrated. Little inconspicuous green flowers, the males in clusters, appear in spring and are followed by enduring leathery fruit. This fully hardy species prefers cool weather, open spaces and some wind protection. Plant in deep, damp, well-drained soil and allow full sun. Propagate from seed in autumn/fall. The timber is highly regarded in Japan.

ZIZIPHUS
jujuba

syn. *Zizyphus jujuba*
CHINESE DATE, JUJUBE

This tree is native to an area stretching from south-eastern Europe to China. It grows quickly up to 15 m (about 50 ft) and ranges in habit from compact and shrubby to open and spreading. The leaves are rectangular to elliptical with angled teeth. Little creamy flowers develop in clusters in spring, succeeded by the lush, reddish orange fruit. Edible and sweet, they ripen in winter. Plant this frost-tender tree in light porous soil with full sun or partial shade and water frequently. Prune to encourage dense growth and propagate from seed or cuttings. 'Chinese dates' are a delicacy in Middle Eastern countries and are delicious cooked or uncooked.

Zelkova serrata

Virgilia oroboides

Weinmannia racemosa

Tristaniopsis laurina

Ulmus procera 'Louis Van Houtte'

Umbellularia californica

Ziziphus jujuba

CHAPTER 5

Bulbs, Corms & Tubers

*T*he history of bulbs and how they came to western Europe to be hybridized into the plants we grow today makes fascinating reading. Most of the bulbs we think of as being indigenous to Europe can be traced back to their native habitat much further east in the mountainous regions of Asia Minor, while others were gathered initially from southern Africa.

In the centuries of European worldwide exploration, bulbs, as well as other exotic plants, were prized by naturalists and form the basis of modern strains of the bulbs marketed today. Narcissus for instance were grown by the ancient Egyptians, tulips came from Turkestan while gladiolus and nerines originated in the mountains of the southwestern Cape of South Africa.

As bulbs have differing flowering times, there is no limit to the type and number which can be included in the garden to provide for almost year-round colour. The term bulb, horticulturally speaking, includes true bulbs, corms and tubers.

Bulbs

True bulbs, of which the onion is an easily identified example, are made up of a series of scales joined at the base which enclose and protect a central bud. These scales collect and store food for the following year's growth and flowering and it's for this reason that it is necessary to allow the leaves of true bulbs to die down naturally as they continue to manufacture and store food for the following season, well after the flower has finished. This process also makes it possible for true bulbs such as hyacinths, narcissus and tulips to flower successfully in pots or jars as they use this stored energy to produce the current season's flowers. True bulbs reproduce by forming bulbils around the base of the plant and these can be easily removed when bulbs are lifted, even though they may take several years to flower.

Corms

A corm has a swollen base of solid storage tissue. Once flowering is over a new corm develops on top and the original one dies, often producing new corms or pips around the perimeter before it withers completely. Gladiolus and freesias are good examples of a corm.

Tubers

Again a food storage system, a tuber can be formed from stems or roots. 'Eyes' are produced from these swollen areas and form new plants. Dahlias are easily identified as being this type of bulb as is the common potato which will produce eyes if it is stored for a long time.

Creating Effects with Bulbs

Basically bulbs have evolved in the above ways because of environmental factors. They are able to store food for long, dry, dormant periods, then, in very quick time when the climate is

The elegant flower of the tulip has made it one of the most popular bulbs in the world.

right, shoot, flower then gather enough food for the following year. Some northern hemisphere bulbs like crocus and fritillaria wait for the watering they receive as the snow melts to suddenly burst upon the scene. These and many other bulbs are very particular regarding their environment as many temperate climate gardeners have realized when they have omitted to 'refrigerate' their tulip bulbs to chill them before planting. Other bulbs are far more accommodating and will often naturalize in the most unlikely places because the soil, combined with the surrounding ecosystem is to their liking.

Even in small gardens a natural effect can be created, especially under lightly foliaged deciduous trees as the roots of the trees ensure adequate drainage and there's less competition from grass. These woodland companions need to be chosen with consideration to their dormant period. Choose bulbs like trilliums and scillas and many of the narcissus species which are early to shoot and bloom; as their dormancy approaches the overhead canopy is beginning its active growth.

The informality of a woodland bulb display relies to a great extent on the naturalistic way in which the bulbs are planted. Planting in drifts, random scatterings of the bulbs, whereby they are left to grow where they land when thrown by the handful, is the best method of ensuring this. Size of the drift is governed by available space, of course, yet it is the very randomness of the display rather than its size that is the eye-catching element. Often a gardener in cold areas relies on bulb drifts to give a welcome colour display in early spring and is tempted to mix different species and colours, however a more pleasing effect is achieved by having drifts of different colour or species flowering on from one drift to the next rather than a 'hundreds and thousands' look. Bluebells look good in such a design with the blue species in the lighter, more open areas and the white flowering ones grouped closer to say the dark green background of evergreen shrubs.

There are many hardy bulbs which we often associate with 'old' gardens. Long left to their own devices they surprise us each year with their colourful appearance amid the shrubbery. Some of these, like *Amaryllis belladonna*, send up tall, single stems holding clusters of pale pink trumpets at the cusp of the summer–autumn/fall season

The sunny narcissus flowers are ideal for indoor decoration.

while the snowflake with its dainty green-tipped white bells lets us know when spring is almost here.

Planting bulbs among shrubs usually needs careful consideration because we can very easily lose track of where they are while they are dormant, and gardeners everywhere always have the tendency to fill any vacant space with something new which takes their fancy. As discussed earlier, competition from overhanging shrubs also has to be taken into account.

Many of the more delicate bulbs are overpowered by surrounding plants and are ideally suited to rock gardens where individual pockets can be given over to one particular species. Rockeries really need to be placed on an existing slope or where a change of level is being designed into the garden, otherwise dwarf bulbs can be placed in a brick or stone paved outdoor area where they can pop up in unpaved pockets from under a fine gravel scree. Provided drainage has been catered for, these pockets are ideal for dwarf tulips, crocus, freesias, ixias, sparaxis, babianas, lachenalias and other delicate bulbs which would be lost in the general shrubbery.

Raised beds filled with good quality, free-draining soil, are a sure way of providing the bulbs with the freedom from competition and drainage they need. These beds can be made using treated logs, railway sleepers or a couple of rows of old bricks. For a gardener wishing to perfect the hobby

of growing prized, delicate bulbs rather than opting for a general garden display, these beds may well be the answer. Alternatively these raised beds can be filled with free-draining sand and pots of bulbs plunged into them to ensure they don't dry out, then when the flowers appear each individual pot can be taken indoors or placed in a prominent position in the garden or on the patio where the blooms can be appreciated.

Growing Conditions

Generally bulbs prefer well-drained, slightly acidic soil. Most have evolved in areas with prolonged dry periods followed in the growing season by melting snow or good rains. Therefore, most are unable to withstand prolonged periods of waterlogged soil, but there are always exceptions to the rule and the arum lily thrives in moist sites as do the Japanese and flag iris.

Similarly there are very few bulbs which can be grown in really shady areas and still flower well. Again, luckily for the gardener looking to highlight a shady spot with yearly colour there is *Clivia miniata* which produces bright orange flowers each spring, or the more delicate lily of the valley and snowflakes providing that wonderful flowering highlight of white blooms against green foliage so often employed by professional landscapers to such good effect.

Allium christophii

Albuca canadensis

Amaryllis belladonna

Allium moly

Anemone blanda

Allium narcissiflorum

green stripe on each petal. This species is half-hardy. The large bulbs should be planted in autumn/fall fairly close to the surface, in full sun or slight shade. They can be propagated from offsets or from seed.

ALLIUM

Garlic and onions belong to this large genus of over 300 species, native to Asia, Africa and America. There are many very attractive ornamental species as well as edible ones. Many species have a pungent onion or garlic scent but this is usually only noticeable when parts of the plant are bruised or crushed. Most are frost-hardy and easy to grow; some are so vigorous they can become difficult to control. They vary greatly in size: from 4–5 cm (about 2 in) high to 1 m (about 3 ft). Smaller species are ideal in a rockery. Bulbs should be planted in autumn/fall in well-drained soil, 4–10 cm (about 2–4 in) deep, depending on the size of the bulb. Flowering time is late spring to early autumn/fall. Propagation can be from offsets, which multiply freely, or from seed.

A. christophii
syn. A. albopilosum

This attractive, hardy species grows up to 60 cm (about 24 in) high. The broad leaves are green and shiny on top and white beneath. The sturdy stem bears a rounded umbel of flowers up to 30 cm (about 12 in) wide. The individual violet flowers borne in spring are star-shaped. They turn black as the seeds ripen and are very useful for dried flower arrangements. Bulbs should be planted in autumn/fall, 6 cm (about 2½ in) deep in well-drained soil. *A. christophii* grows best in full sun. Propagate by dividing offsets.

A. moly
GOLDEN GARLIC

Native to Spain, *A. moly* grows up to 35 cm (about 14 in). Broad, grey-green basal leaves surround stems which each bear an umbel of up to 40 flowers. The bright yellow, star-shaped flowers appear in summer. It is very hardy and can be planted in full sun or partial shade. Bulbs or seeds should be planted in autumn/fall in well-drained soil. Propagate by division of bulbs. The Spanish once regarded this plant as a sign of prosperity if they discovered it in their gardens.

A. narcissiflorum

This delightful species grows up to 30 cm (about 12 in) high. Slender, grey-green leaves surround a stem bearing an umbel of up to 12 nodding flowers. The purple, bell-

ALBUCA
canadensis
SENTRY-IN-THE-BOX

This genus is native to southern and tropical Africa, even though its name suggests it is from Canada. *A. canadensis* grows up to 1 m (about 3 ft) high and the grey-green leaves grow to 15 cm (about 6 in) long. The pendulous flowers, which appear in late spring, are about 2.5 cm (about 1 in) long. The inner petals appear joined, as if forming a tube; the outer petals are yellow, with a

shaped flowers appear in summer. Plant bulbs and seeds in autumn/fall in well-drained soil. This hardy species grows well in full sun. Propagate by division of bulbs.

AMARYLLIS
belladonna
MARCH LILY, BELLADONNA LILY

This outstanding plant is a gardener's dream: half- to frost-hardy, easy to grow and, as the name *belladonna* ('beautiful lady') implies, very beautiful. Native to South Africa, it is an autumn/fall flowering bulb. A sturdy, fast-growing stem up to 50 cm (about 20 in) high is topped with a glorious display of rosy pink, lily-like flowers. The strap-like basal leaves appear after the long flowering period. Plant large bulbs in late summer at soil level or just below, in well-drained soil. A fairly sunny position is best in cool areas, but they may need light shade in very warm areas. Cut down flower stalks once flowering is finished but ensure the plant is well watered through winter. Grown easily from seed, it often self-sows freely. The genus *Amaryllis* once contained many species, including hippeastrums. Now, *A. belladonna* is considered to be the only true *Amaryllis* and other species have been reclassified.

ANEMONE
WINDFLOWER

This highly varied genus is mainly native to southern Europe and the Middle East. Size and flower colour vary greatly, as do flowering times; the planting of tubers can be staggered to provide a succession of glorious blooms. Most species are fairly hardy and do well in rich, well-drained soil in a sunny or lightly shaded situation. Take care that the tubers are not upside down. Flowers usually appear about 4 months after planting. Grow from seed planted in summer, being careful to protect the seedlings from hot sun. Plant new tubers each year for best results, as they become weakened after blooming. *Anemos* is Greek for 'wind', hence the common name.

A. blanda
WOOD ANEMONE

This delicate-looking species is frost-hardy. Native to Greece, it grows to 20 cm (about 8 in) with green, oval, toothed leaves. The star-shaped flowers which appear in spring can be white, pink or blue and are about 3 cm (about 1½ in) wide. *A. blanda* self-seeds freely and, given moist, slightly shaded conditions, should spread into a beautiful display of flowers.

Anomatheca laxa

Aristea ensifolia

Anemone × hybrida 'Honorine Jobert'

Arum italicum

Anemone nemorosa

Asphodeline lutea

Anemone coronaria

A. coronaria
WIND POPPY

Many hybrids have evolved from this fully hardy species, the most commonly planted anemone. It grows up to 25 cm (about 10 in). The poppy-like flowers are up to 10 cm (about 4 in) wide and can range in colour from red to purple to blue. A. coronaria is usually treated as an annual. 'De Caen' is a single and 'St Brigid' is a popular semi-double, with colours ranging from pink to purple to scarlet to blue. Excellent as a cut flower.

A. × hybrida
syn. A. Japonica, A. hupehensis
JAPANESE WINDFLOWER

One of the most elegant plants for growing under trees or shrubs, these vigorous branching perennials grow to a height of 60 cm to 1 m (about 2–3 ft) and width of 60 cm (about 24 in). Leaves are deeply divided and dark green, and tall, erect flower stems bear many large saucer-shaped flowers in late summer and early autumn/fall. Flowers are white, pink or carmine red, single, semi-double or double. Plant in humus rich, well-drained soil in full light or semi-shade. These plants adapt themselves to almost any position. Fully hardy. Cut back stems as they fade. Propagate by division of an established clump in winter when the plant is dormant, or from seed sown in late summer. Fertilize in late winter.

A. nemorosa

This hardy, spreading species grows to 15 cm (about 6 in). The green leaves are deeply toothed and the delicate white flowers are star-shaped, about 3 cm (about 1½ in) wide. Plant in fairly moist soil.

ANOMATHECA
laxa
syn. Lapeirousia laxa
SCARLET FREESIA

This freesia-like native of South Africa grows to 60 cm (about 24 in) with long, narrow basal leaves and produces one-sided spikes bearing up to 12 flowers. The tubular, star-shaped red to scarlet flowers, 3 cm (about 1½ in) wide (although there is a form only half that size), appear in spring. Corms should be planted in autumn/fall in well-drained soil in a sunny or partially shaded situation. Water regularly during summer. If left undisturbed, it should self-seed freely. It can be propagated from offsets or from seed sown in late summer, which may flower the next spring but will usually produce a much better display in the second year. It is half hardy.

ARISTEA
ensifolia

This elegant summer-flowering native of South Africa grows up to 1.5 m (about 4½ ft) tall. Iris-like leaves surround a stem with a raceme covered in purple to blue 2cm (about 1 in) flowers, which close at night. Rhizomes should be planted in well-drained soil in full sun or partial shade. Half-hardy, they need to be kept moist and do well beside a pond or stream. Propagate from seed in autumn/fall or spring. Very young plants can be divided as long as the rhizomes are not allowed to dry out. Older plants do not transplant well.

ARUM
italicum
ITALIAN ARUM, JACK IN THE PULPIT, LORDS AND LADIES

Although many plants are commonly called arums, only a few truly belong to this genus. Frost-hardy, A. italicum grows to 30 cm (about 12 in). Broad, arrow-shaped, marbled leaves appear in autumn/fall. The flower is a light green, hooded spathe with a yellow spadix. It appears in early spring and is followed by orange berries which last until late summer. Tubers should be planted in autumn/fall in rich, moist soil in partial shade, with plenty of water during the growing season. Although frost-hardy, they need protection in cold areas. They can be divided once foliage has died, or propagated from seed in autumn/fall.

ASPHODELINE
lutea
ASPHODEL

A native of the Mediterranean, this fragrant, frost-hardy plant grows to 60 cm (about 24 in). Furrowed, grey-green leaves appear below spear-like stems bearing racemes of yellow, star-shaped flowers, some 3 cm (about 1½ in) long. Plant in full sun in well-drained soil and keep moist before the flowering period in spring. Can be propagated by dividing the roots carefully in late winter, or from seed in autumn/fall or spring.

BABIANA
stricta

BABOON FLOWER, BOBBEJAANTJIE

Baboons seem to find the bulbs of this delightful South African plant very tasty and early Dutch settlers often saw them digging up the plants. These half-hardy plants grow to 20 cm (about 8 in). The hairy, slender leaves are strongly ribbed and spikes bearing up to 10 cup-shaped flowers appear above the foliage. The freesia-like flowers, which appear in spring, are blue to violet but there are pale coloured forms of white or cream; some are fragrant. Plant the corms in autumn/fall in sandy soil in a sunny position. They look best planted in large clumps. Provide plenty of water during the growing season. Propagate from offsets or seed in autumn/fall.

BEGONIA
BEGONIA

These immensely popular plants are grown worldwide for their exotic summer blooms and beautiful foliage.

Large-flowered, tuberous begonias are usually called *B.* × *tuberhybrida*. They are available with flowers in every colour of the rainbow, as singles or doubles, with many variations of frills and ruffles. They like temperate to warm conditions and are frost tender. The tubers should be planted in spring in partial shade in a rich, moist soil. Sometimes they are planted in pots and started indoors in winter and transferred outside when the weather is warmer. They may need to be staked as the large flowers are heavy. Water should be decreased after flowering, and when the leaves have started to yellow the tuber should be lifted and dried very carefully before storage. Propagate from seed or from stem or leaf cuttings, but this is best done in a greenhouse.

B. × *tuberhybrida*
'Camellia' and 'Rose' flowered types

TUBEROUS BEGONIA

The most popular of the tuberous begonias, these bear large to enor-

mous, 25 cm (about 10 in) or more, double flowers in every colour but blue. To have the biggest flowers they should be disbudded, sacrificing the small female flowers that grow on either side of the central male. There are many named varieties in an ever-changing selection.

B. × *tuberhybrida multiflora*

Usually single flowered, these are grown not so much for the individual flowers as for the massed effect. They are available in the same range of colours as the others and are grown in the same way, except that they need no disbudding. Plants can be floppy and will benefit from staking.

B. × *tuberhybrida pendula*

BASKET BEGONIA

The basket begonias carry their flowers in pendent sprays, which look very good cascading from hanging baskets. The flowers are single or double, and usually smaller than the large-flowered types. They come in the same range of colours and are grown in the same way.

BELAMCANDA
chinensis

LEOPARD LILY, BLACKBERRY LILY

This little known native of China and Japan is a member of the Iridaceae family, along with irises. Growing to 1 m (about 3 ft), the foliage is sword-shaped like that of an iris. Branched spikes of orange-red, spotted flowers appear in summer, giving it the name 'leopard lily'. The flower produces clusters of black,

shiny seeds, hence the other name, 'blackberry lily'. Tubers should be planted in spring, just below the soil level in rich, well-drained soil in full sun or partial shade. Water well in summer. They are frost-hardy but need some protection in very cold winters. Propagate by division or from seed.

BRIMEURA
amethystina

syn. *Hyacinthus amethystinus*

This hyacinth-like, frost-hardy native of Spain grows to 25 cm (about 10 in). Slender, strap-like foliage surrounds stems which bear up to eight delicate, 1 cm (about ½ in), bell-shaped flowers ranging in colour from white to blue. Plant bulbs in autumn/fall in rich, well-drained soil in full sun or partial shade. Propagate by division or from seed in autumn/fall.

BRUNSVIGIA

Members of this South African genus are similar in character to the belladonna lily. However, they are far more tender and can be quite difficult to grow. Tall stems bear a dazzling mass of flowers in autumn/fall. The scented flowers radiate from the top of the stem like a candelabra. The bulbs are huge, up to 25 cm (about 10 in). They should be planted in rich, sandy soil in full sun. Water well in the growing season but keep dry when dormant. Propagation is slow. Seedlings can take up to 4 years to flower. Offsets must be fairly large before division and may take years to flower.

Begonia × *tuberhybrida*

Begonia × *tuberhybrida pendula*

Belamcanda chinensis

Babiana stricta

Begonia × *tuberhybrida multiflora*

Brimeura amethystina

Bulbine bulbosa

B. josephinae
JOSEPHINE'S LILY

The beautiful Josephine's lily grows up to 75 cm (about 30 in). The stout stem bears a mass of bright pinkish red, funnel-shaped flowers in autumn/fall. The 5 cm (about 2 in) wide flowers are scented and radiate out from the top of the stem. Strap-like leaves appear after flowering. The large bulbs are very expensive.

B. orientalis
CANDELABRA FLOWER

The sturdy stem grows up to 75 cm (about 30 in) and bears a flowerhead which can be up to 50 cm (about 20 in) wide. The small crimson flowers appear in autumn/fall before the leaves. The foliage often lies flat on the ground and is tender to frost.

BULBINE
bulbosa
syn. **Bulbinopsis bulbosa**
MAORI ONION, BULBINE LILY

This attractive plant is widely distributed in Australia and New Zealand. It grows to 50 cm (about 20 in). Spikes of starry, yellow flowers are borne throughout winter and sometimes into spring. It has light green, grassy foliage. Half-hardy, it is very tolerant to most conditions. Water well when growing. Propagate from seed or by division.

BULBINELLA
floribunda
CAT'S-TAIL

This native of South Africa produces 60 cm (about 24 in) flower stalks in late winter to early spring. The stalk is topped with a 10 cm (about 4 in) spike crammed with tiny yellow to orange flowers. Long, narrow basal leaves appear in autumn/fall. The plant disappears completely in summer. Bulbs should be planted in well-drained soil with the top of the bulb at soil level. Quite hardy to frost, it likes a sunny situation and plenty of water during the growing season. Propagate from seed or by division. Excellent as a long-lasting cut flower.

Bulbinella floribunda

Calochortus venustus

Brunsvigia orientalis

CALOCHORTUS
MARIPOSA TULIP, MARIPOSA LILY

Mariposa is Spanish for butterfly, and this aptly describes this richly varied genus with its beautifully coloured and patterned flowers. Native to the west coast of the USA and Mexico, they produce goblet-shaped flowers above grass-like foliage in spring and summer. They are not easy to grow and require care and attention. They are frost-hardy and do well in a temperate climate in a sunny situation. Bulbs should be planted in autumn/fall in a gritty, well-drained soil. A raised bed is ideal as good drainage is essential. Water through the growing season but allow them to dry out for the summer. Can be propagated by division or from seed.

C. albus
FAIRY LANTERN

A delightful, spring-flowering species growing up to 50 cm (about 20 in). White or pink, nodding,

Camassia esculenta

Calochortus albus

bell-shaped flowers, about 2.5 cm (about 1 in) wide, can sometimes have a brownish blotch.

C. venustus

A late spring/early summer flowering species. The wiry, branched flower stem grows to 50 cm (about 20 in) and bears up to 4 poppy-like, 3-petalled flowers, usually white, cream or yellow, with a maroon blotch in the centre. There are also some in violet and red.

CALOSTEMMA
purpureum
AUSTRALIAN BELL, GARLAND LILY

This half-hardy Australian native has a circle of stamens which looks like a golden crown, hence its name from the Greek, *kalos*, beautiful and *stemma*, crown. In late summer a sturdy stem is topped with a mass of small, bell-shaped flowers in purple, pink or red. Bulbs should be planted in late autumn/fall in well-

Calostemma purpureum

Brunsvigia josephinae

drained soil in full sun. Water well through the growing period and then allow to dry out. Propagation by division or from seed is easy.

CAMASSIA
esculenta
syn. *C. quamash*
QUAMASH

This North American native grows to 90 cm (about 36 in) and produces a densely covered flower spike above an erect stem and slender basal leaves. The blue, star-shaped flowers which appear in summer have 6 petals and measure 2.5 cm (about 1 in). Bulbs should be planted in late autumn/fall in loamy, rich, moist soil. Position in partial shade or full sun if the soil is very moist. Frost-hardy, it does well in cool temperatures. Propagate by division or from seed, the latter may take up to five years to produce flowers. North American Indians once ate the large bulbs of quamash.

Chasmanthe aethiopica

Cardiocrinum giganteum

Chlidanthus fragrans

Clivia nobilis

Chasmanthe floribunda var. floribunda

CARDIOCRINUM
giganteum
syn. *Lilium giganteum*
GIANT LILY

A magnificent, summer-flowering plant reaching up to 4 m (about 12 ft). Unfortunately, the giant lily is not for the gardener who needs to see overnight results. A small bulb planted today is unlikely to flower for 5 years. The tall, sturdy stem bears up to twenty 25 cm (about 10 in) flowers, tubular at the base and trumpet-shaped at the top. The cream flowers are striped with maroon-red blotches at the throat and are heavily scented. The large bulbs should be planted in rich, acid soil in partial shade. Water and fertilize well once shoots appear. The main bulb dies after flowering but propagation is possible from offsets (which flower in 3 or 4 years) and seed. A good plan is to buy 3 sizes of bulbs, to ensure some flowers each year.

CHASMANTHE

This genus consists of about 10 species of corms native to tropical Africa and South Africa, grown for their flowers. They are half-hardy to frost-tender. Plant corms in autumn/fall in sun or partial shade and a moist, well-drained soil. Keep moist during the growing season and allow to dry out after flowering. Propagate from offsets or from seeds sown in autumn/fall.

C. aethiopica

This half-hardy South African native shares some characteristics with gladiolus. Ribbed, sword-shaped leaves fan out from the base and the

Clivia miniata

stems rise to 1.5 m (about 4½ ft). Yellow to red, slender, tubular flowers, 2.5 cm (about 1 in) long, are borne fan-like on one side of the stem in late spring and early summer. They are quite tender to frost.

C. floribunda var. floribunda
FLAMES, SUURKANOLPYPIE

Found wild in the south-western Cape area of South Africa, this perennial, branched herb has sword-shaped leaves up to 50 cm (about 20 in) long, and 5 cm (about 2 in) wide. Curved, almost hood-shaped, orange-red flowers, alternately arranged on flat spikes, are borne in late winter and early spring. Must be left undisturbed for several years.

CHIONODOXA
luciliae
syn. *C. gigantea*
GLORY-OF-THE-SNOW

These delicate-looking flowers are seen emerging from the melting snow in Europe and parts of Asia, giving the name *Chionodoxa*, Greek

for snow glory. Ideal for a rock garden in a cool climate, they grow to 15 cm (about 6 in), flowering in early spring. Narrow, basal leaves surround a slender stem which bears up to six, 1 cm (about ½ in), mauve to blue star-shaped flowers with white centres. Bulbs should be planted in cool to cold areas only, in well-drained soil, dressed with a layer of mulch, in autumn/fall. They will spread well of their own accord and can be propagated from seeds or offsets in autumn/fall.

CHLIDANTHUS
fragrans

SEA DAFFODIL, FAIRY LILY, PERUVIAN LILY

This little known South American bulb is frost-tender and ideal for coastal areas. Growing to 25 cm (about 10 in), the bare stem carries up to 5 bright yellow, sweetly scented, trumpet-shaped blooms about 7 cm (about 3 in) long. Basal foliage is like that of a daffodil. Plant the late spring-flowering bulbs in autumn/fall in loose, well-drained soil in a sunny position;

Chionodoxa luciliae

plant in pots in cool areas. Given the right conditions, the bulbs increase rapidly. Propagation is from offsets. This fragrant species is a good cut flower.

CLIVIA

BUSH LILY, FIRE LILY

These South African natives produce a glorious display of funnel-shaped flowers in spring or summer. They are quite easy to grow in all but frost-prone areas. Plant in a sheltered position in rich, well-drained soil. Keep fairly dry in winter and increase watering in spring and summer. Propagate by division after flowering. Seed can also be used but this can be slow to flower. In cooler areas they can be grown in pots; when quite pot bound they flower best.

C. miniata
FIRE LILY, BUSH LILY

This showy species grows up to 45 cm (about 18 in). A cluster of up to 12 funnel-shaped flowers appear in spring. The 8 cm (about 3 in) flowers are orange-red, paler at the throat. The foliage is glossy, thick and strap-like. It does well in a shaded area. Yellow and cream varieties are also available. Hybrids of *C. miniata* are becoming very popular.

C. nobilis
DROOPING CLIVIA, NATAL CLIVIA

This attractive species grows up to 40 cm (about 16 in). The pendulus, tubular flowers, orange and tipped with green, are borne in clusters, up to 30 on each stem. The leaves are glossy and strap-like.

COLCHICUM

AUTUMN CROCUS

This genus of flowering corms is native mainly to Europe and Asia. Masses of crocus-like flowers appear in autumn/fall, followed by the strap-like basal foliage. Frost-hardy, they are very easy to grow. However, they are not suitable for very hot areas. Plant the corms in late summer in well-drained soil in sun or partial shade. Corms will also usually flower without any soil, so they can be kept inside for display and planted after flowering. Propagate from seed or by division in summer. The plants are poisonous, although their active ingredient colchicine is used in the treatment of certain forms of cancer.

C. autumnale

The best known of the species, this grows to 15 cm (about 6 in) and has rosy pink to white, goblet-shaped flowers up to 10 cm (about 4 in) long. Each corm produces masses of flowers and multiplies freely. There is also a double-flowered form.

C. 'Lilac Wonder'

As the name suggests, this hardy cultivar produces large, up to 20 cm (about 8 in) long, lilac flowers. The tulip-like flowers appear in autumn/fall, followed by the strap-like foliage.

CONVALLARIA

majalis

LILY-OF-THE-VALLEY

Renowned for its glorious perfume, this beautiful plant is native to the northern hemisphere, and does best in cool climates. It is low-growing, up to 20 cm (about 8 in), with thick, oval to oblong, dark green leaves. The dainty, white, bell-shaped flowers appear in spring. The rhizomes, or 'pips' as they are commonly known, should be planted in autumn/fall in a partially shaded position in a cool or cold area. Soil should be rich and moist, and a dressing of mulch will give good results. Water well during the growing period. Given the right conditions, C. majalis spreads freely, sometimes becoming overcrowded when it will need to be divided.

CRINUM

These natives of South America, Asia, Africa and Australia are valued for their large, lily-like flowers and the ease with which they grow. Up to 20 scented flowers are borne on a tall, thick stem, usually in summer to early autumn/fall. The large bulbs should be planted in rich moist soil with the neck of the bulb above ground level. Partial shade is best, particularly in very hot areas. Propagation is best from seed as dividing

the plants is difficult. Flowers usually take a few seasons to develop with either method. They are tender to frost and susceptible to caterpillars, slugs and snails.

C. bulbispermum

ORANGE RIVER LILY

This species reaches up to 1.2 m (about 4 ft). Glossy, oblong leaves are borne on a thick leaf stalk. The sturdy scape rises beside the stem and is topped with a cluster of large, 25 cm (about 10 in), funnel-shaped flowers in white to pink, sometimes striped with dark pink. Does well in damp soil.

C. moorei

MOORE'S CRINUM, BUSH LILY

This popular species grows up to 75 cm (about 30 in). The strong stem bears a cluster of 10 cm (about 4 in) funnel-shaped flowers. The semi-pendent blooms are pale pink with white at the throat. The foliage is glossy and strap-like.

C. × powellii

CAPE LILY

This well-known and easily grown hybrid between C. bulbispermum and C. moorei grows up to 1 m (about 3 ft). Strap-like foliage is produced on a thick stalk and the bare scape is crowned with up to 10 scented, pink flowers. There is also a white form.

CROCOSMIA

MONTBRETIA

These half- to fully hardy South African natives bear attractive displays of flowers in summer. Tall, pleated leaves form a fan of foliage, similar to a gladiolus. A branched spike of brightly coloured flowers sits atop the tall stem. Plant the corms in winter in rich soil with adequate drainage in a position which receives morning sun. Water well through summer. They will multiply freely and should not be divided unless overcrowded. This should be done in spring if necessary.

C. aurea

A 90 cm (about 36 in) stem bears a branching spike of yellow to orange, 7 cm (about 3 in), tubular flowers. The slender leaves are sword-shaped. It likes a shaded position. Makes a good cut flower.

C. crocosmiiflora

Growing to 75 cm (about 30 in), the stem bears a branching spike of up to 40 orange-red, gladiolus-like flowers of about 2.5 cm (about 1 in). Bayonet-shaped foliage forms a fan from the base of the plant. This species is frost-hardy but needs a warm situation in cold climates.

Colchicum autumnale

Crinum moorei

Colchicum 'Lilac Wonder'

Crinum × powellii

Crinum bulbispermum

Crocosmia crocosmiiflora

Convallaria majalis

Crocosmia aurea

Crocus, Dutch hybrids

Crocus flavus

Crocosmia masonorum

Crocus vernus

Crocosmia 'Lucifer'

Crocus tomasinianus

Cyclamen coum subsp. caucasicum

Cyclamen coum subsp. coum

C. crocosmiiflora hybrids

Recently, larger flowered hybrids in a wider range of colours (yellow to red) have been raised in England. They have names like 'Bressingham Blaze' and 'Lucifer'. They are a little hardier than the species itself.

C. masonorum

A tall species, growing up to 1.2 m (about 4 ft). The branched stem is topped with an arched display of tangerine flowers. The 6-petalled flowers are quite large, up to 7 cm (about 3 in) wide. The narrow, bayonet-shaped foliage is pleated. It is useful as a cut flower.

CROCUS
CROCUS

Heralding the beginning of spring in Europe, crocuses pop up through the snow, the cheerful displays a sign that winter is over. The goblet-shaped flowers vary greatly in colour. The foliage is grass-like, with a silver-white stripe along the centre of the leaf. Fully hardy, they do best in a cool to cold area. In warm areas the corms

may flower in the first season but may not flower again. They can be grown in pots in warmer areas, in a cool spot. Corms should be planted in early autumn/fall in moist, well-drained soil in full sun or partial shade. Keep well watered until the foliage begins to die. They do not spread very fast but clumps can be divided if they are overcrowded. Seed can be planted in autumn/fall, but plants grown from seed usually will not flower for three years.

C., Dutch hybrids

The Dutch hybrids are vigorous plants with large flowers up to 15 cm (about 6 in) long. The colour range is varied, white to yellow to purple to blue. There are also some striped varieties. Many of these hybrids derive from *C. vernus*. They should be planted in autumn/fall in well-drained soil at a depth of about 10 cm (about 4 in).

C. flavus
syn. *C. aureus*

A profusion of 10 cm (about 4 in) goblet-shaped flowers in spring.

The scented flowers are orange-yellow, with an orange throat. Increases easily from seed. Grows more readily in a warmer climate than most other yellow species.

C. tomasinianus

Grows to 10 cm (about 4 in) with lavender to purple, sometimes white-throated, goblet-shaped flowers. One of the more easily grown species, it does well in a rockery, or naturalized under deciduous trees. There is also a purple-maroon form.

C. vernus
DUTCH CROCUS

The chalice-shaped flowers of this variable species can be white, lilac, blue, purple or striped. Suitable for rock gardens or under a deciduous tree. Flowering in spring, it grows to 10 cm (about 4 in).

CYCLAMEN
CYCLAMEN

The flower of the cyclamen must be one of the most elegant of all plants. These winter-flowering natives of

the Mediterranean region are often used in pots indoors but can also be grown in the garden. Florist's cyclamen (*C. persicum*) is usually bought already in flower for an indoor display. Keep the pot in good light but out of direct sun in an unheated room. It is rather frost tender, although the other species are rated frost- to fully hardy. Tubers should be planted in light, fibrous soil, rich in organic matter with excellent drainage in partial shade. Water regularly during growth but allow to dry out during summer. The tubers are best left undisturbed and should grow larger each year, flowering more abundantly each season. Propagate from seed in autumn/fall. Plants should flower in a year.

C. coum subsp. caucasicum

This popular, Middle Eastern species grows to 10 cm (about 4 in). The leaves are dark green, round to heart-shaped and marbled with silver. The abundant, dark pink flowers which are stained crimson at the base are 2 cm (about 1 in) long.

C. coum subsp. coum

Profusely blooming species popular for its elegant, pink to crimson flowers. The dark green leaves are round to heart-shaped. It grows to a height of 10 cm (about 4 in). There is also a delightful white form, stained crimson at the base of the petals.

C. hederifolium
syn. *C. neapolitanum*

This autumn/fall-flowering species can produce corms up to 15 cm

Eranthis hyemalis

Dracunculus vulgaris

Cyrtanthus macowanii

Cypella herbertii

Cyrtanthus mackenii

Cyclamen hederifolium

(about 6 in) wide. Growing to 10 cm (about 4 in) it has dark green, marbled, ivy-shaped foliage. The flowers are white to rose-pink, darker at the base and some strains are perfumed.

CYPELLA
herbertii

This iris-like cousin of the *Tigridia* is native to the cooler parts of South America. The unusual flowers bloom only for a day, but new flowers appear through most of the summer months. The branched flower stem grows to 90 cm (about 36 in) bearing 7 cm (about 3 in) triangular blooms. The large, pointed, outside petals are copper to tan; the much smaller inner petals are purple and gold. The green foliage is like that of an iris, sword-shaped and pleated. This half-hardy species should be planted in full sun in light, well-drained soil. Water well through the growing season and allow to dry out in winter. The bulbs should be lifted in areas which have very wet winters. Propagation is from offsets or from seed planted in winter/spring.

CYRTANTHUS
IFAFA LILY

This large genus of about 50 species is native to South Africa. The brightly coloured flowers are tubular and curved, nodding down from the top of a hollow stem. The scented flowers bloom at various times, depending on the species. The grass-like foliage usually dies down over winter. Most are tender to frost and they do best in areas where winters

are mild. Although some species have been found growing in swamps, they are best planted in rich, well-drained soil in a sunny situation. The neck of the bulb should be at ground level. Water well through the growing season. The bulbs are best left undisturbed but may need dividing if over-crowding occurs. They can be propagated from seed planted in spring. They do well planted in pots and they also make a long-lasting, perfumed cut flower. They hybridize very freely, and nurseries usually offer them by colour rather than under specific names.

C. mackenii
IFAFA LILY

The most popular species as it is one of the easiest to grow. Narrow, green, basal leaves surround hollow stems which grow to 40 cm (about 16 in). The curved, tubular flowers which appear in spring are white, about 5 cm (about 2 in) long.

C. macowanii
FIRE LILY

Slightly larger than *C. mackenii* and usually flowering a week or two later, this species has brilliant scarlet or coral red flowers. It is almost evergreen in mild climates. The two species interbreed readily.

DRACUNCULUS
vulgaris
syn. *Arum dracunculus*
STINK LILY, DRAGON LILY

This relative of the arum is not a plant you would want to grow beside your front door. It emits a potent,

foul odour which attracts flies for pollinating. A native of the Mediterranean region, it grows to about 90 cm (about 36 in). The large leaves are red-veined and deeply divided. In late spring, a thick stem bears one or more large, up to 40 cm (about 16 in) spathes, like that of the arum, green on the outside and red to purple to black on the inside, with a purple to black spadix. Plant the large tubers in winter in well-drained soil in partial shade. Water well through the growing season but allow to dry out after flowering. In cold areas, protect with a dressing of mulch in winter, although the plant is rated frost-hardy. Propagate from seed or offsets in autumn/fall.

ERANTHIS
hyemalis
syn. *E. cilicicus*
WINTER ACONITE

This delightful, ground-hugging native of Asia and Europe flowers in late winter to early spring. Sunny yellow, goblet-shaped flowers about 3 cm (about 1½ in) wide are

perched on a ruff of green, divided leaves. Plant the tubers in early autumn/fall in rich, slightly damp soil. The species likes full sun to partial shade and is fully hardy. It does best in cooler areas, naturalized under a deciduous tree or in a rock garden where it will spread quite rapidly. Propagate by division in summer or from seed in autumn/fall.

ERYTHRONIUM
DOG-TOOTH-VIOLET

Native to Asia, Europe and North America, these little plants bear delicate, reflexed, star-shaped flowers in spring. The dark green foliage is often attractively mottled. *Erythronia* are fully hardy and do best in cooler areas. Plant the tubers in autumn/fall in well-drained soil which is rich in organic matter. Keep plants moist in partial to full shade. They multiply easily and should be left undisturbed until overcrowding occurs. Propagate from offsets in summer or from seed in autumn/fall.

Freesia, Florist's hybrids

Freesia alba

Fritillaria imperialis

Erythronium 'Pagoda'

Eucomis comosa

Erythronium dens-canis

E. dens-canis
DOG'S TOOTH VIOLET

The most widely grown species, reaching to 20 cm (about 8 in), it has beautiful, oval, marbled foliage. The reflexed, star-shaped flowers are white to lilac, about 5 cm (about 2 in) wide. The common name refers to the shape of the corm.

E. 'Pagoda'

This hardy cultivar grows to 30 cm (about 12 in) and has marbled green foliage. The creamy yellow flowers are star-shaped, reflexed and nodding, about 5 cm (about 2 in) across.

EUCOMIS
comosa
syn. *E. punctata*
PINEAPPLE LILY

This native of South Africa has a spike of flowers which looks very similar to a pineapple; it is even topped with a tuft of pineapple-like leaves. It grows to 70 cm (about 28 in). Dark green, crinkly, strap-like leaves surround the tall, purple spotted scapes. The hundreds of star-shaped flowers, white to green and sometimes spotted with purple, are borne on a spike in autumn/fall. Plant bulbs in spring in full sun in well-drained soil. Half-hardy, it may need to be lifted in very cold winters. Water well through the growing season. Propagate by division in winter or from seed in spring, but it takes a long time to flower. Makes an excellent, long-lasting cut flower.

FREESIA
FREESIA

These South African natives are extensively grown for their brightly coloured and deliciously scented spring flowers. They are rather tender but easily grown in most areas except those that suffer heavy frost. Slender, sword-shaped leaves surround wiry stems which bear spikes of goblet-shaped flowers. The weight of the flowers can be too much for the stems so they may need to be supported by twigs or wire. Plant the corms in autumn/fall in full sun in well-drained soil. They look best in a massed display. Water well through the growing season but allow to dry out once flowering is finished. The clumps are best left undisturbed for three years; they can then be divided in autumn/fall. Seed should be sown in late summer. In cold climates, they grow very well in pots in a cool greenhouse.

F. alba
syn. *F. refracta alba*

This widely grown species flowers in early spring. The creamy white, goblet-shaped flowers are 5 cm (about 2 in) long and are borne on a spike. Slender, bayonet-shaped leaves surround wiry stems up to 30 cm (about 12 in) long. This highly scented species makes an excellent cut flower.

F., Florist's hybrids

There are many named strains of hybrid freesias available; they come in shades of white, pink, blue, red or yellow, and grow from 15–35 cm (about 6–14 in) in height. Some have semi-double flowers whose weight makes the plant top-heavy enough to need staking. None is difficult to grow, although they need glasshouse culture in frosty climates or if blooms outside of their natural spring season are desired. Some strains are well scented, others almost scentless.

FRITILLARIA
FRITILLARY

These relatives of the lily and tulip are native to Asia, Europe and North America. Fully hardy, they do best in areas with cold winters. They are not easy to grow, but their nodding, bell to goblet-shaped flowers which appear in spring are worth the trouble. Plant bulbs in early autumn/fall in partial shade in well-drained soil rich in organic matter. Water well through the growing season but allow to dry out after flowering. In areas which have high summer rainfall, the bulbs will need to be lifted. Handle the rather soft bulbs gently, and keep them out of the ground for as short a time as possible. Propagate from offsets in summer, but clumps are best left undisturbed for a few years. Seed can be sown in autumn/fall but will take 4 or 5 years to bloom.

F. imperialis
CROWN IMPERIAL

This is the tallest species and also the easiest to grow. The stems reach up to 1 m (about 3 ft) or more and the leaves are borne in whorls along the stem. The flowers are also arranged in a whorl or crown at the top of the scape, and above the flowers is a bunch of leaves. The bell-shaped flowers are 3 cm (about 1½ in) long and can be yellow to orange to red; they have a heavy, rather unpleasant odour.

F. meleagris
SNAKE'S HEAD LILY, LEPER'S LILY

Slender stems reaching to 35 cm (about 14 in) each bear one nodding, goblet-shaped bloom. The maroon, green or white flowers are 2.5 cm (about 1 in) long and are blotched or checkered. A few slender leaves are found along the stem. Does well naturalized under deciduous trees or in a rock garden, provided it has plenty of moisture while growing.

F. persica

This Mediterranean species can be grown in warmer areas than most other species. It grows to about 1 m (about 3 ft) and bears up to 25 nodding, bell-shaped flowers on a spike. The 2.5 cm (about 1 in) flowers which appear in spring are dark purple to brown to blackish purple. Dozens of narrow, green leaves appear along the stem.

GALANTHUS
SNOWDROPS

These natives of Europe and western Asia flower in late winter and herald the coming of spring. Fully hardy they do best in cold areas. Delightful, white, nodding flowers appear above daffodil-like foliage. Plant bulbs in autumn/fall in rich, moist soil in partial shade. In very cold areas they may be planted in full sun. They are best divided or transplanted immediately after flowering, before the leaves start to die off. They can be grown from seed which will bloom a few years after sowing. Snowdrops do well in a rockery and are an excellent cut flower.

G. ikariae
syn. *G. latifolius*

Fine stems reaching to 10 cm (about 4 in), each bear one delicate, 2.5 cm (about 1 in), nodding, bell-shaped flower. The outer petals are pure white, the inner petals are green at the throat. The blue-green foliage is narrow and strap-like. It does well in a rock garden.

G. nivalis

This most commonly grown species reaches about 22 cm (about 9 in). The slender, blue-green leaves are strap-shaped. Each fine stem bears one nodding, bell-shaped, 2.5 cm (about 1 in) flower. The outer petals are white and the tubular inner petals green and white. There are many cultivars derived from this species, including a double-flowered one.

GALTONIA
candicans
BERG LILY, SUMMER HYACINTH

This South African native produces delightful bell-shaped flowers for 6 weeks in the middle of summer. The flower spike bears up to 20 white blooms which are sometimes green at the tips. Broad, blue-green, strap-shaped leaves surround stems which can reach up to 2 m (about 6 ft). Plant bulbs in late autumn/fall about 15 cm (about 6 in) deep in well-drained, compost-rich soil in a sunny position. It is half-hardy. Water well through the growing season and allow to dry out after flowering. Propagate from offsets in autumn/fall or from seed which will usually bloom in three years. Protect from slugs and snails.

GLADIOLUS
GLADIOLUS

Gladioli are native to Africa, Europe and the Middle East. They vary greatly in size, colour, flowering time and even the arrangement of the blooms on the flower spike.

Most of the widely cultivated hybrids originate in South Africa. The hybrids are divided into 3 main groups—Large-flowered, Primulinus and Butterfly. The Large-flowered types are those that are usually seen in florist's arrangements, sometimes with ruffled flowers which are arranged alternately either side of the 2 m (about 6 ft) long stem. The Primulinus group have smaller flowers, often blotched, arranged irregularly on a 30 cm (about 12 in) stem. The Butterfly group have blotched, ruffled flowers on 90 cm (about 36 in) stems. Corms should be planted about 12 cm (about 5 in) deep in very well-drained, sandy soil in a sunny position. In cool areas, plant in early spring; in warm areas, plant from autumn/fall until spring for a succession of blooms. The tall stems may need staking. Water well through summer and cut off spent flower stems. Corms will need to be lifted in cold areas and Large-flowered gladioli are best lifted in all areas, especially those with a high winter rainfall. Make sure they are pefectly dry before storing. Can be propagated from offsets although these may take a few years to bloom.

G. alatus
KALKOENTJIE

This small species grows to about 30 cm (about 12 in). Flowers are red to orange and yellow at the base. Good drainage is essential. It is excellent in a rockery.

G., Butterfly hybrids

These resemble the Large-flowered hybrids (see below) but have slightly smaller, ruffled flowers, usually with contrasting blotches in the throat. They come in the same range of colours and are grown in the same way.

G. byzantinus

A Mediterranean species reaching to about 1 m (about 3 ft). The slender stem bears up to 15 pink to magenta blooms.

Gladiolus, Butterfly hybrids

Galanthus ikariae

Fritillaria persica

Gladiolus byzantinus

Galanthus nivalis

Fritillaria meleagris

Galtonia candicans

Gladiolus alatus

Haemanthus coccineus

Gladiolus callianthus

Habranthus robustus

Gloriosa superba

Herbertia drummondii

Gladiolus tristis

Gladiolus carneus

Gladiolus × colvillei

Gladiolus, Large-flowered hybrids

G. callianthus
syn. *Acidanthera bicolor*
PEACOCK FLOWER

This scented species grows to about 90 cm (about 36 in). The mainly white flowers often have a crimson blotch at their base. The 10 cm (about 4 in) long flowers have 6 outer petals and the inner petals appear to form a tube. Half-hardy, it flowers in autumn/fall. Protect from thrips, and water lavishly while in growth.

G. carneus
syn. *G. blandus*
PAINTED LADY

A lovely, spring-flowering plant with arching spikes of white, funnel-shaped flowers stained with purple or yellow blotches. It is half-hardy and easily grown, multiplying vigorously.

G. × colvillei
syn. *G. nanus*

Up to 10, elegant, 7 cm (about 3 in) dark pink, yellow or white blooms on a 45 cm (about 18 in) spike. Usually flowers in late spring.

G., Large-flowered hybrids

These are the familiar gladioli of the flower shops. They grow up to 1.5 m (about 4½ ft) tall with one-sided flower spikes that can carry up to 24 wide open flowers. The individual flowers are normally about 10 cm (about 4 in) wide, although they may be as large as 14 cm (about 5½ in). Every colour but blue is available. Half-hardy, they are best planted in spring and lifted in late autumn/fall to be stored for the winter. Rich soil, sun, and vigilant protection from thrips are needed. Propagate by growing on offsets, which take 3 years to flower.

G. tristis
YELLOW MARSH AFRIKANER

Each 60 cm (about 24 in) slender stem carries up to 6 highly scented, bright yellow flowers, about 7 cm (about 3 in) wide. It prefers a richer soil than the sandy soil favoured by most species. Many spring-flowering hybrids derive from this popular species.

GLORIOSA
superba
GLORY LILY, TIGER'S CLAWS

This is a tropical species from Africa, only suitable for the garden where there is no chance whatever of frost. However, it does grow very well as a pot plant and greenhouse grown flowers are popular with florists. They resemble tigerlilies but are brilliant in red and gold. The plants climb by means of tendrils on the ends of the leaves and need support. Plant the tubers in autumn/fall, taking care as the plant is very poisonous. *G. rothschildiana* is very similar and some authorities consider it merely a variety of *G. superba.*

HABRANTHUS
robustus
PAMPAS LILY

This beautiful plant is a relative of the *Hippeastrum* and comes from the Argentine pampas. A trumpet-shaped flower about 10 cm (about 4 in) long appears on each 30 cm (about 12 in) stem. The flowers, which appear in summer, are rose-pink, often fading to white. The glossy, green basal foliage is strap-like. Tender to frost, it is easily grown in warm to temperate areas. Plant the bulbs in a sunny position in autumn/fall in well-drained soil rich in organic matter. Water well through the growing season. Can be propagated from offsets when dormant or from seed, which will usually flower in the third year.

HAEMANTHUS
coccineus
BLOOD LILY

The half-hardy *Haemanthus* genus, with its brightly coloured flowers, originates in Africa and prefers mild to warm conditions. This autumn/fall-flowering species grows to 35 cm (about 14 in). The two broadly oval, dark green leaves are hairy on the underside, and they lie on the soil. A sturdy, purple-spotted stem bears a cluster of slender, bright red flowers enclosed by scarlet to pink bracts and followed by red berries. Plant bulbs in autumn/fall or spring in partial shade in a compost-rich, well-drained soil. Water and feed well during the growing season, but allow it to get completely dry during its summer dormancy. The plants are best left undisturbed for a few years when they can then be propagated from offsets, or from seed, which takes a few years to flower. The common name has no sinister connotations, it merely refers to the colour of the flowers.

HERBERTIA
drummondii
BLUE TIGER FLOWER

This spring-flowering South American native is a relative of the *Tigridia* and the iris. The foliage is like that of an iris, sword-shaped and pleated. The stems reach to 30 cm (about 12 in) and bear short-lived, triangular flowers about 5 cm (about 2 in) wide. The outer petals are violet-blue and the smaller inner petals are often spotted. It is frost-tender and does best in temperate to warm areas. Plant the corms in autumn/fall in a sunny to

Hyacinthoides hispanica

Hippeastrum 'Red Lion'

Hyacinthus orientalis

Hippeastrum 'Apple Blossom'

Hyacinthoides non-scripta

Hippeastrum advenum

Hermodactylus tuberosus

partially shaded position. The soil should be light and well drained but enriched with compost. Water well through the growing season but allow to dry out after flowering. Propagate by dividing corms in winter or from seed in autumn/fall.

HERMODACTYLUS
tuberosus
syn. *Iris tuberosa*
SNAKE'S HEAD IRIS, WIDOW IRIS

This frost-hardy relative of the iris gets its common names from the appearance and unusual colours (often black and green) of its flowers. Native to the Middle East and Mediterranean region, it grows to 40 cm (about 16 in). The tall, blue-green foliage is slender and squarish. The perfumed, iris-like flowers, yellow-green and purple-black, appear in early spring. Plant the tubers in early autumn/fall in very well-drained soil in a sunny spot. Leave clumps undisturbed for a few years, then divide in spring or summer. Alternatively, grow from seed, but this may be difficult to obtain.

HIPPEASTRUM

BARBADOS LILY

These magnificent plants with their showy, trumpet-shaped flowers are native to tropical South America. They have been widely hybridized and it is these cultivars which are usually grown by the average gardener. Half-hardy, in cold areas they will need to be protected from frost. They can also be grown in a glasshouse or inside as a pot plant. A single bulb in a pot will produce a

display that any florist would be hard pressed to match. Bulbs should be planted in autumn/fall in well-drained soil rich in organic matter, with just the tip of the bulb exposed, in full sun or partial shade. Water and feed well through the growing season and allow the bulb to dry out after the foliage dies down. Clumps are best left undisturbed for a few years when they can then be divided. They can also be grown from seed sown in spring. Protect from snails.

H. advenum
syn. *Rhodolphiala bifurcata*
CHILEAN LILY

Up to 6 dark red, trumpet-shaped flowers about 5 cm (about 2 in) long are borne on a 30 cm (about 12 in) stem. The stem and flowers appear in summer before the blue-green, slender, strap-like foliage appears. There is also a bright red form and a yellow form.

H. 'Apple Blossom'

This is the most popular of all the Dutch-bred hybrid hippeastrums. A sturdy stem reaching up to 45 cm (about 18 in) bears clusters of up to 6 stunning pale pink and white blooms. Trumpet-shaped flowers, up to 20 cm (about 8 in), appear in spring, followed by slender foliage. It is frost-tender.

H. 'Red Lion'

Up to 6 blood-red, trumpet-shaped flowers appear in spring on a thick, 50 cm (about 20 in) stem. The very showy blooms can be 20 cm (about 8 in) long. Slender, blue-green foliage appears after the flowers.

HYACINTHOIDES
syn. *Endymion, Scilla*
BLUEBELLS

The hardy, European bluebells with their attractive, scented flowers are popular with gardeners all over the world. Equally at home in a rock garden, naturalized under deciduous trees or in the flower border, they thrive in moist, partially shaded conditions. Bulbs should be planted in autumn/fall in rich, moist soil. Water well until the flowers start to die. They should multiply freely but are best left undisturbed for a few years, then divided in late summer.

H. hispanica
syn. *Endymion hispanica,*
Scilla campanulata
SPANISH BLUEBELL

The most popular and most easily grown species, it grows to about 30 cm (about 12 in) and flowers in spring. The 2.5 cm (about 1 in) nodding, bell-shaped flowers are lilac to blue. The bright green foliage is strap-like. It multiplies freely.

H. non-scripta
syn. *Endymion non-scripta,*
Scilla non-scripta
ENGLISH BLUEBELL

The English bluebell flowers in early spring and can continue flowering into summer. The very fragrant, nodding, bell-shaped flowers in lavender-blue, pink or white are about 1 cm (about ½ in) long on fine stems reaching to about 30 cm (about 12 in). The slender, strap-like foliage is glossy green.

HYACINTHUS
orientalis
HYACINTH

Popular with gardeners all over the world, the popular named varieties of hyacinth are cultivars of *H. orientalis* which originally comes from the Middle East and Mediterranean region. A spike of flowers is massed on top of a 30 cm (about 12 in) stem. The sweetly perfumed spring flowers vary enormously in colour. 'King of the Blues' is a favourite, but many others are available in white, pale yellow, pink, red or purple.

The glossy green foliage is strap-like. Plant the bulbs in clumps in autumn/fall in rich, well-drained soil in full sun or partial shade. Frost-hardy, hyacinths do best in cool areas, as well as in pots. It is best to buy new bulbs each year, as the flowers are never so magnificent as in that first spring; but, planted in a congenial spot, they will continue to bloom each spring for years.

HYMENOCALLIS

SPIDER LILY, FILMY LILY

The unusual, beautiful, flowers of the spider lily resemble daffodils except for the delicate, spider-like petals surrounding the inner bloom. Mainly native to South America, they are not too fussy about conditions; but are usually frost-tender and do best in temperate or warm areas. Bulbs should be planted in winter, about 15 cm (about 6 in) deep in well-drained soil. A partially shaded position is best. Water very well during growth and never allow

to dry out completely. Offsets form quickly and should be divided in winter.

H. × festalis

This half-hardy to frost-tender plant grows to about 50 cm (about 20 in) and has deliciously scented flowers. The glossy green foliage is slender and strap-like. Each stem bears up to five 10 cm (about 4 in) white flowers. The inner trumpet-shaped cup of petals is surrounded by 6 slender, spider-like petals.

H. littoralis

Pure white, trumpet-shaped flowers surrounded by 6 thread-like petals are borne on 75 cm (about 30 in) stems. The almost strap-like foliage is bright green. This species is frost-tender.

IRIS

IRIS

This wide-ranging genus, named for the Greek goddess of the rain-

bow, is valued all over the world for its beautiful and distinctive flowers. Size, colour and growing conditions vary greatly but the unusual flowers are easily recognized. Each flower has 6 petals: 3 outer petals, called 'falls', droop away from the centre and alternate with the inner petals, called 'standards'. Irises are divided into 2 main groups, rhizomatous (which we have included in the chapter on annuals and perennials) and bulbous. The bulbous irises are divided into 3 groups, which some botanists raise to the status of 3 new genera: *Xiphium*, which includes the Dutch irises of the florist shops as well as the species *I. xiphium, latifolia, lusitania* and *tingitana* from which they have been derived (they are mostly native to Spain, Portugal and North Africa); *Iridodictyum*, which bear small, winter and spring flowers and are mainly native to the Middle East; and *Juno*, also from the Middle East and Central Asia, which are noteworthy for their handsome leaves and spectacular flowers, with diminutive standards but well-developed falls. All are fully hardy, and enjoy a sunny position with ample moisture during growth but very little during their summer dormancy. All are planted in autumn/fall.

IRIDODICTYUM

RETICULATA IRISES

The best known species is *I. reticulata* from Central Asia. It grows to about 10 cm (about 4 in) high in flower, and has flowers in various shades of blue: several named varieties are available, differ-

ing mainly in the precise colour of the flowers. Foliage is short during the late winter/early spring flowering time, becoming longer after bloom. It likes sun and perfectly drained soil and is propagated from seed or by division. Other species in the group, all fully hardy, include: *I. histrio* and *I. histrioides*, both blue; *I. bakeriana*, blue and purple; and *I. danfordiae*, yellow. The whole group does best in cold-winter climates. All species make delightful pot plants.

JUNO

Mainly native to Central Asia, the Junos have a reputation for being difficult to grow, but where winters are cold and summers dry they are easy enough to grow in a sunny, perfectly drained position. Most species have fleshy roots attached permanently to the bulbs and great care must be taken never to damage these. The species all have handsome foliage.

I. bucharica

syn. I. orchiodes

This iris grows to about 45 cm (about 18 in). The 6 cm (about 2½ in) scented flowers can be varied in colour. Standards and falls can both be white or yellow, or standards can be white and falls yellow. It requires a rich soil and is slow to increase. Take care not to damage the thick lateral roots when transplanting.

XIPHIUM

These are the best known of the bulbous irises, and best known among them are the Dutch hybrids. They grow to about 80 cm (about 32 in) in flower, with rather straggly grey-green leaves and bear one or two flowers on long stems. Fully hardy and easy to grow, they like rich, well-drained soil and sun. Water freely while they are in growth, and keep them dry in summer. They are propagated by division in autumn/fall. Handle the bulbs gently as they bruise easily. The so-called English and Spanish irises, mainly derived from *I. latifolia*, are similar to Dutch hybrids but flower later in spring.

Hymenocallis × festalis

Iris reticulata

Iris 'Professor Blauw' (Dutch hybrid)

Iris 'Symphony' (Dutch hybrid)

Iris bucharica

Hymenocallis littoralis

I., Dutch hybrids

These are familiar flower-shop flowers; florists keep them in bloom just about all year by chilling the bulbs and planting in greenhouses. There are many named varieties, in shades of white, blue, violet, or yellow. The blue 'Professor Blaauw' and yellow and white 'Symphony' are typical. In the garden they flower in mid-spring.

I. latifolia
syn. I. xiphioides

Most of the bulbous English irises (so-called because of their great popularity in eighteenth-century England) are derived from this species from Spain. It grows to 75 cm (about 30 in), and the 10 cm (about 4 in) flowers which appear in summer are purple-blue or white. The falls are 'winged' and often have a golden blotch.

I. tingitana

This magnificent species from northern Africa has 15 cm (about 6 in) wide, light blue flowers. It is temperamental in cultivation and is normally represented in gardens by its cultivar 'Wedgwood', a hybrid with a Dutch iris. This grows to 70 cm (about 28 in) tall, and has 12 cm (about 5 in) light blue flowers. It is cultivated the same way as the Dutch hybrids.

IXIA
AFRICAN CORN LILY

The South African corn lily produces masses of delightful, star-shaped flowers on wiry stems in spring. These flowers close in the evening and on cloudy days. The tallest species grows to about 60 cm (about 24 in). The leaves are usually long and slender. They are sensitive to frost but easy to grow in temperate to warm areas. The bulbs should be planted in early autumn/fall in well-drained soil. Blood and bone mixed into the soil before planting will help produce good blooms. A sunny position is ideal except in warm areas where they will need protection from hot sun. Water well through winter and spring but allow to dry out after flowering. Propagate from offsets in autumn/fall. Seed can be used and this should flower in the third year.

I. maculata
YELLOW IXIA

This is the most commonly grown species. The wiry stems grow to about 45 cm (about 18 in), with 5 cm (about 2 in) flowers clustered along the top, with brown centres, and orange to yellow petals, sometimes with pinkish red undersides; garden forms come in white, yellow, pink, orange or red.

I. paniculata
syn. Morphixia paniculata
BUTT IXIA

The slender stems grow to about 60 cm (about 24 in) and are topped with spikes of buff to pale pink blooms. The 5 cm (about 2 in) flowers, star-shaped and tubular at the base, appear in late spring.

I. viridiflora
GREEN IXIA

The exquisite, jewel-like flowers make this a popular species. The 5 cm (about 2 in) flowers are borne on a spike atop the 60 cm (about 24 in) stem. The star-shaped flowers are turquoise with a purple-black centre.

IXIOLIRION
tataricum
syn. I. montanum, I. pallasii
TARTAR LILY

Popular in Europe and America, this native of the Middle East and central Asia flowers in spring. The slender stem reaches to about 45 cm (about 18 in) and bears clusters of up to six tubular, star-shaped, violet to blue flowers. The foliage is slender and grass-like. Plant bulbs in autumn/fall in full sun in well-drained soil. A protective layer of mulch will be needed in cool areas. Plant in a pot in areas with severe frost. Water well during growth and allow to dry out after flowering. Propagate from offsets or seed in autumn/fall.

LACHENALIA
CAPE COWSLIP, SOLDIER BOYS, YIOOLTJIE

Massed in clumps or planted in window boxes, these South African natives make a striking display. Spikes of pendulous, tubular flowers stand erect above narrow, sometimes marbled, strap-like foliage. Plant bulbs in autumn/fall in well-drained soil enriched with organic matter. They like a sunny position and lots of water until the foliage begins to die off. They need to be kept dry when dormant and may need to be lifted in areas with a high summer rainfall. They are sensitive to frost and can be planted in pots or window boxes in cool areas. They spread quite freely and can be divided in autumn/fall.

L. aloides var. aloides
syn. L. tricolour
CAPE COWSLIP

This species grows to about 30 cm (about 12 in). Flowers appear on a spike in winter to spring above strap-like foliage. The nodding, tubular flowers flare out at the tips, and are usually golden yellow and green at the tips. The base of the petals is sometimes red to orange. There are various forms and many hybrids derived from this species.

Ixia maculata

Iris tingitana 'Wedgwood'

Lachenalia aloides var. *aloides*

Iris latifolia

Ixiolirion tataricum

Ixia viridiflora

Ixia paniculata

Lilium, Asiatic hybrid

Leucojum aestivum

Lachenalia orchioides var. glaucina

Lachenalia bulbifera

Leucocoryne ixioides odorata

Lilium 'Royal Gold' (Trumpet)

Lilium 'Bright Star' (Aurelian)

L. bulbifera
syn. L. pendula
RED LACHENALIA

This species grows to about 25 cm (about 10 in), with a spike of flowers appearing in winter to spring. The pendulous, tubular flowers are pink to red to yellow and the flared tips are violet to purple. The green foliage is strap-like.

L. orchioides var. glaucina
syn. L. glaucina

Each 30 cm (about 12 in) spike bears up to 25 bell-shaped blooms. The 2.5 cm (about 1 in) flowers are usually pale blue to violet and are scented. The strap-like leaves are often spotted with purple.

LEUCOCORYNE
ixioides odorata
GLORY OF THE SUN

This native of Chile is a bit of a gamble for the gardener. One year you may get a magnificent display of blooms and the next spring it may refuse to flower at all. Flowers are borne in clusters on wiry stems up to 45 cm (about 18 in) tall. The 5 cm (about 2 in), sweetly scented flowers are reflexed and star-shaped, white in the centre, graduating to blue at the tips with prominent yellow anthers. The foliage is long and slender. Plant bulbs in autumn/fall in full sun in light, well-drained soil with plenty of water in winter and spring and allow to dry out over summer. Half-hardy, it does best in temperate areas. Propagate from seed or offsets in autumn/fall, but this is difficult.

LEUCOJUM
aestivum
SNOWFLAKE

These dainty, spring-flowering bulbs are native to Europe and Asia. They multiply freely year after year and large clumps of the bell-shaped, nodding blooms make a glorious display. The fragrant flowers are white with a green spot near the tip of each petal and are borne in clusters atop 50 cm (about 20 in) stems. The blue-green leaves are long and slender. Frost-hardy, the small bulbs should be planted in autumn/fall in a sunny position, but need protection from hot sun in warm areas. Under a deciduous tree is ideal. The soil should be rich, moist and well-drained. Propagate from seed or the freely forming offsets in autumn/fall or spring, but clumps are best left undisturbed for a few years.

LILIUM
LILY

Many plants are commonly called lilies but the 'true' lilies are the many species and hybrids of the magnificent Lilium genus. The elegant flowers possess a breathtaking beauty often accompanied by a glorious perfume. The flowers have 6 petals arranged in a variety of ways, and 6 stamens. The scaly bulbs should be planted in autumn/fall, but in cold areas they are best planted in spring. The soil should be rich with excellent drainage and the bulbs planted fairly deep as they like a cool root run. A dressing of mulch in spring helps keep the roots cool. A partially shaded position is best as the flowers need protection from hot afternoon sun. Tall species may need staking. Dead flowers should be removed but leaves and stems should not be cut back until autumn/fall. Clumps are best left undisturbed for a few years; they can then be lifted and divided. In recent years, many hybrids, easier to grow than most true lilies, have been created, and have become very popular. The most important groups are the Asiatic or Mid-Century hybrids, the Trumpet hybrids, the Aurelians which have trumpet or bowl shaped flowers, and the spectacular Oriental hybrids. They need lime-free soil, although L. candidum prefers an alkaline soil and L. regale and L. lancifolium will put up with a little lime.

Asiatic hybrids

Raised from L. lancifolium, bulbiferum, croceum and other Asiatic species. These are summer flowering and mostly grow to about 1 m (about 3 ft) tall. Most have upward-facing, flat flowers in shades from white through yellow and pink to orange and russet-red. They have no scent. Fully hardy, they do best in a sunny position and are first-rate cut flowers, much grown in greenhouses by florists for out-of-season bloom. Propagate by division. There are many named varieties: the yellow 'Connecticut King' and orange 'Enchantment' are popular and typical.

Trumpet hybrids

Deriving from L. regale, the trumpet hybrids flower in late summer. They can reach 2 m (about 6 ft) and carry as many as 30 outward facing trumpets in shades from white through pink to yellow, usually with purple shadings on the outside. They are usually fragrant and are easily grown in light shade and lime free, well-drained soil.

Aurelian hybrids
syn. L. aurelianense

The name comes from the Latin name for Orléans in France where the earliest varieties were bred. They derive from crosses between the

Chinese *L. henryi* and trumpet lilies and resemble the Trumpet hybrids except the flowers may be flat or bowl shaped. Some cultivars are well scented, others scentless. They are fully hardy.

Oriental hybrids

Most glamorous of all lilies, the Oriental hybrids grow to 2 m (about 6 ft) tall and bear many bowl-shaped flowers as much as 25 cm (about 10 in) wide in shades from white to crimson. They are power-fully scented and very desirable (and expensive) cut flowers. De-rived from crosses of *U. auratum*, *speciosum* and *ribellum*, they like a temperate climate, light shade and perfectly drained very acid soil. They are subject to virus and care needs to be taken to obtain clean stock. There are many cultivars.

SPECIES

L. auratum
GOLDEN-RAYED LILY OF JAPAN

This magnificent species grows up to 2 m (about 6 ft). Each stem bears up to eight open-faced blooms, about 20 cm (about 8 in) wide. The flow-ers are white, sometimes red spot-ted, and have a yellow or red stripe along each petal.

L. candidum
MADONNA LILY

This beautifully scented species is thought to be the oldest lily in cul-tivation. It grows to 2.3 m (about 7 ft) and bears up to 20 trumpet-shaped blooms in summer. The pure white flowers can be 15 cm (about 6 in) wide and slightly reflexed. It is sometimes tricky to grow, being very subject to virus. Cool climates and mildly alkaline soils suit it best. Plant with the nose of the bulb almost at ground level.

L. formosanum

This is an elegant lily which grows to 2 m (about 6 ft). The flowers which appear in late summer are trumpet-shaped and reflexed. The petals are pure white on the inside and pink to purple-brown on the outside. It is easily grown from seed. Mature bulbs are prone to viruses and often do not give a good display of blooms, so they should be replaced every few years. It is half-hardy.

L. henryi

This lily from Central China grows to about 2 m (about 6 ft), with each stem bearing as many as 40 reflexed flowers in pale apricot. The bulbs can be as much as 20 cm (about 8 in) in diameter, an indication of the great vigour of the species. It tolerates lime and is resistant to viruses. Fully hardy, it is the chief parent of the Aurelian hybrids.

L. lancifolium
syn. *L. tigrinum*
TIGER LILY

One of the most popular species and also one of the oldest in culti-vation, the tiger lily grows to about 1.5 m (about 4½ ft). It produces masses of bright orange, trumpet-shaped, sharply reflexed flowers. The 18 cm (about 7½ in) blooms are spotted with purple and are usually pendent. The tiger lily can harbour viruses without showing any ill effects and for this reason is best grown away from other lilies. It is much grown in its native China for the edible bulbs.

L. longiflorum
EASTER LILY, ST JOSEPH LILY, BERMUDA LILY, CHRISTMAS LILY

A lovely, pure white lily which grows to 1.2 m (about 4 ft). Up to 8 slender, trumpet-shaped flowers are borne on each stem. The fragrant blooms, 20 cm (about 8 in) long, appear in summer. It is half-hardy, and one of the best lilies for warm-winter climates.

L. martagon
TURK'S CAP LILY

Native to Europe, this species flow-ers in summer and bears many reflexed flowers in mauve-pink or white, with a strong fragrance. Fully hardy, it does best in cool climates. The name, 'Child of Mars', dates from a time when even gar-dening was governed by astrology.

Lilium auratum

Lilium henryi

Lilium martagon

Lilium 'Wildfire' (Oriental hybrid)

Lilium lancifolium   *Lilium candidum*   *Lilium longiflorum*   *Lilium formosanum* (white form)

A Field Trip to Darling and Malmesbury

South-western Cape Province, in the southern tip of Africa, is known to botanists worldwide as the 'Cape Floral Kingdom'. Unlike the rest of sub-Saharan Africa this region has a Mediterranean climate—cold, wet winters and hot, dry summers. It is also geologically and topographically diverse—a coastal plain of largely sand or limestone and, further inland, a gently undulating landscape made up of shale and clay. Rising abruptly from this are the rugged parallel ranks of the Cape Fold Mountains, whose jagged and forbidding slopes dominate the skyline. The soil here is deficient in nutrients due to the acid sandstone formation of the mountains. *Gladiolus* is one of many genera of plants that have adapted and thrive in this region of contrast.

Gladiolus species are bewildering in their variety and have been beloved by colonists from the earliest days of European settlement. A number of species common in the vicinity of Cape Town have acquired picturesque names, and one of the best loved of these is the kalkoentjie or little turkey (*Gladiolus alatus*). This delightful little plant derives its name from the appearance of the flowers, which resemble a brilliantly hued turkey head, resplendent with wattles. The flowers are predominantly bright reddish orange, but the lower two petals are yellowish green with orange tips. Other similar species,

also sharing the common name of kalkoentjie, are variously coloured in greens and browns and all have a delightful scent, but none has quite the impact of *G. alatus*. You cannot see a colony of these plants without feeling a little cheerier for the experience.

G. alatus is a small plant, usually 15–25 cm (about 6–10 in) tall, with four strap-shaped leaves. The spike bears up to six flowers 3–5 cm (about 1–2 in) in diameter. The dorsal petal is the largest and forms a shallow hood arching forward, while broad lateral petals curve back like wings. The three stamens, arched together in front of the flower, are pollinated by long-tongued bees of the Anthophoridae family.

Although it is widespread in the south-western Cape, one of the best places for a field trip to see the kalkoentjie is only half an hour's drive from Cape Town. And the best time to see them in bloom is spring, particularly September. As the flowers of a number of showy plants, particularly the annual daisies and the bulbs *Oxalis* and *Romulea*, close in the late afternoon and only open again in the warmth and light of mid-morning, you need not rush off early in the morning to start your trip.

With your back to the splendid massif of Table Mountain, which guards Table Bay and Cape Town harbour, drive towards Malmesbury on the N7 national road. Soon you will see the narrow flats of the west coast and, inland, the gently rolling country of the Swartland. In winter much of this flat, sandy land near the coast is inundated with water. Snowy white arums (*Zantedeschia aethiopica*), thrusting their heads out of clumps of dark, arrow-shaped leaves, are a common sight along drainage lines and roadside ditches.

Clay soil on the rising ground in this area supports a natural vegetation dominated by a grey, small-leaved shrublet which is covered by a confetti of small white flowers in winter, followed by a similar scattering of fluffy white seeds. This is known as the renosterbos or rhinoceros bush (*Elytropappus rhinocerotis*), and as the name suggests, it was once a favourite food of the (now rare) rhinoceros. During spring, annuals

In springtime the meadows near Cape Town are a beautiful sight.

The little turkey, or kalkoentjie

Gladiolus dalenii

Gladiolus priorii

and bulbous plants emerge in abundance, and along the road verges and in patches of undisturbed veld a haze of colour greets your eyes. Some introduced Australian mimosas, the Sydney golden wattle (*Acacia longifolia*) and the golden wattle (*A. cyclopis*), create a magnificent sea of fragrant, yellow blossom in spring but, unfortunately, also form impenetrable woodlands, almost suffocating all other plant growth.

Continue along the N7 towards Malmesbury for 35 km (about 22 miles), and when you reach the turnoff to Atlantis and Mamre stop the car and breathe in the beauty around you. On either side of the road, bordering a small stream, are meadows as resplendent with flowers as an oriental rug. Tall orange bugle lilies (*Watsonia meriana*) stand at attention in serried ranks along the road. Beyond them in the meadows, *Gladiolus alatus* forms orange patches among the velvet blue of bobbejaantjie or little baboon (*Babiana angustifolia*), and the glistening pink of the large sundew (*Drosera cistiflora*). Some 35 km (about 22 miles) to the north-west, a blood red form of *D. cistiflora* grows near the village of Darling, which holds a justifiably famous wildflower show each spring. A host of smaller species are scattered about with profligate generosity, including various sorrels (*Oxalis*) of different colours, the brick red form of the small iris (*Moraea tricolor*), the quaintly formed orchids, *Holothrix villosa* and *Satyrium odorum*, and the heavenly scented *Gladiolus tenellus*—this one is a favourite with the local children, who gather it for their posies.

Further north in Namaqualand, also well known for its spectacular displays of spring flowers, you will see another orange-flowered kalkoentjie (*Gladiolus equitans*). This species is not nearly as common as *G. alatus*, and is a larger plant with much broader leaves. Also, the green kalkoentjie (*G. orchidiflorus*), a taller and more slender species with lovely dove-grey flowers marked with maroon, is common here.

Seeing the kalkoentjie or little turkey in its natural environment, surrounded by other equally colourful flora, is a pleasure you are unlikely to forget.

Gladiolus

The genus *Gladiolus*, which includes many popular commercially cultivated plants, boasts some 220 species. While some *Gladiolus* species are native to western Asia and southern Europe, the great majority are African, with an overwhelming concentration of species in South Africa, where also are found all the largest and brightest flowered species, with the little turkey (*G. alatus*) a fine example. They belong to the 'Cape bulbs', a tremendously diverse and colourful assortment of bulbs from the southern tip of Africa. These have contributed more to the gene pool of garden and florists' bulbs than the plants of any other region. Many (including *Gladiolus*) are members of the iris family, Iridaceae, which are not true bulbs but, for the most part, are corms.

Gladiolus flowers are often regarded as too large and gaudy. If you share this view of the traditional large hybrid varieties, you may be surprised at the graceful forms of many of the wild species and some of the 'old-fashioned' hybrids, which have flowers that are more delicately coloured and loosely arranged.

Gladiolus alatus

L. regale
REGAL LILY

Growing up to 2.3 m (about 7 ft), this easily grown lily from western China bears from 3 to 20 fragrant blooms on each stem. The trumpet-shaped flowers, up to 15 cm (about 6 in) long, appear in summer. The inside of the petals is white, the outside is carmine. There is also a pure white form.

L. speciosum

This popular, fragrant species grows up to 1.5 m (about 4½ ft). The 'Turk's cap' (reflexed) flowers are pendent, up to 10 cm (about 4 in) long. There are many forms, varying from white to crimson, some spotted. It flowers late summer to early autumn/fall. It is half-hardy.

LITTONIA
modesta
CLIMBING LILY, CLIMBING BELL

In summer this native of South Africa produces masses of blooms on a climbing stem. It reaches to about 2 m (about 6 ft), climbing up stakes or other plants by means of leaf tendrils which wind around the supports. The 3 cm (about 1½ in) yellow-orange flowers are produced at the leaf axils and are bell-shaped and nodding. Plant the tubers in late winter to early spring in rich soil with good drainage. Frost-tender, it needs a sunny position. Water well through spring and summer but allow to dry out when dormant. Propagate by division in late winter or from seed in spring.

LYCORIS
SPIDER LILY, SURPRISE LILY

The spider-like flowers of these natives of China and Japan appear in late summer to early autumn/fall. The 50 cm (about 20 in) flower stems appear before the foliage. Each scape carries 4 or 5 blooms. The flowers are trumpet-shaped but the petals are very slender and sharply reflexed. It has slender, strap-like leaves. Plant the bulbs in a sunny position in rich, well-drained soil. They like plenty of water during growth but need warm, dry conditions when dormant. They are half- to moderately hardy. Clumps are best left undisturbed for a few years; they can then be divided when dormant at the end of summer. This genus is named for Marc Antony's actress mistress.

L. aurea
GOLDEN SPIDER LILY

This lily grows to 40 cm (about 16 in) and bears a cluster of 4 or 5 tea-rose yellow flowers. The 7 cm (about 3 in) flowers have narrow, sharply recurved petals and prominent stamens. The slender leaves are strap-like.

L. radiata
RED SPIDER LILY

This is the most common species. The 40 cm (about 16 in) stems bear clusters of 4 or 5 red blooms. The 10 cm (about 4 in) flowers have slender, sharply reflexed petals, with prominent red stamens.

MORAEA

These beautiful, iris-like plants are native mainly to southern Africa. The genus contains about 50 species but only a few are in cultivation. The flowers are often short-lived, usually only lasting a couple of days. They vary greatly in size, flowering time and colour. The bulbs should be planted in full sun, although in warm areas they may need some protection from hot afternoon sun. Half-hardy, they like a fairly rich soil and good drainage is essential. They need plenty of water during growth but must be kept dry when dormant. Propagate from offsets when dormant or from seed.

M. neopavonia
PEACOCK IRIS

This attractive species grows to about 45 cm (about 18 in). The 4 cm (about 2 in) flowers which appear in spring have 3 large outer petals and 3 tuft-like inner petals. The outer petals can be white or orange and each has a bright blue 'peacock eye' which is outlined in black. The foliage is long and narrow. It is frost-tender.

M. spathulata
syn. M. spathacea
LARGE YELLOW TULIP

This half-hardy species grows to 1.2 m (about 4 ft). It has bayonet-shaped foliage which often lays on the ground. The bright yellow, iris-like flowers, about 8 cm (about 3 in) wide, appear in spring.

MUSCARI
GRAPE HYACINTH

The popular grape hyacinths are natives of the Mediterranean region. A short spike bears grape-like clusters of bright blue or white flowers in early spring. Fully to half-hardy, they do best in cool areas. They look best planted in clumps and need a rich, well-drained soil. Plant the bulbs in autumn/fall in a sunny position, but protect from hot sun in warm areas. The slender, strap-like leaves appear soon after planting, as the summer dormancy period is very short. The clumps should spread freely and are

Lilium speciosum

Lycoris aurea

Lilium regale

Moraea spathulata

Lycoris radiata

Moraea neopavonia

Littonia modesta

Muscari plumosum 'Comosum'

Muscari armeniacum 'Blue Spike'

Narcissus (Unnamed) (Div. 3)

Narcissus 'Tahiti' (Div. 4)

best left undisturbed for a few years. Divide the bulbs if they become overcrowded. They can also be grown from seed.

M. armeniacum
GRAPE HYACINTH

Growing to about 5 cm (about 2 in), this is one of the best loved of spring bulbs. The flowers may be blue or white, and there are several named cultivars of which 'Heavenly Blue' is the best known.

M. armeniacum 'Blue Spike'

This fairly new species grows to 20 cm (about 8 in). The flower spikes bear clusters of rounded, bell-shaped double blooms. The flowers are blue, sometimes rimmed with white. The foliage is slender and strap-like.

M. plumosum 'Comosum'
syn. *Leopoldia plumosa*
FEATHERED HYACINTH

This unusual plant grows to 30 cm (about 12 in). It has strap-shaped leaves and curious flowers whose petals are so elongated that the inflorescence looks like a plume of lavender feathers. Frost-hardy, it is as easily grown as other *Muscari* but multiplies less quickly.

NARCISSUS
DAFFODIL, JONQUIL, NARCISSUS

The sunny yellow spring flowers of the daffodil are popular all over the world. They are easy to grow, multiply freely and bloom year after year. Native to the northern hemisphere, the genus is extremely varied, but all flowers have 6 petals which surround a cup or corona. They are grouped into 10 'divisions' or classes, the most important of which are: the Trumpet narcissi (Div. 1) which have trumpets as long as the outer petals or perianth, the Large-cupped narcissi (Div. 2), with trumpets from one-third to two-thirds as long; Small-cupped narcissi (Div. 3), with trumpets less than one-third the length of the petals; and Double-flowered narcissi (Div. 4) with double flowers, either one or several per stem. The remaining groups cover hybrids of

Narcissus 'Fortune' (Div. 2)

important species such as *N. tazetta*, *triandrus*, *cyclaminius* and *poeticus*; these are listed here under their species. Div. 10 consists of miscellaneous species. Colour ranges from white to yellow, although individual varieties may have white, yellow, red, orange or pink trumpets and each group is further sub-divided according to colours. They are usually fully hardy and grow best in cool areas. Bulbs are usually planted in autumn/fall, 10–15 cm (about 4–6 in) deep in rich, well-drained soil. Full sun is fine in cool areas, but they will need some shade in warmer areas. Water well during growth and allow to dry out once the leaves die down. Remove spent flowers but let the leaves die off naturally. Clumps will multiply freely and should be left undisturbed for a few years. Lift and divide them in autumn/fall. The common names daffodil, jonquil and narcissus are rather loosely applied, usage varying widely from place to place.

N., Trumpet hybrids (Div. 1)

These are the best known of all daffodils with their large flowers

and long trumpets. There are innumerable named cultivars, which may be all yellow, white with yellow trumpets, all white, or white with pale pink trumpets. They are the first of the big daffodils to flower. The all-gold 'King Alfred', raised in 1890, is the classic cultivar but its name has been very loosely applied, and some authorities consider the original variety may be extinct.

N., Large-cupped daffodils (Div. 2)

Flowering a week or two later than the trumpets, this is a large class with many named varieties. The popular pink-cupped cultivars with their white perianths mostly belong here but there are many others, in various combinations of white or yellow perianths with cups in white, yellow, orange or red.

N., Small-cupped daffodils (Div. 3)

These resemble the first two groups except for their smaller cups, and like them come in many named cultivars. They flower at the same time as the Div. 2 types.

Muscari armeniacum

Narcissus 'Ptolemy' (Div. 1)

N., Double-flowered daffodils (Div. 4)
DOUBLE NARCISSI

These can have either a solitary large flower or several smaller ones, and either the whole flower can be double, with extra petals with segments of the corona intermixed; or the corona is doubled, like a pompom set against the outer perianth. Some of the most ancient cultivars are double flowered, but as a group they are less popular than the others. They tend to be late flowering and must not suffer drought when the buds are developing or they will not open properly.

Narcissus tazetta

Narcissus × odorus

Narcissus jonquilla

Narcissus 'Tête-à-Tête'

Narcissus cyclamineus

Narcissus 'Silver Chimes'

Narcissus papyraceus

Narcissus bulbocodium

Narcissus poeticus

SPECIES

N. bulbocodium

HOOP-PETTICOAT DAFFODIL

This species grows to 15 cm (about 6 in) and has many forms. Bright yellow flowers, with a long corona and shaped like a petticoat hoop, appear in spring. The petals are usually insignificant.

N. cyclamineus

This species grows to about 20 cm (about 8 in). A native of Portugal, it is slow to increase. It flowers from late winter to early spring. The yellow flowers are pendent and have sharply reflexed petals. The corona is frilled. There are many garden hybrids.

N. jonquilla

JONQUIL

This species grows up to 45 cm (about 18 in). Three to six flowers are borne in a cluster, the yellow petals are star-like and the corona is green to gold. The fragrant flowers appear in spring. N. jonquilla is very easy to grow.

N. × odorus

CAMPERNELLE, JONQUIL

This species grows to 45 cm (about 18 in). The large, 5 cm (about 2 in), fragrant flowers are bright yellow. It flowers in late spring and is very easy to grow. There is a double form.

N. papyraceus

PAPER WHITE, JOSS FLOWER

This species grows to 40 cm (about 16 in). The pure white, fragrant flowers have pointed petals, the corona is frilled and the stamens are orange-yellow. It flowers in late winter to spring. Half-hardy, it makes an attractive display indoors

grown in a bowl of gravel. In China it is grown in pots to celebrate the new year.

N. poeticus

POET'S DAFFODIL

This species grows to about 38 cm (about 15 in). The fragrant flowers appear in late spring. The petals are usually white and the small cup is pale yellow, fringed with green or red. It is a highly variable species, and there are several named cultivars.

N. 'Silver Chimes'

This fine hybrid of N. triandrus can grow to 25 cm (about 10 in). The fragrant flowers appear in late spring, up to 10 per stem. The star-shaped petals are creamy white and the small cup is white also. A good cultivar for warm areas, it is much more widely available than the species itself, which is very similar but smaller.

N. tazetta

This is the most widespread species, growing wild from Europe to China and the best for warmer climates. It grows to about 60 cm (about 24 in) tall, and bears clusters of small flowers with small cups. There are several varieties of which the yellow and orange 'Soleil d'or' is the best known; others come in the usual range of colours and several are double flowered. All are scented and best classed as half-hardy. They flower early, in late winter.

N. 'Tête-à-Tête'

This hybrid of N. cyclamineus grows to 30 cm (about 12 in). The flowers appear in early spring and it tends to produce more than one flower per stem. The golden yellow petals are sharply reflexed, the corona is orange and frilled.

NECTAROSCORDUM
siculum subsp. *bulgaricum*
syn. *N. dioscoridis,*
Allium bulgaricum

The genus name means 'nectar-bearing onion', and this is a relative of the *Allium* (onion) genus. In spring it bears elegant, pendent, bell-shaped flowers; pale pink tinged with purple and green. The upright foliage dies off quickly. A frost-hardy plant, it likes most soil and semi-shade. Keep drier in summer. Propagate from offsets in summer. It makes a lovely cut flower.

NERINE
GUERNSEY LILY

Although the common name might suggest otherwise, these are native to South Africa. They were originally found in Guernsey, but these were the result of bulbs washed up onto the island after a shipwreck. The pretty, spider-like flowers are borne in clusters at the top of tall stems, usually in autumn/fall. The foliage is strap-like. The bulbs should be planted in sandy soil with good drainage in a sunny position. Water well during growth but allow to dry out over the summer dormancy period. They are not suitable for areas with high summer rainfall or severe frosts. They can be propagated from seed or offsets, but the plants do not like being disturbed and may take a couple of years to flower. They are good plants for pots, and can be brought inside when in flower. Half-hardy, they need a warm, sheltered spot in cool climates.

N. bowdenii
PINK SPIDER LILY, LARGE PINK NERINE

A sturdy stem of 60 cm (about 24 in) bears up to 12 pink blooms. The flowers are trumpet-shaped but the narrow petals are split and reflexed. They have a crimson rib running along their centre and the edges are frilled. There is also a white form.

N. filifolia
SPIDER LILY, GRASS-LEAVED NERINE

This plant grows to 25 cm (about 10 in) and bears a 10 cm (about 4 in) cluster of rosy pink blooms. The flowers are trumpet-shaped with slender, reflexed petals. The foliage is grass-like and almost evergreen.

N. flexuosa 'Alba'

A sturdy stem up to 60 cm (about 24 in) bears a cluster of up to 15 white flowers. The trumpet-shaped flowers have narrow, reflexed petals. The foliage is narrow and strap-like and appears before the flowers.

N. sarniensis
GUERNSEY LILY, RED NERINE

This delightful species grows up to 60 cm (about 24 in). The sturdy stem bears up to 20 bright red, 7 cm (about 3 in) blooms. The trumpet-shaped flowers have sharply reflexed petals and prominent stamens. The strap-shaped leaves usually appear after flowering.

NOMOCHARIS
pardanthina
syn. *N. mairei*

These elegant, fully hardy plants come from the Himalayas, western China and Burma and are related to liliums. A slender stem grows to about 1 m (about 3 ft) and bears whorls of leaves and up to 12 blooms in summer. The 10 cm (about 4 in) wide, nodding flowers are white to rose and spotted with crimson. Plant the bulbs in a partially shaded area in rich, well-drained soil. It does best in cool,

moist conditions and acid soil, and can be propagated by division or from seed, although seed may take many years to flower. It is not easy to propagate, and expensive to buy, but it is a glorious plant where conditions suit.

NOTHOLIRION
thomsonianum
FALSE LILY

This frost-hardy native of the Himalayas closely resembles a lilium. Blooming in spring, the main bulb dies after flowering, although it first produces a number of offspring. A tall spike up to 1 m (about 3 ft) emerges from a rosette of basal leaves and bears up to 40 nodding, funnel-shaped blooms in pink to lilac. Bulbs should be planted in autumn/fall in rich, well-drained soil. It likes cool, but not too cold, moist conditions, Water well except when dormant. Propagate from seed or offsets in autumn/fall, but offsets may take a few years to flower.

Nectaroscordum s. subsp. *bulgaricum*

Nerine filifolia

Nerine bowdenii

Nerine flexuosa 'Alba'

Notholirion thomsonianum

Nerine sarniensis

Rhodohypoxis baurii

Ornithogalum thyrsoides

Ornithogalum saundersiae

Pinellia ternata

Romulea bulbocodium

Ranunculus asiaticus

Polianthes tuberosa

ORNITHOGALUM

This large genus of spring- to summer-flowering plants is native to Asia, Africa and Europe. Clusters of star- to cup-shaped flowers are borne along the top of tall stems. They are easy to grow. Half- to fully hardy. Plant bulbs in autumn/fall or spring in well-drained soil. They like full sun but will need partial shade in warm areas. Keep the plants moist until the leaves begin to die off. They need to be kept dry when dormant. Frost-tender species should be lifted in winter. They multiply quite freely and clumps should be divided every one to two years to prevent overcrowding. Also grow them from seed sown in autumn/fall or spring.

O. saundersiae
GIANT CHINCHERINCHEE

This fairly hardy species from South Africa grows to 1.5 m (about 4½ ft). The tall stem bears a flat-topped cluster of creamy white blooms. The waxy flowers are star- to cup-shaped and have a black to green centre. The basal foliage is glossy and strap-shaped.

O. thyrsoides
CHINCHERINCHEE

This frost-tender species from South Africa grows to 45 cm (about 18 in). A cluster of up to 20 star- to cup-shaped, white flowers is borne on a spike. The basal leaves are strap-shaped. The cut flowers last for weeks, even out of water. The flowers absorb dye and bunches of chincherinchees are sold in a myriad of colours.

PINELLIA
ternata

This native of eastern Asia is valued for its unusual, broad leaves which are split into three, and interesting flowers. The pale green spathes curl at the tip and are borne on a leafless stem in late summer. It is half-hardy and should be grown in acidic, humus-rich soil in shade. It likes moisture so water well, particularly during growth, and the clump size should increase. Propagate from offsets in spring.

POLIANTHES
tuberosa
TUBEROSE

This native of Mexico produces a mass of sweetly scented blooms in summer or early autumn/fall. A tall stem up to 1 m (about 3 ft) is topped with a spike bearing clusters of tubular, star-shaped, creamy white flowers. A double variety, 'The Pearl', is more widely available than the single. The slender leaves are strap-shaped. The tubers should be planted

in spring when there is no chance of frost, in a sheltered, sunny position. This frost-tender plant needs a rich soil with good drainage. Water well once leaves appear and allow to dry out when the leaves start to die off. The tubers only bloom once, so they should be lifted in autumn/fall and the offsets stored for planting in spring. Tuberoses are first-rate cut flowers.

RANUNCULUS
asiaticus
PERSIAN BUTTERCUP

This frost-hardy native of the Mediterranean region is parent to many hybrids and cultivars popular all over the world. Masses of single or double flowers are borne on 35 cm (about 14 in) stems in spring. The gorgeous blooms are available in many colours, yellow, orange, red, pink, white and more. The corms should be planted in autumn/fall in a sunny position in well-drained soil enriched with organic matter. Water well through the growing season and allow to dry out after flowering. The rhizomes are usually lifted after flowering and should be stored in a cool dry place. Propagation is by division or from seed sown in spring.

RHODOHYPOXIS
baurii
RED STAR

This charming dwarf plant comes from the mountains of South Africa and is frost-hardy, although it appreciates a warm spot in cold areas. It produces masses of star-shaped flowers in late spring to early summer. The small stems grow to about 10 cm (about 4 in) and each bears one 6-petalled, red, pink or white flower. The hairy foilage is grass-like. The bulb-like tubers should be planted in early spring in rich, acidic, well-drained soil. It needs plenty of water during the growing season but must be kept dry in winter. Plant in full sun, but protect from direct hot afternoon sunlight. Propagate by division or from seed in spring. It is excellent for rockeries.

ROMULEA
bulbocodium
SATIN FLOWER

This dainty little plant is native to southern Europe and northern Africa and is excellent in a rock garden. The fine stems grow to about 10 cm (about 4 in) and each bears up to 6 upward-facing, trumpet-shaped blooms in spring. The 5 cm (about 2 in) long flowers are usually violet with white to yellow centres. The flowers close in the evening or on dull days. Plant the corms in light, well-drained soil in a

Sprekelia formosissima

Scilla peruviana

Sandersonia aurantiaca

Sparaxis tricolor

Scadoxus puniceus

Sternbergia lutea

sunny position. It needs plenty of water during the growing season but must be kept dry when dormant. In areas with wet summers the corms will need to be lifted. It is half-hardy. Propagation is usually from seed as it is quite slow to increase.

SANDERSONIA
aurantiaca
CHRISTMAS BELLS,
GOLDEN LILY OF THE VALLEY

This beautiful South African native blooms in mid-summer. The climbing stems grow to about 60 cm (about 24 in). The ribbed leaves have tendrils at their tips which cling to supports. The nodding, 3 cm (about 1½ in), yellow to orange, flowers are borne at the leaf axils, and have a delicate chinese lantern or chef's hat shape. Plant the tubers in late autumn/fall in well-drained soil enriched with leafmould. Partial shade is ideal. Water well once shoots appear, but keep dry when dormant. It is frost-tender so plant in spring in cool areas. Propagate from offsets or from seed sown in spring.

SCADOXUS
puniceus
syn. *Haemanthus magnificus*,
H. natalensis
PAINTBRUSH LILY, SNAKE LILY

This unique plant is native to South Africa and used to be classed as a species of *Haemanthus*. However, unlike *Haemanthus* species, it has a number of erect leaves. In spring it has masses of orange and red flowers wrapped in red bracts and borne

on marbled stems. Frost-tender, it grows best in rich, well-drained soil in the sun. Water well, but keep dry in winter. It makes an attractive potted plant. Propagate from offsets in spring.

SCILLA
peruviana
CUBAN LILY, WILD HYACINTH, SQUILL

This plant, actually native to south-west Europe, has a dense cluster of up to 50 star-shaped flowers which are borne in summer on a 30 cm (about 12 in) stem. The 2 cm (about 1 in) flowers are usually blue, sometimes white or purple. The dark to olive-green foliage is glossy and strap-like. Plant bulbs in autumn/fall in well-drained soil. It will need partial shade in warm areas. It is quite hardy to frost, but needs sun in cool climates. Water well during the growing season. Clumps are best left undisturbed for a few years. Propagate by division or from seed in autumn/fall.

SPARAXIS
tricolor
VELVET FLOWER, HARLEQUIN FLOWER

This frost-tender native of South Africa is easily grown in warm areas. The 30 cm (about 12 in) wiry, drooping stems bear a spike of up to 5 funnel- to star-shaped blooms in spring. The 5 cm (about 2 in) flowers are red to pink or orange. The centre is usually yellow, outlined in black. The flowers close at night and on dull days. The stiff leaves are lance-shaped. Plant corms in autumn/fall in a sunny spot in well-drained soil.

Water well during the growing season, but allow to dry out when dormant. The corms should be lifted in areas which have wet summers. Propagate from the freely produced offsets or from seed in early autumn/fall.

SPREKELIA
formosissima
JACOBEAN LILY, MALTESE CROSS LILY,
AZTEC LILY

This beautiful Mexican native grows to 45 cm (about 18 in). In summer it produces bright red, 12 cm (about 5 in) long flowers. The lower 3 petals form an open tube and the upper petals curve upwards and outwards. The green leaves are strap-shaped. Plant the bulbs in autumn/fall in sun in cool areas, in partial-shade in warm climates. The flowers will need protection from hot sun. The soil should be rich with good drainage. Water well during the growing season but keep dry when dormant. It is sensitive to severe frosts and should be grown in pots in cold

areas. It does not like being disturbed, so clumps should be left for a few years, then divided in autumn/fall. The flower resembles the red cross borne by the Spanish religious order of St Jacob of Calatrava; hence the common name.

STERNBERGIA
lutea
AUTUMN CROCUS, AUTUMN DAFFODIL

The delightful autumn/fall-flowering lily-of-the-field is native to the Mediterranean region. The buttercup-yellow, crocus-like flowers are 5 cm (about 2 in) long and are borne singly on 15 cm (about 6 in) stems. The slender leaves are strap-shaped. Bulbs should be planted in spring in rich, well-drained soil in a sunny position. It is only just frost-hardy and needs warm, dry conditions when dormant in summer; it is best grown in pots in areas with wet summers. Clumps should be left undisturbed and only divided (in summer) when they are overcrowded. Makes an excellent plant in a rock garden.

Tritonia crocata

Triteleia laxa 'Queen Fabiola'

Tricyrtis hirta

Tigridia pavonia

Tulbaghia violacea

Tristagma uniflora

TIGRIDIA
pavonia

TIGER FLOWER, JOCKEY'S CAP LILY

This brightly coloured Mexican native blooms in summer. The triangular flowers are short-lived, often lasting for only a day, but a succession of new blooms will keep appearing for weeks. The 13 cm (about 5 in) flowers are usually red with a yellow centre spotted with purple, borne on 60 cm (about 24 in) stems. The foliage is iris-like, sword-shaped and pleated. Plant bulbs in spring in a sunny position in rich, well-drained soil. Water well during the growing season, but allow to dry out when dormant. Lift in cool areas or those with high winter rainfall, as they are half-hardy. Propagate from freely formed offsets or seed sown in spring.

TRICYRTIS
hirta

TOAD LILY

Native to cool, mountainous areas of Asia, the toad lily produces trumpet- to star-shaped flowers in late summer to autumn/fall. The 1 m (about 3 ft) branching stems have hairy, stem-clasping leaves and the flowers are borne at the axils of these upper leaves. The 5 cm (about 2 in) flowers are white, spotted with purple. It is frost-hardy. Plant the bulbs in spring in rich, moist, sandy soil in a partially shaded spot. It can also be propagated from offsets in spring or from seed sown in autumn/fall.

TRISTAGMA
uniflora

syn. *Ipheion uniflorum, Triteleia uniflora*

SPRING STARFLOWER

This delightful native of Argentina is very easy to grow and produces masses of star-shaped, pale blue flowers in spring. The 3 cm (about 1½ in) flowers are borne singly on leafless stems. It grows to about 20 cm (about 8 in). The slender, grey-green foliage has an oniony scent, particularly when it is crushed. The small bulbs should be planted in autumn/fall in full sun or

partial shade in well-drained soil. It is frost-hardy and likes plenty of water through winter and spring. It will spread rapidly and the clumps can be divided after a couple of years in autumn/fall. The plant has suffered many name changes over the past 40 years; let us hope the new one, *Tristagma,* will stick.

TRITELEIA
laxa 'Queen Fabiola'

ITHURIEL'S SPEAR, CALIFORNIAN BLUEBELL

This native of California and Oregon, USA, grows to 45 cm (about 18 in). In late spring it produces a scape of up to 30 pink to lilac-blue blooms. The 5 cm (about 2 in) flowers are funnel-shaped; the leaves are slender and grass-like. Plant the corms in a sunny position in well-drained soil. In very warm areas it should be planted in partial shade. Water well during the growing season, less during the summer dormancy period. It is hardy except to severe frost and should be grown in pots in cold areas. Propagate from offsets in autumn/fall.

TRITONIA
crocata

syn. *T. hyalina*

BLAZING STAR, ROOIKALKOENTJIE

The freesia-like plant is native to South Africa. The wiry stems grow to 50 cm (about 20 in) and bear a spike of pretty, cup-shaped blooms. The 5 cm (about 2 in) flowers which appear in late spring to summer are bright orange to red with yellow throats and purple anthers. The erect green leaves are sword-

shaped. Plant the corms in autumn/fall in a sunny position in light, well-drained soil. Water well during the growing season but allow to dry out after flowering. It is half-hardy and needs protection from frost. It multiplies quite freely and can be divided in autumn/fall, or grown from seed. It make a good cut flower.

TULBAGHIA
violacea

SWEET GARLIC, WILD GARLIC

This easily grown South African native is delightful to look at but smells strongly of garlic. A tall 60 cm (about 24 in) stem bears a round cluster of tubular, star-shaped, mauve flowers. The lilac to pink flowers appear in summer to autumn/fall. The masses of evergreen leaves are slender and grass-like. The rhizomes should be planted at the end of winter in rich, moist soil in partial shade. It is half-hardy and could be grown in a pot in cold areas. Clumps are best left undisturbed for a few years. Propagate by division in late winter or by sowing seed in spring. It is good as a border plant or in a rockery. The bulbs are edible.

TULIPA

TULIP

The elegant flower of the tulip has, with good reason, made it one of the most popular bulbs in the world. Tulips originated in the Middle East and Asia and have been cultivated for hundreds of years. The genus contains about 100 species, but the most commonly grown tulips are the highly developed cultivars grouped under *T. gesneriana* which vary in colour, shape and flowering time. There are very many cultivars which were formerly grouped into a large number of classes. Recently the classification has been simplified, the main groups being: Single Early, Double Early, Single late, Double late, and the Parrot tulips. The Single Late tulips are themselves subdivided, and there are also important groups of garden varieties derived from *T. fosteriana*, *greigii* and *kaufmanniana*. The other species are grouped as 'botanical tulips'. Tulips do best in cool areas but can be grown in pots in warm climates. Nearly all are fully hardy. The bulbs should be planted in late autumn/fall, about 15 cm (about 6 in) deep, in a sunny position in rich, limed, and well-drained soil. Water well during the growing season. Spent flowers can be removed but allow the leaves to die off naturally. It is essential to lift the bulbs in areas with a wet summer, and store in a cool, well ventilated spot. Propagate by division in autumn/fall.

GARDEN TULIPS
T. gesneriana

These are of complex hybrid origin, and grouped into a number of classes, which follow. They are very popular and delightful for cutting, but must have a cold climate. In mild-winter areas they are best treated as annuals, by chilling the bulbs for 3 to 6 weeks in the vegetable drawer of the refrigerator before planting in late autumn/fall. They come in a vast range of colours, everything but true blue; the virus-infected striped varieties are now less popular than they used to be.

SINGLE EARLY TULIPS

These are the first of the garden tulips to flower, and bear their flowers on stems about 40 cm (about 16 in) tall. They are the best varieties for forcing for early bloom in a greenhouse and come in the full range of colours.

DOUBLE EARLY TULIPS

These have mostly arisen as sports of single varieties and flower at the same time. The range of colours is wide, but it is a matter of taste whether you like these multi-petalled flowers. They are long-lasting cut flowers.

SINGLE LATE TULIPS

These are the most widely grown tulips flowering in late spring. They are taller, to 65 cm (about 26 in), than the early varieties and divided as follows:

Darwin tulips

Most popular group, growing about 60 cm (about 24 in) tall with flowers almost rectangular in profile and coming in the full range of colours. There is a sub-group with fringed petals. All are excellent for cutting.

Cottage tulips

These are more egg-shaped than the Darwins, and include the lily-flowered tulips with their pointed petals as well as a group called 'viridiflora' tulips with green markings on the petals. They open wider than the Darwins, to give a more graceful effect. Most are about 60 cm (about 24 in) tall.

Darwin hybrid tulips

Derived from crosses between the Darwins and *T. fosteriana*, these tulips grow to about 60 cm (about 24 in), and despite their rather limited colour range—red, yellow and orange—rival their parents in popularity. The flowers can be very large, though they are not as long lasting as the Darwins. They are more reliable in mild-winter areas.

PARROT TULIPS

Sports of Darwin and Cottage tulips, these are grown for their fantastically fringed and ruffled flowers. They grow to about 50 cm (about 20 in) and are available in the usual colours.

Double early tulip, 'Peach Blossom'

Single late tulips

Single early tulip, 'Kees Nellis'

Cottage tulips

Darwin hybrid tulip, 'Golden Oxford'

Tulipa gesneriana

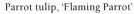
Parrot tulip, 'Flaming Parrot'

Darwin hybrid tulip, 'Queen of Night'

Double late tulips

Tulipa saxatilis

Tulipa clusiana

Tulipa fosteriana

Rembrandt tulips

Tulipa tarda

Tulipa acuminata

Tulipa greigii   Urceolina peruviana

white, the outside petals and inside base stained dark pink. It flowers in mid-spring.

T. fosteriana

This low-growing, mid-season tulip from Central Asia is rarely grown, but it has a number of garden varieties much admired for their enormous, 25 cm (about 10 in) wide flowers. They are almost all red.

T. greigii

This early to mid-season species has given rise to a popular group of hybrids, which mostly grow about 30 cm (about 12 in) tall, with wide-open flowers in the usual tulip colours, often with contrasting edges to the petals. The foliage is variegated with red-brown or purple on a green background.

T. kaufmanniana
WATER LILY TULIP

This early flowering species is admired for the elegant form of its pale yellow flowers, strongly marked with red on the outside. There are several named varieties in shades of red, pink and yellow. They mostly grow about 25 cm (about 10 in) tall.

T. saxatilis
syn. *T. bakeri*
ROCK TULIP

A species originating in Crete, it does well in warmer climates. The 45 cm (about 18 in) stems bear up to 3 goblet-shaped flowers which eventually open out almost flat. The purple-pink flowers have bright yellow centres. It flowers in early spring.

T. tarda
syn. *T. dasystemon of gardens*

This small tulip grows to 15 cm (about 6 in). Each stem bears up to 6 white flowers with yellow centres. The pointed petals sometimes have a red or greenish tinge. It flowers in early spring.

URCEOLINA
peruviana
syn. *U. miniata*
LITTLE URN PLANT

This easily grown native of the Peruvian Andes has red, nodding, urn-shaped flowers with protruding yellow anthers. The 38 cm (about 15 in) slender stems each bear up to 6 blooms in spring, before the glossy, strap-like leaves. Plant bulbs in late autumn/fall in a sunny position in well-drained soil. Water well during the growing season. It is not hardy to severe frosts and could be planted in a pot in cold areas. Clumps may be left undisturbed for a few years. Propagate from offsets in autumn/fall. The name comes from the Latin, *urceolian*, meaning 'small pitcher'.

REMBRANDT TULIPS

Though the great Dutch master is not known to have painted tulips, his name is attached to all the striped tulips. These striped or broken flowers were indeed very popular in Holland in his time, so much so that speculation in tulip bulbs nearly upset the Dutch economy and the government of the day had to step in to stop the 'tulipomania'. Since discovering that the stripes are caused by a virus, they have become less popular and they should be grown apart from other tulips lest the virus spread. Nonetheless, an evenly broken flower in red or pink and white can be very pretty.

DOUBLE LATE TULIPS

These have their admirers, but they are less desirable than the Double Earlies, the many petalled flowers often proving too heavy for the 60 cm (about 24 in) tall stems. They are essentially cut flowers.

SPECIES OR BOTANICAL TULIPS
T. acuminata
HORNED TULIP

A most curious tulip, thought not to be a true species but an ancient cultivar of Turkish origin. It grows about 40 cm (about 16 in) tall, and is distinguished by its curious long, narrow petals in red and yellow.

T. clusiana
syn. *T. aitchisonii*
LADY TULIP

This tulip has 25 cm (about 10 in) stems which bear one or two cup-shaped blooms which eventually open out almost flat. The flowers are

VALLOTA
speciosa
syn. *Cyrtanthus purpureus*
SCARBOROUGH LILY

This beautiful plant, with its showy red flowers, is originally from South Africa. The stout, 30 cm (about 12 in) stem bears up to 5 orange-red, trumpet-shaped blooms. The flowers appear in summer to autumn/fall and are about 10 cm (about 4 in) wide. The thick, green leaves are strap-shaped. It is half-hardy. Plant the bulbs in late winter in rich, well-drained soil, and in partial shade in very warm areas. Water well through the growing season but allow to dry out over winter. Remove spent flowerheads. The small offsets can be removed from the parent bulb and planted out in late winter. It makes a glorious display as an indoor pot plant.

VELTHEIMIA
VELDT LILY, FOREST LILY

These unusual natives of South Africa produce a dense spike of pendent, tubular flowers in winter or spring. Bulbs should be planted in autumn/fall in moist, rich, well-drained soil in partial shade. Reduce watering when flowering is finished. They are frost-tender and should be grown in pots in cold areas. Propagate from offsets in autumn/fall.

V. bracteata
syn. *V. viridifolia*
FOREST LILY

Found in the wild in the eastern Cape area of South Africa, *V. bracteata* has wavy, glossy green leaves growing in a rosette. Rocket-like inflorescences on strong, erect peduncles are produced in spring and early summer. The drooping, tubular flowers are pink, red or pale yellow. It thrives in semi-shade beneath trees or shrubs, and also makes a good potted specimen. Plant in rich, well-drained soil and water occasionally.

V. capensis
syn. *V. glauca*

A strong stem growing up to 45 cm (about 18 in) bears a dense spike of pendent, tubular, 2.5 cm (about 1 in) blooms. The rosy pink to red flowers are sometimes tipped with green. The glossy, dark green leaves have wavy edges.

WATSONIA

These beautiful natives of South Africa produce fragrant flowers in spring and summer. They appear quite similar to the gladiolus and have lance-shaped leaves and a tall flowering spike. The corms should be planted in autumn/fall in light, well-drained soil in a sunny spot. They

like plenty of water during the growing season. They are half-hardy. Clumps are best left undisturbed and they should spread freely. They can be propagated from seed or by division when clumps become overcrowded.

W. beatricis
BEATRICE WATSONIA

This evergreen species grows to 1.2 m (about 4 ft). The flower spike bears 8 cm (about 3 in) long, tubular, star-shaped flowers which are salmon pink. The green foliage is sword-shaped. Hardier than other species, it can withstand some frost. There is some doubt about whether this plant, common in nurseries under this name, is the true wild species, which is now correctly known as *W. pillansii*.

W. borbonica subsp. *borbonica*
syn. *W. pyramidata*
PINK WATSONIA

This delightful species grows to 1.5 m (about 4½ ft). The stem bears a spike of lilac to pink, 5 cm (about 2 in), funnel-shaped flowers. The slender green leaves are sword-shaped. It flowers in spring.

ZEPHYRANTHES
STORM LILY, RAIN LILY

These charming natives of central and southern America often appear quite suddenly after summer rain. The widely trumpet-shaped flowers are borne singly on short stems. They are easy to grow and should be planted in late autumn/fall to early winter in a sunny position. Soil should be rich with excellent drainage. Give plenty of water during the growing season but reduce this after flowering. They are frost- to half-hardy, but should be grown in pots in very cold areas. Clumps are best left undisturbed for a few years. Propagate from offsets in autumn/fall or from seed sown in spring. They are excellent in rockeries or borders.

Z. candida
syn. *Argyropsis candida*
FLOWER OF THE WEST WIND

This vigorous species grows to 15 cm (about 6 in). The starry, cup-shaped, white flowers are 5 cm (about 2 in) wide and are borne singly on the slender stems. The grass-like foliage is evergreen and hardy.

Z. grandiflora
syn. *Z. carinata, Z. rosea*
PINK STORM LILY

This popular species grows to 25 cm (about 10 in). The 10 cm (about 4 in) flowers are dusky pink. The slender leaves are strap-shaped. There are many forms, some with smaller flowers.

Vallota speciosa

Veltheimia capensis

Watsonia beatricis

Zephyranthes grandiflora

Veltheimia bracteata

Zephyranthes candida

Watsonia borbonica subsp. *borbonica*

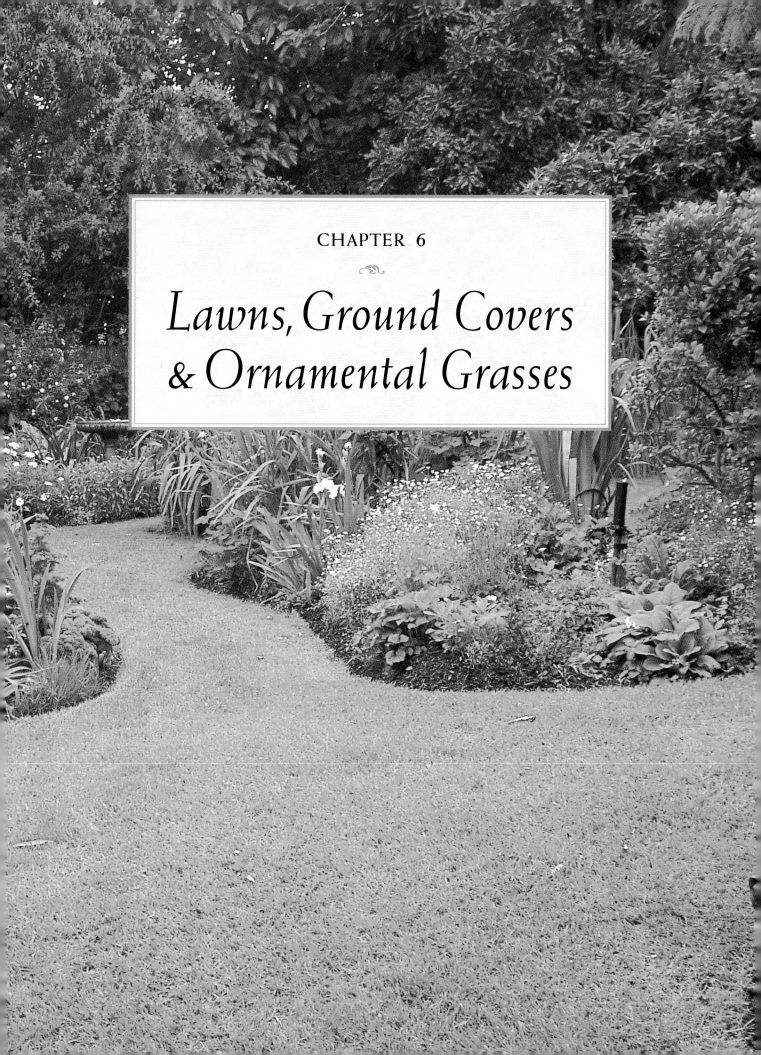

CHAPTER 6

Lawns, Ground Covers
& Ornamental Grasses

*T*he soil is the mother of the garden, and a gardener treats it with all due respect; but bare earth, mud when it rains and dust when it does not, makes a most unsuitable floor for a garden. We can, of course, lay paving or gravel, but they are hard, expensive, and reflective of heat and glare. The universal favourite for flooring the main part of a garden is lawn. It is soft and quiet underfoot, it doesn't reflect glare, and its greenness is the most flattering backdrop imaginable for plants and flowers.

No one species will give a perfect, year-round sward—the finest lawns are the result of careful blending. Every area has its favourite lawn grass species, and these are the ones you should choose. We do suggest that if you choose the finest, slow-growing types you'll have less work to do in the long run, even if they are more trouble to establish than the faster growing meadow and pasture grasses.

Looking After a Lawn

Nonetheless the meadow grasses can become an acceptable lawn if they are regularly shorn, and that brings us to the least loved of all gardening tasks—mowing. No one enjoys it, and many shortcuts are devised by the lazy in the hope of having to take the mower out less frequently. Most common is cutting too short or leaving it to grow too long. Alas, none works. All weaken the grass and encourage the weeds: and so the time saved is spent (with interest) on weeding. A weedy lawn actually needs mowing more frequently than a clean one—the weeds grow faster than the grass so that unacceptable shagginess sets in sooner.

It's best to encourage a good, dense growing turf, by watering as needed, fertilizing at least once a year (in spring) and cutting short enough for neatness but not so short as to scalp the grass. With most fine grasses, 2 or 3 cm (about 1 in) is short enough, and it is desirable not to let the grass get more than about twice as long as that so it won't be unduly shocked when it is cut. When you come to mow, you'll be grateful for

having kept the lines of the lawn simple—getting the mower around wriggly edges and island flowerbeds is time consuming and frustrating. Whether you choose a rotary mower or a reel-cut type is up to you; the reel does give a more velvety finish (and is the only way to get that smart striped effect, caused by the way it 'lays' the grass like the pile of a carpet) but it is more trouble to maintain. Untidy edges will spoil the effect of the most immaculate mowing; allow time for trimming them, either with shears or a powered edging clipper. And don't be careless about safety. Turn the mower off whenever you leave it unattended, even for a minute; keep your hands and feet well away from the blades; and usher small children safely out of harm's way.

It can be tempting to allow the clippings to lie, to rot down and return the nourishment they contain; but this doesn't really work. They'll just make half-rooted 'thatch' and clog up the crowns of the grass plants. Off to the compost heap with them!

In nature, grass tends to grow in the spring and then brown off with summer's heat, to return green with the

A well-manicured lawn can provide a flattering backdrop to flowers and foliage plants.

spring; but in gardens we want spring green all year. Except in the moistest of climates, this means watering. It is amazingly easy to do this wastefully— just sprinkle lightly until the lawn looks refreshed and repeat when it looks tired again. This will be pretty soon; light watering encourages the grass roots to linger near the surface. It is much better to water infrequently—even in the hottest, driest climates, this means no more than every ten days or so—but do it thoroughly so the water penetrates right into the soil and the roots go down deep after it.

The constant removal of foliage from the grass strips it of nutrients, and these ought to be made up to it by occasional fertilizing. This is easy; just buy a ready-made lawn fertilizer, sprinkle it on, and water heavily at once to wash it into the soil—if you don't it can burn the leaves. You can apply it at the manufacturer's suggested rate in one go, but it is more effective to divide the quantity in half and give two doses a fortnight apart.

If you started out with clean soil and keep the grass flourishing, weeds should cause little headache. If any get in, just dig them out (an old kitchen knife is a useful implement here) or spot treat them with glyphosate. The lawn should soon grow over the resulting bare patch, especially if you assist it with water and fertilizer.

Meadow Gardens

There is, however, one currently fashionable style of lawn to which all these rules don't apply, and that is the flowering meadow. Here, the grass is deliberately inter-planted with 'weeds'—primroses, small bulbs, cornflowers, Flanders and Californian poppies, daisies and the like—the aim being to create an effect like the carpets of flowers you see in old tapestries. Very pretty and romantic it can be too. Here, you don't want the grass to flourish so much it smothers the flowers, so you start with rather poor soil, apply fertilizer with a sparing hand, water very judiciously, and mow only a few times a year.

Precisely when depends on your chosen flowers: but as a guide, you'll probably mow in late winter to give the spring flowers a setting of short grass; again when they have shed their seeds and died down; and perhaps again in autumn/fall. Always keep the mower as high as it will go.

Miscanthus sinensis is ideal for perennial borders, water gardens and screens.

Ground Covers

It is a short step from the flowering meadow to leaving out the grass and carpeting the ground entirely with low-growing, easy-care plants, known, naturally enough, as ground covers.

You can use annuals as temporary ground cover—nasturtiums are excellent—but the best ground covers are spreading, evergreen perennials or dense, low-growing shrubs. Flowers are a feature of many, but far more important is the ability to make a carpet dense enough to smother weeds without growing too tall—ankle height is about right. Then a good ground cover needs to be presentable all year; to need little in the way of trimming or spraying; and to be easy to propagate to cut down on cost. It is possible to weave patterns with several species, but the stronger will tend to crowd out the weaker—and simplicity usually looks better anyway. Ground covers cannot be walked on.

Prepare your bed as thoroughly as for any other plant, plant at the appropriate season, and mulch at once; the last thing you want is weeds getting in between the young plants. If you like, you can plant some low-growing

annuals between your permanent plants—and they will remind you to water and fertilize. Ground covers may be low, low maintenance when they are established, but when young they need care!

Ornamental Grasses

You can supplement the flowers in your meadow with grasses chosen for their ornamental foliage and flowers rather than their ability to stand cropping into lawn: but you will need to place them with care as many are quite tall. They can be placed anywhere in the garden that you want their airy grace, and it is currently fashionable to include them in plantings with more orthodox annuals and perennials. The important thing is to choose species that stay in sedate clumps; those that run about will turn themselves into weeds as soon as your back is turned. Most retain their form as they die off for the winter, and their golden and brown tints can be a lovely feature of the autumn/fall and winter garden—but if they might be a fire hazard, by all means cut them down when they dry off. (You can use them in dried flower arrangements indoors.)

Agrostis tenuis

Cynodon dactylon

Festuca elatior

Chlorophytum comosum

Dichondra micrantha

LAWNS AND GROUND COVERS

AGROSTIS
tenuis
COLONIAL BENT, BROWN TOP, BENT GRASS, NEW ZEALAND BENT

Regarded highly for its tolerance of the cold, this attractive and durable annual grass is widely grown in New Zealand, the cooler Australian states and in parts of North America. Although frost-resistant, it is drought-tender. Left unmown, this New Zealand native grows to 40 cm (about 16 in) in height. A recommended mowing height is 20 mm (about ³/₄ in). A prodigious spreader, it has a creeping stem, with bright green, narrow leaves. It prefers moist soil that drains well, in a sunny, open location, although it will grow in light shade. Compared with other bent grasses, this more erect species needs less care. Propagate from seed. Watch out for diseases such as brown patch and dollar spot.

CARDAMINE
pratensis 'Flore Pleno'
CUCKOO FLOWER, LADY'S SMOCK

This perennial is suitable for informal and bush gardens. It has a neat habit, forming a clump up to 45 cm (about 18 in) high with a spread of 30 cm (about 12 in). The leaves are mid-green and divided into rounded leaflets; single or double lilac flowers are borne in spring. Fully hardy, it prefers moist to wet soil in a sunny position with some shade in hot climates. Propagate from leaf-tip cuttings in mid-summer, or from seed or by division in autumn/fall.

CHLOROPHYTUM
comosum
SPIDER PLANT, HEN-AND-CHICKENS

Native to South Africa, this tender, dwarf evergreen, tufted perennial is grown for its attractive grass-like foliage. (It is actually a member of the lily family.) In mild climates it forms an attractive ground cover in the shade of deciduous trees, growing to a height of 30 cm (about 12 in) and with an indefinite spread. It is also good as an edging plant or indoors in hanging baskets. Narrow leaves, 45 cm (about 18 in) long, spread from a rosette. Long thin stems carrying racemes of star-shaped white flowers appear throughout the year, and small rosettes of leaves appear on flower stems forming plantlets. Frost-tender, it requires a bright position, away from direct sun, and fertile, well-drained soil. Propagate from seed or plantlets, or by division at any time except winter. 'Vittatum' is a variegated cultivar.

CYNODON
dactylon
COUCH GRASS, BERMUDA GRASS, INDIAN DOAB, SOUTH AFRICAN COUCH

Considered a relatively minor weed in New Zealand and many parts of the USA, this grass is indeed highly regarded for its hardiness and presentation throughout Australia and elsewhere, wherever winters are not too severe. A medium to fine-textured grass, it quickly spreads by underground and surface runners. Couch does not mind soils that are sandy or clayey. Its tolerance of hot, dry weather provides the added benefit of not requiring as much watering as other lawns. To propagate sow seeds. Runners and turfs will also readily take. Not overly vulnerable to diseases, it will, however, suffer from exposure to cold weather and may turn brown in winter; it prefers sun.

DICHONDRA
micrantha
syn. *D. repens*
KIDNEY WEED

A native of New Zealand and Australia, this perennial makes a good, soft green lawn in many parts of the world; it is good for a shady spot under a tree. Although regarded as drought- and frost-resistant, it is not recommended in areas with temperatures below 4°C (about 39°F). It can be walked on but does not take kindly to heavy foot traffic. The species takes root at nodes on stems that spread widely. Its leaves are kidney-shaped, looking a little like miniature water lily pads. In spring it produces small, green, insignificant flowers. It prefers light to medium fertilized soils in an open sunny location with ample watering. Left unmown in a sunny position, the species grows to 10 cm (about 4 in). Propagate by division in spring or autumn/fall.

FESTUCA
FESCUE

A native of Asia and temperate Europe, this genus provides good grassed areas requiring little maintenance and are ideal for playing fields, street-side plantings and parks in cold through to moderate climates. They grow deep roots and forms tufts, with short rhizomes and bright green leaves 6 mm (about ¹/₄ in) wide. The turfs have a loose texture, wear well and tolerate semi-shade. They also withstand drought and frost well. A mowing height of 5 cm (about 2 in) is recommended for these lawns. Disease and pests rarely affect the fescues.

F. elatior
TALL FESCUE

This is a species with a tendency to clump, making it more suited to coarser lawns such as those grown for playing fields. It is also good for controlling erosion. Its leaves are tough and it will grow in compacted soil. As it does not send out runners, sow thickly to ensure a close turf. Lightly fertilize each month through summer, only once or twice in autumn/fall and spring. Sow seeds in autumn/fall.

F. glauca
BLUE FESCUE

This decorative perennial grass grows in clumps to a height and spread of 10 cm (about 4 in). The leaves are narrow, their colour ranges from silvery white to blue-grey. Insignificant flowers bloom in summer. It is not really a good grass for lawns but closely spaced and left untrimmed, it is suitable for use as an edging to flowerbeds and as a ground cover. This is a very easily grown species which thrives in most soils and does not need much water. Propagate by division of clumps in spring.

F. rubra 'Commutata'
NEW ZEALAND FESCUE, CHEWINGS FESCUE

A tuft-forming grass, this species is often sown with bent grasses, with which it shares common needs and preferences. Established on steep slopes and left ungroomed it makes for an appealing cover. Propagate this species from seed.

F. scoparia
BEARGRASS, BEARSKIN GRASS

The leaves on this perennial grass are needle fine. This fully hardy evergreen grows into tufts that form a dark green, spiky ground cover, which needs regular grooming to keep tidy and dense. The flower-heads are slender, appearing in summer. Spreading widely, the species reaches only 15 cm (about 6 in) high. Establish in well-drained soil in full sun.

LOLIUM
perenne
PERENNIAL RYE GRASS

This perennial grass grows in clumps up to 50 cm (about 20 in) high and 30 cm (about 12 in) in spread. The linear leaves are glossy, smooth and dark green. The yellowy green flowers, which appear in late spring and summer, are narrow, spike-like blooms 15 cm (about 6 in) long. It has smooth, whippy stems that tend to lie down under the lawn mower, springing back up later. This fast-sprouting species from Europe thrives in most well-drained soils, in open, sunny locations. Propagate from seed. It is a very coarse grass needing frequent mowing and is best for rough areas rather than for fine lawn.

MENTHA
pulegium
PENNYROYAL, EUROPEAN PENNYROYAL MINT

A native of Asia and Europe, it has small, elliptical leaves which are grey-green and hairy. It grows to 3 cm (about 1½ in) and bears clusters of reddish purple to lilac-blue flowers in autumn/fall. To stop it

wandering and possibly overcoming other plants, trim it back hard at the beginning of spring. The species resists frosts but is drought-tender. It will tolerate light foot traffic. Grow in rich, moist soil in a shaded, protected location. Propagate from seed or by root division. The curative value of pennyroyal has been extolled through the ages for sweating out colds, treating nausea, headaches, nerves, rashes, itches and skin conditions.

OPHIOPOGON
jaburan 'Variegatus'

This evergreen perennial is grown for its neat tufts of white or yellow striped, grass-like foliage. It is popular with landscape gardeners for ground cover in hard or heavily shaded areas, and is often seen growing under deciduous trees. Sometimes grown as a pot plant indoors in shade. Grows to a height and spread of 30 cm (about 12 in). Loose, drooping sprays of bell-shaped, white flowers are borne in early summer, followed by shiny, deep blue berries. Half-hardy, it grows in sun or partial shade and a well-drained fertile soil. Propagate by division in spring or from seed in autumn/fall. Water well in summer to improve growth.

PENNISETUM

This genus consists of about 80 species of annual or perennial grasses found in tropical or subtropical regions. Leaf blades are usually flat; flower clusters are dense and usually brush-like or spike-like.

P. clandestinum
KIKUYU

This half-hardy grass is particularly hard wearing and vigorous. In some regions it is regarded as too uncontrollable as a lawn grass. This is particularly so in the tropics or subtropics where it needs to be well groomed to control it. Kikuyu withstands clayey soils, dry conditions, cold weather, hot weather and most diseases. Propagate from runners or turfs, although seed is available.

Mentha pulegium

Festuca scoparia

Festuca glauca

Ophiopogon jaburan 'Variegatus'

Lolium perenne

Pennisetum clandestinum

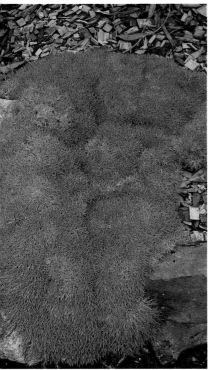

Poa pratensis

Phyla nodiflora

Stenotaphrum secundatum

Scleranthus biflorus

Pennisetum setaceum

P. setaceum
syn. *P. ruppellii*
AFRICAN FOUNTAIN GRASS

Native to tropical Africa, this species belongs to the same genus as many cereal and fodder plants. Arching, coppery spikes with bearded bristles form brush-like flower clusters on this herbaceous perennial grass. Appearing in summer, they last into winter. This half-hardy species grows into tufts comprising very rough stems and long, narrow leaf blades. It grows to 1 m (about 3 ft) with a spread of 50 cm (about 20 in). Plant in moist soil in full sun. It is not suitable as a lawn grass, but makes an attractive tall ground cover (perhaps with some spring bulbs intermixed) or a feature plant in a flower border.

PHYLA
nodiflora
syn. *Lippia repens*
CONDAMINE COUCH

Loose clusters of pink, lilac or white flowers on thin stalks are displayed throughout the year on this vigorous perennial from northern Australia. The species takes root at the nodes and spreads widely into a mat only 5 cm (about 2 in) high. Its cupped, elliptical leaves are green, sometimes tinged with grey. Plant in moist, well-drained soil. It copes with full sun, but will flower more in semi-shade. Although somewhat frost- and drought-tender, it tolerates salt spray. Propagate by division in spring or autumn/fall. It tolerates foot traffic and is often used as a grass substitute in lawns.

POA
pratensis
KENTUCKY BLUE GRASS, MEADOW GRASS

Although producing an appealing blue-green lawn, this native of central Europe will not take the heavy traffic of playgrounds or playing fields and does not survive dry conditions. It does well in cooler climates but is slightly frost-tender. This perennial has smooth, erect stems and small, flat, pointed leaves. If left ungroomed, it will grow to 15 cm (about 6 in) in height and spread. In spring and mid-summer, it bears spikelets in spreading panicles. Establish in light, sandy soil that drains well. Although it tolerates shade, a sunny, open location is best. It needs ample watering. Propagate from seed or by division. It is vulnerable to attack by rust and other diseases, including fusarium blight brought on by a hot summer.

SCLERANTHUS
biflorus
CANBERRA GRASS

Close planting of this perennial (not a true grass but a cousin of the carnation) will give you a mossy, grass-like ground cover, 3–10 cm (about 1½–4 in) deep. The narrow, tightly massed, bright green leaves reach 1 cm (about ½ in) in length. Barely noticeable pale green flowers appear late in spring. Remove any brown patches and spray against fungus. Indigenous to New Zealand and the eastern states of Australia, this frost-hardy species is resistant to the salty atmosphere of seaside

Thymus serpyllum

regions, but not to drought. It will not take foot traffic.

STENOTAPHRUM
secundatum
BUFFALO, ST AUGUSTINE GRASS

Although a coarse-textured grass with wide blades, this spreading perennial makes good lawns in warmer climates, particularly near the sea where its tolerance to salt spray is an asset. Its colour is a light to dark green and it forms a mat by taking root at nodes of runners that spread quickly. It grows up to 15 cm (about 6 in) high if left uncut. Rather frost-tender, it tolerates wet conditions, partial shade and most pests, although it can turn brown while dormant. Propagate from turfs.

THYMUS
serpyllum
WILD THYME, MOTHER-OF-THYME, CREEPING THYME

A smaller plant than garden thyme, this native of Europe grows to a height and spread of 10 cm (about 4 in), to form a useful ground cover. Its creeping stem is woody and branching, and the scented, bright green leaves are elliptical to lanceolate. The bluish purple flowers are small and tubular with two lips, and are borne in spring and summer in dense terminal whorls. This species prefers alkaline soil, and full sun intensifies the aroma of the leaves. Propagate from cuttings or by root division. It will take moderate foot traffic, but needs replanting every few years to maintain a dense cover.

ORNAMENTAL GRASSES

ARUNDO
donax
GIANT REED

This giant perennial grass is one of the most striking of summer foliage plants. Growing to a height of 6 m (about 18 ft) and spread of 1 m (about 3 ft), it is an excellent ornamental plant for large gardens. In mild areas it can grow very vigorously and will need confining. Floppy, blue-green leaves are borne on thick stems, and dense panicles of creamy spikelets appear in summer. It is half-hardy and prefers a sunny situation and moist soil. In winter, when the foliage becomes untidy, it should be cut to the ground, creating luxurious new spring and summer growth. *A. donax* 'Versicolor' is a popular variegated cultivar.

BRIZA
media
QUAKING GRASS

An evergreen, tuft-forming perennial grass that grows to 30–60 cm (about 12–24 in) high, with a spread of 8–10 cm (about 3–4 in). It has mid-green leaves and in summer bears open branched flower clusters of about 30 hanging, brownish purple spikelets. They make very good dried flower decorations and are excellent for dyeing. Fully hardy, plant in full sun in well-drained, poor soil. Propagate from seed in spring or autumn/fall, or by division in spring. Fungus diseases may cause problems.

BUTOMUS
umbellatus
FLOWERING RUSH

This elegant, marginal water plant is the only member of its genus. Related to the lilies, it is a rush-like, deciduous perennial and has razor-sharp, narrow, twisted, mid-green leaves and tall stalks of rose-pink flowers in summer. Fully hardy, it grows to a height of 1 m (about 3 ft) and spread of 45 cm (about 18 in). Plant in a warm, sunny area in a shallow pool or boggy soil. Propagate from seed in spring or late summer, or by division in spring. The plant's name translates as: 'a plant that cuts the mouth of oxen when grazing'.

CAREX
SEDGE

This large genus contains over 1500 temperate perennials with grass-like foliage. Predominately clump-forming and evergreen, they make resilient decorative potted plants. Many species have sharp, pendent leaves and catkin-type flowers. Male and female blooms may appear on the same head or on the same stem. Plant in full sun or partial shade and only water when surface roots seem dry. Propagate by division in spring. These sedges are a characteristic feature of the New Zealand landscape, with more than 70 species native to that country.

C. elata 'Aurea'
syn. C. stricta 'Aurea'
GOLDEN SEDGE

This evergreen, tuft-forming perennial sedge is useful for growing in damp places and beside ponds. It has golden-yellow leaves, and blackish brown flower spikes that are borne in summer. It reaches a height of 40 cm (about 16 in) and spread of 15 cm (about 6 in). Fully hardy, it grows best in a sunny situation in fertile, wet soil.

C. lucida

This is an excellent species for rockeries, pots and for mass planting on banks. The fine grassy foliage is copper coloured and forms dense clumps 30 cm (about 12 in) in height with a spread of 60 cm (about 24 in). This species is hardy and easily grown in most situations except full shade and is drought tolerant once established. Propagate from seed or by division in early spring.

CATANANCHE
caerulea 'Major'
CUPID'S DART

Native to the Mediterranean region, this fully hardy, fast-growing, herbaceous perennial reaches 60 cm (about 24 in) high with a spread of 30 cm (about 12 in). Clump-forming, the leaves are grey-green, and thin, leafless stems topped with daisy-like, lavender-blue flowerheads are borne freely throughout summer. The flowers are suitable for drying. Requiring full sun, it is easily grown in most soil conditions. It is a somewhat untidy plant, and looks its best among long grass in a meadow garden rather than a planting bed. For other meadow garden flowers, turn to the chapters on annuals and perennials, and bulbs—suitable candidates are Shirley and Californian poppies, cornflowers, the species of gladioli and narcissus, primroses, sparaxis, xeranthemum, agrostemma and many others.

Arundo donax

Carex elata 'Aurea'

Briza media

Catananche caerulea 'Major'

Butomus umbellatus

Carex lucida

Cortaderia selloana

Hordeum junceum

Molinia caerulea 'Variegata'

Miscanthus sinensis 'Variegatus'

Coix lacryma-jobi

COIX
lacryma-jobi
JOB'S TEARS

This tuft-forming annual grass is native to east Asia and grows to a height of 50 cm–1 m (about 20–36 in) with a spread of 10–15 cm (about 4–6 in). It has insignificant spikelets, broad green leaves and hard, beady, green fruits that change in autumn/fall to a shiny, greyish mauve colour. Half-hardy, it prefers a sunny situation and well-drained soil. Propagate from seed in spring or autumn/fall. The fruits are used to make bead necklaces.

CORTADERIA
selloana
syn. *C. argentea*
PAMPAS GRASS

Native to Argentina and Brazil, this perennial, clump-forming, stately grass grows to a height of 3 m (about 9 ft) and spread of 1.5 m (about 4½ ft). Its stems are tall and reed-like and the leaves are long and slender, growing outwards from the base. In summer, erect, silvery, plume-like panicles appear above the leaves. Pink varieties are also available. Propagate from seed or by division. It can be invasive, and in some areas is considered a noxious weed.

HORDEUM
junceum
FOXTAIL BARLEY, SQUIRREL GRASS

Growing 30–50 cm (about 12–20 in) tall (depending on the fertility of the soil) this is one of the best grasses for growing in the company of flowers, as it stays sedately in a clump without running about. It has grassy leaves and feathery flower clusters from summer to autumn/fall. Fully hardy, it is officially perennial but old clumps do not always flower freely so many people prefer to grow it as an annual from spring sown seed. The flower clusters retain their silkiness when dried.

MILIUM
effusum 'Aureum'
BOWLES' GOLDEN GRASS, MILLET GRASS

An evergreen, tuft-forming perennial grass grown for its yellow foliage and flowers. Good for growing in perennial borders, water gardens, or as a ground cover, and effective when planted under white variegated shrubs. Its flat leaves are golden-yellow in spring and fade to yellowish green in summer. Panicles of greenish yellow spikelets are produced in summer and these can be cut and used for dried arrangements. It grows to a height of 1 m (about 3 ft) and spread of 30 cm (about 12 in). Fully hardy, it grows best in the shade in a well-drained, rich, moist soil. Propagate from seed in spring or autumn/fall, or by division in spring. It also self-seeds readily. The Bowles in question in the common name was a very influential English gardener of the Edwardian period. He was fond of plants with unusual leaves.

MISCANTHUS
sinensis 'Variegatus'
JAPANESE SILVER GRASS

This large, herbaceous perennial grass grows to a height of 2 m (about 6 ft) with a spread of 50 cm (about 18 in). One of the most popular ornamental grasses, it is grown for its overall plant form and is good for perennial borders, water gardens, naturalized areas, screens and specimen planting. Clump-forming, it has linear leaves with silvery white stripes and margins. Long-lasting beige, red tinged flower heads are borne in autumn/fall—they are good for drying and dyeing. Frost-hardy, it requires a sunny situation and well-drained moist soil. Divide every 5–7 years to keep the plants growing vigorously. Propagate by division in spring.

MOLINIA
caerulea

A native of acid heathlands in Europe, and south-west and northern Asia, this tuft-forming, deciduous perennial grass forms large tussocks growing up to 45 cm (about 18 in) when in flower. It has broad, flat, mid-green leaves and in summer bears panicles of purplish spikelets. It is fully hardy and grows best on acid soils in full sun, tolerating any fertile, neutral soil but disliking chalk. It has swollen stem bases which at times have been used as pipe cleaners and toothpicks. It is one of the most attractive garden grasses, especially in its finest variegated forms. Propagate by division in spring.

PHALARIS
arundinacea var. picta
GARDENER'S GARTERS, REEDY GRASS

This clump-forming perennial grass is easily grown, bearing reed-like leaves with white stripes and, in summer, terminal panicles of purplish or pale green spikelets on stout, upstanding stems. Indigenous to North America and Europe, it can grow to 1.5 m (about 4½ ft) but is generally kept lower in a garden. This fully hardy evergreen likes well-drained soil and semi-shade. It can prove invasive. Propagate by division of the clumps.

PLEIOBLASTUS

pygmaeus

syn. *Arundinaria pygmaea,*
Sasa pygmaea

DWARF BAMBOO

This spreading, rhizomatous bamboo can be used to help control erosion. Left uncut, the dark green foliage (variegated in most of the commonly available strains) of this frost-hardy evergreen will grow to 50 cm (about 20 in) and spread indefinitely. Cut back almost to the ground in early spring to ensure a lush crop of fresh new leaves.

RESTIO

tetraphyllus

The bright green, feathery-looking foliage of this perennial herb is often used as a backdrop in flower arrangements. This frost-hardy, evergreen spreads widely from a creeping rhizome, and the unbranching, erect stems reach 1–1.5 m (about 3–4½ ft) in height. It has brownish flowers in terminal spikes. It is suitable for a damp, sandy position, such as beside a pond, in a sunny, open location. This Australian native is found everywhere in that country except the state of Western Australia.

SASA

This genus consists of over 150 species of rhizomatous, woody grasses. They are found in eastern Asia, especially Japan. They are usually not very tall. Propagate from seed in autumn/fall or by division in spring.

S. palmata

This spreading, evergreen bamboo grows to a height of 2 m (about 6 ft) with an indefinite spread. Its flowers are insignificant but the wide, rich green leaves make it an excellent foliage plant, adding grace and contrast to borders and rock gardens. *S. palmata* does best in a sheltered, not too dry situation in sun or shade. Its hollow stems are streaked with purple and bear one branch at each node.

S. veitchii

syn. *S. albomarginata*

This fully hardy bamboo grows to a height of 1.5 m (about 5 ft) and spreads indefinitely. Its 25 cm (about 10 in) long leaves turn white at the edges. Its stems, which branch from each node, are generally purple with a whitish powder beneath the node. Grow in well-drained soil in full sun.

SCIRPUS

lacustris subsp. *tabernaemontani*
'Zebrinus'

syn. *S. tabernaemontani* 'Zebrinus'

This is an evergreen sedge with white-banded, leafless stems. In summer, it carries brown spikelets. Growing 1.5 m (about 4½ ft) high, this fully hardy perennial spreads widely. It likes full sun, wet soil and is not deterred even by brackish water; however, it is invasive and will need regular division.

STIPA

pennata

WILD OATS

Golden anthers hang from the long-awned, silver spikelets that form delicate, airy panicles on this perennial grass in summer through to winter. The leaves are narrow and 50 cm (about 20 in) or more in length. A frost-hardy species which likes well-drained soil and full sun, it reaches a height of 2.5 m (about 7½ ft).

Restio tetraphyllus

Stipa pennata

Phalaris arundinacea var. *picta*

Sasa palmata

Pleioblastus pygmaeus

Sasa veitchii

CHAPTER 7

Vegetables
& Herbs

There's nothing to quite match the flavour of home-grown vegetables or herbs. They can be picked at the moment of perfection and eaten or preserved within hours to the benefit of both the family's health and budget. What's more, vegetables like spinach and rhubarb, or herbs, are always bunched for sale and we often have to buy more than is immediately needed for a meal. Home grown, these are readily available by the sprig or leaves can be cut as required.

To be grown successfully, vegetables do need to be chosen with consideration to climate. Vegetables such as beans, tomatoes and the ground vine crops like cucumbers and squash are frost-sensitive and therefore need to be planted out when the prospect of frost is over. They like temperatures of around 20°C (about 68°F) to set fruit. On the other hand, many of the root crops (those with the edible parts underground), like spinach and peas, grow well in temperatures of between 12 and 18°C (about 53–64°F) and are not as susceptible to frost. Then there are the cabbages, cauliflowers and brussel sprouts, all members of the same family, which revel in cool temperatures and are quite frost-hardy.

All vegetables must have ample sunlight, and this factor, more than any other, can dictate the positioning of a vegetable garden. Other points to consider include competition from tree or shrub roots, prevailing winds and drainage, although this last factor is usually able to be rectified by raising the beds or by underground piping.

The size of the garden also needs careful thought. Depending on space available and the time you are prepared to spend in the garden, any number of beds can be made, but it's a good idea to begin small. Beds are easily extended or new ones made. A bed of up to 1.2 m (about 3½ ft) wide is easily cultivated from both sides. Length can be determined by available space, but 2 m (about 6 ft) gives ample room for the compact and quick growers. Others, like the vine crops, take up a lot more garden space and need the use of a bed the whole season to complete their cycle. The perennial plants such as rhubarb and asparagus, as well as many of the herbs which occupy the same space for many years, need a bed of their own or to be grouped at one end of a highly cultivated bed so that they are not interfered with when the rest of the garden is being prepared for the new season's crop.

Consider too the choice of vegetables you plan to grow. Yield per plant is a very important factor when space is limited. For instance beans take up relatively little space and their yield is tremendous over a season. Salad vegetables and the leaf crops too are worth considering before, say, a plot given over to potatoes which don't really spoil when left on the greengrocer's shelf.

One very practical way to overcome limited space is to build a trellis towards the back of a garden to hold climbing beans, peas, even cucumbers. Sited correctly, this trellis will not shade the lower growing vegetables and it can act as a windbreak to a row of corn or some tomatoes.

The herb garden—a source of health and wonderful fragrance.

Pots too can be used. They need not be restricted to growing herbs; they are also ideal for such long-cropping vegetables as capsicums, tomatoes, eggplant or the 'bush' varieties of cucumbers or pumpkins. Placed on a sunny patio they can be easily observed and given immediate attention if this is required.

Planting

Some seeds, like the quick growing radish or beans, melons and carrots, can be sown directly into their permanent garden positions. Finer seeds are better planted into seedbeds or frames where germination and early growth can be closely monitored. A seedbed needs to have soil of a fine consistency, perfect drainage and to be placed where it receives adequate sunlight and warmth and is well protected from any drying winds. The surface should be flat so that fine seeds are not washed away. Shallow grooves can be made with a length of dowel or similar, then the seeds carefully dropped into these miniature farrows and covered with a light soil layer. Water with a fine mist or spray, ensuring the surface is neither too wet nor allowed to dry out.

Gardeners in colder areas can sow seeds in frames in protected areas while it is still too early to plant outdoors. These plants are then transplanted into their permanent positions when all possibility of frost is over. When the weather warms up then it may be possible to sow another batch or two in a well-prepared, outdoor seedbed in the successive weeks. By making these regular small sowings the household won't be inundated by a glut of vegetables all maturing at the one time.

Many gardeners prefer to buy their seedlings at the nursery. Transplanting should be done in the cool of the evening. Using a garden knife or small trowel, and holding the plants by their leaves, loosen them gently from the seedbed or punnet and place a bunch of them on a board—covering them with a cloth or damp kitchen paper towel will prevent them drying out. Use a piece of dowel to make a row of holes sufficiently deep so the tiny roots will not be bent or broken, then gently prise the seedlings apart and place single plants in the prepared holes, pushing the soil firmly around them with two fingers. Water each plant to ensure any air pockets are filled with soil. The seed-

Nothing can beat the flavour of home-grown vegetables.

lings do benefit from being given some protection in the form of a leafy branch, cut down milk carton or similar until they have time to become accustomed to their new surroundings.

Planting the same vegetables in the same position each year is not good garden practice as the plants of the same family are often prone to similar diseases and this only accentuates the problem. And, although chemicals can be used, one of the benefits of growing vegetables is that you can decide which, and indeed if any, chemicals to use. Plants of the same family also take up similar nutrients and it was for this reason that crop rotation was first introduced. Today these nutrients can be replaced by commercial fertilizers.

Different crops require different types of fertilizers, the green plants grown for their leaves need a high nitrogen content, while plants grown for their fruit need a more balanced diet. When a garden is as intensively used as it is for vegetable growing it pays to supplement the use of chemical fertilizers with organic material to ensure its continued good health. Organic fertilizers such as compost can be dug into the soil at the changeover of the seasons. Straw or similar material used as a mulch during the growing season is usually sufficiently decomposed to be dug into the garden at the end of summer. You'll be amazed at the difference in soil texture and general health of the soil when this is done.

Vegetables need to be grown quickly to promote maximum quality in both

leaf and fruiting types. To ensure this rapid, uninterrupted development it is necessary to keep soil adequately moist at all times. It follows then that sandy soil, which dries out more rapidly than heavy soil, needs to be watered more frequently. Many of the vine crops and tomatoes are prone to leaf diseases if leaves are subject to continued moisture, so in beds where these types of vegetables are to be grown a trickle hose or a depression running the length of the bed and filled with water each morning could be used instead of sprinklers which spray moisture indiscriminately over foliage and ground alike.

Close planting and mulching are two ways to ensure moisture is conserved. Close planting may produce less vigorous plants or a marginally less prolific crop, but the home gardener can progressively use, and so thin out, rows as plants mature. Mulching saves the gardener time and energy in other ways as well. It helps with soil temperature control at both extremes and stops heavy rain washing away soil from around the fibrous roots that are often very near the surface of many of the annual vegetables. Mulching also limits weed growth. Many gardeners today rely solely on mulched or 'no dig' beds for successful vegetable growing.

Do try gardening with vegetables and herbs as it really is the most satisfying of the stress reducing hobbies and you'll glow with pleasure at the bountiful results of your leisure!

Allium ascalonicum

VEGETABLES

ALLIUM

This is a large genus consisting of more than 700 species of perennials and biennials that grow in temperate climates around the world and range in size from 10–150 cm (about 4–60 in). Some species are edible, including the onions, garlic and chives. The most ornamental species, which are brightly coloured with beautiful flowers, are found in the northern hemisphere. Common to the genus is the oniony smell emitted when the leaves are bruised or pinched. The onion species may need the protection of a cloche if the soil is cold. Both the onion and ornamental species have the same pest and disease enemies such as onion fly, stem eelworm, rust and onion white rot. The name derives from the Celtic, *all*, meaning hot.

A. ascalonicum

SHALLOT

A carefully thinned bed of shallots will self-perpetuate by dropping seeds or generating new clusters of bulbs. Like all onions, shallots like a light, fertile, weed-free soil. They are usually propagated by dividing the clumps of bulbs.

A. cepa

ONION, SPRING ONION, SCALLION

Onions need a cool climate and a sunny, open position in a well-drained bed of soil. Sow the seeds or immature onions in mid-spring in holes 1 cm (about ½ in) deep and 30 cm (about 12 in) apart, and water moderately. Harvest in late

summer when the leaves have begun to yellow. The onion was a popular vegetable among the Greeks and Romans but never eaten by the Egyptians who regarded it as sacred. The spring onion is an immature onion which has not yet made a bulb. It likes the same conditions as other onions. In a warm climate seeds can be sown at any time of the year.

A. cepa var. aggregatum

TREE ONION

Otherwise known as golden shallots or the Egyptian onion, these have a more delicate taste than spring onions and can be used instead of chives. Propagate from the small bulbs that grow among the flowers or by division.

A. porrum

LEEK

Easier to grow than the onion and more suited to cold climates, the leek likes a sunny spot and a moist light soil. Sow seeds in spring or summer or plant seedlings 20 cm (about 8 in) apart with 30 cm (about 12 in) between rows, filling each hole gently with water. Keep clear of weeds and, once the base of the leek is at least 2 cm (about 1 in) thick, harvest as needed.

APIUM

graveolens var. dulce

CELERY

Native to the Mediterranean, this leafy vegetable is a boon to any salad, but a challenge for the home gardener to grow well. It needs a well-prepared, loamy soil that can

Allium cepa var. *aggregatum*

Allium cepa

drain water but still hold the desired amount. It also commands a lot of space and regular doses of liquid fertilizer. Prior to some hard work put in by Italian gardeners some 400 years ago, celery was nothing more than a bitter-tasting weed, and even now its stalks need to be blanched to remove bitterness. This is done by shoring the soil up around them to exclude the light when they reach a height of 30 cm (about 12 in). You can also bundle the plant up in black plastic, and self-blanching varieties are available. Water diligently if the summer is dry. Septoria leaf spot is a serious celery problem.

A. graveolens var. rapaceum
CELERIAC

Easier to grow than celery and with a longer growing season, this is similar to the turnip (often called turnip-rooted celery) but with a celery flavour. Keep well watered even when cool, and harvest the roots when about 10 cm (about 4 in) across. The leaves are edible but inferior to regular celery.

ASPARAGUS
officinalis
ASPARAGUS

A frost-hardy perennial of the lily family this vegetable seems to have been cultivated and eaten all over the world as far back as the ancient Egyptians. Sow seeds in spring or set young plants in winter in 25 cm (about 10 in) deep trenches in a sunny part of the garden. Give asparagus a good 30 cm (about 12 in) between each plant so that its fleshy roots can wander freely. The soil should be well-drained and rich with compost or manure. Do not harvest the young shoots (spears) until the third spring, and always stop in time to allow sufficient shoots to mature to keep the plants going. The red berries should be picked before they go to seed and the plants should be mulched every summer.

BETA
vulgaris
BEETROOT

A relatively easy vegetable to grow, it is fast growing and should be given space and an open position. It needs a deep, fertile soil that has been previously cultivated. Sow seeds in autumn/fall in 2 cm (about 1 in) holes 20 cm (about 8 in) apart. When the first leaves appear weed out the weaker seedlings. Keep the soil moist and pull out the beetroot by hand. In warm climates it can be harvested almost all year round, but in cold climates bulbs will need to be picked and then stored over winter. It is susceptible to boron deficiency and white fly. It was once valued by the Romans and Greeks for its leaves rather than the root itself.

Asparagus officinalis

Apium graveolens var. *dulce*

Beta vulgaris

Apium graveolens var. *rapaceum*

Allium porrum

B. vulgaris var. *cicla*
SILVERBEET, SWISS CHARD

Similar to spinach, but better in warm climates, it has the same requirements as beetroot. It is easy to grow and will tolerate shade or sun. Sow in mid-spring and summer. Snails and slugs are the only real problem. Harvest the leaves, a few at a time, as needed.

BRASSICA

There are 30 species of this annual or biennial vegetable, some grown for cooking, oilseed and mustard, others for animal fodder. It is native to the Mediterranean and parts of Asia. Most of the *Brassica* species love a lime-rich, moist, well-drained soil. Seedlings should be raised in seedbeds and then carefully replanted 6 to 8 weeks later in a sheltered spot in soil that has been prepared previously for an earlier crop. Brassicas are more prone to pests and diseases than other vegetables so ensure all soil is weed-free and not wet. Club root is a common disease in these vegetables, and crop rotation should be practised.

B. campestris var. *rutabaga*
SWEDE, RUTABAGA

Similar to turnips but larger and sweeter, swedes are frost-hardy and prefer a fertile soil. Sow seeds in late spring to early summer in 2 cm (about 1 in) deep holes 45 cm (about 18 in) apart. Harvest in mid-autumn/fall. Watch for slugs and snails.

B. oleracea *gonglyoides*
KOHLRABI

With characteristics of both the turnip and cabbage, this is a versatile vegetable with a slightly nutty flavour that can be eaten raw or cooked. Sow seeds in holes 1 cm (about $\frac{1}{2}$ in) deep and spaced 20 cm (about 8 in) by 80 cm (about 32 in) apart. Weed very lightly as root disturbance will slow growth.

B. oleracea var. *acephala*
KALE

A variety of flat-leafed or curly-leafed, headless cabbage that is prolific in northern Europe because of its tolerance to cold. Plant out the seedlings in 2 cm (about 1 in) holes 45 cm (about 18 in) apart. Sow the flat-leafed variety from seed as they do not tolerate transplanting. In Scotland its broth is a traditional Highland dish.

B. oleracea var. *botrytis*
WHITE CAULIFLOWER

Mark Twain scathingly labelled the cauliflower 'a cabbage with a college education', but time has proved this to be a very popular vegetable with a long history. It prefers a humus-rich soil for large compact head production. Plant seedlings 60 cm (about 24 in) apart and across. Do this with care as they hate being transplanted. Keep the soil moist and with the right amounts of boron, magnesium and potassium.

B. oleracea var. *bullata*
SAVOY CABBAGE

This variety is extremely frost-hardy and will thrive in very cold conditions. It is larger and stronger in flavour than European cabbage, with dark, wrinkled leaves.

B. oleracea var. *capitata*
EUROPEAN CABBAGE

There are many varieties of this very popular cabbage and they range in their seasonal tolerance. This ensures that these cabbages can be grown worldwide in many different climatic zones. Water regularly and mulch well, keeping the soil

Brassica oleracea gonglyoides

Brassica oleracea var. acephala

Beta vulgaris var. *cicla*

Brassica oleracea var. *botrytis*

well drained. Space seedlings between 30–50 cm (about 12–20 in) apart, depending on variety. The Greeks regarded the cabbage, native to southern Europe, as a cure for hangover which may be true considering its high nutritional value. Red cabbage, with its purple leaves, is a slow-maturing cabbage that needs a long growing season. However, its solid, chewy flesh makes it the best of all the cabbage species for pickling and frying.

B. oleracea var. cymosa
BROCCOLI

Broccoli has the same soil needs as other *Brassica* species. Sow seeds in late spring. Plant seedlings in late summer 50 cm (about 20 in) apart in 60 cm (about 24 in) rows, water well and mulch to save weeding work. It is ideally grown in raised beds. Keep clear of weeds and do not allow to flower as it will stop growing. Harvest 10 or 11 weeks after planting. Grubs and water-logging are two major problems.

B. oleracea var. gemmifera
BRUSSELS SPROUTS

Timing is crucial when planting Brussels sprouts since they need to mature in the coldest part of the year in order to form compact hearts. In warm climates sow or plant in summer. In cold climates sow or plant in mid-spring. In autumn/fall remove any yellowing leaves and make sure the soil stays firm around the stem of the plant.

B. pekinsensis
WOM BUK, CHINESE CABBAGE

Resembling lettuce more than cabbage, this fast-growing species is native to China and was only introduced to Europe in the nineteenth century. Sow seeds 10 cm (about 4 in) apart with 40 cm (about 16 in) between rows. This species is easy to grow as long as it is kept moist. Tie the leaves together after they begin to form their heart shape. Harvest the whole plant as you would a regular cabbage.

Brassica oleracea var. *capitata*

Brassica oleracea var. *cymosa*

Brassica oleracea var. *gemmifera*

Brassica oleracea var. *bullata*

Brassica pekinsensis

Capsicum annuum (Chilli pepper)

Brassica rapa

Brassica sinensis

Capsicum annuum (Bell pepper)

B. sinensis
BOK CHOY, CHINESE CABBAGE

This species looks like silverbeet and is also known as Chinese mustard. These run to seed quickly so sow them in small groups every 10 days. Harvest the entire plant or take a few leaves as needed after 6 to 8 weeks.

CAPSICUM

Closely related to the tomato, and like it native to Central America and a lover of hot, humid summers. The genus contains both ornamental species, grown for their brightly coloured fruit—they are far too hot to eat—and edible types, which divide into the sweet or bell peppers. They can be cooked as a vegetable and eaten raw in salads. The chilli peppers are used fresh or dry to add a sharp, hot flavour to cooking.

GROSSUM GROUP

C. annuum
SWEET BELL PEPPER, CAPSICUM

Extremely high in vitamin C and available in lots of different hybrids. Sow the seeds in containers in a compost-rich soil and then leave in a greenhouse for 8 weeks until late spring. This plant is quite frost-tender and, once planted outside, seedlings may need to be covered with cloches to keep warm. Keep plants well watered. Capsicums contain more vitamin C and vitamin A if they are left to mature until they turn a deep red colour, but they are good eating when green. Red spiders and mites are common pests.

LONGUM GROUP

C. annuum
CHILLI PEPPER, CAPSICUM

A much smaller fruit than the sweet bell pepper and a more profuse grower, this plant needs the same conditions as the green capsicum and can be sun dried and stored in jars. Wash your hands after handling, as the 'hot' substance capsicain is present in all parts of the plant.

B. rapa
TURNIP

The turnip was a staple food of the northern European working classes until the potato upstaged it. It is suited more to the cooler regions of the world. In order to produce a quick crop, grow turnips in fertile soil in rows approximately 35 cm (about 14 in) apart. Keep the young plants moist at all times during the growing period. Harvest the turnips when they are a little bigger than a golf ball.

CICHORIUM

This genus of perennials from the Mediterranean and the Middle East is distantly related to the lettuce. The 2 species in gardens, however, have little in common except their family relation—they are grown and used in the kitchen quite differently.

C. endiva
ENDIVE, CURLY ENDIVE

This is a relative of chicory, grown for its leaves. As with most salad vegetables, it needs a humus-rich soil which is kept moist so that it won't run to seed. Sow the seeds 30–35 cm (about 12–14 in) apart in a shaded position in late summer. Use liquid fertilizer every now and then as the plants are growing. The leaves are usually eaten green as a bitter salad; they rather resemble lettuce but are more sharply flavoured. Snails and slugs can be a problem.

C. intybus
CHICORY

The plants are usually grown from spring-sown seed, allowed to grow through the summer and then lifted a few at a time during winter to be replanted in boxes of moist earth in a dark warm place. The resulting shoots (chicons) will be almost pure white and sweet in flavour; they are ready to harvest when they are 25 cm (about 10 in) long; about 3 or 4 weeks from transplanting. The

whole procedure succeeds best in a cool climate; in warm winter areas chicory is a gourmet luxury. Chicory root is used to make caffeine-free coffee and can also be eaten raw or grated. It is a common weed along highways with its bright blue flowers.

COLOCASIA
esculenta
TARO

Widely grown throughout the tropical regions for the edible tubers, it has large, heart-shaped, mid- to dark green leaves often with prominent veins. It likes a well-drained acid soil and will flourish in tropical, hot, wet conditions. Keep the soil around the base of the plant firm to support the slender stem. Propagate from young suckers or sections of tuber. Harvest 8 months after planting. Young shoots can be cooked and eaten like asparagus.

CUCUMIS
sativus cultivars
APPLE CUCUMBER, LONG GREEN CUCUMBER

The cucumber, a native of India, was as popular with Roman emperors as it is today. In cold climates sow seeds in containers and then transfer the seedlings to a greenhouse or cloche. In warm climates sow into high-compost soil in the garden in late spring and cover with a light layer of soil. Ensure seedlings are free of weeds and that the ground is moist and not hot as this

will destroy cucumber vines. The vines have to be trained on a frame or outdoor trellis in warm climates, to keep the fruit away from the soil. Harvest in summer, removing the small cucumbers to encourage further production. Apple cucumber cultivars are compact and can be grown hydroponically, however they are quite vulnerable to downy mildew. Long green cucumbers are more resistant to mildew; pick them when they are a deep green colour. Both vining and compact (bush) cultivars are available.

Cucumis sativus cultivar

Colocasia esculenta

Cichorium endiva

Cichorium intybus

Cynara scolymus

Summer squash

Pumpkin

Courgette

CUCURBITA

This is an ancient vegetable genus that dates back to 7000 BC in Central America and 1000 BC in North America. So hybridized are the 800 species that applying Latin names can be quite arbitrary. There are squashes, pumpkins, marrow, zucchinis, trombones, butternuts and many others. Most species of this genus are easy to raise and have the same need of a warm, rich soil. In warm climates sow from early spring to late summer. In cold climates sow indoors in early summer. To prepare the garden for seedlings dig holes 30 cm (about 12 in) square, 90 cm (about 36 in) apart for bush varieties and 1.2 m (about 3½ ft) apart for the trailing varieties of pumpkin. Fill with a good fertilizer mix. Plant out seedlings in spring, watering well beforehand. Watch for slugs and keep well irrigated as they are water hungry. Harvest in autumn/fall. The genus has been grown and interbred in gardens for so long that its botany is rather confused; most types are

usually given as forms of *C. pepo*, but some authorities loudly disagree. The issue has been sidestepped by simply listing them under the common names used in gardens. However, the common name may also vary from country to country.

Courgette, zucchini, vegetable marrow

Marrow used to be eaten when fully ripe and about the size of a large cucumber; but in recent years the fashion has been to eat them when very small when they are called courgettes (UK) or zucchini. There are varieties selected to be at their best when immature (i.e. as zucchini) and others that are best when mature; but you can in fact eat all of them at either stage. They need fertile soil, sun and lots of moisture so they will grow quickly. Plant seedlings 50 cm (about 20 in) apart and feed with liquid manure as the first fruit forms. Remove any damaged or sick leaves and fruit.

Pumpkin

Food for pigs in much of Europe but a delicious vegetable for the table elsewhere. The pumpkin is a sprawling vine which ripens its fruit in autumn/fall. They will keep all winter if left until cold withers the vine before harvesting, but they can be taken earlier as soon as they are ripe. There are many varieties ranging greatly in size and weight. They like rich soil, warmth, and water while growing. There is an overlap between pumpkin and winter squash in Commonwealth and American terminology—but they are grown and eaten in much the same way.

Summer squash

This is a trailing vine that likes rich, well-drained soil in full sun. Grown during the warm weather, summer squash are eaten while young. Watch for powdery mildew.

Vegetable spaghetti

This delightful marrow cultivar is easy to grow and features bright

yellow fruit whose flesh looks much like spaghetti when boiled.

Winter squash

More hardy than summer squash, this vegetable needs little attention as long as the soil is rich and there is plenty of sunlight. Make sure it has enough space for sunlight to filter through otherwise blossoms may drop. Winter squash are allowed to mature on the vine and eaten in winter.

CYNARA
scolymus
GLOBE ARTICHOKE

Native to the Mediterranean and a distant cousin of the thistle, the globe artichoke is one of many vegetables once considered to be an aphrodisiac. It has delicate, grey-green leaves and is easy to grow in most soils and positions. Make sure it has enough space (one or two plants are enough in a small garden). A rich soil will mean better production. Plant suckers rather than seeds 90 cm (about 36 in) apart in early spring. Remove yellowing leaves and stems in autumn/fall. Cut the plump flower buds from the plants in spring and summer before the flowers begin to open. Watch for septoria leaf spot.

DAUCUS
carota
CARROT

This famous root vegetable is native to Afghanistan and was introduced to Europe 600 years ago. Sow in deep, warm, aerated soil that is loamy, in rows 25 cm (about 10 in) apart, making sure the earth is firmly compacted around the seeds. Keep the earth moist around the seedlings and thin the rows out when they are 2 cm (about 1 in) high. The carrot gives a high yield even in a small garden and can be stored easily in bins or boxes between layers of sand. Once they are big enough to pick, avoid leaving them in the ground during wet weather as the root will split. The carrot is vulnerable to carrot-fly, greenfly and aphids.

HELIANTHUS
tuberosus
JERUSALEM ARTICHOKE

A relative of the sunflower, this plant has nothing whatsoever to do with Jerusalem, and is in fact a native of North America. It is grown for its pleasant flavoured tubers. This is a very enthusiastic plant which in some conditions may need controlling. It will grow in any soil as long as it is well watered and should be placed in a sunny corner. Plant divisions of the tuber 15 cm (about 6 in) deep and 30 cm (about 12 in) apart in late winter. Hoe when necessary during the year and harvest when the tops have died, usually the following autumn/fall. Dig out all the tubers otherwise they will sprout up and take over the garden.

HIBISCUS
esculentus
OKRA, GUMBO

Sometimes known as *Abelmoschus esculentus*, this attractive plant with pale yellow flowers with a red heart is similar to the ornamental hibiscus. The edible part of the plant is the starchy seed pod which is used for general flavouring as well as in Indian curries and Cajun cooking. It does best in warm climates. Sow 3 or 4 seeds together in early summer in aerated, fertilized soil. Ensure there are 40 cm (about 16 in) between each clump of seeds and that rows are 70 cm (about 28 in) apart. Thin seedlings out and weed soil throughout the year. Pick the pods after the flowers have opened (late

summer through to autumn/fall) or when they are 10 cm (about 4 in) long. Do not leave mature pods on the plants. Watch for aphids and caterpillars.

IPOMOEA
batatas
SWEET POTATO

This native of Central America and the Pacific islands comes in both a white-fleshed or, more recently, orange-fleshed variety. Plant cuttings in rows 1 m (about 3 ft) apart in soil that has been fertilized and dug thoroughly. In a frost-free climate sweet potato can be planted at any time, but it is not recommended for planting in cool climates. Keep the young plants clear of weeds until the vines are big enough to cover the ground. Keep the soil moist while the tubers grow. Harvesting depends on the variety of sweet potato and ranges from 16 weeks to 40 weeks after planting. After digging them out let the tubers dry in the sun for half a

day before storage. Watch for potato moth, potato scab and aphids.

LACTUCA
sativa
LETTUCE

From the Latin, *lac*, meaning milk, referring to its milky white sap, this biennial originated in the Middle East and the Mediterranean. Praised through history for its healthy or sleep-inducing properties, lettuce is a salad plant with a very delicate root system. It grows up to 1 m (about 3 ft) high. Sow lettuce seeds in spring or summer in the open ground or sow in seed boxes for later transplanting. Ensure that the seed is right for the climate as there are many kinds of lettuce to suit different climates. The soil must be humus-rich and evenly moist. Thin the seedlings gradually until they are 30 cm (about 12 in) apart. Sudden changes in temperature can leave the lettuce open to disease. Ensure they do not flower. Water regularly over summer, avoiding

excessive water on leaves. Winter growers will need little water. Watch for slugs, grey mould and greenfly. Popular types include the common iceberg with globular heads like pale green cabbages, cos lettuce with more open darker heads, and mignonette with ruffled pink-tinted leaves. All come in an array of cultivars.

Hibiscus esculentus

Daucus carota

Ipomoea batatas

Helianthus tuberosus

Lactuca sativa (mignonette type)

Lycopersicon esculentum

Nasturtium officinale

Phaesolus vulgaris

Pastinacea sativa

Phaesolus coccineus

Pisum sativum

L. sativa var. *asparagina*
CELTUCE

A native of the Far East, this vegetable features an edible stem similar to a celery stalk and edible bright green, curled leaves. Sow seeds in late summer and autumn/fall. Ensure that the soil is rich in organic manure. Water the plants to keep them tender and hoe well. They will be ready to harvest 10 weeks after sowing.

LYCOPERSICON
esculentum
TOMATO

This native of South America was regarded with suspicion for centuries because of its infamous relative, the deadly nightshade. Its basic needs are sunshine, moist, well-drained soil and a frost-free area. In cold climates use a cloche to keep the soil warm. In open ground plant seedlings in rows 1 m (about 3 ft) apart and keep 30–60 cm (about 12–24 in) between each plant. Seedlings can be grown in windowsill pots and then gently planted out when 12 cm (about 5 in) high. It is essential that tomatoes are supported by stakes as they grow and are sheltered from strong winds. Prune secondary shoots and keep soil moist, mulching if necessary. Pick tomatoes when they are ripe. Beware of slugs and birds eating the ripe fruit.

NASTURTIUM
officinale
WATERCRESS

An aquatic plant, watercress will flourish in a damp, shaded corner of the garden as well as in a pond. Plant from cuttings 10 square cm (about 4 square in) apart in early autumn/fall. Make sure the soil has been thoroughly and deeply fertilized. Water thoroughly and constantly and prune the shoots to keep growth thick. Cut back any flowers that appear.

PASTINACEA
sativa
syn . *Peucadeneum officinale, P. sativum*
PARSNIP

A hardy root vegetable which is related to the carrot, parsnip is nutritious and sweet and able to be grown year round in warm climates and mid-spring in cold climates. It needs a sunny position and deep, fertile soil. The roots tend to divide in stony soil so ensure that the soil is stone free before sowing. Water well in dry weather and thin out the weak seedlings. Hoe or mulch to keep weeds off. Harvest when the leaves start to yellow. Watch for slugs, canker, celery fly or greenfly.

PHAESOLUS
BEANS

This genus, native to the warm-temperate to tropical regions of the Americas, contains more than 20 species of mostly twining climbers. Beans are grown for their edible pods and seeds. Frost-tender, they grow best in enriched, well-drained soil. They are also suitable for planting in tubs and flowerbeds.

P. coccineus
SCARLET RUNNER BEANS

This vigorous climber comes in different varieties and can grow up to 3.5 m (about 10½ ft) high. It needs a rich, deep, slightly acid soil in a sheltered position. Sow seeds in late spring in double rows 5 cm (about 2 in) deep and 30 cm (about 12 in) apart. Water well in dry weather. Pick the bean pods when they reach 12–17 cm (about 5–7 in) long. Watch for slugs. The plants are perennial and can be kept for several years, though they bear most heavily in their first year.

P. vulgaris
FRENCH BEANS

The annual French beans, known as kidney beans, string beans or haricot beans, come in dwarf or climbing varieties that need staking. They prefer a warm, rich soil in a sunny, sheltered spot. Mulch with straw to keep off weeds and to keep the soil moist. Harvest 10 to 12 weeks after sowing, picking every 2 to 3 days. Watch for slugs. There are many varieties available, with strings and without.

PISUM
sativum
PEA, BUSH AND CLIMBING VARIETIES

There is an enormous range of peas, from the bush type which is good for humid climates; tall climbing plants which need trellising to the newer snap pea that can be eaten when immature or fully developed. Peas need a sunny, well-drained, rich, previously manured soil bed that contains some lime and dolomite for a good yield. Plant seedlings 5 cm (about 2 in) apart in rows 10 cm (about 4 in) apart. When the seedlings are 8 cm (about 3 in) high stake them with short twigs. The tall varieties will need wire or plastic netting to support them as they grow. Keep weeds down and water when dry. Pick the pods from the lower stems. Watch for mildew, mites and blight.

P. sativum var. *macrocarpum*
SNOW PEA, MANGETOUT PEA

This variety prefers a temperate climate and a moist sandy soil. Sow 5 cm (about 2 in) deep when the garden is likely to be frost-free. Use a trellis for climbing varieties. Pick the pods when they are still immature. The pod as well as the peas are eaten.

PSALLIOTA
campestris
syn. *Agaricus campestris*
MUSHROOM

This common fungus is happy to grow indoors or outdoors, under houses or in sheds, as long as it is dark, dry and the temperature is constant, ideally between 10–13°C (about 50–55°F). The mushroom lives on different sorts of compost, and home gardeners can either buy a mushroom kit or prepare their own compost full of well-rotted manure. Plant mushroom spawn in lumps 2 cm (about 1 in) deep and 25 cm (about 10 in) apart. Keep moist and humid at this stage. After 2 weeks cover the compost with a layer of soil (this is called casing) which must be pre-sterilized to avoid the lethal fungus diseases that prey on mushrooms. Do not firm it down, keep it moist but not soaking. Mushrooms will appear 3 weeks after casing. Pick them by twisting out, not pulling.

RAPHANUS
sativus
RADISH

Eaten by Egyptian slaves, the ancient Chinese and much favoured by the modern Japanese, the well-travelled radish has a winter variety, usually cooked, and a summer variety which is used in salads. The summer radish is easily and quickly grown in a rich, moist soil out of full sun. Sow directly into rows 30 cm (about 12 in) apart and thin out seedlings so that the roots aren't competing. In hot weather keep well watered. Harvest 4 weeks after sowing in warm climates. In cooler climates wait for a further 3 weeks. Don't leave in the ground too long as they turn woody. Keep birds away from the young leaves.

RHEUM
rhabarbarum
RHUBARB

There are numerous varieties of this plant that can supply the home gardener with edible stems for a good 4 to 10 years. It is best grown from roots in a fertile, phosphorous-rich soil. Choose a cool position and plant the roots firmly with 90 cm (about 36 in) between each row and each plant. Leave it to get established in the first year and start harvesting in the second and third years, making sure not to pull off too many sticks as this will weaken further production. Ensure that all flowers are removed and feed with

fertilizer after harvesting. Eat only the stalks as the leaves are poisonous. Watch for brown rot.

RUMEX
acetosella
SORREL

This is a low-growing perennial with pale green, oval-shaped leaves and yellow-red flowers. French sorrel used to be eaten in the same way as spinach, but sorrel's tart flavour is more suitable for sauces, salads or in soups. Sow in spring or plant from divisions, leaving 30 cm (about 12 in) between each plant. Remove flowers to encourage new growth. Do not eat too much sorrel as it contains oxalic acid which is toxic in large amounts.

SOLANUM

A Central and South American genus of great horticultural importance. *Solanum* includes the egg-plant and the potato, and used to include the tomato too, though it is now usually given a genus of its own *Lycopersicon*. There are several ornamental species and many tropical weeds, but they should be approached with caution as it is the exception rather than the rule for them to be edible.

S. melongena
AUBERGINE, EGGPLANT

This tropical vegetable native to Asia has large, purple fruit. It is a relative of the potato and tomato, and needs warm conditions and low level humidity. Cloches should be used in cold climates to protect young plants. Plant seedlings in spring in well-drained soil which is frost-free. The rows should be 1 m (about 3 ft) apart with 60 cm (about 24 in) between each seedling. Feed young plants with liquid fertilizer but stop as soon as fruit develops. Prune away any secondary shoots to increase fruit size. Harvest the fruit if it gives slightly when squeezed. Watch for verticillium wilt.

S. tuberosum
POTATO

Native to South America and one of the most widely eaten vegetables, the potato was preceded to the Western world by the sweet potato. It was grown as a delicacy until the nineteenth century but can now be bought in all sorts of varieties. Potatoes can be scatter grown throughout the garden. Prepare the soil with well-rotted manure or compost. Plant tubers when the soil is frost-free, usually late summer in cool climates or late winter in hot climates. If planting in rows keep them 30 cm (about 12 in) apart and cover with 8 cm (about 3 in) of soil.

For best results plant in sloped mounds for good drainage. Protect shoots from frost with straw or soil. Do not expose potatoes to the light as they will turn green and toxic. (They can be restored by putting them in the dark for a couple of weeks.) Harvest in dry conditions with a fork when foliage turns yellow. Watch for aphids.

Solanum melongena

Rheum rhabarbarum

Pisum sativum var. *macrocarpum*

Solanum tuberosum

Rumex acetosella

Psalliota campestris

Raphanus sativus

Zea mays

Valerianella locusta

Spinacia oleracea

Taraxacum officinale

Tetragonia expansa

Vicia faba

Tragopogon porrifolius

SPINACIA
oleracea
ENGLISH SPINACH

Native to the Middle-East and partial to cool climates, spinach can be a challenge to grow well. It prefers well-drained soil and a cool position in the garden, so find a spot in part-shade and dig in generous amounts of manure. Sow in autumn/fall or in spring in cool climates, spacing plants 10 cm (about 4 in) apart. Keep the soil free of weeds and well watered so that the plant will not run to seed. Harvest the first leaves 8 weeks after sowing and then as needed. Watch for chewing insects and downy mildew.

TARAXACUM
officinale
DANDELION

Regarded highly in Europe, but as an uninteresting weed in Australia, these plants feature toothed leaves, large yellow flowers and round seed heads. The roots, flowers and leaves are all edible. Grow scattered in the lawn or any corner of the garden. For a good, juicy plant ensure the soil is rich and moist. Sow in early summer 30 cm (about 12 in) apart. Cut off the flowers when plants have matured and harvest the roots in autumn/fall.

TETRAGONIA
expansa
syn. T. tetragonioides
NEW ZEALAND SPINACH

Sir Joseph Banks brought this plant back to England from New Zea-

land, but it became more popular in the USA and Europe. Unlike true spinach, it prefers warm summers and a humus-rich soil. Soften the seeds overnight and sow them in groups of 3 in spring, making sure to leave 90 cm (about 36 in) between each group. Thin the weaker seedlings out and keep weeds away from the remaining young plants. Water regularly and harvest the leaves as they are needed.

TRAGOPOGON
porrifolius
SALSIFY

Also known as the oyster plant, this plant belongs to the daisy family and is valued for its edible, white tap roots. It prefers a light soil free from stones. It grows best in temperate climates. Sow the large seeds in lots of 3 in spring. Keep 20 cm (about 8 in) between each group and 30 cm (about 12 in) between each row. Mulch with compost to keep weeds down and water to maintain moisture. Harvest the root from autumn/fall onwards. It can be baked, roasted, boiled or made into soup. It is fairly pest and disease free.

VALERIANELLA
locusta
CORN SALAD

Rampant in corn fields in cool to cold climates and a hardy grower, this is a good substitute for lettuce in winter. Sow the seeds in late summer and early autumn/fall in a sunny spot in the garden. Place seeds 25 cm (about 10 in) apart.

Make sure the soil is lightly raked and forked. Ideally it should be situated where another crop was previously grown. Keep the soil moist and harvest the leaves as they are needed. Watch for slugs. There are two types, not always labelled distinctly by seedsmen: one forms loose hearts like a small lettuce, the other just makes clumps of loose leaves. Both are equally good eating.

VICIA
faba
BROAD BEANS

A good source of protein, the broad bean is native to the Mediterranean and Far East. It prefers a temperate climate and a sunny position in rich, well-drained soil, preferably where no beans were previously grown. Ensure good bean production by digging in organic fertilizer some weeks before sowing. Sow seeds in mid-autumn/fall in double rows 20 cm (about 8 in) apart and leave 10 cm (about 4 in) between each plant. In cold climates sowing can be left until early spring. Shelter seedlings from the wind with stakes.

Make sure that the soil is not too wet as this may encourage root rot. Beans are ready to be picked 2 or 3 months after planting. Do not wait until the pods are too large or they will be tough and unappetizing. Broad beans are vulnerable to aphids.

ZEA
mays
SWEET CORN, MAIZE, MEALY

With its origins in ancient Mexico, sweet corn has had an uphill battle to win a place on the dinner table in Europe, where it has been seen more as fodder than human fare. Corn needs an open, spacious position and is a dramatic addition to the home garden. It likes a nitrogen and lime-rich soil and needs hot weather to grow well. Sow in early summer in short rows 60 cm (about 24 in) apart. Weed gently and water thoroughly in really dry weather. Tie the stems to stakes as they grow taller and be sure to keep the soil firm around the plant base. Harvest when the corn kernels are yellow by twisting the cobs firmly from the stem.

HERBS

ALLIUM

See genus entry under Vegetables, page 336.

A. sativum
GARLIC

There are two main types of garlic. The mauve flowered variety known as 'Giant Russian' (*A. giganteum*) or 'Jumbo' is very much larger and milder than the more potent, small or common garlic (*A. sativum*), which has dainty white flowers. Individual cloves are planted 5 cm (about 2 in) deep in autumn/fall in warmer areas or in spring where there is a frost-risk. Good drainage, a rich organic soil and a sunny position are its requirements. Garlic will take up to 5 or 6 months to mature. Tall flower stalks should be removed for better flavour. Harvest when the leaves have turned yellow and fallen over. Handle gently to avoid bruising and allow to dry off and harden thoroughly before storage. Garlic planted near roses enhances their perfume and helps to keep aphids away. For at least 5000 years garlic has been used for culinary, medicinal and strength-giving purposes as well as a plague preventative and charm against vampires and witchcraft.

A. schoenoprasum
CHIVES

Chives are grown for their narrow, cylindrical leaves which are used for flavouring and garnishing savoury dishes. It is a hardy, perennial plant which grows up to 25 cm (about 10 in) high in small, neat clumps. It bears numerous balls of mauve flowers in late spring and summer which are edible and can be added to salads. Chives do best in a fertile, well-drained soil in full sun or part-shade and should be kept well watered. They are easily grown by seed or division of small bulbs. Bulbs should be spaced about 10 cm (about 4 in) apart because they will quickly multiply and develop into clumps. Lift and divide the clumps every 2 or 3 years to invigorate the tufts. Chives make an attractive edging for the herb garden and can be grown in window boxes, troughs and flower pots. Frequent cutting stimulates fresh, bushy growth and tenderer leaves.

ALOYSIA
triphylla
syn.   *Lippia citriodora*
LEMON VERBENA

This wonderfully fragrant perennial shrub from South America is valued for its delicious, lemon scented leaves. It grows up to 3 m (about 9 ft) and is partly deciduous in winter. Very small, white or lilac flowers are borne at the ends of the stems in late summer and autumn/fall. Half-hardy, it is best positioned in full sun in a warm, sheltered position. It prefers a well-drained, fertile soil and needs regular watering in summer. Propagate from soft tip cuttings in spring or semi-hardwood cuttings in summer. Lemon verbena is commercially cultivated for its fragrant oil used in the cosmetics industry. The leaves are also used to flavour tea. Dried leaves retain their scent exceptionally well and are an excellent potpourri ingredient.

ANDROPOGON
nardus
syn.   *Cymbopogon citratus*
LEMON GRASS

This aromatic, grass-like plant has very long, grey-green leaves reaching to 2 m (about 6 ft). From the tropics, it does best in warm climates where it will multiply readily and quickly form large clumps, so allow plenty of space for spreading. A rich soil, good drainage, full sun and plenty of water are its requirements. It is frost-tender. Propagate by division. The fleshy white part at the base of the plant is used in South-East Asian cooking and is best when fresh. The leaves are used fresh or dried to make a herbal tea.

ANETHUM
graveolens
DILL

This deliciously aromatic annual grows to about 1.5 m (about 4½ ft) high with pretty, feathery, thread-like leaves. Yellow flowers are borne on umbels in summer followed by the pungent dill seeds. Fully hardy, dill requires a humus-rich, well-drained soil and a sunny position. The seed is best sown in spring where it is to grow, as seedlings are difficult to transplant. Both the leaves and seeds are used as flavourings. Since earliest times the seeds have been used to aid digestion.

ANGELICA
archangelica
ANGELICA

A fast-growing, robust biennial, angelica grows to 2 m (about 6 ft) high and will live longer if emerging flowerheads are removed before the seed develops. It has handsome, deeply divided, bright green leaves and umbels of small, green or white flowers in late summer. It is frost-hardy. Soil should preferably be rich, moist and well-drained. It does best in filtered sunlight with protection from strong winds. Propagate from seed in late summer. The roots, leaves, stalks and seeds of angelica are all used in cooking and for flavouring. The young stems are crystallized for confectionery decoration. The seeds, stems and roots are used to flavour liqueurs such as chartreuse, Benedictine and vermouth.

Allium schoenoprasum

Anethum graveolens

Aloysia triphylla

Angelica archangelica

Andropogon nardus

Allium sativum

ARTEMISIA
dracunculus
TARRAGON

Essential in French cuisine, tarragon is grown for its narrow, aromatic leaves which have a delicate, peppery aniseed flavour. Halfhardy, it grows up to 1 m (about 3 ft) high in the warmer months then dies back to a perennial rootstock over winter. Full sun and a fertile, well-drained soil are its requirements. As it produces no seed,

Coriandrum sativum

propagate by division in early spring. The tarragon seed sometimes offered is the flavourless *A. dracunculordes* known as Russian tarragon. Tarragon loses most of its flavour during drying. Before the plant dies down for a winter's rest, gather the leaves and make tarragon vinegar and butter.

BORAGO
officinalis
BORAGE

This decorative, annual herb is grown for its cucumber flavoured leaves and pretty, lilac, star-shaped flowers. It grows to around 75 cm (about 30 in) high and bears clusters of nodding flowers in spring and summer. Fully hardy, it requires full sun to part-shade, good drainage and a light, porous soil. Propagate from seed in spring. Protect from snails. The fresh young leaves are used raw in salads and cool drinks or cooked with vegetables. The edible, blue flowers have been used to decorate salads from the early seventeenth century. Flowers may also be crystallized for cake decoration. It used to be said that eating borage flowers gave you courage.

CARUM
carvi
CARAWAY

Since ancient Egyptian times, caraway has been cultivated for its condiment and medicinal properties. It is an attractive biennial plant growing to 60 cm (about 24 in) high

with finely cut, lacy leaves rather like its relative the parsley. In its second year small, white flowers are produced in umbels, followed in late summer by a crop of seeds. Fully hardy, it will grow well in a light, moist, but well-drained soil in full sun. Propagate from seed in early autumn/fall in mild winter areas or in spring. The small black seeds are used to flavour cakes, breads, sauces and pickles. Their flavour is best when dried. Caraway has also been used as an ingredient of love potions, to prevent pigeons from straying and as protection from witches.

CHAMAEMELUM
nobile
CHAMOMILE

This is a delightfully aromatic, matforming perennial which grows to 30 cm (about 12 in) tall and has fine, bright green leaves and masses of small, white daisies in spring, summer and autumn/fall. Nonflowering varieties are used in chamomile lawns. Fully hardy, it grows best in full sun in a moist, but well-drained fertile soil. It creeps along the ground by runners which take root as they spread. Propagate by division or from seed in spring. Dried chamomile flowers can be used in potpourri, sleep pillows, hair rinses and facials. Renowned as a herbal tea, chamomile has been credited with the power to treat dyspepsia, flatulent colic, fever, stomach cramps, wounds, swelling and also calluses.

CORIANDRUM
sativum
CORIANDER

This herb is grown mainly for its seed and aromatic leaves, although in Thai cuisine the whole of the coriander plant, including the roots, is used. Coriander is a fast-growing annual reaching to 75 cm (about 30 in) high with parsley-like leaves and umbels of tiny, white flowers in summer. The flowers are followed by small, round, aromatic seeds. Fully hardy, it requires a light, welldrained soil and full sun. Propagate from seed in early spring. Fresh leaves will provide an exotic tang in Asian dishes. The dried seeds are used in curry powders, chutneys, confectionery, cakes and sauces.

CUMINUM
cyminum
CUMIN

Cumin is grown commercially in India, China, Japan and the Middle East for its powerfully flavoured seeds. It is a small annual which grows to 30 cm (about 12 in) high with finely divided leaves and small, white flowers in summer, followed by aromatic seeds. It is frost-tender and grows best in warm climates. Grow in a light, well-drained soil in a sunny position. Propagate from seed sown in spring in a warm situation. The dried seed is an important ingredient in curry powders. Both the Dutch and Germans flavour cheese with it, and it is used in many Mexican and Middle Eastern dishes.

Artemisia dracunculus

Carum carvi

Chamaemelum nobile

Borago officinalis

CURCUMA
domestica
syn. *C. longa*
TURMERIC

A tropical member of the ginger family, turmeric is grown for its bright orange, underground stems or rhizomes. This perennial herb can grow to 1 m (about 3 ft) in hot areas. It forms clumps of lance-shaped leaves and dense clusters of pale yellow flowers in summer. Frost-tender, it prefers the warmth of tropical regions but can be successfully grown in warm-temperate areas. It requires a rich, moist, well-drained soil and lots of sun. Propagate by division. Turmeric has been used in the East since antiquity. The dried root provides colour and pungent fragrance to chutneys, pickles and curry powders; it is harvested when the foliage begins to dry off in autumn/fall. It is used as a substitute for saffron (*Crocus sativas*) the world's most expensive spice and one very rarely grown in home gardens.

ELETTARIA
cardamomum
CARDAMOM

An important and pungent oriental spice, cardamom seeds come from a perennial shrub which originated in southern India. It grows to 3 m (about 9 ft) tall and has large, dark green, lance-shaped leaves. The flowering stems spread horizontally near the ground and bear small, yellow flowers during spring. These are followed by grey-green, oblong pods which contain dark reddish brown seeds. Frost-tender, cardamom is for tropical and warm regions only where it requires a rich, moist soil and a shaded position. The seed pods are gathered before they ripen and are then dried before storage. Seeds should be left in the pods until required for use. Propagate by division. Cardamom is used in curry powders, pastries, baked apples and fruit salads. It is often served in coffee in the Middle East.

FOENICULUM
vulgare
FENNEL

Common fennel is a tall, graceful perennial which grows to 2 m (about 6 ft) with thick, glossy stems, masses of feathery foliage and flat clusters of yellow flowers on tall, erect stems during summer. The flowers are followed by aromatic, brown seeds. Bronze fennel is similar but has rich bronzy green leaves and grows to around 1.5 m (about 4½ ft) high. Half-hardy, in cool climates it will die back to the roots over winter and is sometimes grown as an annual. It prefers full

Foeniculum vulgare var. *dulce*

Hyssopus officinalis

sun to part-shade, a rich, alkaline, well-drained soil and regular watering during dry periods. Propagate from seed in mid- to late spring. Both the leaves and seeds have a pleasant aniseed flavour and are used for flavouring fish and other savoury dishes. The seeds are also used in breads and biscuits.

F. vulgare var. dulce
FLORENCE FENNEL, FINOCCHIO

Florence fennel is distinct from common fennel in having a pronounced swelling at the base of the leaves where the stems overlap. It is an annual and needs to be grown from seed each year. Culture conditions are similar to common fennel. The crisp, white bulb, with the texture of celery, is cooked as a vegetable or grated raw for salads.

GLYCYRRHIZA
glabra
LIQUORICE

This perennial, native to southern Europe, is grown commercially for the juice of its sweet roots, used in the production of liquorice. The plant has large, mid-green leaves

Foeniculum vulgare

and bears pea-like, bluish purple and white flowers on short upright spikes in late summer. It grows to a height and spread of 1 m (about 3 ft). Fully hardy, it requires a sunny position and a deep, rich, moist but well-drained soil. Propagate from seed in autumn/fall or spring, or by division in spring.

HYSSOPUS
officinalis
HYSSOP

This bushy perennial grows to 60 cm (about 24 in) and has narrow, pointed, dark green leaves. Spikes of rich blue flowers, that are attractive to bees and butterflies, are borne in late summer. White and pink flowering forms are also available. Fully hardy, hyssop is evergreen in mild climates; in cool areas it dies down for the winter. It prefers a light, well-drained, alkaline soil and full sun. Propagate from seed, cuttings or by division in spring. The slightly bitter leaves are used in small quantities with fatty meats and fish. A tea made from the leaves is taken for respiratory complaints and to aid digestion.

Curcuma domestica

Elettaria cardamomum

Mentha × piperita

Mentha 'Citrata'

Levisticum officinale

Laurus nobilis

Lavandula angustifolia

Melissa officinalis

Juniperus communis

JUNIPERUS
communis
JUNIPER

An evergreen, bushy shrub or small tree, juniper grows to 3 m (about 9 ft). There are a number of ornamental forms in varying shapes, sizes and foliage colour. It has sharply pointed, needle-like leaves, small, yellow flowers and bears fleshy, green berries that take up to 3 years to ripen to black. To ensure berry production grow both male and female plants. Fully hardy, juniper requires excellent drainage and a sunny position. In warm climates provide a cool, moist root run. Propagate from semi-hardwood cuttings in late summer or early autumn/fall. The berries have a resinous flavour and are used to flavour gin. A few berries make an excellent addition to stews and stuffings for poultry.

LAURUS
nobilis
BAY

This medium-sized, evergreen tree which reaches 7 m (about 21 ft) is slow growing and can be kept in a pot for a number of years. It withstands clipping and makes an excellent topiary subject. Half-hardy, it can be grown in a tub and brought indoors where winters are frosty. In warm areas grow in a humus-rich, well-drained, sunny position. Protect from both dry winds and scorching sun in hot areas. Propagate from cuttings. Watch for scale insects. Bay leaves are best used fresh in cooking to flavour marinades, soups, sauces, stews and

meat dishes. Dried leaves may be used in cooking, though they lose flavour quickly; they add scent to potpourri.

LAVANDULA
angustifolia
syn. *L. officinalis*
LAVENDER

This beautiful, small, rounded shrub, native to southern Europe, is valued for its perfumed, lavender flowers and aromatic grey-green foliage. Fully hardy, it thrives in cool-temperate areas in a light, rather alkaline, well-drained soil. Grow in an open, sunny position to avoid fungal disease. Propagate from cuttings in autumn/fall or spring. The best quality essential oil is extracted from this plant, but many other species and varieties of lavender can be grown for their fragrant flowers. Dried lavender flowers are used in potpourri mixtures, lavender bags and moth repellent sachets. The herb can be used sparingly in cooking, but it is an acquired taste.

LEVISTICUM
officinale
LOVAGE

From southern Europe, this robust, coarse-growing perennial reaches 2 m (about 6 ft) tall and looks and tastes like a large celery. It has deeply lobed, dark green leaves, umbels of small, yellow flowers in summer and brown seeds which ripen in late summer or early autumn/fall. Fully hardy, it prefers a fairly cool climate and does best in full sun or part-shade in a rich, moist soil. Propagate by root division in spring or from seed in late summer. The stems are cooked and eaten and tender young leaves can be added to salads and savoury dishes. *Levisticum americanum* and *Ligusticum scoticum* are also called lovage.

MELISSA
officinalis
LEMON BALM

A native of southern Europe, this hardy perennial, 60 cm (about

24 in) high, is grown for its fresh, lemony scented and flavoured leaves. Small, white flowers that appear in late summer attract pollinating bees into the garden. Lemon balm will thrive in a rich, moist soil in full sun or part-shade. It is very hardy and spreads rapidly. It will die down in winter but shoot again in spring. Propagate from cuttings or by root division. The lemon-scented leaves are valued as a calming herbal tea. They will give a light, lemon flavour to fruit salads, jellies, iced tea and summer drinks, and can be used as an emergency substitute for lemon in cooking.

MENTHA
MINT

This is a large genus of herbs, some evergreen and some deciduous, from just about all the continents. They vary in size from tiny creeping ground covers to bushy plants about 40 cm (about 16 in) high, and in flavour from refreshing to so strong they must be used with circumspection. As a rule, they are frost-hardy, like sunshine and rich soil and need lots of moisture (poor drainage matters not at all) and are invasive growers, spreading rapidly by runners. To keep them from taking over, try growing them in large pots, watering regularly and repotting annually.

M. 'Citrata'
EAU DE COLOGNE MINT

Of garden origin and thought to be a variety of peppermint, this mint is too strong and bitter to use in cooking. It is grown for the delicious fragrance of its dark green leaves; perhaps the sweetest and most flower-like of any scented-leafed plant. It has purplish stems and mauve flowers in early summer. Like all the tribe it is a rampant spreader by underground runners.

M. × piperita
PEPPERMINT

This spreading perennial, grown for its aromatic foliage and culinary uses, grows to a height and spread of 60 cm (about 24 in). Spreading by means of underground stems, it forms a carpet of oval, toothed, mid-green and reddish green leaves. Purple flowers appear in spring. Plant this fully hardy herb in sun or shade in moist, well-drained soil. Propagate by division in spring or autumn/fall.

M. spicata
SPEARMINT

This fast-growing perennial, reaching 60 cm (about 24 ft), is the most popular mint used in cooking. It has crinkly, dark green leaves and as it has a tendency to put down roots all over the garden is often best grown in a separate bed or container. Fully hardy, it thrives in a sunny or partially shaded position in a moist, but well-drained soil. Plants should be cut back regularly to encourage fresh growth. Propagate by root division. This is the mint used in mint sauce, mint jelly and to flavour new potatoes and green peas. Fresh sprigs are used as a garnish in fruit drinks or desserts.

MONARDA
didyma
BERGAMOT, BEE BALM

Native to North America, this herb was used by the American Indians and early colonists as a tea. With its spidery flowers in white, pink or red borne in late summer, bergamot is one of the showiest of the culinary herbs. The showiest variety is 'Cambridge Scarlet'. It is a hardy perennial growing to 1 m (about 3 ft) tall with dark green, slightly toothed leaves that when crushed or brushed against emit an exotic, citrus-like scent. It prefers part-shade and a rich, moist soil with a cool root run in hot climates. Cut plants back periodically to keep compact. Propagate by division in spring. The young leaves may be used in salads, but mainly it is used as a soothing tea. Add a few leaves to China or Indian tea for an Earl Grey flavour.

NEPETA
cataria
CATNIP, CATMINT

A native of Europe, catnip is a hardy perennial with branching, upright stems growing up to 1 m (about 3 ft). It has aromatic, grey-green leaves and whorls of white flowers from late spring through to autumn/fall. Provide a light, rich soil in sun or part-shade and moderate water for best results. Cut back each year to prevent the plant from becoming straggly. Propagate by root division or from seed in spring. Cats are attracted to this plant and will lie in it or play in it and sometimes dig it up. Fortunately, their interest is only in the spring growth; once the plants start to flower they

lose interest. Its tea is said to be relaxing.

OCIMUM
basilicum
BASIL

A favourite with cooks, basil is one of the most widely used herbs in Mediterranean cooking. It is a tender, annual plant growing to 30 cm (about 12 in) with light green, oval leaves that have a delicious, warm, spicy fragrance. Small white flowers are carried in whorls towards the ends of the stems in late summer. Full sun and a moderately rich, moist, but well-drained soil are its requirements. Grow in a warm protected position. There are a number of varieties of basil including a compact small-leaf type; a crinkled, lettuce leaf variety and the beautiful 'Dark Opal' with rich purple stems and leaves. There are perennial varieties also, but their flavour is inferior. Regularly pinch back all basil plants to encourage bushy growth and to prevent them going to seed quickly. Propagate from seed sown when there is no frost. Watch for chewing insects or snails. Fresh leaves are best; freeze it for the winter; it loses flavour when dried.

ORIGANUM

Native to the Mediterranean region and parts of Europe and India, these frost-tender perennials are often grown as annuals in cooler climates. They like sun and rich, well-drained soil. Trim regularly and propagate from seed in spring or by root division.

O. hortensis
syn.   *Majorana hortensis*
SWEET MARJORAM

A highly aromatic plant up to 60 cm (about 24 in) high, marjoram is grown for its sweet and spicy, small, grey-green leaves. The flowers consist of tiny, white, knot-like clusters from which the plant gets another common name, knotted marjoram. Leaves are used fresh or dried for savoury foods and are said to aid digestion. Marjoram has a special affinity with tomatoes and goes well with many meats.

O. vulgare
OREGANO, WILD MARJORAM

A close relative of marjoram, oregano has a sharper, more pungent flavour. It has a sprawling habit and grows to 60 cm (about 24 in) high with dark green, oval leaves and small, white or pink flowers in summer. The leaves, fresh or dried, are used in many Mediterranean-inspired dishes. In Italy oregano is used in pizza toppings and pasta dishes.

Ocimum basilicum

Mentha spicata

Nepeta cataria

Monarda didyma

Origanum vulgare

Origanum hortensis

Salvia officinalis

Polygonum persicaria

Salvia elegans

Ruta graveolens

Rosmarinus officinalis

Petroselinum crispum

PETROSELINUM
crispum
PARSLEY

Cultivated for thousands of years for its flavour and health-giving properties, parsley is still one of the most popular herbs grown. It is a biennial plant which grows to 30 cm (about 12 in) high. The most commonly used are the curly-leaved form and the stronger, flat-leaved Italian variety. Parsley does best in full sun or light shade in warm climates. It likes a moist, well-drained position and regular feeding. For best flavour, harvest the leaves before the plant flowers. Propagate from seed. To speed up germination soak the seeds in warm water overnight before planting.

POLYGONUM
persicaria
VIETNAMESE MINT

A native of Indochina, this half-hardy, fast-growing perennial, 60 cm (about 24 in) high, has long, dark green leaves with a distinct hot, spicy taste. Pink flowers in slender spikes appear in late summer and autumn/fall. Vietnamese mint prefers partial shade, a rich soil and plenty of moisture. It can die back in winter frosts but will reshoot in spring. Propagate from cuttings or by division. The leaves are used as a garnish in many Vietnamese dishes including salads and soups. It is also used in other South-East Asian cooking.

ROSMARINUS
officinalis
ROSEMARY

A beautiful, aromatic shrub, rosemary has been cultivated for centuries for flavouring food and for medicine. It will grow to 1 m (about 3 ft) high, has resinous, narrow, needle-like leaves and small flowers in shades of mauve-blue, off and on all year. Half-hardy rosemary can be grown outdoors in warm climates, but should be taken in for winter where temperatures fall much below zero. In the garden it will flourish in a light, well-drained soil in a sheltered position with plenty of sun. It will withstand salt-laden air. Propagate from cuttings or by layering. Rosemary leaves can be used fresh or dried to flavour meat dishes, chicken, fish and vegetables. Dried branches can be used in wreath-making and leaves in potpourri.

RUTA
graveolens
RUE

One of the bitter herbs used for warding off insects and disease, rue is also one of the most decorative herbs with its very pretty, grey-green, lacy leaves. It is a hardy perennial growing 60 cm (about 24 in) high with clusters of small yellow-green flowers in summer. Grow in a slightly alkaline, well-drained soil in full sun. Protect from strong winds and severe frost in cold climates. Trim after flowering. Propagate by division in spring or from stem cuttings in late summer. The leaves and flowers are used in small posies. Rue has been used in the past for medicinal purposes, but can be dangerous if taken in large doses and during pregnancy.

SALVIA

This mainly northern hemisphere genus includes an enormous number of species. Almost all are aromatic and many are grown just for their brightly coloured flowers (see chapter 'Annuals & Perennials'). The following are the most important kitchen species.

S. elegans
syn. S. rutilans
PINEAPPLE SAGE

This half-hardy shrub reaches 1 m (about 3 ft) and is grown for its light green foliage which has a distinct pineapple scent and flavour. Its whorls of red flowers are borne in late summer and autumn/fall. This species is frost-tender so winter protection is needed in cool climates. It likes full sun and a moist, well-drained soil. Propagate from cuttings. Leaves are used in fruit salads, summer drinks and tea.

S. officinalis
SAGE

Sage is a decorative, frost-hardy perennial plant which grows to 60 cm (about 24 in) high, with downy, grey-green, oval leaves and mauve-blue flowers on tall spikes during summer. There are several forms of sage, those with plum-red leaves, greenish-purple variegated leaves, tricoloured leaves and golden variegated leaves. All are attractive and edible. Grow in an open, sunny, well-drained position. In hot areas plants are best in light shade. Trim frequently, but never into hard wood, to keep shapely. Propagate from cuttings. Sage is highly valued for its medicinal qualities and has been used for centuries for curing all manner of ailments and is reputed to give longevity to those who use it.

SATUREJA

Native to the Mediterranean, savory was much loved by the Ancient Greeks and Romans for the refreshing flavour. Among many of its uses savory is added to dishes featuring mildly flavoured meats like chicken and pork.

S. hortensis
SUMMER SAVORY

This bushy annual grows 40 cm (about 16 in) high and has narrow, dark green leaves and pale lavender flowers in late summer. Grow in a humus-rich, well-drained soil in full sun and provide plenty of water. Propagate from seed in spring where it is to grow. The leaves have a sweet, spicy flavour with a hint of thyme and are traditionally used as a flavouring for bean dishes. Use also to flavour vinegar, salad dressings and butter.

S. montana
WINTER SAVORY

A low, spreading perennial which grows to 30 cm (about 12 in), winter savory has dark green, pointed leaves and tiny white flowers with pink markings in summer. Winter savory prefers a light, well-drained, alkaline soil and less moisture than summer savory. It may need winter protection in cold climates. It benefits from regular cutting back to stimulate fresh growth and prevent legginess. Propagate by division or from cuttings. It makes a good edging or border plant and is often grown to attract bees. The leaves, sharper and more peppery than summer savory, are used to flavour meat casseroles and roasts.

SYMPHYTUM
officinale
COMFREY

This robust, clump-forming perennial grows to 1 m (about 3 ft) with large, lance-shaped leaves and clusters of pretty, mauve, pendent flowers in late spring and summer. Grow in part-shade and a humus-rich, well-drained soil. It may die down to the roots in cold areas. Propagate by root division. It is an excellent companion plant in the garden, where it keeps the surrounding soil rich and moist. Wilted leaves are used as a mulch and when added to the compost heap will help activate decomposition. In the Middle Ages, comfrey's chief claim to fame was its ability to aid in knitting fractured and broken bones. It is mildly poisonous if eaten in sufficient quantities.

THYMUS
THYME

No herb garden should be without at least one variety of thyme. There are many species and varieties, all are perennials with tiny, aromatic leaves and small flower spikes that appear at the end of the stems during summer. Thyme likes a light, well-drained soil and full sun if possible. It is generally hardy once established but may need winter protection in very cold areas. Keep well trimmed for compact growth. Propagate by division or layer stems. Historically thyme has been associated with courage, strength, happiness and well-being.

T. × citriodorus
LEMON-SCENTED THYME

This delightful, rounded shrub grows 30 cm (about 12 in) high and has tiny, oval, lemon-scented leaves and pale lilac flowers. Leaves are used fresh or dry in poultry stuffings or to add lemon flavour to fish, meat and vegetables.

T. vulgaris
COMMON THYME

This is the most popular culinary thyme, producing the strongest aromatic leaves. It grows to 30 cm (about 12 in) high. The tiny, mid-green leaves are used in vinegars, butters and to flavour a variety of meat or vegetable dishes. Thyme tea is used to aid digestion, sore throats and coughs.

ZINGIBER
officinale
GINGER

Originating in southern Asia, this tender, perennial plant is grown for its spicy, tuberous roots. It can reach up to 2 m (about 6 ft) high in hot areas, has long, lance-shaped leaves and bears spikes of white flowers with purple streaks in summer. Ginger prefers the warmth of tropical regions but can be successfully grown outdoors in warm, frost-free, temperate areas. A humus-rich, well-drained soil and light shade are its requirements. Propagate from small pieces of root cuttings. The fresh root is peeled and finely chopped or grated and used to flavour many Asian dishes, curries and chutneys. Dried and powdered ginger is used in sweet dishes and cakes. It is often recommended as a therapeutic infusion for colds and travel sickness, and was once thought to safeguard against marauding tigers.

Zingiber officinale

Thymus × citriodorus

Satureja hortensis

Symphytum officinale

Thymus vulgaris

Saturëja montana

CHAPTER 8

*Fruit Trees, Nut Trees
& Other Fruits*

*S*cholars have been arguing for centuries over the identity of the most famous fruit tree of all, the one that caused so much trouble for Adam and Eve. Tradition says it was an apple; some learned people say no, it was an apricot; still others point out that it was called the Tree of Knowledge, a species rarely met with now.

Let us leave them to it and content ourselves with the thought that the author of *Genesis* knew what he was about when he described the chief attraction of the garden of Eden as its fruit trees, with no mention of lawns, flowers or other frivolities.

There are few things so delightful as picking your own fruit, and if it comes from a tree you planted yourself the pleasure is all the greater. The delight won't be just at harvest time either: fruit trees tend to be comely in habit and often beautiful in flower. And few are large, so they take up little space.

Choosing a Fruit Tree

They can be classed into two broad groups: the tropical fruits, members of several plant families, mainly evergreen, and often rather stately growers; and the temperate fruits, deciduous and almost all cousins of the rose. The citrus are a kind of link between the two; evergreen and with members that like hot climates and others that don't mind it coolish. Which to choose? Your own favourite, that goes without saying; but you need to take your climate into account. There is no joy in pining after mangoes if you suffer frost or cherries if you can't provide them with the cold winters they need. Then, there is no point in growing just any sort of variety. Just about all types of fruit have been bred and improved by gardeners for centuries, and come in a bewildering number of varieties. Some of the tropical types (citrus too) can be easily grown from seed, but seedling trees almost always turn out inferior. Insist on a top-quality named cultivar, and check that it is suited to your purpose. (Apples, for

instance, come in 'dessert' and 'cooking' varieties, and so do mangoes, cherries and bananas.) It sometimes happens that the very choicest varieties are rather weak growers and therefore not popular with orchardists; but why grow an ordinary pear that you can buy at the greengrocer's when you could have the incomparable 'Doyenne du Comice'?

The named varieties are almost always grafted, and you may be offered the same one on several different understocks. Usually this is because by choice of a more or less vigorous stock you can tailor the final size of the tree, but sometimes one stock will be better than another in different soils. If in doubt, ask your supplier for advice, bearing in mind that bigger isn't necessarily better—you may prefer to have two smaller trees instead of one large one. That way you might have both a dessert and a cooking apple, or have an early-ripening variety and one that ripens later to spread your crop. (You can indeed buy ultra-dwarf strains of such fruit as apples and peaches, which are great if your gardening is confined

Malus domestica 'Red Delicious', an excellent dessert apple.

to containers on an apartment balcony: but their crop is proportionately tiny too.)

With some of the temperate fruits, notably apples, pears and sweet cherries, you need two trees in any case, as they are not 'self-fertile'—the flowers must receive the pollen of a different variety or there will be no fruit. Not that pollinating insects respect fences; the spouse tree could be in the garden of a co-operative neighbour. Or you might graft a branch of a compatible variety onto your main tree, being careful not to accidentally prune it off later.

Then, before you make your final choice, check with your local Department or Ministry of Agriculture whether your favourites are subject to pests or diseases which you are required by law to spray against. Alas, the number of enemies of fruit is legion (indeed, in different countries there are different enemies), and neglected backyard fruit trees can be a potent source of infestation not only to the neighbours' trees but to commercial orchards—which is why the law takes an interest. The Agriculture people can give you all the details, but take heart—the job isn't as burdensome as all that, and there will be some fruit that you can grow that doesn't suffer unduly from problems.

'Valencia' is the best known variety of Citrus sinensis, *the sweet orange.*

Growing Fruit Trees

Almost all fruit trees need sun and fertile soil, and are best if they don't suffer undue drought while the fruit is ripening. They benefit too from some fertilizer in spring, but there is no need to grow them in mulched beds like vegetables; they can be grown in association with flowers and shrubs, in any way that suits your garden design. Careful and regular pruning will control the size of the tree and increase its fruitfulness, but you only have to come across some ancient apple tree, untouched by the shears for years yet groaning with fruit, to realize that pruning is optional. Most warm climate fruits need little pruning in any case. A specialised form of pruning is training the tree espalier, that is flat against a wall. The idea was originally that the warmth reflected from the masonry encourages the fruit to ripen earlier. It is a lot of work, as you will need to prune each year, but worth doing if you are short on space or want to grow a variety which is on the borderline of hardiness in your climate. (Peaches and figs, for instance, are

almost always grown against walls in Britain, and mangoes and loquats are trained similarly elsewhere.) Choose a tree grafted on a 'dwarfing' rootstock or it will be too vigorous.

All the above applies to nut trees too; after all they are just fruit trees, but we eat a different part of the fruit—the seeds rather than the fleshy covering. They aren't so popular, perhaps because we tend to regard nuts as an occasional luxury, but they are well worth growing, and the crop keeps without having to be preserved. As a group, they are less subject to pests and need less care generally.

Not all fruit grows on trees. There are those that grow on vines, of which the grape is the supreme example, others being the kiwifruit or Chinese gooseberry and the granadilla, sometimes called the passionfruit and a great favourite in warm climates. All are great for covering fences and pergolas, and all are handsome plants. However selection of varieties is just as important as ever, especially with grapes; not only are varieties specially designed for wine, for

eating fresh or for making raisins, they have very marked likes and dislikes about climate. All the vine fruit need regular pruning to keep them under control, but no more than any other vigorous climber does.

Then there are the bush fruits, fruit shrubs rather than fruit trees. They can be the answer if you are short on space (although most like cool climates) and they are well worth growing, as their fruit tends to be soft and easily damaged on the way to market. Grow your own, and you can have the very best. This is particularly true of strawberries, everyone's favourite—and everyone can grow them, for this is a creeping perennial, to be tucked in at the front of any convenient bed or even in containers.

When is a fruit not a fruit? When it is a vegetable. The tomato is a fruit, but the plant is an annual to be grown in the vegetable patch rather than the orchard; and the fruit a savoury one, for main course dishes rather than dessert. The same is true of zucchini, capsicums, squashes, even melons. Everyone calls them vegetables, and so shall we.

Annona squamosa

Ceratonia siliqua

FRUIT TREES AND NUT TREES

ANNONA
squamosa
CUSTARD APPLE, SUGAR APPLE

There are many varieties of the custard apple, a popular fruit that originated in the tropical regions of Africa, Asia and the Americas. Its flowers are pale green and pleasantly scented. The large fruit has a custard-like texture and is delicious when eaten fresh. This is a semi-deciduous tree growing to 5 m (about 15 ft). Plant in a warm, sheltered position as the fruit yield may be damaged by low temperatures and the tree itself is frost-tender. Propagate by grafting.

ARAUCARIA
bidwillii
BUNYA BUNYA

From a genus of conifers native only to the South Pacific region, this 25 m (about 80 ft) tall tree has a short, stout trunk and massive, scaly branches that make it too large for a small city garden. The fruit grows high up, is the size of a pineapple and has the appearance of a fat, green pine cone. Keep young trees moist at the base and clear of weeds and grass. This is a slow-growing, frost-hardy tree which will fruit only after 10 or more years. Australian Aborigines considered its dark red seeds to be a delicacy. Propagate from seed (germination takes 12 months). Eat the nuts fresh, roasted or boiled or they may be ground into flour for cakes.

CARICA
papaya
PAWPAW

This is an evergreen, frost-tender tree, native to South and Central America, which grows to 8 m (about 24 ft) high and is topped with a cluster of large, deep-lobed leaves that drop away as the soft stem grows up. Plant where it will receive lots of warmth and shelter in a well-drained, moist, organic soil.

Carya illinoinensis

Castanea sativa

Araucaria bidwillii

Carica papaya

The large fruit, which weighs up to 2 kg (about 4½ lb), will reduce in size after 4 years of harvesting. Before picking the fruit let it ripen as long as possible on the branch. Propagate from seed and plant the seedlings in summer, watering regularly. Watch for powdery mildew, fruit rot (especially if the tree is in a warm-temperate climate and exposed position) and fruit bugs.

CARYA
illinoinensis
PECAN

A native of the USA, and from the same family as the walnut, the pecan tree's large size may make it impractical for the average garden. The nuts have a smooth, brown shell and a large kernel. Moderately frost-hardy, these trees prefer a dry-summer climate and because of their large taproot need deep, well-drained soil. The fruit will fall early if there is insufficient water or nutrition. Prune the young tree to encourage it to grow to a single, upright stem. Once they are collected, nuts should dry out for several weeks before they are stored. Watch for elephant beetle, bark weevil or pecan scab.

CASTANEA
sativa
SPANISH CHESTNUT, SWEET CHESTNUT

This fully hardy, deciduous Mediterranean native is valued for its timber, shade and edible fruit which is delicious roasted. It grows slowly to 15 m (about 50 ft), with dark green foliage and an open crown. The leaves, which turn brown in autumn/fall, are egg-shaped and heavily serrated, 12–20 cm (about 5–8 in) long, with a hairy underside. Creamy golden, malodorous flowers bloom in early to mid-spring. In late summer to early spring, glossy brown chestnuts develop inside spiny, spherical pods. This species enjoys warm summers and a rich, well-drained, acid soil, otherwise it can be prone to root rot. Propagate mainly from seed in autumn/fall. It is prone to chestnut blight and has a tendency to sucker. The tree is very long lived and some English specimens were reputedly planted by the Romans.

CERATONIA
siliqua
CAROB

Native to the eastern Mediterranean, this evergreen tree or shrub can grow to 13 m (about 40 ft) but can be pruned to a more suitable garden size. It has glossy, green leaves and long, brown, bean-like pods 25 cm (about 10 in) long. It prefers full sun but can tolerate light shade. It requires hot summers to perform well. Fertilizing is usually not necessary and the tree is remarkably resistant to summer drought. The carob pods are ready to be picked in autumn/fall when they are dark brown. When eaten fresh they are sweet and chewy. Roasting and powdering them for use as a chocolate substitute can be arduous but rewarding, and the branches can be used as emergency fodder for stock in times of drought. Do not plant the tree too close to the house as many people find the odour of the flowers objectionable.

CITRUS

Native to South-East Asia, it is thought citrus fruit trees were introduced to the Middle East and Europe in the time of the Romans. They are half-hardy to frost-tender and do best in a warm, humid climate with mild winters. The attractive white flowers in spring and fruit in winter make them a valued tree. A nitrogen-rich, well-drained soil and a sunny position are their requirements. Water and fertilize well. They are attacked by a number of pests including scale insects, aphids, holy cross bug, fruit-fly and fungus. Although citrus are more reliable when grown from seed than most fruit trees, they are almost always budded to ensure the perpetuation of the desired variety. Understocks vary with type, but the most common is *Poncirus trifoliata* which gives greater resistance to cold and to certain viruses.

C. aurantifolia
LIME

Known as the West Indian or key lime, this is a small, slender, thorny evergreen which reaches 3 m (about 9 ft) high and wide. Native to Malaysia this tree can only be grown in tropical and subtropical areas as it is frost-tender. It makes a perfect tub tree when put in a sheltered, sunny spot and will produce lots of fruit. The fruit is best in cool drinks and is acidic and strongly flavoured. Propagate by grafting or budding. Watch for citrus scab and brown scale.

C. auriantium
SOUR ORANGE, SEVILLE ORANGE

These half-hardy small trees originated in China and are grown as ornamental shrubs or providers of fruit for marmalade and jelly. The heavy-fruiting 'Seville' and 'Chinotto' orange trees with their glossy, dark-green leaves and small growth habit are excellent in containers or as border growers. The dwarf variety 'Bouquet de Fleurs' is a more fragrant, ornamental shrub, smooth-stemmed and showy. Propagate from seed. Watch for melanose (dark brown spots on the wood and fruit) and citrus scab.

C. limon
LEMON

Native to Pakistan and India, this only just half-hardy tree or shrub is an attractive evergreen that grows to 4 m (about 12 ft) high and 3 m (about 9 ft) wide. The most common cultivar is 'Eureka' which is a smooth-stemmed tree with an all-year-round display of fruit and flowers if grown in frost-free climates. 'Meyer' is smaller than most lemons with a less acidic flavour, and is rather hardier than other lemons. Plant in well-drained soil and fertilize regularly with nitrogen. Propagate by budding. The lemon is less prone to disease than other citrus trees, but be careful of the fungus, melanose (dark brown spots), which must be pruned off once it appears on the wood.

Citrus medica

Citrus paradisi

Citrus aurantifolia

C. medica
CITRON

The fruit is like a lemon, but has a rougher, highly fragrant skin. Young foliage has a purplish tinge as do the flowers. Propagate by budding. Use for marmalade and candied peel as it has little juice. The tree is about as hardy as a sour orange.

C. paradisi
GRAPEFRUIT

Native to the West Indies where it was called forbidden fruit, grapefruit is relatively large for a citrus tree at 5 m (about 15 ft) high. The fruit is prominently displayed on the tree's outer section, hanging in golden yellow clusters that should be left until fully ripe before being picked. The tree is half-hardy. If it is grown in a cool climate the fruit takes up to 18 months to ripen. The Australian 'Wheeny' variety can be grown in a temperate climate but other varieties such as 'Marsh Seedless', 'Thompson' and 'Ruby' need very warm summers in order to ripen. Propagate by budding. Watch for stem pit virus, spread by the black citrus aphid.

Citrus auriantium

Citrus limon

C. reticulata

MANDARIN, TANGERINE

This is the largest citrus group and has a wide range of climate tolerance among its varieties: the hardiest can take an occasional light frost. It grows to 3 m (about 9 ft) high and is a good fruit tree for the suburban garden. The fruit is similar to oranges, but smaller and looser skinned. It is slow-growing and hardy, with heavily perfumed flowers. Prune to remove dead wood. Propagate by budding. As with most citruses, watch for citrus scab and melanose fungus.

C. sinensis

SWEET ORANGE

The sweet orange travelled the trade routes as far back as the mid-fifteenth century and was introduced to the Western world by Arab traders. A large, half-hardy evergreen, it is grown commercially in subtropical climates. It can be grown in cooler climates if it is grafted *Poncirus trifoliata* rootstock

which helps it tolerate cold winters and also gives it greater resistance to certain virus diseases. Propagate by budding. Humidity encourages fungal diseases. Orange blossom is traditionally worn by brides in their hair. 'Valencia' is the best known variety of sweet orange, much grown commercially.

C. sinensis 'Washington Navel'

NAVEL ORANGE

This small, slow-growing tree grows best away from humid-summer coastal areas as this climate does not suit it. It has a distinctive, button-like growth on its seedless fruit, which many consider superior in mildness and sweetness to 'Valencia'. It is a mutation of the sweet orange.

C. × tangelo

TANGELO

An evergreen tree growing up to 4 m (about 12 ft) high and 3 m (about 9 ft) wide, it is derived from a cross between mandarin and

grapefruit. Tangelo is renowned for its juicing properties and as a superb dessert fruit with its tart, yet sweet, flavour. Plant in well-drained soil in a warm spot sheltered from frost. As with all citrus trees, regular watering is essential, especially when the tree is fruiting. Apply nitrogen fertilizer from early spring until mid-summer. Propagate by budding. Watch for citrus scab and fungi.

CORYLUS
avellana

HAZELNUT, FILBERT

A hardy, deciduous, small tree that grows up to 4 m (about 12 ft) high and wide. It will grow in a wide range of climates, is frost-hardy and prefers mild summers. The tree should be placed in full light where it is sheltered from strong winds. It produces the best crop of nuts, which grow in clusters and ripen in autumn/fall, in fertile, well-drained soil. Propagate by layering or from cuttings. The hazelnut has long

been steeped in mystic lore; parts of the plant were supposedly used for rituals in ancient times. In modern days it is eaten as a dessert and much used in the making of sweets and chocolates.

CYDONIA
oblonga

QUINCE

Native to the Middle East, this is a moderately frost-hardy, deciduous tree growing 3–4 m (about 9–12 ft) high and 3 m (about 9 ft) wide. Its soft green leaves turn an attractive golden yellow before falling and it is not fussy about soil, making it an ideal ornamental for potting or for borders. Its highly aromatic fruit can be left on the tree for a few weeks after it ripens without harm. Pick with care as it bruises easily. Prune minor branches or shoots which have produced fruit. Propagate from cuttings. It is vulnerable to fruit-fly and the fungus quince fleck. Quinces cannot be eaten raw and are best cooked for jellies or sauces. Quinces are thought to be the 'golden apples' that feature in Greek mythology.

CYPHOMANDRA
betacea

TAMARILLO, TREE TOMATO

This is an evergreen shrub or small, shrubby tree from South America with large, green leaves and, depending on the variety, dark red or yellow-orange fruit. Train it up against a wire fence or stake it to protect from the wind, as it is very

Corylus avellana

Citrus sinensis 'Washington Navel'

Citrus reticulata

Cydonia oblonga

Citrus × tangelo

Citrus sinensis

inclined to top-heaviness. This is a shallow-rooted plant which prefers a subtropical or temperate climate and moist, but not wet soil. It grows to 3 m (about 9 ft) in height. Prune lightly after fruiting and take cuttings at 1 m (about 3 ft) high to encourage more shoots. Propagate from cuttings and plan to replace the trees after 5 years or so as they are short lived. The fruit will mature throughout the year and can be used for jam or on ice-cream.

DIOSPYROS
kaki
PERSIMMON

This attractive, deciduous tree is common in Japan and China and grows to 5 m (about 15 ft) high and wide. The leaves are dark green and glossy, changing colour in autumn/fall to a handsome russet and gold. The tree can be kept in a large container and even if pruned will continue to fruit happily. The fruit is golden orange and is either astringent (in which case it should be eaten when quite ripe), or non-astringent (eat while still firm and crunchy or dry for future use, as is done in Japan). The tree is vulnerable to root rot so plant in well-drained soil. Beware of mealy bug, cinnamon fungus and collar rot. No pruning is needed.

ERIOBOTRYA
japonica
LOQUAT

In its natural state this subtropical tree will grow to 7 m (about 21 ft) high but in domesticity can be kept quite small by regular post-harvest pruning. Large, dark green leaves have a silver-grey underside and the scented, creamy coloured flowers form in multiple clusters. It prefers a temperate to subtropical climate. Its fruit is pear-shaped, small and sweet. Prune the more fragile shoots after the first fruiting; this will improve future harvests and make the tree more compact. Fruit-fly and birds can be a problem. Remove the bitter seeds and stew for jam or eat the fruit raw in salads. The tree can be propagated easily from seed, but grafted, named varieties give superior fruit.

FEIJOA
sellowiana
FEIJOA, PINEAPPLE GUAVA

Native to Brazil and Argentina, this evergreen grows to 3–4 m (about 9–12 ft) high and wide, and features green foliage and, in early summer, attractive red and white flowers. It is reasonably frost-hardy and makes a good windbreak or can be pruned to make a tall hedge. Don't let the soil dry out and water

well while fruiting. The fruit is large and pale green, with a similar taste to pineapple and should not be stored for too long before consumption. Plant in pairs of different varieties to ensure pollination. 'Unique' is a good cultivar for the domestic garden, being self-fertile. Its worst enemy is fruit-fly.

FICUS
carica
FIG

Originally from the Mediterranean and Asia, this deciduous tree varies in height from 3–9 m (about 9–27 ft). It flourishes in deep, lime-rich soils and a mild, dry climate and ideally should bear fruit twice a year. A distinguishing feature of this plant is the way the flower is formed and held within the fruit itself. May be trained as a wall plant. The yield is greater when its root range is limited, or containerized. Propagate from cuttings. Figs have few natural enemies although wasps and birds might find the near-ripe fruit very tempting. There are several named varieties, varying in their tolerance of cold and whether their fruit are best eaten fresh or dried. 'Brown Turkey' is usually thought the most luscious. Little pruning is needed, though old trees may be pruned hard to rejuvenate them.

Diospyros kaki

Cyphomandra betacea

Ficus carica

Feijoa sellowiana

Eriobotrya japonica

Juglans regia

Malus domestica 'Golden Delicious'

Fortunella japonica

Macadamia tetraphylla

Litchi chinensis

FORTUNELLA
japonica
KUMQUAT

This small, evergreen, ornamental shrub made the journey from the Orient to the West in the nineteenth century. It is excellent in a large tub and its glossy, green foliage and small, golden fruit can also be a highlight in a flower border. There is a pretty variety with variegated leaves also. Half-hardy, it will survive fairly open spaces on patios and courtyards. Propagate from seed. Kumquats are used in marmalades and liqueurs.

JUGLANS
regia
WALNUT

A forest tree, this species grows 10–25 m (about 30–80 ft) high and 20 m (about 65 ft) wide. It can take several years before the tree starts to bear any nuts so patience is required. The variety 'Wilson's Wonder' fruits young, although its nuts are not thought to be of the very highest quality. A silver-grey trunk ends in a canopy of arching branches, making this a good source of shade in a spacious garden. Prune early to form a central branch and a well-spaced system of boughs. It is cold- and wind-hardy, although young trees may be damaged by harsh frost. Ensure that the soil is deep, loamy and well drained. Water well to increase nut production and pick the nuts from the ground after they have fallen. Large birds can be a problem as well as the erinose mite and nut-boring beetles.

LITCHI
chinensis
LYCHEE

A large, graceful, evergreen tree native to south-eastern China that grows from 7–15 m (about 21–50 ft) high. Bright green, compound leaves form a dense, bushy crown and the fruit hangs in grape-like clusters which turn red when ripe. Although a tropical tree, it can stand a certain amount of light frost but the young tree will need shelter from wind and cold. It is not fussy about soil, even if quite damp, as the lychee is not affected by root rot. Prune lightly to ensure there are only 4 to 5 main branches. There are several named varieties, mostly of Chinese origin, and they are to be preferred to seedlings which are often very unreliable bearers.

MACADAMIA
tetraphylla
MACADAMIA, QUEENSLAND OR CALIFORNIA NUT

This half-hardy evergreen grows to 8 m (about 24 ft) high. Native to Australia and grown commercially in Hawaii and South Africa, it produces attractive, snow-white or pink blossoms. A handsome, shapely tree, it is suitable for a medium-sized, subtropical or warm-temperate garden. Plant in a warm, sunny, sheltered spot in deep, slightly acidic soil. It is worth the 6-year wait for these delicious and nutritious nuts which are released from their green outer husk after 9 months' maturing time. The fruit and flowers are susceptible to attack by moth larvae. The macadamia was once known as *M. ternifolia,* a named which was misapplied to the species.

MALUS

A member of the Rose family, this genus contains the crab apple and the garden apple (*M. domestica*); there are many species and varieties of both. The genus is extremely hardy, tolerating subtropical to subarctic conditions, though they do best in temperate climates with cold winters. Well-drained soil is essential for growth. They prefer deep, humus-rich, sandy loams in full light, although shade is tolerated. Plant in early spring in colder climates and autumn/fall in warmer areas. Pruning consists basically of thinning out branches to allow plenty of air and light around the fruit, though the fruiting apples are subjected to various detailed systems. Once established, it is rarely necessary to do more than shorten (in summer) the current season's over-long shoots. Thrips, mites, aphids moth larvae and fruit-fly are just some among quite a few unwelcome guests. Apple trees are not fertile to their own pollen, so it is necessary to grow two or more varieties to have a crop. The size of the tree depends on the understock, and in most gardens trees grafted on a 'dwarfing' stock will be best.

M. domestica 'Delicious'

'Golden Delicious' is a hardy, prolific tree with juicy golden fruit and

'Red Delicious' is an excellent dessert apple. Neither keeps very well after being picked.

M. domestica 'Granny Smith'

This Australian-bred apple was a lucky seedling in the garden of a woman called Granny Smith. The pale green fruit keeps well and is excellent for cooking or eating fresh. It is vulnerable to apple scab (black spot).

M. domestica 'Gravenstein'

A medium to large aromatic apple native to Germany which is striped red and yellow. This is a large tree which should be placed with care in the home garden. Partly self-fertile, it is the best choice where only one apple tree is grown, though fruit will be more abundant if it has a mate.

M. domestica 'Johnathon'

This American-raised cultivar is very popular in that country and also in Australia and New Zealand for its sweet bland flavour and bright red colour. It is sometimes a rather weak-growing tree.

M. 'Gorgeous'

The 'Gorgeous' crab apple was developed in New Zealand and has showy white flowers that are followed by glossy, dark red fruit in autumn/fall. They are first rate for making crab apple jelly as well as being highly ornamental.

M. 'John Downie'

This large English crab apple grows to 5 m (about 15 ft). It yields an abundant crop of red fruit in autumn/fall. The spring flowers are white, and it is a rather smaller tree than 'Gorgeous'.

M. pumila

CRAB APPLE

This tree grows to 4–5 m (about 12–15 ft) high and its branches spread to 2 m (about 6 ft). Its lance-shaped leaves have serrated margins. Pink and white flowers are produced in spring. The small, attractive fruit of the crab apple tree is ideal for stewing and has for generations been used to make jellies and jams.

MANGIFERA
indica

MANGO

Native to South-East Asia, the mango is a large, evergreen tree with a full canopy of, deep green leaves. The small flowers grow in clusters at the end of the shoots. It will tolerate both wet and dry climates and its roots flourish even in soil that is prone to waterlogging.

However, rainfall during flowering time will reduce the fruit crop and make it prone to disease. Give it lots of room when planting and protect the young tree from frost and sunburn. The 'common' mango, which is virtually unknown over much of New Zealand, is popular for domestic gardens. Mangoes are easily propagated from seed, and seedling mangoes are common in Australia, but grafted, named varieties are immeasurably superior. They usually do not grow so large. Fruit-fly and anthracnose are two major threats to mango production.

Malus 'Gorgeous'

Malus 'John Downie'

Malus domestica 'Granny Smith'

Malus domestica 'Johnathon'

Malus pumila

Malus domestica 'Gravenstein'

Mangifera indica

Morus nigra

Musa paradisiaca 'Lady Finger'

Musa paradisiaca 'Cavendish'

Musa paradisiaca

Mespilus germanica

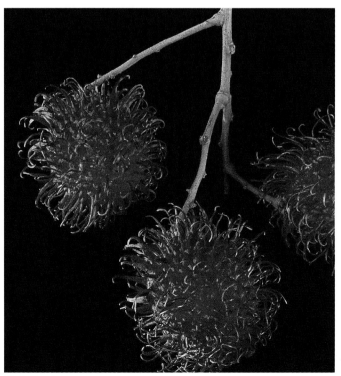

Nephelium lappaceum

MESPILUS
germanica
MEDLAR

A deciduous tree native to the Balkans that grows from 3–5 m (about 9–15 ft) in height. It has handsome foliage that turns a lovely red in autumn/fall. Its showy spring flowers are white and are followed by odd looking, small, brown fruit that resemble acorns. A hardy tree requiring full sun, it is not popular or well known as a fruit-bearer and may be planted solely for display. If grown for its fruit, harvest only when the medlar comes away easily from the stalk and leave to ripen until the flesh is brown and soft. Medlar may be either cooked and used in pies or eaten raw, once the pips are removed, though the fruit must be almost rotten-ripe before being palatable. Pick them when the leaves fall and store them for after-ripening.

MORUS
nigra
BLACK MULBERRY

From the same family as the fig tree, the deciduous mulberry has a 5–10 m (about 15–30 ft) tall trunk and wide-spreading branches. This slow-growing species is native to Iran and is valued for its ornamental, heart-shaped leaves and black fruit. This tree commands a lot of space in the garden but can be grown in tubs or trained *espalier* as long as it has been pruned and shaped from early growth. It loves a temperate climate and the fruit will ripen in early summer, becoming

easy prey for passing birds. Propagate from seedlings. The white mulberry (*M. alba*) is more suitable for warm-winter climates however, fruit is not quite as good. Its leaves are fed to silkworms. Do not plant either *M. nigra* or *M. alba* where the fruit can fall on paving, as it will stain it.

MUSA
paradisiaca
BANANA

The banana tree is not really a tree but a herbaceous perennial which needs frost-free tropical or subtropical areas. It has a palm-like appearance, exotic, orange-yellow or red flowers and the leaves can grow to 2 m (about 6 ft) long. It needs a lot of water for fruit production, loamy soil and a spacious position away from the wind, which can shred the gigantic leaves to ribbons. It is important to feed it regular doses of nitrogenous fertilizer. Propagate from suckers or by a bud from part of the tuber. Cut down the bananas when semi-ripe and let them ripen in a warm place indoors. Watch for the banana weevil borer and for the disease bunchy top, which destroys any chance of fruit. There are many varieties, designed either for cooking or eating fresh, and with red, green or yellow fruit, although very few are available outside South-East Asia.

M. paradisiaca 'Cavendish'

This small banana tree, growing to 2–3 m (about 6–9 ft) high, bears fruit reliably. However, it is unfortunately susceptible to the bunchy top virus.

M. paradisiaca 'Lady Finger'

This tree grows up to 5 m (about 15 ft) in height and is particularly well suited for the domestic garden as it is less vulnerable to bunchy top than other banana trees. It also tolerates cooler, more temperate weather than other species. The fruit is smaller than that of 'Cavendish' but very sweet.

NEPHELIUM
lappaceum
RAMBUTAN

This tropical tree grows to a height of 5 m (about 15 ft) with clusters of white flowers in spring, followed by orange-red fruit in summer. The fruit are similar to lychees with a translucent pulp encased in a skin covered in soft spikes. Frost-tender, it is best grown in rich, well-drained soil in a sunny position. Propagate from seed, although its native South-East Asian named varieties (propagated by grafting) are generally preferred to seedling fruit.

OLEA

europaea subsp. *europaea*
OLIVE

This is a hardy, evergreen tree that grows to 7 m (about 21 ft) high and originates in the eastern Mediterranean where it is grown mostly for its oil but also for eating, either green or ripe but always pickled. It has glossy, narrow, green leaves, small yellow-white flowers and attractive spreading branches. It prefers warm summers and cool winters. It should be potted and grown in a greenhouse for protection in colder climates and tolerates most soils as long as they are well-drained. Water thoroughly in summer to ensure good fruiting. Fruit will not appear for at least 8 years but the tree is ornamental in its own right, developing an interesting gnarled trunk as it ages. There are several named varieties, some being better for eating, others for oil. 'Virgin' olive oil is that from the first pressing of the fruit, and is the best quality.

PERSEA

americana
syn. *P. gratissima*
AVOCADO

Native to Central America and reaching a height of 8 m (about 24 ft) and 6 m (about 18 ft) wide this large, evergreen tree has glossy, dark green leaves and tiny spring flowers. It prefers warmth and shelter in the garden (young trees are frost-tender) and may be grown indoors providing it is exposed to 4 hours of sunlight each day. Water regularly and ensure the soil is salt-free and aerated. Avocados are not self-pollinating and it is best to plant more than one. Pollinate the flowers by hand if only one tree is growing. Thrips, fruit-fly and red scale are the main invading insects and root rot is common. The best-known varieties are 'Fuerte', with large, green-skinned fruit in summer and early autumn/fall; and 'Hass', which bears dark-skinned fruit in winter and spring. Gardeners with room for both can have avocados virtually all year round. Other, newer varieties are also becoming available.

PINUS

pinea
PINE NUT, ITALIAN STONE PINE

This tall pine tree is a native of Italy and one of the most popular nut bearers there, the pine nuts (pignons or pignolias) being much used in cooking. They are very rich in protein. The tree is easily grown in a subtropical or temperate climate. The pines contain an average of 100 nuts and should be picked when slightly green and left to open in a warm, dry spot. When the pine opens out, the nuts can be shaken out. Propagate from seed or cuttings. Eat them raw or roasted.

PISTACIA

vera
PISTACHIO

Belonging to the same family as the mango and cashew, this tree is valued as an ornamental garden tree as well as a nut bearer. It features red-gold leaves in autumn/fall, and red male and white female flowers on separate trees; at least one of each is needed for a crop of nuts although bisexual, grafted trees are sometimes available and grafted trees of known sex are always to be preferred to seedlings. It prefers hot, dry summers and mild to cold winters. Loamy, organic soil is best for quick growth of the tree. The pistachio's long, deep roots make it drought tolerant but it should be well watered to ensure a good crop. *Pistacia chinensis*, the Chinese pistachio, is grown solely for its dazzling autumn/fall colours, its fruit being too small to be worth eating.

PRUNUS

This genus contains over 400 species of deciduous and evergreen

Pistacia vera

Olea europaea subsp. *europaea*

shrubs or trees grown for their fruits or nuts and as ornamentals. Most species are half- to fully hardy and prefer a well-drained soil. Propagate from seed in summer, from cuttings, or by grafting or budding. Prune regularly.

P. armeniaca
APRICOT

This deciduous tree grows to 6 m (about 18 ft) high and 5 m (about 15 ft) wide. Dwarf varieties are now available which may be grown in pots. Apricot trees flourish in warm-summer areas with well-drained, alkaline soil. A wet spring will mean a smaller crop. Prune for the first 4 years to a vase shape with 6 or 7 main branches. Light brown apple moth, fruit-fly, and fungal diseases can be a threat. In areas with spring frost, the tree is best given the shelter of a warm wall.

Prunus armeniaca

Pinus pinea

Persea americana

P. avium
SWEET CHERRY

This tree grows to 10 m (about 30 ft) tall and has white blossoms. Dwarf hybrids that grow to only a few metres high are available and these will live and fruit happily in tubs. It is suited to fan training against a high wall or fence. Otherwise, prune gradually to an open vase shape with 10 or so main branches. Do not prune in winter or during wet weather as cherry wood is prone to fungus. While cherries are ripening, cover the tree with plastic netting to keep birds away. Watch for root weevil and moth larvae. Cherries are not self-fertile (except for the new variety 'Stella'), so two trees will be necessary. They need a cold winter to fruit. The Japanese flowering cherry (P. serrulata) bears no fruit.

P. cerasus
SOUR CHERRY

This species is suitable for the domestic garden, being smaller, more compact and naturally self-fertilizing. The fruit ripens in late summer, but is acidic and needs to be cooked or preserved. Like the sweet cherry, it needs cold winters.

P. domestica and P. salicifolia
PLUM

The plums are of mixed origin but the European varieties are usually assigned to P. domestica and the Japanese (many of which were bred in the USA) to P. salicifolia. The main distinction is that the European plums are lovers of cooler climates than the Japanese. Both types come in many named varieties, but whereas just about all the Japanese plums are dessert fruit, the European plums include varieties best suited to cooking (jam making, pies, etc.) or drying for prunes. Damsons are European plums with rather small but very sweet fruit; greengages are similar but green-yellow even when ripe. Plum blossoms are quite lovely and some species of trees are grown purely for their display of beautiful red leaves.

Plum trees are generally very easy to grow and will tolerate different soil types; these species prefer a potash-rich mixture which is well watered. They like a temperate climate with dry summers and should be planted in a sunny sheltered position. Prune regularly in summer to slow growth and pick the plums only when fully ripe. Use netting to protect the trees from birds. Aphids, scales and mites can be a problem, as can brown rot, bacterial spot and plum mosaic virus.

P. dulcis
syn.   P. amygdalus
ALMOND

A deciduous tree from South-East Asia that grows to 6 m (about 18 ft) high and 5 m (about 15 ft) wide. This is a stone fruit which is closely related to the peach. However the flesh of the fruit is inedible while the kernel is sweet. Pink blossoms grow in clusters of 5 and 6. Ideally, this tree should be grown in a dry-summer climate in a well-drained, salt-free soil. Young trees are frost-tender. As with other stone fruit, weed the base area well and feed the young tree nitrogen. Prune to an open vase shape encouraging 3 or 4 main branches. It is prone to shot-hole disease which appears on the fruit as purple spots, spoiling the nut inside. Almonds are not self-fertile and two varieties that blossom at the same time are needed to produce fruit.

P. persica
PEACH

This deciduous tree grows to 5 m (about 15 ft) high and wide, and is the most commonly grown of the stone fruit. Most feature pink-tinged blossoms, yellowish red-skinned fruit and should be grown in a warm climate. Cultivated dwarf varieties are perfect for placing in tubs or among flower beds and shrubberies. Peach trees must be planted in well-drained soil as waterlogging can be fatal. Plant where the tree, including the interior branches, will receive the most light and shelter from frosts. If new shoots aren't pruned the tree will overbear and the fruit will be small and of poor quality. Pick the peaches when they just start to soften. Propagate from seed. Peaches are susceptible to a number of diseases including peach leaf curl and brown rot. They are officially self-fertile, but crops will be better if two varieties are grown. The trees are not long lived, 25 years or so.

P. persica var. nectarina
NECTARINE

The nectarine is almost identical to the peach in habit and flowers but needs more attention as it is less hardy than the peach. Its fruit is usually smaller and smooth skinned. There are several named varieties; seedlings often give rise to normal peaches.

PSIDIUM
cattleianum
CHERRY GUAVA, STRAWBERRY GUAVA

Native to tropical Central and South America, this medium-sized, hardy evergreen is related to the feijoa. It is fast growing with a smooth trunk and large, white flowers. Its pear-shaped fruit has dark red flesh which is high in vitamin C. It prefers a warm, frost-free climate, plenty of water for good fruit production and some shelter from the wind when it is young. The tree should be pruned to encourage prolific flowering, with old wood and lower branches being removed. Propagate from cuttings, or by grafting or budding. It is susceptible to fruit-fly. Guavas are excellent for juicing, or for using in jams and jellies.

Prunus avium

Prunus cerasus

Prunus domestica

Prunus persica var. nectarina

Prunus persica

Prunus dulcis

PUNICA
granatum
POMEGRANATE

This very attractive, compact but very thorny tree is from the Middle East where about 20 named varieties, varying in flavour from acid to very sweet, are grown. It is valued not only for its sweet fruit but for its large, red blooms which appear in late spring and early summer. It grows to 5 m (about 15 ft) and its glossy leaves, showy scarlet flowers and orange fruit make it popular as an ornamental, long-living shrub. Pomegranate requires hot summer conditions to produce good crops. Prune lightly in winter to encourage new growth. Pomegranates start to bear fruit after 5 to 6 years; the fruit should be harvested when it becomes an orange-brown colour. Do not leave it too long on the tree as it tends to split. Propagate from cuttings or rooted suckers. Watch out for fungal rot. Use the fruit kernels in salads or desserts and eat the pulp fresh. A warm summer is needed for the fruit to ripen, and the double-flowered varieties (red, pink or white) are mostly sterile. There is also available a miniature variety, *P. granatum* 'Nana', which only grows to approximately1 m (about 3 ft) with small, decorative flowers and fruit.

PYRUS
PEAR

Thousands of years of cultivation have produced many different shapes, sizes and fruit of pear trees, some more suitable for the domestic garden than others. Usually a large tree, it is thought to have originated in the Mediterranean. It flourishes in a moist, mild climate. Plant in a warm, protected spot where it will receive maximum sunlight. In a small garden, train it to grow on a lattice or wire frame. Alternatively, pear trees grafted onto quince stock are good for home gardens. It can stand a reasonable amount of water and responds well to loamy soil with the occasional boost of nitrogen-rich fertilizers. Cross-pollination is needed for productive fruiting. The main enemies of the pear are scale, mites, blossom blight and stony pit.

P. communis 'Buerre Bosc'

This is popular worldwide for its large, soft, sweet pears that are ideal for baking. It is prone to the pear scab fungus.

P. communis 'William's Bon Chrétien'
BARTLETT PEAR

This is a sweet, musky flavoured, medium-sized pear which bears the name of an English schoolteacher but is thought by some to have been cultivated by the Ancient Romans. It is the most widely grown Bartlett pear cultivar for canning. The red-skinned cultivar is known as 'Red Bartlett'.

P. pyrifolia
NASHI PEAR

Native to China but also much cultivated in Japan, this tree is an excellent, compact, fruit bearer. Plant among garden shrubs where its white blossoms and glossy, green leaves can be seen to advantage. It has two types, the Japanese nashi, which is more apple-shaped with green or brown skin, and the Chinese nashi, which is more traditionally pear-shaped. The nashi pear is easier to grow than the European pear in mild-winter areas, and more suited to domestic use. Grow on a trellis and prune excess shoots. It is more disease hardy than the European pear, and not so dependent on cross-pollination for fruit, although crops will be better if the tree does have a mate; a European pear will be perfectly adequate.

THEOBROMA
cacao
CACAO TREE, COCOA TREE

Native to tropical South and Central America, this widely cultivated tree grows quickly to 8 m (about 24 ft), with a thick convex crown that spreads in maturity. The long-stalked foliage matures from red to a leathery, lustrous green. In late spring long racemes of pink, yellow or white flowers grow straight out of the limbs and trunk. These are followed by angular, prominently ribbed seed pods, as big as a soccer ball, encasing a gummy mass of numerous elliptical seeds. This frost-tender tree thrives best in peaty, damp soil and shelter from the wind. Propagate the cacao tree from seed or by grafting. The seeds are used to make chocolate and cocoa.

Pyrus pyrifolia

Pyrus communis 'Buerre Bosc'

Thoebroma cacao

Pyrus communis 'William's Bon Chrétien'

Psidium cattleianum

Punica granatum

OTHER FRUITS

ACTINIDIA
chinensis
syn.   A. deliciosa
KIWIFRUIT, CHINESE GOOSEBERRY

This deciduous vine is native to the Yangtze Valley in China and is now grown in warm areas around the world. It should be planted on a sturdy trellis or pergola (as it grows quickly and quite wildly) in deep soil which is high in nitrogen. It prefers a sheltered spot away from the winds, early frosts and hot sun that can damage the fruit. Prune regularly in summer and winter to ensure large, good quality fruit. Water abundantly in summer. The first fruit will appear after 4 to 5 years. Kiwifruit's main enemies are light brown apple moth larvae, fruit-fly, root rot and the leaf-roller caterpillar. You must have a male and a female (named varieties are superior) to produce fruit; grafted plants carrying both sexes are often available. Prune in the same manner as grapes.

ANANAS
comosus
syn. A. sativas
PINEAPPLE

Cultivated by Central American Indians for centuries, the pineapple was praised by early European visitors as the finest of all fruit and shipped back to the Old World. To offer the expensive exotic to a guest was a great compliment; hence the use of pineapple motifs in architecture to symbolize hospitality. A member of the bromeliad family, the plant makes a bushy, 1 m (about 3 ft) tall clump of sword-shaped leaves from which the flower stems arise, the clustered flowers developing into a single aggregate fruit. The leaves are viciously edged with tiny thorns, but recently smooth-leaved cultivars have been developed. Suited only to gardens in the tropics and subtropics, it needs a greenhouse in temperate and cool climates to provide the constant warmth it needs to fruit. Sunshine, regular watering, and the richest possible soil are essential. Named varieties are occasionally available, but the easiest way to acquire a plant is to make a cutting from the shoot atop a choice fruit. It will, if happy, fruit in about two years. Once established, faster and heavier crops will come from plants propagated from side shoots, which should be done every few years as old plants do not fruit prolifically. There is a cultivar with variegated leaves, grown mainly for ornamental purposes, as its fruit is rather small.

ARACHIS
hypogaea
PEANUT

This is a herbaceous annual with bright green, clover-like leaves and yellow flowers that blossom in summer. It can be planted to good effect in flower borders or in containers, but is frost-tender so grow only where it will enjoy a long hot summer. In mild-summer areas the nuts will not ripen, and peanuts are not much of a success in southern Australia and much of New Zealand. The peanuts themselves are actually seeds which grow underground, so make sure that the soil (which should be slightly acid) is loose enough for the peanut to grow productively. If the soil is too damp the peanuts will rot, therefore keep well-drained. They need a long growing season with consistently warm soil and are not very successful over much of New Zealand. Peanut plants should be ready to pull up when the foliage turns yellow in autumn/fall. Cure nuts for a few weeks before eating.

CITRULLUS
lanatus
syn.   C. vulgaris
WATERMELON

This is a large, heat-loving vine with crinkled leaves similar to rather large ivy leaves. Sow seeds in spring in rich, well-drained soil in a sunny position. (Mostly it grows rampantly, and without much encouragement, from compost heaps in the back garden.) Watch for cucumber beetles. The rind can be pickled and of course the sugary, red-pink flesh inside is delicious, but the longer and hotter the summer the better the crop will be.

CUCUMIS
MELON

Native to Africa where there are 40 species, most melons grow on vines

Arachis hypogaea

Actinidia chinensis

Ananas comosus

Cucumis melo (rock melon)

Citrullus lanatus

and are grouped according to the characteristics of their fruit. They need a long, hot growing season to produce sweet fruit, and in a cooler climate the vines should be encouraged to grow over concrete or rocks, or trained over black plastic in order for heat to circulate around the plant. Plant in humus-rich soil and water generously but not too much. A dry climate is preferable, as humid conditions can affect the quality of the fruit and make the plant more prone to the fungus, anthracnose. Hand pollinate if growing melons on a small scale. Propagate from seed.

CANTALUPENSIS GROUP

C. melo

CANTALOUPE, ROCK MELON

This is a compact plant with oval-shaped or round fruit with netted rinds and orange flesh.

INDORUS GROUP

C. melo

HONEYDEW MELON

A small, bushy plant with a harder rind than most melons, making it suitable for long storage. The skin is usually smooth and the flesh is pale green or yellow.

RETICULATUS GROUP

C. melo

NETTED MELON

This melon has net markings on the rind, orange flesh and is widely grown in the USA.

FRAGARIA

STRAWBERRY

This small, frost-hardy perennial grows no more than 20 cm (about 8 in) high and 40 cm (about 16 in) wide. These plants are capable of growing all over the world in all sorts of climates, including the Arctic. The strawberry itself is a false fruit made up of tiny pips. Modern, more robust strawberry plants can produce fruit for 6 months if grown properly; some will bear fruit year round in a warm climate. Plant in tubs, pots, garden beds or even boxes that have been lined with straw, potting mix and fertilizer. Ensure the soil is free draining and acidic. The plants need sun and protection from wind, and in cold climates should be grown in slits in sheets of plastic. Propagate from runners and replant with fresh, virus-free stock every few years. Snails, strawberry aphids and birds are a nuisance. There are many named varieties of the garden strawberry, varying in their preferred climates and especially in flavour. Each area has its own favourites.

F. alpina

ALPINE STRAWBERRY

The fruit from this variety is small and hardy and tastes very tangy. Alpine strawberries make a good ground cover under trees or near walls and are less susceptible to attack by birds. The fruit can be red or yellow, and plants usually don't make runners. They are propagated from seed.

F. vesca

WOODLAND STRAWBERRY

Native to Europe, this was originally a wild woodland berry whose fruit is larger than the alpine strawberry.

PASSIFLORA

This genus contains over 400 species of evergreen or semi-evergreen tendril-climbing vines, primarily, though not exclusively, native to tropical America. They are grown as ornamentals or for their pulpy fruit. Flowers range from pale pink to purple-red and fruits from pale yellow through to purple-black, depending on the species. Plant in rich, well-drained soil in full sun and provide support. Propagate from seed or cuttings. Most species are frost-tender and are susceptible to nematodes.

P. edulis

PASSIONFRUIT

This species of passionfruit vine is a common sight in gardens in temperate climates and is valued for its glossy, bright green leaves, purple-white flowers and flavoursome fruit. Train on a pergola or trellis and prune into shape to prevent tangling, which encourages insect infestation. It is hardy and likes a well-drained, sandy soil and occasional doses of nitrogen fertilizer. The fruit will grow quickly and should be picked when its skin has turned purple and is still smooth. This species is self-fertile. Propagate

from seed or better still by grafting a selected, named variety; seedlings can be unreliable. The Spanish conquistadors regarded the flower of the passionfruit as a symbol of the crucifixion.

P. mollissima

syn. *Tacsonia mollissima*

BANANA PASSIONFRUIT

This attractive, fast-growing vine does well in cool climates and features pink flowers and long, golden yellow fruit. Train against a trellis or

Fragaria vesca

Passiflora edulis

Fragaria alpina

Rubus 'Boysen'

Passiflora mollissima

Ribes nigrum

Ribes grossularia

Ribes sativum

Physalis peruviana

fence, or over a supporting tree where the fruit and flowers can be seen to advantage. Drought-hardy and generous in its crop, it often fruits in the first year. The fruit is not as sweet as the ordinary passionfruit but can still be used for cakes and fruit salads. Banana passionfruit spreads like a weed in South Africa and is best not cultivated there.

PHYSALIS
peruviana
CAPE GOOSEBERRY

This edible species of *Physalis* is an attractive bush with grey-green leaves and gold berries. It is frost-tender so it is best grown in the shelter of another bush or tree. Hot weather usually means that the fruit will be sweet, while a cooler, temperate climate can lead to sour-tasting berries. Propagate from cuttings. Use for chutney or jam or in fruit salads.

RIBES

A member of the Grossulariaceae family, this genus contains about 150 species of deciduous fruit-bearing shrubs. They grow to a height of 1–2 m (about 3–6 ft) and spread of 1–1.5 m (about 3–4½ ft). Frost-hardy, they are unsuited to warm-winter climates. Most species prefer deep, rich, well-drained, slightly acidic soil. Plant in sun or partial shade, and water well during summer. Prune annually to shape as required by the species. Diseases, insects and birds can be a problem.

R. grossularia
GOOSEBERRY

The thorny-stemmed gooseberry bush grows to 1 m (about 3 ft) high. It can tolerate quite poor soil as long as it is salt-free and grows best in cool, moist positions in sun or partial shade. The thorny stems should be kept in mind when placing it in a small garden. Shape as a

short-stemmed bush or tie the shoots against a fan-shaped wire support. Pick the fruit while it is still hard if using for cooking, but wait until it is soft if eating it fresh. Propagate from cuttings. Botrytis, birds, caterpillars and mildew are problems; only mildew-resistant varieties should be grown.

R. nigrum
BLACKCURRANT

This very popular garden shrub reaches up to 2 m (about 6 ft) and produces green-white flowers and sweet, black fruit high in vitamin C. Frost-hardy, it prefers a rich, loamy soil which can hold water. Plant it deep in the soil and enrich wood growth with potash and nitrogen-rich fertilizer. Weeds must be controlled and preferably eradicated before planting the blackcurrant bush. Prune old shoots to encourage new growth. The fruit should be picked when the upper berries are starting to fall from the cluster.

Propagate from cuttings. Watch for currant borer moth, mites and leaf spot.

R. sativum
REDCURRANT

This is very similar to the blackcurrant and prefers the same conditions. Its beautiful, glossy, red berries ripen earlier and are less likely to fall prematurely. They are usually used in cooking. White currants are a form of the red, and are grown in exactly the same way.

RUBUS

This genus includes a large number of the berry fruits, including raspberries and blackberries. The plants produce long, trailing shoots known as canes which bear fruit in their second season and then die. These plants need supporting frames to keep the fruit away from the ground, and to keep the plants under control—any shoot that lies on the ground will take root. In a small garden the plants can be trained against a wall or trellis. Cool climates are best and an acidic, well-drained soil that holds water well. Make sure that the ground is well clear of weeds before planting. Propagate from pieces of root or root suckers.

R. 'Boysen'
BOYSENBERRY

Like all bramble berries this is a rampant grower with long canes that are either thorny or smooth, the thornless variety being much easier to manage. It prefers a warm-temperate climate and depending on the fertility of the soil it may need vigorous pruning. The large, purple-red berries take 6 weeks to ripen, when they can be quite black. The best variety is 'Thornless', the merits of which are indicated by its name. Another variety, *R.* 'Young' (the youngberry), is rather similar but thorny.

R. idaeus
RASPBERRY

R. idaeus from Europe (especially it is said from Mt Ida in Greece where Zeus was born) is the main parent of the garden raspberries, though most modern cultivars have various American species in their background. All make tall lax bushes with delicious red fruit, much used for jam but also eaten fresh. There are both summer and autumn/fall fruiting varieties; be sure to buy certified virus-free stocks and control aphids, which spread virus diseases.

R. 'Logan'
syn. *R. loganobaccus*
LOGANBERRY

This is a hybrid between a blackberry and a garden raspberry, said to have originated in the garden of Judge Logan in California in 1881. It has a crimson, tart fruit highly suitable for cooking. The plant is raspberry-like in growth.

SECHIUM
edule
CHOKO

Native to South America and from the same family as the melon and cucumber, this is strictly a perennial fruit that grows on a strong, bright green vine. It requires sun, and plenty of space to grow as its tendrils will grip onto and climb almost anything. In a temperate climate chokos are frost-tender. Propagate from a shooting choko fruit in spring. The large, hairy green fruit can be boiled, baked or stewed but not overcooked or it will be tasteless. Steamed choko with white sauce is a pleasing accompaniment to meat; and choko pie, with plenty of sugar and cinnamon, rivals apple pie.

VACCINIUM
corymbosum
BLUEBERRY

A fast-growing, deciduous shrub with lovely, small white flowers and handsome autumn/fall colours. It looks best when planted as a thick hedge so that the flowers and berries form a mass of white or blue, depending on the season. It does well in cold climates and prefers a well-drained but constantly moist, loamy, acidic soil. It is self-fertile. Clear away weak branches in winter

and shape so that light and air can reach the inner bush. The cooler the climate the tastier the fruit will be. Propagate from cuttings. The blueberry is harder to reproduce than other berry fruit. Aphids, caterpillars and apple moth can sometimes pay a destructive visit.

VITIS
vinifera
GRAPE

V. vinifera is native to Europe and the Mediterranean and has been cultivated since remote antiquity. A vigorous, frost-hardy, deciduous vine, it has given rise to a multitude of varieties with either black or white (pale green or yellow) fruit, some being designed for wine, others for eating fresh or dried. They need cool winters and low summer humidity or mildew will be a major worry; in humid-summer coastal climates hybrid American varieties like 'Isabella' or 'Concord' are the most reliable. Train on a pergola or fence where it is sunny, and in deep soil so that the vine can dig its roots down. Pruning depends on grape type and upon the way the vine is being grown. For pergola vines, train on a single trunk until it reaches the horizontal beams, then allow it to spread out. Birds are a problem, so cover the vines with bird netting or put paper bags around the grape clusters. Cut the grapes with sharp scissors when fully ripe. Grapes need annual pruning after the leaves have fallen to control the vine's growth and encourage heavy fruiting. They are traditionally propagated by cuttings but where there is the slightest chance of phylloxera, an insect that feeds on the roots, being present they are best grafted on resistant understocks.

Vitis vinifera

Vaccinium corymbosum

Sechium edule

Rubus idaeus

Rubus 'Logan'

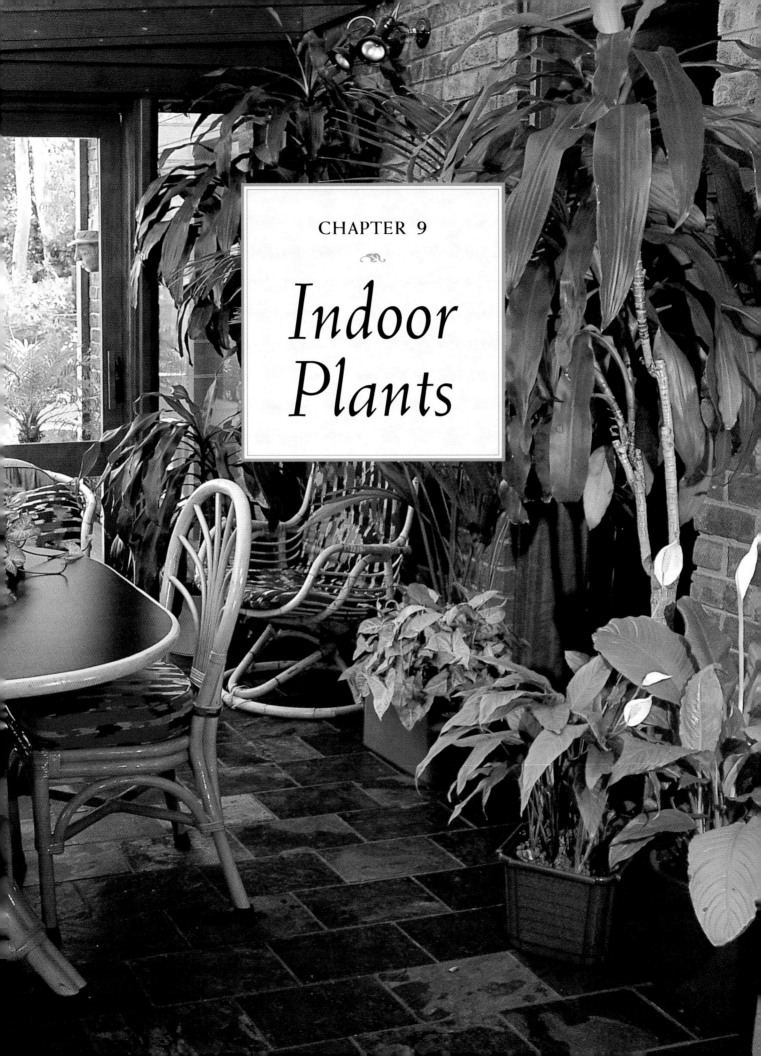

CHAPTER 9

Indoor Plants

*Y*ou'd be forgiven for thinking that in an art as ancient as gardening, there was nothing new; yet house plants are quite a recent idea. True, the Victorians grew fuchsias on their window sills and ferns in miniature greenhouses called Wardian cases; but the idea of using growing plants as major features in interior design—and growing a large range of species too—had to wait for several things to happen.

First, modern architecture had to increase the size of our windows, so that rooms would be bright enough for plants to flourish. Then, electric light had to supersede gas, whose fumes will kill off just about anything except aspidistras and parlour palms. Even now, if you cook with gas you may well find plants don't flourish in your kitchen. Finally, central heating had to make our houses consistently warm enough for tropical plants, for tropical forests are among the few natural environments where decorative plants grow in gloom comparable to the interior of a building.

The Importance of Light

We humans can adjust our eyes to an extraordinary range of brightness; but then we don't need light to photosynthesize. Plants do; and the first rule in growing any plant in the house is to give it adequate light. We almost always place our furniture in the best lit places in the room—and why not, rooms are designed for our own comfort first of all—but that often means that the corners where plants fit the decor best are the darkest in the room. The brightest place is in front of or just next to a window, but if you habitually keep your curtains drawn during the day for privacy, your room can be dim no matter how large your windows. There are plants that can take very low levels of light, but the range is limited, and pretty well confined to plants with plain green leaves. (Variegated leaves are almost always short on chlorophyll, and flowering takes a lot of energy which the plant can only derive from light.) It is a matter of cutting your cloth according to your measure, but remember that a flourishing plant, no matter how plain, is an asset to a room; a struggling one, all weak, pale and drawn, isn't. You can overcome the forces of darkness by placing the plant under a lamp, but it will have to be fitted with a special bulb (a 'grow-light' or fluorescent bulb, to be bought at most plant nurseries) that maximizes the frequencies of light that plants use—ordinary lights are of little use. Alternatively, have two plants and rotate them weekly or fortnightly between the garden or greenhouse.

Humidity

The next requirement is adequate humidity, and here there can be real conflict between our ideas of comfort and those of our plants, many of which would be happiest in a Turkish bath rather than the average living room. If

It's very important to provide adequate light for indoor plants.

you have a well-lit bathroom or kitchen they can be good places for plants, but you can assist by growing several plants together—they will help humidify the air for each other—and by standing your pots on saucers filled with pebbles which you keep constantly moist (on, not in; you don't want the roots standing in water).

Air-conditioning and central heating can dry the air out to desert-like levels. It is often said that house plants dislike air-conditioning, but this isn't strictly true. If they are standing on wet pebbles, they should be fine—and you'll be more comfortable too, and the piano will stay in better tune, for their presence. But you must keep your rooms at a reasonably even temperature. If you save energy by setting your system to come on and adjust the temperature by 10°C (about 18°F) in the half-hour before you come home, your plants will resent it. Happily, the 18–21°C (about 64–70°F) that most people find comfortable will suit most plants too, and if it falls by a couple of degrees during the night they'll appreciate it.

Watering

More house plants drown than die of thirst—water with care. Just about all should be allowed to dry out a little between waterings: but if you can't be so hard-hearted, pot them in terracotta pots, whose porosity makes it harder to over-water than impervious plastic. It looks better too. You can then use the best method of testing: tap the pot and if it rings, the plant needs water; if you hear a dull thud, it doesn't. This doesn't work with plastic! Alternatively, try one of the various self-watering pots, which allow the plants to draw just the water they need from a reservoir in the bottom. Or try concentrating on spathiphyllums, which are among the very few house plants that like constant damp feet!

Temporary Plants

It is all very well to say that happiness comes from concentrating on the easy plants, but you would be less than human if you were not to fall sometimes for one of the difficult but spectacular flowering types like cyclamen, gloxinias or poinsettias. They aren't impossible— just difficult, needing warmer or cooler conditions than usual, high humidity and great care in watering—but they

The peace lily (Spathiphyllum *'Mauna Loa'*), *one of the most popular indoor plants.*

really aren't happy in the average room. Unless you have a greenhouse or sheltered, totally frost-free place in the garden to use as a convalescent home, resign yourself to their being temporary delights. They'll still last longer than a bunch of cut flowers.

Fertilizing and Repotting

Sooner or later, if a plant flourishes the question of fertilizing or repotting will arise. The advent of slow-release fertilizers has made fertilizing easy. Just buy one formulated for indoor plants, and apply it in spring as growth begins (it's astonishing how, even indoors, plants remain aware of the seasons) according to the directions on the packet. As always, don't overdo the dosage. Fertilizer will usually allow you to at least put off the decision about repotting: but if you feel the plant's shoes really are getting too tight, do the job in spring, handle the plant gently, and don't go up to a pot more than a size bigger than the old one. If you like, you can tease off some of the old soil from the roots to allow more fresh soil, which should be the best, premium grade potting mix you can buy. Naturally, you won't be tempted to put your plant in a container, no matter how beautiful, which has no drainage holes. If you can't

resist, put some pebbles in the bottom, and use it purely as a decorative mask for the holey-bottomed one in which the plant is actually growing.

Pests

Alas, pests sometimes follow house plants indoors. The worst are mildew and root rot (almost always a result of over-watering), red spider and mealy bug. All can be controlled by spraying with insecticides and fungicides, but who would be crazy enough to spray such poisons indoors, quite apart from the mess? If you can't take the plant outside to spray, you can use a systemic insecticide which is stirred into the soil. Fungi are more difficult, and if a plant really is severely infested, it might be wise to consider disposing of it, soil and all. (Wash the pot out with bleach and you can re-use it.)

A final word—dust. This settles invisibly on house plants and robs the leaves of light. Wipe it off regularly with a damp cloth, and, better yet, stand your plants out in the summer rain every so often. If you can bear to forego their company, a few weeks outside in the shadiest place in the garden each summer will do them a power of good; but bring them back in the instant you sense autumn/fall in the air.

Anthurium scherzerianum

Aspidistra elatior

Alocasia macrorrhiza

ALOCASIA
macrorrhiza
GIANT ELEPHANT'S EAR, CUNJEVOL, GIANT TARO

This is a member of a genus of plants from Sri Lanka and tropical South-East Asia which are grown for their spectacular foliage of large leaves with highlighted veins on long stalks. This species has 1 m (about 3 ft) long stalks which carry the broad, arrowhead-shaped, glossy green leaves which grow to 1 m (about 3 ft) in length. It produces insignificant but fragrant flowers on a spadix enclosed in a leaf-like, yellowish-green spathe. It can be grown outdoors only in warmer climates as it is frost-tender, and does best indoors in cool climates. If potted, grow in a rich, peaty mixture. Outdoors, grow in well-drained soil in a shady position with

high humidity. Water heavily and feed regularly with diluted fertilizer. May be propagated from suckers which root easily or by division of rhizomes or stem cuttings planted in spring.

ANTHURIUM
scherzerianum
FLAMINGO FLOWER

Grown for its attractive flowers and foliage, this tropical plant from Columbia grows to 60–80 cm (about 24–32 in), often in a greenhouse or indoors, but given the right conditions will grow outdoors. Anthuriums have long-stalked, heart-shaped leaves and long-lasting, graceful, glossy, bright red or pink spathes with yellow or red spadices. Indoors, they need bright light, high humidity and constant warmth and moisture to flower. *A.*

Aphelandra squarrosa 'Louisae'

scherzerianum has red flowers and curled orange to yellow spadices. Plant outdoors in a humid position, in well-drained, peaty soil in full or part-shade out of the wind. Water well, keeping the soil moist but not soggy. The temperature must not fall below 15°C (about 59°F). Propagate from rhizomes in early spring. Potted plants need dividing and repotting every few years. *A. andraenum* and its hybrids are larger and warmer growing.

APHELANDRA
squarrosa 'Louisae'
ZEBRA PLANT

Native to South America, this popular indoor plant takes its common name from its large, glossy, dark green leaves, heavily striped by white veins. It grows to 1 m (about 3 ft). It is sometimes called 'Saffron spike' due to the bright yellow flower bracts which surround the tiny white flowers and which appear in spring. Needs bright light, but not direct sunlight, and warm, reasonably humid conditions, especially when flowering. For high humidity stand the pot on a tray of pebbles and water. It is best in a rich, porous soil and can be grown in relatively small pots as it prefers to be slightly pot-bound. Keep well watered in the warmer months and less in winter, but never let soil ball dry out, and fertilize regularly. As it tends to become leggy, prune back after flowering, leaving one or two pairs of leaves. Propagate by cutting off side shoots that have roots. Leaf-drop can be caused by dry roots, low or sudden

drops in temperature, or by direct sun. Browning of leaf tips or brown leaf spots may be caused by low humidity.

ASPIDISTRA
elatior
CAST-IRON PLANT

This is a species of evergreen perennials from Japan, China and the Himalayas, and was one of the most famous house plants of the Victorian era. The tough, long, narrow, dark green leaves are pointed at the tips and arch elegantly on a clump of 15 cm (about 6 in) stems to a length of 60 cm (about 24 in). There is also a handsome variegated form. The cream to dark purple, bell-shaped flowers grow at soil level and are screened from view by the leaves; it is something of an event to see them, as indoor plants seldom flower. It is known, for good reason, as the 'cast-iron plant' as its ability to withstand neglect makes it one of the toughest and most adaptable house plants. It can be kept in bright to very low light, but direct sunlight burns the leaves. Water lightly when soil is dry and do not stand the pot in water. Feed occasionally and regularly wipe leaves with a damp cloth to maintain the gloss. When the plant becomes very crowded, divide the root crown and repot in late winter to early spring.

BEGONIA
BEGONIA

Begonias are native to all tropical regions except Australia and there are over 1500 known species. They are prized for their beautifully coloured foliage and attractive flowers, making an ideal indoor plant with a number of varieties readily available. This diverse group includes rhizomatous, fibrous-rooted and tuberous plants. They all have waxy leaves and a succulent form. They do well in indoor potting mix with either peat moss, leafmould or decomposed cow manure added to increase acidity. Grow in bright to moderate light, with fresh air, above average humidity and temperatures of 16–30°C (about 60–85°F). Humidity can be maintained by standing the pot on a tray of pebbles and water. Keep soil moist but not soggy. Fertilize in the spring growing season. Pinch back young plants to stop them becoming gangly and to encourage flowers. Most begonias can be propagated from stem and leaf cuttings in spring, by division of rhizomes or from seed. Begonias are susceptible to grey mould, powdery mildew and botrytis from late spring to early autumn/fall if conditions are too damp.

B. auriculata
CATHEDRAL WINDOWS

This evergreen rhizomatous begonia grows to 30–35 cm (about 12–14 in) high and the spreading trunk to a width of 40 cm (about 16 in). The green and red leaves are thick and ear-shaped. It has tall spikes of pink flowers.

B. X *cheimantha* 'Gloire de Lorraine'
CHRISTMAS BEGONIA, LORRAINE BEGONIA

The single, white to pale pink flowers appear in winter on this round-leafed plant. The leaves are bright green and it grows to a height of 30 cm (about 12 in).

B. 'Cleopatra'

This is a popular, easy-to-grow plant with 5 cm (about 2 in) wide, star-shaped leaves. The yellow-green leaves have brown markings with a reddish underside. Clusters of pale pink flowers bloom in early spring.

B. masoniana
IRON CROSS BEGONIA

This plant's name is derived from the bold, brown, iron cross mark on the bright green, puckered leaves. This evergreen, rhizomatous plant grows to a height of 45–60 cm (about 18–24 in) and a spread of 30–45 cm (about 12–18 in). The single, pinkish white flowers are insignificant.

B. rex 'Merry Christmas'
syn. *B. ruhrtal*

Rex are the most common foliage begonias and are available in many cultivars. This evergreen, creeping, rhizomatous variety has a band of emerald green with a rose-red centre and silver highlights on the leaf. The leaves are 15–20 cm (about 6–8 in) long with the plant growing to 25–30 cm (about 10–12 in) high.

BILLBERGIA
VASE PLANT

This genus, comprising about 50 species and many garden varieties, was originally from the jungles of the American tropics where most grew on rocks or suspended in trees. With their exotic foliage of long, thin, stiff leaves, often edged with small teeth, and showy flowers, they are easy to grow and make an ideal indoor plant. The flower displays appear at many times of the year. The rosette of leaves form a cup and it is by filling this cup that the plant should be watered. A porous, fast-draining soil mix is required, but they will grow sitting in a pot of stones. The plant multiplies quickly and can be propagated by division. Scale and mealy bug can be a problem, and brown leaves

may be due to too much sun. Ensure the pot is heavy enough as the weight of the foliage may cause the plant to fall over.

B. leptopoda

The striking grey-green leaves are heavily powdered with silver and framed by small spines or teeth. Dark blue flowers enclosed in salmon-pink bracts appear in winter. A height of 30 cm (about 12 in) is reached. This is one of a number of similar species, all spectacular.

B. nutans
QUEEN'S TEARS, FRIENDSHIP PLANT

Almost hardy, this species can be grown out of doors in shady places where it will only have to endure the occasional light frost. Indoors it likes a rich potting mix and good light. The leaves are long and narrow, plain olive green, and the pendent clusters of flowers appear in spring. They are a unique combination of pale green and navy blue, but it is the pink bracts that grow along the flower stems that catch the eye.

B. pyramidalis var. concolor

A showy, erect spike of pyramid-shaped, rose-red and purple-tipped flowers appears from late summer to mid-winter. Broad, apple-green leaves form rosettes, sometimes with silver banding. It grows to 30–50 cm (about 12–20 in).

Begonia 'Cleopatra'

Begonia rex 'Merry Christmas'

Billbergia nutans

Begonia X *c.* 'Gloire de Lorraine'

Begonia masoniana

Billbergia pyramidalis var. *concolor*

Begonia auriculata

Billbergia leptopoda

Costus speciosus

Calathea makoyana

Codiaeum variegatum

Cordyline terminalis 'Imperialis'

Calathea zebrina

Callisia navicularis

frequently or standing the pot on a tray of pebbles and water. Clean the leaves with a damp cloth. Do not allow to dry out completely and feed with half-strength fertilizer every 4 to 5 weeks, when conditions are warm and growth is active. A standard potting mix, with sand added to the mix for good drainage, is needed. Repot annually as they exhaust the soil and do not like to be overcrowded. Propagate by division in early spring. These plants are occasionally bothered by aphids, mealy bugs, red spider mites and thrips.

C. makoyana
PEACOCK PLANT

This dwarf species has oval, pale yellow-green leaves with a feathery design of darker green markings. The underside has the same markings in purple.

C. zebrina
ZEBRA PLANT

The large, velvety, floppy leaves on short stems are deep green, marked by parallel stripes or bars of pale chartreuse. The undersides are purplish red. In winter the leaves turn yellow and can be removed to reveal clusters of chocolate brown bracts which are the spring flowers.

CALLISIA
navicularis
syn. *Tradescantia navicularis*

Grown for its decorative foliage, this low-growing perennial reaches 5–8 cm (about 2–3 in) high and has creeping shoots which root where they touch the soil. Two rows of oval, keeled, reddish green leaves enclose the stem. In summer to autumn/fall clusters of small, stalkless, 3-petalled, pink to purple flowers appear in the leaf axils. Grow in well-drained, moist, fertile soil in full light but not direct sunlight. If grown outdoors it is frost-tender to a minimum of 10–15°C (about 50°–59°F). Propagate from tip cuttings inserted into light compost in mid-spring or summer.

CODIAEUM
variegatum
CROTON

Originally from Malaysia and Polynesia, this tropical, well-known indoor plant is grown for its brilliantly coloured foliage. The glossy, leathery leaves come in a range of shapes and are variegated in red, yellow, pink and orange, with only the new leaves in green. The small flowers are insignificant. It reaches a height of 1–2 m (about 3–6 ft). Grow outdoors only in warm climates in half- to full shade with a minimum temperature of 10–13°C

(about 50–55°F). If grown indoors it requires bright light, a moist atmosphere and rich, well-drained soil. Water well during the warm season but allow to dry out between waterings when the temperature is low. To encourage branching, remove tips from very young plants. Repot in spring in a peaty compost. Propagate from stem cuttings in spring or summer. Mealy bug or soft scale can be a problem.

CORDYLINE
terminalis 'Imperialis'
TI TREE, TI PLANT, HAPPY PLANT

From Polynesia, this is the only species of *Cordyline* not native to Australia and New Zealand. Most plants are started from 'logs', which are small sections of mature branches imported from Hawaii. It resembles a palm with lance-shaped leaves on cane-like stems. The ti tree needs plenty of room indoors to grow to its full height of 2–4 m (about 6–12 ft). It prefers filtered sunlight and needs higher temperatures and humidity than others of the genus. To increase humidity, stand the plant on a tray of pebbles and water, but do not mist the leaves. It can be allowed to dry out in winter, but keep moist during the growing season from spring to autumn/fall. Problems arise from aphids, mealy bugs, scale and thrips. Fluoride in the water or perlite in the potting mix can cause browning of the leaves.

COSTUS
SPIRAL FLAG, SPIRAL GINGER

This genus of clump-forming perennials comprises 150 species scattered throughout the tropics, particularly Asia and South America. They have attractive flowers carried in heads whose bracts are arranged rather like a pine cone. Preferring temperatures above 18°C (about 64°F), they are suitable for planting outdoors only in tropical or subtropical regions, but they make a showy indoor plant. Grow in humus-rich soil in a well-lit position, but not direct sunlight, and a humid atmosphere. It requires an abundance of water. Propagate by division or from seed in spring. Plants grown indoors may be bothered by red spider mite. *C. speciosus* bear white, sometimes pinkish, flowers with yellow centres.

CRYPTANTHUS
zonatus
ZEBRA PLANT, EARTH STAR

Cryptanthus have earned the name 'earth star' because of the unusual shape of the low-growing rosettes. *C. zonatus* is a native of Brazil, growing to 10–15 cm (about 4–

CALATHEA
PRAYER PLANT

Native to South America and the West Indies, this large genus of plants are grown for their decorative foliage. The long-stalked, mostly upright leaves are usually large with beautiful colourings in shades of green, white, pink, purple and maroon, with contrasting markings. Many leaves have purple undersides. Calatheas require moderate to bright light, but never full sun, and high humidity achieved by misting

6 in) high. The attractive foliage resembles a zebra skin with sepia-green leaves that are wavy edged and banded crosswise with ivory and tannish brown markings. In summer, a cluster of tubular, white flowers appears in each rosette. It is very easy to grow indoors. Grow in a standard potting mix with some sphagnum moss or peat added. Water regularly, maintain humidity and give the plants moderate to bright light. Propagate from offsets which are liberally produced in late spring to summer.

CTENANTHE
lubbersiana
BAMBURANTA

Originally from Brazil, this splendidly marked, foliage plant is an erect, leafy perennial. It produces insignificant flowers. The most commonly grown Ctenanthe,'this variegated species grows to 75 cm (about 30 in) or more. The lance-shaped, green leaves are patterned in irregularly shaded bands of pale yellow-green with pale green undersides. The attractive leaves grow on tall, branching stems. Small, white flowers on one-sided spikes are produced intermittently. Grow in a standard potting mix; add coarse sand to aid drainage. A humid atmosphere is important, so mist foliage occasionally. Keep evenly moist and do not allow to dry out completely. Propagate by division or from basal offsets in spring, but do not repot too often as it likes to be crowded. Give bright to moderate light but direct sunlight may cause the leaves to curl. Low humidity may result in poor growth.

CYCLAMEN
persicum
FLORIST'S CYCLAMEN

From the woodlands of the Middle East, this is the most common species grown indoors and is readily available. From the heart-shaped leaves, which are often marbled light and dark green with silver markings, rise waxy flowers in shades of white and pink, sometimes ruffled or edged with a contrasting tone. There is profuse flowering over a long period in winter. Needs high humidity so stand on a tray of pebbles. To continue flowering it must be kept cool at night. Thoroughly water, avoiding getting water in among the bases of the leaves for fear of rot, then let the surface become just dry. In summer leave in the pot but do not water. Repot in autumn/fall in potting mix with a sprinkling of lime and blood and bone; resume watering. Often flowers are not as good after the second year. Susceptible to black root rot.

Cyperus involucratus

Dieffenbachia 'Amoena'

CYPERUS
involucratus
syn. C. flabelliformis

Grass-like plants, *Cyperus* come from both American continents, Europe and Africa. *C. involucratus* grows to about 1 m (about 3 ft) and sends up triangular, hollow stalks crowned by a whorl of leaf-like bracts. The green flower spikes appear in summer. Grow in rich compost and water well by standing the pot in a dish of water. Direct sunlight is tolerated. Repot when the plant fills the container. If the tips brown, the atmosphere may be too dry. A lack of new stems may be due to too little light.

DIEFFENBACHIA
DUMB CANE

These decorative foliage plants from tropical America reach ceiling height when mature. The large, variegated leaves are oval-shaped. Popular indoor plants, they are easy to maintain, provided humidity is maintained by mist spraying, and extremes of temperatures are minimized by keeping them away from windows in winter. Bright to moderate light suits them. Allow the surface soil to become dry in between thorough waterings as root rot may occur if over watered. Propagate in spring or summer from cuttings or stems laid horizontally in compost, but be careful to wash

Cyclamen persicum

Cryptanthus zonatus

your hands. The common name is due to the poisonous sap which causes the mouth and tongue to swell, rendering speech impossible.

D. 'Amoena'
syn. D. seguine 'Amoena'

This robust plant of up to 2 m (about 6 ft) has large, sword-like, deep green leaves marked with cream-white bars and blotches along the lateral veins. It has insignificant, greenish white flowers and flourishes in poor light.

Ctenanthe lubbersiana

Drosera capensis

Episcia cupreata

Episcia 'Pink Brocade'

Epipremnum aureum

Dizygotheca elegantissima

Dieffenbachia s. 'Rudolph Roehrs'

D. seguine 'Rudolph Roehrs'
syn. *D. seguine* 'Roehrsii'

Slightly smaller, growing to 1 m (about 3 ft) or more, this plant has sword-like, chartreuse leaves with mid-rib and edges in green.

DIZYGOTHECA
elegantissima
syn. *Aralia elegantissima*
FALSE ARALIA, FINGER ARALIA

An elegant, erect plant from the New Hebrides which can grow to 2 m (about 6 ft) indoors. When young, the leaves are bronze-green changing to a lustrous, dark green with maturity. Between 7 and 10 thin, finger-like leaflets with saw-toothed edges grow from slender, mottled green stems. Grow in an all-purpose soil mix in bright, indirect light with no direct sun. Water well during growing period, and at other times only when the top soil is dry—it is extremely sensitive to the level of moisture in the soil, developing leaf drop if it is too high. Difficult to propagate, it prefers to be pot-bound; repot every 2–3 years in spring. Susceptible to whitefly, red spider mite and mealy bug. It can be grown outdoors in warm, frost-free climates, where it grows to a 6 m (about 18 ft) tree with coarse adult foliage—very different from the way it looks indoors.

DROSERA
capensis
CAPE SUNDEW

This insect-eating plant grows to 15 cm (about 6 in) with small rosettes of narrow leaves covered in sensitive, red, glandular hairs which secrete fluid. It attracts insects which get stuck to the leaves and are digested by enzyme secretions. In summer there are many small, purple flowers on leafless stems. Frost-tender and delicate to grow, it should be planted in a pot, preferably in a greenhouse, in a mixture of peat and sphagnum moss, standing the pot on a saucer of water. If grown outdoors plant in the sun in a similar mixture; do not let the soil dry out. Water only with rainwater as it is very sensitive to the impurities found in tapwater. Propagate from seed or by division of rhizomes in spring.

EPIPREMNUM
aureum
syn. *Scindapsus aureus*
POTHOS, DEVIL'S IVY

This evergreen root climber is sometimes mistaken for a philodendron. It is a fast-growing plant which can be kept in water for months or planted in good, rich, moisture-retentive soil. The apple-green, heart-shaped leaves are marbled with creamy white or gold. It needs bright, indirect light and a humid and draught-free location. Water regularly during spring and summer, less in winter. Pinch out shoot tips to encourage branching. Propagate in late spring from leaf-bud or stem cuttings, which are kept in barely moist soil in a dark position until they have rooted. Poor light may cause a lack of variegation.

EPISCIA

From the jungles of tropical America and the West Indies, this relative of the African violet makes an ideal plant for hanging baskets. The attractive, ornamental leaves cascade from runners down the sides of the pot or basket with, given the right conditions, long-lasting, colourful flowers. Plant in African violet mix or porous, peaty, indoor plant mix in bright light (no direct sun). They require constant warmth and humidity, so are well suited to a sunny bathroom or glassed area. Keep moist at all times, but take care not to over water as it leads to rotting. Pinch back stems after flowering to encourage branching, and repot every year in spring. Propagate in summer by laying runners in compost, from stem cuttings or by division. Lack of flowers may be due to poor light.

E. cupreata
FLAME VIOLET

The attractive, felted, bronze leaves have silver veins. This plant intermittently produces tubular, scarlet flowers with yellow centres.

E. 'Pink Brocade'

The runners bear deep, copper-green leaves variegated in silver and pink. Small pink flowers appear in summer but not freely.

Ferns

Their love of shady places makes ferns eligible for indoor culture, and many species do very well. For recommendations, check the chapter, 'Ferns, Palms & Cycads'.

FICUS

A genus of great variety, with some of the most reliable and adaptable house plants, grown for their foliage and tropical effect. Their leathery leaves allow them to tolerate a dry atmosphere. They need bright light, but will tolerate low light and an average room temperature and a winter temperature of at least 13°C (about 55°F). Water moderately, keeping moist in the warmer months, and very little when the temperature is low. Over watering may lead to leaf drop. Sponge leaves with a damp cloth. Propagate from stem or leaf-bud cuttings and repot when roots fill the pot, but remember, figs like to be slightly cramped. They are generally pest free, but red spider mite may cause problems.

F. elastica 'Decora'
INDIA RUBBER TREE, RUBBER PLANT

One of the most foolproof of all indoor plants, this strong-growing *Ficus* has broad, leathery, glossy, deep green leaves 20–30 cm (about 8–12 in) long. Variegated-leaved cultivars are also available. New leaves are encased in rosy pink sheaths that wither and drop, the emerging leaves having a pinkish bronze hue. They can grow to 3 m (about 9 ft) or more and tolerate less light than most plants of this size. If it gets too lanky, prune and stop the flow of the sap with powdered charcoal or chalk.

F. lyrata
FIDDLE-LEAF FIG

A handsome indoor plant, particularly when young, it has huge, lustrous, dark green leaves shaped like a fiddle. The leaves are 30 cm (about 12 in) or more long and are prominently veined. It may grow to 3 m (about 9 ft) indoors and will tolerate low light. Older specimens often appear scraggy and need pruning to make the plant bushy.

GESNERIA
cuneifolia
FLORAL FIRE CRACKER

The genus *Gesneria* is native to the islands of the Caribbean and are

ideal for growing in terrariums. The dark green leaves with light green underside are spoon-shaped and serrated, and can grow to a length of 15 cm (about 6 in). The bright orange, tubular flowers appearing from leaf axils are the size of small Chinese crackers. They bloom mostly in summer and the duration of the bloom depends on temperature. They like a well-drained, leaf-rich soil, bright light and high humidity. Keep well watered and propagate in spring from leaf cuttings or by division of rooted runners.

GRAPTOPHYLLUM
pictum
CARICATURE PLANT

This evergreen shrub grows to over 1 m (about 3 ft) tall and has oval, pointed, green leaves with yellow variegation in the centre. In spring and summer red to purple tubular flowers appear on terminal spikes. Plant in well-drained, fertile soil in part-shade. It can be grown outdoors in subtropical climates. Give plenty of water when growing in the warmer months and less in cooler weather. It requires temperatures above 16°C (about 61°F). To promote branching, tip prune young plants and cut back hard after flowering. Propagate from semi-ripe cuttings in spring or summer.

GUZMANIA

The plants in this genus of bromeliads are known for their formation of rosettes of smooth leaves and attractive flowers. The long-lasting bracts in red, green or

yellow surround a spike of white flowers. Grow in a pot of open, rubble-filled compost. Water moderately during the growing season, less at other times, but always keep the leaf vases filled with water. Propagate in spring or summer from suckers on the parent stem; the original plant usually dies after flowering. *G. lingulata* is the most common of the genus, with basal rosettes of broadly strap-shaped, apple-green leaves growing to a height of 30–45 cm (about 12–18 in). The much showier orange-red bracts surround the clusters of tubular, white to yellow flowers. There are varieties with red-tinted or variegated leaves available also.

HEDERA
COMMON ENGLISH IVY

There are several species of ivy, but the most famous and the only one to thrive indoors is *H. helix*, which is available in many named varieties. As a trailing plant it makes an excel-

lent hanging basket, but it can also be trained to climb almost any kind of support. It comes in a wide array of leaf shapes and colours. Use an all-purpose potting soil and place in a cool, bright spot. It will tolerate some direct weak sun, and likes extra humidity by misting or placing on a tray of pebbles and water. Keep moist, but not soggy, and do not let the soil dry out completely. In spring, prune to encourage bushy growth. Propagate from stem cuttings or rooted runners. Spider mites, scale, thrips and aphids might be a problem. If the plant is not doing well place outdoors for the summer.

H. helix 'Cripsii'
VARIEGATED IVY

There are many cultivars of ivy with variegated leaves, suitable for growing indoors. 'Cripsii' has attractive marblings of dark grey-green with cream; 'Glacier' and 'Gloire de Marengo' are similar in colour. 'Goldheart' is perhaps the best of the green-and-gold cultivars.

Gesneria cuneifolia

Guzmania lingulata

Graptophyllum pictum

Hedera helix 'Crispii'

Ficus elastica 'Decora'

Ficus lyrata

A Field Trip to Fortin de las Flores

The little town of Fortin de las Flores is about a one-day drive east from Mexico City. Set in lush tropical jungle, Fortin is a mecca for bromeliad lovers in general, and more particularly a major native habitat for the epiphytic bromeliad, *Tillandsia ionantha*. This is one of the 'air plants', so-called because they do not use roots to obtain nutrients and appear to survive on nothing but air. The trip to Fortin takes you comfortably along the toll roads that radiate from Mexico City to outlying areas. You will pass through a wide variety of landscapes—green valleys, desert vegetation, mountain country, tropical jungle and pine forests—in abrupt and striking succession.

The toll road following highway F190 and then F150 takes you through the states of Puebla and Veracruz in the heart of Mexico, a region rich in churches and pyramids as well as orchids and bromeliads. On the way you will have the rewarding experience of seeing four of the country's most famous mountains (Popocatepetl, Ixtaccihuatl, Malinche and Orizaba), all snow-capped and in stark contrast to the surrounding jungle.

This route also takes you through the city of Puebla, one of Mexico's oldest and yet most progressive centres. Continuing on past the Tehuacan turn-off, the road climbs the Sierra Madre Oriental mountain range, at an altitude of 2200 m (about 7200 ft), and there are spectacular views of the valley of Acultzingo. At the peak you can find broad leaf air plants of the genus *Tillandsia* thriving in the moist and cloudy

atmosphere. Soon however, you will quickly descend to an oak forest which is home to the succulents *Echeveria nuda* and coral-beads (*Sedum stahlii*).

If you have time, a side trip to the Tehuacan Valley provides an ideal opportunity for cactus lovers. In areas uncleared by farming you can find many huge cacti colonies of the genera *Opuntia*, *Stenocereus*, *Ferocactus* and *Mammillaria*, and also various *Agave* species. It is also home to some of the drier-growing air plants, including the ball moss (*Tillandsia recurvata*) and several related species.

On the road to Fortin is the home of Dr Alfred Lau, an evangelist and leading world cacti expert whose interests extend to the conservation of orchids, bromeliads, passion flower vines and other tropical plants. A visit to his garden is a must. There you can wander through 1.2 ha (3 acres) of landscaped garden, featuring epiphytes landscaped on to citrus and other trees. A nearby motel, the Posada Loma, is the usual stopping point for bromeliad enthusiasts, as it too has an excellent garden.

The town of Fortin de las Flores is a beehive of people, bars, open-style shops, livestock, and even a resort hotel. The town is surrounded by jungle, and trails run into it from the edges of town. It is possible to walk these trails, starting at the edge of the tropical fruit orchards or roadsides, to study the rich variety of flora, bird life and, occasionally, animals. It is a delight to sit quietly and watch the humming birds feeding from the flowers and you may even catch sight of the elusive toucan or bands of spider monkeys.

In the jungle around Fortin the blushing bride (*Tillandsia ionantha*) can be found growing on the trees both above and in front of you. Fallen branches make the best studies as recently fallen branches will still have plants intact and alive. Usually no more than 5 cm (about 2 in) across, *T. ionantha* grows either singly or in clumps, forming a rosette of fleshy pointed leaves frosted with silver scales. Its common name, blushing bride, refers to the way the leaves turn red when the plant is in bloom, in contrast to the blue of its flowers.

Mexican landscapes vary from desert to jungle to mountainsides.

Tillandsias growing on tree trunks in the jungle.

Tillandsia ionantha

Ball moss (*T. recurvata*) grows here too, with other air plants. This small, clumping plant with small blue flowers grows in ball formations on trees, power lines and house roofs. Another air plant that grows in association with *T. ionantha* is Spanish moss (*T. usneoides*), which has long, grey strands and small, scented, green flowers. Its habit of tangling around tree branches makes it popular as bird nest material.

Be careful when examining the larger air plants. They hold quantities of water between their leaves, and a plant tipped on to the ground is likely to reveal cockroaches, salamanders, frogs, spiders and other insects that could sting and bite. As well, watch out for paper wasp nests in the trees as even a slight tap on these can disturb the wasps.

A short trip north on highway F139 will bring you to the town of Huatusco, where *T. ionantha* was first recorded in 1898. The jungle in this area is also home to many beautiful broad leaf air plants including *T. deppeana*, *T. multicaulis* and *T. lieboldiana,* which has bright red bracts and blue tubular flowers which attract pollinating birds and butterflies. If you study the moss-covered branches you will also find many different orchids, cacti and ferns, as well as various *Columnea* and *Anthurium* species. On the floor of the jungle grow giant *Spathiphyllum* species, including elephant ears, which are used as rain hats by the Indian children. Fruit salad plant (*Monstera deliciosa*) is common in all its trailing and compact forms. The colour-changing chameleon and brightly coloured iguana are among the many lizards seen scuttling across the roads and walking tracks. The jaguar and ocelot, both magnificent cats, can occasionally be spotted in the area.

The best time to visit this area is during the earlier months of the year, when the average temperature is around 18°C (about 64°F), and before the rainy season which lasts from June to September.

The whole region covered in this field trip is botanically very rich, but for those who love bromeliads, particularly the epiphytic ones, the jungle around Fortin is the botanic equivalent of heaven.

Tillandsia

Tillandsias are members of the Bromeliaceae family. With 1500 or more species divided among about 60 genera, the family is almost entirely confined to the Americas, the majority South American.

Tillandsia is the largest bromeliad genus, and it is best represented in Mexico and the adjacent countries. Its over 400 species include the most extreme epiphytes, or 'air plants', which appear literally to subsist on nothing but air. Most tillandsias have leaves clothed in minute silvery scales which behave like sponges, soaking up water from rain or mist and absorbing it into the plant's tissues. The scales also trap dust and fine organic debris, from which the plants derive their nutrient minerals; rainwater also contributes essential nitrogen, converted to soluble form by tropical thunderstorms. Successful cultivation of tillandsias requires high humidity combined with high light levels.

Many new forms of *T. ionantha* are emerging, especially from countries in which they are grown for the commercial horticultural market. Popular for its unusual appearance and its adaptability, *T. ionantha* is exported in huge quantities from Mexico and other Central American countries to satisfy a growing world market.

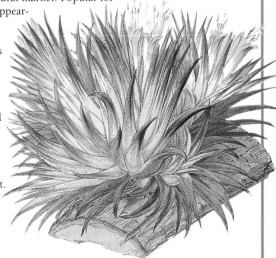

Tillandsia ionantha

Hoya carnosa

Hedera helix 'Pittsburgh'

Hoya bella

Hemigraphis alternata

Nematanthus gregarius

Monstera deliciosa

Maranta leuconeura

H. helix 'Pittsburgh'
syn. H. helix 'Hahn's Self-branching'

A dense, branching plant, this cultivar has closely set, small, deep green leaves.

HEMIGRAPHIS
alternata
RED IVY

This creeping or trailing plant has wonderful foliage of ivy-like, heart-shaped or oblong, deeply puckered, metallic, purplish grey leaves with wine-red undersides and stems. The white summer flowers hardly show at all. Grow in an all-purpose potting mix in bright light, but not direct sunlight. They like average room temperature and humidity. Keep moist and water frequently in the growing season, less in winter. Cut back the spindly stems and pinch off the growing tips to encourage a bushy shape. Propagate from stem cuttings in spring or summer. It is rarely bothered by pests.

HOYA

Twining and/or root climbers with waxy foliage, native to Malaysia, China, India and tropical Australia. They all bear clusters of scented, star-shaped flowers in summer. If the plant is supported on a frame and also slightly pot-bound it is more likely to flower, but may not do so for several years. Plant in any potting soil that drains well, in bright to very bright light, with moderate temperatures and humidity. Allow the soil surface to become quite dry between waterings. As the new flowers come from the same spurs as the old ones it is best not to prune or pick. Propagate from semi-ripe cuttings in summer. Be careful where you place the plant as sticky honeydew drips from the flowers.

H. bella
BEAUTIFUL HONEY PLANT

From India, this shrubby species has pendulous stems and bright green, narrow, lance-shaped leaves. It looks best when grown in a hanging pot or basket where the summer flowers can be easily admired. The star-shaped white flowers, with red or purplish pink centres, hang in flattened clusters.

H. carnosa
WAX PLANT

Native to Queensland, Australia, this twining plant can be grown against a small framework. From summer to autumn/fall, it has dark green, glossy, oval leaves and scented, star-shaped flowers, white to pink in colour and with dark pink centres.

MARANTA
leuconeura var. kerchoviana
RABBIT TRACKS, PRAYER PLANT

Maranta is a genus from tropical America, containing plants grown for their strongly patterned, coloured foliage. Variety kerchoviana has oval, light green leaves with brown blotches on either side of the central vein. The insignificant white to mauve flowers appear intermittently. Maranta in general are called 'prayer plants' because they fold their leaves into a vertical or upright position, as in prayer, to funnel the condensing dew down to the roots. Grow in humus-rich, well-drained soil, using a shallow container, in moderate to low light. They need even, warm temperature and high humidity, but avoid mist spraying as the leaves are easily marked. Keep continually moist. Propagate from stem cuttings or by division in spring or summer. Dry soil or low humidity may cause browning of leaf tips.

MONSTERA
deliciosa
FRUIT SALAD PLANT, SWISS-CHEESE PLANT

A close relative of Philodendron and a native of the West Indies and tropical America, the huge, broad, glossy, perforated and deeply-cut leaves of M. deliciosa grow from woody stems with aerial roots. Mature plants bear thick, cream spathes, followed by sweet-smelling, cone-like, edible fruits, that take about a year to ripen, and usually only outdoors. They are easy to grow and adjust to all but the coldest indoor conditions. Plant in an all-purpose mix in large containers with a stout support for the aerial roots. Some roots can be planted back into the container to help support the plant. Requires bright, indirect light and a high degree of humidity. Water when soil is dry to touch, and feed monthly with a soluble plant food during warm conditions. As M. deliciosa prefer to be pot-bound, repot every 2–3 years in spring. Prune tops off tall plants to limit growth. The lower leaves will drop, but serious leaf drop may result if the plant is moved or there is a sudden environmental change.

NEMATANTHUS
gregarius
syn. N. radicans, Hypocyrta radicans
CLOG PLANT

A relatively easy to grow, trailing plant, it has closely set, glossy, dark green leaves. The dark yellow or orange flowers look puffy and bloom throughout the year, especially if it is slightly pot-bound. It prefers an African violet potting soil

Nidularium fulgens

Neoregelia carolinae 'Tricolor'

Pedilanthus tithymaloides

mix, and bright light with some cool morning sun. Keep the soil moist and the atmosphere humid by placing on a tray of pebbles and water, or mist frequently. It can be grown outdoors in partial shade but is frost-tender. Mealy bug, red spider mite, whitefly and scale may cause problems.

NEOREGELIA

About 50 species and many varieties comprise this spectacular genus of bromeliads. They produce some of the largest rosettes of colourful, thick, shiny leaves, designed to attract fertilizing insects to the tiny flowers blooming deep within the vase. They need bright light with some direct sunlight to maintain colour, and a humid atmosphere. Water regularly and keep the rosette centres full at all times. Propagate from offsets in spring or summer.

N. carolinae
HEART OF FLAME, BLUSHING BROMELIAD

A spreading rosette of 40–60 cm (about 16–24 in) across, composed of light olive-green, strap-shaped, saw-toothed leaves. Just before flowering, which can be at any time of the year, the youngest, inner leaves turn crimson. The cluster of small, inconspicuous, blue-purple flowers is surrounded by crimson-red bracts. The cultivar 'Tricolor', with cream-striped leaves, is seen more often than the species itself.

N. marmorata

Spreading to 50–60 cm (about 20–24 in), the rosettes of red-tipped, pale green leaves are mottled in reddish brown. White flowers bloom deep in the vase in spring to summer.

NEPENTHES
PITCHER PLANT

These insectivorous plants have adapted leaves which form pendulous, coloured pitchers with lids. Insects are attracted to these and drown in the liquid in the pitcher before being absorbed into the plant as food. In rainforests, plants climb via tendrils on the leaf ends. They

Peperomia caperata

are suitable for hanging baskets in a garden where the minimum temperature is 18°C (about 64°F), or for a greenhouse in a temperate climate. Grow as an indoor plant in moist, fertile soil with peat and moss added, in filtered sun and a very humid atmosphere. Propagate from stem cuttings in spring or summer, or from seed in spring.

NIDULARIUM
fulgens
BIRD'S NEST BROMELIAD

Sometimes called 'friendship plants' and resembling the genus *Neoregelia*, *N. fulgens* has dense rosettes of strap-shaped, saw-toothed, glossy, yellow-green foliage with dark green spots. A rosette of scarlet bracts surrounds the white and violet flowers, which appear mainly in summer. The plant is happy in any open, fibrous mix. Position in an area of bright light for good foliage and colour. Water regularly, keeping the rosettes full at all times. Propagate from offsets in spring or summer.

Palms

Many of the smaller species of palm—and some of the larger, at least in their youth—grow very happily indoors. For recommendations, check the chapter, 'Ferns, Palms & Cycads'.

PEDILANTHUS
tithymaloides
ZIGZAG PLANT, DEVIL'S BACKBONE, JACOB'S LADDER

Popular as a greenhouse plant in Britain in the nineteenth century,

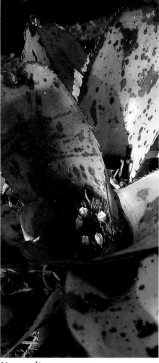

Neoregelia marmorata

this slow-growing succulent from the West Indies, usually grows to about 45 cm (about 18 in). The fleshy, erect stems change direction at each node, hence the name 'zigzag plant'. Leaves are mid-green and sprout from the stems in two rows, resembling ribs on a backbone. (Variegated cultivars are popular.) Showy red bracts shaped like a bird's head, encase small, scarlet flowers, but such flowers are rarely produced indoors. Water sparingly, allowing the soil surface to dry out between waterings. The plant needs very bright light with some direct sun and a dry atmosphere, so it is well suited to wintering in heated rooms. Propagate from seed or summer cuttings, hardened thoroughly. The stems, when cut, secrete poisonous, milky sap. Mildew may be caused by a humid atmosphere.

PEPEROMIA
RADIATOR PLANT

Most of these small plants come from the tropical rainforests of Cen-

Nepenthes, hybrid

tral and South America. Ideal in terrariums or dish gardens, they have diverse and beautifully marked and shaped leaves. They produce long-stemmed spikes of flowers. Well suited to the average home environment, peperomias like bright light (but not direct sun), especially near a window, with high humidity in summer. Keep moist in warm weather, and be sure to water the plants from below as the leaves mark easily; in winter it is best to allow the plants to dry out between waterings. Use a half-strength, soluble fertilizer once a month in spring and summer. Peperomias are easily propagated from leaf or stem cuttings in spring or summer. Re-pot annually. May be pestered by mealy bugs, red spider mites and whitefly.

P. caperata
EMERALD RIPPLE

From the pinkish stems of this species grow oval, deeply corrugated and veined, dark green leaves. Tight clusters of white flower spikes appear irregularly.

Pisonia umbellifera 'Variegata'

Philodendron selloum

Peperomia obtusifolia 'Royal Gold'

Philodendron bipennifolium

Philodendron oxycardium

Peperomia 'Sweetheart'

P. obtusifolia
BABY RUBBER PLANT

This is a bushy perennial with fleshy leaves and occasional spikes of minute flowers. The plain green species is a handsome plant growing about 30 cm (about 12 in) tall. More common are the variegated cultivars with the leaves marbled in grey-green and cream or gold. Good light but not direct sun is needed. Cut back if the plants grow straggly and propagate from cuttings.

P. 'Sweetheart'

Typical of the hybrid peperomias, that appear from time to time, 'Sweetheart' is named for its heart-shaped leaves. *P. marmorata*, the silver-heart peperomia, resembles it except that the leaves have silver markings. Both are a shade larger than *P. caperata*.

PHILODENDRON
PHILODENDRON

Shrubs or climbers native to the tropical forests of Central and South America, these are adaptable, strong plants with handsome leaves and a long life expectancy, making them successful and popular indoors. Arum-like flowers are produced on mature plants in optimum conditions. Grow in bright light with a warm, moist atmosphere, as high humidity improves growth. Water when the surface soil dries out and sponge any dust from the leaves. They need support by tying the aerial roots to a stout pole or moss-covered netting. Remove young stem tips to encourage branching. Philodendrons like to be crowded, so do not plant in too large a pot. Most will drop their lower leaves. Propagate from stem or leaf-bud cuttings in summer. They are free from pests and diseases.

P. bipennifolium
syn. *P. panduriforme*
FIDDLE-LEAF PHILODENDRON

This climber attaches itself to suitable supports by means of aerial roots. A decorative plant, it is unusual for the guitar-like shape of the lobed, bright green leaves. It likes medium light, and in a large pot will grow 2–3 m (about 6–9 ft) tall. Cut back if necessary.

P. oxycardium
syn. *P. scandens*
SWEETHEART VINE, MONEY PLANT

A rapid climber with glossy, heart-shaped, rich green leaves. It may either grow up a column or trail down. The aerial roots on the trailing stems will attach to anything. This is the most common and popular of the genus.

P. selloum

Officially a climber, but in effect a clumpy perennial with a short stem from which the huge, deeply lobed leaves are carried on stalks 60 cm (about 24 in) or more long. It is a magnificent specimen plant, though as a full-grown specimen it can reach 1.5 m (about 4½ ft) high and wide, a bit big for all but the largest rooms. Several cultivars are available, some smaller than usual, others with variegated leaves, and there are several even larger hybrids of which 'Sao Paolo' is most notable. The flowers are insignificant.

PISONIA
umbellifera 'Variegata'
BIRDCATCHER TREE, MAP PLANT

Known in its native New Zealand as 'Para para', this plant is also found in Australia and neighbouring Norfolk and Lord Howe Islands. The 30–40 cm (about 12–16 in), oval leaves are beautifully patterned in tones of pale to dark green and creamy white, resembling a map (hence the common name). The small, greenish flowers rarely appear indoors. The fruit that forms when grown in its native habitat gave it the other common name of 'birdcatcher tree'. Grow in a standard indoor mix in warm temperature and bright light, but keep out of direct sun, wind or warm draughts. Water freely and regularly during the growing season, but in winter allow to dry out between waterings. Mist the plant, and wipe the leaves with milk and water when dull. To encourage bushing, pinch out the growing tips while the plant is young. Propagate from semi-ripe cuttings in summer.

POLYSCIAS
filicifolia
FERN-LEAF ARALIA, MING ARALIA

P. filicifolia, from tropical Asia and
Polynesia, is an unusual house
plant with large, 30 cm (about
12 in) long leaves divided into
bright green, serrated leaflets. They
are not easy to grow as they are
fussy plants. Grow in a container of
standard peaty mix with sand and a
little charcoal added. It needs bright
light (but not direct sunlight) and
warm temperature—keep away
from glass windows in cool climates. Keep humidity high by misting or standing on a tray of pebbles
and water, and keep out of
draughts. Water freely in summer;
keep drier at other times. Feed
monthly with half-strength, soluble
fertilizer during the warm months.
P. filicifolia is at its best when the
plants are young as the stems tend
to grow straggly. These, however,
can be cut back in spring. It prefers
to be pot-bound so repot only
when roots emerge from the pot
hole. Propagate from stem-tip or
stem-section cuttings in summer.
Watch for two-spotted mites and
scale.

PROTASPARAGUS
syn. *Asparagus*
ASPARAGUS FERN

These climbers are grown for their
foliage. They are related to the asparagus of the kitchen table, but
their shoots are too skinny to eat.
They need a fertile, well-drained
soil. Propagate in spring by division
or from seed.

P. densiflorus 'Sprengeri'

This is a sprawling, trailing perennial which grows from small tubers.
Its stems grow about 80 cm (about
32 in) long and, being well clad
with bright green leaves, they look
charming trailing from a hanging
basket, despite the occasional sharp
thorns. In early spring it bears
abundant tiny, white, heavily
scented, flowers, usually followed
by red berries. Remove spent stems
for neatness. Requires good light
and regular watering.

P. setaceus
syn. *Asparagus plumosus*

A slender, climbing perennial with
leaves divided many times into tiny
segments, giving an ultra-ferny
appearance. It is very easy to grow,
provided it is never allowed to
quite dry out and receives good
light. Old leaves need to be removed for neatness, and over-long
stems can be cut to the base in early
spring to encourage new growth.
Handle with care as the plant has
some hooked and razor-sharp
thorns.

SAINTPAULIA
AFRICAN VIOLET

A native of East Africa, saintpaulias
were originally collected in the late
nineteenth century by Baron von
Saint Paul. The several thousand
varieties are some of the most popular flowering indoor plants because
of their attractive foliage, compact
nature, long flowering periods and
wide range of flower colours. Although African violets have a reputation for being difficult to grow,
given the right conditions this is
generally not the case. They do
demand certain soil, however, so it
is easiest to plant in commercial
African violet mix. Constant temperature, moderate humidity and
maximum, bright, indirect light will
ensure prolonged flowering. In
winter this may need to be supple-
mented with artificial light. Use
room temperature water, allowing
the surface soil to dry out a little
between waterings. Avoid splashing
the foliage. Feed once a month in
the warm season with half-strength,
soluble fertilizer. If the plant is
overleafy, flowers may not appear,
so remove some of the leaves. African violets prefer to be slightly pot-
bound to bloom well, but repot
when very leafy and no longer flowering well. They are easy to propagate from leaf cuttings stuck in a
layer of pebbles on top of a moist
sand and peat mixture, so that
leaves do not rot. African violets
are vulnerable to attack by cyclamen mite, mealy bug or powdery
mildew.

S. ionantha

Ionantha means 'with violet-like
flowers' in Greek, and this species
has clusters of tubular, 5-lobed,
violet-blue flowers of semi-succulent texture, growing on the stems
above the leaves. The mid-green
leaves, with reddish green undersides, are scalloped, fleshy and
usually have a hairy surface. There
are thousands of cultivars available,
now far removed from the species.
The flowers can be single or double,
usually 2–5 cm (about 1–2 in)
across, and come in shades from
white through mauve and blue to
purple, and pale and deep pink to
crimson. Some cultivars are parti-
coloured and others have ruffled,
scalloped or variegated leaves.
Named cultivars are available, but
they change constantly and most
growers simply offer a selection by
colour and flower type. Fully grown
plants are normally 25 cm (about
10 in) wide.

S. miniature and trailing types

These African violets are derived
from crosses of *S. ionantha* and
other lesser known *Saintpaulia*
species. They can be compact ro-

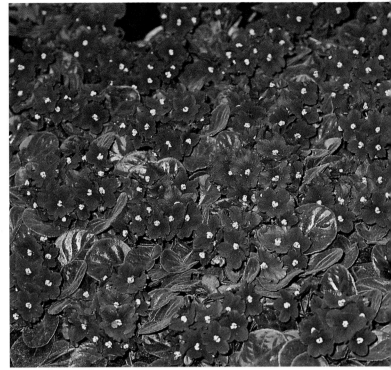
Saintpaulia ionantha

Protasparagus densiflorus 'Sprengeri'

Polyscias filicifolia

Saintpaulia (miniature)

settes, no more than 8 cm (about
3 in) across with leaves and flowers
in proportion—effectively miniatures of the *S. ionantha* cultivars
and available in the same range of
colours—or trailing types, which
may develop stems as much as 10
cm (about 4 in) long. The leaves
and flowers are equally tiny; some
flowers are bell shaped rather than
flat. These miniature types have the
reputation of being easier to grow
than the large ones, but their tiny
pots dry out quickly and they do
need regular watering.

Protasparagus setaceus

SANSEVIERIA
BOWSTRING HEMP,
MOTHER-IN-LAW'S TONGUE

Native to India, and to southern and tropical Africa, these popular and resilient indoor plants are grown for their stiff, fleshy, patterned 30–60 cm (about 12–24 in) tall leaves. Stems of greenish white flowers appear in late spring if conditions have been warm enough during the previous year. The flowers have a slight fragrance. Grow in standard, indoor potting soil with a deep layer of pot rubble for drainage. For good growth, place in bright light with average house temperature and humidity. Sansevierias look their best, however, when the humidity is high, so mist occasionally. Water enough to moisten the soil but allow to dry between waterings in warm weather and, in cool weather, only enough to prevent the soil drying out completely. Over watering may cause rotting at the base of the leaves and roots. Feed monthly in spring and summer with half-strength, soluble plant food. Repot only when the plant fills the pot. Propagate from leaf cuttings or by division in spring or summer. In Africa the fibres are a source of hemp.

S. trifasciata

From the central rosette emerge stiff, lance-shaped leaves, 60–120 cm (about 24–48 in) long, and 4 cm (about 2 in) or more wide. The dark green leaves are banded with grey-green and yellow. The plant sometimes has racemes of tubular, green flowers but rarely when grown indoors.

S. trifasciata 'Hahnii'

This plant has rosettes of banded, grey and green leaves, and is smaller than the other two sansevierias mentioned.

S. trifasciata 'Laurentii'

The narrow upright leaves resemble *S. trifasciata* but they have broad, yellow margins. It sometimes has pale green flowers. Propagate by division.

SCHEFFLERA
syn. *Brassaia, Heptapleurum*

These attractive, subtropical and tropical trees can grow to 2–4 m (about 6–12 ft) indoors and much taller outdoors. The glossy foliage is split into leaflets. They are easy to grow (but rarely flower) indoors. Plant in a standard indoor potting soil, in bright light but no direct sunlight, with average to warm temperatures. Keep humidity high by misting or placing on a tray of pebbles and water. Water freely when in full growth, less at other times, allowing the top of the soil to dry out between waterings. Feed every 6 to 8 weeks in warmer weather, with soluble plant food. Propagate by taking 10 cm (about 4 in) long stem cuttings from just below the node in early spring. Falling leaves may be due to low temperature or too little water. Usually pest free, but occasionally there are problems with red spider mites, mealy bugs and aphids.

S. actinophylla
QUEENSLAND UMBRELLA TREE

The most common indoor species, its glossy foliage resembles segments of an umbrella. Long green stalks are crested by light green leaves divided into 5 to 16 leaflets, the whole being as much as 50 cm (about 20 in) wide. In summer spikes of small red flowers arise from the top of the tree, but this rarely happens indoors where it usually grows to about 2 m (about 6 ft) tall. If the plant gets too big, cut it back in spring.

S. arboricola
MINIATURE UMBRELLA TREE

This plant resembles *S. actinophylla*, but the leaves are only about 12 cm (about 5 in) wide, and it grows into a bushy shrub approximately 80 cm (about 32 in) tall and wide. It can be cut back if it grows straggly. (Outdoors in tropical climates it becomes a 10 m [about 30 ft] tree.) Variegated-leaved cultivars are available. The insignificant flowers and brown-orange fruit are rarely seen indoors.

S. digitata

This is the only species in the genus native to New Zealand. It has rich green leaves that are shaped like a hand and divided into 5 to 10 oval leaflets. In spring there are tiny greenish flowers followed in autumn/fall by small, globular, dark violet fruit, but this happens rarely indoors.

SERISSA
foetida

From South-East Asia, this evergreen shrub has small, oval, deep green leaves that have an unpleasant smell if they are bruised. From spring to autumn/fall 4- or 5-lobed, funnel-shaped, white flowers appear. Cultivars with double flowers or variegated leaves are available also. It is a most attractive garden shrub for frost-free areas; indoors it needs high humidity and good light. Water moderately when growing and less at other times. After flowering, the shape can be retained by trimming. Propagate from semi-ripe cuttings in summer.

SPATHIPHYLLUM

Most species of this genus come from tropical America, but some are native to Malaysia. They are lush, with dark green, oval leaves that stand erect or arch slightly, and beautiful white, cream or green flowers, resembling arum lilies, that bloom reliably indoors. Grow in loose and fibrous, porous potting soil in filtered light away from the sun. To re-create tropical conditions, increase the humidity by placing the plant on a tray of pebbles and water or mist regularly; sponge any dust from the leaves. Water regularly, keeping the soil moist but not soggy, and allow it to dry out a little in winter. Feed every 4 to 6 weeks with half-strength, soluble fertilizer in spring and summer. Propagate by division in spring or summer. Generally pest free, yellowing of foliage may be caused by too much light.

Schefflera actinophylla

Serissa foetida

Schefflera arboricola

Schefflera digitata

Sansevieria trifasciata 'Laurentii'

Sansevieria trifasciata

Sansevieria trifasciata 'Hahnii'

S. 'Mauna Loa'
PEACE LILY

The leathery, lance-shaped, glossy, mid-green leaves reach lengths of 45–60 cm (about 18–24 in). Oval, white, papery spathes, surrounding white spadices, are borne intermittently, turning green with age. It is the best known of a fairly large number of large-flowered cultivars; others are 'Clevelandii', which is shorter, and 'Aztec'.

S. wallisii
WHITE SAILS

This is a dwarf species with clusters of glossy green, lance-shaped leaves on reed-like stems growing to 30 cm (about 12 in). A white spathe encloses tiny, creamy white spadices of fragrant flowers tightly packed around an upright spike. The colour changes to green with age.

SYNGONIUM
podophyllum
syn. *Nephthytis triphylla*
ARROWHEAD VINE

This plant closely resembles its relative, the climbing *Philodendron*, with its handsome climbing or trailing foliage. It has an unusual feature of changing leaf shape with maturity. The young, arrowhead-shaped leaves on the end of erect stalks become, with age, lobed with 7 to 9 glossy leaflets growing to 30 cm (about 12 in) long. There are several varieties with variegated leaves in cream or pink. Grow in an all-purpose potting soil in a warm moist environment. This species tolerates fairly low to bright light, but no direct sunlight. Water thoroughly, allowing the surface to dry out between waterings. Feed when conditions are warm, every 4 to 6 weeks with half-strength, liquid fertilizer. Propagate from stem cuttings in spring or summer. To encourage branching and more young leaves, pinch off long stems.

TILLANDSIA

This genus contains over 350 species of mainly epiphytic plants. Commonly called 'air plants', these bromeliads are grown for their unusual flowers. The flowers are usually carried on spikes, heads or panicles and range in colour from white to purple and green to red. Plant in well-drained sphagnum moss or they may be grown on slabs of bark or driftwood. They are often positioned high up in hanging baskets in order to catch the rising heat. Mist regularly and water moderately in summer and sparingly at other times. Propagate from offsets or by division in spring to summer.

T. cyanea
PINK QUILL

Dense rosettes of grass-like, arching leaves are usually deep green and often reddish brown when new. In summer to autumn/fall the spectacular, paddle-shaped flowerheads rise on tall stems from among the foliage. They consist of overlapping pink or red bracts with deep violet-blue flowers emerging. This variety needs maximum humidity and is best grown in a compost of tree fern fibre, peat and sand.

T. lindenii

The thin, smooth, pointed, arching leaves with red-brown lines grow in a typical rosette. In autumn/fall a large flower spike of crimson or pink-tinted bracts overlaps dense clusters of pansy-shaped, deep blue or purple-blue flowers arising just above the leaves.

TOLMIEA
menziesii
PICK-A-BACK PLANT, PIGGYBACK PLANT, MOTHER-OF-THOUSANDS, YOUTH-ON-AGE

Native to the west coast of the USA, this popular house plant is suitable for both pots and hanging baskets. Bright green, hairy leaves that are ivy shaped with toothed edges, send out new plantlets at the junction of the leaf and stalk. There is also a form with variegated leaves. In spring there are spikes of nodding, tubular to bell-shaped, rich brown and green flowers. Hot, dry air can harm these plants so grow in a cool area in bright to moderate light in an all-purpose potting mix. Keep soil moist but not soggy, and water sparingly in winter. Feed every two months in the warmer season with half-strength, soluble fertilizer. Propagate by planting leaf cuttings or plantlets in spring or summer. Frequent attacks by spider mite create brown or brittle leaves, requiring immediate treatment.

Tillandsia lindenii

Syngonium podophyllum

Spathiphyllum 'Mauna Loa'

Tolmiea menziesii

Tillandsia cyanea

Spathiphyllum wallisii

CHAPTER 10

Cacti &
Succulents

*O*ne of the most intriguing of horticultural statistics comes from Britain. There, nurseries sell more cacti during the school holidays than at any other time of year. The industry interprets that to mean that they appeal strongly to what used to be known (rather pretentiously) as 'junior gardeners'. And why not? A collection of cacti (and other succulents) is just as much fun as a collection of stamps.

You don't have to be an adolescent to find them different and appealing. Nor do you have to have hectares of garden to indulge. Sure, there are giants in the succulent world; but there are many beautiful species that will happily spend their entire lives in a small flower pot.

Some might find them an example of that beauty that resides in grotesqueness; but no one can deny that they are wonderful examples of how life adapts to flourish in the most unpromising of environments. While there are a few

cacti that have migrated to the forests where they live as epiphytes in the manner (and often in the company) of orchids, most of these are plants of the desert, where their lifestyle revolves around the need to conserve water from the rare but copious desert rains.

The cacti, a family from the Americas and distantly related (believe it or not) to the carnation, show the succulent habit at perhaps its most wonderful. They have dispensed with leaves which would only transpire precious water, carrying out the vital business of photosynthesis in the green skin that covers their stems. The stems themselves are enormously swollen and spongy, often being almost spherical so they provide nearly as much light-catching area as leaves would. Many have developed ribbed forms, the ribs ensuring that at least part of the plant is in its own shade. A fat and tender plant full of stored water would be irresistible to thirsty desert animals (at least some of the stories of people lost in the desert saving themselves by breaking open a cactus and sucking the water from it are

true) so the typical cactus has given itself an armory of thorns. Some have so many that they also serve to shade the body of the plant from the sun, almost as though the plant were aware that its thorns were the last vestiges of its leaves.

Handling the plants may put one in mind of the old joke about how porcupines make love (very carefully); but you don't have to be a devoted cactophile to admire their often dazzlingly beautiful flowers. Dazzling is literally true: they need their brilliant sheen and colour to show up in the bleaching desert light.

Other Succulents

The Cactaceae are not the only family of succulent plants, although perhaps they are the only one to be comprised exclusively of succulents. There are succulent members of such well-known garden families as the lilies (agaves, aloes, gasterias) and even the daisies (kleinias, the succulent senecios) as well as families like the Crassulaceae and Mesembryanthemaceae which are

Echinopsis species are highly valued for their brilliant flowers.

predominantly succulents. Most depart from the cacti in preferring to store their reserves of water in succulent leaves rather than stems, and these are often wonderfully shaped, coloured and marked. Their habit varies from shrubby to just a few leaves on ground hugging stems, and their flowers vary from the sheer brilliance of the mesembryanthemums and aloes to almost complete insignificance.

Growing Cacti and Succulents

For all their diversity, cacti and succulents are surprisingly uniform in their cultural needs, and their built-in tolerance of extreme drought makes them invaluable in arid climates. They ask only to be given sun, the more the better; perfectly drained but rich soil (desert soils are usually very fertile, as the prodigious crops they can yield under artificial irrigation show); and to be allowed to dry out completely while they are dormant in winter. Never mind that then they may shrivel alarmingly; they will recover almost fast enough to watch when you water them again in spring. Most can take a degree or two of frost as long as they are dry, but they are best considered tender and grown outdoors only in mild-winter climates. They differ so much in appearance from conventional plants that they need careful placement in the garden. Most people find it easiest to grow them on their own, but you don't have to grow them as single specimens; mass and group them, taking their different heights and colours into account just as you would in creating a border of more conventional perennials or shrubs. If you care to add a few desert-type (xerophytic) shrubs like *Cassia artemisioides* as background and some carpeting annuals like portulacas, you'll find it easier to integrate the planting with the rest of the garden; but you need to exercise restraint—such lush growers as petunias would simply look silly.

Succulents grow perfectly happily in pots and, climate permitting, they can be the ideal answer for a pot placed where it is troublesome to water it frequently—on a roof or balcony for instance. In cold climates, especially those with wet winters, pot culture is the only way most people can grow succulents, either indoors or in a frost-proof greenhouse. Suit the size of the

Notocactus are ideal for beginners as they are very easy to grow.

pot to the plant, and avoid plastic pots if you can—terracotta allows the soil to dry out faster. An open but still rich potting mix is best—you can try adding sand to a regular commercial mix, and mulching the plants with gravel to keep their collars dry. Give the plants as much sun and fresh air as you can, water and fertilize (artificial fertilizer is best) lavishly in spring and early summer while the plants are growing; and then tail off the watering until by the return of cold weather the plants are bone dry.

Almost all can be very easily propagated from cuttings of side shoots, spring being the best time; the only thing to watch is that you don't over-water until the new roots are well developed. Indeed, over-watering is the main thing you can do wrong; it encourages the botrytis fungus to rot the roots and even the bases of the plants, and you can't always save them by making

cuttings of unaffected parts of the plant after drenching everything in a strong fungicide. Mealy bug is the other main pest; it can eat out the growing point of a cactus but can also infest the roots of just about any succulent. As soon as you see it, spray the top and soak the roots in a powerful insecticide.

The only exception to this regime is the epiphytic forest cacti—the epiphyllums, the Christmas cacti, and their ilk. These are definitely tender, needing winter temperatures no lower than about 8°C (about 46°F), and are best grown in hanging baskets, as their usually flattened leaf like-stems tend to weep. They like a fertile, well-drained soil and to be watered in warm weather, but, again, don't water in winter.

All indoor grown cacti and succulents will benefit greatly from being taken outdoors for the summer, but bring them in the moment the weather forecast hints of cold and damp.

Adenium multiflorum

Agave victoriae-reginae

Aeonium arboreum 'Schwarzkopf'

Agave americana 'Variegata'

Aeonium canariense

Adenium obesum

ADENIUM

Originating in tropical and sub-tropical Africa and the Middle East, these semi-succulent shrubs have dense, bloated trunks with woody bases and bright, deep green leaves. The foliage sheds naturally during the dry season but endures for at least another year on cultivated plants. The cylindrical flowers are vividly coloured and have 5 petals. Total sun or semi-shade, porous soil and warm temperatures are required. Propagate from cuttings in summer or seed in spring. They are susceptible to rot. The genus name is derived from Aden, home of the first recorded species.

A. multiflorum
IMPALA LILY

This deciduous, succulent shrub originated in South Africa and reaches to 3 m (about 9 ft) in height. Whorls of silky, lance-shaped to oval leaves appear at the tips of its multiple branches. The decorative, trumpet-shaped blooms are white with deep pinkish red margins.

A. obesum
DESERT ROSE

Valued for its flowers and foliage, this species grows to 2 m (about 6 ft). Whorls of shiny, green, leathery leaves (downy when immature) develop at the ends of plump stems. In mid- to late winter and spring, terminal clusters of vivid, pink-red, tubular flowers appear. This shrub is frost-tender and should be planted in full sun or partial shade. Water sparingly as the species is inclined to rot. Propagate from seed or cuttings in summer.

AEONIUM

Native to the Canary Islands, the Mediterranean and northern Africa, this genus contains 40 short-lived, perennial or evergreen succulents. The species develop either as one large (or several smaller), compact, stemless rosette, or as several long, leathery stalks with rosettes on top. The lush, egg-shaped foliage ranges from vivid green to greenish blue and sometimes purple. Attractive, star-shaped, pink, red, white or yellow flowers appear from the centre of the leaf whorls, usually in spring. These succulents prefer full sun or partial shade, light, well-drained soil and warmer temperatures. Prune stems after the bloom although the flowering rosette will usually die and single-rosette species will die out completely. Propagate from seed or leaf stem cuttings in spring and summer.

A. arboreum 'Schwarzkopf'

This shrubby plant from southern Europe, grows up to 60 cm (about 24 in) in height and 1 m (about 3 ft) in width. Its striking, stemmed rosettes have lance-shaped, purple-black leaves. In spring, after 2 or 3 years, little, starry, golden yellow flowers develop from the centre of each rosette.

A. canariense

This low-growing, frost-tender perennial is native to the Canary Islands where it is typically found growing on rocky outcrops. The species reaches 15 cm (about 6 in) in height and spreads to 50 cm (about 20 in) in diameter. Each rosette has lush green, spoon-shaped leaves with red-tinted edges. After 2 or 3 years, the centre rises to form a flower stem. In spring, yellow, starry flowers develop in a terminal cluster; after blooming the whole plant expires.

AGAVE

This genus consists of over 300 species native to South and Central America. The small species flower after 5 to 10 years; the tall species may not flower until they are 20 to 40 years old. They all like well-drained, gritty soil, but will grow in poor soil. Although they need a very sunny position, young plants should be sheltered if in a frost area. They are drought tolerant, but need regular watering. Propagate from offsets or from seed in spring or summer.

A. americana
CENTURY PLANT

This large succulent makes a very good accent plant in the garden, with a 3 m (about 9 ft) high and wide rosette of thick, fleshy, strap-shaped, grey-green leaves edged with sharp spines and pointed tips; a variety with variegated leaves is popular. It flowers when 10 or more years old with a stalk up to 7 m (about 21 ft) of yellow flowers. The plant dies after flowering, leaving offsets which can be used for propagation.

A. victoriae-reginae
ROYAL AGAVE

Originating in Central America, this slow-growing succulent is considered by many to be the most beautiful of all. Stalkless and up to 60 cm (about 24 in) in height and breadth, its single rosette has dense, narrow, keeled foliage with white edges and surface lines. After 20 years, creamy yellow flowers develop in spring and summer. This extremely resilient species is seldom attacked by pests and requires full sun. Only just half-hardy; a frost-free climate is preferred. If grown in a tub make sure it is a good size, otherwise the species will refuse to bloom and the foliage will be stunted. Plant in rich, well-drained soil and water sparingly. Propagate from seed in spring or from offsets after the rosette has perished.

ALOE
ALOE

This diverse genus of rosetted plants is native to Africa and the Middle East. They range widely in habit, from low and shrubby, to tall and tree-like, with several types of vines and creepers also included.

The whorled, lush, greyish green foliage is usually lanceolate and marked with white lines or patches. In spring and summer, attractive, red, yellow or orange, cylindrical flowers appear in long-stemmed racemes. These plants prefer moderate temperatures and are almost all half-hardy. The larger types prefer full sun, while the dwarf species enjoy semi-shade. Plant in rich, extremely porous soil and only water when the roots appear dry. In spring or summer propagate from seed or stem cuttings.

A. arborescens
KRANTZ ALOE

This popular, South African species has a shrubby habit and reaches up to 2–3 m (about 6–9 ft) in height when in flower. Its short-stemmed rosettes are composed of lush, greyish blue leaves up to 60 cm (about 24 in) long, slightly inward-curving and thorny-edged. Thick clusters of scarlet-red or yellow, cylindrical flowers develop along an upright stem in late winter to early spring. This tough aloe is both salt and drought resistant, and is half-hardy.

A. aristata
TORCH PLANT, LACE ALOE

Native to South Africa, this enduring, stemless species forms a single, basal rosette, 10 cm (about 4 in) tall, and up to 30 cm (about 12 in) wide. Its long, deep green, lanceolate leaves have white surface spots, soft, serrated margins and a curved, short spike on each tip. Clusters of orange-red flowers develop in racemes, in spring. It is half-hardy.

A. barbadensis
syn. *A. vera*
UNGUENTINE CACTUS, MEDICINAL ALOE, MEDICINE PLANT, BURN PLANT

Renowned for its medicinal qualities, this widely cultivated, short-stemmed species is thought to have originated in the Middle East or northern Africa. It grows up to 60 cm (about 24 in) in height and develops dense rosettes composed of long, thick, lance-shaped, greyish green leaves with thorny margins. In summer, small yellow flowers appear in racemes up to 90 cm (about 36 in) in height. This frost-tender species is excellent in window boxes. The flesh of the foliage has soothing qualities and is used in the treatment of scalds.

A. ciliaris
DUNNY VINE

The common name comes from the popular use of this climbing species for hiding outhouses in the Australian outback; it is one of the few climbing plants able to resist semi-desert drought. It prejudices gardeners in more favoured climates against the plant, but it is an attrac-

tive evergreen, half-hardy climber with bright green leaves and scarlet and yellow flowers from spring to autumn/fall. It is easily propagated from cuttings.

A. ferox
TAP ALOE, BITTER ALOE

Originating in South Africa, this lofty, frost-hardy species may grow up to 5 m (about 15 ft) tall. Its single, woody stem produces a dense rosette composed of lance-shaped leaves up to 1 m (about 3 ft) long. These bluish green leaves have a spiny surface with reddish brown spines on the margins. In spring, vivid orange-red blooms appear in a thick, terminal cluster atop a single, slender stalk.

A. variegata
TIGER ALOE, PARTRIDGE-BREASTED ALOE

Native to South Africa, this thicket-forming species grows up to 30 cm (about 12 in) tall and 15 cm (about 6 in) in diameter. The overlaying, pyramidal leaves are boldly marked with white, horizontal bands and have slightly serrated margins. In spring, clusters of funnel-shaped, rose-orange flowers appear at the ends of slender stems.

APTENIA
cordifolia

This mat-forming, enduring succulent is quick growing and up to 5 cm (about 2 in) in height. The creeping stems are covered with lustrous, green, oval leaves. Small, vivid, pink flowers bloom in summer and are daisy-like in appearance with dense stamens. There is also a red-flowered form, and one with variegated leaves. This species is frost-tender and makes good ground cover. It requires extremely porous soil with full sun and should not be watered in cold weather. Propagate from seed or cuttings in spring or summer.

ARGYRODERMA
delaetii
syn. *A. blandum*
LIVING STONES

This bizarre species has two succulent, frosted-green leaves, joined at the base. It appears as a rectangular mass 3 cm (about 1½ in) high with a scooped out centre. In winter a single, deep crimson, daisy-like flower emerges from the middle of the plant, often completely covering the leaves. Plants are half-hardy and require total sun and extremely porous soil. Too much moisture will result in leaf splitting and/or plant rot. Propagate by careful division or from seed in summer. The name comes from the Greek, *derma*: skin and *argyros*: silver, in reference to the foliage.

Argyroderma delaetii

Aloe ciliaris

Aloe variegata

Aptenia cordifolia

Aloe aristata

Aloe ferox

Aloe arborescens

Aloe barbadensis (*Echinocereus* behind)

ASTROPHYTUM

This popular genus contains 6 diverse species of slow-growing cacti, native to Mexico. They range widely in size and their form varies from star-shaped, hence the Greek genus name, to elongated and globular. The plants are divided into 5 to 10 prominent ribs, some with a smooth appearance, some covered in thick hair, others patterned with white, tufty areoles. Individual, large, yellow or red, trumpet-shaped flowers appear from the top of the plant in summer or autumn/fall. The species vary from frost-tender to frost-hardy and prefer porous, alkaline soil. Full sun and dry conditions are also preferred, except during mid-summer. Propagate by grafting and from seed in spring and summer.

A. asterias
SEA URCHIN CACTUS, SAND DOLLAR CACTUS

Looking very much like a sea urchin, this highly valued, greyish green, globular cactus grows to

8 cm (about 3 in) in height and 10 cm (about 4 in) in diameter. It is alternately divided by smooth, vertical ribs and bands of little white areoles. Completely covered with fine, white scales, this cactus is unusual because it has no spikes. Yellow flowers with red interiors bloom in summer. It is frost-tender and should not be watered in winter.

A. myriostigma
BISHOP'S CAP, BISHOP'S MITRE

This odd-looking, half-hardy species grows up to 30 cm (about 12 in) in height and 10 cm (about 4 in) in diameter. It has a greyish green, globular body, divided into 4 to 8 prominent ribs and covered with tiny, white scales. Glossy, yellow blooms appear in summer.

AZUREOCEREUS
hertlingianus
syn. *Browningia hertlingianus*

Native to Peru, this erect, cactus is tree-like in habit, growing up to 4 m

Borzicactus celsianus

Astrophytum myriostigma

Astrophytum asterias

Carnegia gigantea

Azureocereus hertlingianus

(about 12 ft) when cultivated. A slow-developing species, it has a column-shaped, frosted, greyish blue stem with up to 20 ribs and numerous, tufted areoles sprouting rust-coloured spikes. White, tubular, night-blooming flowers appear in summer on larger specimens. This half-hardy species requires full sun and rich, porous soil. Propagate from seed or cuttings in spring and summer.

BESCHORNERIA
yuccoides
MEXICAN LILY

A spectacular member of the lily family, this plant makes clumps of sword-shaped, grey-green leaves about 80 cm (about 32 in) long, rather like a yucca but much less prickly. In spring it sends up 1.5–2 m (about 4½ –6 ft) tall flower stems with pendent, apple-green flowers and bright pink bracts. As the flower stalk is itself pink, it is a spectacular sight. Half-hardy, it prefers full sun and rich but perfectly drained soil. Propagate from seed or offsets.

BORZICACTUS
celsianus
syn. *Oreocereus celsianus*, *Pilocereus celsianus*
OLD MAN OF THE ANDES, OLD MAN OF THE MOUNTAINS

Native to South America, this slow-growing cactus reaches heights of up to 1.5 m (about 4½ ft). The body and branches have 10–18 ribs and rust-coloured spikes. Elliptical

Carpobrotus edulis

Beschorneria yuccoides

areoles sprout long, white hairs which completely cover the younger cacti. Older specimens produce reddish pink summer flowers that close up at night. The species is simple to grow if allowed full sun, porous soil and occasional water. Propagate in spring or summer from seed.

CARNEGIA
gigantea
syn. *Cereus giganteus*
SAGUARO

This is the most famous of all cacti—the 6 m (about 18 ft) tall one that raises single or branched columns in the background of just about every early cowboy movie. It is native to the deserts of California and New Mexico (USA), where changes to the ecology and the depredations of tourists are seriously endangering its future as a wild plant. It grows very slowly, and a seedling will take many years to be tall enough (3 m [about 9 ft]) to flower; but the white, sweetly scented, night-blooming, summer flowers are worth seeing. In cultivation it needs a perfectly drained alkaline soil and lots of sun. It is moderately frost-hardy and may be left to dry out in winter.

CARPOBROTUS

Valued for their abundance of vivid flowers, the 30 species in this genus of carpet-forming succulents are predominantly native to South Africa, with some found in Australia, North America and the Pacific Islands. The vigorous, 2-angled stems vary in length up to 2 m (about 6 ft) and become leathery with age. The deep green, extremely pulpy leaf pairs vary from cylindrical to triangular, and often have serrated margins and clear surface markings. The large, daisy-like flowers are borne individually in varying shades of purple, and occasionally yellow. These are followed by lush, sometimes edible fruit from which the genus name is derived—*karpos*: fruit and *brota*: edible. These half-hardy species are easy to grow, requiring full light and porous soil. They are suited to hanging baskets and make excellent sandbinders. Propagate from stem cuttings or seed in spring to early autumn/fall.

C. edulis
HOTTENTOT FIG

Originating in South Africa, this prostrate, mat-forming, perennial succulent is an excellent sandbinder. It produces long, spreading, narrow stems covered with deep green, erect foliage with serrated, reddish margins. In spring and summer, bright yellow, red or purple flowers appear. Edible, brown, fig-like fruit follows the bloom. This half-hardy species prefers mild temperatures and is ideal for a hanging basket. It requires full sun, porous soil and light water. Propagate from seed or cuttings from spring until late summer.

C. muirii
REAL SOUR FIG

This fast-growing species is native to South Africa and in spring bears pinkish purple flowers up to 9 cm (about 3½ in) in diameter, followed by tasty fruit, the most edible of the genus.

CEPHALOCEREUS
senilis
OLD MAN CACTUS

This erect, South American cactus grows slowly to 13 m (about 40 ft) tall in the wild but only 50 cm (about 20 in) in pots. It has up to 30 ribs, fine, short, yellowy white spines and a profusion of grey-white fleecy hair (hence the common name) which completely covers the body and can be washed and combed similarly to one's own. Mature plants develop thorny crowns from where trumpet-shaped, reddish pink spring flowers appear, but not usually on cultivated specimens. This frost-tender cactus is suitable for the greenhouse and requires full sun or partial shade and sandy, slightly alkaline soil. Water sparingly and propagate from seed or cuttings.

CEREUS
peruvianus
PERUVIAN APPLE, PERUVIAN TORCH

Originating in South America, this popular cactus grows up to 5 m (about 15 ft) in height. It has an erect habit, deep green-blue stems with up to 10 ribs and brown downy areoles with yellow spines. Scented, brown-green flowers open at night during summer and are followed by red, globular fruit. This half-hardy species prefers total sun and porous soil. Propagate from seed or stem cuttings in spring. It is a declared weed in South Africa.

CHAMAECEREUS
silvestrii
PEANUT CACTUS

This well-known Argentine cactus has a prostrate carpeting habit and reaches to 10 cm (about 4 in) in height. It is composed of clusters of initially erect peanut-shaped 'finger' stems with numerous, soft, white bristles. Readily flowering indoors from an early age, this half-hardy species produces vivid, orange-red flowers in spring and summer. It requires porous soil and full sun or

partial shade. Propagate by planting the small 'fingers', which are easily broken off at their joints, in spring and summer.

CLEISTOCACTUS
strausii
SILVER TORCH

This erect columnar cactus is native to Bolivia and reaches to 3 m (about 9 ft) in height. Quick and simple to grow, it has numerous, ribbed, grey-blue stems that distinctively taper toward the base. These are covered with areoles sprouting fine white hair. An abundance of deep red, cylindrical flowers develop straight from the stems in late summer, but only on older cacti. This half-hardy species likes full sun and extremely porous soil. Propagate from seed or cuttings in summer. Older plants may need staking or they tend to fall over.

COPIAPOA

This genus of cacti, all native to Chile, are slow-developing and vary in habit from single and erect, to multi-stemmed and spreading, and from grey to light green with brown shadings. All species have numerous areoles sprouting long spines, and fleecy crowns from where the blooms emerge. These yellow or red flowers are wide and trumpet- or bell-shaped. Ranging from frost-hardy to frost-tender, the cacti require a cold, dry period during winter. Plant in extremely porous soil and water sparingly. Some enjoy full sun, while others prefer semi-shade. Propagate from seed in spring, offsets in summer, or by grafting in summer and spring. The name comes from Copiapo, a province in Chile.

C. cinerea

This unusual species is single-stemmed up to 60 cm (about 24 in) when young, forming colonies up to 2 m (about 6 ft) wide in maturity. Grey, downy areoles sprouting pointed spines cover silver-grey stems. These stems have numerous ribs and a thick, fleecy, white crown from where the flowers emerge. The wide, yellow blooms develop only on cacti 10 cm (about 4 in) or more in diameter, which is unlikely under cultivation. Frost-tender, it requires full sun.

C. echinoides

Reaching a height of up to 15 cm (about 6 in) and 10 cm (about 4 in) in diameter, this solitary-stemmed, frost-tender perennial has a flat, globe-shaped appearance. Its green-grey body has ten outstanding ribs and large areoles producing seven whorls and a central spine. Light, yellowish green flowers bloom in summer.

Carpobrotus muirii

Cereus peruvianus

Copiapoa echinoides

Copiapoa cinerea

Chamaecereus silvestrii

Cleistocactus strausii

Cephalocereus senilis

Dioscorea elephantipes

Cyphostemma juttae

Crassula portulacea

Crassula arborescens

Crassula coccinea

COTYLEDON
orbiculata
PIG'S EAR

This evergreen, succulent shrub is native to northern Africa and reaches to 50 cm (about 20 in) in height and breadth. Egg-shaped, grey-green leaves with a white, wax coating and occasionally red margins form in opposite pairs along plump, multiple stems. In autumn/fall terminal clusters of orange, cylindrical or bell-shaped, hanging flowers appear. Frost-tender, this succulent requires total sun or partial shade and very porous soil. Avoid watering flowers from the top. Propagate from seed or cuttings in summer.

CRASSULA

This large, diverse genus comprises about 300 species of annual and perennial, mostly evergreen, succulent shrubs. Predominantly native to South Africa, they range widely in habit from prostrate and carpet-forming to tall and erect. The op-

Cotyledon orbiculata

posing leaves vary from oval to narrow, with star-shaped flowers forming in terminal clusters. Species range from half-hardy to frost-tender and require full sun or partial shade, very porous soil and slight watering only in winter. Propagate from cuttings or by division in spring and summer, from seed in spring.

C. arborescens
SILVER JADE PLANT, SILVER DOLLAR

Reaching up to 4 m (about 12 ft) in height and 2 m (about 6 ft) in diameter, this perennial succulent has strong, thick stems that develop broad, pulpy, silver-grey leaves with contrasting red margins. This frost-tender succulent requires full sun and well-drained soil. It makes an excellent potted specimen but is then unlikely to flower.

C. coccinea

This evergreen succulent from South Africa reaches 60 cm (about 24 in) in height. Its numerous, upright, leathery stems produce pairs of pulpy, flat green leaves with

red undersides and downy edges. In summer to autumn/fall, an abundance of cylindrical, deep red flowers appear in thick, terminal sprays. This succulent needs warmer temperatures, total sun and porous soil. Prune back stems to just above the base in late winter. This species is easily cultivated from seed or cuttings in spring and summer.

C. portulacea
syn. C. ovata, C. argentea
JADE TREE, FRIENDSHIP TREE, MONEY TREE

This quick-growing, shrubby, perennial succulent grows to 4 m (about 12 ft) in height and 2 m (about 6 ft) in diameter. It has thick, leathery stems that are covered with shiny, pulpy, egg-shaped leaves edged with red. In autumn/fall and winter, small, pink, starry flowers appear. This half-hardy species prefers full sun, and makes a good potted plant.

CYPHOSTEMMA
juttae
syn. Cissus juttae

Native to southern Africa, this deciduous, perennial succulent grows to 2 m (about 6 ft) in height when mature. The Greek name, Cyphostemma: swelling crown, refers to its distinctively bloated trunk which branches near the top and is covered with yellow, peeling bark. The wide, shiny, green foliage is roughly saw-toothed and has a downy underside that emits droplets of resin. Small, greenish yellow flowers appear in summer, followed by red or yellow fruit which look very much like small bunches of

grapes. This frost-tender species requires porous soil, full sun and should not be watered in winter. Propagate from seed in spring.

DIOSCOREA
elephantipes
ELEPHANT'S FOOT, HOTTENTOT BREAD

Many species of the genus, *Dioscorea*, are cultivated for yams, which make up the tuberous storage roots. Although this species was originally cooked and eaten by the Hottentots of southern Africa, it is now grown primarily as a decorative garden plant. *D. elephantipes* is a twining plant with circular to kidney-shaped leaves abruptly pointed at the ends, but its most striking feature is the truly enormous rootstock. Requiring deep soil, good drainage and ideally, semi-arid conditions, it is also suitable as a greenhouse plant. Propagate from seeds, cuttings or root section at any time of the year.

DROSANTHEMUM

This genus contains approximately 95 species of perennial succulents native to South Africa. They have a spreading habit and vary in height, some reaching 1 m (about 3 ft). The leaves are densely covered in bright papillae and flowers range in colour from pink and yellow to deep purple. Frost-tender, they require bright sunlight for the flowers to open fully. Potted specimens can be kept indoors in winter in a warm, sunny position. Plant in well-drained, compost-enriched soil. Water sparingly in summer and keep fairly dry in winter. Propagate from seed or cuttings and replace plants about every 3 years.

D. bicolor
BICOLORED ICE-PLANT

This fast-growing but short-lived perennial has a stiffly branched, thick, rounded form. Spectacular, golden centred, purplish red-tipped flowers are borne in spring.

D. floribundum

This small, cushion-forming plant reaches to 15 cm (about 6 in) in height. Its creeping branches take root as they grow and are covered with pairs of pale, grey-green, cylindrical leaves. A profusion of little, pink, daisy-like flowers are borne in summer. Excellent for hanging baskets or pots.

ECHEVERIA
HEN AND CHICKS

Native to the Americas, this large genus contains over 150 species of ornamental, perennial succulents valued for their habit, foliage and flowers. The species form in perfectly symmetrical, basal rosettes or in multi-stemmed bushes up to 1 m (about 3 ft) tall. These plants have pulpy, sleek-edged leaves which are particularly vivid during the colder months. Bell-shaped to cylindrical flowers bloom at different times of the year. Half-hardy to frost-tender, the succulents require full sun or semi-shade, very porous soil and light watering. Propagate from seed, offsets or cuttings, or by division in spring and summer. The genus

takes its name from Athanasia Echeveria Godoy, an eighteenth century, Spanish, botanical artist.

E. elegans
PEARL ECHEVERIA

This half-hardy succulent develops in a thickly foliaged, basal rosette up to 5 cm (about 2 in) tall and 50 cm (about 20 in) in diameter. Its lush leaves are frosted, blue-green with red margins. The bell-shaped, pinky red flowers have yellow petal tips.

E. pulvinata
PLUSH PLANT, CHENILLE PLANT

This shrubby perennial produces multiple, brown, downy stems crowned with open rosettes up to 10 cm (about 4 in) in diameter. These whorls are composed of dense, inversely egg-shaped leaves, silky soft and covered with white down. In winter to spring red or yellowish red flowers appear along stems up to 30 cm (about 12 in) tall. It is rather frost-tender.

ECHINOCACTUS
grusonii
GOLDEN BARREL CACTUS

Originating in Mexico, this popular, slow-growing cactus reaches up to 2 m (about 6 ft) in height and breadth. It has a single, globe-shaped, pale green body that stretches upwards in maturity, becoming barrel-shaped. This stem is heavily ribbed with numerous areoles sprouting radial, yellow spines. In summer, larger cacti produce a circle of vivid, yellow flowers

from a crown at the top of the plant. Drought-resistant and frost-tender, the species requires well-drained soil and warmer temperatures. Full sun maintains the lustre of the spines and longevity of the flowers. This easily grown cactus is propagated from seed in spring.

ECHINOCEREUS

This large and popular genus of small, North American cacti has a varying habit. The stems are numerously ribbed and spiny with new stems bursting forth from inside existing ones. In spring to summer large, brightly coloured, trumpet-shaped, enduring blooms appear, followed by small thorny, globular fruit. Species range from half-hardy to frost-tender and need extremely porous soil with full sun or semi-shade. Propagate from seed or cuttings in spring and summer. The genus name comes from the Greek echinos: hedgehog.

E. reichenbachii
LACY CACTUS

Native to southern USA and to Mexico, this typically single-

stemmed, half-hardy cactus is globe-shaped when immature, becoming elongated and cylindrical with age. It reaches a height of up to 20 cm (about 8 in) and 10 cm (about 4 in) in diameter. Close-set areoles sprout abundant yellow or white spines, giving the species a lacy appearance. In spring, large, vivid, rose-pink to purple flowers appear.

E. subinervis

This attractive species from New Mexico (USA) grows about 30 cm (about 12 in) in height, usually as a single, fluted grey-green plant. It bears lovely cream or yellow flowers in spring. C. subinervis is half-hardy.

E. viridiflorus

This thicket-forming, globe-shaped cactus is native to southern USA and to Mexico. The shortest species in the genus, its 7 cm (about 3 in) high stems spread in colonies up to 15 cm (about 6 in). The stems are covered in red-brown or white, radial spines with up to 16 ribs. Vivid, green flowers bloom in spring.

Echinocereus viridiflorus

Echinocereus subinervis

Echeveria elegans

Echinocactus grusonii

Drosanthemum floribundum

Echeveria pulvinata

Echinocereus reichenbachii

Drosanthemum bicolor

ECHINOPSIS

This popular genus contains over 35 species of cacti, native to South America, and growing up to 30 cm (about 12 in) tall. Ranging from single, basal, globe-shaped stems to readily colonizing, tubular and erect, these cacti are densely covered with spines and have pronounced ribs. Species are highly valued for their funnel-shaped, brilliantly coloured flowers which are up to 20 cm (about 8 in) long. The blooms open at night and are very short-lived. Half-hardy to frost-tender, these plants will survive in varying degrees of shade and require rich, well-drained soil and light water. Propagate in spring and summer from seed and readily produced offsets. Numerous hybrids have been developed by crossing this genus with *Lobivia*.

E. arachnacantha
syn. *Lobivia arachnacantha*

This short, spherical, frost-tender cactus is up to 3 cm (about 1½ in) tall and 5 cm (about 2 in) in diameter. Numerous undulating, cream-white ribs cover the deep green stem. An abundance of downy, golden yellow flowers 5 cm (about 2 in) in diameter bloom from the crown.

E. 'Green Gold'

While the most ardent cactiphiles prefer to grow pure-bred species, most cactus will hybridize in cultivation and the resulting hybrids are often very pretty, easily grown plants. *E.* 'Green Gold' is one such: a neat, clump-forming cactus about 20 cm (about 8 in) high with abundant lime-yellow flowers in summer. It is half-hardy.

E. multiplex
EASTER LILY CACTUS, BARREL CACTUS

Originating in Brazil, this spherical, multi-branched cactus grows to 15 cm (about 6 in) in maturity and forms dense thickets up to 1 m (about 3 ft) in diameter. Long, slender, tapering, ribbed branches are covered with brown, black-tipped spines. These asparagus-like stems are inwardly curving and sprout fragrant, pinkish blue flowers from the tips.

EPIPHYLLUM
ORCHID CACTUS

This genus from tropical South America and Mexico contains 35 species and over 3000 hybrid, epiphytic cacti. The species have a shrubby, prostrate or pendent habit and are virtually spineless in maturity. Multiple flattened stems develop from a leathery base with heavily undulated margins often mistaken for leaves. In spring or summer, large, funnel-shaped, flowers bloom. These appear from the edges of the stems and vary from nocturnal to daytime-opening. The species require a dry, cold spell during winter, light, sandy soil and full sun for optimum flowering. These cacti are ideal hanging basket plants, their trailing stems seeming to grow better if the roots are restricted. Propagate from seed in spring, stem cuttings in summer.

E. hybrids

Growing usually to 60 cm (about 24 in) in height and width, these frost-tender plants come in a wide range of flower colours—white through pink to red and through yellow to orange. The flowers can be as much as 15 cm (about 6 in) across, and open during the day. They are first-rate hanging basket plants. Named cultivars are available, though often the plants are simply sold by flower colour.

E. oxypetalum
DUTCHMAN'S PIPE, BELLE DE NUIT

Native to Mexico and Guatemala, this popular species has an upright habit to 2 m (about 6 ft) in height, arching in maturity. Its multiple stems are up to 10 cm (about 4 in) wide and tapering. The night-opening, 15 cm (about 6 in) wide, white flowers have slightly curved tubes, hence the common name Dutchman's pipe. They are most intensely fragrant.

EUPHORBIA
SPURGE, MILKWEED

This massive genus contains over 2000 species of shrubs, perennials and succulents naturally occurring worldwide. These slow-growing species have distinctive yet diverse forms and are popular as house plants. The succulents have complex, cup-shaped bracts which encase two to three male flowers and a single 3-toothed female ovary. These are followed by leathery, 3-lobed seed pods which burst open to disperse the seeds. The plants range from half-hardy to frost-tender and require a cool, dry resting period. Plant in damp, porous soil with full sun or partial shade. Propagate from seed or dry cuttings, or by division. Many types contain a milky white, toxic sap which is extremely skin-irritant, and it is by this, as well as the insignificant flowers, that they can be distinguished from the true cacti which many of them superficially resemble.

E. caput-medusae
MEDUSA'S HEAD

This South African, half-hardy, perennial succulent has a thick, leathery base up to 15 cm (about 6 in) tall, out of which develop a number of grey-green, pulpy stems 45 cm (about 18 in) long that look like the tentacles of an octopus. Short-lived, narrow, lance-shaped leaves grow only at the branch extremities, where green flowers with white, lacy margins appear in summer. It is best propagated from seed or offsets; cuttings often fail to develop the distinctive 'gorgon's head' habit.

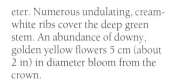

Echinopsis arachnacantha

Echinopsis 'Green Gold'

Echinopsis multiplex

Epiphyllum 'Pink Nymph'

Epiphyllum oxypetalum

Euphorbia caput-medusae

Furcraea foetida

Fenestraria aurantiaca

Faucaria tigrina

Euphorbia obesa

Gasteria verrucosa

Ferocactus hamatacanthus

Euphorbia trigona

E. obesa

GINGHAM GOLF BALL, BASEBALL PLANT

Perfectly spherical, becoming elongated, this unusual and popular, frost-tender, perennial succulent is native to South Africa. It grows up to 20 cm (about 8 in) tall and 15 cm (about 6 in) in diameter, and is spineless. The pale green stem has eight depressed ribs and red-brown, horizontal and vertical lines, making a check pattern similar to gingham. Little, yellow-green, cup-shaped bracts bloom from the apex in summer.

E. trigona

AFRICAN MILK TREE

This 1 m (about 3 ft) tall cactus-like succulent from eastern Africa is a popular indoor plant—it looks prehistoric with its bolt-upright, 3-angled stems and oval leaves standing horizontally at intervals from the angles. By the end of summer, most of the leaves drop. The insignificant green flowers are not often seen on indoor plants. It is frost-tender and needs good light indoors, light shade in the garden.

FAUCARIA
tigrina

TIGER'S JAW

Clump-forming, this easy to cultivate, attractive succulent is native to South Africa. It grows to 10 cm (about 4 in) and spreads out to 50 cm (about 20 in). The triangular, vivid, grey-green leaves form in rosettes and are dense and pulpy with a keeled reverse. They are covered with white dots, occasion-

ally tinted red and bear up to 10 erect, white teeth on their margins—hence the common name. Large, deep yellow, daisy-like flowers bloom in autumn/fall, only opening in the afternoon. This frost-tender species likes full sun, little water in winter and porous soil. Propagate from seed in spring, cuttings in summer.

FENESTRARIA
aurantiaca

WINDOW PLANT

This small, clump-forming succulent, native to South Africa, grows up to 5 cm (about 2 in) tall and 20 cm (about 8 in) across. The basal rosettes are composed of upright, club-shaped, shiny, grey-green foliage approximately 3 cm (about 1 ½ in) long. These slender, smooth leaves have a curved underside and permeable, grey tips, from which both the common and botanical names are derived. Large, vivid, yellow, daisy-like flowers appear from late summer to autumn/fall or in winter. The distinctive leaves enjoy full sun, porous soil and scant water. Propagate from seed in spring and summer or by careful division in spring.

FEROCACTUS
hamatacanthus
syn. *Hamatocactus hamatacanthus*

TURK'S HEAD

Originating in Mexico, this fiercely spined, globe-shaped cactus reaches 60 cm (about 25 in) in height and diameter. Elongating with age, it has up to 20 prominent

ribs and numerous tubercles sprouting extremely sharp, brownish red spines with yellow tips. In spring to summer, a single, yellow flower, with red interior, blooms from the crown, followed by a pulpy, globe-shaped seed pod. Plant in full sun and porous soil. This fully hardy cactus may develop black areoles as a result of fungus or poor air circulation. Propagate from seed in spring and summer.

FURCRAEA
foetida
syn. *F. gigantea*

This giant false agave is the largest of the *Furcraea* genus and, like the agave, is a perennial succulent. It has a rosette of broad, sword-shaped, fleshy, green leaves and in summer fragrant, bell-shaped, white-centred, green flowers on an 8 m (about 24 ft) stem appear. Grow in well-drained soil in full

sun. Frost-tender to a minimum of 6°C (about 42°F). Propagate from bulbils which grow on the lower stem of the flower.

GASTERIA
verrucosa

WARTY ALOE, OX TONGUE

Native to South Africa, this fan-shaped, perennial succulent grows up to 10 cm (about 4 in) in height and 30 cm (about 12 in) wide. Its long, sharply pointed, lance-shaped leaves are deep green and coated with white, wart-like tubercles. They form in two opposing ranks and have slightly furled edges. In spring, racemes of cup-shaped, orange and green flowers appear from the centre. This succulent is half-hardy and simple to cultivate, requiring well-drained soil with full sun or partial shade. Propagate in spring and summer from leaf cuttings or seed, or by division.

A Field Trip to the Anza-Borrego Desert State Park

The Anza-Borrego Desert State Park in southern California is part of a remarkable landscape—and the setting for many a Hollywood western. The park lies in a rain shadow shielded from the coast by the Sierra Nevada Mountains, and takes in an area of high desert approximately 80 km (about 50 miles) east of San Diego.

The road from the San Diego–Carlsbad area, where your trip begins, to Mount Palomar, takes in a breathtaking array of mountain and desert scenery. Leaving the urban areas near the coast you wind through willows and oaks along shaded watercourses. The canyons and hills are home to a number of bulbs and perennials such as blue dicks (*Dichelostemma* sp.), various *Allium*, *Lilium* and *Penstemon* species, the spectacular red delphinium (*Delphinium cardinale*) and many others. As you travel further into the foothills, the area is dominated by chaparral vegetation (dense, tangled brushwood). An outstanding feature here is the manzanita (*Arctostaphylos* sp.), a shrub or small tree which has a beautiful, smooth, rusty coloured bark and clusters of white to pink bell-shaped flowers in spring. If you get out of the car you may be joined by roadrunner birds (made famous by the cartoon character).

Continue along the highway to Mount Palomar; it reaches an imposing 3000 m (about 10000 ft). Here you can walk through the tranquil conifer forests. The atmosphere will be

slightly damp, as this area on the coastal side of the Sierra Nevada is subject to mists from the Pacific Ocean. The walking trails around Mount Palomar are delightful and the conifer forest provides a majestic backdrop for mountain wildflowers such as wild roses, liliums, columbines (*Aquilegia formosa*) and a host of other bulbs and perennials. You are also likely to hear and see the famous woodpecker bird.

Crossing to the other side of the mountains you wind your way down fairly steep roads and, as you travel further east, the vegetation changes rather dramatically—trees give way to cacti, yuccas and agaves. The air is drier, and is accompanied by strong winds whipping off the mountains. Any plant that thrives here is extraordinarily tough.

The visitors' centre at the Anza-Borrego Desert State Park is a suitable place to start a walk which takes you to the most interesting flora and fauna in this unique area. The centre is near Borrego Springs on the floor of the desert and is surrounded by hills and canyons. The '3–4 km (about 2–3 miles) Palm Canyon walk winds through a mountain chasm and rises to 120 m (about 400 ft). The mountains are predominantly granite which, as they erode, forms a sandy and, in places, gravelly soil, providing an ideal medium for the various cacti and other plants that grow here.

The desert of the Anza-Borrego experiences extremes of temperature and low rainfall. The average annual rainfall is 125 mm (about 5 in) but this is erratic and there are years when there is virtually no rain. During the winter period, from November through to April, temperatures go down to 0°C (32°F). Spring arrives in April and lasts a fairly short time, the floral display depending very much on the rainfall. Various ephemerals such as sunflowers and godetias (satin flowers) as well as the perennials ocotillo, agave, and various barrel cactus species can also be found in flower at this time. During the long, hot, desert summer temperatures can reach over 43°C (about 110°F) for days or even weeks on end. Hot dry winds often lash the countryside.

Plants can grow even in this harsh desert environment.

A variety of desert plants in rocky soil.

Ferocactus acanthodes

As you walk along the trail you gradually climb up the canyon, and here the red barrel cactus (*Ferocactus acanthodes*) can be found thriving on the sandy, gravelly slopes. The best time of year to see the red barrel cactus is when it flowers, in spring. One of the most spectacular of the cactus species in the area, it can grow up to 1.5 m (about 4½ ft) tall, which makes for an impressive plant, especially when in flower. Its preference for growing on sloping gravelly ground gives it an almost surreal quality, as if perched ready to roll down the hill. The plant itself is fascinating, with rows of curved spine clusters presumably standing guard to intercept any predator foolish enough to try to feed on it. The curved spines were once used as fish hooks by the local Indians. Arachnophobics should be wary of getting too close to the plant as colonies of tarantula spiders are often found at the base.

While a number of animals such as the mountain lion and kit fox inhabit this area, you are unlikely to encounter them. However, you can occasionally hear the howls of coyotes. The silence of the is desert also sometimes broken by the terrifying sound of the rattlesnake. Although this is rare, if you see one treat it with respect as they have been known to aggressively pursue people.

On the same slopes as the red barrel cactus are other interesting plants such as the ocotillo (*Fouquieria splendens*). In spring it bears tight clusters of spectacular red flowers. The cholla (pronounced choya) cactus and prickly pear (*Opuntia* sp.) grow here in abundance, producing pleasing floral displays. Agaves can also be found with their tall, stout stems and clusters of yellow flowers on the branches. The ubiquitous yuccas are also here and are reminiscent of agaves in their overall form.

A trip to the Anza-Borrego Desert is a unique experience for the plant lover. It certainly does not have the lushness of a tropical rainforest or the wildflower displays of the prairie meadows, but there is an exhilarating feeling of wilderness in the desert, an experience not easily forgottem.

Ferocactus

The 20 to 30 North American species of *Ferocactus* show characteristics typical of many cacti—the stem is a fleshy, succulent, vertically ribbed cylinder, armed with very fierce spines arranged in small radiating groups. The term cacti refers to members of the large plant family Cactaceae. Nearly all the species of Cactaceae are succulent plants, or 'succulents', but there are many succulents which are not cacti, such as euphorbias, aloes and agaves.

The family Cactaceae consists of at least 1000 species, divided among 80 or more genera. They occur as natives only in the Americas (including the West Indies and the Galapagos Islands), except for a few rainforest epiphytes in West Africa and Madagascar. Their popular image as desert plants is a very incomplete picture: in fact they are rare or absent in the driest American deserts, while on the other hand they may be common in other habitats, for example North American prairies, Brazilian rainforests, West Indian vine thickets, and high Andean hillsides. It is true, though, that cacti are adapted for survival in places where a deficiency of moisture is regularly experienced.

Ferocactus acanthodes

Gymnocalycium mihanovichii

Gymnocalycium andreae

Hylocereus undatus

Haworthia fasciata

Hatiora salicornioides

Haageocereus versicolor

Graptopetalum bellum

Haworthia bolusii

GRAPTOPETALUM
bellum
syn. *Tacitus bellus*

Recently discovered in Mexico, this little, perennial succulent grows to 3 cm (about 1½ in) tall and 15 cm (about 6 in) wide. Valued for its foliage and flowers, the species forms in basal rosettes composed of dull grey, triangular leaves. Small, starry, crimson or pink flowers appear from the leaf axils in spring to summer. This frost-tender succulent is suitable for the greenhouse and makes an ideal window-sill specimen. Allow full sun, occasional water and propagate from leaf and stem cuttings from spring to summer.

GYMNOCALYCIUM
CHIN CACTI

Native to South America, these small cacti grow to 25 cm (about 10 in) in height and vary in habit, from single and globe-shaped to clump-forming and cylindrical. All are distinguished by a chin-like prominence just below the areoles, hence the common name. In spring and summer, numerous, trumpet-shaped flowers appear from the crown. The cacti range from frost-hardy to frost-tender and grow well indoors, requiring a winter cool spell. Plant in porous soil with full sun or semi-shade. Propagate from seed in spring or offsets in summer. The genus name comes from the Greek *gymnos*: naked, and *kalyx*: bud, referring to the sessile flowers.

G. andreae

From Argentina, this colonizing cactus reaches 5 cm (about 2 in) in height and spreads to 10 cm (about 4 in). The shiny, green-blue stems are globe-shaped and usually bear eight ribs. Seven yellowish, radial spines and three upwardly curving, central spines sprout from whitish areoles. Vivid yellow, trumpet-shaped flowers appear from the flat crown in spring and summer. This species is frost-tender and requires total sun.

G. mihanovichii
PLAID CACTUS

This species, native to Paraguay, has flattened, greyish green, globular stems up to 5 cm (about 2 in) in diameter. These have eight ribs and horizontal grooves above and below the areoles. Brownish, yellow spines develop in whorls but there are no central spines. Numerous light-yellow tinted, green flowers appear early on. A number of red and yellow, natural varieties occur, which are without chlorophyll and so require grafting onto green specimens to survive; the best known is the scarlet 'Hibotan'.

HAAGEOCEREUS
versicolor

Under cultivation, this Peruvian cactus forms in clumps of upright, tubular stems to 1.5 m (about 4½ ft) tall and 8 cm (about 3 in) in diameter. The compact, downy stems have about 20 light ribs and are thickly covered with areoles bearing up to 30 golden yellow-red, whorled spines. At night during summer, long, white, trumpet-like flowers appear. This cactus is frost-tender and requires porous soil with full sun and light water. Propagate from cuttings in summer, or from seed in spring.

HATIORA
salicornioides
DRUNKARD'S DREAM, BOTTLE PLANT

Native to Brazil, this little, perennial, epiphytic cactus has a narrow, shrubby habit and reaches 40 cm (about 16 in) in height and spread. The slender, jointed, tubular stems readily branch and are totally spineless. In spring, tiny, deep-yellow, cup-shaped flowers appear at the bloated stem tips. This frost-tender species needs extremely porous soil and semi-shade. Maintain moisture during the hotter months and only water occasionally during winter. Propagate from cuttings in spring and summer.

HAWORTHIA

This genus of 150 dense, dwarf-like, perennial succulents originated in South Africa and grows to 30 cm (about 12 in) tall. They are predominantly thicket-forming, developing in basal or short-stemmed rosettes. The decorative, lush foliage is lanceolate to triangular and marked with distinctive, white spots. Racemes of rather insignificant white, or occasionally yellow, six-lobed flowers appear in summer. Ranging from frost-hardy to frost-tender, these succulents require semi-shade to maintain healthy leaves. Keep slightly moist during the hotter months and totally dry in winter. Propagate by division or from offsets during spring to autumn/fall.

H. bolusii

Growing to 6 cm (about 2½ in) in height and 10 cm (about 4 in) in diameter, this extremely attractive succulent develops in a compact, stemless rosette. The plentiful, silvery, grey-blue leaves are triangular and slightly serrated. Slender racemes of typically white flowers appear from spring to autumn/fall.

H. fasciata

This more or less stemless succulent is grown for its interesting leaves, which stand upright in neat rosettes, the better to show off the white dots on their undersides—the whole effect is of grey and white. The tiny white flowers are carried in early summer on 40 cm (about 16 in) tall, bare stems but are not very interesting. Half hardy, it is propagated by removing offsets in spring.

HYLOCEREUS

undatus

NIGHT-BLOOMING CEREUS, MOON FLOWER, HONOLULU QUEEN, QUEEN OF THE NIGHT

Of unknown origin, this tropical, scaling cactus develops long, multiple stems up to 5 m (about 15 ft) in length. These fragile, vivid green stems have two to three angles and tough, undulating margins with widely spread, single-spined areoles. In late spring to summer, enormous, creamy white, fragrant flowers appear at the leaf tips. These are followed by red, edible, egg-shaped fruit. This frost-tender cactus requires warmer temperatures, moist, fertile soil and partial shade. Propagate from stem cuttings in spring and summer. The species is easy to cultivate and will readily climb trees if allowed to grow freely.

KALANCHOE

This genus comprises approximately 200 species of perennial succulents native mostly to southern Asia and tropical and subtropical Africa. The species range in habit from erect and bushy to spreading and prostrate, and grow up to 3 m (about 9 ft) in height and width. The succulent pairs of opposing leaves vary from slender to rounded. The tubular or bell-shaped flowers have four petals and appear in branched terminal clusters. These succulents only require light watering in the colder months and range from frost-hardy to frost-tender. Propagate from stem or leaf cuttings in late spring to summer, seed at the end of spring, or pot up plantlets that may form along leaf margins.

K. blossfeldiana

FLAMING KATY

This small, shrubby perennial is native to Africa and reaches 30 cm (about 12 in) in height and width. Its multiple, upstretched branches are covered with round to rectangular, deep green leaves with red margins and notched tips. Thick racemes of little, deep red, cylindrical flowers appear from winter to early summer; cultivated strains may be pink, yellow or orange also. The species is frost-tender and requires partial shade. It is a very popular florist's pot plant.

K. fedtschenkoi

SOUTH AMERICAN AIR PLANT

This compact succulent of uncertain origin grows to 30–50 cm (about 12–20 in) in height and width, readily producing multiple branches and trailing stems. The glossy, blue-green leaves are rounded to rectangular and have deeply undulating margins; a form with cream edges is very popular. Terminal panicles of reddish orange, bell-shaped flowers appear in late winter. This frost-tender species requires warm temperatures and total sun.

K. tomentosa

PANDA PLANT

This small, shrubby African native grows gradually up to 50 cm (about 20 in) tall. It has dense, spoon-shaped, light green leaves that are covered with white felt and often have brown, rounded tips. Creamy yellow flowers appear in autumn/fall, though flowering is very rare in cultivation.

LAMPRANTHUS

These small, perennial succulents originated in South Africa and have an erect habit, spreading in maturity. Full sun and a well-drained soil are preferred and dry conditions are withstood; however the plants become straggly after several years and should be replaced. Simple to grow, these succulents are propagated from cuttings in late spring and summer, and from seed in spring.

L. aurantiacus

Reaching to 50 cm (about 20 in) in height and 70 cm (about 30 in) in width, this species has small, green-grey, tubular foliage which narrows towards the tip. In summer, an abundance of vivid, dark orange, daisy-like flowers with a spot of purple at their centres appear.

L. aureus

ORANGE VYGIE

Native to South Africa, this upright, perennial, succulent shrub reaches to 40 cm (about 16 in) tall. The bluish green leaves are up to 5 cm (about 2 in) in length and are covered with clear spots. In summer, vivid yellow or orange, daisy-like flowers up to 6 cm (about 2½ in) in diameter appear.

L. coccineus

This spectacular South African plant resembles *L. aurantiacus* except that the leaves are a little shorter; in its late spring season it is a dazzling sight—literally so, as the red flowers are iridescent and flash purple or pink or orange as the sun strikes them. It is half-hardy.

Kalanchoe blossfeldiana

Lampranthus aureus

Lithops dorotheae

Lampranthus coccineus

Kalanchoe fedtschenkoi

Kalanchoe tomentosa

Lampranthus aurantiacus

LITHOPS

LIVING STONES, STONEFACE

Originating in South Africa, this fascinating genus contains over 50 perennial succulents which develop singularly or in colonies. They are composed of pairs of extremely lush, upright leaves compressed together to form a hemispherical mass with a deep crevice running across the top. New growth and white or yellow, daisy-like flowers grow up through the fissure. The plants look like smooth river stones, explaining the genus and common names, and have translucent upper surfaces. These half- to frost-hardy succulents are easy to grow and drought resistant. Plant in light soil and allow full sun. Water only in spring and propagate in summer from seed or by dividing bodies and treating like cuttings.

L. dorotheae

This cushion-forming species is up to 3 cm (about 1½ in) tall and 10 cm (about 4 in) in diameter. Its light, grey-blue, egg-shaped body is

made up of two pulpy, asymmetrical leaves. The top surface has deep green 'windows', red and white markings and a deep, transversal slit. Yellow flowers appear from this crevice in summer to autumn/fall.

L. glesinae

Not a common species, but typical in the way the egg-shaped, spotted leaves mimic the stones among which they grow—particularly if the cultivator has selected matching pebbles for mulch! A pebble or gravel mulch is appreciated by just about all succulents; it keeps their crowns dry.

L. karasmontana var. bella
syn. L. bella

This cluster-forming perennial has egg-shaped bodies up to 3 cm (about 1½ in) tall and 2 cm (about 1 in) in diameter. These are composed of yellowish brown compressed leaves with dark brown lines on the markedly curving crown. In summer to autumn/fall, snow white flowers appear from the crown's crevice.

L. turbiniformis

This South African succulent forms in small clumps of paired leaves. Egg-shaped and orange-brown in colour, these lush leaves grow to 2.5 cm (about 1 in) in height. The flattened surface is scored with a shallow, transverse crevice and brown, linear markings. Vivid yellow flowers up to 4 cm (about 2 in) in diameter bloom from white buds.

LOBIVIA

COB CACTUS, HEDGEHOG CACTUS

This genus contains over 70 species of thicket-forming cacti ranging in habit from basal and globular to erect and cylindrical, up to 30 cm (about 12 in) in height. Large, bell-shaped or funnel-like flowers are borne on short, downy stems and are short-lived, though freely replaced. These decorative blooms come in vivid orange, yellow, purple or red and frequently have deeper-coloured throats. Species vary from frost-hardy to frost-tender and need porous soil, total sun or semi-shade, and light water. They are simple to grow and make beautiful pot plants. Propagate from seed or stem cuttings in spring and autumn/fall. *Lobivia* is an anagram of Bolivia from where many of these plants originate.

L. backebergii

A smaller growing species, with an almost spherical body, tufts of whitish spines, and profuse, magenta flowers in spring. It sometimes refuses to make clumps.

L. bruchii

GOLDEN BARREL OF THE ANDES

This is one of the larger species, the many-ribbed stems growing to be as much as 30 cm (about 12 in) thick. The spines are yellow, the flowers brilliant red.

LOPHOCEREUS
schottii

WHISKER CACTUS

Native to Mexico and southern USA, this erect cactus grows up to 5 m (about 15 ft) tall. Its sallow to bright green stem tends to branch out from below after several years. The body has five to seven ribs and varying areoles. The higher, flowering areoles sprout bristly, grey spines radiating around one central spine. The smaller, non-flowering areoles bear up to 10 dense, cone-shaped, greyish black spines. Small, tubular, night-opening flowers appear in spring and summer, followed by globular fruit. This frost-tender species enjoys full sun and porous soil. Propagate from seed in spring, cuttings in summer.

LOPHOPHORA
williamsii

PEYOTE, MESCAL BUTTONS, DUMPLING CACTUS

This famous (or infamous) flat-crowned cactus is native to Mexico and southern USA. It is extremely slow-growing up to 5 cm (about 2 in) tall and may be singular or colonizing. The dumpling-like, bluish green, ribbed stem is lightly covered with areoles sprouting short, bristly, white hair. Beautiful, light pink flowers sprout from the crown centre in summer. This frost-hardy cactus, perhaps the most cold-tolerant of the tribe, needs full sun and porous soil. Lightly water only in winter as it is susceptible to rot. Propagate from seed in spring and summer. It is the source of the dangerous and illegal drug mescaline. Consumption of the cactus induces hallucinations and it has been used for thousands of years by American Indians in their spiritual ceremonies.

Lobivia backebergii

Lobivia bruchii

Lophophora williamsii

Lithops glesinae

Lithops karasmontana var. *bella*

Lophocereus schottii

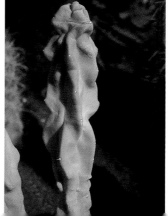

Lithops turbiniformis

MAMMILLARIA
PINCUSHION CACTI

This is one of the largest genus of cacti, containing over 300 dwarf-like species native to Mexico and south-western USA. The short, globular or clump-forming, erect columns up to 30 cm (about 12 in) tall have stems with raised, horny tubercles and downy areoles sprouting either silky bristles or tough, curving spines. In spring and summer, funnel- or bell-shaped flowers appear near the crown, followed by reddish pink fruit. These cacti range from frost-hardy to frost-tender and require full sun to maximize flowering. Easy to grow, they prefer light, sandy soil and occasional water. Propagate from seed in spring and summer, or from offsets in summer. Mealy bug and red spider mite can be a problem.

M. bombycina
SILK PINCUSHION

Native to Mexico, this single, spherical cactus has short, pillar-like stems that grow up to 20 cm (about 8 in) tall, and have spirally arranged tubercles with numerous whorls of white spines and yellowish brown, central spines. If allowed full sun, purple-pink flowers bloom around the fleecy crown from winter to spring.

M. elegans

This Mexican species is singular and globular, later clustering in short columns up to 20 cm (about 8 in) in height. Four black-pointed, central spines and numerous shorter, white bristles densely cover the blue-green stems. In spring, this half-hardy cactus develops vivid, deep reddish purple flowers.

M. plumosa
FEATHER CACTUS

This curious cactus is native to Mexico, and readily forms a thick, woolly, mound-like cluster 15 cm (about 6 in) high and 40 cm (about 16 in) wide. The stems are blanketed with feather-like, overlaying, radial spines which sprout from downy areoles. In winter, creamy green, pink or yellow flowers appear, but rarely under cultivation. This cactus will easily grow given a fertile, alkaline soil.

M. zeilmanniana
ROSE PINCUSHION

Originating in Mexico, this half-hardy cactus has globular stems up to 15 cm (about 6 in) in height and colonizing out to 30 cm (about 12 in). Silky brown and white, radial spines and reddish brown, central spines cover the green stems. Rings of dark purple flowers appear around the crown in spring.

MESEMBRYANTHEMUM
crystallinum

This annual, carpet-forming succulent grows to 10 cm (about 4 in) high and has dense, pulpy foliage with undulating edges. Glossy glands cover the leaves, flower stems and cups. Groups of 4 white flowers appear in summer. This frost-tender species requires extremely light soil and total sun. Propagate from seed in spring.

NOPALXOCHIA

This genus of epiphytic cacti is native to Central America. The species have flat, ribbon-like, spineless stems with heavily undulating margins. Pinkish red flowers appear from the edges of the stems, then both flower and stem perish. These frost-tender species are readily cultivated, provided temperatures do not drop below 5°C (about 41°F), and require porous, fertile soil in semi-shade. Propagate from stem cuttings in spring and summer.

N. ackermannii
syn. *Epiphyllum ackermannii*
RED ORCHID CACTUS

Originating in southern Mexico, this freely branching cactus grows up to 30 cm (about 12 in) tall and spreads up to 60 cm (about 24 in). Its succulent, arching stems are up to 40 cm (about 16 in) long with notched margins. Bright red, trumpet-shaped flowers, that close up at night, bloom from these notches in spring to summer. It is a parent of many epiphyllum hybrids.

N. phyllanthoides 'Deutsche Kaiserin'
syn. *Epiphyllum* × 'Deutsche Kaiserin'

This epiphytic cactus grows up to 60 cm (about 24 in) tall and spreads to 1 m (about 3 ft). The cylindrical base bears vivid green, pendulous stems with wavy margins. Numerous pink, tubular-stemmed flowers bloom in spring.

NOTOCACTUS
apricus
SUN CUP

This small, ball-shaped cactus is native to South America and grows up to 10 cm (about 4 in) in diameter. Its single, multi-ribbed, light green stem has deep, transverse grooves and downy areoles. Colourful, yellow-brown, radial spines and red, central spines completely cover the cactus. In summer, rich yellow flowers with purple stamen readily appear from the crown. This frost-tender plant likes porous soil, semi-shade and occasional water at all times. Propagate from seed in spring and summer.

Nopalxochia phyllanthoides 'Deutsche Kaiserin'

Mammillaria zeilmanniana

Mammillaria elegans

Mammillaria plumosa

Notocactus apricus

Mammillaria bombycina

Mesembryanthemum crystallinum

Nopalxochia ackermannii

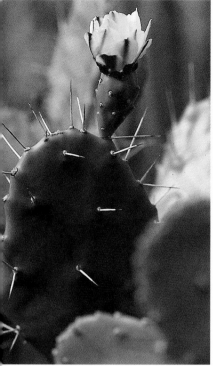

Opuntia ficus-indica

Orbea variegata

Pachypodium lamerei

Pachyphytum oviferum

Parodia formosa

Pachypodium baronii var. windsori

Opuntia verschaffeltii

under cultivation) in spring and summer. These are followed by the frequently edible fruit. Fully hardy to frost-tender, they require total sun and porous soil. Propagate from seed or cuttings in spring and summer; however, cultivation is prohibited in some countries, particularly Australia.

O. ficus-indica
syn. *O. engelmannii*, *O. megacantha*
INDIAN FIG

With an upright, open habit, becoming compact and multistemmed in maturity, this popular species reaches 5 m (about 15 ft) in height and breadth. It has jointed stems composed of grey, oval pads up to 45 cm (about 18 in) long and usually covered with spines. Funnel-like, vivid yellow flowers appear from the stem tips in summer, followed by reddish yellow-purple, bristly but edible fruit. A useful hedge cactus in its native South America. Spineless varieties are cultivated (where legal) for the delicious fruit.

O. verschaffeltii

Native to Bolivia, this clustering, short cactus grows up to 30 cm (about 12 in) in height and spreads up to 1–2 m (about 3–6 ft). Its typically spineless, green, stems are covered with brown tubercles and tipped with small, tubular leaves from spring until autumn/fall. Large attractive, yellow to scarlet-orange flowers bloom from the stem tips in spring.

ORBEA
variegata
TOAD CACTUS, STAR FLOWER, STARFISH FLOWER

Highly valued for its stunning flowers, this South African colonizing, perennial succulent has multiple, finger-shaped, upright stems up to 10 cm (about 4 in) tall. These deep green-grey stems are often marked with purple and have 4 notched angles. From summer to autumn/fall, striking, starfish-shaped flowers appear individually or in clusters with a kaleidoscopic pattern of reddish brown, yellow and purple. The beauty of the flower contrasts with its unpleasant smell. Porous soil is preferred with full sun or partial shade. This frost-tender plant is propagated from seed or stem division in spring or summer.

PACHYPHYTUM
oviferum
SUGAR ALMOND PLANT, MOONSTONES

Originating in Mexico, this beautiful, perennial succulent colonizes in stemless rosettes of bloated, spoon-shaped, blue-green leaves with a whitish red, powdery coating. Deep

red-orange flowers appear in short-stemmed, pendent clusters from the end of winter to early spring. This frost-tender succulent requires full sun, porous soil and light water. Propagate in late spring or summer from stem and leaf cuttings.

PACHYPODIUM

These upright, perennial succulents reach heights up to 6 m (about 18 ft); most species have spines and swollen stems and are native to Madagascar. They are frost-tender and require full sun, porous soil, occasional water during summer months and a dry spell during winter. Propagate from seed in spring and summer.

P. baronii var. windsori

This is a most attractive small species, with an almost spherical main stem and short, spiny branches. The flowers are distinct and a beautiful shade of scarlet.

P. lamerei

This species has a spiny, triangular, light green trunk and develops multiple stems which readily divide after each flowering. Slender leaves sprout from the crown and white, scented, summer flowers appear from the stem tips on taller specimens.

PARODIA
BALL CACTUS

Mostly native to the mountains of equatorial South America, the species in this genus vary from singular and globe-shaped, to colonizing in dense clusters of short cylindrical stems. These stems are ribbed with transverse rows of prominent tubercles with fleecy areoles sprouting brilliantly coloured, curving spines. From a relatively young age, red, yellow and orange, trumpet-shaped flowers bloom from the crown. Species range from frost-hardy to frost-tender, some preferring full sun, others semi-shade. Easy to grow, these cacti mostly require well-drained soil and plentiful water during the summer months, with a dry spell during winter. Propagate from seed in spring, cuttings in summer.

P. formosa

A rather pleasing cactus from South America, less flamboyant in bloom than other species of the genus—the orange flowers are small in comparison with the 30 cm (about 12 in) diameter body—but noteworthy for its spiral ribs and short, white spines. It is half-hardy.

P. mutabilis

Originating in Argentina, this quick-growing, frost-tender cactus

OPUNTIA
PRICKLY PEAR

This large, diverse genus is native to the USA, South America and the West Indies. Varying from prostrate to erect, and typically compact and branching, these cacti either develop flat, pad-like, jointed stems or branches with little tubular or three-angled leaves. Most species are covered with sharp spines and soft, hooked, bristles, called 'glochids'. Open-petalled, mostly yellow flowers appear on larger plants (except has a spherical stem that reaches 8 cm (about 3 in) in diameter and height. The lightly ribbed, green body is covered with white, downy areoles producing numerous, fine, whorled spines and longer, extremely sharp, red central spines with brown tips. Vivid, yellow summer flowers grow out of the fleecy crown. A fertile, neutral to acid soil is recommended.

P. nivosa

This multi-ribbed, egg-shaped cactus reaches up to 15 cm (about 6 in) in height and 10 cm (about 4 in) in diameter. The stem is covered with white, fluffy areoles sprouting rigid, white spines. Brilliant, red flowers appear from the crown in summer. This frost-tender cactus enjoys full sun and porous soil.

PILOSOCEREUS
palmeri

This upright, pillar-like cactus is native to Mexico and grows to 3–6 m (about 9–18 ft) tall and up to

1 m (about 3 ft) in diameter. The silvery, blue-green stem readily branches and is prominently ribbed. Areoles sprouting brown spines line the ribs and white, radially spined areoles cover the apex. Glossy, pink, nocturnal flowers develop near the crown on taller trees. This frost-tender species requires total sun, porous soil and plentiful water only during the hotter months. Propagate from seed and stem cuttings in spring or summer.

PORTULACARIA
afra

JADE PLANT, ELEPHANT FOOD

This small, succulent shrub has an upright habit, reaching up to 3 m (about 9 ft) tall, and a dense rounded crown. The stiff, level branches are covered with little, oval, blue-green leaves. This succulent prefers a sunny location (though it will grow in light shade) with porous soil and will not tolerate the slightest frost. Lightly water during the hotter months and

propagate from semi-ripe cuttings in summer. Like all shrubs, it can be pruned if its shape needs adjusting. It makes a fine pot plant. The common name comes from the popular belief that the shrub is eaten by elephants in Africa where it grows wild.

REBUTIA

CROWN CACTUS, HEDGEHOG CACTUS

This genus, native to South America, contains over 25 very small, predominantly cluster-forming species varying from hemispherical to erect and cylindrical. The plants develop tubercles around their bases from where the flower buds emerge after one or two years. Relatively large, vivid orange, pink, purple, red, yellow or white flowers readily bloom in late spring to early summer. Easily grown in most soil types, the species require total sun and adequate water only during the budding and blooming period. Propagate from seed and cuttings in spring or summer.

R. aureiflora

Originating in Argentina, this mound-forming, half-hardy cactus averages 4 cm (about 2 in) in height. Its deep green-purple body is covered with lateral rows of tubercles and rigid, brownish white radial and central spines. At the end of spring, an abundance of yellow, or occasionally purple, flowers with white interiors bloom in abundance around the base.

R. muscula

Native to Argentina, this globular, deep green cactus has a mound-forming habit spreading out to 15 cm (about 6 in). White, silky, short spines and light green tubercles thickly cover the body. Vivid orange flowers blossom at the end of spring to early summer.

R. pseudodeminuta

WALLFLOWER CACTUS

This is one of the most desirable of all miniature cacti. The plant is just a cluster of 3 cm (about 1½ in) thick, 10 cm (about 4 in) or so tall stems with whitish prickles; but in early summer it disappears under the scarlet flowers with their prominent golden stamens. Yellow-flowered forms are also grown.

RHIPSALIDOPSIS
gaetneri

EASTER CACTUS

This pendent cactus with its leaf-like, thornless stems resembles the popular Christmas cactus (*Schlumbergera* x *buckleyi*) and is grown in the same way. The points of difference are that the Easter cactus has symmetrical, starry flowers instead of asymmetrical ones; that it is a rather smaller plant, rarely more than 30 cm (about 12 in) high and wide; and that it flowers later, in early spring. Garden varieties come in a great range of colours—white, light and deep rose pink, salmon, orange and red. Propagate from cuttings in summer.

Rebutia aureiflora

Rebutia pseudodeminuta

Pilosocereus palmeri

Rebutia muscula

Parodia mutabilis

Parodia nivosa

Rhipsalidopsis gaetneri

Portulacaria afra

Sedum x *rubrotinctum*

Sedum acre

Sedum morganianum

Schlumbergera x *b.* 'White Christmas'

Sedum aizoon

RHIPSALIS

paradoxa

Native to South America, this epiphytic cactus has a compact habit up to 1 m (about 3 ft) tall, then developing multiple, trailing, chain-like stems. In winter to spring, little, trumpet-like, white flowers appear along the margins of the 'chains' followed by resinous, spherical fruit. This frost-tender species requires a dry rest during autumn/fall and should be planted in fertile, porous soil with partial shade. It prefers a warm, damp atmosphere and only needs watering in spring. This pendent cactus makes an ideal hanging basket specimen and is propagated from cuttings in summer, or from seed in spring or summer. The very similar *R. houlettii* is called the 'snowdrop cactus'.

SCHLUMBERGERA

x buckleyi
syn. *Zygocactus truncatus*
CHRISTMAS CACTUS

Originating in Brazil, these epiphytic, readily branching cacti produce upright stems, which arch in maturity. They are composed of flat, rectangular pads or lush, cylindrical links, covered with bristly areoles, often with notched edges. Prominent, cylindrical flowers, bloom from the tops of the stems in autumn/fall and winter. These frost-tender species need porous, fertile soil and full sun or partial shade. They make ideal hanging baskets

Selenicereus grandiflorus

and should only be watered when the surface roots completely dry out. Propagate in summer from stem cuttings. *S.* 'White Christmas', with its white flowers tinged with reddish purple, is a popular cultivar but there are many others, with flowers in the white–pink–coral–red–purple range.

SEDUM

STONECROP

This extremely large genus contains over 500 species of predominantly evergreen succulents native to the northern hemisphere. These quick-growing plants widely vary in habit from carpet-forming to upright up to 1 m (about 3 ft) tall. Their lush, whole leaves may be tubular, lanceolate, egg-shaped or elliptical and the five-petalled flowers appear in terminal sprays. Species range from fully hardy to frost-tender and make excellent hanging basket or pot plants. Fertile, porous soil is preferred; however some types are extremely robust and will grow in most soil types. Propagate from

seed in spring, stem cuttings in summer, or by division in spring or summer.

S. acre
STONECROP, GOLD MOSS

This little plant is one of the hardiest of all succulents. It is native to Europe and eastern Asia and grows abundantly in England, its creeping stems hugging the ground between rocks or growing in the chinks of old walls. The whole plant is only about 3 cm (about 1 1/2 in) high and, with its bright green leaves, looks like a lush patch of moss—until it covers itself in spring with zillions of tiny yellow flowers. Give it sunshine and sharp drainage and propagate by removing offsets.

S. aizoon

Native to Siberia and Japan, this is a fully hardy plant, differing from the usual run of succulents in not being evergreen—it dies down each winter, to return in spring with 50 cm (about 20 in) tall stems with fleshy leaves and crowned with clusters of yellow flowers in summer. There

Rhipsalis paradoxa

are red-flowered forms also; all are grown just as any regular hardy perennial would be.

S. morganianum
DONKEY'S TAIL, BURRO TAIL

Native to Mexico, this popular, readily branching, evergreen succulent has a compact, upright habit, becoming weeping as the stems lengthen. Growing up to 1 m (about 3 ft), the attractive stems are composed of bluish green, interlocking leaves that have a plump, lanceolate form. In cultivation, clusters of long, pinkish red, starry flowers may bloom at the stem tips in summer. This pendent, frost-tender species makes an ideal hanging basket but should be handled with care as leaves readily detach.

S. x rubrotinctum
PORK AND BEANS, JELLY BEANS

Little and semi-evergreen, this fully hardy succulent grows up to 20 cm (about 8 in) in height and has yellow winter blooms. Readily branching, its slender, multiple stems are wide spreading and develop vivid green, pulpy, obovate leaves in grape-like bunches, that turn red and yellow under arid conditions. A cold, damp climate will maintain the leaf lustre.

S. spathulifium

This fully hardy, evergreen succulent has a carpet-forming habit with tiny rosettes to 5 cm (about 2 in) high, composed of plump, circular, green or frosted grey, intermingled with brownish red leaves. In summer, star-shaped yellow flowers appear on short stems.

SELENICEREUS
grandiflorus
QUEEN OF THE NIGHT

This vine-like, climbing cactus reaches up to 3 m (about 9 ft) in height and is native to Jamaica and Cuba. It is highly valued for the large, pure white, nocturnal flowers, up to 30 cm (about 12 in) in diameter, to which the common name refers. They are very sweetly scented. Quick-growing and readily branching, its deep bluish green, slender stems bear needle-shaped, short yellow spines. This half-hardy species likes full sun and fertile, porous soil. Propagate from seed or stem cuttings in summer.

SENECIO
articulatus
syn. *Kleinia articulata*
HOT DOG CACTUS, CANDLE PLANT

Native to South Africa, this deciduous, succulent shrub grows up to 60 cm (about 24 in) tall. Its multiple, greyish blue stems are tubular and weakly jointed. Terminal sprays of yellow-white flowers, similar in appearance to daisies, bloom from spring into summer. This half-hardy species is well-suited to coastal climates and makes an ideal tub or large pot specimen. It prefers full sun (but will tolerate partial shade) and extremely porous soil. Propagate from semi-ripe stem cuttings, simply removed at the joint, in summer.

STAPELIA
leendertziae

Native to South Africa, this species is one of a genus which comprises 90 species of clump-forming, perennial succulents highly valued for their unique flowers. Growing to 30 cm (about 12 in) tall, it has lush, slender, upright stems with 4 angles and indented or winged margins. The hairy, deep purple flowers are bell-shaped and bloom in summer on tubes up to 6 cm (about 2½ in) long. While extremely beautiful, the flowers unfortunately have an unpleasant carrion odour which attracts flies for pollination, making them unsuitable for indoors. The plants are frost-tender and may be grown in the greenhouse. They prefer total light or semi-shade and porous soil. Propagate this species from seed in spring, from cuttings or by division in spring and autumn/fall.

SULCOREBUTIA
arenacea

This extremely attractive, little, globular cactus grows up to 5 cm (about 2 in) in height and the same in diameter. Its greenish brown body is thickly covered with tubercles which are arranged in spirals and bear buff-coloured spines. Beautiful, rich golden yellow flowers, similar to daisies, bloom around the base of the stem. This species is frost-hardy and prefers full sun, though partial shade should be provided in hotter regions. Propagate in summer and spring from stem cuttings.

THELOCACTUS
bicolor
syn. *Ferocactus bicolor*

This perennial cactus is native to Mexico and southern USA. It has a spiny, globe-shaped to erect, pillar-like, singular body up to 20 cm (about 8 in) in height and diameter. This stem has over 10 prominent ribs lined with pronounced tubercles sprouting yellow and red, two-toned, radial spines and four longer, yellow, central spines. Easily flowering, pinkish purple trumpet-shaped flowers bloom from the crown and are up to 6 cm (about 2½ in) long. This frost-tender species enjoys full sun, porous soil and light watering. Propagate from seed in spring and summer.

TRICHOCEREUS

This genus (which is sometimes included in the genus *Echinopsis*) consists of about 25 species of ribbed, cylindrical cacti native to South America. They are half-hardy to frost-tender. Well-drained soil and full sun are required. Propagate in spring and summer from seed or stem cuttings.

T. bridgesii

Originating in the Andes of South America, this cactus has an erect, cylindrical stem up to 4 m (about 12 ft) in height. The greenish blue body freely branches from its base and has up to 8 ribs, sparsely lined with areoles bearing up to 6 spines. In summer, white, trumpet-shaped flowers open widely at night and emit a very strong fragrance.

Spreading only to 1 m (about 3 ft), this cactus makes an excellent conservatory specimen. It is half-hardy and of easy culture, frequently being used for grafting.

T. huascha
syn. *Lobivia huascha*

An example of how imperfect knowledge on the part of botanists can make life difficult for cactus lovers, this Argentine species is found in some books under *Lobivia,* in others under *Trichocereus* or even *Echinopsis*. It is an attractive plant, with stout stems, symmetrically ribbed and spiny, and brilliant red or yellow flowers in summer. They are scentless and open by day.

Trichocereus bridgesii

Senecio articulatis

Sulcorebutia arenacea

Thelocactus bicolor

Trichocereus huascha

Stapelia leendertziae

CHAPTER 11

Orchids

*O*rchids have a reputation for being glamorous, expensive and difficult. Glamorous they certainly are; but new methods of propagation have made plants much more affordable than they used to be—and few are really difficult to grow: wherever you garden, there will be at least a few you can grow just as easily (well, almost) as any other flower.

The family is an enormous one (second only to the grasses as the largest in the plant kingdom) and wild orchids grow just about everywhere except in the Arctic and the Antarctic. The most admired and coveted may be those from the tropics and subtropics of the Old and New Worlds, but the more modest temperate climate orchids are delightful too, and not as well known as they should be.

Growing Orchids in the Garden

Most of these temperate orchids are terrestrial, that is they grow in the ground the way other plants do: but the glamorous warm-climate genera are mostly epiphytes, growing perched in trees (or on rock faces) where they derive nourishment from such debris as they manage to accumulate around their roots—fallen leaves, the odd dead insect, that sort of thing—and storing water from rainy seasons in fleshy, almost succulent, stems called pseudo-bulbs. They can be grown very effectively thus in gardens where the climate is suitable; and it's not difficult to do. A not too shady tree, preferably with rather rough bark to which the roots can cling, is best. (Australian gardeners swear by casuarinas.) Attach the young plant in a suitable fork with twine, and pack sphagnum moss around its roots; water and fertilize as needed. The important thing is to match orchid to climate; but although we always think of epiphytic orchids as tropical plants, many grow in rather cool mountain regions and there is a surprisingly large range that can be grown outdoors wherever the temperature rarely falls to freezing and summer humidity is fairly high.

But most of us will find it more convenient to grow our orchids in the conventional way in pots, which allows us to bring them into the living room when they flower, or to a sunroom for the winter. As long as it has ample drainage holes, the type of pot is immaterial; but terracotta not only looks better than plastic, it makes it easier to control the amount of water the roots receive. This is the most important aspect of growing orchids: most take rest periods both in winter and for a short while after flowering and dislike being over-watered while they are not in active growth. It is critical in coolish climates or in an unheated greenhouse, for orchids can't cope with being both cold and wet—the roots go quite dormant in winter and will rot if they aren't kept dry. (That does mean dry—don't worry if the pseudo-bulbs shrivel a little.) Don't pot them in soil or the roots will suffocate. Rather, choose a specially formulated orchid potting mix. Most of these are based on chopped up bark, the different types varying in how finely it is chopped. (Phalaenopsis and cattleyas, for instance, prefer a coarser mix than cymbidiums or paphiopedilums. If in doubt, choose the coarser mix.) The bark doesn't contain much nourishment for the plant, and you will need to fertilize. You can buy special orchid fertilizers, but a bit of well-rotted manure will be just fine.

Species of the evergreen, epiphytic orchid Zygopetalum *are ideal for cold conditions.*

Fertilize while the plants are growing, either making new leaves or flower buds; but not when the plants are resting. You can divide the plants like any other perennial when they outgrow their pots, after flowering is the best time: but there's no need, just put the plant (pot and all if its roots are clinging to the old one) into a bigger pot. Pests are few: the main ones are snails and caterpillars, which adore orchid flower buds; mealy bugs; and red spider.

Growing Orchids Indoors

If you can arrange the fairly high humidity they enjoy, there is no reason why you can't try orchids as house plants too, although it has to be admitted that out of flower few of them are especially decorative. Don't let direct sun strike them, but give them lots of bright light or they may grow furiously but never flower. Indoors or out, it's best to err on the side of too much light, even if the leaves then look a bit bleached. Lots of fresh air is desirable too—open the windows wide in warm weather.

If the orchid bug bites, you will want to consider a greenhouse. It is hard to do without one in cold climates, but even in mild areas it will considerably enlarge your scope. Whether it be timber or aluminium framed, plain or architecturally elaborate is up to you; but take as many ventilators as the makers offer. Not only do orchids like fresh air, you need to be able to keep the greenhouse temperatures from soaring on warm days, when the humidity should be kept up—spraying the plants with water every couple of days in summer is a good idea. Make sure too that the roof can be shaded from spring to autumn. Heating can be by any means you find economical and convenient, the amount of heat needed depending on the plants. Orchids are classified according to the minimum winter (night-time) temperatures they need, the convention being that 'cool growers' need about 8–10°C (about 46–50°F), 'intermediate growers' about 13–15° (about 55–59°F), 'warm growers' as much as 20°C (about 68°F), with daytime (winter) temperatures about 5°C (about 10°F) higher. (These classes are useful in determining the most suitable types to grow out of doors too, remembering that almost all orchids can take a couple of degrees less if they are kept dry in winter.)

Orchids are grown for their large, showy, often brilliantly coloured flowers.

Propagation

For all their variety, orchid flowers are built to a common pattern—three petal-like sepals and three petals, the lowest (the lip or labellum) being different in size, shape and often in colour too. Above it, the stamens and stigma are fused into a single column, and the often fantastic shapes of column and labellum are designed to ensure that only the orchid's favourite insect gets a chance to pollinate it. Thus orchid hybrids are rare in the wild: but when gardeners perform the act, orchids interbreed with startling freedom and hybrids uniting two, three, or even four genera (unheard of in other families) are common. These are usually given names combining those of their parents; for instance, cattleyas and their close relatives the laelias, brassavolas and sophronitis will cross among themselves, giving rise to brassocattleyas, brassolaeliocattleyas, sophrolaelias and so on. (When all four get into the act, a new name, *Potinara*, is used.) Actually making the pollination is easy, but germinating the seeds is not; it needs laboratory conditions beyond the scope of most of us, who must rely on

division. (Some tall growers such as vandas can be air-layered.)

Still, seed is the best way to propagate orchids in quantity, and this gives rise to a peculiarity in their nomenclature. If a breeder makes a particular cross, all the seedlings of that cross constitute a 'grex' and the grex is given a name, which by convention is not given the usual single quotes. The seedlings will be all of a kind, but some will likely be superior to their fellows; and if one of these is propagated vegetatively, it will be given a further (clone) name of its own, which does get quotes: and thus you get double-barrelled names such as *Brassolaeliocattleya* Sylvia Fry 'Supreme' or *Vuylstekeara* Cambria 'Plush'. (The system is sometimes used for rhododendrons and lilies too, as in *Rhododendron* Loderi 'King George'.) These selected clones used to be frighteningly expensive, propagation by division being slow; but in recent years the technique of tissue culture has been applied to orchids with stunning success, enabling them to be quickly made available in large numbers. More than anything else, this has brought orchids from the gardens of the very rich to being flowers for all of us.

Aerides mitratum

x *Ascocenda* Flambeau

Bifrenaria harrisoniae

Ada aurantiaca, hybrid

x *Angulocaste* Olympus

Ascocentrum curvifolium

Angraecum superbum

ADA
aurantiaca

This cool-growing epiphyte from Colombia is notable both for its lovely clear orange colour and its habit of flowering in late winter and early spring; it has no real rest period and should never be allowed to quite dry out. It is a compact plant, with sprays of small bell-shaped flowers, and grows and looks best when it is allowed to make clumps—do not be in too great a hurry to divide the plants and don't over-pot it. An open, cattleya-type compost suits it best. It will interbreed with odontoglossums, bringing its bright colour, but hybrids are not commonly grown.

AERIDES
FOXTAIL ORCHID

There are about 50 species in this genus from tropical Asia, called foxtail orchids because of the way the sprays of flowers hang down from a rather upright plant which resembles a vanda in growth. They come in several colours, mostly in the delicate white to pink range; are usually very pleasantly scented; and can appear at any time from spring to autumn/fall. They need intermediate to warm conditions and a coarse open compost; a hanging basket shows the pendent flowers to best advantage. They should be allowed to dry out a bit in winter.

ANGRAECUM
COMET ORCHID

There are 200 or so species from tropical Africa and Madagascar, but relatively few are grown in gardens; best known are *A. superbum, A. angraecum* and *A. sesquipedale,* in which last the characteristic nectar spurs can be as much as 35 cm (about 14 in) long; they are pollinated by night-flying moths with exceedingly long tongues. There are several hybrids available too; all are classed as warm-growing and have scented flowers in white or combinations of white and pale green. They grow into metre (about 3 ft) tall plants, and like year-round warmth, humidity and moisture (which makes them difficult house plants) and a coarse potting mix. Give them plenty of light but not direct sunshine, and propagate from offsets.

x ANGULOCASTE HYBRIDS

This hybrid genus is derived from crosses between species of *Lycaste,* from Central America, and the less well known *Anguola,* from South America. The plants are rather like large lycastes in habit, with fat pseudo-bulbs that usually lose their leaves in winter; the large flowers, which may be white, cream or yellow, appear from the bases of the naked pseudo-bulbs at the same time as the new shoots and last for several weeks. The plants are best grown into large clumps, dividing only infrequently. Give them bright, filtered light, and keep them dry in winter. Avoid wetting the leaves, which mark easily. Propagate by division after flowering. They are classed as cool-growing.

x ASCOCENDA HYBRIDS
MINIATURE VANDA

These hybrids, developed from crosses of ascocentrums and vandas, resemble small-growing vandas (to about 60 cm [about 24 in] tall) and have very long lasting flowers about 4 cm (about 2 in) wide in clusters, in just about any colour except green; the blues and purples are especially admired. They are popular with gardeners as they take up less room in the greenhouse than full-size vandas, and they often feature among the bunches of 'Singapore orchids' imported from there and from Thailand and sold in flower shops. Mostly summer-flowering, they are warm-growing and cultivated in the same way as vandas.

ASCOCENTRUM
curvifolium

This is the best known of this genus of 9 or 10 species from South-East Asia. It makes a bushy plant about 35 cm (about 14 in) tall, with leathery leaves and carries its clusters of 2 cm (about 1 in) wide flowers in late spring or summer. Some shade between red and orange, they are very long lasting. The warm-growing genus is closely related to the vandas and will interbreed with them; it is grown in the same way.

BIFRENARIA
harrisoniae

There are 30 or so species in this genus from Central America; *B. harrisoniae* is both typical and the best known. It is an epiphyte, making a single large leaf from the top of each round pseudo-bulb, and the flowers are carried one to a stem but several to a bulb on bare stems from the base in early summer. They look a little like cream-coloured cymbidiums, but the purple labella are delicately fringed. It likes cool to intermediate conditions, an open compost, and to be left undisturbed; though the plants can be propagated by division after flowering, they hate it and take several years to settle down and flower again. Give them plenty of fresh air and a winter rest.

BLETILLA

striata
syn. *B. hyacinthina*
CHINESE GROUND ORCHID

This charming plant from China and Japan is perhaps the prettiest, certainly the easiest to grow, of the temperate climate terrestrial orchids. Frost-hardy, it likes a cool, lightly shaded spot with plenty of organic matter in the soil and ample moisture during the growing season; it shouldn't be allowed to quite dry out even after the leaves have died down for the winter. Midgreen and distinctively pleated, these are an attractive feature in their own right, an unusual characteristic among orchids. In spring, the plant bears 30–40 cm (about 12–16 in) tall sprays of small bright mauve-pink flowers. There is a white variety of great beauty but this is rare and expensive. Propagate by careful division in early spring, but the plants are best left undisturbed to develop into clumps. Plants can be grown in pots, in a cymbidium mix with a little well-rotted manure added.

BRASSAVOLA

nodosa
LADY OF THE NIGHT

This epiphytic orchid from Central America earns its common name from its sweet fragrance, wafted mostly at night. The plant is clumpy, with cylindrical leaves that look like green extensions to the pseudo-bulbs, and the pendent sprays of white (or white and pale green) flowers with their big white labella can appear at any time from spring to autumn/fall. It is coolgrowing and usually grown attached to a piece of tree-fern trunk, but a hanging basket with a coarse, cattleya-style compost suits it also. Give it plenty of light and fresh air and keep it on the dry side during winter, but not so much that the leaves shrivel. Propagate by division in early spring. The glamorous *B. digbyana,* parent of most *Brassocattleya* hybrids, is now officially *Rhyncolaelia digbyana.*

BRASSIA

verrucosa

This is the most popular of this genus of cool-growing epiphytes from South America. It makes a clump of round pseudo-bulbs with strap-shaped leaves, above which the graceful sprays of spidery flowers rise in early summer. These are pale green (or green and cream) and fragrant, though some people find the scent a bit heavy for their taste. Give it coarse compost, fairly bright light and a winter rest, though it shouldn't be allowed to

dry out enough to cause the leaves to shrivel. Propagate by division. There are other species and hybrids available, all rather similar to this one; all are among the easiest of orchids to grow as house plants.

× BRASSOCATTLEYA HYBRIDS

This hybrid genus is derived from crosses between cattleyas and *Rhyncolaelia (Brassavola) digbyana.* The result is usually sumptuous flowers with the rich colourings of the cattleyas and extravagantly frilled and ruffled labella derived from the rhyncolaelia. Often the flowers are fragrant, though usually only at certain times of the day. Cultivation is the same as for cattleyas; most like cool to intermediate conditions.

× BRASSOLAELIOCATTLEYA HYBRIDS

Another hybrid genus, this time derived from *Rhyncolaelia digbyana,* cattleyas and laelias. They resemble the brassocattleyas, the laelia influence showing up in more richly coloured labella and broader petals; the result is some of the most sumptuous of all orchid flowers. They are mostly intermediate growers and are cultivated exactly as cattleyas are. (Often, these multigeneric cattleya hybrids are simply sold as cattleyas.)

CATTLEYA

This large genus of epiphytes from Central and South America is perhaps the most admired of all orchids. The big ruffled hybrids of the flower shop, usually orchid-pink or white, are the best known: but there are more than 60 species and countless hybrids, the flowers ranging from miniatures only 5 cm (about 2 in) or so across to giants of 15 cm (about 6 in) or more. Just about every colour but blue is available, though the brighter yellow-to-red shades tend to have smaller flowers. The genus is divided into two types: the bifoliate cattleyas, which have two thick leaves atop their stem-like pseudo-bulbs and are mostly cool-growing; and the unifoliates, which have only one and tend to prefer intermediate conditions. They mostly grow about 35 cm (about 14 in) tall, though they can spread into clumps as much as a metre (about 3 ft) wide, and the flower sprays (1 or 2 to as many as 10 flowers) arise from the tops of the pseudo-bulbs. They appear, according to variety, in spring or autumn/fall. All prefer good light but not strong sunshine, a coarse potting mix, and a winter rest. They are propagated by division just as growth begins, which

× *Brassocattleya,* unnamed hybrid

Brassia verrucosa

× *Brassolaeliocattleya* Sylvia Fry

Brassavola nodosa

may be either in spring or in early autumn/fall. This can be a messy job, as the roots tend to stick to the pot; if in doubt, simply transfer pot and all to a larger one. The genus hybridizes very easily with the related *Laelia, Rhyncolaelia* and *Sophronitis,* and the resultant hybrids are often sold simply as 'cattleyas'. They are cultivated in the same way. The genus is named after an English orchid fancier, William Cattley, which should be a guide to pronunciation—they are not 'cattle-ay-as'.

Bletilla striata

Cattleya bowringiana, hybrid
Cattleya Bob Betts

Cattleya bifoliate hybrid

Cattleya trianaei

Coelogyne pandurata

Coelogyne cristata

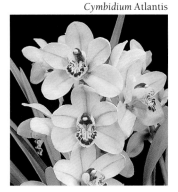

Cymbidium Atlantis

C. bifoliate hybrids
CLUSTER CATTLEYA

There are many of these available, with mostly rather small flowers in clusters, and almost all cool-growing; they can be grown out of doors in any frost-free, humid summer climate. They can be spring or autumn/fall growing, and colours range from white through pink to magenta, with some in the yellow to coral range which carry genes from the dainty orange C. aurantiaca.

C. bowringiana

This delightful autumn/fall-flowering, bifoliate cattleya from Central America is one of the most popular and easy to grow of the cattleya species. It is a cool grower, and looks best when allowed to make a large clump, when it will bear many clusters of 8 cm (about 3 in) wide, orchid-pink flowers of beautiful shape. It is the parent of several hybrids, some of which are rather optimistically described as 'blue'.

C. labiata

The name is now taken to cover a large group of unifoliate cattleyas from South America, including C. mossiae (the national flower of Venezuela), C. warneri, C. trianaei, C. gatskelliana and C. warscewiczii, all pink or white, as well as the yellow C. downiana. They are all intermediate growers with large flowers in spring or autumn/fall, and are collectively the most important parents of the cattleya hybrids of the flower shops. Pure-bred species of the group are not often available, but they are well worth growing.

C. unifoliate hybrids

These are the big, ruffled flowers of the flower shops, mainly in shades of pink or white, the white flowers being especially prized by florists for wedding bouquets and corsages. They prefer intermediate conditions, and can flower either in spring or autumn/fall; some grexes will bloom at both seasons if they are well looked after. The flowers, which can be as much as 14 cm (about 5½ in) wide, are usually borne singly or in twos or threes. Many of these big cattleyas are more or less hybridized with laelias and rhyncolealias, but famous names to look out for among the pure-bred cattleyas are Bow Bells, Suzanne Hye and Bob Betts.

COELOGYNE

There are 120 species of these epiphytic orchids from South-East Asia, Indonesia and the Pacific Islands. Relatively few are grown in gardens, perhaps because they are all best encouraged to grow into large, rather bulky plants and their usual colours—white, pale green or brown—seem tame beside larger and brighter orchids. They are, however, well worth growing, and many are happy in cool conditions. They like a cymbidium-type compost and plenty of water while they are in active summer growth, but they demand a winter rest if they are to flower freely. They can be propagated by division after flowering.

C. cristata
ANGEL ORCHID

This is the most popular of the genus, and one of the loveliest of all orchids. The angel orchid is a specimen plant with dozens of sprays of scented white flowers touched with gold among the glossy leaves; it is a wonderful sight. Cool-growing, it likes summer shade and is one of the easiest orchids to grow as a house plant. It flowers at the end of winter and on into spring.

C. pandurata
BLACK ORCHID

The black is only on the labellum; otherwise the scented flowers are pale green. They are borne on arching, 50 cm (about 20 in) tall sprays in summer, among large leaves which spring from egg-shaped pseudo-bulbs. The black orchid comes from Borneo and prefers intermediate conditions.

CYMBIDIUM

There are nearly 300 species, mostly epiphytic, in the Orient and extending through Indonesia to the east coast of Australia. Relatively few are seen in gardens, though C. ensifolium, a fragrant spring-flowering miniature, is a popular subject with Chinese artists: it is the many showy hybrids that rank among the most widely grown of all orchids. These make rather bulky plants, with clumps of pseudo-bulbs from which spring long, dull green leaves. The leafless flower stems, which can be more than a metre (about 3 ft) tall in the largest hybrids, arise from the foot of the pseudo-bulbs, to carry as many as 30 flowers. Though scentless, these are of elegant form and last for several weeks. They are available in green, yellow, white, pink or dull reds and browns, the labella usually marked in red. They appear mainly in spring, and are excellent for cutting. In recent years, mericlonal propagation has brought the price of the best clones down to the point where plants can be bought in flower at the florist and used as temporary house plants, to be discarded when the flowers are over: but there is no need to do this as the plants are easy to grow, and they do quite well as house plants. They are classed as cool-growing and in frost-free areas can be grown out of doors in the ground in shaded places and lime-free soil liberally enriched with organic matter. In pots, they should be given a fairly coarse, soil-free compost, light shade, and a winter rest, when they can be allowed almost to dry out. They can be divided after flowering. The hybrids are divided into large and miniature types; most species are best classed as miniatures, and some species are fragrant.

C., large-flowered hybrids

These are the best known cymbidiums, and innumerable grexes and clones are available. Atlantis, with 8 cm (about 3 in), cream and pink flowers, is typical. The largest types can have flowers as much as 14 cm (about 5½ in) wide, and their top-heavy flower stems benefit from staking.

Dendrobium falcorostrum

Cypripedium reginae

Dactylorhiza elata

Cypripedium calceolus

C., miniature hybrids

These cymbidiums usually grow about 50 cm (about 20 in) tall, with many flowers about 5 cm (about 2 in) wide or less; some have the broad petals and rounded shape of the larger types, others are more spidery. All are charming, cool-growing plants which look best when allowed to grow into large, many-flowered clumps. Many tend to have weeping flower stems, which may need to be staked.

C. species

There are many of these available from time to time; most grow about 50–60 cm (about 20–24 in) tall, with flowers in various subtle colours. They mainly flower in spring and some are sweetly fragrant. They are mostly cool-growing, and need the same treatment as the hybrids, though some, such as the red and green *C. devonianum*, have pendent flower spikes and look best in hanging baskets. The red-brown *C. caniculatum* is more upright. Like all the cymbidium species, they both look their best grown into large, many-flowered clumps. They are charming cut flowers.

CYPRIPEDIUM

SLIPPER ORCHID

These terrestrial orchids are an exception in the orchid world: they are rarely cultivated in pots but most often in beds, like any other herbaceous plant. They take both their common name and the scientific one which means 'slipper of Venus' from the way the labellum folds over at the end to form a pouch. They come from Europe and North America, and like cool temperate climates, rich, leafy, rather moist soil and a shaded position. They are propagated by division of the tubers in spring, but with care, as like all terrestrial orchids, they resent being disturbed.

C. calceolus

Native to Europe and North America, this herbaceous, frost-hardy perennial has bold bright green leaves and small clusters of yellow and brown (or yellow and

Cymbidium caniculatum

purple) flowers on 1 m (about 3 ft) tall stems in summer.

C. reginae

This rather rare plant is often thought to be one of the most beautiful of all American wildflowers, but though fully hardy it is difficult in cultivation. It must have acid, very leafy, well-drained soil, shade, and a cool position where there is no chance of its drying out; and it is resentful of having its roots disturbed. Where it is happy, it spreads into clumps, their fresh green leaves adorned with large white flowers with rose pink labella, borne singly on 50 cm (about 20 in) tall stems in early summer.

DACTYLORHIZA

syn. *Orchis*
MARSH ORCHID, MAY ORCHID

The genus *Orchis*, native to southern Europe, is the one from which the whole tribe takes its name (from the Greek for a testicle, because of the way the egg-shaped tubers tend to grow in pairs). It has some pretty members, but the most garden worthy are now usually classed in the genus *Dactylorhiza*. They are frost-hardy herbaceous perennials, with bold green leaves and 50 cm (about 20 in) tall spikes of small, magenta or white flowers in early summer. The best known species are *D. latifolia*, which has spotted leaves, and the slightly taller *D. elata*, also known as *D. majalis*, which has plain green ones. Both like a semi-shaded position, in moist leafy but well-drained soil and prefer to be left undisturbed; they hate being

Dendrobium, cane-stemmed hybrid

transplanted and often take 1 or 2 years to recover and start flowering.

DENDROBIUM

This is one of the largest of all the genera of orchids, with some 1500 species ranging from India, to China and Japan, Indonesia, New Guinea, Australia (where there are many) and New Zealand. It is also one of the most diverse, and here we have contented ourselves with illustrating only a few of the more easily grown species, ignoring most of the many hybrids. They can be evergreen or deciduous: most are epiphytic, but they vary in habit from clump-formers, which make fat pseudo-bulbs rather like those of a cattleya, to those whose bulbs have grown long and stem-like and which often carry their flowers in sprays in the axils of the fallen leaves. These last are divided into 'hard' and 'soft-caned' types: but though the hard types tend to be more upright in habit, the soft more floppy, even pendulous, the distinctions are not very consistent. The species and hybrids range from cool- to warm-growing: but in these days of high fuel costs, the warm-growing types are more often seen in bunches of

Cymbidium, miniature hybrid

imported 'Singapore orchids' than in what the orchid trade patronizingly calls 'amateur' greenhouses. There are innumerable hybrids, both natural and man-made.

D., cane-stemmed hybrids

D. nobile gives you an idea of what to expect from these; they are mostly upright growers, bearing sprays of flowers along the canes in spring or summer, in a wide variety of colours, from white and cream through yellow and pink to magenta red. *D. nobile* itself has entered into the parentage of many, but such other species as *D. infundibulum* from India, the purple *D. phalaenopsis* and the yellow *D. signatum* have had great influence too. They are mostly cool- to intermediate-growing and are propagated by division after flowering.

D. falcorostrum

This epiphyte from eastern Australia makes a clump of thick pseudo-bulbs about 20 cm (about 8 in) tall and topped with leathery leaves; in summer, sprays of many dainty flowers, beautifully shaped and fragrant, appear. They are white, often with red on the labellum. It is cool-growing.

D. kingianum

Photographs are apt to make this enchanting plant from eastern Australia look more imposing than it is; it is in fact a miniature, and a clump filling a 15 cm (about 6 in) pot counts as a large one. It will certainly be large enough to carry at least a hundred of its centimetre (about ½ in) wide, beautifully formed flowers, which may be in any shade from white to deep pink. It is cool-growing, and likes shade and an open, well-drained compost. It is a very reliable species for growing out of doors, when it might be described as half-hardy. It flowers in spring.

D. nobile

This species from northern India is one of the most popular of all dendrobiums, both in its own right and as a parent of fine hybrids. Cool-growing, it is classed as a soft-cane type. The pseudo-bulbs shoot up in summer to about 35 cm (about 14 in) high; in winter they lose their leaves and then the following spring are garlanded from top to bottom with shapely flowers, pale pink with maroon and gold on the labellum; some forms are richer and darker in colour, some white and gold. They are fragrant, the scent being stronger at certain times of day. It likes shade in summer, an open compost, and must have a winter rest to flower—don't start watering again until the flower buds are well developed.

D. speciosum
ROCK LILY

Though the individual flowers are quite small—2 cm (about 1 in) across at the most—they are borne in huge sprays of as many as 80 from the big, cattleya-like pseudo-bulbs, and a large clump with many flower clusters of white or cream flowers is a magnificent sight in spring. The flowers are scented too, though they are not very long lasting, fading in a fortnight or so. The plan grows about 45 cm (about 18 in) tall, and does best when allowed to multiply into generous clumps. It comes from eastern Australia, likes cool to intermediate conditions, an open compost, and a complete winter rest. A little summer shade is desirable.

D. thyrsiflorum
BACON AND EGGS

The common name comes from the yolk-yellow labella and white petals of the flowers, which are borne in large, pendent sprays in spring; the bacon is presumably the white pseudo-bulbs and green leaves. It is in fact a species of very great beauty and comes from Indo-China. It is intermediate- to warm-growing.

DISA

This genus of terrestrial orchids comes from central and southern Africa, and is notable for the beauty of its flowers, which are normally borne several to a stem in summer. They have the labellum at the top, and this is normally white or cream, heavily veined with the colour of the remaining petals. Notoriously difficult to grow and propagate, they need mild climates with freedom from extremes of temperature, constant moisture (but perfect drainage), light shade and high humidity. They are classed as cool-growing. Thrips are apt to be a major worry.

D., hybrids

Derived from crosses of *D. uniflora* with several other species, these are considerably easier to grow, and make splendid long lasting cut flowers. The flowers are usually rather smaller than *D. uniflora*, but borne as many as 8 to the stem, in shades of red, pink or lilac with white. They like a cool, shaded, but airy position and as long as they are in no danger of frost there is no need the heat the greenhouse. Pot the tubers in any standard, rather rich orchid compost, and then plunge the pots in damp sphagnum moss to keep them evenly moist—they should never be allowed to dry out, even during their winter dormancy. They can be divided with care in early spring.

D. uniflora
PRIDE OF TABLE MOUNTAIN

Often held to be the most beautiful of all South Africa's native flowers, this orchid with its large scarlet and white, scented flowers on metre (about 3 ft) tall stems is native to the cloud forests of the high mountains of the Cape, whose even temperatures, constant cloud and light rain are far from easy to duplicate in gardens. It is thus a very difficult plant to grow away from its native home, and only very skilled orchid cultivators should attempt it.

DRACULA
bella

The name has nothing to do with Count Dracula of horror-movie fame, but means 'a little dragon', referring to the curious formation of the flowers with their long-tailed sepals and their mahogany red colour. They appear in spring and summer from the base of the 20 cm (about 8 in) tall plant which looks best grown in a hanging basket. Warm-growing, it likes an open

Disa uniflora

Dendrobium kingianum

Dracula bella

Disa, hybrid

Dendrobium thyrsiflorum

Dendrobium nobile

Dendrobium speciosum

Encyclia cochleata

Eulophia speciosa

Gongora galeata

Laelia Coronet

Laelia anceps

Laelia purpurata

Epidendrum ibaguense

compost and regular watering even in winter, as the plant forms no water-storing pseudo-bulbs. Fungus can mark the leaves unless they get plenty of fresh air. Propagate by division after flowering.

ENCYCLIA
cochleata
COCKLE-SHELL ORCHID

This cool-growing epiphyte comes from Central America, and is one of the best orchids to try as a house plant. It makes clumps of strap-shaped leaves attached to round pseudo-bulbs, with flower stems arising from their summits. The flowers themselves are green with purple, shell-shaped labella; each stem carries 3 or 4 at any one time, but continues to open a succession of flowers for months; it is not un-known for a flower stem to bloom continuously for two years, so you can have last year's stems flowering beside this summer's. Give the plant a coarse compost and light shade and do not let it get too dry in winter. Propagate by division, which is best done in spring, even if the plant is still in flower. There are several other desirable species such as the bright orange *E. vitellina* and *E. citrina*, yellow, and *E. mariae*, green and cream. They resemble small cattleyas and are grown in the same way.

EPIDENDRUM
ibaguense
syn. E. radicans
CRUCIFIX ORCHID

This is one of the easiest of all orchids to grow, suiting cool, inter-mediate or warm conditions and flowering profusely out of doors in any frost-free climate in sun or light shade. It is an epiphyte, but will grow happily in the ground if the soil is lavishly enriched with organic matter; as a pot plant it will accept any standard orchid compost. It makes a rather straggly plant, with long thin pseudo-bulbs about 65 cm (about 26 in) tall that have leathery leaves all along them—staking and the occasional trimming back will help keep it neat. The

flowers, which can appear at any time of year, are only about 2 cm (about 1 in) wide, but each flower stem will have up to 20 open at any one time and continues to produce new flowers for months. The com-mon name comes from the shape of the yellow labellum that stands upright in the centre of the orange star of the petals and sepals. There are red and mauve flowered varie-ties available also, but the orange is the commonest. Water and fertilize from spring to autumn/fall, and propagate by division or removing rooted offsets. Less often seen, other species are more like small flowered cattleyas in appearance, and need the same treatment.

EULOPHIA
speciosa

A terrestrial species from Africa, this orchid bears vivid yellow flow-ers in spring, when the new foliage also appears. It is warm-growing, and needs constant moisture and light shade; it can be propagated by division of the dense clumps of tubers in early spring before growth begins. There are over 200 species in the genus, but very few are known in gardens; even *E. speciosa* is something of a rarity.

GONGORA
galeata

There are about 12 species of these Central and South American epi-phytes, of which *G. galeata* is the most likely to be found at specialist growers. It needs to be grown in a hanging basket, as the 5 cm (about

2 in) wide flowers, on their wire-thin, zig-zag stems dangle below the evergreen foliage. Of most intricate and curious form, they are a pleas-ing tawny yellow colour and strongly fragrant. They appear in summer. The plant is cool-growing and likes shade, a coarse compost, and regular summer water and fertilizer, but should be kept dry in winter. Propagate by division in early spring.

LAELIA

The laelias are closely allied to the cattleyas and rather resemble them, both in growth and the shape and colours of their flowers. They have always suffered by comparison with their more glamorous relatives, but are in their own right a most attrac-tive group of South American epi-phytes and many of the 75 species and their hybrids are well worth growing. They interbreed easily with the cattleyas, bringing to the hybrids their richly coloured labella and also a neater flower shape—some of the larger cattleya species have distinctly floppy petals. They may be either cool- or intermediate-growing, and are cultivated in the same way as the cattleyas.

L. anceps

Important in cattleya breeding but a most attractive species in its own right, this cool-growing species resembles a unifoliate cattleya in habit, though its 8 cm (about 3 in) wide lilac pink flowers with their purple labella are carried several together on rather long flower stems; a plant in full autumn/fall bloom can be 65 cm (about 26 in)

tall. There are several named clones available, chosen for their larger or more shapely flowers.

L. Coronet

This is representative of a group of miniature hybrids raised from *L. cinnabarina* (itself well worth culti-vating) which have dainty sprays of 5 cm (about 2 in) wide flowers in shades of deep yellow or orange. The plants grow about 25 cm (about 10 in) tall, and look best when allowed to form generous, many-flowered clumps. Intermedi-ate conditions suit them and they flower in spring or summer. Some have cattleya genes and thus are officially classed as laeliocattleyas, but you usually have to read the label to discover this.

L. purpurata

This orchid well deserves the hon-our of having been selected as the national flower of Brazil, a country with many beautiful wildflowers—its 15 cm (about 6 in) wide flowers with their white or pale mauve petals and vivid purple labella are

x *Laeliocattleya*, hybrid

Masdevallia, unnamed hybrid

Odontoglossum crispum hybrid

Miltoniopsis, hybrid

Odontoglossum grande

Lycaste virginalis

pink, sometimes quite deep in tone. At first sight they seem to be three-petalled, and can be as much as 15 cm (about 6 in) wide; they are carried on bare stems about 35 cm (about 14 in) long which arise from the base of the round pseudo-bulbs, which are often quite naked at the spring flowering time, the broad leaves having fallen during the winter. It is the best known species, but others, such as the bright yellow and intensely fragrant *L. aromatica* and *L. deppei*, are also much admired, and there are a number of handsome hybrids available. All are cool growing, and need a coarse compost; give them light shade and do not overwater—keep them quite dry in winter, and on the dry side in summer after the new growth has finished.

MASDEVALLIA

These epiphytes come from the mountains of South America, and are classed as cool-growing. The dainty, 5 cm (about 2 in) wide flowers are notable for their shape; the petals and labellum are tiny, so the sepals give the effect of a triangular flower, held on a slender stem about 35 cm (about 14 in) above the lowly foliage. Even more strikingly, the petals are iridescent so that as you change your point of view they glitter with different spectrum colours. The effect is seen even in the white varieties, but is still more wonderful in the red and orange types such as *M. coccinea* and *M. veitchii*. There are a number of hybrids available in the red-to-yellow range also. The plants are evergreen and flower from winter to spring. They should not be given a winter rest; it is important therefore that winter temperatures do not fall near freezing or the plants will be damaged. They can be propagated by division after flowering.

MILTONIOPSIS
syn. *Miltonia*
PANSY ORCHID

The several species of *Miltonia* are worth growing, but the popular pansy orchids are now reclassified in a genus of their own. There are about 5 species, but much more commonly grown are the many hybrids. These make round pseudo-bulbs with strap-shaped, rather pale green leaves; and the flowers are carried in small clusters, mostly in mid-summer, a time when there are not many orchids in flower—though they can appear at any time from spring to autumn/fall. Usually about 10 cm (about 4 in) wide, they are quite flat, like pansies; though the colours, white through clear pinks to red with flashes of gold on the labella, are

not really pansy-like. They like an open compost, light shade, and to be kept growing all year—a winter rest is not desirable. Propagate by division after flowering.

ODONTOGLOSSUM

The most widely grown species of this genus of 200 species from Central and South America are epiphytes, though terrestrial species are known. They are admired for their usually ruffled flowers borne in long sprays, and the wonderful variety of colours and markings displayed thereon. Few are difficult to grow: most are cool-growing, and need only the usual orchid cultivation of coarse compost, plenty of water in summer and light shade. They don't need as definite a winter rest as, say, cattleyas do, but should not be overwatered then. They make egg-shaped pseudo-bulbs, from the bases of which the flower stems appear. Flowering is from early spring to autumn/fall, depending on variety. They can be divided after flowering. The closely related genus *Cochlioda* is very similar but has smaller flowers in shades of red; it has been crossed with odonto-glossums to bring in this colour, and some of the more brilliantly coloured hybrid odontoglossums are more properly known as odontiodas. As the two genera are grown in the same way, this only affects orchid breeders with an eye on bloodlines.

O. crispum and hybrids

This species and its many hybrids are the best known of the genus. *O. crispum* itself is white, though it is very common for the flowers to be patterned and marked in shades of red or pink; some of the hybrids are almost striped, in a range of colours that may blend white with cream, yellow, red, pink or purple: or they may be entirely of any of these colours, and the ruffled, flat flowers can be as much as 12 cm (about 5 in) wide and borne 20 to the stem. They don't have a definite flowering season, flowers appearing whenever the plant feels like it: but spring and autumn/fall are the peak periods. They are cool-growing, and dislike too-hot conditions in summer, when they should be given plenty of fresh air.

O. grande

This species differs from the *O. crispum* group in that it definitely flowers in autumn/fall and needs a winter rest, but otherwise its cultivation is similar. The huge (to 15 cm [about 6 in] wide) flowers are a blend of yellow and russet, with white on the labella, and borne half a dozen to the stem. It can be divided in spring.

quite magnificent. They appear in small clusters in early spring and the plant likes intermediate conditions and a winter rest. It has been much used in crossing with cattleyas.

x LAELIOCATTLEYA HYBRIDS

The laelias have been much crossed with the cattleyas, and this hybrid genus has over 2000 named members. They vary from cool- to intermediate-growing, and can have dainty, almost miniature flowers or enormous ruffled ones, in the full range of 'cattleya' colours. They are cultivated in exactly the same way as cattleyas are.

LYCASTE
virginalis
syn. *L. skinneri*

The name *virginalis* might suggest a white flower, but though white varieties do exist, most forms of this Central American epiphyte, the national flower of Guatemala, are

ONCIDIUM

This is a huge and varied genus (over 700 species) from Central and South America, allied to the odontoglossums and miltonias (though different in appearance) and able to be crossed with them to give odontocidiums and such multi-generic hybrids as wilsonaras. The ones usually grown are epiphytes, and vary in their temperature requirements: according to species (or parentage) they can be cool-, intermediate- or warm-growing. They all like light shade and only a short winter rest; open, coarse potting mix and high humidity, but most intensely dislike being overwatered. Many have a tendency to climb up their host tree, and are best potted with a slab of tree-fern trunk to cling to. They can be propagated by division in spring.

O. papilio
BUTTERFLY ORCHID

This much admired species is atypical in that it bears its flowers singly, though the 50 cm (about 20 in) tall flower stem carries several buds which open in succession over many weeks in summer. The flowers are 14 cm (about 5½ in) across, of unusual shape, and marbled with bronze on a gold background. It is warm-growing: give it a very coarse compost and keep it on the dry side, relying on a very humid greenhouse to give it the moisture it needs, and keep vigilant for red spider. It can be propagated by division, but it is so difficult to please that few growers, having persuaded it to grow, would dare.

O. varicosum
DANCING LADIES

This species from South America is typical of a large group that bears small flowers in large branched sprays, which dance in the slightest movement of air. The most prominent feature of each flower is the labellum, the other parts being tiny; in O. varicosum and O. flexuosum this is yellow, but other species can be yellow and chestnut-brown, and some of the hybrids are almost red or pink, though always with a russet tinge. Flowering season runs from spring to autumn/fall. Most are cool-growing, and not at all difficult to grow if given their winter rest and bright light but not direct sun. They are very popular with florists, as the airy sprays last for weeks in water.

PAPHIOPEDILUM
SLIPPER ORCHID

The tropical slipper orchids used to be classed with the temperate ones in the genus Cyprepedium, but now they have been given a genus of their own. There are about 60 species from Indo-China and Indonesia, and though all are distinctive enough to be worth cultivating, the most important is the cool-growing C. insigne. This has been the parent of many hybrids and selected forms, but there are other hybrids available, developed from other species and many of these are intermediate- or even warm-growing. As a general rule, types with spotted leaves need warmer conditions than those with plain green leaves, but none is difficult to grow. All are clump-forming perennials, mostly terrestrial in habit, with no pseudo-bulbs; the leaves hug the ground and the flowers are borne above them, one to a stem. They all like a rich compost and shade and should not be allowed to dry out, even in winter. They are propagated by division; mericlonal propagation does not suit them, so selected clones and hybrids remain expensive.

P., hybrids

The aim in breeding hybrids has been to achieve a rounder flower than the rather spidery one of P. insigne, and the unnamed flower in the picture gives a good idea of the ideal. Colours range from green and bronze to yellow and white, often in combination but always subtle; they are not brilliant.

P. insigne

This cool-growing species comes from Bangladesh and the nearby Himalayas, and is rather variable; there are many different named forms in cultivation. They are normally about 30 cm (about 12 in) tall in flower, and the waxy flowers combine shades of green, russet, cream and white in various patterns and markings; all-green forms are much admired. They all look best when allowed to form generous clumps, and the flowers last for several weeks.

PHAIUS
tankervillae
NUN'S HOOD ORCHID, SWAMP ORCHID

This orchid from northern Australia is perhaps the most magnificent of all terrestrial orchids, its metre (about 3 ft) tall stems of glossy leaves being crowned in spring with clusters of 14 cm (about 5½ in) wide flowers in an unusual and attractive combination of purple, brown and white. It is just half-hardy, and grows quite readily outdoors wherever temperatures rarely fall to freezing. Give it rich, leafy soil, light shade and constant moisture, and propagate by division of the tubers in early spring. In cooler areas, it needs a cool greenhouse, a large pot and a cymbidium-type compost; potted plants can be allowed to dry out a little in winter when the foliage dies down.

PHALAENOPSIS
amabilis
MOTH ORCHID

There are nearly 60 species in this Oriental genus, but by far the most important is P. amabilis from the Philippines and its many garden forms and hybrids. They do not make pseudo-bulbs; rather, the leaves, which may be plain green or spotted, spring directly from the rootstock and the arching flower stems rise clear above them. In the best forms, the stem can be 65 cm (about 26 in) tall and bear as many as 20 shapely, 12 cm (about 5 in) wide flowers, usually shining white but sometimes pale pink. They can appear at almost any time of year. They should be treated as temporary house plants, to be discarded when the flowers fade unless you have a greenhouse to retire them to. Warm-growing, the plants need shade, constant moisture and a rich

Phalaenopsis amabilis

Paphiopedilum, hybrid

Oncidium varicosum

Oncidium papilio

Phaius tankervillae

Paphiopedilum insigne

but open and perfectly drained compost. They are apt to send roots out over the top of the pot which then attach themselves to the greenhouse staging, and these should be left undisturbed if at all possible. Propagation is by division in spring.

PLEIONE
bulbocodioides
syn. P. formosana, P. pricei

This species is the best known of this genus of herbaceous terrestrial

Sarcochilus falcatus

x Sophrolaeliocattleya, hybrid

Sophronitis coccinea

Renanthera coccinea

orchids from China. It is a lovely, dainty plant, bearing its shapely, 8 cm (about 3 in) wide pink flowers in early spring before the new leaves appear. Half-hardy, it will grow out of doors in temperate climate, though it is best given the shelter of a frost-free greenhouse. A cymbidium-type compost suits it, and it looks best when the tubers are allowed to multiply undisturbed to form clumps. Water well in summer while it is growing, hardly at all in winter after the leaves have died down. There are several other, rather similar species and now a range of hybrids, which extend the colour range to white, mauve, yellow and deeper pinks; they are all grown in the same way.

PTEROSTYLIS
GREENHOOD

A fairly large genus of diminutive terrestrial orchids from Australia and New Zealand, notable for their unusually shaped pale green flowers that rise on bare stems about 15 cm

Pterostylis banksii

Pleione bulbocodioides

Rhyncolaelia digbyana

(about 6 in) tall in late spring. The foliage is ground-hugging and dies off for the winter. Cool-growing, they can be grown outdoors in a frost-free climate, in leafy soil and shade; in pots they can be allowed to dry out a bit in winter but should be watered freely while growing. Propagate by careful division after flowering. There are several species, all very much alike.

RENANTHERA
FIRE ORCHID

This is a small genus from the tropical Far East, allied to the vandas and grown in the same way. They make tall, vanda like plants and bear, at various times of the year, branching sprays of as many as 100 small brilliant red or orange flowers. A plant in full cry is a dazzling sight, and as the flowers last very well when cut, they are exported from Singapore and Thailand to appear in high-class flower shops elsewhere. There are several species, of which R. coccinea and R. imschootiana are the best known, and a number of hybrids; they have been crossed with the vandas and ascocentrums to lend them their dazzling colour. They are outdoor plants only in humid tropical climates.

RHYNCOLAELIA
digbyana
syn. Brassavola digbyana

Its reputation for being difficult has cost this orchid from Central America popularity with gardeners, but it is a very beautiful plant and important in orchid breeding. It grows like a large unifoliate cattleya and bears its lemon-scented flowers, one per pseudo-bulb, in summer. They are 12 cm (about 5 in) wide and pale green or pinkish; their outstanding feature is their enormous deeply fringed labella. Crosses with cattleyas are still known as brassocattleyas, the name Rhyncolaelia having been adopted only in 1971; with their splendidly ruffled labella they probably now outnumber the pure-bred cattleyas in gardens. R. digbyana itself is classed as intermediate-growing and is grown in the same way as cattleyas, though it loves bright sunshine and fresh air and must never be overwatered. Keep it quite dry in winter and on the dry side when it is not actually growing or flowering, and propagate by division in spring.

SARCOCHILUS
ORANGE-BLOSSOM ORCHID

This is a genus of very pretty dwarf epiphytic orchids from the rainforests of north-eastern Australia. They

make low clumps of leathery foliage and in spring bear sprays of 2.5 cm (about 1 in) wide flowers which do resemble orange blossom in size and shape, though not in scent. The best known are the white S. falcatus and S. hartmannii, white with a small crimson labellum: S. fitzgeraldii is pink, and there are a number of hybrids and selected forms of all three, of which the white Blue Nob is perhaps the best known. All are cool-growing and like a coarse, open compost and light shade. They appreciate constant moisture, and shouldn't be allowed to get quite dry even in winter.

x SOPHROCATTLEYA AND SOPHROLAELIOCATTLEYA HYBRIDS
RED CATTLEYA

These two hybrid genera derive from infusions of Sophronitis coccinea genes into the cattleya and laeliocattleya breeding lines, creating beautifully coloured red or orange, rather small-flowered 'cattleyas'. We have grouped them together because the laelia influence is not always very obvious without consulting the label and they are grown in the same way—exactly as intermediate-growing cattleyas are, though perhaps with a little more water in winter. When Rhyncolaelia digbyana gets into the act the resultant flowers are not called Sophrobrassolaeliocattleya but Potinara, in honour of the great French horticulturist Julien Potin. Their cultivation is the same.

SOPHRONITIS
coccinea
syn. S. grandiflora

This is a most dainty epiphyte from Brazil. It makes a low-growing clump of dark green leaves, adorned in spring with beautifully shaped, 3 cm (about 1½ in) wide flowers like small cattleyas. They can be pink, orange, red or violet, but it is the scarlet forms that are most admired and which have been crossed with cattleyas to lend them their beautiful colour. It likes intermediate conditions; culture is the same as for cattleyas, but it dislikes being divided and is best left to multiply. Don't let it dry out too much in winter, as it is never quite dormant.

STANHOPEA
wardii
UPSIDE-DOWN ORCHID

There are several species of this South American genus of epiphytes, all rather similar in habit: the cream-flowered S. wardii and the yellow and brown S. tigrina are the best known. (There are several hy-

Vuylstekeara Cambria 'Plush'

Thunia marshalliana

Stanhopea wardii

Vanda Rothschildiana

Wilsonara, unnamed hybrid

Vanda Nellie Morley

Zygopetalum mackayi

brids available also.) All have the peculiarity that the flower buds burrow down through the potting compost, to hang in the air beneath the roots, so they must be grown in hanging baskets. The extraordinarily shaped flowers appear in summer. As orchid flowers go, they are not very long lasting, but they are very strongly fragrant. The pseudo-bulbs are round and the leaves broad and luxuriant. Cool to intermediate conditions suit, and they will grow happily outdoors in a shaded position in frost-free climates. Keep the plants dry in winter, and propagate by division in spring.

THUNIA
marshalliana
BAMBOO ORCHID, ORCHID OF BURMA

This is the most commonly grown of the 9 species which all come from Indo-China. It is a terrestrial, and, having no pseudo-bulbs, is effectively a regular, frost-tender herbaceous plant. The pendent clusters of 13 cm (about 5 in) wide, white flowers with pink and gold veins on the labellum are carried atop the metre (about 3 ft) tall stems. The stems die down after the summer flowering, when the plants can be divided if desired. It likes intermediate conditions, summer shade, and regular watering; it should not be allowed to get quite dry even in winter. Give the plants fairly large pots of any ordinary orchid compost, and allow them to build up into generous, many flowered clumps.

VANDA

The most celebrated species of this epiphytic genus from South-East Asia to northern Australia is *V. caerulea*, the blue orchid from the mountains of Thailand and Burma, where it used to be quite common. Sadly, the greed of Western gardeners has brought it to an endangered state—and it is not often seen in gardens either, its place having been taken by more easily grown hybrids. It is typical of its genus in its metre (about 3 ft) tall, stem-like pseudo-bulbs, with leathery leaves, from which the sprays of as many

as 12, 10 cm (about 4 in) wide flowers appear in early autumn/fall. Some of the 70 or so species are spring or summer flowering, and the colour range is from white through cream and pink to orange—the blue is in fact rare. Many have interesting markings and mottlings of other colours. They are all warm-growing epiphytes, liking a very coarse compost and strong light, though preferably not full sunshine; they are outdoor plants only in the tropics. Keep them warm and watered all year, as they rarely take a winter rest, and propagate by removing rooted offsets. Most will require staking; if this is a piece of tree fern trunk they will cling to it by aerial roots.

V. Nellie Morley

Derived, as so many good vanda hybrids are, from the not now often cultivated (except by orchid breeders) *V. sanderana*, Nellie Morley has become perhaps the most popular of the vanda hybrids, with many named clones available, usually with 10 cm (about 4 in) wide flowers in some shade of rich pink or coral. It has the unusual habit of flowering twice a year, in spring and again in autumn/fall. It likes warm conditions but plenty of fresh air, and an open potting mix; don't dry off in the winter.

V. Rothschildiana
BLUE ORCHID

This hybrid between *V. caerulea* and *V. sanderana* is easier to grow than *V. caerulea* itself, and hence more often encountered in gardens. It bears sprays of 12 cm (about 5 in) or larger flowers in winter; they range in the different clones from light to deep violet-blue, the flowers being distinctly veined with a deeper shade; a well-grown plant can carry several sprays of flowers. Its cultivation is the same as that of Nellie Morley, and it has itself given rise to further hybrids, many of startlingly intense blue.

Vuylstekeara
CAMBRIA 'PLUSH'

There are many other members of this hybrid genus, but Cambria

'Plush' is by far the most famous—and, thanks to mericlonal propagation, one of the most widely available. It is a compact plant, with round pseudo-bulbs each carrying a few long leaves; and the flowers can appear at any time from spring to autumn/fall. They are about 8 cm (about 3 in) wide, carried in sprays of a dozen or so, and an attractive shade of dull red with very pretty white markings on the labellum. Like almost all the group, it adapts to cool, intermediate or warm conditions, likes a coarse compost and regular watering—it needs no winter rest—and flowers even when the plants are very young and small. Propagate by division in spring. The name *Vuylstekeara* honours the Flemish orchid grower C. Vuylsteke who originated the genus early in the twentieth century from crossings of species and hybrids of *Odontoglossum*, *Miltonia* and *Cochlioda*. (The last are like small, red-flowered odontoglossums.)

WILSONARA HYBRIDS

This hybrid genus, which combines the genes of *Oncidium*, *Odontoglossum* and *Cochlioda*, goes in and out of fashion, but does have some rather charming members, rather like vividly red- or chocolate-striped odontoglossums and given such appropriate names as Tiger Talk. They are grown and propagated in the same way as the *Odontoglossum crispum* hybrids are and like them can flower at any time.

ZYGOPETALUM
mackayi
syn. *Z. intermedium*

This is the best known of several rather similar species from Central and South America. It makes a low-growing plant with mid-green leaves and carries its 60 cm (about 24 in) tall flower stems in autumn/fall or early winter. The flowers are chiefly notable for their unusual colour—the petals and sepals are green, spotted with red, and the labellum is purple and white. The effect is much more attractive than it sounds, and the flowers are fragrant. The plant likes intermediate to cool conditions, and needs a winter rest after flowering. Give it good light and plenty of fresh air; if the leaves get damp they will develop unsightly black blotches. Propagate by division in spring.

CHAPTER 12

Ferns, Palms
& Cycads

*T*hat these three groups of plants come together here in this book is a coincidence of horticulture rather than botany—it would be hard to select three groups so unrelated to each other.

Except for moss, cultivated only in Japanese gardens and their imitations elsewhere, ferns are the most ancient, 'primitive' plants we grow. Far more ancient than the flowering plants, they have been around for hundreds of millions of years. The palms on the other hand are among the most recent and highly evolved flowering plants, although their flowers are not such that gardeners take much notice of them. The cycads, often hard to distinguish from palms at a little distance, are a kind of bridge between the ferns and the most primitive flowers, the conifers; they aren't even flowering plants.

Yet they play similar roles in gardens: all are admired mainly for their leaves, characteristically long but divided into small segments (although there are many exceptions); all are invaluable plants for shade; their most glamorous varieties are lovers of warm climates; some species at least provide food in their native lands; and they can find their place among indoor plants.

Ferns

Let us take the ferns first. They are all perennials, mainly growing from creeping or clumpy rootstocks—although the tree ferns array their leaves atop palm-like trunks—and none has flowers. Their sex life is in fact rather complex and interesting. On the underside of their leaves (sometimes on special leaves which differ from the usual) they bear an array of what look like blisters. These are called sori, and they release spores, tiny clusters of cells which blow away on the wind. If they land in a favourable place, they germinate into curious little plants called prothalli, which usually look like little bits of leaf lying on the ground. These in turn bear male and female organs, the male releasing sperm which *swim* to the female ones to fertilize them. Then, and only then, the fern plant grows from the prothallus into its familiar form. The swimming sperm need water to swim in, of course; and that is why ferns are almost all lovers of moist ground and shady places—the sun dries up the needed moisture too fast.

They fall into two broad groups, the tropical and the temperate climate species, in each of which the variety of foliage forms and even colours is staggering. You can have the usual once-divided fronds, twice or three times divided, crested, or even severely plain with no divisions at all. And they can be any shade of green or marked with colour; in some species the sori are silver or gold and so abundant they colour the leaf. The plants can be sedentary in habit or running about by their rhizomes, and they range from just a couple of centimetres in height to over a metre (about 3 ft), with the tree ferns growing to five times that. No wonder the Victorians

Ferns are greatly admired for their beautiful and diverse foliage.

adored them and devoted whole gardens to them. The tree ferns are mostly natives of warm-temperate to tropical climates and dislike frost, but they share the tribe's fondness for shade, fertile soil and moisture. Few have big root systems, which makes them wonderful pot plants, although you need to choose your varieties with care if you want to grow them as house plants—most need more humidity than living rooms offer. They can be propagated from the spores, which are sown in pots of moist soil like seeds, and most can be divided like any other perennial.

Food? The very young leaves of many species can be gathered and cooked as a vegetable—if you see fiddlehead ferns on a restaurant menu, do try them. (The term fiddlehead doesn't designate a species; it refers to the way the young leaves are scrolled like a crosier or the end of the pegboard of a violin.)

Palms

The palms are, by contrast, trees, although usually they grow on a single unbranched trunk, with a crown of large leaves at the top. (Some form clumps of stems, but these are normally unbranched.) These leaves can be long and divided, like giant fern leaves, or they can be rounded and fan shaped, the two types being called 'feather' or 'fan' palms. They mostly grow in the company of other trees, so they like the shade, at least when they are young; but there are few among the taller palms that insist on it. Palms vary enormously in height; some of the clump-formers grow to only about 2 or 3 metres (about 6 or 9 ft) tall and can be placed in the garden like shrubs; others can reach 30 metres (about 90 ft) and are sufficiently stately for the largest gardens. Alas, the most magnificent palms are strictly for frost-free climates, and the delights of a palm avenue is denied to the temperate climate gardener. (There are a few species that will grow even in climates like Britain's, but they aren't very exciting.) He or she will have to be content with growing some of the more modest palms indoors: but they are among the most attractive of all house plants. They are mostly easy to grow; give them reasonable light, don't over-water them, and don't over-pot them—they rather like tight shoes.

There are few groups of trees as useful as palms in the countries where

Palms and ferns can be used to create an oasis in the suburban garden.

they grow; some people make thatch from the leaves, the trunks provide timber, and dates and coconuts are both borne by palms. Some species can have their sap tapped to make palm wine or toddy (which in turn can be distilled into arrack, one of the most head-spinning liquors known); and there are those whose young shoots can be cut out and cooked like cabbage. Not the sort of thing for the backyard vegetable patch, but you can buy canned palm hearts, also known as millionaire's salad. They are usually imported from Brazil.

Cycads

Cycads also produce food; they bear large, nut-like seeds that are very rich in starch. But again they are not for the vegetable plot—the raw seeds contain poisonous alkaloids, which have to be destroyed by long and elaborate preparation. This varies with the species, but may involve pounding the seeds, steeping them in water for long periods or both. This is an art perfected by the indigenous peoples of Australia and Africa, where most species grow. Some species contain a great deal of starch (called sago) in their growing shoots,

although as cycads grow so very slowly it is not economic to harvest the sago. In fact, commercial sago (tapioca) comes from a different, totally unrelated plant.

It is their agonisingly slow growth that limits the popularity of cycads in gardens; sow a seed and it will be years before you are rewarded with a fully developed clump of glossy, palm-like leaves, let alone the curious flower cones, which can be huge, far larger than any pine cone. The plants bear male and female cones, usually on the same plant, and the female cones can be a striking sight when the seeds ripen. Eventually, most will grow up onto a short, thick trunk, but don't hold your breath waiting—the magnificent specimens you see in botanic gardens have almost all been transplanted fully grown from the wild. Cycads must be the most easily transplanted of all woody plants, but we must discourage you from going cycad hunting—they are not exactly abundant and are usually protected by law. If you do acquire one, give it a climate free of frost, or almost so, a place in light shade, and fertile soil. Grow it in a big pot by all means, and if you like you can bring it inside to a sunny room.

Adiantum aethiopicum

Athyrium filix-femina

Asplenium australasicum   *Asplenium bulbiferum*

Adiantum capillus-veneris

FERNS

ADIANTUM

MAIDENHAIR FERN

Common throughout the tropics and subtropics, these half-hardy or tender ferns look delicate but grow vigorously in the right conditions. There are over 200 species worldwide, mostly ground-dwellers with an even greater number of cultivars. They grow well in gardens with filtered sunlight and make perfect ground cover where there is any decaying organic matter such as leaf litter to keep the surface moist. Their fronds vary in length from 5 cm (about 2 in) to 1 m (about 3 ft) and turn from red to green as they grow. They have creeping rhizomes and polished, black-brown leaf stalks. Most species need repeated watering during summer.

A. aethiopicum

COMMON MAIDENHAIR

Originally from Africa and Australasia, this fern is one of the most popular and hardy of the genus. It flourishes in containers and hanging baskets (with frequent repotting) and in gardens, where it spreads via underground runners and forms large showy clumps of feathery fronds. It is half-hardy and grows to a height of nearly 1 m (about 3 ft).

A. capillus-veneris

VENUS-HAIR FERN, EUROPEAN MAIDENHAIR

Found almost worldwide, this species grows to 60 cm (about 18 in) with bipinnate or tripinnate fronds. It does well with a little lime added to its potting mixture. There are several cultivars which grow best away from direct sunlight and, though frost-hardy, they prefer a sheltered position.

ANEIMIA

mexicana

FLOWERING FERN

No ferns have flowers, but this one bears its spores on special fronds which take the form of curly, tufted branches that do look a little like plumes of beige flowers arising from amidst the rich green of the other leaves. It is rather frost-tender and likes the usual fern conditions of shade, fertile soil and regular watering. It grows about 0.5 m (about 1½ ft) tall and in cooler areas dies down for the winter.

ASPLENIUM

SPLEENWORT

Commonly found in rainforests all over the world, this fern genus has approximately 650 species that differ greatly in size and frond shape (simple, pinnate or bipinnate). Many hybrids have developed in the wild. Most of them are fast, hardy growers and tend to grow in clumps with creeping or tufted rhizomes. Species may be ground-dwelling, rock-dwelling or epiphytic. Avoid placing these ferns under direct sun under glass. Propagate from spore or by division.

A. australasicum

syn. A. nidus
BIRD'S-NEST FERN, CROW'S-NEST FERN

A native of Australia's rainforests, this frost-tender fern is much loved by landscape gardeners. It spreads out to 50 cm (about 20 in) in a profuse, nest-like shape of broad, glossy, bright green fronds. In drier forests it grows among rocks. This is one of the easiest ferns to grow provided it is not watered to excess. A lightly shaded position is preferred. Suitable for a moist, protected garden and hanging baskets or tubs, it will also flourish in a fernery.

A. bulbiferum

MOTHER SPLEENWORT, MOKU, HEN-AND-CHICKEN FERN

This large rainforest fern is common to Australia, New Zealand and the islands of East Africa and the Pacific. It generally grows to more than 1 m (about 3 ft) high. It varies greatly in the wild, so there are many widely differing subspecies. It will grow well indoors, as well as in a sheltered garden if the rhizome is placed in a well-drained position. Propagate from the plantlets that grow on the mature fronds.

ATHYRIUM

filix-femina

syn. Asplenium filix-femina
LADY FERN

The lady fern was a great favourite in Victorian ferneries, and a number of garden varieties with variegated or unusually shaped and feathered leaves and names like 'Fritzelliae', 'Pulcherrimum' and 'Victoria' were developed. The wild plant, which comes from Europe and America, is as pretty as any, with much divided leaves in a delicate shade of green. It can vary in height from 35 cm (about 14 in) to 3 times that, according to variety, and gradually spreads into wild clumps. It is frost-hardy and likes the usual fern treatment of shade, fertile soil and moisture.

BLECHNUM

WATER FERNS

This genus is found in temperate to tropical climates, mostly in the southern hemisphere. Size and growth vary according to species. Most are ground-dwellers that prefer moist soil, and propagate via their runners to form clumps. The new fronds on most species are pinnate and fishbone-shaped, and some are brightly coloured. They are mostly frost-tender and happiest in subtropical climates.

B. discolor

CROWN FERN, PUI-PUI

So called because of the attractive crown of bright green fronds radiating from its centre, this New Zealand native has become a common sight in landscaped gardens. Mature plants have a trunk that grows to 30 cm (about 12 in) and a total height of 1 m (about 3 ft). This fern likes lots of water and will grow in sun, although it prefers a shady position.

B. fluviatile

RAY WATER FERN

This colonising, semi-upright, evergreen fern has a squat, leathery crown which has both decorative rosettes of sterile fronds and erect, fertile fronds. These are up to 50 cm (about 20 in) high and 1 m (about 3 ft) in spread. The rigid, slender, pinnate fronds are densely foliaged. Frost-hardy, it requires total shade and light, fertile soil.

B. penna-marina

ALPINE WATER FERN

A native of New Zealand, Australia, South America and the subantarctic islands, this fern is often found where snow and frost are common. Growing in quick bursts in the summer, its slender, dark green

fronds grow up to 20 cm (about 8 in). It prefers bright light and, although not soil-sensitive, needs a temperate climate with cold periods. It makes an ideal ground cover.

B. tabulare

This clump-shaped, attractive species has an upright, leathery, scaly trunk up to 60 cm (about 24 in) in height and is native to Australia, the Falkland Islands, South Africa and the West Indies. Half-hardy, it needs moist soil with plenty of compost and leaf mould.

CYATHEA

syn. *Alsophila, Sphaeropteris*

TREE FERN

These evergreen tree ferns, from tropical to subtropical areas of the world, can reach a height of 15 m (about 50 ft), although they are usually not as tall as that in gardens. Their palm-like trunks, from the summits of which the fronds spring, are composed of knitted-together aerial roots; below ground they have

normal roots. Established plants need care in transplanting—ensure that the normal, subterranean roots are not damaged. The genus is characterized by its arching rosette of weeping or erect, bipinnate or tripinnate fronds. Tree ferns prefer a warm climate but need plentiful water in warm weather and protection from the hot sun. They do well in tubs but eventually need replanting. Propagate from spores.

C. australis

ROUGH TREE FERN

A popular garden plant for mild climates, this majestic fern grows

up to 12 m (about 37 ft) high. The fronds may grow up to 4 m (about 12 ft) long; they are deep green in dark positions and yellowish in open areas. A very adaptable fern which will tolerate sun or shade and a whole range of soil conditions, but requires regular watering.

C. dealbata

SILVER KING, PONGA, SILVER TREE FERN

New Zealand's national emblem, this fern is instantly identifiable by the silver-white underside of the fronds. This is a hardy plant that grows to 5 m (about 15 ft), although it is often taller in the wild.

Blechnum penna-marina

Blechnum fluviatile

Cyathea dealbata

Blechnum discolor

Cyathea australis

Blechnum tabulare

Dicksonia antarctica

Davallia pyxidata

Cyathea dregei

C. dregei

This South African species has pendent fronds, with a deep green surface and pale underside, growing to 1 m (about 3 ft) in length. The 8 cm (about 3 in) long, lance-shaped pinnae have a fleecy underside.

CYRTOMIUM
falcatum

HOLLY FERN

A native of South-East Asia, its common name derives from the small, shiny, holly-shaped leaves that grow upright on wiry stems. Its spores are easily carried by the wind, so it has naturalized in many countries and is widespread on the cliffs of coastal areas. It grows well in greenhouses and indoors in a well-lit position, ideally growing up to 50 cm (about 20 in). Although it is frost-hardy, its upper fronds can burn. If this happens just clip them. The plant will form new growth in warmer weather. It likes shade, although it is one of the most sun-tolerant of the ferns.

DAVALLIA
pyxidata

HARE'S-FOOT FERN

A member of a genus popular among fern enthusiasts, this species is native to northern Australia, where it is found growing among rocks as well as on trees and larger ferns in rainforests. It grows to a height of 30–40 cm (about 12–16 in) with glossy pinnate fronds up to 1 m (about 3 ft) long and has long-creeping, fleshy rhizomes. It is easy to cultivate in hanging baskets or pots. Propagate from spores and rhizome cuttings. The rather similar *D. fijiensis* is also widely grown; it comes from Fiji and is frost-tender.

DICKSONIA

This genus contains 30 large species of evergreen to semi-evergreen tree ferns native to the region stretching from Malaysia to Australia. Reasonably fast-growing, these attractive ferns develop trunks in maturity and have arching, lance-shaped, multi-pinnate fronds with downy bases. The plants range from

Dicksonia squarrosa

frost-hardy to frost-tender and require protection from the wind. Plant in peaty, damp soil with full or partial shade. Withered fronds should be frequently pruned. Propagate from spores in summer. The genus was named after the eighteenth-century British botanist, James Dickson.

D. antarctica

SOFT TREE FERN

Native to south-eastern Australia and the giant of its genus, this tree fern grows to 15 m (about 50 ft) with a trunk diameter of 2 m (about 6 ft). It is a fast and hardy grower that does well in tubs and favours a moist, sheltered position in the garden. Its lance-shaped fronds are long—up to 4.5 m (about 13 ft—and its huge trunk is made of fibrous roots. Sections of trunk are used to make hanging baskets. Possums often make a meal out of the young fronds, and the pith of the trunk is a traditional food source for Australian Aborigines. As the severed trunk will grow when replanted, it is easy for unscrupulous

Cyrtomium falcatum

persons to steal it from its rainforest habitat.

D. squarrosa

WHEKI, ROUGH TREE FERN

One of the most popular tree ferns, this robust New Zealand species develops in colonies, prohibiting the growth of other plants. The trunk is covered in brownish red down and grows to over 5 m (about 15 ft) tall and 3 m (about 9 ft) in diameter. The rough, deep green 3–4 pinnate fronds, forming in a rough crown, have a lighter coloured underside and are over 1 m (about 3 ft) long. This half-hardy fern needs a humid climate, partial shade, damp soil and shelter from frost and wind.

DOODIA

This genus contains 15 thicket-forming, evergreen dwarf ferns native to Sri Lanka, some Pacific islands and Australia. The rough, slender pinnate fronds have heavily serrated leaflets and are vivid red-pink when immature. Species range from fully to half-hardy and prefer a cool, but not cold, climate. Plant in any reasonably fertile, damp soil and avoid direct sunlight. The plants in this genus grow well in an extremely humid atmosphere and are suitable for rockeries or as ground cover. Dry conditions are withstood after they have become well rooted. Do not overwater as they are susceptible to rot. Propagate from spores or by division in spring. The genus was named after English chemist and botanist, Samuel Doody.

Doodia aspera

Doodia media

D. aspera
PRICKLY RASP FERN

Native to Norfolk Island, eastern Australia and New Zealand, this small, hardy fern proliferates in open forests in tropical and temperate climates. Its light green, pinnate fronds are lance-shaped and, as the common name suggests, have a rough, raspy texture. New growth is an attractive pink or red. A moderate grower, this fern does well in shade and sun, provided it is kept moist. It will do well in hanging baskets and makes excellent ground cover for steep banks or slopes. Propagate by division or from spores.

D. media
COMMON RASP FERN

This low-tufted New Zealand fern has upright rhizomes growing 20–30 cm (about 8–12 in) tall and spreading up to 60 cm (about 24 in). The immature, rich reddish pink, lanceolate fronds are covered in scales and hairs. They are at their most vivid in full sun, turning deep

green in maturity. This species prefers a heavy clay soil.

DORYOPTERIS
pedata

HAND FERN

Native to tropical regions in America, this attractive plant is the most commonly grown species in a genus of small, palm-shaped ferns. It is easily identified by its broad, dark green leaf segments. Mature fronds have small buds at the base of the leaf. With an average growth rate, it reaches a height and width of some 30 cm (about 12 in). This is a half-hardy plant which needs warm, moist conditions if grown indoors.

DRYOPTERIS
filix-mas

MALE FERN

Common to the temperate and tropical areas of the northern hemisphere, this fern features lanceolate, pinnate fronds. It grows up to 30 cm (about 12 in) high and

Dryopteris filix-mas

spreads out to the same width. A hardy ground-dweller with short rhizomes, it prefers moist, well-drained soils. The common name survives from the days when herbalists thought that plants came in male and female, the ivy and the oak being one such 'couple'. The lady fern is *Athyrium filix-femina*. It is a graceful plant, similar in culture to the male fern (see entry earlier in this chapter).

HUMATA
tyermannii

SILVER HARE'S-FOOT FERN

Native to the tropical parts of China, this small, hardy fern is easily identified by the small silvery scales on its rhizomes. It has thick, leathery tripinnate fronds. One of the hardiest of its genus, this plant flourishes when maintained in moist soil and placed in a hanging basket. It is rather frost-tender, and is really only a garden plant in subtropical climates, where it makes pleasing ground cover. It grows about 30 cm (about 12 in) tall.

Lycopodium phlegmarioides

LYCOPODIUM
phlegmarioides

LAYERED TASSEL FERN

From a genus of 'fern allies' rather than true ferns, this elegant species features small, shiny, lacquered leaves that grow forward along the stem in 4 rows. Very popular with enthusiasts, these epiphytes form clumps of hanging stems that make them perfect for basket culture. Hang in positions where the air flows well and make sure that the soil is well-drained, as tassel ferns are sensitive to excess water.

MARATTIA

salicina

POTATO FERN

Native to Asia, Australia and New Zealand, this species has a pulpy, multi-branching trunk which produces arching, shiny green fronds which are pinnate when immature, becoming bipinnate with age. The fronds develop into a crown that reaches to 8 m (about 24 ft) across.

The plant develops a very large semi-tuberous root that was once a Maori food source, however the number of wild species has been drastically reduced by feral pigs. A magnificent fern that is readily transplanted. It demands a rich soil, space, shade, ample moisture, humidity and a mild climate with a minimum temperature of 5°C (about 40°F). Propagate by root division.

Nephrolepis exaltata

NEPHROLEPIS

SWORD FERN

Commonly found in the tropics and subtropics on the edges of rainforests or in open forests, this genus of hardy ferns features fishbone-shaped fronds with short, upright rhizomes. They are extremely tolerant to drought and are fast growing, provided they are given enough room to spread out. Since they are sensitive to cold, these ferns are ideal for indoor placement, but be sure to provide lots of water in warm conditions. Propagate from spores or tissue culture, or by division.

N. cordifolia

syn. *N. cordata*

FISHBONE FERN, HERRINGBONE FERN, SWORD FERN, LADDER FERN

Naturally found among rocks at the edge of rainforests this fern can grow in fairly dry and dark positions as well as in full sun. It is one of the toughest species in cultivation. Fronds grow to 1 m (about 3 ft). It is a very easily grown, fast-

Marattia salicina

growing plant—so much so that it can become a pest.

N. exaltata

BOSTON FERN

Native to tropical America, this species is less often grown than its many cultivars, which have more luxuriant foliage that is sometimes lacy or yellow-tinted. These cultivars are sterile and must be propagated by division or from tissue culture. All are suitable for hanging baskets. They are first-rate indoor plants and do well outdoors in frost-free climates. Give them rich soil, light to heavy shade and regular moisture; clean the fronds of outdoor plants occasionally.

ONOCLEA

sensibilis

SENSITIVE FERN

Native to the USA and east Asia, this deciduous, water-loving fern is the only member of its genus. Hardy and quick spreading, with creeping rhizomes, it has two types of fronds, one sterile and one fertile. The sterile bipinnate fronds are large and wide while the fertile fronds look like a small group of green balls growing on the leaf stalk. Suitable for cool climates.

OSMUNDA

regalis

ROYAL FERN, FLOWERING FERN

Native to Asia, the USA, Africa and Europe and varying slightly in each country, this is the largest of its genus and grows to a height of 2 m (about 6 ft) with long bipinnate fronds. Deciduous and frost-hardy,

Onoclea sensibilis

Nephrolepis cordifolia

it is commonly found in large groups in swamps and other boggy areas and so is suitable for wet gardens as long as it is shaded. Propagate from spores. It takes the name 'flowering fern' from the brown, clustered, spore-bearing fronds which grow among the regular ones.

PELLAEA
rotundifolia
BUTTON FERN, ROUND-LEAFED FERN, TARAWERA

Native to New Zealand, this species is very popular as a garden plant in other countries as well. It is a small, dark green, ground-dwelling fern found in damp open forests or drier woodlands. It has pinnate fronds with deep green, glossy round leaflets and long-creeping rhizomes. Suitable for a garden or fernery with filtered sunlight, protected from draughts, it also does well in rock gardens.

PHYMATOSOROS
diversifolius
KOWAOWAO

The most common and variable of its genus, this prostrate, epiphytic species is native to New Zealand and Australia. It has distinctive pulpy green stems covered with brownish black scales. Slender, undivided fronds, becoming woody and pinnate with age, grow to 25 cm (about 10 in) long and bear up to 12 shiny green leaflets with conspicuous veins, smooth or undulating margins and rounded tips. This species grows well in total shade, as ground cover or over logs.

PLATYCERIUM
A genus of epiphytes common to the tropics and subtropics of Africa, South-East Asia and Australia, some species can tolerate quite cool temperatures though not frost. They are valued for their showy, staghorn-like appearance and are easily grown as epiphytes when tied on to the tree on slabs of board, or grown in baskets. The sterile nest leaves are used to catch leaf litter and other vegetable matter so that the roots eventually grow into the debris and are protected from winds. The base of the plant should be kept moist. Fertilize with blood and bone or old manure. Propagate by division in spring. Watch for beetles, moths and lacewings.

P. bifurcatum
ELKHORN FERN

Native to the north-east coast of Australia, to New Guinea and New Caledonia, the elkforn fern is an easily grown plant that does well in sheltered gardens. It grows to a

height and spread of approximately 1 m (about 3 ft).

P. superbum
syn. P. grande
STAGHORN FERN

The enormous size (up to 2 m [about 6 ft] high and wide) that this epiphyte reaches as it clings to a rainforest tree can cause it to fall to the ground from sheer weight; however, usually it is only half that size in gardens. A half-hardy fern, it does well in a fernery or garden.

Osmunda regalis

Phymatosoros diversifolius

Pellaea rotundifolia

Platycerium superbum

Platycerium bifurcatum

Polystichum setiferum

Polystichum proliferum

Polystichum vestitum var. richardii

Polypodium aureum

POLYPODIUM
aureum
RABBIT'S-FOOT FERN

This evergreen fern has creeping rhizomes with golden scales. The mid-green fronds have orange-yellow sporangia on the undersides. The plant grows to 1.5 m (about 4½ ft) high and spreads to 60 cm (about 24 in). Frost-tender, it is happiest in partial shade and a moist, well-drained soil. It is ideal for growing in hanging baskets.

POLYSTICHUM

SHIELD FERN

This genus of ground- or rock-dwelling ferns is found in tropical and subantarctic regions world-wide. Their fronds are either pinnate or simple and ribbon-shaped and they are known as shield ferns because groups of spores are covered with a fragile, shield-shaped growth. Some of these ferns are very ornamental and have become popular with gardeners and enthusiasts. The plants prefer moist soil and partial shade, although some grow well in direct sunlight. There is usually an abundance of small buds on the tips of fronds that become plantlets in their own right when conditions are favourable.

P. proliferum
MOTHER SHIELD FERN

This is one of the most easy growing and reliable of the shield ferns, growing to a height of 1 m (about 3 ft) and lasting for a long time in tubs or the ground.

P. vestitum var. richardii
syn. P. richardii
COMMON SHIELD FERN, PIKOPIKO, TUTOKE

Originating in New Zealand and Fiji, this robust, variable fern has a squat, upright trunk. The deep green, woody fronds have a paler underside and are up to 30 cm (about 12 in) long. These are composed of bluish to sallow green leaflets. This adaptable species will grow in poor quality soil either with total sun or shade. Propagate from spores or by division in spring.

Pteris cretica

P. setiferum
SOFT SHIELD FERN

Native to the damp woodlands and valleys of Europe, this large fern grows to 60 cm (about 18 in) high. With its long, soft bipinnate fronds, it is extremely popular in ferneries or gardens.

PTERIS

BRAKE FERN, BRACKEN

This genus is native to the shady, damp gullies of subtropical and tropical rainforests but can also be found growing out of rock crevices in full sunlight. They are usually hardy and can adapt to various positions but they need a great deal of water during the early growth period and should be kept out of direct sunlight. Some species are frost-tender while others are frost-hardy. Keep an eye out for aphids on the leaf stalks. These ferns are often grown indoors and are generally best propagated from spores. The common bracken is considered a weed, but there are several species which are well worth cultivating.

P. cretica
CRETAN BRAKE FERN

One of the many hardy cultivars of the Cretan brake fern, this grows to 50 cm (about 20 in) high. A bushy yet delicate fern, it prefers a moist, sheltered garden or fernery, and makes a very pretty indoor plant. There are several cultivated varieties, the best known being 'Albo-lineata', which has almost grey leaves with broad central margins of white. They are all very pretty indoor plants.

P. ensiformis
SLENDER BRAKE FERN

This dainty little fern originates in South-East Asia's moist lowland forests. It grows to some 30 cm (about 12 in) high and its small fronds are pinnate or bipinnate, with narrow segments rounded at their tip. Cultivars are variegated. This species prefers a warm climate, so in cool areas it should be well sheltered.

SELAGINELLA
uncinata

The selaginellas are not strictly ferns but what botanists call 'fern allies'. They do, however, resemble ferns in their much-divided feathery leaves and in having no flowers—you can think of them as being half-way between a fern and a giant moss. There are several species grown, of which the most striking is *S. uncinatum* with its leaves of peacock blue. Like all the genus, it is of trailing habit, rather frost-tender and loves shade and moist soil. It is a splendid hanging basket plant. Once any of the species is established in a greenhouse (which they need in frosty climates) it will self-sow all over the place, coming up in pots and under the staging. Unless it is strangling other plants, leave it—it will help keep the air bouyant.

TODEA
barbara
KING FERN

From a genus of large tree ferns, this majestic fern is common in South Africa and some parts of Australia and New Zealand. It features a black, fibrous trunk that grows to 1.5 m (about 4½ ft) and bipinnate, dark green fronds that can reach 2 m (about 6 ft) in length. Although it prefers wet sites such as gullies, creeks and rainforests, it is a tough plant that tolerates some sun and grows well in tubs or gardens, provided the soil is kept moist. Propagate from fresh spores.

PALMS

ARCHONTOPHOENIX
cunninghamiana
BANGALOW OR PICCABEEN PALM

Native to Australia and Malaysia, this tall, slender, pinnate palm grows to 22 m (about 70 ft) high and is popular with landscape gardeners. The leaves are 2–3.5 m (about 6–10 ft) long, upright to spreading, and green to rust-brown at the crown shaft. This palm will tolerate an indoor position and some shade, but humidity must be maintained or its leaftips may go brown. This is the most frost-hardy of the genus. Propagate from seed—germination takes 6 weeks to 3 months. The bright red, 1 cm (about ½ in) fruits of these palms vaguely resemble dates; hence the misleading Greek name *Archontophoenix*, 'chief of the date palms'. The rather more slender *A. alexandrae* from North Queensland, Australia, is also much admired and widely grown.

ARECASTRUM
romanzoffianum
syn. *Syagrus romanzoffianum, Cocos plumosa*
QUEEN PALM, COCOS PALM

In its native South America this palm grows in forests and along rivers. The 25 m (about 80 ft) trunk is smooth, grey and clearly ringed. There is no crown shaft; the crown is dense with leaves that grow to 5 m (about 15 ft). This fast-growing palm is perfect for a large tub in subtropical areas and flourishes in full sun in its mature stages; it is a very popular palm for avenues and clumps in large gardens in frost-free climates, although it grows best where it is sheltered from the wind. Like almost all palms, it transplants easily even when mature. It adapts well to different conditions as long as plenty of water reaches the roots and the climate is not too cool. Seed germination takes 2 months; allow enough room for the roots to run deep. The trunks of the mature plant are sometimes hollowed out and used as irrigation pipes and its leaves provide cattle fodder during droughts.

Todea barbara

Selaginella uncinata   *Archontophoenix cunninghamiana*
Pteris ensiformis

Arecastrum romanzoffianum

Brahea armata

Caryota mitis

Caryota urens

Butia capitata

BRAHEA
armata
BLUE HESPER PALM

Originally found in Mexico on hillsides or in deep gullies, this attractive but very slow-growing palm has a stout trunk, eventually 15 m (about 50 ft) high and 45 cm (about 18 in) in diameter. The tree features bluish grey fan-shaped blades, brown-yellow fruits and yellow flowers clustered in groups of 3 on the branchlets. Avoid rich acidic soils when planting in wet climates. Propagate from seed; germination is slow (up to 6 months).

BUTIA
capitata
syn. *Cocos capitata*
JELLY PALM

Native to central Brazil, Uruguay and Argentina, this species varies in appearance, with a variable trunk height of 1–5 m (about 3–15 ft). It is characterized by its overlapping leaf bases, which make the palm's trunk quite spiky and rough. Its flowers are creamy yellow and the orange-yellow fruits are egg-shaped. This palm grows well in areas of high or low rainfall and is moderately frost-hardy. The sweet flesh of the fruit can be strained and used to make jelly or, when fermented, wine.

CARYOTA
FISHTAIL PALMS

Native to the hill slopes and rocky outcrops of Malaysia, eastern Asia and northern Australia, this genus has bipinnate leaves rather than the pinnate or palmate leaves that are common to most palms. These smaller leaflets are triangular and form a fishtail shape. The flower-bearing branches have a short stalk and numerous pendulous smaller branches. Some species are multi-stemmed and others are taller and single-trunked. *Caryota* are generally fast growers and trouble-free in tropical and subtropical frost-free areas; they are often grown as indoor plants. Fibre from the leaves is used to make brooms. The fruit contain caustic crystals and should not be eaten.

C. mitis
CLUSTERED FISHTAIL PALM

This is one of the smaller, multi-stemmed species which inhabits the forest floor rather than the canopy. It grows to varying heights and has sparse numbers of leaves at the crown. These fleshy, drooping leaves are 2–4 m (about 6–12 ft) long. This palm looks attractive in tubs or pots, indoors or out, and is excellent in the garden; give it

plenty of water and a rich, well-drained soil.

C. urens
WINE PALM, JAGGERY PALM, SOLITARY FISHTAIL PALM

This species has a distinctive grey trunk that grows to 12 m (about 37 ft) and thins out as it gets higher. Once established it grows fast and may reach 20 m (about 65 ft) tall. In some Asian countries it is used to make palm sugar, or jaggery. It flowers only once in its life, but flower clusters follow in succession down the trunk for several years.

CHAMAEDOREA

This genus comprises more than 130 species and most of these are native to Central America. They are slender, ornamental palms with smooth, green, bamboo-like stems that grow to just below the forest canopy rather than towering above it. The stems can grow singly or in clusters. The leaves are slender and green and may be whole or pinnate. When leaflets die they leave bare, gaping leaf veins visible below the palm's apex. These palms make good garden plants in shady positions. Propagate from seed.

C. elegans
PARLOR PALM

Native to Mexico and Guatemala, this dwarf palm has dark green, pinnate leaves that arch upwards, with shiny leaflets up to 50–80 cm (about 20–30 in) long. A popular indoor plant, as the common name implies, it may be grown outside in a cool position if protected from sun and wind. Insignificant yellow flowers are borne, followed by small black fruit. The leaves are frost-sensitive.

C. erumpens
BAMBOO PALM

This palm has sickle-shaped leaflets, which form part of shiny leaves 50 cm (about 20 in) long. Growing up to 4 m (about 12 ft) in height and spreading up to 2 m (about 7 ft), it forms a nice cluster in gardens and does best in tropical and subtropical climates; it grows very well indoors.

CHAMAEROPS
humilis
EUROPEAN FAN PALM

Europe's most widespread native palm (native to southern Europe and the Mediterranean), this single-species genus is varied in its habit: it can have many trunks or one solitary trunk and be small or large, depending on its position. It is very resilient and perfect for temperate regions, being frost-hardy. It has been found covered in snow at high altitudes. It prefers a sunny position and well-drained soil. A big clump makes a good lawn specimen and it can also be grown in a tub for long periods of time. Carpet fibres known as 'African hair' are manufactured from the leaf sheaths, and leaf fibres have also been used as a substitute for flax.

CHRYSALIDOCARPUS
lutescens
syn. *Areca lutescens*
GOLDEN CANE PALM, YELLOW PALM, BUTTERFLY PALM

This multi-trunked plant is native to Madagascar and derives its common name from its golden leaf stalks and stems. Frost-tender, it can be grown indoors and outdoors in pots and reaches a height of up to 10 m (about 30 ft), capped with a crown of yellow-green pinnate fronds. When a specimen is malnourished or getting too much sun the yellow colour increases, although if it is really unhappy this will be at the expense of healthy growth. Propagate from seed but be prepared to wait 4–5 months for germination.

COCOS
nucifera
COCONUT PALM

A palm highly valued as a source of food, drink, and housing and other materials throughout the tropics. The only species in its genus, it has long been a symbol of tranquillity and recreation for exhausted city workers. It grows up to 30 m (about 95 ft) high and has a crown of long pinnate leaves. Male and female flowers grow on the same plant. Despite the popular coastal image, this palm can be grown inland as long as it has an underground water supply and a warm climate. It is not frost-hardy and will not fruit away from tropical or warm subtropical climates.

CYRTOSTACHYS
renda
syn. *C. lakka*
SEALING WAX PALM, MAHARAJAH PALM

The contrast between the rich green of the leaves and the brilliant scarlet of the glossy leaf bases makes this clumping feather palm from Malaysia one of the most ornamental of all palms. Alas, it is rarely a success away from the tropics—although it will grow in subtropical climates, it needs constant hot weather for the colour to develop properly. It likes rich, constantly moist soil, grows to about 4 m (about 12 ft) tall and has the reputation of being rather difficult to transplant. Propagate from absolutely fresh seed.

Cyrtostachys renda

Chamaedorea elegans

Chrysalidocarpus lutescens

Chamaerops humilis

Chamaedorea erumpens

Cocos nucifera

A Field Trip to Tengchong

Near Tengchong in Yunnan Province, China, you can observe the Chusan or Chinese windmill palm (*Trachycarpus fortunei*) in a setting that closely resembles its native origin. This widespread species has been so widely cultivated over the centuries that its origin is now uncertain. However, it was probably native to southern and central China, northern Burma, and possibly the island of Kyushu in southern Japan.

Tengchong is situated in the extreme west of China, and has only been open to tourists since the late 1980s. You start your trek at Kunming, the provincial capital and administrative hub of Yunnan. A short flight from Hong Kong, Kunming is a picturesque city surrounded by mountains and situated on the shores of China's sixth largest lake, Dian Chi. It has a reputation for being the most pleasant of Chinese cities because of its mild, subtropical climate. Tengchong is some 750 km (about 460 miles) to the north-west of Kunming.

Leaving Kunming you then travel along the Burma Road. Dali, the next stop on your trek to Tengchong, is about a twelve-hour drive to the north-west. Along the way you will pass through small villages, over mountain passes and along denuded hillsides. The road is lined with Tasmanian blue gums (*Eucalyptus globulus*) and a relative of the American tupelo or sour gum (*Camptotheca acuminata*). The tree trunks are whitewashed, as guideposts.

Yunnan Province, a region of contrasts.

Dali, like Kunming, is situated on the Yunnan–Guizhou Plateau at about 1900 m (about 6000 ft) above sea level. It has an idyllic setting at the foot of the Cang Shan, or 'Tali Range', which is a 50 km (about 30 miles) long mountain range to the west of Dali, attaining an altitude of about 4100 m (about 13 000 ft).

Numerous collections of plants have been made from the Cang Shan by European and American botanists, but the most extensive collections were made by George Forrest between 1904 and 1932. Of the 30 000 plants he collected, many came from the Cang Shan, and he was responsible for introducing many fine garden plants from this area to the West. Some notable examples include a yellow-flowered orchid (*Pleione forrestii*), the fragrant, white-flowered *Rhododendron edgeworthii*, the silver fir (*Abies delavayi*), and the pink-flowered *Magnolia campbellii*.

Leaving Dali and travelling for about 350 km (about 220 miles), you descend from the crest of the plateau into a broad, open valley. If you go in autumn/fall, the landscape will glow with ripened grain and straw ready for the rice harvest. The only impediment to the view is a sombre range of mountains with some distinctly conical peaks. These are volcanoes, remnants of the county's volatile geological history, and were active as recently as 700 years ago.

Very few tourists have visited this region so, whether you stay at the Tengchong Hotel or choose other accommodation, do not be surprised if you are the object of great interest.

Tengchong has a mild, subtropical climate with a mean annual temperature of about 17°C (about 63°F) and an average annual rainfall of approximately 1100 mm (about 43 in). The south-west monsoon influences the climate, and the rain falls mostly from July to October.

North of Tengchong on the road to the Goaligong Shan, a copse of about twenty Chusan palms grows in an exposed hillside corn field. The soil is a deep, red earth. The palms are very old and most probably have been cultivated for many

Dense vegetation in a valley near Luxi.

The Chusan palm fibres have many uses.

Trachycarpus fortunei

decades. They are 10 m (about 30 ft) high with 10 cm (about 4 in) diameter trunks, the uppermost sections of which are clad in coarse, black-brown fibres which are the remnants of old leaf sheaths. You can sometimes see irregularly shaped, bluish fruits either on the ground or on the upper leaf axils. However, this is unlikely as the flowers of the Chusan palm are considered a culinary delicacy throughout the region and are regularly harvested by the villagers. The immature flower spikes resemble cauliflower and are used in a similar way to bamboo shoots.

From here, drive on to the Goaligong Shan and its botanical treasures. Some plants to be observed there include the pink-flowered *Rhododendron stenaulum*, *Michelia doltsopa* (a white-flowered magnolia relative), and last but not least *Gordonia chrysandra* (a relative of the camellia).

You can also see the Chusan palm near a series of small volanic lakes located on the outskirts of Tenchong, on the way to Mount Yunfeng. Near the lakes is a small village surrounded by well constructed, dry-packed, basalt stone walls. Behind these walls about twelve Chusan palms grow in rich, deep, red-brown loam which is very acidic. Again, it is unlikely that you will find flowers or fruits in evidence. Drive on to Mount Yunfeng, where you can walk to the summit and view a Taoist temple. This involves a climb up 2000 steps which are in places quite steep and precarious. Nevertheless, the walk is worthwhile for the spectacular views and the chance to explore the richness and almost untouched serenity of the forest surrounding the temple. The forest includes Yunnan pine (*Pinus yunnanensis*) and *Quercus*, *Lithocarpus* and *Castanopsis* species.

Whether you visit Yunnan to observe the spectacular scenery or experience its tourist attractions, much of the province's significance lies in the many and varied plants that occur here. By a combination of topographic, geologic and climatic factors, Yunnan has definitely proved its claim to be 'The Kingdom of Plants'.

Trachycarpus

Palms belong to the Arecaceae family, which contains almost 3000 species. These are largely confined to the tropics; only a handful are adapted to moderately cool conditions. Among these are the six species of the small Chinese-Himalayan genus *Trachycarpus*, which all occur in regions receiving winter snow. Most widely grown is the Chusan palm (*Trachycarpus fortunei*); it regularly withstands winter temperatures of minus 10°C and has been known to survive at minus 15°. This palm will grow almost anywhere between these colder limits and a few degrees of latitude short of the tropics (or highlands even within the tropics), thriving in most soils and tolerating both fierce sun and winter gales. However, neither this nor any palm can survive outdoors in climates in which the soil becomes frozen.

Trachycarpus has been prized in China for many centuries, both as an ornamental plant and for its many uses. Apart from a variety of fibre and similar products from the trunk and leaves, there is a high quality wax, used in polishes, obtained from the fruit skin, and a blood-clotting drug, 'hsuen an', extracted from the seed. Both of these are now processed on an industrial scale. *T. fortunei* has been widely cultivated in South-East Asia for its fibre.

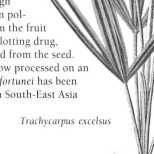

Trachycarpus excelsus

Euterpe edulis

EUTERPE
edulis
ASSAI PALM

Originally from Brazil, this forest-dwelling palm has a tall, slender trunk and a crown of dark green, pinnate fronds. It bears small, round, brown-black fruit. It is easy to grow in a warm, humid climate but be sure to keep the young plant sheltered from direct sunlight for a few years. It prefers well-drained soil. Seeds germinate quickly, especially if leached in warm water for three days. Brazil harvests and exports palmito, the edible, sweet white tissue of the palm hearts; it is taken from the young shoots.

HEDYSCEPE
canterburyana
UMBRELLA PALM, BIG MOUNTAIN PALM

From Lord Howe Island, Australia, this solitary feather palm grows to heights of 4–10 m (about 12–30 ft) and features a thick crown of dark green leaves and a silver crown shaft. It is slow growing but has potential as an ornamental palm, with its dramatic crest of dense leaves and contrasting brown to red fruit. It prefers shade, humidity and subtropical climates. Avoid placing it in full sun, especially when young. Propagate from seed.

HOWEA
syn. Howeia, Kentia

This genus of small palms has only two species, both native to Australia's Lord Howe Island and both widely cultivated. They have feathered leaves on long, smooth stalks and a smooth, ringed, single trunk. Flowers are male (light brown) or female (green). The plants are frost-sensitive and need moist humid conditions and shade if they are to be kept outdoors. They are more commonly grown indoors as they tolerate less light and need less heat than a lot of other palms. They can be kept in the same pot or tub for years, as long as the potting mix is well drained and contains some humus. Provide partial shade while they mature. Lord Howe Islanders successfully export the seeds.

H. belmoreana
CURLY PALM, SENTRY PALM

This is of great value as an indoor palm as it tolerates a substantial amount of neglect. Outdoors, it may grow to 8 m (about 24 ft) high.

Howea forsteriana

Hedyscepe canterburyana

Howea belmoreana

Livistona chinensis

H. forsteriana
THATCH PALM, KENTIA PALM

This is the more popular and faster-growing of the two species in the *Howea* genus. An excellent palm for a small garden, it is widely grown in the USA, Europe and Australia.

JUBAEA
chilensis
COQUITO PALM, CHILEAN WINE PALM

Now very rare in its natural habitat of coastal Chile, this palm grows to 25 m (about 80 ft) with a very thick trunk and a dense mass of long, straight, deep green leaves spanning 4–5 m (about 12–15 ft). Flowers are yellow and 4–5 cm (about 2 in) long. This is a very slow-growing tree, suitable to a temperate climate and full sun. The soil should be well drained and deep. Seeds may take up to 6 months to germinate. Chileans once tapped the trunks of this palm for up to two years, then made wine or palm honey from its sugary sap, but this practice is now banned as it weakens the trees.

LACCOSPADIX
australasica
ATHERTON PALM

An Australian native from the rainforests of north-eastern Queensland, this feathered palm is found either in clumps or standing alone. It has a 2–8 m (about 6–24 ft) trunk and single cascading spikes of yellow to red fruit. It prefers the dense canopies of rainforests and so is best placed in shade in a rich, organic soil. It makes an excellent indoor plant but is also good for landscaping as long as it can be sheltered from full sun. It is moderately frost-hardy. Propagate from seed or divisions of suckers.

LIVISTONA

A genus of medium to tall fan palms found in the wetter parts of Malaysia, south China and Australia. They feature very large, round, pleated fronds 1.5 m (about 4½ ft) across and a dense crown from which

Laccospadix australasica

dead leaves may remain hanging for a short time. The leaf stalks are usually long and edged with sharp teeth. These palms are good for outdoor landscaping: their clusters of purple-black fruit and tapering leaves are shown to great effect. Most species prefer a moderate amount of light and are hardy enough to survive cool and sub-tropical climates, although they do better in mild, frost-free climates. They prefer a deep, sandy soil and are slow growing, especially in the early stages. Propagate from seed.

L. australis
AUSTRALIAN CABBAGE-TREE PALM

This is one of the tallest species, reaching heights of up to 26 m (about 83 ft) in the wild. It does well in coastal areas. Australian Aborigines traditionally ate the fleshy part of this palm's young leaves and made spear-heads from the hard wood.

L. chinensis
FOUNTAIN PALM, CHINESE FAN PALM

A smaller, very attractive palm with glossy green, tapering leaves, this species can be grown in tubs. In the garden it may grow to some 8 m (about 24 ft) and tolerates full sun or partial shade. It is moderately frost-hardy and has been grown outdoors in sheltered gardens in England.

NEODYPSIS
decaryi

This palm is native to Madagascar and has an unusual 3-sided trunk, formed by the leaf bases that ar-

Neodypsis decaryi

Livistona australis

Jubaea chilensis

range themselves in 3 rows. Both the trunk and leaflets feature a chalky white growth. The pinnate leaves grow upright and curve at the tips only. It grows quickly and well in a sun-filled location in tropical and subtropical areas but is not commonly cultivated. Propagate from seed.

PHOENIX
DATE PALM

Tropical Africa, southern China, Asia and the Philippines are where this genus originates. They are feather palms that feature a dense crown of long, pinnate leaves with stiff, sharp spines and a very rough

trunk where the leaf base has broken away and left scarring. The flowers grow in clusters of thousands on some species. The bright red or golden fruit is usually edible. These palms are sun-lovers, very popular as landscape subjects on main streets and in parks and among the hardiest palms in cultivation. They are not commonly grown in containers. They tolerate hot winds and poor soil and the various species hybridize freely when grown together. Propagate from seeds. Species of *Phoenix* are valued not only as ornamental palms, but also as a source of palm sugar, which is widely used in Asian cooking.

Phoenix dactylifera

Rhapis excelsa

Rhopalostylis sapida

Rhopalostylis baueri

Sabal palmetto

Serenoa repens

Phoenix canariensis

P. canariensis

CANARY ISLAND DATE PALM

Native to the Canary Islands, as the name implies, this shorter, heavier species has large, dark green fronds. Its 2 cm (about 1 in) orange fruit is inedible.

P. dactylifera

DATE PALM

Able to make do with less water than almost any other tree, this palm grows to 30 m (about 95 ft) high and grows succulent fruit in dry tropical and subtropical conditions.

RHAPIS
excelsa
LADY PALM, BAMBOO PALM

Native to southern China, this is a dwarf palm with several hundred slender stems that form very large, leafy clumps. Its leaves are 60–70 cm (about 24–28 in) long, pale green, randomly scattered along the stem and divided into rigid, finger-like segments. An excellent tub

plant, it must be kept away from full sunlight as the leaves burn easily. It makes a neat, attractive indoor palm and can live in the same pot for years with infrequent breaks outside. If planted in the garden, it is happiest under a large tree where the ground is more easily kept moist and shady; it is frost-tender. Propagate by division.

RHOPALOSTYLIS

This genus comprises 3 attractive, evergreen feather palms with upright, grey-green, solitary trunks and erect or pendent pinnate fronds. The leaflets have a smooth surface, fleecy underside and scaly mid-rib. Both male and female flowers are borne along semi-upright or arching, branched stems. These are followed by smooth, red, round to elliptical fruit. The species range from frost-hardy to frost-tender, surviving in temperatures down to 3°C (about 37°F). They require a humid atmosphere and reasonably fertile soil with protection from full sun and wind.

Swampy conditions are tolerated and propagation is from seed in spring.

R. baueri
NORFOLK PALM

This palm originates in Norfolk Island and has a grey, closely ringed trunk growing up to 12 m (about 37 ft) high, a wide-spreading crown and leaves that grow to 4 m (about 12 ft) long. The crown shaft of this tree is stout, very pale green and easily recognizable. Young plants have a distinct reddish toning in their leaves. The fruit is small, red and slightly conical. Suited to a moist and frost-free climate, this palm should be kept out of the wind as the leaves very easily become shredded and ragged-looking. Easily propagated from fresh seeds.

R. sapida
NIKAU PALM, FEATHER DUSTER PALM

The only palm native to New Zealand, this slow-growing species reaches 11 m (about 34 ft) in height and 40 cm (about 16 in) in diameter. It has a slender, unbranched trunk encircled by prominent rings. The pinnate, rigid fronds are upstretched and 1–3 m (about 3–9 ft) in length. Light bluish purple-pink to cream flowers are followed by vivid red fruit.

SABAL
palmetto
PALMETTO, CABBAGE PALM

Native to south-eastern USA, this tall, thick palm grows up to 25 m (about 80 ft) tall and 30–45 cm

(about 12–18 in) in diameter. The trunk is covered with continuous, interlaced leaf bases and the fan-shaped leaves have an idiosyncratic twist initiated by the leaf stalk, making this plant easy to recognize. It flowers and bears fruit while it is still young. This is a sun-lover, as are most species of the *Sabal* genus, and should be planted in sandy soil in subtropical and tropical areas. Large group plantings are particularly showy and many of the famous palm avenues in Los Angeles and Miami are of their species. Propagate from seed.

SERENOA
repens
SAW PALMETTO

A single-species dwarf genus, this low-growing fan palm appears in large colonies in the south-eastern USA. It has stiff, spiky, variable-coloured leaves ranging from yellow to bluish green or silvery white and the trunk often grows below the ground. Plant in a sunny position as it can tolerate full sun even when immature and is quite frost-tender. It grows well along coastlines and can withstand salt-laden winds. Its egg-shaped, dark purple fruit was eaten by the local American Indians for its therapeutic properties and is valued now as a health food. Propagate from seed.

TRACHYCARPUS
fortunei
CHUSAN PALM, HEMP PALM, WINDMILL PALM

This is perhaps the most frost-hardy of all the palms, surviving even in English gardens. In a mild climate it can grow 10 m (about 30 ft) tall, its trunk covered in the shaggy, fibrous remains of the old leaf bases and crowned with splendidly slashed, fan-shaped leaves. It is a solitary grower, but looks best in groups; and in China and Japan the fibrous leaf sheaths are made into rope—hence the name 'hemp palm'. The specific name honours Robert Fortune who first brought the plant from China to England in the 1840s; it is said that several of his original specimens are still growing there.

Lepidozamia peroffskyana

Macrozamia spiralis

Washingtonia robusta

WASHINGTONIA

Native to the rocky, dry areas of the southern USA and Mexico, there are only two species in this genus, both large, single-standing fan palms. The trunk is fatter at the base and, in older trees, may be covered with a thick thatch of old leaves which extends almost to the ground. If you dislike the appearance, the palm will come to no harm if the dead leaves are cut off; they can be a fire hazard. The crown is dense with no crown shaft and the stalks of the finely bladed leaves are broad and toothed. The fruit is small, brown and egg-shaped. These are versatile landscaping plants, appropriate for planting in avenues or as potted ornamental palms. Suited to a sun-filled position in warm-temperate areas or dry tropical climates. Ensure soil is well drained. Propagate from seed.

W. filifera

WASHINGTON PALM, AMERICAN COTTON PALM, DESERT FAN PALM, PETTICOAT PALM

The more frost-hardy of the two species, this has long, grey-green leaves and bears small white flowers in summer. It grows up to 15 m (about 50 ft) high. One of the common names refers to the white, cotton-like threads on the leaf segments. This is the palm that lends its name to the city of Palm Springs, California.

W. robusta

WASHINGTON PALM, THREAD PALM, SKYDUSTER

At 25 m (about 80 ft) high this is the taller species, with a more slender trunk and greener leaves. Its flowers are creamy white.

CYCADS

CYCAS
revoluta

SAGO PALM, JAPANESE SAGO CYCAD, JAPANESE FERN PALM

Native to the islands of southern Japan, this half-hardy evergreen suits temperate and subtropical regions. The trunk grows slowly to 3 m (about 10 ft), with a wide, flat

Washingtonia filifera

crown of numerous glossy green leaves. Male cones are narrow cylinders up to 40 cm (about 16 in) long; female cones, brown and hairy, are half as long. The hairy vermilion seeds, 3 cm (about 1½ in) long, appear in autumn/fall. Grow in a glasshouse or outdoors in full sun. Water well in dry weather and fertilize lightly. Propagate from seed, basal suckers or trunk offsets. Widely grown as an ornamental, this is a very popular bonsai subject in Japan.

ENCEPHALARTOS
altensteinii

BREAD TREE

Originating in South Africa, this evergreen cycad forms an attractive, erect fan shape reaching to 2 m (about 6 ft) in height and spread. Its densely foliaged crown appears to grow directly out of the ground and it does not develop a noticeable trunk until well into old age. The rigid palm-like leaves grow to 2 m (about 6 ft) long and have an abundance of saw-toothed, woody, grey leaflets. Vividly coloured cones contain seeds which will only be viable if both male and female plants are present. Prune withered fronds and propagate from seed or potted sucker cuttings; seeds take at least a year to germinate. Susceptible to scale insects and caterpillars.

LEPIDOZAMIA
peroffskyana

There are four species of *Lepidozamia*—two living and two fossil species. This evergreen species is

Encephalartos altensteinii

Cycas revoluta

native to the forests of eastern Australia. Half-hardy, it suits subtropical to warm-temperate regions. It grows very slowly, the trunk eventually reaching 7 m (about 21 ft) with a wide, spreading crown of glossy dark green leaves. Male cones, cylindrical and curved, are up to 60 cm (about 24 in) long; female cones are broad and ovoid, about half as long. The seeds are 5–6 cm (about 2–2½ in) long and bright red. This cycad thrives indoors in tubs in a well-lit position and grows outdoors in sun or shade. Water in dry weather and fertilize regularly. Propagate from seed. The genus was first described in 1857 by a Russian botanist.

MACROZAMIA
spiralis

BURRAWANG

This evergreen cycad is native to eastern Australia, where it grows in

open forests in sandy soils. A stumpy plant, it grows mostly underground, reaching 1 m (about 3 ft) in height above. The spiralling, deep green leaves grow up to 1 m (about 3 ft) long, developing a full crown in fertile conditions, and limited to one or two leaves in poor conditions. The male cones are cylindrical and the female ones are ovoid and bear brilliant scarlet seeds the size of bantam eggs. Both are 15–20 cm (about 6–8 in) long, and appear only sporadically. Suitable for temperate and tropical regions, this plant will thrive best in full or filtered sun and tolerates moderate to heavy frosts. Propagate from seed but be prepared to be patient. Australian Aborigines developed a long, complex method of processing the poisonous, starchy seeds to make them edible. Some early white settlers tried eating the unfamiliar seeds unprocessed, with disastrous results.

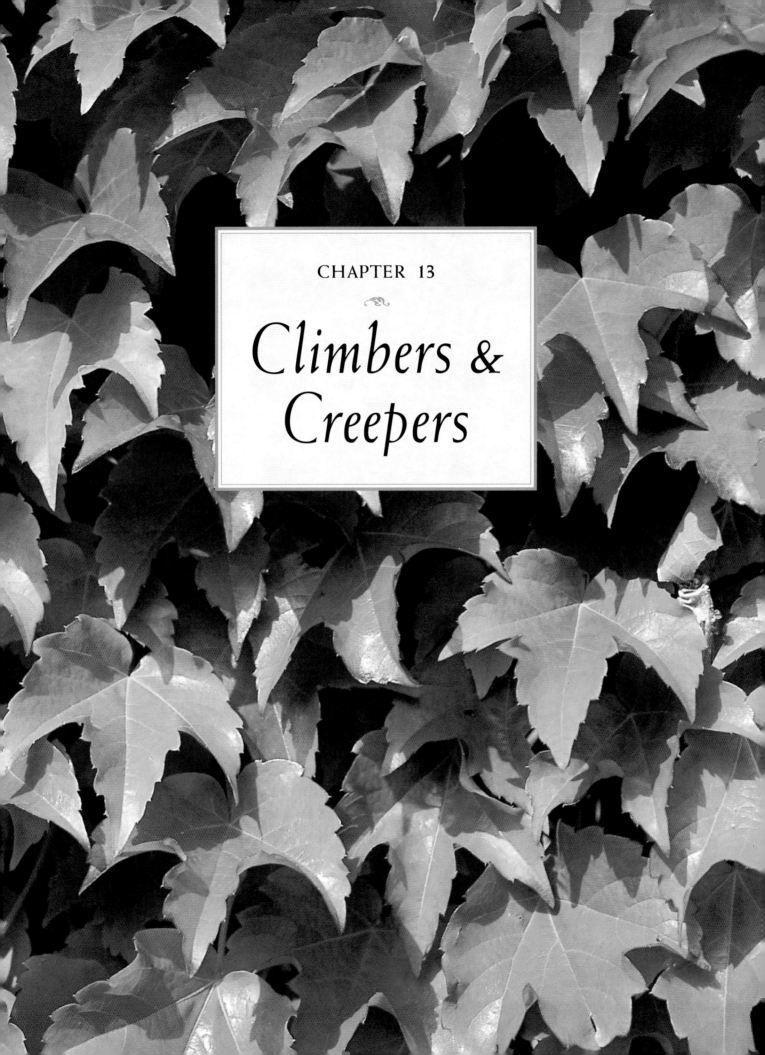

CHAPTER 13

Climbers & Creepers

*T*here's nothing as welcoming as a vine-covered arch over a front gate or a delicate rambler twining its way in and around window shutters to display its perfumed flowers to perfection. In these and other subtle ways climbers play an important role in the overall garden landscape.

By their very nature climbers set out to reach the high spots where there's less competition for light. Some are suited to providing a focal point in a small garden or in a tight spot as they need very little ground or wall space; other more adventurous types will sprawl over a garden shed, camouflaging it in no time. Climbers come mainly from temperate or tropical forests where competition has forced them to evolve various means of ensuring their lax stems reach the light that is essential for manufacturing food. These modifications allow some vines to twine around a host while others have thorns or hooks, tendrils, sucker discs even aerial roots to reach out for an anchorage on supporting plants.

The most common climbing mechanism is simply for a vine to twine; *Pandorea jasminoides*, *Phaseolus caracalla* and the delicate *Sollya heterophylla* are among the most accommodating. All they need is a post or open support such as lattice or a wire frame. Plants with thread-like tendrils such as sweet peas or the wonderful range of clematis need fine supports to allow the slender, modified leaf parts to grip. Those with sucker pads, like parthenocissus, are ideal for solid masonry walls although their position should be chosen with care as the pads will leave unsightly marks on the masonry should they ever need to be removed. *Hydrangea petiolaris*, the climbing hydrangea, and the temperate garden climber *Campsis grandiflora* are two vines which rely on their aerial roots to grip onto a solid surface, as does the true ivy, *Hedera helix*. Be warned though, true ivy is fine contained on walls but its brush-like roots can very soon help in a takeover bid for the complete garden if allowed ground space. The scramblers, like roses and some tropical plants such as bougainvillea, have thorns or hooks by which to hoist their branches even

higher—in a garden with the correct support and a little time spent on training they are docile and most rewarding to grow.

Once these characteristics are known and understood, climbers can be chosen to suit any existing garden situation or be coupled with a new structure to add a wonderful softening effect.

Arbours, Pergolas and Balcony Gardens

Arbours and pergolas are generally firm, solid structures built to last and can take strong growing twiners such as wisteria and the ornamental grapes. Both of these are deciduous, providing shade in summer and allowing the sun to penetrate during the colder months. However, pergolas can be 'double planted' with less vigorous plants to give a combined show. For instance, a delicate, soft look can be achieved by highlighting the single, yellow flowers of the rose 'Mermaid' against the small, starry, white flowers of the dainty potato vine. As well, these delicate twiners can be used on a growing frame such as an established flowering fruit tree and

A climbing rose—the perfect complement to a timber pergola.

when the blossoms synchronize there are few more beautiful sights that a gardener could look forward to.

One of the joys of sitting under a pergola is being able to enjoy the flowers of the covering vine. Those with pendulous sprays such as *Akebia quinata* and *Thunbergia grandiflora* as well as the superb wisterias will certainly delight. However, some other vines will provide a carpet of fallen petals but the flowers remain hidden to all but those looking out from balconies or windows above. For this reason many vines are best grown on a vertical surface such as a trellis or lattice or strands of wire stretched between two vertical posts to form a screen or fence. Here the complete surface area of the plant provides a breathtaking display while taking up very little actual garden space. Aspect needs to be taken into account when growing climbers in this way. In cold areas tender plants can be damaged if frozen tissue is thawed rapidly against a wall receiving early morning sun, while in warmer areas both the last rays of the sun and reflected heat from nearby paved areas can scorch new summer growth on plants which have been trained against a wall.

Often the very reason for choosing to plant a vine against a wall is because it takes up very little space, yet this also could mean the root run is limited. Take care here with soil preparation and fertilizing to provide the best possible conditions for what is to be a feature plant. Often in these conditions, protected by eaves or next to a concrete slab, the climber is best planted away from the house then trained back against it. Then again in cases like this you could consider using a decorative tub filled with a good quality potting mix. Tubs can be used to grow cascading plants like the colourful nasturtiums or dwarf sweet peas with some branches allowed to tumble over the edge while others are trained upwards to camouflage the lower twiggy sections of the main vine.

Many balcony gardens rely solely on tub culture to produce stunning effects with cascading vines and shady canopies. The risk of these tubs overheating and drying out can be greatly reduced by 'mulching' the surface area and sides of the pots with a growing veil. In these often exposed situations care should be taken never to allow the pots to dry out or its contents to become overheated— one cunning method to overcome this is

Clematis montana 'Rubens' provides a spectacular spring display.

to drop a plastic pot containing the plant into a more decorative one so the pot is insulated. Grouping say three or five pots together to generate shade for one another is another way to ensure a successful high-rise or balcony garden.

Soil Preparation and Planting

As most climbers will be permanent, time spent preparing the soil well by digging it over will certainly pay dividends. Like most plants, climbers need good drainage; this is especially important in those pockets against house walls. In these spots it is very often worthwhile to dig deep and wide to unearth any leftover builder's rubble buried just beneath the surface. These positions are often a lot drier than the open garden so be generous with garden compost or animal manure to help with moisture retention.

Pruning

General pruning rules apply equally to climbers as to any other plant. In the very early stage of a climber's growth, finger or tip pruning encourages a single stem to branch out, giving more than one stem to be trained up a trellis—this can become the basis for an informal or stylised espaliered effect say

for a rose growing on stretched wire supports. Then as the climber matures, flowering can be encouraged by pruning; but as in the case of shrubs you have to become aware of the flowering characteristics of your chosen plant. Most will flower at the tips of branches so by pruning at nodes and allowing two or three extra branches to be formed, flowering can be increased. But, it must also be remembered that some vines flower on new or the present season's growth while others take till the next season to produce their blooms, and pruning needs to be carried out keeping this in mind. Of course rambling type roses, for instance, flower on long new canes, and in general these can be cut well back after flowering. However, many of the climbing roses form a permanent mainframe of branches which adhere to horizontal trellising, then each year flowering side shoots appear and in turn these are pruned back to make way for further flowers. Even though they are thorny, roses trained in this way are very easily managed and are very long lived.

If a vine is tied onto a support be sure to check the ties regularly, particularly in the growing season, as they can very easily injure the plant if they become too tight. Vines may take that little bit more of a gardener's time but it is very satisfying to see the end results.

Araujia hortorum

Antigonon leptopus

Akebia quinata

Actinidia chinensis

ACTINIDIA
chinensis
syn. *A. deliciosa*
CHINESE GOOSEBERRY, KIWI FRUIT

Native to China, this deciduous
vine, strong-growing to 9 m (about
27 ft), is valued for its fragrant
creamy flowers in spring and summer, and delicious brown, hairy
fruit which ripen in autumn/fall.
The vine is attractive, with large
velvety leaves and red, hairy stems.
It is extremely vigorous and requires a strong trellis, pergola, wall
or fence to support it. Plant both
male and female vines, or a grafted
bisexual vine, to produce a fruit
crop. It is frost-hardy, but needs
warm summers to ripen the fruit.
Grow in deep, well-drained, humus-rich soil, in a warm, fairly
frost-free position sheltered from
hot drying winds. Prune early in
winter before new growth begins.
A. kolomitka is similar in habit but
grown for its pink and white variegated leaves rather than its fruit.

AKEBIA
quinata
FIVE-LEAF AKEBIA, CHOCOLATE VINE

Deciduous (or semi-evergreen in
warm areas), this decorative, twining climber from China is grown for
its attractive habit, leaves and flowers. The grey-green leaves are divided into 5 leaflets and fragrant,
purple-mauve, drooping flowers
appear in late spring. Male and
female plants are needed for the
female plants to produce interesting
sausage-shaped, edible fruit in mild
climates. Fully hardy, the plant
likes full sun, good drainage and

Allamanda cathartica

plenty of water during summer. It
will grow to 10 m (about 30 ft) or
more and requires a strong support.
Prune after flowering and cut down
to the base every 3 or 4 years to
remove tangled growth. Propagate
from cuttings or by layering in
spring.

ALLAMANDA
cathartica
GOLDEN TRUMPET VINE

Native to South America, this vigorous, evergreen climber, fast-growing
to 5 m (about 15 ft), bears large,
yellow, trumpet-shaped flowers up to
12 cm (about 5 in) across in summer.
It has whorls of lance-shaped leaves
and makes a luxuriant cover for
walls and strong fences in frost-free
areas. It is frost-tender. Grow in full
sun or partial shade in humus-rich
soil and water well during the growing period. Regular tip pruning
improves its appearance. Propagate
from softwood cuttings in spring
and summer, and watch for two-

spotted mite. It will take heavy
pruning and can be grown in a large
container.

AMPELOPSIS
brevipedunculata var.
maximowiczii
syn. *A. heterophylla,*
Vitis heterophylla
TURQUOISE-BERRY VINE

This vigorous, deciduous climber
will twine with the aid of tendrils
5 m (about 15 ft) or more. It has
grape-like, lobed leaves, small
greenish flowers in summer, and in
autumn/fall bunches of berries like
miniature grapes that ripen from pale
green to turquoise, bright blue and
violet. Grow in a sunny or partially
shaded position in a moisture-retentive, but well-drained soil. It is fully
hardy. It grows rapidly and needs
strong support and plenty of room to
spread. Cut back hard to the main
branches when berries have finished.
Propagate from cuttings in summer or
by layering in autumn/fall.

Ampelopsis brevipedunculata var.
maximowiczii

ANTIGONON
leptopus
CORAL VINE, CHAIN OF LOVE

A dainty, fast-growing, showy
creeper that climbs by tendrils and
may grow to 7 m (about 21 ft) or
more. It bears masses of deep pink,
heart-shaped flowers from early
summer to autumn/fall and is easily
grown in warm, frost-free areas. In
cool areas it can be grown as a summer-flowering annual. The plant
does best in a sunny situation in
well-drained, fertile soil. Keep well
watered during spring and summer.
It is ideal for trellises, pergolas and
arbours where a light cover is desirable. Remove spent flowerheads and
cut out old twiggy growth in early
spring. Propagate from seed sown in
spring or from cuttings in late spring.

ARAUJIA
hortorum
syn. *A. sericofera*
CRUEL PLANT, KAPOK VINE

An evergreen twining vine growing
to 7 m (about 21 ft) with broad,
heart-shaped leaves, scented, white
flowers in late summer and green,
pointed seed pods which contain
numerous silky seeds. It is half-hardy,
and thrives in a rich, well-drained soil
in a sunny position. A native of Peru,
this species has become a weed in
warm climates, particularly in South
Africa. The seeds, thought to be
poisonous to poultry and dogs, germinate readily and should be removed and disposed of carefully to
prevent the plant from becoming
invasive.

ARISTOLOCHIA
elegans
CALICO FLOWER

This creeper, fast-growing to 6 m (about 18 ft), is native to Brazil and needs high humidity and protection from frost. It has fleshy, heart-shaped leaves and in summer, bears strangely shaped, maroon flowers with white, thread-like markings. Plant in humus-rich, well-drained soil in a partially shaded position. An interesting plant for verandah columns or a pergola. Propagate from semi-ripe cuttings in late summer, or seed in spring. It can be grown as an annual in cool climates.

ASARINA
erubescens
CLIMBING SNAPDRAGON

This dainty, semi-evergreen climber has velvety, heart-shaped leaves and bears pink, tubular flowers resembling snapdragons in late spring and early summer. It has twining stems up to 3 m (about 9 ft) tall and adapts well to hanging baskets and window boxes. Moderately frost-hardy, it requires full sun, good drainage and regular watering in summer. Easily propagated from seed in spring.

BAUHINIA
corymbosa
syn. B. scandens
CLIMBING BAUHINIA

A spectacular flowering climber with pale pink, orchid-like flowers borne freely during spring and summer. It will reach a height of 3 m (about 9 ft) and is very pretty when trained on a trellis. The distinctive leaves are 2-lobed and almost butterfly shaped. It is frost-tender, growing best in full sun in warm, sheltered sites in humus-rich, well-drained soil. Keep well watered in spring and summer. Pruning is not usually necessary, but vigorous growth may be thinned out after flowering. Propagate from seed sown in spring. In cool areas it can be grown in a frost-free greenhouse.

BEAUMONTIA
grandiflora
HERALD'S TRUMPET

This beautiful, large, woody, evergreen climber growing to 8 m (about 24 ft) needs strong support for its thick twining stems. It is valued for its large, fragrant, white, trumpet flowers, which appear in late spring and summer, and handsome, deep green leaves. Frost-tender, it is best suited to subtropical areas, but it can also be grown in a protected position in warm-temperate districts. Soil should be deep

Aristolochia elegans

Bauhinia corymbosa

and fertile with good drainage. It requires full sun and regular watering in summer. Prune immediately after flowering. Propagate from cuttings in late summer.

BOMAREA
caldasii
syn. B. kalbreyeri
CLIMBING ALSTROEMERIA

This attractive, evergreen, twining climber to 3 m (about 9 ft) bears large clusters of bright orange, pendulous bell flowers in summer. Grow in well-drained, humus-rich soil and water regularly in summer. Half-hardy, it is ideal for a warm, environment in a sunny or partially shaded position. It needs strong support and will form an attractive dense screen on a fence or trellis. Cut back hard after flowering to encourage fresh growth. Propagate by division of underground stems in early spring.

BOUGAINVILLEA
BOUGAINVILLEA

Native to South America, bougainvilleas are valued for their glorious, flamboyant flowers and their ability to cover a large area. There is a large range of different kinds and colours to choose from, but all do best in warm to hot climates in full sun. They are evergreen in the tropics, but may be deciduous in cooler climates. The flowering period is early spring and can extend well into autumn/fall. The true flowers are insignificant, but the surrounding bracts are brilliantly coloured, often changing colour or shade as they age. Only water when needed and do not over

Bomarea caldasii

Asarina erubescens

Beaumontia grandiflora

Bougainvillea 'Hawaiian Gold'

Bougainvillea glabra

fertilize, particularly with nitrogen as this will produce luxuriant leaf growth but very little in the way of colourful bracts. Bougainvilleas need strong support for vigorous growth, but can be controlled by pruning after flowering, when rampant plants can be ruthlessly cut back without harm. Flowers appear on the new wood. Propagate from semi-hardwood cuttings in summer. With regular heavy pruning, they can be grown in large containers.

B. glabra

This is the parent of several varieties. A vigorous shrubby vine growing to 10 m (about 30 ft), with masses of bright purple floral bracts in spring and summer.

B. 'Hawaiian Gold'

A rather frost-tender, evergreen cultivar that will reach up to 7 m (about 21 ft). Floral bracts are a magnificent shade of orange-gold.

Clematis 'Jackmanii'

Celastrus orbiculatus

Cissus antarctica

Clematis aristata

Campsis grandiflora

Cardiospermum halicacabum

Bougainvillea 'Scarlett O'Hara'

B. 'Scarlett O'Hara'

A fast-growing, free-flowering cultivar growing to 8 m (about 24 ft), with spectacular sprays of rosy crimson bracts in summer.

CAMPSIS
grandiflora
syn. *C. chinensis,*
Bignonia grandiflora
CHINESE TRUMPET CREEPER

This vigorous, woody-stemmed climber from China will reach up to 10 m (about 30 ft) with the aid of aerial rootlets clinging to a support. Deciduous and fast-growing, it produces eye-catching clusters of trumpet-shaped scarlet to orange flowers, up to 10 cm (about 4 in) long, in late summer and autumn/fall. Only just frost-hardy, it requires full sun in a well-drained, humus-rich soil. Water generously during the growing season. Prune in spring and propagate from semi-ripe cuttings taken in summer, or from layers or suckers. The cultivar 'Madame Galen' has slightly smaller flowers and is a little more hardy.

CARDIOSPERMUM
halicacabum
BALLOON VINE

Native to Australia, India, Africa and America, this fast-growing, deciduous plant climbs by tendrils, and is usually grown in colder climates as an annual. It has hairy, pale green leaves of 2 oblong, 3-lobed leaflets which are pointed and toothed. In summer there are clusters of inconspicuous, white, scented flowers. These are followed by papery, inflated, straw-coloured fruit enclosing black seeds (balloon seed pods). Grown in full light in any soil or climate with a minimum temperature of 5°C (about 40°F), this plant makes an attractive trellis climber. Propagate from seed in spring.

CELASTRUS
orbiculatus
syn. *C. articulatus*
ORIENTAL BITTERSWEET

From China, this deciduous, vine-like climber is valued for its brilliantly

coloured red and gold, pea-like berries which are retained through winter. Grow in humus-rich, moisture-retentive soil in sun or partial shade and provide good, roomy support for the twining stems as they can reach 6 m (about 18 ft) or more. It is fully hardy. Pruning is only necessary to maintain shape, and is best done in late winter. Propagate from root cuttings or layering in autumn/fall, or from seed sown in spring.

CISSUS
antarctica
KANGAROO VINE

This vigorous inhabitant of Australian rainforests is grown for its handsome, rich green, oval leaves and its ability to cover large areas. When given support, it will climb by tendrils up to 5 m (about 15 ft) or more in the garden. Without support it will effectively scramble over rocky slopes and banks. This plant grows well in partial shade or full shade in humus-rich, well-drained soil with some water reten-

tion. It is frost-tender and in cool areas can be grown as a house plant, as it will accept reasonably dark situations. Regular pruning improves its appearance. Propagate from stem cuttings or fresh seed. In warm areas it can be used as a ground cover, although its tendency to climb any tree or shrub within reach will need to be controlled.

CLEMATIS
VIRGIN'S BOWER, TRAVELLER'S JOY

The generally woody climbers of this romantic genus are from moist temperate regions of the world, but nearly all the popular, larger-flowered garden plants have come from Japan and China. They climb by twisting their tendrils about a support and are a lovely choice for training on verandah posts, arbours, bowers and trellises. Showy, bell-shaped or flattish flowers with 4 to 6 petals are followed by masses of fluffy seed heads, often lasting well into winter, which inspired the common names. The most important requirement for successful cultivation is a well-drained, humus-rich, permanently cool soil with good moisture retention. The plants like to climb up to the sun with their roots in the shade. Prune old, twiggy growth in spring and propagate from cuttings or by layering in summer. In some areas where clematis is a problem, plants are often grafted.

C. aristata
AUSTRALIAN CLEMATIS, GOAT'S BEARD

A native of the Australian bush, this showy evergreen climber, growing to 6 m (about 18 ft), will fare equally well in most temperate gardens if given a deep, cool, humus-rich soil. It is often almost completely covered in masses of white, starry flowers in spring and summer. Large, fluffy seed heads are an additional decorative feature. It will grow in sun and shade and is half-hardy.

C. 'Jackmanii'

Produced in 1862, this is still the most popular large-flowered cultivar. It will climb up to 3 m (about 9 ft), and produces spectacular purple flowers, 15 cm (about 6

Clematis 'Lasurstern'

Clematis 'Nelly Moser'

Clematis tangutica

Clitoria ternatea

Clematis paniculata

Clematis montana

in) across, in summer and autumn/fall. It is deciduous and fully hardy.

C. 'Lasurstern'

A beautiful, large-flowered cultivar with semi-double, lavender-blue flowers in late spring and early summer. It will reach up to 3 m (about 9 ft) and is fully hardy.

C. montana

This vigorous, deciduous species from the Himalayas will reach up to 10 m (about 30 ft) or more. It bears prolific, sweetly perfumed, pure white flowers with yellow anthers in clusters in late spring. Fast-growing and fully hardy, it is ideal for covering a small shed or wall. It was introduced to England in 1831 by Lady Amherst, wife of the Governor-General of India. *C. m.* 'Rubens' is a popular pink form. Prune hard after flowering.

C. 'Nelly Moser'

This cultivar bears large single flowers, pale pink with a deeper pinkish stripe in the centre of each petal.

Grow in a partly shaded position that receives morning sun. It will reach up to 5 m (about 15 ft) and is fully hardy.

C. paniculata

PUAWHANANGA

This frost-hardy, robust, evergreen climber is native to New Zealand and climbs up to 10 m (about 30 ft). Its leathery main stem reaches 10 cm (about 4 in) in diameter and develops woody lustrous green leaves divided into 3 egg- or heart-shaped entire leaflets. In late spring to early summer, male and female flowers appear in open branched clusters on the same plant. These are scented and white with yellow centres, frequently tipped with pinkish purple. The premature blooms are followed by downy seed clusters in autumn/fall.

C. paniculata 'Purity'

The most showy of the evergreen New Zealand native *Clematis* species, this selected male form bears very large, scented white flowers in

spring. It is a vigorous climber that may spread to over 5 m (16 ft) wide. Its height is really only limited by the extent of its support. The foliage is deep green and leathery. Easily grown in any position where the roots can be kept cool and moist. Prune immediately after flowering if growth is to be restricted. Hardy to minus 10°C (about 14°F).

C. tangutica

LEMON PEEL CLEMATIS

This long-flowering species from China grows up to 6 m (about 18 ft). It bears curious, nodding, lantern-shaped flowers, with clear yellow 'thick-skinned' petals, in summer and early autumn/fall. The flowers are followed by decorative silky seed heads.

CLITORIA
ternatea
BUTTERFLY PEA

A lovely evergreen twining up to 4 m (about 12 ft), with slender

stems and fresh green leaves divided into 3 or 5 oval leaflets. Large, dark blue, pea-like flowers with yellow centres bloom in summer, followed by flat pods. There is also a double-flowered form. It is frost-tender, growing best in full sun in warm, sheltered sites in humus-rich, well-drained soil. Provide good support for twining stems and thin out growth with annual spring pruning. Propagate from cuttings in summer or from seed.

Combretum bracteosum

Clytostoma callistegioides

CLYTOSTOMA
callistegioides
VIOLET TRUMPET VINE

This evergreen creeper native to tropical South America is grown for its showy, trumpet-shaped flowers. Fast-growing and densely foliaged, it climbs to 4 m (about 12 ft) by means of tendrils and needs good support. In late spring and summer the pale lavender flowers with purple streaks are carried atop long, drooping stems, making it ideal for training over fences and tall tree stumps in warm areas. Half-hardy, it prefers a sunny position, humus-rich soil, good drainage and regular watering in summer. It is frost-tender. Thin out less vigorous canes after flowering. Propagate from cuttings taken in summer.

COMBRETUM
bracteosum
HICCUP NUT

This climbing, evergreen shrub is native to South Africa, growing to a height and spread of over 3 m (about 9 ft). It has smooth, dull green leaves which are paler underneath, and in summer, bears a profusion of orange-red flowers with rounded heads. The nutty fruit that follows is said to either cause or cure hiccups. Frost-tender, it does best in full sun, in a rich, well-drained, composted soil, with frequent watering in summer. It is ideal as a wall climber or cascading down a bank.

DISTICTIS
buccinatoria
syn. *Phaedranthus buccinatorius*
MEXICAN BLOOD FLOWER, CHERERE

A native of Mexico, this half-hardy, evergreen, woody climber reaching 5 m (about 15 ft) bears large clusters of trumpet flowers in bright shades of red in early spring and summer. This vigorous vine clings with tendrils to surfaces such as rough brick and stone. It grows best in sun or semi-shade in fertile, well-drained soil and needs regular watering in summer. Prune in spring. Propagate from softwood cuttings in early summer.

DOLICHOS
lablab
syn. *Lablab purpureus*
HYACINTH BEAN

This deciduous, twining plant with a spread of about 6 m (about 18 ft) is often grown as an annual for quick cover to hide unattractive fences, walls and sheds. Frost-tender, it will die down in winter. It is easily grown in full sun in any well-drained soil. Pink to mauve pea-like flowers appear from early summer to autumn/fall, followed by many large seed pods which can make the plant unsightly. The plant can be removed and easily replaced by sowing the seed in late winter; in other words, growing it as an annual. In some parts of the world it is grown as a forage or green manure crop.

ECCREMOCARPUS
scaber
CHILEAN GLORY FLOWER

This native of Chile and Peru is a lightweight, sub-shrubby tendril climber grown for its attractive flowers, blooming over a long season from summer into autumn/fall. It is evergreen, with dainty leaves and racemes of small, orange-red, tubular flowers, followed by fruit pods containing winged seeds. Grows sparsely to a height of 2–3 m (about 6–9 ft). Half-hardy, it can be grown as an annual in areas prone to frost. It grows best in full sun in a light, well-drained soil. Keep moist during the growing season and support with small sticks until attached to the main trellis. Propagate from seed in early spring.

FICUS
pumila
CREEPING FIG

From Japan and China, this decorative creeper is a useful evergreen climber for covering walls or fences. It clings by aerial roots along the stems and, although often slow to get started, it later grows very vigorously. It has small, bright green, heart-shaped juvenile leaves and a neat habit. Young growth is an attractive bronze. Remove any mature woody branches that stand out from the support to retain juvenile leaves. Half-hardy, it is best grown in full sun or semi-shade in a well-drained, fertile soil. Propagate from semi-hardwood cuttings. A tiny-leaved form, *F. p.* 'Minima', is less rampant.

GELSEMIUM
sempervirens
CAROLINA JASMINE

A well-behaved, evergreen twiner with glossy green leaves and fragrant, yellow trumpet flowers, which appear for many months in

Distictis buccinatoria

Dolichos lablab

Ficus pumila

spring and again in autumn/fall. Half-hardy, it likes a sunny, warm, sheltered position and a fertile, well-drained soil. It grows quickly but tidily to 3 m (about 9 ft) and can be trained on fences, walls, or a pergola near the house, where the perfume can be enjoyed. All parts of the plant are poisonous and should be kept away from children. Thin out older growth after flowering. Propagate from semi-hardwood cuttings in summer.

HARDENBERGIA
violacea
syn. *H. monophylla*
PURPLE CORAL PEA, FALSE SARSAPARILLA

Used as a ground cover for scrambling over banks or as a climber when given support, this beautiful twining plant from Australia can grow under adverse conditions. It will withstand dry conditions, some frost and will grow in most soils with good drainage. Semi-shade or a fairly sunny position is preferred. Lovely sprays of purple pea flowers are borne in spring. Propagate from presoaked seed. *H. comptoniana* is similar, with slightly larger, pale flowers. It has a pink form also.

HEDERA
IVY

Useful for enhancing many a situation, ivies have long been well-loved, hardy evergreen creepers. Their firmly clasping habit was once considered a lucky love charm. They can be used for ground cover, clothing walls and fences, covering tree stumps and arches, growing up pillars and posts, edging borders and masonry work, trailing from containers and as indoor specimens. In sun or shade they are adaptable to a wide variety of conditions, soils and climates. Regular pruning is recommended so that the attractive, lobed juvenile leaves are retained and no flowers are produced. If the mature growth (which produces tiny green flowers in autumn/fall, followed by black berries) is struck as cuttings, the resultant plants remain as shrubs. This is called 'arborescent ivy'. Propagate from cuttings or rooted stems. The charming fashion of ivy topiary has been revived and wire topiary frames are now available in many garden centres. As the ivy grows over the shape the sideshoots are regularly clipped to produce a dense cover.

H. canariensis 'Variegata'

A handsome, popular ivy with broad, leathery leaves, dark green in the middle shading to silver-grey and bordered with cream or white. Some leaves are completely white or cream. This slightly frost-tender ivy is particularly showy and looks

good covering large areas of walls or fences.

H. helix
ENGLISH IVY, COMMON IVY

This fully hardy species will produce a dense, dark green cover. It is often used as a ground cover in shade where grass has difficulty thriving, and is also excellent for climbing up walls and hiding paling fences. There are innumerable named varieties with unusually shaped and/or variegated leaves. They are often grown as house plants.

HIBBERTIA
scandens
GUINEA FLOWER, GUINEA GOLD VINE

A native of Australia, this soft twining climber or trailing plant can grow up to 4 m (about 12 ft) high or be trained along the ground as an effective ground cover. It has broad, dark green leaves and large, showy buttercup yellow flowers from spring through the warmer months. Any moderately fertile, well-drained soil is suitable. It will grow in full sun or semi-shade and is a good choice for sandy, coastal gardens, as it tolerates salt spray. Half-hardy, it is ideal for warm climates. Lightly prune to shape in spring and propagate from semi-ripe tip cuttings in late summer.

HYDRANGEA
petiolaris
syn. *H. anomala* subsp. *petiolaris*
CLIMBING HYDRANGEA

This deciduous, self-clinging climber grows up to 15 m (about 50 ft) or more and bears beautiful, flattened heads of small white flowers in summer. It has oval, finely toothed leaves, and is fully hardy. Plant in humus-rich, well-drained moist soil in full sun, with some protection from hot afternoon sun, and water regularly in summer. Propagate from semi-hardwood cuttings in summer. Prune after flowering, trimming close to the support.

Hedera canariensis 'Variegata'

Hydrangea petiolaris

Hibbertia scandens

Hedera helix

Gelsemium sempervirens

Hardenbergia violacea

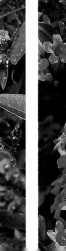

IPOMOEA
MORNING GLORIES

Care should be taken when choosing these ornamental climbers, as some rampant species can become extremely invasive in warm districts. Native to tropical and warm-temperate regions, most species have a twining habit and masses of funnel-shaped flowers which are at their best in the early morning. Half-hardy to frost-tender, they are best suited to warm coastal districts or tropical areas. Any moderately fertile, well-drained soil is suitable and they prefer a sunny position. These plants are useful for covering sheds, fences, trellises and banks. They may also be grown in pots. Propagate in spring from seed which has been gently filed and presoaked to aid germination, or from cuttings (for perennial species).

I. alba
syn. *Calonyction aculeatum*
MOON FLOWER

From tropical America, this fast-growing, soft-stemmed, perennial vine grows up to 7 m (about 21 ft) and is cultivated for its large, white, fragrant flowers, 15 cm (about 6 in) across, which open at night during summer. It is frost-tender, but is easily grown as an annual in cool areas.

I. horsfalliae
CARDINAL CREEPER

Native to the West Indies and other tropical regions, this beautiful flowering vine grows up to 3 m (about 9 ft) and requires warm, frost-free conditions. It bears long, tubular, rosy red flowers from summer through to winter.

I. tuberosa
syn. *Merremia tuberosa*
WOOD ROSE, YELLOW MORNING GLORY

This twining climber, growing up to 6 m (about 18 ft), has delicately lobed leaves and funnel-shaped, yellow flowers in summer. The flowers are followed by brown, satiny, woody fruit that resemble a carved rose. These are popular in dried arrangements.

JASMINUM
JASMINE

These mostly woody stemmed, climbing plants are valued for their showy, fragrant flowers. Most like a sunny or lightly shaded position with a moderately fertile, well-drained soil. They must have adequate water during spring and summer. Some species are easily propagated by layering, others can be raised from semi-ripe cuttings in summer. The flowers of some species are used in making essential oils for perfume, as well as scenting jasmine tea.

J. officinale
COMMON JASMINE, POET'S JASMINE

Introduced to Europe from the East during the Tudor period, this vigorous, deciduous or semi-evergreen climber can reach up to 9 m (about 27 ft) high. Sweetly fragrant, white flowers are borne in terminal clusters throughout summer and autumn/fall. It is moderately frost-hardy. Elizabethan poets referred to its common use on arbours, and it also provides beautiful covering for pergolas, arches, bowers or trellises.

J. polyanthum

This vigorous, scrambling, evergreen climber from China is fast-growing but tender and easy to grow in mild climates only. In cool areas it makes a pretty pot plant. Very fragrant, white flowers with pink buds are produced in spring. It grows to 6 m (about 18 ft) and requires a good pruning after flowering to keep tidy and under control.

J. sambac
ARABIAN JASMINE

A small, fairly weak climber that grows only about 1.5 m (about 5 ft). It has large, glossy green leaves, and bears sweetly perfumed, white flowers for most of the year. It is half-hardy. The flowers are used in China for perfuming tea. There is a double-flowered form called 'Grand Duke of Tuscany'.

KADSURA
japonica

Valued for its bright red berries in autumn/fall, this evergreen, twining climber grows up to 3 m (about 9 ft) tall. It has attractive, rich green, oval leaves and lightly perfumed, small, cream flowers in summer. Fully hardy, this plant does best in semi-shade in a well-drained soil. Male and female flowers grow on separate plants, so both are needed to produce berries. Propagate from cuttings in summer.

Ipomoea alba

Ipomoea horsfalliae

Jasminum polyanthum

Ipomoea tuberosa

Jasminum officinale

Jasminum sambac

Kennedia rubicunda

Kennedia nigricans

Lonicera hildebrandiana

Lonicera caprifolium

Lapageria rosea

Lathyrus latifolius

KENNEDIA

Endemic to Australia, these climbing or scrambling plants were named after John Kennedy, a London nurseryman. They are widely cultivated for their showy, pea-like flowers which attract birds. Half-hardy to frost-tender, they thrive in a light, well-drained soil and a sunny situation, but will tolerate light shade. Plant growth can be very vigorous and a strong climbing support is necessary. In spring or after flowering, invasive growth can be cut back reasonably hard without harming the plant, but keep well watered until new growth is established. Propagate from presoaked seed.

K. nigricans
BLACK CORAL PEA

A robust climber that will quickly cover an area of up to 6 m (about 18 ft) in diameter. It has dark green leaves divided into 3 leaflets and unusual black and yellow pea flowers in spring. It is ideal for covering a large area on a fence or shed in a fairly open position.

K. rubicunda
RUNNING POSTMAN

This extremely vigorous species grows up to 5 m (about 15 ft) and should be kept well away from nearby shrubs and trees, as it will quickly climb over anything in reach. It bears showy, dark red pea flowers in small sprays in spring and early summer.

LAPAGERIA
rosea
CHILEAN BELLFLOWER

Native to Chile (where it is the national flower) this beautiful evergreen climber can reach 5 m (about 15 ft) on support. The oval leaves are bright glossy green. Waxy, pinkish red, bell-like flowers, faintly spotted within, are borne for a long period through summer and autumn/fall. Half-hardy, it needs a warm, sheltered spot in cool climates. Grow in humus-rich, well-drained soil in partial shade, and keep fairly dry in winter. Propagate from presoaked seed in spring or

layers in autumn/fall. Watch for two-spotted mite and thrips.

LATHYRUS
latifolius
PERRENIAL PEA, EVERLASTING PEA

This perennial, tendril climber from Chile grows to about 2 m (about 6 ft) high. It has dull green foliage and dense heads of pink, rose or white, scentless pea flowers in spring and summer. Fully hardy, it is easily grown in a humus-rich, well-drained soil. It needs the support of a sunny fence or trellis. The plant responds to regular feeding and watering when the buds are forming. Propagate from seed or cuttings or by division in spring.

LONICERA
HONEYSUCKLE, WOODBINE

Grown for their masses of perfumed flowers, these are perhaps the most romantic climbers of all. They are perfect for covering arches, arbours and bowers, where they will provide a sweet summer evening

fragrance. Grow in a well-drained, moisture-retentive soil in sun or semi-shade. Propagate from cuttings in summer or late autumn/fall.

L. caprifolium
HONEYSUCKLE, WOODBINE

A deciduous, twining climber growing up to 5 m (about 15 ft) with light green, oval, pointed leaves that are joined at the base. Highly scented, yellow flowers, tinted with pink on the outside appear in summer and autumn/fall. It is frost-hardy. There are many named cultivars with brightly coloured flowers, from pink and white to red and yellow. Alas, the brighter the colour, the less fragrance.

L. hildebrandiana
GIANT HONEYSUCKLE,
BURMESE HONEYSUCKLE

This deciduous climber from Burma reaching up to 20 m (about 65 ft) bears large, creamy flowers in summer that turn orange with age; they are only faintly scented. It needs strong support and is frost-tender.

Mandevilla laxa

Mandevilla × amabilis 'Alice du Pont'

Mandevilla splendens

Macfadyena unguis-cati

Lonicera japonica 'Aurea-reticulata'

Manettia inflata

Lonicera japonica

L. japonica
JAPANESE HONEYSUCKLE

This vigorous climber from east Asia, growing to 10 m (about 30 ft), has glossy, dark green leaves. Pairs of fragrant, white flowers ageing yellow, or sometimes purple-tinged, appear in late summer to autumn/fall. This species is only just frost-hardy, but can become an invasive weed.

L. japonica 'Aurea-reticulata'

This less vigorous, slow-growing cultivar is suited to mild climates and does well in shade. Its leaves have attractive gold veins, but it bears only a few flowers.

MACFADYENA
unguis-cati
syn. *Doxantha unguis-cati*
CAT'S CLAW CREEPER

A beautiful, evergreen vine grown for its large, bright yellow flowers in the shape of a flattened trumpet up to 10 cm (about 4 in) across. These are borne in profusion in late spring. It clings by tiny, 3-pronged tendrils, like little claws, and climbs to a mature height of up to 10 m (about 30 ft). An excellent climber for covering a high fence or garden shed, it likes a sunny, well-drained position and is frost tender. Prune back hard after flowering to keep in check. Propagate from semi-ripe cuttings in late summer.

MANDEVILLA

Native to tropical America, these woody-stemmed climbers are grown for their profusion of showy trumpet-shaped flowers, which are sometimes fragrant. They do best in warm, frost-free climates with partial shade in summer. Soil should be deep, rich and well-drained. Provide ample water on hot days. Propagate from semi-ripe cuttings in summer. In cool areas they grow very well in frost-free greenhouses.

M. × amabilis 'Alice du Pont'
syn. *Dipladenia × amabilis* 'Alice du Pont'

A twining climber growing up to 4 m (about 12 ft) with handsome, oval, glossy leaves and clusters of large, deep pink, scentless, trumpet flowers over a long period in summer. It is frost-tender and needs a warm protected position with light shade.

M. laxa
syn. *M. suaveolens*
CHILEAN JASMINE

From Argentina, this fast-growing, woody vine reaches 6 m (about 18 ft) or more and is deciduous in cool areas. It is half-hardy. In summer it produces heavily perfumed, white trumpet flowers in profusion —these make good cut flowers. The plants can be pruned heavily in early spring to keep it tidy and encourage new growth.

M. splendens
syn. *Dipladenia splendens*

One of the showiest species of its genus, this evergreen twisting climber is native to Brazil and climbs to 3 m (about 9 ft). Its lustrous green leaves are wide and elliptical to rectangular, reaching a length of 20 cm (about 8 in). At the end of spring to the beginning of summer, attractive, deep reddish pink, trumpet-shaped flowers with yellow middles appear. This species prefers temperatures above 10°C (about 50°F).

MANETTIA
inflata
syn. *M. bicolor*
BRAZILIAN FIRECRACKER

This evergreen, light, twining climber reaches 2 m (about 6 ft) and produces small, decorative, tubular flowers, bright red and tipped with gold, in spring and summer. Originally from South America, this plant does best in a warm climate. Soil should preferably be rich, slightly acidic, with good drainage. Provide regular water and some shade in summer. This climber is pretty for training up a pillar, over a trellis or trailing from a hanging basket. Propagate this species from softwood cuttings in late spring. It can be grown as an indoor plant, in which case it should be given plenty of bright light.

Mucuna bennettii

Pandorea jasminoides

Parthenocissus tricuspidata

Pandorea pandorana

Passiflora caerulea

Parthenocissus quinquefolia

Passiflora coccinea

MUCUNA
bennettii

The leaves of this strong, fast-growing tropical climber are divided into 3 oval leaflets, and in summer have large, pendant clusters of pea-like, orange-scarlet flowers. It will only grow in summer in moist, but well-drained, humus-rich soil in partial shade. Frost-tender, it needs abundant water during growth, less at other times. The vigorous growth requires a well-supported, large area for climbing. Crowded stems may be thinned out in spring. Propagate from seed in spring or by layering in late summer.

PANDOREA

Named after Pandora of Greek mythology, this is a small genus of beautiful twining climbers native to Malaysia and Australia. They are grown for their spectacular, long-lasting displays of tubular bell flowers and make excellent pergola or trellis subjects. Frost-tender, they are ideal for warm-temperate or tropical areas; where the temperature reaches freezing, *P. pandorana* may survive if given a warm, sheltered spot. The soil should be well-drained and enriched with humus. Most require abundant moisture and a sunny position protected from strong winds. Propagate from fresh seed in spring or semi-ripe cuttings in summer.

P. jasminoides
syn. *Tecoma jasminoides*
BOWER CLIMBER

This very attractive climber from Australia grows up to 5 m (about 15 ft) and has lush, deep green, glossy leaflets. Showy, pale pink trumpet flowers with a deep carmine throat are borne from late spring to autumn/fall in warm climates. A pure white flowering form is also in cultivation, and there is a form with variegated leaves is available.

P. pandorana
syn. *Tecoma australis*
WONGA-WONGA VINE

Also from Australia, this robust, woody climber up to 6 m (about

18 ft) bears masses of very showy, tubular flowers in spring and summer. The flowers are usually creamy white with reddish throats, but a number of cultivars are available, one with pure white flowers and another with gold and brown flowers. This is a very good climber for covering arches, and pergolas and for disguising unattractive sites such as wire mesh fences.

PARTHENOCISSUS

These charming climbing plants from North America and Asia have deciduous, attractively cut leaves, some with magnificent autumn/fall colouring. The genus name is from the Greek *parthenos*, meaning 'virgin', and *kissos,* 'creeper'. They climb by tendrils with tiny disc-shaped suckers and are the perfect climbers for growing on buildings and walls. They are fully hardy and they will grow best in humus-rich, well-drained soil in filtered sunlight with protection from hot winds. Propagate from hardwood cuttings in late winter or early spring.

P. quinquefolia
syn. *Ampelopsis quinquefolia, Vitis quinquefolia*
VIRGINIA CREEPER

A high climber growing 15 m (about 50 ft) or more. The handsome leaves divided into 5 leaflets make an attractive green wall cover in summer and turn a brilliant red in autumn/fall.

P. tricuspidata
syn. *Ampelopsis veitchii*
BOSTON IVY, JAPANESE IVY

Ideal for covering large walls, this ivy will reach up to 20 m (about 65 ft). The 3-lobed leaves, 20 cm (about 8 in) across, turn spectacular shades of red and purple in autumn/fall.

PASSIFLORA
PASSION FLOWER

Native chiefly to tropical South America, these showy, tendril climbers are treasured for their ornamental blossoms and their delicious fruit, notably the well-known passionfruit. Half-hardy to

frost-tender, they are best suited to warm areas. A humus-rich, well-drained soil and a sunny aspect are preferred. Water regularly in summer and provide good support. Prune congested or overgrown plants in spring. Propagate from seed or semi-ripe cuttings or by layering in summer.

P. caerulea
BLUE PASSION FLOWER

In summer this half-hardy, fast-growing evergreen or semi-evergreen climber to 10 m (about 30 ft) produces beautiful flowers with pale pink petals, banded with blue or purple. There are followed by edible but not especially delicious egg-shaped, yellow fruit.

P. coccinea
RED PASSION FLOWER

A robust, evergreen climber to 4 m (about 12 ft) grown for the brilliant, large, scarlet flowers borne in summer and autumn/fall, set among large, dark green, crinkly leaves. It is frost-tender and also needs protection from hot winds.

Podranea ricasoliana

Phaseolus caracalla

Pyrostegia venusta

Quisqualis indica

Petrea volubilis

Rosa 'Albéric Barbier'

PETREA
volubilis
PURPLE WREATH, SANDPAPER

Native to Central America and the West Indies this bushy, evergreen woody-stemmed climber is grown for the clusters of delightful star-like, violet flowers that appear from late winter to late summer, set among simple, elliptic, rough-textured leaves. It does best in a fertile, moist, well-drained soil in a protected, shady position. Frost-tender it grows to a height of 6 m (about 18 ft) or more. Provide support to maintain its climbing habit and water regularly when in full growth. Propagate from semi-ripe cuttings in summer.

PHASEOLUS
caracalla
syn. *Vigna caracalla*
SNAIL CREEPER

A decorative, evergreen, twining climber with soft green foliage composed of 3 leaflets and curiously twisted, pea-like flowers in shades of purple, white and yellow. The flowers have a delightful perfume and are produced from mid-summer to early autumn/fall. Frost-tender, it is best suited to warm-temperate and tropical areas, where it will grow rapidly to 3 m (about 9 ft), scrambling over everything in reach. Grow in full sun in humus-rich, well-drained soil and protect from drying winds. Prune tangled growth in spring. Propagate from seed sown in spring.

PODRANEA
ricasoliana
syn. *Pandorea ricasoliana,*
Tecoma ricasoliana
PINK TECOMA

Native to South Africa, this compact evergreen climber reaches 4 m (about 12 ft) high and is valued for its scented flowers. It has a leathery twisting stem and dark green, fern-like leaves composed of up to 11 finely serrated, lance-shaped to rounded leaflets. From spring until autumn/fall, beautiful light pink, funnel-shaped flowers, with red markings appear on branched terminal clusters. This climber will withstand light frosts and requires rich, porous soil with full sun. Water liberally during growth period and provide support. Dense foliage may be pruned in winter and the beginning of summer. Propagate from cuttings in summer or seed in spring.

PYROSTEGIA
venusta
FLAME VINE, GOLDEN SHOWER

From South America, this magnificent creeper will reach great heights of 10 m (about 30 ft) or more in warm climates. This climber is grown chiefly for its brilliant display of orange-gold flowers in autumn/fall, winter or spring, depending on the climate. Frost-tender, it will thrive in most well-drained soils but will only flower well in full sun. Water well in summer and grow on a strong pergola or arch where the flowers can droop down freely. After flowering prune out old shoots and spent flowers. Propagate from semi-hardwood cuttings in summer or autumn/fall.

QUISQUALIS
indica
RANGOON CREEPER

This strong-growing creeper can reach 9 m (about 27 ft) in tropical areas. The tubular flowers are strongly fragrant, especially at night, opening white and deepening to pink and then red, throughout summer. Frost-tender, it enjoys warm, humid conditions, full sun and a humus-rich, well-drained soil. Water regularly in spring and summer but keep fairly dry during the cool months. It needs a sturdy support and is useful for covering fences, walls and pergolas. Cut back old stems in spring and remove spent flowers in autumn/fall. Propagate from seed, semi-ripe cuttings or suckers.

ROSA
ROSE

Climbing roses vary greatly in their habit from short-stemmed, rambling or pillar roses to tall vigorous climbers capable of reaching up to 10 m (30 ft) high. They beautifully decorate fences, walls, trellises, pergolas, arches, pillars and columns, and are ideal for small gardens where there is not enough room for a conventional rose bed. Species growing to around 4 m (about 12 ft) are useful for covering walls and fences; those short-stemmed roses held close to the foliage are best for growing on pillars; and. miniature climbers look pretty cascading down retaining walls and tall containers. Most roses are fully hardy and require humus-rich soil, full sun and ample water. Give climbers room to develop and tie back canes as they grow. Some of the pillar roses need only light pruning, but old vigorous climbers may need more severe cutting back. Always remove spent blooms to prolong flowering. Aphids, blackspot and mildew can cause problems.

R. 'Albéric Barbier'

A vigorous, fully hardy rambler growing to 5 m (about 15 ft). Yellow buds open to full double, creamy white blooms in spring. The fragrant flowers are carried in large trusses; foliage is dark and glossy.

Rosa banksiae lutea

Rosa 'Albertine'

Rosa 'Climbing Lady Hillingdon'

Rosa 'Madame Alfred Carrièrre'

Rosa 'Handel'

R. 'Albertine'

A beautiful, vigorous rambler to 6 m (about 18 ft), good for growing over a pergola. Fragrant, double, ruffled, coppery-pink blooms are borne in large trusses in spring. It is fully hardy but a little prone to mildew.

R. banksiae lutea

This extremely vigorous, thornless climber will reach up to 10 m (30 ft). Clusters of small, white or yellow, double flowers are borne in spring. Light green foliage is small and pointed. Half-hardy, it needs warmth and protection. As flowers are borne on permanent spurs produced on older wood, remove only dead wood when pruning.

R. 'Climbing Lady Hillingdon'

A climbing tea rose with rather stiff growth to 4 m (about 12 ft). The large, double, apricot-yellow blooms with pointed petals are borne freely throughout the warmer

months. It is frost-hardy, but appreciates a sunny wall in cold districts.

R. 'Handel'

Ideal for a wall, fence or pillar, this frost-hardy, free-flowering 3 m (about 9 ft) climber bears semi-double, ivory-cream flowers edged and flushed deep pink. They are borne in clusters from spring to autumn/fall. Watch for mildew.

R. 'Lorraine Lee'

A slightly frost-tender, shrubby climber with semi-double, rose-pink, shaded apricot, blooms. Very fragrant, it continues flowering throughout the warmer months.

R. 'Madame Alfred Carrière'

This is the most popular white climber among the old garden roses (it is classed as a Noisette); and bears scented, medium-sized, double flowers, white with faint touches of pink, all season. It grows to about 6 m (about 18 ft).

Rosa 'Mermaid'

R. 'Mermaid'

This extremely vigorous climber, reaching 8 m (about 24 ft), is for large areas only. Its stiff, thorny canes are rather awkward to train and tie. It makes an impressive climber for walls, as its flowers are large, prolific and continuous from spring to autumn/fall. Single pale yellow flowers have prominent stamens. The glossy foliage is oval and dark green. It is frost-hardy, but appreciates a sunny wall in cold districts.

Rosa 'Lorraine Lee'

R. 'Zéphirine Drouhin'

A fully hardy, semi-climbing bourbon rose growing to 2.5 m (about 7½ ft), noted for its lack of thorns and recurrent, fragrant blooms. The long, pointed buds open to semi-double, deep pink blooms from spring to autumn/fall.

SCHIZOPHRAGMA
hydrangeoides
JAPANESE HYDRANGEA

From Japan and Korea, this vigorous, deciduous, woody-stemmed climber clings by aerial roots for support. It will grow to 9 m (about 27 ft) or more and makes a spectacular cover for pergolas and large walls. The large, flattened flowerheads, 30 cm (about 12 in) across, are composed of very small white flowers surrounded by ornamental, white bracts, and are borne in summer. It has attractive, deep green, toothed leaves 12 cm (about 5 in) long on long, red stalks. Grow in a humus-rich, moist, but well-drained soil in full sun. It is frost hardy. Train young plants on the support until established, and remove spent blooms. Propagate from semi-ripe cuttings in summer.

SOLANDRA
maxima
CUP OF GOLD, HAWAIIAN LILY, GOLDEN CHALICE VINE

A giant Mexican climber valued for its huge flowers and ability to cover very large areas. It is a rampant, woody vine growing to 10 m (about 30 ft) or more requiring plenty of space and a sturdy support. The yellow flowers, up to 25 cm (about 10 in) across, with a near purple stripe down the centre of each petal, are produced in spring and summer. Frost-tender, it requires fertile soil, good drainage and full sun. It will tolerate wind, drought and salt spray, making it an excellent plant for seaside gardens. Prune in summer to keep the plant in bounds and promote more flowers. Propagate from semi-ripe cuttings in summer.

SOLANUM

With a worldwide distribution, this very large genus of annuals, perennials, shrubs, trees and climbers includes potatoes, tomatoes and other food plants, as well as a few medicinal and poisonous plants. The climbers are valued for their ornamental flowers, foliage and fruit. They are fast-growing and require fastening to support. They do best in a warm, sunny position in fertile, well-drained soil. Cut back congested growth in spring. Propagate from seed.

S. jasminoides
POTATO VINE

From South America, this quick-growing, semi-evergreen climber reaches 5 m (about 15 ft) and bears showy clusters of pale blue flowers in summer and autumn/fall, followed by small, purple berries. It is half-hardy; in cool areas it can be potted up in autumn/fall to spend the winter under glass. The cultivar 'Album' has masses of star-shaped, white flowers.

S. seaforthianum

A showy vine growing to 6 m (about 18 ft) and bearing large clusters of violet-blue flowers with yellow stamens in summer, followed by small, scarlet berries. It is frost-tender.

STEPHANOTIS
floribunda
WAX FLOWER

This evergreen climber can grow to a height and spread of 3 m (about 9 ft). It is grown for its pleasant fragrance and its attractive foliage of paired, waxy, deep green leaves. The pendulous, tubular, white flowers have widely flared lobes, and appear in clusters of about 4 blooms from spring to autumn/fall. The flowers are very popular as bridal decorations. Plant in well-drained soil in partial shade. This climber is frost-tender, but may be grown indoors and forced into flower throughout the year. Propagate by layering.

Solandra maxima

Solanum jasminoides

Solanum seaforthianum

Stephanotis floribunda

Thunbergia alata

Thunbergia grandiflora

Trachelospermum jasminoides

Strongylodon macrobotrys

Tecomanthe speciosa

STRONGYLODON
macrobotrys
JADE VINE

A large, twining climber up to 20 m (about 65 ft), valued for the spectacular, long, pendulous sprays of blue-green flowers, almost 50 cm (about 20 in) long, borne throughout summer. Native to the Philippines, this species is frost-tender, suitable only to subtropical and warm-temperate areas. Plant in humus-rich, moist, but well-drained soil, with partial shade in summer. Grow over a pergola or large arch where there is freedom for the long racemes of flowers to hang down. Propagate from seed or cuttings.

TECOMANTHE
speciosa

This vigorous twisting climber grows to 10 m (about 30 ft). Its compound leaves consist of up to 5 leaflets. In autumn/fall, lush cream, green-tinged flowers are borne. This frost-tender species requires temperatures above 10°C (about 50°F), peaty soil with good drainage and protection from the summer sun. Water liberally during the growth period and stake stems. Prune closely packed stems in spring. Propagate from seed in spring or semi-ripe cuttings in summer.

THUNBERGIA
CLOCK VINE

This genus contains 200 species of annual twisting climbers and perennial evergreen clump-forming shrubs. These species are native to Africa, Asia and Malagasy. Their leaves, which are entire, have up to 5 lobes. The cylindrical blooms are borne individually from the leaf axils or in trusses. The species range from half-hardy to frost-tender and prefer temperatures above 10°C (about 50°F). They will grow in any reasonably rich soil with adequate drainage. Full sun is preferred, except during the summer months when partial shade and liberal water should be provided. Support stems and prune densely

packed foliage during early spring. Propagate from seed in spring and semi-ripe cuttings in summer. This genus was named after the eighteenth-century Swedish botanist Dr Carl Peter Thunberg who worked in Africa.

T. alata
BLACK-EYED SUSAN

Native to the tropics of Africa, this vigorous annual or perennial twisting climber grows quickly to 3 m (about 9 ft). Its deep green, cordate leaves grow to 8 cm (about 3 in) long. It bears masses of 4 cm (about 2 in) wide orange flowers with black throats all summer. It is perennial in frost-free areas.

T. grandiflora
BLUE TRUMPET VINE, SKY FLOWER

Originally from India, this quick-growing, vigorous climber to 5 m (about 15 ft) is grown for its drooping clusters of large, sky-blue trumpet flowers, borne in summer and autumn/fall. It has large-toothed, heart-shaped leaves up to 20 cm (about 8 in) long and looks best

when grown on a trellis, fence or pergola. It is frost-tender, and requires humus-rich, well-drained soil, lots of water and protection from dry summer winds. Propagate from semi-hardwood cuttings in summer.

TRACHELOSPERMUM
jasminoides
STAR JASMINE

Valued for its perfumed, star-shaped flowers, this attractive, evergreen, twining climber from China grows up to 7 m (about 21 ft) high. It has lance-shaped leaves, and hanging clusters of white flowers are produced in summer. Frost-hardy, this plant does best in a sunny position in well-drained, fertile soil. Although it is slow-growing during the early stages, it will flourish once established and is excellent for training on pillars, pergolas and arches. It can also be used as a ground cover. Prune congested or straggly branches in autumn/fall. Propagate from semi-ripe cuttings in summer or autumn/fall.

Wisteria floribunda 'Alba'   *Wisteria chinensis*   *Wisteria f.* 'Violacea Plena'

TROPAEOLUM
speciosum
FLAME NASTURTIUM

A herbaceous, perennial climber with slender stems reaching up to 3 m (about 9 ft). It has a tuberous rhizome and attractive, bright green foliage composed of 6 oval leaflets. Scarlet flowers in summer are followed by blue fruit. Grow in partial shade in a humus-rich, moist, but well-drained soil. Native to China, this species is frost-hardy. Propagate from seed or by division of tubers.

VITIS

This genus consists of deciduous woody-stemmed, tendril climbers. They are grown for their foliage (on trellises and the like as ornamentals) and fruits (grapes). Grow in humus-rich, moisture-retentive, but well-drained soil in full sun or partial shade. Propagate from hardwood cuttings taken in late autumn/fall or winter.

V. coignetiae
CRIMSON GLORY VINE

A rapid-growing climber reaching 15 m (about 50 ft), with green, slightly lobed leaves which change to deep crimson, orange and scarlet in autumn/fall. Clusters of small, black berries with a glaucous bloom are borne in late summer. Its tendrils coil around supports and need plenty of room to spread. Frost-hardy, the leaf colour is best in cool climates. Prune in winter when the plants are completely dormant.

Wisteria floribunda

V. vinifera 'Ganzin Glory'
syn. *V. v.* 'Tinto'
ORNAMENTAL GRAPE, GLORY VINE

A hybrid originally raised in France for use as a grafting stock, this vigorous, deciduous climber is widely grown for its brilliant crimson autumn/fall foliage which colours reliably, even in mild-winter areas. Tiny pale green spring flowers are fragrant, but it is very rare to see a grape. Other cultivars of *V. vinifera* are grown for ornamental foliage also; 'Brandt' is very well thought of in England. The species is frost-hardy.

WISTERIA
WISTERIA

The deciduous wisteria is one of the most popular plants for pergolas, where the large, drooping sprays of perfumed flowers are best displayed. Providing welcome summer shade, the soft, light green, luxuriant foliage is particularly attractive. Wisterias like a sunny position and a humus-rich, well-drained soil. Although they take some time to establish, they become large, vigorous plants and need strong support for healthy future growth. Prune after flowering and again in late winter; only prune in winter if really necessary to control size. Propagate from cuttings or by layering in late summer. With regular pruning, and some support in the early years, wisteria can be grown as a large, free-standing shrub or standard.

W. chinensis
syn. *W. sinensis*
CHINESE WISTERIA

Native to China, this vigorous, fully hardy, woody-stemmed climber will reach up to 30 m (about 95 ft) high. The sprays of slightly fragrant, lavender-blue flowers up to 30 cm (about 12 in) long appear in spring on bare branches before the leaves, creating a magnificent sight.

W. floribunda
JAPANESE WISTERIA

This vigorous, woody-stemmed climber up to 10 m (about 30 ft) bears pendulous, purple-blue flowers of around 50 cm (about 20 in) or more long. The flowers are fragrant and are often produced after the leaves in spring. This climber is fully hardy.

W. floribunda 'Alba'

A beautiful, white flowering climber with drooping sprays up to 60 cm (about 24 in) long. It is fully hardy.

W. floribunda 'Violacea Plena'

Fragrant, double purple flowers are borne in early summer on this fully hardy climber.

Vitis coignetiae

Vitis vinifera 'Ganzin Glory'

Tables

Keys

The following lists are keys to the Cultivation Guidelines and Seasonal Calendars which follow. If, for example, you wish to find out how to propagate *Ageratum houstonianum*, you simply locate it in the keys below (Annuals, low-growing, summer–autumn flowering), find that group in the Cultivation Guidelines (page 504), then move across the column until you reach the one headed 'Propagation'. For ease of reference, each plant is also listed in the Index to Plants, with page numbers referring to where it occurs in the text and where it occurs in these keys.

ANNUALS & PERENNIALS

The cultivation of annual and perennial plants is rewarding as a large variety of flowering plants can be grown to appear throughout the year. To grow the more unusual annual flowers from seed requires both patience, as germination can be erratic, and constant attention, as seedlings need an even light source and must never be allowed to dry out. In other words, their best chance of healthy development requires daily care.

Perennials, on the other hand, are not called hardy for nothing. Different perennials can be found for cold, mountainous climates, for salt-spray coastal gardens and for excessively dry, wet or shady positions. Simple maintenance practices such as removing spent flowers, checking under leaves for pests and a tidy up during winter are all they need. Regular mulching and fertilizing during the growing and flowering seasons helps maintain their vigour, and before long there will be excess plants to give away to friends.

Annuals, low-growing, summer–autumn flowering

Ageratum houstonianum
Begonia semperflorens group
Begonia semperflorens
Browallia americana
Calceolaria herbeohybrida
Celosia cristata
Convolvulus tricolor
Echium vulgare [dwarf]
Exacum affine
Felicia bergeriana
Gomphrena globosa
Impatiens balsamina
Nierembergia hippomanica var. *violacea* 'Purple Robe'
Petunia 'Bonanza'
Petunia 'Cascade'
Petunia 'Giants of California'
Phacelia campanularia
Phlox drummondii
Portulaca grandiflora
Reseda odorata
Sanvitalia procumbens
Tagetes patula
Torenia fournieri
Xeranthemum annum

Annuals, low-growing, spring–summer flowering

Dianthus barbatus
Dianthus chinensis
Eschscholzia californica
Iberis amara
Iberis umbellata
Lobelia erinus 'Cambridge Blue'
Lobularia maritima
Nemophila insignis
Papaver rhoeas
Tropaeolum majus
Ursinia anthemoides
Ursinia calenduliflora
Verbena × *hybrida*
Verbena laciniata
Viola × *wittrockiana*

Annuals, low-growing, winter–spring flowering

Bellis perennis
Calendula officinalis
Dianthus barbatus
Dianthus chinensis
Dorotheanthus bellidiformis
Erysimum hieraciifolium
Malcolmia maritima
Nemesia strumosa
Papaver nudicaule
Primula malacoides
Viola × *wittrockiana*

Annuals, medium-growing, summer flowering

Agrostemma githago
Anagallis linifolia
Anchusa capensis 'Blue Angel'
Callistephus chinensis
Catharanthus roseus
Centaurea moschata
Coleus blumei
Coreopsis tinctoria
Cosmos sulphureus
Eustoma grandiflorum
Gaillardia pulchella
Gilia capitata
Impatiens wallerana
Kochia scoparia × *trychophylla*
Lindheimera texana
Linum grandiflorum 'Rubrum'
Lunaria annua
Rudbeckia hirta
Salvia farinacea 'Blue Bedder'
Salvia splendens
Scabiosa atropurpurea
Silene coeli-rosa
Tagetes erecta
× *Venidio-arctotis* cultivars
Zinnia angustifolia
Zinnia haageana 'Old Mexico'

Annuals, medium-growing, spring–summer flowering

Annual or marguerite carnations
Antirrhinum majus
Argemone mexicana
Campanula medium
Centaurea cyanus
Cheiranthus cheiri
Cheiranthus mutabilis
Chrysanthemum carinatum
Clarkia amoena
Coreopsis maritima
Dianthus caryophyllus cultivars
Dimorphotheca sinuata
Gypsophila elegans
Helichrysum bracteatum
Limonium sinuatum
Linaria maroccana 'Fairy Bouquet'
Lupinus hartwegii
Lupinus texensis
Matthiola incana
Nigella damascena
Penstemon × *gloxinioides*
Salpiglossus sinuata
Schizanthus pinnatus
Senecio elegans

Annuals, tall-growing, spring–summer flowering

Alcea rosea
Delphinium belladonna
Dephinium elatum hybrids
Delphinium grandiflorum
Digitalis purpurea
Hunnemannia fumariifolia
Lathyrus odoratus
Matthiola 'Mammoth Column'
Moluccella laevis

Annuals, tall-growing, summer flowering

Abelmoschus moschatus 'Mischief'
Amaranthus caudatus
Amaranthus tricolor 'Joseph's Coat'
Calceolaria integrifolia
Canna × *generalis*
Carthamus tinctorius
Cleome hassleriana
Cobaea scandens
Cosmos bipinnatus
Echium wildpretti
Euphorbia marginata
Helianthus annuus
Hibiscus moscheutos
Lavatera trimestris
Malva moschata
Mina lobata
Mirabilis jalapa
Nicotiana alata
Nicotiana × *sanderae*
Oenothera biennis
Papaver somniferum
Rhodochiton atrosanguineum
Thunbergia alata

Tithonia rotundifolia 'Torch'
Tropaeolum peregrinum
Zinnia elegans

Annuals, dahlias

Cactus dahlias
Collarette dahlias
Decorative dahlias
Dwarf or bedding dahlias
Pompon dahlias
Waterlily or Nymphaea dahlias

Perennials, spring–early summer flowering

Adonis aestivalis
Anigozanthos 'Bush Gems'
Border carnations
Centranthus ruber
Chelidonium majus
　'Flore Pleno'
Dianella tasmanica
Dianthus × allwoodii
Dianthus deltoides
Dianthus plumarius
Dietes grandiflora
Dietes iridioides
Euphorbia amygdaloides subsp.
　robbiae
Geum × borisii
Geum 'Mrs Bradshaw'
Kaempferia rotunda
Lupinus, Russell hybrids
Marguerite carnations
Patersonia glabrata
Penstemon barbatus
Plectranthus parviflorus
Potentilla 'Gibson's Scarlet'
Potentilla nepalensis
Sedum rosea
Silene vulgaris subsp. maritima
Sisyrinchium graminoides
Sisyrinchium striatum
Swainsona galegifolia
Tanacetum coccineum 'Brenda'
Viola reichenbachiana
Wachendorfia thyrsiflora

Perennials, spring–early summer flowering, short lived

Actinotus helianthi
Anchusa azurea
Anigozanthos manglesii
Aquilegia caerulea
Aqiulegia, McKana hybrids
Aquilegia vulgaris
Clianthus formosus
Dimorphotheca pluvialis
Dimorphotheca sinuata
Helipterum anthemoides
Myosotis alpestris
Myosotis 'Blue Ball'
Oenothera missouriensis
Papaver alpinum
Papaver orientale

Perennials, summer flowering, sun

Acanthus mollis
Acanthus spinosus
Achillea filipendulina 'Gold Plate'
Achillea millefolium
Agapanthus 'Blue Baby'
Agapanthus praecox subsp.
　orientalis
Alstroemeria aurea
Alstroemeria, Ligtu hybrids
Anaphalis margaritacea
Artemisia lactiflora
Artemisia stelleriana
Blandfordia grandiflora
Centaurea dealbata
Coreopsis verticillata
Crambe maritima
Dictamnus albus
Dierama pulcherrimum
Diplarrhena moraea
Echinacea purpurea
Echinops ritro
Eremurus, Shelford hybrids
Erigeron 'Charity'
Erigeron glaucus
Eryngium agavifolium
Eryngium giganteum
Eryngium × oliverianum
Euphorbia griffithii 'Fireglow'
Gaillardia aristata
Galega officinalis
Gaura lindheimeri
Geranium incanum
Geranium 'Johnson's Blue'
Geranium sanguineum
Gerbera jamesonii
Gypsophila paniculata
　'Bristol Fairy'
Helichrysum hookeri
Hesperis matronalis
Leucanthemum maximum
Liatris spicata
Limonium latifolium
Linum perenne
Lychnis coronaria
Lychnis × haagena
Macleaya cordata
Malva moschata
Oenothera speciosa
Osteospermum ecklonis
Osteospermum jucundum
Oxypetalum caeruleum
Perpetual-flowering carnations
Physostegia virginiana
Platycodon grandiflorus
Salvia azurea
Salvia elegans
Salvia nemorosa
Salvia uliginosa
Scabiosa caucasica
Sidalcea 'Rose Queen'
Stokesia laevis
Telekia speciosa
Tradescantia virginiana

Verbascum olympican
Veronica spicata
Zantedeschia, New Zealand
　Mixed hybrids
Zantedeschia rehmannii

Perennials, summer flowering, shade to part-shade

Aruncus dioicus
Astilbe 'Fanal'
Astilbe chinensis 'Pumila'
Campanula lactiflora
Campanula persicifolia
Diascia barberae
Digitalis × mertonensis
Filipendula vulgaris
Heuchera 'Palace Purple'
Heuchera sanguinea
Libertia grandiflora
Ligularia dentata
　'Desdemona'
Ligularia tussilaginea
　'Aureomaculata'
Liriope spicata
Lobelia 'Vedrariensis'
Lysimachia punctata
Meconopsis betonicifolia
Myosotidium hortensia
Neomarica caerulea
Phlox paniculata
Polemonium caeruleum
Rheum palmatum
　'Atrosanguineum'
Rodgersia podophylla
Roscoea cauteloides
Thalictrum aquilegiifolium
Thalictrum delavayi
Veratrum nigrum

Perennials, winter–early summer flowering

Bergenia cordifolia
Dicentra formosa
Dicentra spectabilis
Helleborus lividus subsp.
　corsicus
Helleborus orientalis
Mertensia virginica
Myosotis colensoi
Paeonia 'Bowl of Beauty'
Paeonia mlokosewitschii
Paeonia officinalis
Paradisea liliastrum
Perpetual-flowering carnations
Pulmonaria angustifolia
Ramonda myconi
Ranunculus aconitifolius
Ranunculus gramineus
Smilacina racemosa
Trillium grandiflorum
Trollius europaeus
Viola odorata
Viola septemtrionalis

Perennials, summer–autumn flowering

Aconitum napellus
Asclepias physocarpa
Aster frikartii 'Mönch'
Aster novae-angliae 'Barr's Pink'
Aster novae-angliae
　'Harrington's Pink'
Aster novi-belgii 'Mulberry'
Cosmos atrosanguineus
Dendranthema grandiflora
Helenium 'Moerheim Beauty'
Helianthus salicifolius
Heliopsis 'Light of Loddon'
Hemerocallis fulva
Hemerocallis, hybrids
Hosta fortunei
Hosta lancifolia
Hosta sieboldiana
Kniphofia ensifolia
Kniphofia 'Maid of Orleans'
Kniphofia praecox
Kniphofia uvaria
Lobelia cardinalis
Rudbeckia fulgida 'Goldsturm'
Rudbeckia laciniata
　'Golden Glow'
Schizostylis coccinea 'Grandiflora'
Sedum spectabile
Solidago 'Golden Wings'
Verbascum nigrum
Yucca filamentosa
Yucca gloriosa

Perennials, ground covers & rock plants, temperate climate

Aethionema 'Warley Rose'
Anthemis tinctoria
Arabis caucasica 'Plena'
Arctotis × hybrida
Armeria maritima
Aubrieta deltoidea
Aurinia saxatilis
Brachycome iberidifolia
Cerastium tomentosum
Convolvulus sabatius
Crepsis incana
Duchesnea indica
Erigeron karvinskianus
Gazania 'Daybreak'
Gazania krebsiana
Gazania, Sunshine hybrids
Globularia cordifolia
Iberis sempervirens
Inula oculis-christi
Lotus berthelotii
Nepeta × faassenii
Phlox subulata
Saponaria ocymoides
Scaevola aemula
Scaevola 'Mauve Clusters'
Sedum spurium
Stachys byzantina
Viola hederacea

Perennials, alpines, ground covers & rock plants, cool climate

Astelia chathamica 'Silver Spear'
Astelia nervosa
Aster alpinus
Celmisia asteliifolia
Celmisia semicordata
Corydalis cashmeriana
Dodecatheon meadia
Epilobium nummularifolium
Epimedium alpinum
Erinus alpinus
Euphorbia amygdaloides subsp.
    robbiae
Galeobdolon argentatum
Gentiana acaulis
Gentiana sino-ornata
Incarvillea delavayi
Mazus radicans
Mimulus luteus
Mimulus moschatus
Nertera granadensis
Ourisia macrophylla
Pachysandra terminalis
Pratia angulata
Prunella grandiflora
Pulsatilla vulgaris
Ranunculus lyallii
Raoulia australis
Saxifraga caespitosa
Saxifraga paniculata
Saxifraga stolinifera
Sempervivum arachnoideum
Sempervivum tectorum
Solidago virgaurea subsp. minuta
Tanacetum ptarmicifolium
Tiarella cordifolia
Veronica prostrata
Wahlenbergia gloriosa

Perennials, sub-shrubs, sun

Argyranthemum frutescens
Artemisia arborescens
Calocephalus brownii
Ceratostigma plumbaginoides
Convolvulus cneorum
Felicia amelloides
Gentiana lutea
Helianthemum nummularium
Hypericum calycinum
Hypericum cerastoides
Leonotis leonurus
Penstemon heterophyllus 'True Blue'
Ptilotus exaltatus
Reinwardtia indica
Romneya coulteri
Solanum pseudocapsicum
Zauschneria californica

Perennials, sub-shrubs, shade to part-shade

Ajuga reptans
Alchemilla mollis
Campanula isophylla

Campanula portenschlagiana
Campanula poscharskyana
Glechoma hederacea
Heterocentron elegans
Lamium maculatum
Mimosa pudica
Parochetus communis
Polygonatum × hybridum
Polygonum affine
Pratia pedunculata
Soleirolia soleirolii
Vinca major
Vinca minor

Perennials, water garden plants

Acorus calamus
Caltha palustris
Cyperus papyrus
Houttuynia cordata 'Chamaeleon'
Lysichiton camtschatcensis
Myosotis scorpioides
Nelumbo nucifera
Nymphaea alba
Nymphaea 'Aurora'
Nymphaea 'Blue Beauty'
Nymphaea nouchali var. caerulea
Peltiphyllum peltatum
Pontederia cordata
Thalia dealbata
Zantedeschia aethiopica

Perennials, for tropical effect

Alpinia purpurata
Alpinia zerumbet
Begonia metallica
Begonia 'Orange Rubra'
Begonia scharfii
Coleus thyrsoideus
Dichorisandra thyrsiflora
Doryanthes excelsa
Hedychium coronarium
Hedychium gardnerianum
Heliconia humilis
Heliconia psittacorum
Impatiens, New Guinea hybrids
Impatiens sodenii
Nicolaia elatior
Phormium 'Dawn'
Phormium tenax 'Bronze Baby'
Phormium tenax 'Purpureum'
Ricinus communis
Sarracenia flava
Strelitzia nicolai
Strelitzia reginae
Xanthorrhoea australis
Zingiber zerumbet

Perennials, irises

Iris, bearded hybrids
Iris ensata
Iris japonica
Iris, Louisiana hybrids
Iris ochroleuca

Iris, Pacific Coast hybrids
Iris pallida 'Variegata'
Iris pseudacorus
Iris spuria hybrids
Iris unguicularis

Perennials, pelargoniums

Pelargonium crispum
Pelargonium cucullatum
Pelargonium × domesticum
Pelargonium echinatum
Pelargonium × fragrans
Pelargonium 'Orange Ricard'
Pelargonium peltatum
Pelargonium rodneyanum
Pelargonium tomentosum
Pelargonium × zonale

Perennials, primulas

Primula denticulata
Primula florindae
Primula japonica
Primula obconica
Primula × polyantha
Primula viallii
Primula vulgaris

SHRUBS

The cultivation of shrubs will only be successful if they are correctly located. A sun-loving shrub will never flower brilliantly in a dark, damp corner; instead, it will sulk for years and produce only one or two flowers.

Always provide adequate water during dry spells as water stress often leaves shrubs vulnerable to insect attack. Using plenty of mulch around plants will help to conserve water. Conversely, planting in water-logged soils may result in shrubs suffering root rot or fungal diseases, so an even balance needs to be found.

Regular, controlled pruning after flowering will result in healthy, well-formed shrubs. Deciduous shrubs should *not* be cut back when the leaves drop off as the next season's flowers may be inadvertently removed as well. If you don't have the time for regular pruning plant the same shrub in groups of three or five, as this will look much better than one straggly individual. Also, lightly fertilize every few months rather than in one big hit; avoid heaping animal manures up around plants' main stems.

Wander through a botanic garden to see shrubs growing in

their prime. At the same time you can discover which shrubs might be suitable for your garden.

Low-growing, frost-hardy, evergreen

Andromeda polifolia
Bauera rubioides
Beaufortia sparsa
Brachyglottis greyi
Brachyglottis monroi
Buxus microphylla var. japonica
Buxus sempervirens
Calluna vulgaris
Cassia artemisioides
Chorizema cordatum
Coleonema pulchrum
Coprosma × kirkii
Daboecia cantabrica
Dampiera diversifolia
Daphne × burkwoodii
Daphne odora
Dillwynia retorta
Epacris impressa
Eremophila glabra
Eriostemon australasius
Eriostemon myoporoides
Euryops pectinatus
Gamolepis chrysanthemoides
Goodenia ovata
Halimium lasianthum
Helichrysum selago
Isopogon anemonifolius
Lambertia formosa
Lechenaultia biloba
Leucadendron 'Safari Sunset'
Leucadendron salignum
Mimulus aurantiacus
Myoporum parvifolium
Myrtus ugni
Nandina domestica 'Nana'
Osmanthus heterophyllus
    'Variegatus'
Pachystegia insignis
Parahebe cataractae
Parahebe lyalli
Parahebe perfoliata
Pernettya mucronata
Philesia magellanica
Phlomis fruticosa
Pimelea prostrata
Polygala chamaebuxus
Potentilla fruticosa 'Tangerine'
Pultenaea pedunculata
Raphiolepis indica
Ruscus aculeatus
Salvia africana-lutea
Santolina chamaecyparissus
Telopea 'Shady Lady'
Telopea speciosissima
Tetratheca ciliata
Thomasia macrocarpa
Thryptomene saxicola
Thuja occidentalis 'Rheingold'
Verticordia plumosa

Low-growing, frost-tender, evergreen

Agapetes serpens
Allamanda neriifolia
Ardisia crispa
Begonia fuchsioides
Bouvardia hybrids
Bouvardia longiflora
Brunfelsia pauciflora
Cantua buxifolia
Cuphea ignea
Drejerella guttata
Heliotropium arborescens
Justicia carnea
Lantana montevidensis
Pentas lanceolata
Russelia juncea
Senecio petasitis
Serruria florida
Streptosolen jamesonii
Wigandia caracasana

Low-growing, frost-hardy, deciduous

Abelia schumannii
Berberis thunbergii
Caryopteris × clandonensis
Cytisus scoparius
Deutzia × rosea
Hypericum patulum
Hypericum 'Rowallane'
Indigofera decora
Prunus glandulosa 'Rosea Plena'
Punica granatum var. nana
Symphoricarpos orbiculatus
Symphoricarpos rivularis

Medium-to tall-growing, frost-hardy, evergreen

Abelia × grandiflora
Abutilon × hybridum
Abutilon megapotamicum
    'Variegatum'
Acokanthera oblongifolia
Alyogyne huegelii
Aucuba japonica
Azara microphylla
Backhousia citriodora
Baeckia virgata
Berberis darwinii
Bursaria spinosa
Carmichaelia odorata
Carpentaria californica
Ceanothus 'Gloire de Versailles'
Ceanothus impressus
Ceratopetalum gummiferum
Chamaelaucium uncinatum
Choisya ternata
Clianthus puniceus
Coprosma repens
Corokia cotoneaster
Corokia × virgata
Coronilla glauca
Corynabutilon vitifolium
Crinodendron hookerianum

Crotolaria agatiflora
Desfontainea spinosa
Dodonaea viscosa
Dryandra spp.
Elaeagnus pungens
Elaeagnus pungens 'Maculata'
Eremophila maculata
Escallonia 'Apple Blossom'
Eucalyptus forrestiana
Eucalyptus macrocarpa
Eucalyptus rhodantha
Euonymus fortunei
Euonymus japonicus
    'Aureomarginatus'
× Fatshedera lizei
Fatsia japonica
Fremontodendron californicum
Garrya elliptica
Gaultheria rupestris
Grewia occidentalis
Greyia sutherlandii
Griselinia littoralis
Hymenolepis parviflora
Hypoestes aristata
Ilex aquifolium
Ilex cornuta
Ilex 'Golden King'
Indigofera australis
Itea ilicifolia
Jasminum mesnyi
Jasminum nudiflorum
Kalmia latifolia
Kunzea baxteri
Ligustrum ovalifolium 'Aureum'
Ligustrum sinense
Lonicera fragrantissima
Lonicera nitida
Lophomyrtus bullata
Loropetalum chinense
Macropiper excelsum
Mahonia aquifolium
Mahonia lomariifolia
Melianthus major
Michelia figo
Mimetes cucullatus
Myrtus communis
Nandina domestica
Notospartium carmichaeliae
Osmanthus fragrans
Persoonia pinifolia
Photinia glabra
Photinia serrulata
Pieris forrestii
Pieris japonica
Pinus mugo
Pisonia brunoniana
Pittosporum eugenioides 'Variegatum'
Pittosporum tenuifolium
Podalyria calyptrata
Polygala myrtifolia 'Grandiflora'
Polygala virgata
Pomaderris apetala
Pomaderris kumeraho
Prostanthera rotundifola
Prunus laurocerasus

Pseudowintera colorata
Pyracantha angustifolia
Pyracantha crenulata
Raphiolepis × delacourii
Rhabdothamnus solandri
Rhamnus alaternus
Rothmannia globosa
Senna corymbosa
Sesbania grandiflora
Skimmia japonica
Spartium junceum
Sutherlandia frutescens
Tecoma stans
Tetrapanax papyriferus
Teucrium fruticans
Viminaria juncea
Westringia fruticosa
Westringia grandifolia

Medium-to tall-growing, frost-tender, evergreen

Bauhinia galpinii
Brugmansia sanguinea
Brugmansia suaveolens
Burchellia bubalina
Caesalpinia pulcherrima
Calliandra tweedii
Carissa macrocarpa
Clerodendrum thomsoniae
Clerodendrum ugandense
Cordyline banksii
Crotolaria capensis
Dais cotinifolia
Dombeya burgessiae
Duranta repens
Eupatorium megalophyllum
Gordonia axillaris
Hovea lanceolata
Iboza riparia
Leucospermum cordifolium
Leucospermum reflexum
Leucospermum tottum
Luculia gratissima
Mackaya bella
Malvaviscus arboreus
Melastoma affine
Murraya paniculata
Mussaenda erythrophylla
Mussaenda frondosa
Ochna serrulata
Plumbago auriculata
Pseudopanax lessonii
Pseudopanax lessonii, hybrids
Rondeletia amoena
Sparmannia africana
Tecomaria capensis
Thevetia peruviana
Tibouchina urvilleana

Medium-to tall-growing, frost-hardy, deciduous

Acer palmatum 'Dissectum
    Atropurpureum'
Acer palmatum 'Dissectum Viridis'

Caesalpinia gilliesii
Callicarpa bodinieri
Chaenomeles speciosa
Chimonanthus praecox
Clerodendrum trichotomum
Clethra alnifolia
Cornus alba
Cornus nuttalli
Corylopsis spicata
Cotinus coggygria
Cytisus × praecox
Dahlia excelsa
Deutzia scabra
Dipelta floribunda
Edgeworthia papyrifera
Enkianthus campanulatus
Erythrina humeana
Euonymus alatus
Euonymus europaeus
Exochorda racemosa
Forsythia × intermedia
Forsythia × intermedia
    'Beatrix Farrand'
Fothergilla major
Kerria japonica
Kolkwitzia amabilis
Lagerstroemia indica
Magnolia quinquepeta
Magnolia stellata
Paeonia lutea
Paeonia suffruticosa
Ribes sanguineum
Sambucus nigra 'Aurea'
Staphylea colchica
Tamarix gallica
Tamarix parviflora
Vitex agnus-castus

Acacia

Acacia acinacea
Acacia boormannii
Acacia cardiophylla
Acacia floribunda
Acacia howittii
Acacia pravissima

Banksia

Banksia coccinea
Banksia ericifolia
Banksia integrifolia

Boronia

Boronia heterophylla
Boronia ledifolia
Boronia mollis
Boronia serrulata

Buddleia

Buddleia davidii
Buddleia globosa
Buddleia salviifolia

Callistemon

Callistemon citrinus
Callistemon 'Harkness'

Callistemon viminalis
Callistemon viminalis 'Hannah Ray'

Camellia

Camellia chrysantha
Camellia granthamiana
Camellia japonica
Camellia japonica 'Adolphe
    Audusson'
Camellia japonica 'Desire'
Camellia japonica 'Elegans'
Camellia japonica 'Kingy-Tsubaki'
Camellia japonica 'Lady Vansittart'
Camellia japonica 'Yamato Nishiki'
Camellia lutchuensis
Camellia reticulata
Camellia sasanqua
Camellia sasanqua 'Hiryu'
Camellia sasanqua 'Yuletide'
Camellia sinensis
Camellia × williamsii
Camellia × williamsii 'Donation'

Cestrum

Cestrum aurantiacum
Cestrum 'Newellii'
Cestrum nocturnum

Cistus

Cistus 'Brilliancy'
Cistus ladanifer
Cistus salviifolius

Correa

Correa alba
Correa 'Dusky Bells'
Correa reflexa

Cotoneaster

Cotoneaster dammeri
Cotoneaster horizontalis
Cotoneaster salicifolius

Erica

Erica bauera
Erica carnea
Erica cerinthoides
Erica cinerea
Erica grandiflora var. grandiflora
Erica mediterranea
Erica regia
Erica speciosa

Euphorbia

Euphorbia fulgens
Euphorbia milii
Euphorbia pulcherrima

Fuchsia

Fuchsia 'Gartenmeister Bonstedt'
Fuchsia magellanica cultivars
Fuchsia magellanica var. gracilis
Fuchsia magellanica var. gracilis
    'Alba'
Fuchsia procumbens

Gardenia

Gardenia augusta 'Florida'
Gardenia augusta 'Radicans'
Gardenia thunbergia

Genista

Genista aetnensis
Genista monosperma
Genista tinctoria

Grevillea

Grevillea banksii
Grevillea biternata
Grevillea 'Boongala Spinebill'
Grevillea glabrata
Grevillea 'Honey Gem'
Grevillea juniperina
Grevillea lavandulacea
Grevillea 'Misty Pink'
Grevillea 'Poorinda Royal Mantle'
Grevillea 'Robyn Gordon'

Hakea

Hakea laurina
Hakea saligna
Hakea sericea

Hebe

Hebe × andersonii 'Variegata'
Hebe × franciscana 'Blue Gem'
Hebe hulkeana
Hebe speciosa

Hibiscus

Hibiscus mutabilis
Hibiscus rosa-sinensis
Hibiscus rosa-sinensis 'Apple
    Blossom'
Hibiscus rosa-sinensis 'Cooperi'
Hibiscus rosa-sinensis 'Madonna'
Hibiscus rosa-sinensis 'Sabrina'
Hibiscus syriacus
Hibiscus syriacus 'Ardens'
Hibiscus syriacus 'Blue Bird'

Hydrangea

Hydrangea aspera var. aspera
Hydrangea macrophylla
Hydrangea macrophylla 'Blue Wave'
Hydrangea paniculata 'Grandiflora'
Hydrangea quercifolia

Juniperus

Juniperus conferta
Juniperus sabina
Juniperus sabina 'Tamariscifolia'

Lavandula

Lavandula angustifolia
Lavandula dentata
Lavandula stoechas

Leptospermum

Leptospermum laevigatum
Leptospermum petersonii

Leptospermum scoparium
    'Red Damask'

Melaleuca

Melaleuca armillaris
Melaleuca fulgens
Melaleuca hypericifolia
Melaleuca incana
Melaleuca nesophylla

Nerium

Nerium oleander
Nerium oleander 'Album'
Nerium oleander 'Punctatum'
Nerium oleander
    'Splendens Variegatum'

Olearia

Olearia arborescens
Olearia macrodonta
Olearia phlogopappa
Olearia traversii

Philadelphus

Philadelphus coronarius
Philadelphus 'Lemoinei'
Philadelphus mexicanus
Philadelphus 'Virginal'

Protea

Protea compacta
Protea cynaroides
Protea grandiceps
Protea neriifolia
Protea 'Pink Ice'
Protea repens 'Guerna'
Protea scolymocephala

Rhododendron

Rhododendron arboreum
Rhododendron augustinii
Rhododendron auriculatum
Rhododendron 'Chrysomanicum'
Rhododendron ciliicalyx
Rhododendron
    'Fragrantissimum'
Rhododendron × gandavense
Rhododendron gumpo azaleas
Rhododendron Hardy hybrids
Rhododendron indica azaleas
Rhododendron jasminiflorum
Rhododendron javanicum
Rhododendron kurume azaleas
Rhododendron lochae
Rhododendron luteum hybrids
Rhododendron maccabeanum
Rhododendron ponticum
Rhododendron trichostomum
Rhododendron yakushimanum

Rosa

Alba roses
Bourbon roses
Centifolia roses
Cluster-flowered bush roses

Damask roses
Ground cover roses
Hybrid Perpetual roses
Large-flowered bush roses
Miniature roses
Modern shrub roses
Moss roses
Patio roses
Polyantha roses
Portland roses
Provence roses
Rosa chinensis
Rosa foetida
Rosa gallica
Rosa glauca
Rosa moyesii
Rosa pimpinellifolia
Rosa rugosa
Rosa virginiana
Tea roses
Wild roses

Spiraea

Spiraea 'Anthony Waterer'
Spiraea cantoniensis
Spiraea thunbergii
Spiraea vanhouttei

Syringa

Syringa 'Maréchal Foch'
Syringa × persica
Syringa 'Souvenir de Louis Spaëth'

Viburnum

Viburnum × burkwoodii
Viburnum carlesii
Viburnum farreri
Viburnum opulus 'Sterile'
Viburnum plicatum 'Mariesii'
Viburnum tinus

Weigela

Weigela florida
Weigela florida 'Eva Ratke'
Weigela florida 'Variegata'

TREES

Choosing the right tree for a
location requires careful consideration—the tiny seedling tree you
admire in a pot may grow to
overwhelm a small garden or cause
major problems to building
foundations and underground
pipes. Always check the mature
height of a tree before purchase
and allow plenty of room for it to
fully develop. Visit an arboretum
to see trees growing at their best
when choosing one for your
garden.

   At planting time dig a hole at
least three times the root volume

and add compost and a complete fertilizer. To help the tree get off to a good start, cut off any coiled or damaged roots, plant firmly and leave a slight depression around the main stem to allow rainwater to collect. Although many trees are drought-tolerant, they still require a good supply of water. As the tree grows, avoid root disturbance at all times and remove any crossing or rubbing branches. Fertilize to the dripline of trees during rainy weather.

When pruning mature trees always cut flush to a branch or trunk, leaving no stubs—these look unsightly and give insect pests and diseases an easy entry to the tree. Seasonal checks for insect pests may be necessary. Small holes or sawdust on the trunk indicate the presence of borers.

Evergreen

Acacia baileyana
Acacia dealbata
Acacia melanoxylon
Acacia pendula
Acacia pycnantha
Agonis flexuosa
Agonis juniperina
Alberta magna
Albizia lophantha
Alectryon excelsa
Alnus jorullensis
Angophora costata
Arbutus menziesii
Arbutus unedo
Banksia serrata
Beaucarnea recurvata
Callicoma serratifolia
Calodendrum capense
Castanospermum australe
Cinnamomum camphora
Citharexylum quadrangulare
Clusia rosea
Cordyline australis
Corynocarpus laevigata
Cussonia spicata
Dombeya tiliacea
Elaeocarpus reticulatus
Ficus rubiginosa
Fuchsia excorticata
Geijera parviflora
Grevillea robusta
Harpephyllum caffrum
Hoheria populnea
Hymenosporum flavum
Lagunaria patersonii
Lophostemon confertus
Magnolia grandiflora
Maytenus boaria
Melaleuca quinquenervia
Metrosideros excelsa

Michelia doltsopa
Nothofagus fusca
Nothofagus moorei
Nothofagus obliqua
Nothofagus solandri
Pittosporum rhombifolium
Pittosporum undulatum
Pseudopanax arboreus
Quercus suber
Quercus virginiana
Rhus pendulina
Rothmannia capensis
Schinus ariera
Schinus terebinthifolia
Schotia brachypetela
Sophora microphylla
Spathodea campanulata
Stenocarpus sinuatus
Stuartia pseudocamellia
Syzygium luehmannii
Syzygium paniculatum
Tamarix aphylla
Toronia toru
Trichilia emetica
Tristaniopsis laurina
Umbellularia californica
Virgilia oroboides
Vitex lucens
Weinmannia racemosa

Semi-deciduous

Bauhinia variegata
Bauhinia variegata 'Candida'
Brachychiton acerifolius
Brachychiton populneus
Citharexylum spinosum
Crataegus pubescens
Erythrina caffra
Erythrina lysistemon
Ficus sur
Firmiana simplex
Jacaranda mimosifolia
Peltophorum africanum
Peltophorum pterocarpum
Plumeria obtusa
Plumeria rubra var. acutifolia
Rauvolfia caffra
Sophora tetraptera
Tipuana tipu

Deciduous, taller than 10 metres

Acer negundo 'Aureo-variegatum'
Acer platanoides 'Crimson King'
Aesculus × carnea
Ailanthus glandulosa
Alnus glutinosa
Betula pendula
Betula pendula 'Dalecarlica'
Catalpa bignonioides
Cedrela sinensis
Cercis canadensis
Cercis siliquastrum
Chorisia speciosa
Cladrastis lutea

Cornus capitata
Cornus florida
Crataegus phaenopyrum
Davidia involucrata
Diospyros kaki
Fagus sylvatica
Fagus sylvaticus f. purpurea
Fraxinus ornus
Fraxinus oxycarpa 'Raywood'
Gleditsia triacanthos 'Sunburst'
Juglans nigra
Laburnum × watereri 'Vossii'
Liquidambar formosana
Liquidambar styraciflua
Liriodendron tulipifera
Maclura pomifera
Magnolia campbellii
Magnolia heptapeta
Magnolia × soulangiana
Melia azedarach
Nyssa sylvatica
Parrotia persica
Paulownia fortunei
Paulownia tomentosa
Phellodendron amurense
Pistacia chinensis
Platanus × acerifolia
Platanus orientalis
Populus alba
Populus deltoides
Populus nigra 'Italica'
Populus tremuloides
Pterocarya fraxinifolia
Quercus lusitanica
Quercus palustris
Quercus robur
Robinia pseudoacacia
Robinia pseudoacacia 'Frisia'
Salix babylonica
Salix 'Chrysocoma'
Salix matsudana 'Tortuosa'
Sassafras albidum
Sophora japonica
Sorbus aria
Sorbus aucuparia
Sorbus hupehensis
Tilia × europaea
Tilia 'Petiolaris'
Ulmus parvifolia
Ulmus procera
Ulmus procera 'Louis van Houtte'
Zelkova serrata

Deciduous, 10 metres or shorter

Acer palmatum
Albizia julibrissin
Aralia elata
Bolusanthus speciosus
Chionanthus virginicus
Corylus avellana 'Contorta'
Crataegus laevigata 'Paul's Scarlet'
Dais cotinifolia
Erythrina crista-galli
Koelreuteria paniculata

Rhus succedanea
Rhus typhina 'Laciniata'
Salix alba
Salix caprea
Sapium sebiferum

Conifers

Abies cephalonica
Abies procera 'Glauca'
Agathis australis
Agathis robusta
Araucaria bidwillii
Araucaria heterophylla
Athrotaxis selaginoides
Calocedrus decurrens
Casuarina cunninghamiana
Casuarina glauca
Cedrus atlantica
Cedrus deodara
Cephalotaxus harringtonia
Chamaecyparis lawsoniana
Chamaecyparis pisifera
Cryptomeria japonica 'Elegans'
Cupressus macrocarpa
Cupressus sempervirens 'Swane's Gold'
Cupressus torulosa
Ginkgo biloba
Juniperus communis
Juniperus virginiana
Lagarostrobus franklinii
Larix decidua
Nageia falcata
Picea pungens 'Koster'
Pinus canariensis
Pinus densiflora
Pinus patula
Pinus pinea
Pinus radiata
Podocarpus henkelii
Podocarpus totara
Pseudotsuga menziesii
Sciadopitys verticillata
Sequoia sempervirens
Sequoiadendron giganteum
Taiwania cryptomerioides
Taxodium distichum
Taxus baccata
Thuja occidentalis
Thuja plicata
Thujopsis dolabrata
Tsuga canadensis

Ornamental, blossom & fruit

Entelea arborescens
Malus 'Aldenhamensis'
Malus floribunda
Malus 'Gorgeous'
Malus ioensis 'Plena'
Prunus × amygdalo-persica
Prunus × blireiana
Prunus campanulata
Prunus cerasifera 'Nigra'
Prunus mume

Prunus serrulata
Prunus serrulata 'Amanogawa'
Prunus serrulata 'Mount Fuji'
Prunus subhirtella 'Pendula'
Prunus × yedoensis
Pyrus calleryana
Pyrus salicifolia 'Pendula'
Pyrus ussuriensis

Tropical & subtropical

Butea monosperma
Cassia fistula
Cassia javanica
Cassia multijuga
Delonix regia
Embothrium coccineum
Kigelia africana
Knightia excelsa
Millettia grandis
Parkinsonia aculeata
Ziziphus jujuba

Eucalyptus species

Eucalyptus citriodora
Eucalyptus ficifolia
Eucalyptus globulus
Eucalyptus haemastoma
Eucalyptus leucoxylon
Eucalyptus mannifera
    subsp. maculosa
Eucalyptus saligna
Eucalyptus torquata

BULBS, CORMS & TUBERS

Bulbs are one of the easiest groups of plants to grow, as they are adaptable to a wide range of climates and growing conditions. Select firm, healthy bulbs when buying and check around the surface or under the outer papery casing for any sign of insects or grubs. Soft, damp spots or grey mould may indicate damage from a fungus. Many bulbs in or near flowering time are now available in pots.

If you live in a warm climate and wish to grow cold-climate bulbs, you may have to give the bulbs an artificial winter in the refrigerator crisper for six weeks before planting. In a cold climate, lift frost-tender bulbs over winter, grow them in pots and plant them out in spring when the danger of frost has passed.

Certain bulbs are known as 'garden escapees'. Freesias in lawns or on roadsides in spring are popular with everyone, however, other bulbs appearing in prime country pasture cause heartache to farmers. Check with a reputable dealer if in doubt about the suitability of any bulb.

Summer flowering, sun

Crinum bulbispermum
Crinum moorei
Crinum × powellii
Cypella herbertii
Eucomis comosa
Galtonia candicans
Gloriosa superba
Hippeastrum advenum
Hymenocallis × festalis
Hymenocallis littoralis
Littonia modesta
Ornithogalum saundersiae
Polianthes tuberosa
Tigridia pavonia
Tulbaghia violacea
Watsonia beatricis

Summer flowering, part-shade

Aristea ensifolia
Belamcanda chinensis
Cardiocrinum giganteum
Nomocharis pardanthina
Pinellia ternata
Sandersonia aurantiaca

Autumn flowering

Amaryllis belladonna
Anemone × hydrida
Colchium autumnale
Colchium 'Lilac Wonder'
Cyclamen hederifolium
Habranthus robustus
Haemanthus coccineus
Nerine bowdenii
Nerine filifolia
Nerine flexuousa 'Alba'
Nerine sarniensis
Sternbergia lutea

Winter flowering

Anemone blanda
Chasmanthe aethiopica
Chasmanthe floribunda var.
    floribunda
Cyclamen coum subsp. caucasicum
Cyclamen coum subsp. coum
Eranthis hyemalis
Galanthus ikariae
Galanthus nivalis

Winter–spring flowering

Bulbine bulbosa
Bulbinella floribunda
Chionodoxa luciliae
Convallaria majalis
Crocus, Dutch hybrids
Crocus flavus
Crocus tomasinianus

Crocus vernus
Erythronium dens-canis
Erythronium 'Pagoda'
Hippeastrum 'Apple Blossom'
Hippeastrum 'Red Lion'
Hyacinthus orientalis
Lachenalia aloides var. aloides
Lachenalia bulbifera
Lachenalia orchioides var. glaucina
Leucojum aestivum
Muscari armeniacum
Muscari armeniacum 'Blue Spike'
Muscari plumosum 'Comosum'
Romulea bulbocodium

Spring flowering, sun

Babiana stricta
Freesia alba
Freesia, Florist's hybrids
Hermodactylus tuberosus
Leucocoryne ixioides odorata
Moraea neopavonia
Moraea spathulata
Sparaxis tricolor
Tristagma uniflora
Tritonia crocata
Watsonia borbonica subsp. borbonica

Spring flowering, shade to part-shade

Anemone coronaria
Arum italicum
Brimeura amethystina
Herbertia drummondii
Hyacinthoides hispanica
Hyacinthoides non-scripta

Summer–autumn flowering

Brunsvigia josephinae
Brunsvigia orientalis
Calostemma purpureum
Crocosmia aurea
Crocosmia crocosmiiflora
Crocosmia crocosmiiflora hybrids
Crocosmia masonorum
Lycoris aurea
Lycoris radiata
Tricyrtis hirta
Vallota speciosa
Zephyranthes candida
Zephyranthes grandiflora

Spring–summer flowering, sun

Albuca canadensis
Anomatheca laxa
Asphodeline lutea
Chlidanthus fragrans
Cyrtanthus mackenii
Cyrtanthis macowanii
Dracunculus vulgaris
Ixia maculata
Ixia paniculata
Ixia viridiflora

Ixiolirion tataricum
Sprekelia formosissima
Triteleia laxa 'Queen Fabiola'
Urceolina peruviana

Spring–summer flowering, shade

Anemone nemorosa
Calochortus albus
Calochortus venustus
Camassia esculenta
Clivia miniata
Clivia nobilis
Nectaroscordum siculum subsp.
    bulgaricum
Notholirion thomsonianum
Ornithogalum thyrsoides
Ranunculus asiaticus
Rhodohypoxis baurii
Scadoxus puniceus
Scilla peruviana
Veltheimia bracteata
Veltheimia capensis

Allium

Allium christophii
Allium moly
Allium narcissiflorum

Begonia

Begonia × tuberhybrida 'Camellia'
    and 'Rose' flowered types
Begonia × tuberhybrida multiflora
Begonia × tuberhybrida pendula

Fritillaria

Fritillaria imperialis
Fritillaria meleagris
Fritillaria persica

Gladiolus

Gladiolus alatus
Gladiolus, Butterfly hybrids
Gladiolus byzantinus
Gladiolus callianthus
Gladiolus carneus
Gladiolus × colvillei
Gladiolus, Large-flowered hybrids
Gladiolus tristis

Iris

Iridodictyum irises
Iris bucharica
Iris, Dutch hybrids
Iris latifolia
Iris tingitana
Juno irises
Xiphium irises

Lilium

Asiatic hybrids
Aurelian hybrids
Lilium auratum
Lilium candidum
Lilium formosanum

Lilium henryi
Lilium lancifolium
Lilium longiflorum
Lilium martagon
Lilium regale
Lilium speciosum
Oriental hybrids
Trumpet hybrids

Narcissus

Narcissus bulbocodium
Narcissus cyclamineus
Narcissus, Double-flowered daffodils
Narcissus jonquilla
Narcissus, Large-cupped daffodils
Narcissus × *odorus*
Narcissus papyraceus
Narcissus poeticus
Narcissus 'Silver Chimes'
Narcissus, Small-cupped daffodils
Narcissus tazetta
Narcissus 'Tête-à-Tête'
Narcissus, Trumpet hybrids

Tulipa

Double early tulips
Double late tulips
Parrot tulips
Rembrandt tulips
Single early tulips
Single late tulips
Tulipa acuminata
Tulipa clusiana
Tulipa fosteriana
Tulipa gesneriana
Tulipa greigii
Tulipa kaufmanniana
Tulipa saxatilis
Tulipa tarda

LAWNS, GROUND COVERS & ORNAMENTAL GRASSES

Cultivating the perfect lawn is the aim of every gardener; it can even develop into an obsession. The key to success is a fine, even, well-drained ground surface that is free from weeds. The chosen grass or ground cover must be suitable for the climate and be able to with-stand its intended use. Softer grasses or ground covers are suitable for occasional foot traffic, while tough grasses are more able to withstand sport, children and dogs. Pests and diseases will take hold in lawns if an unsuitable type has been chosen.

Regular watering is essential to keep a nice green surface but is fairly wasteful of a valuable resource. A brown lawn will quickly recover after adequate rain. Light, frequent applications of fertilizer during the growing season will gain the best results.

Always weed and mow on a regular basis, never mowing the lawn to lower than 20 to 30 millimetres in height. Ground cover lawns may just need the occasional once over with a whipper-snipper or hedge shears if the area is small.

Ornamental grasses, sedges and bamboos grow best in garden conditions that are not overly fertile. Add some moisture-retaining compost to the soil and give them plenty of space to develop. However, some form of barrier may be necessary to stop the spread of vigorous species. Few pests worry them.

Propagation is from seed or by division of clumps in spring. When dividing clumps or cultivating soil near them, be sure to wear protective clothing as the sharp leaf blades and fine hairs can irritate the skin.

Lawns & ground covers

Agrostis tenuis
Cardamine pratensis 'Flore Pleno'
Chlorophytum comosum
Cynodon dactylon
Dichondra micrantha
Festuca elatior
Festuca rubra 'Commutata'
Festuca scoparia
Lolium perenne
Mentha pulegium
Ophiopogon jaburan 'Variegatus'
Pennisetum clandestinum
Pennisetum setaceum
Phyla nodiflora
Poa pratensis
Scleranthus biflorus
Stenotaphrum secundatum
Thymus serpyllum

Ornamental grasses, sedges & bamboos

Arundo donax
Briza media
Butomus umbellatus
Carex elata 'Aurea'
Carex lucida
Catananche caerulea 'Major'
Coix lacryma-jobi
Cortaderia selloana
Festuca glauca
Hordeum junceum
Milium effusum 'Aureum'
Miscanthus sinensis 'Variegatus'
Molinia caerulea
Phalaris arundinacea var. *picta*
Pleioblastus pygmaeus
Restio tetraphyllus
Sasa palmata
Sasa veitchii
Scirpus lacustris subsp. *tabernaemontani* 'Zebrinus'
Stipa pennata

VEGETABLES & HERBS

It was not practicable to include vegetables in the Seasonal Calendars and Cultivation Guidelines in this book. For detailed information refer to books specifically dealing with vegetables.

Herbs are ideally suited to cultivation in cool-temperate climates where summers may be hot but not humid. They can tolerate a range of growing conditions within a garden, from dry, gravelly, limy positions in full sun to cool, moist, partly shaded positions.

Herbs don't need a special garden of their own although this is often more convenient. Prepare the garden position by adding plenty of compost and a light application of fertilizer, or else grow in pots with a good-quality potting mix and some slow-release fertilizer.

Annual herbs grown from seed need to be sown regularly to ensure a constant supply for the kitchen. They tend to bolt to seed when fluctuations of temperature occur. Perennial herbs should be tip pruned regularly for compact growth, checked occasionally for invasions of leaf-eating insects or snails and tidied up in late winter before spring growth starts.

Cuttings strike readily during spring and summer, or herbs can be divided during the cooler months. Frost-tender herbs may need to be moved to a sheltered position during winter in cold climates. Otherwise, their demands are few.

Herbs make good companion plants and mix happily with flowers, vegetables and fruit or they can be used as ground cover among shrubs.

Herbs

Allium sativum
Allium schoenoprasum
Aloysia triphylla
Andropogon nardus
Anethum graveolens
Angelica archangelica
Artemisia dracunculus
Borago officinalis
Carum carvi
Coriandrum sativum
Cuminum cyminum
Curcuma domestica
Elettaria cardamomum
Foeniculum vulgare
Foeniculum vulgare var. *dulce*
Glycyrrhiza glabra
Hyssopus officinalis
Juniperus communis
Laurus nobilis
Lavandula angustifolia
Levisticum officinale
Melissa officinalis
Mentha 'Citrata'
Mentha × *pipirata*
Mentha spicata
Monarda didyma
Nepeta cataria
Ocimum basilicum
Origanum hortensis
Origanum vulgare
Petroselinum crispum
Polygonum persicaria
Rosmarinus officinalis
Salvia elegans
Salvia officinalis
Satureja hortensis
Satureja montana
Symphytum officinale
Thymus × *citriodorus*
Thymus vulgaris
Zingiber officinale

FRUIT TREES, NUT TREES & OTHER FRUITS

The basic requirement for fruit and nut trees is a good, deep, fertile soil that is well-drained. Have your soil tested in a laboratory to see if it is deficient in certain elements; this will save a lot of problems later on after planting. As well, check with a reputable dealer for varieties suitable for your area and for the pollination requirements.

Remember to always choose virus-free or organically grown trees. Prune to allow light and air into the tree and to encourage continuous cropping. Keep the area around trees free of weeds and mulch and fertilize regularly.

Pest and disease problems may be numerous, so always seek expert advice on the safest way of dealing with them. Plant companion plants that are beneficial for insect control and fruit and nut production. Do not attempt to grow cool-temperate fruits in warm climates. If you follow these simple procedures you will soon be able to enjoy the 'fruits' of your labour.

Tropical to subtropical

Annona squamosa
Arachis hypogaea
Araucaria bidwillii
Carica papaya
Citrullus lanatus
Cyphomandra betacea
Litchi chinensis
Macadamia tetraphylla
Mangifera indica
Musa paradisiaca
Musa paradisiaca 'Cavendish'
Musa paradisiaca 'Lady Finger'
Nephelium lappaceum
Persea americana
Psidium cattleianum
Theobroma cacao

Cool-temperate

Castanea sativa
Corylus avellana
Cydonia oblonga
Fragaria alpina
Fragaria vesca
Juglans regia
Malus domestica 'Delicious'
Malus domestica 'Granny Smith'
Malus domestica 'Gravenstein'
Malus domestica 'Johnathon'
Malus 'Gorgeous'
Malus 'John Downie'
Malus pumila
Mespilus germanica
Morus nigra
Pyrus communis 'Buerre Bosc'
Pyrus communis
    'William's Bon Chrétien'
Pyrus pyrifolia
Ribes grossularia
Ribes nigrum
Ribes sativum
Rubus 'Boysen'
Rubus idaeus
Rubus 'Logan'
Vaccinium corymbosum

Warm-temperate

Actinidia chinensis
Ananas comosus
Carya illinoinensis
Ceratonia siliqua
Cucumis melo

Diospyros kaki
Eriobotrya japonica
Feijoa sellowiana
Ficus carica
Fortunella japonica
Olea europaea subsp. *europaea*
Passiflora edulis
Passiflora mollissima
Physalis peruviana
Pinus pinea
Pistacia vera
Punica granatum
Sechium edule
Vitis vinifera

Citrus

Citrus aurantifolia
Citrus auriantium
Citrus limon
Citrus medica
Citrus paradisi
Citrus reticulata
Citrus sinensis
Citrus sinensis 'Washington Navel'
Citrus × *tangelo*

Prunus

Prunus armeniaca
Prunus avium
Prunus cerasus
Prunus domestica
Prunus dulcis
Prunus persica
Prunus persica var. *nectarina*
Prunus salicifolia

INDOOR PLANTS

Cultivation of indoor plants is simple if they are given positions with reasonable light and warmth, kept evenly moist (but slightly drier in winter), and have regular weak doses of liquid fertilizer. Check regularly for pests such as mealy bug, scale insects and mites on the stems and undersides of leaves, as these bugs thrive in warm, enclosed conditions. Also, take plants outside occasionally to wash the dust from the leaves, never allowing them to sit in the sun as they will quickly burn.

If you live in a warm climate, don't be tempted to plant indoor plants in the garden if they have become too big—they may grow even bigger outside and cause real problems.

Propagation is fairly easy, particularly from stem or leaf cuttings during the warmer months. Clump-forming types can be divided once they have

outgrown their pots. Seasonal flowering plants such as cyclamen are best discarded after they flower, as they rarely perform as well the next year.

Indoor foliage plants

Alocasia macrorrhiza
Aspidistra elatior
Calathea makoyana
Calathea zebrina
Callisia navicularis
Codiaeum variegatum
Cordyline terminalis 'Imperialis'
Cryptanthus zonatus
Ctenanthe lubbersiana
Cyperus involucratus
Dieffenbachia 'Amoena'
Dieffenbachia seguine
    'Rudolph Roehrs'
Dizygotheca elegantissima
Epipremnum aureum
Ficus elastica 'Decora'
Ficus lyrata
Hedera helix 'Cripsii'
Hedera helix 'Pittsburgh'
Hemigraphis alternata
Maranta leuconeura var. *kerchoviana*
Monstera deliciosa
Neoregelia carolinae
Neoregelia marmorata
Nepenthes species
Nidularium fulgens
Pedilanthus tithymaloides
Peperomia caperata
Peperomia obtusifolia
Peperomia 'Sweetheart'
Philodendron bipennifolium
Philodendron oxycardium
Philodendron selloum
Pisonia umbellifera 'Variegata'
Polyscias filicifolia
Protasparagus densiflorus 'Sprengeri'
Protasparagus setaceus
Sansevieria trifasciata
Sensevieria trifasciata 'Hahnii'
Sansevieria trifasciata 'Laurentii'
Schefflera actinophylla
Schefflera arboricola
Schefflera digitata
Syngonium podophyllum
Tolmiea menziesii

Indoor flowering and foliage plants

Anthurium scherzerianum
Aphelandra squarrosa 'Louisae'
Begonia auriculata
Begonia × *cheimantha*
    'Gloire de Lorraine'
Begonia 'Cleopatra'
Begonia masoniana
Begonia rex 'Merry Christmas'
Billbergia leptopoda
Billbergia nutans

Billbergia pyramidalis var. *concolor*
Billbergia saundersii
Drosera capensis
Episcia cupreata
Episcia 'Pink Brocade'
Graptophyllum pictum
Guzmania lingulata
Nematanthus gregarius
Serissa foetida
Spathiphyllum 'Mauna Loa'
Spathiphyllum wallisii
Tillandsia cyanea
Tillandsia lindenii

Indoor flowering plants

Costus species
Cyclamen persicum
Gesneria cuneifolia
Hoya bella
Hoya carnosa
Saintpaulia ionantha
Saintpaulia, miniature and
    trailing types

CACTI & SUCCULENTS

Most of these weirdly decorative, fascinating plants are native to arid regions of the world and their cultivation requirements are fairly simple; that is, a warm, dry atmosphere and protection from too much moisture. The misconception arising from this, unfortunately, is that they should all be planted in the hottest, most desolate site in a garden or be allowed to languish in pots without any attention. This simply is not true.

Species such as *Epiphyllum*, *Haworthia* and *Kalanchoe* prefer shade and more fertile soil, and they will tolerate humidity. As a general rule, water well only during the growing or flowering periods, then give them a rest.

Propagation is from seed or cuttings in spring and summer. The stored moisture inside leaves and stems is mucilaginous, or jelly-like, and should be allowed to dry out slightly before propagation. Wear thick gloves when handling cacti with sharp spines and protect your eyes. Watch for pests such as scale insects, mealy bugs and aphids, which tend to hide between cacti spines or in the closely packed rosette leaves of succulents.

Cacti and succulents are fun to collect, so join a cacti and succulent society to obtain the more unusual ones or visit a specialist nursery and talk to an expert.

Adenium multiflorum
Adenium obesum
Aeonium arboreum
    'Schwarzkopf'
Aeonium canariense
Agave americana
Agave victoriae-reginae
Aloe arborescens
Aloe aristata
Aloe barbadensis
Aloe ciliaris
Aloe ferox
Aloe variegata
Aptenia cordifolia
Argyroderma delaetii
Astrophytum asterias
Astrophytum myriostigma
Azureocereus hertlingianus
Beschorneria yuccoides
Borzicactus celsianus
Carnegia gigantea
Carpobrotus edulis
Carpobrotus muirii
Cephalocereus senilis
Cereus peruvianus
Chamaecereus silvestrii
Cleistocactus strausii
Copiapoa cinerea
Copiapoa echinoides
Cotyledon orbiculata
Crassula arborescens
Crassula coccinea
Crassula portulacea
Cyphostemma juttae
Dioscorea elephantipes
Drosanthemum bicolor
Drosanthemum floribundum
Echeveria elegans
Echeveria pulvinata
Echinocactus grusonii
Echinocereus reichenbachii
Echinocereus subinervis
Echinocereus viridiflorus
Echinopsis arachnacantha
Echinopsis 'Green Gold'
Echinopsis multiplex
Epiphyllum hybrids
Epiphyllum oxypetalum
Euphorbia caput-medusae
Euphorbia obesa
Euphorbia trigona
Faucaria tigrina
Fenestraria aurantiaca
Ferocactus hamatacanthus
Furcraea foetida
Gasteria verrucosa
Graptopetalum bellum
Gymnocalycium andreae
Gymnocalycium mihanovichii
Haageocereus versicolor
Hatiora salicornioides

Haworthia bolusii
Haworthia fasciata
Hylocereus undatus
Kalanchoe blossfeldiana
Kalanchoe fedtschenkoi
Kalanchoe tomentosa
Lampranthus aurantiacus
Lampranthus aureus
Lampranthus coccineus
Lithops dorotheae
Lithops glesinae
Lithops karasmontana var. bella
Lithops turbiniformis
Lobivia backebergii
Lobivia bruchii
Lophocereus schottii
Lophophora williamsii
Mammillaria bombycina
Mammillaria elegans
Mammillaria plumosa
Mammillaria zeilmanniana
Mesembryanthemum crystallinum
Nopalxochia ackermannii
Nopalxochia phyllanthoides
    'Deutsche Kaiserin'
Notocactus apricus
Opuntia ficus-indica
Opuntia verschaffeltii
Orbea variegata
Pachyphytum oviferum
Pachypodium baronii var. windsori
Pachypodium lamerei
Parodia formosa
Parodia mutabilis
Parodia nivosa
Pilosocereus palmeri
Portulacaria afra
Rebutia aureiflora
Rebutia muscula
Rebutia pseudodeminuta
Rhipsalidopsis gaetneri
Rhipsalis paradoxa
Schlumbergera × buckleyi
Sedum acre
Sedum aizoon
Sedum morganianum
Sedum × rubrotinctum
Sedum spathulifium
Selenicereus grandiflorus
Senecio articulatus
Stapelia leendertziae
Sulcorebutia arenacea
Thelocactus bicolor
Trichocereus bridgesii
Trichocereus huascha

ORCHIDS

There is a large and varied selection of orchids for warm-temperate climates, or cooler climates if extra protection is given over winter. You don't need a special greenhouse to cultivate orchids as they can be successfully grown outdoors in pots, in garden beds or on the trunks and branches of trees.

There is no great mystery to growing orchids, as their requirements are similar to other groups of plants. The correct temperature is the most important factor for success, although lighting, atmosphere, water supply and food should also be taken into consideration. Propagation is usually carried out in spring by division of well-established clumps. Methods of division will vary depending on the species.

Terrestrial orchids grown in gardens or pots need good drainage and plenty of leaf mould and well-rotted cow manure at planting time. Epiphytes can be grown in pots or on trees; if planting on a tree make sure it is one with rough, fibrous bark that does not shed. Pests and diseases will be kept to a minimum if plants are well fertilized and well watered and there is good air circulation around them. Look out for the dendrobium beetle, though, as it is well known for causing havoc.

If you want to include orchids in your garden, try one or two types first before considering a large and expensive collection.

Ada aurantiaca
Aerides
Angraecum
× Angulocaste hybrids
× Ascocenda hybrids
Ascocentrum curvifolium
Bifrenaria harrisoniae
Bletilla striata
Brassavola nodosa
Brassia verrucosa
× Brassocattleya hybrids
× Brassolaeliocattleya hybrids
Cattleya bifoliate hybrids
Cattleya bowringiana
Cattleya labiata
Cattleya unifoliate hybrids
Coelogyne cristata
Coelogyne pandurata
Cymbidium, large-flowered
    hybrids
Cymbidium, miniature hybrids
Cymbidium species
Cypripedium calceolus
Cypripedium reginae
Dactylorhiza
Dendrobium, cane-stemmed
    hybrids
Dendrobium falcorostrum

Dendrobium kingianum
Dendrobium nobile
Dendrobium speciosum
Dendrobium thyrsiflorum
Disa hybrids
Disa uniflora
Dracula bella
Encyclia cochleata
Disa
Epidendrum ibaguense
Eulophia speciosa
Gongora galeata
Laelia anceps
Laelia 'Coronet'
Laelia purpurata
× Laeliocattleya hybrids
Lycaste virginalis
Masdevallia
Miltoniopsis
Odontoglossum crispum and
    hybrids
Odontoglossum grande
Oncidium papilio
Oncidium varicosum
Paphiopedilum hybrids
Paphiopedilum insigne
Phaius tankervillae
Phalaenopsis amabilis
Pleione bulbocodioides
Pterostylis
Renanthera
Rhyncolaelia digbyana
Sarcochilus
× Sophrocattleya hybrids
Sophrolaeliocattleya hybrids
Sophronitis coccinea
Stanhopea wardii
Thunia marshalliana
Vanda Nellie Morley
Vanda Rothschildiana
Vuylstekeara
Wilsonara hybrids
Zygopetalum mackayi

FERNS, PALMS & CYCADS

Ferns thrive in quite unusual places and often appear on moist rock ledges or among rotting tree trunks where no soil seems to be present, which should give an indication of how best to grow them. They need fairly moist conditions, and plenty of leaf humus compost should be added to the soil before planting. Apply a weak solution of liquid fertilizer in the warmer months. During dry spells ferns may brown off or disappear completely, only to reappear after rain. Inspect new fronds for any sign of pests such as caterpillars, aphids or snails, which may congregate around the fresh young foliage and distort their growth before they unravel.

Palm trees promote the image of carefree days on tropical islands. On a practical level, palms are ideal for growing close to swimming pools and structures as their root systems are not extensive or destructive. Add plenty of compost and a slow-release fertilizer at planting time. Mature palms are heavy feeders and enjoy frequent applications of nitrogenous fertilizer along with an adequate water supply. Pest and disease problems are more likely to occur on dry, underfed palms. Certain caterpillars and grasshoppers can sew the leaves of palms together, resulting in a ragged appearance. Control caterpillars with a bacterial pesticide; grasshoppers with a strong insecticide.

To propagate ferns, collect mature spore by placing older fronds in a paper bag until dry, or carefully divide older plants in spring. Propagation of palms is from seed, although this can be slow and erratic. Prune off old or dead fronds of both ferns and palms regularly to create a neat appearance, although many palms are 'self-cleaning'. Frost can cause considerable damage in cold districts, even to mature specimens, and will cause the fronds of ferns to blacken. In these areas choose hardy specimens and plant out in sheltered sites protected from wind.

Ferns

Adiantum aethiopicum
Adiantum capillus-veneris
Aneimia mexicana
Asplenium australasicum
Asplenium bulbiferum
Athyrium filix-femina
Blechnum discolor
Blechnum fluviatile
Blechnum penna-marina
Blechnum tabulare
Cyathea australis
Cyathea dealbata
Cyathea dregei
Cyrtomium falcatum
Davallia pyxidata
Dicksonia antarctica
Dicksonia squarrosa
Doodia aspera
Doodia media
Doryopteris pedata
Dryopteris filix-mas

Humata tyermannii
Lycopodium phlegmarioides
Marattia salicina
Nephrolepis cordifolia
Nephrolepis exaltata
Onoclea sensibilis
Osmunda regalis
Pellaea rotundifolia
Phymatosoros diversifolius
Platycerium bifurcatum
Platycerium superbum
Polypodium aureum
Polystichum proliferum
Polystichum vestitum var.richardii
Polystichum setiferum
Pteris cretica
Pteris ensiformis
Selaginella uncinata
Todea barbara

Palms & cycads

Archontophoenix cunninghamiana
Arecastrum romanzoffianum
Brahea armata
Butia capitata
Caryota mitis
Caryota urens
Chamaedorea elegans
Chamaedorea erumpens
Chamaerops humilis
Chrysalidocarpus lutescens
Cocos nucifera
Cycas revoluta
Cyrtostachys renda
Encephalartos altensteinii
Euterpe edulis
Hedyscepe canterburyana
Howea belmoreana
Howea forsteriana
Jubaea chilensis
Laccospadix australasica
Lepidozamia peroffskyana
Livistonia australis
Livistonia chinensis
Macrozamia spiralis
Neodypsis decaryi
Phoenix canariensis
Phoenix dactylifera
Rhapis excelsa
Rhopalostylis baueri
Rhopalostylis sapida
Sabal palmetto
Serenoa repens
Washingtonia filifera
Washingtonia robusta

CLIMBERS & CREEPERS

Climbers and creepers are adaptable to a wide range of climates, and even exotic-looking subtropical ones may adapt to cold, frosty areas. They will look ragged, tattered or even leafless over winter, but will spring back into growth once the weather warms up.

Be prepared to work hard with climbers and creepers, pruning, training and tying them up to shape them the way you want; even self-clinging types will wander if they are not controlled. Be careful not to leave training for too long, as brittle stems will break.

Carefully prepare the soil before planting climbers and creepers by digging in plenty of compost and a complete fertilizer to ensure healthy results. Adequate water during the growing season and mulching are also essential practices. Check the seasonal calendar for information on propagation and pest and disease problems.

Warm-temperate to cool-temperate

Actinidia chinensis
Akebia quinata
Ampelopsis brevipedunculata var. maximowiczii
Araujia hortorum
Aristolochia elegans
Asarina erubescens
Bomarea caldasii
Campsis grandiflora
Celastrus orbiculatus
Cissus antarctica
Clematis aristata
Clematis 'Jackmanii'
Clematis 'Lasurstern'
Clematis montana
Clematis 'Nelly Moser'
Clematis paniculata
Clematis paniculata 'Purity'
Clematis tangutica
Clitoria ternatea
Clytostoma callistegioides
Dolichos lablab
Eccremocarpus scaber
Gelsemium sempervirens
Hardenbergia violacea
Hedera canariensis 'Variegata'
Hedera helix
Hibbertia scandens
Hydrangea petiolaris
Jasminum officinale
Jasminum polyanthum
Jasminum sambac
Kadsura japonica
Lapageria rosea
Lathyrus latifolius
Lonicera caprifolium
Lonicera hildebrandiana
Lonicera japonica

Lonicera japonica 'Aurea-reticulata'
Mandevilla × amabilis 'Alice du Pont'
Mandevilla laxa
Mandevilla splendens
Parthenocissus quinquefolia
Parthenocissus tricuspidata
Rosa 'Albéric Barbier'
Rosa 'Albertine'
Rosa banksiae lutea
Rosa 'Climbing Lady Hillingdon'
Rosa 'Handel'
Rosa 'Lorraine Lee'
Rosa 'Madame Alfred Carrière'
Rosa 'Mermaid'
Rosa 'Zéphirine Drouhin'
Schizophragma hydrangeoides
Solanum jasminoides
Solanum seaforthianum
Stephanotis floribunda
Trachelospermum jasminoides
Tropaeolum speciosum
Vitis coignetiae
Vitis vinifera 'Ganzin Glory'
Wisteria chinensis
Wisteria floribunda
Wisteria floribunda 'Alba'
Wisteria floribunda 'Violacea Plena'

Tropical to subtropical

Allamanda cathartica
Antigonon leptopus
Bauhinia corymbosa
Beaumontia grandiflora
Bougainvillea glabra
Bougainvillea 'Hawaiian Gold'
Bougainvillea 'Scarlett O'Hara'
Cardiospermum halicacabum
Combretum bracteosum
Distictis buccinatoria
Ficus pumila
Ipomoea alba
Ipomoea horsfalliae
Ipomoea tuberosa
Kennedia nigricans
Kennedia rubicunda
Macfadyena unguis-cati
Manettia inflata
Mucuna bennettii
Pandorea jasminoides
Pandorea pandorana
Passiflora caerulea
Passiflora coccinea
Petrea volubilis
Phaseolus caracalla
Podranea ricasoliana
Pyrostegia venusta
Quisqualis indica
Solandra maxima
Strongylodon macrobotrys
Tecomanthe speciosa
Thunbergia alata
Thunbergia grandiflora

Seasonal Calendars

| | S U M M E R | | |
PLANT	DECEMBER	JANUARY	FEBRUARY
ANNUALS & PERENNIALS			
Annuals, low-growing, summer–autumn flowering	Mulch plants to conserve water • Peak flowering time	Compost spent flowers • Watch for aphids, white fly; spray with pyrethrum • Peak flowering time • Store saved seed in dry place	Check for nematodes • Cut back straggly growth or replant with fresh seedlings • Spray powdery mildew with a fungicide or wettable sulphur
Annuals, low-growing, spring–summer flowering	Add spent plants to compost • Practise crop rotation	Add spent plants to compost • Practise crop rotation	Add spent plants to compost • Practise crop rotation
Annuals, low-growing, winter–spring flowering	Sharpen and oil garden tools	Look for seed suppliers in garden magazines	Sow seed in seed-raising mix in well-lit sheltered position
Annuals, medium-growing, summer flowering	Water and liquid fertilize regularly • Compost to conserve water, suppress weeds and keep roots cool	Remove spent flowers regularly to prolong flowering • Pick zinnia flowers regularly to prolong flowering • Protect *Impatiens* from afternoon sun	Spray powdery mildew with a fungicide • Prune *Coleus* flower heads as these are not required
Annuals, medium-growing, spring–summer flowering	Cut back flowering stems of *Cheiranthus* to prolong flowering into autumn • Allow *Nigella* to produce decorative seed pods	Remove spent flowers of *Helichrysum* to prolong flowering	Sow seed • As seedlings emerge drench soil with a fungicide to prevent damping off
Annuals, tall-growing, spring–summer flowering	Remove spent flowers • Spray rust and powdery mildew with a fungicide or wettable sulphur • Mulch • Break down organic matter with liquid fertilizer	Remove spent plants and add to compost heap • Practise crop rotation	Sow seed in seed-raising mix • Protect seedlings from damping off using a fungicide
Annuals, tall-growing, summer flowering	Mulch garden • Liquid fertilize • Spray black aphids with pyrethrum • Spray leaf spot with a fungicide	Add spent blooms to compost heap • Spray mildew with a fungicide or wettable sulphur • Ensure adequate water for optimum flowering	Cut back over-grown plants to continue flowering • Store saved seed in dry location • Add summer weeds to compost before seed sets
Annuals, dahlias	Mulch around plants to conserve water • Plant marigolds around plants to discourage nematodes	Liquid fertilize before flowering and then at 2-week intervals • Protect plants from strong wind • Restake	Remove spent flowers to encourage continuous flowering • Spray mould/stem rot or mildew with a fungicide
Perennials, spring–early summer flowering	Prune dead flower stems of *Anigozanthos* and liquid fertilize • Take cuttings of *Swainsona* • Divide *Geum*	*Dianella* produces blue berries after flowering—leave for their decorative value	Water *Anigozanthos* sparingly in humid weather to prevent root rot • Collar rot may occur in *Dianthus* • Gravel mulch
Perennials, spring–early summer flowering, short lived	Plants can be allowed to seed—scatter seed to produce new plants	Provide a mulch of compost but keep away from plant stems	Provide gravel mulch for those that need sharp drainage
Perennials, summer flowering, sun	Flowering begins • Liquid fertilize regularly	Remove spent flowers and add to compost • Ensure adequate water • Soak plants once a week if dry	Tidy up plants, removing old foliage • Liquid fertilize to encourage continuous blooming

Seasonal Calendars

	A U T U M N		
MARCH	**APRIL**	**MAY**	**PLANT**
			ANNUALS & PERENNIALS
Liquid fertilize at 2-week intervals • Peak flowering time • Watch out for snails and caterpillars	Add spent flowers to compost• Peak flowering time • Store saved seed in dry place	Practise crop rotation • Use green manure crops • Wear safety equipment if you plan to spray	*Annuals, low-growing, summer–autumn flowering*
Sow seed • Mix seed with sand for even coverage • Dress soil with dolomite/lime; and/or add compost and complete or slow-release fertilizer	Sow large seed direct	Protect seedlings from transplant shock by drenching soil with liquid fertilizer	*Annuals, low-growing, spring–summer flowering*
Protect seedlings with a fungicide • Dress garden beds with compost, complete or slow-release fertilizer • Sow seed direct	Protect young seedlings from snails	Liquid fertilize with weak solution of fertilizer	*Annuals, low-growing, winter–spring flowering*
Allow *Lunaria* to go to seed for decorative seed pods • Sow seed of *Anchusa* and *Eustoma;* keep moist until germination	Cut back salvias and *Catharanthus;* treat as biennials • Add spent annuals to compost heap	Sow seed • Keep sheltered • For hard-to-get seeds contact a reputable seed supply company	*Annuals, medium-growing, summer flowering*
Plant lupins with a minimum of fertilizer to encourage flowers • Plant seedlings • Apply lime when planting out *Matthiola* and *Gypsophila*	*Campanula, Senecio* and *Schizanthus* need cool, semi-shaded positions • Plant seedlings • Plant *Dianthus* with crown above soil level to avoid phytophthora collar rot	Thin seedlings to avoid overcrowding and diseases • Plant seedlings	*Annuals, medium-growing, spring–summer flowering*
Sow seed • Protect from damping off using a fungicide • Lightly apply dolomite/lime to soil; and/or add compost and slow-release fertilizer	Plant seedlings • Give weak solution of liquid fertilizer once established • Protect from snails	Plant seedlings • Give weak solution of liquid fertilizer once established	*Annuals, tall-growing, spring–summer flowering*
Add compost or waste from worm farm • Store saved seeds in dry location	Add spent plants to compost heap • Practise crop rotation • Remove autumn weeds as they appear	Investigate companion planting to reduce spraying with chemicals	*Annuals, tall-growing, summer flowering*
Flowering continues into autumn • Give extra protection to flowers for exhibition	Flowering continues into autumn • Give extra protection to flowers for exhibition	Lift tubers as foliage dies • Dust with fungicide and store in cool dry place • Leave tubers in well-drained soil	*Annuals, dahlias*
Divide *Dietes, Anigozanthos* and *Sisyrinchium* • Take cuttings of *Dianthus* • Sow seed of *Potentilla* or *Geum*	Plant *Lupinus,* Russel hybrids, now but only in a cold climate • Plants begin winter dormancy • Plants may be divided now	Dig in compost and complete fertilizer • Apply low-phosphorus fertilizer to native plants • Divide *Lupinus,* Russel hybrids, every 3–5 years	*Perennials, spring–early summer flowering*
Cut back old foliage of *Aquilegia* and mulch with compost • Liquid fertilize to encourage new growth	Prepare a cool site for *Anchusa, Aquilegia, Myosotis* and *Papaver,* apply compost and a complete fertilizer	Prepare a cool site for *Anchusa, Aquilegia, Myosotis* and *Papaver;* apply compost and a complete fertilizer	*Perennials, spring–early summer flowering, short lived*
Collect seed from flower stems and store in cool dry place	Order new plants for summer flowering • Check heights and spread • Organize a colour scheme	Cut down old flower stems to ground level • Plants may be divided now • Prepare soil as for September	*Perennials, summer flowering, sun*

Seasonal Calendars

PLANT	JUNE	JULY	AUGUST
ANNUALS & PERENNIALS			
Annuals, low-growing, summer–autumn flowering	Sow seed in hot districts • Sharpen and oil garden tools	Join a garden club to discuss your success with others	Sow seed • Lightly apply dolomite/lime to soil; and/or add compost and apply complete or slow-release fertilizer • In shaded positions add extra cocopeat
Annuals, low-growing, spring–summer flowering	In frosty areas protect plants with loose straw or sow seed in protected position then plant when frost is over	In frosty areas protect plants with loose straw or sow seed in protected position then plant when frost is over	In frosty areas protect plants with loose straw or sow seed in protected position then plant when frost is over
Annuals, low-growing, winter–spring flowering	Protect plants with loose straw in frosty areas	Flowering begins in warm districts	Spray with pyrethrum if aphids appear • Check underside of leaves
Annuals, medium-growing, summer flowering	Protect plants in frosty areas	Sow seed in warm districts • Plant a children's summer garden • Do not use sprays in gardens where children play	Sow seed in warm districts • Plant a children's summer garden • Do not use sprays in gardens where children play
Annuals, medium-growing, spring–summer flowering	Use loose straw to protect against frost, or plant seedlings in spring • Sow seed in hot districts • Protect seedlings from wind	Use loose straw to protect against frost, or plant seedlings in spring • Sow seed in hot districts • Protect seedlings from wind	Avoid planting *Argemone* in warm districts where it can be a weed
Annuals, tall-growing, spring–summer flowering	Protect seedlings from frost in cold districts or plant out when danger of frost is over	Apply loose straw around plants to help protect from cold	Protect plants from cold winds • Give weak solution of liquid fertilizer
Annuals, tall-growing, summer flowering	Look for seed suppliers in garden magazines • Sow seed in hot districts	Start a worm farm for valuable humus and summer fishing	Sow seed ensuring good light and even moisture • Lightly apply dolomite/lime to soil; and/or add compost and complete or slow-release fertilizer
Annuals, dahlias	Join a horticultural society and exhibit your dahlias at their meetings and shows	Join a horticultural society and exhibit your dahlias at their meetings and shows	Join a horticultural society and exhibit your dahlias at their meetings and shows
Perennials, spring–early summer flowering	Protect plants over winter with loose straw	Protect plants over winter with loose straw	Cut back old flowering shoots of *Swainsona*
Perennials, spring–early summer flowering, short lived	Take root cuttings of *Papaver orientale*; plant pieces upright in pot	Protect plants in frosty areas with loose straw	Protect plants in frosty areas with loose straw
Perennials, summer flowering, sun	Protect plants with loose straw in frosty areas	Take root cuttings of *Acanthus, Echinops, Eryngium, Gaillardia, Verbascum*	Take root cuttings of *Acanthus, Echinops, Eryngium, Gaillardia, Verbascum*
Perennials, summer flowering, shade to part-shade	Winter dormancy	Winter dormancy	Winter dormancy

Seasonal Calendars

S P R I N G			
SEPTEMBER	**OCTOBER**	**NOVEMBER**	**PLANT**
			ANNUALS & PERENNIALS
Sow seed or plant seedlings • Water regularly • Protect from snails • Apply liquid fertilizer to increase humus level and prevent transplant shock	Thin seedlings if too close • Plant seedlings in cold districts • Protect seedlings from damping off with a fungicide	Collect rainwater to water garden • Tip prune • Liquid fertilize buds at 2-week intervals	*Annuals, low-growing, summer–autumn flowering*
Pinch out growing tips to encourage bushy growth • Liquid fertilize • Spray leaf spot with a fungicide • Plant seedlings in cool districts	Spray caterpillars with a pesticide • Check undersides of leaves	Flowering continues • If growth is poor, check soil for nematode activity	*Annuals, low-growing, spring–summer flowering*
Remove spent flowers to encourage more blooms • Liquid fertilize at 2-week intervals	Flowering continues	Flowering continues	*Annuals, low-growing, winter–spring flowering*
Plant seed in cold areas after frost has passed • Cultivate soil for direct sowing to fine tilth and add sand	Protect young seedlings from snails and slugs • Practise crop rotation	Lightly trim *Kochia* • As flower buds form, liquid fertilize at 2-week intervals	*Annuals, medium-growing, summer flowering*
Check *Senecio* for leaf miner and spray with an insecticide • Sow seed in cold districts	As buds appear liquid fertilize at 2-week intervals	Spray rust on foliage underside with a fungicide • Spray budworm on *Dianthus* buds with an insecticide • Pick flowers for indoor decoration	*Annuals, medium-growing, spring–summer flowering*
Provide support for flower stems using lightweight stakes • Liquid fertilize regularly • Plant seedlings in cold districts	Spray pests with pyrethrum or use biological control • Liquid fertilize to promote flowering	Remove spent flowers • Spray rust and powdery mildew with a fungicide or wettable sulphur • Mulch • Break down organic matter with liquid fertilizer	*Annuals, tall-growing, spring–summer flowering*
Sow seed direct or plant out seedlings when frost is over • Protect from snails • Apply liquid fertilizer when transplanting seedlings	Thin out seedlings and support with stakes or tripods • Spray caterpillars with an insecticide • Liquid fertilize regularly	Spray cutworms with an insecticide • Control weeds to reduce cutworm population • Sow extra seed to fill in gaps of planting	*Annuals, tall-growing, summer flowering*
Order dahlia tubers from a reputable grower • Apply compost, complete fertilizer or slow-release fertilizer. Avoid high nitrogen fertilizer	Plant tubers • Provide a stake at planting time	Tip prune new growth to encourage bushy compact growth • Set traps to control earwigs • Check for snails in foliage	*Annuals, dahlias*
Main flowering season begins • Plant *Centranthus* in or near rock walls so it can establish in cracks or crevices • Divide *Tanacetum*	Take cuttings of *Plectranthus* and *Silene* • Spray budworm on *Dianthus* with an insecticide	Collect seed as it matures • Sow seed of *Patersonia*	*Perennials, spring–early summer flowering*
Main flowering period • Dead-head flowers to encourage continuous blooming • Fresh seed may be sown	Main flowering period • Dead-head flowers to encourage continuous blooming • Fresh seed may be sown	Cut back plants after flowering • Use for cuttings	*Perennials, spring–early summer flowering, short lived*
Take stem cuttings • Divide plants • Lightly dress soil with lime; dig in compost, complete fertilizer or slow-release fertilizer for perennials	Protect new foliage from snails and slugs • Take stem cuttings from established plants	Mulch around plants to conserve water and suppress weeds • Add water-storing granules in dry areas • Side dress plants with blood and bone	*Perennials, summer flowering, sun*
Plant seed and keep moist until germination in warm sheltered place	Side dress with blood and bone as weather warms up	Mulch garden and compost around plants	*Perennials, summer flowering, shade to part-shade*

	S U M M E R		
PLANT	**DECEMBER**	**JANUARY**	**FEBRUARY**
ANNUALS & PERENNIALS (*continued*)			
Perennials, summer flowering, shade to part-shade	Protect plants from hot drying winds • Ensure plentiful supply of water • Pick flowering stems to encourage more blooms	Liquid fertilize regularly • Check plants for snail or slug damage	Take cuttings from flowering stems of *Lobelia* • Remove old flowers of other plants
Perennials, winter–early summer flowering	Ensure adequate water • Provide a leaf compost and light dressing of blood and bone fertilizer • Protect plants from hot winds	Ensure adequate water • Provide a leaf compost and light dressing of blood and bone fertilizer • Protect plants from hot winds	Ensure adequate water • Provide a leaf compost and light dressing of blood and bone fertilizer • Protect plants from hot winds
Perennials, summer–autumn flowering	Mulch around plants to conserve water and suppress weeds • Watch for snails and slugs	Liquid fertilize regularly • Flowering stems appear	Flowering • Provide stakes for tall flower stems
Perennials, ground covers & rock plants, temperate climate	Mulch plants with compost; side dress with blood and bone fertilizer • Remove spent flowers • Cut back hard plants that overgrow others	Ensure adequate water for *Viola*	Provide gravel mulch in humid conditions to prevent root rot diseases of *Gazania*, *Lotus*, *Arctotis* and *Phlox* • Take semi-ripe cuttings
Perennials, alpines, ground covers & rock plants, cool climate	Plan a drystone wall for plants such as *Erinus alpinus*, *Tanacetum* and *Sempervivum* • Cut back spring-flowering plants	Take semi-ripe cuttings • Provide shade and extra water if required • Remove dead sections from rosette plants	Take semi-ripe cuttings • Provide shade and extra water if required • Remove dead sections from rosette plants
Perennials, sub-shrubs, sun	Mulch plants with compost; side dress with blood and bone • Cuttings may be planted out	Spray leaf miner on *Argyranthemum* with an insecticide • Ensure adequate water during dry spells	Keep *Ptilotus* and *Calocephalus* a little dry during humid weather or root rot may occur
Perennials, sub-shrubs, shade to part-shade	Flowering season • Ensure adequate water during summer months • Apply liquid fertilizer regularly	Flowering season • Ensure adequate water during summer months • Apply liquid fertilizer regularly	Spray powdery mildew on *Ajuga* with a fungicide
Perennials, water garden plants	Feed water plants with slow-release fertilizer	Cut back plants which crowd out others • Take softwood cuttings	Collect ripe seed from water plants • Sow and keep covered
Perennials, for tropical effect	Mulch with compost and ensure adequate water for summer flowering • Keep *Sarracenia* wet during summer months	Spray stem borer on *Hedychium* with an insecticide • Remove toxic flowers from *Ricinus*	Spray stem borer on *Hedychium* with an insecticide • Remove toxic flowers from *Ricinus*
Perennials, irises	Fertilize and mulch	Divide and replant bearded irises	Divide and replant bearded irises
Perennials, pelargoniums	Mulch around plants to conserve water • Water only during very dry spells	Spray bud caterpillars on flowers with an insecticide • Water early morning to discourage black stem rot • Treat soil with a fungicide	Spray rust on *P.* × *zonale* and 'Orange Ricard', with a fungicide or wettable sulphur
Perennials, primulas	Liquid fertilize regularly • Remove old leaves around base of plants	Keep plants moist during summer • Shelter from hot winds	Remove plants after 3 years if flowering diminishes • Spray two-spotted mite with an insecticide • Plant seed of *P.* × *polyantha*
SHRUBS			
Low-growing, frost-hardy, evergreen	Provide adequate water during dry spells • Prune after flowering • Mulch and fertilize	Take semi-ripe cuttings • Tip prune regularly	Check for insect pests • Prune after flowering • Mulch and fertilize
Low-growing, frost-tender, evergreen	Check for summer pests • Provide adequate water during dry spells	Mulch • Fertilize	Ensure good drainage in hot, humid weather
Low-growing, frost-hardy, deciduous	Take softwood cuttings • Mulch and fertilize • Check for summer insect pests	Provide adequate water during dry spells • Mulch	Prune after flowering • Mulch and fertilize

A U T U M N			
MARCH	**APRIL**	**MAY**	**PLANT**
			ANNUALS & PERENNIALS *(continued)*
Prepare soil with generous amount of compost, leaf mould, cocopeat • Order new plants • Collect seed and store in cool, dry place	Divide established plants	Tidy up plants of old flowering stems • Allow leaves from deciduous trees to gently cover established plants	*Perennials, summer flowering, shade to part-shade*
Bergenia produces autumn-coloured foliage	Divide plants • Prepare soil with good quantity of compost and complete fertilizer	Plant together for spring display *Mertensia*, *Dicentra*, and *Ranunculus aconitifolius* in cool, shady spot	*Perennials, winter–early summer flowering*
Peak flowering • Cut flower stems for indoor decoration	Peak flowering	Flowering may continue until frosts • Cut down spent flower stems to ground level • Divide established plants	*Perennials, summer– autumn flowering*
Take cuttings of gazanias and place in peat/sand mix in warm position • Second flush of flowers as weather cools	Plants may be divided • Liquid fertilize plants in warm districts • Sow seed of *Globularia*	Reset stones in rock gardens to protect plants during winter	*Perennials, ground covers & rock plants, temperate climate*
Take cuttings now • Sow seed and keep moist until germination	Divide mat- and clump-forming plants	Protect plants from winter wet if necessary • Plan a raised bed to display alpine plants	*Perennials, alpines, ground covers & rock plants, cool climate*
Plant seed collected during summer; keep moist until germination • Light pruning of plants	*Solanum* produces bright decorative fruit • Spot flowering occurs on other plants	*Solanum* produces bright decorative fruit • Spot flowering occurs on other plants	*Perennials, sub-shrubs, sun*
Campanula continues to flower • Cut back rampant growth of *Vinca*	Plants may be divided now	Allow leaves from deciduous trees to protect plants over winter	*Perennials, sub-shrubs, shade to part-shade*
Divide established clumps of waterside plants	Remove all dead or dying foliage from submerged plants	Cover ponds to keep out leaves from deciduous trees • Move frost-tender plants to warm position	*Perennials, water garden plants*
Add plenty of manure and compost to soil • Establish plants in pots then plant in spring	Cut down flowering stems of *Alpinia*, *Heliconia*, *Strelitzia* and *Hedychium* after they have finished flowering • Tidy up plants	Cut down flowering stems of *Alpinia*, *Heliconia*, *Strelitzia* and *Hedychium* after they have finished flowering • Tidy up plants	*Perennials, for tropical effect*
Sow seed and keep moist until germination	Divide overcrowded clumps • Do not damage rhizomes when digging up • Cut foliage down before replanting	Divide overcrowded clumps • Do not damage rhizomes when digging up • Cut foliage down before replanting	*Perennials, irises*
Take cuttings from overgrown summer growth; strike in sand • Keep cuttings in warm, dry location • Flowering of *P. peltatum* continues	Flowering of *P.* × *zonale* continues • Remove spent flowers	Remove old foliage and tidy up plants	*Perennials, pelargoniums*
Apply blood and bone to existing plants • Remove plants that flower poorly	Prepare garden site with compost and old manure • Select site with heavy or clay soil	Set out new plants • Divide old plants; trim old roots and excess foliage • *P.* × *polyantha* begins to flower	*Perennials, primulas*
			SHRUBS
Choose shrub for right location • Prepare planting site with compost and complete fertilizer	Water well until established • Mulch	Water well until established	*Low-growing, frost-hardy, evergreen*
Lightly prune • Mulch • Lightly fertilize	Add compost and complete fertilizer at planting time	Add compost and complete fertilizer at planting time	*Low-growing, frost-tender, evergreen*
Mulch • Lightly fertilize for winter hardiness	Autumn colour on some plants	Autumn colour on some plants	*Low-growing, frost-hardy, deciduous*

	W I N T E R		
PLANT	JUNE	JULY	AUGUST
ANNUALS & PERENNIALS (continued)			
Perennials, winter– early summer flowering	Lift *Dicentra* and divide with sharp knife into pieces with leaf bud and root attached	New foliage begins to appear • *Viola* in flower in warm districts • *Helleborus* in flower • Take root cuttings of *Paeonia officinalis*	New foliage begins to appear • Some may start to flower • Apply a weak solution of liquid fertilizer
Perennials, summer– autumn flowering	Winter dormancy	Winter dormancy	Protect emerging foliage from snail damage
Perennials, ground covers & rock plants, temperate climate	Protect plants with loose straw in frosty areas • Provide minimum water over winter	Protect plants with loose straw in frosty areas • Provide minimum water over winter	Prepare soil for spring planting with compost and general-purpose fertilizer • Prepare heavy soil with gypsum and drainage material
Perennials, alpines, ground covers & rock plants, cool climate	Protect plants from winter wet if necessary • Plan a raised bed to display alpine plants	Apply loamy soil, cocopeat and sharp sand. Provide extra cocopeat for acid-loving plants such as *Corydalis, Gentiana, Ourisa*	Apply loamy soil, cocopeat and sharp sand. Provide extra cocopeat for acid-loving plants such as *Corydalis, Gentiana, Ourisa*
Perennials, sub-shrubs, sun	Take root cuttings of *Romneya*; plant upright in a pot • Protect plants in areas of severe frost	Take root cuttings of *Romneya*; plant upright in a pot • Protect plants in areas of severe frost	Take root cuttings of *Romneya*; plant upright in a pot • Protect plants in areas of severe frost
Perennials, sub-shrubs, shade to part-shade	Allow leaves from deciduous trees to protect plants over winter	Allow leaves from deciduous trees to protect plants over winter	Allow leaves from deciduous trees to protect plants over winter
Perennials, water garden plants	Cover ponds to keep out leaves from deciduous trees • Move frost-tender plants to warm position	Cover ponds to keep out leaves from deciduous trees • Move frost-tender plants to warm position	Clean and drain pond or water garden in preparation for spring planting
Perennials, for tropical effect	*Coleus thyrsoideus* in flower • Reduce watering and allow plants to rest	Do not take plants of *Xanthorrhoea* or *Doryanthes* from bushland areas. Grow from seed or buy from reputable dealers • Supply a well-drained position	Do not take plants of *Xanthorrhoea* or *Doryanthes* from bushland areas. Grow from seed or buy from reputable dealers • Supply a well-drained position
Perennials, irises	Divide overcrowded clumps, if necessary	Divide overcrowded clumps, if necessary	Divide overcrowded clumps, if necessary
Perennials, pelargoniums	Protect plants in frosty areas • Move to warm location over winter • *P. echinatum* loses leaves—keep dry over winter	Prepare soil for summer display • Dig in compost and complete fertilizer • Ensure good drainage	Protect plants from strong winds • *P. echinatum* in flower
Perennials, primulas	Take root cuttings of *P. denticulata* in 5 cm pieces; propagate in sharp sand	*P. obconica* flowering for indoor use; those with sensitive skin may have allergic reaction to this plant	Remove old flowers from *P. obconica* • Move outdoors as weather warms up
SHRUBS			
Low-growing, frost-hardy, evergreen	Protect young plants in frosty areas	Protect young plants in frosty areas	Protect young plants in frosty areas
Low-growing, frost-tender, evergreen	Provide some winter protection if growing in cold districts	Provide some winter protection if growing in cold districts	Prune after flowering in warm districts • Mulch and fertilize
Low-growing, frost-hardy, deciduous	Take hardwood cuttings	Flowering may begin in warm districts	Flowering may begin
Medium- to tall-growing, frost-hardy, evergreen	Protect young plants in frosty areas	Protect young plants in frosty areas	Protect young plants in frosty areas

S P R I N G			
SEPTEMBER	**OCTOBER**	**NOVEMBER**	**PLANT**
			ANNUALS & PERENNIALS (continued)
Divide clumps of *Pulmonaria* • Plants in flower	Collect and sow seed as it ripens • Stake tall-flowering stems • Spray paeony wilt with a fungicide	*Mertensia* dies down • Pot on self-sown seedlings	*Perennials, winter–early summer flowering*
Divide plants • Take root cuttings of *Verbascum* • Take care in handling *Aconitum* as it is very poisonous	Add compost around plants • Side dress established plants with blood and bone	Side dress plants with blood and bone	*Perennials, summer–autumn flowering*
Flowering • Take stem cuttings	Flowering • Remove spent blooms regularly	Flowering • Plants may be divided or cut back after flowering • Liquid fertilize regularly to prolong flowering into summer	*Perennials, ground covers & rock plants, temperate climate*
Plant out rock garden plants • Fertilize lightly with complete plant food or slow-release fertilizer	Plants begin to flower and continue into summer • Plants may be divided now	Flowering continues • Plants may be divided	*Perennials, alpines, ground covers & rock plants, cool climate*
Liquid fertilize as plants come into bud • For planting out choose a sunny, well-drained, light soil	Main flowering period through to late summer • Take cuttings and strike in sand/peat mix	Flowering • Prune after flowering to maintain good shape	*Perennials, sub-shrubs, sun*
Divide overgrown clumps • Replant with addition of compost	Place flat rocks near plants for them to grow over and keep roots cool • *Polygonum* in flower	Mulch around plants with leaf mould compost; side dress with blood and bone	*Perennials, sub-shrubs, shade to part-shade*
Prepare planting site • Use compost and well-rotted cow manure • Plant marginal, shallow, deep water plants	Divide overcrowded plants • Plant water plants in heavy loam with compost and slow-release fertilizer	Provide gravel mulch over water plants if fish are active	*Perennials, water garden plants*
Divide established clumps of *Alpinia, Hedychium, Phormium and Strelitzia* • Take stem cuttings of *Begonia*	Divide established clumps of *Alpinia, Hedychium, Phormium and Strelitzia* • Take stem cuttings of *Begonia*	Liquid fertilize *Impatiens* to produce good flowers • Give plenty of space for *Nicolaia* and a deep, rich soil	*Perennials, for tropical effect*
Fertilize and mulch	Visit a specialist grower to choose correct iris for your garden • Apply generous compost • Check soil pH before planting	Check plants for any sign of pests and disease, especially discoloured or streaked foliage • Iris may suffer from fungus disease	*Perennials, irises*
Flowering • Remove dead flowers	Tip prune regularly • Plant *P. crispum, P. × fragrans* or *P. tomentosum* near a path so they release fragrance when brushed against	Liquid fertilize regularly to encourage flowers • Cut back *P. cucullatum* after flowering • Plant *P. rodneyanum* in rock garden or as ground cover	*Perennials, pelargoniums*
Sow seed in seed-raising mix • *P. vulgaris* in flower • *P. × polyantha* in full flower	Treat grey mould botrytis with a fungicide • *P. viallii* in flower	Mulch around plants • Remove spent flowers • *P. florindae* in flower • Plant seed of *P. × polyantha* in summer months	*Perennials, primulas*
			SHRUBS
Prune after flowering	Sow seed and keep moist until germination	Take semi-ripe cuttings • Mulch • Lightly fertilize	*Low-growing, frost-hardy, evergreen*
Fertilize established shrubs • Add compost and complete fertilizer at planting time	Add compost and complete fertilizer at planting time	Take semi-ripe cuttings • Mulch	*Low-growing, frost-tender, evergreen*
Flowering	Prune after flowering • Mulch and fertilize	Prune after flowering • Mulch and fertilize	*Low-growing, frost-hardy, deciduous*
Prune after flowering • Mulch and fertilize	Prune after flowering • Mulch and fertilize • Sow seed and keep moist until germination	Take semi-ripe cuttings • Mulch • Lightly fertilize	*Medium- to tall-growing, frost-hardy, evergreen*

PLANT	S U M M E R		
	DECEMBER	JANUARY	FEBRUARY
SHRUBS (continued)			
Medium- to tall-growing, frost-hardy, evergreen	Provide adequate water during dry spells • Prune after flowering • Mulch and fertilize	Take semi-ripe cuttings • Tip prune regularly	Check for insect pests • Prune after flowering • Mulch and fertilize
Medium- to tall-growing, frost-tender, evergreen	Check for summer pests • Provide adequate water during dry spells	Mulch • Fertilize	Ensure good drainage in hot, humid weather
Medium- to tall-growing, frost-hardy, deciduous	Take softwood cuttings • Mulch and fertilize • Check for summer insect pests	Ensure adequate water during dry spells • Mulch	Prune after flowering • Mulch and fertilize
Acacia	Check older plants for signs of borer, sawdust or small holes in trunk	Ensure adequate water during dry spells • Remove galls if they appear at ends of stems	Lightly prune to shape
Banksia	Apply a leaf mulch of gum leaves or *Casuarina* needles	Ensure adequate water during dry spells	Plants may suffer root rot disease in very humid weather
Boronia	Place rocks or logs around plants to keep roots cool	Keep soil moist at all times but not wet	Check soil drainage before planting
Buddleia	*B. globosa* in flower	Prune spent flowers regularly to encourage continuous blooming	Ensure adequate water during dry spells, although all are drought-tolerant
Callistemon	Take cuttings of semi-ripe wood • Apply mulch around plants • Fertilize lightly with complete or slow-release plant food	Ensure adequate water during dry spells • Mulch well • Tip bug may cause wilting and death of young shoots	Check for pests; sawfly larvae may defoliate shrubs, thrip damage may cause deformed leaves
Camellia	Sunburn may cause brown patches on leaves; move plant to cooler location	Check for aphids, thrips and mealy bug • Cut out variegated leaves	Check for aphids, thrips and mealy bug • Cut out variegated leaves
Cestrum	Take semi-ripe or softwood cuttings • Main flowering time	Prune old or recently flowered branches • Collect seed from mature specimens	Provide adequate water to encourage continuous flowering
Cistus	Apply gravel mulch to imitate natural habitat	Ensure adequate water during dry spells, although *Cistus* is drought-tolerant	*Cistus* resents humid weather • Ensure soil is well-drained • Allow free air movement around plants
Correa	Keep moist during dry spells	Keep moist during dry spells	Take cuttings now
Cotoneaster	Take cuttings from semi-ripe wood • Flowering now	*Cotoneaster* is drought-tolerant	Ensure adequate water while lightly fertilizing
Erica	*E. cinerea* in flower • Lightly prune after flowering	*E. speciosa* in flower	Take cuttings now
Euphorbia	Take cuttings of semi-ripe wood • Ensure adequate water	Ensure adequate water	Ensure adequate water
Fuchsia	Liquid fertilize regularly to promote continuous flowering	Provide adequate water during dry spells	Cuttings may be taken • Check leaves for spider mite damage
Gardenia	If growth is stunted dig up plants and check roots for nematode infestation; treat soil with a nematicide or plant marigolds	Ensure adequate water during dry spells or buds may drop • Check for scale insects and mealy bug on leaves and stems	Some leaves will turn yellow and drop off • If foliage is yellow or pale green add iron or magnesium
Genista	Take cuttings now	Prune lightly after flowering	Prune lightly after flowering

A U T U M N			
MARCH	**APRIL**	**MAY**	**PLANT**
			SHRUBS (continued)
Choose right shrub for right location • Prepare planting site with compost and complete fertilizer	Water well until established • Mulch	Water well until established	*Medium- to tall-growing, frost-hardy, evergreen*
Mulch • Lightly prune • Lightly fertilize	Add compost and complete fertilizer at planting time	Add compost and complete fertilizer at planting time	*Medium- to tall-growing, frost-tender, evergreen*
Mulch • Lightly fertilize for winter hardiness	Autumn colour on some plants	Autumn colour on some plants	*Medium- to tall-growing, frost-hardy, deciduous*
Top up mulch around plants • Lightly fertilize with blood and bone • Ensure soil is moist before applying fertilizer	Plant new specimens • Prepare soil by digging in compost and slow-release fertilizer	Plant new specimens • Prepare soil by digging in compost and slow-release fertilizer	*Acacia*
Ensure soil is well-drained before planting	Use a low-phosphorus plant food for banksias	Flowers appear on *B. ericifolia*	*Banksia*
Top up gum leaf mulch around plants • Lightly fertilize	Tip prune for compact growth	——	*Boronia*
Prune old flowers • Apply compost around plants	Prune lightly	Prune lightly	*Buddleia*
Sow seed collected from previous season; keep moist until germination • Lightly fertilize with blood and bone	Mulch well and check again for insect pests	Watch for web worm in dry districts	*Callistemon*
Lightly fertilize; water well before and after • Apply compost mulch around plants; keep away from main stem	Debud large flowering varieties to encourage better size and colour • *C. sasanqua* in flower • Established plants may be moved	Debud	*Camellia*
Mulch around plants • Lightly fertilize	Tip prune regularly	Tip prune regularly	*Cestrum*
Prune lightly • Tip prune	*Cistus* tolerates coastal conditions	*Cistus* tolerates coastal conditions	*Cistus*
Mulch with gum leaves • Tip prune regularly • Lightly fertilize with blood and bone	*Correa* are suitable for coastal gardens	Flowering begins and continues to spring	*Correa*
Red fruits appear • Cut branches for indoor decoration	Collect and sow seed; keep moist until germination	Keep seed moist	*Cotoneaster*
Provide well-drained soil for planting • Check soil pH	Cut old flowering stems and lightly prune to shape	——	*Erica*
Mulch around plants and fertilize	Mulch around plants and fertilize	Leaves fall from *E. pulcherrima* as flowers form	*Euphorbia*
Plant in sites sheltered from strong wind • Apply compost and complete fertilizer before planting • Lightly fertilize established plants	Flowering continues in warm districts	Flowering may continue in warm districts	*Fuchsia*
Tip prune regularly • Lightly fertilize with blood and bone	Second flush of flowers may occur	Second flush of flowers may occur	*Gardenia*
Sow seed now; keep moist until germination	Keep seed moist	——	*Genista*

PLANT	W I N T E R		
	JUNE	JULY	AUGUST
SHRUBS (continued)			
Medium- to tall-growing, frost-tender, evergreen	Provide some winter protection if growing in cold districts	Provide some winter protection if growing in cold districts	Prune after flowering in warm districts • Mulch and fertilize
Medium- to tall-growing, frost-hardy, deciduous	Take hardwood cuttings	Remove dead wood • Flowering may begin in warm districts	Flowering may begin
Acacia	Flowering begins	Flowering	Flowering
Banksia	*B. integrifolia* flowering till September	Provide a gravel mulch around plants in very cold districts	Provide a gravel mulch around plants in very cold districts
Boronia	—	—	Flowering begins
Buddleia	Plants may be deciduous in very cold districts	*B. salviifolia* in flower in warm districts	Cut out old or woody stems
Callistemon	Watch for web worm in dry districts	—	—
Camellia	Select camellias while in flower • Sun may damage flowers in morning if wet with dew	Prepare planting site • Dig in plenty of compost • Add cocopeat • Ensure soil is well-drained to deter root rot	Prune while blooming to remove dead, diseased or straggling branches
Cestrum	Protect plants in very cold districts from frost damage with hessian	Protect plants in very cold districts from frost damage with hessian	Prune frost-damaged stems when all danger of frost is over
Cistus	Protect from very cold winds	Protect from very cold winds	Protect from very cold winds
Correa	Flowering	Flowering	Flowering
Cotoneaster	*C. horizontalis* is deciduous in cold climates	*C. horizontalis* is deciduous in cold climates	*C. horizontalis* is deciduous in cold climates
Erica	—	*E. carnea* in flower • Tolerates a position with some lime	*E. mediterranea* in flower
Euphorbia	Protect flowering stems from strong winds	Protect flowering stems from strong winds	Protect flowering stems from strong winds
Fuchsia	Provide some shelter from cold winter winds	Frost may damage some stems but growth will recommence in spring	Frost may damage some stems but growth will recommence in spring
Gardenia	Provide shelter from cold winds • Move plants in pots to warm location in frosty areas	Provide shelter from cold winds • Move plants in pots to warm location in frosty areas	Provide shelter from cold winds • Move plants in pots to warm location in frosty areas
Genista	—	—	—
Grevillea	Protect young plants in frosty areas; provide gravel mulch and hessian cover at night	Protect young plants in frosty areas; provide gravel mulch and hessian cover at night	Protect young plants in frosty areas; provide gravel mulch and hessian cover at night
Hakea	Protect plants when young in frosty areas; provide gravel mulch and hessian cover at night	Protect plants when young in frosty areas; provide gravel mulch and hessian cover at night	Protect plants when young in frosty areas; provide gravel mulch and hessian cover at night

SEPTEMBER	OCTOBER	NOVEMBER	PLANT
			SHRUBS (continued)
Fertilize established shrubs • Add compost and complete fertilizer at planting time	Add compost and complete fertilizer at planting time	Mulch • Take semi-ripe cuttings	*Medium- to tall-growing, frost-tender, evergreen*
Flowering	Prune after flowering • Mulch and fertilize	Prune after flowering • Mulch and fertilize	*Medium- to tall-growing, frost-hardy, deciduous*
Flowering	Collect ripe seed as covering turns brown • Treat with boiling water before sowing	Lightly prune • Apply mulch • Side dress with slow-release fertilizer	*Acacia*
Flowering	Apply iron chelate for banksias with yellow leaf tips and margins	Treat seed cones with heat to release seed • Lightly prune to shape	*Banksia*
Main flowering period	Main flowering period • Lightly prune after flowering • Use pruned material for cuttings	Sow seed and take cuttings	*Boronia*
Cut back plants • Add compost and complete fertilizer	Give plenty of space when planting	*B. davidii* begins to flower	*Buddleia*
Flowering period	Flowering period	Prune off all spent flowers; retain some for seed collection	*Callistemon*
Test soil pH if growth is unsatisfactory	Prune long or straggly growth • Lightly fertilize with azalea/camellia food	Mulch around plants as weather warms up • Spray scale insect attack with white oil	*Camellia*
Sow seed in seed-raising mix; keep moist until germination • Cut back old or woody shrubs hard to encourage new growth	Mulch around plants • Apply light application of complete fertilizer	Tip prune regularly to encourage bushy shape	*Cestrum*
Ensure perfect drainage when planting • Dig in compost and slow-release fertilizer	Flowering • Prune lightly after flowering	Take cuttings • Apply light application of fertilizer	*Cistus*
Sow seed; keep moist until germination	Prune over lightly	Mulch well and keep moist during dry spells	*Correa*
Lightly prune • Fertilize with complete fertilizer	When planting ensure soil is well drained	Mulch plants to conserve water	*Cotoneaster*
Dig in plenty of compost and complete fertilizer before planting	Sow seed; keep moist until germination	Fertilize and mulch	*Erica*
Choose a warm, sunny location for planting • Prune as flowers fade	Mulch and fertilize • Prune as flowers fade	Ensure adequate water, although most are drought-tolerant	*Euphorbia*
Prune • Fertilize with complete fertilizer	Tip prune young plants for good shape	Mulch around plants with compost	*Fuchsia*
Dig in plenty of compost and complete or slow-release fertilizer • Check soil pH: it should be slightly acid	Prune old or woody plants hard • Fertilize and mulch	Remove spent flowers regularly	*Gardenia*
Prune lightly • Fertilize lightly with complete fertilizer	*Genista* are suitable for coastal conditions	Ensure soil is well-drained • Avoid root disturbance; do not cultivate around *Genista*	*Genista*
Prepare planting site with compost and slow-release, low-phosphorus fertilizer • Ensure excellent drainage	Tip prune regularly or pick bunches of flowers • Fertilize established plants • Sow seed; keep moist until germination	Choose *G. banksii* for salt spray site on coast • Mulch plants with gum leaf mulch	*Grevillea*
Prepare planting site with compost and slow-release, low-phosphorus fertilizer	Sow seed • Avoid root disturbance of established plants; do not cultivate around roots	Mulch plants with gum leaves or leaf litter	*Hakea*

	S U M M E R		
PLANT	**DECEMBER**	**JANUARY**	**FEBRUARY**
SHRUBS (continued)			
Grevillea	Check leaves for caterpillar larvae, especially on tip growth • Spray with pyrethrum • Tip prune regularly	Check plants for scale insects; spray with white oil • Take cuttings of semi-ripe wood	G. 'Robyn Gordon' may develop leaf spot disease in humid weather
Hakea	Take cuttings of semi-ripe wood • Fungal leaf spot may occur	Spray caterpillar larvae with pyrethrum	Root rot diseases may occur • Ensure sharp drainage
Hebe	Ensure adequate water during dry spells, although most are drought-tolerant	Check for damage by scale insects or leaf miner	Downy mildew may occur in humid weather; spray with a fungicide
Hibiscus	Check for insect pests but spray only when necessary	Hibiscus spray will control aphids, caterpillars	Do not apply mulch around stem or collar rot may occur
Hydrangea	Protect from hot dry winds, as foliage and flowers may burn	Provide adequate water and mulch well • Two-spotted mite may cause silvery leaves	Powdery mildew may occur in humid weather; spray with a fungicide • Take cuttings
Juniperus	——	Check for aphids and scale insects	Check for aphids and scale insects
Lavandula	Take semi-ripe cuttings • Provide gravel mulch	Ensure good drainage and air flow around plants • Fertilize lightly	Stems may blacken and die in humid weather • Prune out dead wood
Leptospermum	Take semi-ripe cuttings	Watch out for scale insects which may result in sooty mould on stems	Web-spinning moth larvae may cause damage; remove affected branches
Melaleuca	Sawfly larvae may defoliate plants; spray with pyrethrum • Take semi-ripe cuttings	Ensure adequate water during dry spells, although most will tolerate dry weather	Spray scale insects with white oil • Root rot diseases may occur in humid weather
Nerium	Take semi-ripe cuttings • Striped orange caterpillars may be present; leave to watch turn into butterflies	Nerium are drought-tolerant but provide adequate water for good flowering	Prune as flowers fade • Spray wax or brown scale on stems with white oil
Olearia	Take semi-ripe cuttings	Provide adequate water during dry spells • Prune old flowerheads after flowering	Check for summer pests
Philadelphus	Take softwood cuttings	Provide some shade in warm districts	Ensure adequate water • Mulch • Lightly fertilize
Protea	Take semi-ripe cuttings	Take semi-ripe cuttings	Ensure good drainage in humid conditions
Rhododendron	Apply compost or leaf litter around plants • Supply adequate water • Do not dig around plants as root system may be damaged	Protect plants from hot afternoon sun • Propagation may be carried out by layering	Remove unsprayed plants badly damaged by insect attack • Check for mildew during humid weather; spray with a fungicide
Rosa	Soak plants heavily once a week • Spray scale insects on stems with white oil plus an insecticide; 10:2 ml per litre of water	Spray rust spores with sulphur; remove affected leaves • Prune back sucker growth from base rootstocks • Propagate by budding	Mildew may be a problem on R. 'Souvenir de la Malmaison' • Spray black spot at 2-week intervals • Allow good air movement
Spiraea	Provide adequate water during dry spells • Take softwood cuttings	Provide adequate water during dry spells • Take softwood cuttings	Provide adequate water during dry spells • Take softwood cuttings
Syringa	Mulch around plants and keep moist during dry spells	Take softwood cuttings or buy grafted specimens for greater hardiness	Lightly prune to shape
Viburnum	Take softwood cuttings of deciduous plants • Take semi-ripe cuttings of evergreens • Prune old flower stems • Mulch and fertilize	Ensure adequate water during dry spells • Mulch and fertilize	Two-spotted mite may cause silvering on leaves of V. tinus; control may be difficult
Weigela	Take softwood cuttings • Prune after flowering	Ensure adequate water during dry spells • Mulch • Lightly fertilize	Ensure adequate water during dry spells

A U T U M N			
MARCH	**APRIL**	**MAY**	**PLANT**
			SHRUBS (continued)
Top up mulch after summer and lightly fertilize	Flowering most of the year • Lightly prune regularly	Flowering most of the year • Lightly prune regularly	*Grevillea*
Top up mulch after summer and lightly fertilize	Top up mulch after summer and lightly fertilize	——	*Hakea*
Mulch • Lightly fertilize with complete fertilizer	Some species flowering	Some species flowering	*Hebe*
Select a warm location for planting • Ensure good drainage • Dig in compost • Fertilize once established	Flowering continues	Flowering continues	*Hibiscus*
Flowering	Remove spent flowerheads	Remove spent flowers • Prune out dead wood	*Hydrangea*
——	——	Foliage may start to change colour	*Juniperus*
Some species still flowering	Some species still flowering	Prune off dead flowers to encourage continuous blooming of *L. dentata*	*Lavandula*
Top up mulch • Lightly fertilize	Tip prune regularly	——	*Leptospermum*
Top up mulch • Lightly fertilize	Prune out any old or woody growth	——	*Melaleuca*
Prune old or faded flowers	——	——	*Nerium*
Mulch and fertilize regularly	Some species flowering	Some species flowering	*Olearia*
——	——	Some species may be deciduous over winter	*Philadelphus*
Prepare planting site • Ensure good drainage • Dig in compost • Check soil pH	Main flowering period for many species	Main flowering period for many species	*Protea*
Apply light application of fertilizer and water in well • Take cuttings of semi-ripe wood • Pot on layer-grown plants	Apply mulch of compost or well-rotted animal manure	Spot flowering occurs	*Rhododendron*
Lightly dress soil with dolomite/lime; and/or dig in compost or well-rotted manure, especially in sandy soil • Improve drainage in heavy soil	Allow rose hips to develop on *R. rugosa* • Pick rose hip stems for decoration • Check rose catalogues for varieties suitable for your area	Do not prune old-fashioned roses • Clip annually; shorten back flowering canes • Take cuttings	*Rosa*
Prune lightly to shape	In cold districts autumn leaf colour may occur	In cold districts autumn leaf colour may occur	*Spiraea*
Mulch around established plants with compost	Mulch around established plants with compost	Prepare soil for planting with light application of dolomite/lime and/or compost • Ensure good drainage	*Syringa*
Mulch and fertilize lightly	Autumn leaf colour may occur in deciduous species • Berries may remain on some species	Autumn leaf colour may occur in deciduous species	*Viburnum*
——	Plants begin to lose leaves	Plants continue to lose leaves	*Weigela*

| PLANT | WINTER | | |
	JUNE	JULY	AUGUST
SHRUBS (continued)			
Hebe	Some species flowering	Some species flowering	Some species flowering
Hibiscus	In warm districts cut back by half deciduous hibiscus, *H. mutabilis* and *H. syriacus* • After pruning mulch and fertilize with complete fertilizer	As for June in cooler districts • Use prunings for cutting material	——
Hydrangea	Frost may cause some damage in cold districts; wait until spring to prune	Prune *H. macrophylla* in warm climates; prune to flowering buds	Prune *H. macrophylla* in cool climates; prune to flowering buds
Juniperus	Foliage may change colour	Take hardwood cuttings	Take hardwood cuttings
Lavandula	*L. dentata* produces purple bracts with its flowers	*L. dentata* produces purple bracts with its flowers	*L. dentata* produces purple bracts with its flowers
Leptospermum	——	——	——
Melaleuca	Give some protection to young plants in frosty areas	Give some protection to young plants in frosty areas	Give some protection to young plants in frosty areas
Nerium	Give some protection to young plants in frosty areas	Give some protection to young plants in frosty areas	Give some protection to young plants in frosty areas
Olearia	Some species flowering	Some species flowering	Some species flowering
Philadelphus	Protect *P. mexicanus* from frost; grow in pot and move to sheltered location	Protect *P. mexicanus* from frost; grow in pot and move to sheltered location	Some species may be deciduous
Protea	Provide protection for young plants in frosty areas	Main flowering period for some species	Pick flowers for indoor decoration
Rhododendron	Protect young plants in frosty areas • Move vireyas into warm, sheltered position if in pots	Ensure adequate water if cold dry winds occur	Flowering in warm districts
Rosa	Main pruning time for hybrid Tea and Floribunda roses • Prune back dead, weak or spindly growth • Prune to outward pointing bud	Pruning continues • Bare-rooted roses may be purchased • Water well after planting • When planting, do not allow roots to be bent	Spray scale insects with 25 ml white oil per litre of water • To exhibit roses, join a horticultural society
Spiraea	——	——	——
Syringa	Select grafted, bare-rooted, healthy specimens for planting	Prune out dead or weak shoots on established plants	Some species may flower again
Viburnum	*V. tinus* begins to flower	*V. tinus* flowering	*V. tinus* flowering
Weigela	Deciduous	Deciduous	Deciduous

	S P R I N G		
SEPTEMBER	**OCTOBER**	**NOVEMBER**	**PLANT**
			SHRUBS (continued)
Some species flowering	Prune back old flowering stems • Fertilize and water well	Mulch around plants • Take semi-ripe cuttings	*Hebe*
In warm districts prune *H. rosa-sinensis* • Prune by a third; use for cuttings • Mulch and fertilize after pruning	In warm districts prune *H. rosa-sisensis* • Prune by a third; use for cuttings • Mulch and fertilize after pruning	Flowering season November to May • Fertilize regularly with a high-potassium fertilizer • Mulch well but keep away from stem	*Hibiscus*
Prune *H. paniculata* 'Grandiflora' and *H. quercifolia* by a half • Mulch and fertilize well	Select a cool, moist location for planting • Dig in plenty of compost and complete fertilizer • Take cuttings	Liquid fertilize as buds develop • Take cuttings	*Hydrangea*
Choose a sunny, well-drained site for planting • Sandy soil and coastal conditions are fine	Prune regularly and lightly but growth is naturally compact • Fertilize lightly with complete plant food	——	*Juniperus*
When planting add light application of dolomite/lime to soil; and/or compost and complete fertilizer	Tip prune young plants to ensure compact habit	Prune lightly after or during flowering	*Lavandula*
Sow seed; keep moist until germination	Ensure good drainage • Fertilize and mulch	Tip prune regularly or use hedge shears over plants	*Leptospermum*
Ensure good drainage; all enjoy some moisture in soil • Lightly fertilize with blood and bone	Tip prune regularly, especially young plants • Prune old flowering stems and collect seed • Sow seed; keep moist until germination	Mulch around plants to conserve water	*Melaleuca*
Leaves and flowers are poisonous • Sow seed; keep moist until germination • Prune to shape • Mulch and fertilize	Tip prune young plants to promote compact growth or train as a standard	Old plants may be cut back hard	*Nerium*
Prune to shape; cut out old or dead wood	Mulch and fertilize lightly	Some species flowering	*Olearia*
Prepare planting site • Dig in compost and complete fertilizer	Provide part-shade in hot districts	Prune after flowering, especially older shoots • Mulch and fertilize	*Philadelphus*
Prune lightly • Some species flowering	Fertilize only with fertilizer recommended for proteas	Keep mulch away from main stem	*Protea*
Main flowering period • Apply compost or well-rotted animal manure and a complete plant food for rhododendrons • Water well before planting	Main flowering period • Do not water directly onto flowers • Spray petal blight with a fungicide • Take cuttings 6 weeks after flowering	Prune lightly after flowering • If growth is poor, check soil pH • Use a systemic insecticide regularly to combat insect damage on leaves	*Rhododendron*
Protect new foliage from wind damage • In warmer districts some roses begin to flower • Choose roses by perfume	Use commercial preparations on insect pests and diseases; or plant garlic or onion chives and encourage birds • Prune after flowering	Mulch thickly with straw or old cow manure; keep mulch away from plant stems • Lightly apply fertilizer every 6 weeks	*Rosa*
Cut out old or dead wood	Prune after flowering • Cut out old or dead wood	Fertilize and mulch well	*Spiraea*
——	Fertilize young plants with complete fertilizer once established	Prune old flowers; prune to shape after flowering	*Syringa*
Prepare planting site • Dig in plenty of compost and complete fertilizer	Ensure adequate water as flower buds develop	Prune out any old or dead wood • Pick flowering branches for indoor decoration	*Viburnum*
Hard prune overgrown or straggly specimens • Mulch and fertilize	Prepare planting site • Dig in plenty of compost and complete fertilizer	Tip prune young plants regularly	*Weigela*

| PLANT | S U M M E R | | |
	DECEMBER	JANUARY	FEBRUARY
TREES			
Evergreen	Take semi-ripe cuttings	Watch for summer insect pests	Watch for summer insect pests
Semi-deciduous	Take semi-ripe cuttings	Mulch and fertilize	Watch for summer insect pests
Deciduous, all heights	Mulch and lightly fertilize	Watch for summer insect pests	Watch for summer insect pests
Conifers	Ensure adequate water during dry spells • Check stems for scale insect damage	Thrips may cause brown or dead foliage in patches • Check *Picea* for mite damage in warm climates	Thrips may cause brown or dead foliage in patches • Check *Picea* for mite damage in warm climates
Ornamental, blossom & fruit	Provide cool, moist conditions over summer • Mulch and fertilize	Prune back suckers near ground level • Watch for insect pests during warm weather	Watch for insect pests during warm weather
Tropical & subtropical	Prune young trees to shape • Mulch	Mulch to conserve water	Watch for summer insect pests
Eucalyptus species	Provide adequate water during dry spells	Watch for summer insect pests • Prune young trees of unwanted branches	Watch for summer insect pests • Ensure soil is well-drained or root rot diseases may occur
BULBS, CORMS & TUBERS			
Summer flowering, sun	Provide adequate water during summer months while plants are in active growth and producing flowers	Flowering • Provide adequate water	Flowering • Provide adequate water
Summer flowering, part-shade	Flowering	Flowering	*Cardiocrinum* produce decorative seed pods after flowering • Save seed of *Nomocharis* for spring planting • Collect bulbils from *Pinella* for planting
Autumn flowering	Allow summer sun to bake bulbs in the ground	Plant bulbs • Prepare soil with plenty of compost and slow-release fertilizer for bulbs • Select *Colchium* for a cool climate	Foliage dies down • Reduce watering • Plant bulbs just below ground in hot districts or with neck exposed in cool districts
Winter flowering	—	—	Order bulbs from a reputable grower • Sow seed of *Cyclamen* in compost seed-raising mix • Pot on when large enough
Winter-spring flowering	Dormancy	Plant out *Bulbinella* with top at ground level in humus-rich soil • Plant *Hippeastrum* in a similar way	Dig in plenty of compost and well-rotted cow manure • Make sure soil is well-drained or bulbs may rot • Order bulbs
Spring flowering, sun	Dry off over summer • Bulbs may be lifted and stored in a cool, dry place or left to naturalize	Dry off (bake) bulbs in ground	Divide clumps of *Hermodactylus* • Sow seed of *Freesia* • Add light dressing of lime/dolomite compost and blood and bone fertilizer to soil
Spring flowering, shade to part-shade	—	—	Sow *Anemone* seed in sandy loam or seed-raising mix • Add compost, leaf mould and a low-nitrogen fertilizer to soil
Summer-autumn flowering	Maintain adequate water during dry spells	Bulbs begin main flowering season and continue to autumn	Plant *Lycoris* bulbs 100 mm deep, 150 mm apart; choose a part-shaded site

A U T U M N

MARCH	APRIL	MAY	PLANT
			TREES
Plant new trees in areas of autumn rains • Lightly fertilize established trees	Plant new trees in areas of autumn rains • Lightly fertilize established trees	Plant new trees in areas of autumn rains • Lightly fertilize established trees	*Evergreen*
Prepare planting site for new trees; dig in plenty of compost and complete fertilizer • Be sure soil is well-drained	Water well until established if no rain is present	Leaves may fall in cool districts	*Semi-deciduous*
Prepare planting site 2 months ahead if planting bare-rooted young trees	Dig in plenty of compost and complete fertilizer	Transplant established trees	*Deciduous, all heights*
Prepare soil for planting; dig in compost and complete fertilizer	Water new plants until established	Take hardwood cuttings from young plants	*Conifers*
Prepare planting site 2 months ahead for bare-rooted trees	Dig in plenty of compost and complete fertilizer	Ornamental fruit appear on *Malus* • Leave on tree for winter or until fallen	*Ornamental, blossom & fruit*
Mulch and lightly fertilize	Prune out dead or diseased limbs • Plant new trees during rainy weather	Prune out dead or diseased limbs • Plant new trees during rainy weather	*Tropical & subtropical*
Plant if autumn rains occur	Plant if autumn rains occur	Plant if autumn rains occur	*Eucalyptus species*
			BULBS, CORMS & TUBERS
Plant *Eucomis* bulbs just below soil surface • Plant *Ornithogalum* 75 mm deep, 150 mm apart • Divide established clumps of *Tulbaghia*	Plant *Crinum* bulbs in warm climates or divide clumps and plant offsets • Plant just below soil surface • Plant *Watsonia* 90 mm deep	Plant *Cypella* bulbs or divide established clumps • Divide clumps of *Polianthes* and store in dry sand • Reduce watering of *Littonia*	*Summer flowering, sun*
Plant *Belamcanda* bulbs 50 mm deep, 200 mm apart • Choose a cold site to plant *Nomocharis* 50 mm deep, 200 mm apart • Do not divide	Divide *Aristea* roots • Plant 300 mm apart • Plant *Sandersonia* just below soil surface 300 mm apart	Mulch planting area with compost or allow leaves from deciduous trees to gently cover bulbs	*Summer flowering, part-shade*
Flowering • Top dress areas of naturalized bulbs with compost • Liquid fertilize regularly	Flowering • Divide established clumps • Replant healthiest bulbs • Plant *Nerine filifolia* in a rock garden	Flowering • Fertilize bulbs as foliage begins to die down • *Nerine* foliage appears after flowering	*Autumn flowering*
Select a cool, moist, part-shaded site under deciduous trees or shrubs • Add compost, leaf mould and slow-release fertilizer • Plant bulbs 50 mm deep	Select a cool, moist, part-shaded site under deciduous trees or shrubs • Add compost, leaf mould and slow-release fertilizer • Plant bulbs 50 mm deep	—	*Winter flowering*
Keep *Bulbinella* moist • Plant *Crocus* under deciduous trees in cold climates • In warm areas plant in pots of bulb fibre	Plant *Lachenalia* and *Muscari* in rock garden or as path edging • Plant *Muscari* and *Lachenalia* together for brilliant colour combination	Divide *Convallaria* when over-crowded • Plant *Romulea* in pots if a weed problem	*Winter-spring flowering*
Bulb planting time • Keep moist during growing season • Plant *Babiana*, *Freesia* and *Hermodactylus*	Bulb planting time • Plant *Leucocoryne*, *Moraea*, *Sparaxis*, *Tritonia* and *Watsonia*	Bulb planting time • Divide established clumps of *Moraea*	*Spring flowering, sun*
Plant *Brimeura* in mountain rock gardens • Choose a cool, moist spot for *Cyclamen*, *Arum* and *Hyacinthoides*	Plants left in ground may be divided • Plant *Anemone*, *Arum*, *Brimeura*, *Cyclamen* and *Hyacinthoides*	Spot flowering of *Anemone* occurs if plants have been left in ground • Allow deciduous leaves to fall over bulb planting area	*Spring flowering, shade to part-shade*
Choose a sunny spot, well-drained soil enriched with compost and low-nitrogen bulb fertilizer for bulb planting • Plant *Brunsvigia* bulbs	Water bulbs well once foliage appears • Liquid fertilize when flower buds appear • Protect from snails	Plant *Calostemma* bulbs 100 mm deep, 150 mm apart • Plant *Zephyranthes* bulbs 100 mm deep, 75 mm apart	*Summer-autumn flowering*

| PLANT | W I N T E R | | |
	JUNE	JULY	AUGUST
TREES			
Evergreen	Mulch around young trees with gravel to protect from frost, or cover with hessian tent overnight	Mulch around young trees with gravel to protect from frost, or cover with hessian tent overnight	Mulch around young trees with gravel to protect from frost, or cover with hessian tent overnight
Semi-deciduous	Some loss of leaves in all districts	Some loss of leaves in all districts	Some loss of leaves in all districts
Deciduous, all heights	Protect young trees with gravel mulch in frosty areas	Take hardwood cuttings	Remove old or dead branches • Shape trees if not flowering species
Conifers	Frost damage may occur on young plants of *Abies* and *Picea*	Take hardwood cuttings	Take hardwood cuttings
Ornamental, blossom & fruit	Purchase bare-rooted trees • Do not let roots turn up when planting • Prune branches lightly after planting	Water well until established, but not excessively	Water well until established, but not excessively
Tropical & subtropical	Protect trees from cold wind if growing in cooler climates	Protect trees from cold wind if growing in cooler climates	Protect trees from cold wind if growing in cooler climates
Eucalyptus species	Protect young trees with gravel mulch in frosty areas	Protect young trees with gravel mulch in frosty areas	Protect young trees with gravel mulch in frosty areas
BULBS, CORMS & TUBERS			
Summer flowering, sun	Bulbs are hardy but give some protection in areas of severe frost with mulch of loose straw or dry leaves	As for June • Plant *Hymenocallis* bulbs in warm climates 150 mm deep, 200 mm apart; add compost and slow-release bulb food	Plant *Tigridia* corms 75 mm deep, 150 mm apart • Divide established clumps after several years
Summer flowering, part-shade	Protect *Sandersonia* in frosty areas or wait until spring to plant • Keep in pots over winter	Protect *Sandersonia* in frosty areas or wait until spring to plant • Keep in pots over winter	Protect *Sandersonia* in frosty areas or wait until spring to plant • Keep in pots over winter
Autumn flowering	Flowers die down • Allow leaves from deciduous trees to cover areas of naturalized bulbs	Protect bulbs with loose straw in areas of severe frost	Protect bulbs with loose straw in areas of severe frost
Winter flowering	Main flowering period • Pick flowering stems of *Chasmanthe*	Main flowering period • Do not allow to seed as it may escape to native bushland areas	Leave bulbs to naturalize
Winter-spring flowering	Protect *Hippeastrum* and *Lachenalia* bulbs in frosty areas with mulch of loose straw • Bulb flowering time from now until October	Protect *Hippeastrum* and *Lachenalia* bulbs in frosty areas with mulch of loose straw	Protect *Hippeastrum* flower buds from snails • Liquid fertilize regularly • Plant in pots for indoor decoration
Spring flowering, sun	Provide shelter from cold winds • Protect bulbs in frosty areas with mulch of loose straw or dry leaves	Provide shelter from cold winds • Protect bulbs in frosty areas with mulch of loose straw or dry leaves	Flowering may start in warm climates • Pick naturalized flowers from roadsides and bushland areas
Spring flowering, shade to part-shade	Protect *Anemone* in frosty areas with mulch of loose straw	*Arum* foliage looks good in association with snowdrops	Ensure adequate moisture if cold dry winds occur
Summer-autumn flowering	Plant *Crocosmia* bulbs 100 mm deep, 150 mm apart; confine bulbs as they may be invasive	Protect *Lycoris* bulbs in frosty areas • They are in leaf during winter and rest during summer	Plant *Vallota* bulbs 50 mm deep, 150 mm apart
Spring-summer flowering, sun	Plant *Dracunculus* tubers in sheltered position • Plant *Urceolina* just below soil surface	In frost-prone areas grow potted bulbs in sheltered positions; plant out in spring • If left in ground protect with straw	Divide *Asphodeline*'s thick, fleshy roots • Divide and separate corms of *Herbertia*

S P R I N G			
SEPTEMBER	**OCTOBER**	**NOVEMBER**	**PLANT**
			TREES
Sow tree seed and keep moist until germination	Mulch well as weather warms up • Fertilize during periods of good rain	Mulch well as weather warms up • Fertilize during periods of good rain	*Evergreen*
Prune new trees to shape or after flowering	Mulch and fertilize • Water well	Sow seed and keep moist until germination	*Semi-deciduous*
Plant container specimens	Prune blossom trees after flowering • Mulch and fertilize	Ensure adequate water during dry spells	*Deciduous, all heights*
Prune new growth (not old wood) to shape • Sow seed after giving cold treatment if necessary	Mulch and fertilize	Mulch and fertilize	*Conifers*
Cut flowering branches for indoor decoration	Mulch and fertilize well	Prune after flowering except *Prunus* × *blireiana* and *P. cerasifera* 'Nigra'; shorten interior branches only	*Ornamental, blossom & fruit*
Mulch and fertilize • Plant seed and keep moist until germination	Prune established trees after flowering • Take cuttings	Prepare planting site if good rains have fallen • Dig in compost and complete fertilizer	*Tropical & subtropical*
Prepare ground for planting; dig large hole and incorporate compost and fertilizer suitable for *Eucalyptus*	Planting continues if rain is present	Fertilize young trees with slow-release fertilizer • Mulch	*Eucalyptus species*
			BULBS, CORMS & TUBERS
Plant *Eucomis* bulbs just below soil surface • Add compost and blood and bone fertilizer • Plant *Polianthes tuberosa* 50 mm deep, 125 mm apart	Plant *Crinum* bulbs or seed in cool climates; seed may take several years to flower • Protect plants from snails and slugs	Mulch bulbs with compost and liquid fertilize regularly • Give *Crinum* plenty of room to grow • Support *Littonia* with stakes or canes	*Summer flowering, sun*
Plant *Cardiocrinum* just below soil surface • Allow plenty of space for it to develop • Divide *Pinellia* and plant offsets	Liquid fertilize as weather warms up and plants emerge or grow • Plant seed of *Nomocharis*	Keep soil evenly moist over summer	*Summer flowering, part-shade*
Divide bulbs if overcrowded • Sow seed from previous autumn flowering	Plant fresh bulbs	Provide adequate water while foliage is growing; reduce watering once foliage has died down	*Autumn flowering*
Allow bulbs to dry off after flowering • Mulch area with compost • Bulbs may be divided	—	—	*Winter flowering*
Cut off old flower stalks of *Convallaria* • Divide *Lachenalia* after flowering • Thin and replant healthiest bulbs	Buy fresh *Hyacinthus* bulbs each year as quality may decline • Sprinkle over blood and bone fertilizer as bulbs die down	Dormancy	*Winter-spring flowering*
Main flowering period • Pick flowers regularly for indoor decoration	Main flowering period	Cut off flower stems after flowering • Collect seed for autumn sowing • Destroy surplus bulbs if growing close to bushland areas	*Spring flowering, sun*
Bulbs in full flower • Pick flowers for indoor decoration	Flowering continues • When flowering finishes lift *Anemone* and store in a cool, dry place	Leave bulbs in ground to die off • Mulch with compost • Leave flowering stems of *Arum* to produce berries for decoration	*Spring flowering, shade to part-shade*
Plant *Tricyrtis* bulbs 50 mm deep, 300 mm apart; choose a cool, humus-rich site	Sow seed of bulbs in pots until planted out • Divide large clumps of bulbs if overcrowded • Give away excess bulbs	Maintain adequate water during dry spells	*Summer-autumn flowering*
Sow seed of *Albuca* and keep moist until germinated • Plant bulbs of *Sprekelia*	Main flowering period begins and continues into summer	*Dracunculus* flowers emit a strong odour; do not plant near open windows	*Spring-summer flowering, sun*

	S U M M E R		
PLANT	**DECEMBER**	**JANUARY**	**FEBRUARY**
BULBS, CORMS & TUBERS (continued)			
Spring-summer flowering, sun	Allow bulbs to dry off during summer • A hot dry summer will help bulbs mature	Allow bulbs to dry off during summer • A hot dry summer will help bulbs mature	Allow bulbs to dry off during summer • A hot dry summer will help bulbs mature
Spring-summer flowering, shade	Keep *Notholirion* dry over summer • Plant offsets of *Nectaroscordum*	Sow seed of *Ranunculus* and keep in a cool, moist position until ready to plant • Reduce watering of *Veltheimia* over summer	In warm climates choose *Ranunculus*, *Ornithogalum* and *Scadoxus* for autumn planting • Add plenty of compost and fertilizer to soil
Allium	*A. moly* and *A. narcissiflorum* in flower through summer	Leave foliage to die down • Pick flowers for indoor decoration	Divide plants of *A. christophii*
Begonia	Liquid fertilize regularly • Do not water foliage if possible, just fine spray occasionally • Support flowering stems with thin wire stakes	Plan a visit to begonia festivals	Plan a visit to begonia festivals
Fritillaria	Store bulbs in a cool, dry place	Store bulbs in a cool, dry place	In cold climates prepare part-shaded, moist sites with compost, cocopeat and leaf mould • *Fritillaria* tolerate slightly limy soil
Gladiolus	*G. × colvillei* in flower • Leave 3 or 4 leaves when flowers are cut	Lift when foliage starts to fade • Cut off stems when dry	Add compost and complete fertilizer • Dig sandy loam into heavy soils • *G. callianthus* in flower
Iris	*I. bucharica* requires a hot, dry summer	Order bulbs • Deeply cultivate and add compost, old manure and bulb fertilizer to soil	Chill bulbs in refrigerator if planting in warm climates
Lilium	*L. formosanum* in flower until April • Mulch with compost and fertilizer • Cut flower stems for decoration • Remove seed capsules as flowers fade	*L. longiflorum* the most reliable in warm climates • *L. regale* and *L. martagon* in flower • Take scales from flowering plants for propagation	Plant bulbs in a sunny spot in well-drained, rich, neutral soil • Allow plants to die down naturally after flowering
Narcissus	Cut down yellow foliage • Lift bulbs and store in cool, dry place in warm climates	Order bulbs from catalogue of reputable grower	Planting may start in cool districts • Lightly dress soil with dolomite/lime; and/or add compost, well-rotted manure and small amount of complete fertilizer
Tulipa	Check stored bulbs for any insect damage • Keep only large healthy bulbs • Use insecticide granules to control insect attack	Order bulbs from reputable grower • Plan a garden display keeping same variety together for mass planting	In warm climates store bulbs in refrigerator before planting • Lightly dress soil with dolomite/lime; and/or add compost and well-rotted manure
LAWNS, GROUND COVERS & ORNAMENTAL GRASSES			
Lawns & ground covers	Mow on a regular basis and never lower than 20-30 mm	Insect pests active	Fungal diseases common during humid weather
Ornamental grasses, sedges & bamboos	Cut out dead or overcrowded stems • Cut back vigorous creeping grasses	If planting out, restrict growth around bamboos by placing barrier	If planting out, restrict growth around bamboos by placing barrier • Sow annual grasses
HERBS	Harvest and dry leaf herbs • Place paper bag over annual herbs to collect seed	Mulch garden to conserve water • In cooler districts semi-woody cuttings may be taken of *Aloysia*, *Laurus* and *Thymus*	Take cuttings of all perennial herbs • Plant seed of *Borago*, *Carum*, *Coriandrum*, *Cuminum* and *Satureja hortensis* for autumn harvest

A U T U M N			
MARCH	**APRIL**	**MAY**	**PLANT**
			BULBS, CORMS & TUBERS (continued)
Divide *Cyrtanthus* clumps • They thrive in warm climates and suit rock gardens or edges • Sow bulb seed in seed-raising mix	Plant bulbs of *Ixia, Anomatheca* and *Ixiolirion* 75 mm deep • Lightly apply compost, but average soil is tolerated	Plant *Triteleia* 75 mm deep • Plant *Chlidanthus* 125 mm deep	*Spring-summer flowering, sun*
Plan a woodland garden in a part-shaded site with plenty of leaf compost for *Anemone, Calochortus, Nectaroscordum* and *Scilla*	Plant out *Ranunculus* tubers with claws pointing downwards; mass plant in large groups in sunny position • Main bulb planting time	Plant bulbs • Foliage on *Ranunculus* should be glossy green • Plant *Veltheimia* in warm climates, place in pots in cold climates	*Spring-summer flowering, shade*
Plant all seed varieties; sow in seed-raising mix and pot when ready • Top dress with blood and bone as flowering dies down	Plant bulbs of all varieties when available	Plant bulbs of all varieties when available	*Allium*
Plan a visit to begonia festivals	Lift tubers and allow to dry off in a cool position • Do not remove soil from around tuber until dry	Glasshouse-grown plants are available for indoor use most of the year • Store dry tubers in sand or dry peat moss	*Begonia*
In cold climates only plant *Fritillaria* 100 mm deep, 200 mm apart • Choose *F. persica* for warmer climates	—	—	*Fritillaria*
Plant *G. carneus* for spring flowering	Plant *G. alatus* and *G.* × *colvillei* in a rock garden	Corms can be planted in subtropical or warm climates • Plant at intervals to flower over a long period	*Gladiolus*
Plant bulbs 100 mm deep, 100 mm apart	Plant bulbs 100 mm deep, 100 mm apart	Plant bulbs 100 mm deep, 100 mm apart	*Iris*
Sow seed in seed-raising mix mulched with organic matter • Raise in pots • Divide and plant new bulbs in conditioned soil	Try growing *L. auratum* and *L. speciosum* from bulblets found around the main underground stem • Plant bulbs immediately; do not store	Avoid using garden forks as bulbs damage easily • Glasshouse-grown plants available in flower • After flowering, plant out in spring	*Lilium*
Plant *N. bulbocodium* and *N. cyclamineus* in rock gardens or pots 50 mm deep, 30 mm apart • Plant others 80 mm deep, 100 mm apart	Lightly fertilize bulbs with blood and bone if naturalized in garden position	Overwatering bulbs may cause bulb rot • Watch for aphids when buds form • Otherwise few problems	*Narcissus*
Planting time • Overplant with violas, forget-me-nots or virginian stock • Plant same varieties en masse • Add slow-release bulb fertilizer	Planting time	Planting time	*Tulipa*
			LAWNS, GROUND COVERS & ORNAMENTAL GRASSES
Lightly fertilize in warm districts or prepare site for planting	Lightly fertilize in warm districts or prepare site for planting	Check for appearance of winter weeds	*Lawns & ground covers*
If planting out, restrict growth around bamboos by placing barrier • Sow annual grasses	Remove flowerheads if grass presents a weed problem	Collect seed when fully ripe for sowing	*Ornamental grasses, sedges & bamboos*
Continue to take cuttings • Harvest ripening seed • Cut back flowering stems and old foliage of *Petroselinum*	Harvest and dry last of summer herbs • Remove spent annual herbs and add to compost heap	Cut back overgrown plants • Dig up and pot *Andropogon, Curcuma, Elettaria* and *Zingiber* in frosty areas • Shelter over winter	**HERBS**

PLANT	W I N T E R		
	JUNE	JULY	AUGUST
BULBS, CORMS & TUBERS (continued)			
Spring-summer flowering, shade	Plant *Notholirion* in a cool, sheltered site • *Veltheimia* requires water during winter to ensure good flowering • Reduce watering of *Clivia* to encourage flower production	Keep *Rhodohypoxis* dry over winter • Protect *Scadoxus* from frost in cold districts; keep in a dry, sheltered position	Liquid fertilize as buds develop in spring
Allium	──	──	──
Begonia	Turn potted specimens on their sides to dry off	Prepare a soil mix for begonias with equal parts loamy soil, leaf mould or cocopeat, cow manure and blood and bone	Tubers available until November; begin in pots of sand/peat before transferring to garden; ensure tubers are firm
Fritillaria	Watch for winter weeds	Watch for winter weeds	Watch for winter weeds
Gladiolus	Lift bulbs in cold areas or wet areas • Dust bulbs with sulphur fungicide and store in a cool, dry place	Store bulbs in a cool, dry place	Store bulbs in a cool, dry place
Iris	Watch for winter weeds	Provide shelter from strong winds as bulbs sprout • Mulch with compost • Liquid fertilize regularly	Mosaic virus may cause yellow-green streaks on new foliage; destroy bulbs/rhizomes • Spray for aphids with an insecticide • Bulbs begin to flower
Lilium	Do not water bulbs over winter	Frost-hardy over winter	Frost-hardy over winter
Narcissus	Protect plants from strong wind • Odd flowers of *N. jonquilla* and *N. papyraceus* may appear in warm climates	Liquid fertilize as flower stems appear • *N. papyraceus* and *N. tazetta* in flower	*N. cyclamineus* and *N. jonquilla* in flower
Tulipa	Watch for winter weeds	Watch for winter weeds	──
LAWNS, GROUND COVERS & ORNAMENTAL GRASSES			
Lawns & ground covers	Warm-climate grasses may lose green colour in cool winters • Oversow with cool-climate grass	Warm-climate grasses may lose green colour in cool winters • Oversow with cool-climate grass	Warm-climate grasses may lose green colour in cool winters • Oversow with cool-climate grass
Ornamental grasses, sedges & bamboos	Leave flowers for winter decoration in cold districts	Leave flowers for winter decoration in cold districts	Leave flowers for winter decoration in cold districts
HERBS	*Allium* and *Artemisia* go dormant • Divide established clumps of *Glycyrrhiza*, *Melissa* and *Symphytum*	Mulch plants with loose straw over winter	Sow annual seeds under glass or in protected position • Lightly apply dolomite/lime to soil; and/or dig in compost and complete fertilizer
FRUIT TREES, NUT TREES & OTHER FRUITS			
Tropical to subtropical	Protect plants from cold winds if growing in warm-temperate climates	Protect plants from cold winds if growing in warm-temperate climates	Protect plants from cold winds if growing in warm-temperate climates

S P R I N G			
SEPTEMBER	**OCTOBER**	**NOVEMBER**	**PLANT**
			BULBS, CORMS & TUBERS (continued)
Flowering time begins and continues to early summer	Pick flowers regularly for indoor decoration	Remove spent plants of *Ranunculus*; save the best tubers for replanting next autumn	*Spring-summer flowering, shade*
A. christophii in flower	Divide clumps of *A. moly* and *A. narcissiflorum*	Provide adequate water for summer flowering species	*Allium*
Sow seed with fine sand for even distribution; sow in moist, fine compost and cover with thin layer of sand	Pot seedlings in sand/peat; mix 50:50 with slow-release fertilizer • Don't overpot • Keep in greenhouse or warm position	If planting out acclimatize plants gradually • Prepare position with well-rotted cow manure and compost	*Begonia*
Flowering in cold climates	Flowering	Lift bulbs from areas with high summer rain or bulbs may rot • Store in cool, dry place	*Fritillaria*
Plant bulbs in cool climates • Add compost and lightly apply blood and bone fertilizer • Discard insect-damaged bulbs	*Gladiolus* hybrids flowering in warm climates • *G. carneus* and *G. tristis* in flower	Thrips may cause silver streaks on leaves and deformed flowers • Spray with an insecticide • Stake flowering stems in windy sites	*Gladiolus*
Main flowering period • Pick flowers in early morning	Main flowering period • Remove spent flowers	Flowering continues in cold districts • Leave bulbs in ground for 3–5 years or lift and store in cool, dry place	*Iris*
Avoid overwatering as bulbs may rot • Mulch soil with compost and water infrequently • Apply a liquid fertilizer once growth starts	*L. candidum* in flower • Protect flower stems from snail damage • Stake tall flower stems	*L. longiflorum* and *L. lancifolium* in flower • Cucumber mosaic virus may cause reflexing and streaking of leaves; destroy affected plants	*Lilium*
N. bulbocodium and *N.* 'Silver Chimes' in flower • Pick flower stems just before they open	*N. odorus* in flower • Main flowering period for hybrids	Liquid fertilize as bulbs die down • Tie up untidy foliage • Divide bulbs every 2–3 years • Reduce watering	*Narcissus*
Rock garden tulips *T. clusiana, T. saxitalis* and *T. tarda* in flower • Save seed of species tulips for sowing	Spray aphids with an insecticide • Spray tulip fire botrytis with a fungicide • Do not water overhead • Practise crop rotation	Remove spent flowers and let bulbs die down naturally • Lift bulbs and store in cool, dry place	*Tulipa*
			LAWNS, GROUND COVERS & ORNAMENTAL GRASSES
Lightly fertilize • Ensure adequate water	Prepare planting site • Ensure good drainage • Cultivate to fine tilth and even surface • Water well until established	Top dress with sandy loam • Lightly fertilize • Check for appearance of summer weeds	*Lawns & ground covers*
Clumps may be divided and planted out • Sow annual grasses	Cut out dead or overcrowded stems • Cut back vigorous creeping grasses	Cut out dead or overcrowded stems • Cut back vigorous creeping grasses	*Ornamental grasses, sedges & bamboos*
Lightly apply dolomite/lime; and/or dig in compost and fertilize with complete or slow-release fertilizer • Prune dead wood • Sow seed of annuals in seed-raising mix	Plant out established plants in pots • Harvest young, fresh leaves • Apply a weak solution of liquid fertilizer	Tip prune plants regularly to ensure compact growth • Give extra water to *Andropogon* during dry spells	*HERBS*
			FRUIT TREES, NUT TREES & OTHER FRUITS
Provide adequate water during dry spells • Mulch well	Ensure good pollination of flowers	Apply mulch • Suppress weeds • Plant companion plants	*Tropical to subtropical*

| | S U M M E R | | |
PLANT	DECEMBER	JANUARY	FEBRUARY
FRUIT TREES, NUT TREES & OTHER FRUITS			
Tropical to subtropical	Establish plants during or after good summer rain • Add plenty of compost and a complete fertilizer to soil	Fertilize established plants • Buy virus-free stock, or from an organic grower	Check for seasonal pests • Identify common problems and treat with safe methods
Cool-temperate	Practise fruit thinning so that branches are able to support crop • Mulch well to inhibit summer weeds	Use trickle irrigation in dry spells • Summer prune where appropriate to encourage fruit • Bud graft tree fruits onto suitable rootstocks • Take softwood cuttings of *Vaccinium*	Bud graft tree fruits onto suitable rootstocks • Take softwood cuttings of *Vaccinium* • Check for branches rubbing against stakes
Warm-temperate	Use netting to protect developing fruit from birds • Mulch well with compost to inhibit summer weeds	Fertilize regularly with appropriate fertilizer • Water well during dry spells • Summer prune where appropriate to encourage regular crops of high yields	Check for pests and diseases weekly • Allow good air circulation to discourage mildew in humid weather
Citrus	Check for pests • If leaves discoloured check for signs of deficiency in soil	Leaf miner a common problem; cut off damaged section or spray weekly with an insecticide in cool of day	Mulch and fertilize
Prunus	Provide adequate water during dry spells	Clear summer weeds away from trees	Clear summer weeds away from trees
CACTI & SUCCULENTS	Check for pests on spines or under leaves	Protect tender specimens from really hot sun	Root rot diseases occur in humid weather • Top up gravel mulch and ensure good drainage
ORCHIDS	Mist spray daily • Water daily as required in late afternoon • Fertilize weekly with weak solution of orchid food	Control pests and diseases as noticed • Allow air circulation around pots • Fertilize weekly with weak solution of orchid food	Ensure plants are dry before watering • Check for fungal diseases in humid weather
FERNS, PALMS & CYCADS			
Ferns	Provide cool, misty water during dry spells • Mulch around plants with leaf litter • Lightly apply liquid fertilizer	Protect fronds from hot dry winds • Check under leaf hairs for insect pests; use weak strength insecticides or hand remove	Aphids may cause deformed fronds • Check stems for scale insects
Palms & cycads	Transplant palms during rainy weather • Clean up old fronds	Ensure adequate water during dry spells	Ensure adequate water during dry spells
CLIMBERS & CREEPERS			
Warm-temperate to cool-temperate	Mulch around climbers as weather heats up • Ensure adequate water during dry spells • Frequent wilting indicates dryness	Cut overgrowth back drastically • Fertilize, mulch, water well and growth should recommence • Spray caterpillars on large-leafed climbers with a pesticide	Prune back early summer-flowering climbers • Lightly apply complete fertilizer • If soil is badly drained root rot diseases may occur
Tropical to subtropical	Plant evergreen climbers especially during or after rain periods • Check foliage for damage by caterpillars; spray with a pesticide	Mulch around plants	Prune back excess or rampant growth regularly

A U T U M N			
MARCH	**APRIL**	**MAY**	**PLANT**
			FRUIT TREES, NUT TREES & OTHER FRUITS
Prune to allow light into tree or shape for good fruiting	Mulch • Fertilize lightly	Mulch • Fertilize lightly	*Tropical to subtropical*
Prepare ground for planting bare-rooted trees and soft fruit canes • Dig in compost or well-rotted manures • Check soil pH, ideal 6–6.5 except *Vaccinium*, 4–4.5	Check pollination requirements of new plants • Provide stakes or trellis support where appropriate • Take hardwood cuttings from established plants	Check pollination requirements of new plants • Take hardwood cuttings from established plants	*Cool-temperate*
Prepare ground for planting container grown speciments • Dig in compost or well-rotted manure • Avoid over-rich soil • Check pollination requirements	Provide sturdy trellis or stake where necessary • Take hardwood cuttings from established plants • Remove spent annual summer fruit plants and add to compost	Check pollination requirements • Take hardwood cuttings from established plants • Remove spent annual summer fruit plants and add to compost	*Warm-temperate*
Mulch and fertilize	Ensure adequate water at all times	Ensure adequate water at all times	*Citrus*
Prepare planting site for new trees several months in advance	Dig in compost and a complete fertilizer • Ensure soil is well-drained	Check with a reputable dealer for trees suitable for your area • Spray bacterial canker with a fungicide at leaf fall	*Prunus*
Root rot diseases occur in humid weather • Ensure perfect drainage	Remove old dry leaves around succulents • Repot crowded specimens	Tidy up plants and move to a sunny location • Give weak solution of liquid fertilizer for those with flower buds	***CACTI & SUCCULENTS***
Provide a well-lit position but not direct sunlight	Protect flower spikes from insect damage	Reduce watering in deciduous species	***ORCHIDS***
			FERNS, PALMS & CYCADS
Check for caterpillars on young fronds • Lightly fertilize	Remove old fronds • Tidy up plants	Reduce watering during cooler weather	*Ferns*
Mulch and fertilize	Check leaf tips of potted specimens—they turn brown if humidity is low • Spray foliage	If trying palms in cold districts, protect well when young • Move potted specimens to warm, sheltered location	*Palms & cycads*
			CLIMBERS & CREEPERS
Check undersides of leaves for snails • Spray scale insects with white oil • Ants climbing up stems indicates presence of scale insects	Deciduous climbers show autumn colour • Prune after all leaves have dropped or growth may recommence while weather is still warm	Dig plenty of compost and a complete fertilizer into soil • Allow adequate space and strong support • Ensure soil is well-drained	*Warm-temperate to cool-temperate*
Summer flowering species continue to flower in warm districts	Second flush of flowers for spring flowering species	Mulch well around plants and ensure adequate water during dry spells	*Tropical to subtropical*

PLANT	**W I N** JUNE	**T E** JULY	**R** AUGUST
FRUIT TREES, NUT TREES & OTHER FRUITS (continued)			
Cool-temperate	Soak bare-rooted plants well, before planting out; do not plant below graft level • Protect young plants from severe frost with hessian tent • Prune established plants to maintain high yields	Protect young plants from severe frost with hessian tent • Prune established plants to maintain high yields • Prune to open structure to allow light to reach ripening fruit	Protect young plants from severe frost with hessian tent • Prune established plants to maintain high yields • Prune to open structure to allow light to reach ripening fruit
Warm-temperate	Prune young trees to shape, selecting three main branches to form a framework • Cut back current season's fruited shoots	Cut back current season's fruited shoots • Remove crossing or rubbing branches or dead wood • Protect young plants from cold winds or frosty spells	Remove crossing or rubbing branches or dead wood • Protect young plants from cold winds or frosty spells
Citrus	Choose citrus species by cold tolerance; some are frost-tender	Cold winds and frost can cause foliage to curl up	Fertilize and mulch
Prunus	Buy virus-free stock from an organic grower	Buy virus-free stock from an organic grower	Water young plants well until established but not excessively • Check for blossom diseases on established trees
CACTI & SUCCULENTS	Some are frost-hardy but most will require protection over winter • Move pots to sheltered location	Reduce watering for all except those in flower	Bring potted specimens indoors for brief periods and place in a well-lit location
ORCHIDS	Maintain warmth during winter months where appropriate • Reduce watering	Maintain warmth during winter months where appropriate • Reduce watering	Maintain warmth during winter months where appropriate • Reduce watering
FERNS, PALMS & CYCADS			
Ferns	Protect ferns in very cold districts • Fronds may blacken when frost damaged	Protect from cold dry winds in all districts	Protect from cold dry winds in all districts
Palms & cycads	Check for appearance of scale insects • Use very weak solution of white oil or an insecticide	Water containerised plants sparingly	Water containerised plants sparingly
CLIMBERS & CREEPERS			
Warm-temperate to cool-temperate	Add gypsum to badly drained heavy soil or use gravel at bottom of planting hole • Protect frost-tender species with hessian	Planting time for deciduous climbers • Prune climbing roses and *Vitis* • Prune *Wisteria* to flowering buds	Wait until all frost danger is passed before cutting back damaged climbers
Tropical to subtropical	Mulch well around plants and ensure adequate water during dry spells • Protect with hessian blanket if growing in cold districts	Frost may kill tropical species or damage subtropical ones • Growth may recommence from base in spring	Prune back cold- or wind-damaged stems in warm districts • Side dress established plants with blood and bone or complete fertilizer

S P R I N G

SEPTEMBER	OCTOBER	NOVEMBER	PLANT
			FRUIT TREES, NUT TREES & OTHER FRUITS (continued)
Plant out container grown fruit/nuts; choose healthy sturdy plants, less than 2 years old • Spread a balanced fertilizer just beyond where branches grow • Check weekly for signs of pest or disease problems	Mulch established plants with compost and manure • Check for leaf discolouration as a nutrient deficiency may be present • Protect buds and developing fruit from birds	Spread a balanced fertilizer just beyond where branches grow • Check weekly for signs of pest or disease problems • Protect buds and developing fruit from birds	*Cool-temperate*
Plant out annual fruits of *Cucumis*, *Physalis* and *Sechium* • Fertilize established plants to encourage fruit • Mulch heavily as weather warms up with compost or manure	Fertilize established plants to encourage fruit • Lightly prune *Ficus* and *Fortunella* to shape • Take softwood cuttings where appropriate	Check for any sign of aphids or scale insects and take necessary action • Lightly prune *Ficus* and *Fortunella* to shape • Take softwood cuttings where appropriate	*Warm-temperate*
Choose a sheltered position for planting • Prepare site with compost and a complete fertilizer • Ensure good drainage	Mulch and fertilize • Keep away from main trunk	Keep trunk free from weeds	*Citrus*
Check for blossom diseases on established trees	Check for blossom diseases on established trees	Mulch and fertilize	*Prunus*
Sow seed or take cuttings • In garden, build up soil to allow good drainage; add sand, gravel and slow-release fertilizer	Divide established clumps and repot or replant • Give weak solution of liquid fertilizer	Cut off old flowering stems • Watch for snails—they enjoy the fleshy leaves	**CACTI & SUCCULENTS**
Repot overcrowded specimens • Trim dead or damaged roots from plants if repotting	Water regularly during growing period • Fertilize regularly • Divide established plants	Apply extra leaf mould and well-rotted cow manure on garden specimens	**ORCHIDS**
			FERNS, PALMS & CYCADS
Prepare planting site with plenty of compost and leaf litter • Use slow-release fertilizer at planting time	Propagate spore from mature fronds under moist conditions • Side dress established plants with blood and bone • Divide established ferns with rhizomes	Remove dead fronds • Cut them up and use as mulch around ferns • Lightly apply liquid fertilizer	*Ferns*
Mulch well • Fertilize	Collect fresh seed when ripe and sow; for successful germination high temperatures and high humidity are required	Mulch well and apply nitrogenous fertilizer • Dig in plenty of compost and a slow-release fertilizer when planting new palms	*Palms & cycads*
			CLIMBERS & CREEPERS
Prepare evergreen climbers planting position as for May • Spring climbers in flower • Cut back frost-damaged shoots and leaves on tender plants	Plant evergreen climbers • Prune established climbers after flowering • Side dress with blood and bone • Sow fresh climbers seed in seed-raising mix	Tie new growth into growing position • Spray aphids with pyrethrum • Take semi-hardwood cuttings from vigorous plants • Strike in coarse sand/peat mix 3:1	*Warm-temperate to cool-temperate*
Sow fresh seed in seed-raising mix • Prune summer–autumn flowering climbers • Apply blood and bone or complete fertilizer	Dig plenty of compost and a complete fertilizer into soil • Ensure strong support for holding growth • Tip prune regularly	Take semi-hardwood cuttings from vigorous young plants • Train climbers where you want them to grow • Tie up with soft material	*Tropical to subtropical*

Cultivation Guidelines

PLANT	ORIGIN	LIGHT	MINIMUM WINTER TEMP. °C	SOIL PREPARATION	MAINTENANCE	PLANT PROTECTION	PROPAGATION
ANNUALS & PERENNIALS							
Annuals, low-growing, summer–autumn flowering	Warm to cool-temperate	Sun or part-shade in all districts	0	Light application of dolomite/lime; and/or add compost and fertilizer	Water by trickle irrigation • Tip prune to encourage compact habit • Liquid fertilize to prolong flowering	Snails, slugs, mildew, nematodes, aphids, white fly	Seed, seedlings
Annuals, low-growing, spring–summer flowering	Temperate	Sun; part-shade in hot districts	-5	Dolomite/lime; and/or compost and fertilizer	Pick flowers to encourage more blooms • Liquid fertilize regularly • Mulch	Aphids, caterpillars, snails, slugs, damping off, leaf spot, root rot	Seed, seedlings
Annuals, low-growing, winter–spring flowering	Temperate	Sun; part-shade in hot districts	-5	Light application of dolomite/lime; and/or compost and fertilizer	Protect with loose straw in cold districts • Remove spent flowers • Liquid fertilize regularly • Mulch	Snails, aphids, damping off, mildew	Seed, seedlings
Annuals, medium-growing, summer flowering	Cool to warm-temperate	Sun or part-shade	0 to 5	Light application of dolomite/lime; and/or compost and fertilizer	Pick flowers to encourage continuous blooming • Liquid fertilize regularly • Mulch	Snails, mildew, caterpillars, aphids	Seed, seedlings
Annuals, medium-growing, spring–summer flowering	Cool-temperate to warm-temperate	Sun; part-shade in hot districts	0	Light application of dolomite/lime; and/or compost and fertilizer	Shelter from strong winds • Pick flowers regularly to encourage continuous flowering • Liquid fertilize regularly • Mulch	Rust, aphids, snails, mites, budworm, leaf miner	Seed, seedlings
Annuals, tall-growing, spring–summer flowering	Temperate	Sun; part-shade in hot districts	0	Light application of dolomite/lime; and/or compost and fertilizer	Provide tripods if necessary or stakes • Remove spent flowers • Liquid fertilize at regular intervals • Mulch	Rust, mildew, aphids, snails, two-spotted mite	Seed, seedlings
Annuals, tall-growing, summer flowering	Cool-temperate to warm-temperate	Sun or part-shade in all districts	0	Light application of dolomite/lime; and/or compost and fertilizer	Provide tripods if necessary • Shelter from wind • Remove spent flowers • Liquid fertilize regularly • Mulch	Mildew, aphids, leaf-eating insects, snails, cutworms, leaf spot	Seed, seedlings • Rhizome for *Canna*
Annuals, dahlias	Warm-temperate	Sun	0	Well-drained, moderately rich soil	Stake plants • Remove spent flowers	Snails, slugs, mites, earwigs, wilt, stem rot, mildew, mould, nematodes	Tuber
Perennials, spring–early summer flowering	Temperate	Sun	0 to -5	Compost • Fertilizer • Drainage material	Remove spent flowers	Few problems	Division, seed, cuttings
Perennials, spring–early summer flowering, short lived	Warm-temperate	Part-shade	0 to 5	Compost • Fertilizer • Sharp sand or grit for drainage	Remove plants after several seasons or allow to self-seed	Root rot diseases	Cuttings, seed, root cuttings
Perennials, summer flowering, sun	Temperate	Sun; part-shade in hot districts	0 to 15	Dolomite/lime; and/or compost and complete fertilizer • Well-drained soil	Stake tall-flowering plants • Dead-head old flowers	Snails, slugs, few problems	Division, seed, root cuttings, stem cuttings
Perennials, summer flowering, shade to part-shade	Cool-temperate	Part-shade to shade in all districts	0 to -15	Moist, humus-rich soil	Divide every few years	Snails, slugs	Division, seed, stem cuttings
Perennials, winter–early summer flowering	Temperate	Part-shade to shade	0 to -15	Moist, humus-rich soil	Divide every few years	Snails, slugs, wilt disease	Division, seed, root cuttings

PLANT	ORIGIN	LIGHT	MINIMUM WINTER TEMP. °C	SOIL PREPARATION	MAINTENANCE	PLANT PROTECTION	PROPAGATION
ANNUALS & PERENNIALS (continued)							
Perennials, summer–autumn flowering	Temperate	Sun or part-shade	-5	Compost • Fertilizer	Remove spent flowers • Divide every few year	Snails, slugs, few problems	Division, seed, root cuttings
Perennials, ground covers & rock plants, temperate climate	Cool-temperate to warm	Sun	0 to -5	Tolerant of average well-drained soil conditions	Prune overgrown plants	Few problems	Cuttings, division
Perennials, alpines, ground covers & rock plants, cool climate	Cold-temperate	Sun or part-shade	0 to 15	Garden loam with a little compost and sharp sand in a 3:2:1 ratio • Fertilizer	Winter protection from wet	Few problems	Seed, cuttings
Perennials, sub-shrubs, sun	Cool to warm-temperate	Sun	0 to 5	Average garden soil enriched with compost and a complete fertilizer	Remove spent flowers • Prune to shape	Few problems, leaf miner on *Argyranthemum*	Cuttings, seed, root cuttings for *Romneya*
Perennials, sub-shrubs, shade to part-shade	Temperate	Part-shade to shade	0 to -15	Humus-rich, cool, moist soil	Cut back overgrown plants	Mildew, root rot	Division, cuttings
Perennials, water garden plants	Cool to warm-temperate	Sun or part-shade	0 to 5	Moist or wet conditions as recommended	Divide every 3–5 years	Few problems	Division, seed
Perennials, for tropical effect	Tropical to subtropical	Sun or part-shade	10	Moist, humus-rich soil	Remove spent flower stems	Stem borer, snails	Division, cuttings, seed
Perennials, irises	Cool-temperate	Sun, part-shade or shade	-15	Soil requirements as specified for species or variety in plant description	Remove spent flowers • Divide when overcrowded	Mosaic virus, rust, collar rot	Division in autumn to spring, seed in autumn
Perennials, pelargoniums	Warm-temperate	Sun or part-shade	0 to -5	Average garden soil enriched with compost and complete fertilizer	Regular pruning	Caterpillars, rust, stem rot	Cuttings, seed
Perennials, primulas	Temperate	Part-shade	0	Moisture-retaining, humus-rich soil	Frequent liquid fertilizer • Cool site required • Mulch	Snails, mould, mites	Division, seed, root cuttings for *P. denticulata*
SHRUBS							
Low-growing, frost-hardy, evergreen	Warm-temperate to cool-temperate	Sun or part-shade	0 to -5	Well-drained, humus-rich soil, pH adjustment likely	Mulch regularly • Prune regularly • Some protection for young specimens in very cold conditions	Occasional insect damage; less in fertile, well-drained soils	Seed, cuttings, layering
Low-growing, frost-tender, evergreen	Subtropical to warm-temperate	Sun or part-shade	5	Average, fertile, humus-rich soil	Prune to shape or after flowering • Mulch	Occasional insect damage; less in fertile, well-drained soils	Seed, cuttings
Low-growing, frost-hardy, deciduous	Cool-temperate	Sun or part-shade	-5	Well-drained, fertile, humus-rich soil	Mulch regularly • Prune regularly	Occasional insect damage; less in fertile soils	Seed, cuttings
Medium- to tall-growing, frost-hardy, evergreen	Warm-temperate to cool-temperate	Sun, part-shade or shade	0 to -5	Well-drained, fertile, humus-rich soil	Mulch regularly • Prune regularly • Some are able to withstand dry periods	Occasional insect damage; less in fertile soils	Seed, cuttings
Medium- to tall-growing, frost-tender, evergreen	Subtropical to warm-temperate	Sun or part-shade	5	Average, fertile, humus-rich soil	Prune to shape or after flowering • Mulch	Occasional insect damage; less in fertile, well-drained soils	Seed, cuttings
Medium- to tall-growing, frost-hardy, deciduous	Temperate	Sun or part-shade	0	Compost • Complete fertilizer • Well-drained soil	Prune regularly • Mulch	Occasional pest damage; less in fertile soils	Cuttings, grafting

PLANT	ORIGIN	LIGHT	MINIMUM WINTER TEMP. °C	SOIL PREPARATION	MAINTENANCE	PLANT PROTECTION	PROPAGATION
SHRUBS (continued)							
Acacia	Temperate	Sun or part-shade	0 to -5	Average, well-drained soil	Tip prune regularly • Leaf mulch	Borers, galls	Seed, cuttings
Banksia	Cool-temperate to warm-temperate	Sun or part-shade	0	Well-drained soil, low pH	Fertilize with low-phosphorus fertilizer • Leaf mulch	*Phytophthora* root rot	Seed
Boronia	Cool-temperate to warm-temperate	Sun or part-shade	0	Moist, well-drained, light soil	Gum leaf mulch • Tip prune	*Phytophthora* root rot	Seed, cuttings
Buddleia	Temperate	Sun	-5	Average soil	Prune	Few problems	Cuttings
Callistemon	Temperate	Sun	0	Compost • Complete fertilizer • Moisture-retaining soil	Prune after flowering	Sawfly, tip bugs, thrips, borers	Seed, cuttings
Camellia	Temperate	Sun or part-shade	0	Moist, well-drained, humus-rich soil	Provide shelter from weather extremes • Debud	Scale insects, mites	Cuttings
Cestrum	Warm-temperate	Sun	0 to 5	Average, well-drained soil	Tip prune regularly	Few problems	Seed, cuttings
Cistus	Warm-temperate	Sun	0	Well-drained, light soil	Prune after flowering	Few problems	Cuttings
Correa	Temperate	Sun or part-shade	0	Well-drained, light soil	Tip prune regularly	Few problems	Cuttings
Cotoneaster	Temperate	Sun or part-shade	-5	Average, well-drained soil	Prune regularly	Few problems	Seed, cuttings
Erica	Temperate	Sun	0	Acid, well-drained soil	Prune after flowering	Few problems	Cuttings
Euphorbia	Warm-temperate to subtropical	Sun	5	Average, well-drained soil	Prune regularly	Few problems	Cuttings
Fuchsia	Temperate	Part-shade	0	Moist, well-drained, humus-rich soil	Protect from strong winds	Thrips, mites, mealy bug	Cuttings
Gardenia	Warm-temperate	Sun or part-shade	5	Moist, well-drained, humus-rich soil, acid pH	Prune and fertilize regularly • Correct iron or magnesium deficiency	Mealy bug, scale insects, nematodes	Cuttings
Genista	Temperate	Sun	-5	Average, well-drained soil	Prune after flowering	Snails	Cuttings
Grevillea	Warm-temperate to subtropical	Sun	0 to 5	Acid, well-drained soil, low pH	Tip prune	Borer, caterpillars, plant bugs	Cuttings
Hakea	Warm-temperate	Sun	0 to 5	Acid, well-drained, soil, sandy, gravelly	Tip prune	Borer, caterpillars, plant bugs	Seed, cuttings
Hebe	Temperate	Sun	0	Average soil	Prune regularly	Scale insects, leaf miner, downy mildew	Cuttings
Hibiscus	Warm-temperate to subtropical	Sun	5	Well-drained, fertile soil	Prune regularly	Aphids, scale insects, mealy bug, hibiscus beetle, collar rot	Cuttings
Hydrangea	Temperate	Part-shade	0	Cool, moist humus-rich soil	Prune regularly	Mildew, two-spotted mite	Cuttings
Juniperus	Temperate	Sun	-5	Average, well-drained soil	Prune to shape	Few problems	Cuttings
Lavandula	Temperate	Sun	-5	Well-drained, fertile soil	Tip prune regularly	Few problems	Cuttings

PLANT	ORIGIN	LIGHT	MINIMUM WINTER TEMP. °C	SOIL PREPARATION	MAINTENANCE	PLANT PROTECTION	PROPAGATION
SHRUBS (continued)							
Leptospermum	Temperate	Sun	0	Light, well-drained soil	Tip prune regularly	Web moth, borer, manuka blight	Seed, cuttings
Melaleuca	Warm-temperate	Sun	0	Moist, well-drained, soil	Tip prune regularly	Sawfly, wax scale	Seed, cuttings
Nerium	Warm-temperate	Sun	0	Average soil	Prune after flowering	Scale insects	Cuttings
Olearia	Temperate to cool-temperate	Sun or part-shade	0	Fertile, well-drained soil	Tip prune regularly	Borer, wax scale, leaf miner	Cuttings
Philadelphus	Temperate	Sun or part-shade	0	Moist, humus-rich soil	Prune hard after spring flowering	Few problems	Cuttings
Protea	Warm-temperate	Sun	0	Well-drained, organic-rich, acid soil	Water in winter • Prune after flowering	Contact a reputable dealer about *Protea* diseases and their control	Cuttings
Rhododendron	Temperate	Sun, part-shade to shade	0 to -5	Well-drained, humus-rich soil, acid pH	Water regularly • Mulch	Two-spotted mite, lace bug, thrips, caterpillar, leaf miner, petal blight, mildew	Layering, cuttings
Rosa	Temperate	Sun	0 to -5	Well-drained, organic, humus-rich soil	Water regularly • Lightly apply fertilizer • Remove dead or unproductive branches • Mulch with straw or old animal manure • Allow good air circulation	Thrips, aphids, scale insects, mildew, rust, blackspot, caterpillars	Buds, cuttings
Spiraea	Temperate	Sun	-5	Average soil	Prune straggly growth to shape	Few problems	Cuttings
Syringa	Cool-temperate	Sun	-5	Alkaline, rich, cool soil	Remove sucker growth	Keep under cool conditions	Graft on *Privet* rootstock
Viburnum	Temperate	Sun or part-shade	-5	Fertile, humus-rich soil	Prune after flowering	Two-spotted mite, thrips	Cuttings
Weigela	Temperate	Sun	-5	Fertile, humus-rich soil	Prune older branches	Few problems	Cuttings
TREES							
Evergreen	Subtropical to cool-temperate	Sun to part-shade	0 to -5	Well-drained, humus-rich, fertile soil	Regular pruning when young to shape • Mulch • Fertilize on drip line	Seasonal insect pests, root rot diseases on poorly drained soils	Seed, cuttings, grafting
Semi-deciduous	Subtropical to cool-temperate	Sun to part-shade	0 to 10	Well-drained, humus-rich, fertile soil	Regular pruning when young to shape • Mulch • Fertilize on drip line	Seasonal insect pests, root rot diseases on poorly drained soils	Seed, cuttings, grafting
Deciduous, taller than 10 metres	Temperate	Sun to part-shade	-5	Well-drained, humus-rich, fertile soil	Regular pruning when young to shape • Mulch • Fertilize on drip line	Seasonal insect pests, root rot diseases on poorly drained soils	Seed, cuttings, grafting
Deciduous, 10 metres or shorter	Temperate	Sun to part-shade	-5	Well-drained, humus-rich, fertile soil	Regular pruning when young to shape • Mulch • Fertilize on drip line	Seasonal insect pests, root rot diseases on poorly drained soils	Seed, cuttings, grafting
Conifers	Temperate	Sun	-5	Well-drained, humus-rich, soil	Prune to shape if necessary • Mulch • Fertilizer	Thrips, two-spotted mite, beetles	Seed, cuttings, grafting
Ornamental, blossom & fruit	Temperate	Sun	-15	Well-drained, humus-rich, deep soil	Prune after flowering to shape • Mulch • Fertilizer	Shot hole, rust, leaf curl, pear and cherry slug, aphids	Cuttings, grafting

PLANT	ORIGIN	LIGHT	MINIMUM WINTER TEMP. °C	SOIL PREPARATION	MAINTENANCE	PLANT PROTECTION	PROPAGATION
TREES (continued)							
Tropical & subtropical	Tropical to subtropical	Sun to part-shade	10	Well-drained, humus-rich, fertile soil	Regular pruning when young to shape • Mulch • Fertilize on drip line	Seasonal insect pests, root rot diseases on poorly drained soils	Seed, cuttings
Eucalyptus species	Warm-temperate to cool-temperate	Sun	0	Well-drained, humus-rich, fertile to average soil	Prune to shape when young • Gum leaf mulch	Various insect pests, root rot diseases	Seed
BULBS, CORMS & TUBERS							
Summer flowering, sun	Warm-temperate to cool-temperate	Sun or part-shade	0	Rich, organic, well-drained soil	Provide adequate water during growing season • Protect plants with loose straw in frosty areas	Few problems; slugs on *Galtonia*	Seed, division, offsets
Summer flowering, part-shade	Cool-temperate	Part-shade	0 to -5	Cool, moist, humus-rich soil	Mulch with compost once or twice a year	Few problems	Seed, division
Autumn flowering	Temperate	Sun or part-shade	0 to -5	Well-drained, humus-rich soil• Add compost, fertilizer or bulb food	Leave to naturalize or lift and store when dormant	Aphid, snails, bacterial rot	Seed, division
Winter flowering	Temperate	Sun or part-shade	-5	Composty, humus-rich soil	Leave to naturalize	Few problems	Division
Winter-spring flowering	Cool-temperate	Sun or part-shade in warm districts	0 to 5	Prepare soil with compost and complete fertilizer • Soil should be well-drained	Remove spent flowers • Lift and divide every 3–5 years	Snails	Seed in autumn, or offsets, divide clumps
Spring flowering, sun	Warm-temperate	Sun	0	Average well-drained soil • Add compost before planting and complete fertilizer or bulb food	Keep moist during growing season; dry off in summer • Protect with loose straw in frosty areas	Few problems	Seed, division, offsets
Spring flowering, shade to part-shade	Temperate to cool-temperate	Part-shade to shade	0 to -5	Moist, humus-rich soil • Add compost and complete fertilizer or bulb food	Annual compost	Few problems	Seed, division
Summer-autumn flowering	Temperate	Sun or part-shade	0	Average garden soil enriched with compost and complete fertilizer or bulb food	Water during growing season • Allow to dry out when dormant	Snails	Seed, division
Spring-summer flowering, sun	Warm-temperate to cool-temperate	Sun or part-shade in all districts	0 to 5	Average, well-drained soil enriched with compost or bulb food	Protect bulbs with straw in frosty areas • Lift and store in areas with wet, humid summers	Few problems	Seed, offsets, root division for *Asphodeline*
Spring-summer flowering, shade	Temperate	Sun, but most prefer cool shade	0 to 5	Well-drained, fertile soil enriched with compost and bulb food	Naturalize or replant each year • Protect bulbs with loose straw in frosty areas	Few problems	Seed, bulbs, tuber-claw
Allium	Temperate	Sun	-5	Well-drained, fertile soil	Remove spent flowers	Few problems	Seed, division
Begonia	Subtropical	Part-shade or bush house	5	Moist, gritty compost in pots or garden • Position not overwet	Keep dry over winter • Liquid fertilize regularly	Damping off, bulb rot	Seed or tubers in spring
Fritillaria	Cold-temperate	Sun or part-shade	-15	Lime/dolomite • Deep, rich, well-drained soil	Summer moisture	Bulb rot	Seed, offsets

PLANT	ORIGIN	LIGHT	MINIMUM WINTER TEMP. °C	SOIL PREPARATION	MAINTENANCE	PLANT PROTECTION	PROPAGATION
BULBS, CORMS & TUBERS *(continued)*							
Gladiolus	Warm-temperate	Sun	0 to -5	Well-drained, light, sandy loam	Lift and divide every few years	Thrips	Corm, cormlets
Iris	Cold-temperate	Sun	-5	Well-drained soil; compost added	Lift and divide every 3–5 years	Mosaic virus, stem rot	Division
Lilium	Temperate	Sun or, preferably, part-shade	-5	Well-drained, fertile soil; neutral pH	Minimal disturbance of established plants • Mulch in spring/summer • Allow stems to die down before removal	Bulb rot, cucumber mosaic virus	Seed, offsets, bulb scales
Narcissus	Temperate	Sun or part-shade	-5	Well-drained soil • Dolomite/lime; and/or compost and low-nitrogen fertilizer	Provide shelter from strong winds • Lift and divide in warm climates	Bulb rot, aphids	Offsets
Tulipa	Temperate	Sun	-5	Well-drained • Lightly apply dolomite/lime; and/or add compost and blood and bone fertilizer • Add coarse sand in heavy soils	Disease control in spring	Tulip fire botrytis, mosaic virus, aphids	Seed, division
LAWNS, GROUND COVERS & ORNAMENTAL GRASSES							
Lawns & ground covers	Warm-temperate to cool-temperate	Sun or part-shade	5 to -5 depending on species	Drainage material • Fine tilth; even surface	Mowing • Fertilizing • Spraying • Rolling • Aerating	Insect and fungal diseases as per plant description	Runners, seed, turf
Ornamental grasses, sedges & bamboos	Cool-temperate to warm-temperate	Sun to part-shade	0 to -5	Average soil plus compost; dry to poorly drained depending on species	Remove seed heads before dispersal • Restrict spread of bamboos using a barrier	Few problems	Seed, division
HERBS	Warm-temperate to cool-temperate	Sun or part-shade	0	Dolomite/lime; and/or compost and fertilizer	Tip prune regularly • Harvest spring and summer	Few problems	Cuttings, seed, division
FRUIT TREES, NUT TREES & OTHER FRUITS							
Tropical to subtropical	Tropical to subtropical	Full sun	10 to 15	Topsoil at least 600 mm deep • Compost • Fertilizer	Training • Pruning • Fertilizing • Shelter	Seasonal pest problems, root rot diseases	Seed, cuttings, grafting
Cool-temperate and warm-temperate	Temperate	Sun	Chilling requirements as necessary	Well-drained, humus-rich soil	Regular pruning for maximum fruit production • Mulch • Fertilizer • Weed control • Check pollination requirements	Root rot diseases, insects, various bacteria canker	Grafting, budding, cuttings
Citrus	Warm-temperate to cool-temperate	Sun	-5 to 5 depending on variety	Humus-rich, well-drained soil	Regular fertilizer • Mulch • Prune	Scale insects, leaf miner, aphids, caterpillars	Grafting, *trifoliata* or *citronelle* root stocks
Prunus	Warm-temperate to cool-temperate	Sun	-5; check cold tolerance of variety	Humus-rich, well-drained soil	Correct pruning for maximum fruit production • Check pollination requirements • Weed control • Mulch	Leaf curl, silver leaf, brown rot, rust, bacterial canker, various insects	Grafting

PLANT	ORIGIN	LIGHT	MINIMUM WINTER TEMP, °C	SOIL PREPARATION	MAINTENANCE	PLANT PROTECTION	PROPAGATION
INDOOR PLANTS							
Indoor foliage plants	Subtropical to temperate	Good light to part-shade • Warm to humid conditions	10	Humus-rich or loamy soil	Even moisture; less in winter • Liquid fertilize regularly • Remove dead foliage	Mealy bug, mites, scale insects	Seed, cuttings
Indoor flowering plants	Cool to warm-temperate	Part-shade	10	Humus-rich, well-drained soil	Remove spent flowers • Liquid fertilize regularly	Root rot, mealy bug, scale insects	Seed, cuttings
Indoor flowering & foliage plants	Subtropical to warm-temperate	Good light to part-shade	10	Humus-rich soil	Keep soil evenly moist • Dry in winter • Warm conditions • Remove dead flowers/foliage	Mealy bug, mites, scale insects	Seed, cuttings
CACTI & SUCCULENTS	Tropical to subtropical	Sun or part-shade	5	Light, gritty soil • Sharp drainage essential	Water during flowering, then rest	Root rot diseases, mealy bugs, scale insects, aphids	Seed, cuttings
ORCHIDS	Tropical to subtropical, temperate	Part-shade	5 to 10	Open free-draining soil containing bark/leaf litter/ charcoal peatmoss mixture for epiphytes and terrestrials	Regular fertilizer when not in flower • Maintain high humidity where appropriate • Good air circulation	Aphids, scale, mealy bug, beetles, bulb rot	Seed, seedlings, division
FERNS, PALMS & CYCADS							
Ferns	Subtropical to cool-temperate	Sun or part-shade	0 to 5	Well-drained, humus-rich, moist soil	Cut back old fronds • Leaf litter mulch • Regular application of weak solution of liquid fertilizer	Aphids, mealy bug, scale insects, snails, staghorn, fern beetle	Spores, cuttings, division
Palms & cycads	Tropical to warm-temperate	Sun or part-shade	Variable to species	Compost • Humus-rich, moist, well-drained soil • Complete or slow-release fertilizer	Some wind protection when young • Nitrogenous fertilizer• Mulch • Prune old fronds	Mealy bug, mites, palm dart caterpillars, scale insects, grasshoppers	Seed
CLIMBERS & CREEPERS							
Warm-temperate to cool-temperate	Warm-temperate to cool-temperate	Sun or part-shade	0 to -5	Compost • Complete fertilizer	Regular pruning • Mulch	Few problems	Seed, cuttings
Tropical to subtropical	Tropical to subtropical	Sun or part-shade	5	Compost • Complete fertilizer	Regular pruning • Mulch	Few problems	Seed, cuttings

Glossary

× (multiplication sign) A sign placed in front of the name of plants with Latin names to show that they are not true wild species but are of hybrid origin, whether natural or artificial; as in Camellia × williamsii or × Brassolaeliocattleya Sylvia Fry.

+ (plus sign) Though grafts do not usually hybridize, it does happen on very rare occasions, and the resulting plant is designated with the + sign, as with + Laburnocytisus adamii, a freak that occurred in a Paris nursery last century when a purple broom was grafted to laburnum stock to create a standard broom.

Acid (of soils) Containing relatively little lime, to give a pH reaction of less than 7, the sort of soil needed to grow such plants as azaleas, camellias, rhododendrons and the like, and in which hydrangeas flower blue. A very acid soil is described as 'sour'.

Aerial root A root that springs from the stem of a plant above ground. The aerial roots of ivy are short and used by the plant to cling to its support. In such plants as monsteras, philodendrons or some of the tropical figs they eventually reach the ground; before they do they draw moisture from the air.

Air-layering A method of propagation applicable to a wide range of trees and shrubs which involves wounding the stem and then packing the wound with damp sphagnum moss. This is all held in place with string and polythene. When roots show, the new plant can be severed and transplanted.

Alkaline (of soils) Containing a great deal of calcium (lime) to give a pH reaction of more than 7. It is the sort of soil preferred by such plants as bearded irises and the cabbage tribe, and in which hydrangeas flower pink. Some gardeners refer to alkaline soils as 'sweet'.

Alternate (of leaves) Springing, one by one, from first one side of the stem and then the other. Whether the leaves are alternate or opposite is an important aid in plant identification.

Annual A plant that lives for only a year—often less—or which is customarily treated as such in gardens.

Anther The part of the stamen that actually produces the pollen, usually carried on a thin stalk called the filament. Lilium auratum has the largest anthers of any flower.

Apex The growing tip of a shoot, or the very end of a leaf, which may take a variety of shapes.

Arbour A structure, usually free-standing, designed to be covered with climbing plants to provide shade. The term is more or less interchangeable with pergola.

Areole The swelling on the stem of a cactus which bears the spines. It is actually the vestigial remains of a shoot.

Axil The 'armpit' of a leaf, where it joins the stem, and where there is usually a growth bud to be found.

Bedding plant A plant, usually low growing, suitable for a mass planting display of flowers or foliage. Most are annuals or short-lived perennials.

Berry In normal use, a small juicy fruit which is eaten entire and unpeeled; to the botanist, a fleshy fruit containing several seeds which does not open when ripe—including citrus fruits and the tomato.

Biennial A plant which flowers and dies in its second year after germination, producing only roots and leaves in the first. Parsley is the best known example.

Bifoliate (of cattleyas and their hybrids) Plants which have two leaves per pseudo-bulb.

Bipinnate (of leaves) Twice pinnate, as in many ferns and such tropical trees as the jacaranda.

Blade The flat part of a leaf, where most photosynthesis occurs.

Bloom A general term for a flower, much used in flower show schedules. Also, a waxy or powdery coating on the skins of leaves or fruits, as on a grape.

Bole The lowest part of the trunk of a tree, from the ground to the lowest branches.

Bract A leaf-like organ, usually associated with a flower or cluster of flowers, but not part of the flower itself. Bracts are smaller and a different shape to ordinary leaves, as in roses; or they may be brightly coloured and resemble petals, as in bougainvilleas and poinsettias.

Bud An immature, unopened flower. Also, an embryo shoot, usually small and pointed, found normally in the axils of the leaves or at the ends of shoots, but also occurring on rootstocks, tubers and the like. It is usually protected by small, waxy scales.

Budding A form of grafting, where the scion consists of a piece of bark carrying a single growth bud, inserted into the bark of the understock. It is used especially for the propagation of roses and fruit trees.

Bulb An underground (usually) organ, consisting of a reduced stem (the base plate) surrounded by modified leaves that store food for the plant's dormancy. The onion is the classic example.

Bulbil A small bulb, carried in the axil of a leaf, as in certain lilies. It offers a convenient means of propagation.

Bulblet A small bulb developing from the base of a mature one and used for propagation. The

term 'offset' is sometimes used.

Cactus The most significant family of succulent plants, all perennial and native to the Americas.

Calyx The outermost part of a flower, which encloses and protects the rest while in bud. It is made up of sepals, usually small, green and leaf like, but sometimes coloured and the showiest part of the flower, as in clematis and anemones.

Capsule A fruit which when ripe dries and opens to release the seeds, such as the fruits of lilies and petunias.

Carpel The female organ of the flower, also known as the pistil. A flower may have several or only one.

Catkin The type of flower cluster, usually pendulous, found on such plants as willows or alders. The individual flowers, usually one sex only, are tiny and generally have no petals, being pollinated by the wind.

Caudex The thickened base of the stem of certain plants such as some ferns and Dioscorea elephantipes.

Cladode A flattened stem rather like a leaf and performing the same functions, as in the butcher's broom (Ruscus aculeatus). Similar organs in acacias are called phyllodes.

Climber A plant with stems too long and flexible to be self supporting and which raises itself to the light by climbing into and over other plants. It may attach itself to its support by twining around it, as jasmine or honeysuckle do; by means of tendrils (grapes, peas); by short aerial roots (ivy); or by suckers (Virginia creeper). The latter two need no trellis and are termed self-clinging climbers. Some climbers attach themselves only loosely to their supports and need to be tied in place. The term 'vine', while applicable only to the grape, is often used for any climbing plant, especially in the USA.

Cloche A miniature, portable greenhouse placed over crops in the open ground to protect them from cold or encourage early development. Traditionally made from two or four pieces of glass in a wire frame, but can be simply a wire frame clad in transparent polythene.

Clone A group of plants propagated asexually (that is, by cuttings, grafting, division, etc.) from a single individual and thus genetically all identical, such as roses and fruit trees.

Common names The names by which plants are commonly known, as distinct from their Latin or scientific ones (which, unlike common names, are universally recognized). Sometimes the two coincide and, as a plant can have several common names, it is usual for books to list the plants they describe under their scientific names. The American nursery industry has for some years been attempting to standardize common names, by no means an easy task.

Composite The botanist's term for a daisy, from the way the 'flowers' are in fact made up of many small flowers.

Compost The most effective of all fertilizers, it is made from organic matter such as leaves, grass clippings and manure which has been allowed to rot for a few weeks or months until it has turned black and crumbly; in orchid growing, the soil-free medium, which may or may not contain compost from the compost heap, in which the plants are grown.

Compound (of leaves) Subdivided into several leaflets, as in a rose or palm leaf. Leaves not so subdivided are called 'simple'.

Cone The structure that encloses the primitive flowers and then the seeds of conifers (pines, cypresses, etc.) and cycads. It is made up of overlapping scales, which become woody when the seeds ripen.

Conifer A member of a primitive order of flowering plants (the Gymnospermae), characterized by their cones and usually needle-like leaves. They are all shrubs or trees, usually evergreen, and the hardiest trees in cold climates; they supply the bulk of the world's timber. Pines, cypresses, sequoias and junipers are examples.

Cordate (of leaves) Heart shaped, as in the European lime (*Tilia cordata*).

Corm A bulb-like organ, usually growing underground but without the scales (fleshy modified leaves) of a bulb, and often simply called a bulb by gardeners, such as gladiolus and freesias. When a corm flowers the old corm dies and the plant creates a new one on top of it; bulbs are usually more or less permanent structures.

Cormlet A small corm that grows from around the base of a corm, usually in fair numbers and used for propagation.

Corolla The whole collection of petals that forms the eye-catching part of most flowers. The petals can be separate, as in the rose, or fused together in a bell or trumpet, as in rhododendrons or campanulas.

Corona The cup or trumpet-shaped out-growth in the centre of the flower of narcissi and its relatives, such as *Hymenocallis festalis*. It is formed from the bases of the stamens.

Creeper A plant that makes long shoots that grow along the ground, usually rooting as it goes, such as *Convolvulus sabaticus*. The distinction between a climber and a creeper is not clear cut—many creepers will climb if given the chance, and some climbers will creep if there is nothing to climb on, such as ivy and Virginia creeper.

Crown The more or less permanent base of a

herbaceous plant from which the leaves and flower stems grow upwards and the roots downwards; the upper part of a tree, consisting of the branches and top section of the trunk; the corona of a narcissus or narcissus-like plant.

Cultivar A variety of plant which has arisen as the result of cultivation, that is, not naturally, usually by means of hybridization. It may be propagated by any suitable means, and the rules of botany state that it must not be named in Latin but should be given in Roman type with single quotes, for example 'Queen Elizabeth', 'Model of Perfection'. Cultivars that arose before these rulings and were given Latin names are treated similarly, giving rise to such names as *Acer palmatum* 'Dissectum Atropurpureum'.

Cutting A piece of stem or root cut from a plant and used for propagation. According to the state of maturity of the stem from which it is taken, a cutting may be classed as a softwood, semi-mature or hardwood cutting.

Dead-head To remove dead flowers, with the twofold aim of tidying up the plant and preventing it wasting energy in unwanted seed.

Deciduous (of trees and shrubs) Losing all the leaves each year, growing a fresh set later. Typically the leaves fall in autumn/fall, sometimes assuming brilliant colours before they do so, and new leaves grow in spring. Many tropical trees drop at any time of the year in anticipation of a prolonged dry season. A tree that doesn't drop all its leaves is called semi-deciduous.

Die-back The death of the tips of shoots or branches, sometimes followed by the death of the entire shoot. It can be caused by frost or by disease.

Diffuse Growing into many branches, usually used of shrubs to suggest an open, rangy habit of growth rather than a compact one.

Division The simplest method of propagation, whereby a clump of plants is dug up and broken up into several pieces which are then replanted.

Dorsal Situated on the back of an organ.

Double (of flowers) Having more than the 'natural' number of petals. The extra petals are formed from stamens, and where these are completely transformed the flower is apt to be sterile. A flower with only a few extra petals and enough stamens for fertility is described as 'semi-double'.

Elliptic (of leaves) More or less oval in shape.

Entire (of leaves) Having smooth margins, that is, without lobes or serrations, such as an aspidistra or privet leaf.

Epiphyte A plant that grows on, and usually in the branches of, another, but does not steal

nourishment from its host, many orchids are examples.

Espalier The technique of training a tree or shrub, most typically a fruit tree such as a peach or a fig, to grow flat against a wall or trellis. It was originally designed to encourage earlier ripening by holding the fruit close to the reflected warmth of the wall, but can also be used for decorative effect.

Evergreen Any plant that retains foliage all year. Evergreen trees and shrubs do drop old leaves, though not until after the new ones have been formed and usually only a few at a time.

F1 hybrid A hybrid strain created by pollinating two very carefully selected parents. The resulting seedlings usually show great vigour and uniformity and many strains of annuals and vegetables are F1 hybrids. It is useless to save seeds from these, as the original cross must be made afresh every time seed is wanted.

Fall The American (and antique English) term for autumn; the lower three petals of an iris, which project out and down (the upright ones are called 'standards').

Family A group of genera which are considered to be closely related. The cacti (family Cactaceae) are one such; the rose family (Rosaceae) includes not only the rose but such fruits as the peach, blackberry, strawberry and apple.

Fan palm A palm with roughly circular (palmate) leaves, so called because they can be used to make fans. A palm with pinnate leaves is called a 'feather palm'.

Fertilizer Anything added to the soil to maintain or increase its fertility. Fertilizers may be organic, that is, derived from once-living matter, as are manure, compost, and blood and bone; or inorganic (artificial), such as sulphate of ammonia or superphosphate, which are prepared in chemical factories.

Fibrous root A fine, young root, usually one of very many. These are the roots that take up moisture and nourishment from the soil.

Filament The stalk of a stamen, which carries the anther.

Floret A single, small flower in a head or cluster of many, as in a delphinium or cluster-flowered rose.

Flower The organ of reproduction, basic in determining to what genus and species the plant belongs. They are normally composed of three parts: the calyx, the corolla, and the sexual organs proper, the male stamens and the female carpels. Not all may be present in any given flower (clematis, for instance have no petals), and they may be, as in orchids or cannas, modified into the most fantastic forms.

Flowerhead A cluster of flowers, which may be so compact as to look like a single flower, as in a daisy.

Frame A miniature greenhouse, designed mainly for propagation. The traditional style is an enclosed bed with wood to a height of about 40 cm (about 16 in) with an old window across the top. A hot frame is heated, a cold one not.

Frond The leaves of a fern. Fronds carrying spore-bearing organs (sori) are called 'fertile' fronds; if not, they are called 'sterile' fronds. In some species the two types are of different appearance. The term frond is also used for the leaves of feather palms; the Latin *frondosa* when applied to many plants means 'leafy'.

Fruit The part of the plant which carries the seed or seeds, and which arises after the flower is pollinated. It may or may not be edible.

Fungus A very large group of evolutionary primitive plants, of which the most relevant to gardeners are mushrooms and the many parasitic fungi that cause most plant diseases.

Genus A group of species which have sufficient in common to be classed as closely related; the name is always Latin. For example, roses are members of the genus *Rosa,* and both the smoking and ornamental tobaccos are of the genus *Nicotiana.*

Glabrous (of leaves and stems) Smooth and non-hairy; a hairy plant is described as 'hispid'.

Glasshouse A structure, traditionally roofed and clad with glass but now often with polythene sheeting, designed to trap the sun's heat and thus allow warmth loving plants to be grown in cool climates. Supplementary heating may be provided.

Glaucous (of leaves) Bluish grey, a more accurate description for the many conifers sold as having 'blue' leaves.

Grafting A method of propagation which involves the uniting of a piece of stem of a desirable plant, the 'scion', to that of a less desirable one, the 'stock' or 'understock', to give a stronger root system than the scion would have naturally. Many different techniques for grafting have been employed.

Greenhouse Originally a lavishly windowed structure where evergreen plants were placed to keep them from winter cold; but now synonymous with 'glasshouse'.

Green manure A crop of annual plants grown to be dug into the soil at maturity to improve or restore its fertility, for instance legumes such as clover, alfalfa or lupins.

Grex A group of hybrid plants of the same parentage; the term is used mainly in the context of orchid breeding. Grex names are given without quotes, such as Vanda Nellie Morley.

Ground cover An extensive planting of a single species of low-growing plants, intended to carpet the ground with foliage and suppress weeds. Also, a plant suitable for such use.

Habit The complete picture of the way a plant grows; a species may be described as being of 'compact', 'weeping' or 'upright' habit, for instance.

Hanging basket A container designed to be suspended in order to show trailing plants such as ivy, Christmas cactus or fuchsias to their best advantage.

Heel A sliver of old wood retained at the base of a cutting. It is traditional in taking cuttings of carnations and roses.

Herb In botany, any plant that does not have permanent woody stems, such as petunias and zinnias. In gardening, a plant whose leaves or shoots are added to food to enhance its flavour or used in the preparation of medicines.

Herbaceous A perennial plant which dies down to the ground each year; a herbaceous border is a planting composed entirely of such plants, for example delphiniums and chrysanthemums.

Humus The final product of rotting organic matter, whether of plant or animal origin.

Hybrid A plant originating from the cross-pollination, either in the wild or as the result of match-making by the gardener, of two different species. If hybrids are crossed, the resulting plants may carry the genes of several species. Hybrids between plants of different genera are rare, though quite common among orchids.

Inflorescence The structure that carries the flowers. It may take any one of a number of forms—a spike (as in gladioli), a raceme (as in delphiniums), a panicle (as in lilacs), an umbel (as in onions); gardeners often refer simply to a 'cluster'. Inflorescences are described as 'terminal' when they grow at the ends of shoots, or axillary, when they arise in the axils of the leaves.

Insectivorous plant The strict term for carnivorous plants; they trap and digest insects to supply them with extra nitrogen, which is difficult to obtain from the swampy soils where they usually grow.

Irregular (of flowers) Having the petals arranged in some way other than radial symmetry, though almost always bilaterally symmetrical, such as on orchids and violets. The scientific term is 'zygomorphic'.

Labellum The lowest of the three petals of an orchid, usually larger or more elaborately shaped and coloured than the others. Also called a 'lip'.

Lanceolate (of leaves) Long and narrow; lance or sword shaped, such as gladiolus and iris leaves.

Lateral A side shoot, growing from the axil of a leaf of the main stem. In many fruit trees it is these shoots that bear the flowers and ultimately the fruit.

Lax Of rather floppy habit, for instance *Philadelphus mexicanus*, the opposite of upright or stiff.

Layering A method of propagation by which a branch of a plant is bent down to the ground where it takes root; the rooted section can then be severed from its parent and transplanted. It is most useful for plants that can be slow or reluctant to root from cuttings; some plants will layer themselves naturally.

Leaflet One of the several leaves in which a compound leaf such as a rose leaf is divided. A leaf has a bud in its axil; a leaflet does not.

Legume A member of the large pea family, which includes peas, beans, clover, lupins, wisteria, acacias, the various brooms, and some trees such as the cassias. They all share the ability to draw nitrogen straight from the air, by courtesy of bacteria that live in nodules on their roots.

Lime A compound of calcium added to soil to make it more alkaline, and also to improve the structure of clay soil; a tropical fruit of the genus *Citrus;* deciduous trees of the genus *Tilia,* also known as lindens.

Linear (of leaves) Very long and narrow, so that they look as though they could be drawn with a single line, such as the leaves of chives.

Lip See *Labellum*

Lithophytic (of orchids and some primitive plants) Growing on the naked surfaces of rocks and deriving nourishment from any litter they can accumulate around their roots.

Lobe One of the divisions in which a scalloped leaf, such as a maple or ivy leaf, is not quite divided; similarly in the corollas of flowers with united petals such as campanulas.

Manure The dung of animals, used as fertilizer. Like all materials of organic origin it adds humus to the soil.

Marginal plant One which in the wild grows in the swampy margins of ponds or lakes, and which can be cultivated in similar positions around a garden pond, such as *Iris ensata*. Most don't mind having their roots submerged for at least part of the year.

Midrib The main central vein of a leaf; the central stalk to which the leaflets of a pinnate leaf are attached.

Monocarpic A plant which flowers only once in its life and then dies, for example *Agave americana* and the fishtail palm (*Caryota urens*).

Monopodial (of orchids) One that does not naturally form a clump of shoots growing from a creeping rhizome, for example the vandas. (Clump-forming orchids such as cattleyas and cymbidiums are described as 'sympodial'.)

Moss A large group of species of primitive non-flowering plants which need moist soil to grow. Most are of very diminutive stature; some are cultivated as ground cover.

Mulch A blanket spread over the bare surface of soil to block the loss of moisture and to discourage the growth of weeds. Most mulches are of such organic matter as manure, compost, straw, bark chips, etc. which eventually rot and add humus to the soil, thus enhancing its fertility. Inorganic materials are also used.

Nectar The sweet, sugary liquid secreted by glands at the base of the petals of some flowers. Bees gather it and concentrate it into honey.

Neutral (of soils) Neither acid nor alkaline, that is having a pH of 7.

Node The point on a stem where a leaf and its axillary bud grows. It is the place to cut when pruning, and also where the base of a cutting should be cut.

Obovate (of leaves) More or less oval in shape.

Offset A shoot arising from the base of a plant which can be detached and used for propagation.

Opposite (of leaves) Arising in pairs, one on either side of the stem. See also *Alternate*.

Organic matter Material derived from things that were once alive, such as manure and compost, and which breaks down to form humus. The addition of organic matter improves the structure and fertility of any soil.

Ovary The lowest part of a carpel where the embryo seeds are. Ovaries found above the calyx are called 'superior', while those found below the calyx are called 'inferior'.

Ovate, ovoid (of leaves and petals) Oval in shape.

Palm Members of the family Palmae or Arecaceae, that is, trees characterized by a normally unbranched trunk topped by a bunch of large leaves and a distinct preference for warm climates.

Palmate (of leaves) Divided into lobes or leaflets that spread out from the end of the leaf stalk like the fingers of a hand, as in a maple leaf.

Panicle A type of inflorescence, strictly a compound raceme, as typified by that of the lilac.

Parasite A plant which grows upon another, stealing moisture and nourishment from its host. Mistletoe is an example; more common and less welcome are the parasitic fungi that cause plant diseases.

Pendent Hanging, the way the flower sprays of the wisteria do.

Perennial A plant that lives for three years or more. In botany, the term includes trees and shrubs, while in horticulture it is normally limited to plants that do not produce permanent woody stems, such as irises, peonies or ginger lilies.

Persistent A structure that stays on the plant after it serves its purpose, instead of falling off. The sepals of the rose which stay on the ripening rose hip are an example.

Petal The colourful part of most flowers. Petals are in fact modified leaves, and there are some flowers that have green petals, for example the green zinnia 'Envy'.

Petiole The stalk of a leaf.

pH The scale on which the acidity or alkalinity of soil is measured. It ranges from 1, an acid of fear-some strength, to 14, an alkali of equal ferocity, with 7 being the neutral point. Most garden soils fall somewhere between about pH 5.5 to about 8.6.

Phyllode See *Cladode*

Pinch out The operation of removing the tip of a growing shoot, usually with the fingers, to encourage lateral shoots to grow and make the plant bushier.

Pinna, pinnule Another term for the leaflet of a pinnate or bipinnate leaf.

Pinnate A leaf divided into leaflets arranged on either side of the leaf stalk, as in a rose leaf or those of many palms and ferns.

Pollen The tiny grains of plant substance containing DNA which unite with the embryo seeds contained in the ovary to create the fruit and hence a new generation of flowering plants—a process termed pollination. The transfer is usually carried out by insects, but can also be carried out by nectar-eating birds and sometimes by the wind.

Prostrate A plant of low-growing, ground-hugging habit, such as the prostrate junipers.

Pruning The art of cutting off parts of a plant to encourage more of the sort of growth the gardener desires, or to maintain a compact habit of growth.

Pseudo-bulb The fleshy, bulb-like stem found on many orchids.

Raceme A type of inflorescence, where the flowers are arranged on a long, usually upright stem, each flower having a separate flower stalk as in delphiniums.

Revert To return to normal, as when a variegated plant starts producing plain green leaves. **Rhizomatous** A plant that grows from rhizomes.

Rhizome A creeping stem, growing either at ground level, or just below, and swollen with starch and nutrients to nourish the shoots and roots that grow from it. The rhizomes are the edible part of the ginger plant.

Root The underground parts of a plant which anchor the plant and draw up water and nourishment from the soil.

Rootstock The understock of a grafted plant; the base of a perennial where the roots grow.

Rosette A group of leaves radiating from the same point on a short stem, to give an effect like a green flower, as in sempervivums.

Runner A horizontally growing stem that roots at each node where it touches the ground, as in strawberries and violets.

Scape A leafless flower stem that arises directly from the base of the plant, especially common in bulbs. Narcissi and agapanthus are examples.

Scarify To break or soften the hard coat on the seeds of certain plants, especially legumes such as sweet peas and wattles, to allow water to penetrate and thus speed up germination. It can be done by rubbing carefully with fine sandpaper or soaking the seed for a little while in hot water.

Scientific name The internationally recognized Latin name of a plant which often gives a potted description of the plant or commemorates some person connected with it. The name consists of two parts, the genus name and the species name. The system was first devised by the Swedish botanist Linnaeus in 1753.

Seed The organ of propagation of flowering plants. Seeds are not immortal, and it is not worth saving left-over seeds of vegetables and flowers for the following year; the percentage that will germinate decreases markedly.

Seed head A general term for a dry, inedible fruit that contains seeds.

Seed leaf The leaves contained in the seed which are the first to appear when a seedling germinates; they are different from those that follow. Plants are classified according to whether there are one or two.

Self sow, self seed A plant's habit of shedding seeds around itself which germinate without the gardener's assistance.

Sepal One of the parts of the calyx, usually green, leaf like and sometimes coloured and showy, as in hellebores and clematis. In many one-seed-leaf plants the sepals are almost indistinguishable from the petals, as in lilies and tulips.

Series (also **strain**) A group of plants raised from seed and thus not genetically identical but sufficiently alike to be treated as a garden variety, for example most cultivars of annuals and vegetables.

Sessile Having no stalk, as the flowers of most camellias for example.

Sheath An organ, usually vaguely leaf like, that encloses another, such as a shoot or cluster of flower buds. The sheath that encloses the buds of an agapanthus is an example.

Shoot Any aerial part of a plant that bears leaves.

Shrub A plant with several permanent woody stems that arise from ground level. A tree has only one, but in gardening the distinction is not quite clear cut—many plants such as the larger cotoneasters or bottlebrushes can be treated equally well as large shrubs or small, multi-stemmed trees.

Spadix A fleshy flower stalk which bears many tiny flowers—a speciality of the arum family.

Species A population of wild plants which are sufficiently alike to carry the same name, and which will freely breed with one another to give rise to offspring like themselves. The honour of naming a species goes to the scientist who discovers or describes it.

Sphagnum A type of rather luxuriant growing moss, normally an inhabitant of boggy ground and much used when dried as an ingredient in potting mixes, especially for orchids. Live plants often grow from spores in the dried material, and are welcomed by orchid growers as a sign that conditions are right.

Spike A type of inflorescence where the flowers are borne on a long, usually upright stem. Unlike a raceme, a spike has no separate flower stalks, as in gladioli.

Spikelet The basic unit of the flowers of grasses, consisting of one or more petal-less flowers and an accompanying bract or two.

Spore The equivalent of a seed in non-flowering plants such as ferns and fungi. Much tinier than seeds, they are produced in great numbers and blow about on the wind.

Spreading A plant which grows much wider than it does tall, perhaps with mainly horizontal branches, perhaps by rooting in the ground and making an ever-expanding clump.

Spur A hollow projection from a petal, often containing nectar; the short flowering shoots on such plants as apples, pears or hoyas, which normally continue to flower and fruit for several years.

Stalk, stem The two terms are almost interchangeable, but in horticulture a stem usually has leaves growing from its sides while a stalk does not.

Standard The big petal that stands up at the back of a pea flower; a tree or shrub with a single, rather tall stem before the branches begin. Many trees grow thus naturally; shrubs like roses or fuchsias have to be trained to the form artificially. A half-standard has a shorter stem than usual.

Sterile Incapable of bearing seeds or pollen or both (flowers) or spores (the fronds of ferns).

A plant may produce perfectly normal flowers but not mature fertile seed due to some aberration in its genetic make-up, something which often occurs in hybrids; or the reproductive parts of the flower may have been transformed into the extra petals of a double flower.

Stigma The business part of a carpel, where the pollen lands and is captured.

Stipule Leafy outgrowths that grow at the base of a leaf stalk, as in roses, and on the leaves of sucker shoots.

Stratify A technique used to break the dormancy of seeds of such plants as roses and apples, which need a period of cold before they can germinate. In its simplest form, it involves bundling them up in damp sphagnum moss and putting them in a refrigerator for a few weeks.

Striate (of leaves) Ridged or fluted down the length, as in *Sisyrinchium striatum*.

Sub-shrub A perennial with more or less permanent but not woody stems, such as geraniums or *Phlomis fruticosa*.

Subspecies A group of plants within a species, different from the norm but not sufficiently so to rank them as a species in their own right.

Succulent A plant which has evolved swollen water-filled organs, either stems or leaves, which help it to survive in arid climates. Cacti are the extreme example, but other plants show succulence to a lesser degree, as most orchids do in their pseudo-bulbs.

Sucker A shoot or stem that arises from the roots of a tree or shrub or, undesirably, from the understock of a grafted specimen.

Synonym (usually abbreviated to 'syn.') A scientific name which, though no longer valid, still lingers in use, for example *Cyrtostachys renda* syn. *C. lakka*.

Taproot The main root of a plant, which plunges straight down to anchor it; the swollen taproots of carrots are the most familiar. Most trees have them too, and resent their being damaged.

Tendril A string-like structure which some climbing plants wrap around a branch or trellis to support themselves. Peas have them, as do grapes.

Terminal (of inflorescences and flowers) Appearing at the end of a shoot, as with roses, marigolds and poinsettias.

Terrestrial (of orchids) Growing in the ground, the way most plants do, rather than perched in trees.

Throat The inside part of a trumpet- or tube-shaped flower, often carrying, as in foxgloves and gloxinias, a different pattern or colour to guide insects.

Tooth, teeth The serrations on the edges of a leaf or leaflet, as in rose leaves.

Topiary The art of clipping suitable trees or shrubs such as yew, privet or box into artificial shapes, such as pyramids, globes, peacocks, etc.

Tree A woody plant, often very tall and large but not always, with only one main stem and very rarely more. See also *Shrub*.

Tri- In compound words, indicating three, as trifoliate, tripinnate, etc.

Tuber A fat, starchy underground organ designed to store food for a plant during its dormancy. Many tubers, such as those of the potato, provide food for humans too.

Umbel A type of inflorescence where several flower stalks arise from one point, as in onions, agapanthus and parsley.

Upright A growth habit whereby main branches grow more or less vertically.

Variegated Variegated plants have patterns of other colours as well as green on their leaves, and usually grow less strongly than their plain leaved counterparts as they have less chlorophyll. They are usually the result of cultivation and are sometimes caused by viruses though some species, notably *Coleus blumei*, are variegated naturally.

Variety Strictly speaking, a group of plants arising in the wild which though not sufficiently different from the norm of their species to be of great interest to botanists (they may only differ in flower colour, for instance) are different enough to be of interest to gardeners. A variety is designated as, for instance, *Acacia longifolia* var. *sophorae*, the var. being short for *varietas*. Varieties created by gardeners are supposed to be called cultivars and not given Latin names.

Ventral Situated on the front of an organ.

Virus A disease in plants which is incurable and may be fatal. However, some viruses are relatively benign, such as the one that makes tulips 'break' into stripes.

Whorl Usually of leaves, an arrangement where three or more arise at the same node, as in rhododendrons. Flowers can grow in whorls around the stalk also, as in *Primula malacoides*.

Wood, woody A stem which may not be big enough to use as timber but which contains hardened cells and is more or less permanent. It is characteristic of trees and shrubs, but some climbers, such as the grape, are also woody.

General Index

Numbers in *italic* type refer to photographs.

Index to Plants

Photography Credits

The publishers wish to thank the following photographers for the use of their photographs. Each photograph has been referenced by a column number and if necessary, a letter of the alphabet; the letter gives the photograph's position in the column, 'a' being for the one at the top of the column.

Ardea, London: p. 100, col. 3c.
Tony Bomford: p. 88.
Geoff Bryant: back flap e; p. 76, cols 1–2; p. 77, col. 4a; p. 82, col. 4a; p. 86, col. 4; p. 100, cols 1–2; p. 104, cols 1–2; p. 106, cols 2–3; p. 117, cols 1–2b; p. 153, col. 4; p. 159, col. 4b; p. 164, col. 2a, col. 2b; p. 169, cols 3–4; p. 176, col. 1; p. 189, cols 3–4b; p. 197, col. 3b; p. 213, col. 2b, cols 3–4a; p. 214, col. 1b, col. 2b, col. 2c; p. 216, col. 4; p. 217, col. 2; p. 219, col. 4; p. 221, col. 2a, col. 4a, col. 4b; p. 222, col. 1b; p. 234, col. 2; p. 239, col. 4b; p. 240, cols 1–2a, cols 1–2c; p. 247, col. 4b; p. 249, cols 3–4; p. 257, col. 3b; p. 264, col. 1; p. 271, col. 3, col. 4b; p. 275, col. 3b; p. 284, cols 1–2; p. 288, col. 2a; p. 289, col. 4a; p. 305, col. 2b; p. 312, col. 4; p. 388, col. 3a; p. 424, col. 2a; p. 431, col. 2b, cols 3–4a, p. 432, col. 3; p. 434, col. 3; p. 435, cols 2–4; p. 436, cols 1–2b, cols 1–2c; p. 453, cols 3–4b; p. 463, col. 4.
Brinsley Burbidge: p. 125.
Claver Carroll: p. 12, cols 1–3.
Andy Clements: p. 140.
Densey Clyne: p. 64; p. 65.
Tony Curry: p. 440, p. 441.
John Forlonge: p. 210, col. 1, col. 2, col. 3; p. 211.
Denise Grieg: p. 31, col. 3; p. 38, col. 1, col. 2, col. 3; p. 49, col. 2a, col. 2b, col. 3a, col. 3b; p. 50, col. 1, col. 2a, col. 2b, col. 2c, col. 3a, col. 3b, col. 3c; p. 51. col. 1a, col. 1b, col. 2a, col. 2b, col. 3a, col. 3b, col. 3c; p. 52, col. 1, col. 2, col. 3; p. 53, col. 2, col. 3; p. 54, col. 1a, col. 1b, col. 2a, col. 2b, col. 3a, col. 3b; p. 55, col. 1a, col. 1b, col. 2, cols 2–3, col. 3; p. 56; p. 57; p. 58, cols 1–2; p. 90, col. 3a; p. 339, cols 1–2b; p. 346, col. 3a; p. 357; p. 420, cols 1–2; p. 433, cols 1–2.
Joanne Van Gruisen: p. 141, col. 2a.
Sarah Guest: p. 111, col. 2.
Ivy Hansen: back flap d, g; p. 3, col. 4a; p. 40, col. 2, col. 3; p. 300, col. 2, col. 4a; p. 313, col. 4b; p. 314, col. 4; p. 322; p. 323; p. 324; p. 325; p. 344, col. 2c; p. 350, cols 1–2, col. 2a, cols 3–4; p. 366, col. 3b; p. 368, cols 1–2; p. 369, col. 4a; p. 371, col. 2, col. 3a; p. 375; p. 448; p. 449; p. 451, cols 3–4; p. 458, col. 4b; p. 459, col. 4; p. 460, col. 1a; p. 463, cols 3–4.
Joy Harland: back flap a, b, c, f; p. 2, col. 1b, col. 1c, col. 1d, col. 4a, col. 4b, col. 4c, col. 4d; p. 3, col. 1a, col. 1c, col. 1d, col. 4c, col. 4d; p. 10; p. 11, cols 1–2a, col. 2, cols 1–2b; p. 12, col. 1; p. 13, cols 1–2, col. 3a, col. 3b; p. 14, cols 1–2a, cols 1–2b; p. 15, col. 2a; p. 16; p. 18, cols 1–3, col. 3b; p. 19, cols 2–3a, cols 2–3b; p. 20; p. 22; p. 23; p. 24, col. 2; p. 25; p. 26, cols 1–2a, cols 1–2b; p. 27; p. 28, col.1, cols 1–3; p. 29, cols 1–2b; p. 30, col. 3; p. 31, cols 1–3; p. 33; p. 34; p. 36; p. 37; p. 39; p. 41, col. 1, cols 2–3; p. 42; p. 43; p. 44; p. 45; p. 46; p. 58, cols 1–3; p. 59; p. 60; p. 61, cols 1–3; p. 62, col. 1a; p. 63; p. 66–67; p. 68; p. 70, cols 1–2, cols 3–4, col. 3; p. 71, cols 3–4b; p. 72, cols 1–2, col. 2, col. 3b; p. 73, cols 3–4; p. 74, col. 1b, col. 3a, col. 3b; p. 75, col. 3a, cols 3–4, col. 4a, col. 4c; p. 77, col. 1a, col. 4c; p. 78, col. 1a, cols 1–2; p. 79, cols 3–4; p. 80, cols 1–2, cols 3–4b; p. 81, col. 4b; p. 82, cols 1–2, col. 3a; p. 83, cols 1–2, cols 3–4, col. 4a; p. 85, col. 1, col. 2a, cols 3–4; p. 86, cols 1–2, col. 1a; p. 87, cols 2–3, col. 4b; p. 90, col. 1, col. 2; p. 91, cols 2–4, col. 3a, col. 4a; p. 92, cols 1–2, col. 3b, col. 4a, col. 4c; p. 93, cols 3–4, col. 4c; p. 94, cols 1–2, col. 3b; p. 95, col. 2a, cols 3–4b; p. 96, col. 1b, col. 2a; p. 97, col. 2b, col. 3, cols 3–4, col. 4c; p. 98, cols 1–2, col. 3, cols 3–4, col. 4; p. 99, col. 4a, col. 4b; p. 100, col. 1, col. 2; p. 101, col. 2a; p. 102, cols 2–3, cols 3–4; p. 103, col. 1b, col. 3, col. 4a, col. 4c; p. 104, col. 3b, col. 4b; p. 105, cols 1–2; p. 106, col. 1a, col. 1b; p. 107, cols 3–4a; p. 110, cols 1–2a, col. 1b, col. 3; p.111, col. 3c, col. 4a, col. 4b; p. 112, cols 1–2, col. 1a, col. 1b, col. 2b; p. 115, cols 2–3, col. 4b; p. 116, cols 1–2, col. 4a; p. 117, cols 1–2a; p. 119, cols 3–4, col. 4b; p. 120, col. 4b; p. 121, col. 1, cols 2–3, col. 4a; p. 122, col. 3b; p. 123, cols 3–4a; p. 126, col. 1b, col. 1c, cols 2–3a, cols 2–3b; p. 128, col. 2, cols 3–4, col. 4b; p. 129, col. 1, col. 3; p. 130, cols 1–2b, col. 4a; p. 131, cols 1–2; p. 132, cols 1–2a, cols 1–2b, col. 1a; p. 133, col. 2a, cols 3–4, col. 4a; p. 134, cols 1–2; p. 136, col. 1b, cols 2–3, col. 4; p. 137, col. 1a, col. 1b, cols 3–4, col. 3, col. 4b; p. 138, cols 1–2; p. 139, cols 3–4, col. 4; p. 142, cols 2–3, cols 3–4, col. 4; p. 143, cols 1–2, cols 3–4; p. 144, cols 1–2a; p. 145, cols 3–4, col. 3b, col. 4b; p. 146, cols 1–2, col. 4; p. 148, cols 1–2a; p. 149, cols 3–4b; p. 150, cols 1–2, cols 3–4a, cols 3–4b; p. 151, cols 1–2a, cols 1–2b; p. 152, cols 2–3, cols 3–4, col. 3a, col. 3b; p. 153, cols 3–4a, cols 3–4b; p. 154; p. 155; p. 157, p. 161, col. 2c, cols 3–4; p. 164, cols 1–2, col. 2c; p. 165, col. 1a; p. 166, col. 3b; p. 168, cols 3–4, col. 4a, col. 4b; p. 170, cols 3–4a; p. 171, col. 1a, cols 3–4a; p. 172, cols 1–2, col. 1c, col. 2c; p. 173, col. 3a, p. 176, cols 3–4b; p. 178, cols 1–2, col. 4b, col. 4c; p. 179, cols 1–2; p. 180, cols 1–2a; p. 181, cols 3–4a; p. 184, cols 1–2a, cols 1–2b; p. 186, cols. 1–2, cols 3–4; p. 187, cols 3–4b; p. 188, col. 4; p. 189, cols 1–2b; p. 190, cols 1–2b; p. 191, cols 3–4; p. 197, cols 3–4, col. 3c, col. 4a; p. 198, cols 1–3, col. 4d; p. 199, cols 2–4, cols 2–3; p. 200, col. 4a; p. 202, cols 1–2; p. 203, col. 1, cols 2–3, col. 4a, col. 4b; p. 204, col. 4; p. 205, cols 2–3; p. 206, cols 1–2, col. 1a; p. 207, cols 2–4, col. 4; p. 209, col. 4a; p. 212, cols 1–3, col. 1, col. 4a; p. 214, cols 1–2; p. 216, cols 1–2; p. 217, cols 3–4a; p. 218, cols 1–2, cols 3–4a; p. 219, cols 1–2; p. 222, cols 1–2; p. 223, cols 1–3; p. 225, cols 2–4, cols 3–4; p. 229, cols 3–4, p. 230, col. 2; p. 231, cols 3–4a, col. 3b, col. 4b; p. 232, cols 1–2, cols 3–4; p. 233. cols 2–4; p. 234, cols 1–3, col. 4a; p. 235, cols 2–4; p. 236, cols 1–2a; p. 237, cols 3–4, col. 4a; p. 239, cols 2–4; p. 242; p. 243; p. 244; p. 246, col. 1a, cols 2–3; p. 247, col. 3a, cols 3–4, col. 4a, col. 4c; p. 248, cols 1–2a, col. 1a, cols 1–2b; p. 250, col. 1a, col. 1c; p. 251, cols 3–4, col. 4b; p. 252, cols 2–3; p. 253, col. 3; p. 254, cols 1–2, col. 3a, col. 3b, col. 4; p. 255, col. 3; p. 257, cols 3–4, col. 4b; p. 258, col. 3b, col. 4; p. 262, col. 1a, col. 1b, col. 1c, cols 1–2; p. 263, col. 2, col. 3a, cols 3–4; p. 264, col. 3a, col. 4a, col. 4b; p. 265, cols 3–4, col. 4; p. 266, cols 1–2, col. 1a, col. 1b; p. 269, cols 1–2, col. 3a, col. 3b, col. 3c, col. 4a, col. 4b; p. 270, cols 1–2a, cols 1–2b; p. 274, col. 1a, col. 1b, col. 2c; p. 275, cols 3–4, col. 3c, col. 4b; p. 278, cols 2–3; p. 280, cols 1–2; p. 281, col. 2b, cols 3–4; p. 282, col. 1b, col. 2b; p. 283, col. 1, col. 2a, cols 3–4, col. 4b; p. 285, cols 2–3b, col. 4a; p. 286, cols 1–2, col. 3b; p. 287, cols 2–3, col. 4a; p. 288, col. 1a, col. 2b; p. 289, col. 3b, col. 4b; p. 292; p. 293; p. 294, col. 2a; p. 295, cols 3–4b; p. 296, col. 1; p. 298, cols 2–3; p. 299, cols 3–4a, cols 3–4b; p. 300, col. 1, col. 3b; p. 302, cols 1–2a, col. 1–2b; p. 303, cols 3–4a; p. 304, col. 1a, col. 1d, col. 2a, col. 2e; p. 305, col. 1a, col. 2a, cols 3–4; p. 306, col. 1, cols 1–2; p. 307, cols 2–3, col. 3a, col. 4a; p. 308, cols 1–2, col. 3a; p. 312, cols 1–2, col. 2; p. 313, cols 2–3, col. 3, col. 4a, col. 4c; p. 315, col. 1, cols 3–4, col. 4; p. 316, col. 1a; p. 317, cols 3–4; p. 318, cols 1–2; p. 319, col. 1, col. 3a, cols 3–4, col. 4a, col. 4b; p. 320, cols 2–3; p. 321, cols 3–4, col. 4c; p. 327, cols 3–4a; p. 328, cols 2–3; p. 330, cols 1–2, col. 1a; p. 332; p. 333; p. 335; p. 336, cols 1–2a, cols 1–2b, cols 3–4; p. 337, cols 3–4a, cols 3–4b; p. 338, cols 1–2, cols 1–3, cols 2–3; p. 340, cols 1–2a; p. 341, cols 1–2; p. 342, cols 1–3, cols 1–2, col. 3; p. 343, cols 2–4; p. 344, col. 1a, col. 1b; p. 345, col. 4b, col. 4c; p. 346, cols 1–2; p. 347, cols 3–4, col. 3a, col. 4a, col. 4b; p. 348, col. 1, cols 3–4a, cols 3–4b; p. 349, col. 2b, cols 3–4a; p. 351, cols 3–4, col. 3a, col. 3b, col. 3c, col. 4b; p. 352, col. 2c; p. 353, col. 3a, cols 3–4b, col. 4; p. 354; p. 355; p. 356; p. 358, cols 1–2; p. 360, cols 1–2; p. 361, cols 2–3b, cols 3–4, col. 4a; p. 362, cols 1–2a, cols 1–2b, cols 3–4; p. 363, col. 1a, cols 1–2, cols 3–4a, cols 3–4b; p. 364, col. 1a, cols 2–3; p. 365, col. 2b, cols 3–4a; p. 366, cols 1–2, col. 1, col. 2; p. 367, col. 3a, col. 3b, cols 3–4; p. 368, cols 2–3, p. 369, cols 1–3; p. 371, cols 3–4a, col. 4a; p. 376, cols 1–2, col. 1; p. 378, cols 1–2, col. 1c; p. 379, cols 3–4, col. 4; p. 380, cols 1–2a, cols 1–2b; p. 384, cols 1–2; p. 385, col. 1; p. 386, col. 2; p. 389, col. 2, cols 3–4, col. 4a; p. 390; p. 391; p. 394, col. 1a, col. 1b, col. 2a; p. 395, col. 3a, col. 3b, col. 3e, col 4b, col. 4c; p. 396, col. 1a, col. 1b, col. 2a, col. 2c; p. 397, col. 3a, col. 3b, col. 4a, col. 4c; p. 398, col. 1a, cols 2–3; p. 399, col. 3a, col. 4a, col. 4b; p. 400, col. 1; p. 401, col. 3, cols 3–4, col. 4; p. 404, cols 1–2, col. 1a, col. 1b; p. 405, cols 3–4, col. 3a, col. 3b, col. 4a, col. 4b, col. 4c; p. 406, col. 1, cols 1–2, col. 2a, col. 3b; p. 407, cols 3–4, col. 3a, col. 3b, col. 3c, col. 4a, col. 4b; p. 408, col. 1c; p. 409, col. 1b, cols 1–2, col. 3a, col. 3b, col. 4; p. 411, col. 1b, cols 2–3a, col. 4a; p. 412; p. 413; p. 414; p. 415, p. 417, cols 3–4, col. 4b; p. 418, col. 1a, col. 2c; p. 419, col. 4b; p. 421, col. 4b; p. 422, col. 1a, col. 1b; p. 423, col. 3a, cols 3–4, col. 4a; p. 425, col. 4a, col. 4c; p. 428; p. 430, cols 1–2a; p. 433, cols 3–4; p. 435, cols 2–3b; p. 438, cols 1–2b; p. 439, col. 4; p. 443, cols 3–4; p. 446; p. 447; p. 451, col. 2a; p. 453, col. 1, cols 3–4, col. 4; p. 456, cols 1–2; p. 457, cols 1–2, cols 2–4; p. 458, cols 1–2a, cols 3–4, col. 4a; p. 459, col. 2a, cols 3–4; p. 461, col. 1a, cols 2–4, cols 2–3; p. 462, cols 3–4; p. 464, cols 1–2, col. 1a.
James Hyett, ARPS: p. 124.
Maurice Kellett: p. 382, p. 383, cols 1–2, cols 3–4.
Stirling Macoboy: p. 15, col. 2b; p. 17; p. 18, col. 3a; p. 21, col. 2b; p. 24, cols 2–3, col. 3; p. 29, cols 2–3a; p. 30, cols 1–2; p. 35; p. 48; p. 61, cols 2–3; p. 62, col. b; p. 70, col. 1, col. 4; p. 71, col. 1, col. 2b, col. 2c; p. 72, col. 1, col. 3a; p. 73, col. 2a, col. 2c, col. 3, col. 4a; p. 74, col. 1a, col. 2; p. 75, col. 3b, col. 3c, col. 4b; p. 76, col. 1, col. 3a, col. 3b; p. 77, col. 1b, col. 4b; p. 78, col. 1b, col. 1c, col. 2a, col. 2c; p.79, col. 1, cols 1–2, col. 2; p. 80, cols 3–4b; p. 81, col. 1, col. 2a, col. 3, cols 3–4, col. 4a; p. 83, col. 2, col. 4b; p. 84, col. 2a, col. 2b, col. 2c; p. 85, col. 2b; p. 86, col. 1b, col. 1c, col. 2, col. 3; p. 87, col. 1a, col. 1b, cols 3–4; p. 90, cols 1–2, col. 3b, col. 4a, col. 4b; p. 91, col. 3b, col. 4b; p. 92, col. 3a, col. 3c, col. 4b; p. 93, col. 3a, col. 3b; p. 94, col.1, col. 2, col. 4a, col. 4b; p. 95, col. 1a, col. 2b, cols 3–4a; p. 96, col. 1a, col. 1c, col. 2b; p. 97, col. 2a, col. 4a, col. 4b; p. 98, col. 1, col. 2; p. 99, col. 2b, col. 3, cols 3–4; p. 100, col. 3a, col. 4; p. 101, col. 2b, cols 3–4b, col. 4; p. 102, col. 1a, col. 1b, col. 4a, col. 4b; p. 103, cols 2–3; p. 104, col. 4a, col. 4c; p. 105, col. 1, col. 2, col. 3a; p. 106, col. 1c, col. 2a; p. 107, col. 2a, col. 2c, cols 3–4b; p. 110, col. 1a, col. 2a, col. 2b; p. 111, col. 1, col. 3a, col. 3b, col. 4c; p. 112, col. 2a; p. 113, col. 1a, col. 1b, cols 2–3, col. 4a, col. 4b; p. 114, col. 1, cols 1–2, col. 2, col. 3a, col. 3b; p. 115, col. 1, col. 3; p. 116, col. 3a, col. 3b, col. 3c, col. 4b; p. 117, col. 2, cols 3–4; p. 118, cols 1–2, col. 3a, col. 3b, col. 4a, col. 4b, col. 4c; p. 119, col. 3a, col. 3b, col. 3c, col. 4a; p. 120, col. 1a, col. 1b, cols 2–3b, col. 4a; p. 122, col. 3a, col. 3c, col. 4b, col. 4d; p. 123, col. 1, cols 3–4b, cols 3–4c; p. 126, col. 1a, col. 4a, col. 4b; p. 127, col. 1a, col. 1b, col. 2, cols 3–4; p. 128, col. 1, col. 3a, col. 3b; p. 129, col. 2, cols 3–4a, col. 4; p. 130, col. 3a, col. 3b, col. 3c, col. 4b; p. 131, col. 1, col. 2, col. 3, cols 3–4, col. 4; p. 132, col. 1b, col. 2a, col. 2b; p. 133, col. 1, col. 2b, col. 2c; p. 134, col. 1, col. 2, col. 3a, col. 3b, col. 4a, col. 4b; p. 135, col. 1, col. 2b, cols 3–4b; p. 136, col. 1a, col. 2; p. 137, col. 2b, col. 4a; p. 138, col. 1, col. 2, cols 3–4a, cols 3–4b; p. 139, col. 2a, col. 2b; p. 142, col. 1, cols 1–2, col. 3; p. 143, col. 1, col. 2, cols 2–3, col. 4; p. 144, cols 1–2b, col. 2, col. 4; p. 145, col. 3a, col. 2; p. 146, col. 1, col. 3a, col. 3c; p. 147, col. 1, cols 1–2, col. 2a, col. 2b, cols 3–4; p. 148, col. 3a, col. 3b, col. 4a, col. 4b; p. 149, col. 1, col. 2, cols 3–4a; p. 150, col. 1, col. 2; p. 151, cols 3–4a, cols 3–4b, col. 4; p. 152, col. 1; p. 153, col. 1, cols 1–2, col. 2; p. 158, col. 3; p. 159, col. 3a, col. 3b, col. 4c; p. 161, col. 2a; p. 162, cols 2–3, col. 3; p. 163, cols 1–2b, col. 3, col. 4a; p. 165, col. 1b; p. 166, col. 2; p. 167, col. 1, col. 2b, col. 3a, col. 3b, col. 4; p. 168, col. 1, col. 3a, col. 3b; p. 169, col. 1b, col. 2a, col. 2b; p. 170, col. 1, cols 1–2, col. 2; p. 171, col. 1b, col. 2b; p. 172, col. 1.a, col. 2a, col. 2b; p. 173, col. 3b, col. 3c, col. 4c; p. 176, col. 2; p. 177, col. 3a, col. 3b, col. 4a, col. 4b; p. 178, col. 4a; p. 179, col. 4b; p. 180, col. 2, col, 3; p. 181, col. 3a, col. 3b; p. 182, cols 1–2; p. 183, col. 2; p. 184, col. 2, col. 3; p. 185, col. 2a, col. 2b, cols 2–3, cols 3–4; p. 186, col. 2, col. 3, col.4; p. 187, col. 3, cols 3–4a; p. 188, col. 2, col. 3; p. 189, cols 3–4a; p. 190, cols 1–2c, col. 3a, col. 4; p. 191, col. 2a, col. 2b, col. 2c; p. 194, cols 1–2, col. 2, col. 3; p. 195, col. 1b, col. 4; p. 196, col. 1a, col. 1b, cols 1–2b, cols 3–4; p. 197, col. 3a, col. 4b; p. 198, col. 3, col. 4b, col. 4c, col. 4e; p. 199, col. 1b, col. 4b; p. 200, col. 3b, col. 3c; p. 201, col. 2a, col. 2b, cols 3–4a; p. 202, cols 2–3; p. 204, col. 3a, col. 3c; p. 205, col. 2, col. 3, col. 4b; p. 206, col. 1b, col. 2a; p. 207, col. 1, col. 3a, col. 3b; p. 208, col. 1b, col. 2, col. 3a; p. 209, col. 1, col. 3a; p. 212, col. 3, col. 4c; p. 213, col. 1, cols 1–2, col. 2a, cols 3–4b; p. 214, col. 1a, col. 2a, col. 3; p. 215, col. 2a, cols 3–4b; p. 216, col. 1, col. 2, col. 3a; p. 218; col. 1, col. 2; p. 219, col. 1, col. 2; p. 221, col. 2b, col. 3; p. 222, col. 2a; p. 223, col. 1a, col. 1b, col. 2, cols 3–4; p. 224, col.2, col. 3b, cols 3–4, col. 4; p. 225, col. 2, col. 3a, col. 3b, col. 4a; p. 228, cols 2–3; p. 229, cols 1–2a, cols 1–2b, col. 3, col. 4; p. 230, col. 1, cols 1–3, col. 3, col. 4a, col. 4b, col. 4c; p. 231, col. 3a, col. 4a; p. 232, col. 2; p. 233, col. 1, col. 3b; p. 234, col.3, col. 4b; p. 235, col. 1a, cols 2–3; p. 236, col. 1, cols 1–3, cols 2–3; p. 237, col. 3b; p. 238, col. 1, cols 3–4, col. 3; p. 239, cols 2–3, col. 4a, col. 4c; p. 240, col. 3; p. 241, col. 1b, col. 1c, col. 2; p. 248, col. 1b, col. 2b; p. 249, col. 3a, col. 3b; p. 250, col. 1b, col. 2a, col. 2c; p. 251, col. 4a; p. 252, col. 1c, col. 4; p. 255, col. 2a, col 2b; p. 256, col. 2a, col. 2b; p. 257, col. 4a; p. 258, col. 3a; p. 259, col. 2, col. 3a, col. 3b col. 4a; p. 262, col. 2b; p. 263, col. 3c, col. 4b; p. 265, col. 2; p. 266, col. 2b, col. 2c; p. 267, col. 2a, col. 2b, col. 4; p. 268, col. 1a, col. 2a, col. 2b; p. 269, col. 2; p. 270, col. 1a, col. 2b; p. 271, col. 1a, col. 4a; p. 272, col. 1c; p. 273, cols 2–3, col. 4b, col. 4c; p. 275, col. 4a; p. 278, col. 1a, col. 1b, col. 4a; p. 279, col. 1, col. 2a, col. 4b; p. 281, col. 3; p. 282, col. 2a; p. 283, col. 3; p. 284, col. 2, col. 3b; p. 285, col. 1, col. 4b; p. 286, col. 3a; p. 287, col. 3; p. 288, col. 1c; p. 289, col. 4c; p. 294, col. 1a, col. 1b, col. 1c, col. 2b; p. 295, col. 1, col. 2a, col. 3, col. 4; p. 296, cols 1–2, col. 2, col. 3a, col. 3b; p. 297, col. 1, col. 2a, col. 2b, col. 3a, col. 3b, col. 4b; p. 298, col.1a, col. 2, col. 3, col. 4b; p. 299, col. 3b; p. 300, cols 1–2, col. 3c, col. 4b; p. 301, col. 1a, col. 1b, cols 2–3, col. 3, col. 4b; p. 302, col. 1a, col. 1b, col. 2a, col. 2b; p. 303, col. 1b, col. 2a, col. 3, col. 4; p. 304, col. 1c, col. 2b, col. 2c; p. 305, col. 1b, col. 3; p. 306, col. 2, col. 3a, col. 3b; p. 307, col. 1, col. 2, col. 3b, col. 4b; p. 308, col. 1, col. 2, col. 3b, col. 3c, col. 4; p. 309, col. 1b, col. 2, cols 2–3, col. 3; p. 312, col. 3a; p. 313, col. 1, col. 2; p. 314, col. 1a, col. 1b, col. 1c, col. 2a, col. 2b, col. 2c, cols 2–3; p. 315, col. 2a, col. 2b, col. 3; p. 316, col. 1b, cols 1–2, col. 2c, col. 2d; p. 317, col. 1, col. 2b; p. 318, col. 1, col. 2; p. 319, col. 2b, col. 3b; p. 120, col. 1a, col. 1b, col. 1c, col. 1d, col. 2a, col. 2b, col. 2c, col. 3; p. 321, col. 3a, col. 3b, col. 3c, col. 4a; p. 326, col. 1b, cols 1–2; p. 327, col. 3, cols 3–4b; p. 328, col. 1, col. 2, cols 3–4; p. 329, col. 1, col. 2, col. 3a, col. 3b, col. 4; p. 330, col. 2a; p. 331, cols 1–2a, cols 1–2b, col.3, cols 3–4b, col. 4; p. 337, col. 1, cols 1–2, col. 2; p. 338, col. 1; p. 339, col. 3a, col. 3b; p. 340, cols 1–2b, col. 3; p. 341, col. 4; p. 343, cols 3–4; p. 344, col. 2a, col. 2b; p. 345, col. 3a, col. 3b, col. 3c, cols 3–4; p. 346, col. 3b, col. 3c, col. 4a; p. 347, col. 3c; p. 348, cols 1–2a, cols 1–2b; p. 349, col. 2a; p. 350, col. 1, col. 3a, col. 3b; p. 352, cols 1–2, col. 2a, col. 2b; p. 353, col. 3b, cols 3–4a; p. 358, col. 1a, col. 1b, col. 2a, col. 2b; p. 359, col. 2c; p. 360, col. 1, cols 2–3, col. 3a, col. 3b, col. 4; p.363, col. 1b, col. 2a, col. 2b; p. 364, col. 1b, col. 1c, col. 2a, col. 2b; p. 365, col. 2a, cols 3–4b, cols 3–4c; p. 366, col. 3a, p. 368, col. 3, cols 3–4; p. 369, col. 4b; p. 370, col. 1, cols 1–2, col. 3b, col. 4; p. 371, cols 3–4b; p. 374; p. 376, col. 3; p. 377, col. 2, cols 2–3, col. 3a, col. 3b, col. 3c, col. 4a, col. 4b, col. 4c; p. 378, col. 1a, col. 1b, col. 2a, col. 2b; p. 379, col. 2b, col. 3; p. 380, col. 3a, col. 4a, col. 4b; p. 381, col. 3a, col. 3b, cols 3–4, col. 4a; p. 384, col. 1b, col. 1c, col. 2b, col. 2c; p. 385, col. 2, col. 4a, col. 4b; p. 386, cols 1–2, cols 3–4, col. 4; p. 387, col. 3a, col. 3b, cols 3–4, col. 4b; p. 388, col. 2a; p. 389, col. 3a, col. 3b, col. 4b; p. 394, col. 1c, col. 2b; p. 396, col. 2a, col. 3a; p. 397, col. 4b; p. 398, col. 1b, col. 4b; p. 399, col. 1b, col. 3b; p. 400, cols 1–2, col. 2, col. 3a, col. 3b, col. 3c; p. 401, col. 1b, col. 2a, col. 2b; p. 404, col. 2a, col. 2b, col. 2c, col. 2d; p. 405, col. 3c; p. 406, col. 2b, col. 3a; p. 407, col. 4c; p. 408, col. 2a, col. 2b, col. 2c, col. 2d; p. 409, col. 1a, col. 2b; p. 410, col. 1a, col. 1b, col. 2, cols 2–3, col. 4b; p. 416, col. 1a, col. 1b, col. 1c, cols 1–2, col. 2a, col. 2b, col. 2c; p. 417, col. 3a, col. 3b, col. 4a; p. 418, col. 1b, col. 1c, col. 1d, col. 2a, col. 2b; p. 419, col. 1, col. 2a, col. 2b, col. 3a, col. 3b, col. 4a; p. 420, col. 1, col. 2, col. 4a; p. 421, col. 1, col. 2b, col. 3a, col. 3b, col. 4a; p. 422, col. 1c, col. 2a, col. 2b, col. 2c; p. 423, col. 3b, col. 3c; p. 424, col. 1a, col. 1b, col. 1c, col. 1d, col. 2c; p. 425, col. 1, col. 2, col. 3a, col. 3b, col. 4b; p. 430, col. 1, col. 3; p. 431, col. 1; p. 433, col. 3, col. 4; p. 434, cols 1–2b; p. 435, cols 2–3a, cols 3–4; p. 436, cols 1–2a, col. 3, col. 4; p. 437, col. 2, col. 3, cols 3–4a, cols 3–4b; p. 438, col. 1; p. 439, cols 1–2, col. 2, cols 3–4a, cols 3–4b; p. 443, cols 2–3, col. 4a; p. 444, col. 1a, col. 1b, col. 3; p. 445, col. 2; p. 450, col. 1b, cols 3–4, col. 4; p. 451, col. 3a, col. 3b, col. 4b; p. 452, col. 1, col. 2, col. 3b; p. 453, col. 2; p. 454, col. 1, p. 456, col. 2, col. 3a; p. 457, col. 1a, col. 1b, col. 3, col. 4; p. 458, col. 3a; p. 459, col. 1, col. 2b, col. 3; p. 460, col. 2b; p. 461, col. 1b, col. 3, col. 4a, col. 4b; p. 463, col. 3; p. 464, col. 1b, col. 2a.
Brett McKay: p. 185, col. 1a; p. 277.
Leo Meier: p. 108; p. 109.
Geoff Moon: p. 276.
Kristo Pienaar: p. 100, col. 3b; p. 122, cols 1–2; p. 127, cols 2–3; p. 128, cols 1–2; p. 148, cols 1–2b; p. 165, col. 4; p. 169, col. 1a; p. 178, col. 3b; p. 181, cols 3–4b; p. 183, col. 1, cols 3–4a, cols 3–4b; p. 184, col. 1, cols 3–4; p. 192; p. 193, cols 1–2, cols 3–4; p. 195, col. 1a; p. 199, col. 4a, col. 4c; p. 205, col. 4a, col. 4c; p. 208, col. 4; p. 218, cols 3–4b; p. 219, cols 3–4; p. 220, col. 1, cols 1–2a, cols 1–2b; p. 233, col. 4a, col. 4b; p. 235, col. 1b; p. 251, col. 3b; p. 256, col. 2c; p. 258, col. 1, cols 1–2; p. 262, col. 2a; p. 264, cols 1–2; p. 272, col. 1a, cols 2–3; p. 275, col. 3a; p. 280, col. 1a; p. 281, col. 1, col. 4a; p. 282, col. 1a; p. 286, col. 1b; p. 288, col. 1b; . 297, cols 2–3; p. 298, col. 1b, col. 4a; p. 299, col. 3a, col. 4c; p. 303, cols 3–4b; p. 310; p 311, col. 1, col. 2, col. 3; p. 321, col. 4b; p. 394, cols 1–2; p. 395, col. 4a; p. 397, cols 3–4; p. 399, col. 2b; p. 406, col. 4; p. 411, col. 4b; p. 420, col. 3a; p. 421, col. 2a; p. 430, cols 1–2b; p. 431, cols 3–4b; p. 432, cols 1–2b; p. 445, col. 4; p. 454, cols 1–2a; p. 458, cols 1–2b; p. 460, cols 1–2b; p. 463, cols 1–2a.
Gordon Roberts: p. 119, col. 2; p. 123, col. 2; p. 135, col. 2a; p. 190, col. 3b.
Tony Rodd: p. 3, col. 1b; p. 70, col. 2; p. 71, col. 2a; p. 72, col. 4; p. 73, col. 2b, col. 4b; p. 76, col. 2, col. 4; p. 77, col. 4d; p. 78, col. 2b; p. 79, col. 4a, col. 4b; p. 80, col. 3, col. 4; p. 81, col. 2b; p. 82, col. 3b, cols 3–4; p. 83, col. 3; p. 84, cols 1–2a, cols 1–2b; p. 85, col. 3, col. 4; p. 91, col. 4c; p. 93, col. 4a, col. 4b; p. 95, col. 1b; p. 96, col. 2c; p. 99, col. 2a; p. 101, col. 2c, cols 3–4a; p. 103, col. 1a, col. 4b; p. 105, col. 3b, col. 4a; p. 106, col. 1d, col. 2b; p. 107, col. 2b; p. 112, col. 2c; p.113, cols 3–4; p. 114, col. 4; p. 115, col. 4a, col. 4c; p. 116, col. 4c; p. 117, col. 4; p.121, col. 4b, col. 4c; p. 122, col. 4a; p. 128, col. 4a; p. 133, col. 3, col. 4b; p. 135, cols 1–2, cols 3–4a; p. 136, cols 3–4; p. 137, col. 2a; p. 139, col. 1a, col. 1b; p. 144, col. 1, col. 3; p. 146, col. 2, col. 3b; p. 147, col. 3, col.4; p. 149, cols 1–2; p. 150, col. 3; p. 152, cols 1–2; p. 158, col. 4b; p. 159, col. 2, col. 3c, cols 3–4; p. 160, col. 1a, col. 1b, cols 2–3, cols 3–4, col. 4; p. 161, col. 2b, col. 3a, col. 3b, col. 4; p. 162, col. 1a, cols 1–2; p. 163, cols 1–2a, cols 3–4, col. 4b; p. 164, col. 1a, col. 1b; p. 165, col. 2a, col. 2b; p. 166, col. 1, col. 3a, col. 3c, col. 4; p. 167, col. 2a, cols 3–4; p. 168, cols 1–2, col. 2; p. 169, cols 1–2; p. 170, cols 3–4b; p. 171, col. 2a, cols 3–4b; p. 172, col. 1b; p. 173, cols 3–4, col. 4a, col. 4b; p. 175, cols 1–2; p. 176, cols 1–2, col 3, cols 3–4a; p. 177, cols 2–3; p. 178, col. 3a, col. 3c; p. 179, col. 3a, col. 3b, cols 3–4, col. 4a; p. 180, col. 1, cols 1–2b, cols 3–4; p. 181, col. 4a, col. 4b; p. 182, col. 1, col. 2, col. 3, col. 4; p. 183, cols 1–2a, cols 1–2b; p. 186, col. 1; p. 187, col. 4; p. 188, col. 1; p. 189, cols 1–2a, col. 4; p. 190, cols 1–2a; p. 191, col. 1a, col. 1b, col. 1c; p. 194, cols 2–3; p. 195, cols 3–4; p. 196, cols 1–2a, col. 2; p. 197, col. 2; p. 200, col. 3a, col. 4b; p. 201, col. 1a, cols 3–4b; p. 202, col. 1, col. 3a, col. 3b; p. 203, col. 4d; p. 204, cols 1–2a, col. 3b; p. 205, col. 4d; p. 206, col. 2b; p. 208, col. 1a, col. 3b; p. 212, col. 2, col. 4b; p. 215, col. 2b, col. 3, col. 4; p. 216, col. 3b; p. 217, cols 1–2, col. 3, col. 4; p. 219, col. 3; p. 220, col. 2, col. 3a, col. 3b; p. 221, col. 1, cols 3–4; p. 222, col. 1a, col. 2b; p. 224, cols 1–2; p. 225, col. 4b; p. 228, col. 1a, col. 1b; p. 232, col. 1, col. 3; p. 233, col. 3a, col. 4c; p. 235, col. 4; p. 236, cols 1–2b; p. 237, col. 2, col. 3a, col. 4b; p. 238, cols 1–2, col. 2, col. 4; p. 240, cols 1–2b, cols 3–4; p. 241, col. 1a, cols 2–4, cols 3–4; p. 246, col. 1b, col. 2, col. 3, col. 4b; p. 247, col. 3b; p. 249, col. 4b; p. 250, col. 2b; p. 251, col. 3a, col. 3c; p. 252, col. 1a, col. 1b, col. 2; p. 253, col. 4a, col. 4b, cols 3–4b; p. 254, col. 1, col. 2; p. 255, col. 1a, col. 1b, cols 1–2; p. 256, col. 1a, cols 1–2, col. 1b; p. 257, col. 3a; p. 258, col. 2; p. 259, cols 3–4, col. 4b; p. 260; p. 261, cols 1–2, cols 3–4; p. 263, col. 4a; p. 264, col. 3b; p. 265, col. 3b; p. 266, col. 2a; p. 267, col. 1, col. 3; p. 268, col. 1b, col. 1c, cols 1–2; p. 270, col. 1b, col. 2a; p. 271, col. 1b, cols 2–3, col. 4c; p. 272, col. 1b, col. 2, col. 3; p. 273, col. 1, col. 3, col. 4a; p. 274, col. 2a, col. 2b; p. 278, col. 2, col. 4b; p. 279, col. 2b, col. 3, cols 3–4a, col. 4a; p. 280, col. 1b, col. 2, col. 3; p. 281, col. 2a, col. 4b; p. 282, cols 1–2, col. 2c; p. 283, col. 2b, col. 4a; p. 284, col. 1, col. 3a, col. 4a, col. 4a, col. 4b; p. 285, cols 2–3a; p. 286, col. 1a, col. 2; p. 287, col. 1a, col. 1b, col. 4b; p. 288, cols 1–2; p. 289, col. 3a, col. 4d; p. 294, cols 1–2; p. 295, col. 2b, cols 3–4a; p. 299, col. 3c, col. 4a, col. 4b; p. 300, col. 3a; p. 301, col. 4a; p. 303, col. 1a, col. 2b; p. 304, col. 2a; p. 305, col. 4; p. 306, col. 4; p. 309, col. 1a, cols 1–2, cols 3–4, col. 4; p. 312, col. 1, col. 3b, col. 3c; p. 314, col. 1d; p. 316, col. 2a, col. 2b; p. 317, col. 2a, col. 3, col. 4; p. 318, col. 3a; p. 319, col. 2a; p. 326, col. 2; p. 327, col. 2, col. 4; p. 328, col. 3, col. 4; p. 330, col. 1b, col 2b; p. 331, cols 3–4a; p. 339, cols 1–2a, col. 3c; p. 340, col. 1; p. 341, cols 3–4a; p. 343, cols 1–2, col. 4; p. 346, col. 4b, col. 4c; p. 349, cols 3–4b; p. 350, col. 2b; p. 352, col. 1b; p. 353, col. 3; p. 358, cols 2–3; p. 359, col. 2a, col. 2b, cols 3–4a, cols 3–4b; p. 361, col. 4b; p. 362, col. 3, col. 4; p. 366, col. 3c; p. 367, cols 2–3, col. 4b; p. 368, col. 1; p. 370, cols 2–3, col. 3a; p. 376, col. 2; p. 380, col. 3b; p. 381, cols 1–2, col. 4b; p. 384, col. 2a; p. 385, cols 2–3, col. 3; p. 386, col. 1, col. 3; p. 387, col. 4a; p. 388, col. 1b, col. 2b, col. 2c, col. 3b; p. 393; p. 395, col. 3d; p. 396, col. 3b; p. 398, col. 2; p. 399, col. 1a, col. 2a; p. 401, col. 1a; p. 407, col. 3d; p. 408, col. 1b; p. 409, col. 2a; p. 410, col. 4a; p. 411, col. 1a, cols 2–3b; p. 420, col. 3b, col. 4b; p. 423, col. 4b; p. 424, col. 2b; p. 430, col. 2; p. 432, cols 3–4; p. 434, cols 1–2a, cols 3–4; p. 437, col. 4; p. 438, col. 2; p. 439, col. 3; p. 441. cols 2–3, col. 4; p. 442, col. 1, cols 1–2, col. 2, cols 3–4; p. 443, col. 1, col. 4b; p. 444, col. 2b, cols 2–3, col. 4; p. 445, col. 1, cols 2–3, col. 3; p. 450, col. 1a, col. 2; p. 451, col. 2b, col. 4a; p. 452, col. 3a; p. 454, col. 2, cols 2–3; p. 455, cols 2–3, col. 3, col. 4b; p. 456, col. 1, col. 3b, col. 4; p. 458, col. 3b; p. 459, col. 2c; p. 460, col. 2a; p. 462, cols 1–2, col. 3, col. 4; p. 464, col. 2b, col. 3.
Lorna Rose: p. 334; p. 372; p. 373.
Paul Sterry: p. 89.
Oliver Strewe: p. 2, col. 1a; p. 367, col. 4a.
Ben Wallace: p. 175, cols 3–4.
Gerry Whitmont: p. 402; p. 403 cols 1–2, 3–4a
Brent Wilson: p. 69; p. 71, cols 3–4a; p. 74, cols 1–2; p. 77, cols 2–3; p. 82, col. 4b; p. 87, col. 4a; p. 94, col. 3a; p. 96, cols 1–2; p. 104, col. 3a; p. 105, col. 4b; p. 110, cols 1–2b; p. 120, cols 2–3a; p. 122, col. 4c; p. 127, col. 4; p. 129, cols 3–4b; p. 130, cols 1–2a; p. 145, col. 4a; p. 158, cols 1–2, cols 3–4, col. 4a; p. 159, col. 4a; p. 162, col. 1b, col. 1c; p. 165, col. 3, cols 3–4; p. 166, cols 1–2; p. 177, cols 3–4; p. 182, cols 3–4; p. 187, cols 1–2; p. 188, cols 1–2; p. 194, col. 1, cols 1–3; p. 195, cols 2–4; p. 198, col. 2, col. 4a; p. 199, col. 1a; p. 200, cols 1–2; p. 201, col. 1b; p. 202, col. 4; p. 203, col. 4c; p. 204, cols 1–2b; p. 207, col. 2; p. 208, cols 1–2; p. 209, cols 2–4, col. 3b, col. 4b; p. 215, cols 3–4a; p. 217, cols 3–4b; p. 224, col. 1; p. 231, cols 3–4b; p. 232, col. 4; p. 234, col. 1; p. 246, col. 4a; p. 248, col. 2a; p. 249, col. 4a; p. 253, cols 3–4a; p. 255, col. 4; p. 257, col. 1, col. 2; p. 263, col. 3b; p. 265, col. 3a; p. 267, cols 3–4; p. 274, cols 1–2; p. 279, cols 3–4b; p. 289, cols 3–4; p. 296, col. 4; p. 297, col. 4a; p. 304, col. 1b; p. 318, col. 3b, col. 4; p. 326, col. 1a, col. 1c; p. 327, cols 3–4c; p. 329, cols 1–2; p. 341, cols 3–4b; p. 342, col. 4; p. 344, col. 1c, cols 1–2; p. 345, col. 4a; p. 347, col. 3b; p. 349, col. 4; p. 351, col. 4a; p. 352, col. 1a; p. 361, cols 2–3a; p. 379, col. 2a; p. 384, col. 1a; p. 388, col. 1a; p. 397, col. 3c; p. 408, col. 1a; p. 431, col. 2a, col. 2c; p. 432, cols 1–2a, col. 4; p. 435, col. 4; p. 438, cols 1–2a; p. 444, col. 2a; p. 445, cols 3–4; p. 450, cols 2–3; p. 452, cols 1–2, col. 3c, col. 4; p. 453, cols 1–2; p. 454, cols 1–2b; p. 455, cols 3–4a, cols 3–4b, col. 4a; p. 460, cols 1–2a, col. 1b; p. 463, cols 1–2b;
Australian Picture Library: p. 174.
Random House Picture Library: p. 3, col. 4b; p. 226; p. 245; p. 392; p. 395, col. 3c; p. 398, col. 4a; p. 404, col. 1c; p. 410, col. 3; p. 426; p. 427; p. 429.
State Library of New South Wales: p. 311 cols 3–4b; p. 441 cols 3–4b

© text Random House (Australia) Pty Ltd 1994
© photographs with individual photographers as listed above, 1994